ELEMENTS
OF LITERATURE

ELEMENTS
OF LITERATURE

Second Canadian Edition

ROBERT SCHOLES
Brown University

NANCY R. COMLEY
City University of New York

CARL H. KLAUS
University of Iowa

DAVID STAINES
University of Ottawa

OXFORD
UNIVERSITY PRESS

OXFORD
UNIVERSITY PRESS

70 Wynford Drive, Don Mills, Ontario M3C 1J9
www.oupcan.com

Oxford   New York
Athens   Auckland   Bangkok   Bogotá   Buenos Aires
Calcutta   Cape Town   Chennai   Dar es Salaam
Delhi   Florence   Hong Kong   Istanbul   Karachi
Kuala Lumpur   Madrid   Melbourne   Mexico City
Mumbai   Nairobi   Paris   São Paulo   Singapore
Taipei   Tokyo   Toronto   Warsaw

and associated companies in
Berlin   Ibadan

Oxford is a trademark of Oxford University Press

Canadian Cataloguing in Publication Data

Main entry under title:
Elements of literature

2nd Canadian ed.
0–19–540786–5

1. Literature.   2. Canadian literature (English).*
I. Scholes, Robert, 1929–

PN6014.E44 1990   808.8   C90–093188–4

Cover painting: James Wilson Morrice, sketch for "At a Country Fair", c. 1905.
Art Gallery of Ontario, Toronto

4 5 6 7 — 02 01 00 99

Printed in Canada by Best Book Manufacturers Inc.

Acknowledgments

Sherwood Anderson. "I'm a Fool" from *The Portable Sherwood Anderson*. Reprinted by permission of Harold Ober Assoicates Incorporated. Copyright 1922 by Dial Pub. Co. Copyright renewed 1949 by Eleanor Copenhaver Anderson.

Margaret Atwood. "At the Tourist Centre in Boston" and "Death of a Young Son by Drowning" from *Selected Poems* © Margaret Atwood 1976. "Variations on the Word *Love*," "Variation on the Word *Sleep*," and "Interlunar" from *Selected Poems II: Poems Selected & New 1976–1986* © Margaret Atwood 1986. All poems used by permission of Oxford University Press Canada.

W.H. Auden. "The Unknown Citizen," "In memory of W.B. Yeates," "Musée des Beaux Arts," "Lullaby," "As I Walked Out One Evening," and "Who's Who". Reprinted by permission of Faber and Faber Ltd from *Collected Poems* by W.H. Auden.

Margaret Avison. "Snow," "New Year's Poem," "The Swimmer's Moment," and "Butterfly Bones: or Sonnet Against Sonnet" from *Winter Sun/The Dumbfounding* by Margaret Avison. Used by permission of the Canadian Publishers, McClelland and Stewart, Toronto. "In a Season of Unemployment" is reprinted from *The Dumbfounding* by Margaret Avison, by permission of W.W. Norton & Company, Inc. Copyright © 1966 by Margaret Avison.

Samuel Beckett. *Krapp's Last Tape*. Copyright © 1957 by Samuel Beckett. Copyright © 1958, 1959, 1960 by Grove Press, Inc. Reprinted by permission of Grove Press, Inc. All rights reserved.

Earle Birney. "Bushed," "Can. Lit.," "A Walk in Kyoto," and "The Bear on the Delhi Road" from *Collected Poems* by Earle Birney. Used by permission of the Canadian Publishers, McClelland and Stewart, Toronto.

Elizabeth Bishop. "First Death in Nova Scotia," "In the Waiting Room," "One Art," and "The Map" from *The Complete Poems, 1927-1979* by Elizabeth Bishop. Copyright © 1979, 1983 by Alice Helen Methfessel. Reprinted by permission of Farrar, Straus and Giroux, Inc.

Elizabeth Bowen. "The Demon Lover" copyright 1946 and renewed 1974 by Elizabeth Bowen. Reprinted from *The Collected Stories of Elizabeth Bowen*, by permission of Alfred A. Knopf, Inc.

Morley Callaghan. "A Cap for Steve" from *Morley Callaghan's Stories* © 1959 by Morley Callaghan. Reprinted by permission of Macmillan of Canada, A Division of Canada Publishing Corporation.

John Cheever. "The Swimmer" copyright © 1964 by John Cheever. Reprinted from *The Stories of John Cheever* by permission of Alfred A. Knopf, Inc.

E.E. Cummings. "pity this busy monster, manunkind," and "my father moved through dooms of love" are reprinted from *Complete Poems, 1913-1962*, by E.E. Cummings. Copyright © 1923, 1925, 1931, 1935, 1938, 1939, 1940, 1944, 1945, 1946, 1947, 1948, 1949, 1950, 1951, 1952, 1953, 1954, 1955, 1956, 1957, 1958, 1959, 1960, 1961, 1962 by the Trustees for the E.E. Cummings Trust. Copyright © 1961, 1963, 1968 by Marion Morehouse Cummings. "Spring is like a perhaps hand" and "Buffalo Bill 's" are reprinted from *Tulips & Chimneys* by E.E. Cummings, Edited by George James Firmage. Copyright 1923, 1925 and renewed 1951, 1953 by E.E. Cummings. Copyright © 1973, 1976 by the Trustees for the E.E. Cummings Trust. Copyright © 1973, 1976 by George James Firmage. "somewhere i have never travelled, gladly beyond" is reprinted from *ViVa*, poems by E.E. Cummings, Edited by George James Firmage. Copyright 1931, 1959 by E.E. Cummings. Copyright © 1979, 1973 by the Trustees for the E.E. Cummings Trust. Copyright © 1979, 1973 by George James Firmage. All reprinted by permission of Liveright Publishing Corporation.

T.S. Eliot. "Journey of the Magi," "The Hollow Men," "The Love Song of J. Alfred Prufrock," and "Marina". Reprinted by permission of Faber and Faber Ltd from *Collected Poems 1909-1962* by T.S. Eliot.

William Faulkner. "A Rose for Emily" copyright 1930 and renewed 1958 by William Faulkner. Reprinted from *Collected Stories of William Faulkner*, by permission of Random House, Inc.

Larry Fineberg. "Death" copyright Larry Fineberg. Reprinted by permission of the author.

F. Scott Fitzgerald. "Babylon Revisited". Reprinted with permission of Charles Scribner's Sons, an imprint of Macmillan Publishing Company from *Taps at Reveille* by F. Scott Fitzgerald. Copyright 1931 by The Curtis Publishing Company; copyright renewed 1959 by Frances Scott Fitzgerald Lanahan.

Robert Frost. "Mending Wall," "After Apple-Picking," "Stopping by Woods on a Snowy Evening," "Design," "Provide, Provide," and "Birches" from *The Poetry of Robert Frost* edited by Edward Connery Latham. Copyright © 1969 by Holt, Rinehart and Winston, Inc. Copyright © 1962 by Robert Frost. Copyright © 1975 by Lesley Frost Ballantine. Reprinted by permission of Henry Holt and Company, Inc.

Mavis Gallant. "The Ice Wagon Going Down the Street" from *Home Truths*. Copyright © 1963 by Mavis Gallant. Reprinted by permission of Georges Borchardt, Inc. This Story appeared originally in *The New Yorker*.

Ernest Hemingway. "Hills Like White Elephants". Reprinted with permission of Charles Scribner's Sons, an imprint of Macmillan Publishing Company from *Men Without Women* by Ernest Hemingway. Copyright 1927 by Charles Scribner's Sons; copyright renewed 1955 by Ernest Hemingway.

Henrik Ibsen. "A Doll's House" from *Ibsen's Plays Two* translated by Michael Meyer. Reprinted by permission of David Higham Associates Limited.

James Joyce. "Araby" from *Dubliners*. Copyright 1916 by B.W. Heubsch, Inc. Definitive Text Copyright © 1967 by the Estate of James Joyce. All rights reserved. Reprinted by permission of Viking Penguin, a division of Penguin Books USA, Inc.

A.M. Klein. "Soire of Velvel Kleinberg," "The Rocking Chair," and "Portrait of the Poet as Landscape," from *The Collected Poems of A.M. Klein*. Copyright © McGraw-Hill Ryerson Limited, 1974. Reprinted by permission.

Margaret Laurence. "The Loons" from *A Bird in the House*. Used by permission of the Canadian Publishers, McClelland and Stewart, Toronto.

Irving Layton. "Keine Lazarovich," "Whatever Else Poetry Is Freedom," "Berry Picking," "The Cold Green Element" from *Collected Poems* by Irving Layton. Used by permission of the Canadian Publishers, McClelland and Stewart, Toronto.

Stephen Leacock. "The Marine Excursion of the Knights of Pythias" from *Sunshine Sketches of a Little Town* by Stephen Leacock. Used by permission of the Canadian Publishers, McClelland and Stewart, Toronto.

Doris Lessing. "Sunrise On the Veld' from *This Was the Old Chief's Country* by Doris Lessing. Copyright 1951 Doris Lessing. Reprinted by permission of Jonathan Clowes Ltd., London, on behalf of Doris Lessing.

Robert Lowell. "For the Union Dead" and "Water" from *For the Union Dead* by Robert Lowell. Copyright © 1960, 1962 by Robert Lowell. "Skunk Hour" and "To Speak of Woe That is in Marriage" from *Life Studies* by Robert Lowell. Copyright © 1956, 1959 by Robert Lowell. Renewal copyright © 1987 by Harriet Lowell. All reprinted by permission of Farrar, Straus and Giroux, Inc.

Bernard Malamud. "The Magic Barrel" from *The Magic Barrel* by Bernard Malamud. Copyright © 1954 and renewal copyright © 1982 by Bernard Malamud. Reprinted by permission of Farrar, Straus and Giroux, Inc.

Marianne Moore. Reprinted with permission of Macmillan Publishing Company from *Collected Poems* by Marianne Moore: "Nevertheless" copyright 1944, and renewed 1972, by Marianne Moore; "Fish" and "Poetry" copyright 1935 by Marianne Moore, renewed 1963 by Marianne Moore and T.S. Eliot. Reprinted by permission of Viking Penguin Inc.: "A Jellyfish" from *The Complete Poems of Marianne Moore*. Copyright © 1959 by Marianne Moore.

Bharati Mukherjee. "The Lady from Lucknow" from *Darkness* by Bharati Mukherjee. Copyright © Bharati Mukherjee, 1985. Reprinted by permission of Penguin Books Canada Limited.

Alice Munro, "The Stone in the Field" copyright © 1982 by Alice Munro from the collection *The Moons of Jupiter* published by Macmillan of Canada and Penguin Canada. Reprinted by permission of Virginia Barber Literary Agency Inc. All rights reserved.

Flannery O'Connor. "Everything That Rises Must Converge" from *Everything That Rises Must Converge* by Flannery O'Connor. Copyright © 1961, 1965 by the Estate of Mary Flannery O'Connor.

Michael Ondaatje. All poems reprinted by permission of the author.

P.K. Page. All poems reprinted by permission of the author.

Dorothy Parker. "You Were Perfectly Fine" from *The Portable Dorothy Parker*. Copyright 1929, renewed 1957 by Dorothy Parker. This selection appeared originally in *The New Yorker*. Reprinted by permission of Viking Penguin, Inc.

Sylvia Plath. "Sheep in Fog," "Daddy," "Kindness," "Edge," and "Words," from *Collected Poems* by Sylvia Plath, published by Faber & Faber Ltd, London, copyright Ted Hughes 1965 and 1981. Reprinted by permission of Olwyn Hughes.

Sharon Pollock. "Doc" © Sharon Pollock. Reprinted by permission of the author.

Adrienne Rich. "Rape," "Moving in Winter," "Night-Pieces: For a Child," "Novella," and "The Afterwake" reprinted from *Poems, Selected and New, 1950-1974*, by Adrienne Rich, by permission of W.W. Norton & Company, Inc. Copyright © 1975, 1973, 1971, 1969, 1966 by W.W. Norton & Company, Inc. Copyright © 1967, 1963, 1962, 1961, 1960, 1959, 1958, 1957, 1956, 1955, 1954, 1953, 1952, 1951 by Adrienne Rich.

George Ryga. "Ecstasy of Rita Joe" from *Rita Joe and Other Plays* by George Ryga. Reprinted by permission of Stoddart Publishing Co. Limited.

George Bernard Shaw. "Major Barbara". Copyright 1907, 1913, 1930, 1941, George Bernard Shaw. Copyright © 1957, The Public Trustee as Executor of the Estate of George Bernard Shaw. Copyright © 1971, The Trustees of the British Museum, The Governors and Guardians of The National Gallery of Ireland and Royal Academy of Dramatic Art. Reprinted by permission of Dodd, Mead & Company, Inc. and The Society of Authors on behalf of the Estate of Bernard Shaw.

William Shakespeare. Glosses are from the New Clarendon Shakespeare edition of *King Lear* edited by R.E.C. Houghton, © Oxford University Press 1959. Used by permission.

Sophocles. *The Oedipus Rex of Sophocles: An English Version* by Dudley Fitts and Robert Fitzgerald, copyright 1949 by Harcourt Brace Jovanovich, Inc. and renewed 1977 by Cornelia Fitts and Robert Fitzgerald, reprinted by permission of the publisher.
    Caution. All rights, including professional, amateur, motion picture, recitation, lecturing, public reading, radio broadcasting, and television are strictly reserved. Inquires on all rights should be addressed to Harcourt Brace Jovanovich, Inc., Copyrights and Permissions Department, Orlando, Florida 32887.

Wallace Stevens. From *The Collected Poems of Wallace Stevens*: "Sunday Morning," "Anecdote of the Jar," "Thirteen Ways of Looking at a Blackbird," "The Snow Man," and "A High-Toned Old Christian Woman" copyright 1923 and renewed 1951 by Wallace Stevens; "Of Modern Poetry" copyright 1942 by Wallace Stevens and renewed 1970 by Holly Stevens. All reprinted by permission of Alfred A. Knopf, Inc.

Dylan Thomas. "Do Not Go Gentle Into That Good Night," "Fern Hill," "A Refusal to Mourn," and "The Force That Through the Green Fuse" from *The Poems of Dylan Thomas*. Reprinted by permission of David Higham Associates Limited.

Guy Vanderhaeghe. "Lazarus" from *The Trouble With Heroes and Other Stories*. Reprinted by permission of the author.

Sheila Watson. "Antigone" used by permission of the author.

Phyllis Webb. All poems reprinted by permission of the author.

Eudora Welty. "Why I Live at the P.O." copyright 1941 and renewed 1969 by Eudora Welty, reprinted from her volume *A Curtain of Green and Other Stories* by permission of Harcourt Brace Jovanovich, Inc.

Rudy Wiebe. "The Naming of Albert Johnson" from *Where Is the Voice Coming From* is used by permission of the author.

Tennessee Williams. "The Glass Menagerie" from *The Glass Menagerie*, by Tennessee Williams. Copyright 1945 and renewed 1973 by Tennessee Williams. Reprinted by permission of Random House, Inc.

William Carlos Williams. Reprinted by permission of New Directions Publishing Corporation: "The Last Words of My English Grandmother," "The Yachts," "Flowers of the Sea," "Spring and All," "The Widow's Lament in Springtime," "The Red Wheelbarrow" from William Carlos Williams *Collected Poems Volume I, 1909–1939*. Copyright 1938 by New Directions Publishing Corporation; and "Landscape with the Fall of Icarus" from William Carlos Williams *Collected Poems Volume II, 1939–1962*. Copyright © 1960 by William Carlos Williams

Ethel Wilson. "Till Death Us Do Part" from *Mrs. Golightly and Other Stories* by Ethel Wilson © 1961. Reprinted by permission of Macmillan of Canada, A Division of Canada Publishing Corporation.

Preface

In making this anthology we have tried to do two things: get as many out-standing works of fiction, poetry, and drama as we can between the covers of a single book; and give as much help as we can to people who want to learn how to understand and enjoy works of literature. To these ends we have gathered together here a collection of stories, poems, and plays by major writers from the classical period to the contemporary period. And for each of these forms of literature we have prepared separate explanatory discussions. Beyond these guides to understanding we have provided biographical head-notes for each author in the collection and a glossary of critical terms after the text of the book. Thus we have no further explanations to offer in this preface. But we do have a number of people to thank for helping us to put this book together.

For their good advice about the table of contents and the critical apparatus, we are grateful to Professors Stephen V. Armstrong (University of Alabama), Ronald L. Ballard (Hagerstown Junior College), David E. Boudreaux (Nicholls State University), Luana F. Clayton (Jackson State University), Robert Cox (University of the Pacific), Robert R. Craven (New Hampshire College), Joan B. Crawford (Garrett Community College), Robert W. Crone (Garrett Community College), William R. Epperson (Oral Roberts University), Diane Turner Everson (Frederick Community College), Miriam Gilbert (University of Iowa), Eric Gould (University of Denver), Paula Johnson (New York University), William Rea Keast (University of Texas), Robert T. Knighton (University of the Pacific), Frank McHugh (Eastern Michigan University), John Means (Hagers-town Junior College), Marguerite H. Norris (Nicholls State University), Evelyn D. Pace (Virginia Wesleyan College), Bobby L. Smith (Kent State University), Idelle Sullens (Monterey Peninsula College), Donald P. Veith (California State University—Chico), Fred White (Goucher College), and Christopher Zinn (New York University). For his fine theatrical drawings, we are grateful to Professor A.G. Smith (University of Windsor). And for their expert work in bringing this book into print, we are indebted to all the good people at Oxford University Press.

R.S.
C.H.K.
N.C.
D.S.

Contents

FICTION

POETRY

DRAMA

Contexts of Drama, 689

Drama, Literature, and Representational Art, 689
Drama and Theatrical Performance, 690
Drama and Other Literary Forms, 692
Drama and Narration, 692
Drama and Meditation, 694
Drama and Persuasion, 696

Modes of Drama, 697

FICTION

The Elements of Fiction

FICTION, FACT, AND TRUTH

A fiction is a made-up story. This definition covers a lot of territory. It includes the homemade lies we tell to protect ourselves from annoying scrutiny, and the casual jokes we hear and re-tell as polite (or impolite) conversation, as well as great visionary works of literature like Milton's *Paradise Lost* or the Bible itself. Yes, I am saying that the Bible is fiction; but before you either bristle with smug piety or nod with complacent skepticism, read a few words more. The Bible is fiction because it is a made-up story. This does not mean that it necessarily lacks truth. Nor does it mean that the Bible may not contain fact. The relation between fact and fiction is by no means as simple as one might think; and, since it is very important to an understanding of fiction, it must be considered with some care.

Fact and fiction are old acquaintances. They are both derivatives of Latin words. Fact comes from *facere*—to make or do. Fiction comes from *fingere*—to make or shape. Plain enough words, one would think—not necessarily loaded with overtones of approval or disapproval. But their fortunes in the world of words have not been equal. Fact has prospered. In our ordinary conversation, "fact" is associated with those pillars of verbal society, "reality" and "truth." "Fiction," on the other hand, is known to consort with such suspicious characters as "unreality" and "falsehood." Still, if we look into the matter, we can see that the relation of "fact" and "fiction" with "the real" and "the true" is not exactly what appears on the surface. Fact still means for us quite literally "a thing done." And fiction has never lost its meaning of "a thing made." But in what sense do things done or things made partake of truth or reality? A thing done has no real existence once it has been done. It may have consequences, and there may be many records that point to its former existence (think of the Spanish Civil War, for

3

example); but once it is done its existence is finished. A thing made, on the other hand, exists until it decays or is destroyed. Once it is finished, its existence begins (think of a Spanish Civil War story like Ernest Hemingway's *For Whom the Bell Tolls*, for example). Fact, finally, has no real existence, while fiction may last for centuries.

We can see this rather strange relation between fact and fiction more clearly if we consider one place where the two come together: the place we call history. The word "history" itself hides a double meaning. It comes from a Greek word that originally meant inquiry or investigation. But it soon acquired the two meanings that interest us here: on the one hand, history can mean "things that have happened"; on the other, it can refer to "a recorded version of things that are supposed to have happened." That is, history can mean both the events of the past and the story of these events: fact—or fiction. The very word "story" lurks in the word "history," and is derived from it. What begins as investigation must end as story. Fact, in order to survive, must become fiction. Seen in this way, fiction is not the opposite of fact, but its complement. It gives a more lasting shape to the vanishing deeds of men.

But this is, in fact, only one aspect of fiction. We *do* think of it also as something quite different from historical records or mere data. We think of it not just as made but as made-up, a non-natural, unreal product of the human imagination. It is helpful to see fiction in both the ways outlined here. It can be very factual, maintaining the closest possible correspondence between its story and things that have actually happened in the world. Or it can be very fanciful, defying our sense of life's ordinary possibilities.

Taking these two extremes as the opposite ends of a whole spectrum of fictional possibilities, between the infra-red of pure history and the ultra-violet of pure imagination, we can distinguish many shades of coloration. But all are fragments of the white radiance of truth, which is present in both history books and fairy tales, but only partly present in each—fragmented by the prism of fiction, without which we should not be able to see it at all. For truth is like ordinary light, present everywhere but invisible, and we must break it to behold it. To fracture truth in a purposeful and pleasing way—that is the job of the writer of fiction, with whatever shades from the spectrum he or she chooses to work.

FICTION: EXPERIENCE AND ANALYSIS

Though fiction itself has a real existence—a book has weight and occupies space—our experience of fiction is unreal. When we are reading a story we are not "doing" anything. We have stopped the ordinary course of our existence, severed our connections with friends and family, in order to withdraw temporarily into a private and unreal world. Our experience of fiction is more like dreaming than like our normal waking activity. It makes us physically inert yet exercises our imagination. In terms of our performing any action in it, this special world is absolutely unreal, whether we are reading a history book or a science fiction story. We can do nothing to affect either the Battle of Waterloo or the War of the Worlds. And yet, in a way, we participate. We are engaged and involved in the events we are reading about, even though powerless to alter them. We *experience* the events of a story, but without the consequences—emerging from Rudy Wiebe's *The Temptations of Big Bear,* for example, without a scratch on our bodies. Emotionally, however, and intellectually, we are different. We have experienced something.

All discussion of literature, all classes and instruction in literary matters, can have only one valid end: to prepare us for our part in the literary experience. Just as the dull routine exercises and repetitious practice for an athletic event or a dramatic performance are devoted to the end of physical and mental readiness for the actual game or play, exercises in literature are preparations for the act of reading. The successful athlete must do much "instinctively," moving faster than thought to make the most of his time. The painstaking analysis of "game movies" by football coach and players, the searching criticism of each player's reactions to every situation, the drill to counteract past errors—all these wait upon the test of the game itself. Then ability, experience, and training will reveal their quality. It is similar with reading. Classroom, teacher, the artificially assembled anthology—all these must give place to that final confrontation between individual reader and story. Except that this is not a struggle like an athletic contest, but something more intimate and more rewarding. Ideally, it is a kind of consummation—an embrace.

Everything that follows in this section is intended to help readers toward an enriched experience of fiction. Such special terminology as is presented is presented not because critical terminology is an important object of study. Its acquisition is not an end in itself. We learn terminology in order to analyze more accurately. We learn the process of analysis in order to read better.

THE SPECTRUM OF FICTION

The fictional spectrum mentioned earlier can be of use in the analysis of fiction, so long as we remember that it is just a metaphor, a handy linguistic tool to be discarded when it becomes more of a hindrance to understanding than a help. In terms of this metaphor, you will remember, it was possible to think of fiction as resembling the spectrum of color to be found in ordinary light, but in the fictional spectrum the ends were not infra-red and ultra-violet but history and fantasy.

Now only a recording angel, taking note of all the deeds of men without distorting or omitting anything, could be called a "pure" historian. And only a kind of deity, creating a world out of his own imagination, could be called a "pure" fantasist. Both ends of the spectrum are invisible to mortal eyes. All history recorded by men becomes fictional. All human fantasy involves some resemblance—however far-fetched—to life. For the student of fiction, then, the *combination* of historical and imaginative materials becomes crucial. This is so because our understanding of fiction depends on our grasping the way in which any particular work is related to life.

Life itself is neither tragic nor comic, neither sentimental nor ironic. It is a sequence of sensations, action, thoughts, and events that we try to tame with language. Every time we say a word about our existence we are engaged in this taming process. An art like fiction is a highly developed method of domestication, in which life is not merely subdued but is asked to perform tricks as well. The tricks, if well done, please us in a very complicated way. In the first place they *please* because their order and intelligibility are a welcome relief from the confusions and pressures of daily existence. In the second place this artificial order may be mastered by us and used to help *make sense of our own experience*. Having read Hemingway, Lawrence or Munro, we will begin to recognize certain situations in our existence as having a family resemblance to situations we have encountered in the pages of Lawrence, Munro or Hemingway.

Literature offers us an "escape" from life, but also provides us with new equipment for our inevitable return. It offers us an "imitation" of life. It helps us understand life, and life helps us understand fiction. We recognize aspects of ourselves and our situations in the more ordered perspectives of fiction, and we also see ideal and debased extremes of existence—both possible and impossible—that are interesting in themselves and interestingly different from our own experience. Fiction interests us because of the complicated ways in which it is at once like and unlike life—which is what we mean when we call it an "imitation." Our experience of fiction, then, involves both pleasure and understanding. We may think of understanding either as a result of the pleasurable experience of fiction or as a necessary preliminary to that pleasure. But no matter how we view the complicated relation between pleasure and understanding, we must recognize that the two are inseparable in the reading of fiction.

Now it happens that education has more to do with understanding than with pleasure. This is regrettable, perhaps, but unavoidable. In our study of fiction, then, we must concentrate on understanding, and hope that plea-- sure will follow because of the connection between the two. Understanding a work of fiction begins with recognizing what kind of fiction it is. This is where the notion of a spectrum becomes useful. We can adjust to the special qualities of any given work more readily if we begin it with a clear and flexible view of fictional possibilities.

Any attempt to give every shade of fiction a place would be cumbersome and misleading. What we want is a rough scale only, with the primary possibilities noted and located in relation to one another. Between the extremes of history and fantasy on such a scale we might locate two major points of reference something like this:

history   realism   romance   fantasy

"Realism" and "romance" are names of the two principal ways that fiction can be related to life. Realism is a matter of perception. The realist presents his impressions of the world of experience. A part of his vocabulary and other technical instruments he shares with the social scientists—especially the psychologists and sociologists. The realistic writer seeks always to give the reader a sense of the way things are, but he feels that a made-up structure of character and event can do better justice to the way things are than any attempt to copy reality directly. The realist's truth is a bit more general and typical than the reporter's fact. It may also be more vivid and memorable.

Romance is a matter of vision. The romancer presents not so much his impressions of the world as his ideas about it. The ordinary world is seen at a greater distance, and its shape and color are deliberately altered by the lenses and filters of philosophy and fantasy. In the world of romance, ideas are allowed to play less encumbered by data. Yet, though "what is" often gives way in romance to "what ought to be" or "might be," *ought* and *might* always imply what *is* by their distortion of it.

Realism and romance are not absolutely different: they share some qualities between them. Realism itself is more romantic than history or journalism. (It is not reality, after all, but real*ism*.) And romance is more realistic than fantasy. Many important works of fiction are rich and complicated blends of romance and realism. In fact, it is possible to say that the greatest works are those that successfully blend the realist's perception and the romancer's vision, giving us fictional worlds remarkably close to our sense of the actual, but skillfully shaped so as to make us intensely aware of the meaningful potential of existence.

FICTIONAL MODES AND PATTERNS

The usefulness of the concept of a fictional spectrum will depend upon our ability to adapt it to various works of fiction. Such adaptation will inevitably require a certain amount of complication. The additional concepts of fictional modes and patterns will be a step in that direction. The spectrum assumed that romance diverges from realism in one way only, along that line which leads from history to fantasy. But it is possible to see this divergence in a more complete way by observing that there are actually two quite different modes of what we have been calling romance.

We may begin by noting that there are two obvious ways that reality can be distorted by fiction, that it can be made to appear better or worse than we actually believe it to be. These distortions are ways of seeing certain aspects of reality more clearly at the expense of others. They can present a "true" picture of either the heroic or the debased side of human existence. A fictional work that presents a world better than the real world is in the mode of romance. A work that presents a fictional world worse than the real world is in the mode of anti-romance, or satire. Because they represent certain potentialities that we recognize as present in our world, both these distorted views depend on our sense of the actual to achieve their effects.

The world of romance emphasizes beauty and order. The world of satire emphasizes ugliness and disorder. The relations between individual characters and these distorted worlds constitute a crucial element of fiction, for these relations determine certain patterns or master plots that affect the shaping of the particular plot of every story. One of these master patterns deals with the kind of character who begins out of harmony with his world and is gradually educated or initiated into a harmonious situation in it. This pattern may operate in either the ordered world of romance or the chaotic world of satire, but the same pattern will have a quite different effect on us when we observe it working out in such different situations. Education that adapts the inept or foolish character for a role in the orderly world presents a comic rise that we observe with approval and pleasure. An initiation into a world of ugliness and disorder, however, amounts to corruption, an ironic rise to what Milton called a "bad eminence"; and we react with disapproval and disgust. (For some reason we find both reactions pleasurable.)

Another master pattern reverses this process of accommodation and presents us with change of another sort: the character who begins in harmony with his world but is finally rejected or destroyed by it. Again, depending on our view of the world presented, we react differently. The heroic figure who falls from his position in the orderly world through some flaw in his character is *tragic*. The lowly creature whose doom is the result of his unfortunate virtue or delicacy is *pathetic*. His fall is, ironically, a kind of rise. (It is traditionally assumed, for complicated reasons, that tragedy is superior to pathos. That assumption is not made here. These patterns are presented as descriptions only, not evaluations.)

The *comic* rise and the *tragic* fall are straightforward because the values of the orderly world represent human virtue raised to a heroic power. The *satiric* rise and *pathetic* fall are ironic because of the inverted values of the debased world. Satire and pathos debase the world in order to criticize it. Tragedy and comedy elevate it to make it acceptable. The two romantic patterns promote resignation. The two satiric patterns promote opposition.

One other pair of fictional patterns may be added to the two already considered. When characters begin and end in a harmonious relation to their respective worlds, the fictional pattern is one not of change but of movement. The characters will have adventures or encounters but will not make any fundamental change in themselves or their relation to the world around them. In this kind of story the hero himself will not be as important as the things he meets. In the romantic world the adventures of the hero will take the form of a quest or voyage that ends with his triumphant return and/or his marriage to the heroine. This pattern moves us to admiration of the wonderful, offering us more of an escape from the actual than a criticism of it. In the satiric world the adventures of a born anti-hero or rogue will parody the quest pattern, often reflecting the chaos of the debased world by becoming endless themselves. Stories of this kind are likely to end when the rogue heads for new territory or another tour of the familiar chaos. This picaresque pattern moves us to recognition and acceptance of the chaotic.

Thus, we have distinguished three pairs of fictional patterns, or six kinds in all: the comic and the satiric rise; the tragic and the pathetic fall; the heroic (romantic) and the anti-heroic (picaresque) quest. But we have done this only with regard to the fantasy worlds of romance and satire, leaving open the question of what happens as these patterns are introduced into a more realistic fictional universe. What happens is, naturally, very complicated indeed. These neat, schematic distinctions fade; the various patterns combine and interact; and values themselves are called into question: rise and fall, success and failure—all become problematic. And this problematic quality is one of the great sources of interest in realistic fiction. Realism uses the familiar patterns of education, expulsion, and quest, but often in such a way as to call into question the great issues of whether the education is beneficial, the expulsion or death justified, the quest worthwhile. Our recognition of the traces of traditional patterns in realistic fiction will be of use, then, mainly in helping us to see what questions are being raised.

Viewed historically, realism developed later than romance and satire; thus it will be useful for us to see realistic fiction as combining the elements of its predecessors in various ways. It would be a mistake, however, to think of realism as superseding the earlier forms just because it uses some of their elements in a new way. In fact, the development of realism has led to a kind of counterflow of realistic elements into the older forms of fiction, reinvigorating them with its problematical qualities. The reader of contemporary fiction in particular will require the flexibility of response that can be attained by careful attention to the workings of traditional patterns in modern fiction. But our discernment of these patterns in any work of fiction will depend on our grasp of the specific elements of that work. We must be alert to the way that *its* characters, *its* plot, and *its* point of view adapt the traditional elements we have been considering.

PLOT

Fiction is movement. A story is a story because it tells about a process of change. A person's situation changes. Or the person is changed in some way. Or our understanding of the person changes. These are the essential movements of fiction. Learning to read stories involves learning to "see" these movements, to follow them, and to interpret them. In the classroom we often—perhaps too often—put our emphasis on interpretation. But you cannot interpret what you cannot see. Thus, before getting into more complicated questions of interpretation, we want to give the plainest and most direct advice possible about how to perceive and follow fictional plotting. This advice includes things to be done while reading and things to be done after a first reading. A good story may be experienced pleasurably many times, and often a second or third reading will be more satisfying in every respect than the first time through.

1. *Look at beginnings and endings.* Movement in fiction is always movement *from* and *to*. A grasp of the start and the finish should lead to a sense of the direction taken to get *from* start *to* finish.

2. *Isolate the central characters.* The things that happen in fiction happen *to* somebody. A few major characters or even a single central character may be the real focus of our concern. Explore the situation of the major characters (or central character) at the beginning and at the end of the story. The nature of the changes revealed by this exploration should begin to suggest what the story is all about.

3. *Note the stages in all important changes.* If a character has moved from one situation to another, or one state of mind to another, the steps leading to the completed change should be illuminating. Through them the reader can get to "how" and "why." But, as always, "what" comes first.

4. *Note the things working against the movement of the story.* Usually, the interest of a story may be seen as the product of two forces: the things that work to move it toward its end, and those that work against that movement, delaying its completion. If the story moves toward a marriage, for example, consider what things delay the happy occasion. When we see the obstacles clearly, we should have a better sense of the direction of the plot itself.

5. *In a long story or novel, consider the various lines of action.* A complex fiction is likely to involve a number of actions, each with its own central character. The actions may or may not interact. The central character in one line of action may be insignificant in another. By isolating the various lines of action and separating them from one another in our

thoughts, we should gain a better sense of those things that connect them. Often these connections will lead us to thematic relations that cast a direct light on the meaning of the whole fiction.

6. *Note carefully characters or events that seem to make no contribution to plot or movement.* This negative advice is a way of moving from the plot to the meaning of a story. Often elements that are not important in the plot have a special thematic importance.

CHARACTER

The greatest mistake we can make in dealing with characters in fiction is to insist on their "reality." No character in a book is a real person. Not even if he is in a history book and is called Louis Riel. Characters in fiction are *like* real people. They are also unlike them. In realistic fiction, which includes most novels and short stories, writers have tried to emphasize the lifelikeness of their characters. This means that such writers have tried to surround these characters with details drawn from contemporary life. And they have tried to restrict the events of their narrative to things likely to happen in ordinary life. As a result, the writers of realistic fiction have had to abandon certain kinds of plots that are too fanciful for characters supposed to typify ordinary life. Such writers have tried to draw the reader away from his interest in the movement of fiction and to lead him toward an interest in character for its own sake.

Using the newly developed ideas we have learned to call psychology and sociology, the realistic writers have offered us instruction in human nature. The motivation of characters, the workings of conscience and consciousness, have been made the focal point of most novels and short stories. Perhaps the most extreme movement in this direction has been the development of the stream of consciousness technique, through which fiction writers offer us a version of mental process at the level where impressions of things seen and heard converge with confused thoughts and longings arising from the subconscious mind. In reading this kind of fiction we must check the validity of its characterization against our own sense of the way people behave. The best realists always offer us a shock of recognition through which we share their perception of human behavior.

It may be useful for us to think of character as a function of two impulses: the impulse to individualize and the impulse to typify. Great and memorable characters are the result of a powerful combination of these two impulses. We remember the special, individualizing quirks—habitual patterns of speech, action, or appearance—and we remember the way the character represents something larger than himself. These individualizing touches are part of the storyteller's art. They amuse us or engage our sympathy for the character. The typifying touches are part of a story's meaning. In realistic fiction a character is likely to be representative of a social class, a race, a profession; or he may be a recognizable psychological type, analyzable in terms of this or that "complex" or "syndrome." Or he may be a mixture of social and psychological qualities. In allegorical fiction the characters are more likely to represent philosophical positions. In a story of adventure we will encounter types belonging to the traditional pattern of romantic quest: hero, heroine, villain, monster.

The important thing for a reader to remember about characterization is that there are many varieties—and many combinations of the varieties. An adventure story may have an important realistic or allegorical dimension that will be observable in its characterizations. Characters in realistic novels may also be meaningful as illustrations of philosophical ideas or attitudes. As readers we must be alert and ready to respond to different kinds of characterization on their own terms. A story by Jorge Luis Borges and a story by James Joyce are not likely to yield equally to the same kind of reading. It is the reader's business to adapt himself to whatever fictional world he enters. It is the writer's business to make such adaptation worthwhile.

MEANING

More often than not, when we talk about a story after our experience of it, we talk about its meaning. In the classroom, "What is the theme of this work?" is a favorite question. This interpretive aspect of literary analysis is the most difficult, we should say, for the reason that in order to attempt it we must not only look carefully at the work itself but also look away from the work toward the world of ideas and experiences. Discovering themes or meanings in a work involves us in making connections between the work and the world outside it. These connections *are* the meaning. The great problem for the interpreter, then, becomes that of the validity of the thematic materials he discovers. Are these ideas *really* there? we want to know. Are they being "read out" of the story or "read into" it? Is any given set of connections between story and world necessarily implied by the story itself or are they arbitrarily imposed by an overly clever interpreter?

A story is always particular, always an instance. How do we properly move from any given instance to a general notion? When is it legitimate to conclude from the presence of a husband and wife in a story (for example) that the story is "about" marriage—that it makes a statement or raises a question about this aspect of human relations? It is impossible to provide a single method that will always work. In fact, as T. S. Eliot once observed, "There is no method except to be very intelligent." But there are certain procedures that will frequently prove helpful, even for the very intelligent.

If we isolate everything that is not just narration, description, or dialogue, some clues are likely to appear in a story. The title of a work is often a striking instance of this kind of material. Sometimes it will point our thinking about the work in a particular direction, or it will emphasize for us the importance of a particular element in the work. Like the title, passages in the writing that are themselves commentary or interpretation are of especial importance for thematic discussion.

Often, however, interpretive passages will not be presented directly by a narrator, with all his authority behind them. They will be spoken instead by a character, and this means that we must assess the reliability of the character before we decide to accept his interpretation as valid. Sometimes the narrator will be characterized to the extent that we must question even *his* reliability. In similar ways narration and description may also be colored by thematic materials. A character or a scene may be presented by the author so as to lead us toward a certain way of thinking about the materials presented. A school called "Dotheboys Hall" or a teacher named "Gradgrind" is presented to us with a name that carries some not too subtle advice as to how we are to understand the presentation.

In less obvious cases, where the author refrains from direct commentary, we must look for subtler clues. Patterns of repetition, ironic juxtaposition, the tone of the narration—devices like these must lead us to the connections between the particular world of the book and the generalized world of ideas. And the more delicate and subtle the story is, the more delicate our interpretation must be. Thus, taking care that our interpretation is rooted in the work itself is only one aspect of the problem.

The other aspect involves the outside knowledge that the interpreter brings to the work. If the story is realistic it will be understood best by those readers whose experience has equipped them with information about the aspect of reality toward which the story points. This does not mean that one must have lived the life of a Canadian trapper to understand "The Naming of Albert Johnson." But these stories do depend on the reader's having some understanding of injustice and prejudice, and some sense of the way impersonal social forces can act destructively upon individuals and even whole groups of human beings.

Often a realistic story may point to an aspect of life we have encountered but never understood, and the fiction may help us clarify and order that experience. D. H. Lawrence's story "The Rocking-Horse Winner" can teach us something about personal relations, but Lawrence requires us to bring some experience of family life to that story, for without that it must remain virtually meaningless for the reader. Fantasy and adventure are the principal ingredients of the child's literary diet, for the reason that the child lacks the experience that would make realism meaningful to him, and he lacks the learning necessary for the interpretation of complex allegorical fiction.

Often, however, allegorical fiction takes the form of fantasy or adventure, so that it can be read by the child "at one level" and by the adult on two.

Jonathan Swift's *Gulliver's Travels* has been read in that way for over two centuries. D. H. Lawrence's "The Rocking-Horse Winner" is an exciting story about a boy with a kind of magical power, but it is also a criticism of an excessively materialistic society. We call such modern allegories "fabulation," and we recognize their ancient ancestors in the simple fable and the homely parable. These two early forms of fiction will be discussed in the next part of this section, and a number of examples of modern fabulation will be found in the anthology of short stories that concludes our study of fiction.

Fiction generates its meanings in innumerable ways, but always in terms of some movement from the particular characters and events of the story to general ideas or human situations suggested by them. The reader comes to an understanding of a fictional work by locating the relevant generalities outside the work and fitting them to the specific instances within the work. The process of understanding can be crudely represented as a sequence something like this:

1. The reader determines whether the work points mainly toward experience itself (i.e., is "realistic"), or toward ideas about experience (i.e., is "allegorical"), or is self-contained.

2. Using the clues in the work, the reader sifts his or her store of general notions drawn from experience or systematic thought to find those appropriate to the specific materials of the story.

3. He or she checks back against the story to test the relevance of the general notions summoned up.

4. He or she seeks for the way the story refines, qualifies, questions, or reinforces those notions.

Something like the process described—performed not a single time but in rapid oscillation into the work and back out—should leave the reader with an understanding of the story and with an enriched store of general notions that he has been led to develop in order to understand. In addition to acquiring new notions, the reader may have refined his attitudes toward his old notions and toward experience itself. Fiction is justified not as a means of conveying ideas but as a means of generating attitudes toward ideas. The meaning of fiction must finally be seen in terms of emotions directed toward impressions of experience or toward ideas about life.

POINT OF VIEW: PERSPECTIVE AND LANGUAGE

Point of view is a technical term for the way a story is told. A stage play normally has no particular point of view: no one stands between the audience and the action. But if we *read* a play, the stage directions—the words of someone who is not a character—provide the beginnings of a special point of view. A story told all in dialogue would be similarly without a point of view. But as soon as a descriptive phrase is added—such as "he said *cruelly*" or "she *whined viciously*"—we begin to have a special viewpoint. A voice outside the action is reaching us, shaping our attitude toward the events being presented. In our experience of fiction, the attitude we develop toward the events presented, and our understanding of those events, will usually be controlled by the author through his or her technical management of point of view.

For convenience we may divide the subject of fictional viewpoint into two related parts—one dealing with the nature of the storyteller in any given fiction, the other dealing with his language. Obviously the two are not really separate. Certain kinds of narration require certain kinds of language— Duddy Kravitz must talk like Duddy Kravitz—but we may consider them apart for analytical purposes.

The nature of the storyteller is itself far from a simple matter. It involves such things as the extent to which he is himself a character whose personality affects our understanding of his statements, and the extent to which his view of events is limited in time and space or in his ability to see into the minds of various characters. The complications and refinements in fictional point of view can be classified at considerable length. But for the reader the classifications themselves are less important than his awareness of many possibilities. The reader's problem comes down to knowing how to take the things presented to him. This means paying special attention to any limitations in the narrator's viewpoint. If the viewpoint in the story is "partial"—in the sense of incomplete or in the sense of biased—the reader must be ready to compensate in appropriate ways.

The language of narration presents a similar problem for the reader—that is, a problem of adjustment and compensation. Of all the dimensions of language that can be considered, two are especially important for the reader of fiction. Both these dimensions may be seen as ways in which wit—or artistic intelligence—operates through language. One has to do with *tone*, or the way unstated attitudes are conveyed through language. The other has to do with *metaphor*, or the way language can convey the richest and most delicate kinds of understanding by bringing together different images and ideas. Consider first this small passage from Virginia Woolf's novel *Mrs. Dalloway:*

> But Sir William Bradshaw stopped at the door to look at a picture. He looked in the corner for the engraver's name. His wife looked too. Sir William Bradshaw was so interested in art.

What is the tone of this? Sarcastic, I should say. The paragraph asks us to be critical of the Bradshaws, but it does not do so directly. It uses the indirection of verbal irony in which the real meaning is different from the apparent sense of the words. The last sentence might be read aloud with a drawn-out emphasis on the word "soooo." How do we know this? How do we supply the appropriate tone of voice for words that we see on the page but do not hear prounounced? We pay attention to the clues given. In *Mrs. Dalloway* the Bradshaws appear in a similar light several times; so that by this, their last appearance, we have been prepared to regard them unsympathetically. But just on the strength of these four sentences we should be able to catch the tone.

The banal "Dick and Jane" sentence patterns reinforce the banality of an approach to art by way of the artist's name. Sir William looks not at the picture itself but at the signature. The implication of this action is that (a) he cannot tell who the artist is by considering the work alone, and (b) he attaches too much importance to the name. His interest in art is fraudulent. Thus, the statement that he is "so" interested in art conflicts with both the actions narrated and the tone of the narration. We resolve the conflict by reading the sentence as *ironic*, meaning the opposite of what it seems to say, and acquiring thereby a sarcastic tone. The way his wife's behavior mechanically mimics his own adds another satiric dimension to the little scene. As an earlier passage in the novel has revealed, she has no life of her own but has been reduced by him to the status of an object:

> Fifteen years ago she had gone under. It was nothing you could put your finger on; there had been no scene, no snap; only the slow sinking, water-logged, of her will into his.

Thus, the short sentence—"His wife looked too"—picks up the earlier statement about the "submersion" of her will in his, and reminds us of it with satiric brevity. Catching the tone of a passage is a matter of paying attention to clues in sentence pattern and choice of words, and also of keeping in mind the whole context of the story we are reading. The more we read a particular author, the better we become at catching her tone—at perceiving the emotional shades that color the sense of her words.

The second passage quoted from *Mrs. Dalloway* (which comes first in the book) is also a good introductory example of a writer's use of metaphor. The expression "gone under" has been used often enough to refer to defeat or failure—so often, in fact, that it is quite possible to use it without any sense that it is metaphorical. But actually the notion of drowning—going under water to the point of death—is present in the expression. A writer who, like

Virginia Woolf, is sensitive to metaphor, can pick up the submerged (!) implications of such an expression and use them to strengthen her meaning: "the slow sinking, water-logged, of her will into his." The metaphor—which implicitly compares her to a floating object and him to the engulfing waters—conveys a sense of how slowly and inexorably this process has taken place, and it generates in us an appropriate feeling of horror at a human being's lingering destruction.

Similar metaphors can be used in different ways. In another part of the same novel, Virginia Woolf employs the metaphor of drowning in a related but distinct context. When Peter Walsh, who wanted to marry Clarissa Dalloway in his youth, returns from India to tell her that he is in love with a young woman whom he intends to marry, Mrs. Dalloway reacts in this way:

> "In love!" she said. That he at his age should be sucked under in his little bow-tie by that monster! And there's no flesh on his neck; his hands are red; and he's six months older than I am! her eye flashed back to her; but in her heart she felt, all the same, he is in love. He has that, she felt; he is in love.

Love is seen here as a monstrous whirlpool that sucks people under. It is dangerous and destructive: one loses one's identity when sucked in by that monster. But it is also heroic to be involved in such dangerous matters. While her "eye" tells Mrs. Dalloway that Peter is unheroic and even ridiculous, with his little bow tie and skinny neck, her "heart" accepts the heroism of this venture. It is absurd to "be sucked under" in a "little bow-tie," but it is also intensely real: "He has that, she felt; he is in love." By comparing these two metaphors of drowning we can see more accurately certain dimensions of Virginia Woolf's view of marriage: it involves a submergence or submission, but a violent conquest by an emotional whirlpool is superior to a "slow sinking, water-logged," of one will into another. We need not go outside the novel to understand this discrimination, but when we learn or remember that in a state of depression Ms. Woolf took her own life by drowning, we get a hint of why this metaphor has such intensity in her hands.

These uses of the metaphor of drowning are actually just brief examples of the way metaphorical possibilities can be exploited in the language of fiction. We present now a fuller example of metaphorical development, for the student to explore. Marcel Proust's multi-volume novel, *The Remembrance of Things Past*, is constructed upon the recovery of the past in the memory of the central character and narrator, Marcel. The process of recollection is described in a famous passage in which, on being given a piece of cake (a *madeleine*) dipped in tea, Marcel suddenly finds that the taste of this morsel has brought to mind much that he had forgotten. In the part of this passage quoted here, Marcel first discusses the persistence of sensations of taste and smell, and then considers the manner in which recollection can emerge from these sensations. The passage should be read with an eye to the metaphors (including similes) operative in it:

> But when from a long-distant past nothing subsists, after the people are dead, after the things are broken and scattered, still, alone, more fragile, but with more vitality, more unsubstantial, more persistent, more faithful, the smell and taste of things remain poised a long time, like souls, ready to remind us, waiting and hoping for their moment, amid the ruins of all the rest; and bear unfaltering, in the tiny and almost impalpable drop of their essence, the vast structure of recollection.
>
> And once I had recognised the taste of the crumb of madeleine soaked in her decoction of lime-flowers which my aunt used to give me (although I did not yet know and must long postpone the discovery of why this memory made me so happy) immediately the old grey house upon the street, where her room was, rose up like the scenery of a theatre, to attach itself to the little pavilion, opening on to the garden, which had been built out behind it for my parents (the isolated panel which until that moment had been all that I could see); and with the house the town, from morning to night and in all weathers, the Square where I was sent before luncheon, the streets along which I used to run errands, the country roads we took when it was fine. And just as the Japanese amuse themselves by filling a porcelain bowl with water and steeping in it little crumbs of paper which until then are without character or form, but, the moment they become wet, stretch themselves and bend, take on colour and distinctive shape, become flowers or houses or people, permanent and recognisable, so in that moment all the flowers in our garden and in M. Swann's park, and the water-lilies on the Vivonne and the good folk of the village and their little dwellings and the parish church and the whole of Combray and of its surroundings, taking their proper shapes and growing solid, sprang into being, town and gardens alike, from my cup of tea.

While it is not my intention to encroach too much on what should be matter for the student's consideration and discussion, I should point out two of the principal metaphors in the passage and offer a suggestion or two about them. The first is the comparison of the smell and taste of things to "souls" in whose "essence" a shape or structure is housed. Proust is here using an ancient Greek notion of the soul as an essence that gives its shape to the body it inhabits. The second, the final metaphor of the passage, takes the form of an extended analogy: "*just as* the Japanese . . . *so* in that moment. . . ." In examining Proust's use of this particular metaphor, the student might begin by considering the ways in which the metaphor is appropriate to the situation—that is, to both the eating of a cake dipped in tea and the ensuing recovery of the past. Beyond that, he might consider how the Japanese paper metaphor is related to the soul metaphor, and how both of these are related to the theatrical simile ("like the scenery") that links them.

Finally, this consideration of metaphor should lead back to an awareness of tone. Though this passage is a translation from the original French, it captures the tone of the original with high fidelity. How would you describe this tone? How should the passage sound if read aloud? What is the function of the repeated use of "and" in the last sentence (which is the last sentence in a whole section of the book)? How is the tone related to the metaphoric structure and the meaning of the passage? In sum, how do these two most important dimensions of the art of language—tone and metaphor—operate in this passage to control the response of a sensitive and careful reader?

In getting at this question the student might try to paraphrase the passage without its metaphors and tonal qualities. Considering such a paraphrase, he might then ask to what extent the meaning *is* paraphrasable, and to what extent the meaning requires the images and rhythms of the passage itself.

DESIGN: JUXTAPOSITION AND REPETITION IN THE STRUCTURE OF FICTION

When we look at a painting up close, we can see its details clearly and the texture of its brush strokes, but we cannot really see it as a whole. When we back away, we lose our perception of these minute qualities but gain, with this new perspective, a sense of its design. Similarly, as we read a story, we are involved in its details. And in a story we are involved especially because we experience it as a flow of words in time, bringing us impressions and ideas, moving us emotionally and stirring us intellectually. It is natural to back away from a painting and see it as a whole. But it is less natural and more difficult to get a similar perspective on a book. We can never "see" it all at once. Yet design is an important part of the writer's art, and a sense of design is essential to a full reading experience.

Design in fiction takes many forms, but these may be seen as mainly of two kinds. One has to do with juxtaposition: with what is put next to what in the arrangement of the story. The other has to do with repetition: with images, ideas, or situations that are repeated—often with interesting variations—in the course of the narrative. Juxtaposition is more important in some kinds of fiction than it is in others. If a single action is presented in a simple, chronological arrangement, the order of events is not likely to assume any special significance. But if the action is rearranged in time so that we encounter events out of their chronological sequence—through flashbacks or some other device—the order should be given some attention. We must look for reasons behind this manipulation of chronology by the author. Why has he chosen to place this particular scene from the "past" next to this particular scene in the "present"? Similarly, if we are following two actions in one story, now one and now the other, we should look for reasons why an incident from one sequence should be placed next to a particular incident in the other.

Often we will find interesting parallels: similar situations that amount to a kind of repetition with variation. If character A gets into a situation and takes one kind of action, while character B, in a similar situation, takes a different action, we should be able to compare the two and contrast their distincitve behavior, thus learning more about both. This kind of comparison can also lead us quite properly to generalizations about the meaning of a work.

Significant kinds of repetition occur also in sections of a story that are not placed next to one another. This kind of repetition is an important element of design, and serves to tie separate parts of a story together, enriching and strengthening the whole structure. Structure in fiction is a very complicated notion, because it involves so many factors. We can think of structure in one sense as the elements that shape our experience as we move through the story. In this sense structure is close to plot. We can also think of structure as the elements that enable us to see a meaningful pattern in the whole work. In this sense structure is close to design. For if plot has to do with the dynamics or movement of fiction, design has to do with the statics of fiction—the way we see a whole story after we have stopped moving through it. When we become aware of design in reading, so that one part of a story reminds us of parts we have read earlier, we are actually involved in a movement counter to our progress through from beginning to end. Plot wants to move us along; design wants to delay our movement, to make us pause and "see." The counteraction of these two forces is one of the things which enrich our experience of fiction.

Design is often a matter of the repetition of images or metaphors. In considering the metaphors of drowning in *Mrs. Dalloway*, we have already begun an examination of the way metaphoric design can tie together quite different characters and situations. Now we present a striking example of a rather different use of repetition in the design of a story. This is a case in which two episodes in the life of the same character—separated both by pages of our reading and by weeks in the life of the character—are brought together into powerful contrast by means of repetition with variation.

At the end of the second chapter of James Joyce's novel *A Portrait of the Artist as a Young Man*, the young man of the title, Stephen Dedalus, has been led by the urgings of physical desire into the arms of a prostitute. This is the last paragraph of that chapter:

> With a sudden movement she bowed his head and joined her lips to his and he read the meaning of her movements in her frank uplifted eyes. It was too much for him. He closed his eyes, surrendering himself to her, body and mind, conscious of nothing in the world but the dark pressure of her softly parting lips. They pressed upon his brain as upon his lips as though they were the vehicle of vague speech; and between them he felt an unknown and timid pressure, darker than the swoon of sin, softer than sound or odour.

By the end of the third chapter, Joyce has taken Stephen Dedalus through a period of disgust, remorse, and repentance. In the last paragraphs of the chapter we find Stephen receiving Holy Communion:

He knelt before the altar with his classmates, holding the altar cloth with them over a living rail of hands. His hands were trembling, and his soul trembled as he heard the priest pass with the ciborium from communicant to communicant.

—*Corpus Domini nostri.*

Could it be? He knelt there sinless and timid: and he would hold upon his tongue the host and God would enter his purified body.

—*In vitam eternam. Amen.*

Another life! A life of grace and virtue and happiness! It was true.

—*Corpus Domini nostri.*

The ciborium had come to him.

In the last sentence of the second chapter, Stephen felt the woman's tongue, pressing through her kiss—"an unknown and timid pressure." In the last lines of the third chapter, his tongue receives the body of Our Lord. Could the contrast be made more striking, or more rich in emotional and intellectual implications? Design here is powerfully carrying out Joyce's intention, which is to make us see Stephen poised between sinful and holy extremes, both of which attract him powerfully but neither of which can hold him finally—as the later chapters demonstrate. The focus on tongues in these two episodes is the crucial repeated element that makes the contrast Joyce wishes. And in the context of the whole story, it reminds us that tongues are not only for kissing or receiving the sacrament. They are also instruments of expression. Stephen ultimately must strive to express himself as an artist of languages, using his gift of tongues. In these two episodes, Stephen has been passive, the receiver. Later he will learn to speak out.

What we have been considering is the way that an object—in this case the tongue—can by its use in a fictional design acquire a metaphorical value that points in the direction of meaning. When this happens, the object becomes a symbol.

A Collection of
Modern Fiction

Fabulation, Realism, Metafiction

FABULATION: *INTRODUCTION*

Modern fabulation looks back to the ancient forms of fable and parable, but instead of leading us toward a clear moral or spiritual conclusion, modern fabling may simply raise a question or play with an idea. Thus, Kafka's parables bear upon the impossibility of reaching final interpretations: they grow out of the gap between literal and figurative levels of meaning, a gap crossed so easily in the fables of Aesop or the parables of Jesus. What all the works of fabulation here collected have in common is a concern for ideas and values rather than for the social surface of existence or the psychological depths of character—or even our notion of what is possible or impossible in this world. Some of these modern tales and fables approach realism in one way or another. There is a good deal of social detail in "The Rocking-Horse Winner," for instance, or in "The Magic Barrel." In fact, each one of them has its realistic dimensions. But in every case there is at least one break with what we recognize as normal or probable; there is some moving away from realism for the sake of ideas that may ordinarily be concealed by the surface of reality.

The justification for this kind of fabling lies precisely in the way that it can open up questions of value for us, and prompt us to consider the assumptions upon which we act. Where ancient fables tried to settle questions of behavior, modern fables try to unsettle, to disturb, patterns of thought and action that have become so habitual that they conceal important

23

dimensions of existence. In studying or discussing such tales it is most important to ask what ideas and values are called into question by the tale in question. Often, the best way to do that is to locate the most *fabulous* elements in each work and ask why the author chose to break with ordinary probabilities or possibilities at this particular point. With this question in mind, it should be possible to examine the way any given feature of a fable relates to the larger concerns of the whole story.

NATHANIEL HAWTHORNE
1804–1864

Born in Salem, Massachusetts, at a time when the American revolution was still living history and the Puritan heritage of Salem was very much alive, Hawthorne absorbed its preoccupation with sin and its remembrance of witch-hunts. Four years at Bowdoin College in Maine, a job at the Boston Custom House, and a short stay at Brook Farm—an idealistic commune that ran into practical problems—broadened his horizons, but his best work came from brooding over the past more than from observation of the present. He called his short fiction "tales" and his longer works "romances," insisting that his imagination have a certain latitude in which to work. He knew what he was about. *The Scarlet Letter* (1850) has become a classic of world literature and many of his shorter tales have proved equally durable.

My Kinsman, Major Molineux

After the kings of Great Britain had assumed the right of appointing the colonial governors, the measures of the latter seldom met with the ready and generous approbation which had been paid to those of their predecessors, under the original charters. The people looked with most jealous scrutiny to the exercise of power which did not emanate from themselves, and they usually rewarded their rulers with slender gratitude for the compliances by which, in softening their instructions from beyond the sea, they had incurred the reprehension of those who gave them. The annals of Massachusetts Bay will inform us, that of six governors in the space of about forty years from the surrender of the old charter, under James II, two were imprisoned by a popular insurrection; a third, as Hutchinson inclines to believe, was driven from the province by the whizzing of a musket-ball; a fourth, in the opinion of the same historian, was hastened to his grave by continual bickerings with the House of

Representatives; and the remaining two, as well as their successors, till the Revolution, were favored with few and brief intervals of peaceful sway. The inferior members of the court party, in times of high political excitement, led scarcely a more desirable life. These remarks may serve as a preface to the following adventures, which chanced upon a summer night, not far from a hundred years ago.[1] The reader, in order to avoid a long and dry detail of colonial affairs, is requested to dispense with an account of the train of circumstances that had caused much temporary inflammation of the popular mind.

It was near nine o'clock of a moonlight evening, when a boat crossed the ferry with a single passenger, who had obtained his conveyance at that unusual hour by the promise of an extra fare. While he stood on the landing-place, searching in either pocket for the means of fulfilling his agreement, the ferryman lifted a lantern, by the aid of which, and the newly risen moon, he took a very accurate survey of the stranger's figure. He was a youth of barely eighteen years, evidently country-bred, and now, as it should seem, upon his first visit to town. He was clad in a coarse gray coat, well worn, but in excellent repair; his under garments were durably constructed of leather, and fitted tight to a pair of serviceable and well-shaped limbs; his stockings of blue yarn were the incontrovertible work of a mother or a sister; and on his head was a three-cornered hat, which in its better days had perhaps sheltered the graver brow of the lad's father. Under his left arm was a heavy cudgel formed of an oak sapling, and retaining a part of the hardened root; and his equipment was completed by a wallet, not so abundantly stocked as to incommode the vigorous shoulders on which it hung. Brown, curly hair, well-shaped features, and bright, cheerful eyes were nature's gifts, and worth all that art could have done for his adornment.

The youth, one of whose names was Robin, finally drew from his pocket the half of a little province bill of five shillings, which, in the depreciation in that currency, did but satisfy the ferryman's demand, with the surplus of a sexangular piece of parchment, valued at three pence. He then walked forward into the town, with as light a step as if his day's journey had not already exceeded thirty miles, and with as eager an eye as if he were entering London city, instead of the little metropolis of a New England colony. Before Robin had proceeded far, however, it occurred to him that he knew not whither to direct his steps; so he paused, and looked up and down the narrow street, scrutinizing the small and mean wooden buildings that were scattered on either side.

"This low hovel cannot be my kinsman's dwelling," thought he,

1. The time of this tale is the eve of the American revolution. The place is Boston.

"nor yonder old house, where the moonlight enters at the broken casement; and truly I see none hereabouts that might be worthy of him. It would have been wise to inquire my way of the ferryman, and doubtless he would have gone with me, and earned a shilling from the Major for his pains. But the next man I meet will do as well."

He resumed his walk, and was glad to perceive that the street now became wider, and the houses more respectable in their appearance. He soon discerned a figure moving on moderately in advance, and hastened his steps to overtake it. As Robin drew nigh, he saw that the passenger was a man in years, with a full periwig of gray hair, a wide-skirted coat of dark cloth, and silk stockings rolled above his knees. He carried a long and polished cane, which he struck down perpendicularly before him at every step; and at regular intervals he uttered two successive hems, of a peculiarly solemn and sepulchral intonation. Having made these observations, Robin laid hold of the skirt of the old man's coat, just when the light from the open door and windows of a barber's shop fell upon both their figures.

"Good evening to you, honored sir," said he, making a low bow, and still retaining his hold of the skirt. "I pray you tell me whereabouts is the dwelling of my kinsman, Major Molineux."

The youth's question was uttered very loudly; and one of the barbers, whose razor was descending on a well-soaped chin, and another who was dressing a Ramillies wig, left their occupations, and came to the door. The citizen, in the mean time, turned a long-favored countenance upon Robin, and answered him in a tone of excessive anger and annoyance. His two sepulchral hems, however, broke into the very centre of his rebuke, with most singular effect, like a thought of the cold grave obtruding among wrathful passions.

"Let go my garment, fellow! I tell you, I know not the man you speak of. What! I have authority, I have—hem, hem—authority; and if this be the respect you show for your betters, your feet shall be brought acquainted with the stocks[2] by daylight, tomorrow morning!"

Robin released the old man's skirt, and hastened away, pursued by an ill-mannered roar of laughter from the barber's shop. He was at first considerably surprised by the result of his question, but, being a shrewd youth, soon thought himself able to account for the mystery.

"This is some country representative," was his conclusion, "who has never seen the inside of my kinsman's door, and lacks the

2. The stocks were an outdoor engine of imprisonment.

breeding to answer a stranger civilly. The man is old, or verily—I might be tempted to turn back and smite him on the nose. Ah, Robin, Robin! even the barber's boys laugh at you for choosing such a guide! You will be wiser in time, friend Robin."

He now became entangled in a succession of crooked and narrow streets, which crossed each other, and meandered at no great distance from the water-side. The smell of tar was obvious to his nostrils, the masts of vessels pierced the moonlight above the tops of the buildings, and the numerous signs, which Robin paused to read, informed him that he was near the centre of business. But the streets were empty, the shops were closed, and lights were visible only in the second stories of a few dwelling-houses. At length, on the corner of a narrow lane, through which he was passing, he beheld the broad countenance of a British hero swinging before the door of an inn, whence proceeded the voices of many guests. The casement of one of the lower windows was thrown back, and a very thin curtain permitted Robin to distinguish a party at supper, round a well-furnished table. The fragrance of the good cheer steamed forth into the outer air, and the youth could not fail to recollect that the last remnant of his travelling stock of provision had yielded to his morning appetite, and that noon had found and left him dinnerless.

"Oh, that a parchment three-penny might give me a right to sit down at yonder table!" said Robin, with a sigh. "But the Major will make me welcome to the best of his victuals; so I will even step boldly in, and inquire my way to his dwelling."

He entered the tavern, and was guided by the murmur of voices and the fumes of tobacco to the public-room. It was a long and low apartment, with oaken walls, grown dark in the continual smoke, and a floor which was thickly sanded, but of no immaculate purity. A number of persons—the larger part of whom appeared to be mariners, or in some way connected with the sea—occupied the wooden benches, or leather-bottomed chairs, conversing on various matters, and occasionally lending their attention to some topic of general interest. Three or four little groups were draining as many bowls of punch, which the West India trade had long since made a familiar drink in the colony. Others, who had the appearance of men who lived by regular and laborious handicraft, preferred the insulated bliss of an unshared potation, and became more taciturn under its influence. Nearly all, in short, evinced a predilection for the Good Creature in some of its various shapes, for this is a vice to which, as Fast Day sermons of a hundred years ago will testify, we have a long hereditary claim. The only guests to whom Robin's sympathies inclined him were two or three sheepish countrymen, who were using the inn somewhat after the fashion of a Turkish caravansary; they had gotten themselves into the darkest corner of the room, and heedless of the Nicotian atmosphere, were supping on the bread of their own ovens, and the bacon cured in their own chimney-smoke. But though Robin felt a sort of brotherhood with these strangers, his eyes were attracted from them to a person who stood near the door, holding whispered conversation with a group of ill-dressed associates. His features were separately striking almost to grotesqueness, and the whole face left a deep impression on the memory. The forehead bulged out into a double prominence, with a vale between; the nose came boldly forth in an irregular curve, and its bridge was of more than a finger's breadth; the eyebrows were deep and shaggy, and the eyes glowed beneath them like fire in a cave.

While Robin deliberated of whom to inquire respecting his kinsman's dwelling, he was accosted by the innkeeper, a little man in a stained white apron, who had come to pay his professional welcome to the stranger. Being in the second generation from a French Protestant, he seemed to have inherited the courtesy of his parent nation; but no variety of circumstances was ever known to change his voice from the one shrill note in which he now addressed Robin.

"From the country, I presume, sir?" said he, with a profound bow. "Beg leave to congratulate you on your arrival, and trust you intend a long stay with us. Fine town here, sir, beautiful buildings, and much that may interest a stranger. May I hope for the honor of your commands in respect to supper?"

"The man sees a family likeness! the rogue has guessed that I am related to the Major!" thought Robin, who had hitherto experienced little superfluous civility.

All eyes were now turned on the country lad, standing at the door, in his worn three-cornered hat, gray coat, leather breeches, and blue yarn stockings, leaning on an oaken cudgel, and bearing a wallet on his back.

Robin replied to the courteous innkeeper, with such an assumption of confidence as befitted the Major's relative. "My honest friend," he said, "I shall make it a point to patronize your house on some occasion, when"—here he could not help lowering his voice— "when I may have more than a parchment three-pence in my pocket. My present business," continued he, speaking with lofty confidence, "is merely to inquire my way to the dwelling of my kinsman, Major Molineux."

There was a sudden and general movement in the room, which Robin interpreted as expressing the eagerness of each individual to become his guide. But the innkeeper turned his eyes to a written paper on the wall, which he read, or seemed to read, with occasional recurrences to the young man's figure.

"What have we here?" said he, breaking his speech into little dry fragments. " 'Left the house of the subscriber, bounden servant, Hezekiah Mudge,—had on, when he went away, gray coat, leather breeches, master's third-best hat. One pound currency reward to whosoever shall lodge him in any jail of the providence.' Better trudge, boy; better trudge!"

Robin had begun to draw his hand towards the lighter end of the oak cudgel, but a strange hostility in every countenance induced him to relinquish his purpose of breaking the courteous innkeeper's head. As he turned to leave the room, he encountered a sneering glance from the bold-featured personage whom he had before noticed; and no sooner was he beyond the door, than he heard a general laugh, in which the innkeeper's voice might be distinguished, like the dropping of small stones into a kettle.

"Now, is it not strange," thought Robin, with his usual shrewdness,—"is it not strange that the confession of an empty pocket should outweigh the name of my kinsman, Major Molineux? Oh, if I had one of those grinning rascals in the woods, where I and my oak sapling grew up together, I would teach him that my arm is heavy though my purse be light!"

On turning the corner of the narrow lane, Robin found himself in a spacious street, with an unbroken line of lofty houses on each side, and a steepled building at the upper end, whence the ringing of a bell announced the hour of nine. The light of the moon, and the lamps from the numerous shop-windows, discovered people promenading on the pavement, and amongst them Robin had hoped to recognize his hitherto inscrutable relative. The result of his former inquiries made him unwilling to hazard another, in a scene of such publicity, and he determined to walk slowly and silently up the street, thrusting his face close to that of every elderly gentleman, in search of the Major's lineaments. In his progress, Robin encountered many gay and gallant figures. Embroidered garments of showy colors, enormous periwigs, gold-laced hats, and silver-hilted swords glided past him and dazzled his optics. Travelled youths, imitators of the European fine gentlemen of the period, trod jauntily along, half dancing to the fashionable tunes which they hummed, and making poor Robin ashamed of his quiet and natural gait. At length, after many pauses to examine the gorgeous display of goods in the shop-windows, and after suffering some rebukes for the impertinence of his scrutiny into people's faces, the Major's kinsman found himself near the steepled building, still unsuccessful in his search. As yet, however, he had seen only one side of the thronged street; so Robin crossed, and continued the same sort of inquisition down the opposite pavement, with stronger hopes than the philosopher seeking an honest man, but with no better fortune. He had arrived about midway towards the lower end, from which his course began, when he overheard the approach of some one who struck down a cane on the flag-stones at every step, uttering at regular intervals, two sepulchral hems.

"Mercy on us!" quoth Robin, recognizing the sound.

Turning a corner, which chanced to be close at his right hand, he hastened to pursue his researches in some other part of the town. His patience now was wearing low, and he seemed to feel more fatigue from his rambles since he crossed the ferry, than from his journey of several days on the other side. Hunger also pleaded loudly within him, and Robin began to balance the propriety of demanding, violently, and with lifted cudgel, the necessary guidance from the first solitary passenger whom he should meet. While a resolution to this effect was gaining strength, he entered a street of mean appearance, on either side of which a row of ill-built houses was straggling towards the harbor. The moonlight fell upon no passenger along the whole extent, but in the third domicile which Robin passed there was a half-opened door, and his keen glance detected a woman's garment within.

"My luck may be better here," said he to himself.

Accordingly, he approached the door, and beheld it shut closer as he did so; yet an open space remained, sufficing for the fair occupant to observe the stranger, without a corresponding display on her part. All that Robin could discern was a strip of scarlet petticoat, and the occasional sparkle of an eye, as if the moonbeams were trembling on some bright thing.

"Pretty mistress," for I may call her so with a good conscience, thought the shrewd youth, since I know nothing to the contrary,— "my sweet pretty mistress, will you be kind enough to tell me whereabouts I must seek the dwelling of my kinsman, Major Molineux?"

Robin's voice was plaintive and winning, and the female, seeing nothing to be shunned in the handsome country youth, thrust open the door, and came forth into the moonlight. She was a dainty little figure, with a white neck, round arms, and a slender waist, at the extremity of which her scarlet petticoat jutted out over a hoop, as if she were standing in a balloon. Moreover, her face was oval and pretty, her hair dark beneath the little cap, and her bright eyes possessed a sly freedom, which triumphed over those of Robin.

"Major Molineux dwells here," said this fair woman.

Now, her voice was the sweetest Robin had heard that night, yet he could not help doubting whether that sweet voice spoke Gospel truth. He looked up and down the mean street, and then surveyed the house before which they stood. It was a small, dark edifice of two stories, the second of which projected over the lower floor, and the front apartment had the aspect of a shop for pretty commodities.

"Now, truly, I am in luck," replied Robin, cunningly, "and so indeed is my kinsman, the Major, in having so pretty a house-keeper. But I prithee trouble him to step to the door; I will deliver him a message from his friends in the country, and then go back to my lodgings at the inn."

"Nay, the Major has been abed this hour or more," said the lady of the scarlet petticoat; "and it would be to little purpose to disturb him to-night, seeing his evening draught was of the strongest. But he is a kind-hearted man, and it would be as much as my life's worth to let a kinsman of his turn away from the door. You are the good old gentleman's very picture, and I could swear that was his rainy-weather hat. Also he has garments very much resembling those leather small-clothes. But come in, I pray, for I bid you hearty welcome in his name."

So saying, the fair and hospitable dame took our hero by the hand; and the touch was light, and the force was gentleness, and though Robin read in her eyes what he did not hear in her words, yet the slender-waisted woman in the scarlet petticoat proved stronger than the athletic country youth. She had drawn his half-willing footsteps nearly to the threshold, when the opening of a door in the neighborhood startled the Major's housekeeper, and, leaving the Major's kinsman, she vanished speedily into her own domicile. A heavy yawn preceded the appearance of a man, who, like the Moonshine of Pyramus and Thisbe, carried a lantern, need-lessly aiding his sister luminary in the heavens. As he walked sleepily up the street, he turned his broad, dull face on Robin, and displayed a long staff, spiked at the end.

"Home, vagabond, home!" said the watchman, in accents that seemed to fall asleep as soon as they were uttered. "Home, or we'll set you in the stocks by peep of day!"

"This is the second hint of the kind," thought Robin. "I wish they would end my difficulties, by setting me there to-night."

Nevertheless, the youth felt an instinctive antipathy towards the guardian of midnight order, which at first prevented him from ask-ing his usual question. But just when the man was about to vanish behind the corner, Robin resolved not to lose the opportunity, and shouted lustily after him,—

"I say, friend! will you guide me to the house of my kinsman, Major Molineux?"

The watchman made no reply, but turned the corner and was gone; yet Robin seemed to hear the sound of drowsy laughter steal-ing along the solitary street. At that moment, also, a pleasant titter saluted him from the open window above his head; he looked up, and caught the sparkle of a saucy eye; a round arm beckoned to him, and next he heard light footsteps descending the staircase within. But Robin, being of the household of a New England clergyman, was a good youth, as well as a shrewd one; so he resisted temptation, and fled away.

He now roamed desperately, and at random, through the town, almost ready to believe that a spell was on him, like that by which a wizard of his country had once kept three pursuers wandering, a whole winter night, within twenty paces of the cottage which they sought. The streets lay before him, strange and desolate, and the lights were extinguished in almost every house. Twice, however, little parties of men, among whom Robin distinguished individuals in outlandish attire, came hurrying along; but, though on both occasions, they paused to address him, such intercourse did not at all enlighten his perplexity. They did but utter a few words in some language of which Robin knew nothing, and perceiving his inability to answer, bestowed a curse upon him in plain English and hastened away. Finally, the lad determined to knock at the door of every mansion that might appear worthy to be occupied by his kinsman, trusting that perseverance would overcome the fatality that had hitherto thwarted him. Firm in this resolve, he was passing beneath the walls of a church, which formed the corner of two streets, when, as he turned into the shade of its steeple, he encountered a bulky stranger, muffled in a cloak. The man was proceeding with the speed of earnest business, but Robin planted himself full before him, holding the oak cudgel with both hands across his body as a bar to further passage.

"Halt, honest man, and answer me a question," said he, very resolutely. "Tell me, this instant, whereabouts is the dwelling of my kinsman, Major Molineux!"

"Keep your tongue between your teeth, fool, and let me pass!" said a deep, gruff voice, which Robin partly remembered. "Let me pass, or I'll strike you to the earth!"

"No, no, neighbor!" cried Robin, flourishing his cudgel, and then thrusting its larger end close to the man's muffled face. "No, no, I'm not the fool you take me for, nor do you pass till I have an answer to my question. Whereabouts is the dwelling of my kinsman, Major Molineux?"

The stranger, instead of attempting to force his passage, stepped back into the moonlight, unmuffled his face, and stared full into that of Robin.

"Watch here an hour, and Major Molineux will pass by," said he.

Robin gazed with dismay and astonishment on the unprecedented physiognomy of the speaker. The forehead with its double prominence, the broad hooked nose, the shaggy eyebrows, and fiery eyes were those which he had noticed at the inn, but the man's complexion had undergone a singular, or more properly, a twofold change. One side of the face blazed an intense red, while the other was black as midnight, the divison line being in the broad bridge of the nose; and a mouth which seemed to extend from ear to ear was black or red, in contrast to the color of the cheek.[3] The effect was as if two individual devils, a fiend of fire and a fiend of darkness had united themselves to form this infernal visage. The stranger grinned in Robin's face, muffled his party-colored features, and was out of sight in a moment.

"Strange things we travellers see!" ejaculated Robin.

He seated himself, however, upon the steps of the church-door, resolving to wait the appointed time for his kinsman. A few moments were consumed in philosophical speculations upon the species of man who had just left him; but having settled this point shrewdly, rationally, and satisfactorily, he was compelled to look elsewhere for his amusement. And first he threw his eyes along the street. It was of more respectable appearance than most of those into which he had wandered; and the moon, creating, like the imaginative power, a beautiful strangeness in familiar objects, gave something of romance to a scene that might not have possessed it in the light of day. The irregular and often quaint architecture of the houses, some of whose roofs were broken into numerous little peaks, while others ascended, steep and narrow, into a single point, and others again were square; the pure snow-white of some of their complexions, the aged darkness of others, and the thousand sparklings, reflected from bright substances in the walls of many; these matters engaged Robin's attention for a while, and then began to grow wearisome. Next he endeavored to define the forms of distant objects, starting away, with almost ghostly indistinctness, just as his eye appeared to grasp them; and finally he took a minute survey of an edifice which stood on the opposite side of the street, directly in front of the church-door, where he was stationed. It was a large, square mansion, distinguished from its neighbors by a balcony, which rested on tall pillars, and by an elaborate Gothic window, communicating therewith.

"Perhaps this is the very house I have been seeking," thought Robin.

Then he strove to speed away the time, by listening to a murmur which swept continually along the street, yet was scarcely audible, except to an unaccustomed ear like his; it was a low, dull, dreamy sound, compounded of many noises, each of which was at too great

3. The disguise of an Indian in war paint was much used by the early revolutionaires, as in the Boston tea party.

a distance to be separately heard. Robin marvelled at this snore of a sleeping town, and marvelled more whenever its continuity was broken by now and then a distant shout, apparently loud where it originated. But altogether it was a sleep-inspiring sound, and, to shake off its drowsy influence, Robin arose, and climbed a window-frame, that he might view the interior of the church. There the moonbeams came trembling in, and fell down upon the deserted pews, and extended along the quiet aisles. A fainter yet more awful radiance was hovering around the pulpit, and one solitary ray had dared to rest upon the open page of the great Bible. Had nature, in that deep hour, become a worshipper in the house which man had builded? Or was that heavenly light the visible sanctity of the place,—visible because no earthly and impure feet were within the walls? The scene made Robin's heart shiver with a sensation of loneliness stronger than he had ever felt in the remotest depths of his native woods; so he turned away and sat down again before the door. There were graves around the church, and now an uneasy thought obtruded into Robin's breast. What if the object of his search, which had been so often and so strangely thwarted, were all the time mouldering in his shroud? What if his kinsman should glide through yonder gate, and nod and smile to him in dimly passing by?

"Oh that any breathing thing were here with me!" said Robin.

Recalling his thoughts from this uncomfortable track, he sent them over forest, hill, and stream, and attempted to imagine how that evening of ambiguity and weariness had been spent by his father's household. He pictured them assembled at the door, beneath the tree, the great old tree, which had been spared for its huge twisted trunk and venerable shade, when a thousand leafy brethen fell. There, at the going down of the summer sun, it was his father's custom to perform domestic worship, that the neighbors might come and join with him like brothers of the family, and that the wayfaring man might pause to drink at that fountain, and keep his heart pure by freshening the memory of home. Robin distinguished the seat of every individual of the little audience; he saw the good man in the midst, holding the Scriptures in the golden light that fell from the western clouds; he beheld him close the book and all rise up to pray. He heard the old thanksgivings for daily mercies, the old supplications for their continuance, to which he had so often listened in weariness, but which were now among his dear remembrances. He perceived the slight inequality of his father's voice when he came to speak of the absent one; he noted how his mother turned her face to the broad and knotted trunk; how his elder brother scorned, because the beard was rough upon his upper lip to permit his features to be moved; how the younger sister drew down a low hanging branch before her eyes; and how the little one of all, whose sports had hitherto broken the decorum of the scene, understood the prayer for her playmate, and burst into clamorous grief. Then he saw them go in at the door; and when Robin would have entered also, the latch tinkled into its place, and he was excluded from his home.

"Am I here, or there?" cried Robin, starting; for all at once, when his thoughts had become visible and audible in a dream, the long, wide, solitary street shone out before him.

He aroused himself, and endeavored to fix his attention steadily upon the large edifice which he had surveyed before. But still his mind kept vibrating between fancy and reality; by turns, the pillars of the balcony lengthened into the tall, bare stems of pines, dwindled down to human figures, settled again into their true shape and size, and then commenced a new succession of changes. For a single moment, when he deemed himself awake, he could have sworn that a visage—one which he seemed to remember, yet could not absolutely name as his kinsman's—was looking towards him from the Gothic window. A deeper sleep wrestled with and nearly overcame him, but fled at the sound of footsteps along the opposite pavement. Robin rubbed his eyes, discerned a man passing at the foot of the balcony, and addressed him in a loud, peevish, and lamentable cry.

"Hallo, friend! must I wait here all night for my kinsman, Major Molineux?"

The sleeping echoes awoke, and answered the voice; and the passenger, barely able to discern a figure sitting in the oblique shade of the steeple, traversed the street to obtain a nearer view. He was himself a gentleman in his prime, of open, intelligent, cheerful, and altogether prepossessing countenance. Perceiving a country youth, apparently homeless and without friends, he accosted him in a tone of real kindness, which had become strange to Robin's ears.

"Well, my good lad, why are you sitting here?" inquired he. "Can I be of service to you in any way?"

"I am afraid not, sir," replied Robin, despondingly; "yet I shall take it kindly, if you'll answer me a single question. I've been searching, half the night, for one Major Molineux; now, sir, is there really such a person in these parts, or am I dreaming?"

"Major Molineux! The name is not altogether strange to me," said the gentleman, smiling. "Have you any objection to telling me the nature of your business with him?"

Then Robin briefly related that his father was a clergyman, settled on a small salary, at a long distance back in the country, and that he and Major Molineux were brothers' children. The Major, having inherited riches, and acquired civil and military rank, had visited his cousin, in great pomp, a year or two before; had manifested much interest in Robin and an elder brother, and, being childless himself, had thrown out hints respecting the future establishment of one of them in life. The elder brother was destined to succeed to the farm which his father cultivated in the interval of sacred duties; it was therefore determined that Robin should profit by his kinsman's generous intentions, especially as he seemed to be rather the favorite, and was thought to possess other necessary endowments.

"For I have the name of being a shrewd youth," observed Robin, in this part of his story.

"I doubt not you deserve it," replied his new friend, good-naturedly; "but pray proceed."

"Well, sir, being nearly eighteen years old, and well grown, as you see," continued Robin, drawing himself up to his full height, "I thought it high time to begin in the world. So my mother and sister put me in handsome trim, and my father gave me half the remnant of his last year's salary, and five days ago I started for this place, to pay the Major a visit. But, would you believe it, sir! I crossed the ferry a little after dark, and have yet found nobody that would show me the way to his dwelling; only, an hour or two since, I was told to wait here, and Major Molineux would pass by."

"Can you describe the man who told you this?" inquired the gentleman.

"Oh, he was a very ill-favored fellow, sir," replied Robin, "with two great bumps on his forehead, a hook nose, fiery eyes; and, what struck me as the strangest, his face was of two different colors. Do you happen to know such a man, sir?"

"Not intimately," answered the stranger, "but I chanced to meet him a little time previous to your stopping me. I believe you may trust his word, and that the Major will very shortly pass through this street. In the mean time, as I have a singular curiosity to witness your meeting, I will sit down here upon the steps and bear you company."

He seated himself accordingly, and soon engaged his companion in animated discourse. It was but of brief continuance, however, for a noise of shouting, which had long been remotely audible, drew so much nearer that Robin inquired its cause.

"What may be the meaning of this uproar?" asked he. "Truly, if your town be always as noisy, I shall find little sleep while I am an inhabitant."

"Why, indeed, friend Robin, there do appear to be three or four riotous fellows abroad to-night," replied the gentleman. "You must not expect all the stillness of your native woods here in our streets. But the watch will shortly be at the heels of these lads and"—

"Ay, and set them in the stocks by peep of day," interrupted Robin, recollecting his own encounter with the drowsy lantern-bearer. "But, dear sir, if I may trust my ears, an army of watchmen would never make head against such a multitude of rioters. There were at least a thousand voices went up to make that one shout."

"May not a man have several voices, Robin, as well as two complexions?" said his friend.

"Perhaps a man may; but Heaven forbid that a woman should!" responded the shrewd youth, thinking of the seductive tones of the Major's housekeeper.

The sounds of a trumpet in some neighboring street now became so evident and continual, that Robin's curiosity was strongly excited. In addition to the shouts, he heard frequent bursts from many instruments of discord, and a wild and confused laughter filled up the intervals. Robin rose from the steps, and looked wistfully towards a point whither people seemed to be hastening.

"Surely some prodigious merry-making is going on," exclaimed he. "I have laughed very little since I left home, sir, and should be sorry to lose an opportunity. Shall we step round the corner by that darkish house, and take our share of the fun?"

"Sit down again, sit down, good Robin," replied the gentleman, laying his hand on the skirt of the gray coat. "You forget that we must wait here for your kinsman; and there is reason to believe that he will pass by, in the course of a very few moments."

The near approach of the uproar had now disturbed the neighborhood; windows flew open on all sides; and many heads, in the attire of the pillow, and confused by sleep suddenly broken, were protruded to the gaze of whoever had leisure to observe them. Eager voices hailed each other from house to house, all demanding the explanation, which not a soul could give. Half-dressed men hurried towards the unknown commotion, stumbling as they went over the stone steps that thrust themselves into the narrow foot-walk. The shouts, the laughter, and the tuneless bray, the antipodes of music, came onwards with increasing din, till scattered individuals, and then denser bodies, began to appear round a corner at the distance of a hundred yards.

"Will you recognize your kinsman, if he passes in this crowd?" inquired the gentleman.

"Indeed, I can't warrant it, sir; but I'll take my stand here, and keep a bright lookout," answered Robin, descending to the outer edge of the pavement.

A mighty stream of people now emptied into the street, and came rolling slowly towards the church. A single horseman wheeled the corner in the midst of them, and close behind him came a band of fearful wind-instruments, sending forth a fresher discord now that no intervening buildings kept it from the ear. Then a redder light disturbed the moon-beams, and a dense multitude of torches shone along the street, concealing, by their glare, whatever object they illuminated. The single horseman, clad in a military dress, and bearing a drawn sword, rode onward as the leader, and, by his fierce and variegated countenance, appeared like war personified; the red of one cheek was an emblem of fire and sword; the blackness of the other betokened the mourning that attends them. In his train were wild figures in the Indian dress, and many fantastic shapes without a model, giving the whole march a visionary air, as if a dream had broken forth from some feverish brain, and were sweeping visibly through the midnight streets. A mass of people, inactive, except as applauding spectators, hemmed the procession in; and several women ran along the sidewalk, piercing the confusion of heavier sounds with their shrill voices of mirth or terror.

"The double-faced fellow has his eye upon me," muttered Robin, with an indefinite but an uncomfortable idea that he was himself to bear a part in the pageantry.

The leader turned himself in the saddle, and fixed his glance full upon the country youth, as the steed went slowly by. When Robin had freed his eyes from those fiery ones, the musicians were passing before him, and the torches were close at hand; but the unsteady brightness of the latter formed a veil which he could not penetrate. The rattling of wheels over the stones sometimes found its way to his ear, and confused traces of a human form appeared at intervals, and then melted into the vivid light. A moment more, and the leader thundered a command to halt: the trumpets vomited a horrid breath, and then held their peace; the shouts and laughter of the people died away, and there remained only a universal hum, allied to silence. Right before Robin's eyes was an uncovered cart. There the torches blazed the brightest, there the moon shone out like day, and there, in tar-and-feathery dignity,[4] sat his kinsman, Major Molineux!

He was an elderly man, of large and majestic person, and strong, square features, betokening a steady soul; but steady as it was, his enemies had found means to shake it. His face was pale as death, and far more ghastly; the broad forehead was contracted in his agony, so that his eyebrows formed one grizzled line; his eyes were red and wild, and the foam hung white upon his quivering lip. His whole frame was agitated by a quick and continual tremor, which his pride strove to quell, even in those circumstances of overwhelm-

---

4. In this rough punishment a man was stripped naked, covered with hot tar, and sprinkled with feathers. It was frequently visited upon those suspected of resisting the revolution.

ing humiliation. But perhaps the bitterest pang of all was when his eyes met those of Robin; for he evidently knew him on the instant, as the youth stood witnessing the foul disgrace of a head grown gray in honor. They stared at each other in silence, and Robin's knees shook, and his hair bristled, with a mixture of pity and terror. Soon, however, a bewildering excitement began to seize upon his mind; the preceding adventures of the night, the unexpected appearance of the crowd, the torches, the confused din and the hush that followed, the spectre of his kinsman reviled by that great multitude,—all this, and more than all, a perception of tremendous ridicule in the whole scene, affected him with a sort of mental inebriety. At that moment a voice of sluggish merriment saluted Robin's ears; he turned instinctively, and just behind the corner of the church stood the lantern-bearer, rubbing his eyes, and drowsily enjoying the lad's amazement. Then he heard a peal of laughter like the ringing of silvery bells; a woman twitched his arm, a saucy eye met his, and he saw the lady of the scarlet petticoat. A sharp, dry cachinnation appealed to his memory, and, standing on tiptoe in the crowd, with his white apron over his head, he beheld the courteous little innkeeper. And lastly, there sailed over the heads of the multitude a great, broad laugh, broken in the midst by two sepulchral hems; thus, "haw, haw, haw,—hem, hem,—haw, haw, haw, haw!"

The sound proceeded from the balcony of the opposite edifice, and thither Robin turned his eyes. In front of the Gothic window stood the old citizen, wrapped in a wide gown, his gray periwig exchanged for a nightcap, which was thrust back from his forehead, and his silk stockings hanging about his legs. He supported himself on his polished cane in a fit of convulsive merriment, which manifested itself on his solemn old features like a funny inscription on a tombstone. Then Robin seemed to hear the voices of the barbers, of the guests of the inn, and of all who had made sport of him that night. The contagion was spreading among the multitude, when all at once, it seized upon Robin, and he sent forth a shout of laughter that echoed through the street,—every man shook his sides, every man emptied his lungs, but Robin's shout was the loudest there. The cloud-spirits peeped from their silvery islands, as the congregated mirth went roaring up the sky! The Man in the Moon heard the far bellow. "Oho," quoth he, "the old earth is frolicsome tonight!"

When there was a momentary calm in that tempestuous sea of sound, the leader gave the sign, the procession resumed its march. On they went, like fiends that throng in mockery around some dead potentate, mighty no more, but majestic still in his agony. On they went, in counterfeited pomp, in senseless uproar, in frenzied merriment, trampling all on an old man's heart. On swept the tumult, and left a silent street behind.

.   .   .   .

"Well, Robin, are you dreaming?" inquired the gentleman, laying his hand on the youth's shoulder.

Robin started, and withdrew his arm from the stone post to which he had instinctively clung, as the living stream rolled by him. His cheek was somewhat pale, and his eye not quite as lively as in the earlier part of the evening.

"Will you be kind enough to show me the way to the ferry?" said he, after a moment's pause.

"You have, then, adopted a new subject of inquiry?" observed his companion, with a smile.

"Why, yes, sir," replied Robin, rather dryly. "Thanks to you, and to my other friends, I have at last met my kinsman, and he will scarce desire to see my face again. I begin to grow weary of a town life, sir. Will you show me the way to the ferry?"

"No, my good friend Robin,—not to-night, at least," said the gentleman. "Some few days hence, if you wish it, I will speed you on your journey. Or, if you prefer to remain with us, perhaps, as you are a shrewd youth, you may rise in the world without the help of your kinsman, Major Molineux."

EDGAR ALLAN POE
1809–1849

Born in Boston into a theatrical family, he became an orphan at an early age and was adopted and raised by John Allan, a Virginia tobacco-exporter. He began school in England, then returned to the United States to attend the University of Virginia. Expelled for drinking and gambling, he entered the army for two years, and later attended the United States Military Academy at West Point, from which he was also expelled. Poet and short-story writer, critic and editor, he aimed for a "unity of effect" in all his writings. In his essay "The Poetic Principle," he suggests that brevity, a sense of mystery, some degree of verbal magic, and immediate emotional effect are the qualities he seeks in poetry. Such too are the qualities he brings to his own short fiction. He made the mystery story his own unique creation, and he became a major influence on the detective story.

The Purloined Letter

Nil sapienatiæ odiosius acumine nimio.[1]
Seneca

At Paris, just after dark one gusty evening in the autumn of 18—, I was enjoying the twofold luxury of meditation and a meerschaum, in company with my friend, C. Auguste Dupin, in his little back library, or book-closet, *au troisième*, No. 33 *Rue Dunôt, Faubourg St. Germain*.[2] For one hour at least we had maintained a profound silence; while each, to any casual observer, might have seemed intently and exclusively occupied with the curling eddies of smoke that oppressed the atmosphere of the chamber. For myself, however, I was mentally discussing certain topics which had formed matter for conversation between us at an earlier period of the evening; I mean the affair of the Rue Morgue, and the mystery attending the murder of Marie Rogêt.[3] I looked upon it, therefore, as something of a coincidence, when the door of our apartment was thrown open and admitted our old acquaintance, Monsieur G——, the Prefect of the Parisian police.

We gave him a hearty welcome; for there was nearly half as much of the entertaining as of the contemptible about the man, and we had not seen him for several years. We had been sitting in the dark, and Dupin now arose for the purpose of lighting a lamp, but sat down again, without doing so, upon G.'s saying that he had called to consult us, or rather to ask the opinion of my friend, about some official business which had occasioned a great deal of trouble.

"If it is any point requiring reflection," observed Dupin, as he forbore to enkindle the wick, "we shall examine it to better purpose in the dark."

"That is another of your odd notions," said the Prefect, who had the fashion of calling everything "odd" that was beyond his comprehension, and thus lived amid an absolute legion of "oddities."

"Very true," said Dupin, as he supplied his visitor with a pipe, and rolled toward him a comfortable chair.

"And what is the difficulty now?" I asked. "Nothing more in the assassination way I hope?"

"Oh, no; nothing of that nature. The fact is, the business is *very* simple indeed, and I make no doubt that we can manage it sufficiently well ourselves; but then I thought Dupin would like to hear the details of it because it is so excessively *odd*."

"Simple and odd," said Dupin.

1. Nothing is more offensive to the wise than an excess of trickery.
2. On the third floor above the ground in a fashionable district in Paris.
3. These are the subjects of previous detective stories by Poe.

"Why, yes; and not exactly that either. The fact is, we have all been a good deal puzzled because the affair *is* so simple, and yet baffles us altogether."

"Perhaps it is the very simplicity of the thing which puts you at fault," said my friend.

"What nonsense you *do* talk!" replied the Prefect, laughing heartily.

"Perhaps the mystery is a little *too* plain," said Dupin.

"Oh, good heavens! who ever heard of such an idea?"

"A little *too* self-evident."

"Ha! ha! ha!—ha! ha! ha!—ho! ho! ho!" roared our visitor, profoundly amused, "oh, Dupin, you will be the death of me yet!"

"And what, after all, *is* the matter on hand?" I asked.

"Why, I will tell you," replied the Prefect, as he gave a long, steady, and contemplative puff, and settled himself in his chair. "I will tell you in a few words; but, before I begin, let me caution you that this is an affair demanding the greatest secrecy, and that I should most probably lose the position I now hold, were it known that I confided it to any one."

"Proceed," said I.

"Or not," said Dupin.

"Well, then; I have received personal information, from a very high quarter, that a certain document of the last importance has been purloined from the royal apartments. The individual who purloined it is known; this beyond a doubt; he was seen to take it. It is known, also, that it still remains in his possession."

"How is this known?" asked Dupin.

"It is clearly inferred," replied the Prefect, "from the nature of the document, and from the non-appearance of certain results which would at once arise from its passing *out* of the robber's possession—that is to say, from his employing it as he must design in the end to employ it."

"Be a little more explicit," I said.

"Well, I may venture so far as to say that the paper gives its holder a certain power in a certain quarter where such power is immensely valuable." The Prefect was fond of the cant of diplomacy.

"Still I do not quite understand," said Dupin.

"No? Well; the disclosure of the document to a third person, who shall be nameless, would bring in question the honor of a personage of most exalted station; and this fact gives the holder of the document an ascendancy over the illustrious personage whose honor and peace are so jeopardized."

"But this ascendancy." I interposed, "would depend upon the robber's knowledge of the loser's knowledge of the robber. Who would dare—"

"The thief," said G., "is the Minister D——, who dares all things, those unbecoming as well as those becoming a man. The method of the theft was not less ingenious than bold. The document in question—a letter, to be frank—had been received by the personage robbed while in the royal *boudoir*. During its perusal she was suddenly interrupted by the entrance of the other exalted personage from whom especially it was her wish to conceal it. After a hurried and vain endeavor to thrust it in a drawer, she was forced to place it, open as it was, upon a table. The address, however, was uppermost, and, the contents thus unexposed, the letter escaped notice. At this juncture enters the Minister D——. His lynx eye immediately perceives the paper, recognizes the handwriting of the address, observes the confusion of the personage addressed, and fathoms her secret. After some business transactions, hurried through in his ordinary manner, he produces a letter somewhat similar to the one in question, opens it, pretends to read it, and then places in in close juxtaposition to the other. Again he converses, for some fifteen minutes, upon the public affairs. At length, in taking leave, he takes also from the table the letter to which he had no claim. Its rightful owner saw, but, of course, dared not call attention to the act, in the presence of the third personage who stood at her elbow. The minister decamped; leaving his own letter—one of no importance—upon the table."

"Here, then," said Dupin to me, "you have precisely what you demand to make the ascendancy complete—the robber's knowledge of the loser's knowledge of the robber."

"Yes," replied the Prefect; "and the power thus attained has, for some months past, been wielded, for political purposes, to a very dangerous extent. The personage robbed is more thoroughly convinced, every day, of the necessity of reclaiming her letter. But this, of course, cannot be done openly. In fine, driven to despair, she has committed the matter to me."

"Than whom," said Dupin, amid a perfect whirlwind of smoke, "no more sagacious agent could, I suppose, be desired, or even imagined."

"You flatter me," replied the Prefect; "but it is possible that some such opinion may have been entertained."

"It is clear," said I, "as you observe, that the letter is still in the possession of the minister; since it is this possession, and not any employment of the letter, which bestows the power. With the employment the power departs."

"True," said G.; "and upon this conviction I proceeded. My first care was to make thorough search of the minister's hotel;[4] and here

4. "Hotel" in the French sense: a large building; in this case a private house in the city.

my chief embarrassment lay in the necessity of searching without his knowledge. Beyond all things, I have been warned of the danger which would result from giving him reason to suspect our design."

"But," said I, "you are quite *au fait* in these investigations. The Parisian police have done this thing often before."

"Oh, yes; and for this reason I did not despair. The habits of the minister gave me, too, a great advantage. He is frequently absent from home all night. His servants are by no means numerous. They sleep at a distance from their master's apartment, and, being chiefly Neapolitans, are readily made drunk. I have keys, as you know, with which I can open any chamber or cabinet in Paris. For three months a night has not passed, during the greater part of which I have not been engaged, personally, in ransacking the D—— Hotel. My honor is interested, and, to mention a great secret, the reward is enormous. So I did not abandon the search until I had become fully satisfied that the thief is a more astute man than myself. I fancy that I have investigated every nook and corner of the premises in which it is possible that the paper can be concealed."

"But is it not possible," I suggested, "that although the letter may be in possession of the minister, as it unquestionably is, he may have concealed it elsewhere than upon his own premises?"

"This is barely possible," said Dupin. "The present peculiar condition of affairs at court, and especially of those intrigues in which D——is known to be involved, would render the instant availability of the document—its susceptibility of being produced at a moment's notice—a point of nearly equal importance with its possession."

"Its susceptibility of being produced?" said I.

"That is to say, of being *destroyed*," said Dupin.

"True," I observed; "the paper is clearly then upon the premises. As for its being upon the person of the minister, we may consider that as out of the question."

"Entirely," said the Prefect. "He has been twice waylaid, as if by footpads, and his person rigidly searched under my own inspection."

"You might have spared yourself this trouble," said Dupin. "D——, I presume, is not altogether a fool, and, if not, must have anti-cipated these waylayings, as a matter of course."

"Not *altogether* a fool," said G., "but then he is a poet, which I take to be only one remove from a fool."

"True," said Dupin, after a long and thoughtful whiff from his meerschaum, "although I have been guilty of certain doggerel myself."

"Suppose you detail," said I, "the particulars of your search."

"Why, the fact is, we took our time, and we searched *everywhere*. I have had long experience in these affairs. I took the entire building, room by room; devoting the nights of a whole week to each.

We examined, first, the furniture of each apartment. We opened every possible drawer; and I presume you know that, to a properly trained police-agent, such a thing as a 'secret' drawer is impossible. Any man is a dolt who permits a 'secret' drawer to escape him in a search of this kind. The thing is so plain. There is a certain amount of bulk—of space—to be accounted for in every cabinet. Then we have accurate rules. The fiftieth part of a line could not escape us. After the cabinets we took the chairs. The cushions we probed with the fine long needles you have seen me employ. From the tables we removed the tops."

"Why so?"

"Sometimes the top of a table, or other similarly arranged piece of furniture, is removed by the person wishing to conceal an article; then the leg is excavated, the article deposited within the cavity, and the top replaced. The bottoms and tops of bedposts are employed in the same way."

"But could not the cavity be detected by sounding?" I asked.

"By no means, if, when the article is deposited, a sufficient wadding of cotton be placed around it. Besides, in our case, we were obliged to proceed without noise."

"But you could not have removed—you could not have taken to pieces all articles of furniture in which it would have been possible to make a deposit in the manner you mention. A letter may be compressed into a thin spiral roll, not differing much in shape or bulk from a large knitting-needle, and in this form it might be inserted into the rung of a chair, for example. You did not take to pieces all the chairs?"

"Certainly not; but we did better—we examined the rungs of every chair in the hotel, and, indeed, the jointings of every description of furniture, by the aid of a most powerful microscope. Had there been any traces of recent disturbance we should not have failed to detect it instantly. A single grain of gimlet-dust, for example, would have been as obvious as an apple. Any disorder in the gluing—any unusual gaping in the joints—would have sufficed to insure detection."

"I presume you looked to the mirrors, between the boards and the plates, and you probed the beds and the bedclothes, as well as the curtains and carpets."

"That of course; and when we had absolutely completed every particle of furniture in this way, then we examined the house itself. We divided its entire surface into compartments, which we numbered, so that none might be missed; then we scrutinized each individual square inch throughout the premises, including the two houses immediately adjoining, with the microscope, as before."

"The two houses adjoining!" I exclaimed; "you must have had a great deal of trouble."

"We had; but the reward offered is prodigious."

"You included the *grounds* about the houses?"

"All the grounds are paved with brick. They gave us comparatively little trouble. We examined the moss between the bricks, and found it undisturbed."

"You looked among D——'s papers, of course, and into the books of the library?"

"Certainly; we opened every package and parcel; we not only opened every book, but we turned over every leaf in each volume, not contenting ourselves with a mere shake, according to the fashion of some of our police officers. We also measured the thickness of every book-*cover*, with the most accurate admeasurement, and applied to each the most jealous scrutiny of the microscope. Had any of the bindings been recently meddled with, it would have been utterly impossible that the fact should have escaped observation. Some five or six volumes, just from the hands of the binder, we carefully probed, longitudinally, with needles."

"You explored the floors beneath the carpets?"

"Beyond doubt. We removed every carpet, and examined the boards with the microscope."

"And the paper on the walls?"

"Yes."

"You looked into the cellars?"

"We did."

"Then," I said, "you have been making a miscalculation, and the letter is *not* upon the premises, as you suppose."

"I fear you are right there," said the Prefect. "And now, Dupin, what would you advise me to do?"

"To make a thorough research of the premises."

"That is absolutely needless," replied G——. "I am not more sure that I breathe than I am that the letter is not at the hotel."

"I have no better advice to give you," said Dupin. "You have, of course, an accurate description of the letter?"

"Oh, yes!"—And here the Prefect, producing a memorandum-book, proceeded to read aloud a minute account of the internal, and especially of the external, appearance of the missing document. Soon after finishing the perusal of this description, he took his departure, more entirely depressed in spirits than I had ever known the good gentleman before.

In about a month afterward he paid us another visit, and found us occupied very nearly as before. He took a pipe and a chair and entered into some ordinary conversation. At length I said:

"Well, but G., what of the purloined letter? I presume you have at last made up your mind that there is no such thing as overreaching the Minister?"

"Confound him, say I—yes; I made the re-examination, however, as Dupin suggested—but it was all labor lost, as I knew it would be."

"How much was the reward offered, did you say?" asked Dupin.

"Why, a very great deal—a *very* liberal reward—I don't like to say how much, precisely; but one thing I *will* say, that I wouldn't mind giving my individual check for fifty thousand francs to any one who could obtain me that letter. The fact is, it is becoming of more and more importance every day; and the reward has been lately doubled. If it were trebled, however, I could do no more than I have done."

"Why, yes," said Dupin, drawlingly, between the whiffs of his meerschaum, "I really—think, G., you have not exerted yourself—to the utmost in this matter. You might—do a little more, I think, eh?"

"How?—in what way?"

"Why—puff, puff—you might—puff, puff—employ counsel in the matter, eh?—puff, puff, puff. Do you remember the story they tell of Abernethy?"

"No; hang Abernethy!"

'To be sure! hang him and welcome. But, once upon a time, a certain rich miser conceived the design of spunging upon this Abernethy for a medical opinion. Getting up, for this purpose, an ordinary conversation in a private company, he insinuated his case to the physician, as that of an imaginary individual.

" 'We will suppose,' said the miser, 'that his symptoms are such and such; now, doctor, what would *you* have directed him to take?'

" 'Take!' said Abernethy, 'why, take *advice*, to be sure.' "

"But," said the Prefect, a little discomposed, "I am *perfectly* willing to take advice, and to pay for it. I would *really* give fifty thousand francs to any one who would aid me in the matter."

"In that case," replied Dupin, opening a drawer, and producing a check-book, "you may as well fill me up a check for the amount mentioned. When you have signed it, I will hand you the letter."

I was astounded. The Prefect appeared absolutely thunderstricken. For some minutes he remained speechless and motionless, looking incredulously at my friend with open mouth, and eyes that seemed starting from their sockets; then apparently recovering himself in some measure, he seized a pen, and after several pauses and vacant stares, finally filled up and signed a check for fifty thousand francs, and handed it across the table to Dupin. The latter examined it carefully and deposited it in his pocket-book; then, unlocking an *escritoire*, took thence a letter and gave it to the prefect. This functionary grasped it in a perfect agony of joy, opened it with a trembling hand, cast a rapid glance at its contents, and then, scrambling and struggling to the door, rushed at length unceremoniously from the room and from the house, without having uttered a syllable since Dupin had requested him to fill up the check.

When he had gone, my friend entered into some explanations.

"The Parisian police," he said, "are exceedingly able in their way. They are persevering, ingenious, cunning, and thoroughly versed in the knowledge which their duties seem chiefly to demand. Thus, when G—— detailed to us his mode of searching the premises at the Hotel D——, I felt entire confidence in his having made a satisfactory investigation—so far as his labors extended."

"So far as his labors extended?" said I.

"Yes," said Dupin. "The measures adopted were not only the best of their kind, but carried out to absolute perfection. Had the letter been deposited within the range of their search, these fellows would, beyond a question, have found it."

I merely laughed—but he seemed quite serious in all that he said.

"The measures, then," he continued, "were good in their kind, and well executed; their defect lay in their being inapplicable to the case and to the man. A certain set of highly ingenious resources are, with the Prefect, a sort of Procrustean bed, to which he forcibly adapts his designs. But he perpetually errs by being too deep or too shallow for the matter in hand; and many a school-boy is a better reasoner than he. I knew one about eight years of age, whose success at guessing in the game of 'even and odd' attracted universal admiration. This game is simple, and is played with marbles. One player holds in his hand a number of these toys, and demands of another whether that number is even or odd. If the guess is right, the guesser wins one; if wrong, he loses one. The boy to whom I allude won all the marbles of the school. Of course he had some principle of guessing; and this lay in mere observation and admeasurements of the astuteness of his opponents. For example, an arrant simpleton is his opponent, and holding up his closed hand, asks, 'Are they even or odd?' Our school-boy replies, 'Odd,' and loses; but upon the second trial he wins, for he then says to himself: 'The simpleton had them even upon the first trial, and his amount of cunning is just sufficient to make him have them odd upon the second; I will therefore guess odd';—he guesses odd, and wins. Now, with a simpleton a degree above the first, he would have reasoned thus: 'This fellow finds that in the first instance I guessed odd, and, in the second, he will propose to himself, upon the first impulse, a simple variation from even to odd, as did the first simpleton; but then a second thought will suggest that this is too simple a variation, and finally he will decide upon putting it even as before. I will therefore guess even';—he guesses even, and wins. Now this mode of reasoning in the school-boy, whom his fellows termed 'lucky,'—what, in its last analysis, is it?"

"It is merely," I said, "an identification of the reasoner's intellect with that of his opponent."

"It is," said Dupin; "and, upon inquiring of the boy by what means he effected the *thorough* identification in which his success consisted, I received answer as follows; 'When I wish to find out how wise, or how stupid or how good, or how wicked is any one, or what are his thoughts at the moment, I fashion the expression of my face, as accurately as possible, in accordance with the expression of his, and then wait to see what thoughts or sentiments arise in my mind or heart, as if to match or correspond with the expression.' This response of the school-boy lies at the bottom of all the spurious profundity which has been attributed to Rochefoucault, to La Bougive, to Machiavelli, and to Campanella."

"And the identification," I said, "of the reasoner's intellect with that of his opponent, depends, if I understand you aright, upon the accuracy with which the opponent's intellect is admeasured."

"For its practical value it depends upon this," replied Dupin; "and the Prefect and his cohort fail so frequently, first, by default of this identification and, secondly, by ill-admeasurement, or rather through non-admeasurement, of the intellect with which they are engaged. They consider only their *own* ideas of ingenuity; and, in searching for any thing hidden, advert only to the modes, in which *they* would have hidden it. They are right in this much—that their own ingenuity is a faithful representative of that of the *mass;* but when the cunning of the individual felon is diverse in character from their own, the felon foils them, of course. This always happens when it is above their own, and very usually when it is below. They have no variation of principle in their investigations; at best, when urged by some unusual emergency—by some extraordinary reward—they extend or exaggerate their old modes of *practice,* without touching their principles. What, for example, in this case of D— —, has been done to vary the principle of action? What is all this boring, and probing, and sounding, and scrutinizing with the microscope, and dividing the surface of the building into registered square inches—what is it all but an exaggeration *of the application* of the one principle or set of principles of search, which are based upon the one set of notions regarding human ingenuity, to which the Prefect, in the long routine of his duty, has been accustomed? Do you not see he has taken it for granted that *all* men proceed to conceal a letter, not exactly in a gimlet-hole bored in a chair-leg, but, at least, in *some* out-of-the-way hole or corner suggested by the same tenor of thought which would urge a man to secrete a letter in a gimlet-hole bored in a chair-leg? And do you not see also, that such *recherchés* nooks for concealment are adapted only for ordinary occasions, and would be adopted only by ordinary intellects; for, in all cases of concealment, a disposal of the article concealed—a dis-posal of it in this *recherché* manner,—is, in the very first instance, presumable and presumed; and thus its discovery depends, not at all upon the acumen, but altogether upon the mere care, patience, and determination of the seekers; and where the case is of impor-tance—or, what amounts to the same thing in the political eyes, when the reward is of magnitude,—the qualities in question have *never* been known to fail. You will now understand what I meant in suggesting that, had the purloined letter been hidden anywhere within the limits of the Prefect's examination—in other words, had the principle of its concealment been comprehended within the principles of the Prefect—its discovery would have been a matter altogether beyond question. This functionary, however, has been thoroughly mystified; and the remote source of his defeat lies in the supposition that the Minister is a fool, because he has acquired renown as a poet. All fools are poets; this the Prefect *feels*; and he is merely guilty of a *non distributio medii* in thence inferring that all poets are fools."

"But is this really the poet?" I asked. "There are two brothers, I know; and both have attained reputation in letters. The Minister I believe has written learnedly on the Differential Calculus. He is a mathematician, and no poet."

"You are mistaken; I know him well; he is both. As poet *and* mathematician, he would reason well; as mere mathematician, he could not have reasoned at all, and thus would have been at the mercy of the Prefect."

"You surprise me," I said, "by these opinions, which have been contradicted by the voice of the world. You do not mean to set at naught the well-digested idea of centuries. The mathematical reason has long been regarded as *the* reason *par excellence.*"

" 'Il y a à parier,' " replied Dupin, quoting from Chamfort, " '*que toute idée publique, toute convention reçue, est une sottise, car elle a convenu au plus grand nombre.*'[5] The mathematicians, I grant you, have done their best to promulgate the popular error to which you allude, and which is none the less an error for its promulgation as truth. With an art worthy a better cause, for example, they have insinuated the term 'analysis' into application to algebra. The French are the originators of this particular deception; but if a term is of any importance—if words derive any value from applicability—then 'analysis' conveys 'algebra' about as much as, in Latin, '*ambitus*' implies 'ambition,' '*religio*' 'religion,' or '*homines honesti*' a set of *honorable* men."

5. "The odds are that any public idea or accepted opinion is stupid, because it has suited the majority of people."

"You have a quarrel on hand, I see," said I, "with some of the algebraists of Paris; but proceed."

"I dispute the availability, and thus the value, of that reason which is cultivated in any especial form other than the abstractly logical. I dispute, in particular, the reason educed by mathematical study. The mathematics are the science of form and quantity; mathematical reasoning is merely logic applied to observation upon form and quantity. The great error lies in supposing that even the truths of what is called *pure* algebra are abstract or general truths. And this error is so egregious that I am confounded at the universality with which it has been received. Mathematical axioms are *not* axioms of general truth. What is true of *relation*—of form and quantity—is often grossly false in regard to morals, for example. In this latter science it is very usually *un*true that the aggregated parts are equal to the whole. In chemistry also the axiom fails. In the consideration of motive it fails; for two motives, each of a given value, have not, necessarily, a value when united, equal to the sum of their values apart. There are numerous other mathematical truths which are only truths within the limits of *relation*. But the mathematician argues from his *finite truths*, through habit, as if they were of an absolutely general applicability—as the world indeed imagines them to be. Bryant, in his very learned 'Mythology,' mentions an analogous source of error, when he says that 'although the pagan fables are not believed, yet we forget ourselves continually, and make inferences from them as existing realities.' With the algebraists, however, who are pagans themselves, the 'pagan fables' *are* believed and the inferences are made, not so much through lapse of memory as through an unaccountable addling of the brains. In short, I never yet encountered the mere mathematician who would be trusted out of equal roots, or one who did not clandestinely hold it as a point of his faith that $x2 + px$ was absolutely and unconditionally equal to q. Say to one of these gentlemen, by way of experiment, if you please, that you believe occasions may occur where $x2 + px$ is *not* altogether equal to q, and, having made him understand what you mean, get out of his reach as speedily as convenient, for, beyond doubt, he will endeavor to knock you down.

"I mean to say," continued Dupin, while I merely laughed at his last observations, "that if the Minister had been no more than a mathematician, the Prefect would have been under no necessity of giving me this check. I knew him, however, as both mathematician and poet, and my measures were adapted to his capacity, with reference to the circumstances by which he was surrounded. I knew him as a courtier, too, and as a bold *intriguant*. Such a man, I considered, could not fail to be aware of the ordinary policial modes of action. He could not have failed to anticipate—and events have proved that he did not fail to anticipate—the waylayings to which he was subjected. He must have foreseen, I reflected, the secret investigations of his premises. His frequent absences from home at night, which were hailed by the Prefect as certain aids to his success, I regarded only as *ruses*, to afford opportunity for thorough search to the police, and thus the sooner to impress them with the conviction to which G——, in fact, did finally arrive—the conviction that the letter was not upon the premises. I felt, also, that the whole train of thought, which I was at some pains in detailing to you just now, concerning the invariable principle of policial action in searches for articles concealed—I felt that this whole train of thought would necessarily pass through the mind of the minister. It would imperatively lead him to despise all the ordinary *nooks* of concealment. *He* could not, I reflected, be so weak as not to see that the most intricate and remote recess of his hotel would be as open as his commonest closets to the eyes, to the probes, to the gimlets, and to the microscopes of the Prefect. I saw, in fine, that he would be driven, as a matter of course, to *simplicity*, if not deliberately induced to it as a matter of choice. You will remember, perhaps, how desperately the Prefect laughed when I suggested, upon our first interview, that it was just possible this mystery troubled him so much on account of its being so *very* self-evident."

"Yes," said I, "I remember his merriment well. I really thought he would have fallen into convulsions."

"The material world," continued Dupin, "abounds with very strict analogies to the immaterial; and thus some color of truth has been given to the rhetorical dogma, that metaphor, or simile, may be made to strengthen an argument as well as to embellish a description. The principle of the *vis inertiæ*, for example, seems to be identical in physics and metaphysics. It is not more true in the former, that a large body is with more difficulty set in motion than a smaller one, and that its subsequent *momentum* is commensurate with this difficulty, than it is, in the latter, that intellects of the vaster capacity, while more forcible, more constant, and more eventful in their movements than those of inferior grade, are yet the less readily moved, and more embarrassed, and full of hesitation in the first few steps of their progress. Again: have you ever noticed which of the street signs, over the shop doors, are the most attractive of attention?"

"I have never given the matter a thought," I said.

"There is a game of puzzles," he resumed, "which is played upon a map. One party playing requires another to find a given word—the name of town, river, state, or empire—any word, in short, upon the motley and perplexed surface of the chart. A novice in the game generally seeks to embarrass his opponents by giving them the most minutely lettered names; but the adept selects such words as stretch, in large characters, from one end of the chart to the other. These, like the over-largely lettered signs and placards of the street, escape observation by dint of being excessively obvious; and here the physical oversight is precisely analogous with the moral inapprehension by which the intellect suffers to pass unnoticed those considerations which are too obtrusively and too palpably self-evident. But this is a point, it appears, somewhat above or beneath the understanding of the Prefect. He never once thought it probable, or possible, that the minister had deposited the letter immediately beneath the nose of the whole world, by way of best preventing any portion of that world from perceiving it.

"But the more I reflected upon the daring, dashing, and discriminating ingenuity of D——; upon the fact that the document must always have been *at hand*, if he intended to use it to good purpose; and upon the decisive evidence, obtained by the Prefect, that it was not hidden within the limits of the dignitary's ordinary search—the more satisfied I became that, to conceal this letter, the minister had resorted to the comprehensive and sagacious expedient of not attempting to conceal it at all.

"Full of these ideas, I prepared myself with a pair of green spectacles, and called one fine morning, quite by accident, at the Ministerial hotel. I found D—— at home, yawning, lounging, and dawdling, as usual, and pretending to be in the last extremity of *ennui*. He is, perhaps, the most really energetic human being now alive—but that is only when nobody sees him.

"To be even with him, I complained of my weak eyes, and lamented the necessity of the spectacles, under cover of which I cautiously and thoroughly surveyed the whole apartment, while seemingly intent only upon the conversation of my host.

"I paid especial attention to a large writing-table near which he sat, and upon which lay confusedly, some miscellaneous letters and other papers, with one or two musical instruments and a few books. Here, however, after a long and very deliberate scrutiny, I saw nothing to excite particular suspicion.

"At length my eyes, in going the circuit of the room, fell upon a trumpery filigree card-rack of pasteboard, that hung dangling by a dirty blue ribbon, from a little brass knob just beneath the middle of the mantelpiece. In this rack, which had three or four compartments, were five or six visiting cards and a solitary letter. This last was much soiled and crumpled. It was torn nearly in two, across the middle—as if a design, in the first instance, to tear it entirely up as worthless, had been altered, or stayed, in the second. It had a large black seal, bearing the D—— cipher *very* conspicuously, and was addressed, in a diminutive female hand, to D——, the minister himself. It was thrust carelessly, and even, as it seemed, contemptuously, into one of the uppermost divisions of the rack.

"No sooner had I glanced at this letter than I concluded it to be that of which I was in search. To be sure, it was, to all appearance, radically different from the one of which the Prefect had read us so minute a description. Here the seal was large and black, with the D—— cipher; there it was small and red, with the ducal arms of the S—— family. Here, the address, to the minister, was diminutive and feminine; there the superscription, to a certain royal personage, was markedly bold and decided; the size alone formed a point of correspondence. But, then, the *radicalness* of these differences, which was excessive; the dirt; the soiled and torn condition of the paper, so inconsistent with the *true* methodical habits of D——, and so suggestive of a design to delude the beholder into an idea of the worthlessness of the document;—these things, together with the hyperobtrusive situation of this document, full in the view of every visitor, and thus exactly in accordance with the conclusions to which I had previously arrived; these things, I say, were strongly corroborative of suspicion, in one who came with the intention to suspect.

"I protracted my visit as long as possible, and, while I maintained a most animated discussion with the minister, upon a topic which I knew well had never failed to interest and excite him, I kept my attention really riveted upon the letter. In this examination, I committed to memory its external appearance and arrangement in the rack; and also fell, at length, upon a discovery which set at rest whatever trivial doubt I might have entertained. In scrutinizing the edges of the paper, I observed them to be more *chafed* than seemed necessary. They presented the *broken* appearance which is manifested when a stiff paper, having been once folded and pressed with a folder, is refolded in a reversed direction, in the same creases or edges which had formed the original fold. This discovery was sufficient. It was clear to me that the letter had been turned, as a glove, inside out, re-directed and re-sealed. I bade the minister good-morning, and took my departure at once, leaving a gold snuff-box upon the table.

"The next morning I called for the snuff-box, when we resumed, quite eagerly, the conversation of the preceding day. While thus engaged, however, a loud report, as if of a pistol, was heard immediately beneath the windows of the hotel, and was succeeded by a series of fearful screams, and the shoutings of a terrified mob. D—— rushed to a casement, threw it open, and looked out. In the meantime I stepped to the card-rack, took the letter, put it in my pocket, and replaced it by a *fac-simile*, (so far as regards externals) which I had carefully prepared at my lodgings—imitating the D—— cipher, very readily, by means of a seal formed of bread.

"The disturbance in the street had been occasioned by the frantic behavior of a man with a musket. He had fired it among a crowd of women and children. It proved, however, to have been without ball, and the fellow was suffered to go his way as a lunatic or a drunkard. When he had gone, D—— came from the window, whither I had followed him immediately upon securing the object in view. Soon afterward I bade him farewell. The pretended lunatic was a man in my own pay."

"But what purpose had you," I asked, "in replacing the letter by a *fac-simile*? Would it not have been better, at the first visit, to have seized it openly, and departed?"

"D——," replied Dupin, "is a desperate man, and a man of nerve. His hotel, too, is not without attendants devoted to his interests. Had I made the wild attempt you suggest, I might never have left the Ministerial presence alive. The good people of Paris might have heard of me no more. But I had an object apart from these considerations. You know my political prepossessions. In this matter, I act as a partisan of the lady concerned. For eighteen months the Minister has had her in his power. She has now him in hers—since, being unaware that the letter is not in his possession, he will proceed with his exactions as if it was. Thus will he inevitably commit himself, at once, to his political destruction. His downfall, too, will not be more precipitate than awkward. It is all very well to talk about the *facilis descensus Averni;*[6] but in all kinds of climbing, as Catalani said of singing, it is far more easy to get up than to come down. In the present instance I have no sympathy—at least no pity—for him who descends. He is that *monstrum horrendum*, an unprincipled man of genius. I confess, however, that I should like very well to know the precise character of his thoughts, when, being defied by her whom the Prefect terms 'a certain personage,' he is reduced to opening the letter which I left for him in the card-rack."

"How?" did you put any thing particular in it?"

"Why—it did not seem altogether right to leave the interior blank—that would have been insulting. D——, at Vienna once, did me an evil turn, which I told him, quite good-humoredly, that I should remember. So, as I knew he would feel some curiosity in regard to the identity of the person who had outwitted him, I thought it a pity not to give him a clew. He is well acquainted with

6. 'The easy descent to Hell" as described by Vergil in *The Aeneid*.

my MS.,[7] and I just copied into the middle of the blank sheet the words—

" '——   ——Un dessein si funeste,
S'il n'est digne d'Atrée, est digne de Thyeste.'[8]

They are to be found in Crébillon's 'Atrée.' "

7. MS—handwriting.
8. "A scheme so horrible,/If it is unworthy of Atreus, is worthy of Thyestes." The allusion is to a particularly revolting episode of revenge in Greek mythology.

HERMAN MEVILLE
1819–1891

Born in New York City, he attended the Albany Academy and the Albany Classical School, then worked as a bank clerk and as a schoolteacher before deciding to seek his fortune at sea. He signed on a packet ship bound for Liverpool in 1839; the experience, however, proved disillusioning and he went back to teaching. But in 1841 he returned to life on the sea, signing on the whaler *Acushnet* bound for the South Seas. He jumped ship there, lived in Tahiti, an finally returned as a sailor to the United States. In his fiction he often sought to record and recreate his experiences at sea; among his novels of the sea are *White-Jacket* (1850), *Moby-Dick* (1851), and the posthumously published *Billy Budd*. Deeply distressed, like his contemporary Walt Whitman, by the American Civil War, he turned to poetry to record his reflections in the collection *Battle-Pieces* (1866). He published three more volumes of poetry. His writings met with little critical and even less popular success, and he never made enough money to support himself and his family.

Bartleby, the Scrivener: A Story of Wall-Street

I am a rather elderly man. The nature of my avocations, for the last thirty years, has brought me into more than ordinary contact with what would seem an interesting and somewhat singular set of men, of whom, as yet, nothing, that I know of, has ever been written—I mean, the law-copyists, or scriveners. I have known very many of them professionally and privately, and, if I pleased, could relate divers histories, at which good-natured gentlemen might smile, and sentimental souls might weep. But I waive the biographies of all other scriveners, for a few passages in the life of Bartleby, who was a scrivener, the strangest I ever saw, or heard of. While, of other law-copyists, I might write the complete life, of Bartleby nothing of that sort can be done. I believe that no materials exist, for a full and satisfactory biography of this man. It is an irreparable loss to literature. Bartleby was one of those beings of whom nothing is ascertainable, except from the original sources, and, in his case, those are very small. What my own astonished eyes saw of Bartleby, *that* is all I know of him, except, indeed, one vague report, which will appear in the sequel.

Ere introducing the scrivener, as he first appeared to me, it is fit I make some mention of myself, my *employés*, my business, my chambers, and general surroundings; because some such description is indispensable to an adequate understanding of the chief character about to be presented. Imprimis: I am a man who, from his youth upwards, has been filled with a profound conviction that the easiest way of life is the best. Hence, though I belong to a profession proverbially energetic and nervous, even to turbulence, at times, yet nothing of that sort have I ever suffered to invade my peace. I am one of those unambitious lawyers who never address a jury, or in any way draw down public applause; but, in the cool tranquillity of a snug retreat, do a snug business among rich men's bonds, and mortgages, and title-deeds. All who know me, consider me an eminently *safe* man. The late John Jacob Astor, a personage little given to poetic enthusiasm, had no hesitation in pronouncing my first grand point to be prudence; my next, method. I do not speak it in vanity, but simply record the fact, that I was not unemployed in my profession by the late John Jacob Astor, a name which, I admit, I love to repeat; for it hath a rounded and orbicular sound to it, and rings like unto bullion. I will freely add, that I was not insensible to the late John Jacob Astor's good opinion.

Some time prior to the period at which this little history begins, my avocations had been largely increased. The good old office, now extinct in the State of New York, of a Master in Chancery, had been conferred upon me. It was not a very arduous office, but very pleasantly remunerative. I seldom lose my temper; much more seldom indulge in dangerous indignation at wrongs and outrages; but I must be permitted to be rash here and declare, that I consider the sudden and violent abrogation of the office of Master in Chancery, by the new Constitution, as a—premature act; inasmuch as I had counted upon a life-lease of the profits, whereas I only received those of a few short years. But this is by the way.

My chambers were up stairs, at No. — Wall Street. At one end, they looked upon the white wall of the interior of a spacious skylight shaft, penetrating the building from top to bottom.

This view might have been considered rather tame than otherwise, deficient in what landscape painters call "life." But, if so, the view from the other end of my chambers offered, at least, a contrast, if nothing more. In that direction, my windows commanded an unobstructed view of a lofty brick wall, black by age and everlasting shade; which wall required no spy-glass to bring out its lurking beauties, but, for the benefit of all near-sighted spectators, was pushed up to within ten feet of my window-panes. Owing to the great height of the surrounding buildings, and my chambers being on the second floor, the interval between this wall and mine not a little resembled a huge square cistern.

At the period just preceding the advent of Bartleby, I had two persons as copyists in my employment, and a promising lad as an office-boy. First, Turkey; second, Nippers; third, Ginger Nut. These may seem names, the like of which are not usually found in the Directory. In truth, they were nicknames, mutually conferred upon each other by my three clerks, and were deemed expressive of their respective persons or characters. Turkey was a short, pursy Englishman, of about my own age—that is, somewhere not far from sixty. In the morning, one might say, his face was of a fine florid hue, but after twelve o'clock, meridian—his dinner hour—it blazed like a grate full of Christmas coals; and continued blazing—but, as it were, with a gradual wane—till six o'clock, P.M., or there-abouts; after which, I saw no more of the proprietor of the face, which, gaining its meridian with the sun, seemed to set with it, to rise, culminate, and decline the following day, with the like regularity and undiminished glory. There are many singular coincidences I have known in the course of my life, not the least among which was the fact, that, exactly when Turkey displayed his fullest beams from his red and radiant countenance, just then, too, at that critical moment, began the daily period when I considered his business capacities as seriously disturbed for the remainder of the twenty-four hours. Not that he was absolutely idle, or averse to business then; far from it. The difficulty was, he was apt to be altogether too energetic. There was a strange, inflamed, flurried, flighty recklessness of activity about him. He would be incautious in dipping his pen into his inkstand. All his blots upon my documents were dropped there after twelve o'clock, meridian. Indeed, not only would he be reckless, and sadly given to making blots in the afternoon, but, some days, he went further, and was rather noisy. At such times, too, his face flamed with augmented blazonry, as if cannel coal had been heaped on anthracite. He made an unpleasant racket with his chair; spilled his sand-box; in mending his pens, impatiently split them all to pieces, and threw them on the floor in a sudden passion; stood up, and leaned over his table, boxing his papers about in a most indecorous manner, very sad to behold in an elderly man like him. Nevertheless, as he was in many ways a most valuable person to me, and all the time before twelve o'clock, meridian, was the quickest, steadiest creature, too, accomplishing a great deal of work in a style not easily to be matched—for these reasons, I was willing to overlook his eccentricities, though, indeed, occasionally, I remonstrated with him. I did this very gently, however, because, though the civilest, nay, the blandest and most reverential of men in the morning, yet, in the afternoon, he was disposed, upon provocation, to be slightly rash with his tongue—in fact, insolent. Now, valuing his morning services as I did, and resolved not to lose them—yet, at the same time, made uncomfortable by his inflamed ways after twelve o'clock—and being a man of peace, unwilling by my admonitions to call forth unseemly retorts from him, I took upon me, one Saturday noon (he was always worse on Saturdays) to hint to him, very kindly, that, perhaps, now that he was growing old, it might be well to abridge his labors; in short, he need not come to my chambers after twelve o'clock, but, dinner over, had best go home to his lodgings, and rest himself till tea-time. But no; he insisted upon his afternoon devotions. His countenance became intolerably fervid, as he oratorically assured me—gesticulating with a long ruler at the other end of the room—that if his services in the morning were useful, how indispensable, then, in the afternoon?

"With submission, sir," said Turkey, on this occasion, "I consider myself your right-hand man. In the morning I but marshal and deploy my columns; but in the afternoon I put myself at their head, and gallantly charge the foe, thus"—and he made a violent thrust with the ruler.

"But the blots, Turkey," intimated I.

"True; but, with submission, sir, behold these hairs! I am getting old. Surely, sir, a blot or two of a warm afternoon is not to be severely urged against gray hairs. Old age—even if it blot the page—is honorable. With submission, sir, we *both* are getting old."

This appeal to my fellow-feeling was hardly to be resisted. At all events, I saw that go he would not. So, I made up my mind to let him stay, resolving, nevertheless, to see to it that, during the afternoon, he had to do with my less important papers.

Nippers, the second on my list, was a whiskered, sallow, and, upon the whole, rather piratical-looking young man, of about five-and-twenty. I always deemed him the victim of two evil powers—ambition and indigestion. The ambition was evinced by a certain impatience of the duties of a mere copyist, an unwarrantable usurpation of strictly professional affairs, such as the original drawing up of legal documents. The indigestion seemed betokened in an occasional nervous testiness and grinning irritability, causing the teeth to audibly grind together over mistakes committed in copying; unnecessary maledictions, hissed, rather than spoken, in the heat of business; and especially by a continual discontent with the height of the table where he worked. Though of a very ingenious mechanical turn, Nippers could never get this table to suit him. He put chips under it, blocks of various sorts, bits of pasteboard, and at last went so far as to attempt an exquisite adjustment, by final pieces of folded blotting-paper. But no invention would answer. If, for the sake of easing his back, he brought the table-lid at a sharp angle well up towards his chin, and wrote there like a man using the steep roof of a Dutch house for his desk, then he declared that it stopped the circulation in his arms. If now he lowered the table to his waistbands, and stooped over it in writing, then there was a sore aching in his back. In short, the truth of the matter was, Nippers knew not what he wanted. Or, if he wanted anything, it was to be rid of a scrivener's table altogether. Among the manifestations of his diseased ambition was a fondness he had for receiving visits from certain ambiguous-looking fellows in seedy coats, whom he called his clients. Indeed, I was aware that not only was he, at times, considerable of a ward-politician, but he occasionally did a little business at the Justices' courts, and was not unknown on the steps of the Tombs. I have good reason to believe, however, that one individual who called upon him at my chambers, and who, with a grand air, he insisted was his client, was no other than a dun, and the alleged title-deed, a bill. But, with all his failings, and the annoyances he caused me, Nippers, like his compatriot Turkey, was a very useful man to me; wrote a neat, swift hand; and, when he chose, was not deficient in a gentlemanly sort of deportment. Added to this, he always dressed in a gentlemanly sort of way; and so, incidentally, reflected credit upon my chambers. Whereas, with respect to Turkey, I had much ado to keep him from being a reproach to me. His clothes were apt to look oily, and smell of eating-houses. He wore his pantaloons very loose and baggy in summer. His coats were execrable; his hat not to be handled. But while the hat was a thing of indifference to me, inasmuch as his natural civility and deference, as a dependent Englishman, always led him to doff it the moment he entered the room, yet his coat was another matter. Concerning his coats, I reasoned with him; but with no effect. The truth was, I suppose, that a man with so small an income could not afford to sport such a lustrous face and a lustrous coat at one and the same time. As Nippers once observed, Turkey's money went chiefly for red ink. One winter day, I presented Turkey with a highly respectable-looking coat of my own—a padded gray coat, of a most comfortable warmth, and which buttoned straight up from the knee to the neck. I thought Turkey would appreciate the favor, and abate his rashness and obstreperousness of afternoons. But no; I verily believe that buttoning himself up in so downy and blanket-like a coat had a pernicious effect upon him—upon the same principle that too much oats are bad for horses. In fact, precisely as a rash, restive horse is said to feel his oats, so Turkey felt his coat. It made him insolent. He was a man whom prosperity harmed.

Though, concerning the self-indulgent habits of Turkey, I had my own private surmises, yet, touching Nippers, I was well persuaded that, whatever might be his faults in other respects, he was, at least, a temperate young man. But, indeed, nature herself seemed to have been his vintner, and, at his birth, charged him so thoroughly with an irritable, brandy-like disposition, that all subsequent potations were needless. When I consider how, amid the stillness of my chambers, Nippers would sometimes impatiently rise from his seat, and stopping over his table, spread his arms wide apart, seize the whole desk, and move it, and jerk it, with a grim, grinding motion on the floor, as if the table were a perverse voluntary agent, intent on thwarting and vexing him, I plainly perceive that, for Nippers, brandy-and-water were altogether superfluous.

It was fortunate for me that, owing to its peculiar cause—indigestion—the irritability and consequent nervousness of Nippers were mainly observable in the morning, while in the afternoon he was comparatively mild. So that, Turkey's paroxysms only coming on about twelve o'clock, I never had to do with their eccentricities at one time. Their fits relieved each other, like guards. When Nippers's was on, Turkey's was off; and *vice versa*. This was a good natural arrangement under the circumstances.

Ginger Nut, the third on my list, was a lad, some twelve years old. His father was a carman, ambitious of seeing his son on the bench instead of a cart, before he died. So he sent him to my office, as student at law, errand-boy, cleaner and sweeper, at the rate of one dollar a week. He had a little desk to himself, but he did not use it much. Upon inspection, the drawer exhibited a great array of the shells of various sorts of nuts. Indeed, to this quick-witted youth, the whole noble science of the law was contained in a nut-shell. Not the least among the employments of Ginger Nut, as well as one which he discharged with the most alacrity, was his duty as cake and apple purveyor for Turkey and Nippers. Copying law-papers being proverbially a dry, husky sort of business, my two scriveners were fain to moisten their mouths very often with Spitzenbergs, to be had at the numerous stalls nigh the Custom House and Post Office. Also, they sent Ginger Nut very frequently for that peculiar cake—small, flat, round, and very spicy—after which he had been named by them. Of a cold morning, when business was but dull, Turkey would gobble up scores of these cakes, as if they were mere wafers—indeed, they sell them at the rate of six· or eight for a penny—the scrape of his pen blending with the crunching of the crisp particles in his mouth. Of all the fiery afternoon blunders and flurried rashnesses of Turkey, was his once moistening a ginger-cake between his lips, and clapping it on to a mortgage, for a seal. I came within an ace of dismissing him then. But he mollified me by making an oriental bow, and saying—

"With submission, sir, it was generous of me to find you in stationery on my account."

Now my original business—that of a conveyancer and title hunter, and drawer-up of recondite documents of all sorts—was considerably increased by receiving the Master's office. There was now great work for scriveners. Not only must I push the clerks already with me, but I must have additional help.

In answer to my advertisement, a motionless young man one morning stood upon my office threshold, the door being open, for it was summer. I can see that figure now—pallidly neat, pitiably respectable, incurably forlorn! It was Bartleby.

After a few words touching his qualifications, I engaged him, glad to have among my corps of copyists a man of so singularly sedate an aspect, which I thought might operate beneficially upon the flighty temper of Turkey, and the fiery one of Nippers.

I should have stated before that ground-glass folding-doors divided my premises into two parts, one of which was occupied by my scriveners, the other by myself. According to my humor, I threw open these doors, or closed them. I resolved to assign Bartleby a corner by the folding-doors, but on my side of them, so as to have this quiet man within easy call, in case any trifling thing was to be done. I placed his desk close up to a small side-window in that part of the room, a window which originally had afforded a lateral view of certain grimy back-yards and bricks, but which, owing to subsequent erections, commanded at present no view at all, though it gave some light. Within three feet of the panes was a wall, and the light came down from far above, between two lofty buildings, as from a very small opening in a dome. Still further to a satisfactory arrangement, I procured a high green folding screen, which might entirely isolate Bartleby from my sight, though not remove him from my voice. And thus, in a manner, privacy and society were conjoined.

At first, Bartleby did an extraordinary quantity of writing. As if long famishing for something to copy, he seemed to gorge himself on my documents. There was no pause for digestion. He ran a day and night line copying by sunlight and by candle-light. I should have been quite delighted with his application, had he been cheer-fully industrious. But he wrote on silently, palely, mechanically.

It is, of course, an indispensable part of a scrivener's business to verify the accuracy of his copy, word by word. Where there are two or more scriveners in an office, they assist each other in this exami-nation, one reading from the copy, the other holding the original. It is a very dull, wearisome, and lethargic affair. I can readily imagine that, to some sanguine temperaments, it would be altogether intol-erable. For example, I cannot credit that the mettlesome poet, Byron, would have contentedly sat down with Bartleby to examine a law document of, say five hundred pages, closely written in a crimpy hand.

Now and then, in the haste of business, it had been my habit to assist in comparing some brief document myself, calling Turkey or Nippers for this purpose. One object I had, in placing Bartleby so handy to me behind the screen, was, to avail myself of his services on such trivial occasions. It was on the third day, I think, of his being with me, and before any necessity had arisen for having his own writing examined, that, being much hurried to complete a small affair I had in hand, I abruptly called to Bartleby. In my haste and natural expectancy of instant compliance, I sat with my head bent over the original on my desk, and my right hand sideways, and somewhat nervously extended with the copy, so that, immedi-ately upon emerging from his retreat, Bartleby might snatch it and proceed to business without the least delay.

In this very attitude did I sit when I called to him, rapidly stating what it was I wanted him to do—namely, to examine a small paper with me. Imagine my surprise, nay, my consternation, when, with-out moving from his privacy, Bartleby, in a singularly mild, firm voice, replied, "I would prefer not to."

I sat awhile in perfect silence, rallying my stunned faculties. Im-mediately it occurred to me that my ears had deceived me, or Bart-leby had entirely misunderstood my meaning. I repeated my re-quest in the clearest tone I could assume; but in quite as clear a one came the previous reply, "I would prefer not to."

"Prefer not to," echoed I, rising in high excitement, and crossing the room with a stride. "What do you mean? Are you moon-struck? I want you to help me compare this sheet here—take it," and I thrust it towards him.

"I would prefer not to," said he.

I looked at him steadfastly. His face was leanly composed; his gray eye dimly calm. Not a wrinkle of agitation rippled him. Had there been the least uneasiness, anger, impatience or impertinence in his manner; in other words, had there been anything ordinarily human about him, doubtless I should have violently dismissed him from the premises. But as it was, I should have as soon thought of turning my pale plaster-of-paris bust of Cicero out of doors. I stood gazing at him awhile, as he went on with his own writing, and then reseated myself at my desk. This is very strange, thought I. What had one best do? But my business hurried me. I concluded to forget the matter for the present, reserving it for my future leisure. So, calling Nippers from the other room, the paper was speedily examined.

A few days after this, Bartleby concluded four lengthy documents, being quadruplicates of a week's testimony taken before me in my High Court of Chancery. It became necessary to examine them. It was an important suit, and great accuracy was imperative. Having all things arranged, I called Turkey, Nippers and Ginger Nut, from the next room, meaning to place the four copies in the hands of my four clerks, while I should read from the original. Accordingly, Turkey, Nippers and Ginger Nut had taken their seats in a row, each with his document in his hand, when I called to Bartleby to join this interesting group.

"Bartleby! quick, I am waiting."

I heard a slow scrape of his chair legs on the uncarped floor, and soon he appeared standing at the entrance of his hermitage.

"What is wanted?" said he, mildly.

"The copies, the copies," said I, hurriedly. "We are going to examine them. There"—and I held towards him the fourth quadruplicate.

"I would prefer not to," he said, and gently disappeared behind the screen.

For a few moments I was turned into a pillar of salt, standing at the head of my seated column of clerks. Recovering myself, I advanced towards the screen, and demanded the reason for such extraordinary conduct.

"*Why* do you refuse?"

"I would prefer not to."

With any other man I should have flown outright into a dreadful passion, scorned all further words, and thrust him ignominiously from my presence. But there was something about Bartleby that not only strangely disarmed me, but, in a wonderful manner, touched and disconcerted me. I began to reason with him.

"These are your own copies we are about to examine. It is labor saving to you, because one examination will answer for your four papers. It is common usage. Every copyist is bound to help examine his copy. Is it not so? Will you not speak? Answer!"

"I prefer not to," he replied in a flute-like tone. It seemed to me that, while I had been addressing him, he carefully revolved every statement that I made; fully comprehended the meaning; could not gainsay the irresistible conclusion; but, at the same time, some paramount consideration prevailed with him to reply as he did.

"You are decided, then, not to comply with my request—a request made according to common usage and common sense?"

He briefly gave me to understand, that on that point my judgment was sound. Yes: his decision was irreversible.

It is not seldom the case that, when a man is browbeaten in some unprecedented and violently unreasonable way, he begins to stagger in his own plainest faith. He begins, as it were, vaguely to surmise that, wonderful as it may be, all the justice and all the reason is on the other side. Accordingly, if any disinterested persons are present, he turns to them for some reinforcement for his own faltering mind.

"Turkey," said I, "what do you think of this? Am I not right?"

"With submission, sir," said Turkey, in his blandest tone, "I think you are."

"Nippers," said I, "what do *you* think of it?"

"I think I should kick him out of the office."

(The reader of nice perceptions will here perceive that, it being morning Turkey's answer is couched in polite and tranquil terms, but Nippers replies in ill-tempered ones. Or, to repeat a previous sentence, Nippers's ugly mood was on duty, and Turkey's off.)

"Ginger Nut," said I, willing to enlist the smallest suffrage in my behalf, "what do *you* think of it?"

"I think, sir, he's a little *luny*," replied Ginger Nut, with a grin

"You hear what they say," said I, turning towards the screen, "come forth and do your duty."

But he vouchsafed no reply. I pondered a moment in sore perplexity. But once more business hurried me. I determined again to postpone the consideration of this dilemma to my future leisure. With a little trouble we made out to examine the papers without Bartleby, though at every page or two Turkey deferentially dropped his opinion, that this proceeding was quite out of the common; while Nippers, twitching in his chair with a dyspeptic nervousness, ground out, between his set teeth, occasional hissing maledictions against the stubborn oaf behind the screen. And for his (Nippers's) part, this was the first and the last time he would do another man's business without pay.

Meanwhile Bartleby sat in his hermitage, oblivious to everything but his own peculiar business there.

Some days passed, the scrivener being employed upon another lengthy work. His late remarkable conduct led me to regard his ways narrowly. I observed that he never went to dinner; indeed, that he never went anywhere. As yet I had never, of my personal knowledge, known him to be outside of my office. He was a perpetual sentry in the corner. At about eleven o'clock though, in the morning, I noticed that Ginger Nut would advance toward the opening in Bartleby's screen, as if silently beckoned thither by a gesture invisible to me where I sat. The boy would then leave the office, jingling a few pence, and reappear with a handful of ginger-nuts, which he delivered in the hermitage, receiving two of the cakes for his trouble.

He lives, then, on ginger-nuts, thought I; never eats a dinner, properly speaking; he must be a vegetarian, then, but no; he never eats even vegetables, he eats nothing but ginger-nuts. My mind then ran on in reveries concerning the probable effects upon the human constitution of living entirely on ginger-nuts. Ginger-nuts are so called, because they contain ginger as one of their peculiar constituents and the final flavoring one. Now, what was ginger? A hot, spicy thing. Was Bartleby hot and spicy? Not at all. Ginger, then, had no effect upon Bartleby. Probably he preferred it should have none.

Nothing so aggravates an earnest person as a passive resistance. If the individual so resisted be of a not inhumane temper, and the resisting one perfectly harmless in his passivity, then, in the better moods of the former, he will endeavor charitably to construe to his imagination what proves impossible to be solved by his judgment. Even so, for the most part, I regarded Bartleby and his ways. Poor fellow! thought I, he means no mischief; it is plain he intends no insolence; his aspect sufficiently evinces that his eccentricities are involuntary. He is useful to me. I can get along with him. If I turn him away, the chances are he will fall in with some less indulgent employer, and then he will be rudely treated, and perhaps driven forth miserably to starve. Yes. Here I can cheaply purchase a delicious self-approval. To befriend Bartleby; to humor him in his strange wilfulness, will cost me little or nothing, while I lay up in my soul what will eventually prove a sweet morsel for my conscience. But this mood was not invariable with me. The passiveness of Bartleby sometimes irritated me. I felt strangely goaded on to encounter him in a new opposition—to elicit some angry spark from him answerable to my own. But, indeed, I might as well have essayed to strike fire with my knuckles against a bit of Windsor soap. But one afternoon the evil impulse in me mastered me, and the following little scene ensued:

"Bartleby," said I, "when those papers are all copied, I will compare them with you."

"I would prefer not to."

"How? Surely you do not mean to persist in that mulish vagary?"
No answer.

I threw open the folding-doors near by, and, turning upon Turkey and Nippers, exclaimed:

"Bartleby a second times says, he won't examine his papers. What do you think of it, Turkey?"

It was afternoon, be it remembered. Turkey sat glowing like a brass boiler; his bald head steaming; his hands reeling among his blotted papers.

"Think of it?" roared Turkey. "I think I'll just step behind his screen, and black his eyes for him!"

So saying, Turkey rose to his feet and threw his arms into a pugilistic position. He was hurrying away to make good his promise, when I detained him, alarmed at the effect of incautiously rousing Turkey's combativeness after dinner.

"Sit down, Turkey," said I, "and hear what Nippers has to say. What do you think of it, Nippers? Would I not be justified in immediately dismissing Bartleby?"

"Excuse me, that is for you to decide, sir. I think his conduct quite unusual, and, indeed, unjust, as regards Turkey and myself. But it may only be a passing whim."

"Ah," exclaimed I, "you have strangely changed your mind, then—you speak very gently of him now."

"All beer," cried Turkey; "gentleness is effects of beer—Nippers and I dined together to-day. You see how gentle I am, sir. Shall I go and black his eyes?"

"You refer to Bartleby, I suppose. No, not to-day, Turkey," I replied; "pray, put up your fists."

I closed the doors, and again advanced towards Bartleby. I felt additional incentives tempting me to my fate. I burned to be rebelled against again. I remembered that Bartleby never left the office.

"Bartleby," said I, "Ginger Nut is away; just step around to the Post Office, won't you?" (it was but a three minutes' walk) "and see if there is anything for me."

"I would prefer not to."

"You *will* not?"

"I *prefer* not."

I staggered to my desk, and sat there in a deep study. My blind inveteracy returned. Was there any other thing in which I could procure myself to be ignominousy repulsed by this lean, penniless wight?—my hired clerk? What added thing is there, perfectly reasonable, that he will be sure to refuse to do?

"Bartleby!"

No answer.

"Bartleby," in a louder tone.

No answer.

"Bartleby," I roared.

Like a very ghost, agreeably to the laws of magical invocation, at the third summons, he appeared at the entrance of his hermitage.

"Go to the next room, and tell Nippers to come to me."

"I prefer not to," he respectfully and slowly said, and mildly disappeared.

"Very good, Bartleby," said I, in a quiet sort of serenely-severe self-possessed tone, intimating the unalterable purpose of some terrible retribution very close at hand. At the moment I half intended something of the kind. But upon the whole, as it was drawing towards my dinner-hour, I thought it best to put on my hat and walk home for the day, suffering much from perplexity and distress of mind.

Shall I acknowledge it? The conclusion of this whole business was, that it soon became a fixed fact of my chambers, that a pale young scrivener, by the name of Bartleby, had a desk there; that he copied for me at the usual rate of four cents a folio (one hundred words); but he was permanently exempt from examining the work done by him, that duty being transferred to Turkey and Nippers, out of compliment, doubtless, to their superior acuteness; moreover, said Bartleby was never, on any account, to be dispatched on the most trivial errand of any sort; and that even if entreated to take upon him such a matter, it was generally understood that he would "prefer not to"—in other words, that he would refuse point-blank.

As days passed on, I became considerably reconciled to Bartleby. His steadiness, his freedom from all dissipation, his incessant industry (except when he chose to throw himself into a standing revery behind his screen), his great stillness, his unalterableness of demeanor under all circumstances, made him a valuable acquisition. One prime thing was this—*he was always there*—first in the morning, continually through the day, and the last at night. I had a singular confidence in his honesty. I felt my most precious papers perfectly safe in his hands. Sometimes, to be sure, I could not, for the very soul of me, avoid falling into sudden spasmodic passions with him. For it was exceeding difficult to bear in mind all the time those strange peculiarities, privileges, and unheard-of exemptions, forming the tacit stipulations on Bartleby's part under which he remained in my office. Now and then, in the eagerness of dispatching pressing business, I would inadvertently summon Bartleby, in a short, rapid tone, to put his finger, say, on the incipient tie of a bit of red tape with which I was about compressing some papers. Of course, from behind the screen the usual answer, "I prefer not to," was sure to come; and then, how could a human creature, with the common infirmities of our nature, refrain from bitterly exclaiming upon such perverseness—such unreasonableness? However, every added repulse of this sort which I received only tended to lessen the probability of my repeating the inadvertence.

Here it must be said, that, according to the custom of most legal gentlemen occupying chambers in densely-populated law buildings, there were several keys to my door. One was kept by a woman residing in the attic, which person weekly scrubbed and daily swept and dusted my apartments. Another was kept by Turkey for convenience sake. The third I sometimes carried in my own pocket. The fourth I knew not who had.

Now, one Sunday morning I happened to go to Trinity Church, to hear a celebrated preacher, and finding myself rather early on the ground I thought I would walk round to my chambers for a while. Luckily I had my key with me; but upon applying it to the lock, I found it resisted by something inserted from the inside. Quite surprised, I called out; when to my consternation a key was turned from within; and thrusting his lead visage at me, and holding the door ajar, the apparition of Bartleby appeared, in his shirt-sleeves, and otherwise in a strangely tattered deshabille, saying quietly that he was sorry, but he was deeply engaged just then, and—preferred not admitting me at present. In a brief word or two, he moreover added, that perhaps I had better walk round the block two or three times, and by that time he would probably have concluded his affairs.

Now, the utterly unsurmised appearance of Bartleby, tenanting my law-chambers of a Sunday morning, with his cadaverously gentlemanly *nonchalance*, yet withal firm and self-possessed, had such a strange effect upon me, that incontinently I slunk away from my own door, and did as desired. But not without sundry twinges of impotent rebellion against the mild effrontery of this unaccountable scrivener. Indeed, it was his wonderful mildness chiefly, which not only disarmed me, but unmanned me, as it were. For I consider that one, for the time, is a sort of unmanned when he tranquilly permits his hired clerk to dictate to him, and order him away from his own premises. Furthermore, I was full of uneasiness as to what Bartleby could possibly be doing in my office in his shirt-sleeves, and in an otherwise dismantled condition of a Sunday morning. Was anything amiss going on? Nay, that was out of the question. It was not to be thought of for a moment that Bartleby was an immoral person. But what could he be doing there—copying? Nay again, whatever might be his eccentricities, Bartleby was an eminently decorous person.

He would be the last man to sit down to his desk in any state approaching to nudity. Besides, it was Sunday; and there was something about Bartleby that forbade the supposition that he would by any secular occupation violate the proprieties of the day.

Nevertheless, my mind was not pacified; and full of a restless curiosity, at last I returned to the door. Without hindrance I inserted my key, opened it, and entered. Bartleby was not to be seen. I looked round anxiously, peeped behind his screen; but it was very plain that he was gone. Upon more closely examining the place, I surmised that for an indefinite period Bartleby must have ate, dressed, and slept in my office, and that too without plate, mirror, or bed. The cushioned seat of a rickety old sofa in one corner bore the faint impress of a lean, reclining form. Rolled away under his desk, I found a blanket; under the empty grate, a blacking box and brush; on a chair, a tin basin, with soap and a ragged towel; in a newspaper a few crumbs of ginger-nuts and a morsel of cheese. Yes, thought I, it is evident enough that Bartleby had been making his home here, keeping bachelor's hall all by himself. Immediately then the thought came sweeping across me, what miserable friendlessness and loneliness are here revealed! His poverty is great; but his solitude, how horrible! Think of it. Of a Sunday, Wall Street is deserted as Petra; and every night of every day it is an emptiness. This building, too, which of week-days hums with industry and life, at nightfall echoes with sheer vacancy, and all through Sunday is forlorn. And here Bartleby makes his home; sole spectator of a solitude which he has seen all populous—a sort of innocent and transformed Marius brooding among the ruins of Carthage!

For the first time in my life a feeling of overpowering stinging melancholy seized me. Before, I had never experienced aught but a not unpleasing sadness. The bond of a common humanity now drew me irresistibly to gloom. A fraternal melancholy! For both I and Bartleby were sons of Adam. I remembered the bright silks and sparkling faces I had seen that day, in gala trim, swan-like sailing down the Mississippi of Broadway; and I contrasted them with the pallid copyist, and thought to myself, Ah, happiness courts the light, so we deem the world is gay; but misery hides aloof, so we deem that misery there is none. These sad fancyings—chimeras, doubtless of a sick and silly brain—led on to other and more special thoughts, concerning the eccentricities of Bartleby. Presentiments of strange discoveries hovered round me. The scrivener's pale form appeared to me laid out, among uncaring strangers, in its shivering winding-sheet.

Suddenly I was attracted by Bartleby's closed desk, the key in open sight left in the lock.

I mean no mischief, seek the gratification of no heartless curiosity, thought I; besides, the desk is mine, and its contents, too, so I will make bold to look within. Everything was methodically arranged, the papers smoothly placed. The pigeon-holes were deep, and removing the files of documents, I groped into their recesses. Presently I felt something there, and dragged it out. It was an old bandanna handkerchief, heavy and knotted. I opened it, and saw it was a saving's bank.

I now recalled all the quiet mysteries which I had noted in the man. I remembered that he never spoke but to answer; that, though at intervals he had considerable time to himself, yet I had never seen him reading—no, not even a newspaper; that for long periods he would stand looking out, at his pale window behind the screen, upon the dead brick wall; I was quite sure he never visited any refectory or eating-house; while his pale face clearly indicated that he never drank beer like Turkey, or tea and coffee even, like other men; that he never went anywhere in particular that I could learn; never went out for a walk, unless, indeed, that was the case at present; that he had declined telling who he was or whence he came, or whether he had any relatives in the world; that though so thin and pale, he never complained of ill-health. And more than all, I remembered a certain unconscious air of pallid—how shall I call it?—of pallid haughtiness, say, or rather an austere reserve about him which had positively awed me into my tame compliance with his eccentricities, when I had feared to ask him to do the slightest incidental thing for me, even though I might know, from his long continued motionlessness, that behind his screen he must be standing in one of those dead-wall reveries of his.

Revolving all these things, and coupling them with the recently discovered fact, that he made my office his constant abiding place and home, and not forgetful of his morbid moodiness; revolving all these things, a prudential feeling began to steal over me. My first emotions had been those of pure melancholy and sincerest pity; but just in proportion as the forlornness of Bartleby grew and grew to my imagination, did that same melancholy merge into fear, that pity into repulsion. So true it is, and so terrible, too, that up to a certain point the thought or sight of misery enlists our best affections; but, in certain special cases, beyond that point it does not. They err who would assert that invariably this is owing to the inherent selfishness of the human heart. It rather proceeds from a certain hopelessness of remedying excessive and organic ill. To a sensitive being, pity is not seldom pain. And when at last it is perceived that such pity cannot lead to effectual succor, common sense bids the soul be rid of it. What I saw that morning persuaded me that the scrivener was the victim of innate and incurable disorder. I might give alms to his body; but his body did not pain him; it was his soul that suffered, and his soul I could not reach.

I did not accomplish the purpose of going to Trinity Church that morning. Somehow, the things I had seen disqualified me for the time from church-going. I walked homeward, thinking what I would do with Bartleby. Finally, I resolved upon this—I would put certain calm questions to him the next morning, touching his history, etc., and if he declined to answer them openly and unreservedly (and I supposed he would prefer not), then to give him a twenty dollar bill over and above whatever I might owe him, and tell him his services were no longer required; but that if in any other way I could assist him, I would be happy to do so, especially if he desired to return to his native place, wherever that might be, I would willingly help to defray the expenses. Moreover, if, after reaching home, he found himself at any time in want of aid, a letter from him would be sure of reply.

The next morning came.

"Bartleby," said I, gently calling to him behind his screen.

No reply.

"Bartleby," said I, in a still gentler tone, "come here; I am not going to ask you to do anything you would prefer not to do—I simply wish to speak to you."

Upon this he noiselessly slid into view.

"Will you tell me, Bartleby, where you were born?"

"I would prefer not to."

"Will you tell me *anything* about yourself?"

"I would prefer not to."

"But what reasonable objection can you have to speak to me? I feel friendly towards you."

He did not look at me while I spoke, but kept his glance fixed upon my bust of Cicero, which, as I then sat, was directly behind me, some six inches above my head.

"What is your answer, Bartleby?" said I, after waiting a considerable time for a reply, during which his countenance remained immovable, only there was the faintest conceivable tremor of the white attenuated mouth.

"At present I prefer to give no answer." he said, and retired into his hermitage.

It was rather weak of me I confess, but his manner, on this occasion, nettled me. Not only did there seem to lurk in it a certain calm disdain, but his perverseness seem ungrateful, considering the undeniable good usage and indulgence he had received from me.

Again I sat ruminating what I should do. Mortified as I was at his behavior, and resolved as I had been to dismiss him when I entered my office, nevertheless I strangely felt something superstitious knocking at my heart, and forbidding me to carry out my purpose, and denouncing me for a villain if I dared to breathe one bitter word against this forlornest of mankind. At last, familiarly drawing my chair behind his screen, I sat down and said: "Bartleby, never mind, then, about revealing your history; but let me entreat you, as a friend, to comply as far as may be with the usages of this office. Say now, you will help to examine papers to-morrow or next day: in short, say now, that in a day or two you will begin to be a little reasonable:—say so, Bartleby."

"At present I would prefer not to be a little reasonable," was his mildly cadaverous reply.

Just then the folding-doors opened, and Nippers approached. He seemed suffering from an unusually bad night's rest, induced by severer indigestion than common. He overheard those final words of Bartleby.

"*Prefer not*, eh?" gritted Nippers—"I'd *prefer* him, if I were you, sir," addressing me—"I'd *prefer* him; I'd give him preferences, the stubborn mule! What is it, sir, pray, that he *prefers* not to do now?"

Bartleby moved not a limb.

"Mr. Nippers," said I, "I'd prefer that you would withdraw for the present."

Somehow, of late, I had got into the way of involuntarily using this word "prefer" upon all sorts of not exactly suitable occasions. And I trembled to think that my contact with the scrivener had already and seriously affected me in a mental way. And what further and deeper aberration might it not yet produce? This apprehension had not been without efficacy in determining me to summary measures.

As Nippers, looking very sour and sulky, was departing, Turkey blandly and deferentially approached.

"With submission, sir," said he, "yesterday I was thinking about Bartleby here, and I think that if he would but prefer to take a quart of good ale every day it would do much towards mending him, and enabling him to assist in examining his papers."

"So you have got the word, too," said I, slightly excited.

"With submission, what word, sir?" asked Turkey, respectfully crowding himself into the contracted space behind the screen, and by so doing, making me jostle the scrivener. "What word, sir?"

"I would prefer to be left alone here," said Bartleby, as if offended at being mobbed in his privacy.

"*That's* the word, Turkey," said I—"*that's* it."

"Oh, *prefer*? oh yes—queer word. I never use it myself. But, sir, as I was saying, if he would but prefer—"

"Turkey," interrupted I, "you will please withdraw."

"Oh certainly, sir, if you prefer that I should."

As he opened the folding-door to retire, Nippers at his desk caught a glimpse of me, and asked whether I would prefer to have a certain paper copied on blue paper or white. He did not in the least roguishly accent the word "prefer." It was plain that it involuntarily rolled from his tongue. I thought to myself, surely I must get rid of a demented man, who already has in some degree turned the tongues, if not the heads of myself and clerks. But I thought it prudent not to break the dismission at once.

The next day I noticed that Bartleby did nothing but stand at his window in his dead-wall revery. Upon asking him why he did not write, he said that he had decided upon doing no more writing.

"Why, how now? what next?" exclaimed I, "do no more writing?"

"No more."

"And what is the reason?"

"Do you not see the reason for yourself?" he indifferently replied.

I looked steadfastly at him, and perceived that his eyes looked dull and glazed. Instantly it occurred to me, that his unexampled diligence in copying by his dim window for the first few weeks of his stay with me might have temporarily impaired his vision.

I was touched. I said something in condolence with him. I hinted that of course he did wisely in abstaining from writing for a while; and urged him to embrace that opportunity of taking wholesome exercise in the open air. This, however, he did not do. A few days after this, my other clerks being absent, and being in a great hurry to dispatch certain letters by the mail, I thought that, having nothing else earthly to do, Bartleby would surely be less inflexible than usual, and carry these letters to the post-office. But he blankly declined. So, much to my inconvenience, I went myself.

Still added days went by. Whether Bartleby's eyes improved or not, I could not say. To all appearance, I thought they did. But when I asked him if they did, he vouchsafed no answer. At all events, he would do no copying. At last, in reply to my urgings, he informed me that he had permanently given up copying.

"What!" exclaimed I; "suppose your eyes should get entirely well—better than ever before—would you not copy then?"

"I have given up copying," he answered, and slid aside.

He remained as ever, a fixture in my chamber. Nay—if that were possible—he became still more of a fixture than before. What was to be done? He would do nothing in the office; why should he stay there? In plain fact, he had now become a millstone to me, not only useless as a necklace, but afflictive to bear. Yet I was sorry for him. I speak less than truth when I say that, on his own account, he occasioned me uneasiness. If he would but have named a single relative or friend, I would instantly have written, and urged their taking the poor fellow away to some convenient retreat. But he seemed alone, absolutely alone in the universe. A bit of wreck in the mid-Atlantic. At length, necessities connected with my business tyrannized over all other considerations. Decently as I could, I told Bartleby that in six days' time he must unconditionally leave the office. I warned him to take measures, in the interval, for procuring some other abode. I offered to assist him in this endeavor, if he himself would but take the first step towards a removal. "And when you finally quit me, Bartleby," added I, "I shall see that you go not away entirely unprovided. Six days from this hour, remember."

At the expiration of that period, I peeped behind the screen, and lo! Bartleby was there.

I buttoned up my coat, balanced myself; advanced slowly towards him, touched his shoulder, and said, "The time has come; you must quit this place; I am sorry for you; here is money; but you must go."

"I would prefer not," he replied, with his back still towards me.

"You *must*."

He remained silent.

Now I had an unbounded confidence in this man's common honesty. He had frequently restored to me sixpences and shillings carelessly dropped upon the floor, for I am apt to be very reckless in such shirt-button affairs. The proceeding, then, which followed will not be deemed extraordinary.

"Bartleby," said I, "I owe you twelve dollars on account; here are thirty-two, the odd twenty are yours— Will you take it?" and I handed the bills towards him.

But he made no motion.

"I will leave them here, then," putting them under a weight on the table. Then taking my hat and cane and going to the door, I tranquilly turned and added—"After you have removed your things from these offices, Bartleby, you will of course lock the door—since every one is now gone for the day but you—and if you please, slip your key underneath the mat, so that I may have it in the morning. I shall not see you again; so good-bye to you. If, hereafter, in your new place of abode, I can be of any service to you, do not fail to advise me by letter. Good-bye, Bartleby, and fare you well."

But he answered not a word; like the last column of some ruined temple, he remained standing mute and solitary in the middle of the otherwise deserted room.

As I walked home in a pensive mood, my vanity got the better of my pity. I could not but highly plume myself on my masterly management in getting rid of Bartleby. Masterly I call it, and such it

must appear to any dispassionate thinker. The beauty of my procedure seemed to consist in its perfect quietness. There was no vulgar
bullying, no bravado of any sort, no choleric hectoring, and striding
to and fro across the apartment, jerking out vehement commands for
Bartleby to bundle himself off with his beggarly traps. Nothing of
the kind. Without loudly bidding Bartleby depart—as an inferior
genius might have done—I *assumed* the ground that depart he must;
and upon that assumption built all I had to say. The more I thought
over my procedure, the more I was charmed with it. Nevertheless,
next morning, upon awakening, I had my doubts—I had somehow
slept off the fumes of vanity. One of the coolest and wisest hours a
man has, is just after he awakes in the morning. My procedure
seemed as sagacious as ever—but only in theory. How it would
prove in practice—there was the rub. It was truly a beautiful
thought to have assumed Bartleby's departure; but, after all, that
assumption was simply my own, and none of Bartleby's. The great
point was, not whether I had assumed that he would quit me, but
whether he would prefer so to do. He was more a man of preferences than assumptions.

After breakfast, I walked down town, arguing the probabilities
pro and *con*. One moment I thought it would prove a miserable
failure, and Bartleby would be found all alive at my office as usual;
the next moment it seemed certain that I should find his chair
empty. And so I kept veering about. At the corner of Broadway and
Canal Street, I saw quite an excited group of people standing in
earnest conversation.

"I'll take odds he doesn't," said a voice as I passed.

"Doesn't go?—done!" said I, "put up your money."

I was instinctively putting my hand in my pocket to produce my
own, when I remembered that this was an election day. The words I
had overheard bore no reference to Bartleby, but to the success or
non-success of some candidate for the mayoralty. In my intent frame
of mind, I had, as it were, imagined that all Broadway shared in my
excitement, and were debating the same question with me. I passed
on, very thankful that the uproar of the street screened my momentary absent-mindedness.

As I had intended, I was earlier than usual at my office door. I
stood listening for a moment. All was still. He must be gone. I tried
the knob. The door was locked. Yes, my procedure had worked to a
charm; he indeed must be vanished. Yet a certain melancholy
mixed with this: I was almost sorry for my brilliant success. I was
fumbling under the door mat for the key, which Bartleby was to
have left there for me, when accidentally my knee knocked against a
panel, producing a summoning sound, and in response a voice

came to me from within—"Not yet; I am occupied."

It was Bartleby.

I was thunderstruck. For an instant I stood like the man who, pipe in mouth, was killed one cloudless afternoon long ago in Virginia, by summer lightning; at his own warm open window he was killed, and remained leaning out there upon the dreamy afternoon, till some one touched him, when he fell.

"Not gone!" I murmured at last. But again obeying that wondrous ascendancy which the inscrutable scrivener had over me, and from which ascendancy, for all my chafing, I could not completely escape, I slowly went down stairs and out into the street, and while walking round the block, considered what I should next do in this unheard-of perplexity. Turn the man out by an actual thrusting I could not; to drive him away by calling him hard names would not do; calling in the police was an unpleasant idea; and yet, permit him to enjoy his cadaverous triumph over me—this, too, I could not think of. What was to be done? or, if nothing could be done, was there anything further that I could *assume* in the matter. Yes, as before I had pro-spectively assumed that Bartleby would depart, so now I might re-trospectively assume that departed he was. In the legitimate carry-ing out of this assumption, I might enter my office in a great hurry, and pretending not to see Bartleby at all, walk straight against him as if he were air. Such a proceeding would in a singular degree have the appearance of a home-thrust. It was hardly possible that Bart-leby could withstand such an application of the doctrine of assump-tions. But upon second thoughts the success of the plan seemed rather dubious I resolved to argue the matter over with him again.

"Bartleby," said I, entering the office, with a quietly severe ex-pression, "I am seriously displeased. I am pained, Bartleby. I had thought better of you. I had imagined you of such a gentlemanly organization, that in any delicate dilemma a slight hint would suf-fice—in short, an assumption. But it appears I am deceived. Why," I added, unaffectedly starting, "you have not even touched that money yet," pointing to it, just where I had left it the evening previous.

He answered nothing.

"Will you, or will you not, quit me?" I now demanded in a sud-den passion, advancing close to him.

"I would prefer *not* to quit you," he replied, gently emphasizing the *not*.

"What earthly right have you to stay here? Do you pay any rent? Do you pay my taxes? Or is this property yours?"

He answered nothing.

"Are you ready to go on and write now? Are your eyes recovered?

Could you copy a small paper for me this morning? or help examine a few lines? or step round to the post-office? In a word, will you do anything at all, to give a coloring to your refusal to depart the premises?"

He silently retired into his hermitage.

I was now in such a state of nervous resentment that I thought it but prudent to check myself at present from further demonstrations. Bartleby and I were alone. I remembered the tragedy of the unfortunate Adams and the still more unfortunate Colt in the solitary office of the latter; and how poor Colt, being dreadfully incensed by Adams, and imprudently permitting himself to get wildly excited, was at unawares hurried into his fatal act—an act which certainly no man could possibly deplore more than the actor himself. Often it had occurred to me in my ponderings upon the subject that had that altercation taken place in the public street, or at a private residence, it would not have terminated as it did. It was the circumstance of being alone in a solitary office, up stairs, or a building entirely unhallowed by humanizing domestic associations—an uncarpeted office, doubtless, of a dusty, haggard sort of appearance—this it must have been, which greatly helped to enhance the irritable desperation of the hapless Colt.

But when this old Adam of resentment rose in me and tempted me concerning Bartleby, I grappled him and threw him. How? Why, simply by recalling the divine injunction: "A new commandment give I unto you, that ye love one another." Yes, this it was that saved me. Aside from higher considerations, charity often operates as a vastly wise and prudent principle—a great safeguard to its possessor. Men have committed murder for jealousy's sake, and anger's sake, and hatred's sake, and selfishness' sake, and spiritual pride's sake; but no man, that ever I heard of, ever committed a diabolical murder for sweet charity's sake. Mere self-interest, then, if no better motive can be enlisted, should, especially with high-tempered men, prompt all beings to charity and philanthropy. At any rate, upon the occasion in question, I strove to drown my exasperated feelings towards the scrivener by benevolently construing his conduct. Poor fellow, poor fellow! thought I, he don't mean anything; and besides, he has seen hard times, and ought to be indulged.

I endeavored, also, immediately to occupy myself, and at the same time to comfort my despondency. I tried to fancy, that in the course of the morning, at such time as might prove agreeable to him, Bartleby, of his own free accord, would emerge from his hermitage and take up some decided line of march in the direction of the door. But no. Half-past twelve o'clock came; Turkey began to glow in the face, overturn his inkstand, and become generally obstreperous; Nippers abated down into quietude and courtesy; Ginger Nut munched his noon apple; and Bartleby remained standing at his window in one of his profoundest dead-wall reveries. Will it be credited? Ought I to acknowledge it? That afternoon I left the office without saying one further word to him.

Some days now passed, during which, at leisure intervals I looked a little into "Edwards on the Will," and "Priestley on Necessity." Under the circumstances, those books induced a salutary feeling. Gradually I slid into the persuasion that these troubles of mine, touching the scrivener, had been all predestinated from eternity, and Bartleby was billeted upon me for some mysterious purpose of an all-wise Providence, which it was not for a mere mortal like me to fathom. Yes, Bartleby, stay there behind your screen, thought I; I shall persecute you no more; you are harmless and noiseless as any of these old chairs; in short, I never feel so private as when I know you are here. At last I see it, I feel it; I penetrate to the predestinated purpose of my life. I am content. Others may have loftier parts to enact; but my mission in this world, Bartleby, is to furnish you with office-room for such period as you may see fit to remain.

I believe that this wise and blessed frame of mind would have continued with me, had it not been for the unsolicited and unchari-table remarks obtruded upon me by my professional friends who visited the rooms. But thus it often is, that the constant friction of illiberal minds wears out at last the best resolves of the more gener-ous. Though to be sure, when I reflected upon it, it was not strange that people entering my office should be struck by the peculiar aspect of the unaccountable Bartleby, and so be tempted to throw out some sinister observations concerning him. Sometimes an at-torney, having business with me, and calling at my office, and find-ing no one but the scrivener there, would undertake to obtain some sort of precise information from him touching my whereabouts; but without heeding his idle talk, Bartleby would remain standing im-movable in the middle of the room. So after contemplating him in that position for a time, the attorney would depart, no wiser than he came.

Also, when a reference was going on, and the room full of lawyers and witnesses, and business driving fast, some deeply-occupied le-gal gentleman present, seeing Bartleby wholly unemployed, would request him to run round to his (the legal gentleman's) office and fetch some papers for him. Thereupon, Bartleby would tranquilly decline, and yet remain idle as before. Then the lawyer would give a great stare, and turn to me. And what could I say? At last I was made aware that all through the circle of my professional acquaintance, a whisper of wonder was running round, having reference to the strange creature I kept at my office. This worried me very much. And as the idea came upon me of his possibly turning out a long-lived man, and keep occupying my chambers, and denying my authority; and perplexing my visitors; and scandalizing my professional reputation; and casting a general gloom over the premises; keeping soul and body together to the last upon his savings (for doubtless he spent but half a dime a day), and in the end perhaps outlive me, and claim possession of my office by right of his perpetual occupancy: as all these dark anticipations crowded upon me more and more, and my friends continually intruded their relentless remarks upon the apparition in my room; a great change was wrought in me. I resolved to gather all my faculties together, and forever rid me of this intolerable incubus.

Ere revolving any complicated project, however, adapted to this end, I first simply suggested to Bartleby the propriety of his permanent departure. In a calm and serious tone, I commended the idea to his careful and mature consideration. But, having taken three days to meditate upon it, he apprised me, that his original determination remained the same; in short, that he still preferred to abide with me.

What shall I do? I now said to myself, buttoning up my coat to the last button. What shall I do? what ought I to do? What does conscience say I *should* do with this man, or, rather, ghost. Rid myself of him, I must; go, he shall. But how? You will not thrust him, the poor, pale, passive mortal—you will not thrust such a helpless creature out of your door? you will not dishonor yourself by such cruelty? No, I will not, I cannot do that. Rather would I let him live and die here, and then mason up his remains in the wall. What, then, will you do? For all your coaxing, he will not budge. Bribes he leaves under your own paper-weight on your table; in short, it is quite plain that he prefers to cling to you.

Then something severe, something unusual must be done. What! surely you will not have him collared by a constable, and commit his innocent pallor to the common jail? And upon what ground could you procure such a thing to be done?—a vagrant, is he? What! he a vagrant, a wanderer, who refuses to budge? It is because he will *not* be a vagrant, then, that you seek to count him *as* a vagrant. That is too absurd. No visible means of support: there I have him. Wrong again: for indubitably he *does* support himself, and that is the only unanswerable proof that any man can show of his possessing the means so to do. No more then. Since he will not quit me, I must quit him. I will change my offices; I will move elsewhere, and give him fair notice, that if I find him on my new premises I will then proceed against him as a common trespasser.

Acting accordingly, next day I thus addressed him: "I find these chambers too far from the City Hall; the air is unwholesome. In a word, I propose to remove my offices next week, and shall no longer require your services. I tell you this now, in order that you may seek another place."

He made no reply, and nothing more was said.

On the appointed day I engaged carts and men, proceeded to my chambers, and, having but little furniture, everything was removed in a few hours. Throughout, the scrivener remained standing behind the screen, which I directed to be removed the last thing. It was withdrawn; and, being folded up like a huge folio, left him the motionless occupant of a naked room. I stood in the entry watching him a moment, while something from within me upbraided me.

I re-entered, with my hand in my pocket—and—and my heart in my mouth.

"Good-bye, Bartleby; I am going—good-bye, and God some way bless you; and take that," slipping something in his hand. But it dropped upon the floor, and then—strange to say—I tore myself from him whom I had so longed to be rid of.

Established in my new quarters, for a day or two I kept the door locked, and started at every footfall in the passages. When I returned to my rooms, after any little absence, I would pause at the threshold for an instant, and attentively listen, ere applying my key. But these fears were needless. Bartleby never came nigh me.

I thought all was going well, when a perturbed-looking stranger visited me, inquiring whether I was the person who had recently occupied rooms at No.—Wall Street.

Full of forebodings, I replied that I was.

"Then, sir," said the stranger, who proved a lawyer, "you are responsible for the man you left there. He refuses to do any copying; he refuses to do anything; he says he prefers not to; and he refuses to quit the premises."

"I am very sorry, sir," said I, with assumed tranquillity, but an inward tremor, "but, really, the man you allude to is nothing to me—he is no relation or apprentice of mine, that you should hold me responsible for him."

"In mercy's name, who is he?"

"I certainly cannot inform you. I know nothing about him. Formerly I employed him as a copyist; but he has done nothing for me now for some time past."

"I shall settle him, then—good morning, sir."

Several days passed, and I heard nothing more; and, though I often felt a charitable prompting to call at the place and see poor

Bartleby, yet a certain squeamishness, of I know not what, withheld me.

All is over with him, by this time, thought I, at last, when, through another week, no further intelligence reached me. But, coming to my room the day after, I found several persons waiting at my door in a high state of nervous excitement.

"That's the man—here he comes," cried the foremost one, whom I recognized as the lawyer who had previously called upon me alone.

"You must take him away, sir, at once," cried a portly person among them, advancing upon me, and whom I knew to be the landlord of No.—Wall Street. "These gentlemen, my tenants, cannot stand it any longer; Mr. B——," pointing to the lawyer, "has turned him out of his room, and he now persists in haunting the building generally, sitting upon the banisters of the stairs by day, and sleeping in the entry by night. Everybody is concerned; clients are leaving the offices; some fears are entertained of a mob; something you must do, and that without delay."

Aghast at this torrent, I fell back before it, and would fain have locked myself in my new quarters. In vain I persisted that Bartleby was nothing to me—no more than to any one else. In vain—I was the last person known to have anything to do with him, and they held me to the terrible account. Fearful, then, of being exposed in the papers (as one person present obscurely threatened), I considered the matter, and, at length, said, that if the lawyer would give me a confidential interview with the scrivener, in his (the lawyer's) own room, I would, that afternoon, strive my best to rid them of the nuisance they complained of.

Going up stairs to my old haunt, there was Bartleby silently sitting upon the banister at the landing.

"What are you doing here, Bartleby?" said I.

"Sitting upon the banister," he mildly replied.

I motioned him into the lawyer's room, who then left us.

"Bartleby," said I, "are you aware that you are the cause of great tribulation to me, by persisting in occupying the entry after being dismissed from the office?"

No answer.

"Now one of two things must take place. Either you must do something, or something must be done to you. Now what sort of business would you like to engage in? Would you like to re-engage in copying for some one?"

"No; I would prefer not to make any change."

"Would you like a clerkship in a dry-goods store?"

"There is too much confinement about that. No, I would not like a clerkship; but I am not particular."

"Too much confinement," I cried, "why, you keep yourself confined all the time!"

"I would prefer not to take a clerkship," he rejoined, as if to settle that little item at once.

"How would a bar-tender's business suit you? There is no trying of the eye-sight in that."

"I would not like it at all; though, as I said before, I am not particular."

His unwonted wordiness inspired me. I returned to the charge.

"Well, then, would you like to travel through the country collecting bills for the merchants? That would improve your health."

"No, I would prefer to be doing something else."

"How, then, would going as a companion to Europe, to entertain some young gentleman with your conversation—how would that suit you?"

"Not at all. It does not strike me that there is anything definite about that. I like to be stationary. But I am not particular."

"Stationary you shall be, then," I cried, now losing all patience, and, for the first time in all my exasperating connection with him, fairly flying into a passion. "If you do not go away from these premises before night, I shall feel bound—indeed, I *am* bound—to—to—to quit the premises myself!" I rather absurdly concluded, knowing not with what possible threat to try to frighten his immobility into compliance. Despairing of all further efforts, I was precipitately leaving him, when a final thought occurred to me—one which had not been wholly unindulged before.

"Bartleby," said I, in the kindest tone I could assume under such exciting circumstances, "will you go home with me now—not to my office, but my dwelling—and remain there till we can conclude upon some convenient arrangement for you at our leisure? Come, let us start now, right away."

"No: at present I would prefer not to make any change at all."

I answered nothing; but, effectually dodging every one by the suddenness and rapidity of my flight, rushed from the building, ran up Wall Street towards Broadway, and, jumping into the first omnibus, was soon removed from pursuit. As soon as tranquillity returned, I distinctly perceived that I had now done all that I possibly could, both in respect to the demands of the landlord and his tenants, and with regard to my own desire and sense of duty, to benefit Bartleby, and shield him from rude persecution. I now strove to be entirely care-free and quiescent; and my conscience justified me in the attempt; though, indeed, it was not so successful as I could have wished. So fearful was I of being again hunted out by the incensed landlord and his exasperated tenants, that, surrendering my business to Nippers, for a few days, I drove about the upper part of the town and through the suburbs, in my rockaway; crossed over to Jersey City and Hoboken, and paid fugitive visits to Manhattanville and Astoria. In fact, I almost lived in my rockaway for the time.

When again I entered my office, lo, a note from the landlord lay upon the desk. I opened it with trembling hands. It informed me that the writer had sent to the police, and had Bartleby removed to the Tombs as a vagrant. Moreover, since I knew more about him than any one else, he wished me to appear at that place, and make a suitable statement of the facts. These tidings had a conflicting effect upon me. At first I was indignant; but, at last, almost approved. The landlord's energetic, summary disposition, had led him to adopt a procedure which I do not think I would have decided upon myself; and yet, as a last resort, under such peculiar circumstances, it seemed the only plan.

As I afterwards learned, the poor scrivener, when told that he must be conducted to the Tombs, offered not the slightest obstacle, but, in his pale, unmoving way, silently acquiesced.

Some of the compassionate and curious by-standers joined the party; and headed by one of the constables arm-in-arm with Bartleby, the silent procession filed its way through all the noise, and heat, and joy of the roaring thoroughfares at noon.

The same day I received the note, I went to the Tombs, or, to speak more properly, the Halls of Justice. Seeking the right officer, I stated the purpose of my call, and was informed that the individual I described was, indeed, within. I then assured the functionary that Bartleby was a perfectly honest man, and greatly to be compassionated, however unaccountably eccentric. I narrated all I knew, and closed by suggesting the idea of letting him remain in as indulgent confinement as possible, till something less harsh might be done—though, indeed, I hardly knew what. At all events, if nothing else could be decided upon, the alms-house must receive him. I then begged to have an interview.

Being under no disgraceful charge, and quite serene and harmless in all his ways, they had permitted him freely to wander about the prison, and, especially, in the inclosed grass-platted yards thereof. And so I found him there, standing all alone in the quietest of the yards, his face towards a high wall, while all around, from the narrow slits of the jail windows, I thought I saw peering out upon him the eyes of murderers and thieves.

"Bartleby!"

"I know you," he said, without looking round—"and I want nothing to say to you."

"It was not I that brought you here, Bartleby," said I, keenly pained at his implied suspicion. "and to you, this should not be so vile a place. Nothing reproachful attaches to you by being here. And see, it is not so sad a place as one might think. Look, there is the sky, and here is the grass."

"I know where I am," he replied, but would say nothing more, and so I left him.

As I entered the corridor again, a broad meat-like man, in an apron accosted me, and, jerking his thumb over his shoulder, said— "Is that your friend?"

"Yes."

"Does he want to starve? If he does, let him live on the prison fare, that's all."

"Who are you?" asked I, not knowing what to make of such an unofficially speaking person in such a place.

"I am the grub-man. Such gentlemen as have friends here, hire me to provide them with something good to eat."

"Is this so?" said I, turning to the turnkey.

He said it was.

"Well, then," said I, slipping some silver into the grubman's hands (for so they called him), "I want you to give particular attention to my friend there; let him have the best dinner you can get. And you must be as polite to him as possible."

"Introduce me, will you?" said the grub-man, looking at me with an expression which seemed to say he was all impatience for an opportunity to give a specimen of his breeding.

Thinking it would prove of benefit to the scrivener, I acquiesced; and, asking the grub-man his name, went up with him to Bartleby.

"Bartleby, this is a friend; you will find him very useful to you."

"Your sarvant, sir, your sarvant," said the grub-man, making a low salutation behind his apron. "Hope you find it pleasant here, sir; nice grounds—cool apartments—hope you'll stay with us some time—try to make it agreeable. What will you have for dinner to-day?"

"I prefer not to dine to-day," said Bartleby, turning away. "It would disagree with me; I am unused to dinners." So saying, he slowly moved to the other side of the inclosure, and took up a position fronting the dead-wall.

"How's this?" said the grub-man, addressing me with a stare of astonishment. "He's odd, ain't he?"

"I think he is a little deranged," said I, sadly.

"Deranged? deranged is it? Well, now, upon my word, I thought that friend of yourn was a gentleman forger; they are always pale and genteel-like, them forgers. I can't help pity 'em—can't help it, sir. Did you know Monroe Edwards?" he added, touchingly, and paused. Then, laying his hand piteously on my shoulder, sighed, "He died of consumption at Sing-Sing. So you weren't acquainted with Monroe?"

"No, I was never socially acquainted with any forgers. But I cannot stop longer. Look to my friend yonder. You will not lose by it. I will see you again."

Some few days after this, I again obtained admission to the Tombs, and went through the corridors in quest of Bartleby; but without finding him.

"I saw him coming from his cell not long ago," said a turnkey, "maybe he's gone to loiter in the yards."

So I went in that direction.

"Are you looking for the silent man?" said another turnkey, passing me. "Yonder he lies—sleeping in the yard there. 'Tis not twenty minutes since I saw him lie down."

The yard was entirely quiet. It was not accessible to the common prisoners. The surrounding walls, of amazing thickness, kept off all sounds behind them. The Egyptian character of the masonry weighed upon me with its gloom. But a soft imprisoned turf grew under foot. The heart of the eternal pyramids, it seemed, wherein, by some strange magic, through the clefts, grass-seed, dropped by birds, had sprung.

Strangely huddled at the base of the wall, his knees drawn up, and lying on his side, his head touching the cold stones, I saw the wasted Bartleby. But nothing stirred. I paused; then went close up to him; stooped over, and saw that his dim eyes were open; otherwise he seemed profoundly sleeping. Something prompted me to touch him. I felt his hand, when a tingling shiver ran up my arm and down my spine to my feet.

The round face of the grub-man peered upon me now. "His dinner is ready. Won't he dine to-day, either? Or does he live without dining?"

"Lives without dining," said I, and closed the eyes.

"Eh!—He's asleep, ain't he?"

"With kings and counselors," murmured I.

*   *   *

There would seem little need for proceeding further in this history. Imagination will readily supply the meagre recital of poor Bartleby's interment. But, ere parting with the reader, let me say, that if this little narrative has sufficiently interested him, to awaken curiosity as to who Bartleby was, and what manner of life he led prior to the present narrator's making his acquaintance, I can only reply, that in such curiosity I fully share, but am wholly unable to gratify it. Yet here I hardly know whether I should divulge one little item of rumor, which came to my ear a few months after the scrivener's decease. Upon what basis it rested, I could never ascertain; and hence, how true it is I cannot now tell. But, inasmuch as this vague report has not been without a certain suggestive interest to me, however sad, it may prove the same with some others, and so I will briefly mention it. The report was this: that Bartleby had been a subordinate clerk in the Dead Letter Office at Washington, from which he had been suddenly removed by a change in the administration. When I think over this rumor, hardly can I express the emotions which seize me. Dead letters! does it not sound like dead men? Conceive a man by nature and misfortune prone to a pallid hopelessness, can any business seem more fitted to heighten it than that of continually handling these dead letters, and assorting them for the flames? For by the cart-load they are annually burned. Sometimes from out the folded paper the pale clerk takes a ring—the finger it was meant for, perhaps, moulders in the grave; a bank-note sent in swiftest charity—he whom it would relieve, nor eats nor hungers any more; pardon for those who died despairing; hope for those who died unhoping; good tidings for those who died stifled by unrelieved calamities. On errands of life, these letters speed to death.

Ah, Bartleby! Ah, humanity!

D. H. LAWRENCE
1885 1930

David Herbert Lawrence was born at Eastwood, a coal-mining village in the English Midlands. His father was a miner, his mother a woman from the middle class who never accepted her husband's way of life. Lawrence was torn between them: close to his mother during her life, appreciating his father only after his death. The story of this family struggle is told in one of Lawrence's finest works, his novel *Sons and Lovers* (1913). In 1901 Lawrence nearly died of pneumonia. His health was delicate after this until his death o tuberculosis at the age of forty-five. In 1904 he took the King's Scholarship examination and came out first in all England and Wales. He seems to have been good at all academic subjects from mathematics to botany, painting, and writing. He began a career as a teacher, but trouble with his health and his early success as a writer took him away from teaching. In 1912 he ran off with the wife of a former professor of his at Nottingham University, and in 1914, when her divorce became final, he married her. From then on the Lawrences traveled, staying in England at times, but also living in Germany, Italy, Ceylon, Australia, the United States, and Mexico. After Lawrence died in southern France, his body was cremated and the ashes were brought to the United States and buried on a hill near Taos, New Mexico.

Lawrence's personality has drawn almost as much attention as his books. He spoke and wrote informally with the same vitality that animates all his literary work. And some of the informality of talk and personal correspondence can be found in his poetry and fiction. For a time censorship of his works and controversy over the supposed immorality of his views on sex obscured the seriousness and beauty of his work for many readers. But now his books are in print and his place in English letters is secure.

The Rocking-Horse Winner

There was a woman who was beautiful, who started with all the advantages, yet she had no luck. She married for love, and the love turned to dust. She had bonny children, yet she felt they had been thrust upon her, and she could not love them. They looked at her coldly, as if they were finding fault with her. And hurriedly she felt she must cover up some fault in herself. Yet what it was that she must cover up she never knew. Nevertheless, when her children were present, she always felt the centre of her heart go hard. This troubled her, and in her manner she was all the more gentle and anxious for her children, as if she loved them very much. Only she herself knew that at the centre of her heart was a hard little place that could not feel love, no, not for anybody. Everybody else said of her: "She is such a good mother. She adores her children." Only she herself, and her children themselves, knew it was not so. They read it in each other's eyes.

There were a boy and two little girls. They lived in a pleasant house, with a garden, and they had discreet servants, and felt themselves superior to anyone in the neighbourhood.

Although they lived in style, they felt always an anxiety in the house. There was never enough money. The mother had a small income, and the father had a small income, but not nearly enough for the social position which they had to keep up. The father went into town to some office. But though he had good prospects, these prospects never materialised. There was always the grinding sense of the shortage of money, though the style was always kept up.

At last the mother said: "I will see if I can't make something." But she did not know where to begin. She racked her brains, and tried this thing and the other, but could not find anything successful. The failure made deep lines come into her face. Her children were growing up, they would have to go to school. There must be more money, there must be more money. The father, who was always very handsome and expensive in his tastes, seemed as if he never *would* be able to do anything worth doing. And the mother, who had a great belief in herself, did not succeed any better, and her tastes were just as expensive.

And so the house came to be haunted by the unspoken phrase: *There must be more money! There must be more money!* The children could hear it all the time, though nobody said it aloud. They heard it at Christmas, when the expensive and splendid toys filled the nursery. Behind the shining modern rocking-horse, behind the smart doll's house, a voice would start whispering: "There *must* be more money! There *must* be more money!" And the children would stop playing, to listen for a moment. They would look into each other's eyes, to see if they had all heard. And each one saw in the eyes of the other two that they too had heard. "There *must* be more money! There *must* be more money!"

It came whispering from the springs of the still-swaying rocking-horse, and even the horse, bending his wooden, champing head, heard it. The big doll, sitting so pink and smirking in her new pram, could hear it quite plainly, and seemed to be smirking all the more self-consciously because of it. The foolish puppy, too, that took the place of the teddy-bear, he was looking so extraordinarily foolish for no other reason but that he heard the secret whisper all over the house: "There *must* be more money!"

Yet nobody ever said it aloud. The whisper was everywhere, and therefore no one spoke it. Just as no one ever says: "We are breathing!" in spite of the fact that breath is coming and going all the time.

"Mother," said the boy Paul one day, "why don't we keep a car of our own? Why do we always use uncle's, or else a taxi?"

"Because we're the poor members of the family," said the mother.

"But why *are* we, mother?"

"Well—I suppose," she said slowly and bitterly, "it's because your father has no luck."

The boy was silent for some time.

"Is luck money, mother?" he asked, rather timidly.

"No, Paul. Not quite. It's what causes you to have money."

"Oh!" said Paul vaguely. "I thought when Uncle Oscar said *filthy lucker*, it meant money."

"*Filthy lucre* does mean money," said the mother. "But it's lucre, not luck."

"Oh!" said the boy. "Then what *is* luck, mother?"

"It's what causes you to have money. If you're lucky you have money. That's why it's better to be born lucky than rich. If you're rich, you may lose your money. But if you're lucky, you will always get more money."

"Oh! Will you? And is father not lucky?"

"Very unlucky, I should say," she said bitterly.

The boy watched her with unsure eyes.

"Why?" he asked.

"I don't know. Nobody ever knows why one person is lucky and another unlucky."

"Don't they? Nobody at all? Does *nobody* know?"

"Perhaps God. But He never tells."

"He ought to, then. And aren't you lucky either, mother?"

"I can't be, if I married an unlucky husband."

"But by yourself, aren't you?"

"I used to think I was, before I married. Now I think I am very unlucky indeed."

"Why?"

"Well—never mind! Perhaps I'm not really," she said.

The child looked at her to see if she meant it. But he saw, by the lines of her mouth, that she was only trying to hide something from him.

"Well, anyhow," he said stoutly, "I'm a lucky person."

"Why?" said his mother, with a sudden laugh.

He stared at her. He didn't even know why he had said it.

"God told me," he asserted, brazening it out.

"I hope He did, dear!" she said, again with a laugh, but rather bitter.

"He did, mother!"

"Excellent!" said the mother, using one of her husband's exclamations.

The boy saw she did not believe him; or rather, that she paid no attention to his assertion. This angered him somewhere, and made him want to compel her attention.

He went off by himself, vaguely, in a childish way, seeking for the clue to "luck." Absorbed, taking no heed of other people, he went about with a sort of stealth, seeking inwardly for luck. He wanted luck, he wanted it, he wanted it. When the two girls were playing dolls in the nursery, he would sit on his big rocking-horse, charging madly into space, with a frenzy that made the little girls peer at him uneasily. Wildly the horse careered, the waving dark hair of the boy tossed, his eyes had a strange glare in them. The little girls dared not speak to him.

When he had ridden to the end of his mad little journey, he climbed down and stood in front of his rocking-horse, staring fixedly into its lowered face. Its red mouth was slightly open, its big eye was wide and glassy-bright.

"Now!" he would silently command the snorting steed. "Now, take me to where there is luck! Now take me!"

And he would slash the horse on the neck with the little whip he had asked Uncle Oscar for. He *knew* the horse could take him to where there was luck, if only he forced it. So he would mount again and start on his furious ride, hoping at last to get there. He knew he could get there.

"You'll break your horse, Paul!" said the nurse.

"He's always riding like that! I wish he'd leave off!" said his elder sister Joan.

But he only glared down on them in silence. Nurse gave him up. She could make nothing of him. Anyhow, he was growing beyond her.

One day his mother and his Uncle Oscar came in when he was on one of his furious rides. He did not speak to them.

"Hallo, you young jockey! Riding a winner?" said his uncle.

"Aren't you growing too big for a rocking-horse? You're not a very little boy any longer, you know," said his mother.

But Paul only gave a blue glare from his big, rather close-set eyes. He would speak to nobody when he was in full tilt. His mother watched him with an anxious expression on her face.

At last he suddenly stopped forcing his horse into the mechanical gallop and slid down.

"Well, I got there!" he announced fiercely, his blue eyes still flaring, and his sturdy long legs straddling apart.

"Where did you get to?" asked his mother.

"Where I wanted to go," he flared back at her.

"That's right, son!" said Uncle Oscar. "Don't you stop till you get there. What's the horse's name?"

"He doesn't have a name," said the boy.

"Gets on without all right?" asked the uncle.

"Well, he has different names. He was called Sansovino last week."

"Sansovino, eh? Won the Ascot. How did you know this name?"

"He always talks about horse-races with Bassett," said Joan.

The uncle was delighted to find that his small nephew was posted with all the racing news. Bassett, the young gardener, who had been wounded in the left foot in the war and had got his present job through Oscar Cresswell, whose batman he had been, was a perfect blade of the "turf." He lived in the racing events, and the small boy lived with him.

Oscar Cresswell got it all from Bassett.

"Master Paul comes and asks me, so I can't do more than tell him, sir," said Bassett, his face terribly serious, as if he were speaking of religious matters.

"And does he ever put anything on a horse he fancies?"

"Well—I don't want to give him away—he's a young sport, a fine sport, sir. Would you mind asking him himself? He sort of takes a pleasure in it, and perhaps he'd feel I was giving him away, sir, if you don't mind."

Bassett was serious as a church.

The uncle went back to his nephew and took him off for a ride in the car.

"Say, Paul, old man, do you ever put anything on a horse?" the uncle asked.

The boy watched the handsome man closely.

"Why, do you think I oughtn't to?" he parried.

"Not a bit of it! I thought perhaps you might give me a tip for the Lincoln."

The car sped on into the country, going down to Uncle Oscar's place in Hampshire.

"Honour bright?" said the nephew.

"Honour bright, son!" said the uncle.

"Well, then, Daffodil."

"Daffodil! I doubt it, sonny. What about Mirza?"

"I only know the winner," said the boy. "That's Daffodil."

"Daffodil, eh?"

There was a pause. Daffodil was an obscure horse comparatively.

"Uncle!"

"Yes, son?"

"You won't let it go any further, will you? I promised Bassett."

"Bassett be damned, old man! What's he got to do with it?"

"We're partners. We've been partners from the first. Uncle, he lent me my first five shillings, which I lost. I promised him, honour bright, it was only between me and him; only you gave me that ten-shilling note I started winning with, so I thought you were lucky. You won't let it go any further, will you?"

The boy gazed at his uncle from those big, hot, blue eyes, set rather close together. The uncle stirred and laughed uneasily.

"Right you are, son! I'll keep your tip private. Daffodil, eh? How much are you putting on him?"

"All except twenty pounds," said the boy. "I keep that in reserve."

The uncle thought it a good joke.

"You keep twenty pounds in reserve, do you, you young romancer? What are you betting, then?"

"I'm betting three hundred," said the boy gravely. "But it's between you and me, Uncle Oscar! Honour bright?"

The uncle burst into a roar of laughter.

"It's between you and me all right, you young Nat Gould," he said, laughing. "But where's your three hundred?"

"Bassett keeps it for me. We're partners."

"You are, are you! And what is Bassett putting on Daffodil?"

"He won't go quite as high as I do, I expect. Perhaps he'll go a hundred and fifty."

"What, pennies?" laughed the uncle.

"Pounds," said the child, with a surprised look at his uncle. "Bassett keeps a bigger reserve than I do."

Between wonder and amusement Uncle Oscar was silent. He pursued the matter no further, but he determined to take his nephew with him to the Lincoln races.

"Now, son," he said, "I'm putting twenty on Mirza, and I'll put five on for you on any horse you fancy. What's your pick?"

"Daffodil, uncle."

"No, not the fiver on Daffodil!"

"I should if it was my own fiver," said the child.

"Good! Good! Right you are! A fiver for me and a fiver for you on Daffodil."

The child had never been to a race-meeting before, and his eyes were blue fire. He pursed his mouth tight and watched. A Frenchman just in front had put his money on Lancelot. Wild with excitement, he flayed his arms up and down, yelling "Lancelot! Lancelot!" in his French accent.

Daffodil came in first, Lancelot second, Mirza third. The child, flushed and with eyes blazing, was curiously serene. His uncle brought him four five-pound notes, four to one.

"What am I do with these?" he cried, waving them before the boy's eyes.

"I suppose we'll talk to Bassett," said the boy. "I expect I have fifteen hundred now; and twenty in reserve; and this twenty."

His uncle studied him for some moments.

"Look here, son!" he said. "You're not serious about Bassett and that fifteen hundred, are you?"

"Yes, I am. But it's between you and me, uncle. Honour bright?"

"Honour bright all right, son! But I must talk to Bassett."

"If you'd like to be a partner, uncle, with Bassett and me, we could all be partners. Only, you'd have to promise, honour bright, uncle, not to let it go beyond us three. Bassett and I are lucky, and you must be lucky, because it was your ten shillings I started winning with. . . ."

Uncle Oscar took both Bassett and Paul into Richmond Park for an afternoon, and there they talked.

"It's like this, you see, sir," Bassett said. "Master Paul would get me talking about racing events, spinning yarns, you know, sir. And he was always keen on knowing if I'd made or if I'd lost. It's about a year since, now, that I put five shillings on Blush of Dawn for him: and we lost. Then the luck turned, with that ten shillings he had from you: that we put on Singhalese. And since that time, it's been pretty steady, all things considering. What do you say, Master Paul?"

"We're all right when we're sure," said Paul. "It's when we're not quite sure that we go down."

"Oh, but we're careful then," said Bassett.

"But when are you *sure?*" smiled Uncle Oscar.

"It's Master Paul, sir," said Bassett in a secret, religious voice. "It's as if he had it from heaven. Like Daffodil, now, for the Lincoln. That was as sure as eggs."

"Did you put anything on Daffodil?" asked Oscar Cresswell.

"Yes, sir. I made my bit."

"And my nephew?"

Bassett was obstinately silent, looking at Paul.

"I made twelve hundred, didn't I, Bassett? I told uncle I was putting three hundred on Daffodil."

"That's right," said Bassett, nodding.

"But where's the money?" asked the uncle.

"I keep it safe locked up, sir. Master Paul he can have it any minute he likes to ask for it."

"What, fifteen hundred pounds?"

"And twenty! And *forty*, that is, with the twenty he made on the course."

"It's amazing!" said the uncle.

"If Master Paul offers you to be partners, sir, I would, if I were you: if you'll excuse me," said Bassett.

Oscar Cresswell thought about it.

"I'll see the money," he said.

They drove home again, and, sure enough, Bassett came round to the garden-house with fifteen hundred pounds in notes. The twenty pounds reserve was left with Joe Glee, in the Turf Commission deposit.

"You see, it's all right, uncle, when I'm *sure!* Then we go strong, for all we're worth. Don't we, Bassett?"

"We do that, Master Paul."

"And when are you sure?" said the uncle, laughing.

"Oh, well, sometimes I'm *absolutely* sure, like about Daffodil," said the boy; "and sometimes I have an idea; and sometimes I haven't even an idea, have I, Bassett? Then we're careful, because we mostly go down."

"You do, do you! And when you're sure, like about Daffodil, what makes you sure, sonny?"

"Oh, well, I don't know," said the boy uneasily. "I'm sure, you know, uncle; that's all."

"It's as if he had it from heaven, sir," Bassett reiterated.

"I should say so!" said the uncle.

But he became a partner. And when the Leger was coming on Paul was "sure" about Lively Spark, which was a quite inconsiderable horse. The boy insisted on putting a thousand on the horse, Bassett was for five hundred, and Oscar Cresswell two hundred. Lively Spark came in first, and the betting had been ten to one against him. Paul had made ten thousand.

"You see," he said, "I was absolutely sure of him."

Even Oscar Cresswell had cleared two thousand.

"Look here, son," he said, "this sort of thing makes me nervous."

"It needn't, uncle! Perhaps I shan't be sure again for a long time."

"But what are you going to do with your money?" asked the uncle.

"Of course," said the boy, "I started it for mother. She said she had no luck, because father is unlucky, so I thought if I was lucky, it might stop whispering."

"What might stop whispering?"

"Our house. I *hate* our house for whispering."

"What does it whisper?"

"Why—why"—the boy fidgeted—"why, I don't know. But it's always short of money, you know, uncle."

"I know it, son, I know it."

"You know people send mother writs, don't you, uncle?"

"I'm afraid I do," said the uncle.

"And then the house whispers, like people laughing at you behind your back. It's awful, that is! I thought if I was lucky——"

"You might stop it," added the uncle.

The boy watched him with big blue eyes, that had an uncanny cold fire in them, and he said never a word.

"Well, then!" said the uncle. "What are we doing?"

"I shouldn't like mother to know I was lucky," said the boy.

"Why not, son?"

"She'd stop me."

"I don't think she would."

"Oh!"—and the boy writhed in an odd way—"I *don't* want her to know, uncle."

"All right, son! We'll manage it without her knowing."

They managed it very easily. Paul, at the other's suggestion, handed over five thousand pounds to his uncle, who deposited it with the family lawyer, who was then to inform Paul's mother that a relative had put five thousand pounds into his hands, which sum was to be paid out a thousand pounds at a time, on the mother's birthday, for the next five years.

"So she'll have a birthday present of a thousand pounds for five successive years," said Uncle Oscar. "I hope it won't make it all the harder for her later."

Paul's mother had her birthday in November. The house had been "whispering" worse than ever lately, and, even in spite of his luck, Paul could not bear up against it. He was very anxious to see the effect of the birthday letter, telling his mother about the thousand pounds.

When there were no visitors, Paul now took his meals with his parents, as he was beyond the nursery control. His mother went into town nearly every day. She had discovered that she had an odd knack of sketching furs and dress materials, so she worked secretly in the studio of a friend who was the chief "artist" for the leading drapers. She drew the figures of ladies in furs and ladies in silk and sequins for the newspaper advertisements. This young woman artist earned several thousand pounds a year, but Paul's mother only made several hundreds, and she was again dissatisfied. She so wanted to be first in something, and she did not succeed, even in making sketches for drapery advertisements.

She was down to breakfast on the morning of her birthday. Paul watched her face as she read her letters. He knew the lawyer's letter. As his mother read it, her face hardened and became more expressionless. Then a cold, determined look came on her mouth. She hid the letter under the pile of others, and said not a word about it.

"Didn't you have anything nice in the post for your birthday, mother?" said Paul.

"Quite moderately nice," she said, her voice cold and absent.

She went away to town without saying more.

But in the afternoon Uncle Oscar appeared. He said Paul's mother had had a long interview with the lawyer, asking if the whole five thousand could not be advanced at once, as she was in debt.

"What do you think, uncle?" said the boy.

"I leave it to you, son."

"Oh, let her have it, then! We can get some more with the other," said the boy.

"A bird in the hand is worth two in the bush, laddie!" said Uncle Oscar.

"But I'm sure to *know* for the Grand National; or the Lincolnshire; or else the Derby. I'm sure to know for *one* of them," said Paul.

So Uncle Oscar signed the agreement, and Paul's mother touched the whole five thousand. Then something very curious happened. The voices in the house suddenly went mad, like a chorus of frogs on a spring evening. There were certain new furnishings, and Paul had a tutor. He was *really* going to Eton, his father's school, in the following autumn. There were flowers in the winter, and a blossoming of the luxury Paul's mother had been used to. And yet the voices in the house, behind the sprays of mimosa and almond-blossom, and from under the piles of iridescent cushions, simply trilled and screamed in a sort of ecstasy: "There *must* be more money! Oh-h-h; there *must* be more money. Oh, now, now-w! Now-w-w—there *must* be more money!—more than ever! More than ever!"

It frightened Paul terribly. He studied away at his Latin and Greek with his tutor. But his intense hours were spent with Bassett. The Grand National had gone by: he had not "known," and had lost a hundred pounds. Summer was at hand. He was in agony for the Lincoln. But even for the Lincoln he didn't "know," and he lost fifty pounds. He became wild-eyed and strange, as if something were going to explode in him.

"Let it alone, son! Don't you bother about it!" urged Uncle Oscar. But it was as if the boy couldn't really hear what his uncle was saying.

"I've got to know for the Derby! I've got to know for the Derby!" the child reiterated, his big blue eyes blazing with a sort of madness.

His mother noticed how overwrought he was.

"You'd better go to the seaside. Wouldn't you like to go now to the seaside, instead of waiting? I think you'd better," she said, looking down at him anxiously, her heart curiously heavy because of him.

But the child lifted his uncanny blue eyes.

"I couldn't possibly go before the Derby, mother!" he said. "I couldn't possibly!"

"Why not?" she said, her voice becoming heavy when she was opposed. "Why not? You can still go from the seaside to see the Derby with your Uncle Oscar, if that's what you wish. No need for you to wait here. Besides, I think you care too much about these races. It's a bad sign. My family has been a gambling family, and you won't know till you grow up how much damage it has done. But it has done damage. I shall have to send Bassett away, and ask Uncle Oscar not to talk racing to you, unless you promise to be reasonable about it: go away to the seaside and forget it. You're all nerves!"

"I'll do what you like, mother, so long as you don't send me away till after the Derby," the boy said.

"Send you away from where? Just from this house?"

"Yes," he said, gazing at her.

"Why, you curious child, what makes you care about this house so much, suddenly? I never knew you loved it."

He gazed at her without speaking. He had a secret within a secret, something he had not divulged, even to Bassett or to his Uncle Oscar.

But his mother, after standing undecided and a little bit sullen for some moments, said:

"Very well, then! Don't go to the seaside till after the Derby, if you don't wish it. But promise me you won't let your nerves go to pieces. Promise you won't think so much about horse-racing and *events*, as you call them!"

"Oh no," said the boy casually. "I won't think much about them, mother. You needn't worry. I wouldn't worry, mother, if I were you."

"If you were me and I were you," said his mother, "I wonder what we *should* do!"

"But you know you needn't worry, mother, don't you?" the boy repeated.

"I should be awfully glad to know it," she said wearily.

"Oh, well, you *can*, you know. I mean, you *ought* to know you needn't worry," he insisted.

"Ought I? Then I'll see about it," she said.

Paul's secret of secrets was his wooden horse, that which had no name. Since he was emancipated from a nurse and a nursery-governess, he had had his rocking-horse removed to his own bedroom at the top of the house.

"Surely you're too big for a rocking-horse!" his mother had remonstrated.

"Well, you see, mother, till I can have a *real* horse, I like to have *some* sort of animal about," had been his quaint answer.

"Do you feel he keeps you company?" she laughed.

"Oh yes! He's very good, he always keeps me company, when I'm there," said Paul.

So the horse, rather shabby, stood in an arrested prance in the boy's bedroom.

The Derby was drawing near, and the boy grew more and more tense. He hardly heard what was spoken to him, he was very frail, and his eyes were really uncanny. His mother had sudden strange seizures of uneasiness about him. Sometimes, for half an hour, she would feel a sudden anxiety about him that was almost anguish. She wanted to rush to him at once, and know he was safe.

Two nights before the Derby, she was at a big party in town, when one of her rushes of anxiety about her boy, her first-born, gripped her heart till she could hardly speak. She fought with the feeling, might and main, for she believed in common sense. But it was too strong. She had to leave the dance and go downstairs to telephone to the country. The children's nursery-governess was terribly surprised and startled at being rung up in the night.

"Are the children all right, Miss Wilmot?"

"Oh yes, they are quite all right."

"Master Paul? Is he all right?"

"He went to bed as right as a trivet. Shall I run up and look at him?"

"No," said Paul's mother reluctantly. "No! Don't trouble. It's all right. Don't sit up. We shall be home fairly soon." She did not want her son's privacy intruded upon.

"Very good," said the governess.

It was about one o'clock when Paul's mother and father drove up to their house. All was still. Paul's mother went to her room and slipped off her white fur cloak. She had told her maid not to wait up for her.

She heard her husband downstairs, mixing a whisky and soda.

And then, because of the strange anxiety at her heart, she stole upstairs to her son's room. Noiselessly she went along the upper corridor. Was there a faint noise? What was it?

She stood, with arrested muscles, outside his door, listening. There was a strange, heavy, and yet not loud noise. Her heart stood still. It was a soundless noise, yet rushing and powerful. Something huge, in violent, hushed motion. What was it? What in God's name was it? She ought to know. She felt that she knew the noise. She knew what it was.

Yet she could not place it. She couldn't say what it was. And on and on it went, like a madness.

Softly, frozen with anxiety and fear, she turned the doorhandle.

The room was dark. Yet in the space near the window, she heard and saw something plunging to and fro. She gazed in fear and amazement.

Then suddenly she switched on the light, and saw her son, in his green pyjamas, madly surging on the rocking-horse. The blaze of light suddenly lit him up, as he urged the wooden horse, and lit her up, as she stood, blonde, in her dress of pale green and crystal, in the doorway.

"Paul!" she cried. "Whatever are you doing?"

"It's Malabar!" he screamed in a powerful, strange voice. "It's Malabar!"

His eyes blazed at her for one strange and senseless second, as he ceased urging his wooden horse. Then he fell with a crash to the ground, and she, all her tormented motherhood flooding upon her, rushed to gather him up.

But he was unconscious, and unconscious he remained, with some brain-fever. He talked and tossed, and his mother sat stonily by his side.

"Malabar! It's Malabar! Bassett, Bassett, I *know!* It's Malabar!"

So the child cried, trying to get up and urge the rocking-horse that gave him his inspiration.

"What does he mean by Malabar?" asked the heart-frozen mother.

"I don't know," said the father stonily.

"What does he mean by Malabar?" she asked her brother Oscar.

"It's one of the horses running for the Derby," was the answer.

And, in spite of himself, Oscar Cresswell spoke to Bassett, and himself put a thousand on Malabar: at fourteen to one.

The third day of the illness was critical: they were waiting for a change. The boy, with his rather long, curly hair, was tossing ceaselessly on the pillow. He neither slept nor regained consciousness, and his eyes were like blue stones. His mother sat, feeling her heart had gone, turned actually into a stone.

In the evening, Oscar Cresswell did not come, but Bassett sent a message, saying could he come up for one moment, just one moment?

Paul's mother was very angry at the intrusion, but on second thoughts she agreed. The boy was the same. Perhaps Bassett might bring him to consciousness.

The gardener, a shortish fellow with a little brown moustache and sharp little brown eyes, tiptoed into the room, touched his imaginary cap to Paul's mother, and stole to the bedside, staring with glittering, smallish eyes at the tossing, dying child.

"Master Paul!" he whispered. "Master Paul! Malabar came in first all right, a clean win. I did as you told me. You've made over seventy thousand pounds, you have; you've got over eighty thousand. Malabar came in all right, Master Paul."

"Malabar! Malabar! Did I say Malabar, mother? Did I say Malabar? Do you think I'm lucky, mother? I knew Malabar, didn't I? Over eighty thousand pounds! I call that lucky, don't you, mother? Over eighty thousand pounds! I knew, didn't I know I knew? Malabar came in all right. If I ride my horse till I'm sure, then I tell you, Bassett, you can go as high as you like. Did you go for all you were worth, Bassett?"

"I went a thousand on it, Master Paul."

"I never told you, mother, that if I can ride my horse, and *get there*, then I'm absolutely sure—oh, absolutely! Mother, did I ever tell you? I *am* lucky!"

"No, you never did," said his mother.

But the boy died in the night.

And even as he lay dead, his mother heard her brother's voice saying to her: "My God, Hester, you're eighty-odd thousand to the good, and a poor devil of a son to the bad. But, poor devil, poor devil, he's best gone out of a life where he rides his rocking-horse to find a winner."

ELIZABETH BOWEN
1899–1973

The only child of Henry and Isabel Bowen, of County Cork, Ireland, she was raised at the family mansion, Bowen's Court, in Ireland, until her father went insane, when she moved, with her mother, to East Kent, England. From childhood on she was handicapped by a pronounced stammer. She went to school at Downe House in Westerham (West Kent), where she was quite happy. She began writing fiction early, publishing her first collection of stories in 1923, the year in which she married. She traveled in Europe and America, building a reputation for sensitive, witty fiction with novels like The House in Paris (1938) and The Death of the Heart (1938) and stories, sometimes with a touch of the supernatural like those in The Demon Lover collection of 1945.

The Demon Lover

Towards the end of her day in London Mrs. Drover went round to her shut-up house to look for several things she wanted to take away. Some belonged to herself, some to her family, who were by now used to their country life. It was late August; it had been a steamy, showery day: at the moment the trees down the pavement glittered in an escape of humid yellow afternoon sun. Against the next batch of clouds, already piling up ink-dark, broken chimneys and parapets stood out. In her once familiar street, as in any unused channel, an unfamiliar queerness had silted up; a cat wove itself in and out of railings, but no human eye watched Mrs. Drover's return. Shifting some parcels under her arm, she slowly forced round her latchkey in an unwilling lock, then gave the door, which had warped, a push with her knee. Dead air came out to meet her as she went in.

The staircase window having been boarded up, no light came down into the hall. But one door, she could just see, stood ajar, so she went quickly through into the room and unshuttered the big window in there. Now the prosaic woman, looking about her, was more perplexed than she knew by everything that she saw, by traces of her long former habit of life— the yellow smoke-stain up the white marble mantelpiece, the ring left by a vase on the top of the escritoire; the bruise in the wallpaper where, on the door being thrown open widely, the china handle had always hit the wall. The piano, having gone away to be stored, had left what looked like claw-marks on its part of the parquet. Though not much dust had seeped in, each object wore a film of another kind; and, the only ventilation being the chimney, the whole drawing-room smelled of the cold hearth. Mrs. Drover put down her parcels on the escritoire and left the room to proceed upstairs; the things she wanted were in a bedroom chest.

She had been anxious to see how the house was—the part-time caretaker she shared with some neighbours was away this week on his holiday, known to be not yet back. At the best of times he did not look in often, and she was never sure that she trusted him. There were some cracks in the structure, left by the last bombing, on which she was anxious to keep an eye. Not that one could do anything—

A shaft of refracted daylight now lay across the hall. She stopped dead and stared at the hall table—on this lay a letter addressed to her.

She thought first—then the caretaker *must* be back. All the same, who, seeing the house shuttered, would have dropped a letter in at the box? It was not a circular, it was not a bill. And the post office redirected, to the address in the country, everything for her that came through the post. The caretaker (even if he *were* back) did not know she was due in London to-day—her call here had been planned to be a surprise—so his negligence in the manner of this letter, leaving it to wait in the dusk and the dust, annoyed her. Annoyed, she picked up the letter, which bore no stamp. But it cannot be important, or they would know . . . She took the letter rapidly upstairs with her, without a stop to look at the writing till she reached what had been her bedroom, where she let in light. The room looked over the garden and other gardens: the sun had gone in; as the clouds sharpened and lowered, the trees and rank lawns seemed already to smoke with dark. Her reluctance to look again at the letter came from the fact that she felt intruded upon—and by someone contemptuous of her ways. However, in the tenseness preceding the fall of rain she read it: it was a few lines.

> DEAR KATHLEEN,
> You will not have forgotten that to-day is our anniversary, and the day we said. The years have gone by at once slowly and fast. In view of the fact that nothing has changed, I shall rely upon you to keep your promise. I was sorry to see you leave London, but was satisfied that you would be back in time. You may expect me, therefore, at the hour arranged.
>
> Until then . . .
>
> K.

Mrs. Drover looked for the date: it was to-day's. She dropped the letter on to the bed-springs, then picked it up to see the writing again—her lips, beneath the remains of lipstick, beginning to go white. She felt so much the change in her own face that she went to the mirror, polished a clear patch in it and looked at once urgently and stealthily in. She was confronted by a woman of forty-four, with eyes starting out under a hat-brim that had been rather carelessly pulled down. She had not put on any more powder since she left the shop where she ate her solitary tea. The pearls her husband had given her on their marriage hung loose round her now rather thinner throat, slipping into the V of the pink wool jumper her sister knitted last autumn as they sat round the fire. Mrs. Drover's most normal expression was one of controlled worry, but of assent. Since the birth of the third of her little boys, attended by a quite serious illness, she had had an intermittent muscular flicker to the left of her mouth, but in spite of this she could always sustain a manner that was at once energetic and calm.

Turning from her own face as precipitately as she had gone to meet it, she went to the chest where the things were, unlocked it, threw up the lid and knelt to search. But as rain began to come crashing down she could not keep from looking over her shoulder at the stripped bed on which the letter lay. Behind the blanket of rain the clock of the church that still stood struck six—with rapidly heightening apprehension, she counted each of the slow strokes. "The hour arranged . . . My God," she said, "*what* hour? How should I . . . ? After twenty-five years. . . ."

The young girl talking to the soldier in the garden had not ever completely seen his face. It was dark; they were saying good-bye under a tree. Now and then—for it felt, from not seeing him at this intense moment, as though she had never seen him at all—she verified his presence for these few moments longer by putting out a hand, which he each time pressed, without very much kindness, and painfully, on to one of the breast buttons of his uniform. That cut of the button on the palm of her hand was, principally, what she was to carry away. This was so near the end of a leave from France that she could only wish him already gone. It was August 1916. Being not kissed, being drawn away from and looked at intimidated Kathleen till she imagined spectral glitters in the place of his eyes. Turning away and looking back up the lawn she saw, through branches of trees, the drawing-room window alight: she caught a breath for the moment when she could go running back there into the safe arms of her mother and sister, and cry: "What shall I do, what shall I do? He has gone."

Hearing her catch her breath, her fiancé said, without feeling: "Cold?"

"You're going away such a long way."

"Not so far as you think."

"I don't understand?"

"You don't have to," he said. "You will. You know what we said."

"But that was—suppose you—I mean, suppose."

"I shall be with you," he said, "sooner or later. You won't forget that. You need do nothing but wait."

Only a little more than a minute later she was free to run up the silent lawn. Looking in through the window at her mother and sister, who did not for the moment perceive her, she already felt that unnatural promise drive down between her and the rest of all human kind. No other way of having given herself could have made her feel so apart, lost and foresworn. She could not have plighted a more sinister troth.

Kathleen behaved well when, some months later, her fiancé was reported missing, presumed killed. Her family not only supported her but were able to praise her courage without stint because they could not regret, as a husband for her, the man they knew almost nothing about. They hoped she would, in a year or two, console herself—and had it been only a question of consolation things might have gone much straighter ahead. But her trouble, behind just a little grief, was a complete dislocation from everything. She did not reject other lovers, for these failed to appear: for years she failed to attract men—and with the approach of her thirties she became natural enough to share her family's anxiousness on this score. She began to put herself out, to wonder; and at thirty-two she was very greatly relieved to find herself being courted by William Drover. She married him, and the two of them settled down in this quiet, arboreal part of Kensington: in this house the years piled up, her children were born and they all lived till they were driven out by the bombs of the next war. Her movements as Mrs. Drover were circumscribed, and she dismissed any idea that they were still watched.

As things were—dead or living the letter-writer sent her only a threat. Unable, for some minutes, to go on kneeling with her back exposed to the empty room, Mrs. Drover rose from the chest to sit on an upright chair whose back was firmly against the wall. The desuetude of her former bedroom, her married London home's whole air of being a cracked cup from which memory, with its reassuring power, had either evaporated or leaked away, made a crisis—and at just this crisis the letter-writer had, knowledgeably, struck. The hollowness of the house this evening cancelled years on years of voices, habits and steps. Through the shut windows she only heard rain fall on the roofs around. To rally herself, she said she was in a mood—and, for two or three seconds shutting her eyes, told herself that she had imagined the letter. But she opened them—there it lay on the bed.

On the supernatural side of the letter's entrance she was not permitting her mind to dwell. Who, in London, knew she meant to call at the house to-day? Evidently, however, this had been known. The caretaker, *had* he come back, had had no cause to expect her: he would have taken the letter in his pocket, to forward it, at his own time, through the post. There was no other sign that the caretaker had been in—but, if not? Letters dropped in at doors of deserted houses do not fly or walk to tables in halls. They do not sit on the dust of empty tables with the air of certainty that they will be found. There is needed some human hand—but nobody but the caretaker had a key. Under circumstances she did not care to consider, a house can be entered without a key. It was possible that she was not alone now. She might be being waited for, downstairs. Waited for—until when? Until "the hour arranged." At least that was not six o'clock: six has struck.

She rose from the chair and went over and locked the door.

The thing was, to get out. To fly? No, not that: she had to catch her train. As a woman whose utter dependability was the keystone of her family life she was not willing to return to the country, to her husband, her little boys and her sister, without the objects she had come up to fetch. Resuming work at the chest she set about making up a number of parcels in a rapid, fumbling-decisive way. These, with her shopping parcels, would be too much to carry; these meant a taxi—at the thought of the taxi her heart went up and her normal breathing resumed. I will ring up the taxi now; the taxi cannot come too soon: I shall hear the taxi out there running its engine, till I walk calmly down to it through the hall. I'll ring up—But no: the telephone is cut off . . . She tugged at a knot she had tied wrong.

The idea of flight . . . He was never kind to me, not really. I don't remember him kind at all. Mother said he never considered me. He was set on me, that was what it was—not love. Not love, not meaning a person well. What did he do, to make me promise like that? I can't remember— But she found that she could.

She remembered with such dreadful acuteness that the twenty-five years since then dissolved like smoke and she instinctively looked for the weal left by the button on the palm of her hand. She remembered not only all that he said and did but the complete suspension of *her* existence during that August week. I was not myself—they all told me so at the time. She remembered—but with one white burning blank as where acid has dropped on a photograph: *under no conditions* could she remember his face.

So, wherever he may be waiting, I shall not know him. You have no time to run from a face you do not expect.

The thing was to get to the taxi before any clock struck what could be the hour. She would slip down the street and round the side of the square to where the square gave on the main road. She would return in the taxi, safe, to her own door, and bring the solid driver into the house with her to pick up the parcels from room to room. The idea of the taxi driver made her decisive, bold: she unlocked her door, went to the top of the staircase and listened down.

She heard nothing—but while she was hearing nothing the *passé* air of the staircase was disturbed by a draught that travelled up to her face. It emanated from the basement: down there a door or window was being opened by someone who chose this moment to leave the house.

The rain had stopped; the pavements steamily shone as Mrs. Drover let herself out by inches from her own front door into the empty street. The unoccupied houses opposite continued to meet her look with their damaged stare. Making towards the thoroughfare and the taxi, she tried not to keep looking behind. Indeed, the silence was so intense—one of those creeks of London silence exaggerated this summer by the damage of war—that no tread could have gained on hers unheard. Where her street debouched on the square where people went on living she grew conscious of and checked her unnatural pace. Across the open end of the square two buses impassively passed each other; women, a perambulator, cyclists, a man wheeling a barrow signalized, once again, the ordinary flow of life. At the square's most populous corner should be—and was—the short taxi rank. This evening, only one taxi—but this, although it presented its blank rump, appeared already to be alertly waiting for her. Indeed, without looking round the driver started his engine as she panted up from behind and put her hand on the door. As she did so, the clock struck seven. The taxi faced the main road: to make the trip back to her house it would have to turn—she had settled back on the seat and the taxi *had* turned before she, surprised by its knowing movement, recollected that she had not "said where." She leaned forward to scratch at the glass panel that divided the driver's head from her own.

The driver braked to what was almost a stop, turned round and slid the glass panel back: the jolt of this flung Mrs. Drover forward till her face was almost into the glass. Through the aperture driver and passenger, not six inches between them, remained for an eternity eye to eye. Mrs. Drover's mouth hung open for some seconds before she could issue her first scream. After that she continued to scream freely and to beat with her gloved hands on the glass all around as the taxi, accelerating without mercy, made off with her into the hinterland of deserted streets.

SHEILA WATSON

1909–

Born in New Westminster, British Columbia, where her father was Superintendent of the Provincial Hospital, Sheila Watson, the second of four children, lived with her family in one wing of the hospital until her father died in 1920. After graduating from the University of British Columbia, she taught in elementary and secondary schools on the British Columbia mainland and on Vancouver Island before embarking on part-time graduate studies in English at the University of Toronto after the Second World War. In 1951 she began a two-year residence in Calgary, where she wrote much of her novel *The Double Hook* (1959), now regarded as the beginning of modern Canadian fiction. In the same decade she completed her graduate studies and began a doctoral dissertation on Wyndham Lewis. In 1961 she joined the Department of English at the University of Alberta, where she taught until her retirement in 1975. She now lives in Nanaimo, British Columbia. In addition to her novel, she has published five short stories. "Antigone" (1959) employs classical myth to organize contemporary reality, to distance that reality, and to endow seemingly homely actions with the significance usually associated with myth.

Antigone

My father ruled a kingdom on the right bank of the river. He ruled it with a firm hand and a stout heart though he was often more troubled than Moses, who was simply trying to bring a stubborn and moody people under God's yoke. My father ruled men who thought they were gods or the instruments of gods or, at very least, god-afflicted and god-pursued. He ruled Atlas who held up the sky, and Hermes who went on endless messages, and Helen who'd been hatched from an egg, and Pan the gardener, and Kallisto the bear, and too many others to mention by name. Yet my father had no thunderbolt, no trident, no helmet of darkness. His subjects were delivered bound into his hands. He merely watched over them as the hundred-handed ones watched over the dethroned Titans so that they wouldn't bother Hellas again.

Despite the care which my father took to maintain an atmosphere of sober common sense in his whole establishment, there were occasional outbursts of self-indulgence which he could not control. For instance, I have seen Helen walking naked down the narrow cement path under the chestnut trees for no better reason, I suppose, than that the day was hot and the white flowers themselves lay naked and expectant in the sunlight. And I have seen Atlas forget the sky while he sat eating the dirt which held him up. These were things which I was not supposed to see.

If my father had been as sensible through and through as he was thought to be, he would have packed me off to boarding school when I was old enough to be disciplined by men. Instead he kept me at home with my two cousins who, except for the accident of birth, might as well have been my sisters. Today I imagine people concerned with our welfare would take such an environment into account. At the time I speak of most people thought us fortunate—especially the girls whose father's affairs had come to an unhappy issue. I don't like to revive old scandal and I wouldn't except to deny it; but it takes only a few impertinent newcomers in any community to force open cupboards which have been decently sealed by time. However, my father was so busy setting his kingdom to rights that he let weeds grow up in his own garden.

As I said, if my father had had all his wits about him he would have sent me to boarding school—and Antigone and Ismene too. I might have fallen in love with the headmaster's daughter and Antigone might have learned that no human being can be right always. She might have found out besides that from the seeds of eternal justice grow madder flowers than any which Pan grew in the gardens of my father's kingdom.

Between the kingdom which my father ruled and the wilderness flows a river. It is this river which I am crossing now. Antigone is with me.

How often can we cross the same river, Antigone asks.

Her persistence annoys me. Besides, Heraklitos made nonsense of her question years ago. He saw a river too—the Inachos, the Kephissos, the Lethaios. The name dosen't matter. He said: See how quickly the water flows. However agile a man is, however nimbly he swims, or runs, or flies, the water slips away before him. See, even as he sets down his foot the water is displaced by the stream which crowds along in the shadow of its flight.

But after all, Antigone says, one must admit that it is the same kind of water. The oolichans run in it as they ran last year and the year before. The gulls cry above the same banks. Boats drift toward the Delta and circle back against the current to gather up the catch.

At any rate, I tell her, we're standing on a new bridge. We are standing so high that the smell of mud and river weeds passes under us out to the straits. The unbroken curve of the bridge protects the eye from details of river life. The bridge is foolproof as a clinic's passport to happiness.

The old bridge still spans the river, but the cat-walk with its cracks and knot-holes, with its gap between planking and handrail has been torn down. The center arch still grinds open to let boats up and down the river, but a child can no longer be walked on it or swung out on it beyond the water-gauge at the very center of the flood.

I've known men who scorned any kind of bridge, Antigone says. Men have walked into the water, she says, or, impatient, have jumped from the bridge into the river below.

But these, I say, didn't really want to cross the river. They went Persephone's way, cradled in the current's arms, down the long halls under the pink feet of the gulls, under the booms and towlines, under the soft bellies of the fish.

Antigone looks at me.

There's no coming back, she says, if one goes far enough.

I know she's going to speak of her own misery and I won't listen. Only a god has the right to say: Look what I suffer. Only a god should say: What more ought I to have done for you that I have not done?

Once in winter, she says, a man walked over the river.

Taking advantage of nature, I remind her, since the river had never frozen before.

Yet he escaped from the penitentiary, she says. He escaped from the guards walking round the walls or standing with their guns in the sentry-boxes at the four corners of the enclosure. He escaped.

Not without risk, I say. He had to test the strength of the ice himself. Yet safer perhaps than if he had crossed by the old bridge where he might have slipped through a knot-hole or tumbled out through the railing.

He did escape, she persists, and lived forever on the far side of the river in the Alaska tea and bulrushes. For where, she asks, can a man go farther than to the outermost edge of the world?

The habitable world, as I've said, is on the right bank of the river. Here is the market with its market stalls—the coops of hens, the long-tongued geese, the haltered calf, the bearded goat, the shoving pigs, and the empty bodies of cows and sheep and rabbits hanging on iron hooks. My father's kingdom provides asylum in the suburbs. Near it are the convent, the churches, and the penitentiary. Above these on the hill the cemetery looks down on the people and on the river itself.

It is a world spread flat, tipped up into the sky so that men and women bend forward, walking as men walk when they board a ship at high tide. This is the world I feel with my feet. It is the world I see with my eyes.

I remember standing once with Antigone and Ismene in the square just outside the gates of my father's kingdom. Here from a bust set high on a cairn the stone eyes of Simon Fraser look from his stone face over the river that he found.

It is the head that counts, Ismene said.

It's no better than an urn, Antigone said, one of the urns we see when we climb to the cemetery above.

And all I could think was that I didn't want an urn, only a flat green grave with a chain about it.

A chain won't keep out the dogs, Antigone said.

But his soul could swing on it, Ismene said, like a bird blown on a branch in the wind.

And I remember Antigone's saying: The cat drags its belly on the ground and the rat sharpens its tooth in the ivy.

I should have loved Ismene, but I didn't. It was Antigone I loved. I should have loved Ismene because, although she walked the flat world with us, she managed somehow to see it round.

The earth is an oblate spheroid, she'd say. And I knew that she saw it there before her comprehensible and whole like a tangerine spiked through and held in place while it rotated on the axis of one of Nurse's steel sock needles. The earth was a tangerine and she saw the skin peeled off and the world parceled out into neat segments, each segment sweet and fragrant in its own skin.

It's the head that counts, she said.

In her own head she made diagrams to live by, cut and fashioned after the eternal patterns spied out by Plato as he rummaged about in the sewing basket of the gods.

I should have loved Ismene. She would live now in some prefabricated and perfect chrysolite by some paradigm which made love round and whole. She would simply live and leave destruction in the purgatorial ditches outside her own walled paradise.

Antigone is different. She sees the world flat as I do and feels it tip beneath her feet. She has walked in the market and seen the living animals penned and the dead hanging stiff on their hooks. Yet she defies what she sees with a defiance which is almost denial. Like Atlas she tries to keep the vaulted sky from crushing the flat earth. Like Hermes she brings a message that there is life if one can escape to it in the brush and bulrushes in some dim Hades beyond the river. It is defiance not belief and I tell her that this time we walk the bridge to a walled cave where we can deny death no longer.

Yet she asks her question still. And standing there I tell her that Heraklitos has made nonsense of her question. I should have loved Ismene for she would have taught me what Plato meant when he said in all earnest that the union of the soul with the body is in no way better than dissolution. I expect that she understood things which Antigone is too proud to see.

I turn away from her and flatten my elbows on the high wall of the bridge. I look back at my father's kingdom. I see the terraces rolling down from the red-brick buildings with their barred windows. I remember hands shaking the bars and hear fingers tearing up paper and stuffing it through the meshes. Diktynna, mother of nets and high leaping fear. O Artemis, mistress of wild beasts and wild men.

The inmates are beginning to come out on the screened verandas. They pace up and down in straight lines or stand silent like figures which appear at the same time each day from some depths inside a clock.

On the upper terrace Pan the gardener is shifting sprinklers with a hooked stick. His face is shadowed by the brim of his hat. He moves as economically as an animal between the beds of lobelia and geranium. It is high noon.

Antigone has cut out a piece of sod and has scooped out a grave. The body lies in a coffin in the shade of the magnolia tree. Antigone and I are standing. Ismene is sitting between two low angled branches of the monkey puzzle tree. Her lap is filled with daisies. She slits the stem of one daisy and pulls the stem of another through it. She is making a chain for her neck and a crown for her hair.

Antigone reaches for a branch of the magnolia. It is almost beyond her grip. The buds flame above her. She stands on a small fire of daisies which smoulder in the roots of the grass.

I see the magnolia buds. They brood above me, whiteness feathered on whiteness. I see Antigone's face turned to the light. I hear the living birds call to the sun. I speak private poetry to myself: Between four trumpeting angels at the four corners of the earth a bride stands before the alar in a gown as white as snow.

Yet I must have been speaking aloud because Antigone challenges me: You're mistaken. It's the winds the angels hold, the four winds of the earth. After the just are taken to paradise the winds will destroy the earth. It's a funeral, she says, not a wedding.

She looks toward the building.

Someone is coming down the path from the matron's house, she says.

I notice that she has pulled one of the magnolia blossoms from the branch. I take it from her. It is streaked with brown where her hands have bruised it. The sparrow which she has decided to bury lies on its back. Its feet are clenched tight against the feathers of its breast. I put the flower in the box with it.

Someone is coming down the path. She is wearing a blue cotton dress. Her cropped head is bent. She walks slowly carrying something in a napkin.

It's Kallisto the bear, I say. Let's hurry. What will my father say if he sees us talking to one of his patients?

If we live here with him, Antigone says, what can he expect? If he spends his life trying to tame people he can't complain if you behave as if they were tame. What would your father think, she says, if he saw us digging in the Institution lawn?

Pan comes closer. I glower at him. There's no use speaking to him. He's deaf and dumb.

Listen, I say to Antigone, my father's not unreasonable. Kallisto thinks she's a bear and he thinks he's a bear tamer, that's all. As for the lawn, I say quoting my father without conviction, a man must have order among his own if he is to keep order in the state.

Kallisto has come up to us. She is smiling and laughing to herself. She gives me her bundle.

Fish, she says.

I open the napkin.

Pink fish sandwiches, I say.

For the party, she says.

But it isn't a party, Antigone says. It's a funeral.

For the funeral breakfast, I say.

Ismene is twisting two chains of daisies into a rope. Pan has stopped pulling the sprinkler about. He is standing beside Ismene resting himself on his hooked stick. Kallisto squats down beside her. Ismene turns away, preoccupied, but she can't turn far because of Pan's legs.

Father said we never should
Play with madmen in the wood.

I look at Antigone.

It's my funeral, she says.

I go over to Ismene and gather up a handful of loose daisies from her lap. The sun reaches through the shadow of the magnolia tree.

It's my funeral, Antigone says. She moves possessively toward the body.

An ant is crawling into the bundle of sandwiches which I've put on the ground. A file of ants is marching on the sparrow's box.

I go over and drip daisies on the bird's stiff body. My voice speaks ritual words: Deliver me, O Lord, from everlasting death on this dreadful day. I tremble and am afraid.

The voice of a people comforts me. I look at Antigone. I look her in the eye.

It had better be a proper funeral then, I say.

Kallisto is crouched forward on her hands. Tears are running down her cheeks and she is licking them away with her tongue.

My voice rises again: I said in the midst of my days, I shall not see—

Antigone just stands there. She looks frightened, but her eyes defy me with their assertion.

It's my funeral, she says. It's my bird. I was the one who wanted to bury it.

She is looking for a reason. She will say something which sounds eternally right.

Things have to be buried, she says. They can't be left lying around anyhow for people to see.

Birds shouldn't die, I tell her. They have wings. Cats and rats haven't wings.

Stop crying, she says to Kallisto. It's only a bird.

It has a bride's flower in its hand, Kallisto says.

We shall rise again, I mutter, but we shall not all be changed.

Antigone does not seem to hear me.

Behold, I say in a voice she must hear, in a moment, in the twinkling of an eye, the trumpet shall sound.

Ismene turns to Kallisto and throws the daisy chain about her neck.

Shall a virgin forget her adorning or a bride the ornament of her breast?

Kallisto is lifting her arms toward the tree.

The bridegroom has come, she says, white as a fall of snow. He stands above me in a great ring of fire.

Antigone looks at me now.

Let's cover the bird up, she says. Your father will punish us all for making a disturbance.

He has on his garment, Kallisto says, and on his thigh is written King of Kings.

I look at the tree. If I could see with Kallisto's eyes I wouldn't be afraid of death, or punishment, or the penitentiary guards. I wouldn't be afraid of my father's belt or his honing strap or his bedroom slipper. I wouldn't be afraid of falling into the river through a knot-hole in the bridge.

But, as I look, I see the buds falling like burning lamps and I hear the sparrow twittering in its box: Woe, woe, woe because of the three trumpets which are yet to sound.

Kallisto is on her knees. She is growling like a bear. She lumbers over to the sandwiches and mauls them with her paw.

Ismene stands alone for Pan the gardener has gone.

Antigone is fitting a turf in place above the coffin. I go over and press the edge of the turf with my feet. Ismene has caught me by the hand.

Go away, Antigone says.

I see my father coming down the path. He has an attendant with him. In front of them walks Pan holding the sprinkler hook like a spear.

What are you doing here? my father asks.

Burying a bird, Antigone says.

Here? my father asks again.

Where else could I bury it? Antigone says.

My father looks at her.

This ground is public property, he says. No single person has any right to an inch of it.

I've taken six inches, Antigone says. Will you dig up the bird again?

Some of his subjects my father restrained since they were moved to throw themselves from high places or to tear one another to bits from jealousy or rage. Others who disturbed the public peace he taught to walk in the airing courts or to work in the kitchen or in the garden.

If men live at all, my father said, it is because discipline saves their life for them.

From Antigone he simply turned away.

JOHN CHEEVER

1912–1982

He was born in Quincy, Massachusetts, where his father owned a shoe factory until the economic disaster of 1929 wiped him out. His father's ancestors were seafarers, going back to the Revolution. His mother was English. After the crash she opened a gift shop that was quite successful. He went to school in Massachusetts until he was expelled from Thayer Academy for bad behavior. His first story, "Expelled," appeared in the *New Republic* a few months later in 1930. He was a writer from the beginning, living and working in Boston, New York, and the Yaddo writer's colony in Saratoga Springs. He was poor, surviving with help from his brother and by doing odd jobs. But he had published almost forty stories when he joined the U.S. Army for World War II. His first collection of stories was published during the war, but his first real success came with his second collection, *The Enormous Radio*, in 1953. By then he was writing for the *New Yorker*, where he placed well over a hundred stories since his first acceptance in 1940. He married in 1941 and became the father of three children. He lived in upstate New York. His reputation as a writer had grown steadily, so that the publication of his collected *Stories of John Cheever* in 1979 was a major literary event. He also wrote novels, but the short story was his form.

The Swimmer

It was one of those midsummer Sundays when everyone sits around saying, "I *drank* too much last night." You might have heard it whispered by the parishioners leaving church, heard it from the lips of the priest himself, struggling with his cassock in the *vestiarium*, heard it from the golf links and the tennis courts, heard it from the wild-life preserve where the leader of the Audubon group was suffering from a terrible hangover. "I *drank* too much," said Donald Westerhazy. "We all *drank* too much," said Lucinda Merrill. "It must have been the wine," said Helen Westerhazy. "I *drank* too much of that claret."

This was at the edge of the Westerhazy's pool. The pool, fed by an artesian well with a high iron content, was a pale shade of green. It was a fine day. In the west there was a massive stand of cumulus cloud so like a city seen from a distance—from the bow of an approaching ship—that it might have had a name. Lisbon. Hackensack. The sun was hot. Neddy Merrill sat by the green water, one hand in it, one around a glass of gin. He was a slender man—he seemed to have the especial slenderness of youth—and while he was far from young he had slid down his banister that morning and given the bronze backside of Aphrodite on the hall table a smack, as he jogged toward the smell of coffee in his dining room. He might have been compared to a summer's day, particularly the last hours of one, and while he lacked a tennis racket or a sail bag the impression was definitely one of youth, sport, and clement weather. He had been swimming and now he was breathing deeply, stertorously as if he could gulp into his lungs the components of that moment, the heat of the sun, the intenseness of his pleasure. It all seemed to flow into his chest. His own house stood in Bullet Park, eight miles to the south, where his four beautiful daughters would have had their lunch and might be playing tennis. Then it occurred to him that by taking a dogleg to the southwest he could reach his home by water.

His life was not confining and the delight he took in this observation could not be explained by its suggestion of escape. He seemed to see, with a cartographer's eye, that string of swimming pools, that quasi-subterranean stream that curved across the county. He had made a discovery, a contribution to modern geography; he would name the stream Lucinda after his wife. He was not a practical joker nor was he a fool but he was determinedly original and had a vague and modest idea of himself as a legendary figure. The day was beautiful and it seemed to him that a long swim might enlarge and celebrate its beauty.

He took off a sweater that was hung over his shoulders and dove in. He had an inexplicable contempt for men who did not hurl themselves into pools. He swam a choppy crawl, breathing either with every stroke or every fourth stroke and counting somewhere well in the back of his mind the one-two one-two of a flutter kick. It was not a serviceable stroke for long distances but the domestication of swimming had saddled the sport with some customs and in his part of the world a crawl was customary. To be embraced and sustained by the light green water was less a pleasure, it seemed, than the resumption of a natural condition, and he would have liked to swim without trunks, but this was not possible, considering his project. He hoisted himself up on the far curb—he never used the ladder—and started across the lawn. When Lucinda asked where he was going he said he was going to swim home.

The only maps and charts he had to go by were remembered or imaginary but these were clear enough. First there were the Grahams, the Hammers, the Lears, the Howlands, and the Crosscups. He would cross Ditmar Street to the Bunkers and come, after a short portage, to the Levys, the Welchers, and the public pool in Lancaster. Then there were the Hallorans, the Sachses, the Biswangers, Shirley Adams, the Gilmartins, and the Clydes. The day was lovely, and that he lived in a world so generously supplied with water seemed like a clemency, a beneficence. His heart was high and he ran across the grass. Making his way home by an uncommon route gave him the feeling that he was a pilgrim, an explorer, a man with a destiny, and he knew that he would find friends all along the way; friends would line the banks of the Lucinda River.

He went through a hedge that separated the Westerhazy's land from the Grahams', walked under some flowering apple trees, passed the shed that housed their pump and filter, and came out at the Grahams' pool. "Why, Neddy," Mrs. Graham said, "what a marvelous surprise. I've been trying to get you on the phone all morning. Here, let me get you a drink." He saw then, like any explorer, that the hospitable customs and traditions of the natives would have to be handled with diplomacy if he was ever going to reach his destination. He did not want to mystify or seem rude to the Grahams nor did he have the time to linger there. He swam the length of their pool and joined them in the sun and was rescued, a few minutes later, by the arrival of two carloads of friends from Connecticut. During the uproarious reunions he was able to slip away. He went down by the front of the Graham's house, stepped over a thorny hedge, and crossed a vacant lot to the Hammers'. Mrs. Hammer, looking up from her roses, saw him swim by although she wasn't quite sure who it was. The Lears heard him splashing past the open windows of their living room. The Howlands and the Crosscups were away. After leaving the Howlands' he crossed Ditmar Street and started for the Bunkers', where he could hear, even at that distance, the noise of a party.

The water refracted the sound of voices and laughter and seemed to suspend it in midair. The Bunkers' pool was on a rise and he climbed some stairs to a terrace where twenty-five or thirty men and women were drinking. The only person in the water was Rusty Towers, who floated there on a rubber raft. Oh, how bonny and lush were the banks of the Lucinda River! Prosperous men and women gathered by the sapphire-colored waters while caterer's men in white coats passed them cold gin. Overhead a red de Haviland trainer was circling around and around and around in the sky with something like the glee of a child in a swing. Ned felt a passing affection for the scene, a tenderness for the gathering, as if it was something he might touch. In the distance he heard thunder. As soon as Enid Bunker saw him she began to scream: "Oh, look who's here! What a marvelous surprise! When Lucinda said that you couldn't come I thought I'd *die*." She made her way to him through the crowd, and when they had finished kissing she led him to the bar, a progress that was slowed by the fact that he stopped to kiss eight or ten other women and shake the hands of as many men. A smiling bartender he had seen at a hundred parties gave him a gin and tonic and he stood by the bar for a moment, anxious not to get stuck in any conversation that would delay his voyage. When he seemed about to be surrounded he dove in and swam close to the side to avoid colliding with Rusty's raft. At the far end of the pool he bypassed the Tomlinsons with a broad smile and jogged up the garden path. The gravel cut his feet but this was the only unpleasantness. The party was confined to the pool, and as he went toward the house he heard the brilliant, watery sound of voices fade, heard the noise of a radio from the Bunkers' kitchen, where someone was listening to a ball game. Sunday afternoon. He made his way through the parked cars and down the grassy border of their driveway to Alewives Lane. He did not want to be seen on the road in his bathing trunks but there was no traffic and he made the short distance to the Levys' driveway, marked with a PRIVATE PROPERTY sign and a green tube for *The New York Times*. All the doors and windows of the big house were open but there were no signs of life; not even a dog barked. He went around the side of the house to the pool and saw that the Levys had only recently left. Glasses and bottles and dishes of nuts were on a table at the deep end, where there was a bathhouse or gazebo, hung with Japanese lanterns. After swimming the pool he got himself a glass and poured a drink. It was his fourth or fifth drink and he had swum nearly half the length of the Lucinda River. He felt tired, clean, and pleased at that moment to be alone; pleased with everything.

It would storm. The stand of cumulus cloud—that city—had risen and darkened, and while he sat there he heard the percussiveness of thunder again. The de Haviland trainer was still circling overhead and it seemed to Ned that he could almost hear the pilot laugh with pleasure in the afternoon; but when there was another peal of thunder he took off for home. A train whistle blew and he wondered what time it had gotten to be. Four? Five? He thought of the provincial station at that hour, where a waiter, his tuxedo concealed by a raincoat, a dwarf with some flowers wrapped in newspaper, and a woman who had been crying would be waiting for the local. It was suddenly growing dark; it was that moment when the pinheaded birds seemed to organize their song into some acute and knowledgeable recognition of the storm's approach. Then there was a fine noise of rushing water from the crown of an oak at his back, as if a spigot there had been turned. Then the noise of fountains came from the crowns of all the tall trees. Why did he love storms, what was the meaning of his excitement when the door sprang open and the rain wind fled rudely up the stairs, why had the simple task of shutting the windows of an old house seemed fitting and urgent, why did the first watery notes of a storm wind have for him the unmistakable sound of good news, cheer, glad tidings? Then there was an explosion, a smell of cordite, and rain lashed the Japanese lanterns that Mrs. Levy had bought in Kyoto the year before last, or was it the year before that?

He stayed in the Levys' gazebo until the storm had passed. The rain had cooled the air and he shivered. The force of the wind had stripped a maple of its red and yellow leaves and scattered them over the grass and the water. Since it was midsummer the tree must be blighted, and yet he felt a peculiar sadness at this sign of autumn. He braced his shoulders, emptied his glass, and started for the Welchers' pool. This meant crossing the Lindleys' riding ring and he was surprised to find it overgrown with grass and all the jumps dismantled. He wondered if the Lindleys had sold their horses or gone away for the summer and put them out to board. He seemed to remember having heard something about the Lindleys and their horses but the memory was unclear. On he went, barefoot through the wet grass, to the Welchers', where he found their pool was dry.

This breach in his chain of water disappointed him absurdly, and he felt like some explorer who seeks a torrential headwater and finds a dead stream. He was disappointed and mystified. It was common enough to go away for the summer but no one ever drained his pool. The Welchers had definitely gone away. The pool furniture was folded, stacked, and covered with a tarpaulin. The bathhouse was locked. All the windows of the house were shut, and when he went around to the driveway in front he saw a FOR SALE sign nailed to a tree. When had he last heard from the Welchers—when, that is, had he and Lucinda last regretted an invitation to dine with them? It seemed only a week or so ago. Was his memory failing or had he so disciplined it in the repression of unpleasant facts that he had damaged his sense of the truth? Then in the distance he heard the sound of a tennis game. This cheered him, cleared away all his apprehensions and let him regard the overcast sky and the cold air with indifference. This was the day that Neddy Merrill swam across the county. That was the day! He started off then for his most difficult portage.

Had you gone for a Sunday afternoon ride that day you might have seen him, close to naked, standing on the shoulders of Route 424, waiting for a chance to cross. You might have wondered if he was the victim of foul play, had his car broken down, or was he merely a fool. Standing barefoot in the deposits of the highway—beer cans, rags, and blowout patches—exposed to all kinds of ridicule, he seemed pitiful. He had known when he started that this was a part of his journey—it had been on his maps—but confronted with the lines of traffic, worming through the summery light, he found himself unprepared. He was laughed at, jeered at, a beer can was thrown at him, and he had no dignity or humor to bring to the situation. He could have gone back, back to the Westerhazys', where Lucinda would still be sitting in the sun. He had signed nothing, vowed nothing, pledged nothing, not even to himself. Why, believing as he did, that all human obduracy was susceptible to common sense, was he unable to turn back? Why was he determined to complete his journey even if it meant putting his life in danger? At what point had this prank, this joke, this piece of horseplay become serious? He could not go back, he could not even recall with any clearness the green water at the Westerhazys', the sense of inhaling the day's components, the friendly and relaxed voices saying that they had *drunk* too much. In the space of an hour, more or less, he had covered a distance that made his return impossible.

An old man, tooling down the highway at fifteen miles an hour, let him get to the middle of the road, where there was a grass divider. Here he was exposed to the ridicule of the northbound traffic, but after ten or fifteen minutes he was able to cross. From here he had only a short walk to the Recreation Center at the edge of the village of Lancaster, where there were some handball courts and a public pool.

The effect of the water on voices, the illusion of brilliance and suspense, was the same here as it has been at the Bunkers' but the sounds here were louder, harsher, and more shrill, and as soon as he entered the crowded enclosure he was confronted with regimentation. "ALL SWIMMERS MUST TAKE A SHOWER BEFORE USING THE POOL. ALL SWIMMERS MUST USE THE FOOTBATH. ALL SWIMMERS MUST WEAR THEIR IDENTIFICATION DISKS." He took a shower, washed his feet in a cloudy and bitter solution, and made his way to the edge of the water. It stank of chlorine and looked to him like a sink. A pair of lifeguards in a pair of towers blew police whistles at what seemed to be regular intervals and abused the swimmers through a public address system. Neddy remembered the sapphire water at the Bunkers' with longing and thought that he might contaminate himself—damage his own prosperousness and charm—by swimming in this murk, but he reminded himself that he was an explorer, a pilgrim, and that this was merely a stagnant bend in the Lucinda River. He dove, scowling with distaste, into the chlorine and had to swim with his head above water to avoid collisions, but even so he was bumped into, splashed, and jostled. When he got to the shallow end both lifeguards were shouting at him: "Hey, you, you without the identification disk, get outa the water." He did, but they had no way of pursuing him and he went through the reek of suntan oil and chlorine out through the hurricane fence and passed the hand-ball courts. By crossing the road he entered the wooded part of the Halloran estate. The woods were not cleared and the footing was treacherous and difficult until he reached the lawn and the clipped beech hedge that encircled their pool.

The Hallorans were friends, an elderly couple of enormous wealth who seemed to bask in the suspicion that they might be Communists. They were zealous reformers but they were not Communists, and yet when they were accused, as they sometimes were, of subversion, it seemed to gratify and excite them. Their beech hedge was yellow and he guessed this had been blighted like the Levys' maple. He called hullo, hullo, to warn the Hallorans of his approach, to palliate his invasion of their privacy. The Hallorans, for reasons that had never been explained to him, did not wear bathing suits. No explanations were in order, really. Their nakedness was a detail in their uncompromising zeal for reform and he stepped politely out of his trunks before he went through the opening in the hedge.

Mrs. Halloran, a stout woman with white hair and a serene face, was reading the *Times*. Mr. Halloran was taking beech leaves out of the water with a scoop. They seemed not surprised or displeased to see him. Their pool was perhaps the oldest in the country, a field-stone rectangle, fed by a brook. It had no filter or pump and its waters were the opaque gold of the stream.

"I'm swimming across the county," Ned said.

"Why, I didn't know one could," exclaimed Mrs. Halloran.

"Well, I've made it from the Westerhazys'," Ned said. "That must be about four miles."

He left his trunks at the deep end, walked to the shallow end, and swam this stretch. As he was pulling himself out of the water he heard Mrs. Halloran say, "We've been *terribly* sorry to hear about all your misfortunes, Neddy."

"My misfortunes?" Ned asked. "I don't know what you mean."

"Why, we heard that you'd sold the house and that your poor children . . ."

"I don't recall having sold the house," Ned said, "and the girls are at home."

"Yes," Mrs. Halloran sighed. "Yes . . ." Her voice filled the air with an unseasonable melancholy and Ned spoke briskly. "Thank you for the swim."

"Well, have a nice trip," said Mrs. Halloran.

Beyond the hedge he pulled on his trunks and fastened them. They were loose and he wondered if, during the space of an afternoon, he could have lost some weight. He was cold and he was tired and the naked Hallorans and their dark water had depressed him. The swim was too much for his strength but how could he have guessed this, sliding down the banister that morning and sitting in the Westerhazys' sun? His arms were lame. His legs felt rubbery and ached at the joints. The worst of it was the cold in his bones and the feeling that he might never be warm again. Leaves were falling down around him and he smelled wood smoke on the wind. Who would be burning wood at this time of year?

He needed a drink. Whiskey would warm him, pick him up, carry him through the last of his journey, refresh his feeling that it was original and valorous to swim across the county. Channel swimmers took brandy. He needed a stimulant. He crossed the lawn in front of the Hallorans' house and went down a little path to where they had built a house for their only daughter, Helen, and her husband, Eric Sachs. The Sachses' pool was small and he found Helen and her husband there.

"Oh, *Neddy*," Helen said. "Did you lunch at Mother's?"

"Not *really*," Ned said. "I *did* stop to see your parents." This seemed to be explanation enough. "I'm terribly sorry to break in on you like this but I've taken a chill and I wonder if you'd give me a drink."

"Why, I'd *love* to," Helen said, "but there hasn't been anything in this house to drink since Eric's operation. That was three years ago."

Was he losing his memory, had his gift for concealing painful facts let him forget that he had sold his house, that his children were in trouble, and that his friend had been ill? His eyes slipped from Eric's face to his abdomen, where he saw three pale, sutured scars, two of them at least a foot long. Gone was his navel, and what, Neddy thought, would the roving hand, bed-checking one's gifts at 3 A.M., make of a belly with no navel, no link to birth, this breach in the succession?

"I'm sure you can get a drink at the Biswangers'," Helen said. "They're having an enormous do. You can hear it from here. Listen!"

She raised her head and from across the road, the lawns, the gardens, the woods, the fields, he heard again the brilliant noise of voices over water. "Well, I'll get wet," he said, still feeling that he had no freedom of choice about his means of travel. He dove into the Sachses' cold water and, gasping, close to drowning, made his way from one end of the pool to the other. "Lucinda and I want *terribly* to see you," he said over his shoulder, his face set toward the Biswangers'. "We're sorry it's been so long and we'll call you *very* soon."

He crossed some fields to the Biswangers' and the sounds of revelry there. They would be honored to give him a drink, they would be happy to give him a drink. The Biswangers invited him and Lucinda for dinner four times a year, six weeks in advance. They were always rebuffed and yet they continued to send out their invitations, unwilling to comprehend the rigid and undemocratic realities of their society. They were the sort of people who discussed the price of things at cocktails, exchanged market tips during dinner, and after dinner told dirty stories to mixed company. They did not belong to Neddy's set—they were not even on Lucinda's Christmas card list. He went toward their pool with feelings of indifference, charity, and some unease, since it seemed to be getting dark and these were the longest days of the year. The party when he joined it was noisy and large. Grace Biswanger was the kind of hostess who asked the optometrist, the veterinarian, the real-estate dealer, and the dentist. No one was swimming and the twilight, reflected on the water of the pool, had a wintry gleam. There was a bar and he started for this. When Grace Biswanger saw him she came toward him, not affectionately as he had every right to expect, but bellicosely.

"Why, this party has everything," she said loudly, "including a gate crasher."

She could not deal him a social blow—there was no question about this and he did not flinch. "As a gate crasher," he asked politely, "do I rate a drink?"

"Suit yourself," she said. "You don't seem to pay much attention to invitations."

She turned her back on him and joined some guests, and he went to the bar and ordered a whiskey. The bartender served him but he served him rudely. His was a world in which the caterer's men kept the social score, and to be rebuffed by a part-time barkeep meant that he had suffered some loss of social esteem. Or perhaps the man was new and uninformed. The he heard Grace at his back say: "They went for broke overnight—nothing but income—and he showed up drunk one Sunday and asked us to loan him five thousand dollars. . . ." She was always talking about money. It was worse than eating your peas off a knife. He dove into the pool, swam its length and went away.

The next pool on his list, the last but two, belonged to his old mistress, Shirley Adams. If he had suffered any injuries at the Biswangers' they would be cured here. Love—sexual roughhouse in fact—was the supreme elixir, the pain killer, the brightly colored pill that would put the spring back into his step, the joy of life in his heart. They had had an affair last week, last month, last year. He couldn't remember. It was he who had broken it off, his was the

upper hand, and he stepped through the gate of the wall that surrounded her pool with nothing so considered as self-confidence. It
seemed in a way to be his pool, as the lover, particularly the illicit
lover, enjoys the possessions of his mistress with an authority unknown to holy matrimony. She was there, her hair the color of
brass, but her figure, at the edge of the lighted, cerulean water,
excited in him no profound memories. It had been, he thought, a
lighthearted affair, although she had wept when he broke it off. She
seemed confused to see him and he wondered if she was still
wounded. Would she, God forbid, weep again?

"What do you want?" she asked.

"I'm swimming across the county."

"Good Christ. Will you ever grow up?"

"What's the matter?"

"If you've come here for money," she said, "I won't give you
another cent."

"You could give me a drink."

"I could but I won't. I'm not alone."

"Well, I'm on my way."

He dove in and swam the pool, but when he tried to haul himself
up onto the curb he found that the strength in his arms and
shoulders had gone, and he paddled to the ladder and climbed out.
Looking over his shoulder he saw, in the lighted bathhouse, a
young man. Going out onto the dark lawn he smelled chrysanthe-
mums or marigolds—some stubborn autumnal fragrance—on the
night air, strong as gas. Looking overhead he saw that the stars had
come out, but why should he seem to see Andromeda, Cepheus,
and Cassiopeia? What had become of the constellations of midsummer? He began to cry.

It was probably the first time in his adult life that he had ever
cried, certainly the first time in his life that he had ever felt so
miserable, cold, tired, and bewildered. He could not understand the
rudeness of the caterer's barkeep or the rudeness of a mistress who
had come to him on her knees and showered his trousers with tears.
He had swum too long, he had been immersed too long, and his
nose and his throat were sore from the water. What he needed then
was a drink, some company, and some clean, dry clothes, and while
he could have cut directly across the road to his home he went on to
the Gilmartins' pool. Here, for the first time in his life, he did not
dive but went down the steps into the icy water and swam a hob-
bled sidestroke that he might have learned as a youth. He staggered
with fatigue on his way to the Clydes' and paddled the length of
their pool, stopping again and again with his hand on the curb to
rest. He climbed up the ladder and wondered if he had the strength

to get home. He had done what he wanted, he had swum the county, but he was so stupefied with exhaustion that his triumph seemed vague. Stooped, holding on to the gateposts for support, he turned up the driveway of his own house.

The place was dark. Was it so late that they had all gone to bed? Had Lucinda stayed at the Westerhazys' for supper? Had the girls joined her there or gone someplace else? Hadn't they agreed, as they usually did on Sunday, to regret all their invitations and stay at home? He tried the garage doors to see what cars were in but the doors were locked and rust came off the handles onto his hands. Going toward the house, he saw that the force of the thunderstorm had knocked one of the rain gutters loose. It hung down over the front door like an umbrella rib, but it could be fixed in the morning. The house was locked, and he thought that the stupid cook or the stupid maid must have locked the place up until he remembered that it had been some time since they had employed a maid or a cook. He shouted, pounded on the door, tried to force it with his shoulder, and then, looking in at the windows, saw that the place was empty.

BERNARD MALAMUD
1914–1986

A city boy, of Jewish background, Malamud was born and raised in Brooklyn, New York. He went to City College, for his B.A. and to Columbia University for his M.A. He taught in night school for almost ten years before taking a job at Oregon State University. His experiences in Oregon from 1949 to 1961 became the basis for his novel *A New Life* (1961). As a short story writer he continued the tradition of Babel and Singer. From 1961 he taught at Bennington College in Vermont. Among his most admired works are a novel, *The Assistant* (1957), and the stories in *The Magic Barrel* (1958).

The Magic Barrel

Not long ago there lived in uptown New York, in a small, almost meager room, though crowded with books, Leo Finkle, a rabbinical student in the Yeshivah University. Finkle, after six years of study, was to be ordained in June and had been advised by an acquaintance that he might find it easier to win himself a congregation if he were married. Since he had no present prospects of marriage, after two tormented days of turning it over in his mind, he called in Pinye Salzman, a marriage broker whose two-line advertisement he had read in the *Forward*.

The matchmaker appeared one night out of the dark fourth-floor hallway of the graystone rooming house where Finkle lived, grasping a black, strapped portfolio that had been worn thin with use. Salzman, who had been long in the business, was of slight but dignified build, wearing an old hat, and an overcoat too short and tight for him. He smelled frankly of fish, which he loved to eat, and although he was missing a few teeth, his presence was not displeasing, because of an amiable manner curiously contrasted with mournful eyes. His voice, his lips, his wisp of beard, his bony fingers were animated, but give him a moment of repose and his mild blue eyes revealed a depth of sadness, a characteristic that put Leo a little at ease although the situation, for him, was inherently tense.

He at once informed Salzman why he had asked him to come, explaining that his home was in Cleveland, and that but for his parents, who had married comparatively late in life, he was alone in the world. He had for six years devoted himself almost entirely to his studies, as a result of which, understandably, he had found himself without time for a social life and the company of young women. Therefore he thought it the better part of trial and error—of embarrassing fumbling—to call in an experienced person to advise him on these matters. He remarked in passing that the function of the marriage broker was ancient and honorable, highly approved in the Jewish community, because it made practical the necessary without hindering joy. Moreover, his own parents had been brought together by a matchmaker. They had made, if not a financially profitable marriage—since neither had possessed any worldly goods to speak of—at least a successful one in the sense of their everlasting devotion to each other. Salzman listened in embarrassed surprise, sensing a sort of apology. Later, however, he experienced a glow of pride in his work, an emotion that had left him years ago, and he heartily approved of Finkle.

The two went to their business. Leo had led Salzman to the only clear place in the room, a table near a window that overlooked the lamp-lit city. He seated himself at the matchmaker's side but facing him, attempting by an act of will to suppress the unpleasant tickle in his throat. Salzman eagerly unstrapped his portfolio and removed a loose rubber band from a thin packet of much-handled cards. As he flipped through them, a gesture and sound that physically hurt Leo, the student pretended not to see and gazed steadfastly out the window. Although it was still February, winter was on its last legs, signs of which he had for the first time in years begun to notice. He now observed the round white moon, moving high in the sky through a cloud menagerie, and watched with half-open mouth as it penetrated a huge hen, and dropped out of her like an egg laying itself. Salzman, though pretending through eyeglasses he had just slipped on to be engaged in scanning the writing on the cards, stole occasional glances at the young man's distinguished face, noting with pleasure the long, severe scholar's nose, brown eyes heavy with learning, sensitive yet ascetic lips, and a certain, almost hollow quality of the dark cheeks. He gazed around at shelves upon shelves of books and let out a soft, contented sigh.

When Leo's eyes fell upon the cards, he counted six spread out in Salzman's hand.

"So few?" he asked in disappointment.

"You wouldn't believe me how much cards I got in my office," Salzman replied. "The drawers are already filled to the top, so I keep them now in a barrel, but is every girl good for a new rabbi?"

Leo blushed at this, regretting all he had revealed of himself in a curriculum vitae he had sent to Salzman. He had thought it best to acquaint him with his strict standards and specifications, but in having done so, felt he had told the marriage broker more than was absolutely necessary.

He hesitantly inquired, "Do you keep photographs of your clients on file?"

"First comes family, amount of dowry, also what kind promises," Salzman replied, unbuttoning his tight coat and settling himself in the chair. "After comes pictures, rabbi."

"Call me Mr. Finkle. I'm not yet a rabbi."

Salzman said he would, but instead called him doctor, which he changed to rabbi when Leo was not listening too attentively.

Salzman adjusted his horn-rimmed spectacles, gently cleared his throat and read in an eager voice the contents of the top card:

"Sophie P. Twenty four years. Widow one year. No children. Educated high school and two years college. Father promises eight thousand dollars. Has wonderful wholesale business. Also real estate. On the mother's side comes teachers, also one actor. Well known on Second Avenue."

Leo gazed up in surprise. "Did you say a widow?"

"A widow don't mean spoiled, rabbi. She lived with her husband maybe four months. He was a sick boy she made a mistake to marry him."

"Marrying a widow has never entered my mind."

"This is because you have no experience. A widow, especially if she is young and healthy like this girl, is a wonderful person to marry. She will be thankful to you the rest of her life. Believe me, if I was looking now for a bride, I would marry a widow."

Leo reflected, then shook his head.

Salzman hunched his shoulders in an almost imperceptible gesture of disappointment. He placed the card down on the wooden table and began to read another:

"Lily H. High school teacher. Regular. Not a substitute. Has savings and new Dodge car. Lived in Paris one year. Father is successful dentist thirty-five years. Interested in professional man. Well Americanized family. Wonderful opportunity."

"I knew her personally," said Salzman. "I wish you could see this girl. She is a doll. Also very intelligent. All day you could talk to her about books and theyater and what not. She also knows current events."

"I don't believe you mentioned her age?"

"Her age?" Salzman said, raising his brows. "Her age is thirty-two years."

Leo said after a while, "I'm afraid that seems a little too old."

Salzman let out a laugh. "So how old are you, rabbi?"

"Twenty-seven."

"So what is the difference, tell me, between twenty-seven and thirty-two? My own wife is seven years older than me. So what did I suffer?—Nothing. If Rothschild's daughter wants to marry you, would you say on account her age, no?"

"Yes," Leo said dryly.

Salzman shook off the no in the yes. "Five years don't mean a thing. I give you my word that when you will live with her for one week you will forget her age. What does it mean five years—that she lived more and knows more than somebody who is younger? On this girl, God bless her, years are not wasted. Each one that it comes makes better the bargain."

"What subject does she teach in high school?"

"Languages. If you heard the way she speaks French, you will think it is music. I am in the business twenty-five years, and I recommend her with my whole heart. Believe me, I know what I'm talking, rabbi."

"What's on the next card?" Leo said abruptly.

Salzman reluctantly turned up the third card:

"Ruth K. Nineteen years. Honor student. Father offers thirteen thousand cash to the right bridegroom. He is a medical doctor. Stomach specialist with marvelous practice. Brother in law owns own garment business. Particular people."

Salzman looked as if he had read his trump card.

"Did you say nineteen?" Leo asked with interest.

"On the dot."

"Is she attractive?" He blushed. "Pretty?"

Salzman kissed his finger tips. "A little doll. On this I give you my word. Let me call the father tonight and you will see what means pretty."

But Leo was troubled. "You're sure she's that young?"

"This I am positive. The father will show you the birth certificate."

"Are you positive there isn't something wrong with her?" Leo insisted.

"Who says there is wrong?"

"I don't understand why an American girl her age should go to a marriage broker."

A smile spread over Salzman's face.

"So for the same reason you went, she comes."

Leo flushed. "I am pressed for time."

Salzman, realizing he had been tactless, quickly explained. "The father came, not her. He wants she should have the best, so he looks around himself. When we will locate the right boy he will introduce him and encourage. This makes a better marriage than if a young girl without experience takes for herself. I don't have to tell you this."

"But don't you think this young girl believes in love?" Leo spoke uneasily.

Salzman was about to guffaw but caught himself and said soberly, "Love comes with the right person, not before."

Leo parted dry lips but did not speak. Noticing that Salzman had snatched a glance at the next card, he cleverly asked, "How is her health?"

"Perfect," Salzman said, breathing with difficulty. "Of course, she is a little lame on her right foot from an auto accident that it happened to her when she was twelve years, but nobody notices on account she is so brilliant and also beautiful."

Leo got up heavily and went to the window. He felt curiously bitter and upbraided himself for having called in the marriage broker. Finally, he shook his head.

"Why not?" Salzman persisted, the pitch of his voice rising.

"Because I detest stomach specialists."

"So what do you care what is his business? After you marry her do you need him? Who says he must come every Friday night in your house?"

Ashamed of the way the talk was going, Leo dismissed Salzman, who went home with heavy, melancholy eyes.

Though he had felt only relief at the marriage broker's departure, Leo was in low spirits the next day. He explained it as arising from Salzman's failure to produce a suitable bride for him. He did not care for his type of clientele. But when Leo found himself hesitating whether to seek out another matchmaker, one more polished than Pinye, he wondered if it could be—his protestations to the contrary, and although he honored his father and mother—that he did not, in essence, care for the matchmaking institution? This thought he quickly put out of mind yet found himself still upset. All day he ran around in the woods—missed an important appointment, forgot to give out his laundry, walked out of a Broadway cafeteria without paying and had to run back with the ticket in his hand; had even not recognized his landlady in the street when she passed with a friend and courteously called out, "A good evening to you, Doctor Finkle." By nightfall, however, he had regained sufficient calm to sink his nose into a book and there found peace from his thoughts.

Almost at once there came a knock on the door. Before Leo could say enter, Salzman, commercial cupid, was standing in the room. His face was gray and meager, his expression hungry, and he looked as if he would expire on his feet. Yet the marriage broker managed, by some trick of the muscles, to display a broad smile.

"So good evening. I am invited?"

Leo nodded, disturbed to see him again, yet unwilling to ask the man to leave.

Beaming still, Salzman laid his portfolio on the table. "Rabbi, I got for you tonight good news."

"I've asked you not to call me rabbi. I'm still a student."

"Your worries are finished. I have for you a first-class bride."

"Leave me in peace concerning this subject." Leo pretended lack of interest.

"The world will dance at your wedding."

"Please, Mr. Salzman, no more."

"But first must come back my strength," Salzman said weakly. He fumbled with the portfolio straps and took out of the leather case an oily paper bag, from which he extracted a hard, seeded roll and a small, smoked white fish. With a quick motion of his hand he stripped the fish out of its skin and began ravenously to chew. "All day in a rush," he muttered.

Leo watched him eat.

"A sliced tomato you have maybe?" Salzman hesitantly inquired.

"No."

The marriage broker shut his eyes and ate. When he had finished he carefully cleaned up the crumbs and rolled up the remains of the fish, in the paper bag. His spectacled eyes roamed the room until he discovered, amid some piles of books, a one-burner gas stove. Lifting his hat he humbly asked, "A glass tea you got, rabbi?"

Conscience-stricken, Leo rose and brewed the tea. He served it with a chunk of lemon and two cubes of lump sugar, delighting Salzman.

After he had drunk his tea, Salzman's strength and good spirits were restored.

"So tell me, rabbi," he said amiably, "you considered some more the three clients I mentioned yesterday?"

"There was no need to consider."

"Why not?"

"None of them suits me."

"What then suits you?"

Leo let it pass because he could give only a confused answer.

Without waiting for a reply, Salzman asked, "You remember this girl I talked to you—the high school teacher?"

"Age thirty-two?"

But, surprisingly, Salzman's face lit in a smile. "Age twenty-nine."

Leo shot him a look. "Reduced from thirty-two?"

"A mistake," Salzman avowed. "I talked today with the dentist. He took me to his safety deposit box and showed me the birth certificate. She was twenty-nine years last August. They made her a party in the mountains where she went for her vacation. When her father spoke to me the first time I forgot to write the age and I told you thirty-two, but now I remember this was a different client, a widow."

"The same one you told me about? I thought she was twenty-four?"

"A different. Am I responsible that the world is filled with widows?"

"No, but I'm not interested in them, nor for that matter, in school teachers."

Salzman pulled his clasped hands to his breast. Looking at the ceiling he devoutly exclaimed, "Yiddishe kinder, what can I say to somebody that he is not interested in high school teachers? So what then you are interested?"

Leo flushed but controlled himself.

"In what else will you be interested," Salzman went on, "if you not interested in this fine girl that she speaks four languages and has personally in the bank ten thousand dollars? Also her father guarantees further twelve thousand. Also she has a new car, wonderful clothes, talks on all subjects, and she will give you a first-class home and children. How near do we come in our life to paradise?"

"If she's so wonderful, why wasn't she married ten years ago?"

"Why?" said Salzman with a heavy laugh. "—Why? Because she is *partikiler*. This is why. She wants the *best*."

Leo was silent, amused at how he had entangled himself. But Salzman had aroused his interest in Lily H., and he began seriously to consider calling on her. When the marriage broker observed how intently Leo's mind was at work on the facts he had supplied, he felt certain they would soon come to an agreement.

Late Saturday afternoon, conscious of Salzman, Leo Finkle walked with Lily Hirschorn along Riverside Drive. He walked briskly and erectly, wearing with distinction the black fedora he had that morning taken with trepidation out of the dusty hat box on his closet shelf, and the heavy black Saturday coat he had thoroughly whisked clean. Leo also owned a walking stick, a present from a distant relative, but quickly put temptation aside and did not use it. Lily, petite and not unpretty, had on something signifying the approach of spring She was au courant, animatedly, with all sorts of subjects, and he weighed her words and found her surprisingly sound—score another for Salzman, whom he uneasily sensed to be somewhere around, hiding perhaps high in a tree along the street, flashing the lady signals with a pocket mirror; or perhaps a cloven-hoofed Pan, piping nuptial ditties as he danced his invisible way before them, strewing wild buds on the walk and purple grapes in their path, symbolizing fruit of a union, though there was of course still none.

Lily startled Leo by remarking, "I was thinking of Mr. Salzman, a curious figure, wouldn't you say?"

Not certain what to answer, he nodded.

She bravely went on, blushing, "I for one am grateful for his introducing us. Aren't you?"

He courteously replied, "I am."

"I mean," she said with a little laugh—and it was all in good taste, or at least gave the effect of being not in bad—"do you mind that we came together so?"

He was not displeased with her honesty, recognizing that she meant to set the relationship aright, and understanding that it took a certain amount of experience in life, and courage, to want to do it quite that way. One had to have some sort of past to make that kind of beginning.

He said that he did not mind. Salzman's function was traditional and honorable—valuable for what it might achieve, which, he pointed out, was frequently nothing.

Lily agreed with a sigh. They walked on for a while and she said after a long silence, again with a nervous laugh, "Would you mind if I asked you something a little bit personal? Frankly, I find the subject fascinating." Although Leo shrugged, she went on half embarrassedly, "How was it that you came to your calling? I mean was it a sudden passionate inspiration?"

Leo after a time, slowly replied, "I was always interested in the Law."

"You saw revealed in it the presence of the Highest?"

He nodded and changed the subject. "I understand that you spent a little time in Paris, Miss Hirschorn?"

"Oh, did Mr. Salzman tell you, Rabbi Finkle?" Leo winced but she went on, "It was ages ago and almost forgotten. I remember I had to return for my sister's wedding."

And Lily would not be put off. "When," she asked in a trembly voice, "did you become enamored of God?"

He stared at her. Then it came to him that she was talking not about Leo Finkle, but of a total stranger, some mystical figure, perhaps even passionate prophet that Salzman had dreamed up for her—no relation to the living or dead. Leo trembled with rage and weakness. The trickster had obviously sold her a bill of goods, just as he had him, who'd expected to become acquainted with a young lady of twenty-nine, only to behold, the moment he laid eyes upon her strained and anxious face, a woman past thirty-five and aging rapidly. Only his self-control had kept him this long in her presence.

"I am not," he said gravely, "a talented religious person," and in seeking words to go on, found himself possessed by shame and fear. "I think," he said in a strained manner, "that I came to God not because I loved Him, but because I did not."

This confession he spoke harshly because its unexpectedness shook him.

Lily wilted. Leo saw a profusion of loaves of bread go flying like ducks high over his head, not unlike the winged loaves by which he had counted himself to sleep last night. Mercifully, then, it snowed, which he would not put past Salzman's machinations.

He was infuriated with the marriage broker and swore he would throw him out of the room the minute he reappeared. But Salzman did not come that night, and when Leo's anger had subsided, an unaccountable despair grew in its place. At first he thought this was caused by his disappointment in Lily, but before long it became evident that he had involved himself with Salzman without a true knowledge of his own intent. He gradually realized—with an emptiness that seized him with six hands—that he had called in the broker to find him a bride because he was incapable of doing it himself. This terrifying insight he had derived as a result of his meeting and conversation with Lily Hirschorn. Her probing questions had somehow irritated him into revealing—to himself more than her—the true nature of his relationship to God, and from that it had come upon him, with shocking force, that apart from his parents, he had never loved anyone. Or perhaps it went the other way, that he did not love God so well as he might, because he had not loved man. It seemed to Leo that his whole life stood starkly revealed and he saw himself for the first time as he truly was—unloved and loveless. This bitter but somehow not fully unexpected revelation brought him to a point of panic, controlled only by extraordinary effort. He covered his face with his hands and cried.

The week that followed was the worst of his life. He did not eat and lost weight. His beard darkened and grew ragged. He stopped attending seminars and almost never opened a book. He seriously considered leaving the Yeshivah, although he was deeply troubled at the thought of the loss of all his years of study—saw them like pages torn from a book, strewn over the city—and at the devastating effect of this decision upon his parents. But he had lived without knowledge of himself, and never in the Five Books and all the Commentaries—mea culpa—had the truth been revealed to him. He did not know where to turn, and in all this desolating loneliness there was no *to whom*, although he often thought of Lily but not once could bring himself to go downstairs and make the call. He became touchy and irritable, especially with his landlady, who asked him all manner of personal questions; on the other hand, sensing his own disagreeableness, he waylaid her on the stairs and apologized abjectly, until mortified, she ran from him. Out of this, however, he drew the consolation that he was a Jew and that a Jew suffered. But gradually, as the long and terrible week drew to a close, he regained his composure and some idea of purpose in life: to go on as planned. Although he was imperfect, the ideal was not. As for his quest of a bride, the thought of continuing afflicted him with anxiety and heartburn, yet perhaps with this new knowledge of himself he would be more successful than in the past. Perhaps love would now come to him and a bride to that love. And for this sanctified seeking who needed a Salzman?

The marriage broker, a skeleton with haunted eyes, returned that very night. He looked, withal, the picture of frustrated expectancy—as if he had steadfastly waited the week at Miss Lily Hirschorn's side for a telephone call that never came.

Casually coughing, Salzman came immediately to the point: "So how did you like her?"

Leo's anger rose and he could not refrain from chiding the matchmaker: "Why did you lie to me, Salzman?"

Salzman's pale face went dead white, the world had snowed on him.

"Did you not state that she was twenty-nine?" Leo insisted.

"I give you my word—"

"She was thirty-five, if a day. *At least* thirty-five."

"Of this don't be too sure. Her father told me—"

"Never mind. The worst of it was that you lied to her."

"How did I lie to her, tell me?"

"You told her things about me that weren't true. You made me out to be more, consequently less than I am. She had in mind a totally different person, a sort of semi-mystical Wonder Rabbi."

"All I said, you was a religious man."

"I can imagine."

Salzman sighed. "This is my weakness that I have," he confessed. "My wife says to me I shouldn't be a salesman, but when I have two fine people that they would be wonderful to be married, I am so happy that I talk too much." He smiled wanly. "This is why Salzman is a poor man."

Leo's anger left him. "Well, Salzman, I'm afraid that's all."

The marriage broker fastened hungry eyes on him.

"You don't want any more a bride?"

"I do," said Leo, "but I have decided to seek her in a different way. I am no longer interested in an arranged marriage. To be frank, I now admit the necessity of premarital love. That is, I want to be in love with the one I marry."

"Love?" said Salzman, astounded. After a moment he remarked, "For us, our love is our life, not for the ladies. In the ghetto they—"

"I know, I know," said Leo. "I've thought of it often. Love, I have said to myself, should be a by-product of living and worship rather than its own end. Yet for myself I find it necessary to establish the level of my need and fulfill it."

Salzman shrugged but answered, "Listen, rabbi, if you want love, this I can find for you also. I have such beautiful clients that you will love them the minute your eyes will see them."

Leo smiled unhappily. "I'm afraid you don't understand."

But Salzman hastily unstrapped his portfolio and withdrew a manila packet from it.

"Pictures," he said, quickly laying the envelope on the table.

Leo called after him to take the pictures away, but as if on the wings of the wind, Salzman had disappeared.

March came. Leo had returned to his regular routine. Although he felt not quite himself yet—lacked energy—he was making plans for a more active social life. Of course it would cost something, but he was an expert in cutting corners; and when there was no corners left he would make circles rounder. All the while Salzman's pictures had lain on the table, gathering dust. Occasionally as Leo sat studying, or enjoying a cup of tea, his eyes fell on the manila envelope, but he never opened it.

The days went by and no social life to speak of developed with a member of the opposite sex—it was difficult, given the circumstances of his situation. One morning Leo toiled up the stairs to his room and stared out the window at the city. Although the day was bright his view of it was dark. For some time he watched the people in the street below hurrying along and then turned with a heavy heart to his little room. On the table was the packet. With a sudden relentless gesture he tore it open. For a half-hour he stood by the table in a state of excitement, examining the photographs of the ladies Salzman had included. Finally, with a deep sigh he put them down. There were six, of varying degrees of attractiveness, but look at them long enough and they all became Lily Hirschorn: all past their prime, all starved behind bright smiles, not a true personality in the lot. Life, despite their frantic yoohooings, had passed them by; they were pictures in a brief case that stank of fish. After a while, however, as Leo attempted to return the photographs into the envelope, he found in it another, a snapshot of the type taken by a machine for a quarter. He gazed at it a moment and let out a cry.

Her face deeply moved him. Why, he could at first not say. It gave him the impression of youth—spring flowers, yet age—a sense of having been used to the bone, wasted; this came from the eyes, which were hauntingly familiar, yet absolutely strange. He had a vivid impression that he had met her before, but try as he might he could not place her although he could almost recall her name, as if he had read it in her own handwriting. No, this couldn't be; he would have remembered her. It was not, he affirmed, that she had an extraordinary beauty—no, though her face was attractive enough; it was that *something* about her moved him. Feature for feature, even some of the ladies of the photographs could do better; but she leaped forth to his heart—had *lived*, or wanted to—more than just wanted, perhaps regretted how she had lived—had somehow deeply suffered: it could be seen in the depths of those reluctant eyes, and from the way the light enclosed and shone from her, and within her, opening realms of possibility: this was her own. Her he desired. His head ached and eyes narrowed with the intensity of his gazing, then as if an obscure fog had blown up in the mind, he experienced fear of her and was aware that he had received an impression, somehow, of evil. He shuddered, saying softly, it is thus with us all. Leo brewed some tea in a small pot and sat sipping it without sugar, to calm himself. But before he had finished drinking, again with excitement he examined the face and found it good: good for Leo Finkle. Only such a one could understand him and help him seek whatever he was seeking. She might, perhaps, love him. How she had happened to be among the discards in Salzman's barrel he could never guess, but he knew he must urgently go find her.

Leo rushed downstairs, grabbed up the Bronx telephone book, and searched for Salzman's home address. He was not listed, nor was his office. Neither was he in the Manhattan book. But Leo remembered having written down the address on a slip of paper after he had read Salzman's advertisement in the "personals" column of the *Forward*. He ran up to his room and tore through his papers, without luck. It was exasperating. Just when he needed the matchmaker he was nowhere to be found. Fortunately Leo remembered to look in his wallet. There on a card he found his name written and a Bronx address. No phone number was listed, the reason—Leo now recalled—he had originally communicated with Salzman by letter. He got on his coat, put a hat on over his skull cap and hurried to the subway station. All the way to the far end of the Bronx he sat on the edge of his seat. He was more than once tempted to take out the picture and see if the girl's face was as he remembered it, but he refrained, allowing the snapshot to remain in his inside coat pocket, content to have her so close. When the train pulled into the station he was waiting at the door and bolted out. He quickly located the street Salzman had advertised.

The building he sought was less than a block from the subway, but it was not an office building, nor even a loft, nor a store in which one could rent office space. It was a very old tenement house. Leo found Salzman's name in pencil on a soiled tag under the bell and climbed three dark flights to his apartment. When he knocked, the door was opened by a thin, asthmatic, gray-haired woman, in felt slippers.

"Yes?" she said, expecting nothing. She listened without listening. He could have sworn he had seen her, too, before but knew it was an illusion.

"Salzman—does he live here? Pinye Salzman," he said, "the matchmaker?"

She stared at him a long minute. "Of course."

He felt embarrassed. "Is he in?"

"No." Her mouth, though left open, offered nothing more.

"The matter is urgent. Can you tell me where his office is?"

"In the air." She pointed upward.

"You mean he has no office?" Leo asked.

"In his socks."

He peered into the apartment. It was sunless and dingy, one large room divided by a half-open curtain, beyond which he could see a sagging metal bed. The near side of a room was crowded with rickety chairs, old bureaus, a three-legged table, racks of cooking utensils, and all the apparatus of a kitchen. But there was no sign of Salzman or his magic barrel, probably also a figment of the imagination. An odor of frying fish made Leo weak to the knees.

"Where is he?" he insisted. "I've got to see your husband."

At length she answered, "So who knows where he is? Every time he thinks a new thought he runs to a different place. Go home, he will find you."

"Tell him Leo Finkle."

She gave no sign she had heard.

He walked downstairs, depressed.

But Salzman, breathless, stood waiting at his door.

Leo was astounded and overjoyed. "How did you get here before me?"

"I rushed."

"Come inside."

They entered. Leo fixed tea, and a sardine sandwich for Salzman. As they were drinking he reached behind him for the packet of pictures and handed them to the marriage broker.

Salzman put down his glass and said expectantly, "You found somebody you like?"

"Not among these."

The marriage broker turned away.

"Here is the one I want." Leo held forth the snapshot.

Salzman slipped on his glasses and took the picture into his trembling hand. He turned ghastly and let out a groan.

"What's the matter?" cried Leo.

"Excuse me. Was an accident this picture. She isn't for you."

Salzman frantically shoved the manila packet into his portfolio. He thrust the snapshot into his pocket and fled down the stairs.

Leo, after momentary paralysis, gave chase and cornered the marriage broker in the vestibule. The landlady made hysterical outcries but neither of them listened.

"Give me back the picture, Salzman."

"No." The pain in his eyes was terrible.

"Tell me who she is then."

"This I can't tell you. Excuse me."

He made to depart, but Leo, forgetting himself, seized the matchmaker by his tight coat and shook him frenziedly.

"Please," sighed Salzman. "*Please*."

Leo ashamedly let him go. "Tell me who she is," he begged. "It's very important for me to know."

"She is not for you. She is a wild one—wild, without shame. This is not a bride for a rabbi."

"What do you mean wild?"

"Like an animal. Like a dog. For her to be poor was a sin. This is why to me she is dead now."

"In God's name, what do you mean?"

"Her I can't introduce to you," Salzman cried.

"Why are you so excited?"

"Why, he asks," Salzman said, bursting into tears. "This is my baby, my Stella, she should burn in hell."

Leo hurried up to bed and hid under the covers. Under the covers he thought his life through. Although he soon fell asleep he could not sleep her out of his mind. He woke, beating his breast. Though he prayed to be rid of her, his prayers went unanswered. Through days of torment he endlessly struggled not to love her; fearing success, he escaped it. He then concluded to convert her to goodness, himself to God. The idea alternately nauseated and exalted him.

He perhaps did not know that he had come to a final decision until he encountered Salzman in a Broadway cafeteria. He was sitting alone at a rear table, sucking the bony remains of a fish. The marriage broker appeared haggard, and transparent to the point of vanishing.

Salzman looked up at first without recognizing him. Leo had grown a pointed beard and his eyes were weighted with wisdom.

"Salzman," he said, "love has at last come to my heart."

"Who can love from a picture?" mocked the marriage broker.

"It is not impossible."

"If you can love her, then you can love anybody. Let me show you some new clients that they just sent me their photographs. One is a little doll."

"Just her I want," Leo murmured.

"Don't be a fool, doctor. Don't bother with her."

"Put me in touch with her, Salzman," Leo said humbly. "Perhaps I can be of service."

Salzman had stopped eating and Leo understood with emotion that it was now arranged.

Leaving the cafeteria, he was, however, afflicted by a tormenting suspicion that Salzman had planned it all to happen this way.

Leo was informed by letter that she would meet him on a certain corner, and she was there one spring night, waiting under a street lamp. He appeared, carrying a small bouquet of violets and rosebuds. Stella stood by the lamp post, smoking. She wore white with red shoes, which fitted his expectations, although in a troubled moment he had imagined the dress red, and only the shoes white. She waited uneasily and shyly. From afar he saw that her eyes—clearly her father's—were filled with desperate innocence. He pictured, in her, his own redemption. Violins and lit candles revolved in the sky. Leo ran forward with flowers outthrust.

Around the corner, Salzman, leaning against a wall, chanted prayers for the dead.

GUY VANDERHAEGHE
1951–

Born and raised in Esterhazy, Saskatchewan, he obtained his B.A. and M.A. in history from the University of Saskatchewan; he also pursued graduate studies in education at the University of Regina. Having worked as a teacher, archivist, and researcher, he now devotes his time chiefly to writing. From 1984 until 1986 he was a member of the Department of English at the University of Ottawa. In his two collections of short stories, *Man Descending* (1982) and *The Trouble with Heroes and Other Stories* (1983), and his two novels, *My Present Age* (1984) and *Homesick* (1989), he depicts men and women in their loneliness, capturing our modern plight with vivid realism yet always emphasizing the undying hope for an alternative to alienation and isolation. In two stories from his second collection, "No Man Could Bind Him" and "Lazarus," he recreates biblical times with the same vitality and richness that characterize his delineation of the contemporary world. He currently resides in Saskatoon with his wife, the painter Margaret Vanderhaeghe.

Lazarus

The villagers hear the first dim sounds of the procession, muffled by the heat, distant. Then, the piercing notes of the flutes, trembling and shrill, pricking the air: at last; the words of the song, the Song of Songs.

> What is this coming up from the desert
> like a column of smoke,
> breathing of myrrh and frankincense
> and every perfume the merchant knows?

The bridal party crests the hill that marks the boundary between the country and village. Here on the summit they pause as the bearers shift the poles of the bridal palanquin on their shoulders, making adjustments for the descent. Behind the procession, on the plain, are fields of barley; an occasional cypress scars the bright horizon with an austere, vertical line. No bird wheels in the sky, nothing distracts their eyes from the precipitous rush of sky to earth until the cypresses, like stitches, bind the blue with the dun. Before them there is only disorder, a jumble of houses, a tangle of streets. But here there is also life, and the streets are ripe with the bitter odors of domesticity.

For the watchers at the outskirts of the village this break in the procession symbolizes a bride's indecision: this or that? backward or forward? So when the litter resumes its progress, swaying forward, borne triumphantly and resolutely by a brightly colored human surf, the villagers rush to welcome the bride and applaud her choice.

All but one man, Lazarus, who stands apart from the others, who is somehow distinctive. Like the rest, he has stood for hours intently waiting; but he is not a man given to running and shouting. Instead, he watches the people cast seeds before the litter and sing, and he searches their faces. He is lean and spare, an ascetic perhaps. He stands with his head craned forward. The lower half of his face is covered by his cloak, so that his sharp eyes are dominant; he resembles a great bird poised to strike. Everything about him is bird-like: his frailty, his barely subdued eagerness, the way his body remains motionless while his head flickers and turns, watching.

The procession is at the village now, at the mouth of the narrow street where Lazarus stands. He can see the bride clearly, carried as she is high above the crowd on her litter. Her brown eyes shine behind her veil, her black hair is bound in wires of gold, it glistens with oil. The dust of the roadway, stirred by many feet, rises in a fine cloud about her. The crowd forces its way into the steet and Lazarus is thrust against a wall by the rush.

> Your two breasts are two fawns,
> twins of a gazelle,
> that feed among the lilies,

they sing.

The litter is so close that if he desired he could reach out and touch it. As his hands trace the rough masonry of the wall, searching for a point to brace himself against the press of the crowd, he catches the scent of spikenard. He closes his eyes, almost reels with excitement as he breathes the rich odor. An image rises behind his closed lids. His sister, dark and serious, bends as she anoints the rabbi. The room fills with the heady aroma of spikenard, the shadows drink it in, the guests stir uneasily, feeling something has passed.

His eyes open. "Messiah!" he cries to the tumult. No one hears; his words are lost in the happy song and the dry rumble of many throats. He struggles to breach the crowd, to insinuate himself between the stubborn bodies, to find the face. But he is an old man with little strength, and he can only swirl feebly at the edges of the crowd.

And then he realizes that the spikenard comes from the perfumed bride who rides above him. The girl seems, for a moment, to turn toward him. She laughs, and her eyes, darkened with kohl, seem to take pleasure in his deception. But she is innocent of any malice; she laughs with joy and the wisdom of her choice.

They are past. The commotion winds through the streets, making for the house of the bridegroom, the noise shifting with every turning. Lazarus tightens the cloak across his face, attempting to mask the perfume that lingers in the air with dry, dusty wool. The street is empty now except for a crippled dog who trots, hindquarters askew, in search of the procession. Lazarus turns his attention back to the hill and gazes anxiously at it. He sees nothing, it bobs and shudders in the heat haze.

"Come quickly," he whispers. "I am waiting."

The hill answers back with nothing.

"Come," he pleads. His lids close against the glare. The scent of spikenard is still present. Is this a sign? Like the dog, he turns and trails the wedding party with faltering steps.

It is the second day of the wedding celebrations. The vows have been said beneath the *chuppah*, the canopy, and now the guests are feasting. The aroma of roast kid and dark honey is everywhere, even in the courtyard where Lazarus sits alone in the swiftly falling darkness.

In moments, the stars will swing up in the heavens.

There is a sprinkling of laughter from the house, the lamps are lit. But Lazarus is not drawn to these comforts. He is condemned to wait, a standard which never flutters in the breeze, a point of flesh that is a bearing for the Messiah. The demon told him so.

It happened like this. Eighteen years before the demon had visited him. Lazarus lived alone; his sisters were dead, Martha carried off by a fever years before, and Mary, only months in the grave, killed by a tumor that had swollen her belly to the size of a large basket. The quiet house had been broken, its peace gone; for Lazarus the only pleasure in life that remained was his studies. That night, however, he had fallen asleep over his scrolls and his head lay amid curling parchment.

Seeing him asleep and weakened, the tiny demon of Bethany had perched on his shoulder and whispered into his ear.

"Lazarus," he whispered urgently. "Poor Lazarus! Searching for answers on these dry skins.

"Lazarus the Scholar, that's what the people of Bethany have named you. I hear them call you that while I am in the streets going about my business. Mine is a small precinct so I get to know my charges intimately, all of them. I observe them closely, and I must say that I know none better than I know you, Lazarus. I've taken a special interest in you and your problems, and I know that you're puzzled, and I know why. From the very moment you stalked out of that tomb you've wanted to know why you were raised from the dead, and to what purpose. Of course, you realize you're an extraordinary man, perhaps one of the most extraordinary ever born. You were raised from the dead, you've seen both worlds. You're the great interpreter.

"But why were you given life? You've asked yourself that question many times. Because He loved you? Really, do you think your merits earned you such a love? I don't think so and neither do you. Were you raised from the dead to ease your sisters' grief, to wipe away their tears? What a macabre notion! What joy is there in seeing a dead man's bones jig, or in smelling death whenever you are within sniffing distance of your brother? No, a rabbi of such great power could have taken away their grief in a way that didn't defy the laws of nature, that didn't flout the very statutes of creation. No, these aren't the answers.

"Well, why then?" asked the demon, shifting himself on his perch and puffing himself up. "I know the answer, and I'll let you in on the secret because I've grown fond of you after all these years, and because I believe you deserve to know your fate. You, Lazarus, were chosen to be the eternal man, the man who could never die. All around you men will wither, dry up, and blow away. But not you, Lazarus. Oh no, you will remain, for you see, you've escaped the bondage of death.

"Why? Because when the Messiah comes again he will need a witness. Very likely everyone who once knew him will have died. For this reason you were liberated from death, so that in the fullness of time you might identify him. And what a witness! Absolutely unimpeachable! Who could ever forget a man raised from the dead? Fathers will tell their sons, 'That is Lazarus, the man raised from the dead, the man who cannot die.' And their sons will remember and tell their sons, and their sons will remember and tell their sons, and their sons will tell their sons, and so it will go. No one will ever forget. You will be the signpost of the generations.

"So you must wait, Lazarus. But wait as a man, not as a god. And there's the crux of it. You will be immortal but your flesh will be as weak as your neighbour's. You will feel pain and misery, every accretion of sorrow will bow you closer to the earth. What a prospect! Year in and year out, waiting, never knowing when the great moment will come. And when it does come, everything will rest on your shoulders, there will be only Lazarus. Only poor Lazarus, scotched and scarred by life. Only Lazarus to point and say, 'That is He! I am His witness! I am Lazarus who cannot die! I remember the face!' "

The demon lowered his mouth a little closer to Lazarus's ear. Slyly he said: "Suffering and more suffering, that is what is in store for you. With every terrible year that passes, with every terrible injury done you, you'll naturally come to hate your jailer. And who could blame you?

"You'll want revenge, Lazarus. That desire will grow and grow, until it will be the only warmth you know—this hope for revenge. To be able to punish God! That will be in your power. Think of it! And when the time comes, when the Messiah appears, the people will turn to you, Lazarus, the eternal man, and ask, 'Is this one the Messiah?' Then what will you do, Lazarus? I think I know. I can foresee the outcome. Your lust for revenge will be so boundless you will deny him. You will point your finger at the Saviour and cry, 'Impostor!' And then the mob will turn and rend him, limb from limb, because their hopes will have been crushed again. The people will avenge their dreary history of charlatans and fakes.

"Can you imagine such a thing? You, virtuous Lazarus, a traitor to God, a traitor to man. Humanity doomed because of your hatred. Because, after all, how many times can God submit himself to such indignities?" The devil paused. "What more can I say? I've warned you. Do your best," he chuckled. "Husband your strength and your will. Spend it like a miser. He may come tomorrow or in an eternity."

And then the demon climbed down from Lazarus's shoulder and stole away before he could wake. He was the demon who sows despair and doubt, the liar and seducer, the familiar of Judas. No sooner was he gone than Lazarus awoke, filled with terror. At first he thought he had been dreaming but his shoulder ached where the demon had perched on it, and the demon's bestial odour pervaded the house. Lazarus lit a lamp and searched the corners of the room, even peered under his table, hoping to discover the demon and take him captive. He had questions he wanted to ask him. But his search was fruitless, the demon had disappeared. Where he had gone to Lazarus couldn't possibly know.

It was months before Lazarus could arrive at a decision. He begged the demon for another meeting, a short colloquy, during which he could probe his intentions. Demons, it went without saying, could not be trusted; they laid complicated snares to trap the foolish. But then again might the demon unwittingly have revealed the truth? A rich man, Lazarus reasoned, sometimes proffers to a begger a coin of greater value than he intends. On the other hand, was this a trap to ensnare Lazarus in his own pride, and then, finally, cause him to despair and lose hope? Or had this little devil underestimated his victim, and in plotting his future thereby warned him and given him the strength to bear its vicissitudes?

And if the Messiah desired an ally could Lazarus allow himself to be found wanting? Or again, was he being led into an error that would undo him? Could any man believe that he was indispensable to the Messiah? The demon's words rattled in his ears. He was being forced to cast his lot, to enter a wager that he felt somehow he must inevitably lose. He could not afford to resort to chance, the stakes, as the demon had pointed out, were too high. Lazarus decided that he must wait, and in waiting rule his doubt.

The decision was reached during the winter rains. It seemed fitting to him that he should take up his post of vigilance outside the village of Bethany in a nasty squall, standing alone in bursts of wind and slashing, cold rain. The Messiah would come, even though no man, and he least of all, knew the hour of His coming. That was a matter of fact; it had been promised. So there he waited, as the seasons and years turned on the treadmill of his desire. There were always strangers whose faces had to be searched for a spark of divinity. Tanners that smelled of dung, drovers and shepherds, merchants from the East with spiked beards and rings in their ears, lepers and cripples. Every man who passed the silent figure, his body still quivering with anticipation after so much disappointment, had to be examined.

Yesterday the wedding had meant many strangers and an excess of hope. The scent of spikenard had drawn him here to this courtyard; it had seemed a sign. He had searched the faces, daring to believe, but had found nothing but masks of flesh, undifferentiated and unremarkable.

So now Lazarus sits in the dust of the courtyard and prays. Or is he merely speaking to himself? No matter—he is sure he is overheard.

"Answer me one question," he demands. "Why are You hiding Yourself? Need I remind You of a promise You made once to come again, soon? I know the answers to that one, after all I was, once, something of a scholar. I don't need to be reminded that an eternity in Your sight is little more than the blinking of an eye. Very well, that's fair. But what about me? After all, an eternity is to me just that—an eternity. My bones are aching with waiting. I'm hungry for my reward. I need a little rest.

"You insist on staying hidden. Now a man cannot play hide and seek with God. I can't ferret You out. I've got to sit and wait. What's more, this monstrous game can only be terminated by one of the players. So hurry up!

"Well that may be as it is. As you know, I'm here in Bethany waiting. Whatever the reasons or the outcome I'm here. I hope there's some virtue in that. Do as you will, here I sit."

Lazarus is finished speaking. He shifts his weight and settles his haunches more comfortably in the dust. He thinks wryly of how thin he has grown. Perhaps his buttocks will leave an impression in the loose soil resembling the hoofprint of a cow.

At this moment, two men flushed with heat and wine step outside the house to catch the breeze. The taller and younger of the two, Stephen, is a member of the bride's party. Stephen has flirted with the schools at Sephoris in Galilee and has consorted with Greeks. He is a new man, a modern. He is shaved, and on one of his fingers he wears a ring fashioned with an image. At times, he thinks it unfortunate he was born a Jew. With him is Simeon, bearded and squat, a native of Bethany. The two men have little in common except that they have drunk together, and in the easy cordiality of a wedding have chosen to act the part of friends for the evening.

Stephen, dulled with wine and too much food, scrubs his face with his palms and flavours his breath with anise. Then looking around with a negligent air, he spies Lazarus, a shadowy figure, dark against the darkness, his body slumped forward, his head drooping over the earth.

Stephen nudges Simeon and asks: "Who is that man?"

Simeon strains his eyes at the purple, waving shadows. At last he recognizes him. "Lazarus," he answers. Simeon is not interested in so familiar a figure.

"Why is he sitting in the darkness, so still?"

Simeon smiles. "Old Lazarus is Bethany's madman. He's waiting for his dead rabbi." He pauses doubtfully. "At least that's what I've been told."

"Ah," breathes Stephen, curious now. "A holy man?"

"Hardly. As I said, he's merely mad. One of those who act strangely to give the impression they are sanctified. They despise and hate other men, thinking that their extraordinary behavior finds favor with God."

Stephen, intrigued and eager to impress his new friend with the skills of controversy acquired at Sephoris, wishes to question this provincial holy man. He says: "An interesting type. I'd like to speak with him."

Simeon snorts derisively. "Speak with him? A man like him? He's old, worn out, mad, living in another world. What could he say? Anyway, he talks with no one. It's a wonder he hasn't taken to the desert."

"How does he live?"

"Who knows? Likely he eats with the dogs. Or feasts on air. Perhaps he is a sorcerer who conjures up his bread." This last thought makes Simeon uneasy; he fingers an amulet that wards off the evil eye.

"How was he driven mad? What provoked this?" Stephen gestures vaguely toward Lazarus slumped in the courtyard.

"Whatever it was is forgotten now—if anyone ever knew. My father once said he came back from the dead, although that is scarcely credible. I can remember when he was a scholar. It is likely that too many letters, too many words, addled his brain."

A roar of laughter, a snatch of music, is heard from the house. Stephen turns, and can see, through the open window, people dancing. He turns his attention back to Lazarus. "Better to be dead," he says, "than to sit in the dust and watch life pass you by."

"It won't be long either," Simeon replies, "before he will be dead. The man is a walking ghost. The spirit is staring from his eyes. And his end will be no better than was his life. There'll be no prayers for the dead, no mourners, no tomb ready to receive him. They'll drop him in a hole outside the village—just like that, into a pauper's grave. A bad ending." He shakes his head at the notion of such an ignominious end.

"A bad ending," Stephen repeats in a murmur. They turn back to the house, as if agreed this is no talk for a wedding. The door opens and pours light over them, they are bathed in the smell of meat and wine. Music quivers in the air around them.

Lazarus sits in the dust waiting. The stars have come out at last. They are so large and so bright that their vast distances, so infinite, have shrunk and become comprehensible. They are his *chuppah*, his canopy, and their light lengthens his shadow across the courtyard. Lazarus is a point of stillness in the night; he is fixed, he is a stele of flesh.

Tonight with the sky pressing down upon him pitted with brilliant light, Lazarus feels for a moment that past and present is bound within his flesh and bone. He rules this kingdom of time as a steward rules in his master's absence. He *is* a witness.

Tomorrow of course, he will be tired, hungry, and sore. He will plead for strength to play the demon's role and doubt if he can endure.

But now in this night, he is sure it is not a bad thing to be still, to be silent, and to wait.

REALISM: *INTRODUCTION*

Even the wildest fantasy has something real about it. But works of fiction that we call "realistic" are real in a particular way. They present a world defined by certain ideas about the way social forces work upon individual human beings, and they show us characters whose inner lives conform to certain notions about human psychology. It would be impossible to define exactly what these "certain" ideas and notions are, but it is necessary to say something about them—at least in a rough and tentative way.

In earlier literature, individual characters are often shown struggling against fate or chance to achieve fame or happiness. Realism begins when writers can identify "society" as the thing against which individuals must struggle. When the romantic ideal of a unique and free personality confronts a deterministic view of social forces, realism is born. In realistic fictions we see individuals in conflict with social groups, with the class structure, the family structure, the political system. The short story—as opposed to the larger novel—specializes in loneliness, in the need for love and companionship that is seldom adequately achieved; and in the desire to retain an individual free will in the face of the enormous pressures of an indifferent or actively hostile world.

In a very definite way, realistic writers are the historians of their times—not chroniclers of the deeds of the great and powerful but witnesses to the quality of ordinary life. Two European writers showed the rest of the Western world how realism in short fiction could be achieved: Guy de Maupassant in France and Anton Chekhov in Russia. English, Irish, and American short story writers learned from them. And the Americans, in particular, learned well.

In the short story, skill with language itself counts for more than it needs to in longer fiction. The shorter a story is, the more closely it can draw upon the resources of poetry in its language. But a story, especially a realistic one, is not a poem. It must have a strong narrative structure or design, and it must get to the roots of human feeling and behavior in a way that convinces us of its human truth: truth to the way things are, to the surface of life, as well as truth to the inner lives of individuals, and the social structures in which individual lives grow or are stifled.

The range of tones and techniques employed by the writers represented here is in fact extraordinary. The interaction of individuals which is at the heart of realism can be presented in the detached, behavioral report of a Hemingway—with no interpretive commentary—or in the rich, engaged recital of a Lawrence, in which the commentary explores emotions that the characters feel but could never articulate for themselves. There are light stories with comic touches here, and heavy stories that bring us close to tears. But all these works of realistic fiction are designed to enlarge our sympathies by broadening our understanding. The end of realism is compassion.

GUY DE MAUPASSANT
1850–1893

Born Henri René Albert Guy de Maupassant, he grew up in Normandy, not far from Rouen, and went to school at the Rouen Lycée before entering government service. At the age of twenty he served in the Franco-Prussian War, and many of his finest stories came out of that experience. After the war he apprenticed himself to the older Flaubert. His greatest gifts were for the realistic short story, and he virtually perfected the form, producing nearly three hundred stories in a dozen years. Early in life he had contracted syphilis, for which there was no effective treatment at the time. In his forties he could no longer work, as the disease attacked his brain, ultimately reducing him to insanity before he died at the age of forty-three.

The Diamond Necklace

She was one of those pretty, charming young ladies, born, as if through an error of destiny, into a family of clerks. She had no dowry, no hopes, no means of becoming known, appreciated, loved, and married by a man either rich or distinguished; and she allowed herself to marry a petty clerk in the office of the Board of Education.

She was simple, not being able to adorn herself; but she was unhappy, as one out of her class; for women belong to no caste, no race; their grace, their beauty, and their charm serving them in the place of birth and family. Their inborn finesse, their instinctive elegance, their suppleness of wit are their only aristocracy, making some daughters of the people the equal of great ladies.

She suffered incessantly, feeling herself born for all delicacies and luxuries. She suffered from the poverty of her apartment, the shabby walls, the worn chairs, and the faded stuffs. All these things, which another woman of her station would not have noticed, tortured and angered her. The sight of the little Breton, who made this humble home, awoke in her sad regrets and desperate dreams. She thought of quiet antechambers, with their Oriental hangings, lighted by high, bronze torches, and of the two great footmen in short trousers who sleep in the large armchairs, made sleepy by the heavy air from the heating apparatus. She thought of large drawing-rooms, hung in old silks, of graceful pieces of furniture carrying bric-à-brac of inestimable value, and of the little perfumed coquettish apartments, made for five o'clock chats with most intimate friends, men known and sought after, whose attention all women envied and desired.

When she seated herself for dinner, before the round table where the tablecloth had been used three days, opposite her husband who uncovered the tureen with a delighted air, saying: "Oh! the good potpie! I know nothing better than that—" she would think of the elegant dinners, of the shining silver, of the tapestries peopling the walls with ancient personages and rare birds in the midst of fairy forests; she thought of the exquisite food served on marvelous dishes, of the whispered gallantries, listened to with the smile of the sphinx, while eating the rose-colored flesh of the trout or a chicken's wing.

She had neither frocks nor jewels, nothing. And she loved only those things. She felt that she was made for them. She had such a desire to please, to be sought after, to be clever, and courted.

She had a rich friend, a schoolmate at the convent, whom she did not like to visit, she suffered so much when she returned. And she wept for whole days from chagrin, from regret, from despair, and disappointment.

One evening her husband returned elated bearing in his hand a large envelope.

"Here," he said, "here is something for you."

She quickly tore open the wrapper and drew out a printed card on which were inscribed these words:

> The Minister of Public Instruction and Madame George Ramponneau ask the honor of Mr. and Mrs. Loisel's company Monday evening, January 18, at the Minister's residence.

Instead of being delighted, as her husband had hoped, she threw the invitation spitefully upon the table murmuring:

"What do you suppose I want with that?"

"But, my dearie, I thought it would make you happy. You never go out, and this is an occasion, and a fine one! I had a great deal of trouble to get it. Everybody wishes one, and it is very select; not many are given to employees. You will see the whole official world there."

She looked at him with an irritated eye and declared impatiently:

"What do you suppose I have to wear to such a thing as that?"

He had not thought of that; he stammered:

"Why, the dress you wear when we go to the theater. It seems very pretty to me—"

He was silent, stupefied, in dismay, at the sight of his wife weeping. Two great tears fell slowly from the corners of his eyes toward the corners of his mouth; he stammered:

"What is the matter? What is the matter?"

By a violent effort, she had controlled her vexation and responded in a calm voice, wiping her moist cheeks:

"Nothing. Only I have no dress and consequently I cannot go to this affair. Give your card to some colleague whose wife is better fitted out than I."

He was grieved, but answered:

"Let us see, Matilda. How much would a suitable costume cost, something that would serve for other occasions, something very simple?"

She reflected for some seconds, making estimates and thinking of a sum that she could ask for without bringing with it an immediate refusal and a frightened exclamation from the economical clerk.

Finally she said, in a hesitating voice:

"I cannot tell exactly, but it seems to me that four hundred francs ought to cover it."

He turned a little pale, for he had saved just this sum to buy a gun that he might be able to join some hunting parties the next summer, on the plains at Nanterre, with some friends who went to shoot larks up there on Sunday. Nevertheless, he answered:

"Very well. I will give you four hundred francs. But try to have a pretty dress."

The day of the ball approached and Mme. Loisel seemed sad, disturbed, anxious. Nevertheless, her dress was nearly ready. Her husband said to her one evening:

"What is the matter with you? You have acted strangely for two or three days."

And she responded: "I am vexed not to have a jewel, not one stone, nothing to adorn myself with. I shall have such a poverty-laden look. I would prefer not to go to this party."

He replied: "You can wear some natural flowers. At this season they look very *chic*. For ten francs you can have two or three magnificent roses."

She was not convinced. "No," she replied, "there is nothing more humiliating than to have a shabby air in the midst of rich women."

Then her husband cried out: "How stupid we are! Go and find your friend Mrs. Forestier and ask her to lend you her jewels. You are well enough acquainted with her to do this."

She uttered a cry of joy: "It is true!" she said. "I had not thought of that."

The next day she took herself to her friend's house and related her story of distress. Mrs. Forestier went to her closet with the glass doors, took out a large jewel-case, brought it, opened it, and said: "Choose, my dear."

She saw at first some bracelets, then a collar of pearls, then a

Venetian cross of gold and jewels and of admirable workmanship. She tried the jewels before the glass, hesitated, but could neither decide to take them nor leave them. Then she asked:

"Have you nothing more?"

"Why, yes. Look for yourself. I do not know what will please you."

Suddenly she discovered, in a black satin box, a superb necklace of diamonds, and her heart beat fast with an immoderate desire. Her hands trembled as she took them up. She placed them about her throat against her dress, and remained in ecstasy before them. Then she asked, in a hesitating voice, full of anxiety:

"Could you lend me this? Only this?"

"Why, yes, certainly."

She fell upon the neck of her friend, embraced her with passion, then went away with her treasure.

The day of the ball arrived. Mme. Loisel was a great success. She was the prettiest of all, elegant, gracious, smiling, and full of joy. All the men noticed her, asked her name, and wanted to be presented. All the members of the Cabinet wished to waltz with her. The Minister of Education paid her some attention.

She danced with enthusiasm, with passion, intoxicated with pleasure, thinking of nothing, in the triumph of her beauty, in the glory of her success, in a kind of cloud of happiness that came of all this homage, and all this admiration, of all these awakened desires, and this victory so complete and sweet to the heart of woman.

She went home toward four o'clock in the morning. Her husband had been half asleep in one of the little salons since midnight, with three other gentlemen whose wives were enjoying themselves very much.

He threw around her shoulders the wraps they had carried for the coming home, modest garments of everyday wear, whose poverty clashed with the elegance of the ball costume. She felt this and wished to hurry away in order not to be noticed by the other women who were wrapping themselves in rich furs.

Loisel retained her: "Wait," said he. "You will catch cold out there. I am going to call a cab."

But she would not listen and descended the steps rapidly. When they were in the street, they found no carriage; and they began to seek for one, hailing the coachmen whom they saw at a distance.

They walked along toward the Seine, hopeless and shivering. Finally they found on the dock one of those old, noctural *coupés* that one sees in Paris after nightfall, as if they were ashamed of their misery by day.

It took them as far as their door in Martyr street, and they went wearily up to their apartment. It was all over for her. And on his part, he remembered that he would have to be at the office by ten o'clock.

She removed the wraps from her shoulders before the glass, for a final view of herself in her glory. Suddenly she uttered a cry. Her necklace was not around her neck.

Her husband, already half undressed, asked: "What is the matter?"

She turned toward him excitedly:

"I have—I have—I no longer have Mrs. Forestier's necklace."

He arose in dismay: "What! How is that? It is not possible."

And they looked in the folds of the dress, in the folds of the mantle, in the pockets, everywhere. They could not find it.

He asked: "You are sure you still had it when we left the house?"

"Yes, I felt it in the vestibule as we came out."

"But if you had lost it in the street, we should have heard it fall. It must be in the cab."

"Yes. It is probable. Did you take the number?"

"No. And you, did you notice what it was?"

"No."

They looked at each other utterly cast down. Finally, Loisel dressed himself again.

"I am going," said he, "over the track where we went on foot, to see if I can find it."

And he went. She remained in her evening gown, not having the force to go to bed, stretched upon a chair, without ambition or thoughts.

Toward seven o'clock her husband returned. He had found nothing.

He went to the police and to the cab offices, and put an advertisement in the newspapers, offering a reward; he did everything that afforded them a suspicion of hope.

She waited all day in a state of bewilderment before this frightful disaster. Loisel returned at evening with his face harrowed and pale; and had discovered nothing.

"It will be necessary," said he, "to write to your friend that you have broken the clasp of the necklace and that you will have it repaired. That will give us time to turn around."

She wrote as he dictated.

At the end of a week, they had lost all hope. And Loisel, older by five years, declared:

"We must take measures to replace this jewel."

The next day they took the box which had inclosed it, to the jeweler whose name was on the inside. He consulted his books:

"It is not I, Madame," said he, "who sold this necklace; I only furnished the casket."

Then they went from jeweler to jeweler seeking a necklace like the other one, consulting their memories, and ill, both of them, with chagrin and anxiety.

In a shop of the Palais-Royal, they found a chaplet of diamonds which seemed to them exactly like the one they had lost. It was valued at forty thousand francs. They could get it for thirty-six thousand.

They begged the jeweler not to sell it for three days. And they made an arrangement by which they might return it for thirty-four thousand francs if they found the other one before the end of February.

Loisel possessed eighteen thousand francs which his father had left him. He borrowed the rest.

He borrowed it, asking for a thousand francs of one, five hundred of another, five louis of this one, and three louis of that one. He gave notes, made ruinous promises, took money of usurers and the whole race of lenders. He compromised his whole existence, in fact, risked his signature, without even knowing whether he could make it good or not, and, harassed by anxiety for the future, by the black misery which surrounded him, and by the prospect of all physical privations and moral torture, he went to get the new necklace, depositing on the merchant's counter thirty-six thousand francs.

When Mrs. Loisel took back the jewels to Mrs. Forestier, the latter said to her in a frigid tone:

"You should have returned them to me sooner, for I might have needed them."

She did open the jewel-box as her friend feared she would. If she should perceive the substitution, what would she think? What should she say? Would she take her for a robber?

Mrs. Loisel now knew the horrible life of necessity. She did her part, however, completely heroically. It was necessary to pay this frightful debt. She would pay it. They sent away the maid; they changed their lodgings; they rented some rooms under a mansard roof.

She learned the heavy cares of a household, the odious work of a kitchen. She washed the dishes, using her rosy nails upon the greasy pots and the bottoms of the stewpans. She washed the soiled linen, the chemises and dishcloths, which she hung on the line to dry; she took down the refuse to the street each morning and brought up the water, stopping at each landing to breathe. And, clothed like a woman of the people she went to the grocer's, the butcher's, and the fruiterer's, with her basket on her arm, shopping, haggling to the last sou her miserable money.

Every month it was necessary to renew some notes, thus obtaining time, and to pay others.

The husband worked evenings, putting the books of some merchants in order, and nights he often did copying at five sous a page.

And this life lasted for ten years.

At the end of ten years, they had restored all, all, with interest of the usurer, and accumulated interest besides.

Mrs. Loisel seemed old now. She had become a strong, hard woman, the crude woman of the poor household. Her hair badly dressed, her skirts awry, her hands red, she spoke in a loud tone, and washed the floors with large pails of water. But sometimes, when her husband was at the office, she would seat herself before the window and think of that evening party of former times, of that ball where she was so beautiful and so flattered.

How would it have been if she had not lost that necklace? Who knows? Who knows? How singular is life, and how full of changes! How small a thing will ruin or save one!

One Sunday, as she was taking a walk in the Champs-Elysées to rid herself of the cares of the week, she suddenly perceived a woman walking with a child. It was Mrs. Forestier, still young, still pretty, still attractive. Mrs. Loisel was affected. Should she speak to her? Yes, certainly. And now that she had paid, she would tell her all. Why not?

She approached her. "Good morning, Jeanne."

Her friend did not recognize her and was astonished to be so familiarly addressed by this common personage. She stammered:

"But, Madame—I do not know— You must be mistaken—"

"No, I am Matilda Loisel."

Her friend uttered a cry of astonishment: "Oh! my poor Matilda! How you have changed—"

"Yes, I have had some hard days since I saw you; and some miserable ones—and all because of you—"

"Because of me? How is that?"

"You recall the diamond necklace that you loaned me to wear to the Commissioner's ball?"

"Yes, very well."

"Well, I lost it."

"How is that, since you returned it to me?"

"I returned another to you exactly like it. And it has taken us ten years to pay for it. You can understand that it was not easy for us who have nothing. But it is finished and I am decently content."

Madame Forestier stopped short. She said:

"You say that you bought a diamond necklace to replace mine?"

"Yes. You did not perceive it then? They were just alike."

And she smiled with a proud and simple joy. Madame Forestier was touched and took both her hands as she replied:

"Oh! my poor Matilda! Mine were false. They were not worth over five hundred francs!"

KATE CHOPIN
1851–1904

Kate O'Flaherty was born in St. Louis, Missouri, to an Irish immigrant father and a French mother. She was educated in a Catholic convent school in St. Louis, and married a Louisiana banker named Oscar Chopin when she was nineteen. In Louisiana she had six children before her husband's death in 1882, after which she returned to St. Louis and began writing to help support herself and her family. Her fine novel, *The Awakening*, which has been called an American *Madame Bovary*, was published in 1899 and instantly became the object of attacks by reviewers. It was actually removed from the shelves of the Mercantile Library in St. Louis, and Chopin was denied membership in the Fine Arts Club because the book was, as a local magazine said, "too strong drink for moral babes and should be labeled 'poison.' " Like many another writer, Chopin is getting her due appreciation after her death. Her story reprinted here is the shortest one of this collection, but it is, if not "poison," strong medicine.

The Story of an Hour

Knowing that Mrs. Mallard was afflicted with a heart trouble, great care was taken to break to her as gently as possible the news of her husband's death.

It was her sister Josephine who told her, in broken sentences; veiled hints that revealed in half concealing. Her husband's friend Richards was there, too, near her. It was he who had been in the newspaper office when intelligence of the railroad disaster was received, with Brently Mallard's name leading the list of "killed." He had only taken the time to assure himself of its truth by a second telegram, and had hastened to forestall any less careful, less tender friend in bearing the sad message.

She did not hear the story as many women have heard the same, with a paralyzed inability to accept its significance. She wept at once, with sudden, wild abandonment, in her sister's arms. When the storm of grief had spent itself she went away to her room alone. She would have no one follow her.

There stood, facing the open window, a comfortable, roomy armchair. Into this she sank, pressed down by a physical exhaustion that haunted her body and seemed to reach into her soul.

She could see in the open square before her house the tops of trees that were all aquiver with the new spring life. The delicious breath of rain was in the air. In the street below a peddler was crying his wares. The notes of a distant song which some one was singing reached her faintly, and countless sparrows were twittering in the eaves.

There were patches of blue sky showing here and there through the clouds that had met and piled one above the other in the west facing her window.

She sat with her head thrown back upon the cushion of the chair, quite motionless, except when a sob came up into her throat and shook her, as a child who has cried itself to sleep continues to sob in its dreams.

She was young, with a fair, calm face, whose lines bespoke repression and even a certain strength. But now there was a dull stare in her eyes, whose gaze was fixed away off yonder on one of those patches of blue sky. It was not a glance of reflection, but rather indicated a suspension of intelligent thought.

There was something coming to her and she was waiting for it, fearfully. What was it? She did not know; it was too subtle and elusive to name. But she felt it, creeping out of the sky, reaching toward her through the sounds, the scents, the color that filled the air.

Now her bosom rose and fell tumultuously. She was beginning to recognize this thing that was approaching to possess her, and she was striving to beat it back with her will—as powerless as her two white slender hands would have been.

When she abandoned herself a little whispered word escaped her slightly parted lips. She said it over and over under her breath: "free, free, free!" The vacant stare and the look of terror that had followed it went from her eyes. They stayed keen and bright. Her pulses beat fast, and the coursing blood warmed and relaxed every inch of her body.

She did not stop to ask if it were or were not a monstrous joy that held her. A clear and exalted perception enabled her to dismiss the suggestion as trivial.

She knew that she would weep again when she saw the kind, tender hands folded in death; the face that had never looked save with love upon her, fixed and gray and dead. But she saw beyond that bitter moment a long procession of years to come that would belong to her absolutely. And she opened and spread her arms out to them in welcome.

There would be no one to live for during those coming years; she would live for herself. There would be no powerful will bending hers in that blind persistence with which men and women believe they have a right to impose a private will upon a fellow-creature. A kind intention or a cruel intention made the act seem no less a crime as she looked upon it in that brief moment of illumination.

And yet she had loved him—sometimes. Often she had not. What did it matter! What could love, the unsolved mystery, count for in face of this possession of self-assertion which she suddenly recognized as the strongest impulse of her being!

"Free! Body and soul free!" she kept whispering.

Josephine was kneeling before the closed door with her lips to the keyhole, imploring for admission. "Louise, open the door! I beg; open the door—you will make yourself ill. What are you doing, Louise? For heaven's sake open the door."

"Go away. I am not making myself ill." No; she was drinking in a very elixir of life through that open window.

Her fancy was running riot along those days ahead of her. Spring days, and summer days, and all sorts of days that would be her own. She breathed a quick prayer that life might be long. It was only yesterday she had thought with a shudder that life might be long.

She arose at length and opened the door to her sister's importunities. There was a feverish triumph in her eyes, and she carried herself unwittingly like a goddess of Victory. She clasped her sister's waist, and together they descended the stairs. Richards stood waiting for them at the bottom.

Some one was opening the front door with a latchkey. It was Brently Mallard who entered, a little travel-stained, composedly carrying his grip-sack and umbrella. He had been far from the scene of accident, and did not even know there had been one. He stood amazed at Josephine's piercing cry; at Richards' quick motion to screen him from the view of his wife.

But Richards was too late.

When the doctors came they said she had died of heart disease—of joy that kills.

ANTON CHEKHOV
1860–1904

Born in Taganrog, Russia, Chekhov was the son of a tradesman and grandson of a serf (peasant slave). After attending a local school, he went in 1879 to study medicine at the University of Moscow, where he supported himself by writing comic sketches for newspapers and magazines. After taking his medical degree in 1884, he began writing more seriously, publishing both stories and plays. When he married a young actress in 1901, he was already dying of tuberculosis. He moved to Yalta in the south and continued to write, finishing his dramatic masterpiece *The Cherry Orchard* in the year of his death. His hundreds of short stories made him, along with Maupassant, one of the two masters of the realistic short story in the nineteenth century.

Heartache

"To whom shall I tell my sorrow?"[1]

Evening twilight. Large flakes of wet snow are circling lazily about the street lamps which have just been lighted, settling in a thin soft layer on roofs, horses' backs, peoples' shoulders, caps. Iona Potapov, the cabby, is all white like a ghost. As hunched as a living body can be, he sits on the box without stirring. If a whole snowdrift were to fall on him, even then, perhaps he would not find it necessary to shake it off. His nag, too, is white and motionless. Her immobility, the angularity of her shape, and the sticklike straightness of her legs make her look like a penny gingerbread horse. She is probably lost in thought. Anyone who has been torn away from the plow, from the familiar gray scenes, and cast into this whirlpool full of monstrous lights, of ceaseless uproar and hurrying people, cannot help thinking.

Iona and his nag have not budged for a long time. They had driven out of the yard before dinnertime and haven't had a single fare yet. But now evening dusk is descending upon the city. The pale light of the street lamps changes to a vivid color and the bustle of the street grows louder.

"Sleigh to the Vyborg District!" Iona hears. "Sleigh!"

Iona starts, and through his snow-plastered eyelashes sees an officer in a military overcoat with a hood.

"To the Vyborg District!" repeats the officer. "Are you asleep, eh? To the Vyborg District!"

As a sign of assent Iona gives a tug at the reins, which sends layers of snow flying from the horse's back and from his own shoulders. The officer gets into the sleigh. The driver clucks to the horse, cranes his neck like a swan, rises in his seat and, more from habit than necessity, flourishes his whip. The nag, too, stretches her neck, crooks her sticklike legs and irresolutely sets off.

"Where are you barging in, damn you?" Iona is promptly assailed by shouts from the massive dark wavering to and fro before him. "Where the devil are you going? Keep to the right!"

"Don't you know how to drive? Keep to the right," says the officer with vexation.

A coachman driving a private carriage swears at him; a pedestrian who was crossing the street and brushed against the nag's nose with his shoulder, looks at him angrily and shakes the snow off his sleeve. Iona fidgets on the box as if sitting on needles and pins, thrusts out his

---

1. From an old Russian song comparable to a Negro Spiritual.

elbows and rolls his eyes like a madman, as though he did not know where he was or why he was there.

"What rascals they all are," the officer jokes. "They are doing their best to knock into you or be trampled by the horse. It's a conspiracy."

Iona looks at his fare and moves his lips. He wants to say something, but the only sound that comes out is a wheeze.

"What is it?" asks the officer.

Iona twists his mouth into a smile, strains his throat and croaks hoarsely: "My son, sir . . . er, my son died this week."

"H'm, what did he die of?"

Iona turns his whole body around to his fare and says, "Who can tell? It must have been a fever. He lay in the hospital only three days and then he died. . . . It is God's will."

"Get over, you devil!" comes out of the dark. "Have you gone blind, you old dog? Keep your eyes peeled!"

"Go on, go on," says the officer. "We shan't get there until tomorrow at this rate. Give her the whip!"

The driver cranes his neck again, rises in his seat, and with heavy grace swings his whip. Then he looks around at the officer several times, but the latter keeps his eyes closed and is apparently indisposed to listen. Letting his fare off in the Vyborg District, Iona stops by a teahouse and again sits motionless and hunched on the box. Again the wet snow paints him and his nag white. One hour passes, another . . .

Three young men, two tall and lanky, one short and hunchbacked, come along swearing at each other and loudly pound the pavement with their galoshes.

"Cabby, to the Police Bridge!" the hunchback shouts in a cracked voice. "The three of us . . . twenty kopecks!"

Iona tugs at the reins and clucks to his horse. Twenty kopecks is not fair, but his mind is not on that. Whether it is a ruble or five kopecks, it is all one to him now, so long as he has a fare. . . . The three young men, jostling each other and using foul language, go up to the sleigh and all three try to sit down at once. They start arguing about which two are to sit and who shall be the one to stand. After a long ill-tempered and abusive altercation, they decide that the hunchback must stand up because he is the shortest.

"Well, get going," says the hunchback in his cracked voice, taking up his station and breathing down Iona's neck. "On your way! What a cap you've got, brother! You won't find a worse one in all Petersburg—"

"Hee, hee . . . hee, hee . . ." Iona giggles, "as you say—"

"Well, then, 'as you say,' drive on. Are you going to crawl like this all the way, eh? D'you want to get it in the neck?"

"My head is splitting," says one of the tall ones. "At the Dukmasovs' yesterday, Vaska and I killed four bottles of cognac between us.''

"I don't get it, why lie?" says the other tall one angrily. "He is lying like a trouper."

"Strike me dead, it's the truth!"

"It is about as true as that a louse sneezes."

"Hee, hee," giggles Iona. "The gentlemen are feeling good!"

"Faugh, the devil take you!" cries the hunchback indignantly. "Will you get a move on, you old pest, or won't you? Is that the way to drive? Give her a crack of the whip! Giddap, devil! Giddap! Let her feel it!"

Iona feels the hunchback's wriggling body and quivering voice behind his back. He hears abuse addressed to him, sees people, and the feeling of loneliness begins little by little to lift from his heart. The hunchback swears till he chokes on an elaborate three-decker oath and is overcome by cough. The tall youths begin discussing a certain Nadezhda Petrovna. Iona looks round at them. When at last there is a lull in the conversation for which he has been waiting, he turns around and says: "This week . . . er . . . my son died."

"We shall all die," says the hunchback, with a sigh wiping his lips after his coughing fit. "Come, drive on, drive on. Gentlemen, I simply cannot stand this pace! When will he get us there?"

"Well, you give him a little encouragement. Biff him in the neck!"

"Do you hear, you old pest? I'll give it to you in the neck. If one stands on ceremony with fellows like you, one may as well walk. Do you hear, you old serpent? Or don't you give a damn what we say?"

And Iona hears rather than feels the thud of a blow on his neck.

"Hee, hee," he laughs. "The gentlemen are feeling good. God give you health!"

"Cabby, are you married?" asks one of the tall ones.

"Me? Hee, hee! The gentlemen are feeling good. The only wife for me now is the damp earth . . . Hee, haw, haw! The grave, that is! . . . Here my son is dead and me alive . . . It is a queer thing, death comes in at the wrong door . . . It don't come for me, it comes for my son. . . ."

And Iona turns round to tell them how his son died, but at that point the hunchback gives a sigh of relief and announces that, thank God, they have arrived at last. Having received his twenty kopecks, for a long while Iona stares after the revelers, who disappear into a dark entrance. Again he is alone and once more silence envelops him. The grief which has been allayed for a brief space comes back again and wrenches his heart more cruelly than ever. There is a look of anxiety and torment in Iona's eyes as they wander restlessly over the crowds moving to and fro on both sides of the street. Isn't there someone among those thousands who will listen to him? But the crowds hurry past, heedless of him and his grief. His grief is immense, boundless. If his heart were to burst and his grief to pour out, it seems that it would flood the whole world, and yet no one sees it. It has found a place for itself in such an insignificant shell that no one can see it in broad daylight.

Iona notices a doorkeeper with a bag and makes up his mind to speak to him.

"What time will it be, friend?" he asks.

"Past nine. What have you stopped here for? On your way!"

Iona drives a few steps away, hunches up and surrenders himself to his grief. He feels it is useless to turn to people. But before five minutes are over, he draws himself up, shakes his head as though stabbed by a sharp pain and tugs at the reins . . . He can bear it no longer.

"Back to the yard!" he thinks. "To the yard!"

And his nag, as though she knew his thoughts, starts out at a trot. An hour and a half later, Iona is sitting beside a large dirty stove. On the stove, on the floor, on benches are men snoring. The air is stuffy and foul. Iona looks at the sleeping figures, scratches himself and regrets that he has come home so early.

"I haven't earned enough to pay for the oats," he reflects. "That's what's wrong with me. A man that knows his job . . . who has enough to eat and has enough for his horse don't need to fret."

In one of the corners a young driver gets up, hawks sleepily and reaches for the water bucket.

"Thirsty?" Iona asks him.

"Guess so."

"H'm, may it do you good, but my son is dead, brother . . . did you hear? This week in the hospital. . . . What a business!"

Iona looks to see the effect of his words, but he notices none. The young man has drawn his cover over his head and is already asleep. The old man sighs and scratches himself. Just as the young man was thirsty for water so he thirsts for talk. It will soon be a week since his son died and he hasn't talked to anybody about him properly. He ought to be able to talk about it, taking his time, sensibly. He ought to tell how his son was taken ill, how he suffered, what he said before he died, how he died. . . . He ought to describe the funeral, and how he went to the hospital to fetch his son's clothes. His daughter Anisya is still in the country. . . . And he would like to talk about her, too. Yes, he has plenty to talk about now. And his listener should gasp and moan and keen. . . . It would be even better to talk to women. Though they are foolish, two words will make them blubber.

"I must go out and have a look at the horse," Iona thinks. "There will be time enough for sleep. You will have enough sleep, no fear. . . ."

He gets dressed and goes into the stable where his horse is standing. He thinks about oats, hay, the weather. When he is alone, he dares not think of his son. It is possible to talk about him with someone, but to think of him when one is alone, to evoke his image is unbearably painful.

"You chewing?" Iona asks his mare seeing her shining eyes. "There, chew away, chew away. . . . If we haven't earned enough for oats, we'll eat hay. . . . Yes. . . . I've grown too old to drive. My son had ought to be driving, not me. . . . He was a real cabby. . . . He had ought to have lived. . . ."

Iona is silent for a space and then goes on: "That's how it is, old girl. . . . Kuzma Ionych is gone. . . . Departed this life. . . . He went and died to no purpose. . . . Now let's say you had a little colt, and you were that little colt's own mother. And suddenly, let's say, that same little colt departed this life. . . . You'd be sorry, wouldn't you?"

The nag chews, listens and breathes on her master's hands. Iona is carried away and tells her everything.

STEPHEN LEACOCK

1869–1944

Humorist and humanist, professor and pundit, he was born in the village of Swanmore, Hampshire, England. His family emigrated in 1876 to a farm north of Toronto. Educated at McGill University, he pursued graduate studies in economics at the University of Chicago and studied under Thorstein Veblen, author of *The Theory of the Leisure Class*. After completing his Ph.D. in 1903, he returned to McGill to teach economics; he chaired the Department of Political Science and Economics from 1908 until his retirement in 1936. His most profitable work was the textbook *Elements of Political Science* (1906), which was translated into seventeen languages. The author of nineteen books and countless articles on economics, history, and political science, he turned to the writing of humor as his beloved avocation. His first collection of humorous stories, *Literary Lapses*, appeared in 1910, and from that time until his death he published a volume of humor almost every year. The two finest are the complementary volumes *Sunshine Sketches of a Little Town* (1912), with its now classic account of "The Marine Excursion of the Knights of Pythias," and the urban satire *Arcadian Adventures with the Idle Rich* (1914). He also wrote popular biographies of his two favorite writers, *Mark Twain* (1932) and *Charles Dickens* (1933).

The Marine Excursion of the Knights of Pythias

Half-past six on a July morning! The *Mariposa Belle* is at the wharf, decked in flags, with steam up ready to start.

Excursion day!

Half-past six on a July morning, and Lake Wissanotti lying in the sun as calm as glass. The opal colours of the morning light are shot from the surface of the water.

Out on the lake the last thin threads of the mist are clearing away like flecks of cotton wool.

The long call of the loon echoes over the lake. The air is cool and fresh. There is in it all the new life of the land of the silent pine and the moving waters. Lake Wissanotti in the morning sunlight! Don't talk to me of the Italian lakes, or the Tyrol or the Swiss Alps. Take them away. Move them somewhere else. I don't want them.

Excursion Day, at half-past six of a summer morning! With the boat all decked in flags and all the people in Mariposa on the wharf, and the band in peaked caps with big cornets tied to their bodies ready to play at any minute! I say! Don't tell me about the Carnival of Venice and the Delhi Durbar. Don't! I wouldn't look at them. I'd shut my eyes! For light and colour give me every time an excursion out of Mariposa down the lake to the Indian's Island out of sight in the morning mist. Talk of your Papal Zouaves and your Buckingham Palace Guard! I want to see the Mariposa band in uniform and the Mariposa Knights of Pythias with their aprons and their insignia and their picnic baskets and their five-cent cigars!

Half-past six in the morning, and all the crowd on the wharf and the boat due to leave in half an hour. Notice it!—in half an hour. Already she's whistled twice (at six, and at six fifteen), and at any minute now, Christie Johnson will step into the pilot house and pull the string for the warning whistle that the boat will leave in half an hour. So keep ready. Don't think of running back to Smith's Hotel for the sandwiches. Don't be fool enough to try to go up to the Greek Store, next to Netley's, and buy fruit. You'll be left behind for sure if you do. Never mind the sandwiches and the fruit! Anyway, here comes Mr. Smith himself with a huge basket of provender that would feed a factory. There must be sandwiches in that. I think I can hear them clinking. And behind Mr. Smith is the German waiter from the caff with another basket—indubitably lager beer; and behind him, the bartender of the hotel, carrying nothing, as far as one can see. But of course if you know Mariposa you will understand that why he looks so nonchalant and empty-handed is because he has two bottles of rye whisky under his linen duster. You know, I think, the peculiar walk of a man with two bottles of whisky in the inside pockets of a linen coat. In Mariposa, you see, to bring beer to an excursion is quite in keeping with public opinion. But, whisky—well, one has to be a little careful.

Do I say that Mr. Smith is here? Why, everybody's here. There's Hussell the editor of the *Newspacket*, wearing a blue ribbon on his coat, for the Mariposa Knights of Pythias are, by their constitution, dedicated to temperance; and there's Henry Mullins, the manager of the Exchange Bank, also a Knight of Pythias, with a small flask of Pogram's Special in his hip pocket as a sort of amendment to the constitution. And there's Dean Drone, the Chaplain of the Order, with a fishing-rod (you never saw such green bass as lie among the rocks at Indian's Island), and with a trolling line in case of maskinonge, and a landing-net in case of pickerel, and with his eldest daughter, Lilian Drone, in case of young men. There never was such a fisherman as the Rev. Rupert Drone.

*   *   *

Perhaps I ought to explain that when I speak of the excursion as being of the Knights of Pythias, the thing must not be understood in any narrow sense. In Mariposa practically everybody belongs to the Knights of Pythias just as they do to everything else. That's the great thing about the town and that's what makes it so different from the city. Everybody is in everything.

You should see them on the seventeenth of March, for example, when everybody wears a green ribbon and they're all laughing and glad—you know what the Celtic nature is—and talking about Home Rule.

On St. Andrew's Day every man in town wears a thistle and shakes hands with everybody else, and you see the fine old Scotch honesty beaming out of their eyes.

And on St. George's Day!—well, there's no heartiness like the good old English spirit, after all; why shouldn't a man feel glad that he's an Englishman?

Then on the Fourth of July there are stars and stripes flying over half the stores in town, and suddenly all the men are seen to smoke cigars, and to know all about Roosevelt and Bryan and the Philippine Islands. Then you learn for the first time that Jeff Thorpe's people came from Massachusetts and that his uncle fought at Bunker Hill (anyway Jefferson will swear it was in Dakota all right enough); and you find that George Duff has a married sister in Rochester and that her husband is all right; in fact, George was down there as recently as eight years ago. Oh, it's the most American town imaginable is Mariposa—on the fourth of July.

But wait, just wait, if you feel anxious about the solidity of the British connexion, till the twelfth of the month, when everybody is wearing an orange streamer in his coat and the Orangemen (every man in town) walk in the big procession. Allegiance! Well, perhaps you remember the address they gave to the Prince of Wales on the platform of the Mariposa station as he went through on his tour to the west. I think that pretty well settled that question.

So you will easily understand that of course everybody belongs to the Knights of Pythias and the Masons and Oddfellows, just as they all belong to the Snow Shoe Club and the Girls' Friendly Society.

And meanwhile the whistle of the steamer has blown again for a quarter to seven—loud and long this time, for anyone not here now is late for certain, unless he should happen to come down in the last fifteen minutes.

What a crowd upon the wharf and how they pile onto the steamer! It's a wonder that the boat can hold them all. But that's just the marvellous thing about the *Mariposa Belle.*

I don't know—I have never known—where the steamers like the *Mariposa Belle* come from. Whether they are built by Harland and Wolff of Belfast, or whether, on the other hand, they are not built by Harland and Wolff of Belfast, is more than one would like to say offhand.

The *Mariposa Belle* always seems to me to have some of those strange properties that distinguish Mariposa itself. I mean, her size seems to vary so. If you see her there in the winter, frozen in the ice beside the wharf with a snowdrift against the windows of the pilot house, she looks a pathetic little thing the size of a butternut. But in the summer time, especially after you've *been* in Mariposa for a month or two, and have paddled alongside of her in a canoe, she gets larger and taller, and with a great sweep of black sides, till you see no difference between the *Mariposa Belle* and the *Lusitania.* Each one is a big steamer and that's all you can say.

Nor do her measurements help you much. She draws about eighteen inches forward, and more than that—at least half an inch more, astern, and when she's loaded down with an excursion crowd she draws a good two inches more. And above the water—why, look at all the decks on her! There's the deck you walk onto, from the wharf, all shut in, with windows along it, and the after cabin with the long table, and above that the deck with all the chairs piled upon it, and the deck in front where the band stand round in a circle, and the pilot house is higher than that, and above the pilot house is the board with the gold name and the flag pole and the steel ropes and the flags; and fixed in somewhere on the different levels is the lunch counter where they sell the sandwiches, and the engine room, and down below the deck level, beneath the water line, is the place where the crew sleep. What with steps and stairs and passages and piles of cordwood for the engine—oh, no, I guess Harland and Wolff didn't build her. They couldn't have.

Yet even with a huge boat like the *Mariposa Belle,* it would be impossible for her to carry all of the crowd that you see in the boat and on the wharf. In reality, the crowd is made up of two classes— all of the people in Mariposa who are going on the excursion and all those who are not. Some come for the one reason and some for the other.

The two tellers of the Exchange Bank are both there standing side by side. But one of them—the one with the cameo pin and the long face like a horse—is going, and the other—with the other cameo pin and the face like another horse—is not. In the same way, Hussell of the *Newspacket* is going, but his brother, beside him, isn't. Lilian Drone is going, but her sister can't; and so on all through the crowd.

*   *   *

And to think that things should look like that on the morning of a steamboat accident.

How strange life is!

To think of all these people so eager and anxious to catch the steamer, and some of them running to catch it, and so fearful that they might miss it—the morning of a steamboat accident. And the captain blowing his whistle, and warning them so severely that he would leave them behind—leave them out of the accident! And everybody crowding so eagerly to be in the accident.

Perhaps life is like that all through.

Strangest of all to think, in a case like this, of the people who were left behind, or in some way or other prevented from going, and always afterwards told of how they had escaped being on board the *Mariposa Belle* that day!

Some of the instances were certainly extraordinary.

Nivens, the lawyer, escaped from being there merely by the fact that he was away in the city.

Towers, the tailor, only escaped owing to the fact that, not intending to go on the excursion he had stayed in bed till eight o'clock and so had not gone. He narrated afterwards that waking up that morning at half-past five, he had thought of the excursion and for some unaccountable reason had felt glad that he was not going.

*   *   *

The case of Yodel, the auctioneer, was even more inscrutable. He had been to the Oddfellows' excursion on the train the week before and to the Conservative picnic the week before that, and had decided not to go on this trip. In fact, he had not the least intention of going. He narrated afterwards how the night before someone had stopped him on the corner of Nippewa and Tecumseh Streets (he indicated the very spot) and asked: "Are you going to take in the excursion tomorrow?" and he had said, just as simply as he was talking when narrating it: "No." And ten minutes after that, at the corner of Dalhousie and Brock Streets (he offered to lead a party of verification to the precise place) somebody else had stopped him and asked: "Well, are you going on the steamer trip tomorrow?" Again he had answered: "No," apparently almost in the same tone as before.

He said afterwards that when he heard the rumour of the accident it seemed like the finger of Providence, and he fell on his knees in thankfulness.

There was the similar case of Morison (I mean the one in Glover's hardware store that married one of the Thompsons). He said afterwards that he had read so much in the papers about accidents lately—mining accidents, and aeroplanes and gasoline—that he had grown nervous. The night before his wife had asked him at supper: "Are you going on the excursion?" He had answered: "No, I don't think I feel like it," and had added: "Perhaps your mother might like to go." And the next evening just at dusk, when the news ran through the town, he said the first thought that flashed through his head was: "Mrs. Thompson's on that boat."

He told this right as I say it—without the least doubt or confusion. He never for a moment imagined she was on the *Lusitania* or the *Olympic* or any other boat. He knew she was on this one. He said you could have knocked him down where he stood. But no one had. Not even when he got halfway down—on his knees, and it would have been easier still to knock him down or kick him. People do miss a lot of chances.

Still, as I say, neither Yodel nor Morison nor anyone thought about there being an accident until just after sundown when they—

Well, have you ever heard the long booming whistle of a steamboat two miles out on the lake in the dusk, and while you listen and count and wonder, seen the crimson rockets going up against the sky and then heard the fire bell ringing right there beside you in the town, and seen the people running to the town wharf?

That's what the people of Mariposa saw and felt that summer evening as they watched the Mackinaw lifeboat go plunging out into the lake with seven sweeps to a side and the foam clear to the gunwale with the lifting stroke of fourteen men!

But, dear me, I am afraid that this is no way to tell a story. I suppose the true art would have been to have said nothing about the accident till it happened. But when you write about Mariposa, or hear of it, if you know the place, it's all so vivid and real, that a thing like the contrast between the excursion crowd in the morning and the scene at night leaps into your mind and you must think of it.

*   *   *

But never mind about the accident—let us turn back again to the morning.

The boat was due to leave at seven. There was no doubt about the hour—not only seven, but seven sharp. The notice in the *Newspacket* said: "The boat will leave sharp at seven"; and the advertising posters on the telegraph poles on Missinaba Street that began, "Ho, for Indian's Island!" ended up with the words: "Boat leaves at seven sharp." There was a big notice on the wharf that said: "Boat leaves sharp on time."

So at seven, right on the hour, the whistle blew loud and long, and then at seven-fifteen three short peremptory blasts, and at seven-thirty one quick angry call—just one—and very soon after that they cast off the last of the ropes and the *Mariposa Belle* sailed off in her cloud of flags, and the band of the Knights of Pythias, timing it to a nicety, broke into the "Maple Leaf for Ever!"

I suppose that all excursions when they start are much the same. Anyway, on the *Mariposa Belle* everybody went running up and down all over the boat with deck chairs and camp stools and baskets, and found places, splendid places to sit, and then got scared that there might be better ones and chased off again. People hunted for places out of the sun and when they got them swore that they weren't going to freeze to please anybody; and the people in the sun said that they hadn't paid fifty cents to get roasted. Others said that they hadn't paid fifty cents to get covered with cinders, and there were still others who hadn't paid fifty cents to get shaken to death with the propeller.

Still, it was all right presently. The people seemed to get sorted out into the places on the boat where they belonged. The women, the older ones, all gravitated into the cabin on the lower deck and by getting round the table with needlework, and with all the windows shut, they soon had it, as they said themselves, just like being at home.

All the young boys and the toughs and the men in the band got down on the lower deck forward, where the boat was dirtiest and where the anchor was and the coils of rope.

And upstairs on the after deck there were Lilian Drone and Miss Lawson, the high-school teacher, with a book of German poetry— Gothey I think it was—and the bank teller and the young men.

In the centre, standing beside the rail, were Dean Drone and Dr. Gallagher, looking through binocular glasses at the shore.

Up in front on the little deck forward of the pilot house was a group of the older men, Mullins and Duff and Mr. Smith in a deck chair, and beside him Mr. Golgotha Gingham, the undertaker of Mariposa, on a stool. It was part of Mr. Gingham's principles to take in an outing of this sort, a business matter, more or less—for you never know what may happen at these water parties. At any rate, he was there in a neat suit of black, not, of course, his heavier or professional suit, but a soft clinging effect as of burnt paper that combined gaiety and decorum to a nicety.

*   *   *

"Yes," said Mr. Gingham, waving his black glove in a general way towards the shore, "I know the lake well, very well. I've been pretty much all over it in my time."

"Canoeing?" asked somebody.

"No," said Mr. Gingham, "not in a canoe." There seemed a peculiar and quiet meaning in his tone.

"Sailing, I suppose," said somebody else.

"No," said Mr. Gingham. "I don't understand it."

"I never knowed that you went onto the water at all, Gol," said Mr. Smith, breaking in.

"Ah, not now," explained Mr. Gingham; "it was years ago, the first summer I came to Mariposa. I was on the water practically all day. Nothing like it to give a man an appetite and keep him in shape."

"Was you camping?" asked Mr. Smith.

"We camped at night," assented the undertaker, "but we put in practically the whole day on the water. You see, we were after a party that had come up here from the city on his vacation and gone out in a sailing canoe. We were dragging. We were up every morning at sunrise, lit a fire on the beach and cooked breakfast, and then we'd light our pipes and be off with the net for a whole day. It's a great life," concluded Mr. Gingham wistfully.

"Did you get him?" asked two or three together.

There was a pause before Mr. Gingham answered.

"We did," he said "—down in the reeds past Horseshoe Point. But it was no use. He turned blue on me right away."

After which Mr. Gingham fell into such a deep reverie that the boat had steamed another half-mile down the lake before anybody broke the silence again. Talk of this sort—and after all what more suitable for a day on the water?—beguiled the way.

*   *   *

Down the lake, mile by mile over the calm water, steamed the *Mariposa Belle.* They passed Poplar Point where the high sand-banks are with all the swallows' nests in them, and Dean Drone and Dr. Gallagher looked at them alternately through the binocular glasses, and it was wonderful how plainly one could see the swallows and the banks and the shrubs—just as plainly as with the naked eye.

And a little farther down they passed the Shingle Beach, and Dr. Gallagher, who knew Canadian history, said to Dean Drone that it was strange to think that Champlain had landed there with his French explorers three hundred years ago; and Dean Drone, who didn't know Canadian history, said it was stranger still to think that the hand of the Almighty had piled up the hills and rocks long before that; and Dr. Gallagher said it was wonderful how the French had found their way through such a pathless wilderness; and Dean Drone said that it was wonderful also to think that the Almighty had placed even the smallest shrub in its appointed place. Dr. Gallagher said it filled him with admiration. Dean Drone said it filled him with awe. Dr. Gallagher said he'd been full of it ever since he was a boy and Dean Drone said so had he.

Then a little further, as the *Mariposa Belle* steamed on down the lake, they passed the Old Indian Portage where the great grey rocks are; and Dr. Gallagher drew Dean Drone's attention to the place where the narrow canoe track wound up from the shore to the woods, and Dean Drone said he could see it perfectly well without the glasses.

Dr. Gallagher said that it was just here that a party of five hundred French had made their way with all their baggage and accoutrements across the rocks of the divide and down to the Great Bay. And Dean Drone said that it reminded him of Xenophon leading his ten thousand Greeks over the hill passes of Armenia down to the sea. Dr. Gallagher said that he had often wished he could have seen and spoken to Champlain, and Dean Drone said how much he regretted to have never known Xenophon.

And then after that they fell to talking of relics and traces of the past, and Dr. Gallagher said that if Dean Drone would come round to his house some night he would show him some Indian arrow heads that he had dug up in his garden. And Dean Drone said that if Dr. Gallagher would come round to the rectory any afternoon he would show him a map of Xerxes' invasion of Greece. Only he must come some time between the Infant Class and the Mothers' Auxiliary.

So presently they both knew that they were blocked out of one another's houses for some time to come, and Dr. Gallagher walked forward and told Mr. Smith, who had never studied Greek, about Champlain crossing the rock divide.

Mr. Smith turned his head and looked at the divide for half a second and then said he had crossed a worse one up north back of the Wahnipitae and that the flies were Hades—and then went on playing freezeout poker with the two juniors in Duff's bank.

So Dr. Gallagher realized that that's always the way when you try to tell people things, and that as far as gratitude and appreciation goes one might as well never read books or travel anywhere or do anything.

In fact, it was at this very moment that he made up his mind to give the arrows to the Mariposa Mechanics' Institute—they afterwards became, as you know, the Gallagher Collection. But, for the time being, the doctor was sick of them and wandered off round the boat and watched Henry Mullins showing George Duff how to make a John Collins without lemons, and finally went and sat down among the Mariposa band and wished that he hadn't come.

So the boat steamed on and the sun rose higher and higher, and the freshness of the morning changed into the full glare of noon, and pretty soon the *Mariposa Belle* had floated out onto the lake again and they went on to where the lake began to narrow in at its foot, just where the Indian's Island is—all grass and trees and with a log wharf running into the water. Below it the Lower Ossawippi runs out of the lake, and quite near are the rapids, and you can see down among the trees the red brick of the power house and hear the roar of the leaping water.

The Indian's Island itself is all covered with trees and tangled vines, and the water about it is so still that it's all reflected double and looks the same either way up. Then when the steamer's whistle blows as it comes into the wharf, you hear it echo among the trees of the island, and reverberate back from the shores of the lake.

The scene is all so quiet and still and unbroken, that Miss Cleghorn—the sallow girl in the telephone exchange, that I spoke of said she'd like to be buried there. But all the people were so busy getting their baskets and gathering up their things that no one had time to attend to it.

I mustn't even try to describe the landing and the boat crunching against the wooden wharf and all the people running to the same side of the deck and Christie Johnson calling out to the crowd to keep to the starboard and nobody being able to find it. Everyone who has been on a Mariposa excursion knows all about that.

Nor can I describe the day itself and the picnic under the trees. There were speeches afterwards, and Judge Pepperleigh gave such offence by bringing in Conservative politics that a man called Patriotus Canadiensis wrote and asked for some of the invaluable space of the *Mariposa Times-Herald* and exposed it.

I should say that there were races too, on the grass on the open side of the island, graded mostly according to ages—races for boys under thirteen and girls over nineteen and all that sort of thing. Sports are generally conducted on that plan in Mariposa. It is realized that a woman of sixty has an unfair advantage over a mere child.

Dean Drone managed the races and decided the ages and gave out the prizes; the Wesleyan minister helped, and he and the young student, who was relieving in the Presbyterian Church, held the string at the winning point.

They had to get mostly clergymen for the races because all the men had wandered off, somehow, to where they were drinking lager beer out of two kegs stuck on pine logs among the trees.

But if you've ever been on a Mariposa excursion you know all about these details anyway.

So the day wore on and presently the sun came through the trees on a slant and the steamer whistle blew with a great puff of white steam and all the people came straggling down to the wharf and pretty soon the *Mariposa Belle* had floated out onto the lake again and headed for the town, twenty miles away.

*   *   *

I suppose you have often noticed the contrast there is between an excursion on its way out in the morning and what it looks like on the way home.

In the morning everybody is so restless and animated and moves to and from all over the boat and asks questions. But coming home, as the afternoon gets later and later and the sun sinks beyond the hills, all the people seem to get so still and quiet and drowsy.

So it was with the people on the *Mariposa Belle*. They sat there on the benches and the deck chairs in little clusters, and listened to the regular beat of the propeller and almost dozed off asleep as they sat. Then when the sun set and the dusk drew on, it grew almost dark on the deck and so still that you could hardly tell there was anyone on board.

And if you had looked at the steamer from the shore or from one of the islands, you'd have seen the row of lights from the cabin windows shining on the water and the red glare of the burning hemlock from the funnel, and you'd have heard the soft thud of the propeller miles away over the lake.

Now and then, too, you could have heard them singing on the steamer—the voices of the girls and the men blended into unison by the distance, rising and falling in long-drawn melody: "O—Can-a-da—O—Can-a-da."

You may talk as you will about the intoning choirs of your European cathedrals, but the sound of "O Can-a-da", borne across the waters of a silent lake at evening is good enough for those of us who know Mariposa.

I think that it was just as they were singing like this: "O—Can-a-da", that word went round that the boat was sinking.

If you have ever been in any sudden emergency on the water, you will understand the strange psychology of it—the way in which what is happening seems to become known all in a moment without a word being said. The news is transmitted from one to the other by some mysterious process.

At any rate, on the *Mariposa Belle* first one and then the other heard that the steamer was sinking. As far as I could ever learn the first of it was that George Duff, the bank manager, came very quietly to Dr. Gallagher and asked him if he thought that the boat was sinking. The doctor said no, that he had thought so earlier in the day but that he didn't now think that she was.

After that Duff, according to his own account, had said to Macartney, the lawyer, that the boat was sinking, and Macartney said that he doubted it very much.

Then somebody came to Judge Pepperleigh and woke him up and said that there was six inches of water in the steamer and that she was sinking. And Pepperleigh said it was perfect scandal and passed the news on to his wife and she said that they had no business to allow it and that if the steamer sank that was the last excursion she'd go on.

So the news went all round the boat and everywhere the people gathered in groups and talked about it in the angry and excited way that people have when a steamer is sinking on one of the lakes like Lake Wissanotti.

Dean Drone, of course, and some others were quieter about it, and said that one must make allowances and that naturally there were two sides to everything. But most of them wouldn't listen to reason at all. I think, perhaps, that some of them were frightened. You see the last time but one that the steamer had sunk, there had been a man drowned and it made them nervous.

What? Hadn't I explained about the depth of Lake Wissanotti? I had taken it for granted that you knew; and in any case parts of it are deep enough, though I don't suppose in this stretch of it from the big reed beds up to within a mile of the town wharf, you could find six feet of water in it if you tried. Oh, pshaw! I was not talking about a steamer sinking in the ocean and carrying down its screaming crowds of people into the hideous depths of green water. Oh, dear me, no! That kind of thing never happens on Lake Wissanotti.

But what does happen is that the *Mariposa Belle* sinks every now and then, and sticks there on the bottom till they get things straightened up.

On the lakes round Mariposa, if a person arrives late anywhere and explains that the steamer sank, everybody understands the situation.

You see when Harland and Wolff built the *Mariposa Belle*, they left some cracks in between the timbers that you fill up with cotton waste every Sunday. If this is not attended to, the boat sinks. In fact, it is part of the law of the province that all the steamers like the *Mariposa Belle* must be properly corked—I think that is the word— every season. There are inspectors who visit all the hotels in the province to see that it is done.

So you can imagine now that I've explained it a little straighter, the indignation of the people when they knew that the boat had come uncorked and that they might be stuck out there on a shoal or a mud-bank half the night.

I don't say either that there wasn't any danger; anyway, it doesn't feel very safe when you realize that the boat is settling down with every hundred yards that she goes, and you look over the side and see only the black water in the gathering night.

Safe! I'm not sure now that I come to think of it that it isn't worse than sinking in the Atlantic. After all, in the Atlantic there is wireless telegraphy, and a lot of trained sailors and stewards. But out on Lake Wissanotti—far out, so that you can only just see the lights of the town away off to the south—when the propeller comes to a stop— and you can hear the hiss of steam as they start to rake out the engine fires to prevent an explosion—and when you turn from the red glare that comes from the furnace doors as they open them, to the black dark that is gathering over the lake—and there's a night wind beginning to run among the rushes—and you see the men going forward to the roof of the pilot house to send up the rockets to rouse the town—safe? Safe yourself, if you like; as for me, let me once get back into Mariposa again, under the night shadow of the maple trees, and this shall be the last, last time I'll go on Lake Wissanotti.

Safe! Oh, yes! Isn't it strange how safe other people's adventures seem after they happen? But you'd have been scared, too, if you'd been there just before the steamer sank, and seen them bringing up all the women on to the top deck.

I don't see how some of the people took it so calmly; how Mr. Smith, for instance, could have gone on smoking and telling how he'd had a steamer "sink on him" on Lake Nipissing and a still bigger one, a side-wheeler, sink on him in Lake Abbitibbi.

Then, quite suddenly, with a quiver, down she went. You could feel the boat sink, sink—down, down—would it never get to the bottom? The water came flush up to the lower deck, and then— thank heaven—the sinking stopped and there was the *Mariposa Belle* safe and tight on a reed bank.

Really, it made one positively laugh! It seemed so queer and, any- way, if a man has a sort of natural courage, danger makes him laugh. Danger? pshaw! fiddlesticks! everybody scouted the idea. Why, it is just the little things like this that give zest to a day on the water.

Within half a minute they were all running round looking for sandwiches and cracking jokes and talking of making coffee over the remains of the engine fires.

*   *   *

I don't need to tell at length how it all happened after that.

I suppose the people on the *Mariposa Belle* would have had to settle down there all night or till help came from the town, but some of the men who had gone forward and were peering out into the dark said that it couldn't be more than a mile across the water to Miller's Point. You could almost see it over there to the left—some of them, I think, said "off on the port bow," because you know when you get mixed up in these marine disasters, you soon catch the atmosphere of the thing.

So pretty soon they had the davits swung out over the side and were lowering the old lifeboat from the top deck into the water.

There were men leaning out over the rail of the *Mariposa Belle* with lanterns that threw the light as they let her down, and the glare fell on the water and the reeds. But when they got the boat lowered, it looked such a frail, clumsy thing as one saw it from the rail above, that the cry was raised: "Women and children first!" For what was the sense, if it should turn out that the boat wouldn't even hold women and children, of trying to jam a lot of heavy men into it?

So they put in mostly women and children and the boat pushed out into the darkness so freighted down it would hardly float.

In the bow of it was the Presbyterian student who was relieving the minister, and he called out that they were in the hands of Providence. But he was crouched and ready to spring out of them at the first moment.

So the boat went and was lost in the darkness except for the lantern in the bow that you could see bobbing on the water. Then presently it came back and they sent another load, till pretty soon the decks began to thin out and everybody got impatient to be gone.

It was about the time that the third boat-load put off that Mr. Smith took a bet with Mullins for twenty-five dollars, that he'd be home in Mariposa before the people in the boats had walked round the shore.

No one knew just what he meant, but pretty soon they saw Mr. Smith disappear down below into the lowest part of the steamer with a mallet in one hand and a big bundle of marline in the other.

They might have wondered more about it, but it was just at this time that they heard the shouts from the rescue boat—the big Mackinaw lifeboat—that had put out from the town with fourteen men at the sweeps when they saw the first rockets go up.

I suppose there is always something inspiring about a rescue at sea, or on the water.

After all, the bravery of the lifeboat man is the true bravery—expended to save life, not to destroy it.

Certainly they told for months after of how the rescue boat came out to the *Mariposa Belle.*

I suppose that when they put her in the water the lifeboat touched it for the first time since the old Macdonald Government placed her on Lake Wissanotti.

Anyway, the water poured in at every seam. But not for a moment—even with two miles of water between them and the steamer—did the rowers pause for that.

By the time they were halfway there the water was almost up to the thwarts, but they drove her on. Panting and exhausted (for mind you, if you haven't been in a fool boat like that for years, rowing takes it out of you), the rowers stuck to their task. They threw the ballast over and chucked into the water the heavy cork jackets and lifebelts that encumbered their movements. There was no thought of turning back. They were nearer to the steamer than the shore.

"Hang to it, boys," called the crowd from the steamer's deck, and hang they did.

They were almost exhausted when they got them; men leaning from the steamer threw them ropes and one by one every man was hauled aboard just as the lifeboat sank under their feet.

Saved! by heaven, saved by one of the smartest pieces of rescue work ever seen on the lake.

There's no use describing it; you need to see rescue work of this kind by lifeboats to understand it.

Nor were the lifeboat crew the only ones that distinguished themselves.

Boat after boat and canoe after canoe had put out from Mariposa to the help of the steamer. They got them all.

Pupkin, the other bank teller with a face like a horse, who hadn't gone on the excursion—as soon as he knew that the boat was signalling for help and that Miss Lawson was sending up rockets—rushed for a row boat, grabbed an oar (two would have hampered him)—and paddled madly out into the lake. He struck right out into the dark with the crazy skiff almost sinking beneath his feet. But they got him. They rescued him. They watched him, almost dead with exhaustion, make his way to the steamer, where he was hauled up with ropes. Saved! Saved!

*   *   *

They might have gone on that way half the night, picking up the rescuers, only, at the very moment when the tenth load of people left for the shore—just as suddenly and saucily as you please, up came the *Mariposa Belle* from the mud bottom and floated.

Floated?

Why, of course she did. If you take a hundred and fifty people off a steamer that has sunk, and if you get a man as shrewd as Mr. Smith to plug the timber seams with mallet and marline, and if you turn ten bandsmen of the Mariposa band onto your hand pump on the bow of the lower decks—float? why, what else can she do?

Then, if you stuff in hemlock into the embers of the fire that you were raking out, till it hums and crackles under the boiler, it won't be long before you hear the propeller thud—thudding at the stern again, and before the long roar of the steam whistle echoes over to the town.

And so the *Mariposa Belle*, with all steam up again and with the long train of sparks careering from the funnel, is heading for the town.

But no Christie Johnson at the wheel in the pilot house this time. "Smith! Get Smith!" is the cry.

Can he take her in? Well, now! Ask a man who has had steamers sink on him in half the lakes from Temiscaming to the Bay, if he can take her in? Ask a man who has run a York boat down the rapids of the Moose when the ice is moving, if he can grip the steering wheel of the *Mariposa Belle?* So there she steams safe and sound to the town wharf!

Look at the lights and the crowds! If only the federal census taker could count us now! Hear them calling and shouting back and forward from the deck to the shore! Listen! There is the rattle of the shore ropes as they get them ready, and there's the Mariposa band—actually forming in a circle on the upper deck just as she docks, and the leader with his baton—one—two—ready now—

"O Can-a-da!"

STEPHEN CRANE

1871–1900

Born in Newark, New Jersey, Crane was the fourteenth child of a Methodist minister, who named him after an ancestor who had signed the Declaration of Independence. He was a delicate child, whose health improved
when his family moved to Port Jervis, New York, in 1879. After his father
died he went to the Hudson River Institute at Caverack, New York, and
then to Lafayette College and Syracuse University, shifting his interests
from engineering to literature. He was an excellent baseball player—once
considering a professional career—and a good boxer as well. While in
school he began work as a journalist, a profession which he pursued for
most of his life. But his reporting always suffered from an excess of art. A
poetic image would distract him from journalistic details. He wrote an
ironic novel *(Maggie: A Girl of the Streets)* when he was twenty-two, and a
masterful novel of the Civil War *(The Red Badge of Courage)* two years
later. He had not been to war but had heard the accounts of soldiers and
he had read Tolstoy. Later, he became a war correspondent and confirmed
his guesses first hand. Like many of America's best writers, he was cynical
and sentimental at the same time. His blunt manner and indifference to
public opinion offended many of his contemporaries, but Henry James and
Joseph Conrad admired his work and came to pay their respects to the
younger man as he was dying in England of tuberculosis.

The Bride Comes to Yellow Sky

I

The great Pullman was whirling onward with such dignity of motion that a glance from the window seemed simply to prove that the
plains of Texas were pouring eastward. Vast flats of green grass,
dull-hued spaces of mesquit and cactus, little groups of frame
houses, woods of light and tender trees, all were sweeping into the
east, sweeping over the horizon, a precipice.

A newly married pair had boarded this coach at San Antonio. The
man's face was reddened from many days in the wind and sun, and
a direct result of his new black clothes was that his brick-coloured
hands were constantly performing in a most conscious fashion.
From time to time he looked down respectfully at his attire. He sat
with a hand on each knee, like a man waiting in a barber's shop.
The glances he devoted to other passengers were furtive and shy.

The bride was not pretty, nor was she very young. She wore a
dress of blue cashmere, with small reservations of velvet here and
there, and with steel buttons abounding. She continually twisted

her head to regard her puff sleeves, very stiff, straight, and high. They embarrassed her. It was quite apparent that she had cooked, and that she expected to cook, dutifully. The blushes caused by the careless scrutiny of some passengers as she had entered the car were strange to see upon this plain, under-class countenance, which was drawn in placid, almost emotionless lines.

They were evidently very happy. "Ever been in a parlour-car before?" he asked, smiling with delight.

"No," she answered; "I never was. It's fine, ain't it?"

"Great! And then after a while we'll go forward to the diner, and get a big lay-out. Finest meal in the world. Charge a dollar."

"Oh, do they?" cried the bride. "Charge a dollar? Why, that's too much—for us—ain't it, Jack?"

"Not this trip, anyhow," he answered bravely. "We're going to go the whole thing."

Later he explained to her about the trains. "You see, it's a thousand miles from one end of Texas to the other; and this train runs right across it, and never stops but four times." He had the pride of an owner. He pointed out to her the dazzling fittings of the coach; and in truth her eyes opened wider as she contemplated the sea-green figured velvet, the shining brass, silver, and glass, the wood that gleamed as darkly brilliant as the surface of a pool of oil. At one end a bronze figure sturdily held a support for a separated chamber, and at convenient places on the ceiling were frescos in olive and silver.

To the minds of the pair, their surroundings reflected the glory of their marriage that morning in San Antonio; this was the environment of their new estate; and the man's face in particular beamed with an elation that made him appear ridiculous to the negro porter. This individual at times surveyed them from afar with an amused and superior grin. On other occasions he bullied them with skill in ways that did not make it exactly plain to them that they were being bullied. He subtly used all the manners of the most unconquerable kind of snobbery. He oppressed them; but of this oppression they had small knowledge, and they speedily forgot that infrequently a number of travellers covered them with stares of derisive enjoyment. Historically there was supposed to be something infinitely humorous in their situation.

"We are due in Yellow Sky at 3:42," he said, looking tenderly into her eyes.

"Oh, are we?" she said, as if she had not been aware of it. To evince surprise at her husband's statement was part of her wifely amiability. She took from a pocket a little silver watch; and as she held it before her, and stared at it with a frown of attention, the new husband's face shone.

"I bought it in San Anton' from a friend of mine," he told her gleefully.

"It's seventeen minutes past twelve," she said, looking up at him with a kind of shy and clumsy coquetry. A passenger, noting this play, grew excessively sardonic, and winked at himself in one of the numerous mirrors.

At last they went to the dining-car. Two rows of negro waiters, in glowing white suits, surveyed their entrance with the interest, and also the equanimity, of men who had been forewarned. The pair fell to the lot of a waiter who happened to feel pleasure in steering them through their meal. He viewed them with the manner of a fatherly pilot, his countenance radiant with benevolence. The patronage, entwined with the ordinary deference, was not plain to them. And yet, as they returned to their coach, they showed in their faces a sense of escape.

To the left, miles down a long purple slope, was a little ribbon of mist where moved the keening Rio Grande. The train was approaching it at an angle, and the apex was Yellow Sky. Presently it was apparent that, as the distance from Yellow Sky grew shorter, the husband became commensurately restless. His brick-red hands were more insistent in their prominence. Occasionally he was even rather absent-minded and far-away when the bride leaned forward and addressed him.

As a matter of truth, Jack Potter was beginning to find the shadow of a deed weigh upon him like a leaden slab. He, the town marshal of Yellow Sky, a man known, liked, and feared in his corner, a prominent person, had gone to San Antonio to meet a girl he believed he loved, and there, after the usual prayers, had actually induced her to marry him, without consulting Yellow Sky for any part of the transaction. He was now bringing his bride before an innocent and unsuspecting community.

Of course people in Yellow Sky married as it pleased them in accordance with a general custom; but such was Potter's thought of his duty to his friends, or of their idea of his duty, or of an unspoken form which does not control men in these matters, that he felt he was heinous. He had committed an extraordinary crime. Face to face with this girl in San Antonio, and spurred by his sharp impulse, he had gone headlong over all the social hedges. At San Antonio he was like a man hidden in the dark. A knife to sever any friendly duty, any form, was easy to his hand in that remote city. But the hour of Yellow Sky—the hour of daylight—was approaching.

He knew full well that his marriage was an important thing to his town. It could only be exceeded by the burning of the new hotel. His friends could not forgive him. Frequently he had reflected on the advisability of telling them by telegraph, but a new cowardice had been upon him. He feared to do it. And now the train was hurrying him toward a scene of amazement, glee, and reproach. He glanced out of the window at the line of haze swinging slowly in toward the train.

Yellow Sky had a kind of brass band, which played painfully, to the delight of the populace. He laughed without heart as he thought of it. If the citizens could dream of his prospective arrival with his bride, they would parade the band at the station and escort them, amid cheers and laughing congratulations, to his adobe home.

He resolved that he would use all the devices of speed and plainscraft in making the journey from the station to his house. Once within that safe citadel, he could issue some sort of vocal bulletin, and then not go among the citizens until they had time to wear off a little of their enthusiasm.

The bride looked anxiously at him. "What's worrying you, Jack?"

He laughed again. "I'm not worrying, girl; I'm only thinking of Yellow Sky."

She flushed in comprehension.

A sense of mutual guilt invaded their minds and developed a finer tenderness. They looked at each other with eyes softly aglow. But Potter often laughed the same nervous laugh; the flush upon the bride's face seemed quite permanent.

The traitor to the feelings of Yellow Sky narrowly watched the speeding landscape. "We're nearly there," he said.

Presently the porter came and announced the proximity of Potter's home. He held a brush in his hand, and, with all his airy superiority gone, he brushed Potter's new clothes as the latter slowly turned this way and that way. Potter fumbled out a coin and gave it to the porter, as he had seen others do. It was a heavy and muscle-bound business, as that of a man shoeing his first horse.

The porter took their bag, and as the train began to slow they moved forward to the hooded platform of the car. Presently the two engines and their long string of coaches rushed into the station of Yellow Sky.

"They have to take water here," said Potter, from a constricted throat and in mournful cadence, as one announcing death. Before the train stopped his eye had swept the length of the platform, and he was glad and astonished to see there was none upon it but the station-agent, who, with a slightly hurried and anxious air, was walking toward the water-tanks. When the train had halted, the porter alighted first, and placed in position a little temporary step.

"Come on, girl," said Potter, hoarsely. As he helped her down they each laughed on a false note. He took the bag from the negro, and bade his wife cling to his arm. As they slunk rapidly away, his hang-dog glance perceived that they were unloading the two trunks, and also that the station-agent, far ahead near the baggage-car, had turned and was running toward him, making gestures. He laughed, and groaned as he laughed, when he noted the first effect of his marital bliss upon Yellow Sky. He gripped his wife's arm firmly to his side, and they fled. Behind them the porter stood, chuckling fatuously.

II

The California express on the Southern Railway was due at Yellow Sky in twenty-one minutes. There were six men at the bar of the Weary Gentleman saloon. One was a drummer who talked a great deal and rapidly; three were Texans who did not care to talk at that time; and two were Mexican sheep-herders, who did not talk as a general practice in the Weary Gentleman saloon. The barkeeper's dog lay on the board walk that crossed in front of the door. His head was on his paws, and he glanced drowsily here and there with the constant vigilance of a dog that is kicked on occasion. Across the sandy street were some vivid green grass-plots, so wonderful in appearance, amid the sands that burned near them in a blazing sun, that they caused a doubt in the mind. They exactly resembled the grass mats used to represent lawns on the stage. At the cooler end of the railway station, a man without a coat sat in a tilted chair and smoked his pipe. The fresh-cut bank of the Rio Grande circled near the town, and there could be seen beyond it a great plum-coloured plain of mesquit.

Save for the busy drummer and his companions in the saloon, Yellow Sky was dozing. The new-comer leaned gracefully upon the bar, and recited many tales with the confidence of a bard who has come upon a new field.

"—and at the moment that the old man fell downstairs with the bureau in his arms, the old woman was coming up with two scuttles of coal, and of course—"

The drummer's tale was interrupted by a young man who suddenly appeared in the open door. He cried: "Scratchy Wilson's drunk, and has turned loose with both hands." The two Mexicans at once set down their glasses and faded out of the rear entrance of the saloon.

The drummer, innocent and jocular, answered: "All right, old man. S'pose he has? Come in and have a drink, anyhow."

But the information had made such an obvious cleft in every skull in the room that the drummer was obliged to see its importance. All had become instantly solemn. "Say," said he, mystified, "what is this?" His three companions made the introductory gesture of eloquent speech; but the young man at the door forestalled them.

"It means, my friend," he answered, as he came into the saloon, "that for the next two hours this town won't be a health resort."

The barkeeper went to the door, and locked and barred it; reaching out of the window, he pulled in heavy wooden shutters, and barred them. Immediately a solemn, chapel-like gloom was upon the place. The drummer was looking from one to another.

"But say," he cried, "what is this, anyhow? You don't mean there is going to be a gun-fight?"

"Don't know whether there'll be a fight or not," answered one man, grimly; "but there'll be some shootin'—some good shootin'."

The young man who had warned them waved his hand. "Oh, there'll be a fight fast enough, if any one wants it. Anybody can get a fight out there in the street. There's a fight just waiting."

The drummer seemed to be swayed between the interest of a foreigner and a perception of personal danger.

"What did you say his name was?" he asked.

"Scratchy Wilson," they answered in chorus.

"And will he kill anybody? What are you going to do? Does this happen often? Does he rampage around like this once a week or so? Can he break in that door?"

"No; he can't break down that door," replied the barkeeper. "He's tried it three times. But when he comes you'd better lay down on the floor, stranger. He's dead sure to shoot at it, and a bullet may come through."

Thereafter the drummer kept a strict eye upon the door. The time had not yet called for him to hug the floor, but, as a minor precaution, he sidled near the wall. "Will he kill anybody?" he said again.

The men laughed low and scornfully at the question.

"He's out to shoot, and he's out for trouble. Don't see any good in experimentin' with him."

"But what do you do in a case like this? What do you do?"

A man responded: "Why, he and Jack Potter—"

"But," in chorus the other men interrupted, "Jack Potter's in San Anton."

"Well, who is he? What's he got to do with it?"

"Oh, he's the town marshal. He goes out and fights Scratchy when he gets on one of these tears."

"Wow!" said the drummer, mopping his brow. "Nice job he's got."

The voices had toned away to mere whisperings. The drummer wished to ask further questions, which were born of an increasing anxiety and bewilderment; but when he attempted them, the men merely looked at him in irritation and motioned him to remain silent. A tense waiting hush was upon them. In the deep shadows of the room their eyes shone as they listened for sounds from the street. One man made three gestures at the barkeeper; and the latter, moving like a ghost, handed him a glass and a bottle. The man poured a full glass of whisky, and set down the bottle noiselessly. He gulped the whisky in a swallow, and turned again toward the door in immovable silence. The drummer saw that the barkeeper, without a sound, had taken a Winchester from beneath the bar. Later he saw this individual beckoning to him, so he tiptoed across the room.

"You better come with me back of the bar."

"No, thanks," said the drummer, perspiring; "I'd rather be where I can make a break for the back door."

Whereupon the man of bottles made a kindly but peremptory gesture. The drummer obeyed it, and, finding himself seated on a box with his head below the level of the bar, balm was laid upon his soul at sight of various zinc and copper fittings that bore a resemblance to armour-plate. The barkeeper took a seat comfortably upon an adjacent box.

"You see," he whispered, "this here Scratchy Wilson is a wonder with a gun—a perfect wonder; and when he goes on the war-trail, we hunt our holes—naturally. He's about the last one of the old gang that used to hang out along the river here. He's a terror when he's drunk. When he's sober he's all right—kind of simple—wouldn't hurt a fly— nicest fellow in town. But when he's drunk—whoo!"

There were periods of stillness. "I wish Jack Potter was back from San Anton'," said the barkeeper. "He shot Wilson up once—in the leg—and he would sail in and pull out the kinks in this thing."

Presently they heard from a distance the sound of a shot, followed by three wild yowls. It instantly removed a bond from the men in the darkened saloon. There was a shuffling of feet. They looked at each other. "Here he comes," they said.

III

A man in a maroon-coloured flannel shirt, which had been purchased for purposes of decoration, and made principally by some Jewish women on the East Side of New York, rounded a corner and walked into the middle of the main street of Yellow Sky. In either hand the man held a long, heavy, blue-black revolver. Often he yelled, and these cries rang through a semblance of a deserted village, shrilly flying over the roofs in a volume that seemed to have no relation to the ordinary vocal strength of a man. It was as if the surrounding stillness formed the arch of a tomb over him. These cries of ferocious challenge rang against walls of silence. And his boots had red tops with gilded imprints, of the kind beloved in winter by little sledding boys on the hillsides of New England.

The man's face flamed in a rage begot of whisky. His eyes, rolling, and yet keen for ambush, hunted the still doorways and windows. He walked with the creeping movement of the midnight cat. As it occurred to him, he roared menacing information. The long revolvers in his hands were as easy as straws; they were removed with an electric swiftness. The little fingers of each hand played sometimes in a musician's way. Plain from the low collar of the shirt, the cords of his neck straightened and sank, straightened and sank, as passion moved him. The only sounds were his terrible invitations. The calm adobes preserved their demeanour at the passing of this small thing in the middle of the street.

There was no offer of fight—no offer of fight. The man called to the sky. There were no attractions. He bellowed and fumed and swayed his revolvers here and everywhere.

The dog of the barkeeper of the Weary Gentleman saloon had not appreciated the advance of events. He yet lay dozing in front of his master's door. At sight of the dog, the man paused and raised his revolver humorously. At sight of the man, the dog sprang up and walked diagonally away, with a sullen head, and growling. The man yelled, and the dog broke into a gallop. As it was about to enter the alley, there was a loud noise, a whistling, and something spat the ground directly before it. The dog screamed, and, wheeling in terror, galloped headlong in a new direction. Again there was a noise, a whistling, and sand was kicked viciously before it. Fear-stricken, the dog turned and flurried like an animal in a pen. The man stood laughing, his weapons at his hips.

Ultimately the man was attracted by the closed door of the Weary Gentleman saloon. He went to it and, hammering with a revolver, demanded drink.

The door remaining imperturbable, he picked a bit of paper from the walk, and nailed it to the framework with a knife. He then turned his back contemptuously upon this popular resort and, walking to the opposite side of the street and spinning there on his heel quickly and lithely, fired at the bit of paper. He missed it by a half inch. He swore at himself, and went away. Later he comfortably fusilladed the windows of his most intimate friend. The man was playing with this town; it was a toy for him.

But still there was no offer of fight. The name of Jack Potter, his ancient antagonist, entered his mind, and he concluded that it would be a glad thing if he should go to Potter's house, and by bombardment induce him to come out and fight. He moved in the direction of his desire, chanting Apache scalp-music.

When he arrived at it, Potter's house presented the same still front as had the other adobes. Taking up a strategic position, the man howled a challenge. But this house regarded him as might a great stone god. It gave no sign. After a decent wait, the man howled further challenges, mingling with them wonderful epithets.

Presently there came the spectacle of a man churning himself into deepest rage over the immobility of a house. He fumed at it as the winter wind attacks a prairie cabin in the North. To the distance there should have gone the sound of a tumult like the fighting of two hundred Mexicans. As necessity bade him, he paused for breath or to reload his revolvers.

IV

Potter and his bride walked sheepishly and with speed. Sometimes they laughed together shamefacedly and low.

"Next corner, dear," he said finally.

They put forth the efforts of a pair walking bowed against a strong wind. Potter was about to raise a finger to point the first appearance of the new home when, as they circled the corner, they came face to face with a man in a maroon-coloured shirt, who was feverishly pushing cartridges into a large revolver. Upon the instant the man dropped his revolver to the ground and, like lightning, whipped another from its holster. The second weapon was aimed at the bridegroom's chest.

There was a silence. Potter's mouth seeemed to be merely a grave for his tongue. He exhibited an instinct to at once loosen his arm from the woman's grip, and he dropped the bag to the sand. As for the bride, her face had gone as yellow as old cloth. She was a slave to hideous rites, gazing at the apparitional snake.

The two men faced each other at a distance of three paces. He of the revolver smiled with a new and quiet ferocity.

"Tried to sneak up on me," he said. "Tried to sneak up on me!" His eyes grew more baleful. As Potter made a slight movement, the man thrust his revolver venomously forward "No; don't you do it, Jack Potter. Don't you move a finger toward a gun just yet. Don't you move an eyelash. The time has come for me to settle with you and I'm goin' to do it my own way, and loaf along with no inter- ferin'. So if you don't want a gun bent on you, just mind what I tell you."

Potter looked at his enemy. "I ain't got a gun on me Scratchy," he said. "Honest, I ain't." He was stiffening and steadying, but yet somewhere at the back of his mind a vision of the Pullman floated: the sea-green figured velvet, the shining brass, silver, and glass, the wood that gleamed as darkly brilliant as the surface of a pool of oil— all the glory of marriage, the environment of the new estate. "You know I fight when it comes to fighting, Scratchy Wilson; but I ain't got a gun on me. You'll have to do all the shootin' yourself."

His enemy's face went livid. He stepped forward, and lashed his weapon to and fro before Potter's chest. "Don't you tell me you ain't got no gun on you, you whelp. Don't tell me no lie like that. There ain't a man in Texas ever seen you without no gun. Don't take me for no kid." His eyes blazed with light, and his throat worked like a pump.

"I ain't takin' you for no kid," answered Potter. His heels had not moved an inch backward. "I'm takin' you for a damn fool. I tell you I ain't got a gun, and I ain't. If you're goin' to shoot me up, you better begin now; you'll never get a chance like this again."

So much enforced reasoning had told on Wilson's rage; he was calmer. "If you ain't got a gun, why ain't you got a gun?" he sneered. "Been to Sunday-school?"

"I ain't got a gun because I've just come fron San Anton' with my wife. I'm married," said Potter. "And if I'd thought there was going to be any galoots like you prowling around when I brought my wife home, I'd had a gun, and don't you forget it."

"Married!" said Scratchy, not at all comprehending.

"Yes, married. I'm married," said Potter, distinctly.

"Married?" said Scratchy. Seemingly for the first time, he saw the drooping, drowning woman at the other man's side. "No!" he said. He was like a creature allowed a glimpse of another world. He moved a pace backward, and his arm, with the revolver, dropped to his side. "Is this the lady?" he asked.

"Yes; this is the lady," answered Potter.

There was another period of silence.

"Well," said Wilson at last, slowly, "I s'pose it's all off now."

"It's all off if you say so, Scratchy. You know I didn't make the trouble." Potter lifted his valise.

"Well, I 'low it's off, Jack," said Wilson. He was looking at the ground. "Married!" He was not a student of chivalry; it was merely that in the presence of this foreign condition he was a simple child of the earlier plains. He picked up his starboard revolver, and, placing both weapons in their holsters, he went away. His feet made funnel-shaped tracks in the heavy sand.

SHERWOOD ANDERSON
1876–1941

Born in Camden, Ohio, Anderson grew up in a variety of small towns, as his talkative, unreliable father moved from job to job. The boy also did odd jobs, and was known for a while as "Jobby." He worked in the fields and at race tracks before serving in the Army—in Cuba—during the Spanish American war. Afterward he wrote advertising copy and ran a paint factory before turning seriously to the writing of fiction. After 1912 essays, poems, and stories by Anderson began appearing regularly, but today his reputation rests upon the stories of small-town America that appeared in *Winesburg, Ohio* (1919) and *Horses and Men* (1923). In his later years he influenced and befriended such younger writers as Hemingway and Faulkner, who parodied him for his pains.

I'm a Fool

It was a hard jolt for me, one of the most bitterest I ever had to face. And it all came about through my own foolishness, too. Even yet sometimes, when I think of it, I want to cry or swear or kick myself. Perhaps, even now, after all this time, there will be a kind of satisfaction in making myself look cheap by telling of it.

It began at three o'clock one October afternoon as I sat in the grandstand at the fall trotting and pacing meet at Sandusky, Ohio.

To tell the truth, I felt a little foolish that I should be sitting in the grandstand at all. During the summer before I had left my home town with Harry Whitehead and, with a nigger named Burt, had taken a job as swipe with one of the two horses Harry was campaigning through the fall race meets that year. Mother cried and my sister Mildred, who wanted to get a job as a school teacher in our town that fall, stormed and scolded about the house all during the week before I left. They both thought it something disgraceful that one of our family should take a place as a swipe with race horses. I've an idea Mildred thought my taking the place would stand in the way of her getting the job she'd been working so long for.

But after all I had to work, and there was no other work to be got. A big lumbering fellow of nineteen couldn't just hang around the house and I had got too big to mow people's lawns and sell newspapers. Little chaps who could get next to people's sympathies by their sizes were always getting jobs away from me. There was one fellow who kept saying to everyone who wanted a lawn mowed or a cistern cleaned, that he was saving money to work his way through college, and I used to lay awake nights thinking up ways to injure him without being found out. I kept thinking of wagons running over him and bricks falling on his head as he walked along the street. But never mind him.

I got the place with Harry and I liked Burt fine. We got along splendid together. He was a big nigger with a lazy sprawling body and soft, kind eyes, and when it came to a fight he could hit like Jack Johnson. He had Bucephalus, a big black pacing stallion that could do 2.09 or 2.10, if he had to, and I had a little gelding named Doctor Fritz that never lost a race all fall when Harry wanted him to win.

We set out from home late in July in a box car with the two horses and after that, until late November, we kept moving along to the race meets and the fairs. It was a peachy time for me, I'll say that. Sometimes now I think that boys who are raised regular in houses, and never have a fine nigger like Burt for best friend, and go to high schools and college, and never steal anything, or get drunk a little, or learn to swear from fellows who know how, or come walking up in front of a grandstand in their shirt sleeves and with dirty horsey pants on when the races are going on and the grandstand is full of people all dressed up—What's the use of talking about it? Such fellows don't know nothing at all. They've never had no opportunity.

But I did. Burt taught me how to rub down a horse and put the bandages on after a race and steam a horse out and a lot of valuable things for any man to know. He could wrap a bandage on a horse's leg so smooth that if it had been the same color you would think it was his skin, and I guess he'd have been a big driver, too, and got to the top like Murphy and Walter Cox and the others if he hadn't been black.

Gee whizz, it was fun. You got to a county seat town, maybe say on a Saturday or Sunday, and the fair began the next Tuesday and lasted until Friday afternoon. Doctor Fritz would be, say in the 2.25 trot on Tuesday afternoon and on Thursday afternoon Bucephalus would knock 'em cold in the "free-for-all" pace. It left you a lot of time to hang around and listen to horse talk, and see Burt knock some yap cold that got too gay, and you'd find out about horses and men and pick up a lot of stuff you could use all the rest of your life, if you had some sense and salted down what you heard and felt and saw.

And then at the end of the week when the race meet was over, and Harry had run home to tend up to his livery stable business, you and Burt hitched the two horses to carts and drove slow and steady across the country, to the place for the next meeting, so as to not overheat the horses, etc., etc., you know.

Gee whizz, Gosh amighty, the nice hickorynut and beechnut and oaks and other kinds of trees along the roads, all brown and red, and the good smells, and Burt singing a song that was called Deep River, and the country girls at the windows of houses and everything. You can stick your colleges up your nose for all me. I guess I know where I got my education.

Why, one of those little burgs of towns you come to on the way, say now on a Saturday afternoon, and Burt says, "let's lay up here." And you did.

And you took the horses to a livery stable and fed them, and you got your good clothes out of a box and put them on.

And the town was full of farmers gaping, because they could see you were race-horse people, and the kids maybe never see a nigger before and was afraid and run away when the two of us walked down their main street.

And that was before prohibition and all that foolishness, and so you went into a saloon, the two of you, and all the yaps come and stood around, and there was always someone pretended he was horsey and knew things and spoke up and began asking questions, and all you did was to lie and lie all you could about what horses you had, and I said I owned them, and then some fellow said, "will you have a drink of whisky," and Burt knocked his eye out the way he could say, offhandlike, "Oh well, all right, I'm agreeable to a little nip. I'll split a quart with you." Gee whizz.

But that isn't what I want to tell my story about. We got home late in November and I promised mother I'd quit the race horses for good. There's a lot of things you've got to promise a mother because she don't know any better.

And so, there not being any work in our town any more than when I left there to go to the races, I went off to Sandusky and got a pretty good place taking care of horses for a man who owned a teaming and delivery and storage coal and real estate business there. It was a pretty good place with good eats, and a day off each week, and sleeping on a cot in a big barn, and mostly just shoveling in hay and oats to a lot of big good-enough skates of horses, that couldn't have trotted a race with a toad. I wasn't dissatisfied and I could send money home.

And then, I started to tell you, the fall races comes to Sandusky and I got the day off and I went. I left the job at noon and had on my good clothes and my new brown derby hat, I'd just bought the Saturday before, and a stand-up collar.

First of all I went downtown and walked about with the dudes. I've always thought to myself, "put up a good front" and so I did it. I had forty dollars in my pocket and so I went into the West House, a big hotel, and walked up to the cigar stand. "Give me three twenty-five cent cigars," I said. There was a lot of horsemen and strangers and dressed-up people from other towns standing around in the lobby and in the bar, and I mingled amongst them. In the bar there was a fellow with a cane and a Windsor tie on, that it made me sick to look at him. I like a man to be a man and dress up, but not to go put on that kind of airs. So I pushed him aside, kind of rough, and had me a drink of whisky. And then he looked at me, as though he thought maybe he'd get gay, but he changed his mind and didn't say anything. And then I had another drink of whisky, just to show him something, and went out and had a hack out to the races, all to myself, and when I got there I bought myself the best seat I could get up in the grandstand, but didn't go in for any of these boxes. That's putting on too many airs.

And so there I was, sitting up in the grandstand as gay as you please and looking down on the swipes coming out with their horses, and with their dirty horsey pants on and the horse blankets swung over their shoulders, same as I had been doing all the year before. I liked one thing about the same as the other, sitting up there and feeling grand and being down there and looking up at the yaps and feeling grander and more important, too. One thing's about as good as another, if you take it just right. I've often said that.

Well, right in front of me, in the grandstand that day, there was a fellow with a couple of girls and they was about my age. The young fellow was a nice guy all right. He was the kind maybe that goes to college and then comes to be a lawyer or maybe a newspaper editor or something like that, but he wasn't stuck on himself. There are some of that kind are all right and he was one of the ones.

He had his sister with him and another girl and the sister looked around over his shoulder, accidental at first, not intending to start anything—she wasn't that kind—and her eyes and mine happened to meet.

You know how it is. Gee, she was a peach! She had on a soft dress, kind of a blue stuff and it looked carelessly made, but was well sewed and made and everything. I knew that much. I blushed when she looked right at me and so did she. She was the nicest girl I've ever seen in my life. She wasn't stuck on herself and she could talk proper grammar without being like a school teacher or something like that. What I mean is she was O.K. I think maybe her father was well-to-do, but not rich to make her chesty because she was his daughter, as some are. Maybe he owned a drugstore or a drygoods store in their home town, or something like that. She never told me and I never asked.

My own people are all O.K. too, when you come to that. My grandfather was Welsh and over in the old country, in Wales he was—But never mind that.

The first heat of the first race come off and the young fellow setting there with the two girls left them and went down to make a bet. I knew what he was up to, but he didn't talk big and noisy and let everyone around know he was a sport, as some do. He wasn't that kind. Well, he come back and I heard him tell the two girls what horse he'd bet on, and when the heat was trotted they all half got to their feet and acted in the excited, sweaty way people do when they've got money down on a race, and the horse they bet on is up there pretty close at the end, and they think maybe he'll come on with a rush, but he never does because he hasn't got the old juice in him, come right down to it.

And then, pretty soon, the horses came out for the 2.18 pace and there was a horse in it I knew. He was a horse Bob French had in his string but Bob didn't own him. He was a horse owned by a Mr. Mathers down at Marietta, Ohio.

This Mr. Mathers had a lot of money and owned some coal mines or something, and he had a swell place out in the country, and he was stuck on race horses, but was a Presbyterian or something, and I think more than likely his wife was one, too, maybe a stiffer one than himself. So he never raced his horses hisself, and the story round the Ohio race tracks was that when one of his horses got ready to go to the races he turned him over to Bob French and pretended to his wife he was sold.

So Bob had the horses and he did pretty much as he pleased and you can't blame Bob, at least, I never did. Sometimes he was out to win and sometimes he wasn't. I never cared much about that when I was swiping a horse. What I did want to know was that my horse had the speed and could go out in front, if you wanted him to.

And, as I'm telling you, there was Bob in this race with one of Mr. Mather's horses, was named "About Ben Ahem" or something like that, and was fast as a streak. He was a gelding and had a mark of 2.21, but could step in .08 or .09.

Because when Burt and I were out, as I've told you, the year before, there was a nigger, Burt knew, worked for Mr. Mathers and we went out there one day when we didn't have no race on at the Marietta Fair and our boss Harry was gone home.

And so everyone was gone to the fair but just this one nigger and he took us all through Mr. Mather's swell house and he and Burt tapped a bottle of wine Mr. Mathers had hid in his bedroom, back in a closet, without his wife knowing, and he showed us this Ahem horse. Burt was always stuck on being a driver but didn't have much chance to get to the top, being a nigger, and he and the other nigger gulped that whole bottle of wine and Burt got a little lit up.

So the nigger let Burt take this About Ben Ahem and step him a mile in a track Mr. Mathers had all to himself, right there on the farm. And Mr. Mathers had one child, a daughter, kinda sick, and not very good-looking, and she came home and we had to hustle to get About Ben Ahem stuck back in the barn.

I'm only telling you to get everything straight. At Sandusky, that afternoon I was at the fair, this young fellow with the two girls was fussed, being with the girls and losing his bet. You know how a fellow is that way. One of them was his girl and the other his sister. I had figured that out.

"Gee whizz," I says to myself, "I'm going to give him the dope."

He was mighty nice when I touched him on the shoulder. He and the girls were nice to me right from the start and clear to the end. I'm not blaming them.

And so he leaned back and I give him the dope on About Ben Ahem. "Don't bet a cent on this first heat because he'll go like an oxen hitched to a plow, but when the first heat is over go right down and lay on your pile." That's what I told him.

Well, I never saw a fellow treat anyone sweller. There was a fat man sitting beside the little girl, that had looked at me twice by this time, and I at her, and both blushing, and what did he do but have the nerve to turn and ask the fat man to get up and change places with me so I could set with his crowd.

Gee whizz, craps amighty. There I was. What a chump I was to go and get gay up there in West House bar, and just because that dude was standing there with a cane and that kind of a necktie on, to go and get all balled up and drink that whisky just to show off.

Of course she would know, me setting right beside her and letting her smell of my breath. I could have kicked myself right down out of that grandstand and all around that race track and made a faster record than most of the skates of horses they had there that year.

Because that girl wasn't any mutt of a girl. What wouldn't I have give right then for a stick of chewing gum to chew, or a lozenger, or some liquorice, or most anything. I was glad I had those twenty-five cent cigars in my pocket and right away I give that fellow one and lit one myself. Then that fat man got up and we changed places and there I was, plunked right down beside her.

They introduced themselves and the fellow's best girl, he had with him, was named Miss Elinor Woodbury, and her father was a manufacturer of barrels from a place called Tiffin, Ohio. And the fellow himself was named Wilbur Wessen and his sister was Miss Lucy Wessen.

I suppose it was their having such swell names got me off my trolley. A fellow, just because he has been a swipe with a race horse, and works taking care of horses for a man in the teaming, delivery, and storage business, isn't any better or worse than anyone else. I've often thought that, and said it too.

But you know how a fellow is. There's something in that kind of nice clothes, and the kind of nice eyes she had, and the way she looked at me, awhile before, over her brother's shoulder, and me looking back at her, and both of us blushing.

I couldn't show her up for a boob, could I?

I made a fool of myself, that's what I did. I said my name was

Walter Mathers from Marietta, Ohio, and then I told all three of them the smashingest lie you ever heard. What I said was that my father owned the horse About Ben Ahem and that he had let him out to this Bob French for racing purposes, because our family was proud and had never gone into racing that way, in our own name, I mean. Then I had got started and they were all leaning over and listening, and Miss Lucy Wessen's eyes were shining and I went the whole hog.

I told about our place down at Marietta, and about the big stables and the grand brick house we had on a hill, up above the Ohio River, but I knew enough not to do it in no bragging way. What I did was to start things and then let them drag the rest out of me. I acted just as reluctant to tell as I could. Our family hasn't got any barrel factory, and, since I've known us, we've always been pretty poor, but not asking anything of anyone at that, and my grandfather, over in Wales—But never mind that.

We set there talking like we had known each other for years and years, and I went and told them that my father had been expecting maybe this Bob French wasn't on the square, and had sent me up to Sandusky on the sly to find out what I could.

And I bluffed it through I had found out all about the 2.18 pace, in which About Ben Ahem was to start.

I said he would lose the first heat by pacing like a lame cow and then he would come back and skin 'em alive after that. And to back up what I said I took thirty dollars out of my pocket and handed it to Mr. Wilbur Wessen and asked him, would he mind, after the first heat, to go down and place it on About Ben Ahem for whatever odds he could get. What I said was that I didn't want Bob French to see me and none of the swipes.

Sure enough the first heat come off and About Ben Ahem went off his stride, up the back stretch, and looked like a wooden horse or a sick one, and come in to be last. Then this Wilbur Wessen went down to the betting place under the grandstand and there I was with the two girls, and when that Miss Woodbury was looking the other way once, Lucy Wessen kinda, with her shoulder you know, kinda touched me. Not just tucking down, I don't mean. You know how a woman can do. They get close, but not getting gay either. You know what they do. Gee whizz.

And then they give me a jolt. What they had done, when I didn't know, was to get together, and they had decided Wilbur Wessen would bet fifty dollars, and the two girls had gone and put in ten dollars each, of their own money, too. I was sick then, but I was sicker later.

About the gelding, About Ben Ahem, and their winning their

money, I wasn't worried a lot about that. It come out O.K. Ahem stepped the next three heats like a bushel of spoiled eggs going to market before they could be found out, and Wilbur Wessen had got nine to two for the money. There was something else eating me.

Because Wilbur come back, after he had bet the money, and after that he spent most of his time talking to that Miss Woodbury, and Lucy Wessen and I was left alone together like on a desert island. Gee, if I'd only been on the square or if there had been any way of getting myself on the square. There ain't any Walter Mathers, like I said to her and them, and there hasn't ever been one, but if there was, I bet I'd go to Marietta, Ohio, and shoot him tomorrow.

There I was, big boob that I am. Pretty soon the race was over, and Wilbur had gone down and collected our money, and we had a hack downtown, and he stood us a swell supper at the West House, and a bottle of champagne beside.

And I was with that girl and she wasn't saying much, and I wasn't saying much either. One thing I know. She wasn't stuck on me because of the lie about my father being rich and all that. There's a way you know. . . . Craps amighty. There's a kind of girl, you see just once in your life, and if you don't get busy and make hay, then you're gone for good and all, and might as well go jump off a bridge. They give you a look from inside of them somewhere, and it ain't no vamping, and what it means is—you want that girl to be your wife, and you want nice things around her like flowers and swell clothes, and you want her to have the kids you're going to have, and you want good music played and no rag-time. Gee whizz.

There's a place over near Sandusky, across a kind of bay, and it's called Cedar Point. And after we had supper we went over to it in a launch, all by ourselves. Wilbur and Miss Lucy and that Miss Woodbury had to catch a ten o'clock train back to Tiffin, Ohio, because, when you're out with girls like that you can't get careless like with some kinds of Janes.

And Wilbur blowed himself to the launch and it cost him fifteen cold plunks, but I wouldn't never have knew if I hadn't listened. He wasn't no tin horn kind of a sport.

Over at Cedar Point place, we didn't stay around where there was a gang of common kind of cattle at all.

There was big dance halls and dining places for yaps, and there was a beach you could walk along and get where it was dark, and we went there.

She didn't talk hardly at all and neither did I, and I was thinking how glad I was my mother was all right, and always made us kids learn to eat with a fork at table, and not swill soup, and not be noisy and rough like a gang you see around a race track that way.

Then Wilbur and his girl went away up the beach and Lucy and I sat down in a dark place, where there was some roots of old trees, the water had washed up, and after that the time, till we had to go back in the launch and they had to catch their trains, wasn't nothing at all. It went like winking your eye.

Here's how it was. The place we were setting in was dark, like I said, and there was the roots from that old stump sticking up like arms, and there was a watery smell, and the night was like—as if you could put your hand out and feel it—so warm and soft and dark and sweet like an orange.

I most cried and I most swore and I most jumped up and danced I was so mad and happy and sad.

When Wilbur come back from being alone with his girl, and she saw him coming, Lucy she says, "we got to go to the train now", and she was most crying too, but she never knew nothing I knew, and she couldn't be so all busted up. And then, before Wilbur and Miss Woodbury got up to where we was, she put her face up and kissed me quick and put her head up against me and she was all quivering and—Gee whizz.

Sometimes I hope I have cancer and die. I guess you know what I mean. We went in the launch across the bay to the train like that, and it was dark, too. She whispered and said it was like she and I could get out of the boat and walk on the water, and it sounded foolish, but I knew what she meant.

And then quick we were right at the depot, and there was a big gang of yaps, the kind that goes to the fairs, and crowded and milling around like cattle, and how could I tell her? "It won't be long because you'll write and I'll write to you." That's all she said.

I got a chance like a hay barn afire. A swell chance I got.

And maybe she would write me, down at Marietta that way, and the letter would come back, and stamped on the front of it by the U.S.A. "there ain't any such guy," or something like that, whatever they stamp on a letter that way.

And me trying to pass myself off for a bigbug and a swell—to her, as decent a little body as God ever made. Craps amighty—a swell chance I got!

And then the train come in, and she got on it, and Wilbur Wessen he come and shook hands with me, and that Miss Woodbury was nice too and bowed to me, and I at her, and the train went and I busted out and cried like a kid.

Gee, I could have run after that train and made Dan Patch look like a freight train after a wreck but, socks amighty, what was the use? Did you ever see such a fool?

I'll bet you what—if I had an arm broke right now or a train had run over my foot—I wouldn't go to no doctor at all. I'd go set down and let her hurt and hurt—that's what I'd do.

I'll bet you what—if I hadn't a drunk that booze I'd a never been such a boob as to go tell such a lie—that couldn't never be made straight to a lady like her.

I wish I had that fellow right here that had on a Windsor tie and carried a cane. I'd smash him for fair. Gosh darn his eyes. He's a big fool—that's what he is.

And if I'm not another you just go find me one and I'll quit working and be a bum and give him my job. I don't care nothing for working, and earning money, and saving it for no such boob as myself.

JAMES JOYCE
1882–1941

Joyce was born near Dublin, Ireland, and educated by the Jesuits at Belvedere and University College. He went into self-imposed exile in 1904, taking with him a young woman named Nora Barnacle. "She'll never leave him," said Joyce's father, and she didn't. In Italy and Switzerland Joyce earned a precarious living teaching English while trying to become a great writer. His short stories were all designed for a collection called *Dubliners*, which spent ten years finding a publisher and then sold less than five hundred copies in 1914. His autobiographical novel, *A Portrait of the Artist as a Young Man* (1916) attracted the attention of T S Eliot and Ezra Pound, who helped him get support for his major project, *Ulysses* (1922), which took realism to its logical conclusion and beyond. *Finnegans Wake* (1939) is all beyond—a book to keep the professors busy, as Joyce observed, and busy they are. But, as Joyce's work becomes more familiar, the technical breakthroughs and the difficulties seem less noticeable and the comic spirit and humanity come through more clearly.

Araby

North Richmond Street, being blind, was a quiet street except at the hour when the Christian Brothers' School set the boys free. An uninhabited house of two storeys stood at the blind end, detached from its neighbours in a square ground. The other houses of the street, conscious of decent lives within them, gazed at one another with brown imperturbable faces.

The former tenant of our house, a priest, had died in the back drawing-room. Air, musty from having been long enclosed, hung in all the rooms, and the waste room behind the kitchen was littered with old useless papers. Among these I found a few paper-covered books, the pages of which were curled and damp: *The Abbot*, by Walter Scott, *The Devout Communicant* and *The Memoirs of Vidocq*. I liked the last because its leaves were yellow. The wild garden behind the house contained a central apple-tree and a few straggling bushes under one of which I found the late tenant's rusty bicycle-pump. He had been a very charitable priest; in his will he had left all his money to institutions and the furniture of his house to his sister.

When the short days of winter came dusk fell before we had well eaten our dinners. When we met in the street the houses had grown sombre. The space of the sky above us was the color of ever-changing violet and towards it the lamps of the street lifted their feeble lanterns. The cold air stung us and we played till our bodies glowed. Our shouts echoed in the silent street. The career of our play brought us through the dark muddy lanes behind the houses where we ran the gauntlet of the rough tribes from the cottages, to the back doors of the dark dripping gardens where odors arose from the ashpits, to the dark odorous stables where a coachman smoothed and combed the horse or shook music from the buckled harness. When we returned to the street light from the kitchen windows had filled the areas. If my uncle was seen turning the corner we hid in the shadow until we had seen him safely housed. Or if Mangan's sister came out on the doorstep to call her brother in to his tea we watched her from our shadow peer up and down the street. We waited to see whether she would remain or go in and, if she remained, we left our shadow and walked up to Mangan's steps resignedly. She was waiting for us, her figure defined by the light from the half-opened door. Her brother always teased her before he obeyed and I stood by the railings looking at her. Her dress swung as she moved her body and the soft rope of her hair tossed from side to side.

Every morning I lay on the floor in the front parlour watching her door. The blind was pulled down to within an inch of the sash so that I could not be seen. When she came out on the doorstep my heart leaped. I ran to the hall, seized my books and followed her. I kept her brown figure always in my eye and, when we came near the point at which our ways diverged, I quickened my pace and passed her. This happened morning after morning. I had never spoken to her, except for a few casual words, and yet her name was like a summons to all my foolish blood.

Her image accompanied me even in places the most hostile to romance. On Saturday evenings when my aunt went marketing I had to go to carry some of the parcels. We walked through the flaring streets, jostled by drunken men and bargaining women, amid the curse of laborers, the shrill litanies of shop-boys who stood on guard by the barrels of pigs' cheeks, the nasal chanting of street-singers, who sang a *come-all-you* about O'Donovan Rossa, or a ballad about the troubles in our native land. These noises converged in a single sensation of life for me: I imagined that I bore my chalice safely through a throng of foes. Her name sprang to my lips at moments in strange prayers and praises which I myself did not understand. My eyes were often full of tears (I could not tell why) and at times a flood from my heart seemed to pour itself out into my bosom. I thought little of the future. I did not know whether I would ever speak to her or not or, if I spoke to her, how I could tell her of my confused adoration. But my body was like a harp and her words and gestures were like fingers running upon the wires.

One evening I went into the back drawing-room in which the priest had died. It was a dark rainy evening and there was no sound in the house. Through one of the broken panes I heard the rain impinge upon the earth, the fine incessant needles of water playing in the sodden beds. Some distant lamp or lighted window gleamed below me. I was thankful that I could see so little. All my senses seemed to desire to veil themselves and, feeling that I was about to slip from them, I pressed the palms of my hands together until they trembled, murmuring: "O love! O love!" many times.

At last she spoke to me. When she addressed the first words to me I was so confused that I did not know what to answer. She asked me was I going to *Araby*. I forgot whether I answered yes or no. It would be a splendid bazaar, she said she would love to go.

"And why can't you?" I asked.

While she spoke she turned a silver bracelet round and round her wrist. She could not go, she said, because there would be a retreat that week in her convent. Her brother and two other boys were fighting for their caps and I was alone at the railings. She held one of the spikes, bowing her head towards me. The light from the lamp opposite our door caught the white curve of her neck, lit up her hair that rested there and, falling, lit up the hand upon the railing. It fell over one side of her dress and caught the white border of a petticoat just visible as she stood at ease.

"It's well for you," she said.

"If I go," I said, "I will bring you something."

What innumerable follies laid waste my waking and sleeping thoughts after that evening! I wished to annihilate the tedious intervening days. I chafed against the work of school. At night in my bedroom and by day in the classroom her image came between me and the page I strove to read. The syllables of the word *Araby* were called to me through the silence in which my soul luxuriated and cast an Eastern enchantment over me. I asked for leave to go to the bazaar on Saturday night. My aunt was surprised and hoped it was not some Freemason affair. I answered few questions in class. I watched my master's face pass from amiability to sternness; he hoped I was not beginning to idle. I could not call my wandering thoughts together. I had hardly any patience with the serious work of life which, now that it stood between me and my desire, seemed to me child's play, ugly monotonous child's play.

On Saturday morning I reminded my uncle that I wished to go to the bazaar in the evening. He was fussing at the hallstand, looking for the hat-brush, and answered me curtly:

"Yes, boy, I know."

As he was in the hall I could not go into the front parlor and lie at the window. I left the house in bad humor and walked slowly towards the school. The air was pitilessly raw and already my heart misgave me.

When I came home to dinner my uncle had not yet been home. Still it was early. I sat staring at the clock for some time and, when its ticking began to irritate me, I left the room. I mounted the staircase and gained the upper part of the house. The high cold empty gloomy rooms liberated me and I went from room to room singing. From the front window I saw my companions playing below in the street. Their cries reached me weakened and indistinct and, leaning my forehead against the cool glass, I looked over at the dark house where she lived. I may have stood there for an hour, seeing nothing but the brown-clad figure cast by my imagination, touched discreetly by the lamplight at the curved neck, at the hand upon the railings and at the border below the dress.

When I came downstairs again I found Mrs. Mercer sitting at the fire. She was an old garrulous woman, a pawnbroker's widow, who collected used stamps for some pious purpose. I had to endure the gossip of the tea-table. The meal was prolonged beyond an hour and still my uncle did not come. Mrs. Mercer stood up to go: she was very sorry she couldn't wait any longer, but it was after eight o'clock and she did not like to be out late, as the night air was bad for her. When she had gone I began to walk up and down the room, clenching my fists. My aunt said:

"I'm afraid you may put off your bazaar for this night of Our Lord."

At nine o'clock I heard my uncle's latchkey in the halldoor. I heard him talking to himself and heard the hallstand rocking when it had received the weight of his overcoat. I could interpret these signs. When he was midway through his dinner I asked him to give me the money to go to the bazaar. He had forgotten.

"The people are in bed and after their first sleep now," he said.

I did not smile. My aunt said to him energetically:

"Can't you give him the money and let him go? You've kept him late enough as it is."

My uncle said he was very sorry he had forgotten. He said he believed in the old saying: "All work and no play makes Jack a dull boy." He asked me where I was going and, when I had told him a second time he asked me did I know *The Arab's Farewell to his Steed*. When I left the kitchen he was about to recite the opening lines of the piece to my aunt.

I held a florin tightly in my hand as I strode down Buckingham Street towards the station. The sight of the streets thronged with buyers and glaring with gas recalled to me the purpose of my journey. I took my seat in a third-class carriage of a deserted train. After an intolerable delay the train moved out of the station slowly. It crept onward among ruinous houses and over the twinkling river. At Westland Row Station a crowd of people pressed to the carriage doors; but the porters moved them back, saying that it was a special train for the bazaar. I remained alone in the bare carriage. In a few minutes the train drew up beside an impro- vised wooden platform. I passed out on to the road and saw by the lighted dial of a clock that it was ten minutes to ten. In front of me was a large building which displayed the magical name.

I could not find any sixpenny entrance and, fearing that the bazaar would be closed, I passed quickly through a turnstile, handing a shilling to a weary-looking man. I found myself in a big hall girdled at half its height by a gallery. Nearly all the stalls were closed and the greater part of the hall was in darkness. I recognised a silence like that which per- vades a church after a service. I walked into the centre of the bazaar timidly. A few people were gathered about the stalls which were still open. Before a curtain, over which the words *Café Chantant* were written in colored lamps, two men were counting money on a salver. I listened to the fall of the coins.

Remembering with difficulty why I had come I went over to one of the stalls and examined porcelain vases and flowered tea-sets. At the door of the stall a young lady was talking and laughing with two young gentlemen. I remarked their English accents and listened vaguely to their conversation.

"O, I never said such a thing!"

"O, but you did!"

"O, but I didn't!"

"Didn't she say that?"

"Yes. I heard her."

"O, there's a . . . fib!"

Observing me the young lady came over and asked me did I wish to buy anything. The tone of her voice was not encouraging; she seemed to have spoken to me out of a sense of duty. I looked humbly at the great jars that stood like eastern guards at either side of the dark entrance to the stall and murmured:

"No, thank you."

The young lady changed the position of one of the vases and went back to the two young men. They began to talk of the same subject. Once or twice the young lady glanced at me over her shoulder.

I lingered before her stall, though I knew my stay was useless, to make my interest in her wares seem the more real. Then I turned away slowly and walked down the middle of the bazaar. I allowed the two pennies to fall against the sixpence in my pocket. I heard a voice call from one end of the gallery that the light was out. The upper part of the hall was now completely dark.

Gazing up into the darkness I saw myself as a creature driven and derided by vanity; and my eyes burned with anguish and anger.

DOROTHY PARKER
1893–1967

Born the daughter of J. Henry and Eliza Rothschild in West End, New Jersey, she went to school at Blessed Sacrament Convent in New York City and Miss Dana's School in Morristown, N.J. At twenty she had a job with *Vogue* magazine and had begun to publish light verse. A few years later she married Edwin Parker, keeping his name though divorcing him eleven years later. Writing was her trade from the beginning, and New York City was her territory. She worked for sophisticated magazines like *Vanity Fair* and the *New Yorker*. She wrote plays for Broadway and film scripts for Hollywood. In her youth she was the only woman who belonged to a select circle of New York wits, whose base was a table in the bar of the Algonquin Hotel. She squandered her talent collaborating with clever men who were not her equals. In her later years, she stopped writing and drank too much. But for a brief period in the twenties and thirties she was the talk of the town, and her stories, verse, and even casual remarks will go on being remembered.

You Were Perfectly Fine

The pale young man eased himself carefully into the low chair, and rolled his head to the side, so that the cool chintz comforted his cheek and temple.

"Oh, dear," he said. "Oh, dear, oh, dear, oh, dear. Oh."

The clear-eyed girl, sitting light and erect on the couch, smiled brightly at him.

"Not feeling so well today?" she said.

"Oh, I'm great," he said. "Corking, I am. Know what time I got up? Four o'clock this afternoon, sharp. I kept trying to make it, and every time I took my head off the pillow, it would roll under the bed. This isn't my head I've got on now. I think this is something that used to belong to Walt Whitman. Oh, dear, oh, dear, oh, dear."

"Do you think maybe a drink would make you feel better?" she said.

"The hair of the mastiff that bit me?" he said. "Oh, no, thank you. Please never speak of anything like that again. I'm through. I'm all, all through. Look at that hand; steady as a humming-bird. Tell me, was I very terrible last night?"

"Oh, goodness," she said, "everybody was feeling pretty high. You were all right."

"Yeah," he said. "I must have been dandy. Is everybody sore at me?"

"Good heavens, no," she said. "Everyone thought you were terribly funny. Of course, Jim Pierson was a little stuffy, there for a minute at dinner. But people sort of held him back in his chair, and got him calmed down. I don't think anybody at the other tables noticed it at all. Hardly anybody."

"He was going to sock me?" he said. "Oh, Lord. What did I do to him?"

"Why, you didn't do a thing," she said. "You were perfectly fine. But you know how silly Jim gets, when he thinks anybody is making too much fuss over Elinor."

"Was I making a pass at Elinor?" he said. "Did I do that?"

"Of course you didn't," she said. "You were only fooling, that's all. She thought you were awfully amusing. She was having a marvelous time. She only got a little tiny bit annoyed just once, when you poured the clam-juice down her back."

"My God," he said. "Clam-juice down that back. And every vertebra a little Cabot. Dear God. What'll I ever do?"

"Oh, she'll be all right," she said. "Just send her some flowers, or something. Don't worry about it. It isn't anything."

"No, I won't worry," he said. "I haven't got a care in the world. I'm sitting pretty. Oh, dear, oh, dear. Did I do any other fascinating tricks at dinner?"

"You were fine," she said. "Don't be so foolish about it. Everybody was crazy about you. The maître d'hôtel was a little worried because you wouldn't stop singing, but he really didn't mind. All he said was, he was afraid they'd close the place again, if there was so much noise. But he didn't care a bit, himself. I think he loved seeing you have such a good time. Oh, you were just singing away, there, for about an hour. It wasn't so terribly loud, at all."

"So I sang," he said. "That must have been a treat. I sang."

"Don't you remember?" she said. "You just sang one song after another. Everybody in the place was listening. They loved it. Only you kept insisting that you wanted to sing some song about some kind of fusiliers or other, and everybody kept shushing you, and you'd keep trying to start it again. You were wonderful. We were all trying to make you stop singing for a minute, and eat something, but you wouldn't hear of it. My, you were funny."

"Didn't I eat any dinner?" he said.

"Oh, not a thing," she said. "Every time the waiter would offer you something, you'd give it right back to him, because you said that he was your long-lost brother, changed in the cradle by a gypsy band, and that anything you had was his. You had him simply roaring at you."

"I bet I did," he said. "I bet I was comical. Society's Pet, I must have been. And what happened then, after my overwhelming success with the waiter?"

"Why, nothing much," she said. "You took a sort of dislike to some old man with white hair, sitting across the room, because you didn't like his necktie and you wanted to tell him about it. But we got you out, before he got really mad."

"Oh, we got out," he said. "Did I walk?"

"Walk? Of course you did," she said. "You were absolutely all right. There was that nasty stretch of ice on the sidewalk, and you did sit down awfully hard, you poor dear. But good heavens, that might have happened to anybody."

"Oh, surely," he said. "Mrs. Hoover or anybody. So I fell down on the sidewalk. That would explain what's the matter with my— Yes. I see. And then what, if you don't mind?"

"Ah, now, Peter!" she said. "You can't sit there and say you don't remember what happened after that! I did think that maybe you were just a little tight at dinner—oh, you were perfectly all right, and all that, but I did know you were feeling pretty gay. But you were so serious, from the time you fell down—I never knew you to be that way. Don't you know, how you told me I had never seen your real self before? Oh, Peter, I just couldn't bear it, if you didn't remember that lovely long ride we took together in the taxi! Please, you do remember that, don't you? I think it would simply kill me, if you didn't."

"Oh, yes," he said. "Riding in the taxi. Oh, yes, sure. Pretty long ride, hmm?"

"Round and round and round the park," she said. "Oh, and the trees were shining so in the moonlight. And you said you never knew before that you really had a soul."

"Yes," he said. "I said that. That was me."

"You said such lovely, lovely things," she said. "And I'd never known, all this time, how you had been feeling about me, and I'd never dared to let you see how I felt about you. And then last night—oh, Peter dear, I think that taxi ride was the most important thing that ever happened to us in our lives."

"Yes," he said. "I guess it must have been."

"And we're going to be so happy," she said. "Oh, I just want to tell everybody! But I don't know—I think maybe it would be sweeter to keep it all to ourselves."

"I think it would be," he said.

"Isn't it lovely?" she said.

"Yes," he said. "Great."

"Lovely!" she said.

"Look here," he said, "do you mind if I have a drink? I mean, just medicinally, you know. I'm off the stuff for life, so help me. But I think I feel a collapse coming on."

"Oh, I think it would do you good," she said. "You poor boy, it's a shame you feel so awful. I'll go make you a highball."

"Honestly," he said, "I don't see how you could ever want to speak to me again, after I made such a fool of myself, last night. I think I'd better go join a monastery in Tibet."

"You crazy idiot!" she said. "As if I could ever let you go away now! Stop talking like that. You were perfectly fine."

She jumped up from the couch, kissed him quickly on the forehead, and ran out of the room.

The pale young man looked after her and shook his head long and slowly, then dropped it in his damp and trembling hands.

"Oh, dear," he said. "Oh, dear, oh, dear, oh dear."

F. SCOTT FITZGERALD
1896–1940

Francis Scott Key Fitzgerald was born in St. Paul, Minnesota, to a genteel but ineffectual father and a doting and eccentric mother. A delicate child, he was reluctant to go to school but finally went to a small Catholic school, then to St. Paul Academy, to Newman, and finally to Princeton. He was unpopular at most of these places for most of the time, and unhappy as well, but his talent for writing and his remarkable good looks began to count for more as he grew up; so that at college he received much of the adulation for which he hungered so deeply. He was concerned to the point of obsession with social standing and prestige. Only his gift for writing and his capacity for ruthless self-criticism prevented him from sliding into a life of empty snobbery. He had to marry a beautiful girl, and he did. He had to become rich and famous—and he did. But his wife's mental health was precarious, and the fame and riches were more than he could handle. After a breakdown and painful recovery, that he described with a typical lack of self-protectiveness, he lived and worked in Hollywood, never quite recapturing the grace and beauty of his early work. He was the poet laureate of the jazz age, and in his finest novels *(The Great Gatsby,* 1925, and *Tender is the Night,* 1934) and his remarkable short stories, we can find the best epitaph for that era as well as for Fitzgerald himself.

Babylon Revisited

"And where's Mr. Campbell?" Charlie asked.

"Gone to Switzerland. Mr. Campbell's a pretty sick man, Mr. Wales."

"I'm sorry to hear that. And George Hardt?" Charlie inquired.

"Back in America, gone to work."

"And where is the Snow Bird?"

"He was in here last week. Anyway, his friend, Mr. Schaeffer, is in Paris."

Two familiar names from the long list of a year and a half ago. Charlie scribbled an address in his notebook and tore out the page.

"If you see Mr. Schaeffer, give him this," he said. "It's my brother-in-law's address. I haven't settled on a hotel yet."

He was not really disappointed to find Paris was so empty. But the stillness in the Ritz bar was strange and portentous. It was not an American bar any more—he felt polite in it, and not as if he owned it. It had gone back into France. He felt the stillness from the moment he got out of the taxi and saw the doorman, usually in a frenzy of activity at this hour, gossiping with a *chasseur* by the servants' entrance.

Passing through the corridor, he heard only a single, bored voice in the once-clamorous women's room. When he turned into the bar he traveled the twenty feet of green carpet with his eyes fixed straight ahead by old habit; and then, with his foot firmly on the rail, he turned and surveyed the room, encountering only a single pair of eyes that fluttered up from a newspaper in the corner. Charlie asked for the head barman, Paul, who in the latter days of the bull market had come to work in his own custom-built car—disembarking, however, with due nicety at the nearest corner. But Paul was at his country house today and Alix giving him information.

"No, no more," Charlie said, "I'm going slow these days."

Alix congratulated him: "You were going pretty strong a couple of years ago."

"I'll stick to it all right," Charlie assured him. "I've stuck to it for over a year and a half now."

"How do you find conditions in America?"

"I haven't been to America for months. I'm in business in Prague, representing a couple of concerns there. They don't know about me down there."

Alix smiled.

"Remember the night of George Hardt's bachelor dinner here?" said Charlie. "By the way, what's become of Claude Fessenden?"

Alix lowered his voice confidentially: "He's in Paris, but he doesn't come here any more. Paul doesn't allow it. He ran up a bill of thirty thousand francs, charging all his drinks and his lunches, and usually his dinner, for more than a year. And when Paul finally told him he had to pay, he gave him a bad check."

Alix shook his head sadly.

"I don't understand it, such a dandy fellow. Now he's all bloated up—" He made a plump apple of his hands.

Charlie watched a group of strident queens installing themselves in a corner.

"Nothing affects them," he thought. "Stocks rise and fall, people loaf or work, but they go on forever." The place oppressed him. He called for the dice and shook with Alix for the drink.

"Here for long, Mr. Wales?"

"I'm here for four or five days to see my little girl."

"Oh-h! You have a little girl?"

Outside, the fire-red, gas-blue, ghost-green signs shone smokily through the tranquil rain. It was late afternoon and the streets were in movement; the *bistros* gleamed. At the corner of the Boulevard des Capucines he took a taxi. The Place de la Concorde moved by in pink majesty; they crossed the logical Seine, and Charlie felt the sudden provincial quality of the Left Bank.

Charlie directed his taxi to the Avenue de l'Opéra, which was out of his way. But he wanted to see the blue hour spread over the magnificent façade, and imagine that the cab horns, playing endlessly the first few bars of *Le Plus que Lent*, were the trumpets of the Second Empire. They were closing the iron grill in front of Brentano's Book-store, and people were already at dinner behind the trim little bourgeois hedge of Duval's. He had never eaten at a really cheap restaurant in Paris. Five-course dinner, four francs fifty, eighteen cents, wine included. For some odd reason he wished that he had.

As they rolled on to the Left Bank and he felt its sudden provincialism, he thought, "I spoiled this city for myself. I didn't realize it, but the days came along one after another, and then two years were gone, and everything was gone, and I was gone."

He was thirty-five, and good to look at. The Irish mobility of his face was sobered by a deep wrinkle between his eyes. As he rang his brother-in-law's bell in the Rue Palatine, the wrinkle deepened till it pulled down his brows; he felt a cramping sensation in his belly. From behind the maid who opened the door darted a lovely little girl of nine who shrieked "Daddy!" and flew up, struggling like a fish, into his arms. She pulled his head around by one ear and set her cheek against his.

"My old pie," he said.

"Oh, daddy, daddy, daddy, daddy, dads, dads, dads!"

She drew him into the salon, where the family waited, a boy and a girl his daughter's age, his sister-in-law and her husband. He greeted Marion with his voice pitched carefully to avoid either feigned enthusiasm or dislike, but her response was more frankly tepid, though she minimized her expression of unalterable distrust by directing her regard toward his child. The two men clasped hands in a friendly way and Lincoln Peters rested his for a moment on Charlie's shoulder.

The room was warm and comfortably American. The three children moved intimately about, playing through the yellow oblongs that led to other rooms; the cheer of six o'clock spoke in the eager smacks of the fire and the sounds of French activity in the kitchen. But Charlie did not relax; his heart sat up rigidly in his body and he drew confidence from his daughter, who from time to time came close to him, holding in her arms the doll he had brought.

"Really extremely well," he declared in answer to Lincoln's question. "There's a lot of business there that isn't moving at all, but we're doing even better than ever. In fact, damn well. I'm bringing my sister over from America next month to keep house for me. My income last year was bigger than it was when I had money. You see, the Czechs—"

His boasting was for a specific purpose; but after a moment, seeing a faint restiveness in Lincoln's eye, he changed the subject:

"Those are fine children of yours, well brought up, good manners."

"We think Honoria's a great little girl too."

Marion Peters came back from the kitchen. She was a tall woman with worried eyes, who had once possessed a fresh American loveliness. Charlie had never been sensitive to it and was always surprised when people spoke of how pretty she had been. From the first there had been an instinctive antipathy between them.

"Well, how do you find Honoria?" she asked.

"Wonderful. I was astonished how much she's grown in ten months. All the children are looking well."

"We haven't had a doctor for a year. How do you like being back in Paris?"

"It seems very funny to see so few Americans around."

"I'm delighted," Marion said vehemently. "Now at least you can go into a store without their assuming you're a millionaire. We've suffered like everybody, but on the whole it's a good deal pleasanter."

"But it was nice while it lasted," Charlie said. "We were a sort of royalty, almost infallible, with a sort of magic around us. In the bar this afternoon"—he stumbled, seeing his mistake—"there wasn't a man I knew."

She looked at him keenly. "I should think you'd have had enough of bars."

"I only stayed a minute. I take one drink every afternoon, and no more."

"Don't you want a cocktail before dinner?" Lincoln asked.

"I take only one drink every afternoon, and I've had that."

"I hope you keep to it," said Marion.

Her dislike was evident in the coldness with which she spoke, but Charlie only smiled; he had larger plans. Her very aggressiveness gave him an advantage, and he knew enough to wait. He wanted them to initiate the discussion of what they knew had brought him to Paris.

At dinner he couldn't decide whether Honoria was most like him or her mother. Fortunate if she didn't combine the traits of both that had brought them to disaster. A great wave of protectiveness went over him. He thought he knew what to do for her. He believed in character; he wanted to jump back a whole generation and trust in character again as the eternally valuable element. Everything else wore out.

He left soon after dinner, but not to go home. He was curious to see Paris by night with clearer and more judicious eyes than those of other days. He bought a *strapontin* for the Casino and watched Josephine Baker go through her chocolate arabesques.

After an hour he left and strolled toward Montmartre, up the Rue Pigalle into the Place Blanche. The rain had stopped and there were a few people in evening clothes disembarking from taxis in front of cabarets, and *cocottes* prowling singly or in pairs, and many Negroes. He passed a lighted door from which issued music, and stopped with the sense of familiarity; it was Bricktop's, where he had parted with so many hours and so much money. A few doors farther on he found another ancient rendezvous and incautiously put his head inside. Immediately an eager orchestra burst into sound, a pair of professional dancers leaped to their feet and a maître d'hôtel swooped toward him, crying, "Crowd just arriving, sir!" But he withdrew quickly.

"You have to be damn drunk," he thought.

Zelli's was closed, the bleak and sinister cheap hotels surrounding it were dark; up in the Rue Blanche there was more light and a local, colloquial French crowd. The Poet's Cave had disappeared, but the two great mouths of the Café of Heaven and the Café of Hell still yawned—even devoured, as he watched, the meager contents of a tourist bus—a German, a Japanese, and an American couple who glanced at him with frightened eyes.

So much for the effort and ingenuity of Montmartre. All the catering to vice and waste was on an utterly childish scale, and he suddenly realized the meaning of the word "dissipate"—to dissipate into thin air; to make nothing out of something. In the little hours of the night every move from place to place was an enormous human jump, an increase of paying for the privilege of slower and slower motion.

He remembered thousand-franc notes given to an orchestra for playing a single number, hundred-franc notes tossed to a doorman for calling a cab.

But it hadn't been given for nothing.

It had been given, even the most wildly squandered sum, as an offering to destiny that he might not remember the things most worth remembering, the things that now he would always remember—his child taken from his control, his wife escaped to a grave in Vermont.

In the glare of a *brasserie* a woman spoke to him. He bought her some eggs and coffee, and then, eluding her encouraging stare, gave her a twenty-franc note and took a taxi to his hotel.

II

He woke upon a fine fall day—football weather. The depression of yesterday was gone and he liked the people on the streets. At noon he sat opposite Honoria at Le Grand Vatel, the only restaurant he could think of not reminiscent of champagne dinners and long luncheons that began at two and ended in a blurred and vague twilight.

"Now, how about vegetables? Oughtn't you to have some vegetables?"

"Well, yes."

"Here's *épinards* and *chou-fleur* and carrots and *haricots*."

"I'd like *chou-fleur*."

"Wouldn't you like to have two vegetables?"

"I usually only have one at lunch."

The waiter was pretending to be inordinately fond of children. "*Qu'elle est mignonne la petite! Elle parle exactement comme une Française.*"

"How about dessert? Shall we wait and see?"

The waiter disappeared. Honoria looked at her father expectantly.

"What are we going to do?"

"First, we're going to that toy store in the Rue Saint-Honoré and buy you anything you like. And then we're going to the vaudeville at the Empire."

She hesitated. "I like it about the vaudeville, but not the toy store."

"Why not?'

"Well, you brought me this doll." She had it with her. "And I've got lots of things. And we're not rich any more, are we?"

"We never were. But today you are to have anything you want."

"All right," she agreed resignedly.

When there had been her mother and a French nurse he had been inclined to be strict; now he extended himself, reached out for a new tolerance; he must be both parents to her and not shut any of her out of communication.

"I want to get to know you," he said gravely. "First let me introduce myself. My name is Charles J. Wales, of Prague."

"Oh, daddy!" her voice cracked with laughter.

"And who are you, please?" he persisted, and she accepted a rôle immediately: "Honoria Wales, Rue Palatine, Paris."

"Married or single?"

"No, not married. Single."

He indicated the doll. "But I see you have a child, madame."

Unwilling to disinherit it, she took it to her heart and thought quickly: "Yes, I've been married, but I'm not married now. My husband is dead."

He went on quickly, "And the child's name?"

"Simone. That's after my best friend at school."

"I'm very pleased that you're doing so well at school."

"I'm third this month," she boasted. "Elsie"—that was her cousin—"is only about eighteenth, and Richard is about at the bottom."

"You like Richard and Elsie, don't you?"

"Oh, yes. I like Richard quite well and I like her all right."

Cautiously and casually he asked: "And Aunt Marion and Uncle Lincoln—which do you like best?"

"Oh, Uncle Lincoln, I guess."

He was increasingly aware of her presence. As they came in, a murmur of ". . . adorable" followed them, and now the people at the next table bent all their silences upon her, staring as if she were something no more conscious than a flower.

"Why don't I live with you?" she asked suddenly. "Because mamma's dead?"

"You must stay here and learn more French. It would have been hard for daddy to take care of you so well."

"I don't really need much taking care of any more. I do everything for myself."

Going out of the restaurant, a man and a woman unexpectedly hailed him.

"Well, the old Wales!"

"Hello there, Lorraine. . . . Dunc."

Sudden ghosts out of the past: Duncan Schaeffer, a friend from college. Lorraine Quarrles, a lovely, pale blonde of thirty; one of a crowd who had helped them make months into days in the lavish times of three years ago.

"My husband couldn't come this year," she said, in answer to his question. "We're poor as hell. So he gave me two hundred a month and told me I could do my worst on that. . . . This your little girl?"

"What about coming back and sitting down?" Duncan asked.

"Can't do it." He was glad for an excuse. As always, he felt Lorraine's passionate, provocative attraction, but his own rhythm was different now.

"Well, how about dinner?" she asked.

"I'm not free. Give me your address and let me call you."

"Charlie, I believe you're sober," she said judicially. "I honestly believe he's sober, Dunc. Pinch him and see if he's sober."

Charlie indicated Honoria with his head. They both laughed.

"What's your address?" said Duncan skeptically.

He hesitated, unwilling to give the name of his hotel.

"I'm not settled yet. I'd better call you. We're going to see the vaudeville at the Empire."

"There! That's what I want to do," Lorraine said. "I want to see some clowns and acrobats and jugglers. That's just what we'll do, Dunc."

"We've got to do an errand first," said Charlie. "Perhaps we'll see you there."

"All right, you snob. . . . Good-by, beautiful little girl."

"Good-by."

Honoria bobbed politely.

Somehow, an unwelcome encounter. They liked him because he was functioning, because he was serious; they wanted to see him, because he was stronger than they were now, because they wanted to draw a certain sustenance from his strength.

At the Empire, Honoria proudly refused to sit upon her father's folded coat. She was already an individual with a code of her own, and Charlie was more and more absorbed by the desire of putting a little of himself into her before she crystallized utterly. It was hopeless to try to know her in so short a time.

Between the acts they came upon Duncan and Lorraine in the lobby where the band was playing.

"Have a drink?"

"All right, but not up at the bar. We'll take a table."

"The perfect father."

Listening abstractedly to Lorraine, Charlie watched Honoria's eyes leave their table, and he followed them wistfully about the room, wondering what they saw. He met her glance and she smiled.

"I liked that lemonade," she said.

What had she said? What had he expected? Going home in a taxi afterward, he pulled her over until her head rested against his chest.

"Darling, do you ever think about your mother?"

"Yes, sometimes," she answered vaguely.

"I don't want you to forget her. Have you got a picture of her?"

"Yes, I think so. Anyhow, Aunt Marion has. Why don't you want me to forget her?"

"She loved you very much."

"I loved her too."

They were silent for a moment.

"Daddy, I want to come and live with you," she said suddenly.

His heart leaped; he had wanted it to come like this.

"Aren't you perfectly happy?"

"Yes, but I love you better than anybody. And you love me better than anybody, don't you, now that mummy's dead?"

"Of course I do. But you won't always like me best, honey. You'll grow up and meet somebody your own age and go marry him and forget you ever had a daddy."

"Yes, that's true," she agreed tranquilly.

He didn't go in. He was coming back at nine o'clock and he wanted to keep himself fresh and new for the thing he must say then.

"When you're safe inside, just show yourself in that window."

"All right. Good-by, dads, dads, dads, dads."

He waited in the dark street until she appeared, all warm and glowing, in the window above and kissed her fingers out into the night.

III

They were waiting. Marion sat behind the coffee service in a dignified black dinner dress that just faintly suggested mourning. Lincoln was walking up and down with the animation of one who had already been talking. They were as anxious as he was to get into the question. He opened it almost immediately:

"I suppose you know what I want to see you about—why I really came to Paris."

Marion played with the black stars on her necklace and frowned.

"I'm awfully anxious to have a home," he continued. "And I'm awfully anxious to have Honoria in it. I appreciate your taking in Honoria for her mother's sake, but things have changed now"—he hesitated and then continued more forcibly—"changed radically with me, and I want to ask you to reconsider the matter. It would be silly for me to deny that about three years ago I was acting badly—"

Marion looked up at him with hard eyes.

"—but all that's over. As I told you, I haven't had more than a drink a day for over a year, and I take that drink deliberately, so that the idea of alcohol won't get too big in my imagination. You see the idea?"

"No," said Marion succinctly.

"It's a sort of stunt I set myself. It keeps the matter in proportion."

"I get you," said Lincoln. "You don't want to admit it's got any attraction for you."

"Something like that. Sometimes I forget and don't take it. But I try to take it. Anyway, I couldn't afford to drink in my position. The people I represent are more than satisfied with what I've done, and I'm bringing my sister over from Burlington to keep house for me, and I want awfully to have Honoria too. You know that even when her mother and I weren't getting along well we never let anything that happened touch Honoria. I know she's fond of me and I know I'm able to take care of her and—well, there you are. How do you feel about it?"

He knew that now he would have to take a beating. It would last an hour or two hours, and it would be difficult, but if he modulated his inevitable resentment to the chastened attitude of the reformed sinner, he might win his point in the end.

Keep your temper, he told himself. You don't want to be justified. You want Honoria.

Lincoln spoke first: "We've been talking it over ever since we got your letter last month. We're happy to have Honoria here. She's a dear little thing, and we're glad to be able to help her, but of course that isn't the question—"

Marion interrupted suddenly. "How long are you going to stay sober, Charlie?" she asked.

"Permanently, I hope."

"How can anybody count on that?"

"You know I never did drink heavily until I gave up business and came over here with nothing to do. Then Helen and I began to run around with—"

"Please leave Helen out of it. I can't bear to hear you talk about her like that."

He stared at her grimly; he had never been certain how fond of each other the sisters were in life.

"My drinking only lasted about a year and a half—from the time we came over until I—collapsed."

"It was time enough."

"It was time enough," he agreed.

"My duty is entirely to Helen," she said. "I try to think what she would have wanted me to do. Frankly, from the night you did that terrible thing you haven't really existed for me. I can't help that. She was my sister."

"Yes."

"When she was dying she asked me to look out for Honoria. If you hadn't been in a sanitarium then, it might have helped matters."

He had no answer.

"I'll never in my life be able to forget that morning when Helen knocked at my door, soaked to the skin and shivering and said you'd locked her out."

Charlie gripped the sides of the chair. This was more difficult than he expected; he wanted to launch out into a long expostulation and explanation, but he only said: "The night I locked her out—" and she interrupted, "I don't feel up to going over that again."

After a moment's silence Lincoln said: "We're getting off the subject. You want Marion to set aside her legal guardianship and give you Honoria. I think the main point for her is whether she has confidence in you or not."

"I don't blame Marion," Charlie said slowly, "but I think she can have entire confidence in me. I had a good record up to three years ago. Of course, it's within human possibilities I might go wrong any time. But if we wait much longer I'll lose Honoria's childhood and my chance for a home." He shook his head, "I'll simply lose her, don't you see?"

"Yes, I see," said Lincoln.

"Why didn't you think of all this before?" Marion asked.

"I suppose I did, from time to time, but Helen and I were getting along badly. When I consented to the guardianship, I was flat on my back in a sanitarium and the market had cleaned me out. I knew I'd acted badly, and I thought if it would bring any peace to Helen, I'd agree to anything. But now it's different. I'm functioning, I'm behaving damn well, so far as—"

"Please don't swear at me," Marion said.

He looked at her, startled. With each remark the force of her dislike became more and more apparent. She had built up all her fear of life into one wall and faced it toward him. This trivial reproof was possibly the result of some trouble with the cook several hours before. Charlie became increasingly alarmed at leaving Honoria in this atmosphere of hostility against himself; sooner or later it would come out, in a word here, a shake of the head there, and some of that distrust would be irrevocably implanted in Honoria. But he pulled his temper down out of his face and shut it up inside him; he had won a point, for Lincoln realized the absurdity of Marion's remark and asked her lightly since when she had objected to the word "damn."

"Another thing," Charlie said: "I'm able to give her certain advantages now. I'm going to take a French governess to Prague with me. I've got a lease on a new apartment—"

He stopped, realizing that he was blundering. They couldn't be expected to accept with equanimity the fact that his income was again twice as large as their own.

"I suppose you can give her more luxuries than we can," said Marion. "When you were throwing away money we were living along watching every ten francs. . . . I suppose you'll start doing it again."

"Oh, no," he said. "I've learned. I worked hard for ten years, you know—until I got lucky in the market, like so many people. Terribly lucky. It won't happen again."

There was a long silence. All of them felt their nerves straining, and for the first time in a year Charlie wanted a drink. He was sure now that Lincoln Peters wanted him to have his child.

Marion shuddered suddenly; part of her saw that Charlie's feet were planted on the earth now, and her own maternal feeling recognized the naturalness of his desire; but she had lived for a long time with a prejudice—a prejudice founded on a curious disbelief in her sister's happiness, and which, in the shock of one terrible night, had turned to hatred for him. It had all happened at a point in her life where the discouragement of ill health and adverse circumstances made it necessary for her to believe in tangible villainy and a tangible villain.

"I can't help what I think!" she cried out suddenly. "How much you were responsible for Helen's death, I don't know. It's something you'll have to square with your own conscience."

An electric current of agony surged through him; for a moment he was almost on his feet, an unuttered sound echoing in his throat. He hung on to himself for a moment, another moment.

"Hold on there," said Lincoln uncomfortably. "I never thought you were responsible for that."

"Helen died of heart trouble," Charlie said dully.

"Yes, heart trouble." Marion spoke as if the phrase had another meaning for her.

Then, in the flatness that followed her outburst, she saw him plainly and she knew he had somehow arrived at control over the situation. Glancing at her husband, she found no help from him, and as abruptly as if it were a matter of no importance, she threw up the sponge.

"Do what you like!" she cried, springing up from her chair. "She's your child. I'm not the person to stand in your way. I think if it were my child I'd rather see her—" She managed to check herself. "You two decide it. I can't stand this. I'm sick. I'm going to bed."

She hurried from the room; after a moment Lincoln said:

"This has been a hard day for her. You know how strongly she feels—" His voice was almost apologetic: "When a woman gets an idea in her head."

"Of course."

"It's going to be all right. I think she sees now that you—can provide for the child, and so we can't very well stand in your way or Honoria's way."

"Thank you, Lincoln."

"I'd better go along and see how she is."

"I'm going."

He was still trembling when he reached the street, but a walk down the Rue Bonaparte to the *quais* set him up, and as he crossed the Seine, fresh and new by the *quai* lamps, he felt exultant. But back in his room he couldn't sleep. The image of Helen haunted him. Helen whom he had loved so until they had senselessly begun to abuse each other's love, tear it into shreds. On that terrible February night that Marion remembered so vividly, a slow quarrel had gone on for hours. There was a scene at the Florida, and then he attempted to take her home, and then she kissed young Webb at a table; after that there was what she had hysterically said. When he arrived home alone he turned the key in the lock in wild anger. How could he know she would arrive an hour later alone, that there would be a snowstorm in which she wandered about in slippers, too confused to find a taxi? Then the aftermath, her escaping pneumonia by a miracle, and all the attendant horror. They were "reconciled," but that was the beginning of the end, and Marion, who had seen with her own eyes and who imagined it to be one of many scenes from her sister's martyrdom, never forgot.

Going over it again brought Helen nearer, and in the white, soft light that steals upon half sleep near morning he found himself talking to her again. She said that he was perfectly right about Honoria and that she wanted Honoria to be with him. She said she was glad he was being good and doing better. She said a lot of other things—very friendly things—but she was in a swing in a white dress, and swinging faster and faster all the time, so that at the end he could not hear clearly all that she said.

IV

He woke up feeling happy. The door of the world was open again. He made plans, vistas, futures for Honoria and himself, but suddenly he grew sad, remembering all the plans he and Helen had made. She had not planned to die. The present was the thing—work to do and someone to love. But not to love too much, for he knew the injury that a father can do to a daughter or a mother to a son by attaching them too closely: afterward, out in the world, the child would seek in the marriage partner the same blind tenderness and, failing probably to find it, turn against love and life.

It was another bright, crisp day. He called Lincoln Peters at the bank where he worked and asked if he could count on taking Honoria when he left for Prague. Lincoln agreed that there was no reason for delay. One thing—the legal guardianship. Marion wanted to retain that a while longer. She was upset by the whole matter, and it would oil things if she felt that the situation was still in her control for another year. Charlie agreed, wanting only the tangible, visible child.

Then the question of a governess. Charlie sat in a gloomy agency and talked to a cross Béarnaise and to a buxom Breton peasant, neither of whom he could have endured. There were others whom he would see tomorrow.

He lunched with Lincoln Peters at Griffons, trying to keep down his exultation.

"There's nothing quite like your own child," Lincoln said. "But you understand how Marion feels too."

"She's forgotten how hard I worked for seven years there," Charlie said. "She just remembers one night."

"There's another thing." Lincoln hesitated. "While you and Helen were tearing around Europe throwing money away, we were just getting along. I didn't touch any of the prosperity because I never got ahead enough to carry anything but my insurance. I think Marion felt there was some kind of injustice in it—you not even working toward the end, and getting richer and richer."

"It went just as quick as it came," said Charlie.

"Yes, a lot of it stayed in the hands of *chasseurs* and saxophone players and maîtres d'hôtel—well, the big party's over now. I just said that to explain Marion's feeling about those crazy years. If you drop in about six o'clock tonight before Marion's too tired, we'll settle the details on the spot."

Back at his hotel, Charlie found a *pneumatique* that had been redirected from the Ritz bar where Charlie had left his address for the purpose of finding a certain man.

DEAR CHARLIE: You were so strange when we saw you the other day that I wondered if I did something to offend you. If so, I'm not conscious of it. In fact, I have thought about you too much for the last year, and it's always been in the back of my mind that I might see you if I came over here. We *did* have such good times that crazy spring, like the night you and I stole the butcher's tricycle, and the time we tried to call on the president and you had the old derby rim and the wire cane. Everybody seems so old lately, but I don't feel old a bit. Couldn't we get together some time today for old time's sake? I've got a vile hang-over for the moment, but will be feeling better this afternoon and will look for you about five in the sweatshop at the Ritz.

Always devotedly,

LORRAINE.

His first feeling was one of awe that he had actually, in his mature years, stolen a tricycle and pedaled Lorraine all over the Étoile between the small hours and dawn. In retrospect it was a nightmare. Locking out Helen didn't fit in with any other act of his life, but the tricycle incident did—it was one of many. How many weeks or months of dissipation to arrive at that condition of utter irresponsibility?

He tried to picture how Lorraine had appeared to him then—very attractive; Helen was unhappy about it, though she said nothing. Yesterday, in the restaurant, Lorraine had seemed trite, blurred, worn away. He emphatically did not want to see her, and he was glad Alix had not given away his hotel address. It was a relief to think, instead, of Honoria, to think of Sundays spent with her and of saying good morning to her and of knowing she was there in his house at night, drawing her breath in the darkness.

At five he took a taxi and bought presents for all the Peters—a piquant cloth doll, a box of Roman soldiers, flowers for Marion, big linen handkerchiefs for Lincoln.

He saw, when he arrived in the apartment, that Marion had accepted the inevitable. She greeted him now as though he were a recalcitrant member of the family, rather than a menacing outsider. Honoria had been told she was going; Charlie was glad to see that her tact made her conceal her excessive happiness. Only on his lap did she whisper her delight and the question "When?" before she slipped away with the other children.

He and Marion were alone for a minute in the room, and on an impulse he spoke out boldly:

"Family quarrels are bitter things. They don't go according to any rules. They're not aches or wounds; they're more like splits in the skin that won't heal because there's not enough material. I wish you and I could be on better terms."

"Some things are hard to forget," she answered. "It's a question of confidence." There was no answer to this and presently she asked, "When do you propose to take her?"

"As soon as I can get a governess. I hoped the day after tomorrow."

"That's impossible. I've got to get her things in shape. Not before Saturday."

He yielded. Coming back into the room, Lincoln offered him a drink.

"I'll take my daily whisky," he said.

It was warm here, it was a home, people together by a fire. The children felt very safe and important; the mother and father were serious, watchful. They had things to do for the children more important than his visit here. A spoonful of medicine was, after all, more important than the strained relations between Marion and himself. They were not dull people, but they were very much in the grip of life and circumstances. He wondered if he couldn't do something to get Lincoln out of his rut at the bank.

A long peal at the door-bell; the *bonne à tout faire* passed through and went down the corridor. The door opened upon another long ring, and then voices, and the three in the salon looked up expectantly; Richard moved to bring the corridor within his range of vision, and Marion rose. Then the maid came back along the corridor, closely followed by the voices, which developed under the light into Duncan Schaeffer and Lorraine Quarrles.

They were gay, they were hilarious, they were roaring with laughter. For a moment Charlie was astounded; unable to understand how they ferreted out the Peters' address.

"Ah-h-h-!" Duncan wagged his finger roguishly at Charlie. "Ah-h-h!"

They both slid down another cascade of laughter. Anxious and at a loss, Charlie shook hands with them quickly and presented them to Lincoln and Marion. Marion nodded, scarcely speaking. She had drawn back a step toward the fire; her little girl stood beside her, and Marion put an arm about her shoulder.

With growing annoyance at the intrusion, Charlie waited for them to explain themselves. After some concentration Duncan said:

"We came to invite you out to dinner. Lorraine and I insist that all this shishi, cagy business 'bout your address got to stop."

Charlie came closer to them, as if to force them backward down the corridor.

"Sorry, but I can't. Tell me where you'll be and I'll phone you in half an hour."

This made no impression. Lorraine sat down suddenly on the side of a chair, and focusing her eyes on Richard, cried, "Oh, what a nice little boy! Come here, little boy." Richard glanced at his mother, but did not move. With a perceptible shrug of her shoulders, Lorraine turned back to Charlie:

"Come and dine. Sure your cousins won' mine. See you so sel'om. Or solemn."

"I can't," said Charlie sharply. "You two have dinner and I'll phone you."

Her voice became suddenly unpleasant. "All right, we'll go. But I remember once when you hammered on my door at four A.M. I was enough of a good sport to give you a drink. Come on, Dunc."

Still in slow motion, with blurred, angry faces, with uncertain feet, they retired along the corridor.

"Good night," Charlie said.

"Good night!" responded Lorraine emphatically.

When he went back into the salon Marion had not moved, only now her son was standing in the circle of her other arm. Lincoln was still swinging Honoria back and forth like a pendulum from side to side.

"What an outrage!" Charlie broke out. "What an absolute outrage!"

Neither of them answered. Charlie dropped into an armchair, picked up his drink, set it down again and said:

"People I haven't seen for two years having the colossal nerve—"

He broke off. Marion had made the sound "Oh!" in one swift, furious breath, turned her body from him with a jerk and left the room.

Lincoln set down Honoria carefully.

"You children go in and start your soup," he said, and when they obeyed, he said to Charlie:

"Marion's not well and she can't stand shocks. That kind of people make her really physically sick."

"I didn't tell them to come here. They wormed your name out of somebody. They deliberately—"

"Well, it's too bad. It doesn't help matters. Excuse me a minute."

Left alone, Charlie sat tense in his chair. In the next room he could hear the children eating, talking in monosyllables, already oblivious to the scene between their elders. He heard a murmur of conversation from a farther room and then the ticking bell of a telephone receiver picked up, and in a panic he moved to the other side of the room and out of earshot.

In a minute Lincoln came back. "Look here, Charlie. I think we'd better call off dinner for tonight. Marion's in bad shape."

"Is she angry with me?"

"Sort of," he said, almost roughly. "She's not strong and—"

"You mean she's changed her mind about Honoria?"

"She's pretty bitter right now. I don't know. You phone me at the bank tomorrow."

"I wish you'd explain to her I never dreamed these people would come here. I'm just as sore as you are."

"I couldn't explain anything to her now."

Charlie got up. He took his coat and hat and started down the corridor. Then he opened the door of the dining room and said in a strange voice, "Good night, children."

Honoria rose and ran around the table to hug him.

"Good night, sweetheart," he said vaguely, and then trying to make his voice more tender, trying to conciliate something, "Good night, dear children."

v

Charlie went directly to the Ritz bar with the furious idea of finding Lorraine and Duncan, but they were not there, and he realized that in any case there was nothing he could do. He had not touched his drink at the Peters, and now he ordered a whisky-and-soda. Paul came over to say hello.

"It's a great change," he said sadly. "We do about half the business we did. So many fellows I hear about back in the States lost everything, maybe not in the first crash, but then in the second. Your friend George Hardt lost every cent, I hear. Are you back in the States?"

"No, I'm in business in Prague."

"I heard that you lost a lot in the crash."

"I did," and he added grimly, "but I lost everything I wanted in the boom."

"Selling short."

"Something like that."

Again the memory of those days swept over him like a nightmare—the people they had met travelling; then people who couldn't add a row of figures or speak a coherent sentence. The little man Helen had consented to dance with at the ship's party, who had insulted her ten feet from the table; the women and girls carried screaming with drink or drugs out of public places—

—The men who locked their wives out in the snow, because the snow of twenty-nine wasn't real snow. If you didn't want it to be snow, you just paid some money.

He went to the phone and called the Peters' apartment; Lincoln answered.

"I called up because this thing is on my mind. Has Marion said anything definite?"

"Marion's sick," Lincoln answered shortly. "I know this thing isn't altogether your fault, but I can't have her go to pieces about it. I'm afraid we'll have to let it slide for six months; I can't take the chance of working her up to this state again."

"I see."

"I'm sorry, Charlie."

He went back to his table. His whisky glass was empty, but he shook his head when Alix looked at it questioningly. There wasn't much he could do now except send Honoria some things; he would send her a lot of things tomorrow. He thought rather angrily that this was just money—he had given so many people money. . . .

"No, no more," he said to another waiter. "What do I owe you?"

He would come back some day; they couldn't make him pay forever. But he wanted his child, and nothing was much good now, beside that fact. He wasn't young any more, with a lot of nice thoughts and dreams to have by himself. He was absolutely sure Helen wouldn't have wanted him to be so alone.

WILLIAM FAULKNER
1897–1962

Faulkner was born in Union County, Mississippi. His family had been important in the political, economic, and cultural life of northern Mississippi for three generations, but their power and influence were declining, and for a time it looked as if young William might be its least distinguished member. He spent most of his youth hunting, fishing, and playing baseball. But he was gifted at drawing and telling stories, and maintained from an early age that he wanted to be a writer like his great-grandfather, William Cuthbert Faulkner, whose *White Rose of Memphis* had gone through thirty-five editions after its publication in 1880. During World War I Faulkner was turned down by the U.S. Army Air Corps because he was too short, but was accepted for flight training in the Royal Canadian Air Force. He wanted to fly in combat, but the war ended too soon, and he was injured when he and a friend celebrated Armistice Day by stunting over the field and crashing through a hangar roof.

Returning to Oxford, Mississippi, he continued to read and to write, and took courses at the University of Mississippi. But he was neither a regular nor a successful student. Nor was he having any luck trying to place his fiction and poetry with magazines. Finally, a friend subsidized a private printing of a volume of Faulkner's poetry, *The Marble Faun*, in 1924. In later life Faulkner spoke of himself as a "failed poet," who had turned to fiction only because his poetry was not good enough.

In 1925 he moved to New Orleans, where he was admitted to the circle of writers that gathered around Sherwood Anderson, and began to publish sketches in the Sunday feature section of the New Orleans *Times Picayune*. Then, with the help of Anderson, he was able to get his first novel, *Soldier's Pay*, published in 1926. In his third novel, *Sartoris* (1929), he began to find his proper material and realize his strength as a writer. With this work he began his immense chronicle of an imaginary Mississippi county, based on the history of the area around his home in Oxford, Mississippi. His Yoknapatawpha County has become a permanent feature in the international literary landscape. Among his most highly regarded works are *Light in August* (1932) and *Absalom, Absalom!* (1936), and two collections of short fiction which have the shape and movement of a novel: *The Unvanquished* (1938) and *Go Down, Moses* (1942). In 1950 he received the Nobel Prize for literature.

A Rose for Emily

I

When Miss Emily Grierson died, our whole town went to her funeral: the men through a sort of respectful affection for a fallen monument, the women mostly out of curiosity to see the inside of her house, which no one save an old manservant—a combined gardener and cook—had seen in at least ten years.

It was a big, squarish frame house that had once been white, decorated with cupolas and spires and scrolled balconies in the heavily lightsome style of the seventies, set on what had once been our most select street. But garages and cotton gins had encroached and obliterated even the august names of that neighborhood; only Miss Emily's house was left, lifting its stubborn and coquettish decay above the cotton wagons and the gasoline pumps—an eyesore among eyesores. And now Miss Emily had gone to join the representatives of those august names where they lay in the cedar-bemused cemetery among the ranked and anonymous graves of Union and Confederate soldiers who fell at the battle of Jefferson.

Alive, Miss Emily had been a tradition, a duty, and a care; a sort of hereditary obligation upon the town, dating from that day in 1894 when Colonel Sartoris, the mayor—he who fathered the edict that no Negro woman should appear on the streets without an apron—remitted her taxes, the dispensation dating from the death of her father on into perpetuity. Not that Miss Emily would have accepted charity. Colonel Sartoris invented an involved tale to the effect that Miss Emily's father had loaned money to the town, which the town, as a matter of business, preferred this way of repaying. Only a man of Colonel Sartoris' generation and thought could have invented it, and only a woman could have believed it.

When the next generation, with its more modern ideas, became mayors and aldermen, this arrangement created some little dissatisfaction. On the first of the year they mailed her a tax notice. February came, and there was no reply. They wrote her a formal letter, asking her to call at the sheriff's office at her convenience. A week later the mayor wrote her himself, offering to call or to send his car for her, and received in reply a note on paper of an archaic shape, in a thin, flowing calligraphy in faded ink, to the effect that she no longer went out at all. The tax notice was also enclosed, without comment.

They called a special meeting of the Board of Aldermen. A deputation waited upon her, knocked at the door through which no visitor had passed since she ceased giving china-painting lessons eight or ten years earlier. They were admitted by the old Negro into a dim hall from which a stairway mounted into still more shadow. It smelled of dust and disuse—a close, dank smell. The Negro led them into the parlor. It was furnished in heavy, leather-covered furniture. When the Negro opened the blinds of one window, they could see that the leather was cracked; and when they sat down, a faint dust rose sluggishly about their thighs, spinning with slow motions in the single sun-ray. On a tarnished gilt easel before the fireplace stood a crayon portrait of Miss Emily's father.

They rose when she entered—a small, fat woman in black, with a thin gold chain descending to her waist and vanishing into her belt, leaning on an ebony cane with a tarnished gold head. Her skeleton was small and spare; perhaps that was why what would have been merely plumpness in another was obesity in her. She looked bloated, like a body long submerged in motionless water, and of that pallid hue. Her eyes, lost in the fatty ridges of her face, looked like two small pieces of coal pressed into a lump of dough as they moved from one face to another while the visitors stated their errand.

She did not ask them to sit. She just stood in the door and listened quietly until the spokesman came to a stumbling halt. Then they could hear the invisible watch ticking at the end of the gold chain.

Her voice was dry and cold. "I have no taxes in Jefferson. Colonel Sartoris explained it to me. Perhaps one of you can gain access to the city records and satisfy yourselves."

"But we have. We are the city authorities, Miss Emily. Didn't you get a notice from the sheriff, signed by him?"

"I received a paper, yes," Miss Emily said. "Perhaps he considers himself the sheriff . . . I have no taxes in Jefferson."

"But there is nothing on the books to show that, you see. We must go by the—"

"See Colonel Sartoris." (Colonel Sartoris had been dead almost ten years.) "I have no taxes in Jefferson. Tobe!" The Negro appeared. "Show these gentlemen out."

II

So she vanquished them, horse and foot, just as she had vanquished their fathers thirty years before about the smell. That was two years after her father's death and a short time after her sweetheart—the one we believed would marry her—had deserted her. After her father's death she went out very little; after her sweetheart went away, people hardly saw her at all. A few of the ladies had the temerity to call, but were not received, and the only sign of life about the place was the Negro man—a young man then—going in and out with a market basket.

"Just as if a man—any man—could keep a kitchen properly," the ladies said; so they were not surprised when the smell developed. It was another link between the gross, teeming world and the high and mighty Griersons.

A neighbor, a woman, complained to the mayor, Judge Stevens, eighty years old.

"But what will you have me do about it, madam?" he said.

"Why, send her word to stop it," the woman said. "Isn't there a law?"

"I'm sure that won't be necessary," Judge Stevens said. "It's probably just a snake or a rat that nigger of hers killed in the yard. I'll speak to him about it."

The next day he received two more complaints, one from a man who came in diffident deprecation. "We really must do something about it, Judge. I'd be the last one in the world to bother Miss Emily, but we've got to do something." That night the Board of Aldermen met—three graybeards and one younger man, a member of the rising generation.

"It's simple enough," he said. "Send her word to have her place cleaned up. Give her a certain time to do it in, and if she don't . . ."

"Dammit, sir," Judge Stevens said, "will you accuse a lady to her face of smelling bad?"

So the next night, after midnight, four men crossed Miss Emily's lawn and slunk about the house like burglars, sniffing along the base of the brickwork and at the cellar openings while one of them performed a regular sowing motion with his hand out of a sack slung from his shoulder. They broke open the cellar door and sprinkled lime there, and in all the outbuildings. As they recrossed the lawn, a window that had been dark was lighted and Miss Emily sat in it, the light behind her, and her upright torso motionless as that of an idol. They crept quietly across the lawn and into the shadow of the locusts that lined the street. After a week or two the smell went away.

That was when people had begun to feel really sorry for her. People in our town, remembering how old lady Wyatt, her great-aunt, had gone completely crazy at last, believed that the Griersons held themselves a little too high for what they really were. None of the young men were quite good enough for Miss Emily and such. We had long thought of them as a tableau; Miss Emily a slender figure in white in the background, her father a spraddled silhouette in the foreground, his back to her and clutching a horsewhip, the two of them framed by the back-flung front door. So when she got to be thirty and was still single, we were not pleased exactly, but vindicated; even with insanity in the family she wouldn't have turned down all of her chances if they had really materialized.

When her father died, it got about that the house was all that was left to her; and in a way, people were glad. At last they could pity Miss Emily. Being left alone, and a pauper, she had become humanized. Now she too would know the old thrill and the old despair of a penny more or less.

The day after his death all the ladies prepared to call at the house and offer condolence and aid, as is our custom. Miss Emily met them at the door, dressed as usual and with no trace of grief on her face. She told them that her father was not dead. She did that for three days, with the ministers calling on her, and the doctors, trying to persuade her to let them dispose of the body. Just as they were about to resort to law and force, she broke down, and they buried her father quickly.

We did not say she was crazy then. We believed she had to do that. We remembered all the young men her father had driven away, and we knew that with nothing left, she would have to cling to that which had robbed her, as people will.

III

She was sick for a long time. When we saw her again, her hair was cut short, making her look like a girl, with a vague resemblance to those angels in colored church windows—sort of tragic and serene.

The town had just let the contracts for paving the sidewalks, and in the summer after her father's death they began the work. The construction company came with niggers and mules and machinery, and a foreman named Homer Barron, a Yankee—a big, dark, ready man, with a big voice and eyes lighter than his face. The little boys would follow in groups to hear him cuss the niggers, and the niggers singing in time to the rise and fall of picks. Pretty soon he knew everybody in town. Whenever you heard a lot of laughing anywhere about the square, Homer Barron would be in the center of the group. Presently we began to see him and Miss Emily on Sunday afternoons driving in the yellow-wheeled buggy and the matched team of bays from the livery stable.

At first we were glad that Miss Emily would have an interest, because the ladies all said, "Of course a Grierson would not think seriously of a Northerner, a day laborer." But there were still others, older people, who said that even grief could not cause a real lady to forget noblesse oblige—without calling it noblesse oblige. They just said, "Poor Emily. Her kinsfolk should come to her." She had some kin in Alabama; but years ago her father had fallen out with them over the estate of old lady Wyatt, the crazy woman, and there was no communication between the two families. They had not even been represented at the funeral.

And as soon as the old people said, "Poor Emily," the whispering began. "Do you suppose it's really so?" they said to one another. "Of course it is. What else could . . ." This behind their hands; rustling of craned silk and satin behind jalousies closed upon the sun of Sunday afternoon as the thin, swift clop-clop-clop of the matched team passed: "Poor Emily."

She carried her head high enough—even when we believed that she was fallen. It was as if she demanded more than ever the recognition of her dignity as the last Grierson; as if it had wanted that touch of earthiness to reaffirm her imperviousness. Like when she bought the rat poison, the arsenic. That was over a year after they had begun to say "Poor Emily," and while the two female cousins were visiting her.

"I want some poison," she said to the druggist. She was over thirty then, still a slight woman, though thinner than usual, with cold, haughty black eyes in a face the flesh of which was strained across the temples and about the eye-sockets as you imagine a lighthouse-keeper's face ought to look. "I want some poison," she said.

"Yes, Miss Emily. What kind? For rats and such? I'd recom—"

"I want the best you have. I don't care what kind."

The druggist named several. "They'll kill anything up to an elephant. But what you want is—"

"Arsenic," Miss Emily said. "Is that a good one?"

"Is . . . arsenic? Yes, ma'am. But what you want—"

"I want arsenic."

The druggist looked down at her. She looked back at him, erect, her face like a strained flag. "Why, of course," the druggist said. "If that's what you want. But the law requires you to tell what you are going to use it for."

Miss Emily just stared at him, her head tilted back in order to look him eye for eye, until he looked away and went and got the arsenic and wrapped it up. The Negro delivery boy brought her the package; the druggist didn't come back. When she opened the package at home there was written on the box, under the skull and bones: "For rats."

IV

So the next day we all said, "She will kill herself"; and we said it would be the best thing. When she had first begun to be seen with Homer Barron, we had said, "She will marry him." Then we said, "She will persuade him yet," because Homer himself had remarked—he liked men, and it was known that he drank with the younger men in the Elks' Club—that he was not a marrying man. Later we said, "Poor Emily" behind the jalousies as they passed on Sunday afternoon in the glittering buggy, Miss Emily with her head high and Homer Barron with his hat cocked and a cigar in his teeth, reins and whip in a yellow glove.

Then some of the ladies began to say that it was a disgrace to the town and a bad example to the young people. The men did not want to interfere, but at last the ladies forced the Baptist minister—Miss Emily's people were Episcopal—to call upon her. He would never divulge what happened during that interview, but he refused to go back again. The next Sunday they again drove about the streets, and the following day the minister's wife wrote to Miss Emily's relations in Alabama.

So she had blood-kin under her roof again and we sat back to watch developments. At first nothing happened. Then we were sure that they were to be married. We learned that Miss Emily had been to the jeweler's and ordered a man's toilet set in silver, with the letters H.B. on each piece. Two days later we learned that she had bought a complete outfit of men's clothing, including a nightshirt, and we said, "They are married." We were really glad. We were glad because the two female cousins were even more Grierson than Miss Emily had ever been.

So we were not surprised when Homer Barron—the streets had been finished some time since—was gone. We were a little disappointed that there was not a public blowing-off, but we believed that he had gone on to prepare for Miss Emily's coming, or to give her a chance to get rid of the cousins. (By that time it was a cabal, and we were all Miss Emily's allies to help circumvent the cousins.) Sure enough, after another week they departed. And, as we had expected all along, within three days Homer Barron was back in town. A neighbor saw the Negro man admit him at the kitchen door at dusk one evening.

And that was the last we saw of Homer Barron. And of Miss Emily for some time. The Negro man went in and out with the market basket, but the front door remained closed. Now and then we would see her at a window for a moment, as the men did that night when they sprinkled the lime, but for almost six months she did not appear on the streets. Then we knew that this was to be expected too; as if that quality of her father which had thwarted her woman's life so many times had been too virulent and too furious to die.

When we next saw Miss Emily, she had grown fat and her hair was turning gray. During the next few years it grew grayer and grayer until it attained an even pepper-and-salt iron-gray, when it ceased turning. Up to the day of her death at seventy-four it was still that vigorous iron-gray, like the hair of an active man.

From that time on her front door remained closed, save for a period of six or seven years, when she was about forty, during which she gave lessons in china-painting. She fitted up a studio in one of the downstairs rooms, where the daughters and granddaughters of Colonel Sartoris' contemporaries were sent to her with the same regularity and in the same spirit that they were sent to church on Sundays with a twenty-five-cent piece for the collection plate. Meanwhile her taxes had been remitted.

Then the newer generation became the backbone and the spirit of the town, and the painting pupils grew up and fell away and did not send their children to her with boxes of color and tedious brushes and pictures cut from the ladies' magazines. The front door closed upon the last one and remained closed for good. When the town got free postal delivery, Miss Emily alone refused to let them fasten the metal numbers above her door and attach a mailbox to it. She would not listen to them.

Daily, monthly, yearly we watched the Negro grow grayer and more stooped, going in and out with the market basket. Each December we sent her a tax notice, which would be returned by the post office a week later, unclaimed. Now and then we would see her in one of the downstairs windows—she had evidently shut up the top floor of the house—like the carven torso of an idol in a niche, looking or not looking at us, we could never tell which. Thus she passed from generation to generation—dear, inescapable, impervious, tranquil, and perverse.

And so she died. Fell ill in the house filled with dust and shadows, with only a doddering Negro man to wait on her. We did not even know she was sick; we had long since given up trying to get any information from the Negro. He talked to no one, probably not even to her, for his voice had grown harsh and rusty, as if from disuse.

She died in one of the downstairs rooms, in a heavy walnut bed with a curtain, her gray head propped on a pillow yellow and moldy with age and lack of sunlight.

V

The Negro met the first of the ladies at the front door and let them in, with their hushed, sibilant voices and their quick, curious glances, and then he disappeared. He walked right through the house and out the back and was not seen again.

The two female cousins came at once. They held the funeral on the second day, with the town coming to look at Miss Emily beneath a mass of bought flowers, with the crayon face of her father musing profoundly above the bier and the ladies sibilant and macabre; and the very old men—some in their brushed Confederate uniforms—on the porch and the lawn, talking of Miss Emily as if she had been a contemporary of theirs, believing that they had danced with her and courted her perhaps, confusing time with its mathematical progression, as the old do, to whom all the past is not a diminishing road but, instead, a huge meadow which no winter ever quite touches, divided from them now by the narrow bottle-neck of the most recent decade of years.

Already we knew that there was one room in that region above stairs which no one had seen in forty years, and which would have to be forced. They waited until Miss Emily was decently in the ground before they opened it.

The violence of breaking down the door seemed to fill this room with pervading dust. A thin, acrid pall as of the tomb seemed to lie everywhere upon this room decked and furnished as for a bridal: upon the valance curtains of faded rose color, upon the rose-shaded lights, upon the dressing table, upon the delicate array of crystal and the man's toilet things backed with tarnished silver, silver so tarnished that the monogram was obscured. Among them lay a collar and tie, as if they had just been removed, which, lifted, left upon the surface a pale crescent in the dust. Upon a chair hung the suit, carefully folded; beneath it the two mute shoes and the discarded socks.

The man himself lay in the bed.

For a long while we just stood there, looking down at the profound and fleshless grin. The body had apparently once lain in the attitude of an embrace, but now the long sleep that outlasts love, that conquers even the grimace of love, had cuckolded him. What was left of him, rotted beneath what was left of the nightshirt, had become inextricable from the bed in which he lay; and upon him and upon the pillow beside him lay that even coating of the patient and biding dust.

Then we noticed that in the second pillow was the indentation of a head. One of us lifted something from it, and leaning forward, that faint and invisible dust dry and acrid in the nostrils, we saw a long strand of iron-gray hair.

ERNEST HEMINGWAY
1899 1961

Born in Oak Park, Illinois, the son of a doctor and a music teacher, Ernest Hemingway went to school in Oak Park and spent his summers in the upper peninsula of Michigan, where his father taught him early to hunt and fish. He was a physically active and popular boy, good at writing but bored with school. A couple of times he simply left and went on the road, but he worked on the school newspaper, graduated, and tried to enlist in the Army for World War I. A bad eye prevented that, so he went into newspaper work and then enlisted as an ambulance driver for the Red Cross in Italy, where he saw plenty of combat, was badly wounded and showed genuine heroism under fire. After the war and some newspaper work in Chicago and Toronto, Hemingway moved to Europe where he lived with his first wife, mostly in Paris. There he met Ezra Pound and Gertrude Stein, who christened Hemingway and his young friends a "lost generation." There, too, Hemingway began to write the stories and novels that made his reputation, beginning with *In Our Time* (1925) and *The Sun Also Rises* (1926). In later years he became more of a public figure and less of a writer, as he hardened into a symbol of patriarchal machismo known as "Papa." But he had a fine success with *The Old Man and the Sea* (1952) and won the

Nobel Prize in 1954. In 1961, in ill health and unable to write, he loaded his silver-inlaid double-barreled shotgun, put both barrels in his mouth and pulled the triggers.

Hills Like White Elephants

The hills across the valley of the Ebro were long and white. On this side there was no shade and no trees and the station was between two lines of rails in the sun. Close against the side of the station there was the warm shadow of the building and a curtain, made of strings of bamboo beads, hung across the open door into the bar, to keep out flies. The American and the girl with him sat at a table in the shade, outside the building. It was very hot and the express from Barcelona would come in forty minutes. It stopped at this junction for two minutes and went on to Madrid.

"What should we drink?" the girl asked. She had taken off her hat and put it on the table.

"It's pretty hot," the man said.

"Let's drink beer."

"Dos cervezas," the man said into the curtain.

"Big ones?" a woman asked from the doorway.

"Yes. Two big ones."

The woman brought two glasses of beer and two felt pads. She put the felt pads and the beer glasses on the table and looked at the man and the girl. The girl was looking off at the line of hills. They were white in the sun and the country was brown and dry.

"They look like white elephants," she said.

"I've never seen one," the man drank his beer.

"No, you wouldn't have."

"I might have," the man said. "Just because you say I wouldn't have doesn't prove anything."

The girl looked at the bead curtain. "They've painted something on it," she said. "What does it say?"

"Anis del Toro. It's a drink."

"Could we try it?"

The man called "Listen" through the curtain. The woman came out from the bar.

"Four reales."

"We want two Anis del Toro."

"With water?"

"Do you want it with water?"

"I don't know," the girl said. "Is it good with water?"

"It's all right."

"You want them with water?" asked the woman.

"Yes, with water."

"It tastes like licorice," the girl said and put the glass down.

"That's the way with everything."

"Yes," said the girl. "Everything tastes of licorice. Especially all the things you've waited so long for, like absinthe."

"Oh, cut it out."

"You started it," the girl said. "I was being amused. I was having a fine time."

"Well, let's try and have a fine time."

"All right. I was trying. I said the mountains looked like white elephants. Wasn't that bright?"

"That was bright."

"I wanted to try this new drink. That's all we do, isn't it—look at things and try new drinks?"

"I guess so."

The girl looked across at the hills.

"They're lovely hills," she said. "They don't really look like white elephants. I just meant the coloring of their skin through the trees."

"Should we have another drink?"

"All right."

The warm wind blew the bead curtain against the table.

"The beer's nice and cool," the man said.

"It's lovely," the girl said.

"It's really an awfully simple operation, Jig," the man said. "It's not really an operation at all."

The girl looked at the ground the table legs rested on.

"I know you wouldn't mind it, Jig. It's really not anything. It's just to let the air in."

The girl did not say anything.

"I'll go with you and I'll stay with you all the time. They just let the air in and then it's all perfectly natural."

"Then what will we do afterward?"

"We'll be fine afterward. Just like we were before."

"What makes you think so?"

"That's the only thing that bothers us. It's the only thing that's made us unhappy."

The girl looked at the bead curtain, put her hand out and took hold of two of the strings of beads.

"And you think then we'll be all right and be happy."

"I know we will. You don't have to be afraid. I've known lots of people that have done it."

"So have I," said the girl. "And afterward they were all so happy."

"Well," the man said, "if you don't want to you don't have to. I wouldn't have you do it if you didn't want to. But I know it's perfectly simple."

"And you really want to?"

"I think it's the best thing to do. But I don't want you to do it if you don't really want to."

"And if I do it you'll be happy and things will be like they were and you'll love me?"

"I love you now. You know I love you."

"I know. But if I do it, then it will be nice again if I say things are like white elephants, and you'll like it?"

"I'll love it. I love it now but I just can't think about it. You know how I get when I worry."

"If I do it you won't ever worry?"

"I won't worry about that because it's perfectly simple."

"Then I'll do it. Because I don't care about me."

"What do you mean?"

"I don't care about me."

"Well, I care about you."

"Oh, yes. But I don't care about me. And I'll do it and then everything will be fine."

"I don't want you to do it if you feel that way."

The girl stood up and walked to the end of the station. Across, on the other side, were fields of grain and trees along the banks of the Ebro. Far away, beyond the river, were mountains. The shadow of a cloud moved across the field of grain and she saw the river through the trees.

"And we could have all this," she said. "And we could have everything and every day we make it more impossible."

"What did you say?"

"I said we could have everything."

"We can have everything."

"No, we can't."

"We can have the whole world."

"No, we can't."

"We can go everywhere."

"No, we can't. It isn't ours any more."

"It's ours."

"No, it isn't. And once they take it away, you never get it back."

"But they haven't taken it away."

"We'll wait and see."

"Come on back in the shade," he said. "You mustn't feel that way."

"I don't feel any way," the girl said. "I just know things."

"I don't want you to do anything that you don't want to do—"

"Nor that isn't good for me," she said. "I know. Could we have another beer?"

"All right. But you've got to realize—"

"I realize," the girl said. "Can't we maybe stop talking?"

They sat down at the table and the girl looked across at the hills on the dry side of the valley and the man looked at her and at the table.

"You've got to realize," he said, "that I don't want you to do it if you don't want to. I'm perfectly willing to go through with it if it means anything to you."

"Doesn't it mean anything to you? We could get along."

"Of course it does. But I don't want anybody but you. I don't want any one else. And I know it's perfectly simple."

"Yes, you know it's perfectly simple."

"It's all right for you to say that, but I do know it."

"Would you do something for me now?"

"I'd do anything for you."

"Would you please please please please please please please stop talking?"

He did not say anything but looked at the bags against the wall of the station. There were labels on them from all the hotels where they had spent nights.

"But I don't want you to," he said, "I don't care anything about it."

"I'll scream," the girl said.

The woman came out through the curtains with two glasses of beer and put them down on the damp felt pads. "The train comes in five minutes," she said.

"What did she say?" asked the girl.

"That the train is coming in five minutes."

The girl smiled brightly at the woman, to thank her.

"I'd better take the bags over to the other side of the station," the man said. She smiled at him.

"All right. Then come back and we'll finish the beer."

He picked up the two heavy bags and carried them around the station to the other tracks. He looked up the tracks but could not see the train. Coming back, he walked through the barroom, where people waiting for the train were drinking. He drank an Anis at the bar and looked at the people. They were all waiting reasonably for the train. He went out through the bead curtain. She was sitting at the table and smiled at him.

"Do you feel better?" he asked.

"I feel fine," she said. "There's nothing wrong with me. I feel fine."

MORLEY CALLAGHAN
1903–

Canada's first professional writer, the first to devote his life to the vocation of writing, Toronto-born Morley Callaghan is a graduate of the University of Toronto and Osgoode Hall Law School. In 1928 his first novel, *Strange Fugitive*, was published; the same year he was called to the bar. Fiction, however, commanded his complete attention, and he never practiced law. In April 1929 he traveled with his wife to Paris, where their literary circle of friends included Ernest Hemingway, with whom Callaghan had already worked as a fellow-journalist on the *Toronto Star*, F. Scott Fitzgerald, James Joyce, and many others. The following autumm he returned to Toronto, which has been and remains his physical and literary home. His sojourn in Paris is the subject of his beautiful memoir, *That Summer in Paris* (1963). The author of fourteen novels and more than a hundred shorter pieces of fiction, he focuses his writing on individual lives, often exploring the moral courage and innate dignity of his characters as they confront adverse and demeaning social situations.

A Cap for Steve

Dave Diamond, a poor man, a carpenter's assistant, was a small, wiry, quick-tempered individual who had learned how to make every dollar count in his home. His wife, Anna, had been sick a lot, and his twelve-year-old son, Steve, had to be kept in school. Steve, a big-eyed, shy kid, ought to have known the value of money as well as Dave did. It had been ground into him.

But the boy was crazy about baseball, and after school, when he could have been working as a delivery boy or selling papers, he played ball with the kids. His failure to appreciate that the family needed a few extra dollars disgusted Dave. Around the house he wouldn't let Steve talk about baseball, and he scowled when he saw him hurrying off with his glove after dinner.

When the Phillies came to town to play an exhibition game with the home team and Steve pleaded to be taken to the ball park, Dave, of course, was outraged. Steve knew they couldn't afford it. But he had got his mother on his side. Finally Dave made a bargain with them. He said that if Steve came home after school and worked hard helping to make some kitchen shelves he would take him that night to the ball park.

Steve worked hard, but Dave was still resentful. They had to coax him to put on his good suit. When they started out Steve held aloof, feeling guilty, and they walked down the street like strangers; then Dave glanced at Steve's face and, half-ashamed, took his arm more cheerfully.

As the game went on, Dave had to listen to Steve's recitation of the batting average of every Philly that stepped up to the plate; the time the boy must have wasted learning these averages began to appal him. He showed it so plainly that Steve felt guilty again and was silent.

After the game Dave let Steve drag him onto the field to keep him company while he tried to get some autographs from the Philly players, who were being hemmed in by gangs of kids blocking the way to the club-house. But Steve, who was shy, let the other kids block him off from the players. Steve would push his way in, get blocked out, and come back to stand mournfully beside Dave. And Dave grew impatient. He was wasting valuable time. He wanted to get home; Steve knew it and was worried.

Then the big, blond Philly outfielder, Eddie Condon, who had been held up by a gang of kids tugging at his arm and thrusting their score cards at him, broke loose and made a run for the club-house. He was jostled, and his blue cap with the red peak, tilted far back on his head, fell off. It fell at Steve's feet, and Steve stooped quickly and grabbed it. "Okay, son," the outfielder called, turning back. But Steve, holding the hat in both hands, only stared at him.

"Give him his cap, Steve," Dave said, smiling apologetically at the big outfielder who towered over them. But Steve drew the hat closer to his chest. In an awed trance he looked up at big Eddie Condon. It was an embarrassing moment. All the other kids were watching. Some shouted. "Give him his cap."

"My cap, son," Eddie Condon said, his hand out.

"Hey, Steve," Dave said, and he gave him a shake. But he had to jerk the cap out of Steve's hands.

"Here you are," he said.

The outfielder, noticing Steve's white, worshipping face and pleading eyes, grinned and then shrugged. "Aw, let him keep it," he said.

"No, Mister Condon, you don't need to do that," Steve protested.

"It's happened before. Forget it," Eddie Condon said, and he trotted away to the club-house.

Dave handed the cap to Steve; envious kids circled around them and Steve said, "He said I could keep it, Dad. You heard him, didn't you?"

"Yeah, I heard him," Dave admitted. The wonder in Steve's face made him smile. He took the boy by the arm and they hurried off the field.

On the way home Dave couldn't get him to talk about the game; he couldn't get him to take his eyes off the cap. Steve could hardly believe in his own happiness. "See," he said suddenly, and he showed Dave that Eddie Condon's name was printed on the sweatband. Then he went on dreaming. Finally he put the cap on his head and turned to Dave with a slow, proud smile. The cap was away too big for him; it fell down over his ears. "Never mind," Dave said. "You can get your mother to take a tuck in the back."

When they got home Dave was tired and his wife didn't understand the cap's importance, and they couldn't get Steve to go to bed. He swaggered around wearing the cap and looking in the mirror every ten minutes. He took the cap to bed with him.

Dave and his wife had a cup of coffee in the kitchen, and Dave told her again how they had got the cap. They agreed that their boy must have an attractive quality that showed in his face and that Eddie Condon must have been drawn to him—why else would he have singled Steve out from all the kids?

But Dave got tired of the fuss Steve made over that cap and of the way he wore it from the time he got up in the morning until the time he went to bed. Some kid was always coming in, wanting to try on the cap. It was childish, Dave said, for Steve to go around assuming that the cap made him important in the neighbourhood, and to keep telling them how he had become a leader in the park a few blocks away where he played ball in the evenings. And Dave wouldn't stand for Steve's keeping the cap on while he was eating. He was always scolding his wife for accepting Steve's explanation that he'd forgotten he had it on. Just the same, it was remarkable what a little thing like a ball cap could do for a kid, Dave admitted to his wife as he smiled to himself.

One night Steve was late coming home from the park. Dave didn't realize how late it was until he put down his newspaper and watched his wife at the window. Her restlessness got on his nerves. "See what comes from encouraging the boy to hang around with those park loafers," he said. "I don't encourage him," she protested. "You do," he insisted irritably, for he was really worried now. A gang hung around the park until midnight. It was a bad park. It was true that on one side there was a good district with fine, expensive apartment houses, but the kids from that neighborhood left the park to the kids from the poorer homes. When his wife went out and walked down to the corner it was his turn to wait and worry and watch at the open window. Each waiting moment tortured him. At last he heard his wife's voice and Steve's voice, and he relaxed and sighed; then he remembered his duty and rushed angrily to meet them.

"I'll fix you, Steve, once and for all," he said. "I'll show you you can't start coming into the house at midnight."

"Hold your horses, Dave," his wife said. "Can't you see the state he's in?" Steve looked utterly exhausted and beaten.

"What's the matter?" Dave asked quickly.

"I lost my cap," Steve whispered; he walked past his father and threw himself on the couch in the living-room and lay with his face hidden.

"Now, don't scold him, Dave," his wife said.

"Scold him. Who's scolding him?" Dave asked, indignantly. "It's his cap, not mine. If it's not worth his while to hang on to it, why should I scold him?" But he was implying resentfully that he alone recognized the cap's value.

"So you are scolding him," his wife said. "It's his cap. Not yours. What happened, Steve?"

Steve told them he had been playing ball and he found that when he ran the bases the cap fell off; it was still too big despite the tuck his mother had taken in the band. So the next time he came to bat he tucked the cap in his hip pocket. Someone had lifted it, he was sure.

"And he didn't even know whether it was still in his pocket," Dave said sarcastically.

"I wasn't careless, Dad," Steve said. For the last three hours he had been wandering around to the homes of the kids who had been in the park at the time; he wanted to go on, but he was too tired. Dave knew the boy was apologizing to him, but he didn't know why it made him angry.

"If he didn't hang on to it, it's not worth worrying about now," he said, and he sounded offended.

After that night they knew that Steve didn't go to the park to play ball; he went to look for the cap. It irritated Dave to see him sit around listlessly, or walk in circles, trying to force his memory to find a particular incident which would suddenly recall to him the moment when the cap had been taken. It was no attitude for a growing, healthy boy to take, Dave complained. He told Steve firmly once and for all he didn't want to hear any more about the cap.

One night, two weeks later, Dave was walking home with Steve from the shoemaker's. It was a hot night. When they passed an ice-cream parlour Steve slowed down. "I guess I couldn't have a soda, could I?" Steve said. "Nothing doing," Dave said firmly. "Come on now," he added as Steve hung back, looking in the window.

"Dad, look!" Steve cried suddenly, pointing at the window. "My cap! There's my cap! He's coming out!"

A well-dressed boy was leaving the ice-cream parlor; he had on a blue ball cap with a red peak, just like Steve's cap. "Hey, you!" Steve cried, and he rushed at the boy, his small face fierce and his eyes wild. Before the boy could back away Steve had snatched the cap from his head. "That's my cap!" he shouted.

"What's this?" the bigger boy said. "Hey, give me my cap or I'll give you a poke on the nose."

Dave was surprised that his own shy boy did not back away. He watched him clutch the cap in his left hand, half crying with excitement as he put his head down and drew back his right fist: he was willing to fight. And Dave was proud of him.

"Wait, now," Dave said. "Take it easy, son," he said to the other boy,who refused to back away.

"My boy says it's his cap," Dave said.

"Well, he's crazy. It's my cap."

"I was with him when he got this cap. When the Phillies played here. It's a Philly cap."

"Eddie Condon gave it to me," Steve said. "And you stole it from me, you jerk."

"Don't call me a jerk, you little squirt. I never saw you before in my life."

"Look," Steve said, pointing to the printing on the cap's sweat-band. 'It's Eddie Condon's cap. See? See, Dad?''

"Yeah, You're right, Son. Ever see this boy before, Steve?''

"No," Steve said reluctantly.

The other boy realized he might lose the cap. "I bought it from a guy," he said. "I paid him. My father knows I paid him." He said he got the cap at the ball park. He groped for some magically impressive words and suddenly found them. "You'll have to speak to my father," he said.

"Sure, I'll speak to your father," Dave said. "What's your name? Where do you live?''

"My name's Hudson. I live about ten minutes away on the other side of the park." The boy appraised Dave, who wasn't any bigger than he was and who wore a faded blue windbreaker and no tie. "My father is a lawyer," he said boldly. "He wouldn't let me keep the cap if he didn't think I should.''

"Is that a fact?" Dave asked belligerently. "Well, we'll see. Come on. Let's go." And he got between the two boys and they walked along the street. They didn't talk to each other. Dave knew the Hudson boy was waiting to get to the protection of his home, and Steve knew it, too, and he looked up apprehensively at Dave. And Dave, reaching for his hand, squeezed it encouragingly and strode along, cocky and belligerent, knowing that Steve relied on him.

The Hudson boy lived in that row of fine apartment houses on the other side of the park. At the entrance to one of these houses Dave tried not to hang back and show he was impressed, because he could feel Steve hanging back. When they got into the small elevator Dave didn't know why he took off his hat. In the carpeted hall on the fourth floor the Hudson boy said, "Just a minute," and entered his own apartment. Dave and Steve were left alone in the corridor, knowing that the other boy was preparing his father for the encounter. Steve looked anxiously at his father, and Dave said, "Don't worry, Son," and he added resolutely, "No one's putting anything over on us.''

A tall, balding man in a brown velvet smoking-jacket suddenly opened the door. Dave had never seen a man wearing one of these jackets, although he had seen them in department-store windows. "Good evening," he said, making a deprecatory gesture at the cap Steve still clutched tightly in his left hand. "My boy didn't get your name. My name is Hudson.''

"Mine's Diamond.''

"Come on in," Mr. Hudson said, putting out his hand and laughing good-naturedly. He led Dave and Steve into his living-room. "What's this about that cap?" he asked. "The way kids can get excited about a cap. Well, it's understandable, isn't it?''

"So it is," Dave said, moving closer to Steve, who was awed by the broadloom rug and the fine furniture. He wanted to show Steve he was at ease himself, and he wished Mr. Hudson wouldn't be so polite. That meant Dave had to be polite and affable, too, and it was hard to manage when he was standing in the middle of the floor in his old windbreaker.

"Sit down, Mr. Diamond," Mr. Hudson said. Dave took Steve's arm and sat him down beside him on the chesterfield. The Hudson boy watched his father. And Dave looked at Steve and saw that he wouldn't face Mr. Hudson or the other boy; he kept looking up at Dave, putting all his faith in him.

"Well, Mr. Diamond, from what I gathered from my boy, you're able to prove this cap belonged to your boy."

"That's a fact," Dave said.

"Mr. Diamond, you'll have to believe my boy bought that cap from some kid in good faith."

"I don't doubt it," Dave said. "But no kid can sell something that doesn't belong to him. You know that's a fact, Mr. Hudson."

"Yes, that's a fact," Mr. Hudson agreed. "But that cap means a lot to my boy, Mr. Diamond."

"It means a lot to my boy, too, Mr. Hudson."

"Sure it does. But supposing we called in a policeman. You know what he'd say? He'd ask you if you were willing to pay my boy what he paid for the cap. That's usually the way it works out." Mr. Hudson said, friendly and smiling, as he eyed Dave shrewdly.

"But that's not right. It's not justice," Dave protested. "Not when it's my boy's cap."

"I know it isn't right. But that's what they do."

"All right. What did you say your boy paid for the cap?" Dave said reluctantly.

"Two dollars."

"Two dollars!" Dave repeated. Mr. Hudson's smile was still kindly, but his eyes were shrewd, and Dave knew that the lawyer was counting on his not having the two dollars; Mr. Hudson thought he had Dave sized up; he had looked at him and decided he was broke. Dave's pride was hurt, and he turned to Steve. What he saw in Steve's face was more powerful than the hurt to his pride; it was the memory of how difficult it had been to get an extra nickel, the talk he heard about the cost of food, the worry in his mother's face as she tried to make ends meet, and the bewildered embarrassment that he was here in a rich man's home, forcing his father to confess that he couldn't afford to spend two dollars. Then Dave grew angry and reckless. "I'll give you the two dollars," he said.

Steve looked at the Hudson boy and grinned brightly. The Hudson boy watched his father.

"I suppose that's fair enough," Mr. Hudson said. "A cap like this can be worth a lot to a kid. You know how it is. Your boy might want to sell—I mean be satisfied. Would he take five dollars for it?''

''Five dollars?'' Dave repeated, ''Is it worth five dollars, Steve?'' he asked uncertainly.

Steve shook his head and looked frightened.

''No, thanks, Mr. Hudson,'' Dave said firmly.

''I'll tell you what I'll do,'' Mr. Hudson said. ''I'll give you ten dollars. The cap has a sentimental value for my boy, a Philly cap, a big-leaguer's cap. It's only worth about a buck and a half really,'' he added. But Dave shook his head again. Mr. Hudson frowned. He looked at his own boy with indulgent concern, but now he was embarrassed. ''I'll tell you what I'll do,'' he said. ''This cap—well, it's worth as much as a day at the circus to my boy. Your boy should be recompensed. I want to be fair. Here's twenty dollars,'' and he held out two ten-dollar bills to Dave.

That much money for a cap, Dave thought, and his eyes brightened. But he knew what the cap had meant to Steve; to deprive him of it now that it was within his reach would be unbearable. All the things he needed in his life gathered around him; his wife was there, saying he couldn't afford to reject the offer, he had no right to do it; and he turned to Steve to see if Steve thought it wonderful that the cap could bring them twenty dollars.

''What do you say, Steve?'' he asked uneasily.

''I don't know,'' Steve said. He was in a trance. When Dave smiled, Steve smiled to, and Dave believed that Steve was as impressed as he was, only more bewildered, and maybe even more aware that they could not possibly turn away that much money for a ball cap.

''Well, here you are,'' Mr. Hudson said, and he put the two bills in Steve's hand. ''It's a lot of money. But I guess you had a right to expect as much.''

With a dazed, fixed smile Steve handed the money slowly to his father, and his face was white.

Laughing jovially, Mr. Hudson led them to the door. His own boy followed a few paces behind.

In the elevator Dave took the bills out of his pocket. ''See, Stevie,'' he whispered eagerly. ''That windbreaker you wanted! And ten dollars for your bank! Won't Mother be surprised?''

''Yeah,'' Steve whispered, the little smile still on his face. But Dave had to turn away quickly so their eyes wouldn't meet, for he saw it was a scared smile.

Outside, Dave said, ''Here, you carry the money home, Steve. You show it to your mother.''

''No, you keep it,'' Steve said, and then there was nothing to say. They walked in silence.

''It's a lot of money,'' Dave said finally. When Steve didn't answer him, he added angrily, "I turned to you, Steve. I asked you, didn't I?"

"That man knew how much his boy wanted that cap," Steve said.

"Sure. But he recognized how much it was worth to us."

"No, you let him take it away from us," Steve blurted.

"That's unfair," Dave said. "Don't dare say that to me."

"I don't want to be like you," Steve muttered, and he darted across the road and walked along on the other side of the street.

"It's unfair," Dave said angrily, only now he didn't mean that Steve was unfair, he meant that what had happened in the prosperous Hudson home was unfair, and he didn't know quite why. He had been trapped, not just by Mr. Hudson, but by his own life. Across the road Steve was hurrying along with his head down, wanting to be alone. They walked most of the way home on opposite sides of the street, until Dave could stand it no longer. "Steve," he called, crossing the street. "It was very unfair. I mean, for you to say. . ." but Steve started to run. Dave walked as fast as he could and Steve was getting beyond him, and he felt enraged and suddenly he yelled, "Steve!" and he started to chase his son. He wanted to get hold of Steve and pound him, and he didn't know why. He gained on him, he gasped for breath and he almost got him by the shoulder. Turning, Steve saw his father's face in the street light and was terrified; he circled away, got to the house, and rushed in, yelling, "Mother!"

"Son, Son!" she cried, rushing from the kitchen. As soon as she threw her arms around Steve, shielding him, Dave's anger left him and he felt stupid. He walked past them into the kitchen.

"What happened?" she asked anxiously. "Have you both gone crazy? What did you do, Steve?

"Nothing," he said sullenly.

"What did your father do?"

"We found the boy with my ball cap, and he let the boy's father take it from us."

"No, no," Dave protested. "Nobody pushed us around. The man didn't put anything over us." He felt tired and his face was burning. He told what had happened; then he slowly took the two ten-dollar bills out of his wallet and tossed them on the table and looked up guiltily at his wife.

It hurt him that she didn't pick up the money, and that she didn't rebuke him. "It is a lot of money, Son," she said slowly. "Your father was only trying to do what he knew was right, and it'll work out, and you'll understand." She was soothing Steve, but Dave knew she felt that she needed to be gentle with him, too, and he was ashamed.

When she went with Steve to his bedroom, Dave sat by himself. His son had contempt for him, he thought. His son, for the first time, had seen how easy it was for another man to handle him, and he had judged him and had wanted to walk alone on the other side of the street. He looked at the money and he hated the sight of it.

His wife returned to the kitchen, made a cup of tea, talked soothingly, and said it was incredible that he had forced the Hudson man to pay him twenty dollars for the cap, but all Dave could think of was Steve was scared of me.

Finally, he got up and went into Steve's room. The room was in darkness, but he could see the outline of Steve's body on the bed, and he sat down beside him and whispered, "Look, Son, it was a mistake. I know why. People like us—in circumstances where money can scare us. No, no" he said, feeling ashamed and shaking his head apologetically; he was taking the wrong way of showing the boy they were together; he was covering up his own failure. For the failure had been his, and it had come out of being so separated from his son that he had been blind to what was beyond the price in a boy's life. He longed now to show Steve he could be with him from day to day. His hand went out hesitantly to Steve's shoulder. "Steve, look," he said eagerly. "The trouble was I didn't realize how much I enjoyed it that night at the ball park. If I had watched you playing for your own team—the kids around here say you could be a great pitcher. We could take that money and buy a new pitcher's glove for you, and a catcher's mitt. Steve, Steve, are you listening? I could catch you, work with you in the lane. Maybe I could be your coach. . .watch you become a great pitcher." In the half-darkness he could see the boy's pale face turn to him.

Steve, who had never heard his father talk like this, was shy and wondering. All he knew was that his father, for the first time, wanted to be with him in his hopes and adventures. He said, "I guess you do know how important that cap was." His hand went out to his father's arm. "With that man the cap was—well it was just something he could buy, eh Dad?" Dave gripped his son's hand hard. The wonderful generosity of childhood—the price a boy was willing to pay to be able to count on his father's admiration and approval—made him feel humble, then strangely exalted.

SINCLAIR ROSS
1908–

Born on a homestead near Shelbrooke in northern Saskatchewan, he dropped out of school after grade eleven to work in a bank. His banking career took him to many small-town banks in Saskatchewan before he transferred to a bank in Winnipeg in 1933. Apart from wartime service with the Canadian army in London, England, he remained in banking until his retirement in 1968. In 1941 he published his first novel, *As For Me and My House*, with its stunning depiction of small-town prairie life during the Depression. The prairie is the major setting for his two collections of short fiction, *The Lamp at Noon and Other Stories* (1968) and *The Race and Other Stories* (1982), which also explore the landscape's unique ability to sustain, to suffocate, or to challenge its inhabitants.

The Painted Door

Straight across the hills it was five miles from John's farm to his father's. But in winter, with the roads impassable, a team had to make a wide detour and skirt the hills, so that from five the distance was more than trebled to seventeen.

"I think I'll walk," John said at breakfast to his wife. "The drifts in the hills wouldn't hold a horse, but they'll carry me all right. If I leave early I can spend a few hours helping him with his chores, and still be back by suppertime."

Moodily she went to the window, and thawing a clear place in the frost with her breath, stood looking across the snowswept farmyard to the huddle of stables and sheds. "There was a double wheel around the moon last night," she countered presently. "You said yourself we could expect a storm. It isn't right to leave me here alone. Surely I'm as important as your father."

He glanced up uneasily, then drinking off his coffee tried to reassure her. "But there's nothing to be afraid of—even if it does start to storm. You won't need to go near the stable. Everything's fed and watered now to last till night. I'll be back at the latest by seven or eight."

She went on blowing against the frosted pane, carefully elongating the clear place until it was oval-shaped and symmetrical. He watched her a moment or two longer, then more insistently repeated, "I say you won't need to go near the stable. Everything's fed and watered, and I'll see that there's plenty of wood in. That will be all right, won't it?"

"Yes—of course—I heard you—" It was a curiously cold voice now, as if the words were chilled by their contact with the frosted pane.

245

"Plenty to eat—plenty of wood to keep me warm—what more could a woman ask for?"

"But he's an old man—living there all alone. What is it, Ann? You're not like yourself this morning."

She shook her head without turning. "Pay no attention to me. Seven years a farmer's wife—it's time I was used to staying alone."

Slowly the clear place on the glass enlarged: oval, then round, then oval again. The sun was risen above the frost mists now, so keen and hard a glitter on the snow that instead of warmth its rays seemed shedding cold. One of the two-year-old colts that had cantered away when John turned the horses out for water stood covered with rime at the stable door again, head down and body hunched, each breath a little plume of steam against the frosty air. She shivered, but did not turn. In the clear, bitter light the long white miles of prairie landscape seemed a region strangely alien to life. Even the distant farmsteads she could see served only to intensify a sense of isolation. Scattered across the face of so vast and bleak a wilderness it was difficult to conceive them as a testimony of human hardihood and endurance. Rather they seemed futile, lost. Rather they seemed to cower before the implacability of snow-swept earth and clear pale sun-chilled sky.

And when at last she turned from the window there was a brooding stillness in her face as if she had recognized this mastery of snow and cold. It troubled John. "If you're really afraid," he yielded, "I won't go today. Lately it's been so cold, that's all. I just wanted to make sure he's all right in case we do have a storm."

"I know—I'm not really afraid." She was putting in a fire now, and he could no longer see her face. "Pay no attention to me. It's ten miles there and back, so you'd better get started."

"You ought to know by now I wouldn't stay away," he tried to brighten her. "No matter how it stormed. Twice a week before we were married I never missed—and there were bad blizzards that winter too."

He was a slow, unambitious man, content with his farm and cattle, naïvely proud of Ann. He had been bewildered by it once, her caring for a dull-witted fellow like him; then assured at last of her affection he had relaxed against it gratefully, unsuspecting it might ever be less constant than his own. Even now, listening to the restless brooding in her voice, he felt only a quick, unformulated kind of pride that after seven years his absence for a day should still concern her. While she, his trust and earnestness controlling her again:

"I know. It's just that sometimes when you're away I get lonely. . . . There's a long cold tramp in front of you. You'll let me fix a scarf around your face."

He nodded. "And on my way I'll drop in at Steven's place. Maybe he'll come over tonight for a game of cards. You haven't seen anybody but me for the last two weeks."

She glanced up sharply, then busied herself clearing the table. "It will mean another two miles if you do. You're going to be cold and tired enough as it is. When you're gone I think I'll paint the kitchen woodwork. White this time—you remember we got the paint last fall. It's going to make the room a lot lighter. I'll be too busy to find the day long."

"I will though," he insisted, "and if a storm gets up you'll feel safer, knowing that he's coming. That's what you need, Ann—someone to talk to besides me."

She stood at the stove motionless a moment, then turned to him uneasily. "Will you shave then, John—now—before you go?"

He glanced at her questioningly, and avoiding his eyes she tried to explain, "I mean—he may be here before you're back—and you won't have a chance then."

"But it's only Steven—he's seen me like this—"

"He'll be shaved, though—that's what I mean—and I'd like you too to spend a little time on yourself."

He stood up, stroking the heavy stubble on his chin. "Maybe I should all right, but it makes the skin too tender. Especially when I've got to face the wind."

She nodded and began to help him dress, bringing heavy socks and a big woollen sweater from the bedroom, wrapping a scarf around his face and forehead. "I'll tell Steven to come early," he said, as he went out. "In time for supper. Likely there'll be chores for me to do, so if I'm not back by six don't wait."

From the bedroom window she watched him nearly a mile along the road. The fire had gone down when at last she turned away, and already through the house there was an encroaching chill. A blaze sprang up again when the drafts were opened, but as she went on clearing the table her movements were furtive and constrained. It was the silence weighing upon her—the frozen silence of the bitter fields and sun-chilled sky—lurking outside as if alive, relentlessly in wait, mile-deep between her now and John. She listened to it, suddenly tense, motionless. The fire crackled and the clock ticked. Always it was there. "I'm a fool," she whispered hoarsely, rattling the dishes in defiance, going back to the stove to put in another fire. "Warm and safe—I'm a fool. It's a good chance when he's away to paint. The day will go quickly. I won't have time to brood."

Since November now the paint had been waiting warmer weather. The frost in the walls on a day like this would crack and peel it as it dried, but she needed something to keep her hands occupied, something to stave off the gathering cold and loneliness. "First of all," she said aloud, opening the paint and mixing it with a little turpentine, "I must get the house warmer. Fill up the stove and open the oven door so that all the heat comes out. Wad something along the window sills to keep out the drafts. Then I'll feel brighter. It's the cold that depresses."

She moved briskly, performing each little task with careful and exaggerated absorption, binding her thoughts to it, making it a screen between herself and the surrounding snow and silence. But when the stove was filled and the windows sealed it was more difficult again. Above the quiet, steady swishing of her brush against the bedroom door the clock began to tick. Suddenly her movements became precise, deliberate, her posture self-conscious, as if someone had entered the room and were watching her. It was the silence again, aggressive, hovering. The fire spit and crackled at it. Still it was there. "I'm a fool," she repeated. "All farmers' wives have to stay alone. I mustn't give in this way. I mustn't brood. A few hours now and they'll be here."

The sound of her voice reassured her. She went on: "I'll get them a good supper — and for coffee tonight after cards bake some of the little cakes with raisins that he likes. . . . Just three of us, so I'll watch, and let John play. It's better with four, but at least we can talk. That's all I need — someone to talk to. John never talks. He's stronger — he doesn't understand. But he likes Steven — no matter what the neighbors say. Maybe he'll have him come again, and some other young people too. It's what we need, both of us, to help keep young ourselves. . . . And then before we know it we'll be into March. It's cold still in March sometimes, but you never mind the same. At least you're beginning to think about spring."

She began to think about it now. Thoughts that outstripped her words, that left her alone again with herself and the ever-lurking silence. Eager and hopeful first; then clenched, rebellious, lonely. Windows open, sun and thawing earth again, the urge of growing, living things. Then the days that began in the morning at half-past four and lasted till ten at night; the meals at which John gulped his food and scarcely spoke a word; the brute-tired stupid eyes he turned on her if ever she mentioned town or visiting.

For spring was drudgery again. John never hired a man to help him. He wanted a mortgage-free farm; then a new house and pretty clothes for her. Sometimes, because with the best of crops it was going to take so long to pay off anyway, she wondered whether they mightn't better let the mortgage wait a little. Before they were worn out, before their best years were gone. It was something of life she wanted, not just a house and furniture; something of John, not pretty clothes when she would be too old to wear them. But John of course couldn't understand. To him it seemed only right that she should have the clothes—only right that he, fit for nothing else, should slave away fifteen hours a day to give them to her. There was in his devotion a baffling, insurmountable humility that made him feel the need of sacrifice. And when his muscles ached, when his feet dragged stolidly with weariness, then it seemed that in some measure at least he was making amends for his big hulking body and simple mind. That by his sacrifice he succeeded only in the extinction of his personality never occurred to him. Year after year their lives went on in the same little groove. He drove his horses in the field; she milked the cows and hoed potatoes. By dint of his drudgery he saved a few months' wages, added a few dollars more each fall to his payments on the mortgage; but the only real difference that it all made was to deprive her of his companionship, to make him a little duller, older, uglier than he might otherwise have been. He never saw their lives objectively. To him it was not what he actually accomplished by means of the sacrifice that mattered, but the sacrifice itself, the gesture — something done for her sake.

And she, understanding, kept her silence. In such a gesture, however futile, there was a graciousness not to be shattered lightly. "John," she would begin sometimes, "you're doing too much. Get a man to help you — just for a month — " but smiling down at her he would answer simply, "I don't mind. Look at the hands on me. They're made for work." While in his voice there would be a stalwart ring to tell her that by her thoughtfulness she had made him only the more resolved to serve her, to prove his devotion and fidelity.

They were useless, such thoughts. She knew. It was his very devotion that made him useless, that forbade her to rebel. Yet over and over, sometimes hunched still before their bleakness, sometimes her brush making swift sharp strokes to pace the chafe and rancour that they brought, she persisted in them.

This now, the winter, was their slack season. She could sleep sometimes till eight, and John till seven. They could linger over their meals a little, read, play cards, go visiting the neighbors. It was the time to relax, to indulge and enjoy themselves; but instead, fretful and impatient, they kept on waiting for the spring. They were compelled now, not by labor, but by the spirit of labor. A spirit that pervaded their lives and brought with idleness a sense of guilt. Sometimes they did sleep late, sometimes they did play cards, but always uneasily, always reproached by the thought of more important things that might be done. When John got up at five to attend to the fire he wanted to stay up and go out to the stable. When he sat down to a meal he hurried his food and pushed his chair away again, from habit, from sheer work-instinct, even though it was only to put more wood in the stove, or go down cellar to cut up beets and turnips for the cows.

And anyway, sometimes she asked herself, why sit trying to talk with a man who never talked? Why talk when there was nothing to talk about but crops and cattle, the weather and the neighbors? The neighbors, too — why go visiting them when still it was the same — crops and cattle, the weather and the other neighbors? Why go to the dances in the schoolhouse to sit among the older women, one of them now, married seven years, or to waltz with the work-bent, tired old farmers to a squeaky fiddle tune? Once she had danced with Steven six or seven times in the evening, and they had talked about it for as many months. It was easier to stay home. John never danced or enjoyed himself. He was always uncomfortable in his good suit and shoes. He didn't like shaving in the cold weather oftener than once or twice a week. It was easier to stay at home, to stand at the window staring out across the bitter fields, to count the days and look forward to another spring.

But now, alone with herself in the winter silence, she saw the spring for what it really was. This spring — next spring — all the springs and summers still to come. While they grew old, while their bodies warped, while their minds kept shrivelling dry and empty like their lives. "I mustn't," she said aloud again. "I married him — and he's a good man. I mustn't keep on this way. It will be noon before long, and then time to think about supper. . . . Maybe he'll come early — and as soon as John is finished at the stable we can all play cards."

It was getting cold again, and she left her painting to put in more wood. But this time the warmth spread slowly. She pushed a mat up to the outside door, and went back to the window to pat down the woollen shirt that was wadded along the sill. Then she paced a few times around the room, then poked the fire and rattled the stove lids, then paced again. The fire crackled, the clock ticked. The silence now seemed more intense than ever, seemed to have reached a pitch where it faintly moaned. She began to pace on tiptoe, listening, her shoulders drawn together, not realizing for a while that it was the wind she heard, thin-strained and whimpering through the eaves.

Then she wheeled to the window, and with quick short breaths thawed the frost to see again. The glitter was gone. Across the drifts sped swift and snakelike little tongues of snow. She could not follow them, where they sprang from, or where they disappeared. It was as if all across the yard the snow were shivering awake — roused by the warnings of the wind to hold itself in readiness for the impending storm. The sky had become a sombre, whitish grey. It, too, as if in readiness, had shifted and lay close to earth. Before her as she watched a mane of powdery snow reared up breast-high against the darker background of the stable, tossed for a moment angrily, and then subsided again as if whipped down to obedience and restraint. But another followed, more reckless and impatient than the first. Another reeled and dashed itself against the window where she watched. Then ominously for a while there were only the angry little snakes of snow. The wind rose, creaking the troughs that were wired beneath the eaves. In the distance, sky and prairie now were merged into one another linelessly. All around her it was gathering; already in its press and whimpering there strummed a boding of eventual fury. Again she saw a mane of snow spring up, so dense and high this time that all the sheds and stables were obscured. Then others followed, whirling fiercely out of hand; and, when at last they cleared, the stables seemed in dimmer outline than before. It was the snow beginning, long lancet shafts of it, straight from the north, borne almost level by the straining wind. "He'll be there soon," she whispered, "and coming home it will be in his back. He'll leave again right away. He saw the double wheel — he knows the kind of storm there'll be."

She went back to her painting. For a while it was easier, all her thoughts half-anxious ones of John in the blizzard, struggling his way across the hills; but petulantly again she soon began, "I knew we were going to have a storm — I told him so — but it doesn't matter what I say. Big stubborn fool — he goes his own way anyway. It doesn't matter what becomes of me. In a storm like this he will never get home. He won't even try. And while he sits keeping his father company I can look after his stable for him, go ploughing through snowdrifts up to my knees — nearly frozen — "

Not that she meant or believed her words. It was just an effort to convince herself that she did have a grievance, to justify her rebellious thoughts, to prove John responsible for her unhappiness. She was young still, eager for excitement and distractions; and John's steadfastness rebuked her vanity, made her complaints seem weak and trivial. Fretfully she went on, "If he'd listen to me sometimes and not be so stubborn we wouldn't be living still in a house like this. Seven years in two rooms — seven years and never a new stick of furniture. . . . There — as if another coat of paint could make it different anyway."

She cleaned her brush, filled up the stove again, and went back to the window. There was a void white moment that she thought must be frost formed on the window pane; then, like a fitful shadow through the whirling snow, she recognized the stable roof. It was incredible. The sudden, maniac raging of the storm struck from her face all its pettishness. Her eyes glazed with fear a little; her lips blanched. "If he starts for home now," she whispered silently — "But he won't — he knows I'm safe — he knows Steven's coming. Across the hills he would never dare."

She turned to the stove, holding out her hands to the warmth. Around her now there seemed a constant sway and tremor, as if the air were vibrating with the violent shudderings of the walls. She stood quite still, listening. Sometimes the wind struck with sharp, savage blows. Sometimes it bore down in a sustained, minute-long blast, silent with effort and intensity; then with a foiled shriek of threat wheeled away to gather and assault again. Always the eavestroughs creaked and sawed. She started towards the window again, then detecting the morbid trend of her thoughts, prepared fresh coffee and forced herself to drink a few mouthfuls. "He would never dare," she whispered again. "He wouldn't leave the old man anyway in such a storm. Safe in here — there's nothing for me to keep worrying about. It's after one already. I'll do my baking now, and then it will be time to get supper ready for Steven."

Soon, however, she began to doubt whether Steven would come. In such a storm even a mile was enough to make a man hesitate. Especially Steven, who, for all his attractive qualities, was hardly the one to face a blizzard for the sake of someone else's chores. He had a stable of his own to look after anyway. It would be only natural for him to think that when the storm rose John had turned again for home. Another man would have — would have put his wife first.

But she felt little dread or uneasiness at the prospect of spending the night alone. It was the first time she had been left like this on her own resources, and her reaction, now that she could face and appraise her situation calmly, was gradually to feel it a kind of adventure and responsibility. It stimulated her. Before nightfall she must go the stable and feed everything. Wrap up in some of John's clothes — take a ball of string in her hand, one end tied to the door, so that no matter how blinding the storm she could at least find her way back to the house. She had heard of people having to do that. It appealed to her now because suddenly it made life dramatic. She had not felt the storm yet, only watched it for a minute through the window.

It took nearly an hour to find enough string, to choose the right socks and sweaters. Long before it was time to start out she tried on John's clothes, changing and rechanging, striding around the room to make sure there would be play enough for pitching hay and struggling over snowdrifts; then she took them off again, and for a while busied herself baking the little cakes with raisins that he liked.

Night came early. Just for a moment on the doorstep she shrank back, uncertain. The slow dimming of the light clutched her with an illogical sense of abandonment. It was like the covert withdrawal of an ally, leaving the alien miles unleashed and unrestrained. Watching the hurricane of writhing snow rage past the little house she forced herself, "They'll never stand the night unless I get them fed. It's nearly dark already, and I've work to last an hour."

Timidly, unwinding a little of the string, she crept out from the shelter of the doorway. A gust of wind spun her forward a few yards, then plunged her headlong against a drift that in the dense white whirl lay invisible across her path. For nearly a minute she huddled still, breathless and dazed. The snow was in her mouth and nostrils, inside her scarf and up her sleeves. As she tried to straighten a smothering scud flung itself against her face, cutting off her breath a second time. The wind struck from all sides, blustering and furious. It was as if the storm had discovered her, as if all its forces were concentrated upon her extinction. Seized with panic suddenly she threshed out a moment with her arms, then stumbled back and sprawled her length across the drift.

But this time she regained her feet quickly, roused by the whip and batter of the storm to retaliative anger. For a moment her impulse was to face the wind and strike back blow for blow; then, as suddenly as it had come, her frantic strength gave way to limpness and exhaustion. Suddenly, a comprehension so clear and terrifying that it struck all thoughts of the stable from her mind, she realized in such a storm her puny insignificance. And the realization gave her new strength, stilled this time to a desperate persistence. Just for a moment the wind held her, numb and swaying in its vise; then slowly, buckled far forward, she groped her way again towards the house.

Inside, leaning against the door, she stood tense and still a while. It was almost dark now. The top of the stove glowed a deep, dull red. Heedless of the storm, self absorbed and self-satisfied, the clock ticked on like a glib little idiot. "He shouldn't have gone," she whispered silently. "He saw the double wheel—he knew. He shouldn't have left me here alone."

For so fierce now, so insane and dominant did the blizzard seem, that she could not credit the safety of the house. The warmth and lull around her was not real yet, not to be relied upon. She was still at the mercy of the storm. Only her body pressing hard like this against the door was staving it off. She didn't dare move. She didn't dare ease the ache and strain. "He shouldn't have gone," she repeated, thinking of the stable again, reproached by her helplessness. "They'll freeze in their stalls — and I can't reach them. He'll say it's all my fault. He won't believe I tried."

Then Steven came. Quickly, startled to quietness and control, she let him in and lit the lamp. He stared at her a moment, then flinging off his cap crossed to where she stood by the table and seized her arms. "You're so white — what's wrong? Look at me —" It was like him in such little situations to be masterful. "You should have known better than to go out on a day like this. For a while I thought I wasn't going to make it here myself—"

"I was afraid you wouldn't come—John left early, and there was the stable—"

But the storm had unnerved her, and suddenly at the assurance of his touch and voice the fear that had been gripping her gave way to an hysteria of relief. Scarcely aware of herself she seized his arm and sobbed against it. He remained still a moment, unyielding, then slipped his other arm around her shoulder. It was comforting and she relaxed against it, hushed by a sudden sense of lull and safety. Her shoulders trembled with the easing of the strain, then fell limp and still. "You're shivering,"—he drew her gently towards the stove. "There's nothing to be afraid of now, though. I'm going to do the chores for you."

It was a quiet, sympathetic voice, yet with an undertone of insolence, a kind of mockery even, that made her draw away quickly and busy herself putting in a fire. With his lips drawn in a little smile he watched her till she looked at him again. The smile too was insolent, but at the same time companionable; Steven's smile, and therefore difficult to reprove. It lit up his lean, still-boyish face with a peculiar kind of arrogance: features and smile that were different from John's, from other men's—wilful and derisive, yet naïvely so—as if it were less the difference itself he was conscious of, than the long-accustomed privilege that thereby fell his due. He was erect, tall, square-shouldered. His hair was dark and trim, his young lips curved soft and full. While John, she made the comparison swiftly, was thick-set, heavy-jowled, and stooped. He always stood before her helpless, a kind of humility and wonderment in his attitude. And Steven now smiled on her appraisingly with the worldly-wise assurance of one for whom a woman holds neither mystery nor illusion.

"It was good of you to come, Steven," she responded, the words running into a sudden, empty laugh. "Such a storm to face—I suppose I should feel flattered."

For his presumption, his misunderstanding of what had been only a momentary weakness, instead of angering quickened her, roused from latency and long disuse all the instincts and resources of her femininity. She felt eager, challenged. Something was at hand that hitherto had always eluded her, even in the early days with John, something vital, beckoning, meaningful. She didn't understand, but she knew. The texture of the moment was satisfyingly dreamlike: an incredibility perceived as such, yet acquiesced in. She was John's wife —she knew—but also she knew that Steven standing here was different from John. There was no thought or motive, no understanding of herself as the knowledge persisted. Wary and poised round a sudden little core of blind excitement she evaded him, "But it's nearly dark—hadn't you better hurry if you're going to do the chores? Don't trouble—I can get them off myself—"

An hour later when he returned from the stable she was in another dress, hair rearranged, a little flush of color in her face. Pouring warm water for him from the kettle into the basin she said evenly, "By the time you're washed supper will be ready. John said we weren't to wait for him."

He looked at her a moment, "But in a storm like this you're not expecting John?"

"Of course." As she spoke she could feel the color deepening in her face. "We're going to play cards. He was the one that suggested it."

He went on washing, and then as they took their places at the table, resumed, "So John's coming. When are you expecting him?"

"He said it might be seven o'clock—or a little later." Conversation with Steven at other times had always been brisk and natural, but now suddenly she found it strained. "He may have work to do for his father. That's what he said when he left. Why do you ask, Steven?"

"I was just wondering—it's a rough night."

"He always comes. There couldn't be a storm bad enough. It's easier to do the chores in the daylight, and I knew he'd be tired—that's why I started out for the stable."

She glanced up again and he was smiling at her. The same insolence, the same little twist of mockery and appraisal. It made her flinch suddenly, and ask herself why she was pretending to expect John—why there should be this instinct of defence to force her. This time, instead of poise and excitement, it brought a reminder that she had changed her dress and rearranged her hair. It crushed in a sudden silence, through which she heard the whistling wind again, and the creaking saw of the eaves. Neither spoke now. There was something strange, almost terrifying, about this Steven and his quiet, unrelenting smile; but strangest of all was the familiarity: the Steven she had never seen or encountered, and yet had always known, always expected, always waited for. It was less Steven himself that she felt than his inevitability. Just as she had felt the snow, the silence and the storm. She kept her eyes lowered, on the window past his shoulder, on the stove, but his smile now seemed to exist apart from him, to merge and hover with the silence. She clinked a cup—listened to the whistle of the storm — always it was there. He began to speak, but her mind missed the meaning of his words. Swiftly she was making comparisons again; his face so different to John's, so handsome and young and clean-shaven. Swiftly, helplessly, feeling the imperceptible and relentless ascendancy that thereby he was gaining over her, sensing sudden menace in this new, more vital life, even as she felt drawn towards it.

The lamp between them flickered as an onslaught of the storm sent shudderings through the room. She rose to build up the fire again and he followed her. For a long time they stood close to the stove, their arms almost touching. Once as the blizzard creaked the house she spun around sharply, fancying it was John at the door; but quietly he intercepted her. "Not tonight — you might as well make up your mind to it. Across the hills in a storm like this — it would be suicide to try."

Her lips trembled suddenly in an effort to answer, to parry the certainty in his voice, then set thin and bloodless. She was afraid now. Afraid of his face so different from John's — of his smile, of her own helplessness to rebuke it. Afraid of the storm, isolating her here alone with him in its impenetrable fastness. They tried to play cards, but she kept starting up at every creak and shiver of the walls. "It's too rough a night," he repeated. "Even for John. Just relax a few minutes — stop worrying and pay a little attention to me."

But in his tone there was a contradiction to his words. For it implied that she was not worrying — that her only concern was lest it really might be John at the door.

And the implication persisted. He filled up the stove for her, shuffled the cards — won — shuffled — still it was there. She tried to respond to his conversation, to think of the game, but helplessly into her cards instead she began to ask, Was he right? Was that why he smiled? Why he seemed to wait, expectant and assured?

The clock ticked, the fire crackled. Always it was there. Furtively for a moment she watched him as he deliberated over his hand. John, even in the days before they were married, had never looked like that. Only this morning she had asked him to shave. Because Steven was coming — because she had been afraid to see them side by side — because deep within herself she had known even then. The same knowledge, furtive and forbidden, that was flaunted now in Steven's smile. "You look cold," he said at last, dropping his cards and rising from the table. "We're not playing, anyway. Come over to the stove for a few minutes and get warm."

"But first I think we'll hang blankets over the door. When there's a blizzard like this we always do." It seemed that in sane, commonplace activity there might be release, a moment or two in which to recover herself. "John has nails in to put them on. They keep out a little of the draft."

He stood on a chair for her, and hung the blankets that she carried from the bedroom. Then for a moment they stood silent, watching the blankets sway and tremble before the blade of wind that spurted around the jamb. "I forgot," she said at last, "that I painted the bedroom door. At the top there, see—I've smeared the blankets coming through."

He glanced at her curiously, and went back to the stove. She followed him, trying to imagine the hills in such a storm, wondering whether John would come. "A man couldn't live in it," suddenly he answered her thoughts, lowering the oven door and drawing up their chairs one on each side of it. "He knows you're safe. It isn't likely that he'd leave his father, anyway."

"The wind will be in his back," she persisted. "The winter before we were married — all the blizzards that we had that year — and he never missed—"

"Blizzards like this one? Up in the hills he wouldn't be able to keep his direction for a hundred yards. Listen to it a minute and ask yourself."

His voice seemed softer, kindlier now. She met his smile a moment, its assured little twist of appraisal, then for a long time sat silent, tense, careful again to avoid his eyes.

Everything now seemed to depend on this. It was the same as a few hours ago when she braced the door against the storm. He was watching her, smiling. She dared not move, unclench her hands, or raise her eyes. The flames crackled, the clock ticked. The storm wrenched the walls as if to make them buckle in. So rigid and desperate were all her muscles set, withstanding, that the room around her seemed to swim and reel. So rigid and strained that for relief at last, despite herself, she raised her head and met his eyes again.

Intending that it should be for only an instant, just to breathe again, to ease the tension that had grown unbearable—but in his smile now, instead of the insolent appraisal that she feared, there seemed a kind of warmth and sympathy. An understanding that quickened and encouraged her—that made her wonder why but a moment ago she had been afraid. It was as if the storm had lulled, as if she had suddenly found calm and shelter.

Or perhaps, the thought seized her, perhaps instead of his smile it was she that had changed. She who, in the long, wind-creaked silence, had emerged from the increment of codes and loyalties to her real, unfettered self. She who now felt suddenly an air of appraisal as nothing more than an understanding of the unfulfilled woman that until this moment had lain within her brooding and unadmitted, reproved out of consciousness by the insistence of an outgrown, routine fidelity.

For there had always been Steven. She understood now. Seven years—almost as long as John—ever since the night they first danced together.

The lamp was burning dry, and through the dimming light, isolated in the fastness of silence and storm, they watched each other. Her face was white and struggling still. His was handsome, clean-shaven, young. Her eyes were fanatic, believing desperately, fixed upon him as if to exclude all else, as if to find justification. His were cool, bland, drooped a little with expectancy. The light kept dimming, gathering the shadows round them, hushed, conspiratorial. He was smiling still. Her hands again were clenched up white and hard.

"But he always came," she persisted. "The wildest, coldest nights —even such a night as this. There was never a storm—"

"Never a storm like this one." There was a quietness in his smile now, a kind of simplicity almost, as if to reassure her. "You were out in it yourself for a few minutes. He would have five miles, across the hills. . . . I'd think twice myself, on such a night, before risking even one."

Long after he was asleep she lay listening to the storm. As a check on the draft up the chimney they had left one of the stovelids partly off, and through the open bedroom door she could see the flickerings of flame and shadow on the kitchen wall. They leaped and sank fantastically. The longer she watched the more alive they seemed to be. There was one great shadow that struggled towards her threateningly, massive and black and engulfing all the room. Again and again it advanced, about to spring, but each time a little whip of light subdued it to its place among the others on the wall. Yet though it never reached her still she cowered, feeling that gathered there was all the frozen wilderness, its heart of terror and invincibility.

Then she dozed a while, and the shadow was John. Interminably he advanced. The whips of light still flicked and coiled, but now suddenly they were the swift little snakes that this afternoon she had watched twist and shiver across the snow. And they too were advancing. They writhed and vanished and came again. She lay still, paralysed. He was over her now, so close that she could have touched him. Already it seemed that a deadly tightening hand was on her throat. She tried to scream but her lips were locked. Steven beside her slept on heedlessly.

Until suddenly as she lay staring up at him a gleam of light revealed his face. And in it was not a trace of threat or anger—only calm, and stonelike hopelessness.

That was like John. He began to withdraw, and frantically she tried to call him back. "It isn't true—not really true—listen, John—" but the words clung frozen to her lips. Already there was only the shriek of wind again, the sawing eaves, the leap and twist of shadow on the wall.

She sat up, startled now and awake. And so real had he seemed there, standing close to her, so vivid the sudden age and sorrow in his face, that at first she could not make herself understand she had been only dreaming. Against the conviction of his presence in the room it was necessary to insist over and over that he must still be with his father on the other side of the hills. Watching the shadows she had fallen asleep. It was only her mind, her imagination, distorted to a nightmare by the illogical and unadmitted dread of his return. But he wouldn't come. Steven was right. In such a storm he would never try. They were safe, alone. No one would ever know. It was only fear, morbid and irrational; only the sense of guilt that even her new-found and challenged womanhood could not entirely quell.

She knew now. She had not let herself understand or acknowledge it as guilt before, but gradually through the wind-torn silence of the night his face compelled her. The face that had watched her from the darkness with its stonelike sorrow — the face that was really John — John more than his features of mere flesh and bone could ever be.

She wept silently. The fitful gleam of light began to sink. On the ceiling and wall at last there was only a faint dull flickering glow. The little house shuddered and quailed, and a chill crept in again. Without wakening Steven she slipped out to build up the fire. It was burned to a few spent embers now, and the wood she put on seemed a long time catching light. The wind swirled through the blankets they had hung around the door, and struck her flesh like laps of molten ice. Then hollow and moaning it roared up the chimney again, as if against its will drawn back to serve still longer with the onrush of the storm.

For a long time she crouched over the stove, listening. Earlier in the evening, with the lamp lit and the fire crackling, the house had seemed a stand against the wilderness, against its frozen, blizzard-breathed implacability, a refuge of feeble walls wherein persisted the elements of human meaning and survival. Now, in the cold, creaking darkness, it was strangely extinct, looted by the storm and abandoned again. She lifted the stove lid and fanned the embers till at last a swift little tongue of flame began to lick around the wood. Then she replaced the lid, extended her hands, and as if frozen in that attitude stood waiting.

It was not long now. After a few minutes she closed the drafts, and as the flames whirled back upon each other, beating against the top of the stove and sending out flickers of light again, a warmth surged up to relax her stiffened limbs. But shivering and numb it had been easier. The bodily well-being that the warmth induced gave play again to an ever more insistent mental suffering. She remembered the shadow that was John. She saw him bent towards her, then retreating, his features pale and overcast with unaccusing grief. She re-lived their seven years together and, in retrospect, found them to be years of worth and dignity. Until crushed by it all at last, seized by a sudden need to suffer and atone, she crossed to where the draft was bitter, and for a long time stood unflinching on the icy floor.

The storm was close here. Even through the blankets she could feel a sift of snow against her face. The eaves sawed, the walls creaked. Above it all, like a wolf in howling flight, the wind shrilled lone and desolate.

And yet, suddenly she asked herself, hadn't there been other storms, other blizzards? And through the worst of them hadn't he always reached her?

Clutched by the thought she stood rooted a minute. It was hard now to understand how she could have so deceived herself — how a moment of passion could have quieted within her not only conscience, but reason and discretion too. John always came. There could never be a storm to stop him. He was strong, inured to the cold. He had crossed the hills since his boyhood, knew every creek-bed and gully. It was madness to go on like this — to wait. While there was still time she must waken Steven, and hurry him away.

But in the bedroom again, standing at Steven's side, she hesitated. In his detachment from it all, in his quiet, even breathing, there was such sanity, such realism. For him nothing had happened; nothing would. If she wakened him he would only laugh and tell her to listen to the storm. Already it was long past midnight; either John had lost his way or not set out at all. And she knew that in his devotion there was nothing foolhardy. He would never risk a storm beyond his endurance, never permit himself a sacrifice likely to endanger her lot or future. They were both safe. No one would ever know. She must control herself — be sane like Steven.

For comfort she let her hand rest a while on Steven's shoulder. It would be easier were he awake now, with her, sharing her guilt; but gradually as she watched his handsome face in the glimmering light she came to understand that for him no guilt existed. Just as there had been no passion, no conflict. Nothing but the sane appraisal of their situation, nothing but the expectant little smile, and the arrogance of features that were different from John's. She winced deeply, remembering how she had fixed her eyes on those features, how she had tried to believe that so handsome and young, so different from John's, they must in themselves be her justification.

In the flickering light they were still young, still handsome. No longer her justification — she knew now — John was the man — but wistfully still, wondering sharply at their power and tyranny, she touched them a moment with her fingertips again.

She could not blame him. There had been no passion, no guilt; therefore there could be no responsibility. Suddenly looking down at him as he slept, half-smiling still, his lips relaxed in the conscienceless complacency of his achievement, she understood that thus he was revealed in his entirety—all there ever was or ever could be. John was the man. With him lay all the future. For tonight, slowly and contritely through the day and years to come, she would try to make amends.

Then she stole back to the kitchen, and without thought, impelled by overwhelming need again, returned to the door where the draft was bitter still. Gradually towards morning the storm began to spend itself. Its terror blast became a feeble, worn-out moan. The leap of light and shadow sank, and a chill crept in again. Always the eaves creaked, tortured with wordless prophecy. Heedless of it all the clock ticked on in idiot content.

They found him the next day, less than a mile from home. Drifting with the storm he had run against his own pasture fence and overcome had frozen there, erect still, both hands clasping fast the wire.

"He was south of here," they said wonderingly when she told them how he had come across the hills. "Straight south — you'd wonder how he could have missed the buildings. It was the wind last night, coming every way at once. He shouldn't have tried. There was a double wheel around the moon."

She looked past them a moment, then as if to herself said simply, "If you knew him, though—John would try."

It was later, when they had left her a while to be alone with him, that she knelt and touched his hand. Her eyes dimmed, still it was such a strong and patient hand; then, transfixed, they suddenly grew wide and clear. On the palm, white even against its frozen whiteness, was a little smear of paint.

EUDORA WELTY

1909–

Born in Jackson, Mississippi, where her father was president of an insurance company, she went to schools there, then to the Mississippi College for Women. She broke out of her home region to finish college at the University of Wisconsin in 1929, after which she studied at the Columbia University School of Advertising in 1930 and 1931. She returned to Mississippi and worked for various radio stations and newspapers, as well as for the WPA. She began writing fiction in the 1930's, publishing her first collection, *A Curtain of Green*, in 1941. Since then she has led a quiet life in Mississippi, writing and publishing her uniquely perceptive and humorous stories and novels at regular intervals.

Why I Live at the P.O.

I was getting along fine with Mama, Papa-Daddy and Uncle Rondo until my sister Stella-Rondo just separated from her husband and came back home again. Mr. Whitaker! Of course I went with Mr. Whitaker first, when he first appeared here in China Grove, taking "Pose Yourself" photos, and Stella-Rondo broke us up. Told him I was one-sided. Bigger on one side than the other, which is a deliberate, calculated falsehood: I'm the same. Stella-Rondo is exactly twelve months to the day younger than I am and for that reason she's spoiled.

She's always had anything in the world she wanted and then she'd throw it away. Papa-Daddy gave her this gorgeous Add-a-Pearl necklace when she was eight years old and she threw it away playing baseball when she was nine, with only two pearls.

So as soon as she got married and moved away from home the first thing she did was separate! From Mr. Whitaker! This photographer with the popeyes she said she trusted. Came home from one of those towns up in Illinois and to our complete surprise brought this child of two.

Mama said she like to make her drop dead for a second. "Here you had this marvelous blond child and never so much as wrote your mother a word about it," says Mamma. "I'm thoroughly ashamed of you." But of course she wasn't.

Stella-Rondo just calmly takes off this *hat*, I wish you could see it. She says, "Why, Mama, Shirley-T.'s adopted, I can prove it."

"How?" says Mama, but all I says was, "H'm!" There I was over the hot stove, trying to stretch two chickens over five people and a completely unexpected child into the bargain, without one moment's notice.

"What do you mean—'H'm!'?" says Stella-Rondo, and Mama says, "I heard that, Sister."

I said that oh, I didn't mean a thing, only that whoever Shirley-T. was, she was the spit-image of Papa-Daddy if he'd cut off his beard, which of course he'd never do in the world. Papa-Daddy's Mama's papa and sulks.

Stella-Rondo got furious! She said, "Sister, I don't need to tell you you got a lot of nerve and always did have and I'll thank you to make no future reference to my adopted child whatsoever."

"Very well," I said. "Very well, very well. Of course I noticed at once she looks like Mr. Whitaker's side too. That frown. She looks like a cross between Mr. Whitaker and Papa-Daddy."

"Well, all I can say is she isn't."

"She looks exactly like Shirley Temple to me," says Mama, but Shirley-T. just ran away from her.

So the first thing Stella-Rondo did at the table was turn Papa-Daddy against me.

"Papa-Daddy," she says. He was trying to cut up his meat. "Papa-Daddy!" I was taken completely by surprise. Papa-Daddy is about a million years old and's got this long-long beard. "Papa-Daddy, Sister says she fails to understand why you don't cut off your beard."

So Papa-Daddy l-a-y-s down his knife and fork! He's real rich. Mama says he is, he says he isn't. So he says, "Have I heard correctly? You don't understand why I don't cut off my beard?"

"Why," I says, "Papa-Daddy, of course I understand, I did not say any such of a thing, the idea!"

He says, "Hussy!"

I says, "Papa-Daddy, you know I wouldn't any more want you to cut off your beard than the man in the moon. It was the farthest thing from my mind! Stella-Rondo sat there and made that up while she was eating breast of chicken."

But he says, "So the postmistress fails to understand why I don't cut off my beard. Which job I got you through my influence with the government. 'Bird's nest'—is that what you call it?"

Not that it isn't the next to smallest P.O. in the entire state of Mississippi.

I says, "Oh, Papa-Daddy," I says, "I didn't say any such of a thing, I never dreamed it was a bird's nest, I have always been grateful though this is the next to smallest P.O. in the state of Mississippi, and I do not enjoy being referred to as a hussy by my own grandfather."

But Stella-Rondo says, "Yes, you did say it too. Anybody in the world could of heard you, that had ears."

"Stop right there," says Mama, looking at *me*.

So I pulled my napkin straight back through the napkin ring and left the table.

As soon as I was out of the room Mama says, "Call her back, or she'll starve to death," but Papa-Daddy says, "This is the beard I started growing on the Coast when I was fifteen years old." He would of gone on till nightfall if Shirley-T. hadn't lost the Milky Way she ate in Cairo.

So Papa-Daddy says, "I am going out and lie in the hammock, and you can all sit here and remember my words: I'll never cut off my beard as long as I live, even one inch, and I don't appreciate it in you at all." Passed right by me in the hall and went straight out and got in the hammock.

It would be a holiday. It wasn't five minutes before Uncle Rondo suddenly appeared in the hall in one of Stella-Rondo's flesh-colored kimonos, all cut on the bias, like something Mr. Whitaker probably thought was gorgeous.

"Uncle Rondo!" I says. "I didn't know who that was! Where are you going?"

"Sister," he says, "get out of my way, I'm poisoned."

"If you're poisoned stay away from Papa-Daddy," I says. "Keep out of the hammock, Papa-Daddy will certainly beat you on the head if you come within forty miles of him. He thinks I deliberately said he ought to cut off his beard after he got me the P.O., and I've told him and told him and told him, and he acts like he just don't hear me. Papa-Daddy must of gone stone deaf."

"He picked a fine day to do it then," says Uncle Rondo, and before you could say "Jack Robinson" flew out in the yard.

What he'd really done, he'd drunk another bottle of that prescription. He does it every single Fourth of July as sure as shooting, and it's horribly expensive. Then he falls over in the hammock and snores. So he insisted on zigzagging right on out to the hammock, looking like a half-wit.

Papa-Daddy woke up with this horrible yell and right there without moving an inch he tried to turn Uncle Rondo against me. I heard every word he said. Oh, he told Uncle Rondo I didn't learn to read till I was eight years old and he didn't see how in the world I ever got the mail put up at the P.O., much less read it all, and he said if Uncle Rondo could only fathom the lengths he had gone to to get me that job! And he said on the other hand he thought Stella-Rondo had a brilliant mind and deserved credit for getting out of town. All the time he was just lying there swinging as pretty as you please and looping out his beard, and poor Uncle Rondo was *pleading* with him to slow down the hammock, it was making him as dizzy as a witch to watch it. But that's what Papa-Daddy likes about a hammock. So Uncle Rondo was too dizzy to get turned against me for the time being. He's Mama's only brother and is a good case of a one-track mind. Ask anybody. A certified pharmacist.

Just then I heard Stella-Rondo raising the upstairs window. While she was married she got this peculiar idea that it's cooler with the windows shut and locked. So she has to raise the window before she can make a soul hear her outdoors.

So she raises the window and says, "Oh!" You would have thought she was mortally wounded.

Uncle Rondo and Papa-Daddy didn't even look up, but kept right on with what they were doing. I had to laugh.

I flew up the stairs and threw the door open! I says, "What in the wide world's the matter, Stella-Rondo? You mortally wounded?"

"No," she says, "I'm not mortally wounded but I wish you would do me the favor of looking out that window there and telling me what you see."

So I shade my eyes and look out the window.

"I see the front yard," I says.

"Don't you see any human beings?" she says.

"I see Uncle Rondo trying to run Papa-Daddy out of the hammock," I says. "Nothing more. Naturally, it's so suffocating-hot in the house, with all the windows shut and locked, everybody who cares to stay in their right mind will have to go out and get in the hammock before the Fourth of July is over."

"Don't you notice anything different about Uncle Rondo?" asks Stella-Rondo.

"Why, no, except he's got on some terrible-looking flesh-colored contraption I wouldn't be found dead in, is all I can see," I says.

"Never mind, you won't be found dead in it, because it happens to be part of my trousseau, and Mr. Whitaker took several dozen photographs of me in it," says Stella-Rondo. "What on earth could Uncle Rondo *mean* by wearing part of my trousseau out in the broad open daylight without saying so much as 'Kiss my foot,' *knowing* I only got home this morning after my separation and hung my negligee up on the bathroom door, just as nervous as I could be?"

"I'm sure I don't know, and what do you expect me to do about it?" I says. "Jump out the window?"

"No, I expect nothing of the kind. I simply declare that Uncle Rondo looks like a fool in it, that's all," she says. "It makes me sick to my stomach."

"Well, he looks as good as he can," I says. "As good as anybody in reason could." I stood up for Uncle Rondo, please remember. And I said to Stella-Rondo, "I think I would do well not to criticize so freely if I were you and came home with a two-year-old child I had never said a word about, and no explanation whatever about my separation."

"I asked you the instant I entered this house not to refer one more time to my adopted child, and you gave me your word of honor you would not," was all Stella-Rondo would say, and started pulling out every one of her eyebrows with some cheap Kress tweezers.

So I merely slammed the door behind me and went down and made some green-tomato pickle. Somebody had to do it. Of course Mama had turned both the niggers loose; she always said no earthly power could hold one anyway on the Fourth of July, so she wouldn't even try. It turned out that Jaypan fell in the lake and came within a very narrow limit of drowning.

So Mama trots in. Lifts up the lid and says, "H'm! Not very good for your Uncle Rondo in his precarious condition, I must say. Or poor little adopted Shirley-T. Shame on you!"

That made me tired. I says, "Well, Stella-Rondo had better thank her lucky stars it was her instead of me came trotting in with that very peculiar-looking child. Now if it had been me that trotted in from Illinois and brought a peculiar-looking child of two, I shudder to think of the reception I'd of got, much less controlled the diet of an entire family."

"But you must remember, Sister, that you were never married to Mr. Whitaker in the first place and didn't go up to Illinois to live," says Mama, shaking a spoon in my face. "If you had I would of been just as overjoyed to see you and your little adopted girl as I was to see Stella-Rondo, when you wound up with your separation and came on back home."

"You would not," I says.

"Don't contradict me, I would," says Mama.

But I said she couldn't convince me though she talked till she was blue in the face. Then I said, "Besides, you know as well as I do that that child is not adopted."

"She most certainly is adopted," says Mama, stiff as a poker.

I says, "Why, Mama, Stella-Rondo had her just as sure as anything in this world, and just too stuck up to admit it."

"Why, Sister," said Mama. "Here I thought we were going to have a pleasant Fourth of July, and you start right out not believing a word your own baby sister tells you!"

"Just like Cousin Annie Flo. Went to her grave denying the facts of life," I remind Mama.

"I told you if you ever mentioned Annie Flo's name I'd slap your face," says Mama, and slaps my face.

"All right, you wait and see," I says.

"I," says Mama, "I prefer to take my children's word for anything when it's humanly possible." You ought to see Mama, she weighs two hundred pounds and has real tiny feet.

Just then something perfectly horrible occurred to me.

"Mama," I says, "can that child talk?" I simply had to whisper! "Mama, I wonder if that child can be—you know—in any way? Do you realize," I says, "that she hasn't spoken one single, solitary word to a human being up to this minute? This is the way she looks," I says, and I looked like this.

Well, Mama and I just stood there and stared at each other. It was horrible!

"I remember well that Joe Whitaker frequently drank like a fish," says Mama. "I believed to my soul he drank *chemicals*." And without another word she marches to the foot of the stairs and calls Stella-Rondo.

"Stella-Rondo? O-o-o o-o! Stella-Rondo!"

"What?" says Stella-Rondo from upstairs. Not even the grace to get up off the bed.

"Can that child of yours talk?" asks Mama.

Stella-Rondo says, "Can she what?"

"Talk! Talk!" says Mama. "Burdyburdyburdyburdy!"

So Stella-Rondo yells back, "Who says she can't talk?"

"Sister says so," says Mama

"You didn't have to tell me, I know whose word of honor don't mean a thing in this house," says Stella-Rondo.

And in a minute the loudest Yankee voice I ever heard in my life yells out, "OE'm Pop-OE the Sailor-r-r-r Ma-a-an!" and then somebody jumps up and down in the upstairs hall. In another second the house would of fallen down.

"Not only talks, she can tap-dance!" calls Stella-Rondo. "Which is more than some people I won't name can do."

"Why, the little precious darling thing!" Mama says, so surprised. "Just as smart as she can be!" Starts talking baby talk right there. Then she turns on me. "Sister, you ought to be thoroughly ashamed! Run upstairs this instant and apologize to Stella-Rondo and Shirley-T."

"Apologize for what?" I says. "I merely wondered if the child was normal, that's all. Now that she's proved she is, why, I have nothing further to say."

But Mama just turned on her heel and flew out, furious. She ran right upstairs and hugged the baby. She believed it was adopted. Stella-Rondo hadn't done a thing but turn her against me from upstairs while I stood there helpless over the hot stove. So that made Mama, Papa Daddy and the baby all on Stella-Rondo's side.

Next, Uncle Rondo.

I must say that Uncle Rondo has been marvelous to me at various times in the past and I was completely unprepared to be made to jump out of my skin, the way it turned out. Once Stella-Rondo did something perfectly horrible to him—broke a chain letter from Flanders Field—and he took the radio back he had given her and gave it to me. Stella-Rondo was furious! For six months we all had to call her Stella instead of Stella-Rondo, or she wouldn't answer. I always thought Uncle Rondo had all the brains of the entire family. Another time he sent me to Mammoth Cave, with all expenses paid.

But this would be the day he was drinking that prescription, the Fourth of July.

So at supper Stella-Rondo speaks up and says she thinks Uncle Rondo ought to try to eat a little something. So finally Uncle Rondo said he would try a little cold biscuits and ketchup, but that was all. So *she* brought it to him.

"Do you think it wise to disport with ketchup in Stella-Rondo's flesh-colored kimono?" I says. Trying to be considerate! If Stella-Rondo couldn't watch out for her trousseau, somebody had to.

"Any objections?" asks Uncle Rondo, just about to pour out all the ketchup.

"Don't mind what she says, Uncle Rondo," says Stella-Rondo. "Sister has been devoting this solid afternoon to sneering out my bedroom window at the way you look."

"What's that?" says Uncle Rondo. Uncle Rondo has got the most terrible temper in the world. Anything is liable to make him tear the house down if it comes at the wrong time.

So Stella-Rondo says, "Sister says, 'Uncle Rondo certainly does look like a fool in that pink kimono!' "

Do you remember who it was really said that?

Uncle Rondo spills out all the ketchup and jumps out of his chair and tears off the kimono and throws it down on the dirty floor and puts his foot on it. It had to be sent all the way to Jackson to the cleaners and re-pleated.

"So that's your opinion of your Uncle Rondo, is it?" he says. "I look like a fool, do I? Well, that's the last straw. A whole day in this house with nothing to do, and then to hear you come out with a remark like that behind my back!"

"I didn't say any such of a thing, Uncle Rondo," I says, "and I'm not saying who did, either. Why, I think you look all right. Just try to take care of yourself and not talk and eat at the same time," I says. "I think you better go lie down."

"Lie down my foot," says Uncle Rondo. I ought to of known by that he was fixing to do something perfectly horrible.

So he didn't do anything that night in the precarious state he was in—just played Casino with Mama and Stella-Rondo and Shirley-T. and gave Shirley-T. a nickel with a head on both sides. It tickled her nearly to death, and she called him "Papa." But at 6:30 A.M. the next morning, he threw a whole five-cent package of some unsold one-inch firecrackers from the store as hard as he could into my bedroom and they every one went off. Not one bad one in the string. Anybody else, there'd be one that wouldn't go off.

Well, I'm just terribly susceptible to noise of any kind, the doctor has always told me I was the most sensitive person he had ever seen in his whole life, and I was simply prostrated. I couldn't eat! People tell me they heard it as far as the cemetery, and old Aunt Jep Patterson, that had been holding her own so good, thought it was Judgment Day and she was going to meet her whole family. It's usually so quiet here.

And I'll tell you it didn't take me any longer than a minute to make up my mind what to do. There I was with the whole entire house on Stella-Rondo's side and turned against me. If I have anything at all I have pride.

So I just decided I'd go straight down to the P.O. There's plenty of room there in the back, I says to myself.

Well! I made no bones about letting the family catch on to what I was up to. I didn't try to conceal it.

The first thing they knew, I marched in where they were all playing Old Maid and pulled the electric oscillating fan out by the plug, and everything got real hot. Next I snatched the pillow I'd done the needlepoint on right off the davenport from behind Papa-Daddy. He went "Ugh!" I beat Stella-Rondo up the stairs and finally found my charm bracelet in her bureau drawer under a picture of Nelson Eddy.

"So that's the way the land lies," says Uncle Rondo. There he was, piecing on the ham. "Well, Sister, I'll be glad to donate my army cot if you got any place to set it up, providing you'll leave right this minute and let me get some peace." Uncle Rondo was in France.

"Thank you kindly for the cot and 'peace' is hardly the word I would select if I had to resort to firecrackers at 6:30 A.M. in a young girl's bedroom," I says back to him. "And as to where I intend to go, you seem to forget my position as postmistress of China Grove, Mississippi," I says. "I've always got the P.O."

Well, that made them all sit up and take notice.

I went out front and started digging up some four-o'clocks to plant around the P.O.

"Ah-ah-ah!" says Mama, raising the window. "Those happen to be my four-o'clocks. Everything planted in that star is mine. I've never known you to make anything grow in your life."

"Very well," I says. "But I take the fern. Even you, Mama, can't stand there and deny that I'm the one watered that fern. And I happen to know where I can send in a box top and get a packet of one thousand mixed seeds, no two the same kind, free."

"Oh, where?" Mama wants to know.

But I says, "Too late. You 'tend to your house, and I'll 'tend to mine. You hear things like that all the time if you know how to listen to the radio. Perfectly marvelous offers. Get anything you want free."

So I hope to tell you I marched in and got that radio, and they could of all bit a nail in two, especially Stella-Rondo, that it used to belong to, and she well knew she couldn't get it back, I'd sue for it like a shot. And I very politely took the sewing-machine motor I helped pay the most on to give Mama for Christmas back in 1929, and a good big calendar, with the first-aid remedies on it. The thermometer and the Hawaiian ukulele certainly were rightfully mine, and I stood on the step-ladder and got all my watermelon-rind preserves and every fruit and vegetable I'd put up, every jar. Then I began to pull the tacks out of the bluebird wall vases on the archway to the dining room.

"Who told you you could have those, Miss Priss?" says Mama, fanning as hard as she could.

"I bought 'em and I'll keep track of 'em," I says. "I'll tack 'em up one on each side the post-office window, and you can see 'em when you come to ask me for your mail, if you're so dead to see 'em."

"Not I! I'll never darken the door to that post office again if I live to be a hundred," Mama says. "Ungrateful child! After all the money we spent on you at the Normal."

"Me either," says Stella-Rondo. "You can just let my mail lie there and *rot*, for all I care. I'll never come and relieve you of a single, solitary piece."

"I should worry," I says. "And who you think's going to sit down and write you all those big fat letters and postcards, by the way? Mr. Whitaker? Just because he was the only man ever dropped down in China Grove and you got him—unfairly—is he going to sit down and write you a lengthy correspondence after you come home giving no rhyme nor reason whatsoever for your separation and no explanation for the presence of that child? I may not have your brilliant mind, but I fail to see it."

So Mama says, "Sister, I've told you a thousand times that Stella-Rondo simply got homesick, and this child is far too big to be hers," and she says, "Now, why don't you all just sit down and play Casino?"

Then Shirley-T. sticks out her tongue at me in this perfectly horrible way. She has no more manners than the man in the moon. I told her she was going to cross her eyes like that some day and they'd stick.

"It's too late to stop me now," I says. "You should have tried that yesterday. I'm going to the P.O. and the only way you can possibly see me is to visit me there."

So Papa-Daddy says, "You'll never catch me setting foot in that post office, even if I should take a notion into my head to write a letter some place." He says, "I won't have you reachin' out of that little old window with a pair of shears and cuttin' off any beard of mine. I'm too smart for you!"

"We all are," says Stella-Rondo.

But I said, "If you're so smart, where's Mr. Whitaker?"

So then Uncle Rondo says, "I'll thank you from now on to stop reading all the orders I get on postcards and telling everybody in China Grove what you think is the matter with them," but I says, "I draw my own conclusions and will continue in the future to draw them." I says, "If people want to write their inmost secrets on penny postcards, there's nothing in the wide world you can do about it, Uncle Rondo."

"And if you think we'll ever *write* another postcard you're sadly mistaken," says Mama.

"Cutting off your nose to spite your face then," I says. "But if you're all determined to have no more to do with the U.S. mail, think of this:

What will Stella-Rondo do now, if she wants to tell Mr. Whitaker to come after her?"

"Wah!" says Stella-Rondo. I knew she'd cry. She had a conniption fit right there in the kitchen.

"It will be interesting to see how long she holds out," I says. "And now—I am leaving."

"Good-bye," says Uncle Rondo.

"Oh, I declare," says Mama, "to think that a family of mine should quarrel on the Fourth of July, or the day after, over Stella-Rondo leaving old Mr. Whitaker and having the sweetest little adopted child! It looks like we'd all be glad!"

"Wah!" says Stella-Rondo, and has a fresh conniption fit.

"*He* left *her*—you mark my words," I says. "That's Mr. Whitaker. I know Mr. Whitaker. After all, I knew him first. I said from the beginning he'd up and leave her. I foretold every single thing that's happened."

"Where did he go?" asks Mama.

"Probably to the North Pole, if he knows what's good for him," I says.

But Stella-Rondo just bawled and wouldn't say another word. She flew to her room and slammed the door.

"Now look what you've gone and done, Sister," says Mama. "You go apologize."

"I haven't got time, I'm leaving," I says.

"Well, what are you waiting around for?" asks Uncle Rondo.

So I just picked up the kitchen clock and marched off, without saying "Kiss my foot" or anything, and never did tell Stella-Rondo good-bye.

There was a nigger girl going along on a little wagon right in front.

"Nigger girl," I says, "come help me haul these things down the hill, I'm going to live in the post office."

Took her nine trips in her express wagon. Uncle Rondo came out on the porch and threw her a nickel.

And that's the last I've laid eyes on any of my family or my family laid eyes on me for five solid days and nights. Stella-Rondo may be telling the most horrible tales in the world about Mr. Whitaker, but I haven't heard them. As I tell everybody, I draw my own conclusions.

But oh, I like it here. It's ideal, as I've been saying. You see, I've got everything cater-cornered, the way I like it. Hear the radio? All the war news. Radio, sewing machine, book ends, ironing board and that great big piano lamp—peace, that's what I like. Butter-bean vines planted all along the front where the strings are.

Of course, there's not much mail. My family are naturally the main people in China Grove, and if they prefer to vanish from the face of the earth, for all the mail they get or the mail they write, why, I'm not going to open my mouth. Some of the folks here in town are taking up for me and some turned against me. I know which is which. There are always people who will quit buying stamps just to get on the right side of Papa-Daddy.

But here I am, and here I'll stay. I want the world to know I'm happy.

And if Stella-Rondo should come to me this minute, on bended knees, and *attempt* to explain the incidents of her life with Mr. Whitaker, I'd simply put my fingers in both my ears and refuse to listen.

DORIS LESSING
1919–

Doris Taylor was born in Kermanshah, Persia (now Iran), where her father had a managerial post in the Imperial Bank of Persia. He was an Englishman who had lost a leg in World War I and married his nurse. In 1925 the family moved to Southern Rhodesia (now Zimbabwe), where Alfred Taylor got a loan from the government land bank to buy 3,000 acres of land recently taken away from Africans, who had been put onto reservations. With cheap native labor the Taylors raised corn on the land and never made enough money to get off it. Doris Taylor went to a Catholic convent school and Girls' High School in the small city of Salisbury, but left school at fourteen and worked as a nursemaid and then as a secretary. She was married twice (acquiring the name of Lessing) and had children, before deciding that marriage was not one of her talents. She had been writing for some time but got serious about it only in her late twenties. She left Rhodesia with her first novel and some stories complete, and moved to England, where she joined the Communist Party briefly and began her five-volume sequence of autobiographical novels, *Children of Violence*. Her most ambitious book is *The Golden Notebook* (1962). Recently, her concern for the human future has led her to writing science fiction. She is one of England's most important writers at the present time.

Sunrise on the Veld

Every night that winter he said aloud into the dark of the pillow: Half-past four! Half-past four! till he felt his brain had gripped the words and held them fast. Then he fell asleep at once, as if a shutter had fallen; and lay with his face turned to the clock so that he could see it first thing when he woke.

It was half-past four to the minute, every morning. Triumphantly pressing down the alarm-knob of the clock, which the dark half of his mind had outwitted, remaining vigilant all night and counting the hours as he lay relaxed in sleep, he huddled down for a last warm moment under the clothes, playing with the idea of lying abed for this once only. But he played with it for the fun of knowing that it was a weakness he could defeat without effort; just as he set the alarm each night for the delight of the moment when he woke and stretched his limbs, feeling the muscles tighten, and thought: Even my brain— even that! I can control every part of myself.

Luxury of warm rested body, with the arms and legs and fingers waiting like soldiers for a word of command! Joy of knowing that the precious hours were given to sleep voluntarily!—for he had once stayed awake three nights running, to prove that he could, and then worked all day, refusing even to admit that he was tired; and now sleep seemed to him a servant to be commanded and refused.

The boy stretched his frame full-length, touching the wall at his head with his hands, and the bedfoot with his toes; then he sprang out, like a fish leaping from water. And it was cold, cold.

He always dressed rapidly, so as to try and conserve his night-warmth till the sun rose two hours later; but by the time he had on his clothes his hands were numbed and he could scarcely hold his shoes. These he could not put on for fear of waking his parents, who never came to know how early he rose.

As soon as he stepped over the lintel, the flesh of his soles contracted on the chilled earth, and his legs began to ache with cold. It was night: the stars were glittering, the trees standing black and still. He looked for signs of day, for the greying of the edge of a stone, or a lightening in the sky where the sun would rise, but there was nothing yet. Alert as an animal he crept past the dangerous window, standing poised with his hand on the sill for one proudly fastidious moment, looking in at the stuffy blackness of the room where his parents lay.

Feeling for the grass-edge of the path with his toes, he reached inside another window further along the wall, where his gun had been set in readiness the night before. The steel was icy, and numbed fingers slipped along it, so that he had to hold it in the crook of his arm for safety. Then he tiptoed to the room where the dogs slept, and was fearful that they might have been tempted to go before him; but they were waiting, their haunches crouched in reluctance at the cold, but ears and swinging tails greeting the gun ecstatically. His warning undertone kept them secret and silent till the house was a hundred yards back: then they bolted off into the bush, yelping excitedly. The boy imagined his parents turning in their beds and muttering: Those dogs again! before they were dragged back in sleep; and he smiled scornfully. He always looked back over his shoulder at the house before he passed a wall of trees that shut it from sight. It looked so low and small, crouching there under a tall and brilliant sky. Then he turned his back on it, and on the frowsting sleepers, and forgot them.

He would have to hurry. Before the light grew strong he must be four miles away; and already a tint of green stood in the hollow of a leaf, and the air smelled of morning and the stars were dimming.

He slung the shoes over his shoulder, veld *skoen* that were crinkled and hard with the dews of a hundred mornings. They would be necessary when the ground became too hot to bear. Now he felt the chilled dust push up between his toes, and he let the muscles of his feet spread and settle into the shapes of the earth; and he thought: I could walk a hundred miles on feet like these! I could walk all day, and never tire!

He was walking swiftly through the dark tunnel of foliage that in day-time was a road. The dogs were invisibly ranging the lower travelways of the bush, and he heard them panting. Sometimes he felt a cold muzzle on his leg before they were off again, scouting for a trail to follow. They were not trained, but free-running companions of the hunt, who often tired of the long stalk before the final shots, and went off on their own pleasure. Soon he could see them, small and wild-looking in a wild strange light, now that the bush stood trembling on the verge of colour, waiting for the sun to paint earth and grass afresh.

The grass stood to his shoulders; and the trees were showering a faint silvery rain. He was soaked; his whole body was clenched in a steady shiver.

Once he bent to the road that was newly scored with animal trails, and regretfully straightened, reminding himself that the pleasure of tracking must wait till another day.

He began to run along the edge of a field, noting jerkily how it was filmed over with fresh spiderweb, so that the long reaches of great black clods seemed netted in glistening grey. He was using the steady lope he had learned by watching the natives, the run that is a dropping of the weight of the body from one foot to the next in a slow balancing movement that never tires, nor shortens the breath; and he felt the blood pulsing down his legs and along his arms, and the exultation and pride of body mounted in him till he was shutting his teeth hard against a violent desire to shout his triumph.

Soon he had left the cultivated part of the farm. Behind him the bush was low and black. In front was a long vlei, acres of long pale grass that sent back a hollowing gleam of light to a satiny sky. Near him thick swathes of grass were bent with the weight of water, and diamond drops sparkled on each frond.

The first bird woke at his feet and at once a flock of them sprang into the air calling shrilly that day had come; and suddenly, behind him, the bush woke into song, and he could hear the guinea fowl calling far ahead of him. That meant they would now be sailing down from their trees into thick grass, and it was for them he had come: he was too late. But he did not mind. He forgot he had come to shoot. He set his legs wide, and balanced from foot to foot, and swung his gun up and down in both hands horizontally, in a kind of improvised exercise, and let his head sink back till it was pillowed in his neck muscles, and watched how above him small rosy clouds floated in a lake of gold.

Suddenly it all rose in him: it was unbearable. He leapt up into the air, shouting and yelling wild, unrecognisable noises. Then he began to run, not carefully, as he had before, but madly, like a wild thing. He was clean crazy, yelling mad with the joy of living and a superfluity of youth. He rushed down the vlei under a tumult of crimson and gold, while all the birds of the world sang about him. He ran in great leaping strides, and shouted as he ran, feeling his body rise into the crisp rushing air and fall back surely on to sure feet; and thought briefly, not believing that such a thing could happen to him, that he could break his ankle any moment, in this thick tangled grass. He cleared bushes like a duiker, leapt over rocks; and finally came to a dead stop at a place where the ground fell abruptly away below him to the river. It had been a two-mile-long dash through waist-high growth, and he was breathing hoarsely and could no longer sing. But he poised on a rock and looked down at stretches of water that gleamed through stooping trees, and thought suddenly, I am fifteen! Fifteen! The words came new to him; so that he kept repeating them wonderingly, with swelling excitement; and he felt the years of his life with his hands, as if he were counting marbles, each one hard and separate and compact, each one a wonderful shining thing. That was what he was: fifteen years of this rich soil, and this slow-moving water, and air that smelt like a challenge whether it was warm and sultry at noon, or as brisk as cold water, like it was now.

There was nothing he couldn't do, nothing! A vision came to him, as he stood there, like when a child hears the word "eternity" and tries to understand it, and time takes possession of the mind. He felt his life ahead of him as a great and wonderful thing, something that was his; and he said aloud, with the blood rising to his head: all the great men of the world have been as I am now, and there is nothing I can't become, nothing I can't do; there is no country in the world I cannot make part of myself, if I choose. I contain the world. I can make of it what I want. If I choose, I can change everything that is going to happen: it depends on me, and what I decide now.

The urgency, and the truth and the courage of what his voice was saying exulted him so that he began to sing again, at the top of his voice, and the sound went echoing down the river gorge. He stopped for the echo, and sang again: stopped and shouted. That was what he was!—he sang, if he chose; and the world had to answer him.

And for minutes he stood there, shouting and singing and waiting for the lovely eddying sound of the echo; so that his own new strong thoughts came back and washed round his head, as if someone were answering him and encouraging him; till the gorge was full of soft voices clashing back and forth from rock to rock over the river. And then it seemed as if there was a new voice. He listened, puzzled, for it was not his own. Soon he was leaning forward, all his nerves alert, quite still: somewhere close to him there was a noise that was no joyful bird, nor tinkle of falling water, nor ponderous movement of cattle.

There it was again. In the deep morning hush that held his future and his past, was a sound of pain, and repeated over and over: it was a kind of shortened scream, as if someone, something, had no breath to scream. He came to himself, looked about him, and called for the dogs. They did not appear: they had gone off on their own business, and he was alone. Now he was clean sober, all the madness gone. His heart beating fast, because of that frightened screaming, he stepped carefully off the rock and went towards a belt of trees. He was moving cautiously, for not so long ago he had seen a leopard in just this spot.

At the edge of the trees he stopped and peered, holding his gun ready; he advanced, looking steadily about him, his eyes narrowed. Then, all at once, in the middle of a step, he faltered, and his face was puzzled. He shook his head impatiently, as if he doubted his own sight.

There, between two trees, against a background of gaunt black rocks, was a figure from a dream, a strange beast that was horned and drunken-legged, but like something he had never even imagined. It seemed to be ragged. It looked like a small buck that had black ragged tufts of fur standing up irregularly all over it, with patches of raw flesh beneath . . . but the patches of rawness were disappearing under moving black and came again elsewhere; and all the time the creature screamed, in small gasping screams, and leaped drunkenly from side to side, as if it were blind.

Then the boy understood: it *was* a buck. He ran closer, and again stood still, stopped by a new fear. Around him the grass was whispering and alive. He looked wildly about, and then down. The ground was black with ants, great energetic ants that took no notice of him, but hurried and scurried towards the fighting shape, like glistening black water flowing through the grass.

And, as he drew in his breath and pity and terror seized him, the beast fell and the screaming stopped. Now he could hear nothing but one bird singing, and the sound of the rustling, whispering ants.

He peered over at the writhing blackness that jerked convulsively with the jerking nerves. It grew quieter. There were small twitches from the mass that still looked vaguely like the shape of a small animal.

It came into his mind that he should shoot it and end its pain; and he raised the gun. Then he lowered it again. The buck could no longer feel; its fighting was a mechanical protest of the nerves. But it was not that which made him put down the gun. It was a swelling feeling of rage and misery and protest that expressed itself in the thought: if I had not come it would have died like this: so why should I interfere? All over the bush things like this happen; they happen all the time; this is how life goes on, by living things dying in anguish. He gripped the gun between his knees and felt in his own limbs the myriad swarming pain of the twitching animal that could no longer feel, and set his teeth, and said over and over again under his breath: I can't stop it. I can't stop it. There is nothing I can do.

He was glad that the buck was unconscious and had gone past suffering so that he did not have to make a decision to kill it even when he was feeling with his whole body: this is what happens, this is how things work.

It was right—that was what he was feeling. *It was right and nothing could alter it.*

The knowledge of fatality, of what has to be, had gripped him and for the first time in his life; and he was left unable to make any movement of brain or body, except to say: "Yes, yes. That is what living is." It had entered his flesh and his bones and grown in to the furthest corners of his brain and would never leave him. And at that moment he could not have performed the smallest action of mercy, knowing as he did, having lived on it all his life, the vast unalterable, cruel veld, where at any moment one might stumble over a skull or crush the skeleton of some small creature.

Suffering, sick, and angry, but also grimly satisfied with his new stoicism, he stood there leaning on his rifle, and watched the seething black mound grow smaller. At his feet, now, were ants trickling back with pink fragments in their mouths, and there was a fresh acid smell in his nostrils. He sternly controlled the uselessly convulsing muscles of his empty stomach, and reminded himself: the ants must eat too! At the same time he found that the tears were streaming down his face, and his clothes were soaked with the sweat of that other creature's pain.

The shape had grown small. Now it looked like nothing recognisable. He did not know how long it was before he saw the blackness thin, and bits of white showed through, shining in the sun—yes, there was the sun, just up, glowing over the rocks. Why, the whole thing could not have taken longer than a few minutes.

He began to swear, as if the shortness of the time was in itself unbearable, using the words he had heard his father say. He strode forward, crushing ants with each step, and brushing them off his clothes, till he stood above the skeleton, which lay sprawled under a small bush. It was clean-picked. It might have been lying there years, save that on the white bone were pink fragments of gristle. About the bones ants were ebbing away, their pincers full of meat.

The boy looked at them, big black ugly insects. A few were standing and gazing up at him with small glittering eyes.

"Go away!" he said to the ants, very coldly. "I am not for you—not just yet, at any rate. Go away." And he fancied that the ants turned and went away.

He bent over the bones and touched the sockets in the skull; that was where the eyes were, he thought incredulously, remembering the liquid dark eyes of a buck. And then he bent the slim foreleg bone, swinging it horizontally in his palm.

That morning, perhaps an hour ago, this small creature had been stepping proud and free through the bush, feeling the chill on its hide even as he himself had done, exhilarated by it. Proudly stepping the earth, tossing its horns, frisking a pretty white tail, it had sniffed the cold morning air. Walking like kings and conquerors it had moved through this free-held bush, where each blade of grass grew for it alone, and where the river ran pure sparkling water for its slaking.

And then—what had happened? Such a swift surefooted thing could surely not be trapped by a swarm of ants?

The boy bent curiously to the skeleton. Then he saw that the back leg that lay uppermost and strained out in the tension of death, was snapped midway in the thigh, so that broken bones jutted over each other uselessly. So that was it! Limping into the ant-masses it could not escape, once it had sensed the danger. Yes, but how had the leg been broken? Had it fallen, perhaps? Impossible, a buck was too light and graceful. Had some jealous rival horned it?

What could possibly have happened? Perhaps some Africans had thrown stones at it, as they do, trying to kill it for meat, and had broken its leg. Yes, that must be it.

Even as he imagined the crowd of running, shouting natives, and the flying stones, and the leaping buck, another picture came into his mind. He saw himself, on any one of these bright ringing mornings, drunk with excitement, taking a snap shot at some half-seen buck. He saw himself with the gun lowered, wondering whether he had missed or not; and thinking at last that it was late, and he wanted his breakfast, and it was not worth while to track miles after an animal that would very likely get away from him in any case.

For a moment he would not face it. He was a small boy again, kicking sulkily at the skeleton, hanging his head, refusing to accept the responsibility.

Then he straightened up, and looked down at the bones with an odd expression of dismay, all the anger gone out of him. His mind went quite empty: all around him he could see trickles of ants disappearing into the grass. The whispering noise was faint and dry, like the rustling of a cast snakeskin.

At last he picked up his gun and walked homewards. He was telling himself half defiantly that he wanted his breakfast. He was telling himself that it was getting very hot, much too hot to be out roaming the bush.

Really, he was tired. He walked heavily, not looking where he put his feet. When he came within sight of his home he stopped, knitting his brows. There was something he had to think out. The death of that small animal was a thing that concerned him, and he was by no means finished with it. It lay at the back of his mind uncomfortably.

Soon, the very next morning, he would get clear of everybody and go to the bush and think about it.

MAVIS GALLANT

1922–

Born in Montreal and educated in many schools in Canada and the eastern United States, she is a distinguished journalist, novelist, dramatist, and, above all, short-story writer. In 1944 she published her first two stories and also began work as a journalist with the *Montreal Standard*. During the following six years she wrote more than sixty feature articles for the *Standard* before leaving, in 1950, for Europe. Since that time Paris has been her home, although she retains her Canadian citizenship, and she has devoted herself primarily to the writing of fiction. Her first collection of short stories, *The Other Paris* (1959), explores the lives of exiles and expatriates; here as elsewhere in her fiction Gallant, an acute observer of social customs, examines men and women trapped in exiled lives that fail to satisfy them. She has published two novels, *Green Water, Green Sky* (1959) and *A Fairly Good Time* (1970), seven more collections of short fiction, one play, *What Is to Be Done?* (1982), and a collection of essays and review articles, *Paris Notebooks* (1986). She is a frequent contributor to *The New Yorker*, where "The Ice Wagon Going Down the Street" first appeared in 1963.

The Ice Wagon Going Down the Street

Now that they are out of world affairs and back where they started, Peter Frazier's wife says, "Everybody else did well in the international thing except us."

"You have to be crooked," he tells her.

"Or smart. Pity we weren't."

It is Sunday morning. They sit in the kitchen, drinking their coffee, slowly, remembering the past. They say the names of people as if they were magic. Peter thinks, *Agnes Brusen*, but there are hundreds of other names. As a private married joke, Peter and Sheilah wear the silk dressing gowns they bought in Hong Kong. Each thinks the other a peacock, rather splendid, but they pretend the dressing gowns are silly and worn in fun.

Peter and Sheilah and their two daughters, Sandra and Jennifer, are visiting Peter's unmarried sister, Lucille. They have been Lucille's guests seventeen weeks, ever since they returned to Toronto from the Far East. Their big old steamer trunk blocks a corner of the kitchen, making a problem of the refrigerator door; but even Lucille says the trunk may as well stay where it is, for the present. The Fraziers' future is so unsettled; everything is still in the air.

Lucille has given her bedroom to her two nieces, and sleeps on a camp cot in the hall. The parents have the living-room divan. They have no privileges here; they sleep after Lucille has seen the last television show that interests her. In the hall closet their clothes are crushed by winter overcoats. They know they are being judged for the first time. Sandra and Jennifer are waiting for Sheilah and Peter to decide. They are waiting to learn where these exotic parents will fly to next. What sort of climate will Sheilah consider? What job will Peter consent to accept? When the parents are ready, the children will make a decision of their own. It is just possible that Sandra and Jennifer will choose to stay with their aunt.

The peacock parents are watched by wrens. Lucille and her nieces are much the same—sandy-colored, proudly plain. Neither of the girls has the father's insouciance or the mother's appearance—her height, her carriage, her thick hair, and sky-blue eyes. The children are more cautious than their parents; more Canadian. When they saw their aunt's apartment they had been away from Canada nine years, ever since they were two and four; and Jennifer, the elder, said, "Well, now we're home." Her voice is nasal and flat. Where did she learn that voice? And why should this be home? Peter's answer to anything about his mystifying children is, "It must be in the blood."

On Sunday morning Lucille takes her nieces to church. It seems to be the only condition she imposes on her relations: the children must be decent. The girls go willingly, with their new hats and purses and gloves and coral bracelets and strings of pearls. The parents, ramshackle, sleepy, dim in the brain because it is Sunday, sit down to their coffee and privacy and talk of the past.

"We weren't crooked," says Peter. "We weren't even smart."

Sheilah's head bobs up; she is no drowner. It is wrong to say they have nothing to show for time. Sheilah has the Balenciaga. It is a black afternoon dress, stiff and boned at the waist, long for the fashions of now, but neither Sheilah nor Peter would change a thread. The Balenciaga is their talisman, their treasure; and after they remember it they touch hands and think that the years are not behind them but hazy and marvelous and still to be lived.

The first place they went to was Paris. In the early 'fifties the pick of the international jobs was there. Peter had inherited the last scrap of money he knew he was ever likely to see, and it was enough to get them over: Sheilah and Peter and the babies and the steamer trunk. To their joy and astonishment they had money in the bank. They said to each other, "It should last a year." Peter was fastidious about the new job; he hadn't come all this distance to accept just anything. In Paris he met Hugh Taylor, who was earning enough smuggling gasoline to keep his wife in Paris and a girl in Rome. That impressed Peter, because he remembered Taylor as a sour scholarship student without the slightest talent for life. Taylor had a job, of course. He hadn't said to himself, I'll go over to Europe and smuggle gasoline. It gave Peter an idea; he saw the shape of things. First you catch your fish. Later, at an international party, he met Johnny Hertzberg, who told him Germany was the place. Hertzberg said that anyone who came out of Germany broke now was too stupid to be here, and deserved to be back home at a desk. Peter nodded, as if he had already thought of that. He began to think about Germany. Paris was fine for a holiday, but it had been picked clean. Yes, Germany. His money was running low. He thought about Germany quite a lot.

That winter was moist and delicate; so fragile that they daren't speak of it now. There seemed to be plenty of everything and plenty of time. They were living the dream of a marriage, the fabric uncut, nothing slashed or spoiled. All winter they spent their money, and went to parties, and talked about Peter's future job. It lasted four months. They spent their money, lived in the future, and were never as happy again.

After four months they were suddenly moved away from Paris, but not to Germany—to Geneva. Peter thinks it was because of the incident at the Trudeau wedding at the Ritz. Paul Trudeau was a French-Canadian Peter had known at school and in the Navy. Trudeau had turned into a snob, proud of his career and his Paris connections. He tried to make the difference felt, but Peter thought the difference was only for strangers. At the wedding reception Peter lay down on the floor and said he was dead. He held a white azalea in a brass pot on his chest, and sang, "Oh, hear us when we cry to Thee for those in peril on the sea." Sheilah bent over him and said, "Peter, darling, get up. Pete, listen, every single person who can do something for you is in this room. If you love me, you'll get up."

"I do love you," he said, ready to engage in a serious conversation. "She's so beautiful," he told a second face. "She's nearly as tall as I am. She was a model in London. I met her over in London in the war. I met her there in the war." He lay on his back with the azalea on his chest, explaining their history. A waiter took the brass pot away, and after Peter had been hauled to his feet he knocked the waiter down. Trudeau's bride, who was freshly out of an Ursuline convent, became hysterical; and even though Paul Trudeau and Peter were old acquaintances, Trudeau never spoke to him again. Peter says now that French-Canadians always have that bit of spite. He says Trudeau asked the Embassy to interfere. Luckily, back home there were still a few people to whom the name "Frazier" meant something, and it was to these people that Peter appealed. He wrote letters saying that a French-Canadian combine was preventing his getting a decent job, and could anything be done? No one answered directly, but it was clear that what they settled for was exile to Geneva: a season of meditation and remorse, as he explained to Sheilah, and it was managed tactfully, through Lucille. Lucille wrote that a friend of hers, May Fergus, now a secretary in Geneva, had heard about a job. The job was filing pictures in the information service of an international agency in the Palais des Nations. The pay was so-so, but Lucille thought Peter must be getting fed up doing nothing.

Peter often asks his sister now who put her up to it—what important person told her to write that letter suggesting Peter go to Geneva?

"Nobody," says Lucille. "I mean, nobody in the way *you* mean. I really did have this girl friend working there, and I knew you must be running through your money pretty fast in Paris."

"It must have been somebody pretty high up," Peter says. He looks at his sister admiringly, as he has often looked at his wife.

Peter's wife had loved him in Paris. Whatever she wanted in marriage she found that winter, there. In Geneva, where Peter was a file clerk and they lived in a furnished flat, she pretended they were in Paris and life was still the same. Often, when the children were at supper, she changed as though she and Peter were dining out. She wore the Balenciaga, and put candles on the card table where she and Peter ate their meal. The neckline of the dress was soiled with make-up. Peter remembers her dabbing on the make-up with a wet sponge. He remembers her in the kitchen, in the soiled Balenciaga, patting on the make-up with a filthy sponge. Behind her, at the kitchen table, Sandra and

Jennifer, in buttonless pajamas and bunny slippers, ate their supper of marmalade sandwiches and milk. When the children were asleep, the parents dined solemnly, ritually, Sheilah sitting straight as a queen.

It was a mysterious period of exile, and he had to wait for signs, or signals, to know when he was free to leave. He never saw the job any other way. He forgot he had applied for it. He thought he had been sent to Geneva because of a misdemeanor and had to wait to be released. Nobody pressed him at work. His immediate boss had resigned, and he was alone for months in a room with two desks. He read the *Herald-Tribune*, and tried to discover how things were here—how the others ran their lives on the pay they were officially getting. But it was a closed conspiracy. He was not dealing with adventurers now but civil servants waiting for pension day. No one ever answered his questions. They pretended to think his questions were a form of wit. His only solace in exile was the few happy weekends he had in the late spring and early summer. He had met another old acquaintance, Mike Burleigh. Mike was a serious liberal who had married a serious heiress. The Burleighs had two guest lists. The first was composed of stuffy people they felt obliged to entertain, while the second was made up of their real friends, the friends they wanted. The real friends strove hard to become stuffy and dull and thus achieve the first guest list, but few succeeded. Peter went on the first list straight away. Possibly Mike didn't understand, at the beginning, why Peter was pretending to be a file clerk. Peter had such an air— he might have been sent by a universal inspector to see how things in Geneva were being run.

Every Friday in May and June and part of July, the Fraziers rented a sky-blue Fiat and drove forty miles east of Geneva to the Burleighs' summer house. They brought the children, a suitcase, the children's tattered picture books, and a token bottle of gin. This, in memory, is a period of water and water birds; swans, roses, and singing birds. The children were small and still belonged to them. If they remember too much, their mouths water, their stomachs hurt. Peter says, "It was fine while it lasted." Enough. While it lasted Sheilah and Madge Burleigh were close. They abandoned their husbands and spent long summer afternoons comparing their mothers and praising each other's skin and hair. To Madge, and not to Peter, Sheilah opened her Liverpool childhood with the words "rat poor." Peter heard about it later, from Mike. The women's friendship seemed to Peter a bad beginning. He trusted women but not with each other. It lasted ten weeks. One Sunday, Madge said she needed the two bedrooms the Fraziers usually occupied for a party of sociologists from Pakistan, and that was the end. In November, the Fraziers heard that the summer house had been closed, and that the Burleighs were in Geneva, in their winter flat; they gave no sign. There was no help for it, and no appeal.

Now Peter began firing letters to anyone who had ever known his late father. He was living in a mild yellow autumn. Why does he remember the streets of the city dark, and the windows everywhere black with rain? He remembers being with Sheilah and the children as if they clung together while just outside their small shelter it rained and rained. The children slept in the bedroom of the flat because the window gave on the street and they could breathe air. Peter and Sheilah had the living-room couch. Their window was not a real window but a square on a wall of cement. The flat seemed damp as a cave. Peter remembers steam in the kitchen, pools under the sink, sweat on the pipes. Water streamed on him from the children's clothes, washed and dripping overhead. The trunk upended in the children's room, was not quite unpacked. Sheilah had not signed her name to this life; she had not given in. Once Peter heard her drop her aitches. "You kids are lucky," she said to the girls. "I never 'ad so much as a sit-down meal. I ate chips out of a paper or I 'ad a butty out on the stairs." He never asked her what a butty was. He thinks it means bread and cheese.

The day he heard "You kids are lucky" he understood they were becoming in fact something they had only *appeared* to be until now— the shabby civil servant and his brood. If he had been European he would have ridden to work on a bicycle, in the uniform of his class and condition. He would have worn a tight coat, a turned collar, and a dirty tie. He wondered then if coming here had been a mistake, and if he should not, after all, still be in a place where his name meant something. Surely Peter Frazier should live where "Frazier" counts? In Ontario even now when he says "Frazier" an absent look comes over his hearer's face, as if its owner were consulting an interior guide. What is Frazier? What does it mean? Oil? Power? Politics? Wheat? Real estate? The creditors had the house sealed when Peter's father died. His aunt collapsed with a heart attack in somebody's bachelor apartment, leaving three sons and a widower to surmise they had never known her. Her will was a disappointment. None of that generation left enough. One made it: the granite Presbyterian immigrants from Scotland. Their children, a generation of daunted women and maiden men, held still. Peter's father's crowd spent: they were not afraid of their fathers, and their grandfathers were old. Peter and his sister and his cousins lived on the remains. They were left the rinds of income, of notions, and the memories of ideas rather than ideas intact. If Peter can choose his reincarnation, let him be the oppressed son of a Scottish parson. Let Peter grow up on cuffs and iron principles. Let him make the fortune! Let him flee the manse! When he was small his patrimony was squandered under his nose. He remembers people dancing in his father's house. He remembers seeing and nearly understanding adultery in a guest room, among a pile of wraps. He thought he had seen a murder; he never told. He remembers licking glasses wherever he found them—on window sills, on stairs, in the pantry. In his room he listened while Lucille read Beatrix Potter. The bad rabbit stole the carrot from the good rabbit without saying please, and downstairs was the noise of the party—the roar of the crouched lion. When his father died he saw the chairs upside down and the bailiff's chalk marks. Then the doors were sealed.

He has often tried to tell Sheilah why he cannot be defeated. He remembers his father saying, "Nothing can touch us," and Peter believed it and still does. It has prevented his taking his troubles too seriously. "Nothing can be as bad as this," he will tell himself. "It is happening to me." Even in Geneva, where his status was file clerk, where he sank and stopped on the level of the men who never emigrated, the men on the bicycles—even there he had a manner of strolling to work as if his office were a pastime, and his real life a secret so splendid he could share it with no one except himself.

In Geneva Peter worked for a woman—a girl. She was a Norwegian from a small town in Saskatchewan. He supposed they had been put together because they were Canadians; but they were as strange to each other as if "Canadian" meant any number of things, or had no real meaning. Soon after Agnes Brusen came to the office she hung her framed university degree on the wall. It was one of the gritty, prideful gestures that stand for push, toil, and family sacrifice. He thought, then, that she must be one of a family of immigrants for whom education is everything. Hugh Taylor had told him that in some families the older children never marry until the youngest have finished school. Sometimes every second child is sacrificed and made to work for the education of the next born. Those who finish college spend years paying back. They are white-hot Protestants, and they live with a load of work and debt and obligation. Peter placed his new colleague on scraps of information. He had never been in the West.

She came to the office on a Monday morning in October. The office was overheated and painted cream. It contained two desks, the filing cabinets, a map of the world as it had been in 1945, and the Charter of the United Nations left behind by Agnes Brusen's predecessor. (She took down the Charter without asking Peter if he minded, with the impudence of gesture you find in women who wouldn't say boo to a goose; and then she hung her college degree on the nail where the Charter had been.) Three people brought her in—a whole committee. One of them said, "Agnes, this is Pete Frazier. Pete, Agnes Brusen. Pete's Canadian, too, Agnes. He knows all about the office, so ask him anything."

Of course he knew all about the office: he knew the exact spot where the cord of the venetian blind was frayed, obliging one to give an extra tug to the right.

The girl might have been twenty-three: no more. She wore a brown tweed suit with bone buttons, and a new silk scarf and new shoes. She clutched an unscratched brown purse. She seemed dressed in going-away presents. She said, "Oh, I never smoke," with a convulsive movement of her hand, when Peter offered his case. He was courteous, hiding his disappointment. The people he worked with had told him a Scandinavian girl was arriving, and he had expected a stunner. Agnes was a mole: she was small and brown, and round-shouldered as if she had always carried parcels or younger children in her arms. A mole's profile was turned when she said goodbye to her committee. If she had been foreign, ill-favored though she was, he might have flirted a little, just to show that he was friendly; but their being Canadian, and suddenly left together, was a sexual damper. He sat down and lit his own cigarette. She smiled at him, questioningly, he thought, and sat as if she had never seen a chair before. He wondered if his smoking was annoying her. He wondered if she was fidgety about drafts, or allergic to anything, and whether she would want the blind up or down. His social compass was out of order because the others couldn't tell Peter and Agnes apart. There was a world of difference between them, yet it was she who had been brought in to sit at the larger of the two desks.

While he was thinking this she got up and walked around the office, almost on tiptoe, opening the doors of closets and pulling out the filing trays. She looked inside everything except the drawers of Peter's desk. (In any case, Peter's desk was locked. His desk is locked wherever he works. In Geneva he went into Personnel one morning, early, and pinched his application form. He had stated on the form that he had seven years' experience in public relations and could speak French, German, Spanish, and Italian. He has always collected anything important about himself—anything useful. But he can never get on with the final act, which is getting rid of the information. He has kept papers about for years, a constant source of worry.)

"I know this looks funny, Mr Ferris," said the girl. "I'm not really snooping or anything. I just can't feel easy in a new place unless I know where everything is. In a new place everything seems so hidden."

If she had called him 'Ferris' and pretended not to know he was Frazier, it could only be because they had sent her here to spy on him and see if he had repented and was fit for a better place in life. "You'll be all right here," he said. "Nothing's hidden. Most of us haven't got brains enough to have secrets. This is Rainbow Valley." Depressed by the thought that they were having him watched now, he passed his hand over his hair and looked outside to the lawn and the parking lot and the peacocks someone gave the Palais des Nations years ago. The peacocks love no one. They wander about the parked cars looking elderly, bad-tempered, mournful, and lost.

Agnes had settled down again. She folded her silk scarf and placed it just so, with her gloves beside it. She opened her new purse and took out a notebook and a shiny gold pencil. She may have written

Duster for desk
Kleenex
Glass jar for flowers
Air-Wick because he smokes
Paper for lining drawers

because the next day she brought each of these articles to work. She also brought a large black Bible, which she unwrapped lovingly and placed on the left-hand corner of her desk. The flower vase—empty—stood in the middle, and the Kleenex made a counterpoise for the Bible on the right.

When he saw the Bible he knew she had not been sent to spy on his work. The conspiracy was deeper. She might have been dispatched by ghosts. He knew everything about her, all in a moment: he saw the ambition, the terror, the dry pride. She was the true heir of the men from Scotland; she was at the start. She had been sent to tell him, "You can begin, but not begin again." She never opened the Bible, but she dusted it as she dusted her desk, her chair, and any surface the cleaning staff had overlooked. And Peter, the first days, watching her timid movements, her insignificant little face, felt, as you feel the approach of a storm, the charge of moral certainty round her, the belief in work, the faith in undertakings, the bread of the Black Sunday. He recognized and tasted all of it: ashes in the mouth.

After five days their working relations were settled. Of course, there was the Bible and all that went with it, but his tongue had never held the taste of ashes long. She was an inferior girl of poor quality. She had nothing in her favor except the degree on the wall. In the real world, he would not have invited her to his house except to mind the children. That was what he said to Sheilah. He said that Agnes was a mole, and a virgin, and that her tics and mannerisms were sending him round the bend. She had an infuriating habit of covering her mouth when she talked. Even at the telephone she put up her hand as if afraid of losing anything, even a word. Her voice was nasal and flat. She had two working costumes, both dull as the wall. One was the brown suit, the other a navy-blue dress with changeable collars. She dressed for no one; she dressed for her desk, her jar of flowers, her Bible, and her box of Kleenex. One day she crossed the space between the two desks and stood over Peter, who was reading a newspaper. She could have spoken to him from her desk, but she may have felt that being on her feet gave her authority. She had plenty of courage, but authority was something else.

"I thought—I mean, they told me you were the person . . ." She got on with it bravely: "If you don't want to do the filing or any work, all right, Mr Frazier. I'm not saying anything about that. You might have poor health or your personal reasons. But it's got to be done, so if you'll kindly show me about the filing I'll do it. I've worked in Information before, but it was a different office, and every office is different."

"My dear girl," said Peter. He pushed back his chair and looked at her, astonished. "You've been sitting there fretting, worrying. How insensitive of me. How trying for you. Usually I file on the last Wednesday of the month, so you see, you just haven't been around long enough to see a last Wednesday. Not another word, please. And let us not waste another minute." He emptied the heaped baskets of photographs so swiftly, pushing "Iran—Smallpox Control" into "Irish Red Cross" (close enough), that the girl looked frightened, as if she had raised a whirlwind. She said slowly, "If you'll only show me, Mr Frazier, instead of doing it so fast, I'll gladly look after it, because you might want to be doing other things, and I feel the filing should be done every day." But Peter was too busy to answer, and so she sat down, holding the edge of her desk.

"There," he said, beaming. "All done." His smile, his sunbrust, was wasted, for the girl was staring round the room as if she feared she had not inspected everything the first day after all; some drawer, some cupboard, hid a monster. That evening Peter unlocked one of the drawers of his desk and took away the application form he had stolen from Personnel. The girl had not finished her search.

"How could you *not* know?" wailed Sheilah. "You sit looking at her every day. You must talk about *something*. She must have told you."

"She did tell me," said Peter, "and I've just told you."

It was this: Agnes Brusen was on the Burleighs' guest list. How had the Burleighs met her? What did they see in her? Peter could not reply. He knew that Agnes lived in a bed-sitting room with a Swiss family and had her meals with them. She had been in Geneva three months, but no one had ever seen her outside the office. "You *should* know," said Sheilah. "She must have something, more than you can see. Is she pretty? Is she brilliant? What is it?"

"We don't really talk," Peter said. They talked in a way: Peter teased her and she took no notice. Agnes was not a sulker. She had taken her defeat like a sport. She did her work and a good deal of his. She sat behind her Bible, her flowers, and her Kleenex, and answered when Peter spoke. That was how he learned about the Burleighs—just by teasing and being bored. It was a January afternoon. He said, "*Miss* Brusen. Talk to me. Tell me everything. Pretend we have perfect rapport. Do you like Geneva?"

"It's a nice clean town," she said. He can see to this day the red and blue anemones in the glass jar, and her bent head, and her small untended hands.

"Are you learning beautiful French with your Swiss family?"

"They speak English."

"Why don't you take an apartment of your own?" he said. Peter was not usually impertinent. He was bored. "You'd be independent then."

"I am independent," she said. "I earn my living. I don't think it proves anything if you live by yourself. Mrs Burleigh wants me to live alone, too. She's looking for something for me. It mustn't be dear. I send money home."

Here was the extraordinary thing about Agnes Brusen: she refused the use of Christian names and never spoke to Peter unless he spoke first, but she would tell anything, as if to say, "Don't waste time fishing. Here it is."

He learned all in one minute that she sent her salary home, and that she was a friend of the Burleighs. The first he had expected; the second knocked him flat.

"She's got to come to dinner," Sheilah said. "We should have had her right from the beginning. If only I'd known! But *you* were the one. You said she looked like—oh, I don't even remember. A Norwegian mole."

She came to dinner one Saturday night in January, in her navy-blue dress, to which she had pinned an organdy gardenia. She sat upright on the edge of the sofa. Sheilah had ordered the meal from a restaurant. There was lobster, good wine, and a *pièce-montée* full of kirsch and cream. Agnes refused the lobster; she had never eaten anything from the sea unless it had been sterilized and tinned, and said so. She was afraid of skin poisoning. Someone in her family had skin poisoning after having eaten oysters. She touched her cheeks and neck to show where the poisoning had erupted. She sniffed her wine and put the glass down without tasting it. She could not eat the cake because of the alcohol it contained. She ate an egg, bread and butter, a sliced tomato, and drank a glass of ginger ale. She seemed unaware she was creating disaster and pain. She did not help clear away the dinner plates. She sat, adequately nourished, decently dressed, and waited to learn why she had been invited here—that was the feeling Peter had. He folded the card table on which they had dined, and opened the window to air the room.

"It's not the same cold as Canada, but you feel it more," he said, for something to say.

"Your blood has gotten thin," said Agnes.

Sheilah returned from the kitchen and let herself fall into an armchair. With her eyes closed she held out her hand for a cigarette. She was performing the haughty-lady act that was a family joke. She flung her head back and looked at Agnes through half-closed lids; then she suddenly brought her head forward, widening her eyes.

"Are you skiing madly?" she said.

"Well, in the first place there hasn't been any snow," said Agnes. "So nobody's doing any skiing so far as I know. All I hear is people complaining because there's no snow. Personally, I don't ski. There isn't much skiing in the part of Canada I come from. Besides, my family never had that kind of leisure."

"Heavens," said Sheilah, as if her family had every kind.

I'll bet they had, thought Peter. On the dole.

Sheilah was wasting her act. He had a suspicion that Agnes knew it was an act but did not know it was a joke. If so, it made Sheilah seem a fool, and he loved Sheilah too much to enjoy it.

"The Burleighs have been wonderful to me," said Agnes. She seemed to have divined why she was here, and decided to give them all the information they wanted, so that she could put on her coat and go home to bed. "They had me out to their place on the lake every weekend until the weather got cold and they moved back to town. They've rented a chalet for the winter, and they want me to come there, too. But I don't know if I will or not. I don't ski, and, oh, I don't know—I don't drink, either, and I don't always see the point. Their friends are too rich and I'm too Canadian."

She had delivered everything Sheilah wanted and more: Agnes was on the first guest list and didn't care. No, Peter corrected; doesn't know. Doesn't care and doesn't know.

"I thought with you Norwegians it was in the blood, skiing. And drinking," Sheilah murmured.

"Drinking, maybe," said Agnes. She covered her mouth and said behind her spread fingers, "In our family we were religious. We didn't drink or smoke. My brother was in Norway in the war. He saw some cousins. Oh," she said, unexpectedly loud, "Harry said it was just terrible. They were so poor. They had flies in the kitchen. They gave him something to eat a fly had been on. They didn't have a real toilet, and they'd been in the same house about two hundred years. We've only recently built our own home, and we have a bathroom and two toilets. I'm from Saskatchewan," she said. "I'm not from any other place."

Surely one winter here had been punishment enough? In the spring they would remember him and free him. He wrote Lucille, who said he was lucky to have a job at all. The Burleighs had sent the Fraziers a second-guest list Christmas card. It showed a Moslem refugee child weeping outside a tent. They treasured the card and left it standing long after the others had been given the children to cut up. Peter had discovered by now what had gone wrong in the friendship—Sheilah had charged a skirt at a dressmaker to Madge's account. Madge had told her she might, and then changed her mind. Poor Sheilah! She was new to this part of it—to the changing humors of independent friends. Paris was already a year in the past. At Mardi Gras, the Burleighs gave their annual party. They invited everyone, the damned and the dropped, with the prodigality of a child at prayers. The invitation said "in costume," but the Fraziers were too happy to wear a disguise. They might not be recognized. Like many of the guests they expected to meet at the party, they had been disgraced, forgotten, and rehabilitated. They would be anxious to see one another as they were.

On the night of the party, the Fraziers rented a car they had never seen before and drove through the first snowstorm of the year. Peter had not driven since last summer's blissful trips in the Fiat. He could not find the switch for the windshield wiper in this car. He leaned over the wheel. "Can you see on your side?" he asked. "Can I make a left turn here? Does it look like a one-way?"

"I can't imagine why you took a car with a right-hand drive," said Sheilah.

He had trouble finding a place to park; they crawled up and down unknown streets whose curbs were packed with snow-covered cars. When they stood at last on the pavement, safe and sound, Peter said. "This is the first snow."

"I can see that," said Sheilah. "Hurry, darling. My hair."

"It's the first snow."

"You're repeating yourself," she said. "Please hurry, darling. Think of my poor shoes. My *hair*."

She was born in an ugly city, and so was Peter, but they have this difference: she does not know the importance of the first snow—the first clean thing in a dirty year. He would have told her that this storm, which was wetting her feet and destroying her hair, was like the first day of the English spring, but she made a frightened gesture, trying to shield her head. The gesture told him he did not understand her beauty.

"Let me," she said. He was fumbling with the key, trying to lock the car. She took the key without impatience and locked the door on the driver's side; and then, to show Peter she treasured him and was not afraid of wasting her life or her beauty, she took his arm and they walked in the snow down a street and around a corner to the apartment house where the Burleighs lived. They were, and are, a united couple. They were afraid of the party, and each of them knew it. When they walk together, holding arms, they give each other whatever each can spare.

Only six people had arrived in costume. Madge Burliegh was disguised as Manet's "Lola de Valence," which everyone mistook for Carmen. Mike was an Impressionist painter, with a straw hat and a glued-on beard. "I am all of them," he said. He would rather have dressed as a dentist, he said, welcoming the Fraziers as if he had parted from them the day before, but Madge wanted him to look as if he had created her. "You know?" he said.

"Perfectly," said Sheilah. Her shoes were stained and the snow had softened her lacquered hair. She was not wasted; she was the most beautiful woman here.

About an hour after their arrival, Peter found himself with no one to talk to. He had told about the Trudeau wedding in Paris and the pot of azaleas, and after he mislaid his audience he began to look around for Sheilah. She was on a window seat, partly concealed by a green velvet curtain. Facing her, so that their profiles were neat and perfect against the night, was a man. Their conversation was private and enclosed, as if they had in minutes covered leagues of time and arrived at the place where everything was implied, understood. Peter began working his way across the room, toward his wife, when he saw Agnes. He was granted the sight of her drowning face. She had dressed with comic intention, obviously with care, and now she was a ragged hobo, half tramp, half clown. Her hair was tucked up under a bowler hat. The six costumed guests who had made the same mistake—the ghost, the gypsy, the Athenian maiden, the geisha, the Martian, and the apache— were delighted to find a seventh; but Agnes was not amused; she was gasping for life. When a waiter passed with a crowded tray, she took a glass without seeing it; then a wave of the party took her away.

Sheilah's new friend was named Simpson. After Simpson said he thought perhaps he'd better circulate, Peter sat down where he had been. "Now look, Sheilah," he began. Their most intimate conversations have taken place at parties. Once at a party she told him she was leaving him; she didn't, of course. Smiling, blue-eyed, she gazed lovingly at Peter and said rapidly, "Pete, shut up and listen. That man. The man you scared away. He's a big wheel in a company out in India or someplace like that. It's gorgeous out there. Pete, the *servants*. And it's warm. It never snows. He says there's heaps of jobs. You pick them off the trees like . . . orchids. He says it's even easier now than when we owned all those places, because now the poor pets can't run anything and they'll pay *fortunes*. Pete, he says it's warm, it's heaven, and Pete, they pay."

A few minutes later, Peter was alone again and Sheilah part of a closed, laughing group. Holding her elbow was the man from the place where jobs grew like orchids. Peter edged into the group and laughed at a story he hadn't heard. He heard only the last line, which was, "Here comes another tunnel." Looking out from the tight laughing ring, he saw Agnes again, and he thought, I'd be like Agnes if I didn't have Sheilah. Agnes put her glass down on a table and lurched toward the doorway, head forward. Madge Burleigh, who never stopped moving around the room and smiling, was still smiling when she paused and said in Peter's ear, "Go with Agnes, Pete. See that she gets home. People will notice if Mike leaves."

"She probably just wants to walk around the block," said Peter. "She'll be back."

"Oh, stop thinking about yourself, for once, and see that that poor girl gets home," said Madge. "You've still got your Fiat, haven't you?"

He turned away as if he had been pushed. Any command is a release, in a way. He may not want to go in that particular direction, but at least he is going somewhere. And now Sheilah, who had moved inches nearer to hear what Madge and Peter were murmuring, said, "Yes, go, darling," as if he were leaving the gates of Troy.

Peter was to find Agnes and see that she reached home: this he repeated to himself as he stood on the landing, outside the Burleighs' flat, ringing for the elevator. Bored with waiting for it, he ran down the stairs, four flights, and saw that Agnes had stalled the lift by leaving the door open. She was crouched on the floor, propped on her fingertips. Her eyes were closed.

"Agnes," said Peter. "*Miss* Brusen, I mean. That's no way to leave a party. Don't you know you're supposed to curtsey and say thanks? My God, Agnes, anybody going by here just now might have seen you! Come on, be a good girl. Time to go home."

She got up without his help and, moving between invisible crevasses, shut the elevator door. Then she left the building and Peter followed, remembering he was to see that she got home. They walked along the snowy pavement, Peter a few steps behind her. When she turned right for no reason, he turned, too. He had no clear idea where they were going. Perhaps she lived close by. He had forgotten where the hired car was parked, or what it looked like; he could not remember its make or its color. In any case, Sheilah had the key. Agnes walked on steadily, as if she knew their destination, and he thought, Agnes Brusen is drunk in the street in Geneva and dressed like a tramp. He wanted to say, "This is the best thing that ever happened to you, Agnes; it will help you understand how things are for some of the rest of us." But she stopped and turned and, leaning over a low hedge, retched on a frozen lawn. He held her clammy forehead and rested his hand on her arched back, on muscles as tight as a fist. She straightened up and drew a breath but the cold air made her cough. "Don't breath too deeply," he said. "It's the worst thing you can do. Have you got a handkerchief?" He passed his own handkerchief over her wet weeping face, upturned like the face of one of his little girls. "I'm out without a coat," he said, noticing it. "We're a pair."

"I never drink," said Agnes. "I'm just not used to it." Her voice was sweet and quiet. He had never seen her so peaceful, so composed. He thought she must surely be all right, now, and perhaps he might leave her here. The trust in her tilted face had perplexed him. He wanted to get back to Sheilah and have her explain something. He had forgotten what it was, but Sheilah would know. "Do you live around here?" he said. As he spoke, she let herself fall. He had wiped her face and now she trusted him to pick her up, set her on her feet, take her wherever she ought to be. He pulled her up and she stood, wordless, humble, as he brushed the snow from her tramp's clothes. Snow horizontally crossed the lamplight. The street was silent. Agnes had lost her hat. Snow, which he tasted, melted on her hands. His gesture of licking snow from her hands was formal as a handshake. He tasted snow on her hands and then they walked on.

"I never drink," she said. They stood on the edge of a broad avenue. The wrong turning now could lead them anywhere; it was the changeable avenue at the edge of towns that loses its houses and becomes a highway. She held his arm and spoke in a gentle voice. She said, "In our house we didn't smoke or drink. My mother was ambitious for me, more than for Harry and the others." She said, "I've never been alone before. When I was a kid I would get up in the summer before the others, and I'd see the ice wagon going down the street. I'm alone now. Mrs Burleigh's found me an apartment. It's only one room. She likes it because it's in the old part of town. I don't like old houses. Old houses are dirty. You don't know who was there before.'

"I should have a car somewhere," Peter said. "I'm not sure where we are."

He remembers that on this avenue they climbed into a taxi, but nothing about the drive. Perhaps he fell asleep. He does remember that when he paid the driver Agnes clutched his arm, trying to stop him. She pressed extra coins into the driver's palm. The driver was paid twice.

"I'll tell you one thing about us," said Peter. "We pay everything twice." This was part of a much longer theory concerning North American behavior, and it was not Peter's own. Mike Burleigh had held forth about it on summer afternoons.

Agnes pushed open a door between a stationer's shop and a grocery, and led the way up a narrow inside stair. They climbed one flight, frightening beetles. She had to search every pocket for the latchkey. She was shaking with cold. Her apartment seemed little warmer than the street. Without speaking to Peter she turned on all the lights. She looked inside the kitchen and the bathroom and then got down on her hands and knees and looked under the sofa. The room was neat and belonged to no one. She left him standing in this unclaimed room—she had forgotten him—and closed a door behind her. He looked for something to do—some useful action he could repeat to Madge. He turned on the electric radiator in the fireplace. Perhaps Agnes wouldn't thank him for it; perhaps she would rather undress in the cold. "I'll be on my way." he called to the bathroom door.

She had taken off the tramp's clothes and put on a dressing gown of orphanage wool. She came out of the bathroom and straight toward him. She pressed her face and rubbed her cheek on his shoulder as if hoping the contact would leave a scar. He saw her back and her profile and his own face in the mirror over the fireplace. He thought, This is how disasters happen. He saw floods of sea water moving with perfect punitive justice over reclaimed land; he saw lava covering vineyards and overtaking of dogs and stragglers. A bridge over an abyss snapped in two and the long express train, suddenly V-shaped, floated like snow. He thought amiably of every kind of disaster and thought, This is how they occur.

Her eyes were closed. She said, "I shouldn't be over here. In my family we didn't drink or smoke. My mother wanted a lot from me, more than from Harry and the others." But he knew all that; he had known from the day of the Bible, and because once, at the beginning, she had made him afraid. He was not afraid of her now.

She said, "It's no use staying here, is it?"

"If you mean what I think, no."

"It wouldn't be better anywhere."

She let him see full on her blotched face. He was not expected to do anything. He was not required to pick her up when she fell or wipe her tears. She was poor quality, really—he remembered having thought that once. She left him and went quietly in to the bathroom and locked the door. He heard taps running and supposed it was a hot bath. He was pretty certain there would be no more tears. He looked at his watch: Sheilah must be home, now, wondering what had become of him. He descended the beetles' staircase and for forty minutes crossed the city under a windless fall of snow.

The neighbor's child who had stayed with Peter's children was asleep on the living-room sofa. Peter woke her and sent her, sleep-walking, to her own door. He sat down, wet to the bone, thinking, I'll call the Burleighs. In half an hour I'll call the police. He heard a car stop and the engine running and a confusion of two voices laughing and calling goodnight. Presently Sheilah let herself in, rosy-faced, smiling. She carried his trenchcoat over her arm. She said, "How's Agnes?"

"Where were you?" he said. "Whose car was that?"

Sheilah had gone into the children's room. He heard her shutting their window. She returned, undoing her dress, and said, "Was Agnes all right?"

"Agnes is all right. Sheilah, this is about the worst . . ."

She stepped out of the Balenciaga and threw it over a chair. She stopped and looked at him and said, "Poor old Pete, are you in love with Agnes?" And then, as if the answer were of so little importance she hadn't time for it, she locked her arms around him and said, "My love, we're going to Ceylon."

Two days later, when Peter strolled into his office, Agnes was at her desk. She wore the blue dress, with a spotless collar. White and yellow freesias were symmetrically arranged in the glass jar. The room was hot, and the spring snow, glued for a second when it touched the window, blurred the view of parked cars.

"Quite a party," Peter said.

She did not look up. He sighed, sat down, and thought if the snow held he would be skiing at the Burleighs' very soon. Impressed by his kindness to Agnes, Madge had invited the family for the first possible weekend.

Presently Agnes said, "I'll never drink again or go to a house where people are drinking. And I'll never bother anyone the way I bothered you."

"You didn't bother me," he said. "I took you home. You were alone and it was late. It's normal."

"Normal for you, maybe, but I'm used to getting myself home by myself. Please never tell what happened."

He stared at her. He can still remember the freesias and the Bible and the heat in the room. She looked as if the elements had no power. She felt neither heat nor cold. "Nothing happened," he said.

"I behaved in a silly way. I had no right to. I led you to think I might do something wrong."

"*I* might have tried something," he said gallantly. "But that would be my fault and not yours."

She put her knuckle to her mouth and he could scarcely hear. "It was because of you. I was afraid you might be blamed, or else you'd blame yourself."

"There's no question of any blame," he said. "Nothing happened. We'd both had a lot to drink. Forget about it. Nothing *happened*. You'd remember if it had."

She put down her hand. There was an expression on her face. Now she sees me, he thought. She had never looked at him after the first day. (He has since tried to put a name to the look on her face; but how can he, now, after so many voyages, after Ceylon, and Hong Kong, and Sheilah's nearly leaving him, and all their difficulties—the money owed, the rows with hotel managers, the lost and found steamer trunk, the children throwing up the foreign food?) She sees me now, he thought. What does she see?

She said, "I'm from a big family. I'm not used to being alone. I'm not a suicidal person, but I could have done something after that party, just not to see any more, or think or listen or expect anything. What can I think when I see these people? All my life I heard, Educated people don't do this, educated people don't do that. And now I'm here, and you're all educated people, and you're nothing but pigs. You're educated and you drink and do everything wrong and you know what you're doing, and that makes you worse than pigs. My family worked to make me an educated person, but they didn't know you. But what if I didn't see and hear and expect anything any more? It wouldn't change anything. You'd all be still the same. Only *you* might have thought it was your fault. You might have thought you were to blame. It could worry you all your life. It would have been wrong for me to worry you."

He remembered that the rented car was still along a snowy curb somewhere in Geneva. He wondered if Sheilah had the key in her purse and if she remembered where they'd parked.

"I told you about the ice wagon," Agnes said. "I don't remember everything, so you're wrong about remembering. But I remember telling you that. That was the best. It's the best you can hope to have. In a big family, if you want to be alone, you have to get up before the rest of them. You get up early in the morning in the summer and it's you, you, once in your life alone in the universe. You think you know everything that can happen . . . Nothing is ever like that again."

He looked at the smeared window and wondered if this day could end without disaster. In his mind he saw her falling in the snow wearing a tramp's costume, and he saw her coming to him in the orphanage dressing gown. He saw her drowning face at the party. He was afraid for himself. The story was still unfinished. It had to come to a climax, something threatening to him. But there was no climax. They talked that day, and afterward nothing else was said. They went on in the same office for a short time, until Peter left for Ceylon; until somebody read the right letter, passed it on for the right initials, and the Fraziers began the Oriental tour that should have made their fortune. Agnes and Peter were too tired to speak after that morning. They were like a married couple in danger, taking care.

But what were they talking about that day, so quietly, such old friends? They talked about dying, about being ambitious, about being religious, about different kinds of love. What did she see when she looked at him—taking her knuckle slowly away from her mouth, bringing her hand down to the desk, letting it rest there? They were both Canadians, so they had this much together—the knowledge of the little you dare admit. Death, near-death, the best thing, the wrong thing—God knows what they were telling each other. Anyway, nothing happened.

When, on Sunday mornings, Sheilah and Peter talk about those times, they take on the glamor of something still to come. It is then he remembers Agnes Brusen. He never says her name. Sheilah wouldn't remember Agnes. Agnes is the only secret Peter has from his wife, the only puzzle he pieces together without her help. He thinks about families in the West as they were fifteen, twenty years ago—the iron-cold ambition, and every member pushing the next one on. He thinks of his father's parties. When he thinks of his father he imagines him with Sheilah, in a crowd. Actually, Sheilah and Peter's father never met, but they might have liked each other. His father admired good-looking women. Peter wonders what they were doing over there in Geneva— not Sheilah and Peter, *Agnes* and Peter. It is almost as if they had once run away together, silly as children, irresponsible as lovers. Peter and Sheilah are back where they started. While they were out in world affairs picking up microbes and debts, always on the fringe of disaster, the fringe of a fortune, Agnes went on and did—what? They lost each other. He thinks of the ice wagon going down the street. He sees something he had never seen in his life—a Western town that belongs to Agnes. Here is Agnes—small, mole-faced, round-shouldered because she has always carried a younger child. She watches the ice wagon and the trail of ice water in a morning invented for her: hers. He sees the weak prairie trees and the shadows on the sidewalk. Nothing moves except the shadows and the ice wagon and the changing amber of the child's eyes. The child is Peter. He has seen the grain of the cement sidewalk and the grass in the cracks, and the dust, and the dandelions at the edge of the road. He is there. He has taken the morning that belongs to Agnes, he is up before the others, and he knows everything. There is nothing he doesn't know. He could keep the morning, if he wanted to, but what can Peter do with the start of a summer day? Sheilah is here, it is a true Sunday morning, with its dimness and headache and remorse and regrets and this is life. He says, "We have the Balenciaga." He touches Sheilah's hand. The children have their aunt now, and he and Sheilah have each other. Everything works out, somehow or other. Let Agnes have the start of the day. Let Agnes think it was invented for her. Who wants to be alone in the universe? No, begin at the beginning: Peter lost Agnes. Agnes says to herself somewhere, Peter is lost.

FLANNERY O'CONNOR
1925–1964

Mary Flannery O'Connor was born in Savannah, Georgia. Her parents were
Roman Catholics from families that had lived in the south for generations.
She went to parochial schools in Savannah. When the girls were taught to
sew and told to make clothes for dolls, she made a fancy coat for a pet
chicken and brought him to school to show off his new outfit. When she
was thirteen her father developed a fatal disease called "disseminated lu-
pus," in which antibodies attack the blood vessels, joints, and internal
organs. The family moved to Milledgeville, Georgia, to live with relatives,
and Mary went to Peabody High School and Georgia State College for
Women. She drew cartoons for the college paper and her yearbook. She
also edited the literary magazine and won a fellowship to the Writers
Workshop at the University of Iowa. At Iowa she began to publish her
fiction, deciding to drop the "Mary" from her name. After receiving her
MFA she went to Yaddo, a writers' colony at Saratoga Springs, New York,
where she met people who encouraged her and helped her arrange publication for more of her work. In 1950 she was stricken with the disease that
had killed her father nine years earlier. She moved to a farm near Milledgeville and continued writing there until her death in 1964, with her reputation growing steadily, even after her death. Most of her fiction can be
found in *Collected Stories* (1971), which includes early versions of her two
novels.

Everything That Rises Must Converge

Her doctor had told Julian's mother that she must lose twenty pounds
on account of her blood pressure, so on Wednesday nights Julian had
to take her downtown on the bus for a reducing class at the Y. The
reducing class was designed for working girls over fifty, who weighed
from 165 to 200 pounds. His mother was one of the slimmer ones, but
she said ladies did not tell their age or weight. She would not ride the
buses by herself at night since they had been integrated, and because
the reducing class was one of her few pleasures, necessary for her
health, and *free*, she said Julian could at least put himself out to take
her, considering all she did for him. Julian did not like to consider all
she did for him, but every Wednesday night he braced himself and
took her.

She was almost ready to go, standing before the hall mirror, putting
on her hat, while he, his hands behind him, appeared pinned to the
door frame, waiting like Saint Sebastian for the arrows to begin
piercing him. The hat was new and had cost her seven dollars and a
half. She kept saying, "Maybe I shouldn't have paid that for it. No, I

shouldn't have. I'll take it off and return it tomorrow. I shouldn't have bought it."

Julian raised his eyes to heaven. "Yes, you should have bought it," he said. "Put it on and let's go." It was a hideous hat. A purple velvet flap came down on one side of it and stood up on the other; the rest of it was green and looked like a cushion with the stuffing out. He decided it was less comical than jaunty and pathetic. Everything that gave her pleasure was small and depressed him.

She lifted the hat one more time and set it down slowly on top of her head. Two wings of gray hair protruded on either side of her florid face, but her eyes, sky-blue, were as innocent and untouched by experience as they must have been when she was ten. Were it not that she was a widow who had struggled fiercely to feed and clothe and put him through school and who was supporting him still, "until he got on his feet," she might have been a little girl that he had to take to town.

"It's all right, it's all right," he said. "Let's go." He opened the door himself and started down the walk to get her going. The sky was a dying violet and the houses stood out darkly against it, bulbous liver-colored monstrosities of a uniform ugliness though no two were alike. Since this had been a fashionable neighborhood forty years ago, his mother persisted in thinking they did well to have an apartment in it. Each house had a narrow collar of dirt around it in which sat, usually, a grubby child. Julian walked with his hands in his pockets, his head down and thrust forward and his eyes glazed with the determination to make himself completely numb during the time he would be sacrificed to her pleasure.

The door closed and he turned to find the dumpy figure, surmounted by the atrocious hat, coming toward him. "Well," she said, "you only live once and paying a little more for it, I at least won't meet myself coming and going."

"Some day I'll start making money," Julian said gloomily—he knew he never would—"and you can have one of those jokes whenever you take the fit." But first they would move. He visualized a place where the nearest neighbors would be three miles away on either side.

"I think you're doing fine," she said, drawing on her gloves. "You've only been out of school a year. Rome wasn't built in a day."

She was one of the few members of the Y reducing class who arrived in hat and gloves and who had a son who had been to college. "It takes time," she said, "and the world is in such a mess. This hat looked better on me than any of the others, though when she brought it out I said, 'Take that thing back. I wouldn't have it on my head,' and she said, 'Now wait till you see it on,' and when she put it on me, I said, 'We-ull,' and she said, 'If you ask me, that hat does something for you and you do something for the hat, and besides,' she said, 'with that

hat, you won't meet yourself coming and going.' "

Julian thought he could have stood his lot better if she had been selfish, if she had been an old hag who drank and screamed at him. He walked along, saturated in depression, as if in the midst of his martyrdom he had lost his faith. Catching sight of his long, hopeless, irritated face, she stopped suddenly with a grief-stricken look, and pulled back on his arm. "Wait on me," she said. "I'm going back to the house and take this thing off and tomorrow I'm going to return it. I was out of my head. I can pay the gas bill with the seven-fifty."

He caught her arm in a vicious grip. "You are not going to take it back," he said. "I like it."

"Well," she said, "I don't think I ought . . ."

"Shut up and enjoy it," he muttered, more depressed than ever.

"With the world in the mess it's in," she said, "it's a wonder we can enjoy anything. I tell you, the bottom rail is on the top."

Julian sighed.

"Of course," she said, "if you know who you are, you can go anywhere." She said this every time he took her to the reducing class. "Most of them in it are not our kind of people," she said, "but I can be gracious to anybody. I know who I am."

"They don't give a damn for your graciousness," Julian said savagely. "Knowing who you are is good for one generation only. You haven't the foggiest idea where you stand now or who you are."

She stopped and allowed her eyes to flash at him. "I most certainly do know who I am," she said, "and if you don't know who you are, I'm ashamed of you."

"Oh hell," Julian said.

"Your great-grandfather was a former governor of this state," she said. "Your grandfather was a prosperous landowner. Your grandmother was a Godhigh."

"Will you look around you," he said tensely, "and see where you are now?" and he swept his arm jerkily out to indicate the neighborhood, which the growing darkness at least made less dingy.

"You remain what you are," she said. "Your great-grandfather had a plantation and two hundred slaves."

"There are no more slaves," he said irritably.

"They were better off when they were," she said. He groaned to see that she was off on that topic. She rolled onto it every few days like a train on an open track. He knew every stop, every junction, every swamp along the way, and knew the exact point at which her conclusion would roll majestically into the station: "It's ridiculous. It's simply not realistic. They should rise, yes, but on their own side of the fence."

"Let's skip it," Julian said.

"The ones I feel sorry for," she said, "are the ones that are half white. They're tragic."

"Will you skip it?"

"Suppose we were half white. We would certainly have mixed feelings."

"I have mixed feelings now," he groaned.

"Well let's talk about something pleasant," she said. "I remember going to Grandpa's when I was a little girl. Then the house had double stairways that went up to what was really the second floor—all the cooking was done on the first. I used to like to stay down in the kitchen on account of the way the walls smelled. I would sit with my nose pressed against the plaster and take deep breaths. Actually the place belonged to the Godhighs but your grandfather Chestny paid the mortgage and saved it for them. They were in reduced circumstances," she said, "but reduced or not, they never forgot who they were."

"Doubtless that decayed mansion reminded them," Julian muttered. He never spoke of it without contempt or thought of it without longing. He had seen it once when he was a child before it had been sold. The double stairways had rotted and been torn down. Negroes were living in it. But it remained in his mind as his mother had known it. It appeared in his dreams regularly. He would stand on the wide porch, listening to the rustle of oak leaves, then wander through the high-ceilinged hall into the parlor that opened onto it and gaze at the worn rugs and faded draperies. It occurred to him that it was he, not she, who could have appreciated it. He preferred its threadbare elegance to anything he could name and it was because of it that all the neighborhoods they had lived in had been a torment to him—whereas she had hardly known the difference. She called her insensitivity "being adjustable."

"And I remember the old darky who was my nurse, Caroline. There was no better person in the world. I've always had a great respect for my colored friends," she said. "I'd do anything in the world for them and they'd . . ."

"Will you for God's sake get off that subject?" Julian said. When he got on a bus by himself, he made it a point to sit down beside a Negro, in reparation as it were for his mother's sins.

"You're mighty touchy tonight," she said. "Do you feel all right?"

"Yes I feel all right," he said. "Now lay off."

She pursed her lips. "Well, you certainly are in a vile humor," she observed. "I just won't speak to you at all."

They had reached the bus stop. There was no bus in sight and Julian, his hands still jammed in his pockets and his head thrust forward, scowled down the empty street. The frustration of having to wait on the bus as well as ride on it began to creep up his neck like a hot hand. The presence of his mother was borne in upon him as she gave a pained sigh. He looked at her bleakly. She was holding herself very erect under the preposterous hat, wearing it like a banner of her imaginary dignity. There was in him an evil urge to break her spirit. He suddenly unloosened his tie and pulled it off and put it in his pocket.

She stiffened. "Why must you look like *that* when you take me to town?" she said. "Why must you deliberately embarrass me?"

"If you'll never learn where you are," he said, "you can at least learn where I am."

"You look like a—thug," she said.

"Then I must be one," he murmured.

"I'll just go home," she said. "I will not bother you. If you can't do a little thing like that for me . . ."

Rolling his eyes upward, he put his tie back on. "Restored to my class," he muttered. He thrust his face toward her and hissed, "True culture is in the mind, the *mind*," he said, and tapped his head, "the mind."

"It's in the heart," she said, "and in how you do things and how you do things is because of who you *are*."

"Nobody in the damn bus cares who you are."

"I care who I am," she said icily.

The lighted bus appeared on top of the next hill and as it approached, they moved out into the street to meet it. He put his hand under her elbow and hoisted her up on the creaking step. She entered with a little smile, as if she were going into a drawing room where everyone had been waiting for her. While he put in the tokens, she sat down in one of the broad front seats for three which faced the aisle. A thin woman with protruding teeth and long yellow hair was sitting on the end of it. His mother moved up beside her and left room for Julian besides herself. He sat down and looked at the floor across the aisle where a pair of thin feet in red and white canvas sandals were planted.

His mother immediately began a general conversation meant to attract anyone who felt like talking. "Can it get any hotter?" she said and removed from her purse a folding fan, black with a Japanese scene on it, which she began to flutter before her.

"I reckon it might could," the woman with the protruding teeth said, "but I know for a fact my apartment couldn't get no hotter."

"It must get the afternoon sun," his mother said. She sat forward and looked up and down the bus. It was half filled. Everybody was white. "I see we have the bus to ourselves," she said. Julian cringed.

"For a change," said the woman across the aisle, the owner of the red and white canvas sandals. "I come on one the other day and they were thick as fleas—up front and all through."

"The world is in a mess everywhere," his mother said. "I don't know how we've let it get in this fix."

"What gets my goat is all those boys from good families stealing automobile tires," the woman with the protruding teeth said. "I told my boy, I said you may not be rich but you been raised right and if I ever catch you in any such mess, they can send you on to the reformatory. Be exactly where you belong."

"Training tells," his mother said. "Is your boy in high school?"

"Ninth grade," the woman said.

"My son just finished college last year. He wants to write but he's selling typewriters until he gets started," his mother said.

The woman leaned forward and peered at Julian. He threw her such a malevolent look that she subsided against the seat. On the floor across the aisle there was an abandoned newspaper. He got up and got it and opened it out in front of him. His mother discreetly continued the conversation in a lower tone but the woman across the aisle said in a loud voice, "Well that's nice. Selling typewriters is close to writing. He can go right from one to the other."

"I tell him," his mother said, "that Rome wasn't built in a day."

Behind the newspaper Julian was withdrawing into the inner compartment of his mind where he spent most of his time. This was a kind of mental bubble in which he established himself when he could not bear to be a part of what was going on around him. From it he could see out and judge but in it he was safe from any kind of penetration from without. It was the only place where he felt free of the general idiocy of his fellows. His mother had never entered it but from it he could see her with absolute clarity.

The old lady was clever enough and he thought that if she had started from any of the right premises, more might have been expected of her. She lived according to the laws of her own fantasy world, outside of which he had never seen her set foot. The law of it was to sacrifice herself for him after she had first created the necessity to do so by making a mess of things. If he had permitted her sacrifices, it was only because her lack of foresight had made them necessary. All of her life had been a struggle to act like a Chestny without the Chestny goods, and to give him everything she thought a Chestny ought to have; but since, said she, it was fun to struggle, why complain? And when you had won, as she had won, what fun to look back on the hard times! He could not forgive her that she had enjoyed the struggle and that she thought *she* had won.

What she meant when she said she had won was that she had brought him up successfully and had sent him to college and that he had turned out so well—good looking (her teeth had gone unfilled so that his could be straightened), intelligent (he realized he was too intelligent to be a success), and with a future ahead of him (there was of course no future ahead of him). She excused his gloominess on the grounds that he was still growing up and his radical ideas on his lack of practical experience. She said he didn't yet know a thing about "life," that he hadn't even entered the real world—when already he was as disenchanted with it as a man of fifty.

The further irony of all this was that in spite of her, he had turned out so well. In spite of going to only a third-rate college, he had, on his own initiative, come out with a first-rate education; in spite of growing up dominated by a small mind, he had ended up with a large one; in spite of all her foolish views, he was free of prejudice and unafraid to face facts. Most miraculous of all, instead of being blinded by love for her as she was for him, he had cut himself emotionally free of her and could see her with complete objectivity. He was not dominated by his mother.

The bus stopped with a sudden jerk and shook him from his meditation. A woman from the back lurched forward with little steps and barely escaped falling in his newspaper as she righted herself. She got off and a large Negro got on. Julian kept his paper lowered to watch. It gave him a certain satisfaction to see injustice in daily operation. It confirmed his view that with a few exceptions there was no one worth knowing within a radius of three hundred miles. The Negro was well dressed and carried a briefcase. He looked around and then sat down on the other end of the seat where the woman with the red and white canvas sandals was sitting. He immediately unfolded a newspaper and obscured himself behind it. Julian's mother's elbow at once prodded insistently into his ribs. "Now you see why I won't ride on these buses by myself," she whispered.

The woman with the red and white canvas sandals had risen at the same time the Negro sat down and had gone further back in the bus and taken the seat of the woman who had got off. His mother leaned forward and cast her an approving look.

Julian rose, crossed the aisle, and sat down in the place of the woman with the canvas sandals. From this position, he looked serenely across at his mother. Her face had turned an angry red. He stared at her, making his eyes the eyes of a stranger. He felt his tension suddenly lift as if he had openly declared war on her.

He would have liked to get in conversation with the Negro and to talk with him about art or politics or any subject that would be above the comprehension of those around them, but the man remained entrenched behind his paper. He was either ignoring the change of seating or had never noticed it. There was no way for Julian to convey his sympathy.

His mother kept her eyes fixed reproachfully on his face. The woman with the protruding teeth was looking at him avidly as if he were a type of monster new to her.

"Do you have a light?" he asked the Negro.

Without looking away from his paper, the man reached in his pocket and handed him a packet of matches.

"Thanks," Julian said. For a moment he held the matches foolishly. A NO SMOKING sign looked down upon him from over the door. This alone would not have deterred him; he had no cigarettes. He had quit smoking some months before because he could not afford it. "Sorry," he muttered and handed back the matches. The Negro lowered the paper and gave him an annoyed look. He took the matches and raised the paper again.

His mother continued to gaze at him but she did not take advantage of his momentary discomfort. Her eyes retained their battered look. Her face seemed to be unnaturally red, as if her blood pressure had risen. Julian allowed no glimmer of sympathy to show on his face. Having got the advantage, he wanted desperately to keep it and carry it through. He would have liked to teach her a lesson that would last her a while, but there seemed no way to continue the point. The Negro refused to come out from behind his paper.

Julian folded his arms and looked stolidly before him, facing her but as if he did not see her, as if he had ceased to recognize her existence. He visualized a scene in which the bus having reached their stop, he would remain in his seat and when she said, "Aren't you going to get off?" he would look at her as at a stranger who had rashly addressed him. The corner they got off on was usually deserted, but it was well lighted and it would not hurt her to walk by herself the four blocks to the Y. He decided to wait until the time came and then decide whether or not he would let her get off by herself. He would have to be at the Y at ten to bring her back, but he could leave her wondering if he was going to show up. There was no reason for her to think she could always depend on him.

He retired again into the high-ceilinged room sparsely settled with large pieces of antique furniture. His soul expanded momentarily but then he became aware of his mother across from him and the vision shriveled. He studied her coldly. Her feet in little pumps dangled like a child's and did not quite reach the floor. She was training on him an exaggerated look of reproach. He felt completely detached from her. At that moment he could with pleasure have slapped her as he would have slapped a particularly obnoxious child in his charge.

He began to imagine various unlikely ways by which he could teach her a lesson. He might make friends with some distinguished Negro professor or lawyer and bring him home to spend the evening. He would be entirely justified but her blood pressure would rise to 300. He could not push her to the extent of making her have a stroke, and moreover, he had never been successful at making any Negro friends. He had tried to strike up an acquaintance on the bus with some of the better types, with ones that looked like professors or ministers or lawyers. One morning he had sat down next to a distinguished-looking dark brown man who had answered his questions with a sonorous solemnity but who had turned out to be an undertaker. Another day he had sat down beside a cigar-smoking Negro with a diamond ring on his finger, but after a few stilted pleasantries, the Negro had rung the buzzer and risen, slipping two lottery tickets into Julian's hand as he climbed over him to leave.

He imagined his mother lying desperately ill and his being able to secure only a Negro doctor for her. He toyed with that idea for a few minutes and then dropped it for a momentary vision of himself participating as a sympathizer in a sit-in demonstration. This was possible but he did not linger with it. Instead, he approached the ultimate horror. He brought home a beautiful suspiciously Negroid woman. Prepare yourself, he said. There is nothing you can do about it. This is the woman I've chosen. She's intelligent, dignified, even good, and she's suffered and she hasn't thought it *fun*. Now persecute us, go ahead and persecute us. Drive her out of here, but remember, you're driving me too. His eyes were narrowed and through the indignation he had generated, he saw his mother across the aisle, purple-faced, shrunken to the dwarf-like proportions of her moral nature, sitting like a mummy beneath the ridiculous banner of her hat.

He was tilted out of his fantasy again as the bus stopped. The door opened with a sucking hiss and out of the dark a large, gaily dressed, sullen-looking colored woman got on with a little boy. The child, who might have been four, had on a short plaid suit and a Tyrolean hat with a blue feather in it. Julian hoped that he would sit down beside him and that the woman would push in beside his mother. He could think of no better arrangement.

As she waited for her tokens, the woman was surveying the seating possibilities—he hoped with the idea of sitting where she was least wanted. There was something familiar-looking about her but Julian could not place what it was. She was a giant of a woman. Her face was set not only to meet opposition but to seek it out. The downward tilt of her large lower lip was like a warning sign: DON'T TAMPER WITH ME. Her bulging figure was encased in a green crepe dress and her feet overflowed in red shoes. She had on a hideous hat. A purple velvet flap came down on one side of it and stood up on the other; the rest of it was green and looked like a cushion with the stuffing out. She carried a mammoth red pocketbook that bulged throughout as if it were stuffed with rocks.

To Julian's disappointment, the little boy climbed up on the empty seat beside his mother. His mother lumped all children, black and white, into the common category, "cute," and she thought little Negroes were on the whole cuter than little white children. She smiled at the little boy as he climbed on the seat.

Meanwhile the woman was bearing down upon the empty seat beside Julian. To his annoyance, she squeezed herself into it. He saw his mother's face change as the woman settled herself next to him and he realized with satisfaction that this was more objectionable to her than it was to him. Her face seemed almost gray and there was a look of dull recognition in her eyes, as if suddenly she had sickened at some awful confrontation. Julian saw that it was because she and the woman had, in a sense, swapped sons. Though his mother would not realize the symbolic significance of this, she would feel it. His amusement showed plainly on his face.

The woman next to him muttered something unintelligible to herself. He was conscious of a kind of bristling next to him, muted growling like that of an angry cat. He could not see anything but the red pocketbook upright on the bulging green thighs. He visualized the woman as she had stood waiting for her tokens—the ponderous figure, rising from the red shoes upward over the solid hips, the mammoth bosom, the haughty face, to the green and purple hat.

His eyes widened.

The vision of the two hats, identical, broke upon him with the radiance of a brilliant sunrise. His face was suddenly lit with joy. He could not believe that Fate had thrust upon his mother such a lesson. He gave a loud chuckle so that she would look at him and see that he saw. She turned her eyes on him slowly. The blue in them seemed to have turned a bruised purple. For a moment he had an uncomfortable sense of her innocence, but it lasted only a second before principle rescued him. Justice entitled him to laugh. His grin hardened until it said to her as plainly as if he were saying aloud: Your punishment exactly fits your pettiness. This should teach you a permanent lesson.

Her eyes shifted to the woman. She seemed unable to bear looking at him and to find the woman preferable. He became conscious again of the bristling presence at his side. The woman was rumbling like a volcano about to become active. His mother's mouth began to twitch slightly at one corner. With a sinking heart, he saw incipient signs of recovery on her face and realized that this was going to strike her suddenly as funny and was going to be no lesson at all. She kept her eyes on the woman and an amused smile came over her face as if the woman were a monkey that had stolen her hat. The little Negro was looking up at her with large fascinated eyes. He had been trying to attract her attention for some time.

"Carver!" the woman said suddenly. "Come heah!"

When he saw that the spotlight was on him at last, Carver drew his feet up and turned himself toward Julian's mother and giggled.

"Carver!" the woman said. "You heah me? Come heah!"

Carver slid down from the seat but remained squatting with his back against the base of it, his head turned slyly around toward Julian's mother, who was smiling at him. The woman reached a hand across the aisle and snatched him to her. He righted himself and hung backwards on her knees, grinning at Julian's mother. "Isn't he cute?" Julian's mother said to the woman with the protruding teeth.

"I reckon he is," the woman said without conviction.

The Negress yanked him upright but he eased out of her grip and shot across the aisle and scrambled, giggling wildly, onto the seat beside his love.

"I think he likes me," Julian's mother said, and smiled at the woman. It was the smile she used when she was being particularly gracious to an inferior. Julian saw everything lost. The lesson had rolled off her like rain on a roof.

The woman stood up and yanked the little boy off the seat as if she were snatching him from contagion. Julian could feel the rage in her at having no weapon like his mother's smile. She gave the child a sharp slap across his leg. He howled once and then thrust his head into her stomach and kicked his feet against her shins. "Behave," she said vehemently.

The bus stopped and the Negro who had been reading the newspaper got off. The woman moved over and set the little boy down with a thump between herself and Julian. She held him firmly by the knee. In a moment he put his hands in front of his face and peeped at Julian's mother through his fingers.

"I see yoooooooo!" she said and put her hand in front of her face and peeped at him.

The woman slapped his hand down. "Quit yo' foolishness," she said, "before I knock the living Jesus out of you!"

Julian was thankful that the next stop was theirs. He reached up and pulled the cord. The woman reached up and pulled it at the same time. Oh my God, he thought. He had the terrible intuition that when they got off the bus together, his mother would open her purse and give the little boy a nickel. The gesture would be as natural to her as breathing. The bus stopped and the woman got up and lunged to the front, dragging the child, who wished to stay on, after her. Julian and his mother got up and followed. As they neared the door, Julian tried to relieve her of her pocketbook.

"No," she murmured, "I want to give the little boy a nickel."

"No!" Julian hissed. "No!"

She smiled down at the child and opened her bag. The bus door opened and the woman picked him up by the arm and descended with him, hanging at her hip. Once in the street she set him down and shook him.

Julian's mother had to close her purse while she got down the bus step but as soon as her feet were on the ground, she opened it again and began to rummage inside. "I can't find but a penny," she whispered, "but it looks like a new one."

"Don't do it!" Julian said fiercely between his teeth. There was a streetlight on the corner and she hurried to get under it so that she could better see into her pocketbook. The woman was heading off rapidly down the street with the child still hanging backward on her hand.

"Oh little boy!" Julian's mother called and took a few quick steps and caught up with them just beyond the lamppost. "Here's a bright new penny for you," and she held out the coin, which shone bronze in the dim light.

The huge woman turned and for a moment stood, her shoulders lifted and her face frozen with frustrated rage, and stared at Julian's mother. Then all at once she seemed to explode like a piece of machinery that had been given one ounce of pressure too much. Julian saw the black fist swing out with the red pocketbook. He shut his eyes and cringed as he heard the woman shout, "He don't take nobody's pennies!" When he opened his eyes, the woman was disappearing down the street with the little boy staring wide-eyed over her shoulder. Julian's mother was sitting on the sidewalk.

"I told you not to do that," Julian said angrily. "I told you not to do that!"

He stood over her for a minute, gritting his teeth. Her legs were stretched out in front of her and her hat was on her lap. He squatted down and looked her in the face. It was totally expressionless. "You got exactly what you deserved," he said. "Now get up."

He picked up her pocketbook and put what had fallen out back in it. He picked the hat up off her lap. The penny caught his eye on the sidewalk and he picked that up and let it drop before her eyes into the purse. Then he stood up and leaned over and held his hands out to pull her up. She remained immobile. He sighed. Rising about them on either side were black apartment buildings, marked with irregular rectangles of light. At the end of the block a man came out of a door and walked off in the opposite direction. "All right," he said, "suppose somebody happens by and wants to know why you're sitting on the sidewalk?"

She took the hand and, breathing hard, pulled heavily up on it and then stood for a moment, swaying slightly as if the spots of light in the darkness were circling around her. Her eyes, shadowed and confused, finally settled on his face. He did not try to conceal his irritation. "I hope this teaches you a lesson," he said. She leaned forward and her eyes raked his face. She seemed trying to determine his identity. Then, as if she found nothing familiar about him, she started off with a headlong movement in the wrong direction.

"Aren't you going on to the Y?" he asked.

"Home," she muttered.

"Well, are we walking?"

For answer she kept going. Julian followed along, his hands behind him. He saw no reason to let the lesson she had had go without backing it up with an explanation of its meaning. She might as well be made to understand what had happened to her. "Don't think that was just an uppity Negro woman," he said. "That was the whole colored race which will no longer take your condescending pennies. That was your black double. She can wear the same hat as you, and to be sure," he added gratuitously (because he thought it was funny), "it looked better on her than it did on you. What all this means," he said, "is that the old world is gone. The old manners are obsolete and your graciousness is not worth a damn." He thought bitterly of the house that had been lost for him. "You aren't who you think you are," he said.

She continued to plow ahead, paying no attention to him. Her hair had come undone on one side. She dropped her pocketbook and took no notice. He stooped and picked it up and handed it to her but she did not take it.

"You needn't act as if the world had come to an end," he said, "because it hasn't. From now on you've got to live in a new world and face a few realities for a change. Buck up," he said, "it won't kill you."

She was breathing fast.

"Let's wait on the bus," he said.

"Home," she said thickly.

"I hate to see you behave like this," he said. "Just like a child. I should be able to expect more of you." He decided to stop where he was and make her stop and wait for a bus. "I'm not going any farther," he said, stopping. "We're going on the bus."

She continued to go on as if she had not heard him. He took a few steps and caught her arm and stopped her. He looked into her face and caught his breath. He was looking into a face he had never seen before. "Tell Grandpa to come get me," she said.

He stared, stricken.

"Tell Caroline to come get me," she said.

Stunned, he let her go and she lurched forward again, walking as if one leg were shorter than the other. A tide of darkness seemed to be sweeping her from him. "Mother!" he cried. "Darling, sweetheart, wait!" Crumpling, she fell to the pavement. He dashed forward and fell at her side, crying, "Mamma, Mamma!" He turned her over. Her face was fiercely distorted. One eye, large and staring, moved slightly on the left as if it had become unmoored. The other remained fixed on him, raked his face again, found nothing and closed.

"Wait here, wait here!" he cried and jumped up and began to run for help toward a cluster of lights he saw in the distance ahead of him. "Help, help!" he shouted, but his voice was thin, scarcely a thread of sound. The lights drifted farther away the faster he ran and his feet moved numbly as if they carried him nowhere. The tide of darkness seemed to sweep him back to her, postponing from moment to moment his entry into the world of guilt and sorrow.

MARGARET LAURENCE
1926–1987

The most distinguished Canadian novelist of her generation, she was born in the small prairie town of Neepawa, Manitoba, of Scottish Presbyterian ancestry. She attended United College in Winnipeg, now the University of Winnipeg, where she developed her interest in fiction writing. She spent the early 1950s with her husband, a civil engineer, in Africa, first in Somaliland (now Somali Repulic) and later in the Gold Coast (now Ghana). Her stay in Africa introduced her to that world's culture and art, and she translated some Nigerian literature, wrote critical studies of African writings, and set her first novel, *This Side Jordan* (1960), and her first collection of short stories, *The Tomorrow-Tamer* (1963), in Africa. Even though she returned to Canada in 1957, she continued for five years to set her fiction in Africa. In 1962 she moved to England, where she completed *The Stone Angel* (1964), her first novel set in the fictional prairie town of Manawaka. Three more novels, *A Jest of God* (1966), *The Fire-Dwellers* (1969), and *The Diviners* (1974) as well as a short-story sequence, *The Bird in the House* (1970), which includes "The Loons," continue Laurence's chronicling of Manawaka, each book a close examination of the life of one woman in the town.

The Loons

Just below Manawaka, where the Wachakwa River ran brown and noisy over the pebbles, the scrub oak and grey-green willow and choke-cherry bushes grew in a dense thicket. In a clearing at the center of the thicket stood the Tonnerre family's shack. The basis of this dwelling was a small square cabin made of poplar poles and chinked with mud, which had been built by Jules Tonnerre some fifty years before, when he came back from Batoche with a bullet in his thigh, the year that Riel was hung and the voices of the Metis entered their long silence. Jules had only intended to stay the winter in the Wachakwa Valley, but the family was still there in the thirties, when I was a child. As the Tonnerres had increased, their settlement had been added to, until the clearing at the foot of the town hill was a chaos of lean-tos, wooden packing cases, warped lumber, discarded car tires, ramshackle chicken coops, tangled strands of barbed wire and rusty tin cans.

The Tonnerres were French half-breeds, and among themselves they spoke a *patois* that was neither Cree nor French. Their English was broken and full of obscenities. They did not belong among the Cree of the Galloping Mountain reservation, further north, and they did not belong among the Scots-Irish and Ukrainians of Manawaka, either. They were, as my Grandmother MacLeod would have put it, neither flesh, fowl, nor good salt herring. When their men were not working at odd jobs or as section hands on the C.P.R., they lived on relief. In the summers, one of the Tonnerre youngsters, with a face that seemed totally unfamiliar with laughter, would knock at the doors of the town's brick houses and offer for sale a lard-pail full of bruised wild strawberries, and if he got as much as a quarter he would grab the coin and run before the customer had time to change her mind. Sometimes old Jules, or his son Lazarus, would get mixed up in a Saturday-night brawl, and would hit out at whoever was nearest, or howl drunkenly among the offended shoppers on Main Street, and then the Mountie would put them for the night in the barred cell underneath the Court House, and the next morning they would be quiet again.

Piquette Tonnerre, the daughter of Lazarus, was in my class at school. She was older than I, but she had failed several grades, perhaps because her attendance had always been sporadic and her interest in schoolwork negligible. Part of the reason she had missed a lot of school was that she had had tuberculosis of the bone, and had once spent many months in hospital. I knew this because my father was the doctor who had looked after her. Her sickness was almost the only thing I knew about her, however. Otherwise, she existed for me only as a vaguely embarrassing presence, with her hoarse voice and her clumsy limping walk and her grimy cotton dresses that were always miles too long. I was neither friendly nor unfriendly towards her. She dwelt and moved somewhere within my scope of vision, but I did not actually notice her very much until that peculiar summer when I was eleven.

"I don't know what to do about that kid," my father said at dinner one evening. "Piquette Tonnerre, I mean. The damn bone's flared up again. I've had her in hospital for quite a while now, and it's under control all right, but I hate like the dickens to send her home again."

"Couldn't you explain to her mother that she has to rest a lot?" my mother said.

"The mother's not there," my father replied. "She took off a few years back. Can't say I blame her. Piquette cooks for them, and she says Lazarus would never do anything for himself as long as she's there. Anyway, I don't think she'd take much care of herself, once she got back. She's only thirteen, after all. Beth, I was thinking—what about taking her up to Diamond Lake with us this summer? A couple of months rest would give that bone a much better chance"

My mother looked stunned.

"But Ewen—what about Roddie and Vanessa?"

"She's not contagious," my father said. "And it would be company for Vanessa."

"Oh dear," my mother said in distress, "I'll bet anything she has nits in her hair."

"For Pete's sake," my father said crossly, "do you think Matron would let her stay in the hospital for all this time like that? Don't be silly, Beth."

Grandmother MacLeod, her delicately featured face as rigid as a cameo, now brought her mauve-veined hands together as though she were about to begin a prayer.

"Ewen, if that half-breed youngster comes along to Diamond Lake, I'm not going," she announced. "I'll go to Morag's for the summer."

I had trouble in stifling my urge to laugh, for my mother brightened visibly and quickly tried to hide it. If it came to a choice between Grandmother MacLeod and Piquette, Piquette would win hands down, nits or not.

"It might be quite nice for you, at that," she mused. "You haven't seen Morag for over a year, and you might enjoy being in the city for a while. Well, Ewen dear, you do what you think best. If you think it would do Piquette some good, then we'll be glad to have her, as long as she behaves herself."

So it happened that several weeks later, when we all piled into my father's old Nash, surrounded by suitcases and boxes of provisions and toys for my ten-month-old brother, Piquette was with us and Grandmother MacLeod, miraculously, was not. My father would only be staying at the cottage for a couple of weeks, for he had to get back to his practice, but the rest of us would stay at Diamond Lake until the end of August.

Our cottage was not named, as many were, "Dew Drop Inn" or "Bide-a-Wee," or "Bonnie Doon." The sign on the roadway bore in austere letters only our name, MacLeod. It was not a large cottage, but it was on the lakefront. You could look out the windows and see, through the filigree of the spruce trees, the water glistening greenly as the sun caught it. All around the cottage were ferns, and sharp-branched raspberry bushes, and moss that had grown over fallen tree trunks. If you looked carefully among the weeds and grass, you could find wild strawberry plants which were in white flower now and in another

month would bear fruit, the fragrant globes hanging like miniature
scarlet lanterns on the thin hairy stems. The two grey squirrels were
still there, gossiping at us from the tall spruce beside the cottage, and
by the end of the summer they would again be tame enough to take
pieces of crust from my hands. The broad moose antlers that hung
above the back door were a little more bleached and fissured after the
winter, but otherwise everything was the same. I raced joyfully around
my kingdom, greeting all the places I had not seen for a year. My brother,
Roderick, who had not been born when we were here last summer, sat
on the car rug in the sunshine and examined a brown spruce cone,
meticulously turning it round and round in his small and curious
hands. My mother and father toted the luggage from car to cottage,
exclaiming over how well the place had wintered, no broken windows,
thank goodness, no apparent damage from storm-felled branches or
snow.

Only after I had finished looking around did I notice Piquette. She
was sitting on the swing, her lame leg held stiffly out, and her other
foot scuffing the ground as she swung slowly back and forth. Her long
hair hung black and straight around her shoulders, and her broad
coarse-featured face bore no expression—it was blank, as though she
no longer dwelt within her own skull, as though she had gone
elsewhere. I approached her very hesitantly.

"Want to come and play?"

Piquette looked at me with a sudden flash of scorn.

"I ain't a kid," she said.

Wounded I stamped angrily away, swearing I would not speak to
her for the rest of the summer. In the days that followed, however,
Piquette began to interest me, and I began to want to interest her. My
reasons did not appear bizarre to me. Unlikely as it may seem, I had
only just realized that the Tonnerre family, whom I had always heard
called half-breeds, were actually Indians, or as near as made no difference. My acquaintance with Indians was not extensive. I did not
remember ever having seen a real Indian, and my new awareness that
Piquette sprang from the people of Big Bear and Poundmaker, of
Tecumseh, of the Iroquois who had eaten Father Brebeuf's heart—all
this gave her an instant attraction in my eyes. I was a devoted reader
of Pauline Johnson at this age, and sometimes would orate aloud and
in an exalted voice, *West Wind, blow from your prairie nest; Blow from
the mountains, blow from the west*—and so on. It seemed to me that
Piquette must be in some way a daughter of the forest, a kind of junior
prophetess of the wilds, who might impart to me, if I took the right
approach, some of the secrets which she undoubtedly knew—where
the whippoorwill made her nest, how the coyote reared her young, or
whatever it was that it said in Hiawatha.

I set about gaining Piquette's trust. She was not allowed to go swimming, with her bad leg, but I managed to lure her down to the beach—or rather, she came because there was nothing else to do. The water was always icy, for the lake was fed by springs, but I swam like a dog, thrashing my arms and legs around at such speed and with such an output of energy that I never grew cold. Finally, when I had had enough, I came out and sat beside Piquette on the sand. When she saw me approaching, her hand squashed flat the sand castle she had been building, and she looked at me sullenly, without speaking.

"Do you like this place?" I asked, after a while, intending to lead on from there into the question of forest lore.

Piquette shrugged. "It's okay. Good as anywhere."

"I love it," I said. "We come here every summer."

"So what?" Her voice was distant, and I glanced at her uncertainly, wondering what I could have said wrong.

"Do you want to come for a walk?" I asked her. "We wouldn't need to go far. If you walk just around the point there, you come to a bay where great big reeds grow in the water, and all kinds of fish hang around there. Want to? Come on."

She shook her head.

"Your dad said I ain't supposed to do no more walking than I got to."

I tried another line.

"I bet you know a lot about the woods and all that, eh?" I began respectfully.

Piquette looked at me from her large dark unsmiling eyes.

"I don't know what in hell you're talkin' about," she replied. "You nuts or somethin'? If you mean where my old man, and me, and all them live, you better shut up, by Jesus, you hear?"

I was startled and my feelings were hurt, but I had a kind of dogged perseverance. I ignored her rebuff.

"You know something, Piquette? There's loons here, on this lake. You can see their nests just up the shore there, behind those logs. At night, you can hear them even from the cottage, but it's better to listen from the beach. My dad says we should listen and try to remember how they sound, because in a few years when more cottages are built at Diamond Lake and more people come in, the loons will go away."

Piquette was picking up stones and snail shells and then dropping them again.

"Who gives a good goddamn?" she said.

It became increasingly obvious that, as an Indian, Piquette was a dead loss. That evening I went out by myself, scrambling through the bushes that overhung the steep path, my feet slipping on the fallen spruce needles that covered the ground. When I reached the shore, I walked along the firm damp sand to the small pier that my father had built, and sat down there. I heard someone else crashing through the undergrowth and the bracken, and for a moment I thought Piquette had changed her mind, but it turned out to be my father. He sat beside me on the pier and we waited, without speaking.

At night the lake was like black glass with a streak of amber which was the path of the moon. All around, the spruce trees grew tall and close-set, branches blackly sharp against the sky, which was lightened by a cold flickering of stars. Then the loons began their calling. They rose like phantom birds from the nests on the shore, and flew out onto the dark still surface of the water.

No one can ever describe that ululating sound, the crying of the loons, and no one who has heard it can ever forget it. Plaintive, and yet with a quality of chilling mockery, those voices belonged to a world separated by eons from our neat world of summer cottages and the lighted lamps of home.

"They must have sounded just like that," my father remarked. "before any person ever set foot here."

Then he laughed. "You could say the same, of course, about sparrows, or chipmunks, but somehow it only strikes you that way with the loons."

"I know," I said.

Neither of us suspected that this would be the last time we would ever sit here together on the shore, listening. We stayed for perhaps half an hour, and then we went back to the cottage. My mother was reading beside the fireplace. Piquette was looking at the burning birch log, and not doing anything.

"You should have come along," I said, although in fact I was glad she had not.

"Not me," Piquette said. "You wouldn' catch me walkin' way down there jus' for a bunch of squawkin' birds."

Piquette and I remained ill at ease with one another. I felt I had somehow failed my father, but I did not know what was the matter, nor why she would not or could not respond when I suggested exploring the woods or playing house. I thought it was probably her slow and difficult walking that held her back. She stayed most of the time in the cottage with my mother, helping her with the dishes or with Roddie, but hardly ever talking. Then the Duncans arrived at their cottage, and I spent my days with Mavis, who was my best friend. I could not reach Piquette at all, and I soon lost interest in trying. But all that summer she remained as both a reproach and a mystery to me.

That winter my father died of pneumonia, after less than a week's illness. For some time I saw nothing around me, being completely immersed in my own pain and my mother's. When I looked outward once more, I scarcely noticed that Piquette Tonnerre was no longer at school. I do not remember seeing her at all until four years later, one Saturday night when Mavis and I were having Cokes in the Regal Café. The jukebox was booming like tuneful thunder, and beside it, leaning lightly on its chrome and its rainbow glass, was a girl.

Piquette must have been seventeen then, although she looked about twenty. I stared at her, astounded that anyone could have changed so much. Her face, so stolid and expressionless before, was animated now with a gaiety that was almost violent. She laughed and talked very loudly with the boys around her. Her lipstick was bright carmine, and her hair was cut short and frizzily permed. She had not been pretty as a child, and she was not pretty now, for her features were still heavy and blunt. But her dark and slightly slanted eyes were beautiful, and her skin-tight skirt and orange sweater displayed to enviable advantage a soft and slender body.

She saw me, and walked over. She teetered a little, but it was not due to her once-tubercular leg, for her limp was almost gone.

"Hi, Vanessa." Her voice still had the same hoarseness. "Long time no see, eh?"

"Hi," I said. "Where've you been keeping yourself, Piquette?"

"Oh, I been around," she said. "I been away almost two years now. Been all over the place—Winnipeg, Regina, Saskatoon. Jesus, what I could tell you! I come back this summer, but I ain't stayin'. You kids goin' to the dance?"

"No," I said abruptly, for this was a sore point with me. I was fifteen, and thought I was old enough to go the Saturday-night dances at the Flamingo. My mother, however, thought otherwise.

"Y'oughta come," Piquette said. "I never miss one. It's just about the on'y thing in this jerkwater town that's any fun. Boy, you couldn' catch me stayin' here. I don' give a shit about this place. It stinks."

She sat down beside me, and I caught the harsh over-sweetness of her perfume.

"Listen, you wanna know something, Vanessa?" she confided, her voice only slightly blurred. "Your dad was the only person in Manawaka that ever done anything good to me."

I nodded speechlessly. I was certain she was speaking the truth. I knew a little more than I had that summer at Diamond Lake, but I could not reach her now any more than I had then. I was ashamed, ashamed of my own timidity, the frightened tendency to look the other way. Yet I felt no real warmth towards her—I only felt that I ought to, because of that distant summer and because my father had hoped she would be company for me, or perhaps that I would be for her, but it had not happened that way. At this moment, meeting her again, I had to admit that she repelled and embarrassed me, and I could not help despising the self-pity in her voice. I wished she would go away. I did not want to see her. I did not know what to say to her. It seemed that we had nothing to say to one another.

"I'll tell you something else," Piquette went on. "All the old bitches an' biddies in this town will sure be surprised. I'm gettin' married this fall—my boyfriend, he's an English fella, works in the stockyards in the city there, a very tall guy, got blond wavy hair. Gee, is he ever handsome. Got this real classy name. Alvin Gerald Cummings—some handle, eh? They call him Al."

For the merest instant, then, I saw her. I really did see her, for the first and only time in all the years we had both lived in the same town. Her defiant face, momentarily, became unguarded and unmasked, and in her eyes there was a terrifying hope.

"Gee, Piquette—" I burst out awkwardly, "that's swell. That's really wonderful. Congratulations—good luck—I hope you'll be happy—"

As I mouthed the conventional phrases, I could only guess how great her need must have been, that she had been forced to seek the very things she so bitterly rejected.

When I was eighteen, I left Manawaka and went away to college. At the end of my first year, I came back home for the summer. I spent the first few days in talking non-stop with my mother, as we exchanged all the news that somehow had not found its way into letters—what had happened in my life and what had happened here in Manawaka while I was away. My mother searched her memory for events that concerned people I knew.

"Did I ever write you about Piquette Tonnerre, Vanessa?" she asked one morning.

"No, I don't think so," I replied. "Last I heard of her, she was going to marry some guy in the city. Is she still there?"

My mother looked perturbed, and it was a moment before she spoke, as though she did not know how to express what she had to tell and wished she did not need to try.

"She's dead," she said at last. Then, as I stared at her, "Oh, Vanessa, when it happened, I couldn't help thinking of her as she was that summer—so sullen and gauche and badly dressed. I couldn't help wondering if we could have done something more at that time—but what could we do? She used to be around in the cottage there with me all day, and honestly, it was all I could do to get a word out of her. She didn't even talk to your father very much, although I think she liked him, in her way."

"What happened?" I asked.

"Either her husband left her, or she left him," my mother said, "I don't know which. Anyway, she came back here with two youngsters, both only babies—they must have been born very close together. She kept house, I guess, for Lazarus and her brothers, down in the valley there, in the old Tonnerre place. I used to see her on the street sometimes, but she never spoke to me. She'd put on an awful lot of weight, and she looked a mess, to tell you the truth, a real slattern, dressed any old how. She was up in court a couple of times—drunk and disorderly, of course. One Saturday night last winter, during the coldest weather, Piquette was alone in the shack with the children. The Tonnerres made home brew all the time, so I've heard, and Lazarus said later she'd been drinking most of the day when he and the boys went out that evening. They had an old woodstove there—you know the kind, with exposed pipes. The shack caught fire. Piquette didn't get out, and neither did the children.''

I did not say anything. As so often with Piquette, there did not seem to be anything to say. There was a kind of silence around the image in my mind of the fire and the snow, and I wished I could put from my memory the look that I had seen once in Piquette's eyes.

I went up to Diamond Lake for a few days that summer, with Mavis and her family. The MacLeod cottage had been sold after my father's death, and I did not even go to look at it, not wanting to witness my long-ago kingdom possessed now by strangers. But one evening I went down to the shore by myself.

The small pier which my father had built was gone, and in its place there was a large and solid pier built by the government, for Galloping Mountain was now a national park, and Diamond Lake had been renamed Lake Wapakata, for it was felt that an Indian name would have a greater appeal to tourists. The one store had become several dozen, and the settlement had all the attributes of a flourishing resort—hotels, a dance-hall, cafés with neon signs, the penetrating odors of potato chips and hot dogs.

I sat on the government pier and looked out across the water. At night the lake at least was the same as it had always been, darkly shining and bearing within its black glass the streak of amber that was the path of the moon. There was no wind that evening, and everything was quiet all around me. It seemed too quiet, and then I realized that the loons were no longer here. I listened for some time, to make sure, but never once did I hear that long-drawn call, half mocking and half plaintive, spearing through the stillness across the lake.

I did not know what had happened to the birds. Perhaps they had gone away to some far place of belonging. Perhaps they had been unable to find such a place, and had simply died out, having ceased to care any longer whether they lived or not.

I remembered how Piquette had scorned to come along, when my father and I sat there and listened to the lake birds. It seemed to me now that in some unconscious and totally unrecognized way, Piquette might have been the only one, after all, who had heard the crying of the loons.

ALICE MUNRO
1931–

Born in the rural community of Wingham in southwestern Ontario, she attended the University of Western Ontario. After two years of study at university, she moved to the west coast, living first in Vancouver, where she worked as an assistant in the Vancouver Public Library, and then in Victoria, where she and her husband opened a bookstore. She has set her six volumes of fiction in the rural area where she was born and where she now resides. Her short-story sequence, *Lives of Girls and Women* (1971), studies a young girl's search for her identity as a woman and as a writer; the heroine, Del Jordan, needs to learn that true fiction is rooted in the factual and tactile world that surrounds her. Acknowledging the fiction of Flannery O'Connor and Eudora Welty among the major influences on her own work, Munro writes out of the world she knows well, taking the ordinary, everyday reality around her and transforming it into fiction. She is now regarded as one of the finest short-story writers in the English language.

The Stone in the Field

My mother was not a person who spent all her time frosting the rims of glasses and fancying herself descended from the aristocracy. She was a businesswoman really, a trader and dealer. Our house was full of things that had not been paid for with money, but taken in some complicated trade, and that might not be ours to keep. For a while we could play a piano, consult an Encyclopaedia Britannica, eat off an oak table. But one day I would come home from school and find that each of these things had moved on. A mirror off the wall could go as easily, a cruet stand, a horsehair loveseat that had replaced a sofa that had replaced a daybed. We were living in a warehouse.

My mother worked for, or with, a man named Poppy Cullender. He was a dealer in antiques. He did not have a shop: He too had a house full of furniture. What we had was just his overflow. He had dressers back-to-back and bedsprings upended against the wall. He bought things—furniture, dishes, bedspreads, doorknobs, pump handles, churns, flatirons, anything—from people living on farms or in little villages in the country, then sold what he had bought to antique stores in Toronto. The heyday of antiques had not yet arrived. It was a time when people were covering old woodwork with white or pastel paint as fast as they were able, throwing out spool beds and putting in blond maple bedroom suites, covering patchwork quilts with chenille bedspreads. It was not hard to buy things, to pick them up for next to nothing, but it was a slow business selling them, which was why they might become part of our lives for a season. Just the same, Poppy and my mother were on the right track. If they had lasted, they might have become rich and justified. As it was, Poppy kept his head above water and my mother made next to nothing, and everybody thought them deluded.

They didn't last. My mother got sick, and Poppy went to jail, for making advances on a train.

There were farmhouses where Poppy was not a welcome sight. Children hooted and wives bolted the door, as he came toiling through the yard in his greasy black clothes, rolling his eyes in an uncontrollably lewd or silly way he had and calling in a soft, pleading voice, "Ith anybody h-home?" To add to his other problems he had both a lisp and a stammer. My father could imitate him very well. There were places where Poppy found doors barred and others, usually less respectable, where he was greeted and cheered and fed, just as if he had been a harmless weird bird dropped out of the sky, valued for its very oddity. When he had experienced no welcome he did not go back; instead, he sent my mother. He must have had in his head a map of the surrounding country with every house in it, and just as some maps have dots to show you where the mineral resources are, or the places of historical interest, Poppy's map would have marked the location of every known and suspected rocking chair, pine sideboard, piece of milk glass, mustache cup. "Why don't you run out and take a look at it?" I would hear him say to my mother when they were huddled in the dining room looking at something like the maker's mark on an old pickle crock. He didn't stammer when he talked to her, when he talked business; his voice though soft was not humble and indicated that he had his own satisfactions, maybe his own revenge. If I had a friend with me, coming in from school, she would say, "Is that Poppy *Cullender*?" She would be amazed to hear him talking like an ordinary person and amazed to find him inside somebody's house. I disliked this connection with us so much that I wanted to say no.

Not much was made, really, of Poppy's sexual tendencies. People may have thought he didn't have any. When they said he was queer, they just meant queer; odd, freakish, disturbing. His stammer and his rolling eyes and his fat bum and his house full of throwaways were all rolled up in that one word. I don't know if he was very courageous, trying to make a life for himself in a place like Dalgleish where random insults and misplaced pity would be what was always coming at him, or whether he was just not very realistic. Certainly it was not realistic to make such suggestions to a couple of baseball players on the Stratford train.

I never knew what my mother made of his final disastrous luck, or what she knew about him. Years later she read in the paper that a teacher at the college I was going to had been arrested for fighting in a bar over a male companion. She asked me did they mean he was defending a friend, and if so, why didn't they say so? *Male companion?*

Then she said, "Poor Poppy. There were always those that were out to get him. He was very smart, in his way. Some people can't survive in a place like this. It's not permitted. No."

My mother had the use of Poppy's car, for business forays, and sometimes for a weekend, when he went to Toronto. Unless he had a trailer-load of things to take down, he traveled—unfortunately, as I have said—by train. Our own car had gone so far beyond repair that we were not able to take it out of town; it was driven into Dalgleish and back, and that was all. My parents were like many other people who had entered the Depression with some large possession, such as a car or a furnace, which gradually wore out and couldn't be fixed or replaced. When we could take it on the roads we used to go to Goderich once or twice in the summer, to the lake. And occasionally we visited my father's sisters who lived out in the country.

My mother always said that my father had a very odd family. It was odd because there had been seven girls and then one boy; and it was odd because six of those eight children still lived together, in the house where they were born. One sister had died young, of typhoid fever, and my father had got away. And those six sisters were very odd in themselves, at least in the view of many people, in the time they lived in. They were leftovers, really; my mother said so; they belonged in another generation.

I don't remember that they ever came to visit us. They didn't like to come to a town as big as Dalgleish, or to venture so far from home. It would have been a drive of fourteen or fifteen miles, and they had no car. They drove a horse and buggy, a horse and cutter in the wintertime, long after everyone else had ceased to do so. There must have been occasion when they had to drive into town, because I saw one of them once, in the buggy, on a town street. The buggy had a great high top on it, like a black bonnet, and whichever aunt it was was sitting side-ways on the seat, looking up as seldom as it is possible to do while driving a horse. Public scrutiny seemed to be causing her much pain, but she was stubborn; she held herself there on the seat, cringing and stubborn, and she was as strange a sight, in her way, as Poppy Cullender was in his. I couldn't really think of her as my aunt; the connection seemed impossible. Yet I could remember an earlier time, when I had been out to the farm—maybe more than one time, for I had been so young it was hard to remember—and I had not felt this impossiblity and had not understood the oddity of these relatives. It was when my grandfather was sick in bed, dying I suppose, with a big brown paper fan hanging over him. It was worked by a system of ropes which I was allowed to pull. One of my aunts was showing me how to do this, when my mother called my name from downstairs. Then the aunt and I looked at each other exactly as two children look at each other when an adult is calling. I must have sensed something unusual about this, some lack of what was expected, even necessary, in the way of balance, or barriers; else I would not have remembered it.

One other time with an aunt. I think the same one, but maybe another, was sitting with me on the back steps of the farmhouse, with a six-quart basket of clothespegs on the step beside us. She was making dolls for me, mannikins, out of the round-headed pegs. She used a black crayon and a red, to make their mouths and eyes, and she brought bits of yarn out of her apron pocket, to twist around to make the hair and clothes. And she talked to me; I am certain she talked.

"Here's a lady. She went to church with her wig on, see? She was proud. What if a wind comes up? It would blow her wig right off. See? You blow."

"Here's a soldier. See he only has one leg? His other leg was blown off by a cannonball at the battle of Waterloo. Do you know what a cannonball is, that shoots out of a big gun? When they have a battle? Boom!"

Now we were going out to the farm, in Poppy's car, to visit the aunts. My father said no, he wouldn't drive another man's car—meaning he wouldn't drive Poppy's, wouldn't sit where Poppy had sat—so my mother drove. That made the whole expedition feel uncertain, the weight wrongly distributed. It was a hot Sunday late in the summer.

My mother was not altogether sure of the way, and my father waited until the last moment to reassure her. This was understood to be teasing, and yet was not altogether free of reservations or reproof.

"Is it here we turn? Is it one further? I will know when I see the bridge."

The route was complicated. Around Dalgleish most roads were straight, but out here the roads twisted around hills or buried themselves in swamps. Some dwindled to a couple of ruts with a row of plantain and dandelions running between. In some places wild berry-bushes sent creepers across the road. These high, thick bushes, dense and thorny, with leaves of a shiny green that seemed almost black, reminded me of the waves of the sea that were pushed back for Moses.

There was the bridge, like two railway cars joined together, stripped to their skeletons, one lane wide. A sign said it was unsafe for trucks.

"We'll never make it," my father said, as we bumped on to the bridge floor. "There he is. Old Father Maitland."

My sister said, "Where? Who? Where is he?"

"The Maitland *River*," my mother said.

We looked down, where the guard-rails had fallen out of the side of the bridge, and saw the clear brown water flowing over big dim stones, between cedar banks, breaking into sunny ripples further on. My skin was craving for it.

"Do they ever go swimming?" I said. I meant the aunts. I thought that if they did, they might take us.

"Swimming?" said my mother. "I can't picture it. Do they?" she asked my father.

"I can't picture it either."

The road was going uphill, out of the gloomy cedar bush on the river bank. I started saying the aunts' names.

"Susan. Clara. Lizzie. Maggie. Jennet was the one who died."

"Annie," said my father. "Don't forget Annie."

"Annie. Lizzie. I said her. Who else?"

"Dorothy," said my mother, shifting gears with an angry little spurt, and we cleared the top of the hill, leaving the dark bush hollow behind. Up here were pasture hills covered with purple-flowering milkweed, wild pea blossom, black-eyed Susans. Hardly any trees here, but lots of elderberry bushes, blooming all along the road. They looked as if they were sprinkled with snow. One bald hill reached up higher than any of the others.

"Mount Hebron," my father said. "That is the highest point of land in Huron County. Or so I always was told."

"Now I know where I am all right," my mother said. "We'll see it in a moment, won't we?"

And there it was, the big wooden house with no trees near it, the barn and the flowering brown hills behind. The drive shed was the original barn, built of logs. The paint on the house was not white as I had absolutely believed but yellow, and much of it had peeled away.

Out in front of the house, in a block of shade which was quite narrow at this time of day, several figures were sitting on straightbacked chairs. On the wall of the house, behind them, hung the scoured milk-pails and parts of the separator.

They were not expecting us. They had no telephone, so we hadn't been able to let them know we were coming. They were just sitting there in the shade, watching the road where scarcely another car went by all afternoon.

One figure got up, and ran around the side of the house.

"That'll be Susan," my father said. "She can't face company."

"She'll come back when she realizes it's us," my mother said. "She won't know the strange car."

"Maybe. I wouldn't count on it."

The others stood, and stiffly readied themselves, hands clasped in front of their aprons. When we got out of the car and were recognized, one or two of them took a few steps forward, then stopped, and waited for us to approach them.

"Come on," my father said, and led us to each in turn, saying only the name in recognition of the meeting. No embraces, no touch of hands or laying together of cheeks.

"Lizzie. Dorothy. Clara."

It was no use, I could never get them straight. They looked too much alike. There must have been a twelve- or fifteen-year age span, but to me they all looked about fifty, older than my parents but not really old. They were all lean and fine-boned, and might at one time have been fairly tall, but were stooped now, with hard work and deference. Some had their hair cut short in a plain, childish style; some had it braided and twisted on top of their heads. Nobody's hair was entirely black or entirely gray. Their faces were pale, eyebrows thick and furry, eyes deep-set and bright; blue-gray or green-gray or gray. They looked a good deal like my father though he did not stoop, and his face had opened up in a way that theirs had not, to make him a handsome man.

They looked a good deal like me. I didn't know it at the time and wouldn't have wanted to. But suppose I stopped doing anything to my hair, now, stopped wearing makeup and plucking my eyebrows, put on a shapeless print dress and apron and stood around hanging my head and hugging my elbows? Yes. So when my mother and her cousins looked me over, anxiously turned me to the light, saying, "Is she a Chaddeley? What do you think?" it was the Fleming face they were seeing, and to tell the truth it was a face that wore better than theirs. (Not that they were claiming to be pretty; to look like a Chaddeley was enough.)

One of the aunts had hands red as a skinned rabbit. Later in the kitchen this one sat in a chair pushed up against the woodbox, half hidden by the stove, and I saw how she kept stroking these hands and twisting them up in her apron. I remembered that I had seen such hands before, on one of the early visits, long ago, and my mother had told me that it was because this aunt—was it always the same one? —had been scrubbing the floor and the table and chairs with lye, to keep them white. That was what lye did to your hands. And after this visit, too, on the way home my mother was to say in a tone of general accusation, sorrow, and disgust, "Did you see those hands? They must have got a Presbyterian dispensation to let them scrub on Sundays."

The floor was pine and it was white, gleaming, but soft-looking, like velvet. So were the chairs and the table. We all sat around the kitchen, which was like a small house tacked on to the main house; back and front doors opposite each other, windows on three sides. The cold black stove shone, too, with polishing. Its trim was like mirrors. The room was cleaner and barer than any I have ever been in. There was no sign of frivolity, no indication that the people who lived here ever sought entertainment. No radio; no newspapers or magazines; certainly no books. There must have been a Bible in the house, and there must have been a calendar, but these were not to be seen. It was hard now even to believe in the clothespin dolls, the crayons and the yarn. I wanted to ask which of them had made the dolls; had there really been a wigged lady and a one-legged soldier? But though I was not usually shy, a peculiar paralysis overcame me in this room, as if I understood for the first time how presumptuous any question might be, how hazardous any opinion.

Work would be what filled their lives, not conversation; work would be what gave their days shape. I know that now. Drawing the milk down through the rough teats, slapping the flatiron back and forth on the scorched-smelling ironing board, swishing the scrub-water in whitening arcs across the pine floor, they would be mute, and maybe content. Work would not be done here as it was in our house, where the idea was to get it over with. It would be something that could, that must, go on forever.

What was to be said? The aunts, like those who engage in a chat with royalty, would venture no remarks of their own, but could answer questions. They offered no refreshments. It was clear that only a great effort of will kept them all from running away and hiding, like Aunt Susan, who never did reappear while we were there. What was felt in that room was the pain of human contact. I was hypnotized by it. The fascinating pain; the humiliating necessity.

My father did have some idea of how to proceed. He started out on the weather. The need for rain, the rain in July that spoiled the hay, last year's wet spring, floods long past, the prospects or non-prospects of a rainy fall. This talk steadied them and he asked about the cows, the driving horse whose name was Nelly and the workhorses Prince and Queen, the garden; did the blight get on their tomatoes?

"No it didn't."

"How many quarts did you do down?"

"Twenty-seven."

"Did you make any chili sauce? Did you make some juice?"

"Juice and chili sauce. Yes."

"So you won't starve next winter. You'll be falling into flesh, next."

Giggles broke from a couple of them and my father took heart, continued teasing. He inquired whether they were doing much dancing these days. He shook his head as he pretended to recall their reputation for running around the country to dances, smoking, cutting up. He said they were a bad lot, they wouldn't get married because they'd rather flirt; why, he couldn't hold up his head for the shame of them.

My mother broke in then. She must have meant to rescue them, thinking it cruel to tease them in this way, dwelling on just what they had never had, or been.

"That is a lovely piece of furniture," she said. "That sideboard. I always have admired it."

Flappers, my father said, that's what they were, in their prime.

My mother went on to look at the kitchen dresser, which was pine, and very heavy and tall. The knobs on all the doors and drawers were not quite round but slightly irregular, either from the making, or from all the hands that had pulled on them.

"You could have an antique dealer come in here and offer you a hundred dollars for that," my mother said. "If that ever happens, don't take it. The table and chairs as well. Don't let anybody smooth-talk you into selling them before you find out what they're really worth. I know what I'm talking about." Without asking permission she examined the dresser, fingered the knobs, looked around at the back. "I can't tell you what it's worth myself but if you ever want to sell it I will get it appraised by the best person I can find. That's not all," she said, stroking the pine judiciously. "You have a fortune's worth of furniture in this house. You sit tight on it. You have the old furniture that was made around here, and there's hardly any of that left. People threw it out, around the turn of the century, they bought Victorian things when they started getting prosperous. The things that didn't get thrown out are worth money and they're going to be worth more. I'm telling you."

So she was. But they could not take such telling. They could no more understand her than if she had been spouting lunacy. Possible the word antique was not known to them. She was talking about their kitchen dresser but she was talking about it in terms they had no under-standing of. If a dealer came into the house and offered them money? Nobody came into their house. Selling the dresser was probably as hard for them to imagine as selling the kitchen wall. None of them would look at anything but their aproned laps.

"So I guess that's lucky, for the ones that never got prosperous," my father said, to ease things, but they could not answer him, either. They would know the meaning of prosperous but they would never have used such a word, would never have got their tongues around it, nor their minds around the idea of getting that way. They would have noticed that some people, their neighbors even, were spending money, on tractors and combines and milking machines as well as on cars and houses, and I think this must have seemed to them a sign of an alarming, not enviable, lack of propriety and self-control. They would pity people for it, in a way, the same way they might pity girls who did run around to dances, and smoke and flirt and get married. They might pity my mother, too. My mother looked at their lives and thought of how they could be brightened, opened up. Suppose they sold some furniture and got hydro in the house, bought a washing machine, put linoleum on the floor, bought a car and learned to drive it? Why not? my mother would ask, seeing life all in terms of change and possiblity. She imagined they would yearn for things, not only material things but condi-tions, abilities, which they did not even bother to deplore, did not think to reject, being so perfectly encased in what they had and were, so far beyond imagining themselves otherwise.

When my father was in the hospital for the last time he became very good-humored and loquacious under the influence of the pills they were giving him, and he talked to me about his life and his family. He told me how he had left home. Actually there were two leave-takings. The first occurred the summer he was fourteen. His father had sent him out to split some chunks of wood. He broke the ax-handle, and his father cursed him out and went after him with a pitchfork. His father was known for temper, and hard work. The sisters screamed, and my father, the fourteen-year-old boy, took off down the lane running as hard as he could.

"Could they scream?"

"What? Oh yes. Then. Yes they could."

My father intended to run only as far as the road, hang around, come back when his sisters let him know the coast was clear. But he did not stop running until he was halfway to Goderich, and then he thought he might as well go the rest of the way. He got a job on a lake-boat. He spent the rest of the season working on the boat, and the month before Christmas, after the shipping season ended, he worked in a flour mill. He could do the work there, but he was underage; they were afraid of the inspector, so they let him go. He wanted to go home anyway, for Christmas. He was homesick. He bought presents for his father and his sisters. A watch was what he got for the old man. That and his ticket took every cent he had.

A few days after Christmas he was out in the barn, putting down hay, and his father came looking for him.

"Have you got any money?" his father wanted to know.

My father said he hadn't.

"Well, do you think then me and your sisters are going to spend all summer and fall looking up the arseholes of cows, for you to come home and sponge off us in the winter?"

That was the second time my father left home.

He shook with laughter in the hospital bed, telling me.

"Looking up the arseholes of cows!"

Then he said the funny thing was the old man himself had left home when he was a kid, after a fight with his own father. The father lit into him for using the wheelbarrow.

"It was this way. They always carried the feed to the horses, pail by pail. In the winter, when the horses were in the stalls. So my father took the notion to carry it to them in the wheelbarrow. Naturally it was a lot quicker. But he got beat. For laziness. That was the way they were, you know. Any change of any kind was a bad thing. Efficiency was just laziness, to them. That's the peasant thinking for you."

"Maybe Tolstoy would agree with them," I said. "Gandhi too."

"Drat Tolstoy and Gandhi. They never worked when they were young."

"Maybe not."

"But it's a wonder how those people had the courage once, to get them over here. They left everything. Turned their backs on everything they knew and came out here. Bad enough to face the North Atlantic, then this country that was all wilderness. The work they did, the things they went through. When your great-grandfather came to the Huron Tract he had his brother with him, and his wife and her mother, and his two little kids. Straightaway his brother was killed by a falling tree. Then the second summer his wife and his mother and the two little boys got the cholera, and the grandmother and both the children died. So he and his wife were left alone, and they went on clearing their farm and started up another family. I think the courage got burnt out of them. Their religion did them in, and their upbringing. How they had to toe the line. Also their pride. Pride was what they had when they had no more gumption."

"Not you," I said. "You ran away."

"I didn't run far."

In their old age the aunts rented the farm, but continued to live on it. Some got cataracts in their eyes, some got arthritis, but they stayed on and looked after each other, and died there, all except the last one, Aunt Lizzie, who had to go to the County Home. They lived a long time. They were a hardier clan, after all, than the Chaddeleys, none of whom reached seventy. (Cousin Iris died within six months of seeing Alaska.) I used to send a card at Christmas, and I would write on it: *to all my aunts, love and a Merry Christmas*. I did that because I could not remember which of them were dead and which were alive. I had seen their gravestone when my mother was buried. It was a modest pillar with all their names and dates of birth on it, a couple of dates of death filled in (Jennet, of course, and probably Susan), the rest left blank. By now more dates would be finished.

They would send me a card too. A wreath or a candle on it, and a few sentences of information.

A good winter so far, not much snow. We are all well except Clara's eyes not getting any better. Best wishes of the Season.

I thought of them having to go out and buy the card, go to the Post Office, buy the stamp. It was an act of faith for them to write and send those sentences to any place as unimaginable as Vancouver, to someone of their own blood leading a life so strange to them, someone who would read the card with such a feeling of bewilderment and unexplainable guilt. It did make me guilty and bewildered to think that they were still there, still attached to me. But any message from home, in those days, could let me know I was a traitor.

In the hospital, I asked my father if any of his sisters had ever had a boyfriend.

"Not what you could call that. No. There used to be a joke about Mr. Black. They used to say he built his shack there because he was sweet on Susan. I don't think so. He was just a one-legged fellow that built a shack down in a corner of the field across the road, and he died there. All before my time. Susan was the oldest, you know, she was twenty or twenty-one years old when I was born."

"So, you don't think she had a romance?"

"I wouldn't think so. It was just a joke. He was an Austrian or some such thing. Black was just what he was called, or maybe he called himself. She wouldn't have been let near him. He was buried right there under a big boulder. My father tore the shack down and used the lumber to build our chicken-house."

I remembered that, I remembered the boulder. I remembered sitting on the ground watching my father who was fixing fenceposts. I asked him if this could be a true memory.

"Yes it could. I used to go out and fix the fences when the old man was sick in bed. You wouldn't have been very big.'

"I was sitting watching you, and you said to me, do you know what that big stone is? That's a gravestone. I don't remember asking you whose. I must have thought it was a joke."

"No joke. That would be it. Mr. Black was buried underneath there. That reminds me of another thing. You know I told you, how the grandmother and the little boys died? They had the three bodies in the house at the one time. And they had nothing to make the shrouds out of but the lace curtains they had brought from the old country. I guess it would be a hasty business when it was cholera and in the summer. So that was what they buried them in."

"Lace curtains."

My father looked shy, as if he had given me a present, and said brusquely, "Well, that's the kind of a detail I thought might be interesting to you."

Some time after my father died I was reading some old newspapers on a microfilm reader in the Toronto Library; this was in connection with a documentary script I was working on, for television. The name Dalgleish caught my eyes and then the name Fleming, which I have gone so long without.

HERMIT DIES NEAR DALGLEISH

It is reported that Mr. Black, a man about forty-five years old, Christian name unknown, had died on the farm of Mr. Thomas Fleming, where he has been living for the last three years in a shack which Mr. Fleming allowed him to construct in the corner of a field. He cultivated a few potatoes, subsisting mainly on those and on fish and small game. He was believed to come from some European country but gave the name Black and did not reveal his history. At some point in his life he had parted company with one of his legs, leading some to speculate that he might have been a soldier. He was heard to mutter to himself in a foreign language.

About three weeks ago Mr. Fleming, not having seen any smoke from the recluse's shack, investigated, and found the man very ill. He was suffering from a cancer of the tongue. Mr. Fleming wished to remove him to his own house for care but Mr. Black would not agree, though he finally allowed himself to be taken to Mr. Fleming's barn, where he remained, the weather being mild, and nursing care being provided by the young Misses Fleming, who reside at home. There he died, and was buried at his own request next to his hermits' shack, taking the mystery of his life with him.

I began to think that I would like to see the stone, I would like to see if it was still there. No one related to me lived in that country any more. I drove up on a Sunday in June and was able to bypass Dalgleish completely; the highway had been changed. I expected to have some trouble finding the farm, but I was on it before I could have believed it possible. It was no longer an out-of-the-way place. The back roads had been straightened; there was a new, strong, two-lane concrete bridge; half of Mount Hebron had been cut away for gravel; and the wild-pasture fields had been planted in corn.

The log drive-shed was gone. The house had been covered in pale-green aluminum siding. There were several wide new windows. The cement slab in front, where my aunts had sat on their straight-backed chairs to watch the road, had been turned into a patio, with tubs of salvia and geraniums, a metal table with an awning, and the usual folding furniture with bright plastic webbing.

All this made me doubtful, but I knocked on the door anyway. A young, pregnant woman answered. She asked me into the kitchen, which was a cheerful room with linoleum that looked something like red and brown bricks, and built-in cupboards that looked very much like maple. Two children were watching a television picture whose colors seemed drained by the brightness of the day outside, and a businesslike young husband was working at an adding machine, seemingly unbothered by the noise of the television as his children were unbothered by the sunlight. The young woman stepped over a large dog to turn off a tap at the sink.

They were not impatient of my story, as I had thought they might be. In fact they were interested and helpful, and not entirely in the dark about the stone I was looking for. The husband said that the land across the road had not been sold to his father, who had bought this farm from my aunts; it had been sold previously. He thought it was over there that the stone was. He said his father had told him there was a man buried over there, under a big stone, and they had even gone for a walk once, to look at it, but he hadn't thought of it in years. He said he would go and look for it now.

I had thought we would walk, but we drove down the lane in his car. We got out, and carefully entered a cornfield. The corn was just about to my knees, so the stone should have been in plain sight. I asked if the man who owned this field would mind, and the farmer said no, the fellow never came near it, he hired somebody else to work it for him.

"He's a fellow that has a thousand acres in corn in Huron County alone."

I said that a farmer was just like a businessman nowadays, wasn't he? The farmer seemed pleased that I had said this and began to explain why it was so. Risks had to be undertaken. Expenses were sky-high. I asked him if he had one of those tractors with the air-conditioned cabs and he said yes, he had. If you did well, he said, the rewards, the financial rewards, could be considerable, but there were trials and tribulations most people didn't know a thing about. Next spring, if all went well, he and his wife were going on their first holiday. They were going to Spain. The children wanted them to forget their holiday and put in a swimming pool, but his idea was to travel. He owned two farms now and was thinking of buying a third. He was just sitting working out some figures when I knocked on the door. In a way, he couldn't afford to buy it. In another way, he couldn't afford not to.

While carrying on this conversation we were walking up and down the corn rows looking for the stone. We looked in the corners of the field and it was not there. He said that of course the corner of a field then was not necessarily the corner of a field now. But the truth probably was that when the field got put in corn the stone was in the way, so they would have hauled it out. He said we could go over to the rock-pile near the road and see if we recognized it.

I said we wouldn't bother, I wasn't so sure I would know it, on a rock-pile.

"Me either," he said. He sounded disappointed. I wondered what he had expected to see, or feel.

I wondered the same thing about myself.

If I had been younger, I would have figured out a story. I would have insisted on Mr. Black's being in love with one of my aunts, and on one of them—not necessarily the one he was in love with—being in love with him. I would have wished him to confide in them, in one of them, his secret, his reason for living in a shack in Huron County, far from home. Later, I might have believed that he wanted to, but hadn't confided this, or his love either. I would have made a horrible, plausible connection between that silence of his, and the manner of his death. Now I no longer believe that people's secrets are defined and communicable, or their feelings full-blown and easy to recognize. I don't believe so. Now, I can only say, my father's sisters scrubbed the floor with lye, they stooked the oats and milked the cows by hand. They must have taken a quilt to the barn for the hermit to die on, they must have let water dribble from a tin cup into his afflicted mouth. That was their life. My mother's cousins behaved in another way; they dressed up and took pictures of each other; they sallied forth. However they behaved they are all dead. I carry something of them around in me. But the boulder is gone, Mount Hebron is cut down for gravel, and the life buried here is one you have to think twice about regretting.

BHARATI MUKHERJEE
1940–

Born in Calcutta, she received her B.A. (1959) from the University of Calcutta, M.A. (1961) from the University of Baroda, and M.F.A. (1963) and Ph.D. (1969) from the University of Iowa. She emigrated from the United States to Canada in 1966, and, after living in Montreal and Toronto, returned in 1980 to the United States. She has taught in many universities in Canada and the United States. Her fiction, like her life, is an exploration of cultural displacement as her East Indian protagonists confront personal and social struggles both in India and in North America. The author of two novels and two collections of short stories, she also co-wrote, with her husband, the fiction writer Clark Blaise, *Days and Nights in Calcutta* (1977), an autobiographical account of their return for a year to India.

The Lady from Lucknow

When I was four, one of the girls next door fell in love with a Hindu. Her father intercepted a love note from the boy, and beat her with his leather sandals. She died soon after. I was in the room when my mother said to our neighbor, "The Nawab-*sahib* had no choice, but Husseina's heart just broke, poor dear." I was an army doctor's daughter, and I pictured the dead girl's heart—a rubbery squeezable organ with auricles and ventricles—first swelling, then bursting and coating the floor with thick, slippery blood.

We lived in Lucknow at the time, where the Muslim community was large. This was just before the British took the fat, diamond-shaped subcontinent and created two nations, a big one for the Hindus and a littler one for us. My father moved us to Rawalpindi in Pakistan two months after Husseina died. We were a family of soft, voluptuous children, and my father wanted to protect us from the Hindus' shameful lust.

I have fancied myself in love many times since, but never enough for the emotions to break through tissue and muscle. Husseina's torn heart remains the standard of perfect love.

At seventeen I married a good man, the fourth son of a famous poet-cum-lawyer in Islamabad. We have a daughter, seven, and a son, four. In the Muslim communities we have lived in, we are admired, Iqbal works for IBM, and because of his work we have made homes in Lebanon, Brazil, Zambia, and France. Now we live in Atlanta, Georgia, in a wide, new house with a deck and a backyard that runs into a golf course. IBM has been generous to us. We expect to pass on this good, decent life to our children. Our children are ashamed of the dingy cities where we got our start.

Some Sunday afternoons when Iqbal isn't at a conference halfway across the world, we sit together on the deck and drink gin and tonics as we have done on Sunday afternoons in a dozen exotic cities. But here, the light is different somehow. A gold haze comes off the golf course and settles on our bodies, our new house. When the light shines right in my eyes, I pull myself out of the canvas deck chair and lean against the railing that still smells of forests. Everything in Atlanta is so new!

"Sit," Iqbal tells me. "You'll distract the golfers. Americans are crazy for sex, you know that."

He half rises out of his deck chair. He lunges for my breasts in mock passion. I slip out of his reach.

At the bottom of the backyard, the golfers, caddies, and carts are too minute to be bloated with lust.

But, who knows? One false thwock! of their golfing irons, and my little heart, like a golf ball, could slice through the warm air and vanish into the jonquil-yellow beyond.

It isn't trouble that I want, though I do have a lover. He's an older man, an immunologist with the Center for Disease Control right here in town. He comes to see me when Iqbal is away at high-tech conferences in sunny, remote resorts. Just think, Beirut was once such a resort! Lately my lover comes to me on Wednesdays even if Iqbal's in town.

"I don't expect to live till ninety-five," James teases on the phone. His father died at ninety-three in Savannah. "But I don't want a bullet in the brain from a jealous husband right now."

Iqbal owns no firearms. Jealousy would inflame him.

Besides, Iqbal would never come home in the middle of the day. Not even for his blood-pressure pills. The two times he forgot them last month, I had to take the bottle downtown. One does not rise through the multinational hierarchy coming home in midday, arriving late, or leaving early. Especially, he says, if you're a "not-quite" as we are. It is up to us to set the standards.

Wives who want to be found out will be found out. Indiscretions are deliberate. The woman caught in mid-shame is a woman who wants to get out. The rest of us carry on.

James flatters me indefatigably; he makes me feel beautiful, exotic, responsive. I am a creature he has immunized of contamination. When he is with me, the world seems a happy enough place.

Then he leaves. He slips back into his tweed suit and backs out of my driveway.

I met James Beamish at a reception for foreign students on the Emory University campus. Iqbal avoids these international receptions because he thinks of them as excuses for looking back when we should be looking forward. These evenings are almost always tedious, but I like to go; just in case there's someone new and fascinating. The last two years, I've volunteered as host in the "hospitality program." At Thanksgiving and Christmas, two lonely foreign students are sent to our table.

That first evening at Emory we stood with name tags on lapels, white ones for students and blue ones for hosts. James was by a long table, pouring Chablis into a plastic glass. I noticed him right off. He was dressed much like the other resolute, decent men in the room. But whereas the other men wore white or blue shirts under their dark wool suits, James's shirt was bright red.

His wife was with him that evening, a stoutish woman with slender ankles and expensive shoes.

"Darling," she said to James. "See if you can locate our Palestinian." Then she turned to me, and smiling, peered into my name tag.

"I'm Nafeesa Hafeez," I helped out.

"Na-fee-sa," she read out. "Did I get that right?"

"Yes, perfect," I said.

"What a musical name," she said. "I hope you'll be very happy here. Is this your first time abroad?"

James came over with a glass of Chablis in each hand. "Did we draw this lovely lady? Oops, I'm sorry, you're a *host*, of course." A mocking blue light was in his eyes. "Just when I thought we were getting lucky, dear."

"Darling, ours is a Palestinian. I told you that in the car. This one is obviously not Palestinian, are you dear?" She took a bright orange notebook out of her purse and showed me a name.

I had to read it upside-down. Something Waheed. School of Dentistry.

"What are you drinking?" James asked. He kept a glass for himself and gave me the other one.

Maybe James Beamish said nothing fascinating that night, but he was attentive, even after the Beamishes' Palestinian joined us. Mrs. Beamish was brave, she asked the dentist about his family and hometown. The dentist described West Beirut in detail. The shortage of bread and vegetables, the mortar poundings, the babies bleeding. I wonder when aphasia sets in. When does a dentist, even a Palestinian dentist, decide it's time to cut losses.

Then my own foreign student arrived. She was an Indian Muslim from Lucknow, a large, bold woman who this far from our common hometown claimed me as a countrywoman. India, Pakistan, she said, not letting go of my hand, what does it matter?

I'd rather have listened to James Beamish but I couldn't shut out the woman's voice. She gave us her opinions on Thanksgiving rituals. She said, "It is very odd that the pumpkin vegetable should be used for dessert, no? We are using it as vegetable only. Chhi! Pumpkin as a sweet. The very idea is horrid."

I promised that when she came to our house for Thanksgiving, I'd make sweetmeats out of ricotta cheese and syrup. When you live in as many countries as Iqbal had made me, you can't tell if you pity, or if you envy, the women who stayed back.

I didn't hear from James Beamish for two weeks. I thought about him. In fact I couldn't get him out of my mind. I went over the phrases and gestures, the mocking light in the eyes, but they didn't add up to much. After the first week, I called Amina and asked her to lunch. I didn't know her well but her husband worked at the Center for Disease Control. Just talking to someone connected with the Center made me feel good. I slipped his name into the small talk with Amina and her eyes popped open, "Oh, he's famous!" she exclaimed, and I shrugged modestly. I stayed home in case he should call. I sat on the deck and in spite of the cold, pretended to read Barbara Pym novels. Lines from Donne and Urdu verses about love floated in my skull.

I wasn't sure Dr. Beamish would call me. Not directly, that is. Perhaps he would play a subtler game, get his wife to invite Iqbal and me for drinks. Maybe she'd even include their Palestinian and my Indian and make an international evening out of it. It sounded plausible.

Finally James Beamish called me on a Tuesday afternoon, around four. The children were in the kitchen, and a batch of my special chocolate sludge cookies was in the oven.

"Hi," he said, then nothing for a bit. Then he said, "This is James Beamish from the CDC. I've been thinking of you."

He was between meetings, he explained. Wednesday was the only flexible day in his week, his day for paperwork. Could we have lunch on Wednesday?

The cookies smelled gooey hot, not burned. My daughter had taken the cookie sheet out and put in a new one. She'd turned the cold water faucet on so she could let the water drip on a tiny rosebud burn on her arm.

I felt all the warm, familiar signs of lust and remorse. I dabbed the burn with an ice cube wrapped in paper towel and wondered if I'd have time to buy a new front-closing bra after Iqbal got home.

James and I had lunch in a Dekalb County motel lounge.

He would be sixty-five in July, but not retire till sixty-eight. Then he would live in Tonga, in Fiji, see the world, travel across Europe and North America in a Winnebago. He wouldn't be tied down. He had five daughters and two grandsons, the younger one aged four, a month older than my son. He had been in the navy during the war (*his* war), and he had liked that.

I said, " 'Goodbye, Mama, I'm off to Yokohama.' " It was silly, but it was the only war footage I could come up with, and it made him laugh.

"You're special," he said. He touched my knee under the table. "You've already been everywhere."

"Not because I've wanted to."

He squeezed my knee again, then paid with his MasterCard card.

As we were walking through the parking lot to his car (it was a Cougar or a Buick, and not German or British as I'd expected), James put his arm around my shoulders. I may have seen the world but I haven't gone through the American teenage rites of making out in parked cars and picnic grounds, so I walked briskly out of his embrace. He let his hand slide off my shoulder. The hand slid down my back. I counted three deft little patts to my bottom before he let his hand fall away.

Iqbal and I are sensual people, but secretive. The openness of James Beamish's advance surprised me.

I got in his car, wary, expectant.

"Do up the seatbelt," he said.

He leaned into his seatbelt and kissed me lightly on the lips. I kissed him back, hard. "You don't panic easily, do you?" he said. The mocking blue light was in his eyes again. His tongue made darting little thrusts and probes past my lips.

Yes, I do, I would have said if he'd let me.

We held hands on the drive to my house. In the driveway he parked behind my Honda. "Shall I come in?"

I said nothing. Love and freedom drop into our lives. When we have to beg or even agree, it's already too late.

"Let's go in." He said it very softly.

I didn't worry about the neighbors. In his grey wool slacks and tweed jacket, he looked too old, too respectable, for any sordid dalliance with a not-quite's wife.

Our house is not that different in size and shape from the ones on either side. Only the inside smells of heavy incense, and the walls are hung with rows of miniature paintings from the reign of Emperor Akbar. I took James's big wrinkled hand in mine. Adultery in my house is probably no different, no quieter, than in other houses in this neighborhood.

Afterwards it wasn't guilt I felt (guilt comes with desire not acted), but wonder that while I'd dashed out Tuesday night and bought myself silky new underwear, James Beamish had worn an old T-shirt and lemon-pale boxer shorts. Perhaps he hadn't planned on seducing a Lucknow lady that afternoon. Adventure and freedom had come to him out of the blue, too. Or perhaps only younger men like Iqbal make a fetish of doing sit-ups and dieting and renewing their membership at the racquet club when they're on the prowl.

October through February our passion held. When we were together, I felt cherished. I only played at being helpless, hysterical, cruel. When James left, I'd spend the rest of the afternoon with a Barbara Pym novel. I kept the novels open at pages in which excellent British women recite lines from Marvell to themselves. I didn't read. I watched the golfers trudging over brown fairways instead. I let the tiny golfers—clumsy mummers—tell me stories of ambitions unfulfilled. Golf carts lurched into the golden vista. I felt safe.

In the first week of March we met in James's house for a change. His wife was in Madison to babysit a grandson while his parents flew to China for a three-week tour. It was a thrill to be in his house. I fingered the book spines, checked the color of sheets and towels, the brand names of cereals and detergents. Jane Fonda's Workout record was on the VCR. He was a man who took exceptional care of himself, this immunologist. Real intimacy, at last. The lust of the winter months had been merely foreplay. I felt at home in his house, in spite of the albums of family photographs on the coffee table and the brutish metal vulvas sculpted by a daughter in art school and stashed in the den. James was more talkative in his own house. He showed me the photos he wanted me to see, named real lakes and mountains. His family was real, and not quite real. The daughters were hardy, outdoor types. I saw them hiking in Zermatt and bicycling through Europe. They had red cheeks and backpacks. Their faces were honest and marvellously ordinary. What would they say if they knew their father, at sixty-five, was in bed with a married woman from Lucknow? I feared and envied their jealousy more than any violence in my husband's heart.

Love on the decline is hard to tell from love on the rise. I have lived a life perched on the edge of ripeness and decay. The traveller feels at home everywhere, because she is never at home anywhere. I felt the hot red glow of blood rushing through capillaries.

His wife came back early, didn't call, caught a ride from Hartsfield International with a friend. She had been raised in Saskatchewan, and she'd remained thrifty.

We heard the car pull into the driveway, the loud "thank yous" and "no, I couldn'ts" and then her surprised shout, "James? Are you ill? What're you doing home?" as she shut the front door.

We were in bed, sluggish cozy and still moist under the goosedown quilt that the daughter in Madison had sent them as a fortieth anniversary gift some years before. His clothes were on top of a long dresser; mine were on the floor, the stockings wrinkled and looking legless.

James didn't go to pieces. I had to admire that. He said. "Get in the bathroom. Get dressed. I'll take care of this."

I am submissive by training. To survive, the Asian wife will usually do as she is told. But this time I stayed in bed.

"How are you going to explain me away, James? Tell her I'm the new cleaning woman?" I laughed, and my laugh tinkled flirtatiously, at least to me.

"Get in the bathroom." This was the fiercest I'd ever heard him.

"I don't think so," I said. I jerked the quilt off my body but didn't move my legs.

So I was in bed with the quilt at my feet, and James was by the dresser buttoning his shirt when Kate Beamish stood at the door.

She didn't scream. She didn't leap for James's throat—or mine. I'd wanted passion, but Kate didn't come through. I pulled the quilt over me.

I tried insolence. "Is your wife not the jealous kind?" I asked.

"Let's just get over this as quietly and quickly as we can, shall we?" she said. She walked to the window in her brown Wallabies. "I don't see any unfamiliar cars, so I suppose you'll expect James to drive you home."

"She's the jealous type," James said. He moved towards his wife and tried to guide her out of the bedroom.

"I'm definitely the jealous kind," Kate Beamish said. "I might have stabbed you if I could take you seriously. But you are quite ludicrous lounging like a Goya nude on my bed." She gave a funny little snort. I noticed straggly hairs in her nostrils and looked away.

James was running water in the bathroom sink. Only the panicky ones fall apart and call their lawyers from the bedroom.

She sat on my side of the bed. She stared at me. If that stare had made me feel secretive and loathsome, I might not have wept, later. She plucked the quilt from my breasts as an internist might, and snorted again. "Yes," she said, "I don't deny a certain interest he might have had," but she looked through my face to the pillow behind, and dropped the quilt as she stood. I was shadow without depth or color, a shadow-temptress who would float back to a city of teeming millions when the affair with James had ended.

I had thought myself provocative and fascinating. What had begun as an adventure had become shabby and complex. I was just another involvement of a white man in a pokey little outpost, something that "men do" and then come to their senses while the *memsahibs* drink gin and tonic and fan their faces. I didn't merit a stab wound through the heart.

It wasn't the end of the world. It was humorous, really. Still. I let James call me a cab. That half-hour wait for the cab, as Kate related tales of the grandson to her distracted husband was the most painful. It came closest to what Husseina must have felt. At least her father, the Nawab-*sahib*, had beaten her.

I have known all along that perfect love has to be fatal. I have survived on four of the five continents. I get by because I am at least moderately charming and open-minded. From time to time, James Beamish calls me. "She's promised to file for divorce." Or "Let's go away for a weekend. Let's go to Bermuda. Have lunch with me this Wednesday." Why do I hear a second voice? She has laughed at me. She has mocked my passion.

I want to say yes. I want to beg him to take me away to Hilton Head in his new, retirement Winnebago. The golden light from the vista is too yellow. Yes, *please*, let's run away, keep this new and simple.

I can hear the golfballs being thwocked home by clumsy mummers far away where my land dips. My arms are numb, my breathing loud and ugly from pressing hard against the cedar railing. The pain in my chest will not go away. I should be tasting blood in my throat by now.

METAFICTION: *INTRODUCTION*

Metafiction is really a special case of fabulation. A work of *meta*-fiction is a fictional experiment that either explores or questions the nature and conventions of fiction itself. The very elements of fiction—the relationship of the writer to the text or the text to the world, the concepts of plot, character, setting, and point-of-view—all these are taken not as givens but as questionable or problematic in metafiction.

These experiments in metafiction make an appropriate place to conclude—at least temporarily—a study of the workings of fiction, for they turn the powers of fiction on fiction itself and force us to reconsider fiction, not as something natural and given but as one of humanity's many tools for ordering and shaping the world in human ways.

ETHEL WILSON
1888–1980

Although she published a few stories in the late 1930s, she did not publish her first novel, *Hetty Dorval*, until 1947, and her fiction career ended fourteen years later with the publication of her story collection *Mrs. Golightly and Other Stories*. Yet her fiction influenced such younger writers as Margaret Atwood, Margaret Laurence, and Alice Munro. Born in Port Elizabeth, South Africa, where her father was a missionary, she was taken to England at the age of two when her mother died. Eight years later her father died, and she came to Vancouver, which was to remain her home, to live with her grandmother. She received her teacher's certificate from the Vancouver Normal School in 1907 and taught in many local schools until her marriage in 1921. The settings of her fiction seldom stray beyond her beloved British Columbia. Through her compassionate and often ironic narration she explores the fears and hopes, the despair and sometimes the violence that appear in ordinary human situations.

Till death us do part

I have a friend, well I should say an acquaintance, well anyway someone who works with me in the wool shop that is, and she is a very interesting girl not because she says anything, oh no. She is very silent and I don't know whether she is bad tempered or just silent. I think she is proud. Her name is Kate and she is very efficient in the wool shop. If her expression was happier I would say she is beautiful. She is small with a natural golden coiffure or is it coiffeur, well what I mean hair-do and a very clear complexion but I wish she would respond a bit. She silences me. We never laugh and I am used to laughing when I feel like it.

Kate seems to have got a queer defensive thing, I can't imagine why. Perhaps she *has* to defend herself in some way. Me being older than she is although I am junior in the shop, I've had to knock about a bit and I know things happen sometimes so you *have* to defend yourself but she doesn't need to defend herself against me, I'm not going to do her any harm, or is she jealous? oh surely no. I'd like to like her but as it is she won't let me. I think she's scared of intimacy but heavens I don't want to be intimate. Probably she just doesn't like me. Oh well, you can't like everyone.

If I say, Good morning isn't it a lovely day, she says it's going to rain. And if I say, Did you see that warship come into harbor this morning, she says, That wasn't a warship. At first I used to argue a little but that was silly and got nowhere. She'd be better to say just Yes and No. It would save argument and be pleasanter. And better still I'd be wiser not to make a remark of any kind. However.

The result is that neither of us speaks because it is no fun speaking, except to the customers and we are both lovely to the customers. The owner and manager is away sick and I sure hope she comes back soon and sweetens the atmosphere a little. Perhaps Kate has a secret sorrow. Well so have I.

I began to go home at night pretty ruffled. I knew I was being put in my place and supposed to stay there but couldn't see why this should be. I'm a human being too, aren't I.

Today I was very pleased at a good order of wool to a new customer for bed jackets and I thought why not say so.

Yes, said Kate, I saw you. You didn't sell her enough wool for those bed jackets. I could of told you. Then we'll be out of wool when she wants it.

I was really annoyed and said, I always sell that amount for bed jackets and in my experience—and then I thought, This isn't intelligent, and I said no more.

Then I thought What shall I do about this. Shall I
> Sit on a stile and continue to smile
> That should soften the heart of this cow

but it did not soften the heart. However I had to speak to Kate because the telephone rang and someone asked if Mrs. Physick was there. I said I was sorry but Mrs. Physick was away ill and could I take a message. And the lady said, Oh dear, well I'll get in touch, but say her aunty called.

I said to Kate, That was Mrs. Physick's aunty and I was to say she called.

Kate said, Mrs. Physick hasn't got an aunty.

Well really that attitude made me mad if people have to feed their ego that much, so when I got home at night I rang up Mrs. Physick's place although I didn't really know her and I said to the person who came to the phone, Oh it's Muriel Brown from the shop, and please would you kindly tell Mrs. Physick that her aunty rang up today.

And the person said, Her aunty? Mrs. Physick hasn't got an aunty. Oh you must mean Mrs. Bonaventure, she always calls her aunty. Was there any message?

I felt very small and said, Oh no, she only rang up and will get in touch, and the lady said, Yes she did.

I sat still on the telephone stool and thought So she's right and there isn't any aunty and I can't win.

I had begun to be very introspective because there were ever so many more silly little things like that and I started not sleeping at night. I've got troubles of my own.

One morning Kate came in late to the shop with her right hand bandaged and began to fumble among the boxes. She didn't seem to want to speak about her hand nor about being so late but turned her face away from me and then she dropped a box because she only had her left hand, and the balls of wool rolled all over the floor.

Oh I said, don't try to pick them up! and I began to pick them up. I looked up at her from where I was on my knees and I saw that her face was scarlet and I knew that Kate's pride was hurt to an absurd degree that she should have to be indebted to me, picking up the balls of wool off the floor.

When I had finished I straightened up and looked right at her. I said with authority (a trembling sort of authority I'll tell you, because I had become frightened of Kate and what snub might lie in wait for me), I said, You are not used to letting people do things for you or letting them co-operate with you, but you must let me help you all I can with the boxes and things. It will be a pleasure I assure you except I'm sorry about your hand. Oh what is wrong with your hand?

My hand . . . said Kate turning deathly white, and she had been so scarlet, my hand . . . my hand . . . and a customer came in.

July 7.

I began writing about Kate's hand and her strangeness and then I was much busier for some days and I hadn't time to write down about it. A story has to end and this story hasn't ended yet and I don't know what the end will be.

Kate tried to ignore her hand as much as possible and went back again into her silent way and I went back into my silent way except that I did watch to make things easier if possible, lifting, and boiling the kettle for tea and so on. I do think the shop had the unpleasantest feeling that ever I knew in a place but I decided to go on with it. There's always something.

I got a letter from my sister in Portage la Prairie and she said that when their busy season was over she and Frank would put the boys at his mother's and they might drive to the coast and see how I was getting along, and oh how my heart warmed up under these circumstances. She wrote about Peterborough Edwards too and that was the first time she had mentioned Peterborough Edwards and I found that I didn't mind at all because although it was all on account of Peterborough I had left Portage la Prairie and at first I had felt really badly about it, I found that by this time I was relieved about Peterborough rather than feeling badly. You can go on and on and on with a person till you get past the disappointment point, and then they begin to bore you. I was really just a habit with Peterborough although to my surprise he was awfully shocked when I decided to go off. You never can tell. I like it here in Vancouver except for Kate, it's a change but then I might like to go back to Portage la Prairie sometime but no more Peterborough unless he can make up his mind. It seems that he had rung up my sister to see was there any news from me but she was very airy fairy with him she said and she said I was having a wonderful time in Vancouver.

Ha ha.

After a week Kate had the bandage off her hand and it was really very nasty looking. There were still plasters on it as if there were cuts and it was evidently painful, so I helped all I could but not what you'd call ostentatious. There was once that Kate turned to me with such lovely sweetness and gratitude and her pretty customer smile and oh how my heart warmed as it does, foolishly I expect.

That sweetness did not last only long enough for me to think how lovely it would be, because then Mrs. Physick rang me up.

All my arrangements with Mrs. Physick had been made by mail and so I had not seen her because the doctor said she must have this operation.

But now Mrs. Physick asked me to go and see her in the evening if convenient and take the order book and the old order book too, to compare stocks for ordering. She sounded quite young, I was surprised.

After I hung up I said to Kate, Is Mrs. Physick old or young? She sounds quite young to me.

Kate said coldly, It all depends on what you call young.

Kate was uneasy. At last she said, Why did she ring you not me? Why did she tell *you* to take the order books?

Well really how silly! Mrs. Physick probably wanted to give me the once-over but it was no good entering on a silly argument so I said snappishly Better ask her yourself, and we were quits but the atmosphere was nearly unbearable again.

July 10.

I took the order books to Mrs. Physick's flat where she lived with a woman friend who Mrs. Physick told me had a hat shop. Mrs. Physick was lying on a couch and said she was still taking it easy after the operation. She was pleasant looking, youngish but her hair going grey. She had the nice kind of face with some lines on. We went through the order books and she told me to leave them and she'd run through them again and then Kate or I could come and get them. She looked at me and said, How do you get along with Kate?

I said, Oh I get along. And then I said, But I don't think she likes me.

Mrs. Physick looked worried and she put out her hand. I know, she said, it's not easy. Don't take it personally.

I was afraid of beginning to discuss Kate which would be a disloyal thing to do and anyway I did not think Mrs. Physick would do such a thing, Kate being the senior employee.

Just the same I said, Oh yes it is personal. It would be impossible not to feel that — but I don't take it too seriously. I'll be going now Mrs. Physick, is there anything else?

Mrs. Physick did not speak for a moment and then she looked down and almost whispered, Kate is a very unhappy young woman.

I was standing up to go. I wondered whether I ought to tell her about Kate's right hand or was even that talking too much. However, I blurted out, She hurt her right hand, I think she had an accident, she didn't say, the bandage is off now and it looks nasty but she can manage more easily.

Mrs. Physick stared at me. An accident? she said, an accident to her right hand? It seems to me people always have accidents to their left hand! What kind of accident?

I said, I don't know. She didn't say. It looked to me as if something had hit it.

Mrs. Physick was silent and then spoke sort of unhappily, Oh do be good to her, she said, and I said I'll try. I began to think that Mrs. Physick might be the whole world to Kate and she couldn't bear to have her friendly to any new person.

July 17.

It must have been a few days after I wrote last time and I had been doing what Mrs. Physick said, making every allowance and paying no attention and I thought that perhaps Kate seemed happier and I remember feeling happier myself, and easier, when one day I saw a woman in black standing very still outside the door of the shop. Kate was serving a customer at the back of the shop where the new stock of children's small foreign toys are and I was in the front with a customer who wanted to make some baby outfits. There was the wool and there was the pattern book. The customer was taking a long time looking and making little remarks to herself, and in between I happened to look at the glass front door.

The woman began to peer closely this way and that through the glass as though she was looking for someone. She saw me but paid me no attention. I had to attend to my customer and so I could not keep looking at the woman as I wanted to. But I did see that now she was bending down and gazing in and then it seemed to me that she saw what she was looking for. She looked fixedly and with a very unpleasant expression deep into the shop. Between pleasing my customer and advising with her and looking at the woman and looking to see if Kate had seen her, it was all difficult, but the woman (I could see) remained bent down nearly double and peering in.

Next time I could look away from my customer I saw the woman had gone, and I saw that Kate was moving up the shop with her customer who had in her hand one of those little music boxes that seem so funny in a wool shop.

Oh the woman wore a shabby black coat and had her head tied up like an old peasant woman. Her face was sallow, almost yellow, but although I did not know her, there was something familiar about her face and then I knew that if you can have someone ugly look like someone pretty, this woman looked like Kate.

I was very horrified because I thought could this ever be the mother of Kate who is so pretty and so clean and proud and refined and tension-full and — as Mrs. Physick said — so unhappy. And I thought Oh how terrible, Kate going home every night to perhaps such a mother in a small place and coming back in the morning full of the feeling of it. How terrible! Next day the woman came again and I found myself watching each day for her and each day she came and bent down to peer through the glass but if Kate was in full view, or on the approach of Kate, she always vanished.

I began to make up stories in my head and I think that Kate had forbidden the mother ever to come near the shop, and so shame her who was so proud, but that in order to annoy her the woman came every day and watched, and that was the kind of woman she was.

Sometimes either Kate or I go into the little back place and get out new stock or paper bags or something, and one of these times when Kate was in the back, the woman came to the door. This time she was bolder. She put her hand on the latch and pushed the door open and stood and I saw more clearly her yellow face which seemed to me terrible and without, well, without humanity. I went up to her (and I felt ready to defend Kate) and said, Can I do anything for you? and the sour smell of cheap whiskey came strong right at me. I did not know what to do. She gave me a look only, and then with a kind of derision she looked slowly round the shop, up and down the shelves, as if to fix in her mind the kind of heaven her daughter came to every day.

I said again, Can I do anything for you? and I wondered Is she foreign or what because she doesn't answer, and all the time the reek of whiskey was on her, when Kate came out from the back and suddenly stopped. The peculiar bright scarlet came up on her neck and over her face and then the whiteness and she looked like a frozen woman.

I did not know what was the best thing to do. Everything rushed through my mind in a turmoil about Kate's pride and tension and the hurt right hand and Mrs. Physick saying She is unhappy and there was a kind of yawning terribleness of how unhappy she must be to act like she does. There was also this at the same moment, that I must do something at once and that I must not let Kate think in all her pride that I knew that this woman (a hag if ever I saw one) could be her mother, or the sight of me would always be unbearable to her. So I stepped between them and took the evil-smelling woman gently but firmly by the shoulder and said Let's . . . let's go outside, and I walked her out of the door and shut it.

She was surprised at my action and looked angrily into my face and tried to shake me off.

I got a perfect right, she said, to go into your old shop, and I said, Oh no, you've been drinking, we can't have you in our shop, and she said, I have not so been drinking, and she looked very vicious. Then she spat at me and that made me really mad, a little short and sharp spit.

So I said, You certainly have been drinking and I'll have to get a policeman if you try to come into our shop, there's a policeman at the Bank at the corner, and the woman looked at me like a snake and slipped out of my hand and was gone. There's nothing like the word policeman.

I stood outside in the fresh air for a minute. I felt awful, not just because of this woman but because of Kate. Then I went into the shop but I left the door wide open because it seemed to me the whole place smelled of the stench of that woman. It was lucky there was no customer there, but it would have been just the same if there had been a customer.

Kate was not in the shop. So I wondered What do I do now? It isn't natural for me ever to go to the back and talk to Kate about anything but I'd better do it, casual like, and now. So I went into the back and I think Kate had had her head on the desk but she straightened up and looked at me quite wild.

I didn't seem to notice, I hope, and said, Did you see that woman in the store? She'd been drinking so I took her out and told her not to come in. She said she'd come in if she liked but I said No, not when she'd been drinking, in fact I'd have to call a constable if she came in again and she beat it. I kind of hated to speak to an old wom . . . an old lady like that but what could I do. I hope that was all right? I said, anxious like.

Kate nodded her head, still looking at me in that wild way, and I went back into the shop. When the time came to close up I could not bear to think of Kate going home to what she was going home to, but what can you do?

July 25.

This has been an uncomfortable week. If it weren't for the fact that business is good and us busy (I think those little foreign dolls and houses and things in the window attract people) I don't think I could stick it. Things seem out of control. Kate is the silentest person I ever did see, but more than that she is so unhappy. It would be no good trying to horn in with a little comfort and what's more she looks ill, in herself, I mean. Her hand was very inflamed this morning and she had it bandaged all over again, but badly. Could I help you fix that, I said, and she said, Well just a bit tighter here, and pin it, and then she actually said Thank you.

I'm not one to tell tales but I just felt that it was too much responsibility and I must go and talk to Mrs. Physick after supper. Mrs. Physick came to the door herself and she looked better but she moved slowly and we went into the room and sat down.

I said, I'm very worried Mrs. Physick about Kate, and I told her about the woman and about Kate's reaction to the woman (all out of proportion, I thought, though it sure was bad enough) and how her hand was infected and red and swollen up her arm and what could we do. I said, I am very willing to go and do things up for her at her home but I don't know where she lives.

No no, said Mrs. Physick. That would never never do. Kate is very very proud (I said, I'll say she's proud) and it would spoil your relations together for always if you went into that house and saw it — she'd never forget it. I know it. I'll go. I can drive the car now. You go home. I'll phone later. So I went home.

It was midnight before Mrs. Physick phoned and she didn't waste words.

She said, Can you carry on alone tomorrow? Maybe I'll be down for a bit some time. I got Kate into hospital. She's running a fever. When I got there the mother let me in but Kate's bedroom door was closed. Yes it was locked and I had to knock and knock and call but she was suspicious and it was some time before she'd let me in. To think of her barricaded against that woman! I don't blame her. The place was a dirty shambles. Well goodnight Muriel. Do you know my belief? My belief is that bitch hit her on the hand with a bottle.

July 29.

I'm carrying on at the shop with Mrs. Physick down half days. Kate's been up to the O.R. and they've taken splinters of glass out of her hand. I don't know how I can bear it when Kate comes back, and she will come back, to think of her and that mother going on for ever and ever together and no escape till death comes for one of them, whatever way it comes, but some way death will part them.

There was a letter from Peterborough Edwards tonight when I got home, addressed care of my sister. Peterborough wants to come down to Vancouver on his holiday. He seems upset. I won't answer right away. Do him good to be upset. But my mind turns to Peterborough Edwards as a comfort when I think of Kate and her mother going on until death parts them. I don't say I'd really choose Peterborough Edwards and I never thought I'd turn to Peterborough on account of these circumstances but he might be a comfort and anyway, what can you do.

JOHN BARTH

1930–

John Barth and his twin sister Jill were born in Cambridge, on the eastern shore of Maryland. As a boy he was a serious musician, organizing his own band and starting study at the Juilliard School of Music. His interest shifted to literature and he transferred to Johns Hopkins, where he received his M.A. in 1952. He supported himself, his wife, and children by his music until he got his first teaching job in 1953. He has taught ever since, publishing his first novel in 1956 and establishing himself as a major writer with *The Sot-Weed Factor* in 1960 and his collection of short fiction *Lost in the Funhouse* in 1968.

Lost in the Funhouse

For whom is the funhouse fun? Perhaps for lovers. For Ambrose it is *a place of fear and confusion.* He has come to the seashore with his family for the holiday, *the occasion of their visit is Independence Day, the most important secular holiday of the United States of America.* A single straight underline is the manuscript mark for italic type, *which in turn* is the printed equivalent to oral emphasis of words and phrases as well as the customary type for titles of complete works, not to mention. Italics are also employed, in fiction stories especially, for "outside," intrusive, or artificial voices, such as radio announcements, the texts of telegrams and newspaper articles, et cetera. They should be used *sparingly.* If passages originally in roman type are italicized by someone repeating them, it's customary to acknowledge the fact. *Italics mine.*

Ambrose was "at that awkward age." His voice came out high-pitched as a child's if he let himself get carried away; to be on the safe side, therefore, he moved and spoke with *deliberate calm* and *adult gravity.* Talking soberly of unimportant or irrelevant matters and listening consciously to the sound of your own voice are useful habits for maintaining control in this difficult interval. *Enroute* to Ocean City he sat in the back seat of the family car with his brother Peter, age fifteen, and Magda G——, age fourteen, a pretty girl and exquisite young lady, who lived not far from them on B—— Street in the town of D——, Maryland. Initials, blanks, or both were often substituted for proper names in nineteenth-century fiction to enhance the illusion of reality. It is as if the author felt it necessary to delete the names for reasons of tact or legal liability. Interestingly, as with other aspects of realism, it is an *illusion* that is being enhanced, by purely artificial means. Is it likely, does it violate the principle of verisimilitude, that a thirteen-year-old boy could make such a sophisticated observation? A girl of fourteen is *the psychological coeval* of a boy of fifteen or sixteen; a thirteen-year-old boy, there.ore, even one precocious in some other respects, might be three years *her emotional junior.*

Thrice a year—on Memorial, Independence, and Labor Days—the family visits Ocean City for the afternoon and evening. When Ambrose and Peter's father was their age, the excursion was made by train, as mentioned in the novel *The 42nd Parallel* by John Dos Passos. Many families from the same neighborhood used to travel together, with dependent relatives and often with Negro servants; schoolfuls of children swarmed through the railway cars; everyone shared everyone else's Maryland fried chicken, Virginia ham, deviled eggs, potato salad, beaten biscuits, iced tea. Nowadays (that is, in 19—, the year of our story) the journey is made by automobile—more comfortably and quickly though without the extra fun though without the *camaraderie* of a general excursion. It's all part of the deterioration of American life, their father declares; Uncle Karl supposes that when the boys take *their* families to Ocean City for the holidays they'll fly in Autogiros. Their mother, sitting in the middle of the front seat like Magda in the second, only with her arms on the seat-back behind the men's shoulders, wouldn't want the good old days back again, the steaming trains and stuffy long dresses; on the other hand she can do without Autogiros, too, if she has to become a grandmother to fly in them.

Description of physical appearance and mannerisms is one of several standard methods of characterization used by writers of fiction. It is also important to "keep the senses operating"; when a detail from one of the five senses, say visual, is "crossed" with a detail from another, say auditory, the reader's imagination is oriented to the scene, perhaps unconsciously. This procedure may be compared to the way surveyors and navigators determine their positions by two or more compass bearings, a process known as triangulation. The brown hair on Ambrose's mother's forearms gleamed in the sun like. Though right-handed, she took her left arm from the seat-back to press the dashboard cigar lighter for Uncle Karl. When the glass bead in its handle glowed red, the lighter was ready for use. The smell of Uncle Karl's cigar smoke reminded one of. The fragrance of the ocean came strong to the picnic ground where they always stopped for lunch, two miles inland from Ocean City. Having to pause for a full hour almost within sound of the breakers was difficult for Peter and Ambrose when they were younger; even at their present age it was not easy to keep their anticipation, *stimulated by the briny spume*, from turning into short temper. The Irish author James Joyce, in his unusual novel entitled *Ulysses*, now available in this country, uses the adjectives *snot-green* and *scrotum-tightening* to describe the sea. Visual; auditory; tactile; olfactory; gustatory. Peter and Ambrose's father, while steering their black 1936 LaSalle sedan with one hand, could with the other remove the first cigarette from a white pack of Lucky Strikes and, more remarkably, light it with a match forefingered from its book and thumbed against the flint paper without being detached. The matchbook cover merely advertised U. S. War Bonds and Stamps. A fine metaphor, simile, or other figure of speech, in addition to its obvious "first-order" relevance to the thing it describes, will be seen upon reflection to have a second order of significance: it may be drawn from the *milieu* of the action, for example, or be particularly appropriate to the sensibility of the narrator, even hinting to the reader things of which the narrator is unaware; or it may cast further and subtler lights upon the things it describes, sometimes ironically qualifying the more evident sense of the comparison.

To say that Ambrose's and Peter's mother was *pretty* is to accomplish nothing; the reader may acknowledge the proposition, but his imagination is not engaged. Besides, Magda was also pretty, yet in an altogether different way. Although she lived on B—— Street she had very good manners and did better than average in school. Her figure was very well developed for her age. Her right hand lay casually on the plush upholstery of the seat, very near Ambrose's left leg, on which his own hand rested. The space between their legs, between her right and his left leg, was out of the line of sight of anyone sitting on the other side of Magda, as well as anyone glancing into the rear-view mirror. Uncle Karl's face resembled Peter's—rather, vice versa. Both had dark hair and eyes, short husky statures, deep voices. Magda's left hand was probably in a similar position on her left side. The boys' father is difficult to describe; no particular feature of his appearance or manner stood out. He wore glasses and was principal of a T—— County grade school. Uncle Karl was a masonry contractor.

Although Peter must have known as well as Ambrose that the latter, because of his position in the car, would be the first to see the electrical towers of the power plant at V——, the halfway point of their trip, he leaned forward and slightly toward the center of the car and pretended to be looking for them through the flat pinewoods and tuckahoe creeks along the highway. For as long as the boys could remember, "looking for the Towers" had been a feature of the first half of their excursions to Ocean City, "looking for the standpipe" of the second. Though the game was childish, their mother preserved the tradition of rewarding the first to see the Towers with a candy-bar or piece of fruit. She insisted now that Magda play the game; the prize, she said, was "something hard to get nowadays." Ambrose decided not to join in; he sat far back in his seat. Magda, like Peter, leaned forward. Two sets of straps were discernible through the shoulders of her sun dress; the inside right one, a brassiere-strap, was fastened or shortened with a small safety pin. The right armpit of her dress, presumably the left as well, was damp with perspiration. The simple strategy for being first to espy the Towers, which Ambrose had understood by the age of four, was to sit on the right-hand side of the car. Whoever sat there, however, had also to put up with the worst of the sun, and so Ambrose, without mentioning the matter, chose sometimes the one and sometimes the other. Not impossibly Peter had never caught on to the trick, or thought that his brother hadn't simply because Ambrose on occasion preferred shade to a Baby Ruth or tangerine.

The shade-sun situation didn't apply to the front seat, owing to the windshield; if anything the driver got more sun, since the person on the passenger side not only was shaded below by the door and dashboard but might swing down his sunvisor all the way too.

"Is that them?" Magda asked. Ambrose's mother teased the boys for letting Magda win, insinuating that "somebody [had] a girlfriend." Peter and Ambrose's father reached a long thin arm across their mother to butt his cigarette in the dashboard ashtray, under the lighter. The prize this time for seeing the Towers first was a banana. Their mother bestowed it after chiding their father for wasting a half-smoked cigarette when everything was so scarce. Magda, to take the prize, moved her hand from so near Ambrose's that he could have touched it as though accidentally. She offered to share the prize, things like that were so hard to find; but everyone insisted it was hers alone. Ambrose's mother sang an iambic trimeter couplet from a popular song, femininely rhymed:

> "What's good is in the Army;
> What's left will never harm me."

Uncle Karl tapped his cigar ash out the ventilator window; some particles were sucked by the slipstream back into the car through the rear window on the passenger side. Magda demonstrated her ability to hold a banana in one hand and peel it with her teeth. She still sat forward; Ambrose pushed his glasses back onto the bridge of his nose with his left hand, which he then negligently let fall to the seat cushion immediately behind her. He even permitted the single hair, gold, on the second joint of his thumb to brush the fabric of her skirt. Should she have sat back at that instant, his hand would have been caught under her.

Plush upholstery prickles uncomfortably through gabardine slacks in the July sun. The function of the *beginning* of a story is to introduce the principal characters, establish their initial relationships, set the scene for the main action, expose the background of the situation if necessary, plant motifs and foreshadowings where appropriate, and initiate the first complication or whatever of the "rising action." Actually, if one imagines a story called "The Funhouse," or "Lost in the Funhouse," the details of the drive to Ocean City don't seem especially relevant. The *beginning* should recount the events between Ambrose's first sight of the funhouse early in the afternoon and his entering it with Magda and Peter in the evening. The *middle* would narrate all relevant events from the time he goes in to the time he loses his way; middles have the double and contradictory function of delaying the climax while at the same time preparing the reader for it and fetching him to it. Then the *ending* would tell what Ambrose does while he's lost, how he finally finds his way out, and what everybody makes of the experience. So far there's been no real dialogue, very little sensory detail, and nothing in the way of a *theme*. And a long time has gone by already without anything happening; it makes a person wonder. We haven't even reached Ocean City yet: we will never get out of the funhouse.

The more closely an author identifies with the narrator, literally or metaphorically, the less advisable it is, as a rule, to use the first-person narrative viewpoint. Once three years previously the young people *aforementioned* played Niggers and Masters in the backyard; when it was Ambrose's turn to be Master and theirs to be Niggers Peter had to go serve his evening papers; Ambrose was afraid to punish Magda alone, but she led him to the whitewashed Torture Chamber between the woodshed and the privy in the Slaves Quarters; there she knelt sweating among bamboo rakes and dusty Mason jars, pleadingly embraced his knees, and while bees droned in the lattice as if on an ordinary summer afternoon, purchased clemency at a surprising price set by herself. Doubtless she remembered nothing of this event; Ambrose on the other hand seemed unable to forget the least detail of his life. He even recalled how, standing beside himself with awed impersonality in the reeky heat, he'd stared the while at an empty cigar box in which Uncle Karl kept stone-cutting chisels: beneath the words *El Producto* a laureled, loose-toga'd lady regarded the sea from a marble bench; beside her, forgotten or not yet turned to, was a five-stringed lyre. Her chin reposed on the back of her right hand; her left depended negligently from the bench-arm. The lower half of the scene and lady was peeled away; the words EXAMINED BY ___ were inked there into the wood. Nowadays cigar boxes are made of pasteboard. Ambrose wondered what Magda would have done, Ambrose wondered what Magda would do when she sat back on his hand as he resolved she should. Be angry. Make a teasing joke of it. Give no sign at all. For a long time she leaned forward, playing cow-poker with Peter against Uncle Karl and Mother and watching for the first sign of Ocean City. At nearly the same instant, picnic ground and Ocean City standpipe hove into view; an Amoco filling station on their side of the road cost Mother and Uncle Karl fifty cows and the game; Magda bounced back, clapping her right hand on Mother's right arm; Ambrose moved clear "in the nick of time."

At this rate our hero, at this rate our protagonist will remain in the funhouse forever. Narrative ordinarily consists of alternating dramatization and summarization. One symptom of nervous tension, paradoxically, is repeated and violent yawning; neither Peter nor Magda nor Uncle Karl nor Mother reacted in this manner. Although they were no longer small children, Peter and Ambrose were each given a dollar to spend on boardwalk amusements in addition to what money of their own they'd brought along. Magda too, though she protested she had ample spending money. The boys' mother made a little scene out of distributing the bills; she pretended that her sons and Magda were small children and cautioned them not to spend the sum too quickly or in one place. Magda promised with a merry laugh and, having both hands free, took the bill with her left. Peter laughed also and pledged in a falsetto to be a good boy. His imitation of a child was not clever. The boys' father was tall and thin, balding, fair-complexioned. Assertions of that sort are not effective; the reader may acknowledge the proposition, but. We should be much farther along than we are; something has gone wrong; not much of this preliminary rambling seems relevant. Yet everyone begins in the same place; how is it that most go along without difficulty but a few lose their way?

"Stay out from under the boardwalk," Uncle Karl growled from the side of his mouth. The boys' mother pushed his shoulder in mock annoyance. They were all standing before Fat May the Laughing Lady who advertised the funhouse. Larger than life, Fat May mechanically shook, rocked on her heels, slapped her thighs, while recorded laughter—uproarious, female—came amplified from a hidden loudspeaker. It chuckled, wheezed, wept; tried in vain to catch its breath; tittered, groaned, exploded raucous and anew. You couldn't hear it without laughing yourself, no matter how you felt. Father came back from talking to a Coast-Guardsman on duty and reported that the surf was spoiled with crude oil from tankers recently torpedoed offshore. Lumps of it, difficult to remove, made tarry tidelines on the beach and stuck on swimmers. Many bathed in the surf nevertheless and came out speckled; others paid to use a municipal pool and only sunbathed on the beach. We would do the latter. We would do the latter. We would do the latter.

Under the boardwalk, matchbook covers, grainy other things. What is the story's theme? Ambrose is ill. He perspires in the dark passages; candied apples-on-a-stick, delicious-looking, disappointing to eat. Funhouses need men's and ladies' rooms at intervals. Others perhaps have also vomited in corners and corridors; may even have had bowel movements liable to be stepped in in the dark. The word *fuck* suggests suction and or and or flatulence. Mother and Father; grandmothers and grandfathers on both sides; great-grandmothers and great-grandfathers on four sides, et cetera. Count a generation as thirty years: in approximately the year when Lord Baltimore was granted charter to the province of Maryland by Charles I, five hundred twelve women—English, Welsh, Bavarian, Swiss—of every class and character, received into themselves the penises the intromittent organs of five hundred twelve men, ditto, in every circumstance and posture, to conceive the five hundred twelve ancestors of the two hundred fifty-six ancestors of the et cetera et cetera et cetera et cetera et cetera et cetera et cetera et cetera of the author, of the narrator, of this story, *Lost in the Funhouse*. In alleyways, ditches, canopy beds, pinewoods, bridal suites, ship's cabins, coach-and-fours, coaches-and-four, sultry toolsheds; on the cold sand under boardwalks, littered with *El Producto* cigar butts, treasured with Lucky Strike cigarette stubs, Coca-Cola caps, gritty turds, cardboard lollipop sticks, matchbook covers warning that A Slip of the Lip Can Sink a Ship. The shluppish whisper, continuous as seawash round the globe, tidelike falls and rises with the circuit of dawn and dusk.

Magda's teeth. She *was* left-handed. Perspiration. They've gone all the way, through, Magda and Peter, they've been waiting for hours with Mother and Uncle Karl while Father searches for his lost son; they draw french-fried potatoes from a paper cup and shake their heads. They've named the children they'll one day have and bring to Ocean City on holidays. Can spermatozoa properly be thought of as male animalcules when there are no female spermatozoa? They grope through hot, dark windings, past Love's Tunnel's fearsome obstacles. Some perhaps lose their way.

Peter suggested then and there that they do the funhouse; he had been through it before, so had Magda, Ambrose hadn't and suggested, his voice cracking on account of Fat May's laughter, that they swim first. All were chuckling, couldn't help it; Ambrose's father, Ambrose's and Peter's father came up grinning like a lunatic with two boxes of syrup-coated popcorn, one for Mother, one for Magda; the men were to help themselves. Ambrose walked on Magda's right; being by nature left-handed, she carried the box in her left hand. Up front the situation was reversed.

"What are you limping for?" Magda inquired of Ambrose. He supposed in a husky tone that his foot had gone to sleep in the car. Her teeth flashed. "Pins and needles?" It was the honeysuckle on the lattice of the former privy that drew the bees. Imagine being stung there. How long is this going to take?

The adults decided to forego the pool; but Uncle Karl insisted they change into swimsuits and do the beach. "He wants to watch the pretty girls," Peter teased, and ducked behind Magda from Uncle Karl's pretended wrath. "You've got all the pretty girls you need right here," Magda declared, and Mother said: "Now that's the gospel truth." Magda scolded Peter, who reached over her shoulder to sneak some popcorn. "Your brother and father aren't getting any." Uncle Karl wondered if they were going to have fireworks that night, what with the shortages. It wasn't the shortages, Mr. M____ replied; Ocean City had fireworks from pre-war. But it was too risky on account of the enemy submarines, some people thought.

"Don't seem like Fourth of July without fireworks," said Uncle Karl. The inverted tag in dialogue writing is still considered permissible with proper names or epithets, but sounds old-fashioned with personal pronouns. "We'll have 'em again soon enough," predicted the boys' father. Their mother declared she could do without fireworks: they reminded her too much of the real thing. Their father said all the more reason to shoot off a few now and again. Uncle Karl asked *rhetorically* who needed reminding, just look at people's hair and skin.

"The oil, yes," said Mrs. M____.

Ambrose had a pain in his stomach and so didn't swim but enjoyed watching the others. He and his father burned red easily. Magda's figure was exceedingly well developed for her age. She too declined to swim, and got mad, and became angry when Peter attempted to drag her into the pool. She always swam, he insisted; what did she mean not swim? Why did a person come to Ocean City?

"Maybe I want to lay here with Ambrose," Magda teased.

Nobody likes a pedant.

"Aha," said Mother. Peter grabbed Magda by one ankle and ordered Ambrose to grab the other. She squealed and rolled over on the beach blanket. Ambrose pretended to help hold her back. Her tan was darker than even Mother's and Peter's. "Help out, Uncle Karl!" Peter cried. Uncle Karl went to seize the other ankle. Inside the top of her swimsuit, however, you could see the line where the sunburn ended and, when she hunched her shoulders and squealed again, one nipple's auburn edge. Mother made them behave themselves. "*You* should certainly know," she said to Uncle Karl. Archly. "That when a lady says she doesn't feel like swimming, a gentleman doesn't ask questions." Uncle Karl said excuse *him*; Mother winked at Magda; Ambrose blushed; stupid Peter kept saying "Phooey on *feel like!*" and tugging at Magda's ankle; then even he got the point, and cannon-balled with a holler into the pool.

"I swear," Magda said, in mock *in feigned* exasperation.

The diving would make a suitable literary symbol. To go off the high board you had to wait in a line along the poolside and up the ladder. Fellows tickled girls and goosed one another and shouted to the ones at the top to hurry up, or razzed them for bellyfloppers. Once on the springboard some took a great while posing or clowning or deciding on a dive or getting up their nerve; others ran right off. Especially among the younger fellows the idea was to strike the funniest pose or do the craziest stunt as you fell; a thing that got harder to do as you kept on and kept on. But whether you hollered *Geronimo!* or *Sieg heil!*, held your nose or "rode a bicycle," pretended to be shot or did a perfect jacknife or changed your mind halfway down and ended up with nothing, it was over in two seconds, after all that wait. Spring, pose, splash. Spring, neat-o, splash. Spring, aw fooey, splash.

The grown-ups had gone on; Ambrose wanted to converse with Magda; she was remarkably well developed for her age; it was said that that came from rubbing with a turkish towel, and there were other theories. Ambrose could think of nothing to say except how good a diver Peter was, who was showing off for her benefit. You could pretty well tell by looking at their bathing suits and arm muscles how far along the different fellows were. Ambrose was glad he hadn't gone in swimming, the cold water shrank you up so. Magda pretended to be uninterested in the diving; she probably weighed as much as he did. If you knew your way around in the funhouse like your own bedroom, you could wait until a girl came along and then slip away without ever getting caught, even if her boyfriend was right with her. She'd think *he* did it! It would be better to be the boyfriend, and act outraged, and tear the funhouse apart.

Not act; *be*.

"He's a master diver," Ambrose said. In feigned admiration. "You really have to slave away at it to get that good." What would it matter anyhow if he asked her right out whether she remembered, even teased her with it as Peter would have?

There's no point in going farther; this isn't getting anybody anywhere; they haven't even come to the funhouse yet. Ambrose is off the track, in some new or old part of the place that's not supposed to be used; he strayed into it by some one-in-a-million chance, like the time the roller coaster car left the tracks in the nineteen-teens against all the laws of physics and sailed over the boardwalk in the dark. And they can't locate him because they don't know where to look. Even the designer and operator have forgotten this other part, that winds around on itself like a whelk shell. That winds around the right part like the snakes on Mercury's caduceus. Some people, perhaps, don't "hit their stride" until their twenties, when the growing-up business is over and women appreciate other things besides wisecracks and teasing and strutting. Peter didn't have one-tenth the imagination *he* had, not one-tenth. Peter did this naming-their-children thing as a joke, making up names like Aloysius and Murgatroyd, but Ambrose knew *exactly* how it would feel to be married and have children of your own, and be a loving husband and father, and go comfortably to work in the mornings and to bed with your wife at night, and wake up with her there. With a breeze coming through the sash and birds and mockingbirds singing in the Chinese-cigar trees. His eyes watered, there aren't enough ways to say that. He would be quite famous in his line of work. Whether Magda was his wife or not, one evening when he was wise-lined and gray at the temples he'd smile gravely, at a fashionable dinner party, and remind her of his youthful passion. The time they went with his family to Ocean City; the *erotic fantasies* he used to have about her. How long ago it seemed, and childish! Yet tender, too, *n'est-ce pas?* Would she have imagined that the world-famous whatever remembered how many strings were on the lyre on the bench beside the girl on the label of the cigar box he'd stared at in the toolshed at age ten while she, age eleven. Even then he had felt *wise beyond his years;* he'd stroked her hair and said in his deepest voice and correctest English, as to a dear child: "I shall never forget this moment."

But though he had breathed heavily, groaned as if ecstatic, what he'd really felt throughout was an odd detachment, as though some one else were Master. Strive as he might to be transported, he heard his mind take notes upon the scene: *This is what they call* passion. *I am experiencing it.* Many of the digger machines were out of order in the penny arcades and could not be repaired or replaced for the duration. Moreover the prizes, made now in USA, were less interesting than formerly, pasteboard items for the most part, and some of the machines wouldn't work on white pennies. The gypsy fortune-teller machine might have provided a foreshadowing of the climax of this story if Ambrose had operated it. It was even dilapidateder than most: the silver coating was worn off the brown metal handles, the glass windows around the dummy were cracked and taped, her kerchiefs and silks long-faded. If a man lived by himself, he could take a department-store mannequin with flexible joints and modify her in certain ways. *However:* by the time he was that old he'd have a real woman. There was a machine that stamped your name around a white-metal coin with a star in the middle: A____. His son would be the second, and when the lad reached thirteen or so he would put a strong arm around his shoulder and tell him calmly: "It is perfectly normal. We have all been through it. It will not last forever." Nobody knew how to be what they were right. He'd smoke a pipe, teach his son how to fish and softcrab, assure him he needn't worry about himself. Magda would certainly give, Magda would certainly yield a great deal of milk, although guilty of occasional solecisms. It don't taste so bad. Suppose the lights came on now!

The day wore on. You think you're yourself, but there are other persons in you. Ambrose gets hard when Ambrose doesn't want to, *and obversely.* Ambrose watches them disagree; Ambrose watches him watch. In the funhouse mirror-room you can't see yourself go on forever, because no matter how you stand, your head gets in the way. Even if you had a glass periscope, the image of your eye would cover up the thing you really wanted to see. The police will come; there'll be a story in the papers. That must be where it happened. Unless he can find a surprise exit, an unofficial backdoor or escape hatch opening on an alley, say, and then stroll up to the family in front of the funhouse and ask where everybody's been; *he's* been out of the place for ages. That's just where it happened, in that last lighted room: Peter and Magda found the right exit; he found one that you weren't supposed to find and strayed off into the works somewhere. In a perfect funhouse you'd be able to go only one way, like the divers off the highboard; getting lost would be impossible; the doors and halls would work like minnow traps or the valves in veins.

On account of German U-boats, Ocean City was "browned out": streetlights were shaded on the seaward side; shop-windows and boardwalk amusement places were kept dim, not to silhouette tankers and Liberty-ships for torpedoing. In a short story about Ocean City, Maryland, during World War II, the author could make use of the image of sailors on leave in the penny arcades and shooting galleries, sighting through the crosshairs of toy machine guns at swastika'd subs, while out in the black Atlantic a U-boat skipper squints through his periscope at real ships outlined by the glow of penny arcades. After dinner the family strolled back to the amusement end of the boardwalk. The boys' father had burnt red as always and was masked with Noxema, a minstrel in reverse. The grown-ups stood at the end of the boardwalk where the Hurricane of '33 had cut an inlet from the ocean to Assawoman Bay.

"Pronounced with a long *o*," Uncle Karl reminded Magda with a wink. His shirt sleeves were rolled up; Mother punched his brown biceps with the arrowed heart on it and said his mind was naughty. Fat May's laugh came suddenly from the funhouse, as if she'd just got the joke; the family laughed too at the coincidence. Ambrose went under the boardwalk to search for out-of-town matchbook covers with the aid of his pocket flashlight; he looked out from the edge of the North American continent and wondered how far their laughter carried over the water. Spies in rubber rafts; survivors in lifeboats. If the joke had been beyond his understanding, he could have said: *"The laughter was over his head."* And let the reader see the serious wordplay on second reading.

He turned the flashlight on and then off at once even before the woman whooped. He sprang away, heart athud, dropping the light. What had the man grunted? Perspiration drenched and chilled him by the time he scrambled up to the family. "See anything?" his father asked. His voice wouldn't come; he shrugged and violently brushed sand from his pants legs.

"Let's ride the old flying horses!" Magda cried. I'll never be an author. It's been forever already, everybody's gone home, Ocean City's deserted, the ghost-crabs are tickling across the beach and down the littered cold streets. And the empty halls of clapboard hotels and abandoned funhouses. A tidal wave; an enemy air raid; a monster-crab swelling like an island from the sea. *The inhabitants fled in terror.* Magda clung to his trouser leg; he alone knew the maze's secret. "He gave his life that we might live," said Uncle Karl with a scowl of pain, as he. The fellow's hands had been tattooed; the woman's legs, the woman's fat white legs had. *An astonishing coincidence.* He yearned to tell Peter. He wanted to throw up for excitement. They hadn't even chased him. He wished he were dead.

One possible ending would be to have Ambrose come across another lost person in the dark. They'd match their wits together against the funhouse, struggle like Ulysses past obstacle after obstacle, help and encourage each other. Or a girl. By the time they found the exit they'd be closest friends, sweethearts if it were a girl; they'd know each other's inmost souls, be bound together *by the cement of shared adventure;* then they'd emerge into the light and it would turn out that his friend was a Negro. A blind girl. President Roosevelt's son. Ambrose's former archenemy.

Shortly after the mirror room he'd groped along a musty corridor, his heart already misgiving him at the absence of phosphorescent arrows and other signs. He's found a crack of light—not a door, it turned out, but a seam between the plyboard wall panels—and squinting up to it, espied a small old man, *in appearance not unlike* the photographs at home of Ambrose's late grandfather, nodding upon a stool beneath a bare, speckled bulb. A crude panel of toggle- and knife-switches hung beside the open fuse box near his head; elsewhere in the little room were wooden levers and ropes belayed to boat cleats. At the time, Ambrose wasn't lost enough to rap or call; later he couldn't find that crack. Now it seemed to him that he'd possibly dozed off for a few minutes somewhere along the way; certainly he was exhausted from the afternoon's sunshine and the evening's problems; he couldn't be sure he hadn't dreamed part or all of the sight. Had an old black wall fan droned like bees and shimmied two flypaper streamers? Had the funhouse operator—gentle, somewhat sad and tired-appearing, in expression not unlike the photographs at home of Ambrose's late Uncle Konrad—murmured in his sleep? Is there really such a person as Ambrose, or is he a figment of the author's imagination? Was it Assawoman Bay or Sinepuxent? Are there other errors of fact in this fiction? Was there another sound besides the little slap slap of thigh on ham, like water sucking at the chine-boards of a skiff?

When you're lost, the smartest thing to do is stay put till you're found, hollering if necessary. But to holler guarantees humiliation as well as rescue; keeping silent permits some saving of face—you can act surprised at the fuss when your rescuers find you and swear you weren't lost, if they do. What's more you might find your own way yet, *however belatedly.*

"Don't tell me your foot's still asleep!" Magda exclaimed as the three young people walked from the inlet to the area set aside for ferris wheels, carrousels, and other carnival rides, they having decided in favor of the vast and ancient merry-go-round instead of the funhouse. What a sentence, everything was wrong from the outset. People don't know what to make of him, he doesn't know what to make of himself, he's only thirteen, *athletically and socially inept*, not astonishingly bright, but there are antennae; he has . . . some sort of receivers in his head; things speak to him, he understands more than he should, the world winks at him through its objects, grabs grinning at his coat. Everybody else is in on some secret he doesn't know; they've forgotten to tell him. Through simple *procrastination* his mother put off his baptism until this year. Everyone else had it done as a baby; he'd assumed the same of himself, as had his mother, so she claimed, until it was time for him to join Grace Methodist-Protestant and the oversight came out. He was mortified, but pitched sleepless through his private catechizing, intimidated by the ancient mysteries, a thirteen year old would never say that, resolved to experience conversion like St. Augustine. When the water touched his brow and Adam's sin left him, he contrived by a strain like defecation to bring tears into his eyes—but felt nothing. There was some simple, radical difference about him; he hoped it was genius, feared it was madness, devoted himself to amiability and inconspicuousness. Alone on the seawall near his house he was seized by the terrifying transports he'd thought to find in toolshed, in Communion-cup. The grass was alive! The town, the river, himself, were not imaginary; time roared in his ears like wind; the world was *going on!* This part ought to be dramatized. The Irish author James Joyce once wrote. Ambrose M____ is going to scream.

There is no *texture of rendered sensory detail,* for one thing. The fad ?d distorting mirrors beside Fat May; the impossibility of choosing a mount when one had but a single ride on the great carrousel; the *vertigo attendant on his recognition* that Ocean City was worn out, the place of fathers and grandfathers, straw-boatered men and parasoled ladies survived by their amusements. Money spent, the three paused at Peter's insistence beside Fat May to watch the girls get their skirts blown up. The object was to tease Magda, who said: "I swear, Peter M___, you've got a one-track mind! Amby and me aren't *interested* in such things." In the tumbling-barrel, too, just inside the Devil's-mouth entrance to the funhouse, the girls were upended and their boyfriends and others could see up their dresses if they cared to. Which was the whole point, Ambrose realized. Of the entire funhouse! If you looked around, you noticed that almost all the people on the boardwalk were paired off into couples except the small children; in a way, that was the whole point of Ocean City! If you had X-ray eyes and could see everything going on at that instant under the boardwalk and in all the hotel rooms and cars and alleyways, you'd realize that all that normally *showed,* like restaurants and dance halls and clothing and test-your-strength machines, was merely preparation and intermission. Fat May screamed.

Because he watched the goings-on from the corner of his eye, it was Ambrose who spied the half-dollar on the boardwalk near the tumbling-barrel. Losers weepers. The first time he'd heard some people moving through a corridor not far away, just after he'd lost sight of the crack of light, he'd decided not to call to them, for fear they'd guess he was scared and poke fun; it sounded like roughnecks; he'd hoped they'd come by and he could follow in the dark without their knowing. Another time he'd heard just one person, unless he imagined it, bumping along as if on the other side of the plywood; perhaps Peter coming back for him, or Father, or Magda lost too. Or the owner and operator of the funhouse. He'd called out once, as though merrily: "Anybody know where the heck we are?" But the query was too stiff, his voice cracked, when the sounds stopped he was terrified: maybe it was a queer who waited for fellows to get lost, or a longhaired filthy monster that lived in some cranny of the funhouse. He stood rigid for hours it seemed like, scarcely respiring. His future was shockingly clear, in outline. He tried holding his breath to the point of unconsciousness. There ought to be a button you could push to end your life absolutely without pain; disappear in a flick, like turning out a light. He would push it instantly! He despised Uncle Karl. But he despised his father too, for not being what he was supposed to be. Perhaps his father hated *his* father, and so on, and his son would hate him, and so on. Instantly!

Naturally he didn't have nerve enough to ask Magda to go through the funhouse with him. With incredible nerve and to everyone's surprise he invited Magda, quietly and politely, to go through the funhouse with him. "I warn you, I've never been through it before," he added, *laughing easily;* "but I reckon we can manage somehow. The important thing to remember, after all, is that it's meant to be a *fun*house; that is, a place of amusement. If people really got lost or injured or too badly frightened in it, the owner'd go out of business. There'd even be lawsuits. No character in a work of fiction can make a speech this long without interruption or acknowledgment from the other characters."

Mother teased Uncle Karl: "Three's a crowd, I always heard." But actually Ambrose was relieved that Peter now had a quarter too. Nothing was what it looked like. Every instant, under the surface of the Atlantic Ocean, millions of living animals devoured one another. Pilots were falling in flames over Europe; women were being forcibly raped in the South Pacific. His father should have taken him aside and said: "There is a simple secret to getting through the funhouse, as simple as being first to see the Towers. Here it is. Peter does not know it; neither does your Uncle Karl. You and I are different. Not surprisingly, you've often wished you weren't. Don't think I haven't noticed how unhappy your childhood has been! But you'll un- derstand, when I tell you, why it had to be kept secret until now. And you won't regret not being like your brother and your uncle. *On the contrary!*" If you knew all the stories behind all the people on the boardwalk, you'd see that *nothing* was what it looked like. Husbands and wives often hated each other; parents didn't necessarily love their children; et cetera. A child took things for granted because he had nothing to compare his life to and everybody acted as if things were as they should be. Therefore each saw himself as the hero of the story, when the truth might turn out to be that he's the villain, or the coward. And there wasn't one thing you could do about it!

Hunchbacks, fat ladies, fools—that no one chose what he was was unbearable. In the movies he'd meet a beautiful young girl in the funhouse; they'd have hairs-breadth escapes from real dangers; he'd do and say the right things; she also; in the end they'd be lovers; their dialogue lines would match up; he'd be perfectly at ease; she'd not only like him well enough, she'd think he was *marvelous;* she'd lie awake thinking about *him,* instead of vice versa—the way *his* face looked in different lights and how he stood and exactly what he'd said—and yet that would be only one small episode in his wonderful life, among many many others. Not a *turning point* at all. What had happened in the toolshed was nothing. He hated, he loathed his parents! One reason for not writing a lost-in-the-funhouse story is that either everybody's felt what Ambrose feels, in which case it goes without saying, or else no normal person feels such things, in which case Ambrose is a freak. "Is anything more tiresome, in fiction, than the problems of sensitive adolescents?" And it's all too long and rambling, as if the author. For all a person knows the first time through, the end could be just around any corner; perhaps, *not impossibly* it's been within reach any number of times. On the other hand he may be scarcely past the start, with everything yet to get through, an intolerable idea.

Fill in: His father's raised eyebrows when he announced his decision to do the funhouse with Magda. Ambrose understands now, but didn't then, that his father was wondering whether he knew what the funhouse was *for*—especially since he didn't object, as he should have, when Peter decided to come along too. The ticket-woman, witchlike, mortifying him when inadvertently he gave her his name-coin instead of the half-dollar, then unkindly calling Magda's attention to the birthmark on his temple: "Watch out for him, girlie, he's a marked man!" She wasn't even cruel, he understood, only vulgar and insensitive. Somewhere in the world there was a young woman with such splendid understanding that she'd see him entire, like a poem or story, and find his words so valuable after all that when he confessed his apprehensions she would explain why they were in fact the very things that made him precious to her . . . and to Western Civilization! There was no such girl, the simple truth being. Violent yawns as they approached the mouth. Whispered advice from an old-timer on a bench near the barrel: "Go crabwise and ye'll get an eyeful without upsetting!" Composure vanished at the first pitch: Peter hollered joyously, Magda tumbled, shrieked, clutched her skirt; Ambrose scrambled crabwise, tight-lipped with terror, was soon out, watched his dropped name-coin slide among the couples. Shamefaced he saw that to get through expeditiously was not the point; Peter feigned assistance in order to trip Magda up, shouted "I see Christmas!" when her legs went flying. The old man, his latest betrayer, cackled approval. A dim hall then of black-thread cobwebs and recorded gibber: he took Magda's elbow to steady her against revolving discs set in the slanted floor to throw your feet out from under, and explained to her in a calm, deep voice his theory that each phase of the funhouse was triggered either automatically, by a series of photoelectric devices, or else manually by operators stationed at peepholes. But he lost his voice thrice as the discs unbalanced him; Magda was anyhow squealing; but at one point she clutched him about the waist to keep from falling, and her right cheek pressed for a moment against his belt-buckle. Heroically he drew her up, it was his chance to clutch her close as if for support and say: "I love you." He even put an arm lightly about the small of her back before a sailor-and-girl pitched into them from behind, sorely treading his left big toe and knocking Magda asprawl with them. The sailor's girl was a string-haired hussy with a loud laugh and light blue drawers; Ambrose realized that he wouldn't have said "I love you" anyhow, and was smitten with self-contempt. How much better it would be to be that common sailor! A wiry little Seaman 3rd, the fellow squeezed a girl to each side and stumbled hilarious into the mirror room, closer to Magda in thirty seconds than Ambrose had got in thirteen years. She giggled at something the fellow said to Peter; she drew her hair from her eyes with a movement so womanly it struck Ambrose's heart; Peter's smacking her backside then seemed particularly coarse. But Magda made a pleased indignant face and cried, "All right for *you*, mister!" and pursued Peter into the maze without a backward glance. The sailor followed after, leisurely, drawing his girl against his hip; Ambrose understood not only that they were all so relieved to be rid of his burdensome company that they didn't even notice his absence, but that he himself shared their relief. Stepping from the treacherous passage at last into the mirror-maze, he saw once again, more clearly than ever, how readily he deceived himself into supposing he was a person. He even foresaw, wincing at his dreadful self-knowledge, that he would repeat the deception, at ever-rarer intervals, all his wretched life, so fearful were the alternatives. Fame, madness, suicide; perhaps all three. It's not believable that so young a boy could articulate that reflection, and in fiction the merely true must always yield to the plausible. Moreover, the symbolism is in places heavy-footed. Yet Ambrose M— understood, as few adults do, that the famous loneliness of the great was no popular myth but a general truth— furthermore, that it was as much cause as effect.

All the preceding except the last few sentences is exposition that should've been done earlier or interspersed with the present action instead of lumped together. No reader would put up with so much with such *prolixity*. It's interesting that Ambrose's father, though presumably an intelligent man (as indicated by his role as grade-school principal), neither encouraged nor discouraged his sons at all in any way—as if he either didn't care about them or cared all right but didn't know how to act. If this fact should contribute to one of them's becoming a celebrated but wretchedly unhappy scientist, was it a good thing or not? He too might someday face the question; it would be useful to know whether it had tortured his father for years, for example, or never once crossed his mind.

In the maze two important things happened. First, our hero found a name-coin someone else had lost or discarded: *AMBROSE*, suggestive of the famous lightship and of his late grandfather's favorite dessert, which his mother used to prepare on special occasions out of coconut, oranges, grapes, and what else. Second, as he wondered at the endless replication of his image in the mirrors, second, as he *lost himself in the reflection* that the necessity for an observer makes perfect observation impossible, better make him eighteen at least, yet that would render other things unlikely, he heard Peter and Magda chuckling somewhere together in the maze. "Here!" "No, here!" they shouted to each other; Peter said, "Where's Amby?" Magda murmured. "Amb?" Peter called. In a pleased, friendly voice. He didn't reply. The truth was, his brother was a *happy-go-lucky youngster* who'd've been better off with a regular brother of his own, but who seldom complained of his lot and was generally cordial. Ambrose's throat ached; there aren't enough different ways to say that. He stood quietly while the two young people giggled and thumped through the glittering maze, hurrah'd their discovery of its exit, cried out in joyful alarm at what next beset them. Then he set his mouth and followed after, as he supposed, took a wrong turn, strayed into the pass *wherein he lingers yet.*

The action of conventional dramatic narrative may be represented by a diagram called Freitag's Triangle:

or more accurately by a variant of that diagram:

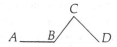

in which *AB* represents the exposition, *B* the introduction of conflict, *BC* the "rising action," complication, or development of the conflict, *C* the climax, or turn of the action, *CD* the dénouement, or resolution of the conflict. While there is no reason to regard this pattern as an absolute necessity, like many other conventions it became conventional because great numbers of people over many years learned by trial and error that it was effective; one ought not to forsake it, therefore, unless one wishes to forsake as well the effect of drama or has clear cause to feel that deliberate violation of the "normal" pattern can better can better effect that effect. This can't go on much longer; it can go on forever. He died telling stories to himself in the dark; years later, when that vast unsuspected area of the funhouse came to light, the first expedition found his skeleton in one of its labyrinthine corridors and mistook it for part of the entertainment. He died of starvation telling himself stories in the dark; but unbeknownst unbeknownst to him, an assistant operator of the funhouse, happening to overhear him, crouched just behind the plyboard partition and wrote down his every word. The operator's daughter, an exquisite young woman with a figure unusually well developed for her age, crouched just behind the partition and transcribed his every word. Though she had never laid eyes on him, she recognized that here was one of Western Culture's truly great imaginations, the eloquence of whose suffering would be an inspiration to unnumbered. And her heart was torn between her love for the misfortunate young man (yes, she loved him, though she had never laid though she knew him only—but how well!—through his words, and the deep, calm voice in which he spoke them) between her love et cetera and her womanly intuition that only in suffering and isolation could he give voice et cetera. Lone dark dying. Quietly she kissed the rough plyboard, and a tear fell upon the page. Where she had written in shorthand *Where she had written in shorthand* Where she had written in shorthand *Where she* et cetera. A long time ago we should have passed the apex of Freitag's Triangle and made brief work of the *dénouement;* the plot doesn't rise by meaningful steps but winds upon itself, digresses, retreats, hesitates, sighs, collapses, expires. The climax of the story must be its protagonist's discovery of a way to get through the funhouse. But he has found none, may have ceased to search.

What relevance does the war have to the story? Should there be fireworks outside or not?

Ambrose wandered, languished, dozed. Now and then he fell into his habit of rehearsing to himself the unadventurous story of his life, narrated from the third-person point of view, from his earliest memory parenthesis of maple leaves stirring in the summer breath of tidewater Maryland end of parenthesis to the present moment. Its principle events, on this telling, would appear to have been A, B, C, and D.

He imagined himself years hence, successful, married, at ease in the world, the trials of his adolescence far behind him. He has come to the seashore with his family for the holiday: how Ocean City has changed! But at one seldom at one ill-frequented end of the boardwalk a few derelict amusements survive from times gone by: the great carrousel from the turn of the century, with its monstrous griffins and mechanical concert band; the roller coaster rumored since 1916 to have been condemned; the mechanical shooting gallery in which only the image of our enemies changed. His own son laughs with Fat May and wants to know what a funhouse is; Ambrose hugs the sturdy lad close and smiles around his pipestem at his wife.

The family's going home. Mother sits between Father and Uncle Karl, who teases him good-naturedly who chuckles over the fact that the comrade with whom he'd fought his way shoulder to shoulder through the funhouse had turned out to be a blind Negro girl—to their mutual discomfort, as they'd opened their souls. But such are the walls of custom, which even. Whose arm is where? How must it feel. He dreams of a funhouse vaster by far than any yet constructed; but by then they may be out of fashion, like steamboats and excursion trains. Already quaint and seedy: the draperied ladies on the frieze of the carrousel are his father's father's mooncheeked dreams; if he thinks of it more he will vomit his apple-on-a-stick.

He wonders: will he become a regular person? Something has gone wrong; his vaccination didn't take; at the Boy-Scout initiation campfire he only pretended to be deeply moved, as he pretends to this hour that it is not so bad after all in the funhouse, and that he has a little limp. How long will it last? He envisions a truly astonishing funhouse, incredibly complex yet utterly controlled from a great central switchboard like the console of a pipe organ. Nobody had enough imagination. He could design such a place himself, wiring and all, and he's only thirteen years old. He would be its operator: panel lights would show what was up in every cranny of its cunning of its multifarious vastness; a switch-flick would ease this fellow's way, complicate that's, to balance things out; if anyone seemed lost or frightened, all the operator had to do was.

He wishes he had never entered the funhouse. But he has. Then he wishes he were dead. But he's not. Therefore he will construct funhouses for others and be their secret operator—though he would rather be among the lovers for whom funhouses are designed.

RUDY WIEBE

1934 –

Born on the family farm in a small Mennonite community near Fairholme, Saskatchewan, he moved at an early age with his family to another farm near Coaldale, Alberta. He was educated at Coaldale's Mennonite High School and at the Universities of Alberta and Tübingen, West Germany. He completed a theological degree at the Mennonite Brethren Bible College in Winnipeg, where he also taught, and a master's degree in English at the University of Alberta, where he currently teaches. Firmly rooted in his Mennonite background, his fiction often explores the conflict between religious vision and a social environment that is increasingly hostile to that vision. His novel *The Blue Mountains of China* (1970) chronicles the wanderings of Mennonites during the twentieth century and recounts the tensions between their religion and the social systems in which they find themselves. The author of seven novels and three collections of short stories, Wiebe is one of the mythmakers of western Canada, frequently recreating the prairie world by transforming historical material into myth. Albert Johnson also features in his latest book, *Playing Dead: A Contemplation Concerning the Arctic* (1989).

The Naming of Albert Johnson

1. *The Eagle River, Yukon:* Wednesday, February 17, 1932
                              Tuesday, February 16

There is arctic silence at last, after the long snarl of rifles. As if all the stubby trees within earshot had finished splitting in the cold. Then the sound of the airplane almost around the river's bend begins to return, turning as tight a spiral as it may up over bank and trees and back down, over the man crumpled on the bedroll, over the frantic staked dogteams, spluttering, down, glancing down off the wind-ridged river. Tail leaping, almost cartwheeling over its desperate roar for skis, immense sound rocketing from that bouncing black dot on the level glare but stopped finally, its prop whirl staggering out motionless just behind the man moving inevitably forward on snow-shoes, not looking back, step by step up the river with his rifle ready. Hesitates, lifts one foot, then the other, stops, and moves forward again to the splotch in the vast whiteness before him.

The pack is too huge, and apparently worried by rats with very long, fine teeth. Behind it a twisted body. Unbelievably small. One outflung hand still clutching a rifle, but no motion, nothing, the airplane dead and only the distant sounds of dogs somewhere, of men moving at the banks of the river. The police rifle points down, steadily extending the police arm until it can lever the body, already stiffening, up. A red crater for hip. As if one small part of that incredible toughness had rebelled at last, exploded red out of itself,

372

splattering itself with itself when everything but itself was at last unreachable. But the face is turning up. Rime, and clots of snow ground into whiskers, the fur hat hurled somewhere by bullets perhaps and the whipped cowlick already a mat frozen above half-open eyes showing only white, nostrils flared, the concrete face wiped clean of everything but snarl. Freezing snarl and teeth. As if the long clenched jaws had tightened down beyond some ultimate cog and openly locked their teeth into their own torn lips in one final wordlessly silent scream.

The pilot blunders up, gasping. "By god, we got the son, of a bitch!" stumbles across the back of the snowshoes and recovers beside the policeman. Gagging a little, "My g—" All that sudden colour propped up by the rifle barrel on the otherwise white snow. And the terrible face.

The one necessary bullet, in the spine where its small entry cannot be seen at this moment, and was never felt as six others were, knocked the man face down in the snow. Though that would never loosen his grip on his rifle. The man had been working himself over on his side, not concerned as it seemed for the bullets singing to him from the level drifts in front of him or the trees on either bank. With his left hand he was reaching into his coat pocket to reload his Savage .30–.30, almost warm on the inside of his other bare hand, and he knew as every good hunter must that he had exactly thirty-nine bullets left besides the one hidden under the rifle's butt plate. If they moved in any closer he also had the Winchester .22 with sixty-four bullets, and closer still there will be the sawed-off shotgun, though he had only a few shells left, he could not now be certain exactly how many. He had stuffed snow tight into the hole where one or perhaps even two shells had exploded in his opposite hip pocket. A man could lose his blood in a minute from a hole that size but the snow was still white and icy the instant he had to glance at it, packing it in. If they had hit him there before forcing him down behind his pack in the middle of the river, he could not have moved enough to pull out of the pack straps, leave alone get behind it for protection. Bullets twitch it, whine about his tea tin like his axe handle snapping once at his legs as he ran from the eastern river bank too steep to clamber up, a very bad mistake to have to discover after spending several minutes and a hundred yards of strength running his snowshoes towards it. Not a single rock, steep and bare like polished planks. But he had gained a little on them, he saw that as he curved without stopping towards the centre of the river and the line of trees beyond it. That bank is easily climbed, he knows because he climbed it that morning, but all the dogs and men so suddenly around the hairpin turn surprised him toward the nearest

bank, and he sees the teams spreading to outflank him, three towards the low west bank. And two of them bending over the one
army radioman he got.

Instantly the man knew it was the river that had betrayed him. He
had outlegged their dogs and lost the plane time and again on glare-
ice and in fog and brush and between the endless trails of caribou
herds, but the sluggish loops of this river doubling back on itself
have betrayed him. It is his own best move, forward and then back,
circle forward and further back, backwards, so the ones following his
separate tracks will suddenly confront each other in cursing bewilderment. But this river, it cannot be named the Porcupine, has out-
doubled him. For the dogs leaping towards him around the bend,
the roaring radioman heaving at his sled, scrabbling for his rifle, this
is clearly what he saw when he climbed the tree on the far bank, one
of the teams he saw then across a wide tongue of land already ahead
of him, as it seemed, and he started back to get further behind them
before he followed and picked them off singly in whatever tracks of
his they thought they were following. These dogs and this driver
rounding to face him as he walks so carefully backwards in his snowshoes on the curve of his own tracks.

Whatever this river is spiralling back into the Yukon hills, his rifle
will not betray him. Words are bellowing out of the racket of teams
hurtling around the bend. His rifle speaks easily, wordlessly to the
army radioman kneeling, sharpshooter position, left elbow propped
on left knee. The sights glided together certain and deadly, and long
before the sound had returned that one kneeling was already flung
back clean as frozen wood bursting at his axe.

He has not eaten, he believes it must be two days, and the rabbit
tracks are so old they give no hope for his snares. The squirrel
burrow may be better. He is scraping curls from tiny spruce twigs,
watching them tighten against the lard pail, watching the flames as it
seems there licking the tin blacker with their gold tongues. The fire
lives with him, and he will soon examine the tinfoil of matches in his
pocket, and the tinfoil bundle in his pack and also the other two
paper-wrapped packages. That must be done daily, if possible. The
pack, unopened, with the .22 laced to its side is between his left
shoulder and the snow hollow; the moose hides spread under and
behind him; the snowshoes stuck erect into the snow on the right,
the long axe lying there and the rifle also, in its cloth cover but on
the moosehide pouch. He has already worked carefully on his feet,
kneading as much of the frost out of one and then the other as he
can before the fire though two toes on the left are black and the heel
of the right is rubbed raw. Bad lacing when he walked backwards,
and too numb for him to notice. The one toe can only be kept

another day, perhaps, but he has only a gun-oily rag for his heel. Gunoil? Spruce gum? Wait. His feet are wrapped and ready to move instantly and he sits watching warmth curl around the pail. Leans his face down into it. Then he puts the knife away in his clothes and pulls out a tiny paper. His hard fingers unfold it carefully, he studies the crystals a moment, and then as the flames tighten the blackened spirals of spruce he pours that into the steaming pail. He studies the paper, the brownness of it; the suggestion of a word beginning, or perhaps ending, that shines through its substance. He lowers it steadily then until it darkens, smiling as a spot of deep brown breaks through the possible name and curls back a black empty circle towards his fingers. He lets it go, feeling warmth like a massage in its final flare and dying. There is nothing left but a smaller fold of pepper and a bag of salt so when he drinks it is very slowly, letting each mouthful move for every part of his tongue to hold a moment this last faint sweetness.

He sits in the small yellow globe created by fire. Drinking. The wind breathes through the small spruce, his body rests motionlessly; knowing that dug into the snow with drifts and spruce tips above him they could see his smokeless fire only if they flew directly over him. And the plane cannot fly at night. They are somewhere very close now, and their plane less than a few minutes behind. It has flown straight in an hour, again and again, all he had overlaid with tangled tracks in five weeks, but the silent land is what it is. He is now resting motionlessly. And waiting.

And the whisky-jacks are suddenly there. He had not known them before to come after dark, but grey and white tipped with black they fluffed themselves at the grey edge of his light, watching, and then one hopped two hops. Sideways. The first living thing he had seen since the caribou. But he reaches for the bits of babiche he had cut and rubbed in salt, laid ready on the cloth of the riflebutt. He throws, the draggle-tail is gone but the other watches, head cocked, then jumps so easily the long space his stiff throw had managed, and the bit is gone. He does not move his body, tosses another bit, and another, closer, closer, and then draggle-tail is there scrabbling for the bit, and he twitches the white string lying beside the bits of babiche left by the rifle, sees the bigger piece tug from the snow and draggle-tail leap to it. Gulp. He tugs, feels the slight weight as the thread lifts from the snow in the firelight, and now the other is gone while draggle-tail comes towards him inevitably, string pulling the beak soundlessly agape, wings desperate in snow, dragged between rifle and fire into the waiting claw of his hand. He felt the bird's blood beat against his palm, the legs and tail and wings thud an instant, shuddering and then limp between his relentless fingers.

Wings. Noiselessly he felt the beautiful muscles shift, slip over bones delicate as twigs. He could lope circles around any dogs they set on his trail but that beast labelled in letters combing the clouds, staring everywhere until its roar suddenly blundered up out of a canyon or over a ridge, laying its relentless shadow like words on the world: he would have dragged every tree in the Yukon together to build a fire and boil that. Steel pipes and canvas and wires and name, that stinking noise. In the silence under the spruce he skims the tiny fat bubbles from the darkening soup; watches them coagulate yellow on the shavings. Better than gunoil, or gum. He began to unwrap his feet again but listening, always listening. The delicate furrow of the bird pointed toward him in the snow.

2. *The Richardson Mountains, N.W.T.:*   Tuesday, February 9, 1932
                                            Saturday, January 30

Though it means moving two and three miles to their one, the best trail to confuse them in the foothill ravines was a spiral zig-zag. West of the mountains he has not seen them; he has outrun them so far in crossing the Richardson Mountains during the blizzard that when he reaches a river he thought it must be the Porcupine because he seems at last to be inside something that is completely alone. But the creeks draining east lay in seemingly parallel but eventually converging canyons with tundra plateaus glazed under wind between them, and when he paused on one leg of his zag he sometimes saw them, across one plateau or in a canyon, labouring with their dogs and sleds as it seems ahead of him. In the white scream of the mountain pass where no human being has ever ventured in winter he does not dare pause to sleep for two days and the long night between them, one toe and perhaps another frozen beyond saving and parts of his face dead, but in the east he had seen the trackers up close, once been above them and watched them coming along his trails towards each other unawares out of two converging canyons with their sleds and drivers trailing, and suddenly round the cliff to face each other in cursing amazement. He was far enough not to hear their words as they heated water for tea, wasting daylight minutes, beating their hands to keep warm.

The police drive the dog teams now, and the Indians sometimes; the ones who best track him on the glazed snow, through zags and bends, always wary of ambush, are the two army radiomen. One of the sleds is loaded with batteries when it should be food, but they sniff silently along his tracks, loping giant circles ahead of the heaving dogs and swinging arms like semaphores when they find a trail leading as it seems directly back towards the sleds they have just left. He would not have thought them so relentless at unravelling his

trails, these two who every morning tried to raise the police on their
frozen radio, and when he was convinced they would follow him as
certainly as Millen and the plane roared up, dropping supplies, it
was time to accept the rising blizzard over the mountains and find at
last, for certain, the Porcupine River.

It is certainly Millen who brought the plane north just before the
blizzard, and it was Millen who saw his smoke and heard him
coughing, whistling in that canyon camp hidden in trees under a cliff
so steep he has to chop handholds in the frozen rock to get out of
there. Without dynamite again, or bombs, they could not dig him
out; even in his unending alert his heart jerks at the sound of what
was a foot slipping against a frozen tree up the ridge facing him. His
rifle is out of its sheath, the shell racking home in the cold like
precise steel biting. There is nothing more; an animal? A tree bursting? He crouches motionless, for if they are there they should be all
around him, perhaps above on the cliff, and he will not move until
he knows. Only the wind worrying spruce and snow, whining
wordlessly. There, twenty yards away a shadow moves, Millen certainly, and his shot snaps as his rifle swings up, as he drops. Bullets
snick from everywhere, their sound booming back and forth along
the canyon. He has only fired once and is down, completely aware,
on the wrong side of his fire and he shoots carefully again to draw
their shots and they come, four harmlessly high and nicely spaced
out: there are two—Millen and another—below him in the canyon
and two a bit higher on the right ridge, one of them that slipped.
Nothing up the canyon or above on the cliff. With that knowledge he
gathered himself and leaped over the fire against the cliff and one on
the ridge made a good shot that cut his jacket and he could fall as if
gut-shot in the hollow or deadfall. Until the fire died, he was almost
comfortable.

In the growing dusk he watches the big Swede, who drove dogs
very well, crawl toward Millen stretched out, face down. He watches
him tie Millen's legs together with the laces of his mukluks and drag
him backwards, plowing a long furrow and leaving the rifle sunk in
the snow. He wastes no shot at their steady firing, and when they
stop there are Millen's words still

You're surrounded. King isn't dead. Will you give

waiting, frozen in the canyon. He lay absolutely motionless behind
the deadfall against the cliff, as if he were dead, knowing they would
have to move finally. He flexed his feet continuously, and his fingers
as he shifted the rifle no more quickly than a clock hand, moving
into the position it would have to be when they charged him. They

almost outwait him; it is really a question between the coming darkness and his freezing despite his invisible motions, but before darkness Millen had to move. Two of them were coming and he shifted his rifle slightly on the log to cover the left one—it must have been the long cold that made him mistake that for Millen—who dived out of sight, his shot thundering along the canyon, but Millen did not drop behind anything. Simply down on one knee, firing. Once, twice bullets tore the log and then he had his head up with those eyes staring straight down his sights and he fired two shots so fast the roar in the canyon sounded as one and Millen stood up, the whole length over him, whirled in that silent unmistakable way and crashed face down in the snow. He hears them dragging and chopping trees for a stage cache to keep the body, and in the darkness he chops handholds up the face of the cliff, step by step as he hoists himself and his pack out of another good shelter. As he has had to leave others.

3. *The Rat River, N.W.T..* Saturday, January 10, 1932
Thursday, December 31, 1931
Tuesday, July 28

In his regular round of each loophole he peers down the promontory toward their fires glaring up from behind the riverbank. They surround him on three sides, nine of them with no more than forty dogs, which in this cold means they already need more supplies than they can have brought with them. They will be making plans for something, suddenly, beyond bullets against his logs and guns and it will have to come soon. In the long darkness, and he can wait far easier than they. Dynamite. If they have any more to thaw out very carefully after blowing open the roof and stovepipe as darkness settled, a hole hardly big enough for one of them—a Norwegian, they were everywhere with their long noses—to fill it an instant, staring down at him gathering himself from the corner out of roof-sod and pipes and snow: the cabin barely stuck above the drifts but that one was gigantic to lean in like that, staring until he lifted his rifle and the long face vanished an instant before his bullet passed through that space. But the hole was large enough for the cold to slide down along the wall and work itself into his trench, which would be all that saved him when they used the last of their dynamite. He began to feel what they had stalked him with all day: cold tightening steadily as steel around toes, face, around fingers.

In the clearing still nothing stirs. There is only the penumbra of light along the circle of the bank as if they had laid a trench-fire to thaw the entire promontory and were soundlessly burrowing in under him. Their flares were long dead, the sky across the river flickering with orange lights to vanish down into spruce and willows again, like the shadow blotting a notch in the eastern bank and he thrust his rifle through the chink and had almost got a shot away when a projectile arced against the sky and he jerked the gun out, diving, into the trench deep under the wall among the moose hides that could not protect him from the roof and walls tearing apart so loud it seemed most of himself had been blasted to the farthest granules of sweet, silent, earth. The sods and foot-thick logs he had built together where the river curled were gone and he would climb out and walk away as he always had, but first he pulled himself up and out between the splinters, still holding the rifle, just in time to see yellow light humpling through the snow toward him and he fired three times so fast it sounded in his ears as though his cabin was continuing to explode. The shadows around the light dance in one spot an instant but come on in a straight black line, lengthening down, faster, and the light cuts straight across his eyes and he gets away the fourth shot and the light tears itself into bits. He might have been lying on his back staring up into night and had the stars explode into existence above him. And whatever darkness is left before him then blunders away, desperately plowing away from him through the snow like the first one who came twice with a voice repeating at his door

I am Constable Alfred King, are you in there?

fist thudding the door the second time with a paper creaking louder than his voice so thin in the cold silence

I have a search warrant now, we have had complaints and if you don't open

and then plowing away in a long desperate scrabble through the sun-shot snow while the three others at the riverbank thumped their bullets hopelessly high into the logs but shattering the window again and again until they dragged King and each other head first over the edge while he placed lead carefully over them, snapping willow bits on top of them and still seeing, strangely, the tiny hole that had materialized up into his door when he flexed the trigger, still hearing the grunt that had wormed in through the slivers of the board he had whipsawn himself. Legs and feet wrapped in moose hide lay a moment across his window, level in the snow, jerking as if barely attached to a body knocked over helpless, a face somewhere twisted in gradually developing pain that had first leaned against his door,

fist banging while that other one held the dogs at the edge of the
clearing, waiting

Hallo? Hallo? This is Constable Alfred King of the Royal Canadian
Mounted Police. I want to talk to you. Constable Millen

and they looked into each other's eyes, once, through his tiny window. The eyes peering down into his—could he be seen from out of
the blinding sun?—squinted blue from a boy's round face with a
bulging nose bridged over pale with cold. King, of the Royal
Mounted. Like a silly book title, or the funny papers. He didn't look
it as much as Spike Millen, main snooper and tracker at Arctic Red
River who baked pies and danced, everybody said, better than any
man in the north. Let them dance hipped in snow, get themselves
dragged away under spruce and dangling traps, asking, laying
words on him, naming things

You come across from the Yukon? You got a trapper's licence? The
Loucheaux trap the Rat, up towards the Richardson Mountains.
You'll need a licence, why not

Words. Dropping out of nothing into advice. Maybe he wanted a
kicker to move that new canoe against the Rat River? Loaded down
as it is. The Rat drops fast, you have to hand-line the portage anyway to get past Destruction City where those would-be Klondikers
wintered in '98. He looked up at the trader above him on the wedge
of gravel. He had expected at least silence. From a trader standing
with the bulge of seven hundred dollars in his pocket; in the south a
man could feed himself with that for two years. Mouths always full
of words, pushing, every mouth falling open and dropping words
from nothing into meaning. The trader's eyes shifted finally, perhaps
to the junction of the rivers behind them, south and west, the united
river clicking under the canoe. As he raised his paddle. The new rifle
oiled and ready with its butt almost touching his knees as he kneels,
ready to pull the canoe around.

4. *Above Fort McPherson, N.W.T.:* Tuesday, July 7, 1931

The Porcupine River, as he thought it was then, chuckled between
the three logs of his raft. He could hear that below him, under the
mosquitoes probing the mesh about his head, and see the gold
lengthen up the river like the canoe that would come toward him
from the north where the sun just refused to open the spiky horizon.
Gilded, hammered out slowly, soundlessly toward him the thick

gold. He sat almost without breathing, watching it come like silence. And then imperceptibly the black spired riverbend grew pointed, stretched itself in a thin straight line double-bumped, gradually spreading a straight wedge below the sun through the golden river. When he had gathered that slowly into anger it was already too late to choke his fire; the vee had abruptly bent toward him, the bow man already raised his paddle; hailed. Almost it seemed as if a name had been blundered into the silence, but he did not move in his fury. The river chuckled again.

" . . . o-o-o-o . . . " the point of the wedge almost under him now. And the sound of a name, that was so clear he could almost distinguish it. Perhaps he already knew what it was, had long since lived this in that endlessly enraged chamber of himself, even to the strange Indian accent mounded below him in the canoe bow where the black hump of the stern partner moved them straight toward him out of the fanned ripples, crumpling gold. To the humps of his raft below on the gravel waiting to anchor them.

"What d'ya want."

"You Albert Johnson?"

It could have been the sternman who named him. The sun like hatchet-strokes across slanted eyes, the gaunt noses below him there holding the canoe against the current, their paddles hooked in the logs of his raft. Two Loucheaux half-faces, black and red kneeling in the roiled gold of the river, the words thudding softly in his ears.

You Albert Johnson?

One midnight above the Arctic Circle to hear again the inevitability of name. He has not heard it in four years, it could be to the very day since that Vancouver garden, staring into the evening sun and hearing this quiet sound from these motionless—perhaps they are men kneeling there, perhaps waiting for him to accept again what has now been laid inevitably upon him, the name come to meet him in his journey north, come out of north around the bend and against the current of the Peel River, as they name that too, to confront him on a river he thought another and aloud where he would have found after all his years, at long last, only nameless silence.

You Albert Johnson?

"Yes," he said finally.

And out of his rage he begins to gather words together. Slowly, every word he can locate, as heavily as he would gather stones on a Saskatchewan field, to hold them for one violent moment against himself between his two hands before he heaves them up and hurls them—but they are gone. The ripples of their passing may have been smoothing out as he stares at where they should have been had they been there. Only the briefly golden river lies before him, what-

ever its name may be since it must have one, bending back somewhere beyond that land, curling back upon itself in its giant, relentless spirals down to the implacable, and ice-choked, arctic sea.

POETRY

POETRY

The Elements of Poetry

INTRODUCTION

The Poetry Game

If you ask a poet, "What good is it? I mean, what earthly good is it?" you may get an answer like Marianne Moore's "I, too, dislike it," or W. H. Auden's "Poetry makes nothing happen." The modern poet is not likely to make grandiose claims for his craft. And we shall try not to betray that honest and tough-minded attitude. Poetry is essentially a game, with artificial rules, and it takes two—a writer and a reader—to play it. If the reader is reluctant, the game will not work.

Physical games have their practical aspects. They help make sound bodies to go with the sound minds so much admired by philosophers of education. A language game like poetry also has uses, but they are by-products rather than its proper ends. Poetry exercises a valuable though perhaps "unsound" side of the mind: imagination. (It takes an exercise of the imagination, for example, to get at what Bob Dylan means by a "hard rain.") Poetry can also be used to develop the student's ability to control and respond to language. But it is a game first of all, where—as Robert Frost said—"the work is play for mortal stakes."

A game can require great exertion, but it must reward that exertion with pleasure or there is no playing it. Anyone who has ever responded to a nursery rhyme, or to a Beatles record, or to Gordon Lightfoot singing a ballad, has experienced the fundamental pleasure of poetry. More complicated and sophisticated poems offer essentially the same kind of pleasure. We labor to understand the rules of the game so that we need not think about them when we are playing. We master technique to make our execution easier. When we are really proficient the work becomes play.

The Qualities of Poetry

Part of the pleasure of poetry lies in its relation to music. It awakens in us a fundamental response to rhythmic repetitions of various kinds. Learning to read poetry is partly a matter of learning to respond to subtle and delicate rhythmic patterns as well as to the most obvious and persistant ones. But poetry is not just a kind of music. It is a special combination of musical and linguistic qualities—of sounds regarded both as pure sound and as meaningful speech. In particular, poetry is expressive language. It does for us what Samuel Beckett's character Watt wanted done for him:

> Not that Watt desired information, for he did not. But he desired words to be applied to his situation, to Mr Knott, to the house, to the grounds, to his duties, to the stairs, to his bedroom, to the kitchen, and in a general way to the conditions of being in which he found himself.

Poetry applies words to our situations, to the conditions of being in which we find ourselves. By doing so, it gives us pleasure because it helps us articulate our states of mind. The poets we value are important because they speak for us and help us learn to speak for ourselves. A revealing instance of a poet's learning to apply words to his own situation, and finding in their order and symmetry a soothing pleasure, has been recorded by James Joyce. Here we see a child of nine years making an important discovery about the nature and uses of poetry:

> [Bray: in the parlour of the house in Martello Terrace]
> MR VANCE (comes in with a stick) . . . O, you know, he'll have to apologise, Mrs Joyce.
> MRS JOYCE O yes . . . Do you hear that, Jim?
> MR VANCE Or else—if he doesn't—the eagles'll come and pull out his eyes.
> MRS JOYCE O, but I'm sure he will apologise.
> JOYCE (under the table, to himself)
> —Pull out his eyes,
> Apologise,
> Apologise,
> Pull out his eyes.
>
> Apologise,
> Pull out his eyes,
> Pull out his eyes,
> Apologise.

The coincidence of sound that links the four-word phrase "pull-out-his-eyes" with the four-syllable word "apologise" offers the child a refuge from Mr Vance far more secure than the table under which he is hiding. In his novel A Portrait of the Artist as a Young Man, Joyce used this moment from his own life to illustrate Stephen's vocation for verbal art.

As a poem the child's effort is of course a simple one, but it achieves a real effect because of the contrast between the meanings of its two basic lines that sound so much alike. Gentle "apologise" and fierce "pull out his eyes" ought not to fit together so neatly, the poem implies; and in doing so it makes an ethical criticism of Mr Vance, who, after all, coupled them in the first place. Young Joyce's deliberate wit has made a poem from the old man's witless tirade.

Marianne Moore qualifies her dislike of poetry this way:

> I, too, dislike it: there are things that are important beyond
>   all this fiddle.
> Reading it, however, with a perfect contempt of it, one
>   discovers in
> it after all, a place for the genuine.
>   Hands that can grasp, eyes
>   that can dilate, hair that can rise
>   if it must, these things are important not because a
>
> high-sounding interpretation can be put upon them but
>   because they are
> useful. . . .

And Auden adds,

> . . . poetry makes nothing happen: it survives
> In the valley of its making where executives
> Would never want to tamper: flows on south
> From ranches of isolation and the busy griefs,
> Raw towns that we believe and die in; it survives,
> A way of happening, a mouth.

He concludes the poem "In Memory of W. B. Yeats," from which these lines are taken, with some advice to poets that suggests the kinds of thing poetry can do:

> Follow, poet, follow right
> To the bottom of the night,
> With your unconstraining voice
> Still persuade us to rejoice;
>
> With the farming of a verse
> Make a vineyard of the curse,
> Sing of human unsuccess
> In a rapture of distress;
>
> In the deserts of the heart
> Let the healing fountain start,
> In the prison of his days
> Teach the free man how to praise.

10

Poetry, then, is a kind of musical word game that we value because of its expressive qualities. Not all poems are equally musical, or equally playful, or equally expressive. Nor are they necessarily musical, playful, or expressive in the same way. But we may consider these three qualities as the basic constituents of poetry so that we may examine some of the various ways in which poets combine and modify them in making different kinds of poems. Recognizing various poetic possibilities is important to the student of poetry because the greatest single problem for the reader of a poem is the problem of tact.

Tact

Tact acknowledges the diversity of poetry. A tactful approach to a poem must be appropriate to the special nature of the poem under consideration. Reading a poem for the first time ought to be a little like meeting a person for the first time. An initial exploratory conversation may lead to friendship, dislike, indifference, or any of dozens of other shades of attitude from love to hate. If the relation progresses, it will gain in intimacy as surface politeness is replaced by exchange of ideas and feelings at a deeper level.

We need, of course, to speak the same language if we are to communicate in any serious way. For most of us, this means we make friends with people who speak English and we read poems written in English. But speaking the same language means more than just inheriting or acquiring the same linguistic patterns. Some poems, like some people, seem to talk to us not merely in our native language but in our own idiom as well. We understand them easily and naturally. Others speak in ways that seem strange and puzzling. With poems, as with people, our first response to the puzzling should be a polite effort to eliminate misunderstanding. We need not adopt any false reverence before the poems of earlier ages. An old poem may be as much of a bore as an old person. But we should treat the aged with genuine politeness, paying attention to their words, trying to adjust to their idiom. This may turn out to be very rewarding, or it may not. But only after we have understood are we entitled to reject—or accept—any utterance.

Since the English language itself has changed considerably over the centuries and continues to change, we must often make a greater effort to understand an older poem than a modern one. Also, notions of what poetry is and should be have changed in the past and continue to change. The poetry game has not always been played with the same linguistic equipment or under the same rules. The difference between a love lyric by an Elizabethan sonneteer and a contemporary poem of love may be as great as the difference between Elizabethan tennis and modern tennis. The Elizabethans played tennis indoors, in an intricately walled court which required great finesse to master all its angles. The modern game is flat and open, all power serves and rushes to the net. Which ought to remind us that Robert Frost likened free verse (verse with unrhymed, irregular lines) to playing tennis with the net down. Such a game would make points easy to score but would not be much fun to play. Poetry, like tennis, depends on artificial rules and hindrances. These arbitrary restrictions are what give it its game-like quality.

Unlike the rules of tennis, however, the rules of poetry have never really been written down. Although critics have frequently tried to produce a "poetics" that would operate like a code of rules, they have always failed because poetry is always changing. In fact poetic "rules" are not really rules but conventions that change perpetually and must change perpetually to prevent poems from being turned out on a mass scale according to formulas. Every poet learns from his predecessors, but any poet who merely imitates them produces flat, stale poems. A poet is above all a man who finds a unique idiom, a special voice for his own poetry. The tactful reader quickly picks up the conventions operating in any particular poem and pays careful attention to the idiom of every poet, so that he can understand and appreciate or criticize each separate poetic performance.

The following parts of this discussion are designed to help the student of poetry to acquire tact. They are arranged to present certain basic elements drawn from the whole system of poetic conventions. Tact itself cannot be taught because it is of the spirit. But if the instinct for it is there, tact can be developed and refined through conscious effort. In the pages that follow, the student may consider consciously and deliberately the kinds of intellectual and emotional adjustments that the expert reader of poetry makes effortlessly and instantaneously.

EXPRESSION

Drama and Narration

Drama usually implies actors on a stage impersonating characters who speak to one another in a sequence of situations or scenes. A short poem with a single speaker, thus, is dramatic only in a limited sense. Nevertheless, *some* poems are very dramatic; the element of drama in them must be grasped if we are to understand them at all. And *all* poems are dramatic to some extent, however slight.

We approach the dramatic element in poetry by assuming that every poem shares some qualities with a speech in a play: that it is spoken aloud by a "speaker" who is a character in a situation which implies a certain relationship with other characters; and we assume that this speech is "overheard" by an audience. We may have to modify these assumptions. The poem may finally be more like a soliloquy or unspoken thought than like a part of a dialogue. Or it may seem more like a letter or a song than a speech. Still, in approaching our poem we must make a tentative decision about who the speaker is, what his situation is, and whom he seems to be addressing. In poems that are especially dramatic, the interest of the poem will depend on the interest of the character and situation presented. But because dramatic poems are very short and compressed in comparison with plays, the reader must usually do a good deal of guessing or inferring in order to grasp the elements of character and situation. The good reader will make plausible inferences; the inadequate reader will guess wildly, breaking the rules of plausibility and spoiling the inferential game.

Consider the following lines from the beginning of a dramatic poem. This imaginary speech is assigned by the title of the poem to a painter who lived in Renaissance Italy. Brother Filippo Lippi was a Carmelite friar and an important painter, whose work was sponsored by the rich and powerful Florentine banker Cosimo de Medici.

Fra Lippo Lippi

I am poor brother Lippo, by your leave!
You need not clap your torches to my face.
Zooks, what's to blame? you think you see a monk!
What, 't is past midnight, and you go the rounds,
And here you catch me at an alley's end
Where sportive ladies leave their doors ajar?
The Carmine's my cloister: hunt it up,
Do,—harry out, if you must show your zeal,
Whatever rat, there, haps on his wrong hole,
10   And nip each softling of a wee white mouse,
Weke, weke, that's crept to keep him company!
Aha, you know your betters! Then, you'll take
Your hand away that 's fiddling on my throat,
And please to know me likewise. Who am I?
Why, one, sir, who is lodging with a friend
Three streets off—he 's a certain . . . how d' ye call?
Master—a . . . Cosimo of the Medici,
I' the house that caps the corner. Boh! you were best!
Remember and tell me, the day you 're hanged,
20   How you affected such a gullet's-gripe!
But you, sir, it concerns you that your knaves
Pick up a manner nor discredit you:
Zooks, are we pilchards, that they sweep the streets
And count fair prize what comes into their net?
He 's Judas to a tittle, that man is!
Just such a face! Why, sir, you make amends.
Lord, I 'm not angry! Bid your hangdogs go
Drink out this quarter-florin to the health
Of the munificent House that harbours me
30   (And many more beside, lads! more beside!)
And all 's come square again. I 'd like his face—
His, elbowing on his comrade in the door
With the pike and lantern,—for the slave that holds

John Baptist's head a-dangle by the hair
With one hand ("Look, you, now," as who should say)
And his weapon in the other, yet unwiped!
It 's not your chance to have a bit of chalk,
A wood-coal or the like? or you should see!
Yes, I'm the painter, since you style me so.

Now consider, in order, each of these questions:

1. From these lines, what can we infer about the situation and its development?

2. Who is Lippo speaking to in the opening lines?

3. At what time of day and in what sort of neighborhood does this scene take place?

4. Would we be justified in making an inference about what Lippo has been up to? What inference might we make?

5. What is Lippo talking about when he says in line 18, "Boh! you were best!"? And whom does he say it to? What produced the action which Lippo refers to here?

6. In line 21 he addresses a different person in "you, sir." Who is he addressing?

7. What kind of man do the details in these lines suggest is speaking in this poem?

8. How would you describe the whole progress of the situation? How might the events presented in these 39 lines be re-told in the form of a story narrated by an observer of the action?

This series of questions—and their answers—should suggest the kind of inferential activity that many dramatic poems require of their readers. The words of such a poem are points of departure, and the actual poem is the one we create with our imaginative but logical response to the poet's words. The poet—Robert Browning—offers us the pleasure of helping to create his poem, and also the pleasure of entering a world remote from our own in time and space. Dramatic poems like Browning's do not so much apply words to our situations as take us out of ourselves into situations beyond our experience. When we speak Lippo's words aloud, or read them imaginatively, we are refreshed by this assumption of a strange role and this expression of a personality other than our own. In a sense, our minds are expanded, and we return to ourselves enriched by the experience. Yet even the strangest characters will often express ideas and attitudes that we recognize as related to our own, related to certain moods or conditions of being in which we have found ourselves. Every citizen who has had to explain an awkward situation to a policeman has something in common with Lippo Lippi as he begins to speak.

The line between the dramatic and narrative elements in a poem is not always clear. But a narrative poem gives us a story as told by a narrator from a perspective outside the action, while a dramatic poem presents a fragment of an action (or story) through the voice (or point of view) of a character involved in that action. The principal speaker in a narrative poem addresses us—the audience—directly, telling us about the situation and perhaps offering us introductions to characters who function as dramatic elements in the poem. In the days when long stories were recited aloud by bardic poets, verse was the natural form for narration, because it provided easily memorizable units of composition and a regular, flowing rhythm into which these units might be fitted. But now that printing has converted most of the audience for fiction from listeners to readers, most stories are told in prose. The only narrative verse form that is really alive today is the ballad, which justifies its use of rhyme and rhythm by being set to music and sung. Verse meant to be sung has its own rules or conventions, which will be discussed later on. But here we can talk about the narrative element in ballads and other forms of fiction in verse, and how versified fiction differs from the kind of story we expect to find in prose.

If we think of a dramatic poem as something like a self-sufficient fragment torn from a play, which through its compression encourages us to fill out its dramatic frame by acts of inference and imagination—then we may think of a narrative poem as related to prose fiction in a similar way. In comparison to stories, narrative poems are compressed and elliptical, shifting their focus, concentrating on striking details, and leaving us to make appropriate connections and draw appropriate conclusions. In fact, there is a strong tendency toward the dramatic in short verse narratives—a tendency to present more dialogue or action in relation to description than we would expect to find in prose fiction dealing with the same subject matter.

Actually, we find poetic elements in much prose fiction and fictional elements in many poems. Here we are concerned mainly with the special problems posed by the compressed and elliptical form taken by fiction in short poems such as this one, by E. A. Robinson:

Reuben Bright

Because he was a butcher and thereby
Did earn an honest living (and did right)
I would not have you think that Reuben Bright
Was any more a brute than you or I;
For when they told him that his wife must die,

He stared at them, and shook with grief and fright,
And cried like a great baby half that night,
And made the women cry to see him cry.

And after she was dead, and he had paid
10   The singers and the sexton and the rest,
He packed a lot of things that she had made
Most mournfully away in an old chest
Of hers, and put some chopped-up cedar boughs
In with them, and tore down the slaughter-house.

The poem is narrative for the reason that the speaker addresses us from a perspective outside the action and undertakes to comment for our benefit on the character and situation presented: Reuben earns an "honest" living; he did "right." Yet the narrator presents just two incidents from the whole of Bright's life, and he makes no final interpretation or commentary on Bright's climactic act. It is left for us to conclude that only by destroying the place of butchery could this butcher express his anguish at the death of his beloved wife. And it is left for us to note the irony involved in this presentation of an act of destructive violence as evidence that the butcher is not "any more a brute than you or I." It is also left for us to note the pathos of this gesture by which the butcher tries to dissociate himself from that death which has claimed his wife. The compactness and brevity characteristic of poetry often move narration in the direction of drama.

Consider the combination of drama and narration in the following poem by D. H. Lawrence:

Piano

Softly, in the dusk, a woman is singing to me;
Taking me back down the vista of years, till I see
A child sitting under the piano, in the boom of the tingling strings
And pressing the small, poised feet of a mother who smiles as she sings.

In spite of myself, the insidious mastery of song
Betrays me back, till the heart of me weeps to belong
To the old Sunday evenings at home, with winter outside
And hymns in the cosy parlour, the tinkling piano our guide.

So now it is vain for the singer to burst into clamour
10   With the great black piano appassionato. The glamour
Of childish days is upon me, my manhood is cast
Down in the flood of remembrance, I weep like a child for the past.

Here the speaker seems to be addressing us directly as a narrator. But he is describing a scene in which he is the central character, and describing it in the present tense as something in progress. Drama is always *now*. Narrative is always *then*. But this scene mingles now *and* then, bringing together two pianos, and two pianists; linking the speaker's childish self with his present manhood. In a sense, the poem depends on its combination of now and then, drama and narration, for its effect—uniting now and then, man and child, in its last clause: "I weep like a child for the past."

Because this is a poem, tightly compressed, it is possible for us to miss an essential aspect of the dramatic situation it presents. Why is it "vain" for the singer to play the piano "appassionato"? Why does he say that his "manhood" is cast down? What does this phrase mean? These elliptical references seem intended to suggest that the woman at the piano is in some sense wooing the man who listens, attempting to arouse his passion through her performance. But ironically, she only reminds him of his mother, casting down his manhood, reducing him from a lover to a son, from a man to a child.

It is interesting to compare this poem by D. H. Lawrence to an early version. Looking at the early draft, we might consider Lawrence's revisions as an attempt to achieve a more satisfactory combination of narrative and drama, and a more intense poem. The early version tells quite a different story from the later one—almost the opposite story. And it contains much that Lawrence eliminated. Examine the revisions in detail. What does each change accomplish? Which changes are most important, most effective?

The Piano
(*Early version*)

Somewhere beneath that piano's superb sleek black
Must hide my mother's piano, little and brown, with the back
That stood close to the wall, and the front's faded silk both torn,
And the keys with little hollows, that my mother's fingers had worn.

Softly, in the shadows, a woman is singing to me
Quietly, through the years I have crept back to see
A child sitting under the piano, in the boom of the shaking strings
Pressing the little poised feet of the mother who smiles as she sings.

The full throated woman has chosen a winning, living song
10 And surely the heart that is in me must belong
To the old Sunday evenings, when darkness wandered outside
And hymns gleamed on our warm lips, as we watched mother's fingers glide.

Or this is my sister at home in the old front room
Singing love's first surprised gladness, alone in the gloom.
She will start when she sees me, and blushing, spread out her hands
To cover my mouth's raillery, till I'm bound in her shame's heartspun bands.

A woman is singing me a wild Hungarian air
And her arms, and her bosom, and the whole of her soul is bare,
And the great black piano is clamouring as my mother's never could clamour
20 And my mother's tunes are devoured of this music's ravaging glamour.

Description and Meditation

Description is the element in poetry closest to painting and sculpture. Poets like Edmund Spenser, Keats, and Tennyson have been very sensitive to this relationship: Spenser maintained that the Poet's wit "passeth Painter farre," while Keats admitted that a painted piece of Greek pottery could "express a flowery tale more sweetly than our rhyme." In fact, describing with words has both advantages and disadvantages in comparison to plastic representation. Words are rich in meaning and suggestion but weak for rendering precise spatial relations and shades of color. Therefore, what descriptive words do best is convey an attitude or feeling through the objects that they describe.

Take a very simple description from a short poem by William Carlos Williams:

a red wheel
barrow

glazed with rain
water

beside the white
chickens.

We sense a word game here in the arbitrary arrangement of the words in lines, as they lead us to consider a visual image dominated by contrasting colors and textures—feathery white and glazed red, animate and inanimate things. But it is hard to sense distinctly any attitude conveyed by the description, which seems like a poor substitute for a painting.

Here is the entire poem:

so much depends
upon

a red wheel
barrow

glazed with rain
water

beside the white
chickens.

Now we can see how the description itself depends upon the assertion "so much depends" for its animation. The assertion directs our search for meaning, and conveys the speaker's attitude toward the objects described. We may wonder how anything at all can "depend" on such insignificant objects, and yet this very response is a response not just to a description but to a poem as well. The poem is created by the distance between this sweeping statement and the apparent insignificance of the objects it refers to. We understand, finally, that the poet is using this distance to make us feel his concern for trivial things, his sense that there is beauty in humble objects; and beyond that, he is encouraging us to share his alertness to the beautiful in things that are neither artful nor conventionally pretty. He is advising us to keep our eyes open, and he does it not with a direct admonition but with a description charged with the vigor of his own response to the visible world.

It is of the essence of poetic description that it come to us charged with the poet's feelings and attitudes. Sometimes these will be made explicit by statement or commentary in the poem. Sometimes they will remain implicit, matters of tone, rhythm, and metaphor. Consider these four opening lines from a poem by Tennyson. What attitudes or emotions are conveyed by them, and how are they conveyed?

The woods decay, the woods decay and fall,
The vapours weep their burthen to the ground,
Man comes and tills the field and lies beneath,
And after many a summer dies the swan.

The topic is decay and death, presented in terms of generalized natural description. In line 1 the continuing process of decay is emphasized by the exact repetition of a whole clause. In line 2 the vapors are presented as sentient creatures who weep. In line 3 the whole adult life of man is compressed into just nine words, few seconds, a patch of earth. In the climactic position, reserved by an inversion of normal syntax for the very last place in the sentence, comes the death of the swan. The life and death of man is thus surrounded by decay and death in other natural things, and in this way is reduced, distanced. It is not horrible but natural, and characterized by a melancholy beauty.

These lines of description serve in the poem as the beginning of a dramatic monologue. The nature of the speaker and his situation (as we come to understand them) help us to refine our grasp of the tone and the attitude these lines convey toward the objects they describe. Here is the opening verse-paragraph of the poem:

Tithonus

The woods decay, the woods decay and fall,
The vapours weep their burthen to the ground,
Man comes and tills the field and lies beneath,
And after many a summer dies the swan.
Me only cruel immortality
Consumes: I wither slowly in thine arms,
Here at the quiet limit of the world,

A white-haired shadow roaming like a dream
The ever-silent spaces of the East,
10   Far-folded mists, and gleaming halls of morn.

The speaker is Tithonus, a mythological prince who became the lover of the dawn goddess; she made him immortal but could not prevent him from growing older throughout eternity. In the light of lines 5 and 6, the first four lines are enriched with the wistful envy of one who is unable to die. At the close of the poem (some seventy lines later) the speaker returns to the images of line 3 in speaking of "happy men that have the power to die" and of "the grassy barrows of the happier dead." He asks for release so that he can become "earth in earth" and forget his unhappy existence.

The melancholy beauty of the opening lines becomes more lovely and less sad as we move toward the conclusion of the poem with its powerful projection of man's return to earth as the most desirable of consummations. Behind the dramatic speaker in the poem—the mythological Tithonus—stands the poet, reminding us that death is natural and the appropriate end of life. In this poem, description and drama collaborate to suggest rather than state a meaning.

Serious English poetry has often embodied in particular poems a movement from description to overt meditation. This movement is frequently found in religious poetry, as poets move from contemplation of created things to an awareness of the Creator. William Wordsworth was a master—prehaps *the* master—of this kind of poetic movement in English. Thus, a selection from Wordsworth makes a fitting conclusion to this discussion of description and meditation. The poem is a sonnet (see the note on this form in the introduction to Shakespeare in our Selection of Poets), in which the first eight lines (the *octet*) are devoted to description of nature and the last six (the *sestet*) take the form of a meditation on Wordsworth's daughter Caroline. The expression "Abraham's bosom" in the poem refers of course to heaven. In the New Testament (Luke 16:22) we are told that the righteous will join the patriarch Abraham in heaven after death.

It is a beauteous evening, calm and free,
The holy time is quiet as a Nun
Breathless with adoration; the broad sun
Is sinking down in its tranquillity;
The gentleness of heaven broods o'er the Sea:
Listen! the mighty Being is awake,
And doth with his eternal motion make
A sound like thunder—everlastingly.
Dear Child! dear Girl! that walkest with me here,
10   If thou appear untouched by solemn thought,
Thy nature is not therefore less divine:
Thou liest in Abraham's bosom all the year;
And worshipp'st at the Temple's inner shrine,
God being with thee when we know it not.

WORD GAMES

Language can be used to help us perceive relations that connect disparate things, or to help us make discriminations that separate similar things. In poetry these two aspects of language take the form of metaphorical comparison and ironic contrast. Metaphor and irony are the twin bases of poetical language. This means that a good reader of poetry must be especially alert and tactful in his responses to metaphorical and ironic language.

It is because poetry places such stress on these crucial dimensions of language that it is of such great use in developing linguistic skills in its readers. It makes unusual demands and offers unusual rewards. The kind of skill it takes to be a first-rate reader of poetry cannot be acquired by reading a textbook like this one, any more than the ability to play the piano can be acquired in a few lessons. Continuing practice is the most important factor in a performing art like piano playing—and reading poetry (even silently, to oneself) has many of the qualities and satisfactions of a performing art.

In the sections that follow on metaphoric and ironic language we have not tried to present an exhaustive list of poetical devices to be carefully noted and memorized. We have tried to examine some of the main varieties of metaphoric and ironic language, with a view toward establishing an awareness of these two crucial varieties of poetical word-play. To move from awareness to expertise, the student must read many poems and consider them carefully.

Some Varieties of Metaphorical Language

SIMILE

This is the easiest form of metaphor to perceive because in it both of the images or ideas being joined are stated and explicitly linked by the word *as* or *like* or a similar linking-word. Similes are often quite simple:

O my Love's like a red, red rose

But even a statement of resemblance as simple and direct as this one of Robert Burns's asks us to consider the ways in which his beloved is like a rose—and not a white or yellow rose, but a red rose. And not just a red rose but a "red, red" rose. What the redness of the rose has to do with the qualities of the speaker's beloved is the first question this simile poses for us. In the poem, the simile is further complicated by a second line:

O my Love's like a red, red rose,
    That's newly sprung in June;

Here we are asked to associate the freshness of the flower and its early blooming with the qualities of the speaker's beloved. In the poem, the next two lines add a second image, compounding the simile:

O my Love's like the melodie
    That's sweetly played in tune.

The first image emphasizes the spontaneous naturalness of the beloved, the second her harmonious composure. Both roses and sweet melodies are pleasing; so that, in a sense, the poet is using his similes to make the simple statement that his beloved is pleasing to behold. But the simile is also saying that she has a complicated kind of appeal: like the rose, to sight and smell; like the melody, to the sense of sound; like the rose, a natural fresh quality; like the melody, a deliberate artfulness which intends to please. The simile also conveys to us the strength of the poet's feeling; his choice of images tells us something about the qualities of his feeling for her, because it is *he* who has found these words—which themselves have some of the qualities of spontaneous freshness and tuneful order.

A single simile can also be elaborated: as in the traditional epic simile, in which the illustrative image is often extensive enough to require the construction as . . . *so*, or *like* . . . *thus*. An extended simile, by multiplying possible points of contact between the thing presented and the illustrative image, can often become very complicated indeed, with the illustrative image itself becoming a thing to be illustrated or developed with other images still. Consider, for example, this epic simile from Book IV of Spenser's *Faerie Queene*:

27

Like as the tide that comes from th' Ocean main,
Flows up the Shanon with contrary force,
And overruling him in his own reign,
Drives back the current of his kindly course,
And makes it seem to have some other source:
But when the flood is spent, then back again
His borrowed waters forced to redisbourse
He sends the sea his own with double gain
And tribute eke withall, as to his Soveraine.

28

Thus did the battle vary to and fro . . .

METAPHOR

The word "metaphor" is used both as a general term for all kinds of poetic linking of images and ideas, and as a specific term for such linking when the thing and image are not presented as a direct analogy (A is *like* B) but by discussing one in terms of the other (A *is* B-ish, or A B's; Albert *is* a dog or Albert *barked* at me). For example, within the epic simile from Spenser, we can find metaphor at work. The simile involves describing a hand-to-hand combat in terms of the ebb and flow of tides where the River Shannon meets the Atlantic Ocean. The ebb and flow of the waters illustrates the shifting tide of battle (as this metaphor become a cliché usually puts it). But this basic simile in Spenser is enriched by the idea of Shannon and Ocean as hostile potentates engaged in a struggle, with the Ocean tide invading the river and "overruling him in his own reign."

The struggle of potentates is itself further complicated by a financial metaphor. The phrase "when the flood is spent" means literally when the incoming tide has expended its force and lost its momentum. But Spenser chooses to use the financial overtones in the word "spent" to further adorn his metaphor. From "spent" he moves to "borrowed" and "redisburse," and the concept of repayment with 100 percent interest in the expression "double gain." This transaction between Ocean and Shannon can be seen as a combat or a loan. Finally, Spenser merges these two metaphors in the last line of the stanza, by calling this double payment the "tribute" of a lesser feudal power to a higher. And here Spenser actually turns his metaphor into a simile within the basic simile, with the expression "as to his Soveraine."

This kind of interweaving of similes and metaphors is playful and decorative in its intent. The metaphors seem to emerge naturally and blend easily with one another. But these graceful arabesques tell us nothing much about the course of the combat of the two warriors, beyond the suggestion that the fight ebbs and flows. Their struggle is not so much described as dignified by this heroic comparison to two sovereign forces of nature.

In poems that depend heavily on metaphoric processes for their interest, the subtle interaction of images and ideas almost defies analysis; yet such poems may depend upon our attempts to follow their metaphoric threads. For us to understand such a poem, to feel it, we must start our thoughts along the lines indicated by the metaphors. Consider Shakespeare's sonnet 73 as an example of this kind of poem:

> That time of year thou may'st in me behold
> When yellow leaves, or none, or few, do hang
> Upon those boughs which shake against the cold—
> Bare ruin'd choirs where late the sweet birds sang.
> In me thou see'st the twilight of such day
> As after Sunset fadeth in the West,
> Which by and by black night doth take away,
> Death's second self, that seals up all in rest.
> In me thou see'st the glowing of such fire
> That on the ashes of his youth doth lie,
> As the death-bed whereon it must expire,

Consumed with that which it was nourish'd by.
This thou perceiv'st, which makes thy love more strong
To love that well which thou must leave ere long.

The images of the first twelve lines are all elaborations of the simple notion that the speaker is getting old. The last two lines are a dramatic assertion, also rather simple. The speaker tells his listener that the listener will love him all the more, precisely because old age and death threaten their relationship. We can infer that the speaker is older than the listener, and in terms of the dramatic situation we are entitled to wonder whether these self-assured words are merely wishful thinking, or an appraisal of the listener's attitude. How does the imagery of the first twelve lines contribute to the situation and to our understanding of it? We have in these lines three separate but related metaphors, each developed for four lines. The speaker says, in effect, "You see in me—autumn; you see in me—twilight; you see in me—embers."

These three metaphors for aging have in common certain qualities: a growing coldness and darkness; suggestions of finality and impending extinction. But each image generates its own attitude and emphasizes a different aspect of the aging process. The first four lines suggest an analogy between an aging person and trees whose leaves have fallen, leaving them exposed to cold winds. And the bare trees suggest, by a further reach of metaphor, a ruined and desolate church. Above all, this complex metaphor generates sympathy for the speaker, a sympathy based on our concern for lost beauty, for destruction of spiritual things, and for victims of the forces of nature.

The next four lines, focusing on the twilight after sunset, emphasize the threat of coming darkness. By another extension of metaphor, "black night" is called "Death's second self." The brevity of the time between sunset and night increases our sense of sympathetic urgency, and the introduction of "Death" takes us full circle through the metaphors back to their object, an aging man. The next four lines also introduce a complex metaphor. The speaker compares himself to the glowing embers of a dying fire which lies upon "the ashes of his youth." The fire becomes human, here, and returns us again to the life of the speaker.

This image is the most intense of the three, because it likens the arrival of age not merely to a seasonal change, worked by the passage of time, but to the consumption or destruction of matter which can never be restored to its original state. The ashes of the fire lying upon its deathbed are forcible reminders that the speaker's body will soon lie upon a deathbed, and will become ashes, to be returned to the ashes and dust of the grave. It is the emotional force of all "This" which the speaker maintains in the next-to-last line that the listener must perceive. And the confidence of the assertion is partly the confidence of a poet who still has his poetical power. He can still sing like a sweet bird and move his hearer with his poetry. The imagery justifies the dramatic situation, and the situation intensifies the significance of the imagery.

THE CONCEIT

It is useful to think of the conceit as an extension of the simile in which aspects of the basic analogy are developed with a kind of relentless ingenuity. The "metaphysical" poets of the late sixteenth and the seventeenth century specialized in witty conceits. Here, for example, John Donne combines a dramatic situation with development of a conceit so that the images become an argument persuading his lady listener to give in.

The Flea

Mark but this flea, and mark in this,
How little that which thou deny'st me is;
Me it sucked first, and now sucks thee,
And in this flea, our two bloods mingled be;
Confess it, this cannot be said
A sin, or shame, or loss of maidenhead,
   Yet this enjoys before it woo,
    And pampered swells with one blood made of two,
    And this, alas, is more than we would do.

10   Oh stay, three lives in one flea spare,
Where we almost, nay more than married are.
This flea is you and I, and this
Our marriage bed, and marriage temple is;
Though parents grudge, and you, we are met,
And cloistered in these living walls of jet.
   Though use make you apt to kill me,
    Let not to this, self murder added be,
    And sacrilege, three sins in killing three.

Cruel and sudden, hast thou since
20   Purpled thy nail, in blood of innocence?
In what could this flea guilty be,
Except in that drop which it sucked from thee?
Yet thou triumph'st, and say'st that thou
Find'st not thyself, nor me the weaker·now;
   'Tis true, then learn how false, fears be;
    Just so much honour, when thou yield'st to me,
    Will waste, as this flea's death took life from thee.

In the first two lines the speaker makes the basic analogy between the flea's having bitten both himself and the lady, and the act of love-making to which he would like to persuade her. In the rest of the poem he develops the analogy as an argument in a changing dramatic context. At the start of stanza two, the lady has threatened to kill the flea. By stanza three she has done so. And meanwhile the speaker has imaginatively transformed the flea into a marriage bed, a temple, a cloister, and a figure of the Holy Trinity (three in one); so that the flea's destruction can be hyperbolically described as murder, suicide, and sacrilege. All in preparation for the turn of the argument in the last three lines of the poem. Donne's conceit is both ingenious and playful in this poem. It is witty in more than one sense.

THE SYMBOL

The symbol can be seen as an extension of the metaphor. In it, instead of saying that A is B-ish, or calling an A a B, the poet presents us with one half of the analogy only, and requires us to supply the missing part. This invites the reader to be creative and imaginative in a situation controlled by the poet. Bob Dylan's "Hard Rain" is a symbolic poem. And here is a symbolic poem by W. B. Yeats:

The Dolls

A doll in the doll-maker's house
Looks at the cradle and bawls:
'That is an insult to us.'
But the oldest of all the dolls,
Who had seen, being kept for show,
Generations of his sort,
Out-screams the whole shelf: 'Although
There's not a man can report
Evil of this place,
10   The man and the woman bring
Hither, to our disgrace,
A noisy and filthy thing.'
Hearing him groan and stretch
The doll-maker's wife is aware
Her husband has heard the wretch,
And crouched by the arm of his chair,
She murmurs into his ear,
Head upon shoulder leant:
'My dear, my dear, O dear,
20   It was an accident.'

This whole incident stands in a metaphoric relation to something else. In other words, the poem is only apparently about dolls and doll-makers. It is really about something symbolized by the incident narrated. What? And how do we go about determining what? We must work very carefully from the situation toward possible analogies in the world of ideas and experience, first exploring the situation and images in the poem. The situation derives from the doll-maker's unique role as creator of two kinds of small, man-shaped objects: dolls and children. The dolls in their lifeless perfection resent the noise and filth produced by an actual human child. The human baby is, in fact, as the doll-maker's wife apologetically points out, not "made" in the same sense as dolls are made. Birth is an "accident"; dolls are deliberately constructed. The situation leads us outward until we see it as an illustration of the opposition between art and life, between the ideal and the real. The doll-maker himself thus symbolizes any artist who is obliged to live in the real world but create idealized objects, or any person who faces the impossible problem of realizing his ideas—or idealizing reality.

Having got this far from the concrete situation of the poem, the reader is in a position to return and consider the ways in which Yeats has used language to control his tone and charge the scene with emotion. How should we react to the various characters in this little drama? What, finally, should our attitude be toward the real/ideal conflict that the drama illustrates?

THE PUN

Often subjected to abuse as a "low" form of wit, the pun is essentially a kind of metaphor that can be used lightly and facetiously or for more serious purposes. Consider some verses by Thomas Hood (selected by William Empson to exemplify punning techniques):

How frail is our uncertain breath!
The laundress seems full hale, but death
Shall her 'last linen' bring;
The groom will die, like all his kind;
And even the stable boy will find
This life no stable thing. . . .

Cook, butler, Susan, Jonathan,
The girl that scours the pot and pan
And those that tend the steeds,
10   All, all shall have another sort
Of service after this—in short
The one the parson reads.

These puns on "stable" and "service" are playful but not funny. They use the basic device of the pun—dissimilar meanings for the same "word" or rather the same sound—to convey an attitude toward an idea. That both the life of a servant and his funeral are somehow included in that one piece of language—"service"—brings home to us the interconnection of life and death—which is the point of the poem.

Shakespeare was a master of the pun as of other metaphorical devices. Hamlet's bitter, punning responses to his uncle's smooth speeches are deadly serious and powerfully dramatic in their witty compression of his resentment.

KING   . . . But now, my cousin Hamlet, and my son—
HAMLET [*Aside*]   A little more than kin and less than kind!
KING   How is it that the clouds still hang on you?
HAMLET   Not so, my lord. I am too much i' the sun.

Hamlet and the King are more than *kin* (twice related: uncle/nephew and stepfather/son) but Hamlet feels they are not kindred spirits, not the same *kind*. And being called *son* by his father's murderer rouses all Hamlet's bitterness, causing him to return the King's metaphorical question about Hamlet's emotional weather with a pun that brings the metaphor back to the literal with a sarcastic bite: I am too much in the *son*.

The Language of Animation and Personification

In addition to their playful or ingenious aspects, the various metaphorical devices help to generate the qualities of compression and intensity that we value in much poetry. Similar qualities are often achieved by other means, such as animation and personification.

ANIMATION
Animation confers on objects or creatures a greater degree of awareness or purposefulness than we normally credit them with. When Tennyson writes, "The vapours weep their burthen to the ground," he gives life to the vapours, animating them with an emotion, sadness, that only living creatures experience. Less lovely scenes can also be intensified by animation. Consider these lines from Samuel Johnson's "Vanity of Human Wishes," which describe the treatment accorded the portraits of a statesman whose power has waned. Those who were honored to gaze at his features, now that no more is to be gained from the man, suddenly find the likeness ugly:

From every room descends the painted face,
That hung the bright palladium of the place;
And, smoked in kitchens, or in auctions sold,
To better features yields the frame of gold;
For now no more we trace in every line
Heroic worth, benevolence divine;
The form distorted justifies the fall,
And detestation rids th' indignant wall.

In that last line Johnson intensifies his satire by animating the very wall on which the picture hangs—it, even, is indignant and wishes to be rid of these odious features. The removal itself is effected by a person who has dwindled into an attitude—"detestation."

PERSONIFICATION

In this example from Dr. Johnson, we have a kind of reverse personification—as a human being becomes an abstract idea. Personification usually works the other way, clothing abstractions with the attributes of personality. Of all the ideas presented as sentient beings, Love has been most frequently selected. In mythology, Love figures as the boy-god Cupid or Eros, offering poets a ready-made personification which they have often used. The mechanical use of traditional personification can be a dull and dreary thing. But observe Sir Philip Sidney as he personifies Love in this sonnet, and finds ways to make concrete a whole range of other abstractions such as reverence, fear, hope, will, memory, and desire. If Love is personified here, these other notions are objectified—turned into material objects.

I on my horse, and Love on me doth try
    Our horsemanships, while by strange work I prove
    A horseman to my horse, a horse to Love;
    And now man's wrongs in me, poor beast, descry.

The reins wherewith my rider doth me tie,
    Are humbled thoughts, which bit of reverence move,
    Curb'd in with fear, but with gilt boss above
    Of hope, which makes it seem fair to the eye.

The wand is will; thou, fancy, saddle art,
10   Girt fast by memory, and while I spur
    My horse, he spurs with sharp desire my heart:

He sits me fast, however I do stir:
    And now hath made me to his hand so right,
    That in the manage my self takes delight.

The dominant image of Love as horseman provides the subordinate imagery for making concrete the other abstractions which serve to amplify this picture of a love-ridden man. The effectiveness of the poem depends on the ingenuity with which the poet has matched the objects and ideas to one another, relating all to the dominant personification of Love. Like Spenser's epic simile, Sidney's personification seems to breed subordinate metaphors easily, gracefully, and naturally.

The Anti-Metaphorical Language of Irony

Verbal irony may be said to start with simple negation of resemblance in situations where resemblance is customarily insisted upon: as in Shakespeare's sonnet 130, which begins,

My mistress' eyes are nothing like the sun;
Coral is far more red than her lips red:
If snow be white, why then her breasts are dun;
If hairs be wires, black wires grow on her head.

The anti-similes of the first three lines serve the same function as the ugly metaphor in line 4. All four lines present attacks on what the speaker will name in the last line as "false compare"—the misuse by poets of the metaphorical dimension of poetical language.

Usually, however, irony is not so straightforward. In fact, we normally think of it as involving some indirection or misleading of the reader—some gap between what the words *seem* to be saying and what they *are* saying. Thus, in this Shakespearean sonnet, after eight more lines of plain speaking about an ordinary human female, the speaker concludes,

And yet, by heaven, I think my love as rare
As any she belied by false compare.

What we might have taken as disparagement of the lady turns out to be praise after all. She is not uglier than the others; she just has a lover who won't exaggerate her beauty with the usual clichés. Thus, there is an irony in the disparity between the apparent disparagement of the lady in the first part of the poem and the praise of her at the end. We can see, then, in those opening lines, a kind of understatement, which works finally to convince us of the lady's beauty more effectively than a conventionally exaggerated simile of "false compare" would have done. (The entire sonnet may be found in our Selection of Poets.)

Understatement and overstatement are two of the most frequently used kinds of verbal irony. When Swift causes a character to observe (in prose), "Last Week I saw a Woman *flay'd*, and you will hardly believe, how much it altered her Person for the worse"—the main thing that strikes us is the awful inadequacy of the sentiment for the event. Disparity, contrast, incongruity—these things are at the heart of verbal irony. And, perhaps at the heart of that heart lies the notion that all words are inadequate for the representation of things. The poet as maker of metaphors may be seen as a genuine magician, bringing new things into the world, or as a charlatan pretending with feeble words to unite things that are essentially separate. Metaphor emphasizes the creative dimension of language, irony its tricky dimension.

For example, in Marvell's "To His Coy Mistress" the exaggerated protestations of the extent that the speaker's love would require "Had we but world enough and time" are all based on the view that of course we do *not* have world enough and time. Even before we get there, we sense the presence of the "But" on which the poem will make its turn:

But at my back I always hear
Time's winged chariot hurrying near;

The contrast between what the speaker *would* do:

Two hundred years should go to praise
Thine eyes, and on thy forehead gaze:
Two hundred to adore each breast:
And thirty thousand to the rest;

and what he *does* urge:

Now let us sport us while we may,

is an ironic one, enhanced by the extreme distance in time between hundreds or thousands of years and "Now." (Marvell's poem may be found in our Selection of Poets.)

Irony can also take the form of metaphorical overstatement, as it does in Alexander Pope's description of coffee being poured into a China cup:

From silver spouts the grateful liquors glide,
While China's earth receives the smoking tide.

These lines are metaphorical in that they present one thing (pouring a cup of coffee) in terms of another image (a kind of burning flood pouring over the mainland of China); but they are ironic in that the equation is made mainly so that we will perceive the disparity between the two images and enjoy their incongruity. Something of this reverse anti-metaphorical wit is present in many metaphors. John Donne's "The Flea" has a witty, ironic dimension derived from the inappropriateness of his basic image. To call a flea a temple is to establish a very far-fetched metaphor. The conceits used by Donne and other "metaphysical" poets of his time often have an ironic dimension.

Samuel Johnson characterized the metaphysical poets precisely in terms of this dimension—a special and extreme form of "wit" based on the "discovery of occult resemblances in things apparently unlike," and resulting in poems in which "the most heterogeneous ideas are yoked by violence together." Johnson's description emphasizes ("yoked by violence") the tension between metaphoric comparison and ironic contrast in many metaphysical conceits. Conceits tend to be witty, cerebral, unnatural; while metaphors are serious, imaginative, and natural. The metaphors of Romantic poetry are perceptions of relationships felt actually to exist. Metaphysical conceits often establish powerful but artificial relationships where one would least expect to find them.

Linking incongruous things is a feature of most kinds of witty poetry. A simple list with one incongruous element can serve to indict a whole way of life, as when Alexander Pope surveys the debris on a lady's dressing table:

Puffs, Powders, Patches, Bibles, Billet-doux

The inclusion of Bibles among love letters and cosmetics suggests a confusion between worldly and spiritual values—a failure to distinguish between true and false worth. The list is funny, but in an ironic and satiric way—as is this list of possible calamities from the same poem:

Whether the nymph shall break Diana's law,
Or some frail China jar receive a flaw;
Or stain her honour or her new brocade;
Forget her prayers or miss a masquerade;
Or lose her heart or necklace at a ball; . . .

Here Pope mixes several serious matters of the spirit with trivial and worldly items. The breaking of Diana's law of chastity is equated with damage to a jar. A single verb, "stain," governs two objects—"honour" and "brocade"—of different qualities and intensities. By this manipulation of grammar Pope makes us forcibly aware of the frivolousness of an attitude toward life which equates things that properly should have different values. He brings those two objects under that one verb so that we will feel a powerful urge to part them in our minds, resolving the incongruity by separating the elements he has brought together.

Another kind of incongruity is that achieved by Byron in such passages as this one, which presents a romantic lover trying to keep his mind on his beloved while his stomach is attacked by seasickness:

"Sooner shall heaven kiss earth—(here he fell sicker)
    Oh, Julia! what is every other woe?—
(For God's sake let me have a glass of liquor;
    Pedro, Battista, help me down below.)
Julia my love—(you rascal, Pedro, quicker)—
    Oh, Julia—(this curst vessel pitches so)—
Beloved Julia, hear me still beseeching!"
(Here he grew inarticulate with retching.)

The irony here is more a matter of drama than of language; but the difference between the language of the speaker's romantic assertions and his cries to his servants, supports the dramatic irony. The narrator points up the contrast by mis-rhyming "retching" with "beseeching" in the last two lines.

Beyond Metaphor and Irony

Much of the best contemporary poetry presents combinations of images and ideas so stretched and disconnected that they go beyond metaphor and yet so serious and appropriate they transcend irony also. The difficulty in understanding many modern poems stems from a profusion of images that seem ironically disconnected, but nevertheless suggest genuine metaphorical connection. We can find a relatively simple illustration in a few lines from a ballad by W. H. Auden entitled "As I Walked Out One Evening":

The glacier knocks in the cupboard,
  The desert sighs in the bed
And the crack in the tea-cup opens
  A lane to the land of the dead.

Here Auden seems to be operating with ironic incongruities—the glacier in the cupboard and so on—but this collection of incongruities adds up to a quite coherent statement about the absurd and empty horror that threatens much of modern life. Such a collection of images seems to combine qualities of conceit and symbol with ironic incongruity, leaving us to resolve the problem of whether these assertions are ironic overstatements or powerful metaphors for our condition.

A poem composed of a number of these high-tension ironic metaphors can be immediately intelligible in a general way and still difficult to reduce to prose sense at every point. But we should make the effort to establish prose sense—or possible prose senses—for each image and situation in such a poem, because even if we do not succeed entirely, we will be testing the ultimate intelligibility of the poem, the durability of its interest. As with certain kinds of modern art, it is sometimes hard to separate the fraudulent from the real in contemporary poetry. If we cannot discover intelligibility and coherence in a poem, if its images and situations do not enhance one another, we are confronted by either a fraudulent poem or a poem that is beyond us—one that we have not as yet learned how to read. Differences in poetic quality cannot be demonstrated conclusively, yet they exist. The following poem by a young American poet, William Knott, is offered as a problem in intelligibility and evaluation. Does it make sense? Does it work? Is it good?

Survival of the Fittest Groceries

The violence in the newspapers is pure genius
A daily gift to the reader
From some poet who wants to keep in good with us
Brown-noser wastepaperbasket-emptier

I shot 437 people that day
2 were still alive when I killed them
Why do people want to be exhumed movie-stars
I mean rats still biting them, the flesh of comets, why do they walk around like that?

I'm going to throw all of you into the refrigerator
10   And leave you to claw it out with the vegetables and meats

MUSIC

The musical element in poetry is the hardest to talk about because it is non-verbal. Our responses to rhythm and to pleasing combinations of sounds are in a sense too immediate, too fundamental to be comprehended in words. Yet music is important in all poetry, and for most poetry written before the last half-century it is crucial. Therefore, we must try to get some sort of verbal grasp of this poetical element, simply in order to do justice to most poetic achievement. Students generally prefer discussing one aspect of poetry to another in an order something like this:

1. ideas
2. situations
3. language
4. metrics

But if we are concerned about what makes poetry poetry rather than another kind of composition, we should probably reverse this order. If a piece of writing is neither especially rhythmical nor especially ironic or metaphorical in its language, it is not poetry, regardless of its dramatic situations or the ideas it presents.

In our experience, students are not only least interested in metrics of all the elements of poetry; they are also least competent in it. To demonstrate this, one need only ask them to translate a few sentences of prose into a simple, versified equivalent. Most will find this very difficult to do. No wonder they don't like poetry. They can't hear it properly. Fortunately, the fundamentals of versification are teachable to some extent, and should be part of any poetical curriculum. In the pages that follow, these fundamentals are presented in a fairly simple way, with a minimum of special terminology.

Metrics

Metrics has to do with all rhythmical effects in poetry. In English versification this means that it is largely a matter of accents and pauses. The pauses are determined by the usual grammatical principles that govern our speech and writing, and are indicated by the usual grammatical symbols: periods, commas, and so on. But one new factor is added. The end of a line of verse is itself a mark of punctuation. If a line ends with a regular mark of punctuation we call it *end-stopped*. If the last word of a line is followed by no punctuation and is part of a continuing grammatical unit like a prepositional phrase, we call the line *run-on*, or *enjambed*. In end-stopped lines, the line-end works *with* the punctuation and reinforces it, making each line a tight unit of thought. In enjambed lines the line-end works *against* the punctuation, throwing certain words into a prominence that they would not ordinarily have. The enjambed line really adds a special kind of poetical punctuation to the language: something at once more and less than a comma. Poets who use free verse forms with no regular rhythm are very dependent on enjambment to give their words a special poetical quality.

Reconsider the little poem by Williams:

so much depends
upon

a red wheel
barrow

glazed with rain
water

beside the white
chickens.

If we write this out as prose we get

So much depends upon a red wheelbarrow, glazed
with rainwater, beside the white chickens.

This is a simple, declarative prose sentence, with a couple of adjectival phrases tacked on, set off with commas. Has anything been lost by this rearrangement of the poem on the page? Decidedly so. The assertion being made is much less convincing in plain prose. The free-verse form of the sentence uses its line-endings to work against the prose movement, slowing it up, and providing a metrical equivalent for the visual highlighting of the images. Just where we would bring the words closest together in prose— making single words out of "wheel" and "barrow," "rain" and "water"— Williams has pulled them apart by breaking the line in mid-word.

The poem may or may not carry us to final agreement with its assertion, but in the free-verse form it certainly convinces us of the speaker's earnestness. We get a sense of how much he cares about what he is saying from the care with which he has spaced out his words. And when we read the poem aloud, with little pauses at line-ends, it carries us further toward conviction than the same sentence in its prosaic form.

That is a simple illustration of how poetry's special line-end punctuation can group words in a rhythm different from the rhythm of normal speech or prose. Here is a further illustration of how a poet can use the line-end to achieve an ironic effect virtually unduplicatable in prose. E. E. Cummings begins a poem this way:

pity this busy monster, manunkind,
not.

The first word of the second line absolutely reverses the meaning of the first line. We pause, with a comma, at the end of line 1. We stop entirely, with a period, after the first word of line 2. We hover, thus, with the wrong meaning until we are given the word that changes it, whereupon we stop to contemplate the admonition offered us in the whole opening sentence. Consider it rearranged as plain prose:

Pity this busy monster, manunkind, not.

or more prosaically,

Do not pity this busy monster, manunkind.

or still more prosaically,

Do not pity this busy, unkind monster, man.

By unraveling the poetical arrangement and combination of the words, we have destroyed the force of the admonition, taking away its suspense and eliminating the recoil in the original last word.

In verse that is not markedly rhythmical, unusual pauses and arrangements of words are the principal metrical device. In verse that is regularly rhythmical, however, the rhythm or meter itself is the crucial metrical element. Poetical arrangement does something to prosaic language, but not so much as does rhythm, which lifts an utterance and moves it in the direction of music. Just as the line-end pauses in a poem can work with or against the normal grammatical pauses of speech and prose, poetic rhythm can work both with and against our normal patterns of pronunciation.

In speech we begin with standard grammatical pronunciations for words. Take the word "defense." Normally we pronounce this word by accenting the first syllable lightly and the second syllable heavily. Indicating light accent by ∪ and heavy accent by —, we pronounce the word this way:

∪ —
defense. That is grammatical accent or grammatical stress. But in certain situations we might change this pronunciation for purposes of emphasis, as in, "It's not offense that's important, it's defense." Here we pronounce the

‾ ⌣
word defense. This is not grammatical stress but rhetorical stress. We have altered the usual pattern of light and heavy accent in order to make a point. (Grammar, or course, keeps changing, and the repeated use of one particular rhetorical pattern can eventually alter standard pronunciation. Broadcasts of football and basketball games, for instance, are helping to

‾ ⌣
make defense the standard way to accent the word.)

Both grammatical and rhetorical stress operate in poetry, where they are complicated by a third kind of accent, which we may call poetical stress. Poetical stress is a regular system of accents which establishes the basic rhythm of a poem. There are only two fundamental systems of poetic stress in English verse, though they have many variations. Most frequently, English verse simply alternates light and heavy accents, giving every other syllable the same stress. Like this:

⌣ ‾ ⌣ ‾ ⌣ ‾ ⌣ ‾ ⌣ ‾
The woods decay, the woods decay and fall

Less frequently, English verse uses two light syllables between each heavy stress. Like this:

⌣ ⌣ ‾ ⌣ ⌣ ‾ ⌣ ⌣ ‾ ⌣ ⌣ ‾
The Assyrian came down like the wolf on the fold
⌣ ⌣ ‾ ⌣ ⌣ ‾ ⌣ ⌣ ‾ ⌣ ⌣ ‾
And his cohorts were gleaming in purple and gold

The rhythm of this second metrical pattern is more insistent than that of the first. The simple da-dum, da-dum of "The woods decay" is more like the spoken language than the da-da-dum, da-da-dum of "like the wolf on the fold."

When discussing metrics it is useful to have a term for the units that are repeated to make the pattern. It is customary to call these units *feet*. In the first example above, we have five repeated units in the line, five feet divided this way:

⌣ ‾ | ⌣ ‾ | ⌣ ‾ | ⌣ ‾ | ⌣ ‾
The woods | decay, | the woods | decay | and fall

In the second example each line has four feet, divided like this:

⌣ ⌣ ‾ | ⌣ ⌣ ‾ | ⌣ ⌣ ‾ | ⌣ ⌣ ‾
And his co | horts were gleam | ing in pur | ple and gold

In describing metrical patterns we usually state the number of feet in the basic line and name the standard foot in each line. The traditional name for the foot used in the first example (da-dum) is the *iamb*. The traditional name for the foot used in the second example (da-da-dum) is the *anapest*. In referring to the number of feet in the basic line of a poem, it is customary to use numerical prefixes derived from the Greek. Thus,

```
one-foot line = mono  + meter = monometer
two-foot line =   di  + meter = dimeter
three-foot line =   tri  + meter = trimeter
four-foot line = tetra + meter = tetrameter
five-foot line = penta + meter = pentameter
six-foot line = hexa  + meter = hexameter
```

We could skip the Greek and talk about such things as "lines with ten syllables that go da-dum" and so on, but it is finally easier to learn the accepted terms and say simply "iambic pentameter."

The iamb and the anapest each have a variant foot which is made by placing the accented syllable at the beginning of each foot rather than at the end. These are called the *trochee* (dum-da) and the *dactyl* (dum-da-da). They are not used very consistently for one good reason. Rhyme in poetry is pleasing only if it includes the last accented syllable in a line *and all the unaccented syllables that follow it.* Thus, if you write:

Upon a mid | night drear | y once

You need find only a one syllable rhyme for your rhyming line, such as:

Upon a midnight dreary once
I tried my hand at kicking punts

But if you use the trochee, and write

Once u | pon a | midnight | dreary

then you must rhyme

Once upon a midnight dreary
Of kicking punts my foot was weary.

The trochaic foot can, in fact, grow quite wearisome if carried through to the rhyme word consistently; so we often get a variation that looks like this:

Tiger, Tiger burning bright

In the forests of the night

These lines first appear trochaic (dum-da) and end by looking iambic (da-dum). (Though, actually the second line is more complicated in a way we will consider later on.) The two lines could be made fully iambic by a very slight change in each:

˘ ‾˘ ‾˘ ‾ ˘
O, Tiger, Tiger burning bright

˘ ‾ ˘ ‾˘ ‾ ˘ ‾
Within the forest of the night

or we could make them fully trochaic by this kind of alteration:

‾˘ ‾˘ ‾ ˘ ‾˘
Tiger, Tiger burning brightly,

‾ ˘ ‾ ˘ ‾˘ ‾˘
Roaming through the forest nightly

In order to name the metrical pattern of "Tiger, Tiger" we must supply an imaginary unaccented syllable at one end of the line or the other, like this:

˘ ‾ | ˘ ‾ | ˘ ‾ | ˘ ‾
x Ti | ger, Ti | ger, burn | ing bright

or this:

‾ ˘ | ‾ ˘ | ‾ ˘ | ‾ ˘
Tiger, | Tiger, | burning | bright x |

These maneuverings strongly suggest that the special terminology of metrical analysis is not important in itself, and that beyond the major distinction between the two-syllable foot and the three-syllable foot, we need not be terribly fussy in classifying. What, then, is the use of all these special terms?

The art of metrics involves a poet's ability to generate and maintain a consistent meter without destroying normal patterns of grammar and syntax. To succeed metrically a poet must make language dance without making it unnatural. And a really crucial aspect of this art is perceptible only when we have the terminology to recognize it. Any absolutely regular meter quickly becomes boring through repetition. But a totally irregular poem is totally without the kind of interest and pleasure that rhythm provides.

All good poets who work in regular meters introduce metrical variations into their poems. The simplest way to understand this is to see the variations as substitutions of a different sort of foot for the one called for by the established meter of the poem. (The second line of Blake's "The Tyger," is not quite the same as the first. Can you devise alternative ways to describe its rhythm? The whole poem may be found in our Selection of Poets.) As an example of metrical variation, consider this stanza from a poem by A. E. Housman:

With rue my heart is laden

  For golden friends I had

For many a rose-lipt maiden

  And many a lightfoot lad.

The meter is basically iambic, complicated a little by the extra syllable of a feminine rhyme in alternate lines (laden, maiden—two-syllable rhymes are called *feminine*). But the basic meter is varied by the addition of one anapestic foot in lines three and four.

    The second (and last) stanza of that poem goes like this:

By brooks too broad for leaping
  The lightfoot boys are laid;
The rose-lipt girls are sleeping
  In fields where roses fade.

This looks almost absolutely regular—iambic trimeter with alternate feminine rhyme—but it is not quite. Both grammar and rhetoric urge us to accent and elongate the sound of the word "too" in the first line. Thus the line must be scanned (analyzed metrically) this way:

by brooks | too broad | for leaping

The second foot of this line has two accented syllables and no unaccented one. This is a kind of foot that is often used as a substitute but never as the metrical basis for a whole poem. Its technical name is *spondee*. Housman has used the spondee here for a slight variation of his rhythm—one that is almost unnoticeable to the analytic eye but works subtly on the ear to prevent the rhythm from becoming monotonous.

    Having noticed that substitution, we might notice also that in both stanzas the words "lightfoot" and "rose-lipt" work gently in a spondaic direction. In both stanzas these words appear so that the heavy accent of the iamb falls on their first syllable. But that second syllable is a word in its own right, and one that might well take a heavy accent in another metrical situation, such as this:

‿ ― ‿ ―‿
My foot is weary,

‿ ― ‿ ―‿
My eye is teary,

‿ ―‿ ― ‿
My lip is beery.

"Foot" and "lip" (or "lipt") can both take heavy accents. In Housman's stanzas the syllables "foot" and "lipt," falling where we would expect light accents, actually result in something between heavy and light.

The basic terminology of metrical analysis establishes only the simple distinction between heavy and light, thus it cannot take us too far into any metrical subtleties. In scansion, however, we need to consider subtleties, and should probably be ready to use at least one more symbol to indicate a stress between heavy and light. Using a combination of the two stress marks we already have in operation to indicate an intermediate stress, we might re-scan the first stanza this way:

‿ ― ‿ ― ‿ ―‿
With rue my heart is laden

‿ ― ‿ ― Y ―
for golden friends I had,

‿ ―‿‿ ― ‿ ― ‿
For many a rose-lipt maiden

‿ ―‿‿ ― ‿ ―
And many a lightfoot lad.

Then we could point out that the intermediate accents on lipt and foot make the last feet of lines 3 and 4 partially spondaic.

Thus far we have considered the metrics of this little poem only in terms of its pleasing variation within a firmly established pattern. We can see how the pattern is established in the first two lines of the first stanza, and then varies subtly in most of the succeeding lines, until the pattern reasserts itself in the perfectly regular last line. Now, we are in a position to deal with the question of the relation of the metrics to the meaning of the poem. The poem makes a simple statement about sadness felt for the death of those who were once agile and pretty. But death is never mentioned. It is evoked metaphorically through words like "laid" and "sleeping." These metaphors are very gentle, suggesting more the peace of the grave than any decay or destruction. In the second stanza the speaker also suggests delicately the frustration and sadness felt by those in the world of the living. The unleapable brooks symbolize things unachievable in life; the fading roses symbolize the impermanence of living things. The peace of the dead is ironically contrasted with the sadness of the living. The speaker is finally rueful not just because his golden friends are dead but because *he* is alive.

How does the meter relate to all this? Iambic trimeter calls for a good deal of rhyme—a rhyming sound every third foot. The addition of feminine rhymes in alternate lines makes for even more rhyming syllables. If we compare this metrical situation with that in another poem (by Ben Jonson) about death and decay, we should notice something about the effect of meter.

Slow, slow, fresh fount, keep time with my salt tears;
   Yet slower, yet; O faintly gentle springs;
List to the heavy part the music bears,
   Woe weeps out her division when she sings:
     Droop herbs and flowers;
     Fall grief in showers;
     Our beauties are not ours.
       O, I could still,
Like melting snow upon some craggy hill,
     Drop, drop, drop, drop,
Since nature's pride is now a withered daffodil.

How should this first line be scanned? Something like this:

$$\text{Slow, slow,} \mid \text{fresh fount,} \mid \text{keep time} \mid \text{with my} \mid \text{salt tears;}$$

Here we have that rarity, a line almost completely spondaic—with only a suggestion of iambs in the third and fourth feet. An iambic pattern establishes itself gradually in the poem, but the verse is dominated by spondees, even in the short lines:

$$\text{Droop herbs and flowers;}$$

$$\text{Fall grief in showers;}$$

$$\text{Our beauties are not ours.}^1$$

In addition to this spondaic domination, the lines are frequently broken by pauses—those indicated by the punctuation, as well as those which naturally follow imperatives like "droop" and "fall." These pauses and the spondees work together to give the poem a slow, hesitant, funereal movement like the sound of muffled drums. This meter works in a metaphoric or harmonious relation to the sense of the poem, which is a direct utterance of grief over seasonal decay and the death it symbolizes.

   Now, how does this compare to the movement of the Housman poem? Housman's iambic trimeter, virtually pauseless except for line-ends, is a much lighter, almost gay meter. The stresses bounce regularly, the lines

1. These rhyme words can all be scanned as either one or two syllables.

flow smoothly, the rhymes chime insistently. This pattern establishes an ironic or contrasting relation to the mournful sense of the words, but is perfectly appropriate because the words themselves are finally ironic. Housman deals with death lightly, easily, if wryly. Jonson works hard to make us respond seriously and sadly. The frequent pauses, the heavy spondees, the varying length of the lines—all these work to reinforce the sadness and seriousness of Jonson's words. Both poems have a pronounced musical dimension, but Housman's is like a spritely ballad meter and Jonson's is like a funeral dirge.

Before considering rhyme and other sound effects further, we need to look at one last important dimension of metrics. The standard line of English verse which is meant to be spoken rather than sung is a line of five iambic feet—iambic pentameter. This is the basic line of Chaucer's *Canterbury Tales*, of Spenser's *Faerie Queene*, of Shakespeare's plays, of Milton's *Paradise Lost*, of the satires of Dryden and Pope, of Byron's *Don Juan*, of Wordsworth's *Prelude*, of Browning's *The Ring and the Book*. This line often appears unrhymed, as in Shakespeare's plays (for the most part), *Paradise Lost*, and *The Prelude*; or in pairs of rhymed lines. Technically, the unrhymed iambic pentameter line is called blank verse; the paired rhymes are called couplets. In both these iambic pentameter lines, an important element is the mid-line pause or *caesura*. Varying the location of the *caesura* is an important way of preventing monotony in blank verse and pentameter couplets. Consider, for example, these opening lines of Book II of *Paradise Lost:*

High on a Throne of Royal State, which far
Outshone the wealth of *Ormus* and of *Ind,*
Or where the gorgeous East with richest hand
Show'rs on her Kings *Barbaric* Pearl and Gold,
Satan exalted sat, by merit rais'd
To that bad eminence; and from despair
Thus high uplifted beyond hope, aspires
Beyond thus high, insatiate to pursue
Vain war with Heav'n, and by success untaught
10   His proud imaginations thus display'd.

If we locate the obvious *caesurae*—those indicated by internal punctuation marks—we find this situation:

line 1 . . . end of 4th foot
line 2 . . . none
line 3 . . . none
line 4 . . . none
line 5 . . . end of 3rd foot
line 6 . . . end of 3rd foot

line 7 . . . end of 4th foot
line 8 . . . end of 2nd foot
line 9 . . . end of 2nd foot
line 10 . . . none

In reading the poem aloud, we will find ourselves pausing slightly, at some point in nearly every line, whether a pause is indicated by punctuation or not. Thus, we can mark the whole passage this way, using a single slash for a slight pause and two for a noticeable one, three for a full stop.

High on a throne of Royal State,// which far
Outshone/ the wealth of *Ormus*/ and of *Ind,*
Or where the gorgeous East/ with richest hand
Show'rs on her kings/ *Barbaric* Pearl and Gold,
Satan exalted sat,// by merit rais'd
To that bad eminence;/// and from despair
Thus high uplifted beyond hope,// aspires
Beyond thus high,// insatiate to pursue
Vain war with Heav'n,// and by success untaught
10   His proud imaginations/ thus display'd.

By varying end-stopped lines with enjambed, and deploying caesurae of varying strengths at different points in his line, Milton continually shifts his pauses to prevent the march of his lines from growing wearisome. He also uses substitute feet frequently—especially a trochee or spondee in the first foot of a line. We count three trochees and one spondee in the first feet of these ten lines. Check this count yourself.

Now consider Alexander Pope's use of enjambment, caesura, and substitution of feet in the following lines. Pope uses a tight form, with punctuation coming nearly always at the end of each couplet. These closed couplets (as opposed to enjambed or open couplets) in iambic pentameter are called "heroic" couplets because they were the standard verse form of Restoration heroic drama (but they might better be called satiric, because they have been most successful in the satiric poems of Dryden, Pope, and Samuel Johnson).

In such a tight form as the heroic couplet, great skill is needed to avoid monotony. When we read only the real masters of such a form, we tend to take such skill for granted, but it is far from easy. Here we find Pope talking about poetic blunders and poetic skill, modulating his own verse deftly to illustrate the points he is making. (The *Alexandrine* referred to is an iambic hexameter line, occasionally used for variety in English iambic pentameter forms.) These two passages from Pope's "Essay on Criticism" are printed here widely spaced, to allow the student to write in his or her own scansion.

These equal syllables alone require,

Though oft the ear the open vowels tire;

While expletives their feeble aid do join;

And ten low words oft creep in one dull line:

While they ring round the same unvaried chimes,

With sure returns of still expected rhymes;

Where'er you find "the cooling western breeze,"

In the next line, it "whispers through the trees:"

If crystal streams "with pleasing murmurs creep,"

10   The reader's threatened (not in vain) with "sleep:"

Then, at the last and only couplet fraught

With some unmeaning thing they call a thought,

A needless Alexandrine ends the song

That, like a wounded snake, drags its slow length along.

True ease in writing comes from art, not chance,

As those move easiest who have learned to dance.

'Tis not enough no harshness gives offence,

The sound must seem an Echo to the sense:

Soft is the strain when Zephyr gently blows,

And the smooth stream in smoother numbers flows;

But when loud surges lash the sounding shore,

The hoarse, rough verse should like the torrent roar:

When Ajax strives some rock's vast weight to throw,

10   The line too labours, and the words move slow;

Not so, when swift Camilla scours the plain,

Flies o'er th' unbending corn, and skims along the main.

Rhyme is an important element in musical poetry, but much less so in dramatic poetry—where it can be too artificial—or in meditative poetry. Associated with rhyme as elements designed to generate a pleasure in sound which is almost purely aesthetic are such devices as alliteration and assonance. Alliteration is the repetition of the same sound at the beginning of words in the same line or adjacent lines. Assonance is the repetition of vowel sounds in the same or adjacent lines. For full rhyme we require the same vowel sounds which end in the same consonantal sounds. "Fight" and "foot" are alliterative. "Fight" and "bike" are assonant. "Fight" and "fire" are both assonant and alliterative but do not make a rhyme. "Fight" and "bite" make a rhyme. Consider the metrical and sonic effects in this stanza of a poem by Swinburne:

Till the slow sea rise and the sheer cliff crumble,
  Till terrace and meadow the deep gulfs drink,
Till the strength of the waves of the high tides humble
  The fields that lessen, the rocks that shrink,
Here now in his triumph where all things falter,
  Stretched out on the spoils that his own hand spread,
As a god self-slain on his own strange altar,
    Death lies dead.

The meter is mainly a mixture of anapests and spondees—an exotic combination of rapid and slow feet. Can you discern any particular pattern in the way the feet are combined? Is there variation in the pattern? What do rhyme, assonance, and alliteration contribute to the pattern?

In addition to its purely aesthetic or decorative effect, designed to charm the reader out of a critical posture and into a receptive one, rhyme can be used for just the opposite effect. In satiric or comic verse, strained rhymes are often used to awaken the reader's wits and give him a comic kind of pleasure. Ogden Nash often combines strained rhymes with lines of awkwardly unequal length for especially absurd effects. But something similar can be achieved within fairly strict formal limits. In the following stanza from Byron's *Don Juan*, we find the poet using feminine and even triple rhyme with deliberate clumsiness:

'Tis pity learned virgins ever wed
  With persons of no sort of education,
Or gentlemen, who, though well born and bred,
  Grow tired of scientific conversation:
I don't choose to say much upon this head,
  I'm a plain man, and in a single station,
But—Oh! ye lords of ladies intellectual,
Inform us truly, have they not hen-peck'd you all?

The last rhyme in particular is surprising, audacious, and deliberately strained—echoing in this way the sense of the stanza. Like imagery and metrics, rhyme can be used harmoniously or ironically, to establish or to break a mood.

Before closing, we should note that it is customary to indicate the rhyme scheme of any given poetic selection by assigning letters of the alphabet to each rhyming sound, repeating each letter as the sound is repeated. The rhyme scheme of the Byron stanza we just considered would be designated this way: *abababcc,* with *a* standing for the sounds in *wed, bred,* and *head; b,* for . . . *ation;* and *c,* for . . . *ectual* and . . . *eck'd you all.* And in the Swinburne quoted just above, the rhyme scheme is simply *ababcdcd.*

Approaching a Poem

We do not, if we are honest, keep in readiness a number of different approaches to poems or to people. We try to keep our integrity. But at the same time we must recognize and accept the otherness that we face. In getting to know a person or a poem we make the kind of accommodation that we have called tact. But we do not pretend, we do not emote falsely, and we try not to make stock responses to surface qualities. We do not judge a man by his clothes or even by his skin. We do not judge a poem by words or ideas taken out of their full poetic context. We do not consider a statement in a poem without attention to its dramatic context, the overtones generated by its metaphors and ironies, the mood established by its metrics. And we try to give each element of every poem its proper weight.

Obviously, there can be no single method for treating every poem with tact. What is required is a flexible procedure through which we can begin to understand the nature of any poem. The suggestions below are intended to facilitate such a procedure. Like everything else in this book they should serve as a scaffolding only—a temporary structure inside of which the real building takes shape. Like any scaffolding, this one must be discarded as soon as it becomes constricting or loses its usefulness. Like good manners learned by rote, this procedure will never amount to anything until it is replaced by naturally tactful behavior. Then it will have served its purpose.

1. Try to grasp the expressive dimension of the poem first. This means especially getting a clear sense of the nature and situation of the speaker. What are the circumstances under which he or she says, writes, or thinks these words? Who hears them? Are they part of an ongoing action which is implied by them?

2. Consider the relative importance of the narrative-dramatic dimension and the descriptive-meditative dimension in the poem. Is the main interest psychological or philosophical—in character or in idea? Or is the poem's verbal playfulness or music its main reason for being? How do the nature of the speaker and the situation in which he speaks color the ideas and attitudes presented?

3. After you have a sense of the poem's larger, expressive dimension, re-read it with particular attention to the play of language. Consider the way that metaphor and irony color the ideas and situations. How does the language work to characterize the speaker or to color the ideas presented with shadings of attitude? How important is sheer word-play

or verbal wit in the poem? How well do the images and ideas fit together and reinforce one another in a metaphoric or ironic way?

4. Re-read the poem yet again with special attention to its musical dimension. To the extent that it seems important, analyze the relation of rhythm and rhyme to the expressive dimension of the poem.

5. Throughout this process, reading the poem aloud can be helpful in establishing emphases and locating problems. Parts of a poem that are not fully understood will prove troublesome in the reading. Questions of tone and attitude will become more insistent in oral performance. Thus, it is advisable to work toward a reading performance as a final check on the degree to which we have mastered situation, ideas, images, attitudes, and music. An expert may be able to read through a piece of piano music and hear in his mind a perfect performance of it. Most of us need to tap out the notes before we can grasp melodies, harmonies, and rhythms with any sureness. Reading poetry aloud helps us to establish our grasp of it—especially if a patient and knowledgeable teacher is there to correct our performance and encourage us to try again.

One last piece of advice, in the form of some lines by the Spanish poet Antonio Machado, translated by Robert Bly:

People possess four things
that are no good at sea
anchor, rudder, oars
and the fear of going down.

A Selection of Poets

INTRODUCTION

The poems collected here are intended as an introduction to the work of thirty-four poets. For each we have provided at least four poems: enough for a student to get some sense of how that poet uses the English language to create poetry. We have not attempted to provide translations from other languages, since a translation into English must either become a new poem or fail utterly. Poetry, as Robert Frost remarked, is what gets lost in translation.

The poets are presented in the chronological order of their birth dates. They range in time and place from William Shakespeare, who wrote his sonnets in England before the year 1590, to Michael Ondaatje, whose first volume of poetry was published in 1967. Still, this is not a "history of poetry in English." What this collection is and what it is not should be clarified here.

These selections do not constitute anyone's choice of the greatest poets writing in English. Some of the greatest, indeed, have been excluded here. Spenser, Milton, and Pope—to name but three—were omitted for the reason that most of their best work is found in long poems, and even their shorter works are inaccessible to the beginning student of poetry without a deadening amount of annotation. (Along with others not anthologized here, these three poets are, however, represented in the discussion of poetic elements just completed; and all poets represented are listed in the index.)

BALLADS

A Note on the Ballad

The ballad comes down to us from a time when few people knew how to read and write. Because ballads were transmitted orally by ballad singers, they had to be easy to remember. Consequently, in most ballads we find a four-line stanza with a simple *abcb* rhyme scheme and regular metrical pattern: usually the first and third lines are iambic tetrameter and the second and fourth are iambic trimeter, as in this stanza from "The Demon Lover":

They had not sailed a league, a league,
   A League but scarcely three,
Till altered grew his countenance,
   And raging grew the sea.

Of the older ballads here, "The Demon Lover" and "The Unquiet Grave" follow this scheme with but few variations, while "Edward" has a more complex rhyme scheme of *aabaab*, with refrains interspersed after the first and fourth lines of each stanza.

The ballad is a narrative about a single event, which is presented in a straightforward manner with attention to action. The most popular themes of the older ballads were tragic love affairs, supernatural events, and various forms of violence usually resulting in death. Some humorous ballads exist, as well as some with religious themes, but these are far outnumbered by the tragic and mournful ballads. Then as now, the news of most interest, and therefore the most likely to be remembered and passed on to be savored by others, tended to be violent or tragic. The story is presented simply and chronologically with each stanza repeating the previous one and adding another new piece to the narrative strand. This characteristic feature is called *incremental repetition*. Dialogue is frequently used to forward the action. Here, "Edward" provides the most dramatic example of the question and answer form of dialogue, while "The Unquiet Grave" and "The Demon Lover" combine narrative and dialogue. In some ballads, such as "The Streets of Laredo," we find a first-person narrator introducing the action, but this "I" is not any one particular person. Rather, this is a communal "I," an objective voice speaking for a group of people. So while the subject of a ballad may deal with a moral issue, very little moralizing occurs; and while the subject may be an emotional one, such as a tragic love affair, we find little expression of feeling.

The question of authorship of early ballads has provoked lively debate. Is "Anonymous" one author, or a group of authors? The answer might well be both; however, it's more likely that a ballad was created by one person, but in its oral transmission from place to place and person to person, each new singer added to, subtracted from, or rearranged the original material.

Consequently, in the most definitive collection of ballads we have, Francis Child's *The English and Scottish Popular Ballads*, we find that most ballads exist in more than one version. For example, there are seven versions of "The Demon Lover" ranging in length from thirty-two stanzas (Version A) to nine stanzas (Versions D and G).

The American folk ballad, represented here by "The Streets of Laredo" and "John Henry," has its roots in the many lands from which America's settlers came, bringing their musical heritages with them. As these groups settled and mingled, their music mingled as well, and the variety of ballad versions increased. Americanized versions of British or continental ballads tended to be a bit more strait-laced than their ancestors, perhaps because of the Puritan heritage of this country. For example, "The Streets of Laredo" is taken from an eighteenth-century English ballad, "The Sailor Cut Down in His Prime." In the American ballad, the dying young cowboy who has been shot knows he's "done wrong," and we can assume that his trips to "the dram house and then to the card house" mean that he got involved in a drunken barroom brawl about gambling, but the ballad is not specific about details here. The cowboy requests a romanticized funeral:

Get six jolly cowboys to carry my coffin,
Get six pretty maidens to bear up my pall,
Put bunches of roses all over my coffin,
Put roses to deaden the sods as they fall.

The English version is more specific about the young sailor's ruin and about his funeral:

His poor old father, his good old mother,
Oft-times had told him about his past life,
When along with those flash girls his money he'd squander,
And along with those flash girls he took his delight.

And now he's dead and he lies in his coffin,
Six jolly sailors shall carry him along,
And six jolly maidens shall carry white roses,
Not for to smell him as they pass him by.

While both ballads use the universal and poignant theme of the untimely death of a young person, the English version takes a more ironically humorous view toward the facts of life than does the more sentimental and melancholy American version, which is based on a very American story, one fairly common in the early West: that of the feisty young cowboy hitting town after some months on the trail, and his search for fun ending in disaster.

Where "The Streets of Laredo" refers to a general theme, "John Henry," on the other hand, has its roots in an actual event: a contest between man and machine at the Big Bend Tunnel in West Virginia about 1870. John Henry, a tall strong black railroad worker, won the contest and achieved legendary status thereby. The original form of this ballad was derived from a Scottish ballad, but in the version we have chosen here (and it is one of many), we can see the influence of West African rhythms transforming the original structure.

After you have studied this group of ballads, you might look at A. E. Housman's "Is My Team Ploughing" and W. H. Auden's "As I Walked Out One Evening" as examples of modern poets who have been influenced by the ballad form. Their use of this form is called the *literary ballad*, and its most noticeable difference lies in the reader's awareness of the shaping imagination of a single poet who is addressing a message to an educated audience.

Edward

"Why does your brand[1] sae drap wi' bluid,
    Edward, Edward,

his sword full of blood

Why does your brand sae drap wi' bluid,
    And why sae sad gang[2] ye, O?"
"O I ha'e killed my hawke sae guid,
    Mither, Mither,
O I ha'e killed my hawke sae guid,

killed something (hawk)

    And I had nae mair but he, O."

"Your hawke's bluid was never sae reid,
10   Edward, Edward,
Your hawke's bluid was never sae reid,
    My dear son I tell thee, O."
"O I ha'e killed my reid-roan steed,
    Mither, Mither,
O I ha'e killed my reid-roan steed,
    That erst was sae fair and free, O."

1. sword
2. go

"Your steed was auld, and ye ha'e got mair,
    Edward, Edward,
Your steed was auld, and ye ha'e got mair,
20   Some other dule ye drie,[3] O."
"O I ha'e killed my fader dear,
    Mither, Mither,
O I ha'e killed my fader dear,
    Alas, and wae is me, O!"

"And whatten penance wul ye drie for that,
    Edward, Edward,
And whatten penance wul ye drie for that,
    My dear son, now tell me, O?"
"I'll set my feet in yonder boat,
30   Mither, Mither,
"I'll set my feet in yonder boat,
    And I'll fare over the sea, O."

"And what wul ye do wi' your towers and your ha',
    Edward, Edward,
And what wul ye do wi' your towers and your ha',
    That were sae fair to see, O?"
"I'll let them stand tul down they fa',
    Mither, Mither,
I'll let them stand tul down they fa',
40   For here never mair maun[4] I be, O."

"And what wul ye leave to your bairns[5] and your wife,
    Edward, Edward,
And what wul ye leave to your bairns and your wife,
    When ye gang over the sea, O?"
"The warldes room,[6] let them beg thrae life,
    Mither, Mither,
The warldes room, let them beg thrae life,
    For them never mair wul I see, O."

"And what wul ye leave to your ain mither dear,
50   Edward, Edward,
And what wul ye leave to your ain mither dear,
    My dear son, now tell me, O."

3. grief you suffer
4. must
5. children
6. world's space

"The curse of hell frae me sall ye bear,
   Mither, Mither,
The curse of hell frae me sall ye bear,
   Sic[7] counsels ye gave to me, O."

7. such

The Unquiet Grave

"The wind doth blow today, my love,
   And a few small drops of rain:
I never had but one true-love,
   In cold grave she was lain.

"I'll do as much for my true-love
   As any young man may;
I'll sit and mourn all at her grave
   For a twelvemonth and a day."

The twelvemonth and a day being up,
10   The dead began to speak:
"Oh who sits weeping on my grave,
   And will not let me sleep?"

"'Tis I, my love, sits on your grave,
   And will not let you sleep;
For I crave one kiss of your clay-cold lips,
   And that is all I seek."

"You crave one kiss of my clay-cold lips;
   But my breath smells earthy strong;
If you have one kiss of my clay-cold lips,
20   Your time will not be long.

"'Tis down in yonder garden green,
   Love, where we used to walk,
The finest flower that ere was seen
   Is withered to a stalk.

"The stalk is withered dry, my love,
   So will our hearts decay;
So make yourself content, my love,
   Till God calls you away."

The Demon Lover

"Where have you been, my long lost lover,
  This seven long years and more?"
"I've been seeking gold for thee, my love,
  And riches of great store.

"Now I've come for the vows you promised me,
  You promised me long ago;"
"My former vows you must forgive,
  For I'm a wedded wife."

"I might have been married to a king's daughter,
10   Far, far ayont the sea;
But I refused the crown of gold,
  And it's all for love of thee."

 "If you might have married a king's daughter,
  Yourself you have to blame;
For I'm married to a ship's carpenter,
  And to him I have a son.

"Have you any place to put me in,
  If I with you should gang?"[1]
"I've seven brave ships upon the sea,
20   All laden to the brim.

"I'll build my love a bridge of steel,
  All for to help her o'er;
Likewise webs of silk down her side,
  To keep my love from the cold."

She took her eldest son into her arms,
  And sweetly did him kiss;
"My blessing go with you, and your father too,
  For little does he know of this."

As they were walking up the street,
30   Most beautiful for to behold,
He cast a glamour[2] o'er her face,
  And it shone like brightest gold.

1. go
2. enchantment, magic spell

As they were walking along the sea-side,
  Where his gallant ship lay in,
So ready was the chair of gold
  To welcome this lady in.

They had not sailed a league, a league,
  A league but scarcely three,
Till altered grew his countenance,
40   And raging grew the sea.

When they came to yon sea-side,
  She set her down to rest;
It's then she spied his cloven foot,
  Most bitterly she wept.

"O is it for gold that you do weep?
  Or is it for fear?
Or is it for the man you left behind
  When that you did come here?"

"It is not for gold that I do weep,
50   O no, nor yet for fear;
But it is for the man I left behind
  When that I did come here.

"O what a bright, bright hill is yon,
  That shines so clear to see?"
"O it is the hill of heaven," he said,
  "Where you shall never be."

"O what a black, dark hill is yon,
  That looks so dark to me?"
"O it is the hill of hell," he said,
60   "Where you and I shall be.

"Would you wish to see the fishes swim
  In the bottom of the sea,
Or wish to see the leaves grow green
  On the banks of Italy?"

"I hope I'll never see the fishes swim
  On the bottom of the sea,
But I hope to see the leaves grow green
  On the banks of Italy."

He took her up to the topmast high,
70   To see what she could see;
He sunk the ship in a flash of fire,
    To the bottom of the sea.

The Streets of Laredo

As I walked out in the streets of Laredo,
As I walked out in Laredo one day,
I spied a poor cowboy wrapped up in white linen,
Wrapped in white linen as cold as the clay.

Oh, beat the drums slowly, and play the fife lowly,
Play the dead march as you carry me along,
Take me to the green valley, there lay the sod o'er me,
For I'm a young cowboy, and I know I've done wrong.

Let sixteen gamblers come handle my coffin,
10   Let sixteen cowboys come sing me a song,
Take me to the graveyard, and lay the sod o'er me,
For I'm a poor cowboy, and I know I've done wrong.

It was once in the saddle I used to go dashing,
It was once in the saddle I used to go gay,
First to the dram house, and then to the card house,
Got shot in the breast, and I'm dying today.

Get six jolly cowboys to carry my coffin,
Get six pretty maidens to bear up my pall,
Put bunches of roses all over my coffin,
20   Put roses to deaden the sods as they fall.

Oh, bury me beside my knife and my six-shooter,
My spurs on my heel, my rifle by my side,
And over my coffin put a bottle of brandy,
That's the cowboy's drink, and carry me along.

We beat the drums slowly and played the fife lowly,
And bitterly wept as we bore him along,
For we all loved our comrade, so brave, young, and handsome,
We all loved our comrade, although he'd done wrong.

John Henry

When John Henry was a little babe,
   A-holding to his mama's hand,
Says, "If I live till I'm twenty-one,
   I'm going to make a steel-driving man, my babe,
   I'm going to make a steel-driving man."

When John Henry was a little boy,
   A-sitting on his father's knee,
Says, "The Big Bend Tunnel on the C. & O. Road
   Is going to be the death of me, my babe,
10   Is going to be the death of me."

John he made a steel-driving man,
   They took him to the tunnel to drive;
He drove so hard he broke his heart,
   He laid down his hammer and he died, my babe,
   He laid down his hammer and he died.

O now John Henry is a steel-driving man,
   He belongs to the steel-driving crew,
And every time his hammer comes down,
   You can see that steel walking through, my babe,
20   You can see that steel walking through.

The steam drill standing on the right-hand side,
   John Henry standing on the left;
He says, "I'll beat that steam drill down,
   Or I'll die with my hammer in my breast, my babe,
   Or I'll die with my hammer in my breast."

He placed his drill on the top of the rock,
   The steam drill standing close at hand;
He beat it down one inch and a half
   And laid down his hammer like a man, my babe,
30   And laid down his hammer like a man.

Johnny looked up to his boss-man and said,
   "O boss-man, how can it be?
For the rock is so hard and the steel is so tough,
   I can feel my muscles giving way, my babe,
   I can feel my muscles giving way."

Johnny looked down to his turner and said,
   "O turner, how can it be?

The rock is so hard and the steel is so tough
  That everybody's turning after me, my babe,
40   That everybody's turning after me."

They took poor Johnny to the steep hillside,
  He looked to his heavens above;
He says, "Take my hammer and wrap it in gold
  And give it to the girl I love, my babe,
  And give it to the girl I love."

They took his hammer and wrapped it in gold
  And gave it to Julia Ann;
And the last word John Henry said to her
  Was, "Julia, do the best you can, my babe,"
50   Was, "Julia, do the best you can."

"If I die a railroad man,
  Go bury me under the tie,
So I can hear old Number Four,
  As she goes rolling by, my babe,
  As she goes rolling by.

"If I die a railroad man,
  Go bury me under the sand,
With a pick and shovel at my head and feet,
  And a nine-pound hammer in my hand, my babe,
60   And a nine-pound hammer in my hand."

WILLIAM SHAKESPEARE
1564–1616

William Shakespeare was born into a middle-class family in the Warwick-shire market town of Stratford-on-Avon. His father, a glover by trade, was a leading citizen, holding the office of bailiff, a position equivalent to mayor. As a boy, Shakespeare attended the very strict Stratford Grammar School, where the curriculum consisted of grammar, reading, writing, and recitation done almost entirely in Latin. In 1582, when he was eighteen, Shakespeare married Anne Hathaway, but not much else is known of him until 1592, by which time he had established himself as author and playwright in the London theater world. He turned to writing poetry when an outbreak of the plague closed the London theaters from the summer of 1592 until June, 1594. Most of Shakespeare's 154 sonnets were written between 1593 and 1599, and about ten were written between then and 1609, the year of their publication. The sonnets were dedicated "To the Onlie Begetter of these ensving Sonnets Mr. W.H.," who was probably Shakespeare's patron but whose identity is not known. Nor have scholars been able to establish identities for the characters found in the sonnets: the poet's young friend of high social position who is addressed in sonnets 1–126; the "dark lady" of sonnets 127–154 who causes joy and pain for the poet; and a rival poet. Though the autobiographical mystery is tantalizing, it is probably wiser to read and enjoy the sonnets for the mastery of language and form which was to inspire so many other poets.

A Note on the Sonnet

The sonnet was invented by Italians to plague Englishmen—or so some poets have maintained. It is a special form of verse that requires a good deal of intricate rhyming—which is easier to do in Italian than in English. Nevertheless, once domesticated in the sixteenth century, the sonnet form has persisted in English poetry with surprising vigor and is still alive today, though at its lowest ebb in four hundred years. Its rules are relatively few. A fourteen-line sequence of iambic pentameter verse has become the norm, even though the early sonneteers did not always adhere to this measure. The tightest rhyme schemes require just four or five sounds, in one combination or another, at the end of all fourteen lines.

In structure, most sonnets may be seen as variations on two basic patterns—and these are patterns of thought as well as of grammar and rhyme. One pattern is called *Italian* (or *Petrarchan* after its first important practitioner), the other *English* (or *Shakespearean*). In the Petrarchan structure the poem is divided into two major units of thought, syntax, and rhyme: the first eight lines, called the *octave*, and the last six, called the *sestet*. Here is an example of a Petrarchan sonnet by an American poet of the nineteenth century: Henry Wadsworth Longfellow's "Milton."

I pace the sounding sea-beach and behold
How the voluminous billows roll and run,
Upheaving and subsiding, while the sun
Shines through their sheeted emerald far unrolled
And the ninth wave, slow gathering fold by fold
All its loose-flowing garments into one,
Plunges upon the shore, and floods the dun
Pale reach of sands, and changes them to gold.
So in majestic cadence rise and fall
The mighty undulations of thy song,
O sightless Bard, England's Mæonides!
And ever and anon, high over all
Uplifted, a ninth wave superb and strong,
Floods all the soul with its melodious seas.

Longfellow uses the octet for a single sentence that flows on—barely slowed by punctuation (a few commas)—until the mighty wave it describes breaks in the seventh and eighth lines. The sestet then turns the wave into an epic simile describing the epic poet Milton's verse. Actually, the sestet is composed of two sentences, each of three lines. The rhyme scheme is very strict. *a bb a a bb a* for the octet, and *c e d c e d* for the sestet. Thus, the rhymes, the sentence-structure, and the thought patterns all reinforce one another

John Milton (1608–1674) himself tended to work in a quite different way. Although he composed sonnets in both Italian and English, following a variety of rhyme schemes, he did not work often or comfortably in this form. His most regular sonnets are on subjects of trivial consequence, and when he wrote on a subject of great importance to him he was apt to set his syntax working against the sonnet form, just as he breaks the iambic line with heavy pauses when writing long narrative poems (as our discussion of a passage from *Paradise Lost* on pp. 420–21 indicates). Here is a sonnet that Milton wrote on his own blindness. While it is less regular than Longfellow's, it concludes with one of those "ninth wave" lines of which Longfellow wrote—a line so memorable that it has become a permanent part of the language.

When I consider how my light is spent
Ere half my days, in this dark world and wide,
And that one talent which is death to hide,
Lodged with me useless, though my soul more bent

To serve therewith my Maker, and present
My true account, lest he returning chide,
"Doth God exact day-labour, light denied?"
I fondly ask; but Patience, to prevent
That murmur, soon replies, "God doth not need
Either man's work or his own gifts; who best
Bear his mild yoke, they serve him best. His state
Is kingly. Thousands at his bidding speed
And post o'er land and ocean without rest:
They also serve who only stand and wait."

In the Shakespearean sonnet the poem's fourteen lines are divided into twelve and two, and end with a rhymed couplet. In the hands of Shakespeare himself the couplet is a potent force: the whole meaning of a poem may turn on it. The first twelve lines, as we saw in sonnet 73 (discussed on pp. 400 –1 above) may be subdivided in various ways, often into three quatrains, so that the whole poem will rhyme *abab cdcd efef gg*, and each of the four rhyming units will be a separate grammatical and conceptual unit as well—either a whole sentence or a major independent clause.

When the English borrowed (or stole) the sonnet from Italy they acquired a special "Petrarchan" subject matter along with the form. A true Petrarchan sonneteer might produce a whole sequence of sonnets—a hundred or more—devoted to a single subject matter: the poet's love for a lady who refuses to accept him as her lover. (See, for example, Sidney's sonnet 49 from *Astrophel and Stella*, quoted above, p. 406) The poet describes his sufferings at great length—his fever, chills, pallor—and the lady's beauties at similar length. Often this description takes the form of a "blazon," which is a formal recounting of said beauties, one by one: eyes, nose, lips, teeth, bosom, and so on. Relics of the blazon are found in many love poems written after the English poets had escaped the domination of Italy. Shakespeare himself toyed with the Petrarchan conventions, writing to a man about his "beauties" and refusing to depict his "mistress" in the conventional way.

The Shakespearean form has been the most popular among English poets, and they have turned it to a variety of uses, serious and frivolous. We shall give one of these poets the last word on the sonnet at this point, after a reminder to watch for the progress of the sonnet throughout this anthology, noting its transformations in the modern poets. Gerard Manley Hopkins wrote sonnets in a slightly disguised form, as the attentive reader will discover. Here is William Wordsworth's view of the sonnet, expressed in Shakespearean form. The names mentioned by Wordsworth include some Italian poets of the Middle Ages and Renaissance, and the Portugese poet Camöens, as well as England's Shakespeare, Spenser, and Milton.

Scorn not the Sonnet; Critic, you have frowned,
Mindless of its just honours; with this key
Shakespeare unlocked his heart; the melody
Of this small lute gave ease to Petrarch's wound;
A thousand times this pipe did Tasso sound;
With it Camöens soothed an exile's grief;
The Sonnet glittered a gay myrtle leaf
Amid the cypress with which Dante crowned
His visionary brow: a glow-worm lamp,
It cheered mild Spenser, called from Faery-land
To struggle through dark ways; and when a damp
Fell round the path of Milton, in his hand
The Thing became a trumpet; whence he blew
Soul-animating strains—alas, too few!

Sonnets

18

Shall I compare thee to a summer's day?
Thou art more lovely and more temperate.
Rough winds do shake the darling buds of May,
And summer's lease hath all too short a date.
Sometime too hot the eye of heaven shines,
And often is his gold complexion dimmed;
And every fair from fair sometimes declines,
By chance, or nature's changing course, untrimmed:
But thy eternal summer shall not fade
10 Nor lose possession of that fair thou ow'st,
Nor shall Death brag thou wand'rest in his shade
When in eternal lines to time thou grow'st.
  So long as men can breathe or eyes can see,
  So long lives this, and this gives life to thee.

29

When, in disgrace with Fortune and men's eyes,
I all alone beweep my outcast state,
And trouble deaf heaven with my bootless cries
And look upon myself and curse my fate,
Wishing me like to one more rich in hope,
Featured like him, like him with friends possessed,

Desiring this man's art, and that man's scope,
With what I most enjoy contented least;
Yet in these thoughts myself almost despising,
10   Haply I think on thee, and then my state,
Like to the lark at break of day arising
From sullen earth, sings hymns at heaven's gate;
　　For thy sweet love remembered such wealth brings
　　That then I scorn to change my state with kings.

35

No more be grieved at that which thou hast done.
Roses have thorns, and silver fountains mud,
Clouds and eclipses stain both moon and sun,
And loathsome canker lives in sweetest bud.
All men make faults, and even I in this,
Authorizing thy trespass with compare,
Myself corrupting, salving thy amiss,
Excusing thy sins more than thy sins are.
For to thy sensual fault I bring in sense —
10   Thy adverse party is thy advocate —
And 'gainst myself a lawful plea commence.
Such civil war is in my love and hate
　　That I an accessary needs must be
　　To that sweet thief which sourly robs from me.

55

Not marble nor the gilded monuments
Of princes shall outlive this powerful rime,
But you shall shine more bright in these contents
Than unswept stone, besmeared with sluttish time.
When wasteful war shall statues overturn,
And broils root out the work of masonry,
Nor Mars his sword nor war's quick fire shall burn
The living record of your memory.
'Gainst death and all oblivious enmity
10   Shall you pace forth; your praise shall still find room
Even in the eyes of all posterity
That wear this world out to the ending doom.
　　So, till the judgment that yourself arise,
　　You live in this, and dwell in lovers' eyes.

65

Since brass, nor stone, nor earth, nor boundless sea,
But sad mortality o'ersways their power,
How with this rage shall beauty hold a plea,
Whose action is no stronger than a flower?
O, how shall summer's honey breath hold out
Against the wrackful siege of batt'ring days,
When rocks impregnable are not so stout,
Nor gates of steel so strong but Time decays?
O fearful meditation: where, alack,
10   Shall Time's best jewel from Time's chest lie hid?
Or what strong hand can hold his swift foot back,
Or who his spoil of beauty can forbid?
    O, none, unless this miracle have might,
    That in black ink my love may still shine bright.

73

That time of year thou mayst in me behold
When yellow leaves, or none, or few, do hang
Upon those boughs which shake against the cold,
Bare ruined choirs, where late the sweet birds sang.
In me thou see'st the twilight of such day
As after sunset fadeth in the west,
Which by and by black night doth take away,
Death's second self, that seals up all in rest.
In me thou see'st the glowing of such fire
10   That on the ashes of his youth doth lie,
As the death-bed whereon it must expire,
Consumed with that which it was nourished by.
    This thou perceiv'st, which makes thy love more strong,
    To love that well which thou must leave ere long.

130

My mistress' eyes are nothing like the sun;
Coral is far more red than her lips' red;
If snow be white, why then her breasts are dun;
If hairs be wires, black wires grow on her head.
I have seen roses damasked, red and white,
But no such roses see I in her cheeks;

And in some perfumes is there more delight
Than in the breath that from my mistress reeks.
I love to hear her speak; yet well I know
10 That music hath a far more pleasing sound:
I grant I never saw a goddess go;
My mistress, when she walks, treads on the ground.
 And yet, by heaven, I think my love as rare
 As any she belied with false compare.

JOHN DONNE
1572–1631

As a young man, Donne appears to have pursued knowledge and women with equal passion—or so his earlier lyrics would have us believe. However, he may well have been more interested in flouting Elizabethan poetic conventions than in displaying his amorous adventures. Certainly he had his share of the latter, when as a young law student he was using his personal charm, wit, and learning to gain preferment in Elizabethan court circles. But his career in state affairs ended abruptly in 1601 when he eloped with the sixteen-year-old niece of Sir Thomas Egerton, whose secretary he was. Elopement was unlawful, Donne hadn't the means to support a wife and family, and until 1615, when Donne's fine sermons had made him well known, he lived on the edge of poverty. At the urging of King James, he became an Anglican priest and was one of the greatest preachers of his time. Though he achieved material security, he was not a happy man. We see in his poetry and devotional writing his constant spiritual struggle worsened by frequent illness. During his lifetime, his eloquent devotional writing was widely read, but the genius of his amorous poetry, published after his death in 1633, with its stunningly unconventional metaphors and the strong, irregular rhythms of ordinary speech, was considered "rough," and not fully appreciated until Herbert Grierson's edition of his poems appeared in 1912.

A Note on Metaphysical Poetry

We have learned to call a certain group of seventeenth-century English poets "metaphysical" because of Dr. Samuel Johnson, the eighteenth-century critic, poet, and lexicographer, who complained that these poets used strained and unnatural language in which heterogeneous ideas were "yoked by violence together." Johnson's adjective has stuck to these poets, even though his criticism of them is not always accepted. Donne, in particular, has been a favorite of modern readers, perhaps because in his work the metaphysical impulse is always colored by strong erotic or religious feeling. His love poetry is no Petrarchan ritual, nor is his religious poetry in any way perfunctory. In Donne's view, God himself, as Creator of this world and Author of the Bible, was a kind of "metaphysical" poet, too, as we can see in this quotation from one of Donne's *Devotions*, a sequence of prose meditations he wrote during a serious illness. Donne's words describe the metaphysical impulse perfectly. They are worth the close attention they require.

From Devotion 19

My God, my God, thou art a direct God, may I not say a literal God, a God that wouldst be understood literally and according to the plain sense of all that thou sayest? but thou art also (Lord, I intend it to thy glory, and let no profane misinterpreter abuse it to thy diminution), thou art a figurative, a metaphorical God too; a God in whose words there is such a height of figures, such voyages, such peregrinations to fetch remote and precious metaphors, such extensions, such spreadings, such curtains of allegories, such third heavens of hyperboles, so harmonious elocutions, so retired and so reserved expressions, so commanding persuasions, so persuading commandments, such sinews even in thy milk, and such things in thy words, as all profane authors seem of the seed of the serpent that creeps, thou art the Dove that flies. O, what words but thine can express the inexpressible texture and composition of thy word, in which to one man that argument that binds his faith to believe that to be the word of God, is the reverent simplicity of the word, and to another the majesty of the word; and in which two men equally pious may meet, and one wonder that all should not understand it, and the other as much that any man should. So, Lord, thou givest us the same earth to labour on and to lie in, a house and a grave of the same earth; so, Lord, thou givest us the same word for our satisfaction and for our inquisition, for our instruction and for our admiration too; for there are places that thy servants Hierom[1] and Augustine would scarce believe (when they grew warm by mutual letters) of one another, that they understood them, and yet both Hierom and Augustine call upon persons whom they knew to be far weaker than they thought one another (old women and young maids) to read the Scriptures, without confining them to these or those places. Neither art thou thus a figurative, a metaphorical God in thy word only, but in thy works too. The style of thy works, the phrase of thine actions, is metaphorical. The institution of thy whole worship in the old law

1. St. Jerome, like St. Augustine, one of the early Fathers of the Church

was a continual allegory; types and figures overspread all, and figures flowed into figures, and poured themselves out into farther figures; circumcision carried a figure of baptism, and baptism carries a figure of that purity which we shall have in perfection in the new Jerusalem. Neither didst thou speak and work in this language only in the time of thy prophets; but since thou spokest in thy Son it is so too. How often, how much more often, doth thy Son call himself a way, and a light, and a gate, and a vine, and bread, than the Son of God, or of man? How much oftener doth he exhibit a metaphorical Christ, than a real, a literal? This hath occasioned thine ancient servants, whose delight it was to write after thy copy, to proceed the same way in their expositions of the Scriptures, and in their composing both of public liturgies and of private prayers to thee, to make their accesses to thee in such a kind of language as thou wast pleased to speak to them, in a figurative, in a metaphorical language, in which manner I am bold to call the comfort which I receive now in this sickness in the indication of the concoction and maturity thereof, in certain clouds and recidences, which the physicians observe, a discovering of land from sea after a long and tempestuous voyage.

Love Poems

The Good Morrow

I wonder, by my troth, what thou and I
Did, till we loved? Were we not weaned till then,
But sucked on country pleasures, childishly?
Or snorted we in the seven sleepers' den?
'Twas so; but this, all pleasures fancies be.
If ever any beauty I did see,
Which I desired, and got, 'twas but a dream of thee.

And now good morrow to our waking souls,
Which watch not one another out of fear;
10   For love all love of other sights controls,
And makes one little room an everywhere.
Let sea-discoverers to new worlds have gone,
Let maps to other, worlds on worlds have shown,
Let us possess one world; each hath one, and is one.

My face in thine eye, thine in mine appears,
And true plain hearts do in the faces rest;
Where can we find two better hemispheres

Without sharp North, without declining West?
Whatever dies was not mixed equally;
20 If our two loves be one, or thou and I
Love so alike that none do slacken, none can die.

The Sun Rising

    Busy old fool, unruly sun,
      Why doest thou thus
Through windows and through curtains call on us?
Must to thy motions lovers' seasons run?
    Saucy pedantic wretch, go chide
    Late schoolboys and sour prentices,
  Go tell court-huntsmen that the king will ride,
  Call country ants to harvest offices;
Love, all alike, no season knows, nor clime,
10 Nor hours, days, months, which are the rags of time.

    Thy beams, so reverend, and strong
      Why shouldst thou think?
I could eclipse and cloud them with a wink,
But that I would not lose her sight so long;
    If her eyes have not blinded thine,
    Look, and tomorrow late tell me
  Whether both the Indias of spice and mine
  Be where thou left'st them, or lie here with me.
Ask for those kings whom thou saw'st yesterday,
20 And thou shalt hear, all here in one bed lay.

    She is all states, and all princes I;
      Nothing else is.
Princes do but play us; compared to this,
All honor's mimic, all wealth alchemy.
    Thou, sun, art half as happy as we,
    In that the world's contracted thus;
  Thine age asks ease, and since thy duties be
  To warm the world, that's done in warming us.
Shine here to us, and thou art everywhere;
30 This bed thy center is, these walls thy sphere.

The Canonization

For God's sake hold your tongue and let me love;
   Or chide my palsy or my gout,
My five gray hairs or ruined fortune flout,
    With wealth your state, your mind with arts improve,
      Take you a course, get you a place,
      Observe His Honour, or His Grace,
Or the King's real, or his stamped face
   Contemplate; what you will, approve,
   So you will let me love.

10   Alas, alas, who's injured by my love?
    What merchant's ships have my sighs drown'd?
Who says my tears have overflow'd his ground?
    When did my colds a forward spring remove?
      When did the heats which my veins fill
      Add one more to the plaguey Bill?[1]
Soldiers find wars, and Lawyers find out still
   Litigious men, which quarrels move,
   Though she and I do love.

Call us what you will, we are made such by love;
20   Call her one, me another fly,
We are tapers too, and at our own cost die,
    And we in us find th' Eagle and the Dove.
      The Phoenix[2] riddle hath more wit
      By us: we two being one, are it.
So to one neutral thing both sexes fit;
   We die and rise the same, and prove
   Mysterious by this love.

We can die by it, if not live by love,
   And if unfit for tombs and hearse
30   Our legend be, it will be fit for verse;
    And if no piece of Chronicle we prove,
      We'll build in sonnets pretty rooms;
      As well a well-wrought urn becomes
The greatest ashes, as half-acre tombs,
   And by these hymns, all shall approve
   Us *Canonized* for Love;

1. List of those dead of the plague
2. Mythical bird of no sex that lived a thousand years,
then burned itself and was reborn from the ashes

And thus invoke us: You whom reverend love
  Made one another's hermitage;
You, to whom love was peace, that now is rage;
40   Who did the whole world's soul contract, and drove
    Into the glasses of your eyes
    (So made such mirrors and such spies
That they did all to you epitomize);
    Countries, Towns, Courts: Beg from above
    A pattern of your love!

The Relic

  When my grave is broke up again
  Some second guest to entertain
  (For graves have learned that womanhead
  To be to more than one a bed)
    And he that digs it spies
A bracelet of bright hair about the bone,
    Will he not let us alone,
And think that there a loving couple lies,
Who thought that this device might be some way
10 To make their souls at the last busy day
Meet at this grave, and make a little stay?

  If this fall in a time or land
  Where mis-devotion doth command,
  Then he that digs us up will bring
  Us to the bishop and the king
    To make us relics; then
Thou shalt be a Mary Magdalen,[1] and I
    A something else thereby.
All women shall adore us, and some men;
20 And since at such time miracles are sought,
I would have that age by this paper taught
What miracles we harmless lovers wrought.

  First, we loved well and faithfully,
  Yet knew not what we loved, nor why;
  Difference of sex no more we knew
  Than our guardian angels do;
    Coming and going, we
Perchance might kiss, but not between those meals;
    Our hands ne'er touched the seals

30 Which nature, injured by late law, sets free.
These miracles we did; but now, alas,
All measure and all language I should pass,
Should I tell what a miracle she was.

1. In Christian tradition Mary Magdalene was a prostitute
who reformed to follow Jesus—which suggests that
the "something else" in the next line refers to Christ.

Holy Sonnets

10

Death, be not proud, though some have calléd thee
Mighty and dreadful, for thou are not so;
For those whom thou think'st thou dost overthrow
Die not, poor Death, nor yet canst thou kill me.
From rest and sleep, which but thy pictures be,
Much pleasure; then from thee much more must flow,
And soonest our best men with thee do go,
Rest of their bones, and soul's delivery.
Thou'art slave to fate, chance, kings, and desperate men,
10 And dost with poison, war, and sickness dwell,
And poppy'or charms can make us sleep as well
And better than thy stroke; why swell'st thou then?
One short sleep past, we wake eternally
And death shall be no more; Death, thou shalt die.

14

Batter my heart, three-personed God; for You
As yet but knock, breathe, shine, and seek to mend;
That I may rise and stand, o'erthrow me, and bend
Your force to break, blow, burn, and make me new.
I, like an usurped town, to another due,
Labor to admit You, but Oh, to no end.
Reason, Your viceroy in me, me should defend,
But is captived, and proves weak or untrue.
Yet dearly I love You, and would be loved fain,
10 But am betrothed unto Your enemy:
Divorce me, untie or break that knot again,
Take me to You, imprison me, for I,
Except You enthrall me, never shall be free,
Nor ever chaste, except You ravish me.

ROBERT HERRICK
1591–1674

Born the son of a prosperous London goldsmith, Robert Herrick was apprenticed to this trade at the age of twelve. Ten years later, however, he
went to Cambridge and received his B.A. degree in 1617. He returned to
London to pursue a literary life as admirer and pupil of the popular playwright Ben Jonson with whom he enjoyed "lyrick Feasts" (conversing and
drinking) in such taverns as The Sun and The Dog. In 1627 he entered the
priesthood of the Church of England, a common career for younger sons of
good family. Two years later, Herrick was named Vicar of Dean Priory in
Devonshire, a locale noted for its brutish peasantry, who lived mostly in
hovels, changed their clothes infrequently, and provided unpleasant subject matter for Herrick's satirical poetry. Pleasanter subjects were such inhabitants of the vicarage as Herrick's maid Prudence, his pet sparrow Phill,
and his beloved spaniel Tracie. But out of this bachelor's imagination
emerged his best subjects: the bewitching and beribboned Julias and Co-
rinnas who grace his most lyrical poetry. They dance through a pastoral
world of happy pagan ritual, gathering rosebuds and strewing them
through the dewy grass in celebration of the joys of this life, a life made the
more poignant by an awareness of the next life fast approaching.

Ousted from his vicarage in 1647 by the Puritans, Herrick returned to
London and published *Hesperides* and *Noble Numbers*. But his light, playful lyrics went unappreciated in such parlous times. When the monarchy
was restored in 1660, Herrick returned to Devonshire to quietly live out his
final years.

A Note on Cavalier Poetry

England in the seventeenth century was deeply divided both politically and
religiously. The same impulse that brought Puritans to the American
Colonies seeking religious freedom led to a Puritan rebellion against the
King and the Church of England. Commanded by Oliver Cromwell, the
Puritans deposed the King of England, Charles I, and later executed him. But
after a few decades his son, who had been in exile in France, returned to be
crowned as Charles II in 1660.

The wars of this era were aspects of a class struggle as well as of a religious
one, and they anticipated the revolutions that came a century later in
America and France. The King's strongest defenders were members of the
hereditary aristocracy, of conservative and Catholic tendencies. His opponents were drawn mainly from the rising middle class, and were more
radically Protestant, often Puritan. The greatest poet of the era was the
Puritan John Milton, but the other side was neither mute nor inglorious
when it came to verse. Those who sympathized with the King, whether they

went into exile or stayed home in England, were called "Cavaliers." Some of them wrote elegant verse, more light than serious, so that the term "Cavalier Poetry" came to refer to a kind of light lyric, often advocating a *carpe diem* attitude.

Carpe diem, a Latin phrase meaning literally "seize the day," is a familiar theme in poetry from ancient times to the present. To "seize the day" means to disregard the future, including any "hereafter," so that one might expect the poets of this theme to ignore religion. But life is not so simple. Some Cavalier poets were also men of strong religious faith, though they wrote neither religious epics nor holy sonnets.

Robert Herrick was such a poet. And the last seventeenth-century poet included in this anthology, Andrew Marvell, managed a blend of Metaphysical and Cavalier attitudes and techniques so neat and elegant that he has been classified under both headings. There is a lesson in this about classification of poetic schools in general. Such conceptual guides must never be applied too rigidly. No good poet will stay put calmly in a box. But let Herrick sum up for us his own approach to poetry, in a little poem he used as preface to a volume of his verse.

I sing of Brooks, of Blossoms, Birds, and Bowers:
Of April, May, of June, and July-Flowers.
I sing of May-poles, Hock-carts, Wassails, Wakes,
Of Bride-grooms, Brides, and of their Bridal-cakes.
I write of Youth, of Love, and have access
By these, to sing of cleanly-wantonness.
I sing of Dews, of Rains, and piece by piece
Of Balm, of Oil, of Spice, and Amber-Greece.
I sing of Times trans-shifting; and I write
10   How Roses first came red, and Lilies white.
I write of Groves, of Twilights, and I sing
The Court of Mab, and of the Fairy-King.
I write of Hell; I sing (and ever shall)
Of Heaven, and hope to have it after all.

Delight in Disorder

A sweet disorder in the dress
Kindles in clothes a wantonness.
A lawn[1] about the shoulders thrown
Into a fine distraction;

1. Fine linen (as a scarf)

An erring lace, which here and there
Enthralls the crimson stomacher[2];
A cuff neglectful, and thereby
Ribbons to flow confusedly;
A winning wave, deserving note,
In the tempestuous petticoat;
A careless shoestring, in whose tie
I see a wild civility
Do more bewitch me than when art
Is too precise in every part.

2. Separate piece for the center front of a bodice

Upon Julia's Clothes

Whenas in silks my Julia goes
Then, then (methinks) how sweetly flows
That liquefaction of her clothes.

Next, when I cast mine eyes and see
That brave vibration each way free;
O how that glittering taketh me!

To the Virgins, to Make Much of Time

Gather ye rosebuds while ye may,
    Old time is still a-flying,
And this same flower that smiles to-day,
    To-morrow will be dying.

The glorious lamp of heaven, the sun,
    The higher he's a-getting,
The sooner will his race be run,
    And nearer he's to setting.

That age is best which is the first,
    When youth and blood are warmer;
But being spent, the worse, and worst
    Times still succeed the former.

Then be not coy, but use your time,
    And while ye may, go marry;
For having lost but once your prime,
    You may for ever tarry.

Corinna's Going A-Maying[1]

Get up, get up for shame, the blooming morn
Upon her wings presents the god unshorn.[2]
    See how Aurora[3] throws her fair
    Fresh-quilted colors through the air:
    Get up, sweet-slug-a-bed, and see
    The dew bespangling herb and tree.
Each flower has wept, and bowed toward the east,
Above an hour since; yet you not drest,
    Nay! not so much as out of bed?
10   When all the birds have matins said,
    And sung their thankful hymns: 'tis sin,
    Nay, profanation to keep in
When as a thousand virgins on this day
Spring, sooner than the lark, to fetch in May.

Rise; and put on your foliage, and be seen
To come forth, like the springtime, fresh and green;
    And sweet as Flora.[4] Take no care
    For jewels for your gown, or hair:
    Fear not; the leaves will strew
20   Gems in abundance upon you:
Besides, the childhood of the day has kept,
Against[5] you come, some orient pearls[6] unwept:
    Come, and receive them while the light
    Hangs on the dew-locks of the night:
    And Titan[7] on the eastern hill
    Retires himself, or else stands still
Till you come forth. Wash, dress, be brief in praying:
Few beads[8] are best, when once we go a-Maying.

Come, my Corinna, come; and coming, mark
30 How each field turns a street; each street a park
    Made green, and trimmed with trees: see how
    Devotion gives each house a bough,
    Or branch: each porch, each door, ere this,

1. May Day observances go
back to pagan times, when
they related to fertility
rites. In Herrick's time
they continued to have a
religious or ritual overtone.
2. Apollo's locks were never cut.

3. The dawn
4. Goddess of flowers
5. Until
6. Dew
7. Sun
8. Rosary beads, prayers

An ark,[9] a tabernacle is
Made up of white-thorn neatly interwove;
As if here were those cooler shades of love.
    Can such delights be in the street,
    And open fields, and we not see 't?
    Come, we'll abroad; and let's obey
40   The proclamation made for May:
And sin no more, as we have done, by staying;
But my Corinna, come, let's go a-Maying.
There's not a budding boy, or girl, this day,
But is got up, and gone to bring in May.
    A deal of youth, ere this, is come
    Back, and with white-thorn laden home.
    Some have dispatched their cakes and cream,
    Before that we have left to dream:[10]
And some have wept, and wooed, and plighted troth,
50 And chose their priest, ere we can cast off sloth:
    Many a green[11] gown has been given;
    Many a kiss, both odd and even:
    Many a glance too has been sent
    From out the eye, Love's firmament:
Many a jest told of the keys betraying
This night, and locks picked, yet we're not a-Maying.

Come, let us go, while we are in our prime;
And take the harmless folly of the time.
    We shall grow old apace, and die
60   Before we know our liberty.
    Our life is short; and our days run
    As fast away as does the sun:
And as a vapor, or a drop of rain
Once lost, can ne'er be found again:
    So when or you or I are made
    A fable, song, or fleeting shade;
    All love, all liking, all delight
    Lies drowned with us in endless night.
Then while time serves, and we are but decaying;
70 Come, my Corinna, come, let's go a-Maying.

9. Hebrew Ark of the Covenant (see Ex. 25: 10–21)
10. Left off dreaming
11. From lying in the grass

JOHN MILTON
1608–1674

One of the most educated and learned of the major English poets, he was born in Cheapside, London, and attended Saint Paul's School, where he studied Latin and Greek and mastered many modern European languages as well as Hebrew. In 1625 he entered Christ's College, Cambridge, where he received his B.A. (1629) and M.A. (1632). Rather than study towards the ministry, he retired to his father's country home to read and to embark on a writing career. He wrote his elegy *Lycidas* in 1637 as a memorial to Edward King, his Cambridge classmate for six years who had drowned that summer. He then traveled for two years on the continent. On his return to England, he became an apologist for Cromwell, defending the decision of parliament to execute Charles I in 1649. Although he went blind in 1651, he continued his work as Latin Secretary to Cromwell's Council of State. With the Restoration of Charles II in 1660, he found himself in political disfavor and was imprisoned. Through the intervention of friends his life was spared. During his last years he completed his epic *Paradise Lost* (1667), his shorter epic *Paradise Regained* (1671), and his tragedy *Samson Agonistes* (1671).

On Shakespeare

What needs my Shakespeare for his honoured bones
The labour of an age in piled stones,
Or that his hallowed relics should be hid
Under a star-ypointing pyramid?
Dear son of memory, great heir of fame,
What need'st thou such weak witness of thy name?
Thou in our wonder and astonishment
Hast built thyself a live-long monument.
For whilst to th' shame of slow-endeavouring art,
10 Thy easy numbers flow, and that each heart
Hath from the leaves of thy unvalued book
Those Delphic lines with deep impression took;
Then thou, our fancy of itself bereaving,
Dost make us marble with too much conceiving;
And so sepùlchered in such pomp dost lie,
That kings for such a tomb would wish to die.

How Soon Hath Time

How soon hath Time, the subtle thief of youth,
   Stolen on his wing my three-and-twentieth year!
   My hasting days fly on with full career,
   But my late spring no bud or blossom show'th.
Perhaps my semblance might deceive the truth
   That I to manhood am arrived so near;
   And inward ripeness doth much less appear,
   That some more timely-happy spirits indu'th.
Yet, be it less or more, or soon or slow,
10   It shall be still in strictest measure even
   To that same lot, however mean or high,
Toward which Time leads me, and the will of Heaven.
   All is, if I have grace to use it so,
   As ever in my great Task-Master's eye.

Lycidas

*In this Monody[1] the Author bewails a learned Friend, unfortunately drowned
in his passage from Chester on the Irish Sea, 1637; and, by occasion, foretells
the ruin of our corrupted Clergy, then in their height.*

Yet once more, O ye laurels, and once more,
Ye myrtles brown, with ivy never sere,
I come to pluck your berries harsh and crude,
And with forced fingers rude
Shatter your leaves before the mellowing year.
Bitter constraint and sad occasion dear
Compels me to disturb your season due;
For Lycidas is dead, dead ere his prime,
Young Lycidas, and hath not left his peer.
10 Who would not sing for Lycidas? he knew
Himself to sing, and build the lofty rhyme.
He must not float upon his watery bier
Unwept, and welter to the parching wind,
Without the meed of some melodious tear.
   Begin, then, Sisters[2] of the sacred well

1. *Monody*: a dirge or elegy sung by a single voice. "Lycidas" was first published in a volume of commemorative verse for Edward King, a friend of Milton's from his student days at Cambridge University.
2. *Sisters . . . well*: the muses, who dance at the altar of Jove at their sacred well, Aganippe, on Mt. Helicon.

That from beneath the seat of Jove doth spring;
Begin, and somewhat loudly sweep the string.
Hence with denial vain and coy excuse:
So may some gentle Muse
20   With lucky words favour my destined urn,
And as he passes turn,
And bid fair peace be to my sable shroud!
For we were nursed upon the self-same hill,
Fed the same flock, by fountain, shade, and rill;
Together both, ere the high lawns appeared
Under the opening eyelids of the Morn,
We drove a-field, and both together heard
What time the grey-fly winds her sultry horn,
Batt'ning our flocks with the fresh dews of night,
30   Oft till the star that rose at evening bright
Toward heaven's descent had sloped his westering wheel.
Meanwhile the rural ditties were not mute,
Tempered to th' oaten flute;
Rough Satyrs danced, and Fauns with cloven heel
From the glad sound would not be absent long;
And old Damaetas[3] loved to hear our song.
   But, oh! the heavy change, now thou art gone,
Now thou art gone, and never must return!
Thee, Shepherd, thee the woods, and desert caves,
40   With wild thyme and the gadding vine o'ergrown,
And all their echoes, mourn.
The willows, and the hazel copses green,
Shall now no more be seen,
Fanning their joyous leaves to thy soft lays.
As killing as the canker to the rose,
Or taint-worm to the weanling herds that graze,
Or frost to flowers, that their gay wardrobe wear,
When first the white-thorn blows;
Such, Lycidas, thy loss to shepherd's ear.
50   Where were ye, Nymphs, when the remorseless deep
Closed o'er the head of your loved Lycidas?
For neither were ye playing on the steep,
Where your old bards, the famous Druids, lie,
Nor on the shaggy top on Mona[4] high,

3. *Damaetas*: conventional pastoral name, referring probably to a Cambridge tutor.
4. *Mona*: also known as Anglesey, an island off the northwest coast of Wales. King's ship apparently went down nearby.

Nor yet where Deva spreads her wizard stream.
Ay me! I fondly dream
Had ye been there, . . . for what could that have done?
What could the Muse[5] herself that Orpheus bore,
The Muse herself, for her enchanting son,

60   Whom universal nature did lament,
When, by the rout that made the hideous roar,
His gory visage down the stream was sent,
Down the swift Hebrus to the Lesbian shore?
    Alas! what boots it with incessant care
To tend the homely, slighted, shepherd's trade,
And strictly meditate the thankless Muse?
Were it not better done, as others use,
To sport with Amaryllis[6] in the shade,
Or with the tangles of Neaera's hair?

70   Fame is the spur that the clear spirit doth raise
(That last infirmity of noble mind)
To scorn delights, and live laborious days;
But the fair guerdon when we hope to find,
And think to burst out into sudden blaze,
Comes the blind Fury[7] with th' abhorred shears,
And slits the thin-spun life. "But not the praise,"
Phoebus[8] replied, and touched my trembling ears:
"Fame is no plant that grows on mortal soil,
Nor in the glistering foil

80   Set off to the world, nor in broad rumour lies,
But lives and spreads aloft by those pure eyes
And perfect witness of all-judging Jove;
As he pronounces lastly on each deed,
Of so much fame in heaven expect thy meed."
    O fountain Arethuse,[9] and thou honoured flood,
Smooth-sliding Mincius,[10] crowned with vocal reeds,
That strain I heard was of a higher mood.
But now my oat proceeds,
And listens to the Herald of the Sea

90   That came in Neptune's plea.
He asked the waves, and asked the felon winds,

5. Calliope the Muse of epic poetry and mother of Orpheus. Angry female votaries of Dionysus tore him to pieces and flung his head into the river Hebrus.

6. *Amaryllis*: conventional female pastoral name.

7. Atropos, third of the Fates, cuts the thread of life that is spun and measured by the other two.

8. *Phoebus*: Apollo, god of poetry.

9. *Arethuse*: fountain in Sicily, emblematic of early pastoral of Theocritus.

10. *Mincius*: river on which Virgil was born.

What hard mishap hath doomed this gentle swain?
And questioned every gust of rugged wings
That blows from off each beaked promontory.
They knew not of his story;
And sage Hippotades[11] their answer brings,
That not a blast was from his dungeon strayed;
The air was calm, and on the level brine
Sleek Panope[12] with all her sisters played,
100 It was that fatal and perfidious bark,
Built in th' eclipse, and rigged with curses dark,
That sunk so low that sacred head of thine.

    Next, Camus,[13] reverend sire, went footing slow,
His mantle hairy, and his bonnet sedge,
Inwrought with figures dim, and on the edge
Like to that sanguine flower inscribed with woe.
"Ah! who hath reft," quoth he, "my dearest pledge?"
Last came, and last did go,
The Pilot of the Galilean Lake;[14]
110 Two massy keys he bore of metals twain
(The golden opes, the iron shuts amain).
He shook his mitred locks, and stern bespake:—
"How well could I have spared for thee, young swain,
Enow of such as, for their bellies' sake,
Creep, and intrude, and climb into the fold!
Of other care they little reck'ning make
Than how to scramble at the shearers' feast,
And shove away the worthy bidden guest.
Blind mouths! that scarce themselves know how to hold
120 A sheep-hook, or have learned aught else the least
That to the faithful herdman's art belongs!
What recks it them? What need they? They are sped;
And, when they list, their lean and flashy songs
Grate on their scrannel pipes of wretched straw;
The hungry sheep look up, and are not fed,
But, swoln with wind and the rank mist they draw,
Rot inwardly, and foul contagion spread:
Besides what the grim wolf with privy paw
Daily devours apace, and nothing said.
130 But that two-handed engine at the door
Stands ready to smite once, and smite no more."

---

11. *Hippotades*: god of winds.
12. *Panope*: one of the Nereids or sea-nymphs.
13. *Camus*: the god of the river Cam, representing Cambridge.
14. St. Peter.

Return, Alpheus,[15] the dread voice is past
That shrunk thy streams; return, Sicilian Muse,[16]
And call the vales, and bid them hither cast
Their bells and flowers of a thousand hues.
Ye valleys low, where the mild whispers use
Of shades, and wanton winds, and gushing brooks,
On whose fresh lap the swart star[17] sparely looks,
Throw hither all your quaint enamelled eyes,
140 That on the green turf suck the honied showers,
And purple all the ground with vernal flowers.
Bring the rathe primrose that forsaken dies,
The tufted crow-toe, and pale jessamine,
The white pink, and the pansy freaked with jet,
The glowing violet,
The musk-rose, and the well-attired woodbine,
With cowslips wan that hang the pensive head,
And every flower that sad embroidery wears:
Bid amaranthus all his beauty shed,
150 And daffadillies fill their cups with tears,
To strew the laureate hearse where Lycid lies.
For so, to interpose a little ease,
Let our frail thoughts dally with false surmise.
Ay me! whilst thee the shores and sounding seas
Wash far away, where'er thy bones are hurled;
Whether beyond the stormy Hebrides,
Where thou perhaps under the whelming tide
Visit'st the bottom of the monstrous world;
Or whether thou, to our moist vows denied,
160 Sleep'st by the fable of Bellerus old,
Where the great Vision of the guarded mount
Looks toward Namancos, and Bayona's hold;
Look homeward, Angel, now, and melt with ruth:
And, O ye dolphins, waft the hapless youth.
Weep no more, woeful shepherds, weep no more,
For Lycidas, your sorrow, is not dead,
Sunk though he be beneath the wat'ry floor.
So sinks the day-star in the ocean bed,
And yet anon repairs his drooping head,
170 And tricks his beams, and with new-spangled ore
Flames in the forehead of the morning sky:
So Lycidas sunk low, but mounted high,

15. *Alpheus*: Greek river god.   pastoral poetry.
16. *Sicilian Muse*: relates to Theocritan   17. Sirius, the Dog Star.

Through the dear might of Him that walked the waves;
Where, other groves and other streams along,
With nectar pure his oozy locks he laves,
And hears the unexpressive nuptial song,
In the blest kingdoms meek of joy and love.
There entertain him all the Saints above,
In solemn troops, and sweet societies,
180   That sing, and singing in their glory move,
And wipe the tears for ever from his eyes.
Now, Lycidas, the shepherds weep no more;
Henceforth thou art the Genius of the shore,
In thy large recompense, and shalt be good
To all that wander in that perilous flood.
   Thus sang the uncouth swain to th' oaks and rills,
While the still morn went out with sandals grey:
He touched the tender stops of various quills,
With eager thought warbling his Doric[18] lay:
190   And now the sun had stretched out all the hills,
And now was dropped into the western bay;
At last he rose, and twitched his mantle blue:
To-morrow to fresh woods, and pastures new.

18. *Doric*: Greek dialect of the pastoral
    poets such as Theocritus.

When I Consider How My Light Is Spent

When I consider how my light is spent,
  Ere half my days in this dark world and wide,
  And that one talent which is death to hide
  Lodged with me useless, though my soul more bent
To serve therewith my Maker, and present
  My true account, lest He returning chide;
  "Doth God exact day-labour, light denied?"
  I fondly ask: but Patience, to prevent
That murmur, soon replies, "God doth not need
10 Either man's work or his own gifts. Who best
  Bear his mild yoke, they serve him best: his state
Is kingly: thousands at his bidding speed,
  And post o'er land and ocean without rest;
  They also serve who only stand and wait."

ANDREW MARVELL
1621–1678

Andrew Marvell is an elusive figure whose life presents as many paradoxes as his poetry does. During his lifetime he was known as a public servant and politician, but not as a poet. However, during this public career he was writing a private kind of poetry, extolling pastoral solitude and the inner life of the mind. He was a Puritan, yet he wrote one of the most erotic proposals of all time, "To His Coy Mistress." Marvell was born in Winestead, near Hull, where his father was rector of the parish church. He went to Trinity College, Cambridge, at the age of twelve, and mastered six ancient languages. After his father died in 1641, we know that Marvell was a clerk in a Hull business house, and that he later travelled to Europe for four years before becoming tutor to the twelve-year-old daughter of Lord Fairfax whose garden at Nun Appleton House probably inspired the "green thoughts" of Marvell's lyrics, for he wrote prolifically during this period. In 1657, Marvell was an assistant to the blind poet John Milton, Cromwell's Latin Secretary, and in 1659, Marvell was elected to Parliament and represented Hull for the rest of his life. When his poems were published in 1681, three years after his death, they were ignored and felt to be out of date. Though his work was appreciated by later poets such as Blake, Wordsworth, and Tennyson, Marvell did not receive full critical attention until the twentieth century.

To His Coy Mistress

Had we but world enough, and time,
This coyness, lady, were no crime.
We would sit down, and think which way
To walk, and pass our long love's day.
Thou by the Indian Ganges' side
Should'st rubies find: I by the tide
Of Humber would complain. I would
Love you ten years before the Flood,
And you should, if you please, refuse
10   Till the conversion of the Jews.
My vegetable love should grow
Vaster than empires, and more slow.
An hundred years should go to praise
Thine eyes, and on thy forehead gaze;
Two hundred to adore each breast,
But thirty thousand to the rest;
An age at least to every part,

And the last age should show your heart.
For, lady, you deserve this state,
20 Nor would I love at lower rate.
    But at my back I always hear
Time's wingèd chariot hurrying near:
And yonder all before us lie
Deserts of vast eternity.
Thy beauty shall no more be found;
Nor, in thy marble vault, shall sound
My echoing song: then worms shall try
That long-preserved virginity.
And your quaint honor turn to dust,
30 And into ashes all my lust.
The grave's a fine and private place,
But none, I think, do there embrace.
    Now, therefore, while the youthful hue
Sits on thy skin like morning dew,
And while thy willing soul transpires
At every pore with instant fires,
Now let us sport us while we may;
And now, like amorous birds of prey,
Rather at once our Time devour,
40 Than languish in his slow-chapt power.
Let us roll all our strength and all
Our sweetness up into one ball,
And tear our pleasures with rough strife
Thorough the iron gates of life.
Thus, though we cannot make our sun
Stand still, yet we will make him run.

The Garden

How vainly men themselves amaze
To win the palm, the oak, or bays;
And their incessant labors see
Crowned from some single herb, or tree,
Whose short and narrow-vergèd shade
Does prudently their toils upbraid;
While all flowers and all trees do close
To weave the garlands of repose!

Fair Quiet, have I found thee here,
10 And Innocence, thy sister dear!
Mistaken long, I sought you then

In busy companies of men.
Your sacred plants, if here below,
Only among the plants will grow;
Society is all but rude
To this delicious solitude.

No white nor red was ever seen
So amorous as this lovely green.
Fond lovers, cruel as their flame,
20   Cut in these trees their mistress' name:
Little, alas! they know or heed
How far these beauties hers exceed!
Fair trees! wheres'e'er your barks I wound
No name shall but your own be found.

When we have run our passion's heat,
Love hither makes his best retreat.
The gods, that mortal beauty chase,
Still in a tree did end their race;
Apollo hunted Daphne so,
30   Only that she might laurel grow;
And Pan did after Syrinx speed,
Not as a nymph, but for a reed.

What wondrous life is this I lead!
Ripe apples drop about my head;
The luscious clusters of the vine
Upon my mouth do crush their wine;
The nectarine, and curious peach,
Into my hands themselves do reach;
Stumbling on melons, as I pass,
40   Ensnar'd with flowers, I fall on grass.

Meanwhile, the mind, from pleasure less,
Withdraws into its happiness:
The mind, that ocean where each kind
Does straight its own resemblance find;
Yet it creates, transcending these,
Far other worlds, and other seas;
Annihilating all that's made
To a green thought in a green shade.

Here at the fountain's sliding foot,
50   Or at some fruit-tree's mossy root,

Casting the body's vest aside,
My soul into the boughs does glide:
There like a bird it sits, and sings,
Then whets and combs its silver wings;
And, till prepared for longer flight,
Waves in its plumes the various light.

Such was that happy garden-state,
While man there walked without a mate:
After a place so pure and sweet,
60   What other help could yet be meet?
But 'twas beyond a mortal's share
To wander solitary there:
Two paradises 'twere in one,
To live in paradise alone.

How well the skillful gardener drew
Of flowers, and herbs, this dial new;
Where, from above, the milder sun
Does through a fragrant zodiac run;
And, as it works, the industrious bee
70   Computes its time as well as we.
How could such sweet and wholesome hours
Be reckoned but with herbs and flowers!

The Fair Singer

To make a final conquest of all me,
Love did compose so sweet an enemy,
In whom both beauties to my death agree,
Joyning themselves in fatal harmony;
That while she with her eyes my heart does bind,
She with her voice might captivate my mind.

I could have fled from one but singly fair:
My dis-intangled soul itself might save,
Breaking the curléd trammels of her hair.
10   But how should I avoid to be her slave,
Whose subtle art invisibly can wreath
My fetters of the very air I breath?

It had been easie fighting in some plain,
Where victory might hang in equal choice.
But all resistance against her is vain,

Who has th' advantage both of eyes and voice.
And all my forces needs must be undone,
She having gainéd both the wind and sun.

The Coronet

When for the thorns with which I long, too long,
    With many a piercing wound,
    My Saviour's head have crown'd
I seek with garlands to redress that wrong:
    Through every garden, every mead,
I gather flow'rs (my fruits are only flow'rs)
    Dismantling all the fragrant tow'rs
That once adorn'd my shepherdess's head.
And now when I have summed up all my store,
10   Thinking (so I my self deceive)
    So rich a chaplet thence to weave
As never yet the King of glory wore:
    Alas I find the serpent old
    That, twining in his speckled breast,
    About the flow'rs disguised does fold,
    With wreaths of fame and interest.
    Ah, foolish man, that would'st debase with them,
    And mortal glory, heaven's diadem!
    But Thou who only could'st the serpent tame
20   Either his slippery knots at once untie,
    And disintangle all his winding snare:
    Or shatter too with him my curious frame:
    And let these wither, so that he may die,
    Though set with skill and chosen out with care.
    That they, while Thou on both their spoils dost tread,
    May crown Thy feet, that could not crown Thy head.

ALEXANDER POPE
1688-1744

Born in London, the son of a linen merchant, he was privately educated. He could not, as a Roman Catholic, attend university, hold public office, or vote. Deformed by tuberculosis of the spine, he was left crookbacked and four-and-a-half feet in height. He taught himself Greek, learned French and Italian, and read extensively in English and Latin poetry. In his verse *Essay on Criticism* (1711), he outlined the ideals of the neoclassical tradition in criticism. With some of his writing friends, including Jonathan Swift and John Gay, all Tories like himself, he formed the Scriblerus Club to satirize all forms of false learning and pedantry. After his translation of the *Iliad* (1715–20), his reputation was established. He often used the epistles of Horace as models for his own verse epistles on the cultural, moral, and political malaise of his time. Translator, editor, and critic, he was a superb poet whose mastery of the heroic couplet confirmed the form as the standard for the time.

Eloïsa to Abelard[1]

Argument

Abelard and Eloisa flourished in the twelfth Century; they were two of the most distinguished persons of their age in learning and beauty, but for nothing more famous than for their unfortunate passion. After a long course of calamities, they retired each to a several Convent, and consecrated the remainder of their days to religion. It was many years after this separation, that a letter of Abelard's to a Friend, which contained the history of his misfortune, fell into the hands of Eloisa. This awakening all her tenderness, occasioned those celebrated letters (out of which the following is partly extracted) which give so lively a picture of the struggles of grace and nature, virtue and passion.

In these deep solitudes and awful cells,
Where heav'nly-pensive contemplation dwells,
And ever-musing melancholy reigns;
What means this tumult in a Vestal's veins?
Why rove my thoughts beyond this last retreat?

---

1. Peter Abelard (1079–1142), a most distinguished scholastic theologian, seduced his pupil Eloisa. She bore him a child, and they secretly married. Enraged by Abelard's actions, Eloisa's uncle had him castrated. The lovers parted, and each entered a monastery and a career of service in the Church. Their Latin letters, translated into English by John Hughes in 1713, are the immediate source of the poem. Modern scholarship has questioned the historical authenticity of the letters.

Why feels my heart its long-forgotten heat?
Yet, yet I love!—From Abelard it came,
And Eloïsa yet must kiss the name.
    Dear fatal name! rest ever unreveal'd,
Nor pass these lips in holy silence seal'd:
Hide it, my heart, within that close disguise,
Where, mix'd with God's, his lov'd Idea lies:
O write it not, my hand—the name appears
Already written—wash it out, my tears!
In vain lost Eloïsa weeps and prays,
Her heart still dictates, and her hand obeys.
    Relentless walls! whose darksome round contains
Repentant sighs, and voluntary pains:
Ye rugged rocks! which holy knees have worn;
Ye grots and caverns shagg'd with horrid thorn!
Shrines! where their vigils pale-ey'd virgins keep,
And pitying saints, whose statues learn to weep!
Tho' cold like you, unmov'd and silent grown,
I have not yet forgot myself to stone.
All is not Heav'ns while Abelard has part,
Still rebel nature holds out half my heart;
Nor pray'rs nor fasts its stubborn pulse restrain,
Nor tears, for ages, taught to flow in vain.
    Soon as thy letters trembling I unclose,
That well-known name awakens all my woes.
Oh name for ever sad! for ever dear!
Still breath'd in sighs, still usher'd with a tear.
I tremble too where'er my own I find,
Some dire misfortune follows close behind.
Line after line my gushing eyes o'erflow,
Led thro' a sad variety of woe:
Now warm in love, now with'ring in my bloom,
Lost in a convent's solitary gloom!
There stern Religion quench'd th'unwilling flame,
There dy'd the best of passions, Love and Fame.
    Yet write, oh write me all, that I may join
Griefs to thy griefs, and echo sighs to thine.
Nor foes nor fortune take this pow'r away;
And is my Abelard less kind than they?
Tears still are mine, and those I need not spare,
Love but demands what else were shed in pray'r;
No happier task these faded eyes pursue;
To read and weep is all they now can do.
    Then share thy pain, allow that sad relief;

50 Ah, more than share it! give me all thy grief.
    Heav'n first taught letters for some wretch's aid,
    Some banish'd lover, or some captive maid;
    They live, they speak, they breathe what love inspires,
    Warm from the soul, and faithful to its fires,
    The virgin's wish without her fears impart,
    Excuse the blush, and pour out all the heart,
    Speed the soft intercourse from soul to soul,
    And waft a sigh from Indus to the Pole.
        Thou know'st how guiltless first I met thy flame,
60 When Love approach'd me under Friendship's name;
    My fancy form'd thee of Angelic kind,
    Some emanation of th'all-beauteous Mind.
    Those smiling eyes, attemp'ring ev'ry ray,
    Shone sweetly lambent with celestial day:
    Guiltless I gaz'd; heav'n listen'd while you sung;
    And truths divine came mended from that tongue.[2]
    From lips like those what precept fail'd to move?
    Too soon they taught me 'twas no sin to love:
    Back thro' the paths of pleasing sense I ran,
70 Nor wish'd an Angel whom I lov'd a Man.
    Dim and remote the joys of saints I see,
    Nor envy them that heav'n I lose for thee.
        How oft, when press'd to marriage, have I said,
    Curse on all laws but those which love has made?
    Love, free as air, at sight of human ties,
    Spreads his light wings, and in a moment flies.
    Let wealth, let honour, wait the wedded dame,
    August her deed, and sacred be her fame;
    Before true passion all those views remove,
80 Fame, wealth, and honour! what are you to Love?
    The jealous God, when we profane his fires,
    Those restless passions in revenge inspires,
    And bids them make mistaken mortals groan,
    Who seek in love for aught but love alone.
    Should at my feet the world's great master fall,
    Himself, his throne, his world, I'd scorn 'em all:
    Not Caesar's empress would I deign to prove;
    No, make me mistress to the man I love;
    If there be yet another name more free,
90 More fond than mistress, make me that to thee!

    2. "He was her Preceptor in Philosophy
       and Divinity" [Pope's note].

Oh happy state! when souls each other draw,
When love is liberty, and nature, law:
All then is full, possessing, and possess'd,
No craving void left aking in the breast:
Ev'n thought meets thought, ere from the lips it part,
And each warm wish springs mutual from the heart.
This sure is bliss (if bliss on earth there be)
And once the lot of Abelard and me.
    Alas how chang'd! what sudden horrors rise!
100 A naked Lover bound and bleeding lies!
Where, where was Eloïse? her voice, her hand,
Her ponyard, had oppos'd the dire command.
Barbarian, stay! that bloody stroke restrain;
The crime was common, common be the pain.
I can no more; by shame, by rage suppress'd,
Let tears, and burning blushes speak the rest.
    Canst thou forget that sad, that solemn day,
When victims at yon altar's foot we lay?
Canst thou forget what tears that moment fell,
110 When, warm in youth, I bade the world farewell?
As with cold lips I kiss'd the sacred veil,
The shrines all trembled, and the lamps grew pale:
Heav'n scarce believ'd the conquest it survey'd,
And Saints with wonder heard the vows I made.
Yet then, to those dread altars as I drew,
Not on the Cross my eyes were fix'd, but you:
Not grace, or zeal, love only was my call,
And if I lose thy love, I lose my all.
Come! with thy looks, thy words, relieve my woe;
120 Those still at least are left thee to bestow.
Still on that breast enamour'd let me lie,
Still drink delicious poison from thy eye,
Pant on thy lip, and to thy heart be press'd;
Give all thou canst—and let me dream the rest.
Ah no! instruct me other joys to prize,
With other beauties charm my partial eyes,
Full in my view set all the bright abode,
And make my soul quit Abelard for God.
    Ah think at least thy flock deserve thy care,
130 Plants of thy hand, and children of thy pray'r.
From the false world in early youth they fled,
By thee to mountains, wilds, and deserts led.

You rais'd these hallow'd walls;[3] the desert smil'd,
And Paradise was open'd in the Wild.
No weeping orphan saw his father's stores
Our shrines irradiate, or emblaze the floors;
No silver saints, by dying misers giv'n,
Here brib'd the rage of ill-requited heav'n:
But such plain roofs as piety could raise,
140   And only vocal with the Maker's praise.
In these lone walls (their days eternal bound)
These moss-grown domes with spiry turrets crown'd,
Where awful arches make a noon-day night,
And the dim windows shed a solemn light;
Thy eyes diffus'd a reconciling ray,
And gleams of glory brighten'd all the day.
But now no face divine contentment wears,
'Tis all blank sadness, or continual tears.
See how the force of others pray'rs I try,
150   (O pious fraud of am'rous charity!)
But why should I on others pray'rs depend?
Come thou, my father, brother, husband, friend!
Ah let thy handmaid, sister, daughter move,
And all those tender names in one, thy love!
The darksome pines that o'er yon rocks reclin'd
Wave high, and murmur to the hollow wind,
The wand'ring streams that shine between the hills,
The grots that echo to the tinkling rills,
The dying gales that pant upon the trees,
160   The lakes that quiver to the curling breeze;
No more these scenes my meditation aid,
Or lull to rest the visionary maid.
But o'er the twilight groves and dusky caves,
Long-sounding isles, and intermingled graves,
Black Melancholy sits, and round her throws
A death-like silence, and a dread repose:
Her gloomy presence saddens all the scene,
Shades ev'ry flow'r, and darkens ev'ry green,
Deepens the murmur of the falling floods,
170   And breathes a browner horror on the woods.
    Yet here for ever, ever must I stay;

3. "He founded the Monastery" [Pope's note]. In 1122 Abelard established the Paraclete, an oratory near Troyes. Seven years later, when the nunnery where Eloisa was prioress was evicted from its lands, he deeded the lands of the Paraclete to her.

Sad proof how well a lover can obey!
Death, only death, can break the lasting chain;
And here, ev'n then, shall my cold dust remain,
Here all its frailties, all its flames resign,
And wait, till 'tis no sin to mix with thine.
　　Ah wretch! believ'd the spouse of God in vain,
Confess'd within the slave of love and man.
Assist me, heav'n! but whence arose that pray'r?
180　Sprung it from piety, or from despair?
Ev'n here, where frozen chastity retires,
Love finds an altar for forbidden fires.
I ought to grieve, but cannot what I ought;
I mourn the lover, not lament the fault;
I view my crime, but kindle at the view,
Repent old pleasures, and sollicit new;
Now turn'd to heav'n, I weep my past offence,
Now think of thee, and curse my innocence.
Of all affliction taught a lover yet,
190　'Tis sure the hardest science to forget!
How shall I lose the sin, yet keep the sense,
And love th'offender, yet detest th'offence?
How the dear object from the crime remove,
Or how distinguish penitence from love?
Unequal task! a passion to resign,
For hearts so touch'd, so pierc'd, so lost as mine.
Ere such a soul regains its peaceful state,
How often must it love, how often hate!
How often hope, despair, resent, regret,
200　Conceal, disdain, — do all things but forget.
But let heav'n seize it, all at once 'tis fir'd;
Not touch'd, but rap't; not waken'd, but inspir'd!
Oh come! oh teach me nature to subdue,
Renounce my love, my life, my self — and you.
Fill my fond heart with God alone, for he
Alone can rival, can succeed to thee.
　　How happy is the blameless Vestal's lot?
The world forgetting, by the world forgot:
Eternal sun-shine of the spotless mind!
210　Each pray'r accepted, and each wish resign'd;
Labour and rest, that equal periods keep;
"Obedient slumbers that can wake and weep;"
Desires compos'd, affections ever ev'n;
Tears the delight, and sighs that waft to heav'n.
Grace shines around her with serenest beams,

And whisp'ring Angels prompt her golden dreams.
For her th'unfading rose of Eden blooms,
And wings of Seraphs shed divine perfumes,
For her the Spouse prepares the bridal ring,
220 For her white virgins Hymenæals sing;
To sounds of heav'nly harps she dies away,
And melts in visions of eternal day.
    Far other dreams my erring soul employ,
Far other raptures, of unholy joy:
When at the close of each sad, sorrowing day,
Fancy restores what vengeance snatch'd away,
Then conscience sleeps, and leaving nature free,
All my loose soul unbounded springs to thee.
O curst, dear horrors of all-conscious night!
230 How glowing guilt exalts the keen delight!
Provoking Dæmons all restraint remove,
And stir within me ev'ry source of love.
I hear thee, view thee, gaze o'er all thy charms,
And around thy phantom glue my clasping arms.
I wake:—no more I hear, no more I view,
The phantom flies me, as unkind as you.
I call aloud; it hears not what I say:
I stretch my empty arms; it glides away.
To dream once more I close my willing eyes;
240 Ye soft illusions, dear deceits, arise!
Alas, no more! methinks we wand'ring go
Thro' dreary wastes, and weep each other's woe,
Where round some mould'ring tow'r pale ivy creeps,
And low-brow'd rocks hang nodding o'er the deeps.
Sudden you mount! you beckon from the skies;
Clouds interpose, waves roar, and winds arise.
I shriek, start up, the same sad prospect find,
And wake to all the griefs I left behind.
    For thee the fates, severely kind, ordain
250 A cool suspense from pleasure and from pain;
Thy life a long, dead calm of fix'd repose;
No pulse that riots, and no blood that glows.
Still as the sea, ere winds were taught to blow,
Or moving spirit bade the waters flow;
Soft as the slumbers of a saint forgiv'n,
And mild as op'ning gleams of promis'd heav'n.
    Come, Abelard! for what hast thou to dread?
The torch of Venus burns not for the dead.
Nature stands check'd; Religion disapproves;

Ev'n thou art cold—yet Eloïsa loves.
260 Ah hopeless, lasting flames! like those that burn
To light the dead, and warm th'unfruitful urn.
     What scenes appear where're I turn my view?
The dear Ideas, where I fly, pursue,
Rise in the grove, before the altar rise,
Stain all my soul, and wanton in my eyes.
I waste the Matin lamp in sighs for thee,
Thy image steals between my God and me,
Thy voice I seem in ev'ry hymn to hear,
270 With ev'ry bead I drop too soft a tear.
When from the Censer clouds of fragrance roll,
And swelling organs lift the rising soul,
One thought of thee puts all the pomp to flight,
Priests, tapers, temples, swim before my sight:
In seas of flame my plunging soul is drown'd,
While Altars blaze, and Angels tremble round.
     While prostrate here in humble grief I lie,
Kind, virtuous drops just gath'ring in my eye,
While praying, trembling, in the dust I roll,
And dawning grace is op'ning on my soul.
280 Come, if thou dar'st, all charming as thou art!
Oppose thyself to heav'n; dispute my heart;
Come, with one glance of those deluding eyes
Blot out each bright Idea of the skies;
Take back that grace, those sorrows, and those tears,
Take back my fruitless penitence and pray'rs,
Snatch me, just mounting, from the blest abode,
Assist the fiends, and tear me from my God!
     No, fly me, fly me, far as Pole from Pole;
290 Rise Alps between us! and whole oceans roll!
Ah, come not, write not, think not once of me,
Nor share one pang of all I felt for thee.
Thy oaths I quit, thy memory resign;
Forget, renounce me, hate whate'er was mine.
Fair eyes, and tempting looks (which yet I view!)
Long lov'd, ador'd ideas, all adieu!
O Grace serene! oh virtue heav'nly fair!
Divine oblivion of low-thoughted care!
Fresh blooming Hope, gay daughter of the sky!
300 And Faith, our early immortality!
Enter, each mild, each amicable guest;
Receive, and wrap me in eternal rest!
     See in her cell sad Eloïsa spread,

Propt on some tomb, a neighbour of the dead.
In each low wind methinks a Spirit calls,
And more than Echoes talk along the walls.
Here, as I watch'd the dying lamps around,
From yonder shrine I heard a hollow sound.
"Come, sister, come! (it said, or seem'd to say)
310   Thy place is here, sad sister, come away!
Once like thyself, I trembled, wept, and pray'd,
Love's victim then, tho' now a sainted maid:
But all is calm in this eternal sleep;
Here grief forgets to groan, and love to weep,
Ev'n superstition loses ev'ry fear:
For God, not man, absolves our frailties here."
   I come, I come! prepare your roseate bow'rs,
Celestial palms, and ever-blooming flow'rs.
Thither, where sinners may have rest, I go,
320   Where flames refin'd in breasts seraphic glow.
Thou, Abelard! the last sad office pay,
And smooth my passage to the realm of day;
See my lips tremble, and my eye-balls roll,
Suck my last breath, and catch my flying soul!
Ah no—in sacred vestments may'st thou stand,
The hallow'd taper trembling in thy hand,
Present the Cross before my lifted eye,
Teach me at once, and learn of me to die.
Ah then, thy once-lov'd Eloïsa see!
330   It will be then no crime to gaze on me.
See from my cheek the transient roses fly!
See the last sparkle languish in my eye!
Till ev'ry motion, pulse, and breath be o'er;
And ev'n my Abelard belov'd no more.
O Death all-eloquent! you only prove
What dust we doat on, when 'tis man we love.
   Then too, when fate shall thy fair frame destroy,
(That cause of all my guilt, and all my joy)
In trance extatic may thy pangs be drown'd,
340   Bright clouds descend, and Angels watch thee round,
From op'ning skies may streaming glories shine,
And Saints embrace thee with a love like mine.
   May one kind grave unite each hapless name,[4]

4. "*Abelard* and *Eloisa* were interr'd in the same grave, or in monuments adjoining, in the Monastery of the *Paraclete*: He died in the year *1142*, she in *1163*" [Pope's note].

And graft my love immortal on thy fame!
Then, ages hence, when all my woes are o'er,
When this rebellious heart shall beat no more;
If ever chance two wand'ring lovers brings
To Paraclete's white walls and silver springs,
O'er the pale marble shall they join their heads,
350   And drink the falling tears each other sheds;
Then sadly say, with mutual pity mov'd,
"Oh may we never love as these have lov'd!"
From the full choir when loud Hosannas rise,
And swell the pomp of dreadful sacrifice,
Amid that scene, if some relenting eye
Glance on the stone where our cold relicks lie,
Devotion's self shall steal a thought from heav'n,
One human tear shall drop, and be forgiv'n.
And sure if fate some future bard shall join
360   In sad similitude of griefs to mine,
Condemn'd whole years in absence to deplore,
And image charms he must behold no more;
Such if there be, who loves so long, so well;
Let him our sad, our tender story tell;
The well-sung woes will sooth my pensive ghost;
He best can paint 'em, who shall feel 'em most.

Epistle IV
To Richard Boyle, Earl of
Burlington

Argument

Of the Use of Riches

The Vanity of Expence in People of Wealth and Quality. The abuse of the word
Taste, v. 13. *That the first principle and foundation, in this as in everything*
else, is Good Sense, v. 40. *The chief proof of it is to* follow Nature, *even in*
works of mere Luxury and Elegance. Instanced in Architecture *and* Garden-
ing, *where all must be adapted to the* Genius *and* Use *of the* Place, *and the*
Beauties not forced into it, but resulting from it, v. 50. How men are disap-
pointed in their most expensive undertakings, for want of this true Foundation,
without which nothing can please long, *if at all; and the best* Examples *and*

Rules *will but be perverted into something* burdensome *or ridiculous, v. 65, &c. to 92. A description of the* false Taste *of* Magnificence; *the first grand Error of which is to imagine that* Greatness *consists in the* Size *and* Dimension, *instead of the* Proportion *and* Harmony *of the* whole, *v. 97, and the second, either in joining together* Parts incoherent, *or too* minutely resembling, *or in the* Repetition *of the* same *too frequently, v. 105, &c. A word or two of false Taste in* Books, *in* Music, *in* Painting, *even in* Preaching *and* Prayer, *and lastly in* Entertainments, *v. 133, &c. Yet* PROVIDENCE *is justified in giving Wealth to be squandered in this manner, since it is dispersed to the Poor and Laborious part of mankind, v. 169 [recurring to what is laid down in the first book, Ep.ii. and in the Epistle preceding this, v. 159, &c.] What are the* proper Objects *of Magnificence, and a proper field for the Expence of* Great Men, *v. 177, &c. and finally, the* Great *and* Public Works *which become a* Prince, *v. 191, to the end.*

My LORD,
The Clamour rais'd about this Epistle could not give me so much pain, as I receiv'd pleasure in seeing the general Zeal of the World in the cause of a Great Man who is Beneficent, and the particular Warmth of your Lordship in that of a private Man who is innocent.

It was not the Poem *that deserv'd this from you; for as I had the Honour to be your friend, I cou'd not treat you quite like a Poet: but sure the* Writer *deserv'd more Candor even from those who knew him not, that to promote a Report which in regard to that Noble Person, was* Impertinent; *in regard to me,* Villainous. *Yet I had no great Cause to wonder, that a Character belonging to* twenty *shou'd be applied to* one; *since, by that means,* nineteen *wou'd escape the Ridicule.*

I was too well content with my Knowledge of that Noble Person's Opinion in this Affair, to trouble the publick about it. But since Malice and Mistake are so long a dying, I take the opportunity of this third Edition to declare His Belief, not only of My Innocence, *but of* Their Malignity, *of the former of which my own Heart is as conscious, as I fear some of theirs must be of the latter. His Humanity feels a Concern for the Injury done to Me, while His Greatness of Mind can bear with Indifference the Insult offer'd to* Himself.

However, my Lord, *I own, that Critics of this Sort can intimidate me, nay half incline me to write no more: It wou'd be making the Town a Compliment which I think it deserves, and which some, I am sure, wou'd take very kindly. This way of Satire is dangerous, as long as Slander rais'd by Fools of the lowest Rank, can find any Countenance from those of a Higher. Even from the Conduct shewn on this occasion, I have learnt there are some who wou'd rather be* wicked *than* ridiculous; *and therefore it may be safer to attack* Vices *than* Follies. *I will leave my Betters in the quiet Possession of their Idols, their Groves, and their* High-Places; *and change my Subject from their* Pride *to their* Meanness, *from their* Vanities *to their* Miseries: *And as the only certain way to avoid*

Misconstruction, to lessen Offence, and not to multiply ill-natur'd Applications,
I may probably in my next make use of Real *Names and not of Fictitious Ones.*
I am,

My Lord,

Your Faithful,

Affectionate Servant,

A. POPE.

'Tis strange, the Miser should his Cares employ,
To gain those Riches he can ne'er enjoy:
Is it less strange, the Prodigal should waste
His wealth, to purchase what he ne'er can taste?
Not for himself he sees, or hears, or eats;
Artists must chuse his Pictures, Music, Meats:
He buys for Topham,[1] Drawings and Designs,
For Pembroke[2] Statues, dirty Gods, and Coins;
Rare monkish Manuscripts for Hearne[3] alone,
10   And Books for Mead, and Butterflies for Sloane.[4]
Think we all these are for himself? no more
Than his fine Wife, alas! or finer Whore.
     For what has Virro painted, built, and planted?
Only to show, how many Tastes he wanted.
What brought Sir Visto's ill got wealth to waste?
Some Daemon whisper'd, "Visto! have a Taste."
Heav'n visits with a Taste the wealthy fool,
And needs no Rod but Ripley[5] with a Rule.
See! sportive fate, to punish aukward pride,
20   Bids Bubo[6] build, and sends him such a Guide:
A standing sermon, at each year's expence,
That never Coxcomb reach'd Magnificence!
     You show us, Rome was glorious, not profuse,[7]

1. "A Gentleman famous for a judicious collection of Drawings" [Pope's note]. Richard Topham (d. 1735), Keeper of the Records in the Tower of London.
2. Thomsa Herbert (c. 1656–1733), eighth Earl of Pembroke and a Whig politician.
3. Thomas Hearne (1678–1735), a famous medievalist and medical scholar.
4. "Two eminent Physicians: the one [Richard Mead 1673–1754] had an excellent Library, the other [Sir Hans Sloane 1660–1753] the finest collection in Europe of natural curiosities; both men of great learning and humanity" [Pope's note].
5. "This man was a carpenter, employ'd by a first Minister [Sir Robert Walopole], who rais'd him to an Architect, without any genius in the art; and after some wretched proofs of his insufficiency in public Buildings, made him Comptroller of the Board of works" [Pope's note].
6. George Bubb (1691–1762), a Whig politician and literary patron.
7. "The Earl of Burlington was then publishing the Designs of Inigo Jones, and the Antiquities of Rome by Palladio" [Pope's note].

And pompous buildings once were things of Use.
Yet shall (my Lord) your just, your noble rules
Fill half the land with Imitating-Fools;
Who random drawings from your sheets shall take,
And of one beauty many blunders make;
Load some vain Church with old Theatric state,
30   Turn Arcs of triumph to a Garden-gate;
Reverse your Ornaments, and hang them all
On some patch'd dog-hole ek'd with ends of wall,
Then clap four slices of Pilaster on't,
That, lac'd with bits of rustic, makes a Front:
Or call the winds thro' long arcades to roar,
Proud to catch cold at a Venetian[8] door;
Conscious they act a true Palladian part,
And if they starve, they starve by rules of art.
    Oft have you hinted to your brother Peer,
40   A certain truth, which many buy too dear:
Something there is, more needful than Expence,
And something previous ev'n to Taste—'tis Sense:
Good Sense, which only is the gift of Heav'n,
And tho' no Science, fairly worth the seven:
A Light, which in yourself you must perceive;
Jones and Le Nôtre have it not to give.[9]
    To build, to plant, whatever you intend,
To rear the Column, or the Arch to bend,
To swell the Terras, or to sink the Grot;
50   In all, let Nature never be forgot.
But treat the Goddess like a modest fair,
Nor over-dress, nor leave her wholly bare;
Let not each beauty ev'ry where be spy'd,
Where half the skill is decently to hide.
He gains all points, who pleasingly confounds,
Surprizes, varies, and conceals the Bounds.
    Consult the Genius of the Place in all;
That tells the Waters or to rise, or fall,
Or helps th'ambitious Hill the heav'ns to scale,
60   Or scoops in circling theatres the Vale;
Calls in the Country, catches op'ning glades,
Joins willing woods, and varies shades from shades;
Now breaks, or now directs, th'intending Lines,

8. "A Door or Window, so called, from being much practised at Venice, by Palladio and others" [Pope's note].
9. "*Inigo Jones* the celebrated Architect, and M. *Le Nôtre* [1613–1700], the designer of the best Gardens of France" [Pope's note].

Paints as you plant, and as you work, designs.
　Still follow Sense, of ev'ry Art the Soul,
Parts answ'ring parts shall slide into a whole,
Spontaneous beauties all around advance,
Start ev'n from Difficulty, strike from Chance;
Nature shall join you; Time shall make it grow
70　A Work to wonder at—perhaps a STOW.[10]
　Without it, proud Versailles! thy glory falls,
And Nero's Terraces desert their walls:
The vast Parterres a thousand hands shall make,
Lo! COBHAM comes, and floats them with a Lake:
Or cut wide views thro' Mountains to the Plain,
You'll wish your hill or shelter'd seat again.
Ev'n in an ornament its place remark,
Nor in an Hermitage set Dr. Clarke.[11]
　Behold Villario's ten-years toil compleat;
80　His Arbours darken, his Espaliers meet;
The Wood supports the Plain, the parts unite,
And strength of Shade contends with strength of light:
A waving Glow the bloomy beds display,
Blushing in bright diversities of day,
With silver-quiv'ring rills mæander'd o'er—
Enjoy them, you! Villario can no more;
Tir'd of the scene Parterres and Fountains yield,
He finds at last he better likes a Field.
　Thro' his young Woods how pleas'd Sabinus stray'd
90　Or sat delighted in the thick'ning shade,
With annual joy the red'ning shoots to greet,
Or see the stretching branches long to meet.
His Son's fine Taste an op'ner Vista loves,
Foe to the Dryads of his Father's groves,
One boundless Green, or flourish'd Carpet views,[12]
With all the mournful family of Yews;[13]

10. "The seat and gardens of the Lord
Viscount Cobham in Buckingham-
shire" [Pope's note].
11. "Dr. S. Clarke's busto placed by the
Queen in the Hermitage, while the
Dr. duely frequented the Court"
[Pope's note]. Samuel Clarke (1675–
1729), a philosopher and divine.
12. "The two extremes in parterres,
which are equally faulty; a *boundless
Green*, large and naked as a field, or
a *flourished* Carpet, where the greatness and nobleness of the piece is
lessened by being divided into too
many parts, with scroll'd works and
beds, of which the examples are frequent" [Pope's note].
13. "Touches upon the ill taste of those
who are so fond of Ever-greens (particularly Yews, which are the most
tonsile) as to destroy the nobler For-
est-trees, to make way for such little
ornaments as Pyramids of darkgreen, continually repeated, not
unlike a Funeral procession" [Pope's
note].

The thriving plants ignoble broomsticks made,
Now sweep those Alleys they were born to shade.
   At Timon's Villa[14] let us pass a day,
100 Where all cry out, "What sums are thrown away!"
So proud, so grand, of that stupendous air,
Soft and Agreeable come never there.
Greatness, with Timon, dwells in such a draught
As brings all Brobdignag before your thought.
To compass this, his building is a Town,
His pond an Ocean, his parterre a Down:
Who but must laugh, the Master when he sees?
A puny insect, shiv'ring at a breeze.
Lo! what huge heaps of littleness around!
110 The whole, a labour'd Quarry above ground.
Two Cupids squirt before: a Lake behind
Improves the keenness of the Northern wind.
His Gardens next your admiration call,
On ev'ry side you look, behold the Wall!
No pleasing Intricacies intervene,
No artful wildness to perplex the scene;
Grove nods at grove, each Alley has a brother,
And half the platform just reflects the other.
The suff'ring eye inverted Nature sees,
120 Trees cut to Statues, Statues thick as trees,
With here a Fountain, never to be play'd,
And there a Summer-house, that knows no shade.
Here Amphitrite sails thro' myrtle bow'rs;
There Gladiators fight, or die, in flow'rs;[15]
Un-water'd see the drooping sea-horse mourn,
And swallows roost in Nilus' dusty Urn.
   My Lord advances with majestic mien,
Smit with the mighty pleasure, to be seen:
But soft—by regular approach—not yet—
130 First thro' the length of yon hot Terrace sweat,[16]
And when up ten steep slopes you've dragg'd your thighs,
Just at his Study-door he'll bless your eyes.

14. "This description is intended to comprize the principles of a false Taste of Magnificence, and to exemplify what was said before, that nothing but Good Sense can obtain it" [Pope's note].

15. "The two statues of the *Gladiator pugnans* and *Gladiator moriens*" [Pope's note].

16. "The *Approaches* and *Communications* of house with garden, or of one part with another, ill judged and inconvenient" [Pope's note].

His Study! with what Authors is it stor'd?[17]
In Books, not Authors, curious is my Lord;
To all their dated Backs he turns you round:
These Aldus[18] printed, those Du Suëil[19] has bound.
Lo some are Vellom, and the rest as good
For all his Lordship knows, but they are Wood.
For Locke or Milton 'tis in vain to look,
140   These shelves admit not any modern book.
    And now the Chapel's silver bell you hear,
That summons you to all the Pride of Pray'r:
Light quirks of Music, broken and uneven,[20]
Make the soul dance upon a Jig to Heav'n.
On painted Cielings you devoutly stare,[21]
Where sprawl the Saints of Verrio or Laguerre,
On gilded clouds in fair expansion lie,
And bring all Paradise before your eye.
To rest, the Cushion and soft Dean invite,
150   Who never mentions Hell to ears polite.[22]
    But hark! the chiming Clocks to dinner call;
A hundred footsteps scrape the marble Hall:
The rich Buffet well-colour'd Serpents grace,[23]
And gaping Tritons spew to wash your face.
Is this a dinner? this a Genial room?[24]
No, 'tis a Temple, and a Hecatomb,

17. "The false Taste in Books; a satyr on the vanity in collecting them, more frequent in men of Fortune than the study to understand them. Many delight chiefly in the elegance of the print, or of the binding; some have carried it so far, as to cause the upper shelves to be filled with painted books of wood; others pique themselves so much upon books in a language they do not understand as to exclude the most useful in one they do" [Pope's note].
18. Aldus Manutio (1450–1515), the Venetian printer who introduced italic type.
19. Abbé Du Suëil (1673–1746), a well-known Paris bookbinder.
20. "The false Taste in Music, improper to the subjects, as of light airs in Churches, often practised by the organists, & c." [Pope's note].
21. "Verrio [1639–1707] painted many cielings, &c. at Windsor, Hampton-court, &c., and Laguerre [1663–1721] at Blenheim-castle, and other Places" [Pope's note].
22. "This is a fact; a reverend Dean [Knightly Chetwood (1650–1720), Dean of Gloucester] preaching at Court, threatned the sinner with punishment in 'a place which he thought it not decent to name in so polite an assembly' " [Pope's note].
23. "Taxes the incongruity of Ornaments (tho' sometimes practised by the ancients) where an open mouth ejects the water into a fountain, or where the shocking images of serpents, &c. are introduced in Grottos or Buffets" [Pope's note].
24. "The proud Festivals of some men are here set forth to ridicule, where pride destroys the ease, and formal regularity all the pleasurable enjoyment of the entertainment" [Pope's note].

A solemn Sacrifice, perform'd in state,
You drink by measure, and to minutes eat.
So quick retires each flying course, you'd swear
160 Sancho's dread Doctor and his Wand were there.[25]
Between each Act the trembling salvers ring,
From soup to sweet-wine, and God bless the King.
In plenty starving, tantaliz'd in state,
And complaisantly help'd to all I hate,
Treated, caress'd, and tir'd, I take my leave,
Sick of his civil Pride from Morn to Eve;
I curse such lavish cost, and little skill,
And swear no Day was ever past so ill.
    Yet[26] hence the Poor are cloath'd, the Hungry fed;
170 Health to himself, and to his Infants bread
The Lab'rer bears: What his hard Heart denies,
His charitable Vanity supplies.
    Another age shall see the golden Ear
Imbrown the Slope, and nod on the Parterre,
Deep Harvests bury all his pride has plann'd,
And laughing Ceres re-assume the land.
    Who then shall grace, or who improve the Soil?
Who plants like BATHURST[27], or who builds like BOYLE.[28]
'Tis Use alone that sanctifies Expence,
180 And Splendor borrows all her rays from Sense.
    His Father's Acres who enjoys in peace,
Or makes his Neighbours glad, if he encrease;
Whose chearful Tenants bless their yearly toil,
Yet to their Lord owe more than to the soil;
Whose ample Lawns are not asham'd to feed
The milky heifer and deserving steed;
Whose rising Forests, not for pride or show,
But future Buildings, future Navies grow:
Let his plantations stretch from down to down,
190 First shade a Country, and then raise a Town.
    You too proceed! make falling Arts your care,

25. "See Don Quixote, chap. xlvii" [Pope's note].
26. "The *Moral* of the whole, where PROVIDENCE is justified in giving Wealth to those who squander it in this manner. A bad Taste employs more hands, and diffuses Expence more than a good one" [Pope's note].
27. Allan, Lord Bathurst (1684–1775), a landscape architect, to whom Pope addressed a later essay on the use of riches.
28. Boyle is the family name of the Earl of Burlington, to whom this poem is dedicated.

Erect new wonders, and the old repair;
Jones and Palladio to themselves restore,
And be whate'er Vitruvius[29] was before:
Till Kings call forth th' Ideas of your mind,
(Proud to accomplish what such hands design'd,)
Bid Harbours open, public Ways extend,
Bid Temples, worthier of the God, ascend,
Bid the broad Arch the dang'rous Flood contain,
200   The Mole projected break the roaring Main;
Back to his bounds their subject Sea command,
And roll obedient Rivers thro' the Land:
These Honours, Peace to happy Britain brings,
These are Imperial Works, and worthy Kings.

29. M. Vitruvius Pollio (b. 88 B.C.), a
    Roman architect and engineer.

WILLIAM BLAKE
1757–1827

Blake's wife once said, "I have very little of Mr. Blake's company. He is always in Paradise." Living with a visionary genius was probably not easy, especially for a woman who had been illiterate until her marriage, when her husband taught her to read and write. Blake, the son of a tradesman interested in the mystical ideas of Swedenborg and Jacob Boehme, was mostly self-taught, and formally schooled only in drawing. At the age of fourteen, he was apprenticed to an engraver for seven years and later supported himself with engraving and printing work. He lived most of his life in London, whose dull and ugly streets infused him with the sense of social injustice so poignantly expressed in such poems as "The Chimney-Sweeper" and "London." For Blake, the world of senses was full of symbols and a source of the metaphors in his poetry. In his earlier poetry, he turned to forms such as the ballad as inspiration for new forms and techniques. Utterly unorthodox in his religious and moral beliefs, he developed a complete mythology of his own, a radically spiritual interpretation of the Bible. He was seeking a vision which would transfigure the natural, or fallen world, revealing its correspondence with an eternal form (see "Auguries of Innocence," below). Much of his poetry was accompanied by his engravings, for he made little distinction between these two expressive forms. In his art, he refused to cater to popular taste, and his work was largely ignored by the public. Like many geniuses, he seemed not to belong to his time or place, and though he battled with poverty much of his life, he died serene and full of joy.

A Note on Romantic Poetry

England's Romantic poets (of whom the greatest are Blake, Wordsworth, Coleridge, Byron, Keats, and Shelley) constitute the most important single influence on later poetry in English. Though the poetic style and the values of each poet may show striking differences, the Romantic poets as a group tended to be radical in their politics (in sympathy with the American and French revolutions, against royalty and slavery) and transcendental in their philosophy, seeing nature as symbolic of the Creator's presence, and natural creation as analogous to the lesser creations of imaginative human beings.

These poets were part of a larger Romantic or transcendental movement, with philosophical roots in Germany and political roots in France. In America, poets and men of letters like Emerson, Bryant, and Thoreau were a part of this same movement of mind, which strongly influenced Whitman and through him most later American poetry. We are all children of the Romantic movement, no matter how rebellious we may be.

The Clod and the Pebble

"Love seeketh not itself to please,
 Nor for itself hath any care,
 But for another gives its ease,
 And builds a heaven in hell's despair."

   So sung a little clod of clay,
   Trodden with the cattle's feet,
   But a pebble of the brook
   Warbled out these metres meet:

"Love seeketh only self to please,
10   To bind another to its delight,
   Joys in another's loss of ease,
   And builds a hell in heaven's despite."

The Chimney-Sweeper

A little black thing among the snow,
Crying "weep, weep" in notes of woe!
"Where are thy father and mother, say?"—
"They are both gone up to church to pray.

"Because I was happy upon the heath,
And smiled among the winter's snow,
They clothed me in the clothes of death,
And taught me to sing the notes of woe.

"And because I am happy, and dance and sing,
10   They think they have done me no injury,
And are gone to praise God and his Priest and King,
Who make up a heaven of our misery."

The Sick Rose

O Rose, thou art sick:
The invisible worm,
That flies in the night,
In the howling storm,

Has found out thy bed
Of crimson joy;
And his dark secret love
Does thy life destroy.

The Tyger

Tyger! Tyger! burning bright
In the forests of the night,
What immortal hand or eye
Could frame thy fearful symmetry?

In what distant deeps or skies
Burnt the fire of thine eyes?
On what wings dare he aspire?
What the hand dare seize the fire?

And what shoulder, and what art,
10 Could twist the sinews of thy heart?
And when thy heart began to beat,
What dread hand? and what dread feet?

What the hammer? what the chain?
In what furnace was thy brain?
What the anvil? what dread grasp
Dare its deadly terrors clasp?

When the stars threw down their spears,
And water'd heaven with their tears,
Did he smile his work to see?
20 Did he who made the Lamb make thee?

Tyger! Tyger! burning bright
In the forests of the night,
What immortal hand or eye,
Dare frame thy fearful symmetry?

The Lamb

Little lamb who made thee
Dost thou know who made thee
Gave thee life & bid thee feed
By the stream & o'er the mead;
Gave thee clothing of delight,
Softest clothing wooly bright;
Gave thee such a tender voice,
Making all the vales rejoice!
Little Lamb who made thee
10 Dost thou know who made thee

Little Lamb I'll tell thee,
Little Lamb I'll tell thee!
He is called by thy name,
For he calls himself a Lamb:
He is meek & he is mild,
He became a little child:
I a child & thou a lamb,
We are called by his name.
Little Lamb God bless thee.
20 Little Lamb God bless thee.

London

I wander through each charter'd[1] street,
Near where the charter'd Thames does flow,
And mark in every face I meet
Marks of weakness, marks of woe.

In every cry of every man,
In every infant's cry of fear,
In every voice in every ban,
The mind-forg'd manacles I hear.

How the chimney-sweeper's cry
10 Every blackening church appalls;
And the hapless soldier's sigh
Runs in blood down palace walls.

But most through midnight streets I hear
How the youthful harlot's curse
Blasts the new born infant's tear,
And blights with plagues the marriage hearse.

1. Pre-empted or rented

Auguries of Innocence

To see a world in a grain of sand
And a heaven in a wild flower,
Hold infinity in the palm of your hand,
And eternity in an hour.

A robin redbreast in a cage
Puts all heaven in a rage.
A dove-house filled with doves and pigeons
Shudders hell through all its regions.
A dog starved at his master's gate
10 Predicts the ruin of the state.
A horse misused upon the road
Calls to heaven for human blood.
Each outcry of the hunted hare
A fiber from the brain does tear.
A skylark wounded in the wing,
A cherubim does cease to sing;

The game cock clipped and armed for fight
Does the rising sun affright.
Every wolf's and lion's howl
20   Raises from hell a human soul.
The wild deer wandering here and there,
Keeps the human soul from care.
The lamb misused breeds public strife
And yet forgives the butcher's knife.
The bat that flits at close of eve
Has left the brain that won't believe.
The owl that calls upon the night
Speaks the unbeliever's fright.
He who shall hurt the little wren
30   Shall never be beloved by men.
He who the ox to wrath has moved
Shall never be by woman loved.
The wanton boy that kills the fly
Shall feel the spider's enmity.
He who torments the chafer's sprite
Weaves a bower in endless night.
The caterpillar on the leaf
Repeats to thee thy mother's grief.
Kill not the moth nor butterfly,
40   For the last judgment draweth nigh.
He who shall train the horse to war
Shall never pass the polar bar.
The beggar's dog and widow's cat,
Feed them and thou wilt grow fat.
The gnat that sings his summer's song
Poison gets from slander's tongue.
The poison of the snake and newt
Is the sweat of envy's foot.
The poison of the honey bee
50   Is the artist's jealousy.
The prince's robes and beggar's rags
Are toadstools on the miser's bags.
A truth that's told with bad intent
Beats all the lies you can invent.
It is right it should be so;
Man was made for joy and woe;
And when this we rightly know,
Through the world we safely go.
Joy and woe are woven fine,
60   A clothing for the soul divine;

Under every grief and pine
Runs a joy with silken twine.
The babe is more than swadling bands,
Throughout all these human lands;
Tools were made, and born were hands,
Every farmer understands.
Every tear from every eye
Becomes a babe in eternity;
This is caught by females bright,
70 And returned to its own delight.
The bleat, the bark, bellow, and roar
Are waves that beat on heaven's shore.
The babe that weeps the rod beneath
Writes revenge in realms of death.
The beggar's rags, fluttering in air,
Does to rags the heavens tear.
The soldier, armed with sword and gun,
Palsied strikes the summer's sun.
The poor man's farthing is worth more
80 Than all the gold on Afric's shore.
One mite wrung from the lab'rer's hands
Shall buy and sell the miser's lands;
Or, if protected from on high,
Does that whole nation sell and buy.
He who mocks the infant's faith
Shall be mocked in age and death.
He who shall teach the child to doubt
The rotting grave shall never get out.
He who respects the infant's faith
90 Triumphs over hell and death.
The child's toys and the old man's reasons
Are the fruits of the two seasons.
The questioner, who sits so sly
Shall never know how to reply.
He who replies to words of doubt
Doth put the light of knowledge out.
The strongest poison ever known
Came from Caesar's laurel crown.
Naught can deform the human race
100 Like to the armour's iron brace.
When gold and gems adorn the plow
To peaceful arts shall envy bow.
A riddle, or the cricket's cry,
Is to doubt a fit reply.

The emmet's inch and eagle's mile
Make lame philosophy to smile.
He who doubts from what he sees
Will ne'er believe, do what you please.
If the sun and moon should doubt,
110   They'd immediately go out.
To be in a passion you good may do,
But no good if a passion is in you.
The whore and gambler, by the state
Licensed, build that nation's fate.
The harlot's cry from street to street
Shall weave Old England's winding sheet.
The winner's shout, the loser's curse,
Dance before dead England's hearse.
Every night and every morn
120   Some to misery are born.
Every morn and every night
Some are born to sweet delight.
Some are born to sweet delight,
Some are born to endless night.
We are led to believe a lie
When we see not through the eye,
Which was born in a night to perish in a night,
When the soul slept in beams of light.
God appears, and God is light,
130   To those poor souls who dwell in night,
But does a human form display
To those who dwell in realms of day.

WILLIAM WORDSWORTH

1770–1850

Wordsworth was born and educated at the edge of the Lake District in Cumberland, England, and spent his youthful days roaming the countryside, absorbing the sights and sounds that would inspire his greatest poetry. The headmaster of his boarding school encouraged Wordsworth's early interest in poetry, an interest which deepened when he attended St. John's College, Cambridge. In 1791, after graduation, he travelled the continent, excited by the possibilities of the French Revolution. In France he met Annette Vallon, on whom he fathered a child. Forced to return to England because of financial problems, and unable to get back to France because war had broken out, his ardor for Vallon eventually cooled, and they never married. Words-worth settled with his sister Dorothy in a cottage at Racedown, and then moved to Alfoxden, Somerset, to be near Samuel Taylor Coleridge, with whom he wrote the *Lyrical Ballads*. The *Ballads* signalled a new trend in poetry, a break with the neoclassical tradition. Subjects for poetry, accord-ing to Wordsworth, should be "incidents and situations from common life," and they should be written in language "really used by men," rather than in the elevated diction found in eighteenth-century poetry. Wordsworth and Dorothy eventually moved back to the Lake District, settling in Grasmere in a little house named Dove Cottage. Wordsworth married a woman he had known since childhood, and steadily acquired a reputation as an outstand-ing poet, as well as financial security. For the young Wordsworth, nature was invested with an almost divine radiance, but such vision was lost as he grew older, and in the *Immortality Ode*, Wordsworth mourns this loss and tries to take comfort "In years that bring the philosophic mind." It is gen-erally agreed that Wordsworth's best poetry was written before 1807 when his youthful experience was the source of his poetry. Much of his later po-etry is prosaic, reflecting the orthodoxy which had replaced his earlier revo-lutionary fervor. He was named poet laureate of England in 1843.

I Wandered Lonely as a Cloud

I wandered lonely as a cloud
That floats on high o'er vales and hills,
When all at once I saw a crowd,
A host, of golden daffodils;
Beside the lake, beneath the trees,
Fluttering and dancing in the breeze.

Continuous as the stars that shine
And twinkle on the milky way,
They stretched in never-ending line
10   Along the margin of a bay:
Ten thousand saw I at a glance,
Tossing their heads in sprightly dance.

The waves beside them danced; but they
Out-did the sparkling waves in glee:
A poet could not but be gay,
In such a jocund company:
I gazed—and gazed—but little thought
What wealth the show to me had brought:

For oft, when on my couch I lie
20　In vacant or in pensive mood,
They flash upon that inward eye
Which is the bliss of solitude;
And then my heart with pleasure fills,
And dances with the daffodils.

Ode

Intimations of Immortality from Recollections
of Early Childhood

> The Child is father of the Man;
> And I could wish my days to be
> Bound each to each by natural piety.

I

There was a time when meadow, grove, and stream,
The earth, and every common sight,
　　To me did seem
　　Apparelled in celestial light,
The glory and the freshness of a dream.
It is not now as it hath been of yore;—
　　Turn whereso'er I may,
　　By night or day,
The things which I have seen I now can see no more.

II

10　　The Rainbow comes and goes,
　　And lovely is the Rose,
　　The Moon doth with delight
Look round her when the heavens are bare,
　　Waters on a starry night
　　Are beautiful and fair;
　The sunshine is a glorious birth;
　But yet I know, where'er I go,
That there hath past away a glory from the earth.

III

Now, while the birds thus sing a joyous song,
20　　And while the young lambs bound
　　　As to the tabor's sound,

To me alone there came a thought of grief:
A timely utterance gave that thought relief,
    And I again am strong:
The cataracts blow their trumpets from the steep;
No more shall grief of mine the season wrong;
I hear the Echoes through the mountains throng,
The Winds come to me from the fields of sleep,
    And all the earth is gay;
30   Land and sea
  Give themselves up to jollity.
    And with the heart of May
Doth every Beast keep holiday;—
    Thou Child of Joy,
Shout round me, let me hear thy shouts, thou happy Shepherd-boy!

      IV

Ye blessèd Creatures, I have heard the call
  Ye to each other make; I see
The heavens laugh with you in your jubilee;
  My heart is at your festival,
40   My head hath its coronal,
The fulness of your bliss, I feel—I feel it all.
    Oh evil day! if I were sullen
    While Earth herself is adorning,
      This sweet May-morning,
    And the Children are culling
      On every side,
    In a thousand valleys far and wide,
    Fresh flowers; while the sun shines warm,
And the Babe leaps up on his Mother's arm:—
50   I hear, I hear, with joy I hear!
    —But there's a Tree, of many, one,
A single Field which I have looked upon,
Both of them speak of something that is gone:
    The Pansy at my feet
    Doth the same tale repeat:
Whither is fled the visionary gleam?
Where is it now, the glory and the dream?

      V

Our birth is but a sleep and a forgetting:
The Soul that rises with us, our life's Star,

60   Hath had elsewhere its setting,
          And cometh from afar:
      Not in entire forgetfulness,
      And not in utter nakedness,
  But trailing clouds of glory do we come
          From God, who is our home:
  Heaven lies about us in our infancy!
  Shades of the prison-house begin to close
          Upon the growing Boy,
  But He beholds the light, and whence it flows,
70   He sees it in his joy;
  The Youth, who daily farther from the east
          Must travel, still is Nature's Priest,
          And by the vision splendid
          Is on his way attended;
  At length the Man perceives it die away,
  And fade into the light of common day.

          VI

  Earth fills her lap with pleasures of her own;
  Yearnings she hath in her own natural kind,
  And, even with something of a Mother's mind,
80   And no unworthy aim,
          The homely Nurse doth all she can
  To make her Foster-child, her Inmate Man,
          Forget the glories he hath known,
  And that imperial palace whence he came.

          VII

  Behold the Child among his new-born blisses,
  A six years' Darling of a pigmy size!
  See, where 'mid work of his own hand he lies,
  Fretted by sallies of his mother's kisses,
  With light upon him from his father's eyes!
90 See, at his feet, some little plan or chart,
  Some fragment from his dream of human life,
  Shaped by himself with newly-learned art;
          A wedding or a festival,
          A mourning or a funeral;
              And this hath now his heart,
          And unto this he frames his song.
              Then will he fit his tongue

To dialogues of business, love, or strife;
  But it will not be long
100   Ere this be thrown aside,
   And with new joy and pride
The little Actor cons another part;
Filling from time to time his "humorous stage"
With all the Persons, down to palsied Age,
That Life brings with her in her equipage;
   As if his whole vocation
   Were endless imitation.

   VIII

Thou, whose exterior semblance doth belie
  Thy Soul's immensity;
110 Thou best Philosopher, who yet dost keep
Thy heritage, thou Eye among the blind,
That, deaf and silent, read'st the eternal deep,
Haunted for ever by the eternal mind, —
   Mighty Prophet! Seer blest!
   On whom those truths do rest,
Which we are toiling all our lives to find,
In darkness lost, the darkness of the grave,
Thou, over whom thy Immortality
Broods like the Day, a Master o'er a Slave,
120 A Presence which is not to be put by;
Thou little Child, yet glorious in the might
Of heaven-born freedom on thy being's height,
Why with such earnest pains dost thou provoke
The years to bring the inevitable yoke,
Thus blindly with thy blessedness at strife?
Full soon thy Soul shall have her earthly freight,
And custom lie upon thee with a weight,
Heavy as frost, and deep almost as life!

   IX

  O joy! that in our embers
130 Is something that doth live,
  That nature yet remembers
  What was so fugitive!
The thought of our past years in me doth breed
Perpetual benediction: not indeed
For that which is most worthy to be blest;

Delight and liberty, the simple creed
Of Childhood, whether busy or at rest,
With new-fledged hope still fluttering in his breast:—
    Not for these I raise
140   The song of thanks and praise:
    But for those obstinate questionings
    Of sense and outward things,
    Fallings from us, vanishings;
    Blank misgivings of a Creature
Moving about in worlds not realised,
High instincts before which our mortal Nature
Did tremble like a guilty Thing surprised:
    But for those first affections,
    Those shadowy recollections,
150   Which, be they what they may,
Are yet the fountain-light of all our day,
Are yet a master-light of all our seeing;
    Uphold us, cherish, and have power to make
Our noisy years seem moments in the being
Of the eternal Silence: truths that wake,
      To perish never:
Which neither listlessness, nor mad endeavour,
      Nor Man nor Boy,
Nor all that is at enmity with joy,
160 Can utterly abolish or destroy!
    Hence in a season of calm weather
      Though inland far we be,
Our Souls have sight of that immortal sea
     Which brought us hither,
    Can in a moment travel thither,
And see the Children sport upon the shore,
And hear the mighty waters rolling evermore.

     x

Then sing, ye Birds, sing, sing a joyous song!
    And let the young Lambs bound
170   As to the tabor's sound!
We in thought will join your throng,
    Ye that pipe and ye that play,
    Ye that through your hearts today
    Feel the gladness of the May!
What though the radiance which was once so bright
Be now for ever taken from my sight,

Though nothing can bring back the hour
Of splendour in the grass, of glory in the flower;
   We will grieve not, rather find
180   Strength in what remains behind;
   In the primal sympathy
   Which having been must ever be;
   In the soothing thoughts that spring
   Out of human suffering;
   In the faith that looks through death,
In years that bring the philosophic mind.

     XI

And O, ye Fountains, Meadows, Hills, and Groves,
Forebode not any severing of our loves!
Yet in my heart of hearts I feel your might;
190 I only have relinquished one delight
To live beneath your more habitual sway.
I love the Brooks which down their channels fret,
Even more than when I tripped lightly as they;
The innocent brightness of a new-born Day
   Is lovely yet;
The Clouds that gather round the setting sun
Do take a sober colouring from an eye
That hath kept watch o'er man's mortality;
Another race hath been, and other palms are won.
200 Thanks to the human heart by which we live,
Thanks to its tenderness, its joys, and tears,
To me the meanest flower that blows can give
Thoughts that do often lie too deep for tears.

Sonnets

4

Composed upon Westminster Bridge,
September 3, 1802

Earth has not anything to show more fair:
Dull would he be of soul who could pass by
A sight so touching in its majesty:
This City now doth, like a garment, wear

The beauty of the morning; silent, bare,
Ships, towers, domes, theatres, and temples lie
Open unto the fields, and to the sky;
All bright and glittering in the smokeless air.
Never did sun more beautifully steep
10 In his first splendour, valley, rock, or hill;
Ne'er saw I, never felt, a calm so deep!
The river glideth at his own sweet will:
Dear God! the very houses seem asleep;
And all that mighty heart is lying still!

14

The world is too much with us; late and soon,
Getting and spending, we lay waste our powers:
Little we see in Nature that is ours;
We have given our hearts away, a sordid boon!
This Sea that bares her bosom to the moon;
The winds that will be howling at all hours,
And are up-gathered now like sleeping flowers;
For this, for everything, we are out of tune;
It moves us not.—Great God! I'd rather be
10 A Pagan suckled in a creed outworn;
So might I, standing on this pleasant lea,
Have glimpses that would make me less forlorn;
Have sight of Proteus rising from the sea;
Or hear old Triton blow his wreathèd horn.

Lines

COMPOSED A FEW MILES ABOVE TINTERN ABBEY ON REVISITING
THE BANKS OF THE WYE DURING A TOUR. JULY 13, 1798

Five years have passed; five summers, with the length
Of five long winters! and again I hear
These waters, rolling from their mountain-springs
With a soft inland murmur. Once again
Do I behold these steep and lofty cliffs,
That on a wild secluded scene impress
Thoughts of more deep seclusion; and connect
The landscape with the quiet of the sky.

The day is come when I again repose
10   Here, under this dark sycamore, and view
These plots of cottage ground, these orchard tufts,
Which at this season, with their unripe fruits,
Are clad in one green hue, and lose themselves
'Mid groves and copses. Once again I see
These hedgerows, hardly hedgerows, little lines
Of sportive wood run wild; these pastoral farms,
Green to the very door; and wreaths of smoke
Sent up, in silence, from among the trees!
With some uncertain notice, as might seem
20   Of vagrant dwellers in the houseless woods,
Or of some Hermit's cave, where by his fire
The Hermit sits alone.

                         These beauteous forms,
Through a long absence, have not been to me
As is a landscape to a blind man's eye;
But oft, in lonely rooms, and 'mid the din
Of towns and cities, I have owed to them,
In hours of weariness, sensations sweet,
Felt in the blood, and felt along the heart;
And passing even into my purer mind,
30   With tranquil restoration—feelings too
Of unremembered pleasure; such, perhaps,
As have no slight or trivial influence
On that best portion of a good man's life,
His little, nameless, unremembered, acts
Of kindness and of love. Nor less, I trust,
To them I may have owed another gift,
Of aspect more sublime; that blessed mood,
In which the burthen of the mystery,
In which the heavy and the weary weight
40   Of all this unintelligible world,
Is lightened—that serene and blessed mood,
In which the affections gently lead us on—
Until, the breath of this corporeal frame
And even the motion of our human blood
Almost suspended, we are laid asleep
In body, and become a living soul;
While with an eye made quiet by the power
Of harmony, and the deep power of joy,
We see into the life of things.

                              If this
50   Be but a vain belief, yet, oh! how oft—
     In darkness and amid the many shapes
     Of joyless daylight; when the fretful stir
     Unprofitable, and the fever of the world,
     Have hung upon the beatings of my heart—
     How oft, in spirit, have I turned to thee,
     O sylvan Wye! thou wanderer through the woods,
     How often has my spirit turned to thee!

        And now, with gleams of half-extinguished thought,
     With many recognitions dim and faint,
60   And somewhat of a sad perplexity,
     The picture of the mind revives again;
     While here I stand, not only with the sense
     Of present pleasure, but with pleasing thoughts
     That in this moment there is life and food
     For future years. And so I dare to hope,
     Though changed, no doubt, from what I was when first
     I came among these hills; when like a roe
     I bounded o'er the mountains, by the sides
     Of the deep rivers, and the lonely streams,
70   Wherever nature led—more like a man
     Flying from something that he dreads than one
     Who sought the thing he loved. For nature then
     (The coarser pleasures of my boyish days,
     And their glad animal movements all gone by)
     To me was all in all.—I cannot paint
     What then I was. The sounding cataract
     Haunted me like a passion; the tall rock,
     The mountain, and the deep and gloomy wood,
     Their colors and their forms, were then to me
80   An appetite; a feeling and a love,
     That had no need of a remoter charm,
     By thought supplied, nor any interest
     Unborrowed from the eye.—That time is past,
     And all its aching joys are now no more,
     And all its dizzy raptures. Not for this
     Faint I, nor mourn nor murmur; other gifts
     Have followed; for such loss, I would believe,
     Abundant recompense. For I have learned
     To look on nature, not as in the hour
90   Of thoughtless youth; but hearing oftentimes
     The still, sad music of humanity,

Nor harsh nor grating, though of ample power
To chasten and subdue. And I have felt
A presence that disturbs me with the joy
Of elevated thoughts; a sense sublime
Of something far more deeply interfused,
Whose dwelling is the light of setting suns,
And the round ocean and the living air,
And the blue sky, and in the mind of man:
100 A motion and a spirit, that impels
All thinking things, all objects of all thought,
And rolls through all things. Therefore am I still
A lover of the meadows and the woods,
And mountains; and of all that we behold
From this green earth; of all the mighty world
Of eye, and ear—both what they half create,
And what perceive; well pleased to recognize
In nature and the language of the sense
The anchor of my purest thoughts, the nurse,
110 The guide, the guardian of my heart, and soul
Of all my moral being.

     Nor perchance,
If I were not thus taught, should I the more
Suffer my genial spirits to decay:
For thou art with me here upon the banks
Of this fair river; thou my dearest Friend,
My dear, dear Friend; and in thy voice I catch
The language of my former heart, and read
My former pleasures in the shooting lights
Of thy wild eyes. Oh! yet a little while
120 May I behold in thee what I was once,
My dear, dear Sister! and this prayer I make,
Knowing that Nature never did betray
The heart that loved her; 'tis her privilege,
Through all the years of this our life, to lead
From joy to joy: for she can so inform
The mind that is within us, so impress
With quietness and beauty, and so feed
With lofty thoughts, that neither evil tongues,
Rash judgments, nor the sneers of selfish men,
130 Nor greetings where no kindness is, nor all
The dreary intercourse of daily life,
Shall e'er prevail against us, or disturb
Our cheerful faith, that all which we behold

Is full of blessings. Therefore let the moon
Shine on thee in thy solitary walk;
And let the misty mountain winds be free
To blow against thee: and, in after years,
When these wild ecstasies shall be matured
Into a sober pleasure; when thy mind
140 Shall be a mansion for all lovely forms,
Thy memory be as a dwelling place
For all sweet sounds and harmonies; oh! then,
If solitude, or fear, or pain, or grief
Should be thy portion, with what healing thoughts
Of tender joy wilt thou remember me,
And these my exhortations! Nor, perchance —
If I should be where I no more can hear
Thy voice, nor catch from thy wild eyes these gleams
Of past existence — wilt thou then forget
150 That on the banks of this delightful stream
We stood together; and that I, so long
A worshiper of Nature, hither came
Unwearied in that service; rather say
With warmer love — oh! with far deeper zeal
Of holier love. Nor wilt thou then forget,
That after many wanderings, many years
Of absence, these steep woods and lofty cliffs,
And this green pastoral landscape, were to me
More dear, both for themselves and for thy sake!

JOHN KEATS
1795–1821

"Here lies one whose name was writ in water," is the epitaph Keats chose
for his gravestone. Though his life was pitifully brief, his name survives as
one of the greatest of English poets. Perhaps his creative fire burned the
more intensely because he knew he would be doomed by the tuberculosis
that had killed other members of his family. His father had died when Keats
was nine; his mother when he was fifteen, and at that time his formal
schooling came to an end. At his school in Enfield, the handsome, small but
tough boy was well-liked by his classmates, and it was during this period
that he became fascinated with the classical mythology that was to structure
much of his poetry. He was apprenticed to an apothecary-surgeon and then
continued his medical studies and was licensed to practice. But his love for
literature made him give up medicine for poetry and what was to be a dif-

ficult life. Yet during the terrible period when he was deeply in love with Fanny Brawne but too poor to marry her, when his brother Tom had just died of tuberculosis and when the symptoms of that awful disease appeared in him, he produced some of his finest poetry: the Odes and his verse romances. He died at the age of twenty-five in Rome, where he had gone in a desperate search for health in a warmer climate.

Bright Star

Bright star! would I were steadfast as thou art—
   Not in lone splendor hung aloft the night
And watching, with eternal lids apart
   Like Nature's patient sleepless Eremite,[1]
The moving waters at their priestlike task
   Of pure ablution round earth's human shores,
Or gazing on the new soft fallen mask
   Of snow upon the mountains and the moors—
No—yet still steadfast, still unchangeable,
10   Pillowed upon my fair love's ripening breast,
To feel forever its soft fall and swell,
   Awake forever in a sweet unrest,
Still, still to hear her tender-taken breath,
And so live ever—or else swoon to death

1. Religious hermit

On the Sonnet

If by dull rhymes our English must be chained,
   And, like Andromeda,[1] the Sonnet sweet
Fettered, in spite of painèd loveliness;
Let us find out, if we must be constrained,
   Sandals more interwoven and complete
To fit the naked foot of poesy;
Let us inspect the lyre, and weigh the stress
Of every chord, and see what may be gained
   By ear industrious, and attention meet;
10   Misers of sound and syllable, no less

1. Ethiopian princess chained as prey for a monster
   and rescued by Perseus, who then married her

Than Midas of his coinage, let us be
　Jealous of dead leaves in the bay-wreath crown;
So, if we may not let the Muse be free,
　She will be bound with garlands of her own.

Ode to a Nightingale

1

My heart aches, and a drowsy numbness pains
　My sense, as though of hemlock I had drunk,
Or emptied some dull opiate to the drains
　One minute past, and Lethe-wards[1] had sunk:
'Tis not through envy of thy happy lot,
　But being too happy in thine happiness,—
　　That thou, light-wingèd Dryad[2] of the trees,
　　In some melodious plot
Of beechen green, and shadows numberless,
10　Singest of summer in full-throated ease.

2

O, for a draught of vintage! that hath been
　Cool'd a long age in the deep-delved earth,
Tasting of Flora[3] and the country green,
　Dance, and Provençal song, and sunburnt mirth!
O for a beaker full of the warm South,
　Full of the true, the blushful Hippocrene,[4]
　　With beaded bubbles winking at the brim,
　　And purple-stained mouth;
That I might drink, and leave the world unseen,
20　And with thee fade away into the forest dim:

3

Fade far away, dissolve, and quite forget
　What thou among the leaves hast never known,
The weariness, the fever, and the fret
　Here, where men sit and hear each other groan;
Where palsy shakes a few, sad, last gray hairs,

1. Toward Lethe, the river of Hades whose waters cause forgetfulness
2. Wood nymph
3. Goddess of flowers: personification for flowers
4. Fountain of the Muses on Mt. Helicon

Where youth grows pale, and spectre-thin, and dies;
  Where but to think is to be full of sorrow
    And leaden-eyed despairs,
Where Beauty cannot keep her lustrous eyes,
30   Or new Love pine at them beyond tomorrow.

     4

Away! away! for I will fly to thee,
  Not charioted by Bacchus[5] and his pards,
But on the viewless wings of Poesy,
  Though the dull brain perplexes and retards:
Already with thee! tender is the night,
  And haply the Queen-Moon is on her throne,
    Cluster'd around by all her starry fays;
    But here there is no light,
Save what from heaven is with the breezes blown
40   Through verdurous glooms and winding mossy ways.

     5

I cannot see what flowers are at my feet,
  Nor what soft incense hangs upon the boughs,
But, in embalmèd darkness, guess each sweet
  Wherewith the seasonable month endows
The grass, the thicket, and the fruit-tree wild;
  White hawthorn, and the pastoral eglantine;
    Fast fading violets cover'd up in leaves;
    And mid-May's eldest child,
The coming musk-rose, full of dewy wine,
50   The murmurous haunt of flies on summer eves.

     6

Darkling I listen; and, for many a time
  I have been half in love with easeful Death,
Call'd him soft names in many a musèd rhyme,
  To take into the air my quiet breath;
Now more than ever seems it rich to die,
  To cease upon the midnight with no pain,
    While thou art pouring forth thy soul abroad
    In such an ecstasy!
Still wouldst thou sing, and I have ears in vain—
60   To thy high requiem become a sod.

5. God of wine, whose chariot is drawn by leopards

7

Thou wast not born for death, immortal Bird!
　No hungry generations tread thee down;
The voice I hear this passing night was heard
　In ancient days by emperor and clown:
Perhaps the self-same song that found a path
　　Through the sad heart of Ruth,[6] when, sick for home,
　　　She stood in tears amid the alien corn;
　　　　The same that oft-times hath
Charm'd magic casements, opening on the foam
70　　Of perilous seas, in faery lands forlorn.

8

Forlorn! the very word is like a bell
　To toll me back from thee to my sole self!
Adieu! the fancy cannot cheat so well
　As she is fam'd to do, deceiving elf.
Adieu! adieu! thy plaintive anthem fades
Past the near meadows, over the still stream,
　　Up the hill-side; and now 'tis buried deep
　　　In the next valley-glades:
Was it a vision, or a waking dream?
80　　Fled is that music:—Do I wake or sleep?

6. In the Bible, Ruth forsook her native land to live in Israel
　with Naomi, her mother-in-law.

Ode on a Grecian Urn

1

Thou still unravish'd bride of quietness,
　Thou foster-child of silence and slow time,
Sylvan historian, who canst thus express
　A flowery tale more sweetly than our rhyme:
What leaf-fring'd legend haunts about thy shape
　Of deities or mortals, or of both,
　　In Tempe[1] or the dales of Arcady?[1]

1. In Greek poetry, symbols of pastoral beauty

What men or gods are these? What maidens loth?
   What mad pursuit? What struggle to escape?
10   What pipes and timbrels?[2] What wild ecstasy?

2

Heard melodies are sweet, but those unheard
   Are sweeter; therefore, ye soft pipes, play on;
Not to the sensual ear, but, more endear'd,
   Pipe to the spirit ditties of no tone;
Fair youth, beneath the trees, thou canst not leave
   Thy song, nor ever can those trees be bare;
      Bold Lover, never, never canst thou kiss,
Though winning near the goal—yet, do not grieve;
   She cannot fade, though thou hast not thy bliss,
20   For ever wilt thou love, and she be fair!

3

Ah, happy, happy boughs! that cannot shed
   Your leaves, nor ever bid the Spring adieu;
And, happy melodist, unwearièd,
   For ever piping songs for ever new;
More happy love! more happy, happy love!
   For ever warm and still to be enjoy'd,
      For ever panting, and for ever young;
All breathing human passion far above,
   That leaves a heart high-sorrowful and cloy'd,
30   A burning forehead, and a parching tongue.

4

Who are these coming to the sacrifice?
   To what green altar, O mysterious priest,
Lead'st thou that heifer lowing at the skies,
   And all her silken flanks with garlands drest?
What little town by river or sea shore,
   Or mountain-built with peaceful citadel,
      Is emptied of this folk, this pious morn?
And, little town, thy streets for evermore
   Will silent be; and not a soul to tell
40   Why thou art desolate, can e'er return.

2. Tambourines

O Attic shape! Fair attitude! with brede
  Of marble men and maidens overwrought,
With forest branches and the trodden weed;
  Thou, silent form, dost tease us out of thought
As doth eternity: Cold Pastoral!
  When old age shall this generation waste,
    Thou shalt remain, in midst of other woe
Than ours, a friend to man, to whom thou say'st,
  "Beauty is truth, truth beauty,"—that is all
50   Ye know on earth, and all ye need to know.

Ode to Autumn

1

Season of mists and mellow fruitfulness!
  Close bosom-friend of the maturing sun;
Conspiring with him how to load and bless
  With fruit the vines that round the thatch-eaves run;
To bend with apples the moss'd cottage-trees,
  And fill all fruit with ripeness to the core;
    To swell the gourd, and plump the hazel shells
  With a sweet kernel; to set budding more
And still more, later flowers for the bees,
10 Until they think warm days will never cease;
  For summer has o'er-brimm'd their clammy cells.

2

Who hath not seen thee oft amid thy store?
  Sometimes whoever seeks abroad may find
Thee sitting careless on a granary floor,
  Thy hair soft-lifted by the winnowing wind;
Or on a half-reap'd furrow sound asleep,
  Drowsed with the fume of poppies, while thy hook
    Spares the next swath and all its twinèd flowers;
  And sometimes like a gleaner thou dost keep
20 Steady thy laden head across a brook;
  Or by a cider-press, with patient look,
  Thou watchest the last oozings, hours by hours.

3

Where are the songs of Spring? Aye, where are they?
  Think not of them,—thou hast thy music too,

While barred clouds bloom the soft-dying day
    And touch the stubble-plains with rosy hue;
Then in a wailful choir the small gnats mourn
    Among the river-sallows, borne aloft
        Or sinking as the light wind lives or dies;
30   And full-grown lambs loud bleat from hilly bourn;
Hedge-crickets sing, and now with treble soft
The redbreast whistles from a garden-croft:
    And gathering swallows twitter in the skies.

La Belle Dame sans Merci:
A Ballad

I

O what can ail thee, knight at arms,
    Alone and palely loitering?
The sedge has wither'd from the lake,
    And no birds sing.

II

O what can ail thee, knight at arms,
    So haggard and so woe-begone?
The squirrel's granary is full,
    And the harvest's done.

III

I see a lily on thy brow
10   With anguish moist and fever dew,
And on thy cheeks a fading rose
    Fast withereth too.

IV

I met a lady in the meads,
    Full beautiful, a fairy's child;
Her hair was long, her foot was light,
    And her eyes were wild.

V

I made a garland for her head,
    And bracelets too, and fragrant zone;
She look'd at me as she did love,
20   And made sweet moan.

VI

I set her on my pacing steed,
  And nothing else saw all day long,
For sidelong would she bend, and sing
    A fairy's song.

VII

She found me roots of relish sweet,
  And honey wild, and manna dew,
And sure in language strange she said—
    I love thee true.

VIII

She took me to her elfin grot,
30   And there she wept, and sigh'd full sore,
And there I shut her wild wild eyes
    With kisses four.

IX

And there she lulled me asleep,
  And there I dream'd—Ah! woe betide!
The latest dream I ever dream'd
    On the cold hill's side.

X

I saw pale kings, and princes too,
  Pale warriors, death pale were they all;
They cried—"La belle dame sans merci
40   Hath thee in thrall!"

XI

I saw their starv'd lips in the gloam
  With horrid warning gaped wide,
And I awoke and found me here
    On the cold hill's side.

XII

And this is why I sojourn here,
  Alone and palely loitering,
Though the sedge is wither'd from the lake,
    And no birds sing.

ALFRED, LORD TENNYSON

1809–1892

Tennyson was the fourth son born into an eccentric but loving family in Lincolnshire, England. Eleven children and many pets, including an owl and a monkey, filled Somersby Rectory, which was presided over by George Clayton Tennyson, a clergyman of erratic moods, and his wife Elizabeth, a gentle and beautiful woman who was so casual a housekeeper that she often forgot to order food for family meals. The house was full of books, and both parents loved poetry and often read it to their children, who at very tender ages started composing their own. Tennyson spent four miserable years at Louth Grammar School, an institution which featured thrashing as an incentive to learning. At the age of eleven he returned home to be tutored by his father. Because George Tennyson was frequently ill, Alfred escaped to roam the countryside, composing and reciting his poetry aloud, a habit he kept for the rest of his life. He went to Trinity College, Cambridge, where he became close friends with Arthur Henry Hallam, whose lively wit complemented Tennyson's shyness and melancholy humor. Hallam's sudden death at the age of twenty-two was a shock from which Tennyson never fully recovered. Some of his greatest poetry, including "Ulysses" and *In Memoriam* resulted from his struggle with grief, and with faith and doubt. After leaving Cambridge, Tennyson, who never wanted to be anything but a poet, assumed a sort of nomadic existence, inviting himself to the homes of friends in London and in the countryside. He would stay for weeks or months at a time, filling the rooms with pungent pipesmoke, composing aloud, and consuming large amounts of port. By 1850, when *In Memoriam* was published to great acclaim, and when he became poet laureate, he finally felt himself financially secure enough to marry Emily Sellwood after a fourteen-year courtship. When he died he was the most popular poet in Victorian England and America, and he was buried with his head crowned with laurel from Virgil's tomb, and a copy of Shakespeare's *Cymbeline*, the last thing he read, in his hand.

The Lady of Shalott

PART I

On either side the river lie
Long fields of barley and of rye,
That clothe the wold and meet the sky;
And through the field the road runs by
    To many-towered Camelot;
And up and down the people go,

Gazing where the lilies blow
Round an island there below,
    The island of Shalott.

10 Willows whiten, aspens quiver,
Little breezes dusk and shiver
Through the wave that runs for ever
By the island in the river
    Flowing down to Camelot.
Four gray walls, and four gray towers,
Overlook a space of flowers,
And the silent isle imbowers
    The Lady of Shalott.

By the margin, willow-veiled,
20 Slide the heavy barges trailed
By slow horses; and unhailed
The shallop flitteth silken-sailed
    Skimming down to Camelot;
But who hath seen her wave her hand?
Or at the casement seen her stand?
Or is she known in all the land,
    The Lady of Shalott?

Only reapers, reaping early
In among the bearded barley,
30 Hear a song that echoes cheerly
From the river winding clearly,
    Down to towered Camelot:
And by the moon the reaper weary,
Piling sheaves in uplands airy,
Listening, whispers " 'Tis the fairy
    Lady of Shalott."

PART II

There she weaves by night and day
A magic web with colours gay.
She has heard a whisper say,
40 A curse is on her if she stay
    To look down to Camelot.
She knows not what the curse may be,
And so she weaveth steadily,
And little other care hath she,
    The Lady of Shalott.

And moving through a mirror clear
That hangs before her all the year,
Shadows of the world appear.
There she sees the highway near
50   Winding down to Camelot;
There the river eddy whirls,
And there the surly village-churls,
And the red cloaks of market girls,
        Pass onward from Shalott.

Sometimes a troop of damsels glad,
An abbot on an ambling pad,
Sometimes a curly shepherd-lad,
Or long-haired page in crimson clad,
        Goes by to towered Camelot;
60   And sometimes through the mirror blue
The knights come riding two and two:
She hath no loyal knight and true,
        The Lady of Shalott.

But in her web she still delights
To weave the mirror's magic sights,
For often through the silent nights
A funeral, with plumes and lights
        And music, went to Camelot;
Or when the moon was overhead,
70   Came two young lovers lately wed:
"I am half sick of shadows," said
        The Lady of Shalott.

PART III

A bow-shot from her bower-eaves,
He rode between the barley-sheaves,
The sun came dazzling through the leaves,
And flamed upon the brazen greaves
        Of bold Sir Lancelot.
A red-cross knight for ever kneeled
To a lady in his shield,
80   That sparkled on the yellow field,
        Beside remote Shalott.

The gemmy bridle glittered free,
Like to some branch of stars we see
Hung in the golden Galaxy.

The bridle bells rang merrily
    As he rode down to Camelot;
And from his blazoned baldric slung
A mighty silver bugle hung,
And as he rode his armour rung,
90   Beside remote Shalott.

All in the blue unclouded weather
Thick-jewelled shone the saddle-leather,
The helmet and the helmet-feather
Burned like one burning flame together,
    As he rode down to Camelot.
As often through the purple night,
Below the starry clusters bright,
Some bearded meteor, trailing light,
    Moves over still Shalott.

100 His broad clear brow in sunlight glowed;
On burnished hooves his war-horse trode;
From underneath his helmet flowed
His coal-black curls as on he rode,
    As he rode down to Camelot.
From the bank and from the river
He flashed into the crystal mirror,
"Tirra lirra," by the river
    Sang Sir Lancelot.

She left the web, she left the loom,
110 She made three paces through the room,
She saw the water-lily bloom,
She saw the helmet and the plume,
    She looked down to Camelot.
Out flew the web and floated wide;
The mirror cracked from side to side;
"The curse is come upon me," cried
    The Lady of Shalott.

PART IV

In the stormy east-wind straining,
The pale yellow woods were waning,
120 The broad stream in his banks complaining.
Heavily the low sky raining
    Over towered Camelot;
Down she came and found a boat

Beneath a willow left afloat,
And round about the prow she wrote
 The Lady of Shalott.

And down the river's dim expanse
Like some bold seër in a trance,
Seeing all his own mischance —
130 With a glassy countenance
  Did she look to Camelot.
And at the closing of the day
She loosed the chain, and down she lay;
The broad stream bore her far away,
 The Lady of Shalott.

Lying, robed in snowy white
That loosely flew to left and right —
The leaves upon her falling light —
Through the noises of the night
140 She floated down to Camelot;
And as the boat-head wound along
The willowy hills and fields among,
They heard her singing her last song.
 The Lady of Shalott.

Heard a carol, mournful, holy,
Chanted loudly, chanted lowly,
Till her blood was frozen slowly,
And her eyes were darkened wholly,
  Turned to towered Camelot.
150 For ere she reached upon the tide
The first house by the water-side,
Singing in her song she died,
 The Lady of Shalott.

Under tower and balcony,
By garden-wall and gallery,
A gleaming shape she floated by,
Dead-pale between the houses high,
  Silent into Camelot.
Out upon the wharfs they came,
160 Knight and burgher, lord and dame,
And round the prow they read her name,
 The Lady of Shalott.

Who is this? and what is here?
And in the lightened palace near
Died the sound of royal cheer;
And they crossed themselves for fear,
 All the knights at Camelot:
But Lancelot mused a little space;
He said, "She has a lovely face;
170 God in his mercy lend her grace,
  The Lady of Shalott."

Ulysses

It little profits that an idle king,
By this still hearth, among these barren crags,
Match'd with an aged wife, I mete and dole
Unequal laws unto a savage race,
That hoard, and sleep, and feed, and know not me.
I cannot rest from travel: I will drink
Life to the lees: all times I have enjoy'd
Greatly, have suffer'd greatly, both with those
That loved me, and alone; on shore, and when
10 Thro' scudding drifts the rainy Hyades
Vext the dim sea: I am become a name;
For always roaming with a hungry heart
Much have I seen and known: cities of men,
And manners, climates, councils, governments,
Myself not least, but honour'd of them all;
And drunk delight of battle with my peers,
Far on the ringing plains of windy Troy.
I am a part of all that I have met;
Yet all experience is an arch wherethro'
20 Gleams that untravell'd world, whose margin fades
For ever and for ever when I move.
How dull it is to pause, to make an end,
To rust unburnish'd, not to shine in use!
As tho' to breathe were life. Life piled on life
Were all too little, and of one to me
Little remains: but every hour is saved
From that eternal silence, something more,
A bringer of new things; and vile it were
For some three suns to store and hoard myself,
30 And this gray spirit yearning in desire
To follow knowledge like a sinking star,

This is a fight the cannot win, against age, death

Beyond the utmost bound of human thought.
    This is my son, mine own Telemachus,
To whom I leave the sceptre and the isle—
Well-lov'd of me, discerning to fulfil
This labour, by slow prudence to make mild
A rugged people, and thro' soft degrees
Subdue them to the useful and the good.
Most blameless is he, centred in the sphere
40   Of common duties, decent not to fail
In offices of tenderness, and pay
Meet adoration to my household gods
When I am gone. He works his work, I mine.
    There lies the port; the vessel puffs her sail:
There gloom the dark broad seas. My mariners,
Souls that have toil'd, and wrought, and thought with me—
That ever with a frolic welcome took
The thunder and the sunshine, and opposed
Free hearts, free foreheads—you and I are old;
50   Old age hath yet his honour and his toil;
Death closes all: but something ere the end,
Some work of noble note, may yet be done,
Not unbecoming men that strove with Gods.
The lights begin to twinkle from the rocks:
The long day wanes: the slow moon climbs: the deep
Moans round with many voices. Come, my friends,
'Tis not too late to seek a newer world.
Push off, and sitting well in order smite
The sounding furrows; for my purpose holds
60   To sail beyond the sunset, and the baths
Of all the western stars, until I die.
It may be that the gulfs will wash us down:
It may be we shall touch the Happy Isles,
And see the great Achilles, whom we knew.
Tho' much is taken, much abides; and tho'
We are not now that strength which in old days
Moved earth and heaven; that which we are, we are;
One equal temper of heroic hearts,
Made weak by time and fate, but strong in will
70   To strive, to seek, to find, and not to yield.

Tears, Idle Tears

Tears, idle tears, I know not what they mean,
Tears from the depth of some divine despair
Rise in the heart, and gather to the eyes,
In looking on the happy Autumn-fields,
And thinking of the days that are no more.

Fresh as the first beam glittering on a sail,
That brings our friends up from the underworld,
Sad as the last which reddens over one
That sinks with all we love below the verge;
10.   So sad, so fresh, the days that are no more.

Ah, sad and strange as in dark summer dawns
The earliest pipe of half-awaken'd birds
To dying ears, when unto dying eyes
The casement slowly grows a glimmering square;
So sad, so strange, the days that are no more.

Dear as remember'd kisses after death,
And sweet as those by hopeless fancy feign'd
On lips that are for others; deep as love,
Deep as first love, and wild with all regret;
20   O Death in Life, the days that are no more.

From **In Memoriam**

7

Dark house, by which once more I stand
    Here in the long unlovely street,
    Doors, where my heart was used to beat
So quickly, waiting for a hand,

A hand that can be clasp'd no more—
    Behold me, for I cannot sleep,
    And like a guilty thing I creep
At earliest morning to the door.

He[1] is not here; but far away
10   The noise of life begins again,

And ghastly thro' the drizzling rain
On the bald street breaks the blank day.

8

A happy lover who has come
    To look on her that loves him well,
    Who 'lights and rings the gateway bell,
And learns her gone and far from home;

He saddens, all the magic light
    Dies off at once from bower and hall,
    And all the place is dark, and all
The chambers emptied of delight:

So find I every pleasant spot
10   In which we two were wont to meet,
    The field, the chamber and the street,
For all is dark where thou are not.

Yet as that other, wandering there
    In those deserted walks, may find
    A flower beat with rain and wind,
Which once she foster'd up with care;

So seems it in my deep regret,
    O my forsaken heart, with thee
    And this poor flower of poesy
Which little cared for fades not yet.

But since it pleased a vanish'd eye,
    I go to plant it on his tomb,
    That if it can it there may bloom,
Or dying, there at least may die.

115

Now fades the last long streak of snow,
    Now burgeons every maze of quick

1. Arthur Henry Hallam, Tennyson's friend,
    whose death inspired a sequence of poems
    entitled *In Memoriam A. H. H.*

About the flowering squares, and thick
By ashen roots the violets blow.

Now rings the woodland loud and long,
  The distance takes a lovelier hue,
  And drown'd in yonder living blue
The lark becomes a sightless song.

Now dance the lights on lawn and lea,
10 The flocks are whiter down the vale,
  And milkier every milky sail
On winding stream or distant sea;

Where now the seamew pipes, or dives
  In yonder greening gleam, and fly
  The happy birds, that change their sky
To build and brood; that live their lives

From land to land; and in my breast
  Spring wakens too; and my regret
  Becomes an April violet,
20 And buds and blossoms like the rest.

ROBERT BROWNING
1812–1889

Browning is a poet of masks. While we know a lot about his life, we don't ever feel that we really know him. He hides behind the faces of the rogues' gallery in his dramatic monologues, allowing his characters to present psychological portraits of themselves, but not of him. His greatest work, *The Ring and the Book*, is a seventeenth-century Roman murder mystery featuring the despicable Count Guido Franceschini, recounted through dramatic monologues in which each character presents a contrasting point of view. Browning's interest in things Italian started when he was a boy living in the London suburb of Camberwell. Largely educated at home by tutors, he all but devoured his father's 6000-volume library, from which he acquired much of his wide knowledge of Italian history, art, and literature. He lived happily with his parents until the age of thirty-four, when he eloped to Italy with the semi-invalid poet, Elizabeth Barrett, rescuing her from her jealous, tyrannical father and a life of languishing on divans covered with lap robes. This love affair was the great romance of its time, and continued for fifteen idyllic years spent mostly in Italy, until Elizabeth Barrett Browning's death in

1861. Like Tennyson, Browning was enormously productive, and also like Tennyson, he was an extremely popular poet. Shortly before his death, the Browning Society was formed. These literary groups blossomed throughout the English-speaking world, revering Browning as the great affirmative voice of the age, a voice which, they sincerely believed, would refute Tennysonian doubt.

Soliloquy of the Spanish Cloister

Gr-r-r—there go, my heart's abhorrence!
    Water your damned flower-pots, do!
If hate killed men, Brother Lawrence,
    God's blood, would not mine kill you!
What? your myrtle-bush wants trimming?
    Oh, that rose has prior claims—
Needs its leaden vase filled brimming?
    Hell dry you up with its flames!

At the meal we sit together;
10   *Salve tibi!*[1] I must hear
Wise talk of the kind of weather,
    Sort of season, time of year:
Not a plenteous cork-crop: scarcely
    Dare we hope oak-galls, I doubt;
What's the Latin name for "parsley"?
    What's the Greek name for Swine's Snout?

Whew! We'll have our platter burnished,
    Laid with care on our own shelf!
With a fire-new spoon we're furnished,
20   And a goblet for ourself,
Rinsed like something sacrificial
    Ere 'tis fit to touch our chaps—
Marked with L. for our initial!
    (He-he! There his lily snaps!)

Saint, forsooth! While brown Dolores
    Squats outside the Convent bank
With Sanchicha, telling stories,
    Steeping tresses in the tank,

1. Greetings to you!

Blue-black, lustrous, thick like horsehairs,
30   —Can't I see his dead eye glow,
Bright as 'twere a Barbary corsair's?
   (That is, if he'd let it show!)

When he finishes refection,
   Knife and fork he never lays
Cross-wise, to my recollection,
   As do I, in Jesu's praise.
I, the Trinity illustrate,
   Drinking watered orange-pulp—
In three sips the Arian[2] frustrate;
40   While he drains his at one gulp!

Oh, those melons! if he's able
   We're to have a feast; so nice!
One goes to the Abbot's table,
   All of us get each a slice.
How go on your flowers? None double?
   Not one fruit-sort can you spy?
Strange!—And I, too, at such trouble,
   Keep them close-nipped on the sly!

There's a great text in Galatians,[3]
50   Once you trip on it, entails
Twenty-nine distinct damnations,
   One sure, if another fails;
If I trip him just a-dying,
   Sure of heaven as sure can be,
Spin him round and send him flying
   Off to hell, a Manichee?[4]

Or, my scrofulous French novel
   On grey paper with blunt type!
Simply glance at it, you grovel
60   Hand and foot in Belial's[5] gripe;
If I double down its pages
   At the woeful sixteenth print,

2. Follower of the heretic Arius, who denied the Trinity
3. One of St. Paul's Epistles
4. Follower of the heretic Mani
5. A devil

When he gathers his greengages,
  Ope a sieve and slip it in't?

Or, there's Satan!—one might venture
  Pledge one's soul to him, yet leave
Such a flaw in the indenture
  As he'd miss till, past retrieve,
Blasted lay that rose-acacia
70   We're so proud of! *Hy, Zy, Hine....*
'St, there's Vespers![6] *Plena gratia*
  Ave, Virgo! Gr-r-r—you swine!

6. Evening prayers. The speaker intones "Hail Virgin, full of grace."

My Last Duchess

Ferrara

That's my last Duchess painted on the wall,
Looking as if she were alive. I call
That piece a wonder, now: Frà Pandolf's hands
Worked busily a day, and there she stands.
Will't please you sit and look at her? I said
"Frà Pandolf" by design, for never read
Strangers like you that pictured countenance,
The depth and passion of its earnest glance,
But to myself they turned (since none puts by
10 The curtain I have drawn for you, but I)
And seemed as they would ask me, if they durst,
How such a glance came there; so, not the first
Are you to turn and ask thus. Sir, 'twas not
Her husband's presence only, called that spot
Of joy into the Duchess' cheek; perhaps
Frà Pandolf chanced to say, "Her mantle laps
Over my lady's wrist too much," or "Paint
Must never hope to reproduce the faint
Half-flush that dies along her throat": such stuff
20 Was courtesy, she thought, and cause enough
For calling up that spot of joy. She had
A heart—how shall I say?—too soon made glad,
Too easily impressed: she liked whate'er
She looked on, and her looks went everywhere.
Sir, 'twas all one! My favour at her breast,
The dropping of the daylight in the West,

He didn't feel respected

The bough of cherries some officious fool
Broke in the orchard for her, the white mule
She rode with round the terrace—all and each
30 Would draw from her alike the approving speech.
Or blush, at least. She thanked men,—good! but thanked
Somehow—I know not how—as if she ranked
My gift of a nine-hundred-years-old name
With anybody's gift. Who'd stoop to blame
This sort of trifling? Even had you skill
In speech—(which I have not)—to make your will
Quite clear to such an one, and say, "Just this
Or that in you disgusts me; here you miss,
Or there exceed the mark"—and if she let
40 Herself be lessoned so, nor plainly set
Her wits to yours, forsooth, and made excuse,
—E'en then would be some stooping; and I choose
Never to stoop. Oh sir, she smiled, no doubt,
Whene'er I passed her; but who passed without
Much the same smile? This grew; I gave commands;
Then all smiles stopped together. There she stands
As if alive. Will't please you rise? We'll meet
The company below, then. I repeat,
The Count your master's known munificence
50 Is ample warrant that no just pretence
Of mine for dowry will be disallowed;
Though his fair daughter's self, as I avowed
At starting, is my object. Nay, we'll go
Together down, sir. Notice Neptune, though,
Taming a sea-horse, thought a rarity,
Which Claus of Innsbruck cast in bronze for me!

The Bishop Orders His Tomb
at Saint Praxed's Church

Rome, 15—

Vanity, saith the preacher, vanity!
Draw round my bed: is Anselm keeping back?
Nephews—sons mine . . . ah God, I know not! Well—
She, men would have to be your mother once,
Old Gandolf envied me, so fair she was!
What's done is done, and she is dead beside,
Dead long ago, and I am Bishop since,
And as she died so must we die ourselves,

And thence ye may perceive the world's a dream.
10 Life, how and what is it? As here I lie
In this state-chamber, dying by degrees,
Hours and long hours in the dead night, I ask,
"Do I live, am I dead?" Peace, peace seems all.
Saint Praxed's ever was the church for peace;
And so, about this tomb of mine. I fought
With tooth and nail to save my niche, ye know:
—Old Gandolf cozened me, despite my care;
Shrewd was that snatch from out the corner South
He graced his carrion with, God curse the same!
20 Yet still my niche is not so cramped but thence
One sees the pulpit o' the epistle-side,
And somewhat of the choir, those silent seats,
And up into the aery dome where live
The angels, and a sunbeam's sure to lurk:
And I shall fill my slab of basalt there,
And 'neath my tabernacle take my rest,
With those nine columns round me, two and two,
The odd one at my feet where Anselm stands:
Peach-blossom marble all, the rare, the ripe
30 As fresh-poured red wine of a mighty pulse.
—Old Gandolf with his paltry onion-stone,
Put me where I may look at him! True peach,
Rosy and flawless: how I earned the prize!
Draw close: that conflagration of my church
—What then? So much was saved if aught were missed!
My sons, ye would not be my death? Go dig
The white-grape vineyard where the oil-press stood,
Drop water gently till the surface sink,
And if ye find . . . Ah God, I know not, I! . . .
40 Bedded in store of rotten fig-leaves soft,
And corded up in a tight olive-frail,
Some lump, ah God, of *lapis lazuli,*
Big as a Jew's head cut off at the nape,
Blue as a vein o'er the Madonna's breast . . .
Sons, all have I bequeathed you, villas, all,
That brave Frascati villa with its bath,
So, let the blue lump poise between my knees,
Like God the Father's globe on both his hands
Ye worship in the Jesus Church so gay,
For Gandolf shall not choose but see and burst!
Swift as a weaver's shuttle fleet our years:
Man goeth to the grave, and where is he?
Did I say basalt for my slab, sons? Black—

'Twas ever antique-black I meant! How else
Shall ye contrast my frieze to come beneath?
The bas-relief in bronze ye promised me,
Those Pans and Nymphs ye wot of, and perchance
Some tripod, thyrsus, with a vase or so,
The Savior at his sermon on the mount,
60   Saint Praxed in a glory, and one Pan
Ready to twitch the Nymph's last garment off,
And Moses with the tables . . . but I know
Ye mark me not! What do they whisper thee,
Child of my bowels, Anselm? Ah, ye hope
To revel down my villas while I gasp
Bricked o'er with beggar's moldy travertine
Which Gandolf from his tomb-top chuckles at!
Nay, boys, ye love me—all of jasper, then!
'Tis jasper ye stand pledged to, lest I grieve.
70   My bath must needs be left behind, alas!
One block, pure green as a pistachio-nut,
There's plenty jasper somewhere in the world—
And have I not Saint Praxed's ear to pray
Horses for ye, and brown Greek manuscripts,
And mistresses with great smooth marbly limbs?
—That's if ye carve my epitaph aright,
Choice Latin, picked phrase, Tully's every word,
No gaudy ware like Gandolf's second line—
Tully, my masters? Ulpian serves his need!
80   And then how I shall lie through centuries,
And hear the blessed mutter of the mass,
And see God made and eaten all day long,
And feel the steady candle-flame, and taste
Good, strong, thick, stupefying incense-smoke!
For as I lie here, hours of the dead night,
Dying in state and by such slow degrees,
I fold my arms as if they clasped a crook,
And stretch my feet forth straight as stone can point,
And let the bedclothes, for a mortcloth, drop
90   Into great laps and folds of sculptor's-work:
And as yon tapers dwindle, and strange thoughts
Grow, with a certain humming in my ears,
About the life before I lived this life,
And this life too, popes, cardinals and priests,
Saint Praxed at his sermon on the mount,
Your tall pale mother with her talking eyes,
And new-found agate urns as fresh as day,
And marble's language, Latin pure, discreet,

—Aha, ELUCESCEBAT[1] quoth our friend?
100   No Tully, said I, Ulpian at the best!
Evil and brief hath been my pilgrimage.
All *lapis*, all, sons! Else I give the Pope
My villas! Will ye ever eat my heart?
Ever your eyes were as a lizard's quick,
They glitter like your mother's for my soul,
Or ye would heighten my impoverished frieze,
Piece out its starved design, and fill my vase
With grapes, and add a visor and a Term,
And to the tripod ye would tie a lynx
110   That in his struggle throws the thyrsus down,
To comfort me on my entablature
Whereon I am to lie till I must ask,
"Do I live, am I dead?" There, leave me, there!
For ye have stabbed me with ingratitude
To death—ye wish it—God, ye wish it! Stone—
Gritstone, a-crumble! Clammy squares which sweat
As if the corpse they keep were oozing through—
And no more *lapis* to delight the world!
Well, go! I bless ye. Fewer tapers there,
120   But in a row: and, going, turn your backs
—Aye, like departing altar-ministrants,
And leave me in my church, the church for peace,
That I may watch at leisure if he leers—
Old Gandolf—at me, from his onion-stone,
As still he envied me, so fair she was!

1. He was famous: not in the pure Latin of Cicero (Tully)
but in the debased style of Ulpian.

Porphyria's Lover

The rain set early in to-night
   The sullen wind was soon awake,
It tore the elm-tops down for spite,
   And did its worst to vex the lake:
   I listen'd with heart fit to break.
When glided in Porphyria; straight
   She shut the cold out and the storm,
And kneel'd and made the cheerless grate
   Blaze up, and all the cottage warm;
10   Which done, she rose, and from her form
Withdrew the dripping cloak and shawl,

And laid her soil'd gloves by, untied
Her hat and let the damp hair fall,
    And, last, she sat down by my side
    And call'd me. When no voice replied,
She put my arm about her waist,
    And made her smooth white shoulder bare,
And all her yellow hair displaced,
    And, stooping, made my cheek lie there,
20   And spread, o'er all, her yellow hair,
Murmuring how she loved me — she
    Too weak, for all her heart's endeavour,
To set its struggling passion free
    From pride, and vainer ties dissever,
    And give herself to me for ever.
But passion sometimes would prevail,
    Nor could to-night's gay feast restrain
A sudden thought of one so pale
    For love of her, and all in vain:
30   So, she was come through wind and rain.
Be sure I look'd up at her eyes
    Happy and proud; at last I knew
Porphyria worshipp'd me; surprise
    Made my heart swell, and still it grew
    While I debated what to do.
That moment she was mine, mine, fair,
    Perfectly pure and good: I found
A thing to do, and all her hair
    In one long yellow string I wound
40   Three times her little throat around,
And strangled her. No pain felt she;
    I am quite sure she felt no pain.
As a shut bud that holds a bee,
    I warily oped her lids: again
    Laugh'd the blue eyes without a stain.
And I untighten'd next the tress,
    About her neck; her cheek once more
Blush'd bright beneath my burning kiss:
    I propp'd her head up as before,
50   Only, this time my shoulder bore
Her head, which droops upon it still:
    The smiling rosy little head,
So glad it has its utmost will,
    That all it scorn'd at once is fled,
    And I, its love, am gain'd instead!

Porphyria's love: she guess'd not how
  Her darling one wish would be heard.
And thus we sit together now,
  And all night long we have not stirr'd,
60 And yet God has not said a word!

WALT WHITMAN
1819–1892

In 1844, Ralph Waldo Emerson called for a truly American poet who would see that "America is a poem in our eyes; its ample geography dazzles the imagination, and it will not wait long for metres." Eleven years later Walt Whitman's "barbaric yawp," as he himself called it, gave answer to Emerson's request. The voice was distinctly American and the form broke away from conventional metrical regularity, its lines swelling and undulating with oceanic rhythm, echoing the biblical psalmists, or declaiming oratorically in the best American political tradition. It was an expansive voice for an expanding America, and Whitman saw himself as prophet and seer celebrating individualism and democratic idealism as it manifested itself in all experience. Whitman would "let nature speak, without check, with original energy," and this energy was sexual, "the procreant urge" of nature and of man and woman. He would speak for all people, and not just for privileged literary circles: "I am your voice—it was tied in you—in me it begins to talk." Emerson was impressed with the first edition of *Leaves of Grass*, but though he realized that Whitman was indeed the poet he sought, he was somewhat shocked at some of Whitman's subject matter. Whitman in his time was not considered respectable, and each new edition of *Leaves of Grass* was inevitably pronounced "obscene."

Whitman was born on Long Island, New York, and grew up in Brooklyn, returning frequently to Long Island and his beloved ocean. Mostly self-educated, he attended school only six years, and then worked variously as an office boy, schoolteacher, newspaper editor, or carpenter. He would roam the streets of the city absorbing sights and sounds, a friend of both artists and laborers. During the Civil War he was a wound dresser in a Washington army hospital, and after the war he lost his job in the Office of Indian Affairs when it was discovered he had written an "indecent" book. Never financially secure, Whitman supported himself as he could, continuing to expand and rearrange the poetry of *Leaves of Grass*. Toward the end of his life, his poetry was becoming accepted, and when he addressed "Poets to come," he could be confident in the immortality of his vision. And rightly so, for it was these poets who would answer him affirmatively, as those of his own time could not.

Crossing Brooklyn Ferry

1

Flood-tide below me! I see you face to face!
Clouds of the west—sun there half an hour high—I see you also face to face.

Crowds of men and women attired in the usual costumes, how curious you are to me!
On the ferry-boats the hundreds and hundreds that cross, returning home, are more curious to me than you suppose,
And you that shall cross from shore to shore years hence are more to me, and more in my meditations, than you might suppose.

2

The impalpable sustenance of me from all things at all hours of the day,
The simple, compact, well-joined'd scheme, myself disintegrated, every one disintegrated yet part of the scheme,
The similitudes of the past and those of the future,
The glories strung like beads on my smallest sights and hearings, on the walk in the street and the passage over the river,
10   The current rushing so swiftly and swimming with me far away,
The others that are to follow me, the ties between me and them,
The certainty of others, the life, love, sight, hearing of others.
Others will enter the gates of the ferry and cross from shore to shore,
Others will watch the run of the flood-tide,
Others will see the shipping of Manhattan north and west, and the heights of Brooklyn to the south and east,
Others will see the islands large and small;
Fifty years hence, others will see them as they cross, the sun half an hour high,
A hundred years hence, or ever so many hundred years hence, others will see them,
Will enjoy the sunset, the pouring-in of the flood-tide, the falling-back to the sea of the ebb-tide.

3

20   It avails not, time nor place—distance avails not,
I am with you, you men and women of a generation, or ever so many generations hence,
Just as you feel when you look on the river and sky, so I felt,

Just as any of you is one of a living crowd, I was one of a crowd,
Just as you are refresh'd by the gladness of the river and the bright flow, I was
    refresh'd,
Just as you stand and lean on the rail, yet hurry with the swift current, I stood yet
    was hurried,
Just as you look on the numberless masts of ships and the thick-stemm'd pipes of
    steamboats, I look'd.

I too many and many a time cross'd the river of old,
Watched the Twelfth-month sea-gulls, saw them high in the air floating with
    motionless wings, oscillating their bodies,
Saw how the glistening yellow lit up parts of their bodies and left the rest in strong
    shadow,
30 Saw the slow-wheeling circles and the gradual edging toward the south,
Saw the reflection of the summer sky in the water,
Had my eyes dazzled by the shimmering track of beams,
Look'd at the fine centrifugal spokes of light round the shape of my head in the
    sunlit water,
Look'd on the haze on the hills southward and south-westward,
Look'd on the vapor as it flew in fleeces tinged with violet,
Look'd toward the lower bay to notice the vessels arriving,
Saw their approach, saw aboard those that were near me,
Saw the white sails of schooners and sloops, saw the ships at anchor,
The sailors at work in the rigging or out astride the spars,
40 The round masts, the swinging motion of the hulls, the slender serpentine
    pennants,
The large and small steamers in motion, the pilots in their pilot-houses,
The white wake left by the passage, the quick tremulous whirl of the wheels,
The flags of all nations, the falling of them at sunset,
The scallop-edged waves in the twilight, the ladled cups, the frolicsome crests and
    glistening,
The stretch afar growing dimmer and dimmer, the gray walls of the granite
    storehouses by the docks,
On the river the shadowy group, the big steam-tug closely flank'd on each side by
    the barges, the hay-boat, the belated lighter,
On the neighboring shore the fires from the foundry chimneys burning high and
    glaringly into the night,
Casting their flicker of black contrasted with wild red and yellow light over the
    tops of houses and down into the clefts of streets.

4

These and all else were to me the same as they are to you,
50 I loved well those cities, loved well the stately and rapid river,

The men and women I saw were all near to me,
Others the same—others who look back on me because I look'd forward to them,
(The time will come, though I stop here to-day and to-night.)

5

What is it then between us?
What is the count of the scores or hundreds of years between us?

Whatever it is, it avails not—distance avails not, and place avails not,
I too lived, Brooklyn of ample hills was mine,
I too walk'd the streets of Manhattan island, and bathed in the waters around it,
I too felt the curious abrupt questionings stir within me,
60 In the day among crowds of people sometimes they came upon me,
In my walks home late at night or as I lay in my bed they came upon me,
I too had been struck from the float forever held in solution,
I too had receiv'd identity by my body,
That I was I knew was of my body, and what I should be I knew I should be of my
    body.

6

It is not upon you alone the dark patches fall,
The dark threw its patches down upon me also,
The best I had done seem'd to me blank and suspicious,
My great thoughts as I supposed them, were they not in reality meagre?
Nor is it you alone who know what it is to be evil,
70 I am he who knew what it was to be evil,
I too knitted the old knot of contrariety,
Blabb'd, blush'd, resented, lied, stole, grudg'd,
Had guile, anger, lust, hot wishes I dared not speak,
Was wayward, vain, greedy, shallow, sly, cowardly, malignant,
The wolf, the snake, the hog, not wanting in me,
The cheating look, the frivolous word, the adulterous wish, not wanting,
Refusals, hates, postponements, meanness, laziness, none of these wanting,
Was one with the rest, the days and haps of the rest,
Was call'd by my nighest name by clear loud voices of young men as they saw me
    approaching or passing,
80 Felt their arms on my neck as I stood, or the negligent leaning of their flesh against
    me as I sat,
Saw many I loved in the street or ferry-boat or public assembly, yet never told
    them a word,
Lived the same life with the rest, the same old laughing, gnawing, sleeping,

Play'd the part that still looks back on the actor or actress,
The same old role, the role that is what we make it, as great as we like,
Or as small as we like, or both great and small.

7

Closer yet I approach you,
What thought you have of me now, I had as much of you—I laid in my stores in
    advance,
I consider'd long and seriously of you before you were born.

Who was to know what should come home to me?
90   Who knows but I am enjoying this?
Who knows, for all the distance, but I am as good as looking at you now, for all you
    cannot see me?

8

Ah, what can ever be more stately and admirable to me than mast-hemm'd
    Manhattan?
River and sunset and scallop-edg'd waves of flood-tide?
The sea-gulls oscillating their bodies, the hay-boat in the twilight, and the belated
    lighter?
What gods can exceed these that clasp me by the hand, and with voices I love call
    me promptly and loudly by my nighest name as I approach?
What is more subtle than this which ties me to the woman or man that looks in my
    face?
Which fuses me into you now, and pours my meaning into you?
We understand then do we not?
What I promis'd without mentioning it, have you not accepted?
100   What the study could not teach—what the preaching could not accomplish is
    accomplish'd, is it not?

9

Flow on, river! flow with the flood-tide, and ebb with the ebb-tide!
Frolic on, crested and scallop-edg'd waves!
Gorgeous clouds of the sunset! drench with your splendor me, or the men and
    women generations after me!
Cross from shore to shore, countless crowds of passengers!

Stand up, tall masts of Mannahatta! stand up, beautiful hills of Brooklyn!
Throb, baffled and curious brain! throw out questions and answers!
Suspend here and everywhere, eternal float of solution!
Gaze, loving and thirsty eyes, in the house or street or public assembly!
Sound out, voices of young men! loudly and musically call me by my nighest
     name!
110 Live, old life! play the part that looks back on the actor or actress!
Play the old role, the role that is great or small according as one makes it!
Consider, you who peruse me, whether I may not in unknown ways be looking
     upon you;
Be firm, rail over the river, to support those who lean idly, yet haste with the
     hasting current;
Fly on, sea-birds! fly sideways, or wheel in large circles high in the air;
Receive the summer sky, you water, and faithfully hold it till all downcast eyes
     have time to take it from you!
Diverge, fine spokes of light, from the shape of my head, or any one's head, in the
     sunlit water!
Come on, ships from the lower bay! pass up or down, white-sail'd schooners,
     sloops, lighters!
Flaunt away, flags of all nations! be duly lower'd at sunset!
Burn high your fires, foundry chimneys! cast black shadows at nightfall! cast red
     and yellow light over the tops of the houses!
120 Appearances, now or henceforth, indicate what you are,
You necessary film, continue to envelop the soul,
About my body for me, and your body for you, be hung out divinest aromas,
Thrive, cities—bring your freight, bring your shows, ample and sufficient rivers,
Expand, being than which none else is perhaps more spiritual,
Keep your places, objects than which none else is more lasting.

You have waited, you always wait, you dumb, beautiful ministers,
We receive you with free sense at last, and are insatiate henceforward,
Not you any more shall be able to foil us, or withhold yourselves from us,
We use you, and do not cast you aside—we plant you permanently within us,
130 We fathom you not—we love you—there is perfection in you also,
You furnish your parts toward eternity,
Great or small, you furnish your parts toward the soul.

I Hear America Singing

I hear America singing, the varied carols I hear,
Those of mechanics, each one singing his as it should be blithe and strong,
The carpenter singing his as he measures his plank or beam,

The mason singing his as he makes ready for work, or leaves off work.
The boatman singing what belongs to him in his boat, the deckhand singing on
    the steamboat deck,
The shoemaker singing as he sits on his bench, the hatter singing as he stands,
The wood-cutter's song, the ploughboy's on his way in the morning, or at noon
    intermission or at sundown,
The delicious singing of the mother, or of the young wife at work, or of the girl
    sewing or washing,
Each singing what belongs to him or her and to none else,
10   The day what belongs to the day—at night the party of young fellows, robust,
    friendly,
Singing with open mouths their strong melodious songs.

The Dalliance of the Eagles

Skirting the river road, (my forenoon walk, my rest,)
Skyward in air a sudden muffled sound, the dalliance of the eagles,
The rushing amorous contact high in space together,
The clinching interlocking claws, a living, fierce, gyrating wheel,
Four beating wings, two beaks, a swirling mass tight grappling,
In tumbling turning clustering loops, straight downward falling,
Till o'er the river pois'd, the twain yet one, a moment's lull,
A motionless still balance in the air, then parting, talons loosing,
Upward again on slow-firm pinions slanting, their separate diverse flight,
10   She hers, he his, pursuing.

A Sight in Camp in the Daybreak Gray and Dim

A sight in camp in the daybreak gray and dim,
As from my tent I emerge so early sleepless,
As slow I walk in the cool fresh air the path near by the hospital tent,
Three forms I see on stretchers lying, brought out there untended lying,
Over each the blanket spread, ample brownish woolen blanket,
Gray and heavy blanket, folding, covering all.

Curious I halt and silent stand,
Then with light fingers I from the face of the nearest the first just lift the blanket;
Who are you elderly man so gaunt and grim, with well-gray'd hair, and flesh all
    sunken about the eyes?
10   Who are you my dear comrade?

Then to the second I step—and who are you my child and darling?
Who are you sweet boy with cheeks yet blooming?

Then to the third—a face nor child nor old, very calm, as of beautiful yellow-white
    ivory;
Young man I think I know you—I think this face is the face of the Christ himself,
Dead and divine and brother of all, and here again he lies.

The Ox-Tamer

In a far-away northern county in the placid pastoral region,
Lives my farmer friend, the theme of my recitative, a famous tamer of oxen,
There they bring him the three-year-olds and the four-year-olds to break them,
He will take the wildest steer in the world and break him and tame him,
He will go fearless without any whip where the young bullock chafes up and down
    the yard,
The bullock's head tosses restless high in the air with raging eyes,
Yet see you! how soon his rage subsides—how soon this tamer tames him;
See you! on the farms hereabout a hundred oxen young and old, and he is the man
    who has tamed them,
They all know him, all are affectionate to him;
10   See you! some are such beautiful animals, so lofty looking;
Some are buff-color'd, some mottled, one has a white line running along his back,
    some are brindled,
Some have wide flaring horns (a good sign)—see you! the bright hides,
See, the two with stars on their foreheads—see, the round bodies and broad backs,
How straight and square they stand on their legs—what fine sagacious eyes!
How they watch their tamer—they wish him near them—how they turn to look
    after him!
What yearning expression! how uneasy they are when he moves away from them;
Now I marvel what it can be he appears to them, (books, politics, poems,
    depart—all else departs,)
I confess I envy only his fascination—my silent, illiterate friend,
Whom a hundred oxen love there in his life on farms,
20   In the northern county far, in the placid pastoral region.

EMILY DICKINSON

1830–1886

Emily Dickinson provided another new voice for American poetry, but one quite the opposite of that of her contemporary, Walt Whitman. She is as coiled and condensed as he is loose and expansive; as private as he is public. She was born in Amherst, Massachusetts, the daughter of a highly respected lawyer. She graduated from Amherst Academy and entered nearby Mount Holyoke Female Seminary. However, less than a year later she returned home because she could not accept the Seminary's rigid brand of Christianity, and because she was homesick. She lived the rest of her life in her father's house, rarely leaving Amherst, and eventually becoming a recluse, seeing only a few visitors a year. Though some biographers have characterized Dickinson as a frail, highly eccentric spinster, hiding from the world and frustrated in life and in love, the power of her poetry and the sheer amount of her literary output belies such a picture. Rather, we might consider her withdrawal from society a choice for the freedom to pursue the career of poet. And poet she was, producing over 1700 poems, of which only seven were published during her lifetime. Though the form of her poetry looks simple, with its patterns of meter and rhyme suggesting her use of nineteenth-century hymnals as models of prosody, there is nothing simplistic in what she says, and her unconventional punctuation forces us to pause with her thoughts as she examines faith and doubt, death, nature, and varieties of love.

[Success Is Counted Sweetest]

Success is counted sweetest
By those who ne'er succeed.
To comprehend a nectar
Requires sorest need.

Not one of all the purple Host
Who took the Flag today
Can tell the definition
So clear of Victory

As he defeated—dying—
10 On whose forbidden ear
The distant strains of triumph
Burst agonized and clear!

[I Never Hear the Word]

I never hear the word "escape"
Without a quicker blood,
A sudden expectation,
A flying attitude!

I never hear of prisons broad
By soldiers battered down,
But I tug childish at my bars
Only to fail again!

[I'm "Wife"—I've Finished That]

I'm "wife"—I've finished that—
That other state—
I'm Czar—I'm "Woman" now—
It's safer so—

How odd the Girl's life looks
Behind this soft Eclipse—
I think that Earth feels so
To folks in Heaven—now—

This being comfort—then
10 That other kind—was pain—
But why compare?
I'm "Wife"! Stop there!

[What Is—"Paradise"]

What is—"Paradise"—
Who live there—
Are they "Farmers"—
Do they "hoe"—
Do they know that this is "Amherst"—
And that I—am coming—too—
Do they wear "new shoes"—in "Eden"—
Is it always pleasant—there—
Won't they scold us—when we're hungry—
10 Or tell God—how cross we are—

You are sure there's such a person
As "a Father"—in the sky—
So if I get lost—there—ever—
Or do what the nurse calls "die"—
I shan't walk the "Jasper"—barefoot—
Ransomed folks—won't laugh at me—
Maybe—"Eden" a'nt so lonesome
As New England used to be!

[I Heard a Fly Buzz]

I heard a Fly buzz—when I died—
The Stillness in the Room
Was like the Stillness in the Air—
Between the Heaves of Storm—

The Eyes around—had wrung them dry—
And Breaths were gathering firm
For that last Onset—when the King
Be witnessed—in the Room—

I willed my Keepsakes—Signed away
10 What portion of me be
Assignable—and then it was
There interposed a Fly—

With Blue—uncertain stumbling Buzz—
Between the light— and me—
And then the Windows failed—and then
I could not see to see—

[The Heart Asks Pleasure—First]

The Heart asks Pleasure—first—
And then—Excuse from Pain—
And then—those little Anodynes
That deaden suffering—
And then—to go to sleep—
And then—if it should be
The will of its Inquisitor
The privilege to die—

[Because I Could Not Stop for Death]

Because I could not stop for Death—
He kindly stopped for me—
The Carriage held but just Ourselves—
And Immortality.

We slowly drove—He knew no haste
And I had put away
My labor and my leisure too,
For His Civility—

We passed the School, where Children strove
10   At Recess—in the Ring—
We passed the Fields of Gazing Grain—
We passed the Setting Sun—

Or rather—He passed Us—
The Dews drew quivering and chill—
For only Gossamer, my Gown—
My Tippet—only Tulle—

We paused before a House that seemed
A Swelling of the Ground—
The Roof was scarcely visible—
20   The Cornice—in the Ground—

Since then—'tis Centuries—and yet
Feels shorter than the Day
I first surmised the Horses' Heads
Were toward Eternity—

THOMAS HARDY
1840–1928

One of the great novelists of English literature, he pursued a writing career in fiction, poetry, and drama that spanned more than six decades. Born near Dorchester in southwestern England, the area that would become Wessex in his writings, he became an architect's apprentice at the age of fifteen. In 1861 he moved to London to continue his architectural work. At the same time he began to write poetry and fiction, his first novel, *Desperate Remedies*, appearing in 1871. His commitment to fiction led him to abandon his architectural career, and he published a total of fifteen novels, including *The Mayor of Casterbridge* (1885), *Tess* of the *D'Urbervilles* (1891), and his last novel, *Jude the Obscure* (1896), and several collections of short fiction. Like his fiction, his poetry explores in naturalistic terms the hapless condition of humankind, caught in a world without design, providence, or God. Unable to return to the religious faith of his Victorian upbringing, he shares with many modern poets a belief in the futility and waste of human existence.

Hap

If but some vengeful god would call to me
From up the sky, and laugh: "Thou suffering thing,
Know that thy sorrow is my ecstasy,
That thy love's loss is my hate's profiting!"
Then would I bear it, clench myself, and die,
Steeled by the sense of ire unmerited;
Half-eased in that a Powerfuller than I
Had willed and meted me the tears I shed.
But not so. How arrives it joy lies slain,
10   And why unblooms the best hope ever sown?
—Crass Casualty obstructs the sun and rain,
And dicing Time for gladness casts a moan. . . .
These purblind Doomsters had as readily strown
Blisses about my pilgrimage as pain.

The Darkling Thrush

I leant upon a coppice gate
    When Frost was spectre-gray
And Winter's dregs made desolate
    The weakening eye of day.
The tangled bine-stems scored the sky
    Like strings of broken lyres,
And all mankind that haunted nigh
    Had sought their household fires.

The land's sharp features seemed to be
10   The Century's corpse outleant,
His crypt the cloudy canopy,
    The wind his death-lament.
The ancient pulse of germ and birth
    Was shrunken hard and dry,
And every spirit upon earth
    Seemed fervourless as I.

At once a voice arose among
    The bleak twigs overhead
In a full-hearted evensong
20   Of joy illimited;
An aged thrush, frail, gaunt, and small,
    In blast-beruffled plume,
Had chosen thus to fling his soul
    Upon the growing gloom.

So little cause for carolings
    Of such ecstatic sound
Was written on terrestrial things
    Afar or nigh around,
That I could think there trembled through
30   His happy good-night air
Some blessed Hope, whereof he knew
    And I was unaware.

The Convergence of the Twain

(*Lines on the loss of the 'Titanic'*)

I

In a solitude of the sea
    Deep from human vanity,
And the Pride of Life that planned her, stilly couches she.

II

Steel chambers, late the pyres
    Of her salamandrine fires,
Cold currents thrid, and turn to rhythmic tidal lyres.

III

Over the mirrors meant
    To glass the opulent
The sea-worm crawls—grotesque, slimed, dumb, indifferent.

IV

10   Jewels in joy designed
    To ravish the sensuous mind
Lie lightless, all their sparkles bleared and black and blind.

V

Dim moon-eyed fishes near
Gaze at the gilded gear
And query: "What does this vaingloriousness down here?" . . .

VI

Well: while was fashioning
This creature of cleaving wing,
The Immanent Will that stirs and urges everything

VII

Prepared a sinister mate
For her—so gaily great—
A Shape of Ice, for the time far and dissociate.

VIII

And as the smart ship grew
In stature, grace, and hue,
In shadowy silent distance grew the Iceberg too.

IX

Alien they seemed to be:
No mortal eye could see
The intimate welding of their later history.

X

Or sign that they were bent
By paths coincident
On being anon twin halves of one august event,

XI

Till the Spinner of the Years
Said "Now!" And each one hears,
And consummation comes, and jars two hemispheres.

The Oxen

Christmas Eve, and twelve of the clock.
   "Now they are all on their knees."
An elder said as we sat in a flock
   By the embers in hearthside ease.

We pictured the meek mild creatures where

They dwelt in their strawy pen,
Nor did it occur to one of us there
    To doubt they were kneeling then.

So fair a fancy few would weave
10   In these years! Yet, I feel,
If someone said on Christmas Eve,
    "Come; see the oxen kneel,

In the lonely barton by yonder coomb
    Our childhood used to know,"
I should go with him in the gloom,
    Hoping it might be so.

During Wind and Rain

They sing their dearest songs—
He, she, all of them—yea,
Treble and tenor and bass,
    And one to play;
With the candles mooning each face. . . .
    Ah, no; the years O!
How the sick leaves reel down in throngs!

They clear the creeping moss—
Elders and juniors—aye,
10   Making the pathways neat
    And the garden gay;
And they build a shady seat. . . .
    Ah, no; the years, the years;
See, the white storm-birds wing across!

They are blithely breakfasting all—
Men and maidens—yea,
Under the summer tree,
    With a glimpse of the bay,
While pet fowl come to the knee. . . .
20   Ah, no; the years O!
And the rotten rose is ript from the wall.

They change to a high new house,
He, she, all of them—aye,

Clocks and carpets and chairs
  On the lawn all day,
And brightest things that are theirs. . . .
  Ah, no; the years, the years;
Down their carved names the rain-drop ploughs.

In Time of "The Breaking of Nations"

I
Only a man harrowing clods
  In a slow silent walk
With an old horse that stumbles and nods
  Half asleep as they stalk.

II
Only thin smoke without flame
  From the heaps of couch-grass;
Yet this will go onward the same
  Though Dynasties pass.

III
Yonder a maid and her wight
10 Come whispering by:
War's annals will fade into night
  Ere their story die.

GERARD MANLEY HOPKINS
1844–1889

Born in Stratford, Essex, the son of a London marine insurance adjuster, Hopkins showed an early interest in poetry, winning a poetry prize at Highgate School in London. He then went on to Balliol College, Oxford, but at this time, he wanted to become a painter. Caught up in the Oxford Movement, a revival of ritualistic Christianity, he converted to Catholicism in 1866. Two years later he joined the Jesuits, was ordained as a priest in 1877, and served as a missionary in the squalid slums of Liverpool. He later took a church at Oxford, and near the end of his life was professor of Greek at University College, Dublin. While studying for the priesthood, Hopkins had burned all his poetry, but in 1875, still struggling with the demands of his faith and with his aesthetic interests, he began writing again, exploring this struggle in his poetry. An intense observer of the natural world, Hopkins saw patterns, which he called "inscapes," in natural phenomena, and his poetry attempts to convey the complex unity of his sensual observation. Yet his is primarily a poetry for the ear. Experimenting in prosody, he drew on rhythms of early English poetry, modeling his "sprung rhythm" on ordinary speech. Wrenching and straining syntax into original and startling forms, he presents us with an inspired vision of the beauty of nature infused with the glory of God.

God's Grandeur

The world is charged with the grandeur of God.
  It will flame out, like shining from shook foil;
  It gathers to a greatness, like the ooze of oil
Crushed. Why do men then now not reck his rod?
Generations have trod, have trod, have trod;
  And all is seared with trade; bleared, smeared with toil;
  And wears man's smudge and shares man's smell: the soil
Is bare now, nor can foot feel, being shod.

And for all this, nature is never spent;
10   There lives the dearest freshness deep down things;
And though the last lights off the black West went
  Oh, morning, at the brown brink eastward, springs—
Because the Holy Ghost over the bent
  World broods with warm breast and with ah! bright wings.

The Windhover

To Christ Our Lord

I caught this morning morning's minion, king-
  dom of daylight's dauphin, dapple-dawn-drawn Falcon, in his riding
  Of the rolling level underneath him steady air, and striding
High there, how he rung upon the rein of a wimpling wing
In his ecstasy! then off, off forth on swing,
  As a skate's heel sweeps smooth on a bow-bend: the hurl and gliding
  Rebuffed the big wind. My heart in hiding
Stirred for a bird,—the achieve of, the mastery of the thing!

Brute beauty and valour and act, oh, air, pride, plume, here
10   Buckle! AND the fire that breaks from thee then, a billion
Times told lovelier, more dangerous, O my chevalier!

No wonder of it: shéer plód makes plough down sillion
Shine, and blue-bleak embers, ah my dear,
    Fall, gall themselves, and gash gold-vermilion.

Pied Beauty

Glory be to God for dappled things—
    For skies of couple-colour as a brinded cow;
        For rose-moles all in stipple upon trout that swim;
Fresh-firecoal chestnut-falls; finches' wings;
    Landscape plotted and pieced—fold, fallow, and plough;
        And áll trádes, their gear and tackle and trim.
All things counter, original, spare, strange;
    Whatever is fickle, freckled (who knows how?)
        With swift, slow; sweet, sour; adazzle, dim;
10   He fathers-forth whose beauty is past change:
                        Praise him.

Spring and Fall: To a Young Child

Márgarét, áre you griev."ng
Over Goldengrove unleaving?
Leáves, líke the things of man, you
With your fresh thoughts care for, can you?
Áh! ás the heart grows older
It will come to such sights <u>colder</u>
By and by, nor spare a sigh
Though worlds of wanwood leafmeal lie;
And yet you *will* weep and know why.
10   Now no matter, child, the name:
Sórrow's spríngs áre the same.
Nor mouth had, no nor mind, expressed
What heart heard of, ghost guessed:
It ís the blight man was born for,
It is Margaret you mourn for.

[handwritten annotations in right margin:]
realication of human mortality
speaker (old) margaret (innocent)
with time, it hurts less
death seems prominent

[Thou Art Indeed Just, Lord]

Justus quidem tu es, Domine, si disputem tecum: verumtamen
justa loquar ad te: Quare via impiorum prosperatur? &c.[1]

Thou are indeed just, Lord, if I contend
With thee; but, sir, so what I plead is just.
Why do sinners' ways prosper? and why must
Disappointment all I endeavor end?

Wert thou my enemy, O thou my friend,
How wouldst thou worse, I wonder, than thou dost
Defeat, thwart me? Oh, the sots and thralls of lust
Do in spare hours more thrive than I that spend,

Sir, life upon thy cause. See, banks and brakes
10   Now, leavèd how thick! lacèd they are again
With fretty chervil, look, and fresh wind shakes

Them; birds build—but not I build; no, but strain,
Time's eunuch, and not breed one work that wakes.
Mine, O thou lord of life, send my roots rain.

1. Quoted from the Biblical prophet Jeremiah, and translated
   in the first three lines of the poem.

ARCHIBALD LAMPMAN
1861–1899

Born in Morpeth, Ontario, of United Empire Loyalist stock, he had rheumatic fever
when he was seven, which left him lame for four years and probably weakened his
health permanently. His early education had to take place at home, although by the
age of nine he was able to attend a private school. He graduated from the University of Toronto in 1882. After teaching high school for four months, he resigned and
joined the Post Office Department in Ottawa, where he worked until his death from
pneumonia. A nature poet, he takes comfort and poetic delight in the variety of the
seasons and their dramatic effect on natural life. Yet his verse, unlike that of many of

his Canadian contemporaries, also ventures into social commentary. "The City of the End of Things," published in 1899, is a startling apocalyptic vision, a denunciation of commercial society. In 1942 the critic E.K. Brown discovered among Lampman's scribblers and notebooks "At the Long Sault: May 1660," a stirring lyrical evocation of a great moment in Canadian history and an indication of new directions that his poetry might have followed had death not cut short his career.

The City of the End of Things

Beside the pounding cataracts
Of midnight streams unknown to us
'Tis builded in the leafless tracts
And valleys huge of Tartarus.[1]
Lurid and lofty and vast it seems;
It hath no rounded name that rings,
But I have heard it called in dreams
The City of the End of Things.

Its roofs and iron towers have grown
10 None knoweth how high within the night,
But in its murky streets far down
A flaming terrible and bright
Shakes all the stalking shadows there,
Across the walls, across the floors,
And shifts upon the upper air
From out a thousand furnace doors;
And all the while an awful sound
Keeps roaring on continually,
And crashes in the ceaseless round
20 Of a gigantic harmony.

Through its grim depths re-echoing
And all its weary height of walls,
With measured roar and iron ring,
The inhuman music lifts and falls.
Where no thing rests and no man is,
And only fire and night hold sway;
The beat, the thunder and the hiss
Cease not, and change not, night nor day.

[1]Infernal abyss below Hades: true hell where Zeus threw rebel Titans.

And moving at unheard commands,
30   The abysses and vast fires between,
Flit figures that with clanking hands
Obey a hideous routine;
They are not flesh, they are not bone,
They see not with the human eye,
And from their iron lips is blown
A dreadful and monotonous cry;
And whoso of our mortal race
Should find that city unaware,
Lean Death would smite him face to face,
40   And blanch him with its venomed air:
Or caught by the terrific spell,
Each thread of memory snapt and cut,
His soul would shrivel and its shell
Go rattling like an empty nut.

It was not always so, but once,
In days that no man thinks upon,
Fair voices echoed from its stones,
The light above it leaped and shone:
Once there were multitudes of men,
50   That built that city in their pride,
Until its might was made, and then
They withered age by age and died.
But now of that prodigious race,
Three only in an iron tower,
Set like carved idols face to face,
Remain the masters of its power;
And at the city gate a fourth,
Gigantic and with dreadful eyes,
Sits looking toward the lightless north,
60   Beyond the reach of memories;
Fast rooted to the lurid floor,
A bulk that never moves a jot,
In his pale body dwells no more,
Or mind or soul,—an idiot!
But sometimes in the end those three
Shall perish and their hands be still,
And with the master's touch shall flee
Their incommunicable skill.
A stillness absolute as death
70   Along the slacking wheels shall lie,
And, flagging at a single breath,

The fires shall moulder out and die.
The roar shall vanish at its height,
And over that tremendous town
The silence of eternal night
Shall gather close and settle down.
All its grim grandeur, tower and hall,
Shall be abandoned utterly,
And into rust and dust shall fall
80   From century to century;
Nor ever living thing shall grow,
Nor trunk of tree, nor blade of grass;
No drop shall fall, no wind shall blow,
Nor sound of any foot shall pass:
Alone of its accursèd state,
One thing the hand of Time shall spare,
For the grim Idiot at the gate
Is deathless and eternal there.

The Death of Tennyson

They tell that when his final hour drew near,
He whose fair praise the ages shall rehearse,
Whom now the living and the dead hold dear;
Our gray-haired master of immortal verse,
Called for his Shakespeare, and with touch of rue
Turned to that page in stormy Cymbeline
That bears the dirge. Whether he read none knew,
But on the book he laid his hand serene,
And kept it there unshaken, till there fell
The last gray change, and from before his eyes,
This glorious world that Shakespeare loved so well,
Slowly, as at a beck, without surprise—
Its woe, its pride, its passion, and its play—
Like mists and melting shadows passed away.

Winter-Solitude

I saw the city's towers on a luminous pale-grey sky;
Beyond them a hill of the softest mistiest green,
With naught but frost and the coming of night between,
And a long thin cloud above it the colour of August rye.

I sat in the midst of a plain on my snowshoes with bended knee
Where the thin wind stung my cheeks,
And the hard snow ran in little ripples and peaks,
Like the fretted floor of a white and petrified sea.

And a strange peace gathered about my soul and shone,
As I sat reflecting there,
In a world so mystically fair,
So deathly silent—I so utterly alone.

February, 1893

At the Long Sault: May, 1660[1]

Under the day-long sun there is life and mirth
    In the working earth,
And the wonderful moon shines bright
    Through the soft spring night,
The innocent flowers in the limitless woods are springing
    Far and away
    With the sound and the perfume of May,
And ever up from the south the happy birds are winging,
    The waters glitter and leap and play
10   While the gray hawk soars.

But far in an open glade of the forest set
    Where the rapid plunges and roars,
Is a ruined fort with a name that men forget,—
    A shelterless pen

[1] On 1 May 1660 Adam Dollard des Ormeaux (sometimes called Daulac), with sixteen companions and forty-four Hurons and Algonkins, laid an ambush for some Iroquois at an abandoned fort on the Ottawa River. The Iroquois were joined by a reinforcement of 500, but it took them ten days to vanquish the Frenchmen and their allies. Until fairly recently this event was considered to have saved the colony of Montreal from Iroquois attack, and the Frenchmen were considered martyrs for the faith.

With its broken palisade,
Behind it, musket in hand,
Beyond message or aid
In this savage heart of the wild,
Mere youngsters, grown in a moment to men,
20   Grim and alert and arrayed,
The comrades of Daulac stand.
Ever before them, night and day,
The rush and skulk and cry
Of foes, not men but devils, panting for prey;
Behind them the sleepless dream
Of the little frail-walled town,[2] far away by the plunging stream.
Of maiden and matron and child,
With ruin and murder impending, and none but they
To beat back the gathering horror
30   Deal death while they may,
    And then die.

Day and night they have watched while the little plain
Grew dark with the rush of the foe, but their host
Broke ever and melted away, with no boast
But to number their slain;
And now as the days renew
Hunger and thirst and care
Were they never so stout, so true,
Press at their hearts; but none
40   Falters or shinks or utters a coward word,
Though each setting sun
Brings from the pitiless wild new hands to the Iroquois horde,
And only to them despair.

Silent, white-faced, again and again
Charged and hemmed round by furious hands,
Each for a moment faces them all and stands
In his little desperate ring; like a tired bull moose
Whom scores of sleepless wolves, a ravening pack,
Have chased all night, all day
50   Through the snow-laden woods, like famine let loose;
And he turns at last in his track
Against a wall of rock and stands at bay;
Round him with terrible sinews and teeth of steel

[2]Montreal.

They charge and recharge; but with many a furious plunge and wheel,
Hither and thither over the trampled snow,
He tosses them bleeding and torn;
Till, driven, and ever to and fro
Harried, wounded, and weary grown,
His mighty strength gives way
60 And all together they fasten upon him and drag him down.

So Daulac turned him anew
With a ringing cry to his men
In the little raging forest glen,
And his terrible sword in the twilight whistled and slew.
And all his comrades stood
With their backs to the pales,[3] and fought
Till their strength was done;
The thews that were only mortal flagged and broke
Each struck his last wild stroke,
70 And they fell one by one,
And the world that had seemed so good
Passed like a dream and was naught.

And then the great night came
With the triumph-songs of the foe and the flame
Of the camp-fires.
Out of the dark the soft wind woke,
The song of the rapid rose alway
And came to the spot where the comrades lay,
Beyond help or care,
80 With none but the red men round them
To gnash their teeth and stare.

All night by the foot of the mountain
    The little town lieth at rest,
The sentries are peacefully pacing;
    And neither from East nor from West
Is there rumor of death or of danger;
    None dreameth tonight in his bed
That ruin was near and the heroes
    That met it and stemmed it are dead.

90 But afar in the ring of the forest,
    Where the air is so tender with May

[3]Row of spiked wooden poles, here the walls of the fort.

And the waters are wild in the moonlight
   They lie in their silence of clay.

The numberless stars out of heaven
   Look down with a pitiful glance;
And the lilies asleep in the forest
   Are closed like the lilies of France.[4]

---

[4]That is, the fleur-de-lis, the emblematic flower of France, often appearing as a heraldic emblem on the shields of warriors.

WILLIAM BUTLER YEATS
1865–1939

Yeats was born at Sandymount, near Dublin, Ireland. His father, John Butler Yeats, was a well-known artist. Yeats was educated at schools in London and Dublin, but was never an outstanding scholar. He went to art school, but left after two years to devote himself to poetry. As a boy, he loved to roam the countryside of County Sligo, listening to folk tales told around peat fires and absorbing the "symbols, popular beliefs, and old scraps of verse that made Ireland romantic to herself." His early poems are full of Irish mythology, with the poet striking a romantic pose and musically intoning in archaic diction. Yeats grew out of this phase, influenced by the movement for Irish nationalism, and he turned to actual events and real people to speak for "the new Ireland, overwhelmed by responsibility, [which] begins to long for psychological truth." In 1899, with the help of Lady Gregory, herself a writer and promoter of Irish literature, he founded the Irish National Theater. He went on to become a public figure, serving from 1922–1928 as Senator of the Irish Free State, and he was at the same time achieving worldwide recognition as a great poet. In 1917, he married Georgie Hyde-Lees, who claimed to have powers as a spiritualist medium. She would fall into trances, and through automatic writing, she produced many of the symbols Yeats used in A Vision, a work which presents his theories of the cyclical patterns of history, human psychology, and the soul's migrations after death. After his death, he was buried as he requested in County Sligo near the mountain that had figured so much both in Irish legend and in Yeats's poetry: "Under bare Ben Bulben's head/ In Drumcliff churchyard Yeats is laid."

The Lake Isle of Innisfree

I will arise and go now, and go to Innisfree,
And a small cabin build there, of clay and wattles made:
Nine bean-rows will I have there, a hive for the honeybee,
And live alone in the bee-loud glade.

And I shall have some peace there, for peace comes dropping slow,
Dropping from the veils of the morning to where the cricket sings;
There midnight's all a glimmer, and noon a purple glow,
And evening full of the linnet's wings.

I will arise and go now, for always night and day
10   I hear lake water lapping with low sounds by the shore;
While I stand on the roadway, or on the pavements grey,
I hear it in the deep heart's core.

The Wild Swans at Coole

The trees are in their autumn beauty,
The woodland paths are dry,
Under the October twilight the water
Mirrors a still sky;
Upon the brimming water among the stones
Are nine-and-fifty swans.

The nineteenth autumn has come upon me
Since I first made my count;
I saw, before I had well finished,
10   All suddenly mount
And scatter wheeling in great broken rings
Upon their clamorous wings.

I have looked upon those brilliant creatures,
And now my heart is sore.
All's changed since I, hearing at twilight,
The first time on this shore,
The bell-beat of their wings above my head,
Trod with a lighter tread.

Unwearied still, lover by lover,
20   They paddle in the cold
Companionable streams or climb the air;

Their hearts have not grown old;
Passion or conquest, wander where they will,
Attend upon them still.

But now they drift on the still water,
Mysterious, beautiful;
Among what rushes will they build,
By what lake's edge or pool
Delight men's eyes when I awake some day
30 To find they have flown away?

The Second Coming

Turning and turning in the widening gyre
The falcon cannot hear the falconer;
Things fall apart; the centre cannot hold;
Mere anarchy is loosed upon the world,
The blood-dimmed tide is loosed, and everywhere
The ceremony of innocence is drowned;
The best lack all conviction, while the worst
Are full of passionate intensity.

Surely some revelation is at hand;
10 Surely the Second Coming is at hand.
The Second Coming! Hardly are those words out
When a vast image out of *Spiritus Mundi*
Troubles my sight: somewhere in sands of the desert
A shape with lion body and the head of a man,
A gaze blank and pitiless as the sun,
Is moving its slow thighs, while all about it
Reel shadows of the indignant desert birds.
The darkness drops again; but now I know
That twenty centuries of stony sleep
20 Were vexed to nightmare by a rocking cradle,
And what rough beast, its hour come round at last,
Slouches towards Bethlehem to be born?

Leda and the Swan[1]

A sudden blow: the great wings beating still
Above the staggering girl, her thighs caressed
By the dark webs, her nape caught in his bill
He holds her helpless breast upon his breast.

How can those terrified vague fingers push
The feathered glory from her loosening thighs?
And how can body, laid in that white rush,
But feel the strange heart beating where it lies?

A shudder in the loins engenders there
10   The broken wall, the burning roof and tower
And Agamemnon dead.
                    Being so caught up,
So mastered by the brute blood of the air,
Did she put on his knowledge with his power
Before the indifferent beak could let her drop?

1. Zeus, in the form of a swan, ravished Leda, who gave birth to Helen, whose desertion of her husband, King Menelaus, caused the Trojan War. Another offspring of this union, Clytemnestra, murdered her husband Agamemnon.

Among School Children

I

I walk through the long schoolroom questioning;
A kind old nun in a white hood replies;
The children learn to cipher and to sing,
To study reading-books and history,
To cut and sew, be neat in everything
In the best modern way—the children's eyes
In momentary wonder stare upon
A sixty-year-old smiling public man.

II

I dream of a Ledaean body, bent
10   Above a sinking fire, a tale that she
Told of a harsh reproof, or trivial event
That changed some childish day to tragedy—

Told, and it seemed that our two natures blent
Into a sphere from youthful sympathy,
Or else, to alter Plato's parable,
Into the yolk and white of the one shell.

III

And thinking of that fit of grief or rage
I look upon one child or t'other there
And wonder if she stood so at that age —
20   For even daughters of the swan can share
Something of every paddler's heritage —
And had that colour upon cheek or hair,
And thereupon my heart is driven wild:
She stands before me as a living child.

IV

Her present image floats into the mind —
Did Quattrocento finger fashion it
Hollow of cheek as though it drank the wind
And took a mess of shadows for its meat?
And I though never of Ledaean kind
30   Had pretty plumage once — enough of that,
Better to smile on all that smile, and show
There is a comfortable kind of old scarecrow.

V

What youthful mother, a shape upon her lap
Honey of generation had betrayed,
And that must sleep, shriek, struggle to escape
As recollection or the drug decide,
Would think her son, did she but see that shape
With sixty or more winters on its head,
A compensation for the pang of his birth,
40   Or the uncertainty of his setting forth?

VI

Plato thought nature but a spume that plays
Upon a ghostly paradigm of things;
Solider Aristotle played the taws
Upon the bottom of the king of kings;
World-famous golden-thighed Pythagoras
Fingered upon a fiddle-stick or strings
What a star sang and careless Muses heard:
Old clothes upon old sticks to scare a bird.

VII

Both nuns and mothers worship images,
50   But those the candles light are not as those
That animate a mother's reveries,
But keep a marble or a bronze repose.
And yet they too break hearts—O Presences
That passion, piety or affection knows,
And that all heavenly glory symbolise—
O self-born mockers of man's enterprise;

VIII

Labour is blossoming or dancing where
The body is not bruised to pleasure soul,
Nor beauty born out of its own despair,
60   Nor blear-eyed wisdom out of midnight oil.
O chestnut tree, great rooted blossomer,
Are you the leaf, the blossom or the bole?
O body swayed to music, O brightening glance,
How can we know the dancer from the dance?

Sailing to Byzantium[1]

That is no country for old men. The young
In one another's arms, birds in the trees
—Those dying generations—at their song,
The salmon-falls, the mackerel-crowded seas,
Fish, flesh, or fowl, commend all summer long
Whatever is begotten, born, and dies.
Caught in that sensual music all neglect
Monuments of unaging intellect.

An aged man is but a paltry thing,
10   A tattered coat upon a stick, unless
Soul clap its hands and sing, and louder sing
For every tatter in its mortal dress,
Nor is there singing school but studying
Monuments of its own magnificence;
And therefore I have sailed the seas and come
To the holy city of Byzantium.

1. Now Istanbul

O sages standing in God's holy fire
As in the gold mosaic of a wall,
Come from the holy fire, perne in a gyre,[2]
20   And be the singing-masters of my soul.
Consume my heart away; sick with desire
And fastened to a dying animal
It knows not what it is; and gather me
Into the artifice of eternity.

Once out of nature I shall never take
My bodily form from any natural thing,
But such a form as Grecian goldsmiths make
Of hammered gold and gold enamelling
To keep a drowsy emperor awake;
30   Or set upon a golden bough to sing
To lords and ladies of Byzantium
Of what is past, or passing, or to come.

2. Revolve in a spiral

After Long Silence

Speech after long silence; it is right,
All other lovers being estranged or dead,
Unfriendly lamplight hid under its shade,
The curtains drawn upon unfriendly night,
That we descant and yet again descant
Upon the supreme theme of Art and Song:
Bodily decrepitude is wisdom; young
We loved each other and were ignorant.

The Circus Animals' Desertion

I

I sought a theme and sought for it in vain,
I sought it daily for six weeks or so.
Maybe at last, being but a broken man,
I must be satisfied with my heart, although
Winter and summer till old age began

My circus animals[1] were all on show,
Those stilted boys, that burnished chariot,
Lion and woman and the Lord knows what.

II

What can I but enumerate old themes?
10 First that sea-rider Oisin led by the nose
Through three enchanted islands, allegorical dreams,
Vain gaiety, vain battle, vain repose,
Themes of the embittered heart, or so it seems,
That might adorn old songs or courtly shows;
But what cared I that set him on to ride,
I, starved for the bosom of his faery bride?

And then a counter-truth filled out its play,
The Countess Cathleen was the name I gave it;
She, pity-crazed, had given her soul away,
20 But masterful Heaven had intervened to save it.
I thought my dear must her own soul destroy,
So did fanaticism and hate enslave it,
And this brought forth a dream and soon enough
This dream itself had all my thought and love.

And when the Fool and Blind Man stole the bread
Cuchulain fought the ungovernable sea;
Heart-mysteries there, and yet when all is said
It was the dream itself enchanted me:
Character isolated by a deed
30 To engross the present and dominate memory.
Players and painted stage took all my love,
And not those things that they were emblems of.

III

Those masterful images because complete
Grew in pure mind, but out of what began?

1. In the course of the poem, Yeats alludes to much of
   his previous work, especially his mythological
   and symbolic figures.

A mound of refuse or the sweeping of a street,
Old kettles, old bottles, and a broken can,
Old iron, old bones, old rags, that raving slut
Who keeps the till. Now that my ladder's gone,
I must lie down where all the ladders start,
40   In the foul rag-and-bone shop of the heart.

ROBERT FROST
1874–1963

Robert Frost was born in San Francisco where his father was a journalist and an aspiring politician. Frost's mother wrote poetry and introduced her son to Scottish poetry and to such poets as Wordsworth, Bryant, and Emerson, whose use of nature in their work undoubtedly influenced Frost. After his father died, the family moved to New England, where Frost's mother taught school. After graduating from high school in Lawrence, Massachusetts, where he was class poet and where he shared the post of valedictorian with Elinor White, whom he later married, Frost attended Dartmouth and Harvard. He did not graduate, but returned home to marry Elinor. They moved to a farm in Derry, New Hampshire, where Frost taught school, wrote poetry, and tried to run a farm. These were years of hardship for the growing family, and discouraged by his inability to interest American publishers in his poetry, Frost sold the farm and the family moved to England. Shortly after his arrival, his first collection of poetry, *A Boy's Will*, was accepted for publication; *North of Boston* followed soon after. Frost met Ezra Pound, who introduced Frost's poetry to American publishers, and three years later, when the family returned because of the outbreak of World War I, Frost had achieved recognition as a major poetic talent. He has always had a wide audience of readers; there are those who read him as a New England nature poet who extols the values of rural America and its work ethic, and those who read him as one who sees nature as other, as a sometimes barren landscape against which human dramas are played out, as they so effectively are in Frost's dramatic narratives. Frost described poetry as "a momentary stay against confusion," but he also said: "The figure a poem makes. It begins in delight and ends in wisdom. The figure is the same as for love."

Mending Wall

Something there is that doesn't love a wall,
That sends the frozen-ground-swell under it
And spills the upper boulders in the sun,
And makes gaps even two can pass abreast.
The work of hunters is another thing:
I have come after them and made repair
Where they have left not one stone on a stone,
But they would have the rabbit out of hiding,
To please the yelping dogs. The gaps I mean,
10 No one has seen them made or heard them made,
But at spring mending-time we find them there.
I let my neighbor know beyond the hill;
And on a day we meet to walk the line
And set the wall between us once again.
We keep the wall between us as we go.
To each the boulders that have fallen to each.
And some are loaves and some so nearly balls
We have to use a spell to make them balance:
'Stay where you are until our backs are turned!'
20 We wear our fingers rough with handling them.
Oh, just another kind of outdoor game,
One on a side. It comes to little more:
There where it is we do not need the wall:
He is all pine and I am apple orchard.
My apple trees will never get across
And eat the cones under his pines, I tell him.
He only says, 'Good fences make good neighbors.'
Spring is the mischief in me, and I wonder
If I could put a notion in his head:
30 'Why do they make good neighbors? Isn't it
Where there are cows? But here there are no cows.
Before I built a wall I'd ask to know
What I was walling in or walling out,
And to whom I was like to give offense.
Something there is that doesn't love a wall,
That wants it down.' I could say 'Elves' to him,
But it's not elves exactly, and I'd rather
He said it for himself. I see him there
Bringing a stone grasped firmly by the top
40 In each hand, like an old-stone savage armed.
He moves in darkness as it seems to me,
Not of woods only and the shade of trees.
He will not go behind his father's saying,

[Handwritten annotations in margins: "Walls define our position is life so we know where we stand. Without them we would walk on eachothers feets" and "I would be coursed the wall to break"]

And he likes having thought of it so well
He says again, 'Good fences make good neighbors.'

After Apple-picking

My long two-pointed ladder's sticking through a tree
Toward heaven still,
And there's a barrel that I didn't fill
Beside it, and there may be two or three
Apples I didn't pick upon some bough.
But I am done with apple-picking now.
Essence of winter sleep is on the night,
The scent of apples: I am drowsing off.
I cannot rub the strangeness from my sight
10 I got from looking through a pane of glass
I skimmed this morning from the drinking trough
And held against the world of hoary grass.
It melted, and I let it fall and break.
But I was well
Upon my way to sleep before it fell,
And I could tell
What form my dreaming was about to take.
Magnified apples appear and disappear,
Stem end and blossom end,
20 And every fleck of russet showing clear.
My instep arch not only keeps the ache,
It keeps the pressure of a ladder-round.
I feel the ladder sway as the boughs bend
And I keep hearing from the cellar bin
The rumbling sound
Of load on load of apples coming in.
For I have had too much
Of apple-picking: I am overtired
Of the great harvest I myself desired.
30 There were ten thousand thousand fruit to touch,
Cherish in hand, lift down, and not let fall.
For all
That struck the earth,
No matter if not bruised or spiked with stubble,
Went surely to the cider-apple heap
As of no worth.
One can see what will trouble
This sleep of mine, whatever sleep it is.
Were he not gone,

40 The woodchuck could say whether it's like his
Long sleep, as I describe its coming on,
Or just some human sleep.

Stopping by Woods on a Snowy Evening

Whose woods these are I think I know.
His house is in the village, though;
He will not see me stopping here
To watch his woods fill up with snow.

My little horse must think it queer
To stop without a farmhouse near
Between the woods and frozen lake
The darkest evening of the year.

He gives his harness bells a shake
10 To ask if there is some mistake.
The only other sound's the sweep
Of easy wind and downy flake.

The woods are lovely, dark, and deep,
But I have promises to keep,
And miles to go before I sleep,
And miles to go before I sleep.

Design

I found a dimpled spider, fat and white,
On a white heal-all, holding up a moth
Like a white piece of rigid satin cloth—
Assorted characters of death and blight
Mixed ready to begin the morning right,
Like the ingredients of a witches' broth—
A snow-drop spider, a flower like a froth,
And dead wings carried like a paper kite.

What had that flower to do with being white,
10 The wayside blue and innocent heal-all?
What brought the kindred spider to that height,
Then steered the white moth thither in the night?
What but design of darkness to appall?—
If design govern in a thing so small.

Provide, Provide

The witch that came (the withered hag)
To wash the steps with pail and rag,
Was once the beauty Abishag,[1]

The picture pride of Hollywood.
Too many fall from great and good
For you to doubt the likelihood.

Die early and avoid the fate.
Or if predestined to die late,
Make up your mind to die in state.

10   Make the whole stock exchange your own!
If need be occupy a throne,
Where nobody can call *you* crone.

Some have relied on what they knew;
Others on simply being true.
What worked for them might work for you.

No memory of having starred
Atones for later disregard,
Or keeps the end from being hard.

Better to go down dignified
20   With boughten friendship at your side
Than none at all. Provide, provide!

1. Biblical beauty brought in to warm dying King David

Birches

When I see birches bend to left and right
Across the lines of straighter darker trees,
I like to think some boy's been swinging them.
But swinging doesn't bend them down to stay.
As ice-storms do. Often you must have seen them
Loaded with ice a sunny winter morning
After a rain. They click upon themselves
As the breeze rises, and turn many-colored
As the stir cracks and crazes their enamel.
10   Soon the sun's warmth makes them shed crystal shells

Shattering and avalanching on the snow-crust—
Such heaps of broken glass to sweep away
You'd think the inner dome of heaven had fallen.
They are dragged to the withered bracken by the load,
And they seem not to break; though once they are bowed
So low for long, they never right themselves:
You may see their trunks arching in the woods
Years afterwards, trailing their leaves on the ground
Like girls on hands and knees that throw their hair
20 Before them over their heads to dry in the sun.
But I was going to say when Truth broke in
With all her matter-of-fact about the ice-storm
I should prefer to have some boy bend them
As he went out and in to fetch the cows—
Some boy too far from town to learn baseball,
Whose only play was what he found himself,
Summer or winter, and could play alone.
One by one he subdued his father's trees
By riding them down over and over again
30 Until he took the stiffness out of them,
And not one but hung limp, not one was left
For him to conquer. He learned all there was
To learn about not launching out too soon
And so not carrying the tree away
Clear to the ground. He always kept his poise
To the top branches, climbing carefully
With the same pains you use to fill a cup
Up to the brim, and even above the brim.
Then he flung outward, feet first, with a swish,
40 Kicking his way down through the air to the ground.
So was I once myself a swinger of birches.
And so I dream of going back to be.
It's when I'm weary of considerations,
And life is too much like a pathless wood
Where your face burns and tickles with the cobwebs
Broken across it, and one eye is weeping
From a twig's having lashed across it open.
I'd like to get away from earth awhile
And then come back to it and begin over.
50 May no fate willfully misunderstand me
And half grant what I wish and snatch me away
Not to return. Earth's the right place for love:
I don't know where it's likely to go better.
I'd like to go by climbing a birch tree,

And climb black branches up a snow-white trunk
Toward heaven, till the tree could bear no more,
But dipped its top and set me down again.
That would be good both going and coming back.
One could do worse than be a swinger of birches.

WALLACE STEVENS
1879–1955

Stevens was born in Reading, Pennsylvania, where his father was an attorney and a schoolteacher with an interest in poetry. After graduating from high school, Stevens attended Harvard for three years as a special student. He was writing poetry at this time, some of which was published in the Harvard *Advocate*, and when he left Harvard, his intention was to pursue a literary career in New York City. He became a reporter for the *Herald Tribune*, but didn't like this job, so he entered law school, was admitted to the bar, but was unsuccessful in private practice. He then joined the legal staff of a bonding company, and feeling himself sufficiently settled, he married Elsie Moll, a young woman from his home town. Seven years later, he joined the Hartford Accident and Insurance Company and in 1916 moved to Hartford, Connecticut, where he lived the rest of his life. Stevens wrote his poetry during his spare time, and though he had some literary friends such as William Carlos Williams and Marianne Moore, his business activities kept him at some remove from literary circles. *Harmonium*, his first volume of poems, appeared in 1923, and though Stevens began to acquire a reputation as one of the outstanding poets of the twentieth century, his coworkers at the insurance company were not aware of this until he won the Bollingen Prize in 1950. This was partly because of Stevens's natural reticence about himself, and partly because he doubtless felt they would not understand. Certainly, it is difficult to reconcile the pragmatics of Stevens's business activities with the gaiety of language and the celebration of the imagination in his poetry.

Sunday Morning

I

Complacencies of the peignoir, and late
Coffee and oranges in a sunny chair,
And the green freedom of a cockatoo
Upon a rug mingle to dissipate
The holy hush of ancient sacrifice.
She dreams a little, and she feels the dark
Encroachment of that old catastrophe,
As a calm darkens among water-lights.
The pungent oranges and bright, green wings
10 Seem things in some procession of the dead,
Winding across wide water, without sound.
The day is like wide water, without sound,
Stilled for the passing of her dreaming feet
Over the seas, to silent Palestine,
Dominion of the blood and sepulchre.

II

Why should she give her bounty to the dead?
What is divinity if it can come
Only in silent shadows and in dreams?
Shall she not find in comforts of the sun,
20 In pungent fruit and bright, green wings, or else
In any balm or beauty of the earth,
Things to be cherished like the thought of heaven?
Divinity must live within herself:
Passions of rain, or moods in falling snow;
Grievings in loneliness, or unsubdued
Elations when the forest blooms; gusty
Emotions on wet roads on autumn nights;
All pleasures and all pains, remembering
The bough of summer and the winter branch.
30 These are the measures destined for her soul.

III

Jove in the clouds had his inhuman birth.
No mother suckled him, no sweet land gave
Large-mannered motions to his mythy mind.
He moved among us, as a muttering king,
Magnificent, would move among his hinds,
Until our blood, commingling, virginal,

With heaven, brought such requital to desire
The very hinds discerned it, in a star.
Shall our blood fail? Or shall it come to be
40 The blood of paradise? And shall the earth
Seem all of paradise that we shall know?
The sky will be much friendlier then than now,
A part of labor and a part of pain,
And next in glory to enduring love,
Not this dividing and indifferent blue.

IV

She says, "I am content when wakened birds,
Before they fly, test the reality
Of misty fields, by their sweet questionings;
But when the birds are gone, and their warm fields
50 Return no more, where, then, is paradise?"
There is not any haunt of prophecy,
Nor any old chimera of the grave,
Neither the golden underground, nor isle
Melodious, where spirits gat them home,
Nor visionary south, nor cloudy palm
Remote on heaven's hill, that has endured
As April's green endures; or will endure
Like her remembrance of awakened birds,
Or her desire for June and evening, tipped
60 By the consummation of the swallow's wings.

V

She says, "But in contentment I still feel
The need of some imperishable bliss."
Death is the mother of beauty; hence from her,
Alone, shall come fulfilment to our dreams
And our desires. Although she strews the leaves
Of sure obliteration on our paths,
The path sick sorrow took, the many paths
Where triumph rang its brassy phrase, or love
Whispered a little out of tenderness,
70 She makes the willow shiver in the sun
For maidens who were wont to sit and gaze
Upon the grass, relinquished to their feet.
She causes boys to pile new plums and pears
On disregarded plate. The maidens taste
And stray impassioned in the littering leaves.

VI

Is there no change of death in paradise?
Does ripe fruit never fall? Or do the boughs
Hang always heavy in that perfect sky,
Unchanging, yet so like our perishing earth,
80   With rivers like our own that seek for seas
They never find, the same receding shores
That never touch with inarticulate pang?
Why set the pear upon those river-banks
Or spice the shores with odors of the plum?
Alas, that they should wear our colors there,
The silken weavings of our afternoons,
And pick the strings of our insipid lutes!
Death is the mother of beauty, mystical,
Within whose burning bosom we devise
90   Our earthly mothers waiting, sleeplessly.

VII

Supple and turbulent, a ring of men
Shall chant in orgy on a summer morn
Their boisterous devotion to the sun,
Not as a god, but as a god might be,
Naked among them, like a savage source.
Their chant shall be a chant of paradise,
Out of their blood, returning to the sky;
And in their chant shall enter, voice by voice,
The windy lake wherein their lord delights,
100   The trees, like serafin, and echoing hills,
That choir among themselves long afterward.
They shall know well the heavenly fellowship
Of men that perish and of summer morn.
And whence they came and whither they shall go
The dew upon their feet shall manifest.

VIII

She hears, upon that water without sound,
A voice that cries, "The tomb in Palestine
Is not the porch of spirits lingering.
It is the grave of Jesus, where he lay."
110   We live in an old chaos of the sun,
Or old dependency of day and night,
Or island solitude, unsponsored, free,
Of that wide water, inescapable.
Deer walk upon our mountains, and the quail

Whistle about us their spontaneous cries;
Sweet berries ripen in the wilderness;
And, in the isolation of the sky,
At evening, casual flocks of pigeons make
Ambiguous undulations as they sink,
120   Downward to darkness, on extended wings.

Anecdote of the Jar

I placed a jar in Tennessee,
And round it was, upon a hill.
It made the slovenly wilderness
Surround that hill.

The wilderness rose up to it,
And sprawled around, no longer wild.
The jar was round upon the ground
And tall and of a port in air.

It took dominion everywhere.
10   The jar was gray and bare.
It did not give of bird or bush,
Like nothing else in Tennessee.

Thirteen Ways of Looking at a Blackbird

I

Among twenty snowy mountains,
The only moving thing
Was the eye of the blackbird.

II

I was of three minds,
Like a tree
In which there are three blackbirds.

III

The blackbird whirled in the autumn winds.
It was a small part of the pantomime.

IV

A man and a woman
Are one.
A man and a woman and a blackbird
Are one.

V

I do not know which to prefer,
The beauty of inflections
Or the beauty of innuendoes,
The blackbird whistling
Or just after.

VI

Icicles filled the long window
With barbaric glass.
The shadow of the blackbird
Crossed it, to and fro.
The mood
Traced in the shadow
An indecipherable cause.

VII

O thin men of Haddam,
Why do you imagine golden birds?
Do you not see how the blackbird
Walks around the feet
Of the women about you?

VIII

I know noble accents
And lucid, inescapable rhythms;
But I know, too,
That the blackbird is involved
In what I know.

IX

When the blackbird flew out of sight,
It marked the edge
Of one of many circles.

X

At the sight of blackbirds
Flying in a green light,
40   Even the bawds of euphony
Would cry out sharply.

XI

He rode over Connecticut
In a glass coach.
Once, a fear pierced him,
In that he mistook
The shadow of his equipage
For blackbirds.

XII

The river is moving.
The blackbird must be flying.

XIII

50   It was evening all afternoon.
It was snowing
And it was going to snow.
The blackbird sat
In the cedar-limbs.

The Snow Man

One must have a mind of winter
To regard the frost and the boughs
Of the pine trees crusted with snow;

And have been cold a long time
To behold the junipers shagged with ice,
The spruces rough in the distant glitter

Of the January sun; and not to think
Of any misery in the sound of the wind,
In the sound of a few leaves,

10   Which is the sound of the land
Full of the same wind
That is blowing in the same bare place

For the listener, who listens in the snow,
And, nothing himself, beholds
Nothing that is not there and the nothing that is.

A High-Toned Old Christian Woman

Poetry is the supreme fiction, madame.
Take the moral law and make a nave of it
And from the nave build haunted heaven. Thus,
The conscience is converted into palms,
Like windy citherns hankering for hymns.
We agree in principle. That's clear. But take
The opposing law and make a peristyle,
And from the peristyle project a masque
Beyond the planets. Thus, our bawdiness,
10   Unpurged by epitaph, indulged at last,
Is equally converted into palms,
Squiggling like saxophones. And palm for palm,
Madame, we are where we began. Allow,
Therefore, that in the planetary scene
Your disaffected flagellants, well-stuffed,
Smacking their muzzy bellies in parade,
Proud of such novelties of the sublime,
Such tink and tank and tunk-a-tunk-tunk,
May, merely may, madame, whip from themselves
20   A jovial hullabaloo among the spheres.
This will make widows wince. But fictive things
Wink as they will. Wink most when widows wince.

Of Modern Poetry

The poem of the mind in the act of finding
What will suffice. It has not always had
To find: the scene was set; it repeated what
Was in the script.
                    Then the theatre was changed
To something else. Its past was a souvenir.
It has to be living, to learn the speech of the place.
It has to face the men of the time and to meet
The women of the time. It has to think about war
And it has to find what will suffice. It has
10   To construct a new stage. It has to be on that stage

And, like an insatiable actor, slowly and
With meditation, speak words that in the ear,
In the delicatest ear of the mind, repeat,
Exactly, that which it wants to hear, at the sound
Of which, an invisible audience listens,
Not to the play, but to itself, expressed
In an emotion as of two people, as of two
Emotions becoming one. The actor is
A metaphysician in the dark, twanging
20   An instrument, twanging a wiry string that gives
Sounds passing through sudden rightness, wholly
Containing the mind, below which it cannot descend,
Beyond which it has no will to rise.
                              It must
Be the finding of a satisfaction, and may
Be of a man skating, a woman dancing, a woman
Combing. The poem of the act of the mind.

E. J. PRATT
1882–1964

Born in Western Bay, Newfoundland, he grew up in the fishing outports of the British colony. Upon graduation from St. John's Methodist College, he served as preacher and teacher in several island communities. In 1907 he entered Victoria College, University of Toronto, to study philosophy, and earned his B.A. (1911), M.A. (1912), and Ph.D. (1917); in 1913 he received a B.D. and was ordained into the Methodist ministry. In 1920 he accepted an appointment in Victoria College's English department, where he taught until his retirement in 1953. His first collection of poetry, *Newfoundland Verse* (1923), began his careful evocations of seascapes and humankind's relentless confrontation with maritime life in its many shapes and moods. In the 1930s he turned to more socially oriented poetic narratives. In such national epics as *Brébeuf and His Brethren* (1940) and *Towards the Last Spike* (1952), he revealed his detailed research in Canadian history and served as his country's poetic mythmaker.

The Shark

He seemed to know the harbor,
So leisurely he swam;
His fin,
Like a piece of sheet-iron,

Three-cornered,
And with knife-edge,
Stirred not a bubble
As it moved
With its base-line on the water.

10   His body was tubular
And tapered
And smoke-blue,
And as he passed the wharf
He turned,
And snapped at a flat-fish
That was dead and floating.
And I saw the flash of a white throat,
And a double row of white teeth,
And eyes of metallic grey,
20   Hard and narrow and slit.

Then out of the harbor,
With that three-cornered fin
Shearing without a bubble the water
Lithely,
Leisurely,
He swam—
That strange fish,
Tubular, tapered, smoke-blue,
Part vulture, part wolf,
30   Part neither—for his blood was cold.

Erosion

It took the sea a thousand years,
A thousand years to trace
The granite features of this cliff,
In crag and scarp and base.

It took the sea an hour one night,
An hour of storm to place
The sculpture of these granite seams
Upon a woman's face.

One Hour of Life

This little face will never know
Cut of wind or bite of snow:
The sea will never wind its sheet
Around those pallid hands and feet.

Nor shall its sleeping heart, grown cold
After a pulse of life, unfold
That futile challenge on the face
Of one who with a last embrace

Could only cheat the earth to save
10   The plunder for another grave:
But in that hour of battle she
Forgot the patience of the sea.

Silences

There is no silence upon the earth or under the earth like the
     silence under the sea;
No cries announcing birth,
No sounds declaring death.
There is silence when the milt is laid on the spawn in the weeds
  and fungus of the rock-clefts;
And silence in the growth and struggle for life.
The bonitoes pounce upon the mackerel,
And are themselves caught by the barracudas,
The sharks kill the barracudas
And the great molluscs rend the sharks,
10 And all noiselessly—
Though swift be the action and final the conflict,
The drama is silent.

There is no fury upon the earth like the fury under the sea.
For growl and cough and snarl are the tokens of spendthrifts who
  know not the ultimate economy of rage.
Moreover, the pace of the blood is too fast.
But under the waves the blood is sluggard and has the same
  temperature as that of the sea.

There is something pre-reptilian about a silent kill.

Two men may end their hostilities just with their battlecries.
"The devil take you," says one.
20   "I'll see you in hell first," says the other.
And these introductory salutes followed by a hail of gutturals and
     sibilants are often the beginning of friendship, for who would
     not prefer to be lustily damned than to be half-heartedly blessed?
No one need fear oaths that are properly enunciated, for they
     belong to the inheritance of just men made perfect, and, for
     all we know, of such may be the Kingdom of Heaven.
But let silent hate be put away for it feeds upon the heart of the
     hater.
Today I watched two pairs of eyes. One pair was black and the
     other grey. And while the owners thereof, for the space of
     five seconds, walked past each other, the grey snapped at the
     black and the black riddled the grey.
One looked to say—"The cat,"
And the other—"The cur."
But no words were spoken;
Not so much as a hiss or a murmur came through the perfect
     enamel of the teeth; not so much as a gesture of enmity.
If the right upper lip curled over the canine, it went unnoticed.
30   The lashes veiled the eyes not for an instant in the passing.
And as between the two in respect to candor of intention or
     eternity of wish, there was no choice, for the stare was mutual
     and absolute.
A word would have dulled the exquisite edge of the feeling,
An oath would have flawed the crystallization of the hate.
For only such culture could grow in a climate of silence, —
Away back before the emergence of fur or feather, back to the
     unvocal sea and down deep where the darkness spills its wash
     on the threshold of light, where the lids never close upon the
     eyes, where the inhabitants slay in silence and are silently
     slain.

The Deed

Where are the roadside minstrels gone who strung
Their fiddles to the stirrup cavalcades?
What happened to the roses oversung
By orchard lovers in their serenades?

A feudal dust that draggle-tailed the plumes
Blinded the minstrels chasing cavaliers:

Moonlight that sucked the color from the blooms
Had soaked the lyrists and the sonneteers.

Where is the beauty still inspired by rhyme,
10   Competing with those garden miracles,
When the first ray conspires with wind to chime
The matins of the Canterbury bells?

Not in the fruit or flower nor in the whir
Of linnet's wings or plaint of nightingales,
Nor in the moonstruck latticed face of her
Who cracked the tenor sliding up his scales.

We saw that beauty once—an instant run
Along a ledge of rock, a curve, a dive;
Nor did he count the odds of ten to one
20   Against his bringing up that boy alive.

This was an arch beyond the salmon's lunge,
There was a rainbow in the rising mists:
Sea-lapidaries started at the plunge
To cut the facets of their amethysts.

But this we scarcely noticed, since the deed
Had power to cleanse a grapnel's rust, transfigure
The blueness of the lips, unmat the weed
And sanctify the unambiguous rigor.

For that embrace had trapped the evening's light,
30   Racing to glean the red foam's harvestings:
Even the seagulls vanished from our sight,
Though settling with their pentecostal wings.

WILLIAM CARLOS WILLIAMS
1883–1963

Born in Rutherford, New Jersey to an English father and a Puerto Rican mother, Williams attended preparatory schools in Switzerland and Paris, and after graduating from Horace Mann High School in New York went to medical school at the University of Pennsylvania. There he was friendly with poets Ezra Pound and Hilda Doolittle and met painter Charles Demuth, with whom he shared a keen interest in modernist painting, over a dish of prunes in a Philadelphia boarding house. Williams did further pediatric study in Leipzig, Germany, and in 1912 he married and began his medical practice in Rutherford, a practice in which he was fully active until he suffered a stroke in 1952. Williams wrote his poetry at night and between professional appointments, for while he was "determined to be a poet," he was convinced that "only medicine, a job I enjoyed, would make it possible for me to live and write as I wanted to." And write he did: in addition to numerous volumes of poetry, he published short stories, essays, novels, and an autobiography. Energetic and feisty, he railed against T. S. Eliot's poetry of literary allusion, stressing that American poets should break with traditional conventions and use the diction and rhythms of American speech. Like Whitman, he celebrated the "vitality of the body" as he saw and felt it in his everyday life as a physician. His most ambitious work, *Paterson*, is an epic giving metaphoric expression to an American city and its people, past and present. *Paterson* also presented new poetic forms which have greatly influenced other American poets.

The Widow's Lament in Springtime

Sorrow is my own yard
where the new grass
flames as it has flamed
often before but not
with the cold fire
that closes round me this year.
Thirtyfive years
I lived with my husband.
The plumtree is white today
10   with masses of flowers.
Masses of flowers
load the cherry branches
and color some bushes
yellow and some red
but the grief in my heart
is stronger than they
for though they were my joy
formerly, today I notice them
and turned away forgetting.
20   Today my son told me
that in the meadows,
at the edge of the heavy woods
in the distance, he saw

trees of white flowers.
I feel that I would like
to go there
and fall into those flowers
and sink into the marsh near them.

Spring and All

By the road to the contagious hospital
under the surge of the blue
mottled clouds driven from the
northeast—a cold wind. Beyond, the
waste of broad, muddy fields
brown with dried weeds, standing and fallen

patches of standing water
the scattering of tall trees

All along the road the reddish
10   purplish, forked, upstanding, twiggy
stuff of bushes and small trees
with dead, brown leaves under them
leafless vines—

Lifeless in appearance, sluggish
dazed spring approaches—

They enter the new world naked,
cold, uncertain of all
save that they enter. All about them
the cold, familiar wind—

20   Now the grass, tomorrow
the stiff curl of wildcarrot leaf
One by one objects are defined—
It quickens: clarity, outline of leaf

But now the stark dignity of
entrance—Still, the profound change
has come upon them: rooted, they
grip down and begin to awaken

Flowers by the Sea

When over the flowery, sharp pasture's
edge, unseen, the salt ocean

lifts its form—chicory and daisies
tied, released, seem hardly flowers alone

but color and the movement—or the shape
perhaps—of restlessness, whereas

the sea is circled and sways
peacefully upon its plantlike stem

The Yachts

contend in a sea which the land partly encloses
shielding them from the too-heavy blows
of an ungoverned ocean which when it chooses

tortures the biggest hulls, the best man knows
to pit against its beatings, and sinks them pitilessly.
Mothlike in mists, scintillant in the minute

brilliance of cloudless days, with broad bellying sails
they glide to the wind tossing green water
from their sharp prows while over them the crew crawls

10 ant-like, solicitously grooming them, releasing,
making fast as they turn, lean far over and having
caught the wind again, side by side, head for the mark.

In a well guarded arena of open water surrounded by
lesser and greater craft which, sycophant, lumbering
and flittering follow them, they appear youthful, rare

as the light of a happy eye, live with the grace
of all that in the mind is fleckless, free and
naturally to be desired. Now the sea which holds them

is moody, lapping their glossy sides, as if feeling
20 for some slightest flaw but fails completely.
Today no race. Then the wind comes again. The yachts

move, jockeying for a start, the signal is set and they
are off. Now the waves strike at them but they are too
well made, they slip through, though they take in canvas.

Arms with hands grasping seek to clutch at the prows.
Bodies thrown recklessly in the way are cut aside.
It is a sea of faces about them in agony, in despair

until the horror of the race dawns staggering the mind,
the whole sea become an entanglement of watery bodies
30   lost to the world bearing what they cannot hold. Broken,

beaten, desolate, reaching from the dead to be taken up
they cry out, failing, failing! their cries rising
in waves still as the skillful yachts pass over.

The Last Words of My English Grandmother

There were some dirty plates
and a glass of milk
beside her on a small table
near the rank, disheveled bed—

Wrinkled and nearly blind
she lay and snored
rousing with anger in her tones
to cry for food,

Gimme something to eat—
10   They're starving me—
I'm all right I won't go
to the hospital. No, no, no

Give me something to eat
Let me take you
to the hospital, I said
and after you are well

you can do as you please.
She smiled, Yes
you do what you please first
20   then I can do what I please—

Oh, oh, oh! she cried
as the ambulance men lifted
her to the stretcher—
Is this what you call

making me comfortable?
By now her mind was clear—
Oh you think you're smart
you young people,

she said, but I'll tell you
30   you don't know anything.
Then we started.
On the way

we passed a long row
of elms. She looked at them
awhile out of
the ambulance window and said,

What are all those
fuzzy-looking things out there?
Trees? Well, I'm tired
40   of them and rolled her head away.

Landscape with the Fall of Icarus[1]

According to Brueghel
when Icarus fell
it was spring

a farmer was ploughing
his field
the whole pageantry

of the year was

1. Second poem from a series based on the paintings
   of the Flemish artist Pieter Brueghel. This painting
   shows the mythical youth Icarus, son of Daedalus,
   falling into the sea after the wings made for him by
   his father had melted. W. H. Auden has also based a
   poem on this painting.

awake tingling
near

10   the edge of the sea
concerned
with itself

sweating in the sun
that melted
the wings' wax

unsignificantly
off the coast
there was

a splash quite unnoticed
20   this was
Icarus drowning

The Red Wheelbarrow

so much depends
upon

a red wheel
barrow

glazed with rain
water

beside the white
chickens.

MARIANNE MOORE
1887–1972

She was born in Kirkwood, Missouri, to a very devout Presbyterian family. Her father abandoned the family after he had suffered a mental breakdown and the collapse of his business. She and her mother moved to Carlisle, Pennsylvania, and Moore attended Metzger Institute, where her mother taught. She went on to Bryn Mawr College, and though she was getting better grades in biology than in literature, she was trying to write poetry. After her graduation in 1909, she taught at the U.S. Indian School in Carlisle, and starting in 1915, her poetry began to be accepted by literary journals. The Moores were a very close family, and when her brother, a Presbyterian minister, took a position in Brooklyn, she and her mother joined him. Moore worked as a tutor and secretary in a girls' school, and as an assistant in a branch library. She was at this time enjoying the company of artists and writers, as well as writing and publishing her poetry. She was editor of *The Dial*, a literary magazine, for three years. After that, she concentrated solely on her writing. In later years, Moore was renowned as probably the most literate baseball fan the Brooklyn Dodgers ever had.

Poetry

I, too, dislike it: there are things that are important beyond
      all this fiddle.
Reading it, however, with a perfect contempt for it, one
      discovers in
it after all, a place for the genuine.
   Hands that can grasp, eyes
   that can dilate, hair that can rise
     if it must, these things are important not because a

high-sounding interpretation can be put upon them but
      because they are
useful. When they become so derivative as to become
      unintelligible,
the same thing may be said for all of us, that we
10   do not admire what
   we cannot understand: the bat
     holding on upside down or in quest of something to

eat, elephants pushing, a wild horse taking a roll, a tireless
     wolf under
a tree, the immovable critic twitching his skin like a

    horse that feels a flea, the base-
ball fan, the statistician—
      nor is it valid
        to discriminate against 'business documents and

school-books';[1] all these phenomena are important. One
      must make a distinction
however: when dragged into prominence by half poets,
      the result is not poetry,
20   nor till the poets among us can be
      'literalists of
      the imagination'[2]—above
        insolence and triviality and can present

for inspection, imaginary gardens with real toads in them,
      shall we have
it. In the meantime, if you demand on the one hand,
the raw material of poetry in
      all its rawness and
      that which is on the other hand
        genuine, then you are interested in poetry.

1. Tolstoy in his *Diary* writes: "Where the boundary between prose and
   poetry lies, I shall never be able to understand. . . . Poetry is verse:
   prose is not verse. Or else poetry is everything with the exception
   of business documents and school books."—*From Miss Moore's notes*
2. W. B. Yeats in his essay "William Blake and the Imagination"
   speaks of Blake as a "too literal realist of the imagination, as
   others are of nature."—*From Miss Moore's notes*

The Fish

wade
through black jade.
    Of the crow-blue mussel-shells, one keeps
    adjusting the ash-heaps;
      opening and shutting itself like

an
injured fan.
    The barnacles which encrust the side
    of the wave, cannot hide
10   there for the submerged shafts of the

sun,
split like spun
   glass, move themselves with spotlight swiftness
   into the crevices—
      in and out, illuminating

the
turquoise sea
   of bodies. The water drives a wedge
   of iron through the iron edge
20   of the cliff; whereupon the stars,

pink
rice-grains, ink-
   bespattered jelly-fish, crabs like green
   lilies, and submarine
      toadstools, slide each on the other.

All
external
   marks of abuse are present on this
   defiant edifice—
30   all the physical features of

ac-
cident—lack
   of cornice, dynamite grooves, burns, and
   hatchet strokes, these things stand
      out on it; the chasm-side is

dead.
Repeated
   evidence has proved that it can live
   on what can not revive
40   its youth. The sea grows old in it.

A Jellyfish

Visible, invisible,
   a fluctuating charm
an amber-tinctured amethyst
   inhabits it, your arm

approaches and it opens
   and it closes; you had meant
to catch it and it quivers;
   you abandon your intent.

Nevertheless

you've seen a strawberry
   that's had a struggle; yet
   was, where the fragments met,

a hedgehog or a star-
   fish for the multitude
   of seeds. What better food

than apple-seeds—the fruit
   within the fruit—locked in
   like counter-curved twin

10   hazel-nuts? Frost that kills
   the little rubber-plant-
   leaves of *kok-saghyz* stalks, can't

harm the roots; they still grow
   in frozen ground. Once where
   there was a prickly-pear-

leaf clinging to barbed wire,
   a root shot down to grow
   in earth two feet below;

as carrots form mandrakes
20   or a ram's-horn root sometimes. Victory won't come

to me unless I go
   to it; a grape-tendril
   ties a knot in knots till

knotted thirty times,—so
   the bound twig that's undergone and over-gone, can't stir.

The weak overcomes its
    menace, the strong over-
30   comes itself. What is there

like fortitude! What sap
    went through that little thread
    to make the cherry red!

T.S. ELIOT
1888–1965

Thomas Stearns Eliot was born in St. Louis, Missouri, the youngest of seven children of a well-to-do family with deep roots in New England. Both parents were cultivated and well-read, and Eliot showed an early interest in literature; his first published poem, an imitation of Ben Jonson, appeared in Smith Academy's literary journal when Eliot was fifteen. Eliot went on to Harvard for his undergraduate and graduate work, absorbing Dante Donne, and discovering the French symbolist poets who would have a strong influence on his early poetry. He went on to Oxford to do further work in Greek and philosophy, finally completing his dissertation on philosopher F. H. Bradley in 1916. But by then he wished to pursue a literary rather than an academic career, and he was achieving a reputation in literary circles with the publication of his "Preludes" and "J. Alfred Prufrock." In 1915, he had entered into what was to prove a disastrous marriage, and was supporting himself and his wife by working in Lloyd's Bank, writing book reviews, and editing journals. Somehow he found time to write, and in 1922, after a struggle with a mental breakdown, and with the editorial help of Ezra Pound, *The Waste Land* was published. This was the most influential poem of its time, partly because of its innovative fragmented structure, and partly because to many it symbolized the enervation and spiritual emptiness of the post-World War I period. The poetry Eliot wrote after *The Waste Land* is generated from a spiritual struggle which culminated in Eliot's joining the Anglican church. He considered the meditative poetry of *The Four Quartets* his finest work, though some critics feel that his Christian orthodoxy dulled his poetic edge. Nevertheless, he was considered the major poet of his generation, and won the Nobel Prize for Literature in 1948.

The Love Song of J. Alfred Prufrock

> S'io credessi che mia risposta fosse
> A persona che mai tornasse al mondo,
> Questa fiamma staria senza più scosse.
> Ma per ciò che giammai de questo fondo
> Non tornò vivo alcun, s'i'odo il vero
> Senza tema d'infamia ti rispondo.[1]

Let us go then, you and I,
When the evening is spread out against the sky
Like a patient etherized upon a table;
Let us go, through certain half-deserted streets,
The muttering retreats
Of restless nights in one-night cheap hotels
And sawdust restaurants with oyster-shells:
Streets that follow like a tedious argument
Of insidious intent

10   To lead you to an overwhelming question....
Oh, do not ask, 'What is it?'
Let us go and make our visit.

In the room the women come and go
Talking of Michelangelo.

The yellow fog that rubs its back upon the window-panes,
The yellow smoke that rubs its muzzle on the window-panes,
Licked its tongue into the corners of the evening,
Lingered upon the pools that stand in drains,
Let fall upon its back the soot that falls from chimneys,

20   Slipped by the terrace, made a sudden leap,
And seeing that it was a soft October night,
Curled once about the house, and fell asleep.

---

1. "If I believed that my answer were to a person who should ever return
   to the world, this flame would stand without further movement;
   but since never one returns alive from this deep, if I hear true,
   I answer you without fear of infamy." *Inferno*, xxvii, 61–66. These words
   are the response a damned soul in Hell makes when a question is put to him.

And indeed there will be time
For the yellow smoke that slides along the street
Rubbing its back upon the window-panes;
There will be time, there will be time
To prepare a face to meet the faces that you meet;
There will be time to murder and create,
And time for all the works and days of hands
30 That lift and drop a question on your plate;
Time for you and time for me,
And time yet for a hundred indecisions,
And for a hundred visions and revisions,
Before the taking of a toast and tea.

In the room the women come and go
Talking of Michelangelo.

And indeed there will be time
To wonder, 'Do I dare?' and, 'Do I dare?'
Time to turn back and descend the stair,
40 With a bald spot in the middle of my hair—
(They will say: 'How his hair is growing thin!')
My morning coat, my collar mounting firmly to the chin,
My necktie rich and modest, but asserted by a simple pin—
(They will say: 'But how his arms and legs are thin!')
Do I dare
Disturb the universe?
In a minute there is time
For decisions and revisions which a minute will reverse.

For I have known them all already, known them all—
50 Have known the evenings, mornings, afternoons,
I have measured out my life with coffee spoons;
I know the voices dying with a dying fall
Beneath the music from a farther room.
So how should I presume?

And I have known the eyes already, known them all—
The eyes that fix you in a formulated phrase,
And when I am formulated, sprawling on a pin,
When I am pinned and wriggling on the wall,
Then how should I begin
60 To spit out all the butt-ends of my days and ways?
And how should I presume?

And I have known the arms already, known them all—

Arms that are braceleted and white and bare
(But in the lamplight, downed with light brown hair!)
Is it perfume from a dress
That makes me so digress?
Arms that lie along a table, or wrap about a shawl.
    And should I then presume?
    And how should I begin?

     .   .   .

70   Shall I say, I have gone at dusk through narrow streets
And watched the smoke that rises from the pipes
Of lonely men in shirt-sleeves, leaning out of windows? . . .

    I should have been a pair of ragged claws
Scuttling across the floors of silent seas.

     .   .   .

And the afternoon, the evening, sleeps so peacefully!
Smoothed by long fingers,
Asleep . . . tired . . . or it malingers,
Stretched on the floor, here beside you and me.
Should I, after tea and cakes and ices,
80   Have the strength to force the moment to its crisis?
But though I have wept and fasted, wept and prayed,
Though I have seen my head (grown slightly bald) brought
       in upon a platter,[2]
I am no prophet—and here's no great matter,
I have seen the moment of my greatness flicker,
And I have seen the eternal Footman hold my coat, and
       snicker,
And in short, I was afraid.

    And would it have been worth it, after all,
After the cups, the marmalade, the tea,
Among the porcelain, among some talk of you and me,
90   Would it have been worth while,
To have bitten off the matter with a smile,
To have squeezed the universe into a ball
To roll it toward some overwhelming question,
To say: 'I am Lazarus, come from the dead,
Come back to tell you all, I shall tell you all'—

2. The head of John the Baptist was "brought in upon a platter" at
   the request of Salome as a reward for her dancing before Herod.

If one, settling a pillow by her head,
    Should say: 'That is not what I meant at all.
    That is not it, at all.'

And would it have been worth it, after all,
100   Would it have been worth while,
After the sunsets and the dooryards and the sprinkled streets,
After the novels, after the teacups, after the skirts that trail
    along the floor—
And this, and so much more?—
It is impossible to say just what I mean!
But as if a magic lantern threw the nerves in patterns on a
    screen:
Would it have been worth while
If one, settling a pillow or throwing off a shawl,
And turning toward the window, should say:
    'That is not it at all,
110   That is not what I meant, at all.'

      . . .

No! I am not Prince Hamlet, nor was meant to be;
Am an attendant lord, one that will do
To swell a progress,[3] start a scene or two,
Advise the prince; no doubt, an easy tool,
Deferential, glad to be of use,
Politic, cautious, and meticulous;
Full of high sentence, but a bit obtuse;
At times, indeed, almost ridiculous—
Almost, at times, the Fool.

120   I grow old. . . . I grow old. . . .
I shall wear the bottoms of my trousers rolled.

    Shall I part my hair behind? Do I dare to eat a peach?
I shall wear white flannel trousers, and walk upon the beach.
I have heard the mermaids singing, each to each.

    I do not think that they will sing to me.

    I have seen them riding seaward on the waves
Combing the white hair of the waves blown back
When the wind blows the water white and black.

---

3. Ceremonial procession at a royal court

We have lingered in the chambers of the sea
130   By sea-girls wreathed with seaweed red and brown
Till human voices wake us, and we drown.

The Hollow Men

Mistah Kurtz — he dead.
A penny for the Old Guy

I

We are the hollow men
We are the stuffed men
Leaning together
Headpiece filled with straw. Alas!
Our dried voices, when
We whisper together
Are quiet and meaningless
As wind in dry grass
Or rats' feet over broken glass
10   In our dry cellar

   Shape without form, shade without colour,
Paralysed force, gesture without motion;

   Those who have crossed
With direct eyes, to death's other Kingdom
Remember us—if at all—not as lost
Violent souls, but only
As the hollow men
The stuffed men.

II

Eyes I dare not meet in dreams
20   In death's dream kingdom
These do not appear:
There, the eyes are
Sunlight on a broken column
There, is a tree swinging
And voices are
In the wind's singing
More distant and more solemn
Than a fading star.

   Let me be no nearer
30   In death's dream kingdom
    Such deliberate disguises

Let me also wear
Rat's coat, crowskin, crossed staves
In a field
Behaving as the wind behaves
No nearer—

Not that final meeting
In the twilight kingdom

III

This is the dead land
This is cactus land
Here the stone images
Are raised, here they receive
The supplication of a dead man's hand
Under the twinkle of a fading star.

Is it like this
In death's other kingdom
Waking alone
At the hour when we are
Trembling with tenderness
Lips that would kiss
Form prayers to broken stone.

IV

The eyes are not here
There are no eyes here
In this valley of dying stars
In this hollow valley
This broken jaw of our lost kingdoms

In this last of meeting places
We grope together
And avoid speech
Gathered on this beach of the tumid river

Sightless, unless
The eyes reappear
As the perpetual star
Multifoliate rose
Of death's twilight kingdom
The hope only
Of empty men.

V

Here we go round the prickly pear
Prickly pear prickly pear
70 *Here we go round the prickly pear*
At five o'clock in the morning.

Between the idea
And the reality
Between the motion
And the act
Falls the Shadow
For Thine is the Kingdom

Between the conception
And the creation
80 Between the emotion
And the response
Falls the Shadow
Life is very long

Between the desire
And the spasm
Between the potency
And the existence
Between the essence
And the descent
90 Falls the Shadow
For Thine is the Kingdom

For Thine is
Life is
For Thine is the

This is the way the world ends
This is the way the world ends
This is the way the world ends
Not with a bang but a whimper.

Journey of the Magi

"A cold coming we had of it,
Just the worst time of the year
For a journey, and such a long journey:
The ways deep and the weather sharp,

The very dead of winter."
And the camels galled, sore-footed, refractory,
Lying down in the melting snow.
There were times we regretted
The summer palaces on slopes, the terraces,
10 And the silken girls bringing sherbet.
Then the camel men cursing and grumbling
And running away, and wanting their liquor and women,
And the night-fires going out, and the lack of shelters,
And the cities hostile and the towns unfriendly
And the villages dirty and charging high prices:
A hard time we had of it.
At the end we preferred to travel all night,
Sleeping in snatches,
With the voices singing in our ears, saying
20 That this was all folly.

   Then at dawn we came down to a temperate valley,
Wet, below the snow line, smelling of vegetation;
With a running stream and a water-mill beating the darkness,
And three trees on the low sky,
And an old white horse galloped away in the meadow.
Then we came to a tavern with vine-leaves over the lintel,
Six hands at an open door dicing for pieces of silver,
And feet kicking the empty wine-skins.
But there was no information, and so we continued
30 And arrived at evening, not a moment too soon
Finding the place; it was (you may say) satisfactory.

   All this was a long time ago, I remember,
And I would do it again, but set down
This set down
This: were we led all that way for
Birth or Death? There was a Birth, certainly,
We had evidence and no doubt. I had seen birth and death,
But had thought they were different; this Birth was
Hard and bitter agony for us, like Death, our death.
40 We returned to our places, these Kingdoms,
But no longer at ease here, in the old dispensation,
With an alien people clutching their gods.
I should be glad of another death.

Marina

Quis hic locus, quae
regio, quae mundi plaga?

What seas what shores what grey rocks and what islands
What water lapping the bow
And scent of pine and the woodthrush singing through the fog
What images return
O my daughter.

Those who sharpen the tooth of the dog, meaning
Death
Those who glitter with the glory of the hummingbird, meaning
Death
10   Those who sit in the sty of contentment, meaning
Death
Those who suffer the ecstasy of the animals, meaning
Death

Are become unsubstantial, reduced by a wind,
A breath of pine, and the woodsong fog
By this grace dissolved in place

What is this face, less clear and clearer
The pulse in the arm, less strong and stronger—
Given or lent? more distant than stars and nearer than the eye

20   Whispers and small laughter between leaves and hurrying feet
Under sleep, where all the waters meet.

Bowsprit cracked with ice and paint cracked with heat.
I made this, I have forgotten
And remember.
The rigging weak and the canvas rotten
Between one June and another September.
Made this unknowing, half conscious, unknown, my own.
The garboard strake leaks, the seams need caulking.
This form, this face, this life
30   Living to live in a world of time beyond me; let me
Resign my life for this life, my speech for that unspoken,
The awakened, lips parted, the hope, the new ships.

What seas what shores what granite islands towards my timbers
And woodthrush calling through the fog
My daughter.

E. E. CUMMINGS

1894–1962

He was born Edward Estlin Cummings, the son of an English professor at Harvard who was later pastor of the Old South Church in Boston. Cummings took his B.A. and M.A. at Harvard, and then joined the Norton Harje Ambulance Corps in France during World War I. Because of the wrongheaded suspicions of a censor regarding "unpatriotic" letters, Cummings was imprisoned in a French concentration camp for three months, a period which is memorably evoked in his novel, *The Enormous Room*, which made him famous. After the war, he lived in Paris and studied painting, then settled in New York's Greenwich Village with other writers and artists, continuing to paint and to write poetry. He developed an innovative, playful poetic style, flaunting the rules of syntax, grammar, and punctuation in order to make us see words and their relationships in a new way. In the form of his poetry and in his themes, he strikes out against conformity, and celebrates the vitality of human love. He is not a poet of ideas, but he is one of our most joyful singers of the traditional themes of love and spring, as well as one of the sharpest satirists in modern poetry.

Buffalo Bill 's

Buffalo Bill 's
defunct
     who used to
     ride a watersmooth-silver
              stallion
and break onetwothreefourfive pigeonsjustlikethat
                 Jesus

he was a handsome man
            and what i want to know is
10   how do you like your blueeyed boy
Mister Death

Spring is like a perhaps hand

Spring is like a perhaps hand
(which comes carefully
out of Nowhere)arranging
a window,into which people look(while

people stare
arranging and changing placing
carefully there a strange
thing and a known thing here)and

changing everything carefully

10   spring is like a perhaps
Hand in a window
(carefully to
and fro moving New and
Old things,while
people stare carefully
moving a perhaps
fraction of flower here placing
an inch of air there)and

without breaking anything.

somewhere i have never travelled

somewhere i have never travelled,gladly beyond
any experience,your eyes have their silence:
in your most frail gesture are things which enclose me,
or which i cannot touch because they are too near

your slightest look easily will unclose me
though i have closed myself as fingers,
you open always petal by petal myself as Spring opens
(touching skilfully,mysteriously)her first rose

or if your wish be to close me,i and
10   my life will shut very beautifully,suddenly,
as when the heart of this flower imagines
the snow carefully everywhere descending;

nothing which we are to perceive in this world equals
the power of your intense fragility:whose texture
compels me with the colour of its countries,
rendering death and forever with each breathing

(i do not know what it is about you that closes

and opens; only something in me understands
the voice of your eyes is deeper than all roses)
20 nobody,not even the rain,has such small hands

my father moved through dooms of love

my father moved through dooms of love
through sames of am through haves of give,
singing each morning out of each night
my father moved through depths of height

this motionless forgetful where
turned at his glance to shining here;
that if(so timid air is firm)
under his eyes would stir and squirm

newly as from unburied which
10 floats the first who,his april touch
drove sleeping selves to swarm their fates
woke dreamers to their ghostly roots

and should some why completely weep
my father's fingers brought her sleep:
vainly no smallest voice might cry
for he could feel the mountains grow.

Lifting the valleys of the sea
my father moved through griefs of joy;
praising a forehead called the moon
20 singing desire into begin

joy was his song and joy so pure
a heart of star by him could steer
and pure so now and now so yes
the wrists of twilight would rejoice

keen as midsummer's keen beyond
conceiving mind of sun will stand,
so strictly(over utmost him
so hugely)stood my father's dream

his flesh was flesh his blood was blood:
30 no hungry man but wished him food;

no cripple wouldn't creep one mile
uphill to only see him smile.

Scorning the pomp of must and shall
my father moved through dooms of feel;
his anger was as right as rain
his pity was as green as grain

septembering arms of year extend
less humbly wealth to foe and friend
than he to foolish and to wise
40   offered immeasurable is

proudly and(by octobering flame
beckoned)as earth will downward climb,
so naked for immortal work
his shoulders marched against the dark

his sorrow was as true as bread:
no liar looked him in the head;
if every friend became his foe
he'd laugh and build a world with snow.

My father moved through theys of we,
50   singing each new leaf out of each tree
(and every child was sure that spring
danced when she heard my father sing)

then let men kill which cannot share,
let blood and flesh be mud and mire,
scheming imagine,passion willed,
freedom a drug that's bought and sold

giving to steal and cruel kind,
a heart to fear,to doubt a mind,
to differ a disease of same,
60   conform the pinnacle of am

though dull were all we taste as bright,
bitter all utterly things sweet,
maggoty minus and dumb death
all we inherit,all bequeath

and nothing quite so least as truth

—i say though hate were why men breathe—
because my father lived his soul
love is the whole and more than all

pity this busy monster

pity this busy monster, manunkind,

not. Progress is a comfortable disease:
your victim(death and life safely beyond)

plays with the bigness of his littleness
—electrons deify one razorblade
into a mountainrange;lenses extend

unwish through curving wherewhen till unwish
returns on its unself.
                          A world of made
10   is not a world of born—pity poor flesh

and trees,poor stars and stones,but never this
fine specimen of hypermagical

ultraomnipotence. We doctors know

a hopeless case if—listen:there's a hell
of a good universe next door;let's go

EARLE BIRNEY

1904–

Born in Calgary, Alberta, he graduated from the University of British Columbia in 1926 and obtained his M.A. and Ph.D. from the University of Toronto, where he lectured from 1936 until 1941. He also served as literary editor of the *Canadian Forum* from 1936 until 1940. After military service during the Second World War, he joined the Department of English at the University of British Columbia and later chaired the Department of Creative Writing. In two novels, *Turvey* (1949) and *Down the Long Table* (1955), many short stories, and more than a dozen volumes of poetry, including his *Collected Poems* (1975), he is the chronicler, the historian, and the interpreter of the Canadian experience. Often with humor and irony, he studies human dislocation in a frequently hostile society and environment. There is some hope for human beings in their natural loyalty and integrity, in those rare moments of human contact that stand in bleak contrast to the indifferent, sometimes malevolent universe. In 1980 Birney published the first volume of his memoirs, *Spreading Time*. He now resides in Toronto.

The Bear on the Delhi Road

Unreal   tall as a myth
by the road the Himalayan bear
is beating the brilliant air
with his crooked arms
About him two men   bare
spindly as locusts   leap

One pulls on a ring
in the great soft nose   His mate
flicks   flicks with a stick
10   up at the rolling eyes

They have not led him here
down from the fabulous hills
to this bald alien plain
and the clamorous world   to kill
but simply to teach him to dance

They are peaceful both   these spare
men of Kashmir   and the bear
alive is their living   too
If   far on the Delhi way
20   around him galvanic they dance
it is merely to wear   wear
from his shaggy body the tranced

wish forever to stay
only an ambling bear
four-footed in berries

It is no more joyous for them
in this hot dust to prance
out of reach of the praying claws
sharpened to paw for ants
30   in the shadows of deodars[1]
It is not easy to free
myth from reality
or rear this fellow up
to lurch   lurch with them
in the tranced dancing of men
Srinagar/Île des Porquerolles 1959

[1]A Himalayan cedar tree; the name means 'divine tree of the gods.'

A Walk in Kyoto

all week   the maid tells me   bowing
her dolls' body at my mat   is Boys' Day
also please Mans' Day   and gravely
bends deeper   the magnolia sprig in my alcove
is it male   the old discretions of Zen
were not shaped for my phallic western eye
there is so much discretion
in this small bowed body of an empire
(the wild hair of waterfalls combed straight
10   in the ricefields   the inn-maid retreating
with the face of a shut flower)   i stand hunched
and clueless   like a castaway in the shoals of my room

when i slide my parchment door to stalk awkward
through lilliput gardens framed & untouchable
as watercolours   the streets look much as everywhere
men are pulled past on the strings
of their engines   the legs of boys
are revolved by a thousand pedals
& all the faces are taut & unfestive as Moscow's
20   or Toronto's   or mine

Lord Buddha help us all there is vigour enough
in these islands & in all islands reefed & resounding
with cities   but the pitch is high   high as the ping

of cicadas (those small strained motors concealed
in the propped pines by the dying river) & only male
as the stretched falsetto of actors mincing the roles
of kabuki women   or female only as the lost heroes
womanized in the Ladies' Opera—
where in these alleys jammed with competing waves
30   of signs in two tongues & three scripts
can the simple song of a man be heard?

by the shoguns' palace   the Important Cultural Property
stripped for tiptoeing schoolgirls   i stare
at the staring penned carp that flail
on each others backs to the shrunk pools edge
for the crumb this non-fish tossed
is this the Day's one parable
or under that peeling pagoda the 500 tons
of hermaphrodite Word?

40   at the inn i prepare to surrender again
my defeated shoes to the bending maid   but suddenly
the closed lotus opens to a smile & she points
to where   over my shoulder   above the sagging tiles
tall in the bare sky & huge as Gulliver
a carp is rising   golden & fighting
thrusting its paper body up from the fist
of a small boy on an empty roof   higher
& higher   into the endless winds of the world

Can. Lit.
(or them able leave her ever[1])

since we'd always sky about
when we had eagles they flew out
leaving no shadow bigger than wren's
to trouble even our broodiest hens

too busy bridging loneliness
to be alone

[1]Word play on 'The Maple Leaf Forever.'

we hacked in railway ties
what Emily[2] etched in bone

we French&English never lost
10   our civil war
endure it still
a bloody civil bore

the wounded sirened off
no Whitman wanted
it's only by our lack of ghosts
we're haunted

                              Spanish Banks, Vancouver 1947/1966

[2]Emily Dickinson.

Bushed

He invented a rainbow but lightning struck it
shattered it into the lake-lap of a mountain
so big his mind slowed when he looked at it

Yet he built a shack on the shore
learned to roast porcupine belly and
wore the quills on his hatband

At first he was out with the dawn
whether it yellowed bright as wood-columbine
or was only a fuzzed moth in a flannel of storm
10   But he found the mountain was clearly alive
sent messages whizzing down every hot morning
boomed proclamations at noon and spread out
a white guard of goat
before falling asleep on its feet at sundown

When he tried his eyes on the lake   ospreys
would fall like valkyries
choosing the cut-throat[1]

[1]Cut-throat: 1. B.C. trout that osprey prey upon; 2. the slain upon the field of
battle who are gathered up by the Valkyries, the spirit-guides to the afterlife
(Valkyries take the form of both women and birds of prey).

He took then to waiting
till the night smoke rose from the boil of the sunset

20   But the moon carved unknown totems
out of the lakeshore
owls in the beardusky woods derided him
moosehorned cedars circled his swamps and tossed
their antlers up to the stars
then he knew   though the mountain slept   the winds
were shaping its peak to an arrowhead
poised

And now he could only
bar himself in and wait
for the great flint to come singing into his heart

                                        Wreck Beach 1951

W. H. AUDEN
1907–1973

Wystan Hugh Auden was born in York, England, the third son of a physician
of comfortable means, who was also interested in archaeology, classical literature, and Icelandic sagas. Auden developed an early interest in geology
during family outings on the Limestone moors of Yorkshire, and evocations
of those barren simple landscapes can be found in much of his poetry.
These outings also took him to the Roman Wall, and to investigations of
pre-Norman churches and crosses. It seems natural that when he was at
Oxford he should study Anglo-Saxon poetry, whose rhythms and alliteration he later emulated. He experimented with many other forms, including
the folk ballad, and was an extremely talented versifier. His first book of
poetry appeared in 1928; this was followed by *September Poems*, and in
1932, *The Orators*. Auden became well-known as one of the major voices of
the thirties, an "age of anxiety" resulting from worldwide depression and
the growing threat of another war. Influenced by Freud, Auden wrote of
the guilt and fears of the human heart; but he wrote just as strongly of the
power of love as the only force which could overcome anxiety. He came to
America in 1939, and taught at a number of colleges and universities, becoming an American citizen in 1946. A prolific writer, he produced a large
number of reviews and essays in addition to his poetry. He also wrote plays
with Christopher Isherwood and opera librettos with Chester Kallmann. In
1957, he bought a farmhouse in Kirchstetten, Austria, where he spent
springs and summers until his death there in 1973.

Who's Who

A shilling life will give you all the facts:
How Father beat him, how he ran away,
What were the struggles of his youth, what acts
Made him the greatest figure of his day:

Of how he fought, fished, hunted, worked all night,
Though giddy, climbed new mountains; named a sea:
Some of the last researchers even write
Love made him weep his pints like you and me.

With all his honours on, he sighed for one
10   Who, say astonished critics, lived at home;
Did little jobs about the house with skill
And nothing else; could whistle; would sit still
Or potter round the garden; answered some
Of his long marvellous letters but kept none.

As I Walked Out One Evening

As I walked out one evening,
  Walking down Bristol Street,
The crowds upon the pavement
  Were fields of harvest wheat.

And down by the brimming river
  I heard a lover sing
Under an arch of the railway:
  'Love has no ending.

'I'll love you, dear, I'll love you
10   Till China and Africa meet,
And the river jumps over the mountain
  And the salmon sing in the street,

'I'll love you till the ocean
  Is folded and hung up to dry
And the seven stars go squawking
  Like geese about the sky.

'The years shall run like rabbits,
  For in my arms I hold

The Flower of the Ages,
20   And the first love of the world.'

But all the clocks in the city
    Began to whirr and chime:
'O let not Time deceive you,
    You cannot conquer Time.

'In the burrows of the Nightmare
    Where Justice naked is,
Time watches from the shadow
    And coughs when you would kiss.

'In headaches and in worry
30   Vaguely life leaks away,
And Time will have his fancy
    To-morrow or to-day.

'Into many a green valley
    Drifts the appalling snow;
Time breaks the threaded dances
    And the diver's brilliant bow.

'O plunge your hands in water,
    Plunge them in up to the wrist;
Stare, stare in the basin
40   And wonder what you've missed.

'The glacier knocks in the cupboard,
    The desert sighs in the bed,
And the crack in the tea-cup opens
    A lane to the land of the dead.

'Where the beggars raffle the banknotes
    And the Giant is enchanting to Jack,
And the Lily-white Boy is a Roarer,
    And Jill goes down on her back.

'O look, look in the mirror,
50   O look in your distress;
Life remains a blessing
    Although you cannot bless.

'O stand, stand at the window

As the tears scald and start;
You shall love your crooked neighbour
   With your crooked heart.'

It was late, late in the evening,
   The lovers they were gone;
The clocks had ceased their chiming,
60   And the deep river ran on.

Lullaby

Lay your sleeping head, my love,
Human on my faithless arm;
Time and fevers burn away
Individual beauty from
Thoughtful children, and the grave
Proves the child ephemeral:
But in my arms till break of day
Let the living creature lie,
Mortal, guilty, but to me
10   The entirely beautiful.

Soul and body have no bounds:
To lovers as they lie upon
Her tolerant enchanted slope
In their ordinary swoon,
Grave the vision Venus sends
Of supernatural sympathy,
Universal love and hope;
While an abstract insight wakes
Among the glaciers and the rocks
20   The hermit's carnal ecstasy.

Certainty, fidelity
On the stroke of midnight pass
Like vibrations of a bell
And fashionable madmen raise
Their pedantic boring cry:
Every farthing of the cost,
All the dreaded cards foretell,
Shall be paid, but from this night
Not a whisper, not a thought,
30   Not a kiss nor look be lost.

Beauty, midnight, vision dies:
Let the winds of dawn that blow
Softly round your dreaming head
Such a day of welcome show
Eye and knocking heart may bless,
Find our mortal world enough;
Noons of dryness find you fed
By the involuntary powers,
Nights of insult let you pass
40 Watched by every human love.

Musée des Beaux Arts[1]

About suffering they were never wrong,
The Old Masters: how well they understood
Its human position; how it takes place
While someone else is eating or opening a window or just walking dully along;
How, when the aged are reverently, passionately waiting
For the miraculous birth, there always must be
Children who did not specially want it to happen, skating
On a pond at the edge of the wood:
They never forgot
10 That even the dreadful martyrdom must run its course
Anyhow in a corner, some untidy spot
Where the dogs go on with their doggy life and the torturer's horse
Scratches its innocent behind on a tree.

In Brueghel's *Icarus*, for instance: how everything turns away
Quite leisurely from the disaster; the ploughman may
Have heard the splash, the forsaken cry,
But for him it was not an important failure; the sun shone
As it had to on the white legs disappearing into the green
Water; and the expensive delicate ship that must have seen
20 Something amazing, a boy falling out of the sky,
Had somewhere to get to and sailed calmly on.

1. Museum of Fine Arts. See also note to William Carlos Williams's poem
   on Brueghel's "Icarus," above.

In Memory of W. B. Yeats

(d. Jan. 1939)

I

He disappeared in the dead of winter:
The brooks were frozen, the airports almost deserted,
And snow disfigured the public statues;
The mercury sank in the mouth of the dying day.
What instruments we have agree
The day of his death was a dark cold day.

Far from his illness
The wolves ran on through the evergreen forests,
The pleasant river was untempted by the fashionable quays;
10   By mourning tongues
The death of the poet was kept from his poems.

But for him it was his last afternoon as himself,
An afternoon of nurses and rumours;
The provinces of his body revolted,
The squares of his mind were empty,
Silence invaded the suburbs,
The current of his feeling failed; he became his admirers.

Now he is scattered among a hundred cities
And wholly given over to unfamiliar affections,
20   To find his happiness in another kind of wood
And be punished under a foreign code of conscience.
The words of a dead man
Are modified in the guts of the living.

But in the importance and noise of to-morrow
When the brokers are roaring like beasts on the floor of the Bourse,
And the poor have the sufferings to which they are fairly
        accustomed,
And each in the cell of himself is almost convinced of his freedom,
A few thousand will think of this day
As one thinks of a day when one did something slightly unusual.
30   What instruments we have agree
The day of his death was a dark cold day.

II

You were silly like us; your gift survived it all:
The parish of rich women, physical decay,
Yourself. Mad Ireland hurt you into poetry.
Now Ireland has her madness and her weather still,
For poetry makes nothing happen: it survives
In the valley of its making where executives
Would never want to tamper, flows on south
From ranches of isolation and the busy griefs,
Raw towns that we believe and die in; it survives,
A way of happening, a mouth.

III

Earth, receive an honoured guest:
William Yeats is laid to rest.
Let the Irish vessel lie
Emptied of its poetry.

In the nightmare of the dark
All the dogs of Europe bark,
And the living nations wait,
Each sequestered in its hate;

Intellectual disgrace
Stares from every human face,
And the seas of pity lie
Locked and frozen in each eye

Follow, poet, follow right
To the bottom of the night,
With your unconstraining voice
Still persuade us to rejoice;

With the farming of a verse
Make a vineyard of the curse,
Sing of human unsuccess
In a rapture of distress;

In the deserts of the heart
Let the healing fountain start,
In the prison of his days
Teach the free man how to praise.

The Unknown Citizen

To JS/07/M/378
This Marble Monument
Is Erected by the State

He was found by the Bureau of Statistics to be
One against whom there was no official complaint,
And all the reports on his conduct agree
That, in the modern sense of an old-fashioned word, he was a saint,
For in everything he did he served the Greater Community.
Except for the War till the day he retired
He worked in a factory and never got fired,
But satisfied his employers, Fudge Motors Inc.
Yet he wasn't a scab or odd in his views,
For his Union reports that he paid his dues,
(Our report on his Union shows it was sound)
And our Social Psychology workers found
That he was popular with his mates and liked a drink.
The Press are convinced that he bought a paper every day
And that his reactions to advertisements were normal in every way.
Policies taken out in his name prove that he was fully insured,
And his Health-card shows he was once in hospital but left it cured.
Both Producers Research and High-Grade Living declare
He was fully sensible to the advantages of the Instalment Plan
And had everything necessary to the Modern Man,
A phonograph, a radio, a car and a frigidaire.
Our researchers into Public Opinion are content
That he held the proper opinions for the time of year;
When there was peace, he was for peace; when there was war, he went.
He was married and added five children to the population,
Which our Eugenist says was the right number for a parent of his generation,
And our teachers report that he never interfered with their education.
Was he free? Was he happy? The question is absurd:
Had anything been wrong, we should certainly have heard.

A.M. KLEIN

1909–1972

Abraham Moses Klein was born in Ratno in the Ukraine. His family emigrated in 1910 to Montreal, where he spent the rest of his life. Raised in an orthodox Jewish family, he abandoned his strict orthodoxy during his high school years and embarked on a passionate and lifelong dedication to Zionism. He graduated from McGill University in 1930 and from the law school of the University of Montreal in 1933. But the practice of law never satisfied him, for writing consumed his attention. He published five volumes of poetry, the novel *The Second Scroll* (1951), several short stories, and numerous literary essays and reviews. His early poetry explores the humor, pathos, and richness of his Jewish heritage. The influence of T.S. Eliot and the symbolist poets is evident in his later colloquial and ironic poems of social commentary, where he decries the absence of human dignity in a commercial world. His final volume of poetry, *The Rocking Chair and Other Poems* (1948), a beautiful evocation of Canada and its traditions, concludes with "Portrait of the Poet as Landscape," which examines the poet's tragic isolation in the secular world. Deeply distressed by the events of the Second World War and its aftermath, he suffered prolonged psychological anxiety in the early nineteen-fifties. For the last two decades of his life, he lived in virtual seclusion, relinquishing any commitment to his writing.

Soirée of Velvel Kleinburger

In back-room dens of delicatessen stores,
In curtained parlours of garrulous barber-shops,
While the rest of the world most comfortably snores
On mattresses, or on more fleshly props,
My brother Velvel vigils in the night,
Not as he did last night with two French whores,
But with a deck of cards that once were white.

He sees three wan ghosts, as the thick smoke fades,
Dealing him clubs, and diamonds, hearts and spades.

His fingers, pricked with a tailor's needle, draw
The well-thumbed cards; while Hope weighs down his jaw.

   O for the ten spade in its proper place,
     Followed by knave in linen lace,
       The queen with her gaunt face,
         The king and mace,
           The ace!

Then Velvel adds a foot-note to his hoax:
I will not have your wherefores and your buts;
For I am for the Joker and his jokes;
I laugh at your alases and tut-tuts,
My days, they vanish into circular smokes,
My life lies on a tray of cigarette-butts.

For it is easy to send pulpit wind
From bellies sumptuously lined;
Easy to praise the sleep of the righteous, when
The righteous sleep on cushions ten,
And having risen from a well-fed wife
Easy it is to give advice on life.

But you who upon sated palates clack a moral,
And pick a sermon from between your teeth,
Tell me with what bay, tell me with what laurel
Shall I entwine the heaven-praising wreath,
I, with whom Deity sets out to quarrel?

But, prithee, wherefore these thumbed cards?

O do not make a pack of cards your thesis
And frame no lesson on a house of cards
Where diamonds go lustreless, and hearts go broken
And clubs do batter the skull to little shards,
And where, because the spade is trump
One must perforce kiss Satan's rump.

For I have heard these things from teachers
With dirty beards and hungry features.

Now, after days in dusty factories,
Among machines that manufacture madness
I have no stomach for these subtleties
About rewards and everlasting gladness;
And having met your over-rated dawns,
Together with milkmen watering their milk,
And having trickled sweat, according to a scale of wages,
Sewing buttons to warm the navels of your business sages,
I have brought home at dusk,
My several bones, my much-flailed husk.

> My meals are grand,
> When supper comes

I feed on canned
Aquariums.

The salmon dies.
The evening waits
As I catch flies
From unwashed plates.

And my true love,
She combs and combs,
The lice from off
My children's domes.

Such is the idyll of my life.
But I will yet achieve
An easier living and less scrawny wife
And not forever will the foreman have
The aces up his sleeve,
But some day I will place the lucky bet.
(Ho! Ho! the social revolutions on a table of roulette!)

Alas, that Velvel's sigh makes eddies in the smoke.
For what's the use?
While the pale faces grin, his brow is hot;
He grasps a deuce . . .

A nicotined hand beyond the smoke sweeps off the pot.

O good my brother, should one come to you
And knock upon the door at mid of night
And show you, writ in scripture, black on white,
That this is no way for a man to do?—
What a pale laughter from these ghosts, and "Who
Are you, my saint, to show us what is right?
Make a fifth hand, and we will be contrite;
Shuffle the cards, be sociable, Reb. Jew."

My brother's gesture snaps; *I spoke.*
His cheeks seek refuge in his mouth.
His nostrils puff superior smoke.
His lips are brown with drouth.

Hum a hymn of sixpence,
A tableful of cards
Fingers slowly shuffling

Ambiguous rewards.
When the deck is opened
The pauper once more gave
His foes the kings and aces
And took himself the knave.

Once more he cuts the cards, and dreams his dream;
A rolls-Royce hums within his brain;
Before it stands a chauffeur, tipping his hat,
"You say that it will rain, Sir; it will rain!"
Upon his fingers diamonds gleam,
His wife wears gowns of ultra-Paris fashion,
And she boasts jewels as large as wondrous eyes
The eyes of Og, the giant-king of Bashan.

So Velvel dreams; dreaming, he rises, and
Buttons his coat, coughs in his raised lapel,
Gropes his way home; he rings a raucous bell.

The Rocking Chair

It seconds the crickets of the province. Heard
in the clean lamplit farmhouses of Quebec,—
wooden,—it is no less a national bird;
and rivals, in its cage, the mere stuttering clock.
To its time, the evenings are rolled away;
and in its peace the pensive mother knits
contentment to be worn by her family,
grown-up, but still cradled by the chair in which she sits.

It is also the old man's pet, pair to his pipe,
10   the two aids of his arithmetic and plans,
plans rocking and puffing into market-shape;
and it is the toddler's game and dangerous dance.
Moved to the verandah, on summer Sundays, it is,
among the hanging plants, the girls, the boy-friends,
sabbatical and clumsy, like the white haloes
dangling above the blue serge suits of the young men.

It has a personality of its own;
is a character (like that old drunk Lacoste,

exhaling amber,[1] and toppling on his pins);
20 it is alive; individual; and no less
an identity than those about it. And
it is tradition. Centuries have been flicked
from its arcs, alternately flicked and pinned.
It rolls with the gait of St Malo.[2] It is act

and symbol, symbol of this static folk
which moves in segments, and returns to base, —
a sunken pendulum: *invoke, revoke;*
loosed yon, leashed hither, motion on no space.
O, like some Anjou ballad, all refrain,[3]
30 which turns about its longing, and seems to move
to make a pleasure out of repeated pain,
its music moves, as if always back to a first love.

[1]Perfume (perhaps, from having drunk bay rum or cologne).
[2]With the walk of sailors. (St Malo is a town on the coast of France.)
[3]Anjou is a former province of western France. What Klein seems to have in mind
is the repetitive quality of those French-Canadian songs that had their roots in
medieval France. About these, Edith Fowke quotes an early traveler in Canada:
'[the song] seems endless. After each short line comes the refrain, and the story
twines itself along like a slender creeping plant' (*The Penguin Book of Canadian Folk
Songs*, 1973).

Portrait of the Poet as Landscape

I

Not an editorial-writer, bereaved with bartlett,[1]
mourns him, the shelved Lycidas.[2]
No actress squeezes a glycerine tear for him.
The radio broadcast lets his passing pass.
And with the police, no record. Nobody, it appears,
either under his real name or his alias,
missed him enough to report.

It is possible that he is dead, and not discovered.
It is possible that he can be found some place
10 in a narrow closet, like the corpse in a detective story,

[1]Bartlett's *Familiar Quotations*.
[2]'Lycidas' (1637) is Milton's pastoral elegy mourning the death by drowning of the
young poet Edward King.

standing, his eyes staring, and ready to fall on his face.
It is also possible that he is alive
and amnesiac, or mad, or in retired disgrace,
or beyond recognition lost in love.

We are sure only that from our real society
he has disappeared; he simply does not count,
except in the pullulation[3] of vital statistics—
somebody's vote, perhaps, an anonymous taunt
of the Gallup poll, a dot in a government table—
20   but not felt, and certainly far from eminent—
in a shouting mob, somebody's sigh.

O, he who unrolled our culture from his scroll—
the prince's quote, the rostrum-rounding roar—
who under one name made articulate
heaven, and under another the seven-circled air,[4]
is, if he is at all, a number, an x,
a Mr Smith in a hotel register,—
incognito, lost, lacunal.[5]

II
The truth is he's not dead, but only ignored—
30   like the mirroring lenses forgotten on a brow
that shine with the guilt of their unnoticed world.
The truth is he lives among neighbours, who, though they will allow
him a passable fellow, think him eccentric, not solid,
a type that one can forgive, and for that matter, forgo.

Himself he has his moods, just like a poet.
Sometimes, depressed to nadir, he will think all lost,
will see himself as throwback, relict,[6] freak,
his mother's miscarriage, his great-grandfather's ghost,
and he will curse his quintuplet senses, and their tutors
40   in whom he put, as he should not have put, his trust.

Then he will remember his travels over that body—

[3]Rapid breeding; teeming.
[4]According to early pre-Copernican versions of the universe, the earth was
surrounded by seven concentric spheres (the sun, the moon, and the five known
planets).
[5]i.e. of a lacuna or empty space.
[6]An organism from a previous age surviving in a changed environment.

the torso verb, the beautiful face of the noun,
and all those shaped and warm auxiliaries!
A first love it was, the recognition of his own.
Dear limbs adverbial, complexion of adjective,
dimple and dip of conjugation!

And then remember how this made a change in him
affecting for always the glow and growth of his being;
how suddenly was aware of the air, like shaken tinfoil,[7]
of the patents of nature, the shock of belated seeing,
the loneliness peering from the eyes of crowds;
the integers of thought; the cube-roots of feeling.

Thus, zoomed to zenith, sometimes he hopes again,
and sees himself as a character, with a rehearsed role:
the Count of Monte Cristo,[8] come for his revenges;
the unsuspecting heir, with papers; the risen soul;
or the chloroformed prince awakening from his flowers;
or—deflated again—the convict on parole.

III
He is alone; yet not completely alone.
60 Pins on a map of a colour similar to his,
each city has one, sometimes more than one;
here, caretakers of art, in colleges;
in offices, there, with arm-bands, and green-shaded;
and there, pounding their catalogued beats in libraries, –

everywhere menial, a shadow's shadow.
And always for their egos—their outmoded art.
Thus, having lost the bevel[9] in the ear,
they know neither up nor down, mistake the part
for the whole, curl themselves in a comma,
70 talk technics, make a colon their eyes. They distort—

such is the pain of their frustration—truth

[7]An echo of the opening lines of Gerard Manley Hopkins' 'God's Grandeur':
The World is charged with the grandeur of God.
It will flame out, like shining from shook foil.
[8]In the novel *The Count of Monte Cristo* (1844-5), by Alexandre Dumas *père*, an
innocent man, imprisoned on trumped-up charges, escapes to the Island of Monte
Cristo, where he finds fabulous riches. He returns to Paris a powerful man, and
under various guises, takes revenge on those responsible for his ill treatment.
[9]A tool for ascertaining angles.

to something convolute and cerebral.
How they do fear the slap of the flat of the platitude!
Now Pavlov's victims, their mouths water at bell,
the platter empty.
                    See they set twenty-one jewels
into their watches; the time they do not tell!

Some, patagonian[1] in their own esteem,
and longing for the multiplying word,
80   join party and wear pins, now have a message,
and ear, and the convention-hall's regard.
Upon the knees of ventriloquists, they own,
of their dandled[2] brightness, only the paint and board.

And some go mystical, and some go mad.
One stares at a mirror all day long, as if
to recognize himself; another courts
angels,—for here he does not fear rebuff;
and a third, alone, and sick with sex, and rapt,
doodles him symbols convex and concave.

90   O schizoid solitudes! O purities
curdling upon themselves! Who live for themselves,
or for each other, but for nobody else;
desire affection, private and public loves;
are friendly, and then quarrel and surmise
the secret perversions of each other's lives.

IV
He suspects that something has happened, a law
been passed, a nightmare ordered. Set apart,
he finds himself, with special haircut and dress,
as on a reservation. Introvert.
100   He does not understand this; sad conjecture
muscles and palls thrombotic on his heart.

He thinks an impostor, having studied his personal biography,
his gestures, his moods, now has come forward to pose
in the shivering vacuums his absence leaves.
Wigged with his laurel, that other, and faked with his face,

---

[1]Gigantic (because the Patagonian Indians of South America are said to be the
tallest human beings).
[2]Moved lightly up and down on the knee.

he pats the heads of his children, pecks his wife,
and is at home, and slippered, in his house.

So he guesses at the impertinent silhouette
that talks to his phone-piece and slits open his mail.
110 Is it the local tycoon who for a hobby
plays poet, he so epical in steel?
The orator, making a pause? Or is that man
he who blows his flash of brass in the jittering hall?

Or is he cuckolded by the troubadour
rich and successful out of celluloid?
Or by the don who unrhymes atoms? Or
the chemist death built up? Pride, lost impostor'd pride,
it is another, another, whoever he is,
who rides where he should ride.

V
120 *Fame,* the adrenalin: to be talked about;
to be a verb; to be introduced as *The:*
to smile with endorsement from slick paper; make
caprices anecdotal; to nod to the world; to see
one's name like a song upon the marquees played;
to be forgotten with embarrassment; to be—
to be.

It has its attractions, but is not the thing;
nor is it the ape mimesis[3] who speaks from the tree
ancestral; nor the merkin joy[4] . . .
130 Rather it is stark infelicity
which stirs him from his sleep, undressed, asleep
to walk upon roofs and window-sills and defy
the gape of gravity.

VI
Therefore he seeds illusions. Look, he is
the nth Adam taking a green inventory
in world but scarcely uttered, naming, praising,
the flowering fiats in the meadow, the
syllabled fur, stars aspirate, the pollen

[3]Imitation; perhaps in reference to the Aristotelian concept of poetry as an
imitation of an action.
[4]A deceptive joy; 'merkin': a wig for the female pubic area.

whose sweet collusion sounds eternally.
140   For to praise

the world—he, solitary man—is breath
to him. Until it has been praised, that part
has not been. Item by exciting item—
air to his lungs, and pressured blood to his heart—
they are pulsated, and breathed, until they map,
not the world's, but his own body's chart!

And now in imagination he has climbed
another planet, the better to look
with single camera view upon this earth—
150   its total scope, and each afflated[5] tick,
its talk, its trick, its tracklessness—and this,
this, he would like to write down in a book!

To find a new function for the *déclassé* craft
archaic like the fletcher's;[6] to make a new thing;
to say the word that will become sixth sense;
perhaps by necessity and indirection bring
new forms to life, anonymously, new creeds—
O, somehow pay back the daily larcenies of the lung!

These are not mean ambitions. It is already something
160   merely to entertain them. Meanwhile, he
makes of his status as zero a rich garland,
a halo of his anonymity,
and lives alone, and in his secret shines
like phosphorus. At the bottom of the sea.

[5]Breathed upon, inspired.
[6]Arrow-makers.

ELIZABETH BISHOP
1911–1979

Though born in Worcester, Massachusetts, she considered herself a Canadian by familial upbringing, if not by birth. She spent her early years in Great Village, Nova Scotia, and many later summers in the Maritimes. In 1930 she entered Vassar College, where, as a senior, she was introduced to Marianne Moore, destined to become a close friend and a formative influence on her career. Their friendship

may well have been the cause of her decision to pursue writing rather than medicine. Throughout her life she was passionately fond of traveling. After graduation
from Vassar in 1934, she moved to New York City and, the following year, to
Europe. France and Florida, Mexico and Brazil — these were her homes for
extended periods. In 1970 she settled in Boston, where she taught at Harvard
University and later at the Massachusetts Institute of Technology. One of the finest
lyric poets of the twentieth century, she does not reveal in her writings any exhaustive philosophy or approach to life. Rather, she shows the rich texture and variety
of the world with its joys and pains, injustices and confusions.

The Map

Land lies in water; it is shadowed green.
Shadows, or are they shallows, at its edges
showing the line of long sea-weeded ledges
where weeds hang to the simple blue from green.
Or does the land lean down to lift the sea from under,
drawing it unperturbed around itself?
Along the fine tan sandy shelf
is the land tugging at the sea from under?

The shadow of Newfoundland lies flat and still.
10   Labrador's yellow, where the moony Eskimo
has oiled it. We can stroke these lovely bays,
under a glass as if they were expected to blossom,
or as if to provide a clean cage for invisible fish.
The names of seashore towns run out to sea,
the names of cities cross the neighboring mountains
—the printer here experiencing the same excitement
as when emotion too far exceeds its cause.
These peninsulas take the water between thumb and finger
like women feeling for the smoothness of yard-goods.

20   Mapped waters are more quiet than the land is,
lending the land their waves' own conformation:
and Norway's hare runs south in agitation,
profiles investigate the sea, where land is.
Are they assigned, or can the countries pick their colors?
—What suits the character or the native waters best.
Topography displays no favorites; North's as near as West.
More delicate than the historians' are the map-makers' colors.

First Death in Nova Scotia

In the cold, cold parlor
my mother laid out Arthur
beneath the chromographs:
Edward, Prince of Wales,
with Princess Alexandra,
and King George with Queen Mary.
Below them on the table
stood a stuffed loon
shot and stuffed by Uncle
10   Arthur, Arthur's father.

Since Uncle Arthur fired
a bullet into him,
he hadn't said a word.
He kept his own counsel
on his white, frozen lake,
the marble-topped table.
His breast was deep and white,
cold and caressable;
his eyes were red glass,
20   much to be desired.

"Come," said my mother,
"Come and say goodbye
to your little cousin Arthur."
I was lifted up and given
one lily of the valley
to put in Arthur's hand.
Arthur's coffin was
a little frosted cake,
and the red-eyed loon eyed it
30   from his white, frozen lake.

Arthur was very small.
He was all white, like a doll
that hadn't been painted yet.
Jack Frost had started to paint him
the way he always painted
the Maple Leaf (Forever).
He had just begun on his hair,
a few red strokes, and then
Jack Frost had dropped the brush
40   and left him white, forever.

The gracious royal couples
were warm in red and ermine;
their feet were well wrapped up
in the ladies' ermine trains.
They invited Arthur to be
the smallest page at court.
But how could Arthur go,
clutching his tiny lily,
with his eyes shut up so tight
50   and the roads deep in snow?

In the Waiting Room

In Worcester, Massachusetts,
I went with Aunt Consuelo
to keep her dentist's appointment
and sat and waited for her
in the dentist's waiting room.
It was winter. It got dark
early. The waiting room
was full of grown-up people,
arctics and overcoats,
10   lamps and magazines.
My aunt was inside
what seemed like a long time
and while I waited I read
the *National Geographic*
(I could read) and carefully
studied the photographs:
The inside of a volcano,
black, and full of ashes;
then it was spilling over
20   in rivulets of fire.
Osa and Martin Johnson
dressed in riding breeches,
laced boots, and pith helmets.
A dead man slung on a pole
—"Long Pig," the caption said.
Babies with pointed heads
wound round and round with string;
black, naked women with necks
wound round and round with wire
30   like the necks of light bulbs.

Their breasts were horrifying.
I read it right straight through.
I was too shy to stop.
And then I looked at the cover:
the yellow margins, the date.

Suddenly, from inside,
cams an *oh!* of pain
— Aunt Consuelo's voice —
not very loud or long.
40   I wasn't at all surprised;
even then I knew she was
a foolish, timid woman.
I might have been embarrassed,
but wasn't. What took me
completely by surprise
was that it was *me*:
my voice, in my mouth.
Without thinking at all
I was my foolish aunt,
50   I — we — were falling, falling,
our eyes glued to the cover
of the *National Geographic*,
February, 1918.

I said to myself: three days
and you'll be seven years old.
I was saying it to stop
the sensation of falling off
the round, turning world
into cold, blue-black space.
60   But I felt: you are an *I*,
you are an *Elizabeth*,
you are one of *them*.
Why should you be one, too?
I scarcely dared to look
to see what it was I was.
I gave a sidelong glance
— I couldn't look any higher —
at shadowy gray knees,
trousers and skirts and boots
70   and different pairs of hands
lying under the lamps.
I knew that nothing stranger

had ever happened, that nothing
stranger could ever happen.
Why should I be my aunt,
or me, or anyone?
What similarities—
boots, hands, the family voice
I felt in my throat, or even
the *National Geographic*
and those awful hanging breasts—
held us all together
or made us all just one?
How—I didn't know any
word for it—how "unlikely" . . .
How had I come to be here,
like them, and overhear
a cry of pain that could have
got loud and worse but hadn't?

The waiting room was bright
and too hot. It was sliding
beneath a big black wave,
another, and another.

Then I was back in it.
The War was on. Outside
in Worcester, Massachusetts,
were night and slush and cold,
and it was still the fifth
of February, 1918.

One Art

The art of losing isn't hard to master;
so many things seem filled with the intent
to be lost that their loss is no disaster.

Lose something every day. Accept the fluster
of lost door keys, the hour badly spent.
The art of losing isn't hard to master.

Then practice losing farther, losing faster:
places, and names, and where it was you meant
to travel. None of these will bring disaster.

10 I lost my mother's watch. And look! my last, or
next-to-last, of three loved houses went.
The art of losing isn't hard to master.

I lost two cities, lovely ones. And, vaster,
some realms I owned, two rivers, a continent.
I miss them, but it wasn't a disaster.

—Even losing you (the joking voice, a gesture
I love) I shan't have lied. It's evident
the art of losing's not too hard to master
though it may look like (*Write* it!) like disaster.

IRVING LAYTON

1912–

Born in Rumania, he emigrated with his family to Montreal as an infant. He graduated from Macdonald College in 1939 and, after military service during the Second
World War, obtained his M.A. in political science and economics from McGill
University. He taught for a while in a Montreal secondary school, and he has
continued to teach literature at many universities in Canada and abroad. Along
with Louis Dudek and John Sutherland, he edited *First Statement* in opposition to
the *Preview* group that included P.K. Page. His first volume of poetry, *Here and
Now*, was published in 1945, and since that time he has been the most prolific poet
in Canada, publishing, on the average, a book of poems every year. Sometimes his
poetry is relentlessly personal in its subject-matter, challenging its Canadian audience to shed the shackles of domestic, sexual, and cultural complacency. At other
times his poetic voice is that of an Old Testament prophet in his own Jewish
tradition, decrying man's inhumanity to man. At still other times his voice has the
refined cadences of a delicate and sensitive lyric poet. Montreal has been and
continues to be his physical and literary home.

The Cold Green Element

At the end of the garden walk
the wind and its satellite wait for me;
their meaning I will not know
          until I go there,
but the black-hatted undertaker

who, passing, saw my heart beating in the grass,
is also going there. Hi, I tell him,

a great squall in the Pacific blew a dead poet
  out of the water,
10 who now hangs from the city's gates.

Crowds depart daily to see it, and return
with grimaces and incomprehension;
if its limbs twitched in the air
  they would sit at its feet
peeling their oranges.

And turning over I embrace like a lover
the trunk of a tree, one of those
for whom the lightning was too much
  and grew a brilliant
20 hunchback with a crown of leaves.

The ailments escaped from the labels
of medicine bottles are all fled to the wind;
I've seen myself lately in the eyes
  of old women,
spent streams mourning my manhood,

in whose old pupils the sun became
a bloodsmear on broad catalpa[1] leaves
and hanging from ancient twigs,
  my murdered selves
30 sparked the air like the muted collisions

of fruit. A black dog howls down my blood,
a black dog with yellow eyes;
he too by someone's inadvertence
  saw the bloodsmear
on the broad catalpa leaves.

But the furies clear a path for me to the worm
who sang for an hour in the throat of a robin,
and misled by the cries of young boys
  I am again
40 a breathless swimmer in that cold green element.

[1]Tree with large heart-shaped leaves.

Berry Picking

Silently my wife walks on the still wet furze
Now darkgreen the leaves are full of metaphors
Now lit up is each tiny lamp of blueberry.
The white nails of rain have dropped and the sun is free.

And whether she bends or straightens to each bush
To find the children's laughter among the leaves
Her quiet hands seem to make the quiet summer hush—
Berries or children, patient she is with these.

I only vex and perplex her; madness, rage
Are endearing perhaps put down upon the page;
Even silence daylong and sullen can then
Enamour as restraint or classic discipline.

So I envy the berries she puts in her mouth,
The red and succulent juice that stains her lips;
I shall never taste that good to her, nor will they
Displease her with a thousand barbarous jests.

How they lie easily for her hand to take,
Part of the unoffending world that is hers;
Here beyond complexity she stands and stares
And leans her marvellous head as if for answers.

No more the easy soul my childish craft deceives
Nor the simpler one for whom yes is always yes;
No, now her voice comes to me from a far way off
Though her lips are redder than the raspberries.

Whatever Else Poetry Is Freedom

Whatever else poetry is freedom.
Forget the rhetoric, the trick of lying
All poets pick up sooner or later. From the river,
Rising like the thin voice of grey castratos[1]—the mist;
Poplars and pines grow straight but oaks are gnarled;
Old codgers must speak of death, boys break windows;
Women lie honestly by their men at last.

---

[1]Historically: males castrated before puberty to retain a soprano or alto singing
voice into adulthood.

And I who gave my Kate a blackened eye
Did to its vivid changing colours
10   Make up an incredible musical scale;
And now I balance on wooden stilts and dance
And thereby sing to the loftiest casements.
See how with polish I bow from the waist.
Space for these stilts! More space or I fail!

And a crown I say for my buffoon's head.
Yet no more fool am I than King Canute,[2]
Lord of our tribe, who scanned and scorned;
who half-deceived, believed; and, poet, missed
The first white waves come nuzzling at his feet;
20   Then damned the courtiers and the foolish trial
with a most bewildering and unkingly jest.

It was the mist. It lies inside one like a destiny.
A real Johah it lies rotting like a lung.
And I know myself undone who am a clown
And wear a wreath of mist for a crown;
Mist with the scent of dead apples,
Mist swirling from black oily waters at evening,
Mist from the fraternal graves of cemeteries.

It shall drive me to beg my food and at last
30   Hurl me broken I know and prostrate on the road;
Like a huge toad I saw, entire but dead,
That Time mordantly had blacked; O pressed
To the moist earth it pled for entry.
I shall be I say that stiff toad for sick with mist
And crazed I smell the odour of mortality.

And Time flames like a paraffin stove
And what it burns are the minutes I live.

At certain middays, I have watched the cars
Bring me from afar their windshield suns;
40   What lay to my hand were blue fenders,

[2]Eleventh-century king of England who is said to have placed his throne on the shore and commanded the tide not to rise. When the tide rolled over him anyway, he explained that he had done this to rebuke his courtiers, who thought or acted as if he had God-like powers.

The suns extinguished, the drivers wearing sunglasses.
And it made me think I had touched a hearse.

So whatever else poetry is freedom. Let
Far off the impatient cadences reveal
A padding for my breathless stilts. Swivel,
O hero, in the fleshy groves, skin and glycerine,
And sing of lust, the sun's accompanying shadow
Like a vampire's wing, the stillness in dead feet—
Your stave[3] brings resurrection, O aggrievèd king.

[3]Rod, lance: but also with the punning meaning of 'stanza'.

Keine Lazarovitch
1870-1959

When I saw my mother's head on the cold pillow,
Her white waterfalling hair in the cheeks' hollows,
I thought, quietly circling my grief, of how
She had loved God but cursed extravagantly his creatures.

For her final mouth was not water but a curse,
A small black hole, a black rent in the universe,
Which damned the green earth, stars and trees in its stillness
And the inescapable lousiness of growing old.

And I record she was comfortless, vituperative,
10   Ignorant, glad, and much else besides; I believe
She endlessly praised her black eyebrows, their thick weave,
Till plagiarizing Death leaned down and took them for his mould.

And spoiled a dignity I shall not again find,
And the fury of her stubborn limited mind;
Now none will shake her amber beads and call God blind,
Or wear them upon a breast so radiantly.

O fierce she was, mean and unaccommodating;
But I think now of the toss of her gold earrings,
Their proud carnal assertion, and her youngest sings
20   While all the rivers of her red veins move into the sea.

DYLAN THOMAS

1914–1953

Born in Swansea, Wales, Thomas attended the Swansea Grammar School where his father was Senior English Master. Never much of a scholar, Thomas did well only in English, and loved to act in school plays and little theater productions. When he left school in 1931, he worked for two newspapers, writing on books and theater, and his explorations of the pubs and streets of his seaport town provided him with material for the short stories he was writing at this time. He was also writing poems in penny exercise books, composing much of his carefully crafted syllabic verse in pubs, with a glass of beer by his notebook. Much of his finest poetry was written before he was twenty, and from 1933 on, he was published regularly. Thomas, who enjoyed playing the role of poet, became known as an extraordinarily fine reader of poetry, doing regular poetry readings for BBC radio. Though he was popular and making a good income, he was always in debt and incapable of managing his money. On his tours to the United States, he was renowned not only for his readings, but for his wild drinking bouts. He died suddenly and prematurely in New York after downing eighteen straight whiskies.

The Force That through the Green Fuse Drives the Flower

The force that through the green fuse drives the flower
Drives my green age; that blasts the roots of trees
Is my destroyer.
And I am dumb to tell the crooked rose
My youth is bent by the same wintry fever.

The force that drives the water through the rocks
Drives my red blood; that dries the mouthing streams
Turns mine to wax.
And I am dumb to mouth unto my veins
10   How at the mountain spring the same mouth sucks.

The hand that whirls the water in the pool
Stirs the quicksand; that ropes the blowing wind
Hauls my shroud sail.
And I am dumb to tell the hanging man
How of my clay is made the hangman's lime.

The lips of time leech to the fountain head;
Love drips and gathers, but the fallen blood

Shall calm her sores.
And I am dumb to tell a weather's wind
20 How time has ticked a heaven round the stars.

And I am dumb to tell the lover's tomb
How at my sheet goes the same crooked worm.

A Refusal to Mourn the Death, By Fire, of a Child in London

Never until the mankind making
Bird beast and flower
Fathering and all humbling darkness
Tells with silence the last light breaking
And the still hour
Is come of the sea tumbling in harness

And I must enter again the round
Zion of the water bead
And the synagogue of the ear of corn
10 Shall I let pray the shadow of a sound
Or sow my salt seed
In the least valley of sackcloth to mourn

The majesty and burning of the child's death.
I shall not murder
The mankind of her going with a grave truth
Nor blaspheme down the stations of the breath
With any further
Elegy of innocence and youth.

Deep with the first dead lies London's daughter,
20 Robed in the long friends,
The grains beyond age, the dark veins of her mother,
Secret by the unmourning water
Of the riding Thames.
After the first death, there is no other.

Do Not Go Gentle into That Good Night[1]

Do not go gentle into that good night,
Old age should burn and rave at close of day;
Rage, rage against the dying of the light.

Though wise men at their end know dark is right,
Because their words had forked no lightning they
Do not go gentle into that good night.

Good men, the last wave by, crying how bright
Their frail deeds might have danced in a green bay,
Rage, rage against the dying of the light.

10   Wild men who caught and sang the sun in flight,
And learn, too late, they grieved it on its way,
Do not go gentle into that good night.

Grave men, near death, who see with blinding sight
Blind eyes could blaze like meteors and be gay,
Rage, rage against the dying of the light.

And you, my father, there on the sad height,
Curse, bless, me now with your fierce tears, I pray.
Do not go gentle into that good night.
Rage, rage against the dying of the light.

1. Like Roethke's "The Waking," this is a villanelle. See above, p. 620.

Fern Hill

Now as I was young and easy under the apple boughs
About the lilting house and happy as the grass was green,
    The night above the dingle starry,
        Time let me hail and climb
    Golden in the heydays of his eyes,
And honoured among wagons I was prince of the apple towns
And once below a time I lordly had the trees and leaves
        Trail with daisies and barley
    Down the rivers of the windfall light.

10   And as I was green and carefree, famous among the barns
About the happy yard and singing as the farm was home,
    In the sun that is young once only,
        Time let me play and be

Golden in the mercy of his means,
And green and golden I was huntsman and herdsman, the calves
Sang to my horn, the foxes on the hills barked clear and cold,
        And the sabbath rang slowly
    In the pebbles of the holy streams.

All the sun long it was running, it was lovely, the hay
Fields high as the house, the tunes from the chimneys, it was air
        And playing, lovely and watery
            And fire green as grass.
        And nightly under the simple stars
As I rode to sleep the owls were bearing the farm away,
All the moon long I heard, blessed among stables, the night-jars
        Flying with the ricks, and the horses
            Flashing into the dark.

And then to awake, and the farm, like a wanderer white
With the dew, come back, the cock on his shoulder: it was all
        Shining, it was Adam and maiden,
            The sky gathered again
        And the sun grew round that very day.
So it must have been after the birth of the simple light
In the first, spinning place, the spellbound horses walking warm
        Out of the whinnying green stable
            On to the fields of praise.

And honoured among foxes and pheasants by the gay house
Under the new made clouds and happy as the heart was long,
        In the sun born over and over,
            I ran my heedless ways,
        My wishes raced through the house high hay
And nothing I cared, at my sky blue trades, that time allows
In all his tuneful turning so few and such morning songs
        Before the children green and golden
            Follow him out of grace,

Nothing I cared, in the lamb white days, that time would take me
Up to the swallow thronged loft by the shadow of my hand,
        In the moon that is always rising,
            Nor that riding to sleep
        I should hear him fly with the high fields
And wake to the farm forever fled from the childless land.
Oh as I was young and easy in the mercy of his means,
        Time held me green and dying
            Though I sang in my chains like the sea.

P.K. PAGE
1916–

Born in Swanage, Dorset, England, Patricia Kathleen Page emigrated with her family to Alberta in 1919. She lived in many areas of Canada before settling in Montreal in 1941, where she edited, along with Patrick Anderson and F.R. Scott, *Preview* magazine, which was designed to "preview" or try out new poetry in a cosmopolitan mode. She engaged in many occupations, including radio actress, research assistant, and scriptwriter for the National Film Board. In 1950 she married W.A. Irwin, Commissioner for the film board; he later served as Canadian High Commissioner to Australia and Ambassador, first to Brazil and then to Mexico. In 1944 Page published her first poems as well as a novel, *The Sun and the Moon*. In addition to several short stories, she has published six collections of poetry, most recently *The Glass Air: Poems Selected and New* (1985). Under her married name, P.K. Irwin, she has also achieved eminence as a painter. "In all essential particulars writing and painting are interchangeable," she has observed. Like the painter that she is, she explores in her poetry an image or a scene by gathering together precise details and impressions in a rich tapestry. Since 1964 the Irwins have lived in Victoria, British Columbia.

The Stenographers

After the brief bivouac of Sunday,
their eyes, in the forced march of Monday to Saturday,
hoist the white flag, flutter in the snow-storm of paper,
haul it down and crack in the mid-sun of temper.

In the pause between the first draft and the carbon
they glimpse the smooth hours when they were children—
the ride in the ice-cart, the ice-man's name,
the end of the route and the long walk home;

remember the sea where floats at high tide
were sea marrows growing on the scatter-green vine
or spools of grey toffee, or wasps' nests on water;
remember the sand and the leaves of the country.

Bell rings and they go and the voice draws their pencil
like a sled across snow; when its runners are frozen
rope snaps and the voice then is pulling no burden
but runs like a dog on the winter of paper.

Their climates are winter and summer—no wind
for the kites of their hearts—no wind for a flight;

a breeze at the most, to tumble them over
20   and leave them like rubbish—the boy-friends of blood.

In the inch of the noon as they move they are stagnant.
The terrible calm of the noon is their anguish;
the lip of the counter, the shapes of the straws
like icicles breaking their tongues, are invaders.

Their beds are their oceans—salt water of weeping
the waves that they know—the tide before sleep;
and fighting to drown they assemble their sheep
in columns and watch them leap desks for their fences
and stare at them with their own mirror-worn faces.

30   In the felt of the morning the calico-minded,
sufficiently starched, insert papers, hit keys,
efficient and sure as their adding machines;
yet they weep in the vault, they are taut as net curtains
stretched upon frames. In their eyes I have seen
the pin men[1] of madness in marathon trim
race round the track of the stadium pupil.

[1]'Stick figures, such as children draw' (Page).

Photos of a Salt Mine

How innocent their lives look,
how like a child's
dream of caves and winter, both combined;
the steep descent to whiteness
and the stope[1]
with its striated walls
their folds all leaning as if pointing to
the greater whiteness still,
that great white bank

10   with its decisive front,
that seam upon a slope,
salt's lovely ice.

And wonderful underfoot the snow of salt
the fine

[1]An excavation in the form of steps made as ore is mined from vertical or steeply
inclined veins.

particles a broom could sweep,
one thinks
muckers might make angels in its drifts
as children do in snow,
lovers in sheets,
20   lie down and leave imprinted where they lay
a feathered creature holier than they.

And in the outworked stopes
with lamps and ropes
up miniature matterhorns
the miners climb
probe with their lights
the ancient folds of rock—
syncline[2] and anticline—
and scoop from darkness an Aladdin's cave:
30   rubies and opals glitter from its walls.

But hoses douse the brilliance of these jewels,
melt fire to brine.
Salt's bitter water trickles thin and forms,
slow fathoms down,
a lake within a cave,
lacquered with jet—
white's opposite.
There grey on black the boating miners float
to mend the stays and struts of that old stope
40   and deeply underground
their words resound,
are multiplied by echo, swell and grow
and make a climate of a miner's voice.

So all the photographs like children's wishes
are filled with caves or winter,
innocence
has acted as a filter,
selected only beauty from the mine.
Except in the last picture,
50   it is shot
from an acute high angle. In a pit
figures the size of pins are strangely lit

---

[2]Low, troughlike fold in stratified rock, the opposite of 'anticline': fold with strata
sloping downwards on both sides away from a common crest.

and might be dancing but you know they're not.
Like Dante's vision of the nether hell[3]
men struggle with the bright cold fires of salt,
locked in the black inferno of the rock:
the filter here, not innocence but guilt.

Arras[1]

Consider a new habit—classical,
and trees espaliered on the wall like candelabra.
How still upon that lawn our sandalled feet.

But a peacock rattling his rattan tail and screaming
has found a point of entry. Through whose eye
did it insinuate in furled disguise
to shake its jewels and silk upon that grass?

The peaches hang like lanterns. No one joins
those figures on the arras.
10   Who am I
or who am I become that walking here
I am observer, other, Gemini,
starred for a green garden of cinema?

I ask, what did they deal me in this pack?
The cards, all suits, are royal when I look.
My fingers slipping on a monarch's face
twitch and grow slack.
I want a hand to clutch, a heart to crack.

No one is moving now, the stillness is
20   infinite. If I should make a break. . . .
take to my springy heels. . . . ? But nothing moves.
The spinning world is stuck upon its poles,
the stillness points a bone[2] at me. I fear
the future on this arras.
                          I confess:

[1]Wall hanging, particularly a tapestry.
[2]'Aboriginal projective magic. A prepared human or kangaroo bone is pointed
by a sorcerer at an intended victim (who may be miles away) to bring about his
death' (from Page's glossary of Australian terms in *Cry Ararat!*).

It was my eye.
Voluptuous it came.
Its head the ferrule[3] and its lovely tail
folded so sweetly; it was strangely slim
30   to fit the retina. And then it shook
and was a peacock—living patina,
eye-bright, maculate!
Does no one care?

I thought their hands might hold me if I spoke.
I dreamed the bite of fingers in my flesh,
their poke smashed by an image, but they stand
as if with a treacle,[4] motionless,
folding slow eyes on nothing. While they stare
another line has trolled the encircling air,
40   another bird assumes its furled disguise.

[3]Metal cap used to reinforce or secure the end of a pole or handle—here belonging to an umbrella.
[4]Molasses or sweet syrup; used here as that which entraps the insects it attracts.

The New Bicycle

All the molecules in the house
re-adjust on its arrival,
make way for its shining presence
its bright dials,
and after it has settled
and the light
has explored its surfaces
—and the night—
they compose themselves again
in another order.

One senses the change at once
without knowing what one senses.
Has somebody cleaned the windows
used different soap
or is there a bowl of flowers
on the mantelpiece?—
for the air makes another shape
it is thinner or denser,

a new design
is invisibly stamped upon it.

How we all adapt ourselves
to the bicycle
aglow in the furnace room,
turquoise where turquoise
has never before been seen,
its chrome gleaming
on gears and pedals,
its spokes glistening.
Lightly resting on the incised
rubber of its airy tires
it has changed us all.

Deaf-mute in the Pear Tree

His clumsy body is a golden fruit
pendulous in the pear tree

Blunt fingers among the multitudinous buds

Adriatic blue the sky above and through
the forking twigs

Sun ruddying tree's trunk, his trunk
his massive head thick-nobbed with burnished curls
tight-clenched in bud

(Painting by Generalić. Primitive.)

I watch him prune with silent secateurs

Boots in the crotch of branches shift their weight
heavily as oxen in a stall

Hear small inarticulate mews from his locked mouth
a kitten in a box

Pear clippings fall
                    soundlessly on the ground
Spring finches sing
                    soundlessly in the leaves

A stone. A stone in ears and on his tongue

Through palm and fingertip he knows the tree's
quick springtime pulse

Smells in its sap the sweet incipient pears

Pale sunlight's choppy water glistens on
his mutely snipping blades

and flags and scraps of blue
above him make regatta of the day

But when he sees his wife's foreshortened shape
sudden and silent in the grass below
uptilt its face to him

then air is kisses, kisses

stone dissolves

his locked throat finds a little door

and through it feathered joy
flies screaming like a jay

ROBERT LOWELL
1917–1977

Robert Lowell's poetry is primarily autobiographical, revealing his deep interest in his family's New England history, as well as his reactions to his lineage. He was born in Boston, the son of a naval officer, attended St. Mark's School (founded by his grandfather), and, as was proper for young men of good family in Boston, he went on to Harvard. But after two years he left and went to study with poet and critic John Crowe Ransom at Kenyon College. He converted to Catholicism in 1940, and during World War II, he tried unsuccessfully to enlist in the navy. He refused to be drafted into the army, and as a conscientious objector, was jailed for six months. His first book of poetry was published in 1944, and in 1947 he won the Pulitzer Prize for *Lord Weary's Castle* and became Consultant in Poetry at the Library of Congress. *Life Studies* (1959) reveals some influence of the self-revelatory mode of the Beat poets, and of William Carlos Williams' colloquial American diction. Lowell's form is highly controlled as he strives for a tone of "heightened conversation" in these complex and personal portraits which many consider his finest poetry. During his career, Lowell taught at several universities, including Harvard, wrote for the theater, and translated European poetry. In his last book, *Day by Day*, he returned to an exploration of his childhood.

"To Speak of Woe That Is in Marriage"

"It is the future generation that presses into being by means of these exuberant feelings and supersensible soap bubbles of ours."

SCHOPENHAUER

"The hot night makes us keep our bedroom windows open.
Our magnolia blossoms. Life begins to happen.
My hopped up husband drops his home disputes,
and hits the streets to cruise for prostitutes,
free-lancing out along the razor's edge.
This screwball might kill his wife, then take the pledge.
Oh the monotonous meanness of his lust. . . .
It's the injustice . . . he is so unjust—
whiskey-blind, swaggering home at five.
My only thought is how to keep alive.
What makes him tick? Each night now I tie
ten dollars and his car key to my thigh. . . .
Gored by the climacteric of his want,
he stalls above me like an elephant."

Skunk Hour

[FOR ELIZABETH BISHOP]

Nautilus Island's hermit
heiress still lives through winter in her Spartan cottage;
her sheep still graze above the sea.
Her son's a bishop. Her farmer
is first selectman in our village;
she's in her dotage.

Thirsting for
the hierarchic privacy
of Queen Victoria's century,
she buys up all
the eyesores facing her shore,
and lets them fall.

The season's ill—

we've lost our summer millionaire,
who seemed to leap from an L. L. Bean
catalogue. His nine-knot yawl
was auctioned off to lobstermen.
A red fox stain covers Blue Hill.

And now our fairy
20   decorator brightens his shop for fall;
his fishnet's filled with orange cork,
orange, his cobbler's bench and awl;
there is no money in his work,
he'd rather marry.

One dark night,
my Tudor Ford climbed the hill's skull;
I watched for love-cars. Lights turned down,
they lay together, hull to hull,
where the graveyard shelves on the town. . . .
30   My mind's not right.

A car radio bleats,
"Love, O careless Love. . . ." I hear
my ill-spirit sob in each blood cell,
as If my hand were at its throat. . . .
I myself am hell;
nobody's here—

only skunks, that search
in the moonlight for a bite to eat.
They march on their soles up Main Street:
40   white stripes, moonstruck eyes' red fire
under the chalk-dry and spar spire
of the Trinitarian Church.

I stand on top
of our back steps and breathe the rich air—
a mother skunk with her column of kittens swills the garbage pail.
She jabs her wedge-head in a cup
of sour cream, drops her ostrich tail,
and will not scare.

Water

It was a Maine lobster town—
each morning boatloads of hands

pushed off for granite
quarries on the islands,

and left dozens of bleak
white frame houses stuck
like oyster shells
on a hill of rock,

and below us, the sea lapped
10   the raw little match-stick
mazes of a weir,
where the fish for bait were trapped.

Remember? We sat on a slab of rock.
From this distance in time,
it seems the color
of iris, rotting and turning purpler,

but it was only
the usual gray rock
turning the usual green
20   when drenched by the sea.

The sea drenched the rock
at our feet all day,
and kept tearing away
flake after flake.

One night you dreamed
you were a mermaid clinging to a wharf-pile,
and trying to pull
off the barnacles with your hands.

We wished our two souls
30   might return like gulls
to the rock. In the end,
the water was too cold for us.

For the Union Dead

"Relinquunt Omnia Servare Rem Publicam."[1]

The old South Boston Aquarium stands
in a Sahara of snow now. Its broken windows are boarded.

The bronze weathervane cod has lost half its scales.
The airy tanks are dry.

Once my nose crawled like a snail on the glass;
my hand tingled
to burst the bubbles
drifting from the noses of the cowed, compliant fish.

My hand draws back. I often sigh still
10   for the dark downward and vegetating kingdom
of the fish and reptile. One morning last March,
I pressed against the new barbed and galvanized

fence on the Boston Common. Behind their cage,
yellow dinosaur steamshovels were grunting
as they cropped up tons of mush and grass
to gouge their underworld garage.

Parking spaces luxuriate like civic
sandpiles in the heart of Boston.
A girdle of orange, Puritan-pumpkin colored girders
20   braces the tingling Statehouse,

shaking over the excavations, as it faces Colonel Shaw[2]
and his bell-cheeked Negro infantry
on St. Gaudens' shaking Civil War relief,
propped by a plank splint against the garage's earthquake.

Two months after marching through Boston,
half the regiment was dead;
at the dedication,
William James could almost hear the bronze Negroes breathe.

Their monument sticks like a fishbone
30   in the city's throat.
Its Colonel is as lean
as a compass-needle.

1. "They give up everything to serve the republic."
2. Robert Gould Shaw led the first northern Negro regiment, the Massachusetts 54th.
   He and many of his men were killed leading an attack on Fort Wagner, South
   Carolina.

He has an angry wrenlike vigilance,
a greyhound's gentle tautness;
he seems to wince at pleasure,
and suffocate for privacy.

He is out of bounds now. He rejoices in man's lovely,
peculiar power to choose life and die—
when he leads his black soldiers to death,
40   he cannot bend his back.

On a thousand small town New England greens,
the old white churches hold their air
of sparse, sincere rebellion; frayed flags
quilt the graveyards of the Grand Army of the Republic.

The stone statues of the abstract Union Soldier
grow slimmer and younger each year—
wasp-waisted, they doze over muskets
and muse through their sideburns . . .

Shaw's father wanted no monument
50   except the ditch,
where his son's body was thrown
and lost with his "niggers."

The ditch is nearer.
There are no statues for the last war here;
on Boylston Street, a commercial photograph
shows Hiroshima boiling

over a Mosler Safe, the "Rock of Ages"
that survived the blast. Space is nearer.
When I crouch to my television set,
60   the drained faces of Negro school-children rise like balloons.

Colonel Shaw
is riding on his bubble,
he waits
for the blesséd break.

The Aquarium is gone. Everywhere,
giant finned cars nose forward like fish;
a savage servility
slides by on grease.

MARGARET AVISON
1918–

Born in Galt (now Cambridge), Ontario, she graduated in English from Victoria College, University of Toronto, in 1940. She studied creative writing at Indiana University (1955) and the University of Chicago (1956–57). Her first collection of poetry, *Winter Sun* (1960), won the Governor General's Award. During the sixties she returned to the University of Toronto to pursue graduate studies. She has been a librarian, a lecturer at Scarborough College, University of Toronto, and a social worker for the Presbyterian Church Mission in Toronto. Her poems are often careful and close observations of physical landscapes, and, like Gerard Manley Hopkins, she delights in the natural world's ability to shadow forth spiritual realities.

Snow

Nobody stuffs the world in at your eyes.
The optic heart must venture: a jail-break
And re-creation. Sedges and wild rice
Chase rivery pewter. The astonished cinders quake
With rhizomes. All ways through the electric air
Trundle candy-bright disks; they are desolate
Toys if the soul's gates seal, and cannot bear,
Must shudder under, creation's unseen freight.
But soft, there is snow's legend: color of mourning
Along the yellow Yangtze where the wheel
Spins an indifferent stasis that's death's warning.
Asters of tumbled quietness reveal
Their petals. Suffering this starry blur
The rest may ring your change, sad listener.

10

New Year's Poem

The Christmas twigs crispen and needles rattle
Along the windowledge.
             A solitary pearl
Shed from the necklace spilled at last week's party
Lies in the suety, snow-luminous plainness
Of morning, on the windowledge beside them.
And all the furniture that circled stately
And hospitable when these rooms were brimmed

With perfumes, furs, and black-and-silver
10   Crisscross of seasonal conversation, lapses
Into its previous largeness.
                    I remember
Anne's rose-sweet gravity, and the stiff grave
Where cold so little can contain;
I mark the queer delightful skull and crossbones
Starlings and sparrows left, taking the crust,
And the long loop of winter wind
Smoothing its arc from dark Arcturus down
To the bricked corner of the drifted courtyard,
20   And the still windowledge.
                    Gentle and just pleasure
It is, being human, to have won from space
This unchill, habitable interior
Which mirrors quietly the light
Of the snow, and the new year.

The Swimmer's Moment

For everyone
The swimmer's moment at the whirlpool comes,
But many at that moment will not say
"This is the whirlpool, then."
By their refusal they are saved
From the black pit, and also from contesting
The deadly rapids, and emerging in
The mysterious, and more ample, further waters.
And so their bland-blank faces turn and turn
10   Pale and forever on the rim of suction
They will not recognize.
Of those who dare the knowledge
Many are whirled into the ominous center
That, gaping vertical, seals up
For them an eternal boon of privacy,
So that we turn away from their defeat
With a despair, not for their deaths, but for
Ourselves, who cannot penetrate their secret
Nor even guess at the anonymous breadth
20   Where one or two have won:
(The silver reaches of the estuary).

Butterfly Bones; or Sonnet Against Sonnets

The cyanide jar seals life, as sonnets move
towards final stiffness. Cased in a white glare
these specimens stare for peering boys, to prove
strange certainties. Plane dogsled and safari
assure continuing range. The sweep-net skill,
the patience, learning, leave all living stranger.
Insect—or poem—waits for the fix, the frill
precision can effect, brilliant with danger.
What law and wonder the museum spectres
10   bespeak is cryptic for the shivery wings,
the world cut-diamond-eyed, those eyes' reflectors,
or herbal grass, sunned motes, fierce listening.
Might sheened and rigid trophies strike men blind
like Adam's lexicon locked in the mind?

In a Season of Unemployment

These green painted park benches are
all new. The Park Commissioner had them
planted.
Sparrows go on
having dust baths at the edge of
the park maple's shadow, just where
the bench is cemented down, planted
and then cemented.

Not a breath moves
10   this newspaper.
I'd rather read it by the Lapland sun at midnight. Here we're
bricked in early by a
stifling dark.

On that bench a man in a
pencil-striped white shirt
keeps his head up and steady.

The newspaper-astronaut says
"I feel excellent under the condition of weightlessness."
And from his bench a
20   scatter of black bands in the hollow air

ray out—too quick for the eye—
and cease.

    "Ground observers watching him on a TV circuit said
    At the time of this report he
    was smiling," Moscow ra-
    dio reported.
I glance across at him, and mark that
he is feeling
excellent too, I guess, and
30   weightless and
"smiling."

We the Poor Who are Always With Us

The cumbering hungry
and the uncaring ill
become too many
try as we will.

Try on and on, still?
In fury, fly
out, smash shards (and quail
at tomorrow's new supply,
and fail anew to find and smash the why?)

10   It is not hopeless.
One can crawling move
in useless recognition
there, still free to love
past use, where none survive.

And there is reason in
the hope that then can shine
when other hope is none.

PHYLLIS WEBB

1927–

Born in Victoria, British Columbia, she graduated from the University of British Columbia in 1949. After running unsuccessfully as a CCF candidate for the provincial legislature, she moved to Montreal in 1950, where she pursued graduate studies at McGill University and came into contact with many of the city's writers, including F.R. Scott. During the sixties she lived in Toronto, where she conceived the CBC radio program "Ideas"; from 1966 until 1969 she served as its executive producer. At the end of the decade she returned to the west coast and settled on Salt Spring Island, which remains her home. Her seamless verses are intense lyrical examinations, often of human loneliness and despair, and the perfect shape of the poems brings an order to the seeming shapelessness of the human condition. Just as love offers some meaning to the chaos of life, so too poetry offers some order to the chaos. Webb has taught at the University of British Columbia and the University of Victoria.

Marvell's Garden

Marvell's garden, that place of solitude,
is not where I'd choose to live
yet is the fixed sundial
that turns me round
unwillingly
in a hot glade
as closer, closer I come to contradiction
to the shade green within the green shade.

The garden where Marvell scorned love's solicitude—
10 that dream—and played instead an arcane solitaire,
shuffling his thoughts like shadowy chance
across the shrubs of ecstasy,
and cast the myths away to flowering hours
as yes, his mind, that sea, caught at green
thoughts shadowing a green infinity.

And yet Marvell's garden was not Plato's
garden—and yet—he *did* care more for the form
of things than for the thing itself—
ideas and visions,
20 resemblances and echoes,
things seeming and being
not quite what they were.

661

- That was his garden, a kind of attitude
struck out of an earth too carefully attended,
wanting to be left alone.
And I don't blame him for that.
God knows, too many fences fence us out
and his garden closed in on Paradise.

On Paradise! When I think of his hymning
30   Puritans in the Bermudas, the bright oranges
lighting up that night! When I recall
his rustling tinsel hopes
beneath the cold decree of steel.
Oh, I have wept for some new convulsion
to tear together this world and his.

But then I saw his luminous plumèd Wings
prepared for flight,
and then I heard him singing glory
in a green tree,
40   and then I caught the vest he'd laid aside
all blest with fire.

And I have gone walking slowly in
his garden of necessity
leaving brothers, lovers, Christ
outside my walls
where they have wept without
and I within.

Lament

Knowing that everything is wrong,
how can we go on giving birth
either to poems or the troublesome lie,
to children, most of all, who sense
the stress in our distracted wonder
the instant of their entry with their cry?

For every building in this world
receives our benediction of disease.
Knowing that everything is wrong
means only that we all know where we're going.

But I, how can I, I
craving the resolution of my earth,
take up my little gang of sweet pretence
and saunter day-dreary down the alleys, or pursue
the half-disastrous night? Where is that virtue
I would claim with tense impersonal unworth,
where does it dwell, that virtuous land
where one can die without a second birth?

It is not here, neither in the petulance
of my cries, nor in the tracers of my active fear,
not in my suicide of love, my dear.
That place of perfect animals and men
is simply the circle we would charm our children in
and why we frame our lonely poems in
the shape of a frugal sadness.

To Friends Who Have Also Considered Suicide

It's still a good idea.
Its exercise is discipline:
to remember to cross the steet without looking,
to remember not to jump when the cars side-swipe,
to remember not to bother to have clothes cleaned,
to remember not to eat or want to eat,
to consider the numerous methods of killing oneself,
that is surely the finest exercise of the imagination:
death by drowning, sleeping pills, slashed wrists,
10   kitchen fumes, bullets through the brain or through
the stomach, hanging by the neck in attic or basement,
a clean frozen death—the ways are endless.
And consider the drama! It's better than a whole season
at Stratford when you think of the emotion of your
family on hearing the news and when you imagine
how embarrassed some will be when the body is found.
One could furnish a whole chorus in a Greek play
with expletives and feel sneaky and omniscient
at the same time. But there's no shame
20   in this concept of suicide.
It has concerned our best philosophers
and inspired some of the most popular
of our politicians and financiers.
Some people swim lakes, others climb flagpoles,
some join monasteries, but we, my friends,

who have considered suicide take our daily walk
with death and are not lonely.
In the end it brings more honesty and care
than all the democratic parliaments of tricks.
30   It is the 'sickness unto death'[1] it is death;
it is not death; it is the sand from the beaches
of a hundred civilizations, the sand in the teeth
of death and barnacles our singing tongue:
and this is 'life' and we owe at least this much
contemplation to our western fact: to Rise,
Decline, Fall, to futility and larks,
to the bright crustaceans of the oversky.

[1]Phrase taken from *The Sickness Unto Death* (1849) by Danish philosopher and theologian Sören Kierkegaard (1813-55); for Kierkegaard, the 'sickness unto death' is despair.

The Days of the Unicorns

I remember when the unicorns
roved in herds through the meadow
behind the cabin, and how they would
lately pause, tilting their jewelled
horns to the falling sun as we shared
the tensions of private property
and the need to be alone.

Or as we walked along the beach
a solitary delicate beast
might follow on his soft paws
until we turned and spoke the words
to console him.

It seemed they were always near
ready to show their eyes and stare
us down, standing in their creamy
skins, pink tongues out
for our benevolence.

As if they knew that always beyond
and beyond the ladies were weaving them
into their spider looms.

I knew where they slept
and how the grass was bent

by their own wilderness
and I pitied them.

It was only yesterday, or seems
like only yesterday when we could
touch and turn and they came
perfectly real into our fictions.
But they moved on with the courtly sun
grazing peacefully beyond the story
horns lowering and lifting and
lowering.

I know this is scarcely credible now
as we cabin ourselves in cold
and the motions of panic
and our cells destroy each other
performing music and extinction
and the great dreams pass on
to the common good.

ADRIENNE RICH

1929–

Born the daughter of a physician in Baltimore, Maryland, Adrienne Rich completed her first book of poetry, *A Change of World* (1952), while still an undergraduate at Radcliffe. W. H. Auden, who had chosen her book for publication in the Yale Series of Younger Poets, described her poems as "very neatly and modestly dressed," as poems which "respect their elders but are not cowed by them." Rich had indeed learned her craft well from her elders: Frost, Thomas, Auden, Stevens, Yeats—all male poets. "I had been taught that poetry should be 'universal,' which meant of course, non-female." In her poetry, one sees her moving from the split between "the girl who wrote poems, who defined herself in writing poems, and the girl who was to define herself by her relationship with men," until she was "able to write for the first time, directly about experiencing myself as a woman." Much of her poetry deals with the separation between men and women, between self and others, though her latest poetry emphasizes the possibility of a "common language" which will transcend such separation. She was married in 1953 to Alfred Conrad, an economist who died in 1970, and with whom she had three sons. She has taught at a number of colleges and universities, and presently teaches at Stanford University.

The Afterwake

Nursing your nerves
to rest, I've roused my own; well,
now for a few bad hours!
Sleep sees you behind closed doors.
Alone, I slump in his front parlor.
You're safe inside. Good. But I'm
like a midwife who at dawn
has all in order: bloodstains
washed up, teapot on the stove,
10 and starts her five miles home
walking, the birthyell still
exploding in her head.

Yes, I'm with her now: here's
the streaked, livid road
edged with shut houses
breathing night out and in.
Legs tight with fatigue,
we move under morning's coal-blue star,
colossal as this load
20 of unexpired purpose, which drains
slowly, till scissors of cockcrow snip the air.

Novella

Two people in a room, speaking harshly.
One gets up, goes out to walk.
(That is the man.)
The other goes into the next room
and washes the dishes, cracking one.
(That is the woman.)
It gets dark outside.
The children quarrel in the attic.
She has no blood left in her heart.
10 The man comes back to a dark house.
The only light is in the attic.
He has forgotten his key.
He rings at his own door
and hears sobbing on the stairs.
The lights go on in the house.
The door closes behind him.
Outside, separate as minds,
the stars too come alight.

Night-Pieces: For a Child

1. *The Crib*

You sleeping I bend to cover.
Your eyelids work. I see
your dream, cloudy as a negative,
swimming underneath.
You blurt a cry. Your eyes
spring open, still filmed in dream.
Wider, they fix me—
—death's head, sphinx, medusa?
You scream.
10   Tears lick my cheeks, my knees
droop at your fear.
Mother I no more am,
but woman, and nightmare.

2. *Her Waking*

Tonight I jerk astart in a dark
hourless as Hiroshima,
almost hearing you breathe
in a cot three doors away.

You still breathe, yes—
and my dream with its gift of knives,
its murderous hider and seeker,
ebbs away, recoils

back into the egg of dreams,
10   the vanishing point of mind.
All gone.

But you and I—
swaddled in a dumb dark
old as sickheartedness,
modern as pure annihilation—

we drift in ignorance.
If I could hear you now
mutter some gentle animal sound!
If milk flowed from my breast again. . . .

Moving in Winter

Their life, collapsed like unplayed cards,
is carried piecemeal through the snow:
Headboard and footboard now, the bed
where she has lain desiring him
where overhead his sleep will build
its canopy to smother her once more;
their table, by four elbows worn
evening after evening while the wax runs down;
mirrors grey with reflecting them,
10   bureaus coffining from the cold
things that can shuffle in a drawer,
carpets rolled up around those echoes
which, shaken out, take wing and breed
new altercations, the old silences.

Rape

There is a cop who is both prowler and father:
he comes from your block, grew up with your brothers,
had certain ideals.
You hardly know him in his boots and silver badge,
on horseback, one hand touching his gun.

You hardly know him but you have to get to know him:
he has access to machinery that could kill you.
He and his stallion clop like warlords among the trash,
his ideals stand in the air, a frozen cloud
10   from between his unsmiling lips.

And so, when the time comes, you have to turn to him,
the maniac's sperm still greasing your thighs,
your mind whirling like crazy. You have to confess
to him, you are guilty of the crime
of having been forced.

And you see his blue eyes, the blue eyes of all the family
whom you used to know, grow narrow and glisten,
his hand types out the details
and he wants them all
20   but the hysteria in your voice pleases him best.

You hardly know him but now he thinks he knows you:
he has taken down your worst moment

on a machine and filed it in a file.
He knows, or thinks he knows, how much you imagined;
he knows, or thinks he knows, what you secretly wanted.

He has access to machinery that could get you put away;
and if, in the sickening light of the precinct,
and if, in the sickening light of the precinct,
your details sound like a portrait of your confessor,
30   will you swallow, will you deny them, will you lie your way home?

SYLVIA PLATH
1932–1963

She was the daughter of Aurelia Plath, a high school teacher of Austrian parentage, and Otto Plath, who had come from Prussia at the age of sixteen, was a professor of biology at Boston University, and an authority on bees. After her father's death in 1940, the family moved to Wellesley, where Aurelia Plath taught high school and encouraged Sylvia and her brother in their literary pursuits. By the time Plath entered Smith College, she was beginning to have her poems and short stories published. She graduated from Smith in 1955 and won a Fulbright Scholarship to Newnham College, Cambridge. There she met, and in 1956 married, British poet Ted Hughes. Except for a year during which Plath taught freshman English at Smith College, the couple lived in England. In 1960, Plath published her first book of poems, *Colossus*, and her first child was born. After the birth of a second child in 1962, Plath and Hughes separated. Plath was frequently ill, working to support herself and her children, and waking before daybreak to write her poetry, turning out two to three poems a day. The strain proved too great, and she took her life in February, 1963.

Sheep in Fog

The hills step off into whiteness.
People or stars
Regard me sadly, I disappoint them.

The train leaves a line of breath.
O slow
Horse the colour of rust,

Hooves, dolorous bells—

All morning the
Morning has been blackening,

10   A flower left out.
My bones hold a stillness, the far
Fields melt my heart.

They threaten
To let me through to a heaven
Starless and fatherless, a dark water.

Daddy

You do not do, you do not do
Any more, black shoe
In which I have lived like a foot
For thirty years, poor and white,
Barely daring to breathe or Achoo.

Daddy, I have had to kill you.
You died before I had time—
Marble-heavy, a bag full of God,
Ghastly statue with one grey toe
10   Big as a Frisco seal

And a head in the freakish Atlantic
Where it pours bean green over blue
In the waters off beautiful Nauset.
I used to pray to recover you.
Ach, du.

In the German tongue, in the Polish town
Scraped flat by the roller
Of wars, wars, wars.
But the name of the town is common.
20   My Polack friend

Says there are a dozen or two.
So I never could tell where you
Put your foot, your root,
I never could talk to you.
The tongue stuck in my jaw.

It stuck in a barb wire snare.

Ich, ich, ich, ich,
I could hardly speak.
I thought every German was you.
30   And the language obscene

An engine, an engine
Chuffing me off like a Jew.
A Jew to Dachau, Auschwitz, Belsen.
I began to talk like a Jew.
I think I may well be a Jew.

The snows of the Tyrol, the clear beer of Vienna
Are not very pure or true.
With my gypsy ancestress and my weird luck
And my Taroc pack and my Taroc pack
40   I may be a bit of a Jew.

I have always been scared of *you*,
With your Luftwaffe, your gobbledygoo.
And your neat mustache
And your Aryan eye, bright blue.
Panzer-man, panzer-man, O You—

Not God but a swastika
So black no sky could squeak through.
Every woman adores a Fascist,
The boot in the face, the brute
50   Brute heart of a brute like you.

You stand at the blackboard, daddy,
In the picture I have of you,
A cleft in your chin instead of your foot
But no less a devil for that, no not
Any less the black man who

Bit my pretty red heart in two.
I was ten when they buried you.
At twenty I tried to die
And get back, back, back to you.
60   I thought even the bones would do.

But they pulled me out of the sack,
And they stuck me together with glue.
And then I knew what to do.
I made a model of you,
A man in black with a Meinkampf look

And a love of the rack and the screw.
And I said I do, I do.
So daddy, I'm finally through.
The black telephone's off at the root,
70   The voices just can't worm through.

If I've killed one man, I've killed two—
The vampire who said he was you
And drank my blood for a year,
Seven years, if you want to know.
Daddy, you can lie back now.

There's a stake in your fat black heart
And the villagers never liked you.
They are dancing and stamping on you.
They always *knew* it was you.
80   Daddy, daddy, you bastard, I'm through.

Kindness

Kindness glides about my house.
Dame Kindness, she is so nice!
The blue and red jewels of her rings smoke
In the windows, the mirrors
Are filling with smiles.

What is so real as the cry of a child?
A rabbit's cry may be wilder
But it has no soul.
Sugar can cure everything, so Kindness says.
10   Sugar is a necessary fluid,

Its crystals a little poultice.
O kindness, kindness
Sweetly picking up pieces!
My Japanese silks, desperate butterflies,
May be pinned any minute, anaesthetized.

And here you come, with a cup of tea
Wreathed in steam.
The blood jet is poetry,
There is no stopping it.
20   You hand me two children, two roses.

Edge

The woman is perfected.
Her dead

Body wears the smile of accomplishment,
The illusion of a Greek necessity

Flows in the scrolls of her toga,
Her bare

Feet seem to be saying:
We have come so far, it is over.

Each dead child coiled, a white serpent,
10 One at each little

Pitcher of milk, now empty.
She has folded

Them back into her body as petals
Of a rose close when the garden

Stiffens and odours bleed
From the sweet, deep throats of the night flower.

The moon has nothing to be sad about,
Staring from her hood of bone.

She is used to this sort of thing.
20 Her blacks crackle and drag.

Words

Axes
After whose stroke the wood rings,
And the echoes!
Echoes travelling
Off from the centre like horses.

The sap
Wells like tears, like the
Water striving
To re-establish its mirror
10 Over the rock

That drops and turns,

A white skull,
Eaten by weedy greens.
Years later I
Encounter them on the road—

Words dry and riderless,
The indefatigable hoof-taps.
While
From the bottom of the pool, fixed stars
20   Govern a life.

MARGARET ATWOOD
1939–

The most prolific writer of her generation, she is the author and editor of more than twenty-five books. Born in Ottawa, Ontario, she spent her early years in the bush country of Quebec and northern Ontario; when she was seven years old, her family settled in Toronto. Atwood graduated from the University of Toronto in 1961, obtained her A.M. from Radcliffe College, and pursued doctoral studies in Victorian literature at Harvard University. Her first volume of poetry, *Double Persephone*, appeared in 1961; her first novel, *The Edible Woman*, appeared in 1967. In addition to more than a dozen volumes of poetry and seven novels, she has published two collections of short fiction, *Dancing Girls* (1977) and *Bluebeard's Egg* (1983), and two volumes of literary criticism, *Survival: A Thematic Guide to Canadian Literature* (1972) and *Second Words* (1982). She sees her work, poetry and fiction, as an artistic lens focused carefully and caringly on contemporary society. Her poetry, which may seem almost prosaic in its stark verse patterns, captures with clinical precision the subjects of her sensitive explorations. An ardent nationalist who is a frequent and articulate speaker for Canada on both the national and international stages, she lives in Toronto with novelist Graeme Gibson and their daughter.

At the Tourist Centre in Boston

There is my country under glass,
a white relief-
map with red dots for the cities,
reduced to the size of a wall

and beside it 10 blownup snapshots
one for each province,
in purple-browns and odd reds,

the green of the trees dulled;
all blues however
of an assertive purity.

Mountains and lakes and more lakes
(though Quebec is a restaurant and Ontario the empty
interior of the parliament buildings),
with nobody climbing the trails and hauling out
the fish and splashing in the water

but arrangements of grinning tourists—
look here, Saskatchewan
is a flat lake, some convenient rocks
where two children pose with a father
and the mother is cooking something
in immaculate slacks by a smokeless fire,
her teeth white as detergent.

Whose dream is this, I would like to know:
is this a manufactured
hallucination, a cynical fiction, a lure
for export only?

I seem to remember people,
at least in the cities, also slush,
machines and assorted garbage. Perhaps
that was my private mirage
which will just evaporate
when I go back. Or the citizens will be gone,
run off to the peculiarly-
green forests
to wait among the brownish mountians
for the platoons of tourists
and plan their old red massacres.

Unsuspecting
window lady, I ask you:

Do you see nothing
watching you from under the water?

Was the sky ever that blue?

Who really lives there?

Death of a Young Son by Drowning

He, who navigated with success
the dangerous river of his own birth
once more set forth

on a voyage of discovery
into the land I floated on
but could not touch to claim.

His feet slid on the bank,
the currents took him;
he swirled with ice and trees in the swollen water

10   and plunged into distant regions,
his head a bathysphere;
through his eyes' thin glass bubbles

he looked out, reckless adventurer
on a landscape stranger than Uranus
we have all been to and some remember.

There was an accident; the air locked,
he was hung in the river like a heart.
They retrieved the swamped body,

cairn of my plans and future charts,
20   with poles and hooks
from among the nudging logs.

It was spring, the sun kept shining, the new grass
lept to solidity;
my hands glistened with details.

After the long trip I was tired of waves.
My foot hit rock. The dreamed sails
collapsed, ragged.

I planted him in this country
like a flag.

Variations on the Word LOVE

This is a word we use to plug
holes with. It's the right size for those warm

blanks in speech, for those red heart-
shaped vacancies on the page that look nothing
like real hearts. Add lace
and you can sell
it. We insert it also in the one empty
space on the printed form
that comes with no instructions. There are whole
magazines with not much in them
but the word *love*, you can
rub it all over your body and you
can cook with it too. How do we know
it isn't what goes on at the cool
debaucheries of slugs under damp
pieces of cardboard? As for the weed-
seedlings nosing their tough snouts up
among the lettuces, they shout it.
Love! Love! sing the soldiers, raising
their glittering knives in salute.

Then there's the two
of us. This word
is far too short for us, it has only
four letters, too sparse
to fill those deep bare
vacuums between the stars
that press on us with their deafness.
It's not love we don't wish
to fall into, but that fear.
This word is not enough but it will
have to do. It's a single
vowel in this metallic
silence, a mouth that says
O again and again in wonder
and pain, a breath, a finger-
grip on a cliffside. You can
hold on or let go.

Variation on the Word *SLEEP*

I would like to watch you sleeping,
which may not happen.
I would like to watch you,
sleeping. I would like to sleep
with you, to enter

your sleep as its smooth dark wave
slides over my head

and walk with you through that lucent
wavering forest of bluegreen leaves
with its watery sun & three moons
towards the cave where you must descend,
towards your worst fear
I would like to give you the silver
branch, the small white flower, the one
word that will protect you
from the grief at the center
of your dream, from the grief
at the center. I would like to follow
you up the long stairway
again & become
the boat that would row you back
carefully, a flame
in two cupped hands
to where your body lies
beside me, and you enter
it as easily as breathing in

I would like to be the air
that inhabits you for a moment
only. I would like to be that unnoticed
& that necessary.

Interlunar

Darkness waits apart from any occasion for it;
like sorrow it is always available.
This is only one kind,

the kind in which there are stars
above the leaves, brilliant as steel nails
and countless and without regard.

We are walking together
on dead wet leaves in the intermoon
among the looming nocturnal rocks
which would be pinkish grey
in daylight, gnawed and softened
by moss and ferns, which would be green,
in the musty fresh yeast smell

of trees rotting, each returning
itself to itself

and I take your hand, which is the shape a hand
would be if you existed truly.
I wish to show you the darkness
you are so afraid of.

Trust me. This darkness
is a place you can enter and be
as safe in as you are anywhere;
you can put one foot in front of the other
and believe the sides of your eyes.
Memorize it. You will know it
again in your own time.
When the appearances of things have left you,
you will still have this darkness.
Something of your own you can carry with you.

We have come to the edge:
the lake gives off its hush;
in the outer night there is a barred owl
calling, like a moth
against the ear, from the far shore
which is invisible.
The lake, vast and dimensionless,
doubles everything, the stars,
the boulders, itself, even the darkness
that you can walk so long in
it becomes light.

MICHAEL ONDAATJE

1943–

Born in Sri Lanka, he moved to England in 1954 and to Canada in 1963. He obtained his B.A. from the University of Toronto and his M.A. from Queen's University; in 1971 he joined the Department of English at Glendon College, York University, where he currently teaches. Poet and novelist, critic and editor, he constantly questions the distinction between poetry and prose and between fact and fiction in writing that challenges his readers' perception and understanding of reality. *The Collected Works of Billy the Kid* (1970), a collage of poetry, prose, and photographs, is a discontinuous narrative of Billy the Kid and Pat Garrett that explores their traditional interpretation as insane outlaw-renegade and sane representative of law and order; *Running in the Family* (1982), also a collage, is the story of Ondaatje's own family, transformed into fiction. Always intensely visual, his poetry eschews formal structures in order to capture with vivid immediacy the dramatic dimensions of a particular character or moment. His five volumes of poetry and his novel, *Coming through Slaughter* (1976), have won international acclaim.

Bearhug

Griffin calls to come and kiss him goodnight
I yell ok. Finish something I'm doing,
then something else, walk slowly round
the corner to my son's room.
He is standing arms outstretched
waiting for a bearhug. Grinning.

Why do I give my emotion an animal's name,
give it that dark squeeze of death?
This is the hug which collects
10   all his small bones and his warm neck against me.
The thin tough body under the pyjamas
locks to me like a magnet of blood.

How long was he standing there
like that, before I came?

Letters & Other Worlds

*'for there was no more darkness for him and, no doubt
like Adam before the fall, he could see in the dark'[1]*

My father's body was a globe of fear
His body was a town we never knew
He hid that he had been where we were going
His letters were a room he seldom lived in
In them the logic of his love could grow

My father's body was a town of fear
He was the only witness to its fear dance
He hid where he had been that we might lose him
His letters were a room his body scared

10   He came to death with his mind drowning.
On the last day he enclosed himself

[1]Translation from Alfred Jarry's *La Dragonne* (1943), cited in *The Banquet Years* by Roger Shattuck (1955).

in a room with two bottles of gin, later
fell the length of his body
so that brain blood moved
to new compartments
that never knew the wash of fluid
and he died in minutes of a new equilibrium.

His early life was a terrifing comedy
and my mother divorced him again and again.
20   He would rush into tunnels magnetized
by the white eye of trains
and once, gaining instant fame,
managed to stop a Perahara[2] in Ceylon
—the whole procession of elephants dancers
local dignitaries—by falling
dead drunk into the street.

As a semi-official, and semi-white at that,
the act was seen as a crucial
turning point in the Home Rule Movement
30   and led to Ceylon's independence in 1948.
(My mother had done her share too—
her driving so bad
she was stoned by villagers
whenever her car was recognized)

For 14 years of marriage
each of them claimed he or she
was the injured party.
Once on the Colombo docks
saying goodbye to a recently married couple
40   my father, jealous
at my mother's articulate emotion,
dove into the waters of the harbour
and swam after the ship waving farewell.
My mother pretending no affiliation
mingled with the crowd back to the hotel.

Once again he made the papers
though this time my mother
with a note to the editor

[2]Religious ceremony celebrated by a parade.

corrected the report—saying he was drunk
50   rather than broken hearted at the parting of friends.
The married couple received both editions
of *The Ceylon Times* when their ship reached Aden.[3]

And then in his last years
he was the silent drinker,
the man who once a week
disappeared into his room with bottles
and stayed there until he was drunk
and until he was sober.

There speeches, head dreams, apologies,
60   the gentle letters, were composed.
With the clarity of architects
he would write of the row of blue flowers
his new wife had planted,
the plans for electricity in the house,
how my half-sister fell near a snake
and it had awakened and not touched her.
Letters in a clear hand of the most complete empathy
his heart widening and widening and widening
to all manner of change in his children and friends
70   while he himself edged
into the terrible acute hatred
of his own privacy
till he balanced and fell
the length of his body
the blood screaming in
the empty reservoir of bones
the blood searching in his head without metaphor

[3]Capital of the British colony of the same name (Aden is now the capital of
Southern Yemen).

Elizabeth

Catch, my Uncle Jack said
and oh I caught this huge apple
red as Mrs Kelly's bum.

It's red as Mrs Kelly's bum, I said
and Daddy roared
and swung me on his stomach with a heave.
Then I hid the apple in my room
till it shrunk like a face
growing eyes and teeth ribs.

10 Then Daddy took me to the zoo
he knew the man there
they put a snake around my neck
and it crawled down the front of my dress.
I felt its flicking tongue
dripping onto me like a shower.
Daddy laughed and said Smart Snake
and Mrs Kelly with us scowled.

In the pond where they kept the goldfish
Philip and I broke the ice with spades
20 and tried to spear the fishes;

we killed one and Philip ate it,
then he kissed me
with raw saltless fish in his mouth.

My sister Mary's got bad teeth
and said I was lucky, then she said
I had big teeth, but Philip said I was pretty.
He had big hands that smelled.

I would speak of Tom, soft laughing,
who danced in the mornings round the sundial
30 teaching me the steps from France, turning
with the rhythm of the sun on the warped branches,
who'd hold my breast and watch it move like a snail
leaving his quick urgent love in my palm.
And I kept his love in my palm till it blistered.

When they axed his shouders and neck
the blood moved like a branch into the crowd.
And he staggered with his hanging shoulder
cursing their thrilled cry, wheeling,
waltzing in the French style to his knees
40 holding his head with the ground,
blood settling on his clothes like a blush;

this way
when they aimed the thud into his back.

And I find cool entertainment now
with white young Essex, and my nimble rhymes.[1]

[1]The 'Elizabeth' of this poem is Elizabeth I (1533-1603), who assumed the throne
of England in 1558 following the reigns of her father, Henry VIII (1491-1547), her
brother, Edward VI (1537-53), and her sister Mary Tudor (1515-58). 'Philip' is
Philip II of Spain (1527-98) who married Mary Tudor in 1554; 'Tom' is Lord
Thomas Seymour of Sudeley (1508?-49), whose repeated attempts to compromise
and marry the adolescent Elizabeth, as well as to overthrow his brother Edward
Seymour, the protector of Edward VI, led to his execution; 'Essex' is the second
Earl of Essex, Robert Devereux (1566-1601), soldier and favourite of Elizabeth,
who was executed for attempting to incite an uprising against the court. 'Uncle
Jack' and 'Mrs Kelly' are characters invented by Ondaatje.

The Cinnamon Peeler

If I were a cinnamon peeler[1]
I would ride your bed
and leave the yellow bark dust
on your pillow.

Your breasts and shoulders would reek
you could never walk through markets
without the profession of my fingers
floating over you. The blind would
stumble certain of whom they approached
10   though you might bathe
under rain gutters, monsoon.

Here on the upper thigh
at this smooth pasture
neighbour to your hair
or the crease
that cuts your back. This ankle.
You will be known among strangers
as the cinnamon peeler's wife.

I could hardly glance at you
20   before marriage

[1]One who peels the cinnamon bark, the source of the spice, from the trees.

never touch you
—your keen nosed mother, your rough brothers.
I buried my hands
in saffron, disguised them
over smoking tar,
helped the honey gatherers . . .

                    *

When we swam once
I touched you in water
and our bodies remained free,
you could hold me and be blind of smell.
You climbed on the bank and said
            this is how you touch other women
the grass cutter's wife, the lime burner's daughter.
And you searched your arms
for the missing perfume
            and knew

        what good is it
to be the lime burner's daughter
left with no trace
as if not spoken to in the act of love
as if wounded without the pleasure of a scar.

You touched
your belly to my hands
in the dry air and said
I am the cinnamon
peeler's wife. Smell me.

DRAMA

Contexts of Drama

DRAMA, LITERATURE, AND REPRESENTATIONAL ART

Drama begins in make-believe, in the play acting of children, in the ritual of primitive religion. And it never forsakes its primitive beginnings, for imitative action is its essence. When an actor appears on stage, he makes believe he is someone other than himself, much as a child does, much as primitive people still do. Thus, like play-acting and ritual, drama creates its experience by doing things that can be heard and seen. "Drama," in fact, comes from a Greek word meaning "thing done." And the things it does, as with play-acting and ritual, create a world apart—a world modeled on ours yet leading its own charmed existence

Drama, of course, is neither primitive ritual nor child's play, but it does share with them the essential quality of *enactment*. This quality should remind us that drama is not solely a form of literature. It is at once literary art *and* representational art. As literary art, a play is a fiction made out of words. It has a plot, characters, and dialogue. But it is a special kind of fiction—a fiction *acted out* rather than narrated. In a novel or short story, we learn about characters and events through the words of a narrator who stands between us and them, but in a play nothing stands between us and the total make-up of its world. Characters appear and events happen without any intermediate comment or explanation. Drama, then, offers us a *direct* presentation of its imaginative reality. In this sense it is representational art.

As students of drama, we are faced with something of a paradox. Because it is literature, a play can be read. But because it is representational art, a play is meant to be witnessed. We can see this problem in other terms. The text of a play is something like the score of a symphony—a finished work, yet only a potentiality until it is performed. Most plays, after all, are written to be performed. Those eccentric few that are not—that are written only to be read—we usually refer to as *closet dramas.* Very little can take place in a closet, but anything is possible in the theater. For most of us, however, the experience of drama is usually confined to plays in print rather than in performance. This means that we have to be unusually resourceful in our study of drama. Careful reading is not enough. We have to be creative readers as well. We have to imagine drama on the stage: not only must we attend to the meanings and implications of words—we also have to envision the words in performance. By doing so, we can begin to experience the understanding *and* pleasure that spectators gain when they attend a play. Their place, of course, is the theater, where our study properly begins.

DRAMA AND THEATRICAL PERFORMANCE

The magic of theater, its ability to conjure up even such incredible characters as the Ghost in *Hamlet,* or the Witches in *Macbeth,* or Death in *Everyman,* depends on the power of *spectacle.* And by spectacle we mean all the sights and sounds of performance—the slightest twitch or the boldest thrust of a sword, the faintest whisper or the loudest cry. Spectacle, in short, is the means by which the fictional world of a play is brought to life in the theater. When we witness a play, our thoughts and feelings are provoked as much by the spectacle as by the words themselves. Thus in reading a play, we should continually seek to create its spectacle in the imaginative theater of our minds. To do so, we must take a special approach to the text of a play.

It is not enough to read the text as simply a sequence of statements made by characters talking to one another or to themselves. We must also read the text as a *script* for performance, as if we were directors and actors involved in staging the play. Once we interpret it as a script, we can then see that the text contains innumerable *cues* from which we can construct a spectacle in our mind's eye. If we are attentive to these cues, they will tell us about the various elements that make up the total spectacle: *setting, costuming, props, blocking* (the arrangement of characters on the stage), *movement, gestures, intonation,* and *pacing* (the tempo and coordination of performance). By keeping those elements continuously in mind, we can imagine what the play looks and sounds like on stage. Then we will truly be entering into the world of the play, and by doing so we will not only understand, but also experience, its meaning.

Some dramatists, such as Ibsen, Shaw, and Williams, provide extensive and explicit directions for performance in parenthetical remarks preceding the *dialogue* and interspersed with it. But no matter how extensive their remarks may be, they are never complete guides to production. They still require us to infer elements of the spectacle from the dialogue itself. Other dramatists such as Sophocles and Shakespeare provide little, if any, explicit guidance about staging. When we read their plays, we must gather our cues almost entirely from the dialogue. Modern directors staging such plays must do the same.

But the *King Lear*, for instance, that we see in a modern theater is not the spectacle Shakespeare's seventeenth-century audiences would have seen when they witnessed the play. The Globe Theater, where Shakespeare's plays were originally produced, was an open-air structure without sets or lights of any kind. Thus the spectators of Shakespeare's time could not have witnessed the "realistic" illusion of a storm such as the one in act III of *King Lear*. They would have seen the action take place in broad daylight on a bare stage without a backdrop. Thus they would have depended wholly upon the language and actors to evoke the setting. Even so, they would have had a more intimate involvement with the characters and the action, for the Globe stage, rather than being set behind an arch, extended out into the audience itself. Their experience of the scene would thus have been quite different from that provided by our modern stage version. In light of that difference, we might well ask which version is valid. Both, in fact, are valid, but for different reasons. The modern version is valid, primarily because it is true to the theatrical conditions of our own time. Most modern theaters, after all, are not designed like the Globe, and if we attend a performance of *King Lear* we should not expect it to duplicate the scene as produced in Shakespeare's day. But when we are reading the play we *can* imagine how it would have been produced in the Globe and thus be true to the theatrical conditions for which Shakespeare created it.

Once we have imagined any play in the context of the theater for which it was written, we can also bring that understanding to any production we may happen to witness. We can compare our imagined production with the production on stage, and by so doing we can recognize how the director and actors have adapted the original context of the play to their own theatrical circumstances. If, for example, we were to attend a production of *King Lear*, we might see the storm scene performed on a bare stage, without sets or props of any kind. Having imagined the play in its original theatrical context, we would then not be surprised or puzzled by that bare stage, but would recognize that the director was attempting to incorporate an important element of seventeenth-century theater in a contemporary production. By being historically informed play-readers, we can also become critically enlightened play-goers.

DRAMA AND OTHER LITERARY FORMS

When we consider drama primarily as a theatrical event—a representational art to be performed and witnessed—we are concerned with the uniquely dramatic experience created by a play in performance. But any performance, moving as it may be, is an *interpretation*—of how the lines should be enacted and delivered. Thus every production of a play stresses some words and minimizes others, includes some meanings and excludes others. No single production can possibly convey all the implications in the language of a play. This should remind us that drama is also a form of literature—an art made out of words—and should be understood in relation not only to the theater but also to the other literary forms: story, poem, and essay.

Each literary form has a unique way of using words and communicating them to the reader. Drama in its pure form uses words to create action through the dialogue of characters talking to one another rather than to the reader: its essential quality is *interaction*. But different forms also share certain similarities. Like a story, drama is concerned with plot and character. Like a poem, it is overheard rather than being addressed to a reader. Like an essay, it is capable of being used to explore issues and propose ideas. Using these relationships as points of departure, we can now examine some of the ways in which drama takes on the characteristics and devices of the other forms.

Drama and Narration

A play is at its most dramatic, of course, when it uses the give-and-take of dialogue to create interaction. But the interaction always takes place within a specific context—a background in time and place without which it cannot be properly understood. To bring about this understanding, drama turns to the narrative techniques of the story. This is not to say we should expect to find storytellers addressing us directly in plays. Occasionally they do turn up, but more often the characters become storytellers in their dialogue with one another. The most obvious form of this storytelling occurs at the beginning of plays, and is appropriately called the *exposition* because it sets forth and explains in a manner typical of narrative.

Exposition is important not only because it establishes the mood of a play but also because it conveys information about the world of that play. Through expository dialogue the dramatist may reveal information about the public state of affairs, as in the opening of *Oedipus Rex*; or exposition may disclose information about the past actions and private relations of the characters. Often the information comes in bits and pieces of dialogue, as in life itself, so that we must put it together on our own. But once we have done so, we have a background for understanding the action that takes place during the play.

Related to exposition is another narrative device, called *retrospection*. Often, during the process of action, characters look back and survey significant events that took place before the time of the play; and when this happens, drama is again using an element of narration. Sometimes retrospection may lead to major revelations about the characters and the motivations for their behavior. Sometimes retrospection may be the principal activity of the play, as in *Oedipus Rex*, where the chief character becomes preoccupied with piecing together elements from the past, and the climax occurs when his retrospection leads him to discoveries about the past that totally reverse his view of himself and his world.

Thus far we have looked at narrative elements referring to pre-play action, but there are also occasions when narration is used to convey the action of the play itself—when narration replaces interaction. Occasions such as these are produced when offstage action is reported rather than represented—for even when characters are offstage they are still doing things that we must know about in order to have a total view of the action. When offstage action is reported, a play becomes most nearly like a story. Words then are being used to develop a view of character and situation rather than to create action through dialogue. This process can be seen most clearly in *Oedipus Rex*, when the Second Messenger tells the Choragus about the death of Iokastê and the self-blinding of Oedipus. The interaction on stage ceases entirely for the length of almost fifty lines, and what we get instead has all the features of a miniature story.

The Messenger first establishes his narrative authority, then moves into his tale, supplying detailed information, offering explanations for facts he cannot provide, reporting dialogue, and concluding with a general reflection on the fate of Oedipus and Iokastê, whose experience he sees as epitomizing the "misery of mankind." In trying to explain why Sophocles has these events reported rather than showing them on stage, we might simply conclude that they are too gruesome to be displayed. But it is also true that through the Messenger's report Sophocles is able to provide a comment on the meaning of the events.

The Messenger's commentary brings us to the last important element of narration in drama—*choric commentary*. When the narrator of a story wishes to comment on characters and events, he can do so at will. But the dramatist, of course, cannot suddenly appear in the play—or on stage—to provide a point of view on the action. The dramatist's alternative is the *chorus*, or *choric characters*—personages, that is, who are relatively detached from the action and can thus stand off from it, somewhat like a narrator, to reflect on the significance of events. In Greek drama the chorus performed this function.

The existence of a chorus, however, is no guarantee that its opinions are always to be trusted. Sometimes it can be as wrongheaded as any of the more involved characters. Sometimes it is completely reliable, as in its concluding remarks in *Oedipus Rex* about the frailty of the human condition. Choric commentary, then, provides a point of view, but not necessarily an authoritative one, or one to be associated necessarily with the dramatist. In each case it has to be judged in the context of the entire play. But whether it is valid, or partially reliable, or completely invalid, the chorus does provoke us to reflect on the meaning of events by providing commentary for us to assess.

After the classical Greek period the formal chorus disappeared almost entirely from drama. Remnants of the chorus can, of course, be found in later plays—even in modern drama. In Bertolt Brecht's *The Threepenny Opera*, for example, several of the songs explicitly comment on the social and political implications of the play. But for us as readers the important matter is to recognize that choric characters persist in drama despite the absence of a formally designated chorus. Minor characters such as messengers, servants, clowns, or others not directly involved in the action, can carry out the functions of a chorus, as does the Doctor at the end of *Everyman*. Characters involved in the action can also function as choric commentators. Ultimately, any character is capable of becoming a commentator of a sort, simply by standing off from the action and viewing it as a spectator rather than as a participant. And their reflections should be taken no less seriously than those of a chorus. After all, like Nora in the last scene of *A Doll's House*, characters can be the most discerning judges of their world.

Drama and Meditation

When we recall that interaction through dialogue is the basis of drama, we can readily see that a play is committed by its very nature to showing us the public side of its characters. Realizing this, we can see as well the artistic problem a dramatist faces when trying to reveal the private side of such characters. The narrator of a story can solve this problem simply by telling us the innermost thoughts of the characters. But a dramatist must turn to the conventions of the poem, using words addressed by a speaker talking or thinking to himself.

When reading a purely lyric poem, we automatically assume that the situation is private rather than public and that we can overhear the words even though they might never be spoken aloud. In reading or witnessing a play, we must make a similar imaginative effort. To assist our efforts, dramatists have traditionally organized their plays so as to make sure that a character thinking to himself is seen in private. That special situation is implied by our term *soliloquy*, which means (literally) to speak alone. But it is also true that we have private thoughts even in the presence of others, and this psychological reality has been recognized by modern dramatists whose characters may often be seen thinking to themselves in the most public situations. Whatever the circumstances, private or public, the soliloquy makes unusual demands on both actors and audience.

As readers we should be aware that the soliloquy can perform a variety of functions, and, since it is so unusual an element in drama, it achieves its purposes with great effectiveness. Customarily, the soliloquy is a means of giving expression to a complex state of mind and feeling, and in most cases the speaker is seen struggling with problems of the utmost consequence.

This accounts for the intensity we often find in the soliloquy. We are all familiar, for example, with Hamlet's predicaments—to be or not to be, to kill or not to kill the king—and these are typical of the weighty issues that usually burden the speaker of a soliloquy. In soliloquy, then, the interaction among characters is replaced by the interaction of a mind with itself.

When a play shifts from dramatic interaction to meditation, its process of events is temporarily suspended, and the soliloquizing character necessarily becomes a spectator of his world. In this way the soliloquy, like choric commentary, offers the dramatist a means of providing a point of view on the action of the play. In reading a soliloquy, then, we should examine it not only as the private revelation of a character but also as a significant form of commentary on other characters and events.

In considering the soliloquy, we have been examining only an element of meditation in drama. It is also possible for plays to become primarily or even exclusively meditative—though at first this probably sounds like a contradiction of dramatic form. If drama depends on the interaction of dialogue, how is it possible for internalized thought and feeling to be the principal subject of a play? Actually, this can happen in a number of ways. One way—a very traditional way—is to create a cast of characters who represent not persons but abstractions—who embody aspects, or qualities, or thoughts, or feelings of a single mind. In *Everyman*, for example, the title character is shown in conversation with other characters named Beauty, Strength, Discretion, and Five Wits. Interaction among characters of that sort is clearly meant to represent the interaction of a mind with itself, and so it constitutes the dramatization of a meditative experience achieved through what we might call an allegory of the mind.

We can also recognize plays dramatizing the life of the mind through methods other than allegory. Many modern plays, such as *Death of a Salesman*, or *A Streetcar Named Desire*, or *Equus*, include not only soliloquies and other kinds of monologue but also imaginary sequences depicting dreams and fantasies. And some contemporary plays, such as *Krapp's Last Tape*, consist exclusively of a single character talking to himself. Plays such as these reflect the influence of modern psychological theories about the behavior of the mind. Writing in 1932, for example, Eugene O'Neill defined the "modern dramatist's problem" as discovering how to "express those profound hidden conflicts of the mind which the probings of psychology continue to disclose to us." Almost fifty years earlier, in 1888, the Swedish dramatist Strindberg anticipated the same idea: "I have noticed that what interests people most nowadays is the psychological action." Looking at their statements side by side, we can see that they share the same concern. O'Neill speaks of "hidden conflicts of the mind," and Strindberg of "psychological action." We might also call it *meditative drama*.

Whatever form a meditative drama may take, we as readers must be alert to the "hidden conflicts" it aims to dramatize. To recognize such conflicts we must be attentive not only to the external action but also to what we might call the internal action. We should examine both plot and dialogue for what they can tell us about the mental life of the characters. And rather than looking for a clearly defined sequence of events, we should expect to find a kind of movement as irregular and hazy as the workings of the mind itself.

Drama and Persuasion

A play could be exclusively a piece of persuasion only if it consisted of a single character—the dramatist!—addressing ideas directly to the audience. In such an event, of course, it would be difficult to distinguish the play from a lecture. This extreme case should remind us that drama is rarely, if ever, simply an exposition or assertion of ideas. Ideas can, of course, be found throughout the dialogue of almost any play, but, as we have seen in the preceding sections, it is best to assume that those ideas are sentiments of the characters rather than the opinions of the dramatist. A character is a character. A dramatist is a dramatist. And dramatists are never present to speak for themselves, except in prefaces, prologues, epilogues, stage directions—and other statements outside the framework of the play.

Although dramatists cannot speak for themselves, their plays can. The essential quality of drama—interaction—may be made to serve the purposes of an essay. Dialogue, plot, and character may be used to expound ideas and sway the opinions of an audience. The desire to persuade usually implies the existence of conflicting ideas, and plays with a persuasive intention customarily seek to demonstrate the superiority of one idea, or set of attitudes, over another. Thus characters may become spokesmen for ideas, dialogue a form of debating ideas, and action a form of testing ideas. Plays of this kind inevitably force audiences and readers to examine the merits of each position and align themselves with one side or the other. In reading such plays, we must be attentive not only to the motives and personalities of characters but also to the ideas they espouse. Similarly, we must be interested not only in the fate of the characters but also in the success or failure of their ideas. Ultimately, then, these plays do not allow us the pleasure of simply witnessing the interaction of characters. Like essays, they seek to challenge our ideas and change our minds.

Because they focus on conflicting beliefs and ideas, plays with a persuasive intention often embody elements similar to a formal argument or debate. Like *Major Barbara*, they usually set up opposing values in their opening scenes. Thus Shaw establishes a conflict between the Salvation Army philosophy of Barbara and the economic-political vision of Undershaft. In defending their ideas, these characters behave so much like contestants in a debate that their dialogue sounds like disputation rather than conversation. And in the process of reading or witnessing the debate, we are clearly invited to take a stand ourselves, to side with one view or the other. The choice, of course, is not an easy one, and the play is designed to keep us from making a simple choice.

Modes of Drama

DRAMA, THE WORLD, AND IMITATION

Drama, as we said at the start, creates a world modeled on our own: its essence is imitative action. But drama is not imitative in the ordinary sense of the word. It does not offer us a literal copy of reality, for the truth of drama does not depend upon reproducing the world exactly as it is. Drama is true to life by being false to our conventional notions of reality.

The sexual sit-down strike in *Lysistrata* is outlandish. The abstract characters of *Everyman* are fantastic. The dialogue in *Krapp's Last Tape* is frequently bizarre. Yet each of these plays creates a world that we recognize as being in some sense like our own. Our problem then is to define the special sense in which drama is imitative. We can begin by recognizing that its mode of imitation must be selective rather than all-inclusive, intensive rather than extensive. It has to be, since time is short and space is limited in the theater. Faced with limitations in stage size and performance time, the dramatist obviously cannot hope to reproduce the world exactly as it is. By selecting and intensifying things, however, the dramatist can emphasize the dominant patterns and essential qualities of human experience. Thus, our understanding of any play requires that we define the principle of emphasis that determines the make-up of its world and the experience of its characters.

In defining the emphasis of any play, we can ask ourselves whether the dramatist has focused on the beautiful or the ugly, on the orderly or the chaotic, on what is best or on what is worst in the world. A play that emphasizes the beautiful and the orderly tends toward an idealized vision of the world—which is the mode we call *romance*. A play focusing on the ugly and chaotic tends toward a debased view of the world, and this we call *satire*. Both these emphases depend for their effect upon extreme views of human nature and existence.

697

In contrast to the extreme conditions of romance and satire, another pair of dramatic processes takes place in a world neither so beautiful as that of romance nor so ugly as that of satire—in a world more nearly like our own. Rather than focusing on essential qualities in the world, these processes—*comedy* and *tragedy*—emphasize the dominant patterns of experience that characters undergo in the world. In comedy the principal characters ordinarily begin in a state of opposition either to one another or to their world—often both. By the end of the play, their opposition is replaced by harmony. Thus the characters are integrated with one another and with their world. In tragedy, however, the hero and his world begin in a condition of harmony that subsequently disintegrates, leaving him by the end of the play completely isolated or destroyed.

With these four possibilities in mind, we might draw a simple diagram such as this:

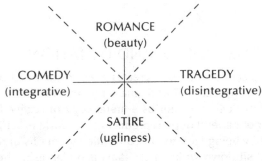

The vertical pair emphasize the essential qualities in the world; the horizontal pair emphasize the dominant patterns of human experience; the point of intersection—the absence of emphasis—refers to the world as it is. In this way we can immediately visualize each of the emphases, its distinguishing characteristics, and its relation to each of the others. Once we have recognized these possibilities, we might be tempted simply to categorize plays in terms of the characteristics we have identified with each emphasis. Yet it should be kept in mind that each emphasis is at best an abstraction—a definition formulated in order to generalize about a great number of plays, not an explanation of any one play in particular. Thus, when we turn to individual plays we should not necessarily expect that they can be accurately described and understood simply by labeling them comedy or tragedy, satire or romance.

As a way of anticipating some of the complexities, we can see in the diagram that each emphasis borders on two others. Comedy, for example, tends toward romance, on the one hand, and satire, on the other. The same is true of tragedy, and the others. Even the antithetical possibilities, as we will see, can interact. But this should hardly surprise us: if the world can incorporate both the beautiful and the ugly, so can a play. Ultimately, then, these categories will serve us best if we use them tactfully as guides to understanding rather than as a rigid system of classification. But before they can serve us as guides, we must familiarize ourselves with their characteristics in greater detail.

TRAGEDY AND COMEDY

Tragedies usually end in death and mourning, comedies in marriage and dancing. That difference accounts for the two familiar masks of drama, one expressing sorrow, the other joy, one provoking tears, the other laughter. That difference also accounts for the commonly held notion that tragedy is serious, and comedy frivolous. But when we consider that both modes are probably descended from primitive fertility rites—tragedy from ritual sacrifice, comedy from ritual feasting—we can recognize that they dramatize equally important dimensions of human experience. Tragedy embodies the inevitability of individual death, comedy the irrepressibility of social rebirth. So, like autumn and spring, tragedy and comedy are equally significant phases in a natural cycle of dramatic possibilities. Indeed, like the seasons of the year and the nature of human experience, they are inextricably bound up with one another.

Every comedy contains a potential tragedy—the faint possibility that harmony may not be achieved, that the lovers may not come together to form a new society. And every tragedy contains a potential comedy—the faint possibility that disaster may be averted, that the hero or heroine may survive. This in turn should remind us that we must be concerned not only with the distinctive endings of tragedy and of comedy, but also with the means by which each brings about its end. Catastrophe in and of itself does not constitute tragedy, nor does marriage alone make for comedy. The unique experience of each mode is produced by the design of its plot and the nature of the characters who take part in it. We can grasp this principle most clearly by looking first at the elements of tragedy, then at the elements of comedy.

Tragedy was first defined by the Greek philosopher Aristotle (384–322 B.C.), who inferred its essential elements from witnessing the plays of his own time. His observations, which he set down in the *Poetics,* cannot be expected to explain all the tragedies that have ever been written; no single theory could possibly do so. But Aristotle's theory has influenced more dramatists—and critics—than any other propounded since his time, and thus it remains the best guide we have to the nature of tragedy.

Aristotle considered *plot* to be the most important element of tragedy, because he believed that "all human happiness or misery takes the form of action," that "it is in our actions—what we do—that we are happy or the reverse." Thus, in discussing tragedy, he emphasized the design of the plot and established several important qualities that contribute to its effect. First, he stressed the *unity* of a tragic plot. By unity he meant that the plot represents a single action, or story, with a definite beginning, middle, and end, and further that all its incidents are "so closely connected that the transposal or withdrawal of any one of them will disjoin or dislocate the whole." By close connection he also meant that the incidents are causally related to one another, so that their sequence is probable and necessary. Ultimately, then, we can see that, in emphasizing the unity of a tragic plot, Aristotle was calling attention to the quality of the inevitable that we associate with tragedy. Thus in reading a tragedy we should attempt to define the chain of cause and effect linking each incident in the plot. In this way we will understand the process that makes its catastrophe inevitable, and thus gain insight into the meaning of the catastrophe.

In examining the plot of a tragedy such as *Oedipus Rex*, we may be tempted to regard its catastrophe as not only inevitable but also inescapable. Aristotle, however, did not see the inevitable change in the fortunes of the tragic hero as being the result of chance, or coincidence, or fate, or even of some profound flaw in the character of the hero. Rather, he saw the change of fortune as being caused by "some error of judgment," a "great error," on the part of the hero. In defining this element of tragedy, Aristotle clearly regarded the hero or heroine, and not some condition beyond human control, as responsible for initiating the chain of events leading to the change of fortune. Even a profound flaw in character, after all, is beyond human control. Accordingly, Aristotle described the tragic hero as an "intermediate kind of personage" in moral character, neither "preeminently virtuous and just," nor afflicted "by vice and depravity"—as someone morally "like ourselves," in whom we can engage our emotional concern. Thus, when we read tragedies such as *Oedipus Rex* or *King Lear* we should not regard their protagonists as victims of absurd circumstances, but rather should seek to identify the sense in which they are agents of their own undoing.

While we seek to understand the nature of their error, we should not forget that most tragic heroes are genuinely admirable characters—persons, as Aristotle tells us, who deservedly enjoy "great reputation and prosperity." And their reputation is a function not simply of their social rank but also of their commitment to noble purposes. Oedipus is not merely a king but also a man committed to discovering the truth and ridding his city of the plague. King Lear is not only a king but a father who loves and trusts his children. Romeo and Juliet are not simply the children of aristocratic families but also persons committed to a love that transcends the pettiness of family squabbles and political factions. Our response to them should thus combine judgment with sympathy and admiration.

Once we make the effort to discover their error, we shall find that we undergo an experience parallel to that of the protagonists themselves. We shall find that we are compelled by the process of events—by the turn of the plot—to recognize how they have undone themselves. The protagonist's act of recognition is defined by Aristotle as the *discovery*, because it entails "a change from ignorance to knowledge." And the discovery, as Aristotle recognized, is caused inevitably by a *reversal,* an incident or sequence of incidents that go contrary to the protagonist's expectations. Reversal and discovery are crucial elements of the tragic experience, because they crystalize its meaning for the protagonist—and for us. When events go contrary to their expectations, when the irony of their situation becomes evident, they—and we—have no choice but to recognize exactly how the noblest intentions can bring about the direst consequences. Thus, in its discovery, as in its entire plot, tragedy affirms both the dignity and the frailty of man.

Discovery scenes take place in comedy as well, but, rather than accounting for an inevitable disaster, comic discoveries reveal information that enables characters to avoid a probable catastrophe. Lost wills may be found, or mistaken identities corrected, or some other fortuitous circumstance may be revealed. Somehow comedy always manages to bring about a happy turn of events for its heroes and heroines—and thus those heroes and heroines are rarely the sole or primary agents of their success. Usually, in fact, they get a large helping hand from chance, or coincidence, or some other lucky state of affairs. Comedy thrives on improbability. And in doing so it defies the mortal imperatives of tragedy.

In this sense comedy embodies the spirit of spring with its eternal promise of rebirth and renewal, and it embodies, too, the festive air and festive activities we associate with spring. The term *comedy,* in fact, is derived from a Greek word, *komoidia,* meaning revel-song, and revelry always finds its way into comedy, whether in the form of feasts and dancing, tricks and joking, sex and loving—or all of them combined, as in *Lysistrata.* So the perils that develop in the world of comedy rarely seem very perilous to us. Although the characters themselves may feel temporarily threatened, the festive air makes us sense that ultimately no permanent damage will be done, and thus we share the perspective of Puck in *A Midsummer Night's Dream,* when he says:

> Jack shall have Jill,
> Naught shall go ill,
> The man shall have his mare again, and all shall be well.

Though comedy avoids the experience of death, it does not evade the significance of life. Comic plots, in fact, usually arise out of conflicts that embody opposing values and beliefs. Thus the conflicts among characters inevitably pit one set of attitudes against another, one kind of social vision against another. In reading comedies, therefore, we should attempt to identify the attitudes that bring characters into conflict. In *Lysistrata,* for example, the wives are committed to peace, their husbands to political honor. In *A Midsummer Night's Dream* the young lovers, Hermia and Lysander, are committed to their vows of true love, but Hermia's father is committed to his parental authority. In *Major Barbara,* Lady Britomart is committed to social tradition, Barbara to social philanthropy, and Undershaft to social engineering. Once we have identified those conflicting values, we will discover that they can help us to understand the meaning of a comic plot.

Comedy usually begins with a state of affairs dominated by one kind of social idea, and thus the resolution of a comic plot—achieved through its scenes of discovery—embodies the triumph of a new social order. Whoever wins out in comedy is invariably on the right side, no matter how improbable the victory may seem. Thus it is that the characters who oppose the new order of things—the blocking figures—are usually subjected to comic ridicule throughout the play. Comedy, after all, expresses an irreverent attitude toward old and inflexible ideas, toward any idea that stifles natural and reasonable impulses in the human spirit. But comedy, as we said earlier, also embodies the generous and abundant spirit of spring. Its heroes and heroines—the proponents of the new society—always seek to include their opponents in the final comic festivities. Comedy seeks not to destroy the old, but rather to reclaim it. And therein is to be seen the ultimate expression of its exuberant faith in life.

TRAGICOMEDY, NATURALISM, AND ABSURDIST DRAMA

Tragedy, comedy, satire, and romance—each of these primary modes embodies its own unique pattern of dramatic experience. Each incorporates distinctly different kinds of plots and characters, distinctly different kinds of conflicts and discovery scenes, and each achieves a distinctly different view of human existence. Thus, when we read or witness a tragedy or comedy, a satire or romance, we undergo an experience that is more or less clear-cut. We feel sorrow or joy, scorn or admiration. We know, in short, exactly how we feel, exactly what we think.

But some plays—many modern plays, especially—do not arouse such clear-cut responses. As we read or witness them, our feelings and judgments may well be confused, or ambiguous, or mixed in one way or another. We may well feel torn between sorrow and joy, scorn and admiration. Indeed, we may not know exactly how we feel, or exactly what we think. When we find ourselves experiencing such mixed feelings, we will probably also discover that the play itself has been designed to leave us in an unresolved state of mind—that it does not embody a clear-cut pattern of catastrophe or rebirth (as in tragedy or comedy) or present clear-cut images of good or evil (as in romance or satire). Many plays, rather than being dominated by a single mode, actually combine differing or opposing modes of dramatic experience. In describing such works we use the term *tragicomedy*—not as a value judgment but as a means of defining the ambiguous experience that we witness in the play and feel within ourselves. Tragicomedy, then, leaves us with a complex reaction, similar to the uncertainty we often feel in response to life itself.

Uncertainty—about the nature of human existence—is a fundamental source of the tragicomic quality we find in many modern and contemporary plays. In some, that quality is produced by a *naturalistic* view of human nature and experience—a view of men and women as influenced by psychological, social, and economic forces so complex that their character and behavior cannot be easily judged or explained. That view of human nature led Strindberg, for example, to create characters whom he describes as being "somewhat 'characterless' "—characters, that is, who are influenced by "a whole series of motives," rather than by any single, or simple, purpose. Like other naturalistic dramatists, Strindberg is unwilling to offer us simple explanations to account for human behavior:

> A suicide is committed. Business troubles, says the man of affairs. Unrequited love, say the women. Sickness, says the invalid. Despair, says the down-and out. But it is possible that the motive lay in all or none of these directions, or that the dead man concealed his actual motive by revealing quite another, likely to reflect more to his glory.

Just as we cannot definitely account for their actions, so too the characters in a realistic drama cannot themselves perceive, much less control, all the forces influencing their behavior. Typically, then, the protagonists of naturalistic drama, such as Nora in *A Doll's House*, are placed in dramatic situations portraying them as being in some sense victims of their environment. They may attempt to alter their circumstances, as does Nora, or they may wilfully deceive themselves about the nature of them, or they may acquiesce in them, or they may sit in judgment upon them; but whatever action they take, it does not lead to a clear-cut resolution of the kind we associate with tragedy and comedy. Nor does their situation allow us to make the clear-cut moral judgment that we do of characters in satire and romance. "Vice has a reverse side very like virtue," as Strindberg reminds us. Thus, naturalistic drama leaves us with a problematic view of human experience, and the most we can hope for is to understand, to the degree that we humanly can, the psychological, social, and economic circumstances that are contributing to the problematic situations of its characters.

In some contemporary plays the problematic situation is produced by conditions that transcend even naturalistic explanations. In these plays we sense the presence of some profound situation that afflicts the characters but is in the end indefinable. In Beckett's *Endgame*, for example, we find the principal characters existing in a world where all the elements of nature seem to be on the verge of extinction; yet the cause of that condition remains a mystery. In *Krapp's Last Tape*, we are faced with a single character, namely Krapp, whose existence is defined almost exclusively by an insatiable appetite for bananas, an unquenchable thirst for soda-water, and an obsessive fixation on his tape-recorded diary. These mysterious, even ridiculous, circumstances lead us to wonder whether there is *any* ultimate source of meaning *at all* in the world of those plays, or for that matter whether there is *any* rational source of explanation *at all* for the experience of the characters. For this reason, such plays are known as *absurdist* drama.

Their absurdity is usually evident not only in plot but in dialogue as well. Often, for example, the conversation of characters in absurdist drama does not make perfect sense, either because they are talking at cross purposes, or because their language has no clear point of reference to anything in their world. Yet even as we read the dialogue we will find it to be at once laughably out of joint and terrifyingly uncommunicative. In much the same way we may be puzzled by the resolution of these plays—wondering whether the characters' situation at the end is in any significant respect different from what it was at the beginning, wondering whether the play is tragic or comic, wondering even whether there is any single word, or concept, such as *tragicomedy*, that can adequately express the possibility that human existence may be meaningless. Ultimately, then, absurdist drama like the other modes does embody a view of human existence; but rather than perceiving existence as dominated by one pattern or another, one quality or another, that view implies that existence may have no pattern or meaning at all.

Elements of Drama

CONTEXTS, MODES, AND THE ELEMENTS OF DRAMA

Characters, dialogue, plot—these are the indispensable elements of drama. Together they make possible the imitative world of every play, for characters are like people, dialogue and plot like the things they say and do. But likeness does not mean identicalness. As we indicated in our discussion of dramatic modes, the truth of drama does not depend upon reproducing the world exactly as it is. For this reason, we should not expect to find characters who talk and act in just the same way that people do, nor should we expect to find plots that develop in just the same way that ordinary events do. The characters who populate romance and satire, for example, are modeled less on specific people than on human potentialities. Similarly, the plots elaborated in comedy and tragedy are based less on real occurrences than on basic patterns of human experience. The elements of drama, then, are highly specialized versions of the elements that make up the world as it is. The particular version we encounter in any single play will be determined by a variety of circumstances—by the mode of the play, the purpose of the play, the literary form of the play, and the design of the theater for which it was written. Thus we should always keep these circumstances in mind when we study the elements of drama.

DIALOGUE

The give-and-take of dialogue is a specialized form of conversation. Designed as it is to serve the needs created by the various contexts and modes of drama, it can hardly be expected to sound like our customary patterns of speech. In ordinary conversation, for example, we adjust our style to meet the needs of the people with whom we are talking, and we reinforce our words with a wide range of facial expressions, bodily gestures, and vocal inflections, many of which we perform unconsciously. If we recognize that we are not being understood, we may stammer momentarily while trying to rephrase our feelings and ideas. Then, before we can get the words out, someone may have interrupted us and completely changed the topic of conversation. Whatever the case, we find ourselves continually adjusting to circumstances that are as random as our thoughts and the thoughts of those with whom we are talking. If we were to transcribe and then listen to the tape of an ordinary conversation, even one that we considered coherent and orderly, we would probably find it far more erratic and incoherent than we had imagined.

Drama cannot afford to reproduce conversation as faithfully as a tape recorder. To begin with, the limitations of performance time require that characters express their ideas and feelings much more economically than we do in the leisurely course of ordinary conversation. The conditions of theatrical performance demand also that dialogue be formulated so that it can be not only heard by characters talking to one another but also overheard and understood by the audience in the theater. Thus the continuity of dialogue must be very clearly marked out at every point. On the basis of what is overheard, the audience—or the reader—must be able to develop a full understanding of the characters and the plot.

Dialogue, then, is an extraordinarily significant form of conversation, for it is the means by which every play conveys the total make-up of its imaginative world. And this is not all. Dialogue must fulfill the needs of not only the audience but also the director, the set designer, and the actors. This means that the dialogue must serve as a script for all the elements of production and performance—for the entire theatrical realization of a play.

Because it has to serve so many purposes all at once, dialogue is necessarily a more artificial form of discourse than ordinary conversation. Thus, in reading any segment of dialogue, we should always keep in mind its special purposes. It is a script for theatrical production, and that means that we should see what it can tell us about the total spectacle: the setting, the arrangement of characters on the stage, their physical movements, gestures, facial expressions, and inflections. It is also a text for conveying the imaginative world of the play, which means that we should see what it can tell us about the character speaking, the character listening, and the other characters not present; about the public and private relations among the characters, the past as well as present circumstances of the characters, and the quality of the world they inhabit; about the events that have taken place prior to the play, the events that have taken place offstage during the play, the events that have caused the interaction of the characters during the dialogue itself, and the events that are likely to follow from their interaction. If we read the dialogue with all these concerns in mind, we will find in the end that it takes us out of ourselves and leads us into the imaginative experience of the play.

PLOT

Plot is a specialized form of experience. We can see just how specialized it is if we consider for a moment what happens during the ordinary course of our daily experience. Between waking and sleeping, we probably converse with a number of people and perform a variety of actions. But most of these events have very little to do with one another, and they usually serve no purpose other than our pleasure, our work, or our bodily necessities. In general, the events that take place in our daily existence do not embody a significant pattern or process. If they have any pattern at all, it is merely the product of habit and routine.

In drama, however, every event is part of a carefully designed pattern and process. And this is what we call plot. Plot, then, is not at all like the routine, and often random, course of our daily existence. Rather it is a wholly interconnected system of events, deliberately selected and arranged for the purpose of fulfilling a complex set of imaginative and theatrical purposes. Plot is thus an extremely artificial element, and it has to be so. Within the limits of a few hours the interest of spectators—and readers—has to be deeply engaged and continuously sustained. That requires a system of events that quickly develops complications and suspense, and leads in turn to a climax and resolution. Interest must also be aroused by events that make up a process capable of being represented on stage. And the totality of events must create a coherent imitation of the world.

In order to understand how plot fulfills these multiple purposes, we should first recognize that it comprises *everything* that takes place in the imaginative world of a play. In other words, plot is not confined to what takes place on stage (the *scenario*): it includes off-stage as well as on-stage action. Thus, if we wish to identify the plot of a play, we have to distinguish it from the scenario. The scenario embodies the plot and presents it to us, but it is not itself the plot.

We can understand this distinction in another way if we realize that in a plot all the events are necessarily arranged *chronologically*, whereas in a scenario events are arranged *dramatically*—that is, in an order that will create the greatest impact on the audience. In some cases that may result in non-chronological order. We may well reach the end of a scenario before we learn about events that took place years before. For this reason, in studying the plot of a play, we must consider not only the events of which it consists but also the order in which those events are presented by the scenario.

The ordering of events can best be grasped if we think of the scenario as being constructed of a series of *dramatic units:* each time a character enters or leaves the stage a new dramatic unit begins. The appearance or departure of a character or group of characters is thus like a form of punctuation that we should take special note of whenever we are reading or witnessing a play. As one grouping of characters gives way to another, the dramatic situation necessarily changes—sometimes slightly, sometimes very perceptibly—to carry the play forward in the evolution of its process and the fulfillment of its plot. Thus we should examine each unit individually, to discover not only what on-stage action takes place within it but also what off-stage action is revealed within it. Then we should determine how the off-stage action that is reported affects the on-stage action, as well as how it shapes our own understanding of the characters and the plot.

In the opening dramatic unit of *Oedipus Rex*, for example, we witness a conversation between Oedipus and a Priest, in which the Priest pleads with Oedipus to rid Thebes of the plague, while Oedipus assures the Priest that he is eager to cure the city of its sickness. During that conversation we also learn from the Priest that, in years past, Oedipus had through his wisdom and knowledge liberated the city from the domination of the Sphinx, and we learn from Oedipus that he has recently sent his brother-in-law, Creon, to seek advice from the oracle at Delphi. These two reports of off-stage action establish the heroic stature of Oedipus, revealing him to be an exceptionally effective and responsible leader. The dramatic unit leads the Priest and Oedipus—and us as spectators—to expect that he will be equally successful in this crisis. In examining the unit we thus see that it not only identifies the motivating problem of the plot but also establishes Oedipus as the hero of the play; and that, moreover, it creates a set of positive expectations about his ability to overcome the problem. (He does, of course, overcome the problem but not without undoing himself in the process.) The unit, then, is crucial in creating a complicated mixture of true and false expectations within both the characters—and us.

In addition to examining dramatic units individually, we should also examine them in relation to one another—in context. Context is important because it is one of the dramatist's major techniques for influencing our perception and understanding of characters and plot. Dramatists usually select and arrange events so as to produce significant parallels or contrasts between them. Thus, if we look at the units in context, we will be able to perceive those relationships and their implications. Finally, of course, we must move beyond pairs and series of units to an overview of all the units together. By doing that we will be able to recognize the dominant process of the play. We will, that is, be able to perceive how it sets up the complications and works toward the discoveries and resolutions of tragedy, comedy, satire, romance, or tragicomedy. By examining the over-all design of the plot, we can thus recognize the dominant view of experience embodied in the play.

On the basis of our discussion, it should be obvious that plot is an extremely complicated element, one that can be understood only through a detailed analysis of dramatic units. Here, then, are some reminders and suggestions to follow in analyzing the plot of any play. Identify *all* the events that take place within the plot and the chronological order in which they occur. In order to do this, examine the scenario closely, paying attention to instances of implied and reported action. Once the details and make-up of the plot have been established, then examine how the plot is presented by the scenario. In order to do this, examine each dramatic unit in detail, beginning with the first and proceeding consecutively through the play. Remember that a single dramatic unit can serve a variety of purposes. Remember, too, that every unit exists within a context of units: within the context of units that immediately precede and follow it, and within the context of all the units of the play.

CHARACTER

Although characters in a play are like real people in some respects, they are by no means identical to people in real life. Real people, after all, exist in the world as it is, whereas characters exist in an imaginative world shaped by the theatrical contexts and imitative purposes of drama. In the classical Greek theater, for example, a character was defined visually by the fixed expression of his or her facial mask. Clearly, it would have been impossible for spectators to regard such characters as identical to complex human personalities. And if we look at Oedipus, we can see that he is conceived in terms of a few dominant traits that could be projected through the bold acting required by the enormous size of the ancient Greek theater.

Because of its sustained interest in psychological behavior, modern drama tends to put a great deal of emphasis on character. Yet even plays—such as *A Doll's House*—that are concerned specifically with the workings of the human mind, do not embody characters who can be taken as identical to real people. It would be misleading to think of Nora, for example, or any other principal character in this play, as a fully developed personality. Although they do represent complex studies in human psychology, they are conceived to dramatize specific ideas about the impact of the family and society upon the individual. In other words, they exhibit patterns of behavior that are *typical* rather than *actual*.

Although dramatic characters are not real people, they are endowed with human capacities. They talk and act and interact with one another. They experience pleasure and endure pain. They feel, and they act on their feelings. They believe, and they act according to their beliefs. It would thus be inhuman of us not to respond to their humanity. But we can only respond appropriately if we know what we are responding to: we have to consider all of the ways in which characters are revealed and defined by dialogue and plot.

The most immediate way to understand a character is to examine in detail everything the character says, in order to identify the important attitudes, beliefs, and feelings of that character. Examine not only the content but also the style of such utterances. Look, for example, at the kinds of words, and images, and sentence structures that mark the character's dialogue, for often these elements of style provide insight into subtle aspects of character. A further source of information is what others in the play say about the character. Since characters, like real people, are repeatedly talking about one another—to their faces and behind their backs—what they have to say often will provide valuable insights into the character. The things a character does may reveal as much as what the character says and what others have to say.

In examining their actions, pay careful attention to context, for characters are likely to behave differently in different situations. The problem in such a case is to determine whether the character has actually changed, for what appears to be a change in character may simply be the result of our knowing the character more fully. Another important key to understanding is to compare and contrast a character with others in the play. A study of this kind often sharpens and intensifies the perceptions we have gained from examining the character in isolation.

Character analysis can be a source of pleasure and understanding in its own right, but it should ultimately lead us more deeply into the play as a whole. For that reason, when we analyze characters, we should always keep in mind the theatrical contexts and imaginative purposes that shape their being. In this way we shall be truly able to appreciate the dramatic imitation of a world created by the wedding of literary and of representational art.

A Collection of Plays

Tragedy in the Classical Greek Theater

THEATER IN CLASSICAL GREECE

The theater of Dionysus at Athens, where *Oedipus Rex* was first produced (c. 425 B.C.), could accommodate an audience of almost fifteen
thousand. So vast a structure could not, of course, be roofed over, but had
to be open-air. This fact alone will take us a long way toward understanding
the nature of a Greek dramatic performance. To begin with, we can see
that the experience must have been very public and communal—nothing at
all like the coziness of our fully enclosed modern theaters, where no more
than five hundred—or a thousand at most—gather in darkened rows of
cushioned seats. The size of the theater also required the drama to be
conceived on a monumental scale and performed in a correspondingly
emphatic style of acting. When Oedipus accused Teiresias of treason, his
impetuous judgment had to be heard and seen by thousands of spectators.
Facial expression obviously would not serve the purpose, nor would a
conversational tone of voice. Instead, the actors wore large, stylized masks
and costumes—an inheritance from primitive ritual—representing character
types; and as their fortunes and emotions changed, they changed their
masks to suit the situation. Further, those masks were probably equipped
with a mouthpiece to aid in projecting the dialogue. In short, we should not
imagine a style of performance corresponding in any way to that of our
present-day ideas about dramatic realism. Exaggerated gestures, bold
movements, declamatory utterances—everything was larger than life and
highly formalized, if only to ensure a clear theatrical impression.

Size alone was not responsible for the highly formal style of Greek drama.

711

The design of the theater, and the religious origin of its design, also had a great deal to do with the ceremonial quality of the production. The Greek theater evolved from places of ritual celebration consisting of a circular area for dancers and singers, surrounded by a hillside to accommodate worshipers. A modified version of that arrangement is what we have in the classical Greek theater illustrated here. The theater consisted of three parts. Its focal element was the *orchestra* (literally, the dancing place), a circular space sixty-four feet in diameter. The *orchestra* was surrounded by the *theatron* (literally, the seeing place), a semicircular terraced hillside equipped with benches. Facing the *theatron* was the *skene* (literally, the hut), a one-story building with three openings entering on to the *orchestra*, wings projecting toward the *orchestra,* and a slightly raised stage-like platform extending between the wings. The classic simplicity of that design is unparalleled in the history of the theater.

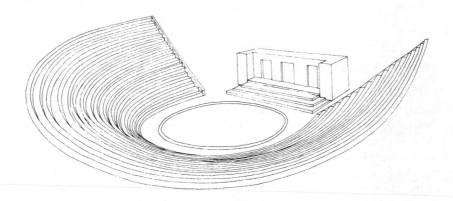

The *skene* was used for storing properties, changing costumes, providing entrances and exits, and serving as a scenic background. Stylized scenes were painted on the areas between the doors to suggest the outlines of a location, and the *skene* itself was understood to represent any structure central to the action (such as the palace in *Oedipus Rex*). Beyond these few hints, the Greek theater provided very little in the way of scenery or props to assist the spectator's imagination. At most, a chariot might be driven in to the *orchestra* to represent the arrival of a hero, or an actor lowered by machine from the roof of the *skene* to depict the intervention of a god, or a tableau wheeled out of the *skene* to suggest off-stage action.

The most important part of the theater was the *orchestra,* for it served as the primary acting area. Within that area the performance of a tragedy such as *Oedipus Rex* adhered to a highly formalized structure. The actors made their initial entrance to the *orchestra* from the *skene* and then performed a brief expository episode, the *prologos*. Then the chorus (of fifteen members) made its entrance—the *parados*—by marching in a stately rhythm through the passageways between the *theatron* and the *skene*. When all the members of the tragic chorus had entered the orchestra, they arranged themselves in rectangular formation and began their choral song and dance to the accompaniment of a flute. The chorus remained in the *orchestra* throughout the play, performing not only during its odes but also during the episodes, sometimes exchanging dialogue with the characters through its leader (the *choragos*), sometimes, no doubt, making gestures and movements in sympathetic response to the action. In this way the chorus provided a sustained point of reference, a source of mediation between the audience and the actors, who moved back and forth between the *orchestra* and the *skene* as their parts dictated.

In imagining the effect produced by the simultaneous presence of actors and chorus, we should remember that the chorus retained the skills inherited from the ritual celebrations of an earlier time, so that its members, like the actors, were accomplished dancers and singers. When we read *Oedipus Rex*, therefore, we should visualize the chorus as moving through a slow and graceful dance appropriate to tragedy. And we should try to hear how it sounded as it chanted its parts accompanied by a flute player. Musically and visually, the total performance must have been as complex as a modern opera—though by no means similar in emphasis, for in opera everything is subordinated to the music, whereas in Greek tragedy everything is subordinated to the action. Taken all in all—the choric singing and dancing, the simplified setting, the bold acting—dramatic productions in ancient Greece must have matched the grand dimensions of the theater and of the tragedies written for it by Sophocles.

SOPHOCLES

496–406 B.C.

Born in Athens, where his father was a wealthy and influential businessman, Sophocles himself became a very influential and admired public figure in Athens during the remarkable century of its rise and fall as a great city-state. During the course of his lifetime, he served his country as an ambassador, general, and treasurer; he served its religion as a priest of the god of healing; and he served its culture as a pre-eminent tragic dramatist. His plays, like those of his Greek contemporaries, were written and produced for an extraordinary drama competition that was held in Athens each spring as the major event in a festival celebrating Dionysus, the Greek god who embodied the power and fertility of nature. Each tragic dramatist who chose to compete submitted a set of three or four plays, known as trilogies or tetralogies, and Sophocles won the contest twenty-four times. He reportedly wrote more than 120 plays, but only 7 of them have survived, all of which show him to have been a masterful dramatist in the conception and elaboration of tragically compelling plots and characters. His best known plays—*Antigone* (c. 440), *Oedipus Rex* (c. 425), and *Oedipus at Colonus* (406)—though written more than thirty years apart, all deal with related characters and themes from the haunting myth of Oedipus and Thebes.

Oedipus Rex

PERSONS REPRESENTED

OEDIPUS	MESSENGER
A PRIEST	SHEPHERD OF LAÏOS
KREON	SECOND MESSENGER
TEIRESIAS	CHORUS OF THEBAN ELDERS
IOKASTÊ	

The Scene. Before the palace of Oedipus, King of Thebes. A central door and two lateral doors open onto a platform which runs the length of the façade. On the platform, right and left, are altars; and three steps lead down into the "orchêstra," or chorus-ground. At the beginning of the action these steps are crowded

An English version by Dudley Fitts and Robert Fitzgerald

*by suppliants who have brought branches and chaplets of olive leaves and who sit
in various attitudes of despair.*

Oedipus enters.

PROLOGUE

OEDIPUS   My children, generations of the living
    In the line of Kadmos, nursed at his ancient hearth:
    Why have you strewn yourselves before these altars
    In supplication, with your boughs and garlands?
    The breath of incense rises from the city
    With a sound of prayer and lamentation.
                             Children,
    I would not have you speak through messengers,
    And therefore I have come myself to hear you—
    I, Oedipus, who bear the famous name.

To a Priest

10   You, there, since you are eldest in the company,
    Speak for them all, tell me what preys upon you,
    Whether you come in dread, or crave some blessing:
    Tell me, and never doubt that I will help you
    In every way I can; I should be heartless
    Were I not moved to find you suppliant here.
PRIEST   Great Oedipus, O powerful King of Thebes!
    You see how all the ages of our people
    Cling to your altar steps: here are boys
    Who can barely stand alone, and here are priests
20   By weight of age, as I am a priest of God,
    And young men chosen from those yet unmarried;
    As for the others, all that multitude,
    They wait with olive chaplets in the squares,
    At the two shrines of Pallas, and where Apollo
    Speaks in the glowing embers.
                      Your own eyes
    Must tell you: Thebes is tossed on a murdering sea
    And can not lift her head from the death surge.
    A rust consumes the buds and fruits of the earth;

The herds are sick; children die unborn,
30   And labor is vain. The god of plague and pyre
Raids like detestable lightning through the city,
And all the house of Kadmos is laid waste,
All emptied, and all darkened: Death alone
Battens upon the misery of Thebes.

You are not one of the immortal gods, we know;
Yet we have come to you to make our prayer
As to the man surest in mortal ways
And wisest in the ways of God. You saved us
From the Sphinx, that flinty singer, and the tribute
40   We paid to her so long; yet you were never
Better informed than we, nor could we teach you:
A god's touch, it seems, enabled you to help us.

Therefore, O mighty power, we turn to you:
Find us our safety, find us a remedy,
Whether by counsel of the gods or of men.
A king of wisdom tested in the past
Can act in a time of troubles, and act well.
Noblest of men, restore
Life to your city! Think how all men call you
50   Liberator for your boldness long ago;
Ah, when your years of kingship are remembered,
Let them not say *We rose, but later fell*—
Keep the State from going down in the storm!
Once, years ago, with happy augury,
You brought us fortune; be the same again!
No man questions your power to rule the land:
But rule over men, not over a dead city!
Ships are only hulls, high walls are nothing,
When no life moves in the empty passageways.
60   OEDIPUS   Poor children! You may be sure I know
All that you longed for in your coming here.
I know that you are deathly sick; and yet,
Sick as you are, not one is as sick as I.
Each of you suffers in himself alone
His anguish, not another's; but my spirit
Groans for the city, for myself, for you.

I was not sleeping, you are not waking me.

No, I have been in tears for a long while
And in my restless thought walked many ways.
70   In all my search I found one remedy,
And I have adopted it: I have sent Kreon,
Son of Menoikeus, brother of the Queen,
To Delphi, Apollo's place of revelation,
To learn there, if he can,
What act or pledge of mine may save the city.
I have counted the days, and now, this very day,
I am troubled, for he has overstayed his time.
What is he doing? He has been gone too long.
Yet whenever he comes back, I should do ill
80   Not to take any action the god orders.
PRIEST   It is a timely promise. At this instant
They tell me Kreon is here.
OEDIPUS   O Lord Apollo!
May his news be fair as his face is radiant!
PRIEST   Good news, I gather: he is crowned with bay,
The chaplet is thick with berries.
OEDIPUS   We shall soon know;
He is near enough to hear us now.

Enter Kreon.

                              O Prince:
Brother: son of Menoikeus:
What answer do you bring us from the God?
KREON   A strong one. I can tell you, great afflictions
90   Will turn out well, if they are taken well.
OEDIPUS   What was the oracle? These vague words
Leave me still hanging between hope and fear.
KREON   Is it your pleasure to hear me with all these
Gathered around us? I am prepared to speak,
But should we not go in?
OEDIPUS   Speak to them all.
It is for them I suffer, more than for myself.
KREON   Then I will tell you what I heard at Delphi.

In plain words
The god commands us to expel from the land of Thebes

100   An old defilement we are sheltering.
It is a deathly thing, beyond cure;
We must not let it feed upon us longer.
OEDIPUS   What defilement? How shall we rid ourselves of it?
KREON   By exile or death, blood for blood. It was
Murder that brought the plague-wind on the city.
OEDIPUS   Murder of whom? Surely the god has named him?
KREON   My lord: Laïos once ruled this land,
Before you came to govern us.
OEDIPUS   I know;
I learned of him from others; I never saw him.
110   KREON   He was murdered; and Apollo commands us now
To take revenge upon whoever killed him.
OEDIPUS   Upon whom? Where are they? Where shall we find a clue
To solve that crime, after so many years?
KREON   Here in this land, he said. Search reveals
Things that escape an inattentive man.
OEDIPUS   Tell me: Was Laïos murdered in his house,
Or in the fields, or in some foreign country?
KREON   He said he planned to make a pilgrimage.
He did not come home again.
OEDIPUS   And was there no one,
120   No witness, no companion, to tell what happened?
KREON   They were all killed but one, and he got away
So frightened that he could remember one thing only.
OEDIPUS   What was that one thing? One may be the key
To everything, if we resolve to use it.
KREON   He said that a band of highwaymen attacked them,
Outnumbered them, and overwhelmed the King.
OEDIPUS   Strange, that a highwayman should be so daring—
Unless some faction here bribed him to do it.
KREON   We thought of that. But after Laïos' death
130   New troubles arose and we had no avenger.
OEDIPUS   What troubles could prevent your hunting down the killers?
KREON   The riddling Sphinx's song
Made us deaf to all mysteries but her own.
OEDIPUS   Then once more I must bring what is dark to light.
It is most fitting that Apollo shows,
As you do, this compunction for the dead.
You shall see how I stand by you, as I should,
Avenging this country and the god as well,
And not as though it were for some distant friend,
140   But for my own sake, to be rid of evil.

Whoever killed King Laïos might—who knows?—
Lay violent hands even on me—and soon.
I act for the murdered king in my own interest.

Come, then, my children: leave the altar steps,
Lift up your olive boughs!
                              One of you go
And summon the people of Kadmos to gather here.
I will do all that I can; you may tell them that.

Exit a Page.

So, with the help of God.
We shall be saved—or else indeed we are lost.
150 PRIEST   Let us rise, children. It was for this we came,
And now the King has promised it.
Phoibos has sent us an oracle; may he descend
Himself to save us and drive out the plague.

Exeunt Oedipus and Kreon into the palace by the central door. The Priest and the Suppliants disperse right and left. After a short pause the Chorus enters the orchêstra.

PÁRODOS

CHORUS   What is God singing in his profound   STROPHE I
    Delphi of gold and shadow?
    What oracle for Thebes, the sunwhipped city?

Fear unjoints me, the roots of my heart tremble.

Now I remember, O Healer, your power and wonder:
Will you send doom like a sudden cloud, or weave it
Like nightfall of the past?

Speak, speak to us, issue of holy sound;
Dearest to our Expectancy: be tender!

10   Let me pray to Athenê, the immortal daughter of Zeus, ANTISTROPHE I
    And to Artemis her sister
    Who keeps her famous throne in the market ring,

And to Apollo, archer from distant heaven—

O gods, descend! Like three streams leap against
The fires of our grief, the fires of darkness;
Be swift to bring us rest!

As in the old time from the brilliant house
Of air you stepped to save us, come again!

Now our afflictions have no end   STROPHE 2
Now all our stricken host lies down
And no man fights off death with his mind;

The noble plowland bears no grain,
And groaning mothers can not bear—

See, how our lives like birds take wing,
Like sparks that fly when a fire soars,
To the shore of the god of evening.

The plague burns on, it is pitiless,   ANTISTROPHE 2
Though pallid children laden with death
Lie unwept in the stony ways,

And old gray women by every path
Flock to the strand about the altars

There to strike their breasts and cry
Worship of Phoibos in wailing prayers:
Be kind, God's golden child!

There are no swords in this attack by fire,   STROPHE 3
No shields, but we are ringed with cries.

Send the besieger plunging from our homes
Into the vast sea-room of the Atlantic
Or into the waves that foam eastward of Thrace—
For the day ravages what the night spares—

Destroy our enemy, lord of the thunder!
Let him be riven by lightning from heaven!

Phoibos Apollo, stretch the sun's bowstring,   ANTISTROPHE 3
That golden cord, until it sing for us,
Flashing arrows in heaven!
                              Artemis, Huntress,
Race with flaring lights upon our mountains!

O scarlet god, O golden-banded brow,
O Theban Bacchos in a storm of Maenads,

Enter Oedipus, center.

Whirl upon Death, that all the Undying hate!
50   Come with blinding torches, come in joy!

SCENE I

OEDIPUS   Is this your prayer? It may be answered. Come,
      Listen to me, act as the crisis demands,
      And you shall have relief from all these evils.

      Until now I was a stranger to this tale,
      As I had been a stranger to the crime.
      Could I track down the murderer without a clue?
      But now, friends,
      As one who became a citizen after the murder,
      I make this proclamation to all Thebans:

10   If any man knows by whose hand Laïos, son of Labdakos,
      Met his death, I direct that man to tell me everything,
      No matter what he fears for having so long withheld it.
      Let it stand as promised that no further trouble
      Will come to him, but he may leave the land in safety.

      Moreover: If anyone knows the murderer to be foreign,
      Let him not keep silent: he shall have his reward from me.
      However, if he does conceal it; if any man
      Fearing for his friend or for himself disobeys this edict,
      Hear what I propose to do:

20   I solemnly forbid the people of this country,
Where power and throne are mine, ever to receive that man
Or speak to him, no matter who he is, or let him
Join in sacrifice, lustration, or in prayer.
I decree that he be driven from every house,
Being, as he is, corruption itself to us: the Delphic
Voice of Apollo has pronounced this revelation.
Thus I associate myself with the oracle
And take the side of the murdered king.

    As for the criminal, I pray to God—
30   Whether it be a lurking thief, or one of a number—
I pray that that man's life be consumed in evil and wretchedness.
And as for me, this curse applies no less
If it should turn out that the culprit is my guest here,
Sharing my hearth.
                You have heard the penalty.

    I lay it on you now to attend to this
For my sake, for Apollo's, for the sick
Sterile city that heaven has abandoned.
Suppose the oracle had given you no command:
Should this defilement go uncleansed for ever?
40   You should have found the murderer: your king,
A noble king, had been destroyed!
                        Now I,
Having the power that he held before me,
Having his bed, begetting children there
Upon his wife, as he would have, had he lived—
Their son would have been my children's brother,
If Laïos had had luck in fatherhood!
(And now his bad fortune has struck him down)—
I say I take the son's part, just as though
I were his son, to press the fight for him
50   And see it won! I'll find the hand that brought
Death to Labdakos' and Polydoros' child,
Heir of Kadmos' and Agenor's line.
And as for those who fail me,
May the gods deny them the fruit of the earth,
Fruit of the womb, and may they rot utterly!
Let them be wretched as we are wretched, and worse!
For you, for loyal Thebans, and for all

Who find my actions right, I pray the favor
Of justice, and of all the immortal gods.

60   CHORAGOS   Since I am under oath, my lord, I swear
I did not do the murder, I can not name
The murderer. Phoibos ordained the search;
Why did he not say who the culprit was?

OEDIPUS   An honest question. But no man in the world
Can make the gods do more than the gods will.

CHORAGOS   There is an alternative, I think—

OEDIPUS   Tell me.
Any or all, you must not fail to tell me.

CHORAGOS   A lord clairvoyant to the lord Apollo,
As we all know, is the skilled Teiresias.

70   One might learn much about this from him, Oedipus.

OEDIPUS   I am not wasting time:
Kreon spoke of this, and I have sent for him—
Twice, in fact; it is strange that he is not here.

CHORAGOS   The other matter—that old report—seems useless.

OEDIPUS   What was that? I am interested in all reports.

CHORAGOS   The King was said to have been killed by highwaymen.

OEDIPUS   I know. But we have no witnesses to that.

CHORAGOS   If the killer can feel a particle of dread,
Your curse will bring him out of hiding!

OEDIPUS   No.
80   The man who dared that act will fear no curse.

Enter the blind seer Teiresias, led by a Page.

CHORAGOS   But there is one man who may detect the criminal.
This is Teiresias, this is the holy prophet
In whom, alone of all men, truth was born.

OEDIPUS   Teiresias: seer: student of mysteries,
Of all that's taught and all that no man tells,
Secrets of Heaven and secrets of the earth:
Blind though you are, you know the city lies
Sick with plague; and from this plague, my lord,
We find that you alone can guard or save us.

90   Possibly you did not hear the messengers?
Apollo, when we sent to him,
Sent us back word that this great pestilence
Would lift, but only if we established clearly
The identity of those who murdered Laïos.

They must be killed or exiled.
                                        Can you use
Birdflight or any art of divination
To purify yourself, and Thebes, and me
From this contagion? We are in your hands.
There is no fairer duty
100   Than that of helping others in distress.
TEIRESIAS   How dreadful knowledge of the truth can be
When there's no help in truth! I knew this well
But did not act on it: else I should not have come.
OEDIPUS   What is troubling you? Why are your eyes so cold?
TEIRESIAS   Let me go home. Bear your own fate, and I'll
Bear mine. It is better so: trust what I say.
OEDIPUS   What you say is ungracious and unhelpful
To your native country. Do not refuse to speak.
TEIRESIAS   When it comes to speech, your own is neither temperate
110   Nor opportune. I wish to be more prudent.
OEDIPUS   In God's name, we all beg you—
TEIRESIAS   You are all ignorant.
No; I will never tell you what I know.
Now it is my misery; then, it would be yours.
OEDIPUS   What! You do know something, and will not tell us?
You would betray us all and wreck the State?
TEIRESIAS   I do not intend to torture myself, or you.
Why persist in asking? You will not persuade me.
OEDIPUS   What a wicked old man you are! You'd try a stone's
Patience! Out with it! Have you no feeling at all?
120 TEIRESIAS   You call me unfeeling. If you could only see
The nature of your own feelings . . .
OEDIPUS   Why,
Who would not feel as I do? Who could endure
Your arrogance toward the city?
TEIRESIAS   What does it matter?
Whether I speak or not, it is bound to come.
OEDIPUS   Then, if 'it' is bound to come, you are bound to tell me.
TEIRESIAS   No, I will not go on. Rage as you please.
OEDIPUS   Rage? Why not!
                                        And I'll tell you what I think:
You planned it, you had it done, you all but
Killed him with your own hands: if you had eyes,
130   I'd say the crime was yours, and yours alone.
TEIRESIAS   So? I charge you, then,
Abide by the proclamation you have made:
From this day forth

Never speak again to these men or to me;
You yourself are the pollution of this country.
OEDIPUS   You dare say that! Can you possibly think you have
Some way of going free, after such insolence?
TEIRESIAS   I have gone free. It is the truth sustains me.
OEDIPUS   Who taught you shamelessness? It was not your craft.
140   TEIRESIAS   You did. You made me speak. I did not want to.
OEDIPUS   Speak what? Let me hear it again more clearly.
TEIRESIAS   Was it not clear before? Are you tempting me?
OEDIPUS   I did not understand it. Say it again.
TEIRESIAS   I say that you are the murderer whom you seek.
OEDIPUS   Now twice you have spat out infamy. You'll pay for it!
TEIRESIAS   Would you care for more? Do you wish to be really angry?
OEDIPUS   Say what you will. Whatever you say is worthless.
TEIRESIAS   I say you live in hideous shame with those
Most dear to you. You can not see the evil.
150   OEDIPUS   Can you go on babbling like this for ever?
TEIRESIAS   I can, if there is power in truth.
OEDIPUS   There is:
But not for you, not for you,
You sightless, witless, senseless, mad old man!
TEIRESIAS   You are the madman. There is no one here
Who will not curse you soon, as you curse me.
OEDIPUS   You child of total night! I would not touch you;
Neither would any man who sees the sun.
TEIRESIAS   True: it is not from you my fate will come.
That lies within Apollo's competence,
As it is his concern.
160   OEDIPUS   Tell me, who made
These fine discoveries? Kreon? or someone else?
TEIRESIAS   Kreon is no threat. You weave your own doom.
OEDIPUS   Wealth, power, craft of statesmanship!
Kingly position, everywhere admired!
What savage envy is stored up against these,
If Kreon, whom I trusted, Kreon my friend,
For this great office which the city once
Put in my hands unsought—if for this power
Kreon desires in secret to destroy me!

170   He has bought this decrepit fortune-teller, this
Collector of dirty pennies, this prophet fraud—
Why, he is no more clairvoyant than I am!
                                              Tell us:
Has your mystic mummery ever approached the truth?

When that hellcat the Sphinx was performing here,
What help were you to these people?
Her magic was not for the first man who came along:
It demanded a real exorcist. Your birds—
What good were they? or the gods, for the matter of that?
But I came by,
180   Oedipus, the simple man, who knows nothing—
I thought it out for myself, no birds helped me!
And this is the man you think you can destroy.
That you may be close to Kreon when he's king!
Well, you and your friend Kreon, it seems to me,
Will suffer most. If you were not an old man,
You would have paid already for your plot.

CHORAGOS   We can not see that his words or yours
Have been spoken except in anger, Oedipus,
And of anger we have no need. How to accomplish
190   The god's will best: that is what most concerns us.

TEIRESIAS   You are a king. But where argument's concerned
I am your man, as much a king as you.
I am not your servant, but Apollo's
I have no need of Kreon's name.

Listen to me. You mock my blindness, do you?
But I say that you, with both your eyes, are blind:
You can not see the wretchedness of your life,
Nor in whose house you live, no, nor with whom.
Who are your father and mother? Can you tell me?
200   You do not even know the blind wrongs
That you have done them, on earth and in the world below.
But the double lash of you parents' curse will whip you
Out of this land some day, with only night
Upon your precious eyes.
Your cries then—where will they not be heard?
What fastness of Kithairon will not echo them?
And that bridal-descant of yours—you'll know it then,
The song they sang when you came here to Thebes
And found your misguided berthing.
210   All this, and more, that you can not guess at now,
Will bring you to yourself among your children.

Be angry, then. Curse Kreon. Curse my words.
I tell you, no man that walks upon the earth
Shall be rooted out more horribly than you.

OEDIPUS   Am I to bear this from him?—Damnation
    Take you! Out of this place! Out of my sight!
TEIRESIAS   I would not have come at all if you had not asked me.
OEDIPUS   Could I have told that you'd talk nonsense, that
    You'd come here to make a fool of yourself, and of me?
220 TEIRESIAS   A fool? Your parents thought me sane enough.
OEDIPUS   My parents again!—Wait: who were my parents?
TEIRESIAS   This day will give you a father, and break your heart.
OEDIPUS   Your infantile riddles! Your damned abracadabra!
TEIRESIAS   You were a great man once at solving riddles.
OEDIPUS   Mock me with that if you like; you will find it true.
TEIRESIAS   It was true enough. It brought about your ruin.
OEDIPUS   But if it saved this town?
TEIRESIAS   *To the Page*   Boy, give me your hand.
OEDIPUS   Yes, boy; lead him away.
                              —While you are here
    We can do nothing. Go; leave us in peace.
230 TEIRESIAS   I will go when I have said what I have to say.
    How can you hurt me? And I tell you again:
    The man you have been looking for all this time,
    The damned man, the murderer of Laïos,
    That man is in Thebes. To your mind he is foreign-born,
    But it will soon be shown that he is a Theban,
    A revelation that will fail to please.
                              A blind man,
    Who has his eyes now; a penniless man, who is rich now;
    And he will go tapping the strange earth with his staff.
    To the children with whom he lives now he will be
240 Brother and father—the very same; to her
    Who bore him, son and husband—the very same
    Who came to his father's bed, wet with his father's blood.

    Enough. Go think that over.
    If later you find error in what I have said,
    You may say that I have no skill in prophecy.

Exit Teiresias, led by his Page. Oedipus goes into the palace.

ODE I

CHORUS   The Delphic stone of prophecies   STROPHE 1
    Remembers ancient regicide
    And a still bloody hand.

That killer's hour of flight has come.
He must be stronger than riderless
Coursers of untiring wind,
For the son of Zeus armed with his father's thunder
Leaps in lightning after him;
And the Furies hold his track, the sad Furies.

10   Holy Parnassos' peak of snow   ANTISTROPHE 1
Flashes and blinds that secret man,
That all shall hunt him down:
Though he may roam the forest shade
Like a bull gone wild from pasture
To rage through glooms of stone.
Doom comes down on him; flight will not avail him;
For the world's heart calls him desolate,
And the immortal voices follow, for ever follow.

But now a wilder thing is heard   STROPHE 2
20   From the old man skilled at hearing Fate in the wing-beat of a bird.
Bewildered as a blown bird, my soul hovers and can not find
Foothold in this debate, or any reason or rest of mind.
But no man ever brought—none can bring
Proof of strife between Thebes' royal house,
Labdakos' line, and the son of Polybos;
And never until now has any man brought word
Of Laïos' dark death staining Oedipus the King.

Divine Zeus and Apollo hold   ANTISTROPHE 2
Perfect intelligence alone of all tales ever told;
30   And well though this diviner works, he works in his own night;
No man can judge that rough unknown or trust in second sight,
For wisdom changes hands among the wise.
Shall I believe my great lord criminal
At a raging word that a blind old man let fall?
I saw him, when the carrion woman faced him of old,
Prove his heroic mind. These evil words are lies.

SCENE II

KREON   Men of Thebes:
    I am told that heavy accusations
    Have been brought against me by King Oedipus.

I am not the kind of man to bear this tamely.

If in these present difficulties
He holds me accountable for any harm to him
Through anything I have said or done—why, then,
I do not value life in this dishonor.

It is not as though this rumor touched upon
10   Some private indiscretion. The matter is grave.
        The fact is that I am being called disloyal
        To the State, to my fellow citizens, to my friends.
CHORAGOS He may have spoken in anger, not from his mind.
KREON But did you not hear him say I was the one
        Who seduced the old prophet into lying?
CHORAGOS The thing was said; I do not know how seriously.
KREON But you were watching him! Were his eyes steady?
        Did he look like a man in his right mind?
CHORAGOS   I do not know.
        I can not judge the behavior of great men.
        But here is the King himself.

Enter Oedipus.

20 OEDIPUS   So you dared come back.
        Why? How brazen of you to come to my house,
        You murderer!
                        Do you think I do not know
        That you plotted to kill me, plotted to steal my throne?
        Tell me, in God's name: am I coward, a fool,
        That you should dream you could accomplish this?
        A fool who could not see your slippery game?
        A coward, not to fight back when I saw it?
        You are the fool, Kreon, are you not? hoping
        Without support or friends to get a throne?
30   Thrones may be won or bought: you could do neither.
KREON Now listen to me. You have talked; let me talk, too.
        You can not judge unless you know the facts.
OEDIPUS You speak well: there is one fact; but I find it hard
        To learn from the deadliest enemy I have.
KREON That above all I must dispute with you.
OEDIPUS That above all I will not hear you deny.
KREON If you think there is anything good in being stubborn
        Against all reason, then I say you are wrong.

OEDIPUS If you think a man can sin against his own kind

40   And not be punished for it, I say you are mad.

KREON I agree. But tell me: what have I done to you?

OEDIPUS You advised me to send for that wizard, did you not?

KREON I did. I should do it again.

OEDIPUS   Very well. Now tell me:

How long has it been since Laïos—

KREON   What of Laïos?

OEDIPUS Since he vanished in that onset by the road?

KREON   It was long ago, a long time.

OEDIPUS   And this prophet,

Was he practicing here then?

KREON   He was; and with honor, as now.

OEDIPUS Did he speak of me at that time?

KREON   He never did;

At least, not when I was present.

OEDIPUS   But . . . the enquiry?

I suppose you held one?

50   KREON   We did, but we learned nothing.

OEDIPUS Why did the prophet not speak against me then?

KREON I do not know; and I am the kind of man

Who holds his tongue when he has no facts to go on.

OEDIPUS There's one fact that you know, and you could tell it.

KREON What fact is that? If I know it, you shall have it.

OEDIPUS If he were not involved with you, he could not say

That it was I who murdered Laïos.

KREON If he says that, you are the one that knows it!—

But now it is my turn to question you.

60   OEDIPUS Put your questions. I am no murderer.

KREON First, then: You married my sister?

OEDIPUS   I married your sister.

KREON And you rule the kingdom equally with her?

OEDIPUS Everything that she wants she has from me.

KREON And I am the third, equal to both of you?

OEDIPUS That is why I call you a bad friend.

KREON No. Reason it out, as I have done.

Think of this first: Would any sane man prefer

Power, with all a king's anxieties,

To that same power and the grace of sleep?

70   Certainly not I.

I have never longed for the king's power—only his rights.

Would any wise man differ from me in this?

As matters stand, I have my way in everything

With your consent, and no responsibilities.

If I were king, I should be a slave to policy.
How could I desire a sceptre more
Than what is now mine—untroubled influence?
No, I have not gone mad; I need no honors,
Except those with the perquisites I have now.
80   I am welcome everywhere; every man salutes me,
And those who want your favor seek my ear,
Since I know how to manage what they ask.
Should I exchange this ease for that anxiety?
Besides, no sober mind is treasonable.
I hate anarchy
And never would deal with any man who likes it.

Test what I have said. Go to the priestess
At Delphi, ask if I quoted her correctly.
And as for this other thing: if I am found
90   Guilty of treason with Teiresias,
Then sentence me to death. You have my word
It is a sentence I should cast my vote for—
But not without evidence!
                    You do wrong
When you take good men for bad, bad men for good.
A true friend thrown aside—why, life itself
Is not more precious!
                    In time you will know this well:
For time, and time alone, will show the just man,
Though scoundrels are discovered in a day.
CHORAGOS   This is well said, and a prudent man would ponder it.
100   Judgments too quickly formed are dangerous.
OEDIPUS   But is he not quick in his duplicity?
And shall I not be quick to parry him?
Would you have me stand still, holding my peace, and let
This man win everything, through my inaction?
KREON   And you want—what is it, then? To banish me?
OEDIPUS   No, not exile. It is your death I want,
So that all the world may see what treason means.
KREON   You will persist, then? You will not believe me?
OEDIPUS   How can I believe you?
KREON   Then you are a fool.
OEDIPUS   To save myself?
110   KREON   In justice, think of me.
OEDIPUS   You are evil incarnate.
KREON   But suppose that you are wrong?
OEDIPUS   Still I must rule.

KREON   But not if you rule badly.

OEDIPUS   O city, city!

KREON   It is my city, too!

CHORAGOS   Now, my lords, be still. I see the Queen,
    Iokastê, coming from her palace chambers;
    And it is time she came, for the sake of you both.
    This dreadful quarrel can be resolved through her.

Enter Iokastê.

IOKASTÊ   Poor foolish men, what wicked din is this?
    With Thebes sick to death, is it not shameful
120   That you should rake some private quarrel up?

To Oedipus

    Come into the house
                    —And you, Kreon, go now:
    Let us have no more of this tumult over nothing.

KREON   Nothing? No, sister: what your husband plans for me
    Is one of two great evils: exile or death.

OEDIPUS   He is right.
                    Why, woman I have caught him squarely
    Plotting against my life.

KREON   No! Let me die
    Accurst if ever I have wished you harm!

IOKASTÊ   Ah, believe it, Oedipus!
    In the name of the gods, respect this oath of his
130   For my sake, for the sake of these people here!

CHORAGOS   STROPHE 1
    Open your mind to her, my lord. Be ruled by her, I beg you!

OEDIPUS   What would you have me do?

CHORAGOS   Respect Kreon's word. He has never spoken like a fool,
    And now he has sworn an oath.

OEDIPUS   You know what you ask?

CHORAGOS   I do.

OEDIPUS   Speak on, then.

CHORAGOS   A friend so sworn should not be baited so,
    In blind malice, and without final proof.

OEDIPUS   You are aware, I hope, that what you say
    Means death for me, or exile at the least.

CHORAGOS

STROPHE 2

140   No, I swear by Helios, first in Heaven!
    May I die friendless and accurst,
The worst of deaths, if ever I meant that!
    It is the withering fields
      That hurt my sick heart:
Must we bear all these ills,
    And now your bad blood as well?

OEDIPUS   Then let him go. And let me die, if I must,
Or be driven by him in shame from the land of Thebes.
It is your unhappiness, and not his talk,
That touches me.

150   As for him—
Wherever he goes, hatred will follow him.
KREON   Ugly in yielding, as you were ugly in rage!
Natures like yours chiefly torment themselves.
OEDIPUS   Can you not go? Can you not leave me?
KREON   I can.
You do not know me; but the city knows me,
And in its eyes I am just, if not in yours.

Exit Kreon.

CHORAGOS

ANTISTROPHE 1

    Lady Iokaste, did you not ask the King to go to his chambers?
IOKASTE   First tell me what has happened.
CHORAGOS   There was suspicion without evidence; yet it rankled
160   As even false charges will.
IOKASTE   On both sides?
CHORAGOS   On both.
IOKASTE   But what was said?

CHORAGOS   Oh let it rest, let it be done with!
Have we not suffered enough?
OEDIPUS   You see to what your decency has brought you:
You have made difficulties where my heart saw none.

CHORAGOS

ANTISTROPHE 2

    Oedipus, it is not once only I have told you—
    You must know I should count myself unwise
To the point of madness, should I now forsake you—
      You, under whose hand,

170   In the storm of another time,
Our dear land sailed out free.
But now stand fast at the helm!

IOKASTÊ   In God's name, Oedipus, inform your wife as well:
Why are you so set in this hard anger?

OEDIPUS   I will tell you, for none of these men deserves
My confidence as you do. It is Kreon's work,
His treachery, his plotting against me.

IOKASTÊ   Go on, if you can make this clear to me.

OEDIPUS   He charges me with the murder of Laïos.

180 IOKASTÊ   Has he some knowledge? Or does he speak from hearsay?

OEDIPUS   He would not commit himself to such a charge,
But he has brought in that damnable soothsayer
To tell his story.

IOKASTÊ   Set your mind at rest.
If it is a question of soothsayers, I tell you
That you will find no man whose craft gives knowledge
Of the unknowable.

Here is my proof:
An oracle was reported to Laïos once
(I will not say from Phoibos himself, but from
His appointed ministers, at any rate)

190   That his doom would be death at the hands of his own son—
His son, born of his flesh and of mine!

Now, you remember the story: Laïos was killed
By marauding strangers where three highways meet;
But his child had not been three days in this world
Before the King had pierced the baby's ankles
And left him to die on a lonely mountainside.

Thus, Apollo never caused that child
To kill his father, and it was not Laïos' fate
To die at the hands of his son, as he had feared.

200   This is what prophets and prophecies are worth!
Have no dread of them.
It is God himself
Who can show us what he wills, in his own way.

OEDIPUS   How strange a shadowy memory crossed my mind,
Just now while you were speaking; it chilled my heart.

IOKASTÊ   What do you mean? What memory do you speak of?

OEDIPUS   If I understand you, Laïos was killed
At a place where three roads meet.

IOKASTÊ   So it was said:
We have no later story.

OEDIPUS   Where did it happen?

IOKASTÊ   Phokis, it is called: at a place where the Theban Way
Divides into the roads toward Delphi and Daulia.

OEDIPUS   When?

IOKASTÊ   We had the news not long before you came
And proved the right to your succession here.

OEDIPUS   Ah, what net has God been weaving for me?

IOKASTÊ   Oedipus! Why does this trouble you?

OEDIPUS   Do not ask me yet.
First, tell me how Laïos looked, and tell me
How old he was.

OEDIPUS   He was tall, his hair just touched
With white; his form was not unlike your own.

OEDIPUS   I think that I myself may be accurst
By my own ignorant edict.

IOKASTÊ   You speak strangely.
It makes me tremble to look at you, my King.

OEDIPUS   I am not sure that the blind man can not see.
But I should know better if you were to tell me—

IOKASTÊ   Anything—though I dread to hear you ask it.

OEDIPUS   Was the King lightly escorted, or did he ride
With a large company, as a ruler should?

IOKASTÊ   There were five men with him in all: one was a herald;
And a single chariot, which he was driving.

OEDIPUS   Alas, that makes it plain enough!
                              But who—
Who told you how it happened?

IOKASTÊ   A household servant,
The only one to escape.

OEDIPUS   And is he still
A servant of ours?

IOKASTÊ   No; for when he came back at last
And found you enthroned in the place of the dead king,
He came to me, touched my hand with his, and begged
That I would send him away to the frontier district
Where only the shepherds go—
As far away from the city as I could send him.
I granted his prayer; for although the man was a slave,
He had earned more than this favor at my hands.

OEDIPUS   Can he be called back quickly?

IOKASTÊ   Easily.
But why?

240 OEDIPUS   I have taken too much upon myself
    Without enquiry; therefore I wish to consult him.
IOKASTÊ   Then he shall come.
                        But am I not one also
    To whom you might confide these fears of yours?
OEDIPUS   That is your right; it will not be denied you,
    Now least of all; for I have reached a pitch
    Of wild foreboding. Is there anyone
    To whom I should sooner speak?

    Polybos of Corinth is my father.
    My mother is a Dorian: Meropê.
250   I grew up chief among the men of Corinth
    Until a strange thing happened—
    Not worth my passion, it may be, but strange.

    At a feast, a drunken man maundering in his cups
    Cries out that I am not my father's son!
    I contained myself that night, though I felt anger
    And a sinking heart. The next day I visited
    My father and mother, and questioned them. They stormed,
    Calling it all the slanderous rant of a fool;
    And this relieved me. Yet the suspicion
260   Remained always aching in my mind;
    I knew there was talk; I could not rest;
    And finally, saying nothing to my parents,
    I went to the shrine at Delphi.

    The god dismissed my question without reply;
    He spoke of other things.
                    Some were clear,
    Full of wretchedness, dreadful, unbearable:
    As that I should lie with my own mother, breed
    Children from whom all men would turn their eyes;
    And that I should be my father's murderer.

270   I heard all this, and fled. And from that day
    Corinth to me was only in the stars
    Descending in that quarter of the sky,
    As I wandered farther and farther on my way
    To a land where I should never see the evil
    Sung by the oracle. And I came to this country
    Where, so you say, King Laïos was killed.

I will tell you all that happened there, my lady.

There were three highways
Coming together at a place I passed;
280   And there a herald came towards me, and a chariot
Drawn by horses, with a man such as you describe
Seated in it. The groom leading the horses
Forced me off the road at his lord's command;
But as this charioteer lurched over towards me
I struck him in my rage. The old man saw me
And brought his double goad down upon my head
As I came abreast.
                          He was paid back, and more!
Swinging my club in this right hand I knocked him
Out of his car, and he rolled on the ground.
                                              I killed him.
290   I killed them all.
Now if that stranger and Laïos were—kin,
Where is a man more miserable than I?
More hated by the gods? Citizen and alien alike
Must never shelter me or speak to me—
I must be shunned by all.
                          And I myself
Pronounced this malediction upon myself!

Think of it: I have touched you with these hands,
These hands that killed your husband. What defilement!

Am I all evil, then? It must be so,
300   Since I must flee from Thebes, yet never again
See my own countrymen, my own country,
For fear of joining my mother in marriage
And killing Polybos, my father.
                                Ah,
If I was created so, born to this fate,
Who could deny the savagery of God?

O holy majesty of heavenly powers!
May I never see that day! Never!
Rather let me vanish from the race of men
Than know the abomination destined me!
310   CHORAGOS   We too, my lord, have felt dismay at this.
But there is hope: you have yet to hear the shepherd.

OEDIPUS   Indeed, I fear no other hope is left me.

IOKASTÊ   What do you hope from him when he comes?

OEDIPUS   This much:
    If his account of the murder tallies with yours,
    Then I am cleared.

IOKASTÊ   What was it that I said
    Of such importance?

OEDIPUS   Why, "marauders," you said,
    Killed the King, according to this man's story.
    If he maintains that still, if there were several,
    Clearly the guilt is not mine: I was alone.

320   But if he says one man, singlehanded, did it,
    Then the evidence all points to me.

IOKASTÊ   You may be sure that he said there were several;
    And can he call back that story now? He cán not.
    The whole city heard it as plainly as I.
    But suppose he alters some detail of it:
    He can not ever show that Laïos' death
    Fulfilled the oracle: for Apollo said
    My child was doomed to kill him; and my child—
    Poor baby!—it was my child that died first.

330   No. From now on, where oracles are concerned,
    I would not waste a second thought on any.

OEDIPUS   You may be right.
                But come: let someone go
    For the shepherd at once. This matter must be settled.

IOKASTÊ   I will send for him.
    I would not wish to cross you in anything,
    And surely not in this.—Let us go in.

Exeunt into the palace.

Ode II

CHORUS   Let me be reverent in the ways of right,   STROPHE 1
    Lowly the paths I journey on;
    Let all my words and actions keep
    The laws of the pure universe
    From highest Heaven handed down.
    For Heaven is their bright nurse,
    Those generations of the realms of light;
    Ah, never of mortal kind were they begot,

Nor are they slaves of memory, lost in sleep:
Their Father is greater than Time, and ages not.

The tyrant is a child of Pride   ANTISTROPHE 1
Who drinks from his great sickening cup
Recklessness and vanity,
Until from his high crest headlong
He plummets to the dust of hope.
That strong man is not strong.
But let no fair ambition be denied;
May God protect the wrestler for the State
In government, in comely policy,
Who will fear God, and on His ordinance wait.

Haughtiness and the high hand of disdain   STROPHE 2
Tempt and outrage God's holy law;
And any mortal who dares hold
No immortal Power in awe
Will be caught up in a net of pain:
The price for which his levity is sold.
Let each man take due earnings, then,
And keep his hands from holy things,
And from blasphemy stand apart—
Else the crackling blast of heaven
Blows on his head, and on his desperate heart.
Though fools will honor impious men,
In their cities no tragic poet sings.

Shall we lose faith in Delphi's obscurities,   ANTISTROPHE 2
We who have heard the world's core
Discredited, and the sacred wood
Of Zeus at Elis praised no more?
The deeds and the strange prophecies
Must make a pattern yet to be understood.
Zeus, if indeed you are lord of all,
Throned in light over night and day,
Mirror this in your endless mind:
Our masters call the oracle
Words on the wind, and the Delphic vision blind!
Their hearts no longer know Apollo,
And reverence for the gods has died away.

SCENE III

Enter Iokastê.

IOKASTÊ   Princes of Thebes, it has occurred to me
To visit the altars of the gods, bearing
These branches as a suppliant, and this incense.
Our King is not himself: his noble soul
Is overwrought with fantasies of dread,
Else he would consider
The new prophecies in the light of the old.
He will listen to any voice that speaks disaster,
And my advice goes for nothing.

She approaches the altar, right.

To you, then, Apollo,
10   Lycéan lord, since you are nearest, I turn in prayer.

Receive these offerings, and grant us deliverance
From defilement. Our hearts are heavy with fear
When we see our leader distracted, as helpless sailors
Are terrified by the confusion of their helmsman.

Enter Messenger.

MESSENGER   Friends, no doubt you can direct me:
Where shall I find the house of Oedipus,
Or, better still, where is the King himself?
CHORAGOS   It is this very place, stranger; he is inside.
This is his wife and mother of his children.
20   MESSENGER   I wish her happiness in a happy house,
Blest in all the fulfillment of her marriage.
IOKASTÊ   I wish as much for you: your courtesy
Deserves a like good fortune. But now, tell me:
Why have you come? What have you to say to us?
MESSENGER   Good news, my lady, for your house and your husband.
IOKASTÊ   What news? Who sent you here?
MESSENGER   I am from Corinth.
The news I bring ought to mean joy for you,
Though it may be you will find some grief in it.
IOKASTÊ   What is it? How can it touch us in both ways?

30 MESSENGER   The word is that the people of the Isthmus
    Intend to call Oedipus to be their king.
IOKASTÊ   But old King Polybos—is he not reigning still?
MESSENGER   No. Death holds him in his sepulchre.
IOKASTÊ   What are you saying? Polybos is dead?
MESSENGER   If I am not telling the truth, may I die myself.
IOKASTÊ   *To a Maidservant*
    Go in, go quickly; tell this to your master.

    O riddlers of God's will, where are you now!
    This was the man whom Oedipus, long ago,
    Feared so, fled so, in dread of destroying him—
40   But it was another fate by which he died.

Enter Oedipus, center.

OEDIPUS   Dearest Iokastê, why have you sent for me?
IOKASTÊ   Listen to what this man says, and then tell me
    What has become of the solemn prophecies.
OEDIPUS   Who is this man? What is his news for me?
IOKASTÊ   He has come from Corinth to announce your father's death!
OEDIPUS   Is it true, stranger? Tell me in your own words.
MESSENGER   I can not say it more clearly: the King is dead.
OEDIPUS   Was it by treason? Or by an attack of illness?
MESSENGER   A little thing brings old men to their rest.
OEDIPUS   It was sickness, then?
50 MESSENGER   Yes, and his many years.
OEDIPUS   Ah!
    Why should a man respect the Pythian hearth, or
    Give heed to the birds that jangle above his head?
    They prophesied that I should kill Polybos,
    Kill my own father; but he is dead and buried,
    And I am here—I never touched him, never,
    Unless he died of grief for my departure,
    And thus, in a sense, through me. No. Polybos
    Has packed the oracles off with him underground.
    They are empty words.
IOKASTÊ   Had I not told you so?
60 OEDIPUS   You had; it was my faint heart that betrayed me.
IOKASTÊ   From now on never think of those things again.
OEDIPUS   And yet—must I not fear my mother's bed?
IOKASTÊ   Why should anyone in this world be afraid,
    Since Fate rules us and nothing can be foreseen?
    A man should live only for the present day.

Have no more fear of sleeping with your mother:
How many men, in dreams, have lain with their mothers!
No reasonable man is troubled by such things.

OEDIPUS   That is true; only—

70   If only my mother were not still alive!
But she is alive. I can not help my dread.

IOKASTÊ   Yet this news of your father's death is wonderful.

OEDIPUS   Wonderful. But I fear the living woman.

MESSENGER   Tell me, who is this woman that you fear?

OEDIPUS   It is Meropê, man; the wife of King Polybos.

MESSENGER   Meropê? Why should you be afraid of her?

OEDIPUS   An oracle of the gods, a dreadful saying.

MESSENGER   Can you tell me about it or are you sworn to silence?

OEDIPUS   I can tell you, and I will.

80   Apollo said through his prophet that I was the man
Who should marry his own mother, shed his father's blood
With his own hands. And so, for all these years
I have kept clear of Corinth, and no harm has come—
Though it would have been sweet to see my parents again.

MESSENGER   And is this the fear that drove you out of Corinth?

OEDIPUS   Would you have me kill my father?

MESSENGER   As for that
You must be reassured by the news I gave you.

OEDIPUS   If you could reassure me, I would reward you.

MESSENGER   I had that in mind, I will confess: I thought

90   I could count on you when you returned to Corinth.

OEDIPUS   No: I will never go near my parents again.

MESSENGER   Ah, son, you still do not know what you are doing—

OEDIPUS   What do you mean? In the name of God tell me!

MESSENGER   —If these are your reasons for not going home.

OEDIPUS   I tell you, I fear the oracle may come true.

MESSENGER   And guilt may come upon you through your parents?

OEDIPUS   That is the dread that is always in my heart.

MESSENGER   Can you not see that all your fears are groundless?

OEDIPUS   Groundless? Am I not my parents' son?

MESSENGER   Polybos was not your father.

100   OEDIPUS   Not my father?

MESSENGER   No more your father than the man speaking to you.

OEDIPUS   But you are nothing to me!

MESSENGER   Neither was he.

OEDIPUS   Then why did he call me son?

MESSENGER   I will tell you:
Long ago he had you from my hands, as a gift.

OEDIPUS   Then how could he love me so, if I was not his?

MESSENGER   He had no children, and his heart turned to you.

OEDIPUS   What of you? Did you buy me? Did you find me by chance?

MESSENGER   I came upon you in the woody vales of Kithairon.

OEDIPUS   And what were you doing there?

MESSENGER   Tending my flocks.

OEDIPUS   A wandering shepherd?

110   MESSENGER   But your savior, son, that day.

OEDIPUS   From what did you save me?

MESSENGER   Your ankles should tell you that.

OEDIPUS   Ah, stranger, why do you speak of that childhood pain?

MESSENGER   I pulled the skewer that pinned your feet together.

OEDIPUS   I have had the mark as long as I can remember.

MESSENGER   That was why you were given the name you bear.

OEDIPUS   God! Was it my father or my mother who did it?
    Tell me!

MESSENGER   I do not know. The man who gave you to me
    Can tell you better than I.

OEDIPUS   It was not you that found me, but another?

120   MESSENGER   It was another shepherd gave you to me.

OEDIPUS   Who was he? Can you tell me who he was?

MESSENGER   I think he was said to be one of Laïos' people.

OEDIPUS   You mean the Laïos who was king here years ago?

MESSENGER   Yes; King Laïos; and the man was one of his herdsmen.

OEDIPUS   Is he still alive? Can I see him?

MESSENGER   These men here
    Know best about such things.

OEDIPUS   Does anyone here
    Know this shepherd that he is talking about?
    Have you seen him in the fields, or in the town?
    If you have, tell me. It is time things were made plain.

130   CHORAGOS   I think the man he means is that same shepherd
    You have already asked to see. Iokastê perhaps
    Could tell you something.

OEDIPUS   Do you know anything
    About him, Lady? Is he the man we have summoned?
    Is that the man this shepherd means?

IOKASTÊ   Why think of him?
    Forget this herdsman. Forget it all.
    This talk is a waste of time.

OEDIPUS   How can you say that,
    When the clues to my true birth are in my hands?

IOKASTÊ   For God's love, let us have no more questioning!
    Is your life nothing to you?

140   My own is pain enough for me to bear.

OEDIPUS   You need not worry. Suppose my mother a slave,
 And born of slaves: no baseness can touch you.
IOKASTÊ   Listen to me, I beg you: do not do this thing!
OEDIPUS   I will not listen; the truth must be made known.
IOKASTÊ   Everything that I say is for your own good!
OEDIPUS   My own good
 Snaps my patience, then; I want none of it.
IOKASTÊ   You are fatally wrong! May you never learn who you are!
OEDIPUS   Go, one of you, and bring the shepherd here.
 Let us leave this woman to brag of her royal name.
150   IOKASTÊ   Ah, miserable!
 That is the only word I have for you now.
 That is the only word I can ever have.

            Exit into the palace.

CHORAGOS   Why has she left us, Oedipus? Why has she gone
 In such a passion of sorrow? I fear this silence:
 Something dreadful may come of it.
OEDIPUS   Let it come!
 However base my birth, I must know about it.
 The Queen, like a woman, is perhaps ashamed
 To think of my low origin. But I
 Am a child of Luck; I can not be dishonored.
160   Luck is my mother; the passing months, my brothers,
 Have seen me rich and poor.
       If this is so,
 How could I wish that I were someone else?
 How could I not be glad to know my birth?

Ode III

CHORUS   If ever the coming time were known   STROPHE
 To my heart's pondering,
 Kithairon, now by Heaven I see the torches
 At the festival of the next full moon,
 And see the dance, and hear the choir sing
 A grace to your gentle shade:
 Mountain where Oedipus was found,
 O mountain guard of a noble race!
 May the god who heals us lend his aid,
10   And let that glory come to pass
 For our king's cradling-ground.

Of the nymphs that flower beyond the years,   ANTISTROPHE
Who bore you, royal child,
To Pan of the hills or the timberline Apollo,
Cold in delight where the upland clears,
Or Hermês for whom Kyllenê's heights are piled?
Or flushed as evening cloud,
Great Dionysos, roamer of mountains,
He—was it he who found you there,
20   And caught you up in his own proud
Arms from the sweet god-ravisher
Who laughed by the Muses' fountains?

SCENE IV

OEDIPUS   Sirs: though I do not know the man,
    I think I see him coming, this shepherd we want:
    He is old, like our friend here, and the men
    Bringing him seem to be servants of my house.
    But you can tell, if you have ever seen him.

Enter Shepherd escorted by servants.

CHORAGOS   I know him, he was Laios' man. You can trust him.
OEDIPUS   Tell me first, you from Corinth: Is this the shepherd
    We were discussing?
MESSENGER   This is the very man.
OEDIPUS   *To Shepherd*
    Come here. No, look at me. You must answer
10   Everything I ask.—You belonged to Laïos?
SHEPHERD   Yes: born his slave, brought up in his house.
OEDIPUS   Tell me: what kind of work did you do for him?
SHEPHERD   I was a shepherd of his, most of my life.
OEDIPUS   Where mainly did you go for pasturage?
SHEPHERD   Sometimes Kithairon, sometimes the hills near-by.
OEDIPUS   Do you remember ever seeing this man out there?
SHEPHERD   What would he be doing there? This man?
OEDIPUS   This man standing here. Have you ever seen him before?
SHEPHERD   No. At least, not to my recollection.
20   MESSENGER   And that is not strange, my lord. But I'll refresh
    His memory: he must remember when we two
    Spent three whole seasons together, March to September,
    On Kithairon or thereabouts. He had two flocks;
    I had one. Each autumn I'd drive mine home

And he would go back with his to Laïos' sheepfold.—

Is this not true, just as I have described it?

SHEPHERD   True, yes; but it was all so long ago.

MESSENGER   Well, then: do you remember, back in those days,

That you gave me a baby boy to bring up as my own?

30   SHEPHERD   What if I did? What are you trying to say?

MESSENGER   King Oedipus was once that little child.

SHEPHERD   Damn you, hold your tongue!

OEDIPUS   No more of that!

It is your tongue needs watching, not this man's.

SHEPHERD   My King, my Master, what is it I have done wrong?

OEDIPUS   You have not answered his question about the boy.

SHEPHERD   He does not know . . . He is only making trouble . . .

OEDIPUS   Come, speak plainly, or it will go hard with you.

SHEPHERD   In God's name, do not torture an old man!

OEDIPUS   Come here, one of you; bind his arms behind him.

40   SHEPHERD   Unhappy king! What more do you wish to learn?

OEDIPUS   Did you give this man the child he speaks of?

SHEPHERD   I did.

And I would to God I had died that very day.

OEDIPUS   You will die now unless you speak the truth.

SHEPHERD   Yet if I speak the truth, I am worse than dead.

OEDIPUS   *To Attendant*

He intends to draw it out, apparently—

SHEPHERD   No! I have told you already that I gave him the boy.

OEDIPUS   Where did you get him? From your house? From somewhere else?

SHEPHERD   Not from mine, no. A man gave him to me.

OEDIPUS   Is that man here? Whose house did he belong to?

50   SHEPHERD   For God's love, my King, do not ask me any more!

OEDIPUS   You are a dead man if I have to ask you again.

SHEPHERD   Then . . . Then the child was from the palace of Laïos.

OEDIPUS   A slave child? or a child of his own line?

SHEPHERD   Ah, I am on the brink of dreadful speech!

OEDIPUS   And I of dreadful hearing. Yet I must hear.

SHEPHERD   If you must be told, then . . .

They said it was Laïos' child:

But it is your wife who can tell you about that.

OEDIPUS   My wife!—Did she give it to you?

SHEPHERD   My Lord, she did.

OEDIPUS   Do you know why?

SHEPHERD   I was told to get rid of it.

OEDIPUS   Oh heartless mother!

60   SHEPHERD   But in dread of prophecies . . .

OEDIPUS   Tell me.

SHEPHERD   It was said that the boy would kill his own father.
OEDIPUS   Then why did you give him over to this old man?
SHEPHERD   I pitied the baby, my King,
    And I thought that this man would take him far away
    To his own country.
                    He saved him—but for what a fate!
    For if you are what this man says you are,
    No man living is more wretched than Oedipus.
OEDIPUS   Ah God!
    It was true!
           All the prophecies!
                  —Now,
70   O Light, may I look on you for the last time!
    I, Oedipus,
    Oedipus, damned in his birth, in his marriage damned,
    Damned in the blood he shed with his own hand!

He rushes into the palace.

ODE IV

CHORUS   Alas for the seed of men.   STROPHE 1

    What measure shall I give these generations
    That breathe on the void and are void
    And exist and do not exist?

    Who bears more weight of joy
    Than mass of sunlight shifting in images,
    Or who shall make his thought stay on
    That down time drifts away?

    Your splendor is all fallen.

10   O naked brow of wrath and tears,
    O change of Oedipus!
    I who saw your days call no man blest—
    Your great days like ghósts góne.

    That mind was a strong bow.   ANTISTROPHE 1

    Deep, how deep you drew it then, hard archer,
    At a dim fearful range,

And brought dear glory down!

You overcame the stranger—
The virgin with her hooking lion claws—
And though death sang, stood like a tower
To make pale Thebes take heart.

Fortress against our sorrow!

True king, giver of laws,
Majestic Oedipus!
No prince in Thebes had ever such renown,
No prince won such grace of power.

And now of all men ever known   STROPHE 2
Most pitiful is this man's story:
His fortunes are most changed, his state
Fallen to a low slave's
Ground under bitter fate.

O Oedipus, most royal one!
The great door that expelled you to the light
Gave at night—ah, gave night to your glory:
As to the father, to the fathering son.

All understood too late.

How could that queen whom Laïos won,
The garden that he harrowed at his height,
Be silent when that act was done?

But all eyes fail before time's eye,   ANTISTROPHE 2
All actions come to justice there.
Though never willed, though far down the deep past,
Your bed, your dread sirings,
Are brought to book at last.

Child by Laïos doomed to die,
Then doomed to lose that fortunate little death,
Would God you never took breath in this air
That with my wailing lips I take to cry:

For I weep the world's outcast.

50   I was blind, and now I can tell why:
        Asleep, for you had given ease of breath
        To Thebes, while the false years went by.

EXODOS

Enter, from the palace, Second Messenger.

SECOND MESSENGER   Elders of Thebes, most honored in this land,
        What horrors are yours to see and hear, what weight
        Of sorrow to be endured, if, true to your birth,
        You venerate the line of Labdakos!
        I think neither Istros nor Phasis, those great rivers,
        Could purify this place of all the evil
        It shelters now, or soon must bring to light—
        Evil not done unconsciously, but willed.

        The greatest griefs are those we cause ourselves
10   CHORAGOS   Surely, friend, we have grief enough already;
        What new sorrow do you mean?
        SECOND MESSENGER   The Queen is dead.
        CHORAGOS   O miserable Queen! But at whose hand?
        SECOND MESSENGER   Her own.
        The full horror of what happened you can not know,
        For you did not see it; but I, who did, will tell you
        As clearly as I can how she met her death.

        When she had left us,
        In passionate silence, passing through the court,
        She ran to her apartment in the house,
        Her hair clutched by the fingers of both hands.
20   She closed the doors behind her; then, by that bed
        Where long ago the fatal son was conceived—
        That son who should bring about his father's death—
        We heard her call upon Laïos, dead so many years,
        And heard her wail for the double fruit of her marriage,
        A husband by her husband, children by her child.

        Exactly how she died I do not know:
        For Oedipus burst in moaning and would not let us
        Keep vigil to the end: it was by him
        As he stormed about the room that our eyes were caught.
30   From one to another of us he went, begging a sword,
        Hunting the wife who was not his wife, the mother

Whose womb had carried his own children and himself.
I do not know: it was none of us aided him,
But surely one of the gods was in control!
For with a dreadful cry
He hurled his weight, as though wrenched out of himself,
At the twin doors: the bolts gave, and he rushed in.
And there we saw her hanging, her body swaying
From the cruel cord she had noosed about her neck.
40   A great sob broke from him, heartbreaking to hear,
As he loosed the rope and lowered her to the ground.

I would blot out from my mind what happened next!
For the King ripped from her gown the golden brooches
That were her ornament, and raised them, and plunged them down
Straight into his own eyeballs, crying, "No more,
No more shall you look on the misery about me,
The horrors of my own doing! Too long you have known
The faces of those whom I should never have seen,
Too long been blind to those for whom I was searching!
50   From this hour, go in darkness!" And as he spoke,
He struck at his eyes—not once, but many times;
And the blood spattered his beard,
Bursting from his ruined sockets like red hail.

So from the unhappiness of two this evil has sprung,
A curse on the man and woman alike. The old
Happiness of the house of Labdakos
Was happiness enough: where is it today?
It is all wailing and ruin, disgrace, death—all
The misery of mankind that has a name—
60   And it is wholly and for ever theirs.
CHORAGOS   Is he in agony still? Is there no rest for him?
SECOND MESSENGER   He is calling for someone to open the doors wide
So that all the children of Kadmos may look upon
His father's murderer, his mother's—no,
I can not say it!
                    And then he will leave Thebes,
Self-exiled, in order that the curse
Which he himself pronounced may depart from the house.
He is weak, and there is none to lead him,
So terrible is his suffering.
                              But you will see:
70   Look, the doors are opening; in a moment
You will see a thing that would crush a heart of stone.

The central door is opened; Oedipus, blinded, is led in.

CHORAGOS   Dreadful indeed for men to see.
     Never have my own eyes
     Looked on a sight so full of fear.

     Oedipus!
     What madness came upon you, what daemon
     Leaped on your life with heavier
     Punishment than a mortal man can bear?
     No: I can not even
80   Look at you, poor ruined one.
     And I would speak, question, ponder,
     If I were able. No.
     You make me shudder.
OEDIPUS   God. God.
     Is there a sorrow greater?
     Where shall I find harbor in this world?
     My voice is hurled far on a dark wind.
     What has God done to me?
CHORAGOS   Too terrible to think of, or to see.

90   OEDIPUS   O cloud of night,   STROPHE 1
     Never to be turned away: night coming on,
     I can not tell how: night like a shroud!

     My fair winds brought me here.
                              O God. Again
     The pain of the spikes where I had sight,
     The flooding pain
     Of memory, never to be gouged out.

CHORAGOS   This is not strange.
     You suffer it all twice over, remorse in pain,
     Pain in remorse.

100   OEDIPUS   Ah dear friend   ANTISTROPHE 1
     Are you faithful even yet, you alone?
     Are you still standing near me, will you stay here,
     Patient, to care for the blind?
                              The blind man!
     Yet even blind I know who it is attends me,
     By the voice's tone—
     Though my new darkness hide the comforter.

CHORAGOS Oh fearful act!
    What god was it drove you to rake black
    Night across your eyes?

110 OEDIPUS Apollo. Apollo. Dear   STROPHE 2
    Children, the god was Apollo.
    He brought my sick, sick fate upon me.
    But the blinding hand was my own!
    How could I bear to see
    When all my sight was horror everywhere?

CHORAGOS Everywhere; that is true.

OEDIPUS And now what is left?
    Images? Love? A greeting even,
    Sweet to the senses? Is there anything?
120 Ah, no, friends: lead me away.
    Lead me away from Thebes.
                                Lead the great wreck
    And hell of Oedipus, whom the gods hate.

CHORAGOS Your misery, you are not blind to that.
    Would God you had never found it out!

OEDIPUS Death take the man who unbound   ANTISTROPHE 2
    My feet on that hillside
    And delivered me from death to life! What life?
    If only I had died,
    This weight of monstrous doom
130 Could not have dragged me and my darlings down.

CHORAGOS I would have wished the same.

OEDIPUS Oh never to have come here
    With my father's blood upon me! Never
    To have been the man they call his mother's husband!
    Oh accurst! Oh child of evil,
    To have entered that wretched bed—
                                the selfsame one!
    More primal than sin itself, this fell to me.

CHORAGOS I do not know what words to offer you.
    You were better dead than alive and blind.

140 OEDIPUS Do not counsel me any more. This punishment

That I have laid upon myself is just.
If I had eyes,
I do not know how I could bear the sight
Of my father, when I came to the house of Death,
Or my mother; for I have sinned against them both
So vilely that I could not make my peace
By strangling my own life.

                     Or do you think my children,
Born as they were born, would be sweet to my eyes?
Ah never, never! Nor this town with its high walls,
Nor the holy images of the gods.

150   For I,
Thrice miserable!—Oedipus, noblest of all the line
Of Kadmos, have condemned myself to enjoy
These things no more, by my own malediction
Expelling that man whom the gods declared
To be a defilement in the house of Laïos.
After exposing the rankness of my own guilt,
How could I look men frankly in the eyes?
No, I swear it,
If I could have stifled my hearing at its source,
160   I would have done it and made all this body
A tight cell of misery, blank to light and sound:
So I should have been safe in my dark mind
Beyond external evil.

               Ah Kithairon!
Why did you shelter me? When I was cast upon you,
Why did I not die? Then I should never
Have shown the world my execrable birth.

Ah Polybos! Corinth, city that I believed
The ancient seat of my ancestors: how fair
I seemed, your child! And all the while this evil
Was cancerous within me!
170   For I am sick
In my own being, sick in my origin.

O three roads, dark ravine, woodland and way
Where three roads met: you, drinking my father's blood,
My own blood, spilled by my own hand: can you remember
The unspeakable things I did there, and the things
I went on from there to do?

                  O marriage, marriage!
The act that engendered me, and again the act

Performed by the son in the same bed—

                                    Ah, the net

Of incest, mingling fathers, brothers, sons,

180   With brides, wives, mothers: the last evil

That can be known by men: no tongue can say

How evil!

                 No. For the love of God, conceal me

Somewhere far from Thebes; or kill me; or hurl me

Into the sea, away from men's eyes for ever.

Come, lead me. You need not fear to touch me.

Of all men, I alone can bear this guilt.

Enter Kreon.

CHORAGOS Kreon is here now. As to what you ask,

    He may decide the course to take. He only

    Is left to protect the city in your place.

190 OEDIPUS Alas, how can I speak to him? What right have I

    To beg his courtesy whom I have deeply wronged?

KREON I have not come to mock you, Oedipus,

    Or to reproach you, either.

    To Attendants   —You standing there:

    If you have lost all respect for man's dignity,

    At least respect the flame of Lord Helios:

    Do not allow this pollution to show itself

    Openly here, an affront to the earth

    And Heaven's rain and the light of day. No, take him

    Into the house as quickly as you can.

200   For it is proper

    That only the close kindred see his grief.

OEDIPUS I pray you in God's name, since your courtesy

    Ignores my dark expectation, visiting

    With mercy this man of all men most execrable:

    Give me what I ask—for your good, not for mine.

KREON And what is it that you turn to me begging for?

OEDIPUS Drive me out of this country as quickly as may be

    To a place where no human voice can ever greet me.

KREON I should have done that before now—only,

210   God's will had not been wholly revealed to me.

OEDIPUS But his command is plain: the parricide

    Must be destroyed. I am that evil man.

KREON That is the sense of it, yes; but as things are,

    We had best discover clearly what is to be done.

OEDIPUS You would learn more about a man like me?

KREON You are ready now to listen to the god.

OEDIPUS   I will listen. But it is to you
    That I must turn for help. I beg you, hear me.

    The woman in there—
220   Give her whatever funeral you think proper:
    She is your sister.
                 —But let me go, Kreon!
    Let me purge my father's Thebes of the pollution
    Of my living here, and go out to the wild hills,
    To Kithairon, that has won such fame with me,
    The tomb my mother and father appointed for me,
    And let me die there, as they willed I should.
    And yet I know
    Death will not ever come to me through sickness
    Or in any natural way: I have been preserved
230   For some unthinkable fate. But let that be.

    As for my sons, you need not care for them.
    They are men, they will find some way to live.
    But my poor daughters, who have shared my table,
    Who never before have been parted from their father—
    Take care of them, Kreon; do this for me.
    And will you let me touch them with my hands
    A last time, and let us weep together?
    Be kind, my lord,
    Great prince, be kind!
                 Could I but touch them,
240   They would be mine again, as when I had my eyes.

Enter Antigone and Ismene, attended.

    Ah, God!
    Is it my dearest children I hear weeping?
    Has Kreon pitied me and sent my daughters?
KREON   Yes, Oedipus: I knew that they were dear to you
    In the old days, and know you must love them still.
OEDIPUS   May God bless you for this—and be friendlier
    Guardian to you than he has been to me!

    Children, where are you?
    Come quickly to my hands: they are your brother's—
250   Hands that have brought your father's once clear eyes
    To this way of seeing—
                Ah dearest ones,

I had neither sight nor knowledge then, your father
By the woman who was the source of his own life!
And I weep for you—having no strength to see you—,
I weep for you when I think of the bitterness
That men will visit upon you all your lives.
What homes, what festivals can you attend
Without being forced to depart again in tears?
And when you come to marriageable age,
Where is the man, my daughters, who would dare
Risk the bane that lies on all my children?
Is there any evil wanting? Your father killed
His father; sowed the womb of her who bore him;
Engendered you at the fount of his own existence!

That is what they will say of you.

                                        Then, whom
Can you ever marry? There are no bridegrooms for you,
And your lives must wither away in sterile dreaming.

O Kreon, son of Menoikeus!
You are the only father my daughters have,
Since we, their parents, are both of us gone for ever.
They are your own blood: you will not let them
Fall into beggary and loneliness;
You will keep them from the miseries that are mine!
Take pity on them; see, they are only children,
Friendless except for you. Promise me this,
Great Prince, and give me your hand in token of it.

Kreon clasps his right hand.

Children:
I could say much, if you could understand me,
But as it is, I have only this prayer for you:
Live where you can, be as happy as you can—
Happier, please God, than God has made your father.
KREON   Enough. You have wept enough. Now go within.
OEDIPUS   I must; but it is hard.
KREON   Time eases all things.
OEDIPUS   You know my mind, then?
KREON   Say what you desire.
OEDIPUS   Send me from Thebes!
KREON   God grant that I may!

OEDIPUS   But since God hates me . . .

KREON   No, he will grant your wish.

OEDIPUS   You promise?

KREON   I can not speak beyond my knowledge.

OEDIPUS   Then lead me in.

KREON   Come now, and leave your children.

OEDIPUS   No! Do not take them from me!

KREON   Think no longer

290   That you are in command here, but rather think
           How, when you were, you served your own destruction.

*Exeunt into the house all but the Chorus; the Choragos chants directly to the
audience.*

CHORAGOS   Men of Thebes: look upon Oedipus.

           This is the king who solved the famous riddle
           And towered up, most powerful of men.
           No mortal eyes but looked on him with envy,
           Yet in the end ruin swept over him.

           Let every man in mankind's frailty
           Consider his last day; and let none
           Presume on his good fortune until he find
300   Life, at his death, a memory without pain.

MORALITY DRAMA ON THE MEDIEVAL STAGE

Permanent theaters did not exist in England during the medieval period. When the morality play *Everyman* was first produced sometime near the end of the fifteenth century, it was probably performed on a makeshift platform set up in a village square or in the great dining hall of a castle. On the platform a couple of small set-like structures known as *mansions* (literally, dwelling places) would have been set up to stand for the two specific locations where action takes place—namely, heaven, from which God speaks at the opening of the play, and the house of salvation, to which Everyman goes in the middle of the play for confession and penance. As the action moved from one mansion to the other, the stage was understood to be an extension of one location and then of the other.

Sometimes, of course, the location of the action was neither specified nor implied, as when Everyman encounters Death, or Fellowship, or Kindred and Cousin. In such instances the stage would have been understood to represent a street or some other open area. And at the end of the play, when Everyman is about to die, he would have moved to the front of the stage, so that after his last speech he could step down from the stage to indicate that he had entered his grave. Thus the medieval method of staging *Everyman* was fundamentally symbolic in its use of space and processional in its movement from one mansion or location to another.

Costuming was also symbolic rather than realistic, and yet at the same time highly vivid. God, for example, might be dressed in the imperial vestments of a Pope, and Goods might be got up in a costume decorated with jewels or gold and silver coins. The audience, then, would have been treated to a spectacle that was at once visually appealing and spiritually significant.

The medieval method of staging brought actors and spectators closer to one another than ever before or since. They were not separated either by distance or by the architecture of a theater. Spectators witnessed the play from only a few feet away, and on occasion—as when Everyman enters his grave—an actor literally moved into the area of the audience. Although that movement into the audience may strike us today as being a violation of theatrical conventions, it would have affected medieval spectators quite differently: it would have shown them the imminence of their own death and the futility of clinging to their worldly possessions. That vision of *Everyman* would have been especially meaningful to medieval spectators, for they had also endured the bubonic plague, the so-called Black Death, which had ravaged England and the Continent during the fourteenth century.

Although we have not witnessed the Black Death, we all know the inescapable facts of death—the physical decay, the loss of consciousness, the end of being in the world—and *Everyman* does show us how those facts might affect a representative human being like ourselves. Everyman's initial denial of death, his desire to postpone it, his attempt to bargain with it, his final acceptance of it, and his ultimate recognition that it can be transcended only by the knowledge of having lived a decent life—the spectacle of these events makes the play as relevant for us as it must have been for its medieval audience.

ANONYMOUS

c. 1485

Everyman

CHARACTERS

MESSENGER	GOOD DEEDS
GOD	KNOWLEDGE
DEATH	CONFESSION
EVERYMAN	BEAUTY
FELLOWSHIP	STRENGTH
KINDRED	DISCRETION
COUSIN	FIVE WITS
GOODS	ANGEL
DOCTOR	

*Here beginneth a treatise how the High Father of Heaven sendeth Death to sum-
mon every creature to come and give account of their lives in this world, and is in
manner of a moral play.*

Enter Messenger

MESSENGER   I pray you all give your audience
     And hear this matter with reverence,
     By figure a moral play:
     The Summoning of Everyman called it is,
     That of our lives and ending shows
     How transitory we be all day.
     This matter is wondrous precious,
     But the intent of it is more gracious
     And sweet to bear away.
10   The story saith: Man, in the beginning
     Look well, and take good heed to the ending,
     Be you never so gay!
     Ye think sin in the beginning full sweet,
     Which in the end causeth the soul to weep,
     When the body lieth in clay.
     Here shall you see how Fellowship and Jollity
     Both, Strength, Pleasure and Beauty
     Will fade from thee as flower in May;

Edited by Kate Franks

For ye shall hear how our Heaven's King
Calleth Everyman to a general reckoning.
Give audience, and hear what he doth say.

Exit Messenger

God speaks.

GOD   I perceive, here in my majesty,
How that all creatures be to me unkind,
Living without dread in worldly prosperity.
Of ghostly sight[1] the people be so blind,
Drowned in sin, they know me not for their God.
In worldly riches is all their mind;
They fear not my righteousness, the sharp rod.
My law that I showed when I for them died
They forget clean, and shedding of my blood red.
I hanged between two thieves, it cannot be denied;
To get them life I suffered to be dead;
I healed their feet, with thorns hurt was my head.
I could do no more than I did, truly;
And now I see the people do clean forsake me.
They use the seven deadly sins damnable,
As pride, covetise, wrath, and lechery
Now in the world be made commendable;
And thus they leave of angels the heavenly company.
Every man liveth so after his own pleasure,
And yet of their life they be nothing sure.
I see the more that I them forbear
The worse they be from year to year.
All that liveth appaireth[2] fast;
Therefore I will, in all the haste,
Have a reckoning of every man's person;
For, if I leave the people thus alone
In their life and wicked tempests,
Verily they will become much worse than beasts;
For now one would by envy another up eat;
Charity they do all clean forget.
I hoped well that every man
In my glory should make his mansion,
And thereto I had them all elect;
But now I see, like traitors deject,

1. Spiritual sight; knowledge of God
2. Worsens

They thank me not for the pleasure that I to them meant,
Nor yet for their being that I them have lent.
I proffered the people great multitude of mercy,
And few there be that asketh it heartily.
60   They be so cumbered with worldly riches
That needs on them I must do justice,
On every man living without fear.
Where art thou, Death, thou mighty messenger?

Enter Death

DEATH   Almighty God, I am here at your will,
Your commandment to fulfill.
GOD   Go thou to Everyman
And show him, in my name,
A pilgrimage he must on him take,
Which he in no wise may escape;
70   And that he bring with him a sure reckoning
Without delay or any tarrying.
DEATH   Lord, I will in the world go run over all
And cruelly search out both great and small.
Every man will I beset that liveth beastly
Out of God's laws, and dreadeth not folly.
He that loveth riches I will strike with my dart,
His sight to blind, and from Heaven to depart—
Except that alms be his good friend—
In hell for to dwell, world without end.

Enter Everyman.

80   Lo, yonder I see Everyman walking.
Full little he thinketh on my coming;
His mind is on fleshly lusts and his treasure,
And great pain it shall cause him to endure
Before the Lord, Heaven's King.
Everyman, stand still! Whither art thou going
Thus gaily? Hast thou thy Maker forgot?
EVERYMAN   Why askest thou?
Wouldest thou know?
DEATH   Yea, sir. I will you show:
90   In great haste I am sent to thee
From God out of his majesty.
EVERYMAN   What, sent to me?

DEATH   Yea, certainly.
    Though thou have forgot him here,
    He thinketh on thee in the heavenly sphere,
    As, ere we depart, thou shalt know.
EVERYMAN   What desireth God of me?
DEATH   That I shall show to thee:
    A reckoning he will needs have

100   Without any longer respite.
EVERYMAN   To give a reckoning longer leisure I crave;
    This blind[3] matter troubleth my wit.
DEATH   On thee thou must take a long journey;
    Therefore thy book of account with thee thou bring,
    For turn again thou cannot, by no way.
    And look thou be sure of thy reckoning,
    For before God thou shalt answer and show
    Thy many bad deeds, and good but a few;
    How thou hast spent thy life, and in what wise,

110   Before the Chief Lord of Paradise.
    Have ado that thou were in that way,
    For know thou well, thou shalt make no attorney.[4]
EVERYMAN   Full unready I am, such reckoning to give.
    I know thee not. What messenger art thou?
DEATH   I am Death that no man dreadeth,[5]
    For every man I rest and no man spareth;
    For it is God's commandment
    That all to me should be obedient.
EVERYMAN   O Death, thou comest when I had thee least in mind!

120   In thy power it lieth me to save;
    Yet of my goods will I give thee, if thou will be kind—
    Yea, a thousand pound shalt thou have!—
    And defer this matter till another day.
DEATH   Everyman, it may not be, by no way.
    I set not by gold, silver, nor riches,
    Nor by pope, emperor, king, duke, nor princes;
    For, if I would receive gifts great,
    All the world I might get;
    But my custom is clean contrary:

130   I give thee no respite. Come hence, and not tarry!
EVERYMAN   Alas, shall I have no longer respite?
    I may say Death giveth no warning!

3. Unknown, obscure
4. You won't be able to plead your case
5. Who fears no man

        To think on thee, it maketh my heart sick,
        For all unready is my book of reckoning.
        But twelve years if I might have abiding,
        My accounting book I would make so clear
        That my reckoning I should not need to fear.
        Wherefore, Death, I pray thee, for God's mercy,
        Spare me till I be provided of remedy.

140 DEATH   Thee availeth not to cry, weep and pray;
        But haste thee lightly[6] that thou were gone that journey,
        And prove thy friends if thou can.
        For know thou well the tide abideth no man,
        And in the world each living creature
        For Adam's sin must die of nature.

    EVERYMAN   Death, if I should this pilgrimage take
        And my reckoning surely make,
        Show me, for sainted charity,
        Should I not come again shortly?

150 DEATH   No, Everyman. If thou be once there
        Thou mayst never more come here,
        Trust me verily.

    EVERYMAN   O gracious God in the high seat celestial,
        Have mercy on me in this most need!
        Shall I have no company from this vale terrestial
        Of mine acquaintance, that way me to lead?

    DEATH   Yea, if any be so hardy
        That would go with thee and bear thee company.
        Hie thee that thou were gone to God's magnificence,
160   Thy reckoning to give before his presence.
        What, thinkest thou thy life is given thee
        And thy worldly goods also?

    EVERYMAN   I had thought so, verily.

    DEATH   Nay, nay, it was but lent thee;
        For as soon as thou art gone,
        Another a while shall have it and then go therefrom,
        Even as thou hast done.
        Everyman, thou art mad! Thou hast thy wits five
        And here on earth will not amend thy life;
170   For suddenly I do come.

    EVERYMAN   O wretchéd caitiff, whither shall I flee,
        That I might escape this endless sorrow?
        Now, gentle Death, spare me till tomorrow,

---

6. Quickly

That I may amend me
With good advisement.
DEATH   Nay, thereto I will not consent,
   Nor no man will I respite;
   But to the heart suddenly I shall smite
   Without any advisement.
180   And now out of thy sight I will me hie.
   See thou make thee ready shortly;
   For thou mayst say this is the day
   That no man living may escape away.

Exit Death.

EVERYMAN   Alas, I may well weep with sighs deep!
   Now have I no manner of company
   To help me in my journey and me to keep;
   And also my writing is full unready.
   How shall I do now for to excuse me?
   I would to God I had never been begot!
190   To my soul a full great profit it had been;
   For now I fear pains huge and great.
   The time passeth. Lord, help, that all wrought!
   For though I mourn it availeth naught.
   The day passeth and is almost ago;
   I know not well what for to do.
   To whom were I best my complaint to make?
   What if I to Fellowship thereof spake
   And showed him of this sudden chance?
   For in him is all mine affiance;[7]
200   We have in the world so many a day
   Been good friends in sport and play.

Enter Fellowship.

   I see him yonder, certainly.
   I trust that he will bear me company;
   Therefore to him will I speak to ease my sorrow.
   Well met, good Fellowship, and good morrow!
FELLOWSHIP   Everyman, good morrow, by this day!
   Sir, why lookest thou so piteously?
   If anything be amiss, I pray thee me say,
   That I may help to remedy.
210 EVERYMAN   Yea, good Fellowship, yea,
   I am in great jeopardy.

7. Faith or trust

FELLOWSHIP   My true friend, show to me your mind.
   I will not forsake thee to my life's end
   In the way of good company.
EVERYMAN   That was well spoken and lovingly.
FELLOWSHIP   Sir, I must needs know your heaviness;
   I have pity to see you in any distress.
   If any have you wronged, ye shall revenged be,
   Though I on the ground be slain for thee,
220   Though that I know before that I should die.
EVERYMAN   Verily, Fellowship, gramercy.
FELLOWSHIP   Tush! By thy thanks I set not a straw.
   Show me your grief, and say no more.
EVERYMAN   If I my heart should to you break,
   And then you to turn your mind from me
   And would not me comfort when ye hear me speak,
   Then should I ten times sorrier be.
FELLOWSHIP   Sir, I say as I will do in deed.
EVERYMAN   Then be you a good friend in need.
230   I have found you true herebefore.
FELLOWSHIP   And so ye shall evermore;
   For, in faith, if thou go to hell,
   I will not forsake thee by the way.
EVERYMAN   Ye speak like a good friend; I believe you well.
   I shall deserve it, if I may.
FELLOWSHIP   I speak of no deserving, by this day!
   For he that will say and nothing do
   Is not worthy with good company to go;
   Therefore show me the grief of your mind,
240   As to your friend most loving and kind.
EVERYMAN   I shall show you how it is:
   Commanded I am to go a journey,
   A long way hard and dangerous,
   And give a straight account without delay
   Before the high judge, Adonai.[8]
   Wherefore, I pray you, bear me company,
   As ye have promised, in this journey.
FELLOWSHIP   That is matter indeed! Promise is duty;
   But if I should take such a voyage on me,
250   I know it well, it should be to my pain;
   Also it maketh me afeared, certain.
   But let us take counsel here as well as we can,
   For your words would fear a strong man.

8. Hebrew name for God

EVERYMAN   Why, ye said if I had need
    Ye would me never forsake, quick nor dead,
    Though it were to hell, truly.
FELLOWSHIP   So I said, certainly,
    But such pleasures be set aside, the sooth to say;
    And also, if we took such a journey
260   When should we again come?
EVERYMAN   Nay, never again till the day of doom.
FELLOWSHIP   In faith, then will not I come there!
    Who hath you these tidings brought?
EVERYMAN   Indeed, Death was with me here.
FELLOWSHIP   Now, by God that all hath bought,
    If Death were the messenger,
    For no man that is living today
    I will not go that loath journey—
    Not for the father that begat me!
270 EVERYMAN   Ye promised otherwise, pardie.
FELLOWSHIP   I know well I said so, truly;
    And yet, if thou wilt eat and drink and make good cheer,
    Or haunt to women the lusty company[9]
    I would not forsake you while the day is clear,
    Trust me verily.
EVERYMAN   Yea, thereto ye would be ready!
    To go to mirth, solace and play
    Your mind will sooner apply
    Than to bear me company in my long journey.
280 FELLOWSHIP   Now, in good faith, I will not that way,
    But if thou will murder or any man kill,
    In that I will help thee with a good will.
EVERYMAN   O, that is a simple advice indeed.
    Gentle fellow, help me in my necessity!
    We have loved long, and now I need;
    And now, gentle Fellowship, remember me.
FELLOWSHIP   Whether ye have loved me or no,
    By Saint John, I will not with thee go!
EVERYMAN   Yet, I pray thee, take the labor and do so much for me
290   To bring me forward, for sainted charity,
    And comfort me till I come without the town.
FELLOWSHIP   Nay, if thou would give me a new gown,
    I will not a foot with thee go;
    But if thou had tarried, I would not have left thee so.

9. Seek women's company for pleasure; go a-whoring

And as now, God speed thee in thy journey,

For from thee I will depart as fast as I may.

EVERYMAN   Whither away, Fellowship? Will thou forsake me?

FELLOWSHIP   Yea, by my faith! To God I betake[10] thee.

EVERYMAN   Farewell, good Fellowship! For thee my heart is sore.

300 Adieu forever! I shall see thee no more.

FELLOWSHIP   In faith, Everyman, farewell now at the ending!

For you I will remember that parting is mourning.

Exit Fellowship.

EVERYMAN   Alack, shall we thus depart indeed—

Ah, Lady, help!—without any more comfort?

Lo, Fellowship forsaketh me in my most need.

For help in this world whither shall I resort?

Fellowship herebefore with me would merry make,

And now little sorrow for me doth he take.

It is said, "In prosperity men friends may find,

310 Which in adversity be full unkind."

Now whither for succor shall I flee,

Since that Fellowship hath forsaken me?

To my kinsmen I will, truly,

Praying them to help me in my necessity.

I believe that they will do so,

For kind will creep where it may not go.[11]

Enter Kindred and Cousin.

I will go say, for yonder I see them.

Where be ye now, my friends and kinsmen?

KINDRED   Here be we now at your commandment.

320 Cousin, I pray you show us your intent

In any wise and not spare.

COUSIN   Yea, Everyman, and to us declare

If ye be disposed to go anywhither;

For know you well, we will live and die together.

KINDRED   In wealth and woe we will with you hold,

For over his kin a man may be bold.

EVERYMAN   Gramercy, my friends and kinsmen kind.

Now shall I show you the grief of my mind:

I was commanded by a messenger,

330 That is a high king's chief officer;

10. Entrust
11. One's kin will crawl where they may not walk;
    i.e., will do what they can.

He bade me go a pilgrimage, to my pain,
And I know well I shall never come again.
Also I must give a reckoning strait,
For I have a great enemy that hath me in wait,
Which intendeth me for to hinder.

KINDRED   What account is that which ye must render?
That would I know.

EVERYMAN   Of all my works I must show
How I have lived and my days spent;

340   Also of ill deeds that I have used
In my time, since life was me lent;
And of all virtues that I have refused.
Therefore, I pray you, go thither with me
To help to make mine account, for saint charity.

COUSIN   What, to go thither? Is that the matter?
Nay, Everyman, I had liefer fast bread and water
All this five years and more.

EVERYMAN   Alas, that ever I was born!
For now shall I never be merry

350   If that you forsake me.

KINDRED   Ah, sir, but ye be a merry man!
Take good heart to you, and make no moan.
But one thing I warn you, by Saint Anne—
As for me, ye shall go alone.

EVERYMAN   My Cousin, will you not with me go?

COUSIN   No, by our Lady! I have the cramp in my toe.
Trust not to me; for, so God me speed,
I will deceive you in your most need.

KINDRED   It availeth not us to entice.

360   Ye shall have my maid with all my heart;
She loveth to go to feasts, there to be nice,
And to dance and abroad to start.
I will give her leave to help you in that journey,
If that you and she may agree.

EVERYMAN   Now show me the very effect of your mind:
Will you go with me, or abide behind?

KINDRED   Abide behind? Yea, that will I, if I may!
Therefore farewell till another day.

Exit Kindred.

EVERYMAN   How should I be merry or glad?

370   For fair promises men to me make,
But when I have most need they me forsake.
I am deceived; that maketh me sad.

COUSIN   Cousin Everyman, farewell now,

For verily I will not go with you.
Also of mine own an unready reckoning
I have to account; therefore I make tarrying.
Now God keep thee, for now I go.

Exit Cousin.

EVERYMAN   Ah, Jesus, is all come hereto?
Lo, fair words maketh fools fain;
380   They promise and nothing will do, certain.
My kinsmen promised me faithfully
For to abide with me steadfastly,
And now fast away do they flee,
Even so Fellowship promised me.
What friend were best me of to provide?
I lose my time here longer to abide.
Yet in my mind a thing there is:
All my life I have loved riches;
If that my Goods now help me might,
390   He would make my heart full light.
I will speak to him in this distress.
Where art thou, my Goods and riches?

Goods revealed in a corner.

GOODS   Who calleth me? Everyman? What, hast thou haste?
I lie here in corners, trussed and piled so high,
And in chests I am locked so fast,
Also sacked in bags. Thou mayst see with thine eye
I cannot stir; in packs, low I lie.
What would ye have? Lightly me say.
EVERYMAN   Come hither, Goods, in all the haste thou may,
400   For of counsel I must desire thee.
GOODS   Sir, if ye in the world have sorrow or adversity,
That can I help you to remedy shortly.
EVERYMAN   It is another disease that grieveth me;
In this world it is not, I tell thee so.
I am sent for, another way to go,
To give a strait account general
Before the highest Jupiter of all;
And all my life I have had joy and pleasure in thee.
Therefore, I pray thee, go with me;
410   For, peradventure, thou mayst before God Almighty
My reckoning help to clean and purify;
For it is said ever among
That "money maketh all right that is wrong."

GOODS   Nay, Everyman, I sing another song.
    I follow no man in such voyages; ·
    For if I went with thee,
    Thou shouldst fare much the worse for me.
    For because on me thou did set thy mind,
    Thy reckoning I have made blotted and blind,
420   That thine account thou cannot make truly—
    And that hast thou for the love of me!
EVERYMAN   That would grieve me full sore,
    When I should come to that fearful answer.
    Up, let us go thither together.
GOODS   Nay, not so! I am too brittle, I may not endure.
    I will follow no man one foot, be ye sure.
EVERYMAN   Alas, I have thee loved, and had great pleasure
    All my life-days in goods and treasure.
GOODS   That is to thy damnation, without lying,
430   For my love is contrary to the love everlasting.
    But if thou had me loved moderately during,
    As to the poor given part of me,
    Then shouldst thou not in this dolor be,
    Nor in this great sorrow and care.
EVERYMAN   Lo, now was I deceived ere I was aware,
    And all I may lay to my spending of time.
GOODS   What, thinkest thou that I am thine?
EVERYMAN   I had thought so.
GOODS   Nay, Everyman, I say no.
440   As for a while I was lent thee;
    A season thou hast had me in prosperity.
    My condition is a man's soul to kill;
    If I save one, a thousand I do spill.
    Thinkest thou that I will follow thee?
    Nay, from this world not, verily.
EVERYMAN   I had thought otherwise.
GOODS   Therefore to thy soul Goods is a thief;
    For when thou art dead, this is my guise—
    Another to deceive in this same wise
450   As I have done thee, and all to his soul's reprief.[12]
EVERYMAN   O false Goods, cursed thou be,
    Thou traitor to God, that hast deceived me
    And caught me in thy snare!
GOODS   Marry, thou brought thyself in care,

12. Harm

Whereof I am glad.
I must needs laugh; I cannot be sad.
EVERYMAN   Ah, Goods, thou hast had long my hearty love;
I gave thee that which should be the Lord's above.
But wilt thou not go with me indeed?
460   I pray thee truth to say.
GOODS   No, so God me speed!
Therefore farewell, and have good day.

Exit Goods.

EVERYMAN   O, to whom shall I make my moan
For to go with me in that heavy journey?
First Fellowship said he would with me go;
His words were very pleasant and gay,
But afterward he left me alone.
Then spake I to my kinsmen, all in despair,
And also they gave me words fair;
470   They lacked no fair speaking,
But all forsook me in the ending.
Then went I to my Goods that I loved best,
In hope to have comfort; but there had I least,
For my Goods sharply did me tell
That he bringeth many into Hell.
Then of myself I was ashamed,
And so I am worthy to be blamed;
Thus may I well myself hate.
Of whom shall I now counsel take?
480   I think that I shall never speed
Till that I go to my Good Deeds.
But, alas, she is so weak
That she can neither go nor speak;
Yet will I venture on her now.
My Good Deeds, where be you?

Good Deeds revealed on the ground.

GOOD DEEDS   Here I lie, cold in the ground.
Thy sins hath me so sore bound
That I cannot stir.
EVERYMAN   O Good Deeds, I stand in fear!
490   I must you pray of counsel,
For help now should come right well.
GOOD DEEDS   Everyman, I have understanding

That ye be summoned account to make
Before Messiah, of Jerusalem King;
If you do by me, that journey with you will I take.
EVERYMAN   Therefore I come to you my moan to make.
I pray you that ye will go with me.
GOOD DEEDS   I would full fain, but I cannot stand, verily.
EVERYMAN   Why, is there anything on you fallen?
500   GOOD DEEDS   Yea, sir, I may thank you of all.
If ye had perfectly cheered me,
Your book of account full ready would be.
Look, the books of your works and deeds eke,[13]
As how they lie under the feet
To your soul's heaviness.
EVERYMAN   Our Lord Jesus help me!
For one letter here I cannot see.
GOOD DEEDS   There is a blind reckoning in time of distress.
EVERYMAN   Good Deeds, I pray you help me in this need,
510   Or else I am forever damned indeed;
Therefore help me to make reckoning
Before the Redeemer of all things,
That King is, and was, and ever shall.
GOOD DEEDS   Everyman, I am sorry of your fall,
And fain would I help you if I were able.
EVERYMAN   Good Deeds, your counsel I pray you give me.
GOOD DEEDS   That shall I do verily.
Though that on my feet I may not go,
I have a sister that shall with you also,
520   Called Knowledge, which shall with you abide
To help you to make that dreadful reckoning.

Enter Knowledge.

KNOWLEDGE   Everyman, I will go with thee and be thy guide,
In thy most need to go by thy side.
EVERYMAN   In good condition I am now in everything
And am wholly content with this good thing;
Thanked be God my Creator.
GOOD DEEDS   And when she hath brought you there,
Where thou shalt heal thee of thy smart,
Then go you with your reckoning and your Good Deeds together
530   For to make you joyful at heart
Before the Blesséd Trinity.

13. Also

EVERYMAN   My Good Deeds, gramercy!
    I am well content, certainly,
    With your words sweet.

Everyman and Knowledge leave Good Deeds.

KNOWLEDGE   Now go we together lovingly
    To Confession, that cleansing river.
EVERYMAN   For joy I weep; I would we were there!
    But, I pray you, give me cognition
    Where dwelleth that holy man, Confession.
540   KNOWLEDGE   In the house of salvation;
    We shall find him in that place
    That shall us comfort, by God's grace.

Knowledge leads Everyman to Confession.

    Lo, this is Confession. Kneel down and ask mercy,
    For he is in good esteem with God Almighty.
EVERYMAN   O glorious fountain, that all uncleaness doth clarify,
    Wash from me the spots of vice unclean,
    That on me no sin may be seen.
    I come with Knowledge for my redemption,
    Redempt with hearty and full contrition;
550   For I am commanded a pilgrimage to take
    And great accounts before God to make.
    Now I pray you, Shrift, mother of salvation,
    Help my Good Deeds for my piteous exclamation.
CONFESSION   I know your sorrow well, Everyman.
    Because with Knowledge ye come to me,
    I will you comfort as well as I can,
    And a precious jewel I will give thee,
    Called penance, voider of adversity;
    Therewith shall your body chastised be,
560   With abstinence and perseverance in God's serviture.
    Here shall you receive that scourge of me
    Which is penance strong that ye must endure,
    To remember thy Saviour was scourged for thee
    With sharp scourges and suffered it patiently;
    So must thou, ere thou escape that painful pilgrimage.

Confession gives scourge to Knowledge.

    Knowledge, keep him in this voyage,

And by that time Good Deeds will be with thee.
But in any wise be sure of mercy,
For your time draweth fast; if ye will saved be,
570   Ask God mercy, and he will grant truly.
When with the scourge of penance man doth him bind,
The oil of forgiveness then shall he find.

Everyman and Knowledge leave Confession.

EVERYMAN   Thanked be God for his gracious work!
For now I will my penance begin.
This hath rejoiced and lighted my heart,
Though the knots be painful and hard within.
KNOWLEDGE   Everyman, look your penance that ye fulfill,
What pain that ever it to you be;
And Knowledge shall give you counsel at will
580   How your account ye shall make clearly.
EVERYMAN   O eternal God, O heavenly figure,
O way of righteousness, O goodly vision,
Which descended down in a virgin pure
Because he would every man redeem,
Which Adam forfeited by his disobedience;
O blesséd Godhead, elect and high divine,
Forgive me my grievous offence!
Here I cry thee mercy in this presence.
O ghostly[14] treasure, O ransomer and redeemer,
590   Of all the world hope and conductor,
Mirror of joy, foundation of mercy,
Which illumineth Heaven and earth thereby,
Hear my clamorous complaint though it late be;
Receive my prayers unworthy in this heavy life!
Though I be a sinner most abominable,
Yet let my name be written in Moses' table.
O Mary, pray to the Maker of all things,
Me for to help at my ending;
And save me from the power of my enemy,
600   For Death assaileth me strongly.
And, Lady, that I may by means of thy prayer
Of your Son's glory to be partner,
By the means of his passion, I it crave;
I beseech you, help my soul to save.

14. Spiritual, as in Holy Ghost

Knowledge, give me the scourge of penance;
My flesh therewith shall give acquittance.
I will now begin if God give me grace.

Knowledge gives scourge to Everyman.

KNOWLEDGE   Everyman, God give you time and space!
Thus I bequeath you in the hands of our Saviour;
610   Now may you make your reckoning sure.
EVERYMAN   In the name of the Holy Trinity,
My body sore punishéd shall be:
Take this, body, for the sins of the flesh!
Also thou delightest to go gay and fresh,
And in the way of damnation thou did me bring;
Therefore suffer now strokes of punishing.
Now of penance I will wade the water clear
To save me from Purgatory, that sharp fire.

Good Deeds rises from the ground.

GOOD DEEDS   I thank God, now I can walk and go
620   And am delivered of my sickness and woe.
Therefore with Everyman I will go and not spare;
His good works I will help him to declare.
KNOWLEDGE   Now, Everyman, be merry and glad!
Your Good Deeds cometh now; ye may not be sad.
Now is your Good Deeds whole and sound,
Going upright upon the ground.
EVERYMAN   My heart is light and shall be evermore;
Now will I smite faster than I did before.
GOOD DEEDS   Everyman, pilgrim, my special friend,
630   Blessed be thou without end!
For thee is prepared the eternal glory.
Ye have me made whole and sound,
Therefore I will bide by thee in every stound.[15]
EVERYMAN   Welcome, my Good Deeds! Now I hear thy voice
I weep for very sweetness of love.
KNOWLEDGE   Be no more sad, but ever rejoice;
God seeth thy living in his throne above.

Knowledge gives Everyman the garment of contrition.

15. Instance, occasion

Put on this garment to thy behove,[16]
Which is wet with your tears,

640   Or else before God you may it miss
When you to your journey's end come shall.

EVERYMAN   Gentle knowledge, what do ye it call?

KNOWLEDGE   It is the garment of sorrow;
From pain it will you borrow.
Contrition it is
That getteth forgiveness;
It pleaseth God passing well.

GOOD DEEDS   Everyman, will you wear it for your heal?[17]

Everyman puts on the garment of contrition.

EVERYMAN   Now blesséd be Jesu, Mary's Son,

650   For now have I on true contrition;
And let us go now without tarrying.
Good Deeds, have we clear our reckoning?

GOOD DEEDS   Yea, indeed, I have it here.

EVERYMAN   Then I trust we need not fear.
Now, friends, let us not part in twain.

KNOWLEDGE   Nay, Everyman, that will we not, certain.

GOOD DEEDS   Yet must thou lead with thee
Three persons of great might.

EVERYMAN   Who should they be?

660   GOOD DEEDS   Discretion and Strength they hight,[18]
And thy Beauty may not abide behind.

KNOWLEDGE   Also ye must call to mind
Your Five Wits as for your counsellors.

GOOD DEEDS   You must have them ready at all hours.

EVERYMAN   How shall I get them hither?

KNOWLEDGE   You must call them all together,
And they will hear you incontinent.[19]

EVERYMAN   My friends, come hither and be present:
Discretion, Strength, my Five Wits, and Beauty.

Enter Discretion, Strength, Five Wits, and Beauty.

670   BEAUTY   Here at your will we be all ready.
What would ye that we should do?

16. Benefit
17. Salvation
18. Are called
19. At once

GOOD DEEDS   That ye would with Everyman go
    And help him in his pilgrimage.
    Advise you, will ye with him or not in that voyage?
STRENGTH   We will bring him all thither
    To his help and comfort, ye may believe me.
DISCRETION   So will we go with him all together.
EVERYMAN   Almighty God, loved may thou be!
    I give thee laud that I have hither brought

680   Strength, Discretion, Beauty and Five Wits. Lack I naught;
    And my Good Deeds, with Knowledge clear,
    All be in company at my will here.
    I desire no more to my business.
STRENGTH   And I, Strength, will by you stand in distress,
    Though thou would in battle fight on the ground.
FIVE WITS   And though it were through the world round,
    We will not depart for sweet nor sour.
BEAUTY   No more will I unto death's hour,
    Whatsoever thereof befall.

690 DISCRETION   Everyman, advise you first of all;
    Go with a good advisement and deliberation.
    We all give you virtuous monition
    That all shall be well.
EVERYMAN   My friends, hearken what I will tell:
    I pray God reward you in his heavenly sphere.
    Now hearken, all that be here,
    For I will make my testament
    Here before you all present:
    In alms, half my goods I will give with my hands twain

700   In the way of charity with good intent,
    And the other half still shall remain
    In queth,[20] to be returned where it ought to be.
    This I do in despite of the fiend of hell,
    To go quite out of his peril
    Ever after and this day.
KNOWLEDGE   Everyman, hearken what I say:
    Go to Priesthood, I you advise,
    And receive of him in any wise
    The holy sacrament and ointment together;

710   Then shortly see ye turn again hither.
    We will all abide you here.
FIVE WITS   Yea, Everyman, hie you that ye ready were.

---

20. As a bequest; though the remainder of the line indicates that it is
    actually a restitution of illegally acquired property.

There is no emperor, king, duke, nor baron
That of God hath commission
As hath the least priest in the world being;
For of the blesséd sacraments pure and benign,
He beareth the keys, and thereof hath the cure
For man's redemption—it is ever sure—
Which God for our soul's medicine
720   Gave us out of his heart with great pine.[21]
Here in this transitory life, for thee and me,
The blessed sacraments seven there be:
Baptism, confirmation with priesthood good,
And the sacrament of God's precious flesh and blood,
Marriage, the holy extreme unction, and penance.
These seven be good to have in remembrance,
Gracious sacraments of high divinity.
EVERYMAN   Fain would I receive that holy body,
And meekly to my ghostly[22] father I will go.
730   FIVE WITS   Everyman, that is the best that ye can do.
God will you to salvation bring,
For priesthood exceedeth all other things:
To us holy scripture they do teach
And converteth man from sin, Heaven to reach;
God hath to them more power given
Than to any angel that is in Heaven.
With five words he may consecrate,
God's body in flesh and blood to make,
And handleth his Maker between his hands.
740   The priest bindeth and unbindeth all bands,
Both in earth and in Heaven.
Thou ministers all the sacraments seven;
Though we kissed thy feet, thou were worthy.
Thou art surgeon that cureth sin deadly;
No remedy we find under God
But all only priesthood.
Everyman, God gave priests that dignity
And setteth them in his stead among us to be;
Thus be they above angels in degree.

                                        Exit Everyman.

750   KNOWLEDGE   If priests be good, it is so, surely.
But when Jesu hanged on the cross with great smart,
There he gave, out of his blesséd heart,

21. Anguish, torment
22. Spiritual

The seven sacraments in great torment;
He sold them not to us, that Lord omnipotent;
Therefore Saint Peter the apostle doth say
That Jesu's curse hath all they
Which God their Saviour do buy or sell,
Or they for any money do take or tell.[23]

760   Sinful priests giveth the sinners example bad;
Their children sitteth by other men's fires, I have heard;
And some haunteth women's company
With unclean life, as lusts of lechery;
These be with sin made blind.

FIVE WITS   I trust to God no such may we find;
Therefore let us priesthood honor
And follow their doctrine for our souls' succour.
We be their sheep, and they shepherds be
By whom we all be kept in surety.
Peace! For yonder I see Everyman come,

770   Which hath made true satisfaction.

GOOD DEEDS   Methinks it is he indeed.

Re-enter Everyman.

EVERYMAN   Now Jesu be your alder speed![24]
I have received the sacrament for my redemption
And then mine extreme unction.
Blesséd be all they that counselled me to take it!
And now, friends, let us go without longer respite.
I thank God that ye have tarried so long.
Now set each of you on this rood your hand
And shortly follow me.

780   I go before where I would be. God be our guide!

They go toward the grave.

STRENGTH   Everyman, we will not from you go
Till ye have done this voyage long.

DISCRETION   I, Discretion, will bide by you also.

KNOWLEDGE   And though this pilgrimage be never so strong,
I will never part you from.

STRENGTH   Everyman, I will be as sure by thee
As ever I did by Judas Maccabee.[25]

---

23. Count out, as in bank teller
24. Help to all of you
25. A Jewish leader of the second century B.C., known for his courage (1 Macc. 3)

They arrive at the grave.

EVERYMAN   Alas, I am so faint I may not stand;
  My limbs under me do fold.
790   Friends, let us not turn again to this land,
  Not for all the world's gold;
  For into this cave must I creep
  And turn to earth, and thereto sleep.
BEAUTY   What, into this grave? Alas!
EVERYMAN   Yea, there shall ye consume, more and less.[26]
BEAUTY   And what, should I smother here?
EVERYMAN   Yea, by my faith, and never more appear.
  In this world live no more we shall,
  But in Heaven before the highest Lord of all.
800   BEAUTY   I cross out all this. Adieu, by Saint John!
  I take my tap in my lap and am gone.[27]
EVERYMAN   What, Beauty, whither will ye?
BEAUTY   Peace! I am deaf. I look not behind me,
  Not if thou wouldest give me all the gold in thy chest.

                                                        Exit Beauty.

EVERYMAN   Alas, whereto may I trust?
  Beauty goeth fast away from me.
  She promised with me to live and die.
STRENGTH   Everyman, I will thee also forsake and deny;
  Thy game liketh me not at all.
810   EVERYMAN   Why, then, ye will forsake me all?
  Sweet Strength, tarry a little space.
STRENGTH   Nay, sir, by the rood of grace!
  I will hie me from thee fast,
  Though thou weep till thy heart to-brast.[28]
EVERYMAN   Ye would ever bide by me, ye said.
STRENGTH   Yea, I have you far enough conveyed.
  Ye be old enough, I understand,
  Your pilgrimage to take in hand.
  I repent me that I hither came.
820   EVERYMAN   Strength, you to displease I am to blame;
  Yet promise is debt, this ye well wot.[29]
STRENGTH   In faith, I care not.

26. The grave devours all, both the great and the small.
27. A tap is an unspun tuft of wool or flax. Hence, like a peasant housewife, Beauty
   is saying, "I'm pocketing my spinning materials and am off."
28. Bursts in two
29. Know

Thou art but a fool to complain;
You spend your speech and waste your brain.
Go thrust thee into the ground!

Exit Strength.

EVERYMAN   I had thought surer I should you have found.
He that trusteth in his Strength,
She him deceiveth at the length.
Both Strength and Beauty forsaketh me;
830   Yet they promised me fair and lovingly.
DISCRETION   Everyman, I will after Strength be gone.
As for me, I will leave you alone.
EVERYMAN   Why, Discretion, will ye forsake me?
DISCRETION   Yea, in faith, I will go from thee;
For when Strength goeth before,
I follow after evermore.
EVERYMAN   Yet, I pray thee, for the love of the Trinity,
Look in my grave once piteously.
DISCRETION   Nay, so nigh will I not come.
840   Farewell, everyone!

Exit Discretion.

EVERYMAN   O, all things faileth, save God alone—
Beauty, Strength and Discretion;
For when Death bloweth his blast,
They all run from me full fast.
FIVE WITS   Everyman, my leave now of thee I take.
I will follow the others, for here I thee forsake.
EVERYMAN   Alas, then may I wail and weep,
For I took you for my best friend.
FIVE WITS   I will no longer thee keep.
850   Now farewell, and there an end.

Exit Five Wits.

EVERYMAN   O Jesu, help! All hath forsaken me.
GOOD DEEDS   Nay, Everyman, I will bide with thee.
I will not forsake thee in deed;
Thou shalt find me a good friend in need.
EVERYMAN   Gramercy, Good Deeds! Now may I true friends see.
They have forsaken me, every one;
I loved them better than my Good Deeds alone.
Knowledge, will ye forsake me also?
KNOWLEDGE   Yea, Everyman, when ye to Death shall go;
860   But not yet, for no manner of danger.
EVERYMAN   Gramercy, Knowledge, with all my heart.
KNOWLEDGE   Nay, yet I will not from hence depart
Till I see where ye shall be come.

EVERYMAN   Methinks, alas, that I must be gone
　　To make my reckoning and my debts pay,
　　For I see my time is nigh spent away.
　　Take example, all ye that this do hear or see,
　　How they that I loved best do forsake me,
　　Except my Good Deeds that bideth truly.
870 GOOD DEEDS   All earthly things is but vanity:
　　Beauty, Strength and Discretion do man forsake,
　　Foolish friends and kinsmen that fair spake—
　　All fleeth save Good Deeds, and that am I.
EVERYMAN   Have mercy on me, God most mighty,
　　And stand by me, thou mother and maid, Holy Mary!
GOOD DEEDS   Fear not, I will speak for thee.
EVERYMAN   Here I cry God mercy.
GOOD DEEDS   Shorten our end, and diminish our pain;
　　Let us go and never come again.

Good Deeds leads Everyman into grave.

880 EVERYMAN   Into thy hands, Lord, my soul I commend;
　　Receive it, Lord, that it be not lost.
　　As thou me boughtest, so me defend
　　And save me from the fiend's boast,
　　That I may appear with that blesséd host
　　That shall be saved at the day of doom.
　　In manus tuas, of mights most
　　Forever, *commendo spiritum meum.*[30]
　　　　　　　　　Exeunt Everyman and Good Deeds.
KNOWLEDGE   Now hath he suffered that we all shall endure;
　　The Good Deeds shall make all sure.
890 　　Now hath he made ending;
　　Methinks that I hear angels sing
　　And make great joy and melody
　　Where Everyman's soul received shall be.

Enter Angel.

THE ANGEL   Come, excellent elect spouse, to Jesu!
　　Here above thou shalt go
　　Because of thy singular virtue.
　　Now thy soul is taken thy body from,
　　Thy reckoning is crystal clear.

30. *In manus tuas . . . commendo spiritum meum:* Into thy hands I commend my spirit.

Now shalt thou into the heavenly sphere,
900   Unto the which all ye shall come
That liveth well before the day of doom.

Exeunt Angel and Knowledge.

Enter Doctor.

DOCTOR   This moral men may have in mind.
Ye hearers, take it of worth, old and young,
And forsake Pride, for he deceiveth you in the end;
And remember Beauty, Five Wits, Strength, and Discretion,
They all at the last do Everyman forsake,
Save his Good Deeds there doth he take.
But beware, for if they be small,
Before God he hath no help at all:
No excuse may be there for Everyman.
910   Alas, how shall he do then?
For after death amends may no man make,
For then mercy and pity doth him forsake.
If his reckoning be not clear when he doth come,
God will say, "*Ite, maledicti, in ignem eternum.*"[31]
And he that hath his account whole and sound,
High in Heaven he shall be crowned;
Unto which place God bring us all thither,
That we may live body and soul together.
Thereto help the Trinity!
920   Amen, say ye, for saint charity.

Exit Doctor.

Thus endeth this moral play of Everyman.

31. Go, sinners, into eternal fire.

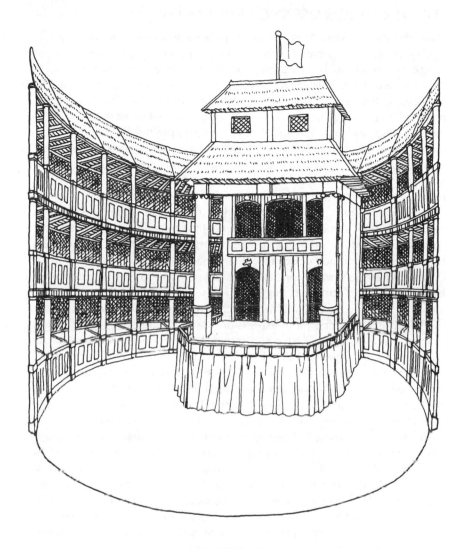

The Globe Theater

THEATER IN RENAISSANCE ENGLAND

The Globe Theater, where Shakespeare's plays were performed in his lifetime, was a public playhouse capable of accommodating between two and three thousand spectators. Despite its large seating capacity, the Globe, like other theaters in Renaissance England, created an intimate experience of drama, as we can tell by considering its physical dimensions and design. The Globe was a circular or polygonally shaped building, approximately eighty-four feet in diameter and thirty-three feet high. Its height was sufficient to accommodate three levels of galleries for spectators. The area enclosed by the galleries was approximately fifty-five feet in diameter. Into this space extended an acting platform approximately forty-three feet wide and about twenty-seven feet deep, leaving a sizable area of ground surrounding the stage for standing spectators.

We can readily see that this arrangement must have created an intimate relationship between actors and members of the audience. Since the actors were surrounded on three sides by spectators in the yard and the galleries, they were in fact much closer to one another than in our smaller modern theaters where actors and spectators are physically set off from one another by the framed and curtained stage. The Renaissance audience could see the actors up close—which meant that the actors had to pay meticulous attention to all their gestures and facial expressions. Most significantly, that physical intimacy necessarily must have aroused in the spectators a very immediate and personal engagement in the action of the play. In another respect, however, drama in the Renaissance English theater was a very public and communal affair, for the yard area was open to the sky, and plays were thus performed in full daylight. As they sat in the galleries or stood in the yard, the spectators could easily see one another, as well as the actors.

The stage itself consisted of two acting levels. The main area was the platform jutting into the yard; at the rear of the platform on each side were doors for entrances and exits. Between the doors was a curtained inner stage for use in "discoveries" and special dramatic situations. Above this inner stage was the second acting level, a gallery, which could be used for balcony scenes such as the one in Romeo and Juliet. The gallery was also used for musicians, or even for spectators when it was not required for the performance. Directly above the gallery was a roof covering the rear half of the acting platform. As we can see from these arrangements, Shakespeare's stage was a remarkably flexible one, allowing action to be set in a number of different areas, and allowing, too, for rapid entrances and exits. Flexibility in staging resulted also from the fact that scenery was not used in the Globe Theater. The stage was understood to stand for whatever setting was implied by the action and from whatever props were placed on the stage.

Even though the English theater of the Renaissance did not create a realistic or by any means complete scenic illusion of the sort we are accustomed to on the modern stage, it set forth a vividly human and symbolic spectacle—a spectacle, in fact, that would have been regarded by the audience as embodying universal significance. For when the actors appeared on stage, they were also understood to be standing between the heavens implied by that roof above them and hell implied by the space beneath the stage. Thus, when the audience witnessed the action of *King Lear*, they would have regarded it not only as representing the catastrophe of a particular man who is undone because he trusts empty flattery more than truth, but also as presenting a spectacle of universal significance about the conflict of good and evil.

WILLIAM SHAKESPEARE

1564–1616

Born and raised in Stratford-upon-Avon, where his father was a glover, tanner, and dealer in hides, Shakespeare was educated locally at the King's New School and there acquired some familiarity with the classics, particularly in Latin language and literature, but did not go on to attend one of the universities. Instead, he went off to London, probably attracted by the touring theatrical companies of the period, to make a career for himself as an actor and dramatist. He made his way to London sometime In the late 1580s, when public theater was just beginning to become a popular enterprise in the city, and no doubt started out as an actor with one of the local companies. By 1590, his earliest plays were being produced, and during his remaining twenty-three years of involvement with the theater he wrote thirty-seven plays, as well as becoming a leading actor and shareholder in one of the major theatrical companies of the period. His plays cover a broad range of dramatic modes, extending from the comedies and history plays that figured largely in his early career, through the problem plays, tragedies, and romances that predominated in his later career. His plays reflect an equally broad range of experience, extending from the English battle scenes and tavern life of *1 Henry IV*, to the Roman and Egyptian court scenes of *Antony and Cleopatra*, to the fantastic island world of *The Tempest*. Like most of his contemporaries he borrowed ideas for many of his works from classical, continental, or—as in the case of *King Lear*—native sources.

King Lear

CHARACTERS

LEAR, King of Britain
KING OF FRANCE
DUKE OF BURGUNDY
DUKE OF CORNWALL
DUKE OF ALBANY
EARL OF KENT
EARL OF GLOUCESTER
EDGAR, Son to Gloucester
EDMUND, Bastard Son to Gloucester
CURAN, a Courtier
OSWALD, Steward to Goneril
OLD MAN, Tenant to Gloucester
DOCTOR
FOOL
AN OFFICER, employed by Edmund
A GENTLEMAN, Attendant on Cordelia
A HERALD
SERVANTS, to Cornwall
GONERIL,
REGAN,   } Daughters to Lear
CORDELIA,

KNIGHTS OF LEAR'S TRAIN, OFFICERS, MESSENGERS, SOLDIERS, ATTENDANTS

SCENE: *Britain*

ACT I

SCENE 1

A Room of State in King Lear's Palace.

Enter Kent, Gloucester, and Edmund.

KENT   I thought the king had more affected[1] the Duke of Albany than Cornwall.

GLOUCESTER   It did always seem so to us; but now, in the division of the kingdom, it appears not which of the dukes he values most; for equalities

---

1. *had ... affected*: was more partial to, preferred

are so weighed[2] that curiosity[3] in neither can make choice of either's
moiety.[4]

KENT   Is not this your son, my lord?

GLOUCESTER   His breeding,[5] sir, hath been at my charge: I have so often blushed
to acknowledge him, that now I am brazed[6] to it.

KENT   I cannot conceive[7] you.

GLOUCESTER   Sir, this young fellow's mother could; whereupon she grew
round-wombed, and had, indeed, sir, a son for her cradle ere she had a
husband for her bed. Do you smell a fault?

KENT   I cannot wish the fault undone, the issue[8] of it being so proper.[9]

GLOUCESTER   But I have a son, sir, by order of law,[10] some year[11] elder than
this, who yet is no dearer in my account:[12] though this knave came
something[13] saucily into the world before he was sent for, yet was his
mother fair; there was good sport at his making, and the whoreson[14]
must be acknowledged. Do you know this noble gentleman, Edmund?

EDMUND   No, my lord.

GLOUCESTER   My Lord of Kent: remember him hereafter as my honourable
friend.

EDMUND   My services to your lordship.

KENT   I must love you, and sue[15] to know you better.

EDMUND   Sir, I shall study deserving.[16]

GLOUCESTER   He hath been out[17] nine years, and away he shall again. The
king is coming.

Sennet.[18] Enter Lear, Cornwall, Albany, Goneril, Regan, Cordelia, and Attendants.

LEAR   Attend[19] the Lords of France and Burgundy, Gloucester.

GLOUCESTER   I shall, my leige.

[*Exeunt Gloucester and Edmund.*

LEAR   Meantime we shall express[20] our darker[21] purpose.
Give me the map there. Know that we have divided
In three our kingdom; and 'tis our fast[22] intent
To shake all cares and business from our age,

2. *equalities . . . weighed*: shares are so carefully equalized. l. 3-4 i.e. neither duke
can find ground for preferring the other's share to his own
3. careful examination
4. part, share (not necessarily half)
5. upbringing
6. hardened (as in one slang sense of
"brass")
7. understand
8. *both* (1) result *and* (2) offspring
9. handsome
10. *son...law*: legitimate, born in wedlock
11. about a year
12. reckoning

13. somewhat
14. rascal (literally "son of a whore" but
often used playfully, like "knave"
above)
15. beg
16. try to be worth (the effort you make)
17. away from home, abroad
18. a set of notes on a trumpet heralding a
procession
19. wait upon (and bring in, cf. l. 188)
20. expound, show
21. hitherto unrevealed (i.e. the details of
the division)
22. firm, fixed

Conferring them on younger strengths, while we
Unburden'd crawl toward death. Our son[23] of Cornwall,
35   And you, our no less loving son of Albany,
We have this hour a constant[24] will to publish
Our daughters' several dowers,[25] that future strife
May be prevented now. The princes, France and Burgundy,
Great rivals in our youngest daughter's love,
40   Long in our court have made their amorous sojourn,[26]
And here are to be answer'd.[27] Tell me, my daughters,—
Since now we will divest us both of rule,
Interest[28] of territory, cares of state,—
Which of you shall we say doth love us most?
45   That we our largest bounty may extend
Where nature[29] doth with merit challenge.[30] Goneril,
Our eldest-born, speak first.

GONERIL   Sir, I love you more than words can wield the matter;
Dearer than eye-sight, space,[31] and liberty;
50   Beyond what can be valu'd, rich or rare;
No less than life, with[32] grace, health, beauty, honour;
As much as child e'er lov'd, or father found;[33]
A love that makes breath poor and speech unable;[34]
Beyond all manner of so much[35] I love you.

55   CORDELIA   [Aside.]   What shall Cordelia do? Love, and be silent.

LEAR   Of all these bounds, even from this line to this,
With shadowy[36] forests and with champains[37] rich'd,
With plenteous rivers and wide-skirted meads,
We make thee lady: to thine and Albany's issue
60   Be this perpetual. What says our second daughter,
Our dearest Regan, wife to Cornwall? Speak.

REGAN   I am made of that self[38] metal[39] as my sister,
And prize me at her worth.[40] In my true heart[41]
I find she names my very deed of love;[42]
65   Only she comes too short: that[43] I profess

---

23. inlaw, Duke of Cornwall
24. firm
25. respective dowries
26. stay for purposes of love (to woo Cordelia)
27. are . . . answer'd: await a decision
28. right, title to (and so possession of)
29. affection
30. claim (it)
31. the world (unless the word simply expands the notion of "liberty")
32. combined with
33. experienced (love)
34. unequal to expressing it

35. all . . . much: all degree of such comparisons
36. shady
37. meadows, open country
38. same
39. (1) material, (2) temperament (in this sense now spelt mettle)
40. prize . . . worth: I count myself equal to her (in my affection for you)
41. In . . . heart: in all sincerity
42. names . . . love: exactly describes my love
43. in that

Myself an enemy to all other joys
Which the most precious square of sense[44] possesses
And find I am alone felicitate[45]
In your dear highness' love.

CORDELIA   [*Aside*] Then, poor Cordelia!
70   And yet not so; since, I am sure, my love's
More richer than my tongue.

LEAR   To thee and thine, hereditary ever,[46]
Remain this ample third of our fair kingdom,
No less in space, validity,[47] and pleasure,
75   Than that conferr'd on Goneril. Now, our joy,
Although our last, not least; to whose young love
The vines of France and milk of Burgundy[48]
Strive to be interess'd;[49] what can you say to draw
A third more opulent than your sisters? Speak.

80   CORDELIA   Nothing, my lord.

LEAR   Nothing?

CORDELIA   Nothing.

LEAR   Nothing will come of nothing: speak again.

CORDELIA   Unhappy that I am, I cannot heave
85   My heart into my mouth: I love your majesty
According to my bond;[50] nor more nor less.

LEAR   How, how, Cordelia! mend your speech a little,
Lest you may mar your fortunes.

CORDELIA   Good my lord,
You have begot me, bred me, lov'd me: I
90   Return those duties back as are right fit,[51]
Obey you, love you, and most honour you.
Why have my sisters husbands, if they say
They love you all?[52] Haply, when I shall wed,
That lord whose hand must take my plight[53] shall carry
95   Half my love with him, half my care and duty:
Sure I shall never marry like my sisters,
To love my father all.

LEAR   But goes thy heart with this?

CORDELIA   Ay, good my lord.

LEAR   So young, and so untender?

100   CORDELIA   So young, my lord, and true.

44. *most . . . sense*: most delicate sense
45. made happy
46. and to your heirs for ever
47. value
48. i.e. the King of F., rich in vineyards, and the Duke of B., rich in pastures
49. concerned, bound up with (interess is an old form of interest, Lat. *interesse*)
50. obligation (cf. "bounden duty and service" of *Prayer Book*)
51. duties right and fit to be returned
52. entirely
53. plighted troth, vows

LEAR   Let it be so; thy truth then be thy dower:[54]
   For, by the sacred radiance of the sun,
   The mysteries of Hecate[55] and the night,
   By all the operation[56] of the orbs[57]
105 From whom we do exist and cease to be,
   Here I disclaim all my paternal care,
   Propinquity[58] and property of blood,[59]
   And as a stranger to my heart and me
   Hold thee from this for ever. The barbarous Scythian,
110 Or he that makes his generation[60] messes[61]
   To gorge his appetite, shall to my bosom
   Be as well neighbour'd,[62] pitied, and reliev'd,
   As thou my sometime daughter.
KENT   Good my liege,—
LEAR   Peace, Kent!
115 Come not between the dragon and his wrath.[63]
   I lov'd her most, and thought to set my rest[64]
   On her kind nursery.[65] Hence, and avoid my sight!
   So be my grave my peace, as here I give
   Her father's heart from[66] her! Call France. Who stirs?[67]
120 Call Burgundy. Cornwall and Albany,
   With my two daughters' dowers digest the third;
   Let pride, which she calls plainness, marry her.[68]
   I do invest you jointly with my power,
   Pre-eminence, and all the large effects[69]
125 That troop with[70] majesty. Ourself by monthly course,[71]
   With reservation of[72] a hundred knights,
   By you to be sustain'd, shall our abode
   Make with you by due turn. Only we shall retain
   The name and all th' addition[73] to a king;
130 The sway, revenue, execution of the rest,
   Beloved sons, be yours: which to confirm,
   This coronet part between you.

54. dowry
55. Hécate (here two syllables)
56. work, influence
57. heavenly bodies
58. *lit.* nearness, so kinship
59. ownership of your blood
60. children
61. dishes
62. *as . . . neighbour'd*: held as near
63. *Come . . . wrath:* i.e. don't try, to stop my (natural) wrath (cf. 165 below)
64. *set . . . rest*: stake my all (a gaming metaphor, but also involving the ordinary sense of ''rest'')
65. nursing
66. away from
67. *Who stirs?* make haste
68. *Let . . . her*: let her pride find her a husband, i.e. let her find one for herself without a dowry
69. manifestations of splendour
70. *troop with*: accompany
71. *by . . . course*: for a month in turn
72. *With . . . of*: i.e. reserving to ourselves (properly a legal word for an *exception*)
73. title

KENT   Royal Lear,
    Whom I have ever honour'd as my king,
    Lov'd as my father, as my master follow'd,
135   As my great patron thought on in my prayers,—
LEAR   The bow is bent and drawn; make from[74] the shaft.
KENT   Let it fall rather, though the fork[75] invade
    The region of my heart: be Kent unmannerly
    When Lear is mad. What wouldst thou do, old man?
140   Think'st thou that duty shall have dread to speak
    When power to flattery bows? To plainness[76] honour's bound
    When majesty falls to folly. Reserve thy state;[77]
    And, in thy best consideration,[78] check
    This hideous rashness: answer my life my judgment,[79]
145   Thy youngest daughter does not love thee least;
    Nor are those empty-hearted whose low sound
    Reverbs[80] no hollowness.
LEAR   Kent, on my life,[81] no more.
KENT   My life I never held[82] but as a pawn
    To wage[83] against thine enemies; nor fear to lose it,
    Thy safety being the motive.
150   LEAR   Out of my sight!
KENT   See better, Lear; and let me still remain
    The true blank of thine eye.[84]
LEAR   Now, by Appollo,—
KENT   Now, by Apollo, king,
    Thou swear'st thy gods in vain.
LEAR   O vassal! miscreant![85]
                          [*Laying his hand on his sword.*
155   ALBANY   } Dear sir, forbear.
     CORNWALL }
KENT   Do;[86]
    Kill thy physician, and the fee bestow
    Upon the foul disease.[87] Revoke thy gift;[88]
    Or, whilst I can vent clamour from my throat,
    I'll tell thee thou dost evil.
160   LEAR   Hear me, recreant!

---

74. *make from*: avoid
75. head, barb
76. plain-speaking
77. regal power
78. *best consideration*: considering the matter more carefully
79. *answer . . . judgment*: let my life answer for (the correctness of) my judg(e)ment
80. echoes back
81. *on . . . life*: as you value your life
82. accounted

83. *pawn to wage*: stake to wager, risk
84. *let . . . eye*: keep me always in view, always with you (*blank* = *white* centre of a target)
85. *vassal! miscreant!* and *recreant!* (159): all used loosely as terms of abuse, "villain"
86. execute your will
87. *the fee . . . disease*: i.e. make things worse for yourself
88. i.e. of Cordelia's share

On thine allegiance, hear me!
Since thou hast sought to make us break our vow,—
Which we durst never yet,—and, with strain'd[89] pride
To come betwixt our sentence and our power,—[90]
165   Which nor our nature nor our place can bear,—
Our potency made good,[91] take thy reward,
Five days we do allot thee for provison
To shield thee from diseases[92] of the world;
And, on the sixth, to turn[93] thy hated back
170   Upon our kingdom: if, on the tenth day following
Thy banish'd trunk[94] be found in our dominions,
The moment is thy death. Away! By Jupiter,
This shall not be revok'd.

KENT   Fare thee well, king; sith[95] thus thou wilt appear,[96]
175   Freedom lives hence, and banishment is here.
[To Cordelia.]   The gods to their dear shelter take thee, maid,
That justly think'st and hast most rightly said!
[To Regan and Goneril.]   And your large[97] speeches may your deeds
approve,[98]
That good effects may spring from words of love.
180   Thus Kent, O princes! bids you all adieu;
He'll shape his old course[99] in a country new.

[Exit.

Flourish.[100] Re-enter Gloucester, with France, Burgundy, and Attendants.

GLOUCESTER   Here's France and Burgundy, my noble lord.
LEAR   My Lord of Burgundy,
We first address toward[101] you, who with this king
185   Hath rivall'd for[102] our daughter. What, in the least,
Will you require in present dower with her,
Or cease your quest of love?
BURGUNDY   Most royal majesty,
I crave no more than hath your highness offer'd,
Nor will you tender[103] less.
LEAR   Right noble Burgundy,
190   When she was dear to us we did hold her so.[104]

89. exaggerated
90. *our power*: the execution of it
91. *potency . . . good*: power shown to be (still) valid
92. discomforts (consequent on lack of preparation for exile)
93. we sentence thee to turn
94. body
95. since
96. show thyself
97. grand
98. make good
99. *shape . . . course*: make his way, old as he is, *or* continues his old habits (of plain-speaking etc.)
100. a blast of trumpets or horns
101. *address* (ourselves) *toward*: speak to
102. entered into rivalry for
103. offer
104. dear (in value), worth a good dowry

But now her price is fall'n. Sir, there she stands:
If aught within that little-seeming substance,[105]
Or all of it, with our displeasure piec'd,[106]
And nothing more, may fitly like[107] your Grace,
She's there, and she is yours.

195 BURGUNDY   I know no answer.

LEAR   Will you, with those infirmities she owes,[108]
Unfriended, new-adopted to our hate,
Dower'd with our curse, and stranger'd with[109] our oath,
Take her, or leave her?

BURGUNDY   Pardon me, royal sir;
200 Election makes not up[110] on such conditions.

LEAR   Then leave her, sir; for, by the power that made me,
I tell you all her wealth.—[*To France.*]   For you,[111] great king,
I would not from your love make such a stray[112]
To[113] match you where I hate; therefore, beseech you
205 To avert[114] your liking a more worthier way[115]
Than on a wretch whom nature is asham'd
Almost to acknowledge hers.

FRANCE   This is most strange,
That she, who even but now was your best[116] object,
The argument[117] of your praise, balm of your age,[118]
210 The best, the dearest, should in this trice[119] of time
Commit a thing so monstrous, to dismantle[120]
So many folds of favour. Sure, her offence
Must be of such unnatural degree
That monsters[121] it, or your fore-vouch'd affection
215 Fall into taint;[122] which to believe of her,
Must be a faith that reason without miracle
Could never plant in me.

CORDELIA   I yet beseech your majesty—
If for[123] I want that glib and oily art
To speak and purpose not;[124] since what I well intend,
220 I'll do't before I speak—that you make known

105. *little-seeming substance*: person of few
     pretensions (sarcastic)
106. pieced out (with), added (to it)
107. please
108. owns
109. made a stranger (to us) by (cf. 108)
110. *Election . . . up*: choice does not decide,
     will not choose
111. as for you
112. *make . . . stray*: depart from, i.e. offend
     against
113. as to
114. turn aside
115. *a . . . way*: in a worthier direction
116. favourite
117. subject
118. *balm . . . age*: see 116–17
119. moment (Spanish)
120. shed off
121. makes it monstrous
122. *your . . . taint*: your previously affirmed
     affection must be discredited
123. If (you are disowning me) because
124. *purpose not*: not intend to carry out

It is no vicious blot nor other foulness,[125]
No unchaste action, or dishonour'd[126] step,
That hath depriv'd me of your grace and favour,
But even for want of[127] that for which I am richer,
225   A still-soliciting[128] eye, and such a tongue
That I am glad I have not, though not to have it
Hath lost me in your liking.

LEAR   Better thou
Hadst not been born than not to have pleas'd me better.

FRANCE   Is it but this? a tardiness in nature[129]
230   Which often leaves the history[130] unspoke
That it intends to do? My Lord of Burgundy,
What say you to the lady?[131] Love is not love
When it is mingled with regards[132] that stand
Aloof from the entire[133] point. Will you have her?
She is herself a dowry.

235   BURGUNDY   Royal Lear,
Give but that portion which yourself propos'd,
And here I take Cordelia by the hand,
Duchess of Burgundy.

LEAR   Nothing: I have sworn; I am firm.

240   BURGUNDY   I am sorry, then, you have so lost a father
That you must lose a husband.

CORDELIA   Peace be with[134] Burgundy!
Since that respects of fortune are his love,
I shall not be his wife.

FRANCE   Fairest Cordelia, that art most rich, being poor;
245   Most choice, forsaken; and most lov'd, despis'd!
Thee and thy virtues here I seize upon:
Be it lawful I take up what's cast away.
Gods, gods! 'tis strange that from their cold'st neglect
My love should kindle to inflam'd respect.[135]
250   Thy dowerless daughter, king, thrown to my chance,[136]
Is queen of us, of ours, and our fair France:
Not all the dukes of waterish[137] Burgundy
Shall buy this unpriz'd[138] precious maid of me.

---

125. i.e. no wickedness, such as murder or fornication
126. dishonourable
127. *even . . . of*: it is just because I lack
128. always begging (for something)
129. *tardiness in nature*: natural slowness (to speak)
130. verbal record
131. *What . . . lady?* How do you like the lady?

132. considerations (so *respects* 242)
133. whole
134. *Peace be with*: good-bye to
135. *inflam'd respect*: ardent esteem
136. lot
137. perhaps literally "well-watered," but certainly implying that the man is as thin-blooded as his country is inferior in wines to France (cf. 77)
138. *either* not (properly) valued *or* priceless

Bid them farewell, Cordelia, though unkind:[139]
255   Thou losest here, a better where[140] to find.
LEAR   Thou hast her, France; let her be thine, for we
Have no such daughter, nor shall ever see
That face of hers again, therefore be gone
Without our grace, our love, our benison.[141]
260   Come, noble Burgundy.
[*Flourish. Exeunt Lear, Burgundy, Cornwall, Albany, Gloucester, and Attendants.*
FRANCE   Bid farewell to your sisters.
CORDELIA   The jewels[142] of our father, with wash'd eyes
Cordelia leaves you: I know you what you are;
And like a sister am most loath to call
265   Your faults as they are nam'd.[143] Use well our father:
To your professed bosoms[144] I commit him:
But yet, alas! stood I within his grace,
I would prefer[145] him to a better place.
So farewell to you both.
REGAN   Prescribe not us our duties.
270   GONERIL   Let your study
Be to content your lord, who hath receiv'd you
At fortune's alms;[146] you have obedience scanted,
And well are worth the want[147] that you have wanted.
CORDELIA   Time shall unfold what plighted[148] cunning hides;
275   Who[149] covers faults, at last shame them derides.
Well may you prosper!
FRANCE   Come, my fair Cordelia.
[*Exit France and Cordelia.*
GONERIL   Sister, it is not little I have to say of what most nearly appertains to
us both. I think our father will hence[150] to night.
REGAN   That's most certain, and with you; next month with us.
280   GONERIL   You see how full of changes his age is;[151] the observation we have
made of it hath not been little: he always loved our sister most; and with
what poor judgment he hath now cast her off appears too grossly.[152]
REGAN   'Tis the infirmity of his age; yet he hath ever but slenderly known
himself.
285   GONERIL   The best and soundest of his time hath been but rash;[153] then, must
we look to receive from his age, not alone the imperfections of long-

---

139. see III. iv. 58
140. place (to parallel "here")
141. blessing
142. *The jewels*: vocative case
143. *as . . . nam'd*: by their true names
144. love
145. advance, recommend
146. *At . . . alms*: as a humble gift of fortune; cf. 250

147. *are . . . wanted*: deserve the destitution that has befallen you
148. folded
149. those who (antecedent to *them*)
150. *will go hence*
151. *full . . . is*: changeable he is now he is old
152. obviously
153. hot-headed

engraffed condition,[154] but, therewithal the unruly waywardness that infirm and choleric years[155] bring with them.

REGAN   Such unconstant starts[156] are we like[157] to have from him as this of
290   Kent's banishment.

GONERIL   There is further compliment[158] of leave-taking between France and him. Pray you, let us hit together:[159] if our father carry[160] authority with such dispositions[161] as he bears, this last surrender[162] of his will but offend[163] us.

295 REGAN   We shall further think on't.

GONERIL   We must do something, and i' the heat.[164]

[*Exeunt.*

SCENE 2

A Hall in the Earl of Gloucester's Castle.

Enter Edmund, with a letter.

EDMUND   Thou, Nature, art my goddess; to thy law
         My services are bound. Wherefore should I
         Stand in the plague of custom,[1] and permit
         The curiosity[2] of nations to deprive me,[3]
5   For that I am some twelve or fourteen moonshines
         Lag of[4] a brother? Why bastard? wherefore base?
         When my dimensions[5] are as well compact,[6]
         My mind as generous,[7] and my shape as true,
         As honest madam's[8] issue? Why brand they us
10   With base? with baseness? bastardy? base, base?
         Who in the lusty stealth[9] of nature[10] take
         More composition and fierce quality
         Than doth, within a dull, stale, tired bed,
         Go to the creating a whole tribe of fops,[11]

154. *long-engraffed condition*: a temperament that has become firmly fixed (ingrafted) by habit
155. *infirm . . . years*: years of physical weakness and proneness to anger
156. *unconstant starts*: fits of waywardness
157. likely
158. formal civility
159. *hit together*: strike a bargain, i.e. make joint plans
160. i.e. still wields
161. moods
162. harm (stronger than nowadays)
163. i.e. of the crown
164. *i' . . . heat*: at once (cf. "strike while the iron is hot")

1. *stand . . . custom*: suffer from the inferior position custom assigns to bastards
2. scrupulousness, squeamishness
3. keep me out of my rights
4. *lag of*: behind (in coming into the world)
5. *my dimensions*: the proportions of my body
6. made
7. high-spirited
8. *honest madam's*: the true wife
9. secret act
10. (sexual) desire
11. fools

15   Got[12] 'tween asleep and wake? Well then,
Legitimate Edgar, I must have your land:
Our fathers' love is to the bastard Edmund
As[13] to the legitimate. Fine word, 'legitimate!'
Well, my legitimate, if this letter speed,
20   And my invention thrive, Edmund the base
Shall top[14] the legitimate: —I grow, I prosper;
Now, gods, stand up for bastards!

Enter Gloucester.

GLOUCESTER   Kent banished thus! And France in choler[15] parted![16]
And the king gone to-night![17] subscrib'd[18] his power!
25   Confin'd to exhibition![19] All this done
Upon the gad![20] Edmund, how now! what news?

EDMUND   So please your lordship, none.

[*Putting up the letter.*

GLOUCESTER   Why so earnestly seek you to put up[21] that letter?

EDMUND   I know no news, my lord.

30   GLOUCESTER   What paper were you reading?

EDMUND   Nothing, my lord.

GLOUCESTER   No? What needed then that terrible[22] dispatch[23] of it into your
pocket? the quality of nothing hath not such need to hide itself. Let's see;
come; if it be nothing, I shall not need spectacles.

35   EDMUND   I beseech you, sir, pardon me;[24] it is a letter from my brother that I
have not all o'er-read, and for[25] so much as I have perused, I find it not fit
for your o'er-looking.[26]

GLOUCESTER   Give me the letter, sir.

EDMUND   I shall offend, either to detain or give it. The contents, as in part I
40   understand them, are to blame.

GLOUCESTER   Let's see, let's see.

EDMUND   I hope, for my brother's justification, he wrote this but as an essay[27]
or taste of my virtue.

GLOUCESTER   *This policy and reverence of age[28] makes the world bitter to the best of*
45   *our times;[29] keeps our fortunes from us till our oldness cannot relish them. I begin*
to find an idle and fond[30] bondage in the oppression of aged tyranny,[31] who

12. begotten	23. haste in putting away
13. as much as	24. excuse me from showing it you
14. get the better of	25. as for
15. anger	26. examination
16. departed	27. trial
17. last night	28. *policy . . . age*: policy of reverence for
18. surrendered	old age
19. an allowance (cf. university use)	29. *the best . . . times*: our best days, i.e.
20. *upon the gad*: suddenly (as if pricked	men in their prime
by a gad, = goad)	30. foolish
21. put away	31. *aged tyranny*: my aged father (abstract
22. frightened (*not* our slang use)	for concrete, as often)

sways,[32] *not as it hath power, but as it is suffered. Come to me, that of this I may speak more. If our father would sleep till I waked him, you should enjoy half his revenue for ever, and live the beloved of your brother,* EDGAR. —Hum! Conspiracy! 'Sleep till I waked him, you should enjoy half his revenue.'—My son Edgar! Had he a hand to write this? a heart and brain to breed it in? When came this to you? Who brought it?

EDMUND   It was not brought me, my lord; there's the cunning of it; I found it thrown in at the casement[33] of my closet.

GLOUCESTER   You know the character[34] to be your brother's?

EDMUND   If the matter were good, my lord, I durst swear it were his; but, in respect of that,[35] I would fain think it were not.

GLOUCESTER   It is his.

EDMUND   It is his hand, my lord; but I hope his heart is not in the contents.

GLOUCESTER   Hath he never heretofore sounded you in this business?

EDMUND   Never, my lord: but I have often heard him maintain it to be fit that, sons at perfect age,[36] and fathers declined,[37] the father should be as ward to the son, and the son manage his revenue.

GLOUCESTER   O villain, villain! His very opinion in the letter! Abhorred villain! Unnatural, detested, brutish villain! worse than brutish! Go, sirrah, seek him; I'll apprehend him. Abominable villain! Where is he?

EDMUND   I do not well know, my lord. If it shall please you to suspend your indignation against my brother till you can derive from him better testimony of his intent, you shall run a certain course;[38] where,[39] if you violently proceed against him, mistaking his purpose, it would make a great gap[40] in your own honour, and shake in pieces the heart of his obedience. I dare pawn[41] down my life for him, that he hath writ this to feel[42] my affection to your honour, and to no other pretence of danger.[43]

GLOUCESTER   Think you so?

EDMUND   If your honour judge it meet, I will place you where you shall hear us confer of this, and by an auricular[44] assurance have your satisfaction; and that without any further delay than this very evening.

GLOUCESTER   He cannot be such a monster—

EDMUND   Nor is not, sure.

GLOUCESTER   —to his father, that so tenderly and entirely loves him. Heaven and earth! Edmund, seek him out; wind me into him,[45] I pray you: frame

32. rules
33. (open) window
34. hand-writing
35. *its* goodness or lack of it, i.e. (in this case) its badness
36. *perfect age*: the prime of life
37. in years
38. *run . . . course*: act safely
39. whereas
40. breach
41. see I. i. 148
42. try
43. *to no . . . danger*: not with a view to any (other) dangerous design
44. through the ear
45. *wind . . . him*: insinuate yourself, get into familiar talk with him, please (*me* is not the object of "wind" but the so-called ethic dative)

the business after your own wisdom. I would unstate myself[46] to be in a
due resolution.[47]

EDMUND   I will seek him, sir, presently;[48] convey[49] the business as I shall find
means, and acquaint you withal.[50]

GLOUCESTER   These late eclipses in the sun and moon portend no good to us:
though the wisdom of nature can reason it thus and thus,[51] yet nature
finds itself scourged by the sequent effects.[52] Love cools, friendship falls
off, brothers divide: in cities, mutinies;[53] in countries, discord; in palaces,
treason; and the bond cracked between son and father. This villain of mine
comes under the prediction; there's son against father: the king falls from
bias of nature;[54] there's father against child. We have seen the best of our
time: machinations,[55] hollowness,[56] treachery, and all ruinous disorders,
follow us disquietly to our graves. Find out this villain, Edmund; it shall
lose thee nothing: do it carefully. And the noble and true-hearted Kent
banished! his offence, honesty! 'Tis strange!   [*Exit.*

EDMUND   This is the excellent foppery[57] of the world, that, when we are sick
in fortune,—often the surfeit[58] of our own behaviour,—we make guilty of
our disasters the sun, the moon, and the stars; as if we were villains by
necessity, fools by heavenly compulsion, knaves, thieves, and treachers[59]
by spherical predominance,[60] drunkards, liars, and adulterers by an enforced obedience of planetary influence; and all that we are evil in, by a
divine thrusting on: an admirable evasion[61] of whoremaster[62] man, to lay
his goatish[63] disposition to the charge of a star! My father compounded
with my mother under the dragon's tail,[64] and my nativity was under *ursa
major*;[65] so that it follows I am rough and lecherous. 'Sfoot! I should have
been that I am had the maidenliest star in the firmament twinkled on my
bastardizing.[66] Edgar—

Enter Edgar.

and pat[67] he comes, like the catastrophe of the old[68] comedy: my cue[69]
is villanous melancholy, with a sigh like Tom o' Bedlam.[70] O, these eclipses

46. *unstate myself*: give up my position
47. *to be . . . resolution*: to have my doubts resolved
48. immediately
49. carry out
50. *acquaint you withal*: inform you of it
51. *the wisdom . . . and thus*: natural philosophy can give good explanations
52. *sequent effects*: effects that follow (eclipses)
53. disturbances
54. *from . . . nature*: away from natural inclination (i.e. of affection towards Cordelia)
55. plots
56. insincerity
57. folly

58. evil result
59. traitors
60. *spherical predominance*: dominance of some special star
61. of responsibility
62. lecherous
63. lascivious
64. *dragon's tail*: in astronomy, "The descending node of the moon's orbit with the ecliptic" (*Shorter O.E.D.*)
65. *Ursa Major*: the Great Bear
66. unlawful begetting
67. just at the right moment
68. any old
69. part
70. *Tom o' Bedlam*: beggar feigning madness

110   do portend these divisions! *Fa, sol, la, mi.*[71]

EDGAR   How now, brother Edmund! What serious contemplation are you in?

EDMUND   I am thinking, brother, of a prediction I read this other day, what[72] should follow these eclipses.

115   EDGAR   Do you busy yourself with that?

EDMUND   I promise you the effects he writes of succeed[73] unhappily; as of unnaturalness between the child and the parent; death, dearth, dissolutions of ancient amities; divisions in state; menaces and maledictions against king and nobles; needless diffidences,[74] banishment of friends,

120   dissipation of cohorts,[75] nuptial breaches, and I know not what.

EDGAR   How long have you been a sectary astronomical?[76]

EDMUND   Come, come; when saw you my father last?

EDGAR   The night gone by.

EDMUND   Spake you with him?

125   EDGAR   Ay, two hours together.

EDMUND   Parted you in good terms? Found you no displeasure in him by word or countenance?

EDGAR   None at all.

EDMUND   Bethink yourself wherein you may have offended him; and at my

130   entreaty forbear[77] his presence till some little time hath qualified[78] the heat of his displeasure, which at this instant so rageth in him that with the mischief of your person it would scarcely allay.[79]

EDGAR   Some villain hath done me wrong.

EDMUND   That's my fear. I pray you have a continent forbearance[80] till the

135   speed of his rage goes slower, and, as I say, retire with me to my lodging, from whence I will fitly[81] bring you to hear my lord speak. Pray you, go; there's my key. If you do stir abroad, go armed.

EDGAR   Armed, brother!

EDMUND   Brother, I advise you to the best; go armed; I am no honest man if

140   there be any good meaning[82] toward you what I have seen and heard; but faintly, nothing like the image and horror[83] of it; pray you, away.

EDGAR   Shall I hear from you anon?

EDMUND   I do serve you in this business.   [*Exit Edgar.*

A credulous father, and a brother noble,

145   Whose nature is so far from doing harms

That he suspects none; on whose foolish honesty

My practices[84] ride easy! I see the business.

---

71. *Fa . . . mi*: Edmund sings or hums a series of musical notes
72. (as to) *what*
73. turn out
74. distrust (of others)
75. *dissipation of cohorts*: just possibly ''troops deserting''
76. *sectary astronomical*: follower of, believer in astrology

77. avoid
78. reduced
79. subside
80. *a . . . forbearance*: the restraint to keep away
81. at a suitable time
82. intentions
83. *image . . . horror*: horrible reality
84. plots

Let me, if not by birth, have lands by wit:
All with me's meet that I can fashion fit.[85]   [*Exit.*

SCENE 3

A Room in the Duke of Albany's Palace.

Enter Goneril and Oswald her Steward.

GONERIL   Did my father strike my gentleman for chiding of his fool?
OSWALD   Ay, madam.
GONERIL   By day and night[1] he wrongs me; every hour
    He flashes into[2] one gross crime[3] or other,
5   That sets us all at odds:[4] I'll not endure it:
    His knights grow riotous, and himself upbraids us
    On every trifle. When he returns from hunting
    I will not speak with him; say I am sick:
    If you come slack of former services,
10   You shall do well; the fault of it I'll answer.[5]
OSWALD   He's coming, madam; I hear him.   [*Horns within.*
GONERIL   Put on what weary negligence you please,
    You and your fellows; I'd have it come to question:[6]
    If he distaste[7] it, let him to my sister,
15   Whose mind and mine, I know, in that are one,
    Not to be over-rul'd. Idle[8] old man,
    That still would manage those authorities[9]
    That he hath given away! Now, by my life,
    Old fools are babes again, and must be us'd
20   With checks as flatteries, when they are seen abus'd.[10]
    Remember what I have said.
OSWALD   Well, Madam.
GONERIL   And let his knights have colder looks among you;
    What grows of it,[11] no matter; advise your fellows so:
    I would breed from hence occasions,[12] and I shall,
25   That I may speak: I'll write straight to my sister
    To hold my very course.[13] Prepare for dinner.   [*Exeunt.*

85. to my purpose
1. *By . . . night*: probably "continually",
    rather than an oath
2. *flashes into*: breaks out into
3. offence
4. *sets . . . odds*: upsets
5. (for), be responsible for
6. *I'd . . . question*: I want it discussed
7. dislike (as Q reads)
8. foolish
9. *manage . . . authorities*: exercise the
    powers
10. *us'd . . . abus'd*: rebuked as well as
    flattered when they are seen to be mis-
    led (by their followers) *or* deluded
11. *grows of it*: results from it
12. opportunities
13. *my . . . course*: exactly my course

SCENE 4

A Hall in the Same.

Enter Kent, disguised.

KENT   If but as well I other accents borrow,
    That can my speech diffuse,[1] my good intent
    May carry through itself to that full issue[2]
    For which I raz'd[3] my likeness. Now, banish'd Kent,
5   If thou canst serve where thou dost stand condemn'd,
    So may it come, thy master, whom thou lov'st,
    Shall find thee full of labours.

Horns within. Enter Lear, Knights, and Attendants.

LEAR   Let me not stay a jot[4] for dinner: go, get it ready. [*Exit an Attendant.*]
    How now! what are thou?
10   KENT   A man, sir.
LEAR   What dost thou profess?[5] What wouldst thou with us?
KENT   I do profess to be no less than I seem; to serve him truly that will put me
    in trust; to love him that is honest; to converse[6] with him that is wise, and
    says little; to fear judgment;[7] to fight when I cannot choose; and to eat no
15   fish.[8]
LEAR   What art thou?
KENT   A very honest-hearted fellow, and as poor as the king.
LEAR   If thou be as poor for a subject as he is for a king, thou art poor enough.
    What wouldst thou?
20   KENT   Service.
LEAR   Whom wouldst thou serve?
KENT   You.
LEAR   Dost thou know me, fellow?
KENT   No, sir; but you have that in your countenance[9] which I would fain call
25   master.
LEAR   What's that?
KENT   Authority.
LEAR   What services canst thou do?
KENT   I can keep honest counsel,[10] ride, run, mar a curious[11] tale in telling it,

1. confuse, disguise
2. *my . . . issue*: I may be able to bring off the purpose
3. erased
4. *stay a jot*: wait a moment
5. *What . . . profess?*: what is your business, job? (But Kent takes the word in the sense of "claim".)
6. have to do with (Lat. *conversari*)
7. here *or* hereafter
8. *eat no fish*: be a loyal subject (not fast like a Papist)
9. bearing
10. *honest counsel*: an honourable secret
11. elaborate, difficult (Kent is only a plain man.)

30 and deliver a plain message bluntly; that which ordinary men are fit for, I
    am qualified in, and the best of me is diligence.

LEAR   How old art thou?

KENT   Not so young, sir, to love[12] a woman for singing, nor so old to dote on
    her for any thing; I have years on my back forty-eight.

35 LEAR   Follow me; thou shalt serve me: If I like thee no worse after dinner I will
    not part from thee yet. Dinner, ho! dinner! Where's my knave?[13] my fool?
    Go you and call my fool hither.   [*Exit an Attendant.*

Enter Oswald.

    You, you, sirrah, where's my daughter?

OSWALD   So please you,[14]—   [*Exit.*

40 LEAR   What says the fellow there? Call the clotpoll[15] back. [*Exit a Knight.*]
    Where's my fool, ho? I think the world's asleep. How now! where's that
    mongrel?[16]

Re-enter Knight.

KNIGHT   He says, my lord, your daughter is not well.

LEAR   Why came not the slave back to me when I called him?

45 KNIGHT   Sir, he answered me in the roundest[17] manner, he would not.

LEAR   He would not!

KNIGHT   My lord, I know not what the matter is; but, to my judgment, your
    highness is not entertained with that ceremonious affection as you were
    wont; there's a great abatement of kindness appears as well in the general
50 dependants as in the duke himself also and your daughter.

LEAR   Ha! sayest thou so?

KNIGHT   I beseech you, pardon me, my lord, if I be mistaken; for my duty
    cannot be[18] silent when I think your highness wronged.

LEAR   Thou but rememberest me of mine own conception: I have perceived
55 a most faint[19] neglect of late; which I have rather blamed as mine own
    jealous curiosity[20] than as a very pretence[21] and purpose of unkindness:
    I will look further into't. But where's my fool? I have not seen him this
    two days.

KNIGHT   Since my young lady's going into France, sir, the fool hath much
60 pined him away.

LEAR   No more of that; I have noted it well. Go you and tell my daughter I
    would speak with her.   [*Exit an Attendant.*
    Go you, call hither my fool.   [*Exit an Attendant.*

---

12. (as) *to love*
13. boy (as in a pack of cards)
14. *So . . . you*: excuse me (as he goes out)
15. clodpate, blockhead
16. i.e. Oswald
17. plainest

18. *my . . . be*: my sense of duty forbids me
    to be
19. slight *or* (possibly) cold
20. watchfulness, suspicion
21. *very pretence*: real intention

Re-enter Oswald.

O! you sir, you, come you hither, sir. Who am I, sir?

65 OSWALD My lady's father.

LEAR 'My lady's father!' my lord's knave: you whoreson dog! you slave! you
cur!

OSWALD I am none of these, my lord; I beseech your pardon.

LEAR Do you bandy[22] looks with me, you rascal?   [*Striking him.*

70 OSWALD I'll not be struck, my lord.

KENT Nor tripped neither, you base football player   [*Tripping up his heels.*

LEAR I thank thee, fellow; thou servest me, and I'll love thee.

KENT Come, sir, arise, away! I'll teach you differences:[23] away, away! If you
will measure your lubber's length again, tarry; but away! Go to;[24] have

75   you wisdom?[25] so.[26]   [*Pushes Oswald out.*

LEAR Now, my friendly knave, I thank thee: there's earnest[27] of thy service.
[*Gives Kent money.*

Enter Fool.

FOOL Let me hire him too: here's my coxcomb.[28]   [*Offers Kent his cap.*

LEAR How now, my pretty knave! how dost thou?

FOOL Sirrah, you were best[29] take my coxcomb.

80 KENT Why, fool?

FOOL Why? for taking one's part that's out of favour. Nay, an[30] thou canst
not smile as the wind sits,[31] thou'lt catch cold shortly: there, take my coxcomb. Why, this fellow has banished two on's[32] daughters, and did the
third a blessing against his will: if thou follow him thou must needs wear

85   my coxcomb. How now, nuncle![33] Would I had two coxcombs and two
daughters!

LEAR Why, my boy?

FOOL If I gave them all my living, I'd keep my coxcombs myself. There's
mine; beg another of thy daughters.

90 LEAR Take heed, sirrah; the whip.

FOOL Truth's a dog must to kennel; he must be whipped out when Lady the
brach[34] may stand by the fire and stink.

LEAR A pestilent gall[35] to me!

22. exchange (orginally in tennis)
23. i.e. of rank (between you and a king)
24. *Go to*: Pshaw! (expression of impa-
    tience)
25. *have . . . wisdom?* are you in your
    senses?
26. good (as Oswald goes out)
27. a pledge (of further reward)
28. fool's cap
29. *you . . . best*: you had better (*literally* it
    were, i.e. would be, best for you)

30. if
31. *smile . . sits*: see which way things are
    going, trim your sail to the breeze
32. of his
33. contracted for "mine uncle," a regular
    address of fools to their master
34. bitch
35. irritant *or* bitterness

FOOL [*To Kent.*]   Sirrah, I'll teach thee a speech.

95 LEAR Do.

FOOL Mark it, nuncle:—

        Have more than thou showest,
        Speak less than thou knowest,
        Lend less than thou owest,[36]

100   Ride more than thou goest,[37]
        Learn more than thou trowest,[38]
        Set less than thou throwest;[39]
        Leave thy drink and thy whore,
        And keep in-a-door,[40]

105   And thou shalt have more
        Than two tens to a score.[41]

KENT This is nothing, fool.

FOOL Then 'tis like the breath of an unfee'd lawyer, you gave me nothing for't. Can you make no use of nothing, nuncle?

110 LEAR Why, no, boy; nothing can be made out of nothing.

FOOL [*To Kent.*]   Prithee, tell him, so much the rent of his land comes to: he will not believe a fool.

LEAR A bitter fool!

FOOL Dost thou know the difference, my boy, between a bitter fool and a

115   sweet fool?

LEAR No, lad; teach me.

FOOL   That lord that counsell'd thee
          To give away thy land,
        Come place him here by me,

120   Do thou for him stand:
        The sweet and bitter fool
          Will presently appear;
        The one in motley[42] here,
          The other found out there.

125 LEAR Dost thou call me fool, boy?

FOOL All thy other titles thou hast given away; that thou wast born with.

KENT This is not altogether fool, my lord.

FOOL No, faith, lords and great men will not let me;[43] if I had a monopoly out,[44] they would have part on't, and ladies too: they will not let me have all fool

130   to myself; they'll be snatching. Nuncle, give me an egg, and I'll give thee two crowns.

LEAR What two crowns shall they be?

---

36. owenest
37. walkest
38. i.e. (probably) don't believe all you hear
39. i.e. stake less than you win (at a throw)
40. indoors

41. *And . . . score*: i.e. you'll do well
42. fool's dress (as I am)
43. *let me*: (be the complete fool)
44. taken out, granted (as often by Stuart kings)

FOOL   Why, after I have cut the egg i' the middle and eat up the meat, the two crowns[45] of the egg. When you clovest thy crown i' the middle, and gavest away both parts, thou borest thine ass on thy back o'er the dirt:[46] thou hadst little wit in thy bald crown when thou gavest thy golden one away. If I speak like myself[47] in this, let him be whipped that first finds it so.

> Fools had ne'er less grace[48] in a year;
> For wise men are grown foppish,[49]
> And know not how their wits to wear,[50]
> Their manners are so apish.

LEAR   When were you wont to be so full of songs, sirrah?

FOOL   I have used it,[51] nuncle, ever since thou madest thy daughters thy mothers; for when thou gavest them the rod and puttest down thine own breeches,

> Then they for sudden joy did weep,
> And I for sorrow sung,
> That such a king should play bo-peep,[52]
> And go the fools among.

Prithee, nuncle, keep a schoolmaster than can teach thy fool to lie: I would fain learn to lie.

LEAR   An you lie, sirrah, we'll have you whipped.

FOOL   I marvel what kin thou and thy daughters are: they'll have me whipped for speaking true, thou'lt have me whipped for lying; and sometimes I am whipped for holding my peace. I had rather be any kind o' thing than a fool; and yet I would not be thee, nuncle; thou hast pared thy wit o' both sides, and left nothing i' the middle:[53] here comes one o' the parings.

Enter Goneril.

LEAR   How now, daughter! what makes[54] that frontlet[55] on? Methinks you are too much of late i' the frown.

FOOL   Thou wast a pretty fellow when thou hadst no need to care for her frowning; now thou art an O without a figure.[56] I am better than thou art now; I am a fool, thou art nothing. [*To Goneril.*]   Yes, forsooth, I will hold my tongue; so your face bids me, though you say nothing.

> Mum, mum;
> He that keeps nor crust nor crumb,

45. i.e. half shells
46. *borest . . . dirt*: reversed the proper order of things (from a fable of Aesop)
47. *like myself*: foolishly
48. *had . . . grace*: were never less in favour
49. foolish
50. *their . . . wear*: show their wisdom
51. *used it*: made it my habit
52. *play bo-peep*: behave like a child
53. *pared . . . middle*: i.e. by giving away both halves of thy kingdom
54. means
55. i.e. frown (*lit.* cloth worn on forehead)
56. *an . . . figure*: a mere cipher, thing of nought

Weary of all, shall want some.
That's a shealed peascod.[57]   [*Pointing to Lear.*

GONERIL   Not only, sir, this your all-licens'd fool,
But other of your insolent retinue
170   Do hourly carp and quarrel, breaking forth
In rank[58] and not-to-be-endured riots. Sir,
I had thought, by making this well known unto you,
To have found a safe redress;[59] but now grow fearful,
By what yourself too late have spoke and done,
175   That you protect this course, and put it on[60]
By your allowance; which if you should, the fault
Would not 'scape censure, nor the redresses sleep,
Which, in the tender of a wholesome weal,[61]
Might in their working do you that offence,
180   Which else was shame,[62] that then necessity
Will call discreet proceeding.[63]

FOOL   For you trow, nuncle,
The hedge-sparrow fed the cuckoo so long,
That it had it head bit off by its young.[64]
185   So out went the candle, and we were left darkling.[65]

LEAR   Are you our daughter?

GONERIL   I would you would make use of your good wisdom,
Whereof I know you are fraught;[66] and put away
These dispositions[67] which of late transform you
190   From what you rightly are.

FOOL   May not an ass know when the cart draws the horse?[68] Whoop, Jug!
I love thee.

LEAR   Does any here know me? This is not Lear:
Does Lear walk thus? speak thus? Where are his eyes?
195   Either his notion[69] weakens, his discernings[70]
Are lethargied.[71] Ha! waking?[72] 'tis not so.
Who is it that can tell me who I am?

FOOL   Lear's shadow.

LEAR   I would[73] learn that; for, by the marks of sovereignty, knowledge and

---

57. *shealed peascod*: pod without peas (provincial form of "shelled")
58. gross
59. *safe redress*: sure remedy
60. *put it on*: encourage it
61. *in . . . weal*: in their regard for a healthy state of affairs
62. *Which . . . shame*: which would be disgraceful if the motive (behind my remedial action) were not good
63. *that . . . proceeding*: i.e. although, considering the need, people would approve my conduct ("that" = "which"

again—an awkward construction)
64. its (as often) apparent young, i.e. the young cuckoo (corresponding to Goneril)
65. in the dark
66. stored
67. moods
68. cf. l. 135.
69. understanding
70. powers of discernment
71. dulled
72. am I awake?
73. I must

200   reason, I should be false[74] persuaded I had daughters.

FOOL   Which[75] they will make an obedient father.

LEAR   Your name, fair gentlewoman?

GONERIL   This admiration,[76] sir, is much o' the favour[77]
        Of other your[78] new pranks. I do beseech you
205   To understand my purposes aright:
        As you are old and reverend, should[79] be wise.
        Here do you keep a hundred knights and squires;
        Men so disorder'd,[80] so debosh'd,[81] and bold,
        That this our court, infected with their manners,
210   Shows like a riotous inn: epicurism[82] and lust
        Make it more like a tavern or a brothel
        Than a grac'd[83] palace. The shame itself doth speak
        For[84] instant remedy; be then desir'd[85]
        By her that else will take the thing she begs,
215   A little to disquantity[86] your train;
        And the remainder, that shall still depend,[87]
        To be[88] such men as may besort[89] your age,
        Which know themselves and you.

LEAR   Darkness and devils!
        Saddle my horses; call my train together.
220   Degenerate bastard! I'll not trouble thee:
        Yet have I left a daughter.

GONERIL   You strike my people, and your disorder'd rabble
        Make servants of their betters.

        Enter Albany.

LEAR   Woe, that[90] too late repents;
                    [*To Albany.*] O! sir, are you come?
225   Is it your will? Speak, sir. Prepare my horses.
        Ingratitude, thou marble-hearted fiend,
        More hideous, when thou show'st thee in a child,
        Than the[91] sea-monster.

ALBANY   Pray, sir, be patient.

LEAR   [*To Goneril.*]   Detested kite! thou liest:

---

74. falsely
75. whom (Lear's shadow)
76. (feigned) surprise
77. nature
78. *other* (of) *your*
79. (you) *should*
80. disorderly
81. debauched
82. epicureanism, luxury
83. honourable

84. *speak for*: demand
85. *be . . . desir'd*: let yourself be requested
86. reduce the number of
87. serve you
88. *the remainder . . . be*: allow the remainder to be
89. suit
90. *Woe, that*: Woe to him who
91. a (generic use, cf. I. ii. 109)

230 My train are men of choice and rarest parts,
     That all particulars of duty know,
     And in the most exact regard[92] support
     The worships[93] of their name. O most small fault,[94]
     How ugly didst thou in Cordelia show!
235 Which, like an engine,[95] wrench'd my frame of nature[96]
     From the fix'd place, drew from my heart all love,
     And added to the gall. O Lear, Lear, Lear!
     Beat at this gate, that let thy folly in,   [Striking his head.
     And thy dear[97] judgment out: Go, go, my people.
240 ALBANY   My lord, I am guiltless, as I am ignorant
     Of what hath mov'd you.
     LEAR   It may be so, my lord.
     Hear, Nature, hear! dear goddess, hear!
     Suspend thy purpose, if thou didst intend
     To make this creature fruitful!
245 Into her womb convey sterility!
     Dry up in her the organs of increase,
     And from her derogate[98] body never spring
     A babe to honour her! If she must teem,[99]
     Create her child of spleen, that it may live
250 And be a thwart[100] disnatur'd[101] torment to her!
     Let it stamp wrinkles in her brow of youth,
     With cadent[102] tears fret[103] channels in her cheeks,
     Turn all her mother's pains and benefits[104]
     To laughter and contempt, that she may feel
255 How sharper than a serpent's tooth it is
     To have a thankless child! Away, away!   [Exit.
     ALBANY   Now, gods that we adore, whereof comes this?
     GONERIL   Never afflict yourself to know the cause;
     But let his disposition have that scope[105]
260 That dotage gives it.

     Re-enter Lear.

     LEAR   What! fifty of my followers at a clap,[106]
     Within a fortnight?

92. *in . . . regard*: with scrupulous care	98. debased
93. honour (plural sometimes used when a plurality of persons is concerned)	99. bear children
	100. cross, perverse
94. *O . . . fault*: i.e. Cordelia's obstinacy	101. unnatural
95. the rack (a torture, wrenching the body apart)	102. falling
	103. wear away
96. *frame of nature*: system of natural affection	104. kindness done to the child
	105. disposition: cf. l. 189
97. precious	106. *at a clap*: at a stroke, all at once

ALBANY   What's the matter, sir?

LEAR   I'll tell thee. [*To Goneril.*]   Life and death! I am asham'd
       That thou hast power to shake my manhood thus,
265   That these hot tears, which break from me perforce,
       Should make thee worth them. Blasts and fogs upon thee!
       Th' untented[107] woundings of a father's curse
       Pierce every sense about thee! Old fond[108] eyes,
       Beweep[109] this cause again, I'll pluck ye out,
270   And cast you, with the waters that you lose,[110]
       To temper[111] clay. Yea, is it come to this?
       Let it be so: I have another daughter,
       Who, I am sure, is kind and comfortable:[112]
       When she shall hear this of thee, with her nails
275   She'll flay thy wolvish visage. Thou shalt find
       That I'll resume the shape which thou dost think
       I have cast off for ever; thou shalt, I warrant thee.
                     [*Exeunt Lear, Kent, and Attendants.*

GONERIL   Do you mark that?

ALBANY   I cannot be so partial, Goneril,
280   To the great love I bear you.[113]—

GONERIL   Pray you, content.[114] What, Oswald, ho! [*To the Fool.*]   You, sir,
       more knave than fool, after your master.

FOOL   Nuncle Lear, nuncle Lear! tarry, and take the fool with thee.
               A fox, when one has caught her,
285   And such a daughter,
               Should sure[115] to the slaughter,
               If my cap would buy a halter;
               So the fool follows after. [*Exit.*

GONERIL   This man[116] hath had good counsel. A hundred knights!
290   'Tis politic and safe to let him keep
       At point[117] a hundred knights; yes, that on every dream,
       Each buzz,[118] each fancy, each complaint, dislike,
       He may enguard[119] his dotage with their powers,
       And hold our lives in mercy.[120] Oswald, I say!

ALBANY   Well, you may fear too far.

---

107. unexplored, deep, and so incurable
     (a surgeon probed a wound with a
     "tent" or roll of lint)
108. foolish
109. if you weep for
110. waste
111. moisten
112. comforting
113. *I cannot . . . you*: i.e. so prejudiced by
     my love for you (as to approve your
     conduct now)

114. (be) *content*: calm, almost "shut up!"
115. should surely go
116. *This man*: Lear (the whole speech is
     ironical)
117. *At point*: armed and ready
118. rumour
119. guard
120. *in mercy*: at his mercy

295 GONERIL   Safer than trust too far.
        Let me still[121] take away the harms I fear,
        Not fear still to be taken:[122] I know his heart.[123]
        What he hath utter'd I have writ my sister;
        If she sustain him and his hundred knights,
        When I have show'd the unfitness,—

        Re-enter Oswald

300   How now, Oswald!
        What![124] have you writ that letter to my sister?
    OSWALD   Ay, madam.
    GONERIL   Take you some company, and away to horse:
        Inform her full[125] of my particular[126] fear;
305   And thereto add such reasons of your own
        As may compact[127] it more. Get you gone,
        And hasten your return. [*Exit Oswald.*] No, no, my lord,
        This milky gentleness and course[128] of yours
        Though I condemn not, yet, under pardon,
310   You are much more attask'd[129] for want of wisdom
        Than prais'd for harmful mildness.[130]
    ALBANY   How far your eyes may pierce I cannot tell:
        Striving to better, oft we mar what's well.
    GONERIL   Nay, then—
315 ALBANY   Well, well; the event.[131]   [*Exeunt.*

SCENE 5

Court before the Same.

Enter Lear, Kent, and Fool.

    LEAR   Go you before to Gloucester[1] with these letters.[2] Acquaint my daughter
        no further with any thing you know than comes from her demand out of[3]
        the letter. If your diligence be not speedy I shall be there before you.
    KENT   I will not sleep, my lord, till I have delivered your letter.   [*Exit.*

121. always
122. overtaken by harm
123. *his heart*: i.e. (perhaps) that he is plot-
    ting to recover his throne
124. Well!
125. fully
126. personal
127. strengthen
128. *gentleness . . . course*: gentleness of your
    course (hendiadys)

129. blamed, held to account
130. *harmful mildness*: a mildness which can
    only prove harmful to us
131. *the event*: (let us see) what turns out
    1. the town, not the Earl
    2. this letter (Latin *litterae*)
    3. *demand out of*: questions arising out of

5 FOOL   If a man's brains were in's heels, were't[4] not in danger of kibes?[5]

LEAR   Ay, boy.

FOOL   Then, I prithee, be merry; thy wit shall not go slip-shod.[6]

LEAR   Ha, ha, ha!

FOOL   Shalt see thy other daughter will use thee kindly;[7] for though she's as
10 like this[8] as a crab[9] is like an apple, yet I can tell what I can tell.

LEAR   What canst tell, boy?

FOOL   She will taste as like this as a crab does to a crab. Thou canst tell why
one's nose stands i' the middle on's face?

LEAR   No.

15 FOOL   Why, to keep one's eyes of either side's[10] nose, that what a man cannot
smell out, he may spy into.

LEAR   I did her wrong,—

FOOL   Canst tell how an oyster makes his shell?

LEAR   No.

20 FOOL   Nor I neither; but I can tell why a snail has a house.

LEAR   Why?

FOOL   Why, to put his head in; not to give it away to his daughters, and leave
his horns without a case.

LEAR   I will forget my nature.[11] So kind a father! Be my horses ready?

25 FOOL   Thy asses[12] are gone about 'em. The reason why the seven stars[13] are
no more than seven is a pretty reason.

LEAR   Because they are not eight?

FOOL   Yes, indeed: thou wouldst make a good fool.

LEAR   To take it again perforce! Monster ingratitude![14]

30 FOOL   If thou wert my fool, nuncle, I'd have thee beaten for being old before
thy time.

LEAR   How's that?

FOOL   Thou shouldst not have been old before thou hadst been wise.

LEAR   O! let me not be mad, not mad, sweet heaven;

35 Keep me in temper; I would not be mad!

Enter Gentleman.

How now! Are those horses ready?

GENTLEMAN   Ready, my lord.

---

4. it, his brain(s)
5. chaps or chilblains
6. in slippers (to ease chilblains on the heel)
7. (1) affectionately, (2) after her kind, or nature (the Fool foresees the second)
8. Goneril
9. (apple)
10. *'s nose*: of one's nose

11. *my nature*: my natural affection (for my daughters)
12. *Thy asses*: those who are fools enough to serve you still
13. *the . . . stars*: the Pleiades
14. *Either* Lear contemplates trying to resume his royal power by force, *or* he is thinking of Goneril's withdrawing the privileges he had been allowed

LEAR   Come, boy.

FOOL   She that's a maid now, and laughs at my departure,

40   Shall not be a maid long, unless things be cut shorter.[15]   [*Exeunt.*

15. *She . . . shorter*: i.e. "The maid who sees only the funny side of the Fool's gibes and does not realize that Lear is going on a tragic journey is such a simpleton that she won't know how to preserve her virginity" (K. Muir)

ACT II

SCENE 1

A Court within the Castle of the Earl of Gloucester.

Enter Edmund and Curan, meeting.

EDMUND   Save thee,[1] Curan.

CURAN   And you, sir. I have been with your father, and given him notice that the Duke of Cornwall and Regan his duchess will be here with him to-night.

EDMUND   How comes that?

5 CURAN   Nay, I know not. You have heard of the news abroad? I mean the whispered ones,[2] for they are yet but ear-kissing arguments?[3]

EDMUND   Not I: pray you, what are they?

CURAN   Have you heard of no likely wars toward,[4] 'twixt the Dukes of Cornwall and Albany?

10 EDMUND   Not a word.

CURAN   You may do then, in time. Fare you well, sir.   [*Exit.*

EDMUND   The duke be here to-night! The better![5] best!

    This weaves itself perforce into my business.

    My father hath set guard to take my brother;

15   And I have one thing, of a queasy question,[6]

    Which I must act. Briefness[7] and fortune, work!

    Brother, a word; descend:[8] brother, I say!

Enter Edgar.

    My father watches: O sir! fly this place;

    Intelligence is given where you are hid;

20   You have now the good advantage of the night.

1. (God) *save thee*
2. news
3. *ear-kissing arguments*: subjects of secret conversation (as with the mouth close to the hearer's ear)
4. in view
5. (all) *the better*
6. *of . . . question*: awkward, ticklish to handle
7. swift action
8. Edgar would have entered on the upper stage

Have you not spoken 'gainst the Duke of Cornwall?
He's coming hither, now, i' the night, i' the haste,[9]
And Regan with him; have you nothing said
Upon his party 'gainst[10] the Duke of Albany?
Advise yourself.

25 EDGAR   I am sure on't, not a word.

EDMUND   I hear my father coming; pardon me;
In cunning[11] I must draw my sword upon you;
Draw; seem to defend yourself; now 'quit you well.
Yield;[12]—come before my father. Light, ho! here!
30 Fly, brother. Torches! torches! So, farewell.

[*Exit Edgar.*

Some blood drawn on me would beget opinion

[*Wounds his arm.*

Of my more fierce endeavour:[13] I have seen drunkards
Do more than this in sport. Father! father!
Stop, stop! No help?

Enter Gloucester, and Servants with torches.

35 GLOUCESTER   Now, Edmund, where's the villain?

EDMUND   Here stood he in the dark, his sharp sword out,
Mumbling of wicked charms, conjuring the moon
To stand auspicious mistress.[14]

GLOUCESTER   But where is he?

EDMUND   Look, sir, I bleed.

GLOUCESTER   Where is the villain, Edmund?

40 EDMUND   Fled this way, sir. When by no means he could—

GLOUCESTER   Pursue him, ho! Go after. [*Exeunt some Servants.*]   ''By no means''
what?

EDMUND   Persuade me to the murder of your lordship;
But that I told him,[15] the revenging gods
'Gainst parricides did all their thunders bend;
45 Spoke with how manifold and strong a bond
The child was bound to the father; sir, in fine,
Seeing how loathly opposite[16] I stood
To his unnatural purpose, in fell motion,[17]

---

9. *i' the haste*: in haste
10. *Upon . . . 'gainst*: about the party formed by him against
11. in pretence (as if we were enemies)
12. said louder, for Gloucester to hear
13. *beget . . . endeavour*: make men think that I have really been fighting seriously

14. *stand . . . mistress*: favour him as if she were his mistress (as she was of Endymion in classical mythology)
15. *But . . . him*: without my telling him (in reply) that
16. *loathly opposite*: opposed, with loathing, to
17. *fell motion*: fierce thrust

With his prepared sword he charges home[18]
50   My unprovided[19] body, lanc'd mine arm:
But when he saw my best alarum'd spirits[20]
Bold in the quarrel's right, rous'd to the encounter,
Or whether gasted[21] by the noise I made,
Full suddenly he fled.

GLOUCESTER   Let him fly far:
55   Not in this land shall he remain uncaught;
And found—dispatch.[22] The noble duke my master,
My worthy arch[23] and patron, comes to-night:
By his authority I will proclaim it,
That he which finds him shall deserve our thanks,
60   Bringing the murderous coward to the stake;
He that conceals him, death.

EDMUND   When I dissuaded him from his intent,
And found him pight[24] to do it, with curst speech
I threaten'd to discover him: he replied,
65   "Thou unpossessing[25] bastard! dost thou think,
If I would[26] stand against thee, would the reposal
Of any trust, virtue, or worth, in thee
Make thy words faith'd? No: what I should deny,—
As this I would; ay, though thou didst produce
70   My very character,[27]—I'd turn it all
To thy suggestion,[28] plot, and damned practice:[29]
And thou must make a dullard of the world,[30]
If they not thought[31] the profits of my death
Were very pregnant[32] and potential spurs[33]
To make thee seek it."

75   GLOUCESTER   Strong and fasten'd[34] villain!
Would he deny his letter? I never got[35] him.   [Tucket within.
Hark! the duke's trumpets. I know not why he comes.
All ports I'll bar; the villain shall not 'scape;
The duke must grant me that: besides, his picture
80   I will send far and near, that all the kingdom

---

18. *charges home*: makes a home (effective) thrust at
19. unprotected
20. *best . . . spirits*: my best spirits stirred up
21. frightened
22. when he is found, the order will be "dispatch him!"
23. chief
24. determined
25. as unable to inherit
26. should
27. handwriting
28. temptation
29. treachery
30. *make . . . world*: suppose people very stupid
31. *not thought*: should not think
32. clear, obvious (of different derivation from the word meaning "with child")
33. *potential spurs*: powerful inducements
34. confirmed
35. begot

May have due note of him; and of my land,
Loyal and natural[36] boy, I'll work the means
To make thee capable.[37]

Enter Cornwall, Regan, and Attendants

CORNWALL   How now, my noble friend! since I came hither, —
85   Which I can call but now, — I have heard strange news.
REGAN   If it be true, all vengeance comes too short
         Which can pursue the offender. How dost, my lord?
GLOUCESTER   O! madam, my old heart is crack'd, it's crack'd.
REGAN   What! did my father's godson seek your life?
90   He whom my father name'd?[38] your Edgar?
GLOUCESTER   O! lady, lady, shame would have it hid.
REGAN   Was he not companion with the riotous knights
         That tend upon my father?
GLOUCESTER   I know not, madam; 'tis too bad, too bad.
95   EDMUND   Yes, madam, he was of that consort.[39]
REGAN   No marvel then though he were ill affected;
         'Tis they have put him on[40] the old man's death,
         To have the expense and waste of[41] his revenues.
         I have this present evening from my sister
100   Been well-inform'd of them, and with such cautions
         That if they come to sojourn at my house,
         I'll not be there.
CORNWALL   Nor I, assure thee, Regan.
         Edmund, I hear that you have shown your father
         A child-like[42] office.
EDMUND   'Twas my duty, sir.
105   GLOUCESTER   He did bewray[43] his practice;[44] and receiv'd
         This hurt you see, striving to apprehend him.
CORNWALL   Is he pursu'd?
GLOUCESTER   Ay, my good lord.
CORNWALL   If he be taken he shall never more
         Be fear'd of doing[45] harm; make your own purpose,
110   How in my strength you please.[46] For you, Edmund,
         Whose virtue and obedience[47] doth this instant

36. true, affectionate (with a glance at the meaning of "born out of wedlock")
37. legally able to inherit (cf. l. 65)
38. in baptism
39. (accent consórt) company
40. *put him on*: egged him on to (attempt)
41. *To . . . of*: that he might be able to spend wastefully
42. truly filial
43. reveal
44. plot
45. *of doing*: lest he should do
46. *make . . . please*: use my authority and resources as you like in carrying out your purpose
47. *virtue and obedience*: virtuous obedience (hence verb in singular)

So much commend itself, you shall be ours:
Natures of such deep trust we shall much need;
You we first seize on.

EDMUND   I shall serve you, sir,
Truly, however else.[48]

115 GLOUCESTER   For him I thank your Grace.
CORNWALL   You know now why we came to visit you, —
REGAN   Thus out of season, threading dark-ey'd[49] night:
Occasions, noble Gloucester, of some prize,[50]
Wherein we must have use of your advice.
120 Our father he hath writ, so hath our sister,
Of differences, which I best thought it fit
To answer from[51] our home; the several messengers
From hence attend dispatch.[52] Our good old friend,
Lay comforts to your bosom, and bestow
125 Your needful counsel to our businesses,
Which craves the instant use.[53]

GLOUCESTER   I serve you, madam.
You Graces are right welcome.   [*Exeunt.*

SCENE 2

Before Gloucester's Castle.

Enter Kent and Oswald, severally.

OSWALD   Good dawning to thee, friend: art of this house?[1]
KENT   Ay.
OSWALD   Where may we set our horses?
KENT   I' the mire.
5 OSWALD   Prithee, if thou lovest me, tell me.
KENT   I love thee not.
OSWALD   Why, then I care not for thee.
KENT   If I had thee in Lipsbury pinfold,[2] I would make thee care for me.
OSWALD   Why dost thou use me thus? I know thee not.
10 KENT   Fellow, I know thee.
OSWALD   What dost thou know me for?
KENT   A knave, a rascal, an eater of broken meats;[3] a base, proud, shallow,

---

48. successfully or not
49. *threading dark-ey'd*: (with a pun on the eye of a needle)
50. *Occasions . . . prize*: incidents of some importance have occurred
51. away from
52. *attend dispatch*: wait to be sent out

53. *craves . . . use*: demands immediate execution
1. *of this house*: a dependant, servant
2. *in Lipsbury pinfold*: possibly "in my jaws"
3. *eater . . . meats*: finisher up of scraps

beggarly, three-suited,[4] hundred-pound,[5] filthy, worsted-stocking[6] knave; a lily-liver'd,[7] action-taking[8] knave; a whoreson, glass-gazing,[9] super-
15   serviceable,[10] finical rogue;[11] one-trunk-inheriting[12] slave; one that wouldst be a bawd, in way of[13] good service, and art nothing but the composition[14] of a knave, beggar, coward, pandar, and the son and heir of a mongrel bitch: one whom I will beat into clamorous whining if thou deniest the least syllable of thy addition.[15]

20   OSWALD   Why, what a monstrous fellow art thou, thus to rail on one that is neither known of thee nor knows thee!

KENT   What a brazen-faced varlet art thou, to deny thou knowest me! Is it two days since I tripped up thy heels and beat thee before the king? Draw, you rogue; for, though it be night, yet the moon shines: I'll make a sop o'
25   the moonshine of you. [*Drawing his sword.*]   Draw, you whoreson, cullionly,[16] barber-monger,[17] draw.

OSWALD   Away! I have nothing to do with thee.

KENT   Draw, you rascal; you come with letters against the king, and take vanity the puppet's[18] part against the royalty of her father. Draw, you rogue, or I'll
30   so carbonado[19] your shanks: draw, you rascal; come your ways.[20]

OSWALD   Help, ho! murder! help!

KENT   Strike, you slave; stand, rogue, stand; you neat[21] slave, strike.

[*Beating him.*

OSWALD   Help, oh! murder! murder!

Enter Edmund with his rapier drawn.

EDMUND   How now! What's the matter?   [*Parting them.*
35   KENT   With you,[22] goodman boy, if you please: come, I'll flesh[23] ye; come on, young master.

Enter Cornwall, Regan, Gloucester, and Servants.

GLOUCESTER   Weapons! arms! What's the matter here?

CORNWALL   Keep peace, upon your lives:
He dies that strikes again. What is the matter?

40   REGAN   The messengers from our sister and the king.

4. the allowance of some servants
5. owning only a hundred pounds (the qualification for a jury then)
6. woollen (as opposed to silk)
7. see IV. ii. 52
8. resorting to legal protection (instead of defending himself)
9. vain
10. *either* above his work, *or* over officious
11. affected
12. whose possessions would all go in one chest
13. *in way of*: in order to perform
14. mixture
15. *thy addition*: these titles
16. rascally
17. frequenter of barbers, fop
18. *Vanity the puppet's*: i.e. Goneril's
19. slice, slash
20. *come . . . ways*: come on
21. dandified *or* utter
22. *With you*: my matter, quarrel is with you *or* I'm your man (for a fight)
23. initiate (into bloodshed)

CORNWALL   What is your difference?[24] speak.

OSWALD   I am scarce in breath, my lord.

KENT   No marvel, you have so bestirred your valour. You cowardly rascal, nature disclaims[25] in thee: a tailor made thee.

45 CORNWALL   Thou art a strange fellow; a tailor make a man?

KENT   Ay, a tailor, sir: a stone-cutter[26] or a painter could not have made him so ill, though they had been but two hours o' the trade.

CORNWALL   Speak yet, how grew your quarrel?

OSWALD   This ancient ruffian, sir, whose life I have spar'd at suit of his grey
50 beard, —

KENT   Thou whoreson zed! thou unnecessary letter! My lord, if you will give me leave, I will tread this unbolted[27] villain into mortar, and daub the wall of a jakes[28] with him. Spare my grey beard, you wagtail?[29]

CORNWALL   Peace, sirrah!
55 You beastly knave, know you no reverence?

KENT   Yes, sir; but anger hath a privilege.

CORNWALL   Why art thou angry?

KENT   That such a slave as this should wear a sword,
Who wears no honesty. Such smiling rogues as these,
60 Like rats, oft bite the holy cords[30] a-twain
Which are too intrinse[31] t'unloose; smooth[32] every passion
That in the natures of their lords rebel;
Bring oil to fire, snow to their colder moods;
Renege,[33] affirm, and turn their halcyon beaks
65 With every gale and vary[34] of their masters,
Knowing nought, like dogs, but following.
A plague upon your epileptic[35] visage!
Smile you[36] my speeches, as I were a fool?
Goose, if I had you upon Sarum[37] plain,
70 I'd drive ye cackling home to Camelot.[38]

CORNWALL   What! art thou mad, old fellow?

GLOUCESTER   How fell you out? say that.

KENT   No contraries hold more antipathy
Than I and such a knave.

75 CORNWALL   Why dost thou call him knave? What is his fault?

KENT   His countenance likes[39] me not.

24. (ground of) quarrel
25. disown (any share)
26. sculptor
27. perhaps "unmitigated" (bolt = sift flour)
28. privy
29. probably "obsequious", from its bouncing or bobbing
30. *the holy cords*: of intimate relationship
31. intricate, tight
32. flatter, fall in with
33. deny
34. *gale and vary*: varying breeze
35. distorted and pale, as in an epileptic fit
36. *Smile you*: do you smile at?
37. Salisbury
38. supposed to be near Winchester
39. pleases

CORNWALL   No more, perchance, does mine, nor his, nor hers.

KENT   Sir, 'tis my occupation[40] to be plain:
    I have seen better faces in my time
80   Than stands on any shoulder that I see
    Before me at this instant.

CORNWALL   This is some fellow,
    Who, having been prais'd for bluntness, doth affect
    A saucy roughness, and constrains the garb
    Quite from his nature:[41] he cannot flatter, he
85   An honest mind and plain, he must speak truth:
    An they will take it, so;[42] if not, he's plain.
    These kind of knaves I know, which in this plainness
    Harbour more craft and more corrupter[43] ends
    Than twenty silly-ducking observants,[44]
90   That stretch their duties nicely.[45]

KENT   Sir, in good sooth, in sincere verity,
    Under the allowance of your grand aspect,[46]
    Whose influence, like the wreath of radiant fire
    On flickering Phoebus' front,—

CORNWALL   What mean'st by this?

95   KENT   To go out of my dialect, which you discommend so much. I know, sir, I
    am no flatterer: he that[47] beguiled you in a plain accent was a plain knave;[48]
    which for my part I will not be, though I should win your displeasure[49] to
    entreat me to 't.[50]

CORNWALL   What was the offence you gave him?

100   OSWALD   I never gave him any:
    It pleas'd the king his master very late
    To strike at me, upon his misconstruction;[51]
    When he, conjunct,[52] and flattering his displeasure,
    Tripp'd me behind; being down, insulted, rail'd,
105   And put upon him such a deal of man,
    That worthied him,[53] got praises of the king
    For him attempting[54] who was self-subdu'd;

---

40. business, habit
41. *constrains ... nature*: is behaving in a manner quite unnatural to him (garb = fashion, manner, but not of *dress* in Shakespeare)
42. well and good
43. *more corrupter*: double comparative, not uncommon in Shakespeare
44. *silly-ducking observants*: obsequious attendants foolishly bowing and scraping (observe = pay court to)
45. *stretch ... nicely*: are over-particular in the performance of
46. power, influence (astrological)

47. *he that*: i.e. the "kind of knaves" referred to in l. 87
48. *a plain knave*: a real knave (which I am not)
49. you, in your displeasure
50. *to 't*: to flatter you
51. *upon his misconstruction*: misunderstanding me; see I. iv. 69
52. joining in with (Lear)
53. *put ... worthied him*: made such a show of valour as to win the reputation of honour
54. *him attempting*: attacking a man

And, in the fleshment[55] of this dread exploit,
Drew on me here again.

110 KENT   None of these rogues and cowards
But Ajax is their fool.[56]

CORNWALL   Fetch forth the stocks!
You stubborn ancient knave, you reverend[57] braggart,
We'll teach you.

KENT   Sir, I am too old to learn,
Call not your stocks for me; I serve the king,
115 On whose employment I was sent to you;
You shall do small respect, show too bold malice
Against the grace and person of my master,
Stocking[58] his messenger.

CORNWALL   Fetch forth the stocks! As I have life and honour,
120 There shall he sit till noon.

REGAN   Till noon! Till night, my lord; and all night too.

KENT   Why, madam, if I were your father's dog,
You should not use me so.

REGAN   Sir, being his knave, I will.

CORNWALL   This is a fellow of the self-same colour[59]
125 Our sister speaks of. Come, bring away[60] the stocks.   [Stocks brought out.

GLOUCESTER   Let me beseech your Grace not to do so.
His fault is much, and the good king his master
Will check him for't: your purpos'd low correction
Is such as basest and contemned'st[61] wretches
130 For pilferings and most common trespasses
Are punish'd with: the king must take it ill,
That he, so slightly valu'd in his messenger,
Should have him thus restrain'd.

CORNWALL   I'll answer[62] that.

REGAN   My sister may receive it much more worse
135 To have her gentleman abus'd, assaulted,
For following her affairs. Put in his legs.

[Kent is put in the stocks.

Come, my good lord, away.

[Exeunt all but Gloucester and Kent.

GLOUCESTER   I am sorry for thee, friend; 'tis the duke's pleasure,
Whose disposition, all the world well knows,
140 Will not be rubb'd[63] nor stopp'd: I'll entreat for thee.

---

55. excitement resulting from first success, see l. 36
56. *their fool*: a fool compared to them
57. grey-headed, old enough to know better
58. putting in stocks
59. complexion, kind
60. bring in
61. most despicable
62. take responsibility for
63. hindered (a "rub" is an obstacle in bowls)

KENT   Pray, do not, sir. I have watch'd[64] and travell'd hard;
 　　　　Some time I shall sleep out, the rest I'll whistle.
 　　　　A good man's fortune may grow out at heels:[65]
 　　　　Give you good morrow!
145   GLOUCESTER   The duke's to blame in this; 'twill be ill taken.
KENT   Good king, that must approve[66] the common saw,[67]
 　　　　Thou out of heaven's benediction com'st
 　　　　To the warm sun.[68]
 　　　　Approach, thou beacon[69] to this under globe,[70]
150   That by thy comfortable beams I may
 　　　　Peruse this letter. Nothing almost sees miracles
 　　　　But misery:[71] I know 'tis from Cordelia,
 　　　　Who hath most fortunately been inform'd
 　　　　Of my obscured course;[72] and shall find time
155   From this enormous state, seeking to give
 　　　　Losses their remedies.[73] All weary and o'er-watch'd,
 　　　　Take vantage,[74] heavy eyes, not to behold
 　　　　This shameful lodging.
 　　　　Fortune, good night, smile once more; turn thy wheel!   [*He sleeps.*

SCENE 3

A Part of the Heath.

Enter Edgar.

EDGAR   I heard myself proclaim'd;[1]
 　　　　And by the happy[2] hollow of a tree
 　　　　Escap'd the hunt. No port is free; no place,
 　　　　That[3] guard, and most unusual vigilance,
5   Does not attend my taking.[4] While I may scape
 　　　　I will preserve myself; and am bethought
 　　　　To take[5] the basest and most poorest shape

64. lain awake at night
65. *out at heels*: a metaphor for "in a bad way", like "out at elbow" or "down at heel"
66. prove (the truth of)
67. proverb
68. *Thou . . . sun*: i.e. from better to worse (a surprising sense, but proved by other examples)
69. *thou beacon*: the sun
70. *this . . . globe*: our world, as opposed to heaven (147)
71. the wretched

72. *my . . . course*: what has happened to me who appear to have disappeared
73. *and shall . . . remedies*: and who will find the opportunity to deliver us from this unnatural state of affairs, putting right what is wrong
74. advantage (of the opportunity)
1. see II. i. 59
2. luckily found
3. i.e. where
4. *attend my taking*: wait to arrest me
5. *am . . . take*: have bethought myself of taking

That ever penury, in contempt of man,
Brought near to beast; my face I'll grime with filth,
10   Blanket my loins, elf[6] all my hair in knots,
And with presented[7] nakedness outface
The winds and persecutions of the sky.
The country gives me proof and precedent
Of Bedlam[8] beggars, who with roaring voices,
15   Strike[9] in their numb'd and mortified bare arms
Pins, wooden pricks,[10] nails, sprigs of rosemary;
And with this horrible object,[11] from low farms,
Poor pelting[12] villages, sheep-cotes,and mills,
Sometime with lunatic bans,[13] sometime with prayers,
20   Enforce their charity. Poor Turlygood![14] poor Tom!
That's something yet: Edgar I nothing am.[15]   [*Exit.*

SCENE 4

Before Gloucester's Castle.
Kent in the stocks.

Enter Lear, Fool, and Gentleman.

LEAR   'Tis strange that they[1] should so depart from home,
And not send back my messenger.
GENTLEMAN   As I learn'd,
The night before there was no purpose in them
Of this remove.[2]
KENT   Hail to thee, noble master!
5   LEAR   Ha!
Mak'st thou this shame thy pastime?
KENT   No, my lord.
FOOL   Ha, ha! he wears cruel[3] garters. Horses are tied by the head, dogs and
bears by the neck, monkeys by the loins, and men by the legs: when a man
is over-lusty at legs, then he wears wooden nether-stocks.[4]
10   LEAR   What's he that hath so much thy place[5] mistook
To set thee here?

---

6. tangle (as an elf might)
7. *either* assumed *or* exposed to view
8. cf. I. ii. 110
9. drive
10. skewers
11. appearance
12. petty
13. curses
14. no certain explanation

15. *Edgar . . . am: either* I am Edgar no
more, *or* As Edgar I no longer exist
1. Cornwall and Regan
2. change of residence
3. with a pun on "crewel" = worsted
yarn
4. stockings (as opposed to "upper
stocks" = breeches)
5. rank, status as my envoy

KENT   It is both he and she,
    Your son and daughter.
LEAR   No.
KENT   Yes.
15 LEAR   No, I say.
KENT   I say, yea.
LEAR   No, no; they would not.
KENT   Yes, they have.
LEAR   By Jupiter, I swear, no.
KENT   By Juno, I swear, ay.
20 LEAR   They durst not do 't;
    They could not, would not do't; 'tis worse than murder,
    To do upon respect[6] such violent outrage.
    Resolve me,[7] with all modest[8] haste, which way
    Thou mightst deserve, or they impose, this usage,
    Coming from us.[9]
25 KENT   My lord, when at their home
    I did commend your highness' letters to them,
    Ere I was risen from the place that show'd
    My duty kneeling, there came a reeking post,[10]
    Stew'd[11] in his haste, half breathless, panting forth
30 From Goneril his mistress salutations;
    Deliver'd letters, spite of intermission,[12]
    Which presently[13] they read: on whose contents
    They summon'd up their meiny,[14] straight took horse;
    Commanded me to follow, and attend
35 The leisure of their answer; gave me cold looks:
    And meeting[15] here the other messenger,
    Whose welcome, I perceiv'd, had poison'd mine,—
    Being the very fellow which of late
    Display'd[16] so saucily against your highness,—
40 Having more man[17] than wit about me,—drew:
    He rais'd the house with loud and coward cries.
    Your son and daughter found this trespass worth
    The shame which here it suffers.
FOOL   Winter's not gone yet,[18] if the wild geese fly that way.

---

6. *upon respect*: deliberately
7. *Resolve me*: explain to me
8. becoming
9. *Coming . . . us*: seeing that you came from me
10. messenger
11. sweating
12. *spite of intermission*: in spite of the fact he was interrupting me
13. immediately
14. household, company
15. And I, meeting
16. showed off
17. courage (cf. II. ii. 105)
18. i.e. We are not out of trouble

45   Fathers that wear rags
              Do make their children blind,[19]
            But fathers that bear bags[20]
              Shall see their children kind.
            Fortune, that arrant whore,
50   Ne'er turns the key[21] to the poor.
      But for all this thou shalt have as many dolours[22] for[23] thy daughters
      as thou canst tell[24] in a year.

LEAR   O! how this mother[25] swells up toward my heart;
      Hysterica passio![26] down, thou climbing sorrow!
55   Thy element's below. Where is this daughter?

KENT   With the earl, sir: here within.

LEAR   Follow me not; stay here.   [*Exit.*

GENTLEMAN   Made you no more offence than what you speak of?

KENT   None.

60   How chance the king comes with so small a number?

FOOL   An thou hadst been set i' the stocks for that question, thou hadst well
      deserved it.[27]

KENT   Why fool?

FOOL   We'll set thee to school to an ant, to teach thee there's no labouring i'
65   the winter. All that follow their noses are led by their eyes but blind men;
      and there's not a nose among twenty but can smell him that's stinking.[28]
      Let go thy hold when a great wheel runs down a hill, lest it break thy neck
      with following it; but the great one that goes up the hill, let him draw thee
      after. When a wise man gives thee better counsel, give me mine again:
70   I would have none but knaves follow it, since a fool gives it.
            That sir[29] which serves and seeks for gain,
              And follows but for form,
            Will pack[30] when it begins to rain,
              And leave thee in the storm.
75   But I will tarry; the fool will stay,
              And let the wise[31] man fly:
            The knave turns fool[32] that runs away;
              The fool[33] no knave, perdy.[34]

---

19. to filial duty
20. of money
21. *turns the key*: to admit
22. griefs (with pun on "dollars" = money)
23. from, because of
24. (1) recount griefs, (2) count money
25. hysteria
26. *Hysterica passio!*: suffering in the "mother" (archaic for womb, Gk. hystera), so-called as commoner in women
27. *And thou . . . it*: i.e. you should know that people desert a losing cause

28. *there's . . . stinking*: i.e. it does not take the keen smell of a blind man to smell out the poor state of Lear's fortunes
29. gentleman
30. clear off
31. i.e. worldly wise
32. *turns fool*: i.e. judged from a higher, less self-interested point of view
33. *The fool*: the Fool, I
34. par Dieu

KENT   Where learn'd you this, fool?

80   FOOL   Not i' the stocks, fool.

Re-enter Lear, with Gloucester.

LEAR   Deny[35] to speak with me! They are sick! they are weary,
      They have travell'd hard to-night! Mere fetches,[36]
      The images[37] of revolt and flying off.[38]
      Fetch me a better answer.

GLOUCESTER   My dear lord,

85   You know the fiery quality[39] of the duke;
      How unremovable and fix'd he is
      In his own course.

LEAR   Vengeance! plague! death! confusion!
      Fiery! what quality? Why, Gloucester, Gloucester,

90   I'd speak with the Duke of Cornwall and his wife.

GLOUCESTER   Well, my good lord, I have inform'd them so.

LEAR   Inform'd them! Dost thou understand me, man?

GLOUCESTER   Ay, my good lord.

LEAR   The king would speak with Cornwall; the dear father

95   Would with his daughter speak, commands her service:
      Are they inform'd of this? My breath and blood!
      Fiery! the fiery duke! Tell the hot[40] duke that—
      No, but not yet; may be he is not well:
      Infirmity[41] doth still neglect all office[42]

100   Whereto our health is bound;[43] we are not ourselves
      When nature, being oppress'd, commands the mind
      To suffer with the body. I'll forbear;
      And am fall'n out with my more headier will,[44]
      To take the indispos'd and sickly fit

105   For the sound man. Death on my state! [*Looking on Kent.*]   Wherefore
      Should he sit here? This act persuades me
      That this remotion[45] of the duke and her
      Is practice[46] only. Give me my servant forth.
      Go, tell the duke and 's wife I'd speak with them

110   Now, presently: bid them come forth and hear me,
      Or at their chamber-door I'll beat the drum

35. refuse
36. tricks, excuses (with pun in l. 84)
37. tokens *or* embodiment (cf. IV. vi. 150)
38. *flying off*: desertion
39. nature
40. hot-tempered
41. a sick man

42. duty
43. *Whereto . . . bound*: which, if well, we
   should feel bound to perform
44. *And . . . will*: i.e. I turn back from my
   overhasty determination
45. removal (from their home)
46. a trick

Till it cry sleep to death.[47]

GLOUCESTER   I would have all well betwixt you.   [*Exit.*

LEAR   O, me! my heart, my rising heart! but, down!

115   FOOL   Cry to it, nuncle, as the cockney[48] did to the eels when she put 'em i' the
paste alive; she knapped[49] 'em o' the coxcombs[50] with a stick, and cried,
"Down, wantons,[51] down!" 'Twas her brother that, in pure kindness to
his horse, buttered his hay.[52]

Enter Cornwall, Regan, Gloucester, and Servants.

LEAR   Good morrow to you both.

CORNWALL   Hail to your Grace!

[*Kent is set at liberty.*

120   REGAN   I am glad to see your highness.

LEAR   Regan, I think you are; I know what reason
I have to think so: if thou shouldst not be glad,
I would divorce me from thy mother's tomb,
Sepulchring[53] an adult'ress.—[*To Kent.*]   O! are you free?

125   Some other time for that. Beloved Regan,
Thy sister's naught: O Regan! she hath tied
Sharp-tooth'd unkindness, like a vulture, here: |*Points to his heart.*
I can scarce speak to thee; thou'lt not believe
With how deprav'd a quality[54]—O Regan!

130   REGAN   I pray you, sir, take patience. I have hope
You less know how to value her desert[55]
Than she to scant[56] her duty.

LEAR   Say, how is that?

REGAN   I cannot think my sister in the least
Would fail her obligation: if, sir, perchance
135   She have restrain'd the riots of your followers,
'Tis on such ground, and to such wholesome end,
As clears her from all blame.

LEAR   My curses on her!

REGAN   O, sir! you are old;
Nature in you stands on the very verge
140   Of her confine:[57] you should be rul'd and led
By some discretion[58] that discerns your state

---

47. *cry . . . death*: drown sleep with its
noise (as Macbeth heard a voice "murder" sleep, Macbeth II. ii. 36–37)
48. (probably) an affected woman
49. rapped, struck
50. heads
51. pert, cheeky creatures
52. *buttered his hay*: i.e. did something
equally silly

53. (as it would then be) the tomb of
54. manner (she treated me)
55. merits
56. *Than she* (knows how) *to scant*: is capable of falling short of
57. boundary, utmost limit
58. discreet people

Better than you yourself. Therefore I pray you
That to our sister you do make return;[59]
Say, you have wrong'd her, sir.

LEAR   Ask her forgiveness?

145 Do you but mark how this becomes the house:[60]
''Dear daughter, I confess that I am old;
Age is unnecessary:[61] on my knees I beg   [*Kneeling.*
That you'll vouchsafe me raiment, bed, and food.''

REGAN Good sir, no more; these are unsightly tricks:
Return you to my sister.

150 LEAR   [*Rising*] Never, Regan.
She hath abated[62] me of half my train;
Look'd black upon me; struck me with her tongue,
Most serpent-like, upon the very heart.
All the stor'd vengeances of heaven fall
155 On her ingrateful top![63] Strike her young bones,
You taking[64] airs, with lameness!

CORNWALL   Fie, sir, fie!

LEAR You nimble lightnings, dart your blinding flames
Into her scornful eyes! Infect her beauty,
You fen-suck'd fogs, drawn by the powerful sun,
160 To fall and blast her pride!

REGAN O the blest gods! So will you wish on me,
When the rash mood[65] is on.

LEAR No, Regan, thou shalt never have my curse:
Thy tender-hefted[66] nature shall not give
165 Thee o'er to harshness: her eyes are fierce, but thine
Do comfort and not burn. 'Tis not in thee
To grudge my pleasures, to cut off my train,
To bandy hasty words, to scant my sizes,[67]
And, in conclusion, to oppose the bolt[68]
170 Against my coming in: thou better know'st
The offices of nature, bond of childhood,
Effects[69] of courtesy, dues of gratitude;
Thy half o' the kingdom hast thou not forgot,
Wherein I thee endow'd.

REGAN   Good sir, to the purpose.[70]

LEAR Who put my man i' the stocks?   [*Tucket within.*

59. *make return*: return
60. *the house*: our family relationship *or* the royal house
61. useless, has no right to exist
62. curtailed
63. head
64. infecting, infectious
65. *the . . . mood*: cf. I. i. 280

66. (probably) set in a delicate bodily frame (heft = haft = handle), womanly
67. allowances (cf. sizar = exhibitioner, sometimes at Cambridge)
68. *oppose the bolt*: bar the door
69. manifestations
70. *to the purpose*: come to the point

175   CORNWALL   What trumpet's that?
REGAN   I know't, my sister's; this approves[71] her letter,
    That she would soon be here. Is your lady come?

Enter Oswald.

LEAR   This is a slave, whose easy-borrow'd[72] pride
    Dwells in the fickle[73] grace of her he follows.
    Out, varlet, from my sight!
180   CORNWALL   What means your Grace?
LEAR   Who stock'd my servant? Regan, I have good hope
    Thou didst not know on't. Who comes here?
    O heavens,

Enter Goneril.

    If you do love old men, if your sweet sway
185   Allow[74] obedience, if yourselves are old,
    Make it your cause;[75] send down and take my part!
    [*To Goneril.*]   Art not asham'd to look upon this beard?
    O Regan, wilt thou take her by the hand?
GONERIL   Why not by the hand, sir? How have I offended?
190   All's not offence that indiscretion[76] finds[77]
    And dotage terms so.
LEAR   O sides! you are too tough;
    Will you yet hold? How came my man i' the stocks?
CORNWALL   I set him there, sir: but his own disorders
    Deserv'd much less advancement.[78]
LEAR   You! did you?
195   REGAN   I pray you, father, being weak, seem so.[79]
    If, till the expiration of your month,
    You will return and sojourn with my sister,
    Dismissing half your train, come then to me:
    I am now from home,[80] and out of that provision
200   Which shall be needful for your entertainment.
LEAR   Return to her? and fifty men dismiss'd!
    No, rather I abjure all roofs, and choose
    To wage against[81] the enmity o' the air;
    To be a comrade with the wolf and owl,

71. confirms
72. assumed without justification
73. unreliable (as not given for merit)
74. approve
75. *Make . . . cause*:   identify yourselves
    with my side
76. cf. 141
77. holds
78. *much . . . advancement*: greater disgrace
79. *seem so*: admit it, behave accordingly
80. away from
81. *wage* (war) *against*: contend with

205   Necessity's sharp pinch![82] Return with her!
       Why, the hot-blooded France, that dowerless took
       Our youngest born, I could as well be brought
       To knee his throne, and squire-like, pension beg
       To keep[83] base life afoot. Return with her!
210   Persuade me rather to be slave and sumpter[84]
       To this detested groom.   [*Pointing at Oswald.*

       GONERIL   At your choice, sir.
       LEAR   I prithee, daughter, do not make me mad:
       I will not trouble thee, my child; farewell.
       We'll no more meet, no more see one another;
215   But yet thou art my flesh, my blood, my daughter;
       Or rather a disease that's in my flesh,
       Which I must needs call mine: thou art a boil,
       A plague-sore, an embossed[85] carbuncle,
       In my corrupted blood. But I'll not chide thee;
220   Let shame come when it will, I do not call it:
       I do not bid the thunder-bearer[86] shoot,[87]
       Nor tell tales of thee to high-judging[88] Jove.
       Mend when thou canst; be better at thy leisure:
       I can be patient; I can stay with Regan,
       I and my hundred knights.
225   REGAN   Not altogether so:
       I look'd not for you yet, nor am provided
       For your fit welcome. Give ear, sir, to my sister;
       For those that mingle reason with your passion[89]
       Must be content to think you old, and so[90]—
       But she knows what she does.
230   LEAR   Is this well spoken?
       REGAN   I dare avouch it, sir: what! fifty followers?
       Is it not well? What should you need of more?
       Yea, or so many, sith[91] that both charge[92] and danger[93]
       Speak 'against so great a number? How, in one house,
235   Should many people, under two commands,
       Hold amity?[94] 'Tis hard; almost impossible.
       GONERIL   Why might not you, my lord, receive attendance

82. *Necessity's . . . pinch*: straits to which need will reduce me (cf. "Necessitie must first pinch you by the throat" in Florio's *Montaîgne*)
83. kneel before
84. beast of burden
85. swollen
86. *the thunder-bearer*: Juppiter tonans
87. strike with lightning
88. supreme judge *or* judge in heaven

89. *mingle . . . passion*: examine your passionate utterances in the light of reason (but the figure is probably from mixing drinks)
90. *and so—*: *sc.* not take you seriously (or something similar)
91. since
92. the expense
93. i.e. of disturbance
94. friendship

From those that she calls servants, or from mine?

REGAN   Why not, my lord? If then they chanc'd to slack you[95]

240   We could control them. If you will come to me,—

For now I spy a danger,—I entreat you

To bring but five-and-twenty; to no more

Will I give place or notice.[96]

LEAR   I gave you all—

REGAN   And in good time you gave it.

245   LEAR   Made you my guardians, my depositaries,[97]

But kept a reservation[98] to be follow'd

With such a number. What! must I come to you

With five-and-twenty? Regan, said you so?

REGAN   And speak 't again, my lord; no more with me.

250   LEAR   Those wicked creatures[99] yet do look well-favour'd,

When others are more wicked; not being the worst

Stands in some rank of praise. [*To Goneril.*]   I'll go with thee:

Thy fifty yet doth double five-and-twenty,

And thou art twice her love.[100]

GONERIL   Hear me, my lord.

255   What need you five-and-twenty, ten, or five,

To follow in a house, where twice so many

Have a command to tend you?

REGAN   What need one?

LEAR   O! reason not[101] the need; our basest beggars

Are in the poorest thing superfluous:[102]

260   Allow not nature[103] more than nature needs,

Man's life is cheap as[104] beast's. Thou art a lady;

If only to go warm were gorgeous,

Why, nature needs not what thou gorgeous wear'st,

Which scarcely keeps thee warm.[105] But, for true need,[106]—

265   You heavens, give me that[107] patience, patience I need!

You see me here, you gods, a poor old man,

As full of grief as age; wretched in both!

If it be you that stir these daughters' hearts

Against their father, fool me not so much

---

95. *slack you*: be negligent in serving you
96. recognition
97. trustees
98. *kept a reservation*: made a saving clause or exception (see I. i. 126)
99. *Those . . . creatures*: i.e. Goneril
100. *art . . . love*: show me twice as much love
101. *reason not*: don't argue about
102. possessing more than they actually need
103. *Allow not nature*: if you don't allow men to possess

104. *cheap as*: of as little value as
105. *If only . . . need*: i.e. If the need for warmth were the only purpose of wearing (fine) clothes, well, your body does not need the fine clothes you wear—which incidentally hardly do keep you warm. (The first "gorgeous" is not the logical word but is effective.)
106. *for . . . need*: as for what I really need most
107. the omission of this word would improve sense and metre

270 To[108] bear it tamely; touch me with noble anger,
And let not women's weapons, water-drops,
Stain my man's cheeks! No, you unnatural hags,
I will have such revenges on you both
That all the world shall—I will do such things,—
275 What they are yet I know not,—but they shall be
The terrors of the earth. You think I'll weep;
No, I'll not weep:
I have full cause of weeping, but this heart
Shall break into a hundred thousand flaws[109]
280 Or ere[110] I'll weep. O fool! I shall go mad.

[*Exeunt Lear, Gloucester, Kent, and fool.*

CORNWALL   Let us withdraw; 'twill be a storm.   [*Storm heard at a distance.*

REGAN   This house is little: the old man and his people
Cannot be well bestow'd.[111]

GONERIL   'Tis his own blame; hath[112] put himself from[113] rest,
285 And must needs taste his folly.

REGAN   For his particular,[114] I'll receive him gladly,
But not one follower.

GONERIL   So am I purpos'd.
Where is my Lord of Gloucester?

CORNWALL   Follow'd the old man forth. He is return'd.

Re-enter Gloucester.

GLOUCESTER   The king is in high rage.
290 CORNWALL   Whither is he going?
GLOUCESTER   He calls to horse; but will I know not whither.
CORNWALL   'Tis best to give him way;[115] he leads himself.[116]
GONERIL   My lord, entreat him by no means to stay.
GLOUCESTER   Alack! the night comes on, and the bleak winds
295 Do sorely ruffle;[117] for many miles about
There's scarce a bush.

REGAN   O! sir, to wilful men,
The injuries that they themselves procure
Must be their schoolmasters. Shut up your doors;
He is attended with[118] a desperate train,
300 And what they may incense him to, being apt

108. *fool . . . To*: do not make me such a fool
as to (perhaps with reference to a Fool
who has to endure what his master
does to him)
109. cracks *and/or* fragments
110. *Or ere*: before (which each word
means)
111. accommodated

112. he hath
113. out of
114. *his particular*: himself alone
115. *give him way*: let him be
116. *leads himself*: insists on his own way
117. bluster
118. by

To have his ear abus'd,[119] wisdom bids fear.
CORNWALL   Shut up your doors, my lord; 'tis a wild night:
My Regan counsels well: come out o' the storm.   [*Exeunt.*

119. misled

ACT III

SCENE 1

A Heath.

A storm, with thunder and lightning. Enter Kent and a Gentleman, meeting.

KENT   Who's here, beside foul weather?
GENTLEMAN   One minded like the weather, most unquietly.
KENT   I know you. Where's the king?
GENTLEMAN   Contending with the fretful elements;
5   Bids the wind blow the earth into the sea,
Or swell the curled waters 'bove the main,[1]
That things[2] might change or cease; tears his white hair,
Which the impetuous blasts, with eyeless[3] rage,
Catch in their fury, and make nothing of;[4]
10   Strives in his little world of man to out-scorn
The to-and-fro-conflicting wind and rain.
This night, wherein the cub-drawn[5] bear would couch,[6]
The lion and the belly-pinched wolf
Keep their fur dry, unbonneted[7] he runs,
And bids what will take all.[8]
15   KENT   But who is with him?
GENTLEMAN   None but the fool, who labours to out-jest[9]
His heart-struck[10] injuries.
KENT   Sir, I do know you;
And dare, upon the warrant of my note,[11]
Commend a dear[12] thing to you. There is division,
20   Although as yet the face of it be cover'd
With mutual cunning, 'twixt Albany and Cornwall;

1. mainland (as in "Spanish main")
2. the order of the world *natura rerum*
3. blind
4. *make . . . of*: show no respect for
5. drained by her cubs (and so ravenous)
6. lie down
7. bare-headed (reminding us also of the *crown* he has given up)
8. *what . . . all*: everything go hang (a gesture of despair)
9. jest him out of
10. which have struck him to the heart (cf. II. iv. 153)
11. *upon . . . note*: on the strength of my knowledge
12. important

Who have—as who have not, that their great stars
Thron'd and set high—servants, who seem no less,[13]
Which are to France the spies and speculations[14]
25   Intelligent of[15] our state; what hath been seen,
Either in snuffs[16] and packings[17] of the dukes,
Or the hard rein[18] which both of them have borne
Against the old kind king; or something deeper,
Whereof perchance these are but furnishings;[19]
30   But, true it is, from France there comes a power[20]
Into this scatter'd[21] kingdom; who already,
Wise in our negligence, have secret feet[22]
In some of our best ports, and are at point[23]
To show their open banner. Now to you:[24]
35   If on my credit you dare build[25] so far
To make your speed to Dover, you shall find
Some that will thank you, making[26] just report
Of how unnatural and bemadding sorrow
The king hath cause to plain.[27]
40   I am a gentleman of blood and breeding,
And from some knowledge and assurance[28] offer
This office to you.
GENTLEMAN   I will talk further with you.
KENT   No, do not.
For confirmation that I am much more
45   Than my out-wall,[29] open this purse, and take
What it contains. If you shall see Cordelia,—
As doubt not but you shall,—show her this ring,
And she will tell you who your fellow[30] is
That yet you do not know. Fie on this storm!
50   I will go seek the king.
GENTLEMAN   Give me your hand. Have you no more to say?
KENT   Few words, but, to effect,[31] more than all yet;
That, when we have found the king,—in which your pain
That way, I'll this,[32]—he that first lights on him
55   Holla the other.   [Exeunt severally.

13. *seem no less*: at any rate appear to be
servants
14. observers, spies (abstract for concrete,
as often)
15. *Intelligent of*: giving information about
16. resentments, quarrels
17. plots
18. *hard rein*: metaphor from curbing a
horse severely
19. the trimmings
20. army
21. divided
22. *secret feet*: landed secretly

23. *at point*: ready
24. *Now to you*: to come to your part
25. *on . . . build*: trust me
26. when you make
27. complain of
28. *knowledge and assurance*: sure knowledge
29. exterior (suggests)
30. (present) companion
31. *to effect*: in importance
32. *your . . . this*: let it be your task to go
that way while I go this way

SCENE 2

Another Part of the Heath. Storm still.

Enter Lear and Fool.

LEAR   Blow winds, and crack your cheeks! rage! blow!
    You cataracts[1] and hurricanoes,[2] spout
    Till you have drench'd our steeples, drown'd the cocks![3]
    You sulphurous and thought-executing[4] fires,
5   Vaunt-couriers[5] to oak-cleaving thunderbolts,
    Singe my white head! And thou, all-shaking thunder,
    Strike flat the thick rotundity o' the world!
    Crack nature's moulds,[6] all germens[7] spill[8] at once
    That make ingrateful man!
10   FOOL   O nuncle, court holy-water[9] in a dry house is better than this rain-water
    out o' door. Good nuncle, in, and ask thy daughters' blessing;[10] here's a
    night pities neither wise man nor fool.
LEAR   Rumble thy bellyful! Spit, fire! spout, rain!
    Nor rain, wind, thunder, fire, are my daughters:
15   I tax[11] not you, you elements, with unkindness;
    I never gave you kingdom, call'd you children,
    You owe me no subscription:[12] then, let fall
    Your horrible pleasure; here I stand, your slave,
    A poor, infirm, weak, and despis'd old man.
20   But yet I call you servile ministers,[13]
    That have with two pernicious daughters join'd
    Your high-engender'd battles[14] 'gainst a head
    So old and white as this. O! O! 'tis foul.
FOOL   He that has a house to put his head in has a good head-piece.[15]

25   The cod-piece[16] that will house
                Before the head has any.[17]
                The head and he shall louse;[18]
                So beggars marry many.[19]

1. waterspouts (from heaven)
2. emphatic form of "hurricanes"
3. weathercocks
4. *either* swift as thought *or* executing Jove's wishes
5. precursors
6. *nature's moulds*: the moulds in which things are made
7. seeds
8. destroy
9. *court holy-water*: flattery (a common phrase at the time)
10. *ask . . . blessing*: apologize to and make peace with

11. charge (cf. I. iv. 310)
12. submission
13. agents
14. *high-engender'd battles*: battalions bred in the sky
15. *both* headcovering *and* brain
16. covering worn by men between legs under close-fitting hose
17. house
18. be lousy, infected with lice
19. *So . . . many*: (perhaps) in that condition many beggars marry

<blockquote>
The man that makes his toe
What he his heart should make,
Shall of a corn cry woe,
And turn his sleep to wake.[20]
</blockquote>

30

For there was never yet fair woman but she made mouths[21] in a glass.

Enter Kent.

LEAR   No, I will be the pattern of all patience;
    I will say nothing.

KENT   Who's there?

FOOL   Marry, here's grace[22] and a cod-piece;[23] that's a wise man and a fool.

KENT   Alas! sir, are you here? things that love night
    Love not such nights as these; the wrathful skies
    Gallow[24] the very wanderers of the dark,
    And make them keep their caves.[25] Since I was man
    Such sheets of fire, such bursts of horrid thunder,
    Such groans of roaring wind and rain, I never
    Remember to have heard; man's nature cannot carry[26]
    The affliction nor the fear.

LEAR   Let the great gods,
    That keep this dreadful pother[27] o'er our heads,
    Find out their enemies now. Tremble, thou wretch,
    That hast within thee undivulged crimes,
    Unwhipp'd of[28] justice; hide thee, thou bloody hand;
    Thou perjur'd,[29] and thou simular of[30] virtue
    That art incestuous; caitiff,[31] to pieces shake,[32]
    That under covert[33] and convenient seeming[34]
    Hast practis'd on[35] man's life; close[36] pent-up guilts,[37]
    Rive your concealing continents,[38] and cry
    These dreadful summoners[39] grace.[40] I am a man
    More sinn'd against than sinning.

KENT   Alack! bare-headed!
    Gracious my lord, hard by here is a hovel;

---

20. *The cod-piece . . . wake*: i.e. the man who prefers a meaner part of his body to the more honourable will get himself into trouble
21. *made mouths*: made faces, preened herself
22. the king's grace
23. *a cod-piece*: something comparatively worthless
24. frighten (now only in dialect)
25. *keep . . . caves*: cf. III. i. 12–14
26. bear
27. disturbance, commotion
28. by
29. *perjur'd* (man)
30. *simular of*: pretender to
31. wretch
32. *to . . . shake*: i.e. with fear and trembling
33. secret
34. pretence, hypocrisy
35. *practis'd on*: plotted against
36. (adjective)
37. crimes (for criminals)
38. *Rive . . . continents*: burst open the receptacles that hide you
39. officers who summon to justice
40. *cry . . . grace*: beg mercy from

Some friendship will it lend[41] you 'gainst the tempest;
Repose you there while I to this hard[42] house, —
60   More harder than the stone whereof 'tis rais'd,[43] —
Which even but now, demanding after you,
Denied me to come in,[44] return and force
Their scanted courtesy.

LEAR   My wits begin to turn.
Come on, my boy. How dost, my boy? Art cold?
65   I am cold myself. Where is this straw, my fellow?
The art of our necessities[45] is strange,
That can make vile[46] things precious. Come, your hovel.
Poor fool and knave, I have one part in my heart
That's sorry yet for thee.

70 FOOL   He that has a little tiny wit,
                           With hey, ho, the wind and the rain,
                        Must make content with his fortunes fit,[47]
                           Though the rain it raineth every day.

LEAR   True, my good boy. Come, bring us to this hovel.

                                             [*Exeunt Lear and Kent.*

75 FOOL   This is a brave[48] night to cool a courtezan.
I'll speak a prophecy ere I go:
                   When priests are more in word than matter;[49]
                   When brewers mar their malt with water;
                   When nobles are their tailors' tutors;[50]
80   No heretics burn'd, but wenches' suitors;[51]
                   When every case in law is right;
                   No squire in debt, nor no poor knight;[52]
                   When slanders do not live in tongues;
                   Nor cutpurses come not to throngs;
85   When usurers tell[53] their gold i' the field;
                   And bawds and whores do churches build;
                   Then shall the realm of Albion[54]
                   Come to great confusion:
                   Then comes the time, who lives[55] to see't,
90   That going shall be us'd with feet.[56]
This prophecy Merlin shall make; for I live before his time.   [*Exit.*

41. afford	50. *are . . . tutors*: teach their tailors the
42. cruel	latest fashions
43. built	51. *wenches' suitors*: i.e. lovers burn with
44. *Denied . . . in*: refused me admittance	lust and its results
45. *The art . . . necessities*: necessity is an	52. *no . . . knight*: no knight poor
art, like alchemy, which can change	53. count out
the nature of things	54. England
46. worthless	55. *who lives*: for whoever lives
47. *make . . . fit*: make content fit his for-	56. *going . . . feet*: feet shall be used to walk
tunes, make the best of what he has	on (the lame conclusion is intentional)
48. fine	
49. *more . . . matter*: preach more than they	
practise	

SCENE 3

A Room in Gloucester's Castle.

Enter Gloucester and Edmund.

GLOUCESTER   Alack, alack! Edmund, I like not this unnatural dealing. When
I desired their leave that I might pity[1] him, they took from me the use of
mine own house; charged me, on pain of their perpetual displeasure,
neither to speak of him, entreat for him, nor any way sustain him.

5   EDMUND   Most savage, and unnatural!

GLOUCESTER   Go to;[2] say you nothing. There is division between the dukes,
and a worse matter[3] than that. I have received a letter this night; 'tis dangerous to be spoken; I have locked the letter in my closet. These injuries
the king now bears will be revenged home;[4] there's part of a power[5] already

10   footed;[6] we must incline to[7] the king. I will seek him and privily relieve him;
go you and maintain talk with the duke, that my charity be not of him
perceived. If he ask for me, I am ill and gone to bed. If I die for it, as no
less is threatened me, the king, my old master, must be relieved. There is
some strange thing toward,[8] Edmund; pray you, be careful.   [*Exit.*

15   EDMUND   This courtesy, forbid thee,[9] shall the duke
Instantly know; and of that letter too:
This seems a fair deserving,[10] and must draw me
That which my father loses; no less than all:
The younger rises when the old doth fall.   [*Exit.*

SCENE 4

The Heath. Before a Hovel.

Enter Lear, Kent, and Fool.

KENT   Here[1] is the place, my lord; good my lord, enter:
The tyranny of the open night's[2] too rough
For nature[3] to endure.   [*Storm still.*

LEAR   Let me alone.

KENT   Good my lord, enter here.

LEAR   Wilt break my heart?[4]

---

1. show pity, i.e. relieve (cf. l. 4 "sustain")
2. *Go to*: come!
3. *a worse matter*: the French landing
4. fully (cf. II. i. 49)
5. force
6. see III. i. 32
7. *incline to*: side with
8. imminent

9. *courtesy, . . . thee*: (bit of) kindness
   which was forbidden you
10. that for which one deserves well,
    service
1. see III. ii. 57
2. *the open night*: night in the open
3. human nature, man
4. *Wilt . . . heart*: explained by 23–25

5   KENT I'd rather break mine own. Good my lord, enter.
     LEAR Thou think'st 'tis much that this contentious[5] storm
          Invades us to the skin: so 'tis to thee;
          But where the greater malady is fix'd,
          The lesser is scarce felt. Thou'dst shun a bear;
10   But if thy flight lay toward the roaring sea,
          Thou'dst meet the bear i' the mouth. When the mind's free[6]
          The body's delicate;[7] the tempest in my mind
          Doth from my senses take all feeling else
          Save what beats there.[8] Filial ingratitude!
15   Is it not as[9] this mouth should tear this hand
          For lifting food to 't? But I will punish home:
          No, I will weep no more. In such a night
          To shut me out! Pour on; I will endure.
          In such a night as this! O Regan, Goneril!
20   Your old kind father, whose frank heart gave all,—
          O! that way madness lies; let me shun that;
          No more of that.
     KENT   Good my lord, enter here.
     LEAR Prithee, go in thyself; seek thine own ease:
          This tempest will not give me leave[10] to ponder
25   On things would hurt me more. But I'll go in.
          [To the Fool.] In, boy; go first. You houseless poverty,[11]—
          Nay, get thee in. I'll pray, and then I'll sleep.   [Fool goes in.
          Poor naked wretches, whereso'er you are,
          That bide[12] the pelting of this pitiless storm,
30   How shall your houseless heads and unfed sides,
          Your loop'd and window'd raggedness,[13] defend you
          From seasons such as these? O! I have ta'en
          Too little care of this. Take physic, pomp;
          Expose thyself to feel what wretches feel,
35   That thou mayst shake the superflux[14] to them,
          And show the heavens more just.
     EDGAR [Within.] Fathom and half,[15] fathom and half! Poor Tom![16]
                                    [The Fool runs out from the hovel.
     FOOL Come not in here, nuncle; here's a spirit.
          Help me! help me!
40   KENT Give me thy hand. Who's there?

---

5. quarrelsome, contending with us
6. at ease
7. fastidious (about its comfort)
8. i.e. in the mind (when the thought that throbs is "Filial ingratitude")
9. as if
10. *will . . . leave*: does not leave me free
11. (abstract for concrete)

12. endure
13. *loop'd . . . raggedness*: clothes full of holes (loop = hole)
14. *the superflux*: your superfluity (metaphor from an overladen tree)
15. *Fathom and half*: suggested by the heavy rain
16. *Poor Tom*: cf. II. iii. 20

FOOL   A spirit, a spirit: he says his name's poor Tom.

KENT   What art thou that dost grumble there i' the straw?
Come forth.

Enter Edgar disguised as a madman.

EDGAR   Away! the foul fiend follows me!
45   Through the sharp hawthorn blow the winds.
Hum! go to thy cold bed and warm thee.

LEAR   Didst thou give all to thy two daughters?
And art thou come to this?

EDGAR   Who gives anything to poor Tom? whom the foul fiend hath led through
50   fire and through flame, through ford and whirlpool, o'er bod and quagmire;
that hath laid knives under his pillow, and halters in his pew; set rats-
bane by his porridge; made him proud of heart, to ride on a bay trotting-
horse over four-inched[17] bridges, to course[18] his own shadow for a traitor.
Bless thy five wits! Toms' a-cold. O! do de, do de, do de.[19] Bless thee from
55   whirlwinds, star-blasting,[20] and taking![21] Do poor Tom some charity, whom
the foul fiend vexes. There[22] could I have him now, and there, and there
again, and there.   [*Storm still.*

LEAR   What! have his daughters brought him to this pass?
Couldst thou save nothing? Didst thou give them all?

60   FOOL   Nay, he reserved a blanket, else we had been all shamed.

LEAR   Now all the plagues that in the pendulous[23] air
Hang fated[24] o'er men's faults light on thy daughters!

KENT   He hath no daughters, sir.

LEAR   Death, traitor! nothing could have subdu'd nature
65   To such a lowness, but his unkind[25] daughters.
Is it the fashion that discarded fathers
Should have thus little mercy on their flesh?
Judicious punishment! 'twas this flesh begot
Those pelican daughters.[26]

70   EDGAR   Pillicock[27] sat on Pillicock-hill:
Halloo, halloo, loo, loo![28]

FOOL   This cold night will turn us all to fools and madmen.

EDGAR   Take heed o' the foul fiend. Obey thy parents; keep thy word justly;
swear not; commit[29] not with man's sworn spouse; set not thy sweet heart

17. four inches wide
18. pursue
19. *do . . . de*: represents chattering teeth
    and shivering
20. being struck by the evil influence of
    stars
21. infection (cf. II. iv. 156)
22. as he pretends to feel the devil biting
    some part of his body, perhaps in the
    form of vermin (see 138)

23. hanging over us
24. full of fate
25. unnatural (also suggesting "cruel")
26. pelicans were supposed to feed their
    young on their life-blood
27. darling, pretty knave (the line, adapted
    from an old one, was suggested by
    the word "pelican")
28. properly a cry to encourage hounds
29. sin

75   on proud array. Tom's a-cold.

LEAR   What hast thou been?

EDGAR   A servingman,[30] proud in heart and mind; that curled my hair, wore
        gloves[31] in my cap, served the lust of my mistress's heart, and did the act
        of darkness with her; swore as many oaths as I spake words, and broke
80   them in the sweet face of heaven; one that slept in the contriving of lust,
        and waked to do it. Wine loved I deeply, dice dearly, and in woman out-
        paramoured the Turk:[32] false of heart, light of ear,[33] bloody of hand; hog
        in sloth, fox in stealth, wolf in greediness, dog in madness, lion in prey.
        Let not the creaking of shoes nor the rustling of silks betray thy poor heart
85   to woman: keep thy foot out of brothels, thy hand out of plackets,[34] thy
        pen from lenders'[35] books, and defy the foul fiend. Still through the
        hawthorn blows the cold wind; says suum, mun ha no nonny.[36] Dolphin[37]
        my boy, my boy; sessa![38] let him trot by.   [Storm still.

LEAR   Why, thou wert better in thy grave than to answer[39] with thy uncovered
90   body this extremity of the skies. Is man no more than this? Consider him
        well. Thou[40] owest the worm no silk, the beast no hide, the sheep no
        wool, the cat no perfume. Ha! here's three on's are sophisticated;[41] thou
        art the thing itself; unaccommodated[42] man is no more but such a poor, bare,
        forked animal as thou art. Off, off, you lendings![43] Come; unbutton here.
                                                    [Tearing off his clothes.

95   FOOL   Prithee, nuncle, be contented; 'tis a naughty[44] night to swim in. Now a
        little fire in a wide field were like an old lecher's heart; a small spark, all
        the rest on's body cold. Look! here comes a walking fire.

Enter Gloucester with a torch.

EDGAR   This is the foul fiend Flibbertigibbet: he begins at curfew, and walks
        till the first cock;[45] he gives the web and the pin,[46] squinies[47] the eye, and
100   makes the harelip; mildews the white[48] wheat, and hurts the poor creature
        of earth.[49]

        Swithold[50] footed thrice the old;[51]

30. *either* lover *or* servant
31. as a favour
32. *the Turk*: the Sultan with his many wives
33. *light of ear*: quick to believe evil
34. openings in petticoats or skirts
35. money lenders
36. *suum . . . nonny*: the refrain of a song
37. perhaps addressing an imaginary horse (but Dolphin = Dauphin of France)
38. an interjection of uncertain meaning (perhaps = cessez, stop!, perhaps "off with you")
39. expose yourself to

40. man (in Edgar's state)
41. adulterated, unnatural
42. without the advantages (*Lat.* commoda) of civilization
43. borrowed articles, things not man's own
44. bad
45. *first cock*: cockrow, see *Hamlet* I. i. 147–57
46. *the web . . . pin*: cataract, an eye disease
47. makes it squint
48. ripening
49. *the . . . earth*: mankind
50. St. Withold
51. wold

He met the night-mare,[52] and her nine-fold;[53]
Bid her alight,
105 　　　　And her troth plight,[54]
And aroint thee, witch, aroint[55] thee!

KENT How fares your Grace?

LEAR What's he?[56]

KENT Who's there? What is't you seek?

110 GLOUCESTER What are you there? Your names?

EDGAR Poor Tom; that eats the swimming frog; the toad, the tadpole, the
wall-newt,[57] and the water;[58] that in the fury of his heart, when the foul
fiend rages, eats cow-dung for sallets;[59] swallows the old rat and the
ditch-dog; drinks the green mantle[60] of the standing pool; who is whipped
115 from tithing[61] to tithing, and stock-punished,[62] and imprisoned; who hath
had three suits to his back, six shirts to his body, horse to ride, and weapon
to wear;

But mice and rats and such small deer[63]
Have been Tom's food for seven long year.

120 Beware my follower.[64] Peace, Smulkin! peace, thou fiend.

GLOUCESTER What! hath your Grace no better company?

EDGAR The prince of darkness is a gentleman;
Modo he's call'd, and Mahu.

GLOUCESTER Our flesh and blood,[65] my lord, is grown so vile,
125 That it doth hate what gets[66] it.

EDGAR Poor Tom's a-cold.

GLOUCESTER Go in with me. My duty cannot suffer[67]
To obey in all[68] your daughters' hard commands:
Though their injunction be to bar my doors,
130 And let this tyrannous night take hold upon you,
Yet have I ventur'd to come seek you out
And bring you where both fire and food is ready.

LEAR First let me talk with this philosopher.
What is the cause of thunder?

135 KENT Good my lord, take his offer; go into the house.

LEAR I'll talk a word with this same learned Theban.
What is your study?[69]

EDGAR How to prevent[70] the fiend, and to kill vermin.

52. incubus, demon (*not* female horse)
53. brood
54. *her . . . plight*: give her pledge (not to vex men)
55. begone
56. i.e. Gloucester
57. lizard
58. newt
59. salads
60. covering, screen
61. hamlet (orginally holding *ten* families)
62. punished by being put in the stocks
63. beasts
64. familiar spirit
65. *Our . . . blood*: our children
66. begets
67. submit, agree
68. *in all*: in everything
69. pursuit, brand of learning
70. anticipate, so defeat

LEAR   Let me ask you one word in private.

140   KENT   Importune him once more to go, my lord;
    His wits begin to unsettle.

GLOUCESTER   Canst thou blame him?   [*Storm still.*
    His daughters seek his death. Ah! that good Kent;
    He said it would be thus, poor banish'd man!

145   Thou sayst the king grows mad; I'll tell thee, friend,
    I am almost mad myself. I had a son,
    Now outlaw'd from my blood;[71] he sought my life,
    But lately, very late; I lov'd him, friend,
    No father his son dearer; true to tell thee.   [*Storm continues.*

150   The grief hath craz'd my wits. What a night's this!
    I beseech your Grace, —

LEAR   O! cry you mercy,[72] sir.
    Noble philosopher, your company.

EDGAR   Tom's a-cold.

GLOUCESTER   In, fellow, there, into the hovel: keep thee warm.

LEAR   Come, let's in all.

KENT   This way, my lord.

155   LEAR   With him;
    I will keep still with my philosopher.

KENT   Good my lord, soothe[73] him; let him take the fellow.

GLOUCESTER   Take him you on.

KENT   Sirrah, come on; go along with us.

LEAR   Come, good Athenian.

160   GLOUCESTER   No words, no words: hush.

EDGAR   Child[74] Rowland[75] to the dark tower came,
    His[76] word was still, Fie, foh, and fum,
    I smell the blood of a British man.   [*Exeunt.*

SCENE 5

A Room in Gloucester's Castle.

Enter Cornwall and Edmund.

CORNWALL   I will have my revenge ere I depart his house.

EDMUND   How, my lord, I may be censured, that nature thus gives way to
    loyalty, something fears me to think of.[1]

---

71. *outlaw'd . . . blood*: disinherited
72. *cry you mercy*: (I) beg your pardon
73. humour
74. Sir (title of a young knight)
75. Roland (Charlemagne's hero)

76. the giant's
1. *How . . . of*: i.e. I am rather afraid what
   people will think of me for allowing
   my natural affection to give way to my
   sense of duty

CORNWALL   I now perceive it was not altogether your brother's evil disposition made him seek his[2] death; but a provoking merit, set a-work by a
reproveable badness in himself.[3]

EDMUND   How malicious is my fortune, that I must repent to be just![4] This is
the letter[5] he spoke of, which approves[6] him an intelligent party[7] to the
advantages of France. O heavens! that this treason were not, or not I the
detector!

CORNWALL   Go with me to the duchess.

EDMUND   If the matter of this paper be certain, you have mighty business in
hand.

CORNWALL   True, or false, it hath made thee Earl of Gloucester. Seek out
where thy father is, that he may be ready for our apprehension.[8]

EDMUND   [*Aside*] If I find him comforting[9] the king, it will stuff his suspicion
more fully.[10] I will persever[11] in my course of loyalty, though the conflict
be sore between that and my blood.[12]

CORNWALL   I will lay trust upon thee; and thou shalt find a dearer father in my
love.   [*Exeunt.*

SCENE 6

A Chamber in a Farmhouse adjoining the Castle.

Enter Gloucester, Lear, Kent, Fool, and Edgar.

GLOUCESTER   Here is better than the open air; take it thankfully. I will piece
out[1] the comfort with what addition I can: I will not be long from you.

KENT   All the power of his wits has given way to his impatience. The gods
reward your kindness!   [*Exit Gloucester.*

EDGAR   Fraretto[2] calls me, and tells me Nero is an angler in the lake of darkness. Pray, innocent,[3] and beware the foul fiend.

FOOL   Prithee, nuncle, tell me whether a madman be a gentleman or a yeoman!

LEAR   A king, a king!

FOOL   No; he's a yeoman that has a gentleman to his son;[4] for he's a mad yeoman that sees his son a gentleman before him.

---

2. Gloucester's
3. *a provoking . . . himself*: i.e. (probably) Gloucester's deserts inviting punishment, which, however, was only brought into action by Edgar's own wickedness
4. *to be just*: of being loyal
5. *the letter*: see III. iii. 7
6. proves
7. *intelligent party*: person giving intelligence, informer
8. arrest
9. supporting, strengthening
10. *stuff . . . fully*: make our suspicion of him more justified
11. persevere
12. natural temperament
1. *piece out*: increase
2. an imaginary familiar spirit; so Hop-dance (24–5) (both from Harsnett)
3. simple man
4. *has . . . son*: has his son a gentleman (i.e. a reversal of nature, like your daughters' conduct)

LEAR   To have a thousand with red burning spits[5]
    Come hizzing[6] in upon 'em,—
EDGAR   The foul fiend bites my back.
FOOL   He's mad that trusts in the tameness of a wolf, a horse's health,[7] a boy's
15   love, or a whore's oath.
LEAR   It shall be done; I will arraign them straight.
    [*To Edgar.*]   Come, sit thou here, most learned justicer;[8]
    [*To the Fool.*]   Thou, sapient sir, sit here. Now, you she foxes!
EDGAR   Look, where he[9] stands and glares! wantest thou eyes[10] at trial,
20   madame?[11] Come o'er the bourn,[12] Bessy, to me,—
FOOL   Her boat hath a leak,
    And she must not speak
    Why she dares not come over to thee.
EDGAR   The foul fiend haunts poor Tom in the voice of a nightingale. Hop-
25   dance cries in Tom's belly for two white[13] herring. Croak[14] not, black angel;
    I have no food for thee.
KENT   How do you, sir? Stand you not so amaz'd:[15]
    Will you lie down and rest upon the cushions?
LEAR   I'll see their trial first. Bring in their evidence.[16]
30   [*To Edgar.*]   Thou robed man of justice, take thy place;
    [*To the Fool.*]   And thou, his yoke-fellow of equity,
    Bench by his side. [*To Kent.*]   You are o' the commission,[17]
    Sit you too.
EDGAR   Let us deal justly.

35   Sleepest or wakest thou, jolly shepherd?
              Thy sheep be in the corn;
            And for one blast of thy minikin[18] mouth,[19]
            Thy sheep shall take no harm.[20]

    Purr! The cat[21] is grey.
40 LEAR   Arraign her first; 'tis Goneril. I here take my oath before this honourable
    assembly, she kicked the poor king her father.
FOOL   Come hither, mistress. Is your name Goneril?

5. Lear is brooding over the very course
   he would like to see the Furies take on
   his daughters
6. a variant of "hissing", perhaps in order
   to sound like "whizzing"
7. *a . . . health*: perhaps as described by
   the vendor; or simply as horses are
   delicate animals
8. judge
9. a fiend *or* (possibly) Lear
10. *wantest . . . eyes*: do you want people
   to look at you? *or* can't you see him?
11. Goneril or Regan (present on trial in
   fancy)
12. stream (the line is a fragment of an old
   song)

13. (probably) fresh
14. in the stomach, from hunger
15. dumbfounded
16. *their evidence*: the witnesses against
   them
17. *o' the commission*: commissioned,
   appointed a justice of the peace
18. dainty
19. i.e. while you turn aside to play us a
   tune
20. perhaps ironical, as the sheep would
   harm the corn more than the corn them
21. *the cat*: a "familiar" again, called
   "Purr" (in Harsnett), or Purr may be
   only the sound

LEAR   She cannot deny it.

FOOL   Cry you mercy, I took you for a joint-stool.[22]

45 LEAR   And here's another,[23] whose warp'd[24] looks proclaim
        What store[25] her heart is made on. Stop her there!
        Arms, arms, sword, fire! Corruption in the place!
        False justicer, why hast thou let her 'scape?

EDGAR   Bless thy five wits!

50 KENT   O pity! Sir, where is the patience now
        That you so oft have boasted to retain?

EDGAR   [*Aside.*]   My tears begin to take his part so much,
        They'll mar my counterfeiting.

LEAR   The little dogs and all,

55   Tray, Blanch, and Sweet-heart, see, they bark at me.

EDGAR   Tom will throw his head at them.
        Avaunt, you curs!
            Be thy mouth or black or[26] white,
            Tooth that poisons if it bite;

60   Mastiff, greyhound, mongrel grim,
            Hound or spaniel, brach or lym;[27]
            Or bobtail tike or trundle-tail;[28]
            Tom will make them weep and wail:
            For, with throwing thus my head,

65   Dogs leap the hatch,[29] and all are fled.
        Do de, de, de. Sessa![30] Come, march to wakes and fairs and market-
        towns. Poor Tom, thy horn[31] is dry.

LEAR   Then let them anatomize[32] Regan, see what breeds about her heart. Is
        there any cause in nature that makes these hard hearts? [*To Edgar.*]   You,

70   sir, I entertain[33] you for one of my hundred; only I do not like the fashion
        of your garments: you will say, they are Persian[34] attire; but let them be
        changed.

KENT   Now, good my lord, lie here and rest awhile.

LEAR   Make no noise, make no noise; draw the curtains:[35] so, so, so. We'll go

75   to supper i' the morning: so, so, so.

FOOL   And I'll go to bed at noon.

Re-enter Gloucester.

GLOUCESTER   Come hither, friend: where is the king my master?

---

22. stool made carefully by a joiner (in fact
    Lear took the stool for Goneril)
23. i.e. Regan
24. crooked, perverse
25. material (but probably a corruption,
    perhaps for ''stone,'' since ''store''
    can hardly mean stuff)
26. *or . . . or*: either . . . or
27. a kind of bloodhound

28. long-tailed
29. *leap the hatch*: make a hurried exit
30. *Do de . . . Sessa*: see III. iv. 54 and 88
31. the Bedlam beggar's drinking flask
32. dissect
33. take on
34. proverbial for ''luxurious'' (here ironical)
35. of old-fashioned beds

KENT   Here, sir; but trouble him not, his wits are gone.
GLOUCESTER   Good friend, I prithee, take him in thy arms;
80   I have o'erheard a plot of death upon[36] him.
           There is a litter ready; lay him in 't,
           And drive toward Dover, friend, where thou shalt meet
           Both welcome and protection. Take up thy master:
           If thou shouldst dally half an hour, his life,
85   With thine, and all that offer[37] to defend him,
           Stand in assured loss.[38] Take up, take up;
           And follow me, that will to some provision[39]
           Give thee quick conduct.[40]
     KENT   Oppress'd nature sleeps:
           This rest might yet have balm'd[41] thy broken sinews,[42]
90   Which, if convenience will not allow,[43]
           Stand in hard cure.[44]—[To the Fool.]   Come, help to bear thy master;
           Thou must not stay behind.
     GLOUCESTER   Come, come, away.
           [Exeunt Kent, Gloucester, and the Fool, bearing away Lear.
     EDGAR   When we our betters see bearing our woes,[45]
           We scarcely think our miseries our foes.
95   Who alone[46] suffers suffers most i' the mind,
           Leaving free[47] things and happy shows[48] behind;
           But then the mind much sufferance doth o'erskip,
           When grief hath mates, and bearing[49] fellowship.
           How light and portable[50] my pain seems now,
100   When that which makes me bend makes the king bow;
           He childed as I father'd:[51] Tom, away!
           Mark the high noises,[52] and thyself bewray[53]
           When false opinion,[54] whose wrong thought defiles thee,
           In thy just proof[55] repeals[56] and reconciles[57] thee.
105   What will hap[58] more to-night, safe 'scape the king!
           Lurk, lurk.[59]   [Exit.

36. against
37. presume, dare
38. Stand . . . loss: are certain to be lost
39. some provision: something provided (1. 81)
40. guidance
41. healed like a balm
42. broken sinews: racked nerves
43. if . . . allow: unless circumstances are favourable
44. Stand . . . cure: are hardly likely to be cured
45. our woes: the same trouble as we have
46. emphasize alone
47. carefree, free from distress
48. sights
49. when suffering (has)
50. easy to bear
51. childed . . . father'd: treated by his children as I by my father
52. high noises: disturbances in the state, in high quarters
53. thyself bewray: only reveal who you really are
54. false opinion: wrong suspicions (felt about you)
55. In . . . proof: when your character is vindicated
56. recalls you (from banishment)
57. restores you to your position and reconciles you to your father
58. What . . . hap: whatever happens
59. hide yourself, lie low

SCENE 7

A Room in Gloucester's Castle.

Enter Cornwall, Regan, Goneril, Edmund, and Servants.

CORNWALL   Post speedily to my lord your husband; show him this letter: the
army of France is landed. Seek out the traitor Gloucester.

[*Exeunt some of the Servants.*

REGAN   Hang him instantly.

GONERIL   Pluck out his eyes.

5   CORNWALL   Leave him to my displeasure. Edmund, keep you our sister company: the revenges we are bound to take upon your traitorous father are
not fit for your beholding. Advise the duke, where you are going, to a
most festinate[1] preparation: we are bound to[2] the like. Our posts[3] shall be
swift and intelligent[4] betwixt us. Farewell, dear sister: farewell, my Lord
10   of Gloucester.[5]

Enter Oswald

How now? Where's the king?

OSWALD   My Lord of Gloucester hath convey'd him hence:
Some five or six and thirty of his knights,
Hot questrists[6] after him, met him at gate;
15   Who, with some other of the lord's dependants,
Are gone with him toward Dover, where they boast
To have well-armed friends.

CORNWALL   Get horses for your mistress.

GONERIL   Farewell, sweet lord, and sister.

CORNWALL   Edmund, farewell.   [*Exeunt Goneril, Edmund, and Oswald.*
Go seek the traitor Gloucester,
20   Pinion him like a thief, bring him before us.   [*Exeunt other Servants.*
Though well we may not pass upon[7] his life
Without the form of justice, yet our power
Shall do a courtesy to[8] our wrath, which men
May blame but not control. Who's there?
25   The traitor?

Re-enter Servants, with Gloucester.

REGAN   Ingrateful fox! 'tis he.

1. speedy
2. *bound to*: purposed to, proposing (so
also, probably in 6)
3. messengers
4. bringing good information

5. see III. v. 14–15
6. seekers (*Lat.* quaero)
7. *pass* (sentence) *upon*
8. *do . . . to*: bow before, give way to

CORNWALL   Bind fast his corky[9] arms.

GLOUCESTER   What mean your Graces? Good my friends, consider
   You are my guests: do me no foul play, friends.

CORNWALL   Bind him, I say.   [*Servants bind him.*

30 REGAN   Hard, hard. O filthy[10] traitor!

GLOUCESTER   Unmerciful lady as your are, I'm none.

CORNWALL   To this chair bind him. Villain, thou shalt find—
                                                  [*Regan plucks his beard.*

GLOUCESTER   By the kind gods, 'tis most ignobly done
   To pluck me by the beard.

REGAN   So white, and such a traitor!

35 GLOUCESTER   Naughty[11] lady,
   These hairs, which thou dost ravish from my chin,
   Will quicken,[12] and accuse thee: I am your host:
   With robbers' hands my hospitable favours[13]
   You should not ruffle[14] thus. What will you do?

40 CORNWALL   Come, sir, what letters had you late[15] from France?

REGAN   Be simple-answer'd,[16] for we know the truth.

CORNWALL   And what confederacy have you with the traitors
   Late footed[17] in the kingdom?

REGAN   To whose hands have you sent the lunatic king?

45   Speak.

GLOUCESTER   I have a letter guessingly set down,[18]
   Which came from one that's of a neutral heart,
   And not from one oppos'd.

CORNWALL   Cunning.

REGAN   And false.

CORNWALL   Where hast thou sent the king?

GLOUCESTER   To Dover.

50 REGAN   Wherefore, to Dover? Wast thou not charg'd at peril—

CORNWALL   Wherefore to Dover? Let him answer that.

GLOUCESTER   I am tied to the stake, and I must stand the course.[19]

REGAN   Wherefore to Dover?

GLOUCESTER   Because I would not see thy cruel nails

55   Pluck out his poor old eyes; nor thy fierce sister
   In his anointed[20] flesh stick boarish fangs.
   The sea, with such a storm as his bare head

---

9. dry (as he is old)
10. beastly, disgraceful
11. wicked (not then a childish word)
12. come to life
13. *my . . . favours*: the features of me, your host
14. disturb, violate (cf. II. iv. 295, where, however, it was intransitive)

15. lately
16. *Be simple-answer'd*: answer straight-forwardly
17. see III. i. 32
18. *guessingly set down*: written from conjecture, not knowledge
19. attack of the dogs in bear-baiting
20. royal

In hell-black night endur'd, would have bouy'd up,[21]
And quench'd the stelled[22] fires;
60   Yet, poor old heart, he holp[23] the heavens to rain.
If wolves had at thy gate howl'd that dern[24] time,
Thou shouldst have said, 'Good porter, turn the key,'[25]
All cruels else[26] subscrib'd:[27] but I shall see
The winged vengeance[28] overtake such children.
65   CORNWALL   See't shalt thou never. Fellows, hold the chair.
Upon these eyes of thine I'll set my foot.
GLOUCESTER   He that will think to live till he be old,
Give me some help! O cruel! O ye gods!   [Gloucester's eye put out.
REGAN   One side will mock another; the other too.[29]
CORNWALL   If you see vengeance—
70   FIRST SERVANT   Hold your hand, my lord:
I have serv'd you ever since I was a child,
But better service have I never done you
Than now to bid you hold.
REGAN   How now, you dog!
FIRST SERVANT   If you did wear a beard upon your chin,
75   I'd shake it[30] on this quarrel. What do you mean?
CORNWALL   My villain![31]   [Draws.
FIRST SERVANT   Nay then, come on, and take the chance of anger.[32]
                    [Draws. They fight. Cornwall is wounded.
REGAN   Give me thy sword. A peasant stand up thus!
                    [Takes a sword and runs at him behind.
FIRST SERVANT   O! I am slain. My lord, you have one eye left
80   To see some mischief on him.[33] O!   [Dies.
CORNWALL   Lest it see more, prevent it.[34] Out, vile jelly!
Where is thy lustre now?
GLOUCESTER   All dark and comfortless. Where's my son Edmund?
Edmund, enkindle all the sparks of nature
To quit[35] this horrid act.
85   REGAN   Out, treacherous villain!
Thou call'st on him that hates thee; it was he
That made the overture[36] of thy treasons to us,

21. risen up, like a buoy
22. *either* starry *or* (more probably) fixed (Middle Eng. stellen = fix), or part of both
23. encouraged (lit. helped)
24. dreary, dread
25. *turn the key*: i.e. admit them
26. *All . . . else*: all other cruel things (except the storm)
27. being admitted
28. *winged vengeance*: vengeance of heaven (as in Jove's arrows)
29. *the other* (eye) *too*
30. *shake it*: i.e. challenge you to fight
31. serf (perhaps also in modern sense as in l. 94)
32. *take . . . anger*: take the chance result where anger, not skill, directs the weapons
33. Cornwall
34. *Lest . . . prevent it*: prevent it from seeing more
35. requite, avenge
36. disclosure

Who is too good to pity thee.

GLOUCESTER   O my follies! Then Edgar was abus'd.[37]

90   Kind gods, forgive me that, and prosper him!

REGAN   Go thrust him out at gates, and let him smell

His way to Dover. [*Exit one with Gloucester.*]

How is't, my lord? How look you?[38]

CORNWALL   I have receiv'd a hurt. Follow me, lady.

Turn out that eyeless villain; throw this slave

95   Upon the dunghill. Regan, I bleed apace:

Untimely comes this hurt. Give me your arm.

[*Exit Cornwall led by Regan.*

SECOND SERVANT   I'll never care what wickedness I do

If this man come to good.

THIRD SERVANT   If she live long,

And, in the end, meet the old[39] course of death,

100   Women will all turn monsters.

SECOND SERVANT   Let's follow the old earl, and get the Bedlam

To lead him where he would:[40] his roguish madness.

Allows itself to any thing.[41]

THIRD SERVANT   Go thou; I'll fetch some flax, and whites of eggs,

105   To apply to his bleeding face. Now, heaven help him!

[*Exeunt severally.*

37. deceived
38. *How look you?*: What do you appear
    like (almost) How do you feel?
39. usual, ordinary
40. like to be led

41. *his . . . any thing*: as he (the Bedlamite,
    Edgar) is a mad vagrant he will lend
    himself to anything, go anywhere he
    is asked, *or* his madness affords him
    licence to do what he likes

ACT IV

SCENE 1

The Heath.

Enter Edgar.

EDGAR   Yet better thus,[1] and known to be contemn'd,[2]

Than still[3] contemn'd and flatter'd. To be worst,

The lowest and most dejected thing of fortune,[4]

1. *Yet* (it is better to be) *thus*
2. *known . . . contemn'd*: known to yourself to be, conscious of being despised

3. all the same
4. *most . . . fortune*: the thing (i.e. creature) cast down lowest by fortune

Stands still in esperance,[5] lives not in fear:
5   The lamentable change is from the best;
The worst returns to laughter.[6] Welcome, then,
Thou unsubstantial air that I embrace:
The wretch that thou hast blown unto the worst
Owes nothing[7] to thy blasts. But who comes here?

Enter Gloucester, led by an old Man.

10   My father, poorly led?[8] World, world, O world!
But that[9] thy strange mutations make us hate thee,
Life would not yield to age.[10]
OLD MAN   O my good lord!
I have been your tenant, and your father's tenant,
These fourscore years.
15   GLOUCESTER   Away, get thee away; good friend, be gone;
Thy comforts can do me no good at all;
Thee they may hurt.
OLD MAN   You cannot see your way.
GLOUCESTER   I have no way, and therefore want no eyes;
I stumbled when I saw. Full oft 'tis seen,
20   Our means secure us,[11] and our mere defects
Prove our commodities.[12] Ah! dear son Edgar,
The food[13] of thy abused[14] father's wrath;
Might I but live to see thee in my touch,
I'd say I had eyes again.[15]
OLD MAN   How now! Who's there?
25   EDGAR   [*Aside*]   O gods! Who is't can say, "I am at the worst?"
I am worse than e'er I was.
OLD MAN   'Tis poor mad Tom.
EDGAR   [*Aside.*]   And worse I may be yet; the worst is not,
So long as we can say, "This is the worst."
OLD MAN   Fellow, where goest?
GLOUCESTER   Is it a beggar-man?
30   OLD MAN   Madman and beggar too.
GLOUCESTER   He has some reason,[16] else he could not beg.

---

5. *Stands . . . esperance*: puts you in a situation of permanent hopefulness
6. *returns to laughter*: may yet see you happy again
7. *Owes . . . to*: has paid his full debt to, and has therefore nothing more to fear from
8. *poorly led*: led by a poor man
9. *But that*: if it were not that
10. *Life . . . age*: we should not be reconciled to old age and death
11. *Our . . . us*: our resources make us careless (Lat. *securus*)
12. *our mere . . . commodities*: it is precisely our weaknesses that turn out to our advantage
13. object
14. misled
15. *I'd . . . again*: i.e. it would be as good as recovering my sight
16. *He . . . reason*: he's not quite mad

I' the last night's storm I such a fellow saw,
Which made me think a man a worm: my son[17]
Came then into my mind; and yet my mind
35   Was then scarce friends with him: I have heard more[18] since.
As flies to wanton[19] boys, are we to the gods;
They kill us for their sport.

EDGAR   [*Aside.*] How should this be?[20]
Bad is the trade that must play fool to sorrow,[21]
Angering itself and others.—[*To Gloucester.*]
40   Bless thee, master!

GLOUCESTER Is that the naked fellow?

OLD MAN   Ay, my lord.

GLOUCESTER Then, prithee, get thee gone. If, for my sake,
Thou wilt o'ertake us, hence a mile or twain,
I' the way toward Dover, do it for ancient love;
45   And bring some covering for this naked soul
Who I'll entreat to lead me.

OLD MAN   Alack, sir! he is mad.

GLOUCESTER 'Tis the times' plague,[22] when madmen lead the blind.
Do as I bid thee, or rather do thy pleasure;
Above the rest,[23] be gone.

50 OLD MAN I'll bring him the best 'parel[24] that I have,
Come on't[25] what will.   [*Exit.*

GLOUCESTER Sirrah, naked fellow,—

EDGAR Poor Tom's a-cold. [*Aside.*] I cannot daub it[26] further.

GLOUCESTER Come hither, fellow.

55 EDGAR [*Aside.*] And yet I must. Bless thy sweet eyes, they bleed.

GLOUCESTER Know'st thou the way to Dover?

EDGAR Both stile and gate, horse-way and footpath. Poor Tom hath been
scared out of his good wits: bless thee, good man's son, from[27] the foul
fiend! Five fiends have been in poor Tom at once; of lust, as Obidicut;
60 Hobbididance, prince of dumbness; Mahu, of stealing; Modo, of murder;
and Flibbertigibbet, of mopping and mowing;[28] who since possesses
chambermaids and waiting-women. So, bless thee, master!

GLOUCESTER Here, take this purse, thou whom the heavens' plagues
Have humbled to[29] all strokes: that I am wretched
65 Makes thee the happier: heavens, deal so still!

---

17. *my son*: see III. iv. 146
18. viz. III. vii. 86–8
19. playful
20. *How . . . be?*: probably refers to second
    half of 35
21. i.e. it's a bad job when we have to
    pretend to folly in the presence of
    sorrow (as I am now doing)
22. *'Tis . . . plague*: the world's in a bad
    way

23. *Above the rest*: above all things
24. apparel
25. *on't*: of it
26. *daub it*: dissemble, pretend (lit. cover
    up with plaster)
27. *bless . . . from*: God preserve thee from
28. *mopping and mowing*: grimacing, mak-
    ing faces (Fr. *moue*)
29. *humbled to*: humbled into bearing

Let the superfluous[30] and lust-dieted[31] man,
That slaves your ordinance,[32] that will not see
Because he doth not feel,[33] feel your power quickly;
So distribution should undo excess,
70   And each man have enough. Dost thou know Dover?
EDGAR   Ay, master.
GLOUCESTER   There is a cliff, whose high and bending[34] head
Looks fearfully[35] in[36] the confined[37] deep;
Bring me but to the very brim of it,
75   And I'll repair the misery thou dost bear
With something rich about me; from that place
I shall no leading need.
EDGAR   Give me thy arm:
Poor Tom shall lead thee.   [*Exeunt.*

SCENE 2

Before the Duke of Albany's Palace.

Enter Goneril and Edmund.

GONERIL   Welcome,[1] my lord; I marvel our mild[2] husband
Not met[3] us on the way. [*Enter Oswald.*]   Now, where's your master?
OSWALD   Madam, within; but never man so chang'd.
I told him of the army that was landed;
5   He smil'd at it: I told him you were coming;
His answer was, "The worse:" of Gloucester's treachery.
And of the loyal service of his son,
When I inform'd him, then he call'd me sot,[4]
And told me I had turn'd the wrong side out:[5]
10   What most he should dislike seems pleasant to him;
What like, offensive.[6]
GONERIL   [*To Edmund.*]   Then, shall you go no further.
It is the cowish[7] terror of his spirit.
That dares not undertake;[8] he'll not feel wrongs

30. having more than he needs (cf. II. iv. 259), spoilt
31. gluttonous or (perhaps) indulgent to his sexual appetite (cf. III. iv. 79 and 81)
32. *salves . . . ordinance*: makes your commands his slaves, enslaves them (esp. the command to charity)
33. (sympathy for others)
34. overhanging
35. frighteningly
36. into

37. bounded by it
1. to our house (see III. vii. 1–7 for their journey together)
2. sarcastic, cf. 12
3. *Not met*: did not meet (so in 53)
4. fool (*not* drunkard)
5. *turn'd . . . out*: got things inside out, inverted right and wrong
6. *What* (he should like, seems) *offensive*
7. cowardly (cf. 50 below and I. iv. 308 "milky gentleness")
8. venture take up enterprises

Which tie him to[9] an answer. Our wishes on the way
15 May prove effects.[10] Back, Edmund, to my brother;[11]
Hasten his musters and conduct his powers:[12]
I must change arms[13] at home, and give the distaff
Into my husband's hands. This trusty servant
Shall pass between us; ere long you are like to hear,
20 If you dare venture in your own behalf,
A mistress's command. Wear this; spare speech;   [*Giving a favour.*
Decline[14] your head: this kiss, if it durst speak,
Would stretch thy spirits up into the air.
Conceive,[15] and fare thee well.
EDMUND   Yours in the ranks of death.
25 GONERIL   My most dear Gloucester!
                                              [*Exit Edmund.*

O! the difference of man and man!
To thee a woman's services are due:
My fool[16] usurps my bed.
OSWALD   Madam, here comes my lord   [*Exit.*

Enter Albany.

GONERIL   I have been worth the whistle.[17]
ALBANY   O Goneril!
30 You are not worth the dust which the rude wind
Blows in your face. I fear[18] your disposition:
That nature, which contemns its origin,
Cannot be border'd certain[19] in itself;
She that herself will sliver[20] and disbranch
35 From her material[21] sap, perforce must wither
And come to deadly use.[22]
GONERIL   No more; the text[23] is foolish.
ALBANY   Wisdom and goodness to the vile seem vile;
Filths savour but themselves.[24] What have you done?
40 Tigers, not daughters, what have you perform'd?

9. *tie him to*: demand, require
10. *Our . . . effects*: What we wished for may be realized (ie. that you should replace him)
11. (-in-law) Cornwall
12. *conduct his powers*: lead his forces
13. *change arms*: i.e. take in exchange (for the distaff) his warlike weapons
14. put down (for a kiss)
15. take my meaning
16. *My fool*: My husband who is a fool
17. *worth the whistle*: worth something to you (cf. proverb "It's a poor dog that is not worth the whistling")

18. fear for (what it may lead to)
19. *border'd certain*: contained within fixed bounds, trusted not to break the limits (of right)
20. tear off (as a twig from a branch)
21. forming the substance of a thing, essential
22. *deadly use*: come to a bad end, the only use for dead wood is burning
23. subject of your moral (cf. 58) discourse, sermons
24. *Filths . . . themselves*: filthy creatures enjoy only things that are filthy

A father, and a gracious aged man,
Whose reverence the head-lugg'd[25] bear would lick,[26]
Most barbarous, most degenerate! have you madded.[27]
Could my good brother suffer you to do it?
45   A man, a prince, by him[28] so benefited!
If that the heavens do not their visible[29] spirits
Send quickly down to tame these vile offences,[30]
It[31] will come,
Humanity must perforce prey on itself,
Like monsters of the deep.

50   GONERIL   Milk-liver'd[32] man!
That bear'st a cheek for blows, a head for wrongs;[33]
Who hast not in thy brows an eye discerning
Thine honour from thy suffering;[34] that not know'st
Fools do those villains[35] pity who are punish'd
55   Ere they have done their mischief. Where's thy drum?
France spreads his banners in our noiseless[36] land,
With plumed helm thy slayer begins threats,[37]
Whilst thou, a moral[38] fool, sitt'st still, and criest
"Alack! why does he so?"

ALBANY   See thyself, devil!
60   Proper[39] deformity seems not in the fiend
So horrid as in woman.

GONERIL   O vain fool!

ALBANY   Thou changed and self-cover'd[40] thing, for shame,
Be-monster not thy feature.[41] Were't my fitness[42]
To let these hands obey my blood,[43]
65   They are apt[44] enough to dislocate and tear
Thy flesh and bones; howe'er[45] thou art a fiend,
A woman's shape doth shield thee.

GONERIL   Marry, your manhood.—Mew![46]

---

25. tugged about by the head ("by the nose" in Harsnett!)
26. *Whose . . . lick*: i.e. whose grey hairs even a beast would respect
27. maddened
28. Lear
29. in visible form
30. offenders
31. punishment
32. cowardly (cf. "the liver white and pale, which is the badge of pusillanimity and cowardice," *2 Henry IV*, IV. iii. 103)
33. *That . . . wrongs*: i.e. you are the sort of man to "turn the other cheek" (Matthew v. 39)
34. *discerning . . . suffering*: able to distinguish between what your honour can let you endure and what it cannot
35. *those villains*: in the case (probably) Lear
36. with no sound of drums or other preparations for war
37. *state . . . threat*: begins to threaten thy power, position
38. moralizing
39. which belongs to him (rightly)
40. veiling thy true (devilish) self
41. appearance
42. *my fitness*: befitting me
43. *my blood*: my instinct
44. ready
45. although
46. pooh! A fig for it

Enter a Messenger.

ALBANY   What news?

70   MESSENGER   O! my good lord, the Duke of Cornwall's dead;
      Slain by his servant, going to put out
      The other eye of Gloucester.

ALBANY   Gloucester's eyes!

MESSENGER   A servant that he bred, thrill'd[47] with remorse,[48]
      Oppos'd against the act, bending[49] his sword
75   To[50] his great master; who, thereat enrag'd.
      Flew on him, and amongst them[51] fell'd him dead;
      But not without that harmful stroke, which since
      Hath pluck'd him after.[52]

ALBANY   This shows you are above,
      You justicers,[53] that these our nether[54] crimes
80   So speedily can venge! But, O poor Gloucester!
      Lost he his other eye?

MESSENGER   Both, both, my lord.
      This letter, madam, craves a speedy answer;
      'Tis from your sister.

GONERIL   [*Aside.*]   One way I like this well;
      But being widow, and my Gloucester with her,[55]
85   May all the building in my fancy pluck
      Upon my hateful life:[56] another way,[57]
      This news is not so tart.[58] [*To Messenger.*]   I'll read and answer.   [*Exit.*]

ALBANY   Where was his son when they did take his eyes?

MESSENGER   Come with my lady hither.

ALBANY   He is not here.

90   MESSENGER   No, my good lord; I met him back[59] again.

ALBANY   Knows he the wickedness?

MESSENGER   Ay, my good lord; 'twas he inform'd against him.
      And quit the house on purpose that their punishment
      Might have the freer course.

ALBANY   Gloucester, I live

---

47. excited
48. pity (as often)
49. directing
50. against
51. *amongst them*: between them they (he and Regan)
52. *pluck'd him after*: snatched away him too (to death)
53. judges (as in III. vi. 17, where it was a conjecture)
54. committee on earth (the *lower* world as opposed to heaven)

55. *But . . . her*: i.e. the fact that Regan is a widow and Gloucester, whom I desire, is with her
56. *May . . . life*: i.e. may pull down all my fine schemes and so make my life hateful to me
57. *another way*: the "one way" cf. 83. Goneril sees a chance of the whole kingdom
58. bitter
59. going back (Edmund had only escorted Goneril home)

95   To thank thee for the love thou show'dst the king,
       And to revenge thine eyes. Come hither, friend:
       Tell me what more thou knowest.   [*Exeunt.*

SCENE 3

The French Camp, near Dover.

Enter Kent and a Gentleman.

KENT   Why the King of France is so suddenly gone back know you the reason?
GENTLEMAN   Something he left imperfect in the state, which since his coming
       forth is thought of; which imports[1] to the kingdom so much fear and
       danger, that his personal return was most required and necessary.
5   KENT   Who hath he left behind him general?
GENTLEMAN   The Marshal of France, Monsieur la Far.
KENT   Did your letters pierce[2] the queen to any demonstration of grief?
GENTLEMAN   Ay, sir; she took them, read them in my presence;
       And now and then an ample tear trill'd down
10   Her delicate cheek; it seem'd she was a queen
       Over her passion;[3] who,[4] most rebel-like,
       Sought to be king o'er her.
KENT   O! then it mov'd her.
GENTLEMAN   Not to a rage; patience and sorrow strove
       Who should express her goodliest.[5] You have seen
15   Sunshine and rain at once; her smiles and tears
       Were like a better way;[6] those happy smilets
       That play'd on her ripe lip seem'd not to know
       What guests were in her eyes; which[7] parted thence.
       As pearls from diamonds[8] dropp'd. In brief,
20   Sorrow would be a rarity most belov'd
       If all could so become[9] it.
KENT   Made she no verbal question?[10]
GENTLEMAN   Faith, once or twice she heav'd the name of 'father'
       Pantingly forth, as if it press'd her heart;
       Cried, ''Sisters! sisters! Shame of ladies! sisters!

---

1. involves, carries, with it
2. wound, excite
3. emotion (*not* anger)
4. which
5. *Who . . . goodliest*: as to which should
   become her best
6. *like . . . way*: like that (sunshine and
   rain together), only better (a comma
   could be inserted after ''like'')

7. the guest, i.e. tears
8. her eyes
9. suit
10. *Made . . . question?*: Didn't she *say*
    anything?

25   Kent! father! sisters! What, i' the storm? i' the night?
    Let pity not be believed!''[11] There she shook
    The holy water from her heavenly eyes,
    And clamour-moisten'd,[12] then away she started
    To deal with grief alone.
  KENT   It is the stars,
30   The stars above us, govern our conditions;[13]
    Else one self mate and make[14] could not beget
    Such different issues. You spoke not with her since?
  GENTLEMAN No.
  KENT Was this before the king[15] return'd?
  GENTLEMAN   No, since.
35 KENT Well, sir, the poor distress'd Lear's i' the town,
    Who sometime,[16] in his better tune,[17] remembers
    What we are come about, and by no means
    Will yield[18] to see his daughter.
  GENTLEMAN   Why, good sir?
  KENT A sovereign[19] shame so elbows him:[20] his own unkindness,
40   That stripp'd her from his benediction, turn'd her
    To foreign casualties,[21] gave her dear rights
    To his dog-hearted daughters,—these things sting
    His mind so venemously that burning shame
    Detains him from Cordelia.
  GENTLEMAN   Alack! poor gentleman.
45 KENT Of Albany's and Cornwall's powers[22] you heard not?
  GENTLEMAN 'Tis so,[23] they are afoot.
  KENT Well, sir, I'll bring you to our master Lear,
    And leave you to attend him. Some dear cause[24]
    Will in concealment wrap me up awhile;
50   When I am known aright, you shall not grieve
    Lending me this acquaintance.[25] I pray you, go
    Along with me.   [*Exeunt.*

---

11. to exist, if people can do such things (but "not believe it" is a likely reading)
12. having her outburst, emotion, calmed by a flood of tears
13. character
14. *one . . . make*: the same husband and wife ("make" comes from a root meaning "equal")
15. *the king* (of France)
16. *sometime*(s)
17. *better tune*: saner moments
18. agree

19. (1) all-powerful, but also (2) worthy of a king
20. *elbows him*: pushes him away (from her)
21. *foreign casualties*: the chances of life abroad
22. forces
23. *'Tis so*: it is true that
24. *dear cause*: important reason (cf. III. i. 19)
25. *Lending . . . acquaintance*: for having got to know me

SCENE 4

The Same. A Tent.

Enter with drum and colours, Cordelia, Doctor, and Soldiers.

CORDELIA   Alack! 'tis he: why, he was met even now
    As mad as the vex'd[1] sea; singing aloud;
    Crown'd with rank[2] fumiter[3] and furrow weeds,[4]
    With burdocks, hemlock, nettles, cuckoo-flowers.[5]
5   Darnel, and all the idle weeds that grow
    In our sustaining[6] corn. A century[7] send forth;
    Search every acre in the high-grown field.
    And bring him to our eye.   *[Exit an Officer.*
                 What can[8] man's wisdom
    In the restoring his bereaved[9] sense?
10   He that helps[10] him take all my outward worth.[11]
DOCTOR   There is means, madam;
    Our foster-nurse of nature[12] is repose,
    The which he lacks; that to provoke[13] in him,
    Are many simples operative,[14] whose power
    Will close the eye of anguish.
15 CORDELIA   All bless'd secrets,
    All you unpublish'd virtues[15] of the earth,
    Spring with[16] my tears! be aidant and remediate[17]
    In the good man's distress! Seek, seek for him,
    Lest his ungovern'd rage dissolve the life
    That wants the means to lead it.[18]

Enter a Messenger.

20 MESSENGER   News, madam;
    The British powers are marching hitherward.
CORDELIA   'Tis known before; our preparation stands
    In expectation of them. O dear father!
    It is thy business that I go about;

1. stirred up (by winds)
2. luxuriant
3. fumitory
4. *furrow weeds*: weeds which grow in ploughed land
5. (uncertain)
6. life-giving
7. a hundred men
8. knows, can do
9. lost
10. heals

11. *outward worth*: possessions
12. *Our . . . nature*: the foster-nurse of our nature
13. induce
14. *simples operative*: effective (medicinal) plants
15. properties, (healing) powers
16. *Spring with*: spring up watered by
17. remedial
18. *That . . . it*: i.e. which lacks the power (sanity) to control it(self)

25   Therefore great France[19]
        My mourning and important[20] tears hath pitied,
        No blown[21] ambition doth our arms incite,
        But love, dear love, and our ag'd father's right,
        Soon may I hear and see him!   [*Exeunt.*

SCENE 5

A Room in Gloucester's Castle.

Enter Regan and Oswald.

REGAN But are my brother's[1] powers set forth?
OSWALD   Ay, madam.
REGAN Himself in person there?
OSWALD   Madam, with much ado:[2]
        Your sister is the better soldier.
REGAN Lord Edmund spake not with your lord at home?
5 OSWALD No, madam.
REGAN What might import[3] my sister's letter to him?
OSWALD I know not, lady.
REGAN Faith, he is posted hence on serious matter.
        It was great ignorance,[4] Gloucester's eyes being out,
10   To let him live; where he arrives he moves
        All hearts against us. Edmund I think, is gone,
        In pity of his misery, to dispatch
        His nighted[5] life; moreover, to descry
        The strength o' the enemy.
15 OSWALD I must needs after him, madam, with my letter.
REGAN Our troops set forth to-morrow; stay with us,
        The ways are dangerous.
OSWALD   I may not, madam;
        My lady charg'd my duty[6] in this business.
REGAN Why should she write to Edmund? Might not you
20   Transport her purposes by word? Belike,[7]
        Something—I know not what. I'll love thee much,
        Let me unseal the letter.
OSWALD   Madam, I had rather[8]—

19. the king of France
20. importunate, urgent
21. proud
1. *brother*(-in-law)'s
2. *with much ado*: i.e. Goneril had great difficulty in getting Albany to take up arms in a bad cause
3. signify
4. folly
5. darkened, blinded
6. *charg'd my duty*: invoked my sense of duty to her (to deliver the letter at once)
7. probably
8. *I had rather*—: s.d. refusing the letter (Johnson)

REGAN   I know your lady does not love her husband;
        I am sure of that: and at her late being here
25   She gave strange œilliades⁹ and most speaking¹⁰ looks
        To noble Edmund. I know you are of her bosom.¹¹
OSWALD I, madam!
REGAN   I speak in understanding; you are, I know't:
        Therefore I do advise you, take this note:¹²
30   My lord is dead; Edmund and I have talk'd,¹³
        And more convenient is he for my hand
        Than for your lady's. You may gather¹⁴ more.
        If you do find him, pray you, give him this,¹⁵
        And when your mistress hears thus much from you,
35   I pray desire her call her wisdom to her:¹⁶
        So, fare you well.
        If you do chance to hear of that blind traitor,
        Preferment falls on him that cuts him off.¹⁷
OSWALD Would I could meet him, madam: I would show
        What party I do follow.
40   REGAN   Fare thee well. [Exeunt.

SCENE 6

The Country near Dover.

Enter Gloucester, and Edgar dressed like a peasant.

GLOUCESTER   When shall I come to the top of that same hill?¹
EDGAR   You do climb up it now; look how we labour.
GLOUCESTER   Methinks the ground is even.
EDGAR   Horrible steep:
        Hark! do you hear the sea?
GLOUCESTER   No truly.
5   EDGAR   Why, then your other senses grow imperfect
        By your eyes' anguish.
GLOUCESTER   So may it be, indeed.
        Methinks thy voice is alter'd, and thou speak'st
        In better phrase and matter than thou didst.
EDGAR   Y'are much deceiv'd; in nothing am I chang'd
        But in my garments.

---

9. glad eyes
10. eloquent of her wishes
11. *of her bosom*: trusted by her
12. *take this note*: (probably) take note of
    this
13. come to an understanding
14. infer

15. a token *or* letter
16. *call her . . . her*: show some sense (re-
    member she has a husband)
17. *Preferment . . . off*: i.e. you will be pro-
    moted if you kill him
1. *that same hill*: see IV. i. 72

10   GLOUCESTER   Methinks you're better spoken.
    EDGAR   Come on, sir; here's the place: stand still.
        How fearful
        And dizzy 'tis to cast one's eyes so low!
        The crows and choughs[2] that wing the midway air
15   Show scarce so gross[3] as beetles; half way down
        Hangs one that gathers samphire,[4] dreadful trade!
        Methinks he seems no bigger than his head.
        The fishermen that walk upon the beach
        Appear like mice, and yond tall anchoring bark
20   Diminish'd to her cock,[5] her cock a buoy
        Almost too small for sight. The murmuring surge,
        That on the unnumber'd[6] idle[7] pebbles[8] chafes,
        Cannot be heard so high. I'll look no more,
        Lest my brain turn, and the deficient sight[9]
        Topple down headlong.
25   GLOUCESTER   Set me where you stand.
    EDGAR   Give me your hand; you are now within a foot
        Of the extreme verge: for all beneath the moon
        Would I not leap upright.[10]
    GLOUCESTER   Let go my hand.
        Here, friend, 's another purse;[11] in it a jewel
30   Well worth a poor man's taking: fairies and gods
        Prosper it with thee![12] Go thou further off;
        Bid me farewell, and let me hear thee going.
    EDGAR   Now fare you well, good sir.
    GLOUCESTER   With all my heart.
    EDGAR   Why I do trifle thus with his despair
        Is done to cure it.[13]
35   GLOUCESTER   O you mighty gods!
        This world I do renounce, and, in your sights,
        Shake patiently my great affliction off;
        If I could bear it longer, and not fall
        To quarrel with[14] your great opposeless[15] wills,
40   My snuff and loathed part of nature should

2. still a cliff bird in Cornwall
3. large
4. a herb used for pickles
5. cock-boat, ship's boat
6. innumerable
7. moved to no purpose
8. (used as plural)
9. *the . . . sight*: I, through failing sight
10. *leap upright*: he is so near the edge that
    even such a movement would be fatal

11. *another purse*: see IV. i. 63
12. *Prosper . . . thee*: make the purse lucky
    for you (perhaps a reference to a belief
    that fairies multiplied treasure trove)
13. *Why . . . it*: i.e. The object of my trifling
    . . . is to cure it (a mixture of con-
    structions)
14. *quarrel with*: rebel against
15. irresistible

Burn itself out.[16] If Edgar live, O, bless him!
Now fellow, fare thee well. [*He falls forward.*]

EDGAR   Gone, sir:[17] farewell.
[*Aside.*]   And yet I know not how[18] conceit[19] may rob
The treasury of life when life itself
45   Yields to the theft;[20] had he been where he thought
By this had thought been past. Alive or dead?
[*To Gloucester.*]   Ho, you sir! friend! Hear you, sir? speak![21]
Thus might he pass indeed; yet he revives.[22]
What are you, sir?

GLOUCESTER   Away and let me die.

50   EDGAR   Hadst thou been aught but gossamer, feathers, air,
So many fathom down precipitating,[23]
Thou'dst shiver'd like an egg; but thou dost breathe,
Hast heavy substance, bleed'st not, speak'st, art sound.
Ten masts at each[24] make not the altitude
55   Which thou hast perpendicularly fell:
Thy life's a miracle. Speak yet again.

GLOUCESTER   But have I fallen or no?

EDGAR   From the dread summit of this chalky bourn.[25]
Look up a-height;[26] the shrill-gorg'd[27] lark so far
60   Cannot be seen or heard: do but look up.

GLOUCESTER   Alack! I have no eyes.
Is wretchedness depriv'd that benefit
To end itself by death? 'Twas yet some comfort,
When misery could beguile[28] the tyrant's rage,
And frustrate his proud will.

65   EDGAR   Give me your arm:
Up: so. How is't? Feel you your legs? You stand.

GLOUCESTER   Too well, too well.

EDGAR   This is above all strangeness.
Upon the crown o' the cliff, what thing was that
Which parted from you?

GLOUCESTER   A poor unfortunate beggar.

70   EDGAR   As I stood here below methought his eyes
Were two full moons; he had a thousand noses,

16. *My . . . out*: i.e. I would let the miserable remnant of my life expire naturally,
instead of seeking my own death
(snuff = the half-burnt wick)
17. *Gone, sir*: answer to 31
18. *I . . . how*: I don't know how it is that
19. imagination
20. *when . . . theft*: when there is no longer
the will to live
21. is spoken in a different voice as if by a
stranger who has found Gloucester at
the foot of the cliff

22. (an aside)
23. falling headlong
24. *at each*: on end
25. the limit of the sea (cf. IV. i. 73)
26. on high
27. shrill-throated, high-voiced
28. cheat (by death)

Horns whelk'd[29] and wav'd like the enridged[30] sea:
It was some fiend; therefore, thou happy father,[31]
Think that the clearest[32] gods, who make them honours
75   Of men's impossibilities, have preserv'd thee.
GLOUCESTER   I do remember now; henceforth I'll bear
Affliction till it do cry out itself
"Enough, enough," and die. That thing you speak of
I took it for a man; often 'twould say
80   "The fiend, the fiend:" he led me to that place.
EDGAR   Bear free[33] and patient[34] thoughts. But who comes here?

Enter Lear, fantastically dressed with flowers.[35]

The safer sense will ne'er accommodate
His master thus.[36]
LEAR   No, they cannot touch[37] me for coining;
85   I am the king himself.
EDGAR   O thou side-piercing[38] sight!
LEAR   Nature's above art[39] in that respect. There's your press-money.[40] That
fellow handles his bow like a crow-keeper:[41] draw me[42] a clothier's yard.[43]
Look, look! a mouse. Peace, peace! this piece of toasted cheese will do't.
90   There's my gauntlet;[44] I'll prove it on a giant. Bring up the brown bills.[45] O!
well flown, bird;[46] i' the clout,[47] i' the clout: hewgh![48] Give the word.[49]
EDGAR   Sweet marjoram.[50]
LEAR   Pass.
GLOUCESTER   I know that voice.
95   LEAR   Ha! Goneril, with a white beard! They flatter'd me like a dog,[51] and told
me I had white hairs[52] in my beard ere the black ones were there. To say
"ay" and "no" to everything I said! "Ay" and "no" too was no good
divinity.[53] When the rain came to wet me once and the wind to make me

29. (probably) twisted
30. ridged, furrowed
31. ambiguous, since it could be addressed to any old man
32. purest, open and righteous
33. free from fear, happy (and so not inclined to suicide) *or* generous towards men and 34. *patient* towards God
35. based on IV. iv. 3–6
36. *The . . . thus*: i.e. a man in his right senses would not get himself up like this ("safer" = saner)
37. get at, punish
38. heart-rending
39. *Nature's . . . art*: (probably) a king's above a coiner (issuer of false money)
40. payment given a man forced into the services (cf. press-gang)
41. scarer of birds

42. for me to see
43. *clothier's yard*: long arrow
44. mailed glove as a challenge
45. *brown bills*: halberds painted brown *or* the bearers of them
46. here used for arrow
47. mark, target
48. the whistling sound of the arrow in the air
49. password
50. used as a remedy for madness
51. *like a dog*: as a dog fawns on people
52. *white hairs*: i.e. the wisdom of age
53. *no . . . divinity*: not sound theologically (in view of St. Paul's words "For the Son of God, Jesus Christ . . . was not yea and nay, but in him was yea," 2 Cor. i. 19)

chatter, when the thunder would not peace at my bidding, there I found
100   'em, there I smelt 'em out. Go to, they are not men o' their words: they
told me I was everything; 'tis a lie, I am not ague-proof.

GLOUCESTER   The trick[54] of that voice I do well remember:
Is't not the king?

LEAR   Ay, every inch a king:
When I do stare, see how the subject quakes.
105   I pardon that man's life. What was thy cause?[55]
Adultery?
Thou shalt not die: die for adultery! No:
The wren goes to't, and the small gilded fly
Does lecher in my sight.
110   Let copulation thrive; for Gloucester's bastard son
Was kinder to his father than my daughters
Got 'tween the lawful sheets.
To't luxury,[56] pell-mell![57] for I lack soldiers.
Behold yond simpering dame,
115   Whose face between her forks presageth snow;[58]
That minces[59] virture, and does shake the head
To hear of pleasure's name;
The fitchew[60] nor the soiled[61] horse goes to't
With a more riotous appetite.
120   Down from the waist they are Centaurs,[62]
Though women all above:
But to[63] the girdle do the gods inherit,[64]
Beneath is all the fiends':
There's hell, there's darkness, there is the sulphurous pit,
125   Burning, scalding, stench, consumption; fie, fie, fie! pah, pah! Give me
an ounce of civet,[65] good apothecary, to sweeten my imagination: there's
money for thee.

GLOUCESTER   O! let me kiss that hand!

LEAR   Let me wipe it first; it smells of mortality.[66]

130   GLOUCESTER   O ruin'd piece[67] of nature! This great world
Shall so[68] wear out to nought. Dost thou know me?

LEAR   I remember thine eyes well enough. Dost thou squiny[69] at me? No, do

---

54. accent
55. crime, subject of accusation
56. lust
57. promiscuously
58. *Whose . . . snow*: i.e. Whose face would make you think she had little sexual desire
59. affects
60. (1) pole-cat, and (2) harlot
61. overfed
62. half men, half horses, in Greek mythology

63. *But to*: only as far as
64. own
65. scent
66. (1) humanity, and perhaps also (2) death
67. (perhaps) masterpiece
68. as you have done
69. squint
70. *blind Cupid*: the sign over brothels (may recall Gloucester's sin)

thy worst, blind Cupid;[70] I'll not love. Read thou this challenge; mark but
the penning of it.

135 GLOUCESTER   Were all the letters suns, I could not see.

EDGAR   [*Aside*.]   I would not take this from report; it is,
And my heart breaks at it.

LEAR   Read.

GLOUCESTER   What! with the case[71] of eyes?

140 LEAR   O, ho! are you there with me?[72] No eyes in your head, nor no money in
your purse? Your eyes are in a heavy case,[73] your purse in a light: yet you
see how this world goes.

GLOUCESTER   I see it feelingly.[74]

LEAR   What! art mad? A man may see how this world goes with no eyes. Look
145 with thine ears: see how yond justice rails upon yon simple[75] thief. Hark,
in thine ear: change places; and, handy-dandy,[76] which is the justice, which
is the thief? Thou hast seen a farmer's dog bark at a beggar?

GLOUCESTER   Ay, sir.

LEAR   And the creature[77] run from the cur? There thou mightst behold the great
150 image[78] of authority; a dog's[79] obey'd in office.[80]
Thou rascal beadle,[81] hold thy bloody hand!
Why dost thou lash that whore? Strip thine own back;
Thou hotly lust'st to use her in that kind[82]
For which thou whipp'st her. The usurer hangs the cozener.[83]
155 Through tatter'd clothes small vices do appear;
Robes and furr'd gowns[84] hide all. Plate sin with gold,[85]
And the strong lance of justice hurtless[86] breaks;
Arm it in rags, a pigmy's straw doth pierce it.
None does offend, none, I say none; I'll able[87] 'em:
160 Take that of me, my friend, who have the power
To seal the accuser's lips. Get thee glass eyes;
And, like a scurvy politician,[88] seem[89]
To see the things thou dost not. Now, now, now, now;
Pull off my boots; harder, harder; so.

165 EDGAR   [*Aside*.]   O! matter[90] and impertinency[91] mix'd;
Reason in madness!

71. sockets	83. *The . . . cozener*: i.e. a magistrate who
72. *are . . . me?*: Is that what you mean?	has a man hanged for a petty theft
73. *in . . . case*: because in a bad way	may himself lend money for interest
74. by my sense of feeling (perhaps also	(condemned by medieval church)
suggests "I feel it deeply")	84. *furr'd gowns*: worn by judges and
75. humble	aldermen
76. take which you like (from a children's	85. *Plate . . . gold*: give the sinner the
game)	armour of riches
77. human being	86. inflicting no wound
78. type, example	87. vouch for, protect
79. even a dog	88. *scurvy politician*: rascally schemer
80. *in office*: in a position of authority	89. pretend
81. parish constable	90. good sense
82. *in that kind*: i.e. lustfully	91. irrelevance, nonsense

LEAR   If thou wilt weep my fortunes, take my eyes;
I know thee well enough; thy name is Gloucester:[92]
Thou must be patient; we came crying hither:
170   Thou know'st the first time that we smell the air
We waul[93] and cry. I will preach to thee: mark.
GLOUCESTER   Alack! alack the day!
LEAR   When we are born, we cry that we are come
To this great stage of fools. This'[94] a good block![95]
175   It were a delicate stratagem to shoe
A troop of horse with felt; I'll put it in proof,[96]
And when I have stol'n upon these sons-in-law,
Then, kill, kill, kill, kill, kill, kill!

Enter Gentleman, with Attendants.

GENTLEMAN   O! here he is; lay hand upon him. Sir, Your most dear daughter—
180   LEAR   No rescue? What! a prisoner? I am even[97]
The natural fool of[98] fortune. Use me well;
You shall have ransom. Let me have surgeons;
I am cut to the brains.[99]
GENTLEMAN   You shall have any thing.
LEAR   No seconds?[100] All myself?
185   Why this would make a man a man of salt,[101]
To use his eyes for garden water-pots,
Ay, and laying autumn's dust.
GENTLEMAN   Good sir,—
LEAR   I will die bravely as a bridegroom.[102] What!
I will be jovial: come, come; I am a king,
190   My masters, know you that?
GENTLEMAN   You are a royal one, and we obey you.
LEAR   Then there's life in it.[103] Nay, an you get it, you shall get it by running.
Sa, sa, sa, sa.[104]   [*Exit. Attendants follow.*
GENTLEMAN   A sight most pitiful in the meanest wretch,
195   Past speaking of in a king! Thou hast one daughter,
Who redeems nature[105] from the general curse
Which twain have brought her to.

---

92. see l. 131
93. wail (cf. caterwaul)
94. This is
95. (perhaps) a felt hat
96. *in proof*: on trial
97. Lear has been found by Cordelia's attendants whom he imagines to be enemies.
98. *The . . . of*: born to be the sport, victim of (bad) fortune
99. *cut . . . brains*: cf. "cut to the heart"
100. supporters
101. *a . . . salt*: all tears (but cf. Lot's wife Genesis xix. 26)
102. *as a bridegroom*: meeting death like a bride
103. *there's . . . it*: there's still hope for me
104. *Sa, sa*: a cry inciting to action, as to hunting dogs
105. human nature, disgraced by Goneril and Regan

EDGAR   Hail, gentle sir!

GENTLEMAN   Sir, speed you:[106] what's your will?

200   EDGAR   Do you hear aught, sir, of a battle toward?[107]

GENTLEMAN   Most sure and vulgar;[108] every one hears that,
    Which can distinguish sound.

EDGAR   But, by your favour,
    How near's the other army?

GENTLEMAN   Near, and on speedy foot; the main descry
    Stands on the hourly thought.[109]

205   EDGAR   I thank you, sir: that's all.

GENTLEMAN   Though that the queen on special cause is here,
    Her army is mov'd on.

EDGAR   I thank you, sir.

                                  [*Exit Gentleman.*

GLOUCESTER   You ever-gentle gods, take my breath from me:[110]
    Let not my worser spirit[111] tempt me again
    To die before you please!

210   EDGAR   Well pray you, father.[112]

GLOUCESTER   Now, good sir, what are you?

EDGAR   A most poor man, made tame to fortune's blows;
    Who, by the art of[113] known and feeling[114] sorrows,
    Am pregnant to[115] good pity. Give me your hand
    I'll lead you to some biding.[116]

215   GLOUCESTER   Hearty thanks:
    The bounty and the benison[117] of heaven
    To boot, and boot![118]

Enter Oswald.

OSWALD   A proclaim'd prize![119] Most happy!
    That eyeless head of thine was first fram'd[120] flesh
    To raise my fortunes. Thou old unhappy traitor,
220   Briefly thyself remember:[121] the sword is out[122]
    That must destroy thee.

GLOUCESTER   Now let thy friendly[123] hand

---

106. (God) *speed you*
107. imminent
108. commonly known
109. *the main . . . thought*: the sight of the main body is expected every hour
110. i.e. let me die in heaven's good time
111. *my . . . spirit*: the worse part of me, my evil genius (a phrase used in Sonnet 144)
112. see 73, and cf. 242 &c.
113. *by . . . of*: taught by
114. heart-felt
115. *pregnant to*: disposed to show
116. abode, resting place
117. blessing
118. *To boot, and boot*: in addition, and may it help you (two meanings of ''boot'')
119. *A . . . prize*: a publish'd traitor (223) for whose arrest a reward had been offered
120. made
121. *thyself remember*: remember your sins, prepare for death
122. unsheathed
123. G. desires to die

Put strength enough to't.   [*Edgar interposes.*

OSWALD   Wherefore, bold peasant,
Dar'st thou support a publish'd traitor? Hence;
Lest that infection of his fortune take
225   Like hold on thee.[124] Let go his arm.

EDGAR   Chill[125] not let go, zur, without vurther 'casion.[126]

OSWALD   Let go, slave, or thou diest.

EDGAR   Good gentleman, go your gait,[127] and let poor volk pass. An chud ha'
bin zwaggered[128] out of my life, 'twould not ha' ben zo long as 'tis by a vort-
230   night. Nay, come not near th' old man; keep out, che vor ye,[129] or ise[130] try
whether your costard[131] or my ballow[132] be the harder. Chill be plain
with you.

OSWALD   Out, dunghill!

EDGAR   Chill pick your teeth,[133] zur. Come; no matter vor your foins.[134]

                    [*They fight and Edgar knocks him down.*

235   OSWALD   Slave, thou hast slain me. Villain,[135] take my purse.
If ever thou wilt thrive, bury my body;
And give the letters which thou find'st about me
To Edmund Earl of Gloucester; seek him out
Upon[136] the English party:[137] O! untimely death.   [*Dies.*

240   EDGAR   I know thee well: a serviceable villain;[138]
As duteous to the vices of thy mistress
As badness would desire.

GLOUCESTER   What! is he dead?

EDGAR   Sit you down, father; rest you.
Let's see his pockets: these letters that he speaks of
245   May be my friends. He's dead; I am only sorry
He hath no other deaths-man. Let us see:
Leave,[139] gentle wax; and, manners, blame us not:
To know our enemies minds, we'd rip their hearts;
Their papers, is more lawful.

250   *Let our reciprocal vows be remembered. You have many opportunities to cut
him[140] off; if your will want not,[141] time and place will be fruitfully offered. There
is nothing done if he return the conqueror; then am I the prisoner, and his bed my
goal; from the loathed warmth whereof deliver me, and supply the place for[142]
your labour.*

124. *Lest . . . thee*: lest the same fate overtake you
125. I will
126. reason
127. way
128. *An . . . zwaggered*: If I could have been
bullied
129. *che vor ye*: I warrant you
130. I shall
131. head (lit. a kind of apple)
132. cudgel
133. *pick . . . teeth*: i.e. fight you
134. thrusts
135. serf
136. on, among
137. *party*: side
138. rascal
139. by your leave
140. Albany
141. *want not*: is not deficient
142. as a reward for

255   *Your—wife, so I would say—*
       Affectionate servant,

                      GONERIL.

O undistinguish'd[143] space[144] of woman's will![145]
A plot upon her virtuous husband's life,
260 And the exchange my brother! Here, in the sands,
Thee I'll rake up,[146] the post[147] unsanctified
Of murderous lechers; and in the mature time[148]
With this ungracious[149] paper strike the sight
Of the death-practis'd[150] duke. For him 'tis well
265 That of thy death and business I can tell.
GLOUCESTER The king is mad: how stiff[151] is my vile sense,
That I stand up, and have ingenious[152] feeling
Of my huge sorrows! Better I were distract:[153]
So should my thoughts be sever'd from my griefs,[154]
270 And woes by wrong imaginations[155] lose
The knowledge of themselves.   *[Drums afar off.*
EDGAR   Give me your hand:
Far off, methinks, I hear the beaten drum.
Come, father, I'll bestow[156] you with a friend.   *[Exeunt.*

SCENE 7

A Tent in the French Camp.

Enter Cordelia, Kent, Doctor, and Gentleman.

CORDELIA O thou good Kent! how shall I live and work
To match[1] thy goodness? My life will be too short,
And every measure[2] fail me.
KENT To be acknowledg'd, madam, is o'erpaid.
5 All my reports[3] go with the modest truth,
Nor more nor clipp'd, but so.[4]
CORDELIA   Be better suited:[5]

---

143. indistinguishable, illimitable
144. range
145. desire, lust (cf. IV. ii. 32–33 with this whole line)
146. *rake up*: bury
147. messenger, postman
148. *in . . . time*: at the right moment
149. disgraceful
150. whose death has been plotted
151. unbending, unfeeling
152. intelligent, conscious
153. *distract*(ed): mad

154. *So . . . grief*: i.e. I should not realize my miseries
155. *wrong imaginations*: illusions
156. lodge
1. come up to, in recompensing it
2. degree (of gratitude, compared with Kent's services)
3. *my reports*: the reports I have given you
4. *Nor more . . . so*: neither exaggerated nor understated but accurate
5. *suited*: dressed

These weeds[6] are memories of those worser hours:
  I prithee, put them off.
KENT   Pardon me, dear madam;
  Yet[7] to be known shortens my made intent;[8]
10 My boon I make it[9] that you know me not
  Till time and I think meet.[10]
CORDELIA   Then be't so, my good lord.—[*To the Doctor.*]   How does the king?
DOCTOR   Madam, sleeps still.
CORDELIA   O you kind gods,
15   Cure this great breach in his abused nature!
  The untun'd and jarring senses, O! wind up[11]
  Of this child-changed[12] father!
DOCTOR   So please[13] your majesty
  That we may wake the king? he hath slept long.
CORDELIA   Be govern'd by your knowledge, and proceed
20   I' the sway of your own will.[14] Is he array'd?

Enter Lear in his chair, carried by Servants.

GENTLEMAN   Ay, madam; in the heaviness of sleep,
  We put fresh garments on him.
DOCTOR   Be by, good madam, when we do awake him;
  I doubt not of his temperance.[15]
CORDELIA   Very well, [*Music.*
25 DOCTOR   Please you, draw near. Louder the music there.
CORDELIA   O my dear father! Restoration,[16] hang
    Thy medicine on my lips, and let this kiss
    Repair those violent harms that my two sisters
    Have in thy reverence made!
KENT   Kind and dear princess!
30 CORDELIA   Had you not been their father, these white flakes[17]
    Had challeng'd pity of[18] them. Was this a face
    To be expos'd against the warring winds?
    To stand against the deep[19] dread-bolted[20] thunder?
    In the most terrible and nimble stroke
35   Of quick cross[21] lightning? to watch[22]—poor perdu!—

6. clothes
7. at present
8. *my . . . intent*: the plan I have made
9. *My . . . it*: the favour I ask is
10. *Till . . . meet*: i.e. Till I think the time ripe
11. *wind up*: tune
12. *child-changed*: (1) changed into a child (in mind), (2) changed by (the cruelty of) his children—very probably *both*
13. may it please
14. *I' . . . will*: as you think best
15. sanity
16. the power of restoring the senses (personified)
17. *white flakes*: his *snowy* hair and beard
18. from
19. deep-voiced
20. armed with the dreaded thunderbolt
21. forked
22. stand exposed

With this thin helm?[23] Mine enemy's dog,
Though he had bit me, should have stood that night
Against[24] my fire. And wast thou fain, poor father,
To hovel thee with swine and rogues forlorn,
40   In short[25] and musty straw? Alack, alack!
'Tis wonder that thy life and wits at once
Had not concluded all.[26] He wakes; speak to him.
DOCTOR   Madam, do you; 'tis fittest.
CORDELIA   How does my royal lord? How fares your majesty?
45   LEAR   You do me wrong to take me out o' the grave;
Thou art a soul in bliss; but I am bound
Upon a wheel of fire, that[27] mine own tears
Do scald[28] like molten lead.
CORDELIA   Sir, do you know me?
LEAR   You are a spirit, I know; when did you die?
50   CORDELIA   Still, still, far wide.[29]
DOCTOR   He's scarce awake; let him alone awhile.
LEAR   Where have I been? Where am I? Fair day-light?
I am mightily abus'd.[30] I should even die with pity
To see another thus. I know not what to say.
55   I will not swear these are my hands: let's see;
I feel this pin prick. Would I were assur'd
Of my condition!
CORDELIA   O! look upon me, sir,
And hold your hands in benediction o'er me.
No, sir, you must not kneel.
LEAR   Pray, do not mock me:
60   I am a very foolish fond[31] old man,
Fourscore and upward, not an hour more or less;
And, to deal plainly,
I fear I am not in my perfect mind.
Methinks I should know you and know this man;
65   Yet I am doubtful: for I am mainly[32] ignorant
What place this is, and all the skill I have
Remembers not these garments; nor I know not
Where I did lodge last night. Do not laugh at me;
For, as I am a man, I think this lady
To be my child Cordelia.
70   CORDELIA   And so I am, I am.
LEAR   Be your tears wet? Yes, faith. I pray, weep not:

23. *thin helm*: unprotected head	28. scald me
24. in front of	29. astray (in mind)
25. cut short (and therefore uncomfortable), and/or scanty	30. deceived, deluded (cf. 77 below)
	31. simple, foolish
26. *concluded all*: entirely ended	32. completely
27. so that	

If you have poison for me, I will drink it.
I know you do not love me; for your sisters
Have, as I do remember, done me wrong:
You have some cause, they have not.

75 CORDELIA   No cause, no cause.
LEAR   Am I in France?
KENT   In your own kingdom, sir.
LEAR   Do not abuse me.
DOCTOR   Be comforted, good madam; the great rage,[33]
You see, is kill'd in him; and yet it is danger
80 To make him even o'er[34] the time he has lost.
Desire him to go in; trouble him no more
Till further settling.[35]
CORDELIA   Will't please your highness walk?[36]
LEAR   You must bear with me.
Pray you now, forget and forgive: I am old and foolish.
                    [Exeunt Lear, Cordelia, Doctor, and Attendants.
85 GENTLEMAN   Holds it true, sir, that the Duke of Cornwall was so slain?
KENT   Most certain, sir.
GENTLEMAN   Who is conductor of his people?
KENT   As 'tis said, the bastard son of Gloucester.
GENTLEMAN   They say Edgar, his banished son, is with the Earl of Kent in
90   Germany.
KENT   Report is changeable. 'Tis time to look about; the powers of the king-
    dom approach apace.
GENTLEMAN   The arbitrement[37] is like to be bloody.
    Fare you well, sir.   [Exit.
95 KENT   My point and period[38] will be throughly wrought,
    Or well or ill, as this day's battle's fought.   [Exit.

---

33. frenzy, madness
34. *even o'er*: smooth over, straighten out,
    make the recollection continuous
35. *Till . . . settling*: till his mind has had
    more time to settle down again
36. withdraw
37. decision (of the war)
38. *point and period*: object and end

ACT V

SCENE 1

The British Camp near Dover.

Enter, with drum and colours, Edmund, Regan, Officers, Soldiers, and Others.

EDMUND   Know[1] of the duke if his last purpose hold,[2]
    Or whether since[3] he is advis'd[4] by aught
    To change the course; he's full of alteration
    And self-reproving; bring his constant pleasure.[5]

                                    [*To an Officer, who goes out.*

5   REGAN   Our sister's man[6] is certainly miscarried.
EDMUND   'Tis to be doubted,[7] madam.
REGAN   Now, sweet lord,
    You know the goodness I intend upon you:[8]
    Tell me, but truly, but then[9] speak the truth,
    Do you not love my sister?
EDMUND   In honour'd[10] love.
10   REGAN   But have you never found my brother's way
    To the forefended[11] place?
EDMUND   That thought abuses[12] you.
REGAN   I am doubtful that you have been conjunct
    And bosom'd with her, as far as we call hers.[13]
EDMUND   No, by mine honour, madam.
15   REGAN   I never shall endure her:[14] dear my lord,
    Be not familiar with her.
EDMUND   Fear[15] me not.
    She and the duke her husband!

Enter with drums and colours, Albany, Goneril, and Soldiers.

GONERIL   [*Aside.*]   I had rather lose the battle than that sister
    Should loosen him and me.
20   ALBANY   Our very loving sister, well be-met.[16]
    Sir, this I heard, the king is come to his daughter,
    With others; whom the rigour of our state[17]
    Forc'd to cry out.[18] Where I could not be honest
    I never yet was valiant: for this business,
25   It toucheth us, as[19] France invades our land,
    Not bolds[20] the king, with others, whom, I fear,

1. find out
2. still holds good
3. since then
4. induced
5. *constant pleasure*: firm decision
6. *Our . . . man*: Oswald (see IV. vi. 239)
7. feared (so "doubtful" in l. 12 = afraid)
8. *goodness I intend* (to confer) *upon you*: i.e. my hand
9. even if it is what I fear
10. honourable, not adulterous
11. forbidden
12. deceives
13. i.e. intimate with her to the fullest degree
14. *endure her*: i.e. bear to see her separate us
15. distrust
16. met
17. *our state*: our rule
18. *cry out*: protest, rebel
19. *toucheth us, as*: concerns me in so far as
20. *Not bolds*: not in so far as the king of France emboldens (supports)

Most just and heavy causes make oppose.[21]

EDMUND   Sir, you speak nobly.

REGAN   Why is this reason'd?[22]

GONERIL   Combine together 'gainst the enemy;

For these domestic and particular[23] broils

Are not the question here.

ALBANY   Let's then determine

With the ancient of war[24] on our proceeding.

EDMUND   I shall attend you presently[25] at your tent.

REGAN   Sister, you'll go with us?

GONERIL   No.

REGAN   'Tis most convenient; pray you, go with us.

GONERIL   [Aside.]   O, ho! I know the riddle.[26] [Aloud.]   I will go.

Enter Edgar, disguised.

EDGAR   If e'er your Grace had speech with man so poor,

Hear me one word.

ALBANY   I'll overtake you. Speak.

[Exeunt Edmund, Regan, Goneril, Officers, Soldiers, and Attendants.

EDGAR   Before you fight the battle, ope this letter.

If you have victory, let the trumpet sound

For him that brought it: wretched though I seem,

I can produce a champion that will prove

What is avouched[27] there. If you miscarry,

Your business of the world[28] hath so an end,

And machination[29] ceases. Fortune love you!

ALBANY   Stay till I have read the letter.

EDGAR   I was forbid it.

When time shall serve, let but the herald cry,

And I'll appear again.

ALBANY   Why, fare thee well: I will o'erlook[30] thy paper.   [Exit Edgar.

Re-enter Edmund.

EDMUND   The enemy's in view; draw up your powers.

Here is the guess[31] of their true strength and forces

By diligent discovery;[32] but your haste

21. *whom . . . oppose*: who, I fear, have good and weighty reasons for taking up arms against us
22. *Why . . . reason'd?*: Why all this argument (about the cause of rebellion)?
23. private
24. *the . . . war*: veteran soldiers
25. at once
26. *the riddle*: i.e what you are after
27. asserted
28. *Your . . . world*: your wordly concerns, your life
29. plotting, i.e. Edmund's
30. look over, peruse
31. estimate
32. inquiry, spying

Is now urg'd on you.

ALBANY   We will greet the time.[33] [*Exit.*

55   EDMUND   To both these sisters have I sworn my love;
        Each jealous[34] of the other, as the stung
        Are of the adder. Which of them shall I take?
        Both? one? or neither? Neither can be enjoy'd
        If both remain alive: to take the widow
60   Exasperates, makes mad her sister Goneril;
        And hardly shall I carry out my side,[35]
        Her husband being alive. Now then, we'll use
        His countenance[36] for the battle; which being done
        Let her who would be rid of him devise
65   His speedy taking off.[37] As for the mercy
        Which he intends to Lear, and to Cordelia,
        The battle done, and they within our power,
        Shall[38] never see his pardon; for my state[39]
        Stands on me[40] to defend, not to debate.   [*Exit.*

SCENE 2

A Field between the two Camps.

*Alarum within. Enter, with drum and colours, Lear, Cordelia, and their Forces;
and exeunt. Enter Edgar and Gloucester.*

EDGAR   Here, father, take the shadow of this tree
        For your good host;[1] pray that the right may thrive.
        If ever I return to you again,
        I'll bring you comfort.
GLOUCESTER   Grace go with you, sir!

                                                        [*Exit Edgar.*

Alarum; afterwards a retreat. Re-enter Edgar.

5   EDGAR   Away, old man! give me thy hand: away!
        King Lear hath lost, he and his daughter ta'en.
        Give me thy hand; come on.
GLOUCESTER   No further, sir; a man may rot even here.

---

33. *greet the time*: go to meet the occasion,
    emergency
34. suspicious
35. *carry . . . side*: attain my object, i.e.
    the throne
36. authority, prestige
37. *taking off*: murder (a euphemism like
    ''liquidation'' today)

38. they shall (grammatical confusion)
39. position
40. *Stands on me*: (it) concerns me, it is up
    to me
 1. shelterer, protection

EDGAR   What! in ill thoughts again? Men must endure[2]
10   Their going hence, even as their coming hither:
          Ripeness is all.[3] Come on.
GLOUCESTER   And that's true too.

                                        [*Exeunt.*

SCENE 3

The British Camp, near Dover.

*Enter, in conquest, with drum and colours, Edmund; Lear and Cordelia, prisoners;
Officers, Soldiers, &c.*

EDMUND   Some officers take them away: good guard,[1]
          Until their greater pleasures first be known
          That[2] are to censure them.[3]
CORDELIA   We are not the first
          Who, with best meaning,[4] have incurr'd the worst.
5   For thee, oppress'd king, am I cast down;
          Myself could else out-frown false Fortune's frown.[5]
          Shall we not see these daughters and these sisters?
LEAR   No, no, no, no! Come, let's away to prison;
          We two alone will sing like birds i' the cage:[6]
10   When thou dost ask me blessing, I'll kneel down,
          And ask of thee forgiveness: so we'll live,
          And pray, and sing, and tell old tales, and laugh
          At gilded butterflies,[7] and hear poor rogues
          Talk of court news; and we'll talk with them too,
15   Who loses and who wins; who's in, who's out;
          And take upon's the mystery of things,
          As if we were God's spies:[8] and we'll wear out,[9]
          In a wall'd prison, packs and sets of great ones
          That ebb and flow by the moon.[10]
EDMUND   Take them away.
20   LEAR   Upon such sacrifices,[11] my Cordelia,

2. wait for, live patiently until
3. *Ripeness is all*: the important thing is to be ready for death when it does come
1. *good guard*: keep good guard over them
2. *their . . . That*: the pleasure (decision as to their fate) of those higher authorities (Albany, &c.) who
3. judge
4. *with . . . meaning*: trying to act for the best
5. *out-frown . . . frown*: defy misfortune
6. *also* meant a prison

7. *gilded butterflies*: court gallants (cf. 1 85)
8. *And . . . spies*: i.e. imagine we understand the ways of God in the world as if we were His agents or saw with His eyes
9. *wear out*: outlast
10. *packs . . . moon*: sets and parties at court who go in and out of favour like the changes of the moon
11. *such sacrifices*: as our imprisonment

The gods themselves throw incense. Have I caught thee?
He that parts us shall bring a brand from heaven,[12]
And fire us hence like foxes.[13] Wipe thine eyes;
The goujeres[14] shall devour them, flesh and fell,[15]
25   Ere they shall make us weep: we'll see 'em starve first.
Come.   [*Exeunt Lear and Cordelia, guarded.*
EDMUND   Come hither, captain; hark,
    Take thou this note; [*Giving a paper.*]   go follow them to prison:
    One step I have advanc'd thee; if thou dost
30   As this instructs thee, thou dost make the way
    To noble fortunes; know thou this, that men
    Are as the time is; to be tender-minded
    Does not become a sword;[16] thy great employment
    Will not bear question;[17] either say thou'lt do't,
    Or thrive by other means.
35   OFFICER   I'll do't, my lord.
EDMUND   About it; and write happy[18] when thou hast done.
    Mark,—I say, instantly, and carry it[19] so
    As I have set it down.
OFFICER   I cannot draw a cart nor eat dried oats;
40   If it be man's work I will do it.   [*Exit.*

Flourish. Enter Albany, Goneril, Regan, Officers, and Attendants.

ALBANY   Sir, you have show'd to-day your valiant strain,[20]
    And fortune led you well; you have the captives
    Who were the opposites of[21] this day's strife;
    We do require them of you, so to use them
45   As we[22] shall find their merits[23] and our safety
    May equally determine.
EDMUND   Sir, I thought it fit.
    To send the old and miserable king
    To some retention, and appointed guard;
    Whose[24] age has charms in it, whose title more,
50   To pluck the common bosom[25] on his side,
    And turn our impress'd lances[26] in our eyes[27]
    Which do command them. With him I sent the queen;

12. *He . . . heaven*: i.e. no power on earth
    shall separate us
13. *like foxes*: as foxes are smoked out of
    their holes
14. *The goujeres*: the Devil
15. skin
16. *a sword*: i.e. a soldier
17. investigation, discussion
18. *write happy*: count yourself happy
19. *carry it* (out)

20. lineage
21. *the opposites of*: our opponents in
22. I and my counsellors
23. deserts, deeds
24. refers back to "king"
25. *the . . . bosom*: the affections of the
    common people
26. *our . . . lances*: the soldiers we had
    conscripted
27. *in our eyes*: against ourselves

My reason all the same; and they are ready
To-morrow, or at further space, to appear
Where you shall hold your session. At this time
We sweat and bleed; the friend hath lost his friend,
And the best quarrels,[28] in the heat,[29] are curs'd
By those that feel their sharpness;
The question of Cordelia and her father
Requires a fitter place.

ALBANY   Sir, by your patience,[30]
I hold you but a subject of this war,
Not as a brother.

REGAN   That's as we list[31] to grace him:
Methinks our pleasure might have been demanded,
Ere you had spoke so far. He led our powers,
Bore the commission of my place[32] and person;
The which immediacy[33] may well stand up,[34]
And call itself your brother.

GONERIL   Not so hot;[35]
In his own grace he doth exalt himself
More than in your addition.[36]

REGAN   In my rights,
By me invested, he compeers the best.

GONERIL   That were the most, if[37] he should husband you.

REGAN   Jesters do oft prove prophets.

GONERIL   Holla, holla!
That eye that told you so look'd but a-squint.

REGAN   Lady, I am not well; else I should answer
From a full-flowing stomach.[38] General,
Take thou my soldiers, prisoners, patrimony;
Dispose of them, of me; the walls[39] are thine;
Witness the world, that I create thee here
My lord and master.

GONERIL   Mean you to enjoy him?

ALBANY   The let-alone[40] lies not in your good will.

EDMUND   Nor in thine, lord.

ALBANY   Half-blooded[41] fellow, yes.

---

28. *the . . . quarrels*: battles in the best causes
29. *in the heat* (of the moment): before passions have cooled
30. *by . . . patience*: if you will excuse me saying so
31. choose
32. rank
33. closeness to me
34. *well . . . up*: i.e. justify him in standing up, &c

35. *Not so hot*: Don't be in such a hurry
36. *your addition*: the position you have claimed for him
37. *the most* (he could do, even) *if*
38. *full-flowing stomach*: the eloquence of passion
39. *the walls*: of my fortress (metaphorically), i.e. I myself
40. power to forbid it
41. bastard

REGAN   [*To Edmund.*]   Let the drum strike, and prove my title thine.

ALBANY   Stay yet; hear reason. Edmund, I arrest thee
　　On capital treason; and, in thy arrest,[42]
85　　This gilded[43] serpent. [*Pointing to Goneril.*]   For your claim, fair sister,
　　I bar it in the interest of my wife;
　　'Tis she is sub-contracted[44] to this lord,
　　And I, her husband, contradict your bans.
　　If you will marry, make your love to me,
　　My lady is bespoke.

90　GONERIL　　　　　　　　An interlude![45]

ALBANY   Thou art arm'd, Gloucester; let the trumpet sound:
　　If none appear to prove upon thy person
　　Thy heinous, manifest, and many treasons,
　　There is my pledge; [*Throws down a glove.*]   I'll prove it on thy heart,
95　　Ere I taste bread, thou art in nothing less
　　Than I have here proclaim'd thee.

REGAN　　　　　　　　　　　Sick! O sick!

GONERIL   [*Aside.*]   If not, I'll ne'er trust medicine.[46]

EDMUND   There's my exchange: [*Throws down a glove.*]   what in the world he is
　　That names me traitor, villain-like he lies.
100　　Call by thy trumpet: he that dares approach,
　　On him, on you, who not? I will maintain
　　My truth and honour firmly.

ALBANY   A herald, ho!

EDMUND　　　　　　　A herald, ho! a herald!

ALBANY   Trust to thy single virtue;[47] for thy soldiers,
105　　All levied in my name, have in my name
　　Took their discharge.

REGAN　　　　　　　　My sickness grows upon me.

ALBANY   She is not well; convey her to my tent.　　　　[*Exit Regan, led.*
Come hither, herald,

Enter a Herald.
　　　　　　　　Let the trumpet sound, —
　　And read out this.

110　OFFICER   Sound, trumpet!　　　　　　　　　　[*A trumpet sounds.*

HERALD   *If any man of quality or degree within the lists[48] of the army will maintain
　　upon Edmund, supposed Earl of Gloucester, that he is a manifold traitor, let him
　　appear at the third sound of the trumpet. He is bold in his defence.*

EDMUND   Sound!　　　　　　　　　　　　　　[*First Trumpet.*

115　HERALD   Again!　　　　　　　　　　　　　[*Second Trumpet.*

42. impeachment
43. gilded-over, fair-seeming
44. betrothed for the second time
45. *An interlude*: (This is as good as) a play

46. euphemism for "poison"
47. valour (*virtus*)
48. role, muster

HERALD Again!

[*Third Trumpet.*
[*Trumpet answers within.*

Enter Edgar, armed, with a Trumpet before him.[49]

ALBANY Ask him his purposes, why he appears
    Upon this call o' the trumpet.
HERALD   What are you?
    Your name? your quality?[50] and why you answer
    This present summons?
120   EDGAR   Know, my name is lost;
    By treason's tooth bare-gnawn[51] and canker-bit:[52]
    Yet am I noble as the adversary
    I come to cope.[53]
ALBANY   Which is that adversary?
EDGAR What's he that speaks for Edmund Earl of Gloucester?
EDMUND Himself: what sayst thou to him?
125   EDGAR   Draw thy sword,
    That, if my speech offend a noble heart,
    Thy arm may do thee justice; here is mine:
    Behold, it[54] is the privilege of mine honours,
    My oath, and my profession:[55] I protest,
130   Maugre[56] thy strength, youth, place, and eminence,
    Despite thy victor[57] sword and fire-new[58] fortune,
    Thy valour and thy heart,[59] thou art a traitor,
    False to thy gods, thy brother, and thy father,
    Conspirant[60] 'gainst this high illustrious prince,
135   And, for the extremest upward[61] of thy head
    To the descent[62] and dust below thy foot,
    A most toad-spotted[63] traitor. Say thou "No,"
    This sword, this arm, and my best spirits are bent
    To prove upon thy heart, whereto I speak,
140   Thou liest.
EDMUND In wisdom I should ask thy name;
    But since thy outside looks so fair and war-like,
    And that thy tongue some say[64] of breeding breathes,

49. *with . . . him*: preceded by a trumpeter
50. rank
51. gnawed bare
52. devoured, as by the canker worm
53. engage
54. to fight, to maintain the truth of my assertion
55. *my profession*: of knighthood
56. in spite of
57. (lately) victorious
58. fresh like coins from the mint. Edmund is a *novus homo*, a *parvenu*
59. courage
60. conspiring *or* a conspirer
61. top
62. lowest part, sole of thy feet
63. covered with shame as a toad with spots
64. suggestion, trace

What[65] safe[66] and nicely[67] I might well delay
145   By rule of knighthood, I disdain and spurn;[68]
Back do I toss these treasons to thy head,[69]
With the hell-hated[70] lie o'erwhelm thy heart,
Which,[71] for[72] they yet glance by and scarcely bruise,
This sword of mine shall give them instant way,[73]
150   Where they shall rest for ever. Trumpets, speak!

> [*Alarums. They fight. Edmund falls.*

ALBANY   Save him, save him!
GONERIL   This is practice,[74] Gloucester:
By the law of arms thou wast not bound to answer
An unknown opposite; thou art not vanquish'd,
But cozen'd[75] and beguil'd.
ALBANY   Shut your mouth, dame,
155   Or with this paper[76] shall I stop it. Hold, sir;[77]
Thou[78] worse than any name, read thine own evil:
No tearing, lady; I perceive you know it.   [*Gives the letter to Edmund.*
GONERIL   Say, if I do, the laws are mine, not thine:
Who can arraign me for't   [*Exit.*
ALBANY   Most monstrous!
Know'st thou this paper?
160   EDMUND   Ask me not what I know.
ALBANY   Go after her: she's desperate; govern her.[79]   [*Exit an Officer.*
EDMUND   What you have charg'd me with, that have I done,
And more, much more; the time will bring it out:
'Tis past, and so am I. But what art thou
165   That hast this fortune on me?[80] If thou'rt noble,
I do forgive thee.
EDGAR   Let's exchange charity.[81]
I am no less in blood than thou art, Edmund;
If more, the more thou hast wrong'd me.
My name is Edgar, and thy father's son.
170   The gods are just, and of our pleasant vices
Make instruments to plague us:

65. i.e. the combat
66. safely (from the point of view of honour)
67. by insisting on the exact code of honour (which only requires me to answer an equal; see 153 below)
68. *I . . . spurn*: viz. to insist on my rights (change of construction)
69. *to thy head*: in thy teeth
70. hated like hell
71. treasons
72. because
73. *give . . . way*: press them urgently back (upon you)

74. treachery
75. tricked
76. *this paper*: the love-letter of Goneril to Edmund (see IV. vi. 263)
77. *Hold, sir*: wait a moment (to Edmund)
78. Goneril
79. *govern her*: control her, e.g. prevent her suicide
80. *fortune on me*: advantage given thee by fortune over me
81. including forgiveness

The dark and vicious place where thee he got[82]
Cost him his eyes.
EDMUND   Thou hast spoken right, 'tis true;
The wheel is come full circle; I am here.

175   ALBANY   Methought thy very gait did prophesy
A royal nobleness; I must embrace thee:
Let sorrow split my heart, if ever I
Did hate thee or thy father.
EDGAR   Worthy prince, I know't.
ALBANY   Where have you hid yourself?
180   How have you known the miseries of your father?
EDGAR   By nursing them, my lord. List a brief tale;
And, when 'tis told, O! that my heart would burst,
The bloody proclamation to escape[83]
That follow'd me so near,—O! our lives' sweetness,[84]
185   That we the pain of death would hourly die
Rather than die at once!—taught me to shift[85]
Into a madman's rags, to assume a semblance
That very dogs disdain'd: and in this habit
Met I my father with his bleeding rings,[86]
190   Their precious stones new lost; became his guide,
Led him, begg'd for him, sav'd him from despair;
Never,—O fault!—reveal'd myself unto him,
Until some half hour past, when I was arm'd;
Not sure, though hoping, of this good success,
195   I ask'd his blessing, and from first to last
Told him my pilgrimage: but his flaw'd[87] heart,—
Alack! too weak the conflict to support;
'Twixt two extremes of passion, joy and grief,
Burst smilingly.
200   EDMUND   This speech of yours hath mov'd me,
And shall perchance do good; but speak you on;
You look as you had something more to say.
ALBANY   If there be more, more woeful, hold it in;
For I am almost ready to dissolve,[88]
Hearing of this.
205   EDGAR   This would have seem'd a period[89]
To such as love not sorrow; but another,[90]
To amplify too much,[91] would make much more,

---

82. *The . . . got*: i.e the act of adultery
    which led to your birth
83. *to escape*: governs "the bloody pro-
    clamation"
84. *our . . . sweetness*: how highly we value
    our lives!
85. change

86. eye-sockets
87. cracked, worn out
88. in tears, melt away
89. limit, ending
90. sorrow *or* tale
91. *To . . . much*: (probably) by increasing
    what is already excessive

And top extremity.[92]
Whilst I was big[93] in clamour came there a man,
210   Who, having seen me in my worst estate,[94]
Shunn'd my abhorr'd society; but then, finding
Who 'twas that so endur'd, with his strong arms
He fasten'd on my neck, and bellow'd out
As[95] he'd burst heaven; threw him on my father;
215   Told the most piteous tale of Lear and him
That ever ear receiv'd; which in recounting
His grief grew puissant,[96] and the strings of life
Began to crack: twice then the trumpet sounded,
And there I left him tranc'd.[97]

ALBANY   But who was this?
220   EDGAR   Kent, sir, the banish'd Kent; who in disguise
Follow'd his enemy[98] king, and did him service
Improper for[99] a slave.

Enter a Gentleman, with a bloody knife.

GENTLEMAN   Help, help! O help!
EDGAR   What kind of help?
ALBANY   Speak man.
EDGAR   What means that bloody knife?
GENTLEMAN   'Tis hot, it smokes;
225   It came even from the heart of—O! she's dead.
ALBANY   Who dead? speak, man.
GENTLEMAN   Your lady, sir, your lady: and her sister
By her is poison'd; she confesses it.
EDMUND   I was contracted[100] to them both: all three
Now marry in an instant.
230   EDGAR   Here comes Kent.
ALBANY   Produce the bodies, be they alive or dead:
This judgment of the heavens, that makes us tremble,
Touches us not with pity.   [*Exit Gentleman.*

Enter Kent.

                    O! is this he?
The time will not allow the compliment[101]
Which very manners urges.

92. *top extremity*: pass the (due) limit
93. loud
94. state
95. as if
96. (too) powerful
97. insensible
98. (turned) hostile
99. *Improper for*: too humble even for
100. engaged, promised
101. formal courtesy (as in I. i. 291)

235 KENT   I am come
     To bid my king and master aye good-night;
     Is he not here?
     ALBANY   Great thing of us forgot!
     Speak, Edmund, where's the king? and where's Cordelia?
     Seest thou this object,[102] Kent?
                              [*The bodies of Goneril and Regan are brought in.*

     KENT Alack! why thus?
240 EDMUND   Yet Edmund was belov'd:
     The one the other poison'd for my sake,
     And after[103] slew herself.
     ALBANY Even so. Cover their faces.
     EDMUND I pant for life:[104] some good I mean to do
245 Despite of mine own nature. Quickly send,
     Be brief in it, to the castle; for my writ[105]
     Is on the life of Lear and on Cordelia.
     Nay, send in time.
     ALBANY   Run, run! O run!
     EDGAR To whom, my lord? who has the office? send
250 Thy token of reprieve.
     EDMUND Well thought on: take my sword,
     Give it the captain.
     ALBANY   Haste thee, for thy life.   [*Exit Edgar.*
     EDMUND He hath commission from thy wife and me
     To hang Cordelia in the prison, and
255 To lay the blame upon her own despair,
     That she fordid[106] herself.
     ALBANY The gods defend her! Bear him hence awhile.   [*Edmund is borne off.*

Enter Lear, with Cordelia dead in his arms: Edgar, Officer, and Others.

     LEAR Howl, howl, howl, howl! O! you are men of stones:[107]
     Had I your tongues and eyes, I'd use them so
260 That heavens' vaults should crack. She's gone for ever.
     I know when one is dead, and when one lives;
     She's dead as earth. Lend me a looking-glass;
     If that her breath will mist or stain the stone,[108]
     Why, then she lives.
     KENT   Is this the promis'd end?[109]

---

102. sight, something thrown in the way
     (Lat. *obicio*)
103. *after*(wards)
104. *pant for life*: struggle to live a little
     longer
105. writing, the order given (1. 28 above)

106. destroyed
107. *men of stones*: unfeeling
108. a mirror of polished stone
109. *the . . . end*: the end of the world fore-
     told (in biblical prophecy)

EDGAR   Or image[110] of that horror?

265   ALBANY   Fall and cease?[111]

LEAR   This feather stirs; she lives! if it be so,
It is a chance which does redeem all sorrows
That ever I have felt.

KENT   [*Kneeling.*]   O, my good master!

LEAR   Prithee, away.

270   EDGAR   'Tis noble Kent, your friend.

LEAR   A plague upon you, murderers, traitors all!
I might have sav'd her; now, she's gone forever!
Cordelia, Cordelia! stay a little. Ha!
What is't thou sayst? Her voice was ever soft,

275   Gentle and low, an excellent thing in woman.
I kill'd the slave[112] that was a hanging thee.

OFFICER   'Tis true, my lord, he did.

LEAR   Did I not, fellow?
I have seen the day, with my good biting falchion[113]
I would have made them skip: I am old now,

280   And these same crosses[114] spoil me.[115] Who are you?
Mine eyes are not o' the best: I'll tell you straight.[116]

KENT   If fortune brag of two she lov'd and hated,[117]
One of them[118] we behold.

LEAR   This is a dull[119] sight. Are you not Kent?

KENT   The same,

285   Your servant Kent. Where is your servant Caius?[120]

LEAR   He's a good fellow, I can tell you that;
He'll strike,[121] and quickly too. He's dead and rotten.

KENT   No, my good lord; I am the very man—

LEAR   I'll see that straight.[122]

290   KENT   That, from your first of difference[123] and decay,
Have followed your sad steps.

LEAR   You are welcome hither.

KENT   Nor no man else;[124] all's cheerless, dark, and deadly:
Your eldest daughters have fordone themselves,

---

110. copy, reproduction (cf. ''great doom's image,'' *Macbeth* II. iii. 61)
111. *Fall and cease!*: (probably) let the heavens fall and all things come to an end!
112. *the slave*: not literal, but abusive
113. a kind of light sword
114. troubles
115. *spoil me*: destroy me (as a fighter)
116. straightway, in a moment
117. *two . . . hated*: one whom she raised up (to the highest) and one whom she put down (to the lowest)
118. *One of them*: in Lear
119. melancholy

120. *Where . . . Caius?*: probably Kent is inviting Lear to recognize in him the former Caius
121. as he did Oswald (I. iv. 69)
122. cf. 281. But Lear is only half conscious of what is going on
123. *your . . . difference*: the commencement of your change of fortunes
124. *Nor . . . else*: *either* neither I nor anyone else can be very welcome (well come?) to this scene (which suits what follows), *or* a continuation of his words at 288

And desperately[125] are dead.

LEAR   Ay, so I think.

295   ALBANY He knows not what he says, and vain it is
That we present[126] us to him.

EDGAR   Very bootless.[127]

Enter an Officer.

OFFICER   Edmund is dead, my lord.

ALBANY   That's but a trifle here.
You lords and noble friends, know our[128] intent;
What comfort to this great decay[129] may come
300   Shall be applied: for us, we will resign,
During the life of this old majesty,
To him our absolute power: —[*To Edgar and Kent.*]   You, to your rights;[130]
With boot and such addition[131] as your honours[132]
Have more than merited. All friends shall taste
305   The wages[133] of their virtue, and all foes
The cup of their deservings. O! see, see!

LEAR   And my poor fool[134] is hang'd! No, no, no life!
Why should a dog, a horse, a rat, have life,
And thou no breath at all? Thou'lt come no more,
310   Never, never, never, never, never!
Pray you, undo this button: thank you, sir.
Do you see this? Look on her, look, her lips,
Look there, look there!   [*Dies.*

EDGAR   He faints!—my lord, my lord!

KENT   Break, heart;[135] I prithee, break.

EDGAR   Look up, my lord.

315   KENT   Vex not his ghost:[136] O! let him pass; he hates him
That would upon the rack[137] of this tough world
Stretch him out longer.

EDGAR   He is gone indeed.

KENT   The wonder is he hath endur'd so long:
He but usurp'd[138] his life.

320   ALBANY   Bear them from hence. Our present business

125. in despair
126. ourselves
127. useless
128. the royal plural, since Albany repre-
     sents those to whom Lear surrendered
     power
129. *great decay*: ruin of greatness (Lear)
130. *to . . . rights*: betake you to, enjoy
     your rights
131. *boot . . . addition*: the profit of such
     additions

132. honourable deeds
133. rewards
134. *poor fool*: (term of endearment) Cordelia
135. *Break, heart*: either to his own heart *or*
     of Lear's
136. spirit
137. metaphor from an instrument of tor-
     ture ("racking" the limbs)
138. kept what was due to death

Is general woe. [*To Kent and Edgar.*]   Friends of my soul, you twain
Rule in this realm,[139] and the gor'd[140] state sustain,
KENT   I have a journey, sir, shortly to go;
My master calls me, I must not say no.
325   ALBANY   The weight of this sad time we must obey;
Speak what we feel, not what we ought to say.[141]
The oldest[142] hath borne most: we that are young,
Shall never see so much, nor live so long.

[*Exeunt, with a dead march.*

139. *this realm*: (probably) that half of Britain which had been Regan's share
140. maimed, injured
141. *Speak . . . say*: i.e. (probably) at present we can only speak from the heart,
not prudently as after reflection

142. *The oldest*: especially Lear
143. In the quarto text of *Lear* the final speech
is attributed to Albany; in the folio text
this speech is attributed to Edgar.

ENGLISH THEATER IN THE RESTORATION AND THE EIGHTEENTH CENTURY

In 1642, at the beginning of the English Civil War, the Puritan Parliament closed all the theaters in London "to appease and avert the wrath of God." Although some small companies of actors struggled to produce plays, drama in effect died in England. In 1644 Parliament ordered the destruction of the Globe Theater, and by 1660, the year of the Restoration of the monarchy, most of the great Elizabethan theaters had been torn down.

Under the direct authority of King Charles II, two acting companies, the King's and the Duke's, were formed in 1660. Drama returned to England, and new theaters were designed to cater to a small audience of leisured courtiers, and not to the public at large. Gone now were the sceneless platform stages of the Elizabethan period. The new playhouses, designed in imitation of Italian theaters, introduced adequate space for machinery to stage scenes and to change them, as well as additional room for musicians. Unlike their continental counterparts, the English theaters retained a large apron-stage. A curtain that stayed open during performances hung from the proscenium arch, dividing the wide apron of the forestage from the deep-scene rearstage.

The spectacle of Restoration theater was greatly enhanced by the introduction of moveable stage flats, which were new to public theater. Such flats could be opened, closed, and moved about, for they were fastened to sets of grooves in the stage floor; they depicted many settings and could add the illusion of depth to the scenery.

The seating plans of the theaters were designed to reflect the social levels of their audiences. Many people sat on mat-covered benches in the pit, the large open area immediately in front of the stage. In the larger theaters, and especially in the new indoor theaters, there were boxes furnished with chairs around the three sides of the house where the wealthy took their seats. Above these boxes were the middle galleries for less wealthy members of the audience, and, still higher, the upper galleries where servants and apprentices sat on bare benches.

The major achievement of Restoration theater was comedy. Dramatists such as William Wycherley (*The Country Wife*, 1673) and William Congreve (*The Way of the World*, 1700) wrote savage satires on the manners and pretensions of the upper class. Often named "comedies of manners" because their purpose was to provoke laughter at the moral and social hypocrisies of their characters, these plays laugh at folly, satirize the morality of the upper class and the wealthy merchant class, and frequently ridicule the lewdness and lethargy of country life, always concealing their serious intentions under the veneer of polished wit.

By the early eighteenth century, theater audiences were composed more of middle-class citizens than of courtiers, new theaters were larger in size, and wit gave way to sentimentality. The comedy of manners was replaced by the sentimental comedy, which espoused faith in the innate goodness of humanity and employed dialogue that was moral rather than witty.

In the later eighteenth century, Richard Brinsley Sheridan recaptured the essence of Restoration comedy with a series of plays whose clever wit and pungent satire rivalled the comedies of a century earlier. And it would be yet another century again before such witty satire returned to the London theater in the sophisticated comedies of Oscar Wilde.

RICHARD BRINSLEY SHERIDAN
1751–1816

Born in Dublin, the Anglo-Irish playwright and politician was raised in a show-business family: his father was an actor and theater manager, his mother a playwright. Educated first by tutors, he was sent to Harrow from 1762 until 1769. *The Rivals*, his first play, opened at Covent Garden in 1775. The following year he became manager of the Drury Lane Theatre. His major plays belong to the period from 1775 to 1779, for in 1780 he entered politics as a Whig member of parliament, and he spent more than three decades in the House of Commons, holding several high offices including Treasurer of the Navy. *The School for Scandal*, universally acknowledged as his comic masterpiece, had its premiere at the Drury Lane Theatre in London on May 8, 1777.

The School for Scandal

A PORTRAIT

ADDRESSED TO A LADY WITH THE COMEDY OF THE
SCHOOL FOR SCANDAL
BY R. B. SHERIDAN, ESQ.

Tell me, ye prim adepts in Scandal's school
Who rail by precept, and detract by rule,
Lives there no character, so tried, so known,
So decked with grace—and so unlike your own—
That even *you* assist her fame to raise,
Approve by envy, and by silence praise?
Attend!—a model shall attract your view—
Daughters of calumny, I summon YOU:—
You shall decide if this a *portrait* prove,
10   Or fond creation of the Muse and Love.
Attend!—ye virgin critics shrewd and sage,
Ye matron censors of this childish age,
Whose peering eye and wrinkled front declare
A fixed antipathy to *young* and *fair*:
By cunning, cautious; or by nature cold,
In maiden malice virulently bold!
Attend!—ye skilled to coin the precious tale,
Creating proof, where innuendos fail!
Whose practised mem'ries, cruelly exact,
20   Omit no circumstance, except the fact!—
Attend!—all ye who boast,—or old or young—
The living libel of a sland'rous tongue!
So shall my theme as far contrasted be

As saints by fiends—or hymns by calumny.
Come, gentle *Amoret* (for 'neath that name
In worthier verse is sung thy beauty's fame),
   Come—for but thee who seeks the Muse?—and while
Celestial blushes check thy conscious smile,
With timid grace, and hesitating eye,
30   The perfect model which I boast—supply!
Vain Muse!—couldst thou the humblest sketch create
Of *her*, or slightest charm could'st imitate—
Could thy blest strain, in kindred colours, trace
The faintest wonder of her form, or face—
Poets would study the immortal line,
And *Reynolds* own his *art* subdued by *thine*!
That art, which well might added lustre give
To nature's best!—and heaven's superlative!—
On *Granby's* cheek might bid new glories rise,
40   Or point a purer beam from *Devon's* eyes!—
   Hard is the task to shape that beauty's praise,
Whose judgement scorns the homage—flatt'ry pays?
But praising *Amoret*—we cannot err:—
No tongue o'ervalues heav'n—nor flatters her!
Yet *she* by fate's perverseness!—she alone
Would doubt out truth, nor deem such praise her *own*!
   Adorning fashion, unadorned by dress,
Simple from taste, and not from carelessness;
Discreet in gesture, in deportment mild,
50   Not stiff with prudence, nor uncouthly wild—
No state has *Amoret*—no studied mien;
She frowns no *goddess*—and she moves no *queen*!
The softer charm that in her manner lies
Is fram'd to captivate, yet not surprise;
It justly suits th' expression of her face,—
'Tis less than dignity, and more than grace!
   On her pure cheek the native hue is such,
That form'd by heav'n to be admir'd so much,
The hand that made her with such partial care
60   Might well have fix'd a fainter crimson there,
And bade the gentle inmate of her breast—
Inshrined Modesty—supply the rest.
   But who the peril of her lips shall paint?—
Strip them of smiles—still, still all words were faint!
But moving—Love himself appears to teach
Their *action*, tho' denied to rule her *speech*!
And thou who *seest* her speak, and dost not *hear*,

Mourn not her distant accents 'scape thine ear,
Viewing those lips—thou still may'st make pretence
70   To judge of what she says—and swear 'tis sense;
Cloth'd with such grace, with such expression fraught,
They move in meaning, and they pause in thought!
But dost thou further watch, with charm'd surprise,
The mild irresolution of her eyes?
Curious to mark—how frequent they repose,
In brief eclipse, and momentary close?
Ah! seest thou not!—an ambushed Cupid there—
Too tim'rous of his charge!—with jealous care
Veils, and unveils those beams of heav'nly light,
80   Too full—too fatal else for mortal sight?
Nor yet, such pleasing vengeance fond to meet—
In pard'ning dimples hope a safe retreat,
What tho' her peaceful breast should ne'er allow
Subduing frowns to arm her alter'd brow,
By Love! I swear—and by his gentle wiles!—
More fatal still—the mercy of her smiles!
    Thus lovely!—thus adorn'd!—possessing all
Of bright, or fair that can to woman fall
The height of vanity might well be thought
90   Prerogative in her,—and Nature's fault.
Yet gentle *Amoret*—in mind supreme
As well as charms—rejects the vainer theme;
And half mistrustful of her beauty's store
She barbs with wit—those darts too keen before.
Read in all knowledge that her sex should reach,
Tho' *Grenville* or the Muse should deign to teach,
Fond to improve—nor tim'rous to discern
How far it is a woman's grace to learn;
In *Millar's* catalogue she would not prove
100   Apollo's *priestess*, but Apollo's *love*,
    Grac'd by those signs—which truth delights to own,
The timid blush, and mild submitted tone:
Whate'er she says—tho' sense appear throughout—
Bears the unartful hue of female doubt.
Deck'd with that charm, how lovely *wit* appears,
How graceful *science* when that robe she wears!
Such too her talents, and her bent of mind
As speak a sprightly heart—by thought refin'd:
A taste for mirth—by contemplation school'd,
110   A turn for ridicule—by candour rul'd,
A scorn of folly—which she tries to hide;

An awe of talent—which she owns with pride.
   Peace, idle Muse!—no more thy strain prolong,
But yield a theme, thy warmest praises wrong,
Just to her merit, tho' thou canst not raise
Thy feeble verse—behold th' acknowledged praise
Has spread conviction thro' the envious train,
And cast a fatal gloom o'er Scandal's reign!
And lo! each pallid hag, with blister'd tongue,
120 Mutters assent to all thy zeal has sung,
Owns all the colours just—the outline true,
Thee my inspirer—and my *model*—CREWE!

PROLOGUE

SPOKEN BY MR. KING
WRITTEN BY D. GARRICK, ESQ.

A School for Scandal! tell me, I beseech you,
Needs there a school this modish art to teach you?
No need to lessons now, the knowing think—
We might as well be taught to eat and drink.
Caus'd by a dearth of scandal, should the vapours
Distress our fair ones—let 'em read the papers;
Their pow'rful mixtures such disorders hit;
Crave what they will, there's *quantum sufficit.*
   "Lord!" cries my Lady Wormwood (who loves tattle,
10 And puts much salt and pepper in her prattle),
Just ris'n at noon, all night at cards when threshing
Strong tea and scandal—"Bless me, how refreshing!
Give me the papers, Lisp—how bold and free! [*sips*]
Last night Lord I.—— [sips] was caught with Lady D——
For aching heads what charming sal volatile! [*sips*]
If Mrs. B—— will still continue flirting,
We hope she'll DRAW, *or we'll* UNDRAW *the curtain.*
Fine satire, poz—in public all abuse it,
But, by ourselves [*sips*], our praise we can't refuse it.
20 Now, Lisp, read *you*—there, at that dash and star."
"Yes, ma'am. —*A certain Lord had best beware,*
Who lives not twenty miles from Grosv'nor Square;
For should he Lady W—— find willing,
WORMWOOD *is bitter*" —"Oh! that's me! the villain!
25 Throw it behind the fire, and never more
Let that vile paper come within my door." —

Thus at our friends we laugh, who feel the dart;
To reach our feelings, we ourselves must smart.
Is our young bard so young, to think that he
30 Can stop the full spring-tide of calumny?
Knows he the world so little and its trade?
Alas! the Dev'l is sooner *rais'd* than *laid*.
So strong, so swift, the monster there's no gagging:
Cut Scandal's head off—still the tongue is wagging.
Proud of your smiles, once lavishly bestow'd,
Again your young Don Quixote takes the road:
To show his gratitude, he draws his pen,
And seeks this hydra, Scandal, in his den.
For your applause, all perils he would through—
40 He'll fight—that's *write*—a cavalliero true,
Till ev'ry drop of blood—that's *ink*—is spilt for you.

CHARACTERS

Men
SIR PETER TEAZLE
SIR OLIVER SURFACE
JOSEPH SURFACE
CHARLES SURFACE
CRABTREE
SIR BENJAMIN BACKBITE
ROWLEY
TRIP
MOSES
SNAKE
CARELESS

and other Companions to CHARLES [SURFACE],
Servants, etc.

Women
LADY TEAZLE
MARIA
LADY SNEERWELL
MRS. CANDOUR

[SCENE: *London*]

ACT I

SCENE I

Lady Sneerwell's house
Lady Sneerwell at the dressing-table—
Snake drinking chocolate

LADY SNEERWELL   The paragraphs, you say, Mr. Snake, were all inserted?

SNAKE   They were, Madam, and as I copied them myself in a feigned hand, there can be no suspicion whence they came. —

LADY SNEERWELL   Did you circulate the report of Lady *Brittle's* intrigue with Captain *Boastall*?

SNAKE   That is in as fine a train as your ladyship could wish. —In the common course of things, I think it must reach Mrs. *Clackit's* ears within four-and-twenty hours and then you know the business is as good as done.

LADY SNEERWELL   Why, truly, Mrs. *Clackit* has a very pretty talent — and a great deal of industry .

SNAKE   True, Madam, and has been tolerably successful in her day. — To my knowledge, she has been the cause of six matches being broken off, and three sons being disinherited, of four forced elopements, as many close confinements, nine separate maintenances, and two divorces.—Nay, I have more than once traced her causing a *Tête-à-Tête* in the *Town and Country Magazine*—when the parties perhaps had never seen each other's faces before in the course of their lives.

LADY SNEERWELL   She certainly has talents, but her manner is gross.

SNAKE   'Tis very true, —she generally designs well, has a free tongue, and a bold invention—but her colouring is too dark and her outline often extravagant. She wants that *delicacy* of *hint*, and *mellowness* of *sneer*, which distinguish your ladyship's scandal.

LADY SNEERWELL   Ah! you are partial Snake.

SNAKE   Not in the least—everybody allows that Lady *Sneerwell* can do more with a *word* or a *look* than many can with the most laboured detail, even when they happen to have a little truth on their side to support it.

LADY SNEERWELL   Yes, my dear Snake, and I am no hypocrite to deny the satisfaction I reap from the success of my efforts. Wounded myself, in the early part of my life by the envenomed tongue of slander, I confess I have since known no pleasure equal to the reducing of others to the level of my own injured reputation.

SNAKE   Nothing can be more natural. But, Lady Sneerwell, there is one affair in which you have lately employed me wherein I confess I am at a loss to guess your motives.

LADY SNEERWELL   I conceive you mean with respect to my neighbour, Sir Peter Teazle, and his family.

SNAKE   I do; here are two young men, to whom Sir Peter has acted as a kind of guardian since their father's death; the elder possessing the most amiable character and universally well spoken of; the other, the most dissipated and extravagant young fellow in the kingdom, without friends or character, — the former an avowed admirer of your ladyship and apparently your favourite; the latter attached to Maria, Sir Peter's ward, and confessedly beloved by her. Now on the face of these circumstances it is utterly unaccountable to me why you, the widow of a city knight, with a good jointure, should not close with the passion of a man of such character and expectations as Mr. *Surface* — and more so why you should be so uncommonly earnest to destroy the mutual attachment subsisting between his brother *Charles* and *Maria*.

LADY SNEERWELL   Then at once to unravel this mystery I must inform you that love has no share whatever in the intercourse between Mr. *Surface* and me.

SNAKE   No!

LADY SNEERWELL   His real attachment is to *Maria* or her fortune — but finding in his brother a favoured rival, he has been obliged to mask his pretensions, and profit by my assistance.

SNAKE   Yet still — I am more puzzled why you should interest yourself in his success.

LADY SNEERWELL   Heav'ns! how dull you are! — Cannot you surmise the weakness which I hitherto through shame have concealed even from *you*? Must I confess that *Charles* — that libertine, that extravagant, that bankrupt in fortune and reputation — that he it is for whom I am thus anxious and malicious, and to gain whom I would sacrifice everything?

SNAKE   Now indeed your conduct appears consistent — but how came you and Mr. *Surface* so confidential?

LADY SNEERWELL   For our mutual interest. I have found him out a long time since — I know him to be artful, selfish, and malicious — in short, a sentimental knave.

SNAKE   Yet, Sir Peter vows he has not his equal in England — and above all, he praises him as a man of sentiment.

LADY SNEERWELL   True and with the assistance of his sentiments and hypocrisy he has brought him entirely into his interest with regard to *Maria*.

Enter Servant

SERVANT   Mr. Surface.

LADY SNEERWELL   Show him up.   *Exit Servant*
   He generally calls about this time — I don't wonder at people's
   giving him to me for a lover. —

Enter Joseph Surface

JOSEPH SURFACE   My dear Lady Sneerwell — how do you do to-day? —
   Mr. Snake, your most obedient.

LADY SNEERWELL   Snake has just been arraigning me on our mutual
   attachment, but I have informed him of our real views—you know
   how useful he has been to us, and believe me the confidence is
   not ill placed.

JOSEPH SURFACE   Madam, it is impossible for me to suspect a man of
   Mr. *Snake's* sensibility and discernment.

LADY SNEERWELL   Well, well, no compliments now; — but tell me when
   you saw your mistress, *Maria*, or what is more material to me,
   your brother?

JOSEPH SURFACE   I have not seen either since I left you—but I can inform
   you that they never meet. Some of your stories have taken a good
   effect on Maria.

LADY SNEERWELL   Ah! my dear Snake the merit of this belongs to you.
   But do your brother's distresses increase?

JOSEPH SURFACE   Every hour—I am told he has had another execution
   in the house yesterday; in short his dissipation and extravagance
   exceed any thing I ever heard of.

LADY SNEERWELL   Poor Charles!

JOSEPH SURFACE   True, Madam; — notwithstanding his vices, one can't
   help feeling for him. — Aye, poor Charles! I'm sure I wish it was
   in *my* power to be of any essential service to him. — For the man
   who does not share in the distresses of a brother, even tho' merited
   by his own misconduct, deserves —

LADY SNEERWELL   O lud! you are going to be moral, and forget that you
   are among friends.

JOSEPH SURFACE   Egad, that's true! — I'll keep that sentiment till I see
   Sir Peter. However it is certainly a charity to rescue Maria from
   such a libertine, who if he is to be reclaimed, can be so only by a
   person of your ladyship's superior accomplishments and
   understanding.

SNAKE   I believe Lady Sneerwell here's company coming, I'll go and
   copy the letter I mentioned to you. — Mr. Surface, your most
   obedient.

Exit Snake

JOSEPH SURFACE   Sir, your very devoted. — Lady Sneerwell, I am sorry you have put any further confidence in that fellow.

LADY SNEERWELL   Why so?

JOSEPH SURFACE   I have lately detected him in frequent conference with old *Rowley*, who was formerly my father's steward and has never, you know, been a friend of mine.

LADY SNEERWELL   And do you think he would betray us?

JOSEPH SURFACE Nothing more likely: take my word for't Lady Sneerwell, that fellow hasn't virtue enough to be faithful even to his own villainy. — Hah! Maria!

Enter Maria

LADY SNEERWELL   Maria, my dear, how do you do? — what's the matter?

MARIA   There is that disagreeable lover of mine, Sir *Benjamin Backbite*, has just called at my guardian's with his odious uncle, *Crabtree* — so I slipped out and run hither to avoid them.

LADY SNEERWELL   Is that all?

JOSEPH SURFACE   If my brother *Charles* had been of the party, Ma'am, perhaps you would not have been so much alarmed.

LADY SNEERWELL   Nay now — you are severe, for I dare swear the truth of the matter is, Maria heard *you* were here — but, my dear, what has Sir Benjamin done that you should avoid him so?

MARIA   Oh he has done nothing — but 'tis for what he has said — his conversation is a perpetual libel on all his acquaintance.

JOSEPH SURFACE   Aye and the worst of it is, there is no advantage in not knowing him; for he'll abuse a stranger just as soon as his best friend — and his uncle's as bad.

LADY SNEERWELL   Nay but we should make allowance, Sir Benjamin is a wit and a poet.

MARIA   For my part, I own, Madam, wit loses its respect with me when I see it in company with malice. — What do you think Mr. Surface?

JOSEPH SURFACE   Certainly, Madam, to smile at the jest which plants a thorn in another's breast is to become a principal in the mischief.

LADY SNEERWELL   Pshaw! there's no possibility of being witty — without a little ill nature: the malice of a good thing is the barb that makes it stick. — What's your opinion Mr. Surface?

JOSEPH SURFACE   To be sure Madam, that conversation where the spirit of raillery is suppressed will ever appear tedious and insipid.

MARIA   Well, I'll not debate how far scandal may be allowable; but in a man, I am sure, it is always contemptible.—We have pride, envy, rivalship, and a thousand motives to depreciate each other; but the male — slanderer — must have the cowardice of a woman before he can traduce one.

Enter Servant

SERVANT Madam, Mrs. Candour is below and if your ladyship's at leisure, will leave her carriage. —
LADY SNEERWELL Beg her to walk in. [*Exit Servant*]
Now Maria however here is a character to your taste for though Mrs. Candour is a little talkative, everybody allows her to be the best-natured and best sort of woman.
MARIA Yes, with a very gross affectation of good nature and benevolence, she does more mischief than the direct malice of old Crabtree. —
JOSEPH SURFACE 'Efaith 'tis very true, Lady Sneerwell. Whenever I hear the current running against the characters of my friends, I never think them in such danger as when Candour undertakes their defence.
LADY SNEERWELL Hush, here she is!

Enter Mrs. Candour

MRS. CANDOUR My dear Lady Sneerwell, how have you been this century?—Mr. Surface, what news do you hear?—tho' indeed it is no matter, for I think one hears nothing else but scandal.
JOSEPH SURFACE Just so, indeed Madam
MRS. CANDOUR Ah, Maria, child! — what, is the whole affair off between you and Charles? His extravagance, I presume — the town talks of nothing else.
MARIA I am very sorry Ma'am, the town has so little to do.
MRS. CANDOUR True, true, child, but there is no stopping people's tongues. I own I was hurt to hear it, as indeed I was to learn, from the same quarter, that your guardian, Sir Peter, and Lady Teazle have not agreed lately so well as could be wished.
MARIA 'Tis strangely impertinent for people to busy themselves so.
MRS. CANDOUR Very true child, but what's to be done? People will talk — there's no preventing it. — Why it was but yesterday I was told that Miss Gadabout had eloped with Sir Fillegree Flirt—but, Lord! there's no minding what one hears — tho' to be sure, I had this from very good authority. —
MARIA Such reports are highly scandalous.
MRS. CANDOUR So they are child—shameful, shameful! But the world

is so censorious, no character escapes. Lord now! — who would have suspected your friend, Miss Prim, of an indiscretion? Yet such is the ill nature of people, that they say her uncle stopped her last week just as she was stepping into the York Diligence with her dancing-master.

MARIA I'll answer for't there are no grounds for the report.

MRS. CANDOUR Oh no foundation in the world I dare swear; no more probably, than for the story circulated last month of Mrs. Festino's affair with Colonel Cassino; — though to be sure that matter was never rightly cleared up.

JOSEPH SURFACE The licence of invention some people take is monstrous indeed.

MARIA 'Tis so. — But in my opinion, those who report such things are equally culpable.

MRS. CANDOUR To be sure they are; tale-bearers are as bad as the tale-makers. — 'Tis an old observation and a very true one—but what's to be done, as I said before? how will you prevent people from talking? — Today Mrs. Clackit assured me Mr. and Mrs. Honeymoon were at last become mere man and wife like the rest of their acquaintances. — She likewise hinted that a certain widow in the next street had got rid of her dropsy and recovered her shape in a most surprising manner—and at the same time Miss Tattle, who was by, affirmed that Lord Buffalo had discovered his lady at a house of no extraordinary fame—and that Sir Harry Bouquet and Tom Saunter were to measure swords on a similar provocation. But Lord, do you think I would report these things? No, no, tale-bearers as I said before are just as bad as tale-makers.

JOSEPH SURFACE Ah! Mrs. Candour — if everybody had your forbearance and good nature!

MRS. CANDOUR I confess, Mr. Surface, I cannot bear to hear people attacked behind their backs, and when ugly circumstances come out against one's acquaintance I own I always love to think the best. — By the by I hope it is not true that your brother is absolutely ruined?

JOSEPH SURFACE I am afraid his circumstances are very bad indeed, Ma'am.

MRS. CANDOUR Ah! — I heard so — but you must tell him to keep up his spirits — everybody almost is in the same way! Lord Spindle, Sir Thomas Splint, Captain Quinze, and Mr. Nickit—all up, I hear, within this week! so if Charles is undone he'll find half his acquaintances ruined too—and that you know is a consolation. —

JOSEPH SURFACE Doubtless Ma'am—a very great one.

Enter Servant

SERVANT   Mr. Crabtree and Sir Benjamin Backbite.

Exit Servant

LADY SNEERWELL   So Maria, you see your lover pursues you — positively you shan't escape.

Enter Crabtee and Sir Benjamin Backbite

CRABTREE   Lady Sneerwell, I kiss your hands. Mrs. Candour, I don't believe you are acquainted with my nephew, Sir Bejamin Backbite. Egad, Ma'am, he has a pretty wit, and is a pretty poet too; isn't he, Lady Sneerwell?

SIR BENJAMIN   O fie, uncle!

CRABTREE   Nay, egad it's true — I'll back him at a rebus or a charade against the best rhymer in the kingdom. Has your ladyship heard the epigram he wrote last week on Lady Frizzle's feather catching fire? — Do, Benjamin, repeat it — or the charade you made last night extempore at Mrs. Drowzie's conversazione. — Come now; your *first* is the name of a fish, your *second* a great naval commander, and—

SIR BENJAMIN   Uncle, now — prithee–

CRABTREE   'Efaith, Ma'am, 'twould surprise you to hear how ready he is at these things.

LADY SNEERWELL   I wonder Sir Benjamin, you never publish anything.

SIR BENJAMIN   To say truth, Ma'am, 'tis very vulgar to print and as my little productions are mostly satires and lampoons on particular people, I find they circulate more by giving copies in confidence to the friends of the parties — however, I have some love elegies, which when favoured with this lady's smiles, I mean to give to the public.

CRABTREE   'Fore heav'n, Ma'am, they'll immortalize you — you'll be handed down to posterity like Petrarch's Laura, or Waller's Sacharissa.

SIR BENJAMIN   Yes, Madam, I think you will like them when you shall see them on a beautiful quarto page, where a neat rivulet of text shall murmur through a meadow of margin. — 'Fore gad they will be the most elegant things of their kind.

CRABTREE   But ladies, that's true — have you heard the news?

MRS. CANDOUR   What, sir, do you mean the report of—

CRABTREE   No, Ma'am, that's not it. — Miss Nicely is going to be married to her own footman.

MRS. CANDOUR   Impossible!

CRABTREE   Ask Sir Benjamin.

SIR BENJAMIN   'Tis very true Ma'am—everything is fixed, and the wedding livery bespoke.

CRABTREE   Yes—and they *do* say there were pressing reasons for't.

LADY SNEERWELL   Why I *have* heard something of this before.

MRS. CANDOUR   It can't be—and I wonder any one should believe such a story of so prudent a lady as Miss Nicely.

SIR BENJAMIN   O lud, ma'am! that's the very reason 'twas believed at once. She has always been so *cautious* and so *reserved* that everybody was sure there was some reason for it at bottom.

MRS. CANDOUR   Why to be sure, a tale of scandal is as fatal to the credit of a prudent lady of her stamp as a fever is generally to those of the strongest constitutions; but there is a sort of puny, sickly reputation that is always ailing, yet will outlive the robuster characters of a hundred prudes.

SIR BENJAMIN   True Madam, there are valetudinarians in reputation as well as constitution, who being conscious of their weak part, avoid the least breath of air and supply their want to stamina by care and circumspection.

MRS. CANDOUR   Well but this may be all a mistake. You know Sir Benjamin very trifling circumstances often give rise to the most injurious tales.

CRABTREE   That they do I'll be sworn Ma'am. Did you ever hear how Miss Piper came to lose her lover and her character last summer at Tunbridge?—Sir Benjamin, you remember it.

SIR BENJAMIN   O to be sure!—the most whimsical circumstance—

LADY SNEERWELL   How was it, pray?

CRABTREE   Why one evening at Mrs. Ponto's assembly, the conversation happened to turn on the difficulty of breeding Nova-Scotia sheep in this country. Says a young lady in company, "I have known instances of it for Miss Letitia Piper, a first cousin of mine, had a Nova-Scotia sheep that produced her twins." "What!" cries the old Dowager Lady Dundizzy (who you know is as deaf as a post), "has Miss Piper had twins?" — this mistake as you may imagine, threw the whole company into a fit of laughing—however, 'twas the next morning everywhere reported and in a few days believed by the whole town, that Miss Letitia Piper had actually been brought to bed of a fine boy and a girl—and in less than a week there were people who could name the father and the farm-house where the babies were put out to nurse!

LADY SNEERWELL   Strange, indeed!

CRABTREE   Matter of fact I assure you.—O lud! Mr. Surface, pray is it true that your uncle, Sir Oliver, is coming home?

JOSEPH SURFACE   Not that I know of, indeed, sir.

CRABTREE   He has been in the East Indies a long time, you can scarcely remember him, I believe. — Sad comfort whenever he returns to hear how your brother has gone on!

JOSEPH SURFACE   Charles has been imprudent sir, to be sure, but I hope no busy people have already prejudiced Sir Oliver against him — he may reform.

SIR BENJAMIN   To be sure he may — for my part I never believed him to be so utterly void of principle as people say — and tho' he has lost all his friends, I am told nobody is better spoken of by the Jews.

CRABTREE   That's true, egad, nephew — if the Old Jewry were a ward I believe Charles would be an alderman, no man more popular there; 'fore gad, I hear he pays as many annuities as the Irish tontine, and that whenever he's sick, they have prayers for the recovery of his health in the Synagogue.

SIR BENJAMIN   Yet no man lives in greater splendour: — they tell me when he entertains his friends, he can sit down to dinner with a dozen of his own securities, have a score tradesmen waiting in the antechamber and an officer behind every guest's chair.

JOSEPH SURFACE   This may be entertainment to you gentlemen, but you pay very little regard to the feelings of a brother.

MARIA   Their malice is intolerable — Lady Sneerwell, I must wish you a good morning — I'm not very well.

Exit Maria

MRS. CANDOUR   O dear! she changes colour very much!

MRS. SNEERWELL   Do, Mrs. Candour, follow her — she may want assistance.

MRS. CANDOUR   That I will with all my soul, Ma'am — poor dear girl! who knows what her situation may be!

Exit Mrs. Candour

LADY SNEERWELL   'Twas nothing but that she could not bear to hear Charles reflected on, notwithstanding their difference.

SIR BENJAMIN   The young lady's *penchant* is obvious.

CRABTREE   But, Benjamin, you mustn't give up the pursuit for that — follow her, and put her into good humour — repeat her some of your own verses. Come, I'll assist you.

SIR BENJAMIN   Mr. Surface, I did not mean to hurt you, but depend upon't your brother is utterly undone.   [*Going*]

CRABTREE   O lud! aye — undone as ever man was — can't raise a guinea.   [*Going*]

SIR BENJAMIN   Any everything sold, I'm told, that was movable.   [*Going*]

CRABTREE   I have seen one that was at his house — not a thing left but some empty bottles that were overlooked, and the family pictures, which I believe are framed in the wainscot. —   [*Going*]

SIR BENJAMIN   And I am very sorry to hear also some bad stories against him.   [*Going*]

CRABTREE   O he has done many mean things, that's certain.   [*Going*]

SIR BENJAMIN   But however, as he's your brother —   [*Going*]

CRABTREE   We'll tell you all another opportunity.

Exeunt Crabtree and Sir Benjamin

LADY SNEERWELL   Ha! ha! ha! 'tis very hard for them to leave a subject they have not quite run down.

JOSEPH SURFACE   And I believe the abuse was no more acceptable to your ladyship than to Maria.

LADY SNEERWELL   I doubt her affections are farther engaged than we imagined; but the family are to be here this evening, so you may as well dine where you are and we shall have an opportunity of observing farther. In the meantime I'll go and plot mischief and you shall study sentiments.

Exeunt

SCENE II

Sir Peter Teazle's house
Enter Sir Peter

SIR PETER   When an old bachelor takes a young wife, what is he to expect? — 'Tis now six months since Lady Teazle made me the happiest of men — and I have been the miserablest dog ever since that ever committed wedlock! — we tift a little going to church and came to a quarrel before the bells were done ringing. I was more than once nearly choked with gall during the honeymoon, and had lost all comfort in life before my friends had done wishing me joy! — yet I chose with caution — a girl bred wholly in the country, who never knew luxury beyond one silk gown, nor dissipation above the annual gala of a race-ball. Yet now she plays her part in all the extravagant fopperies of the fashion and the town with as ready a grace as if she had never seen a bush nor a grass-plot out of Grosvenor Square! I am sneered at by my old acquaintance — paragraphed in the newspapers. She dissipates my fortune, and contradicts all my humours — yet the worst of it is, I doubt I love her, or I should never bear all this. However, I'll never be weak enough to own it.

Enter Rowley

ROWLEY   Oh, Sir Peter, your servant, — how is it with you, sir?

SIR PETER   Very bad, Master Rowley, very bad — I meet with nothing but crosses and vexations.

ROWLEY   What can have happened to trouble you since yesterday?

SIR PETER   A good question to a married man!

ROWLEY   Nay I'm sure your lady, Sir Peter, can't be the cause of your uneasiness.

SIR PETER   Why, has anyone told you she was dead?

ROWLEY   Come, come, Sir Peter, you love her notwithstanding your tempers don't exactly agree.

SIR PETER   But the fault is entirely hers, Master Rowley — I am myself the sweetest-tempered man alive and hate a teasing temper — so I tell her a hundred times a day.

ROWLEY   Indeed!

SIR PETER   Aye and what is very extraordinary in all our disputes she is always in the wrong! but Lady Sneerwell and the set she meets at her house encourage the perverseness of her disposition. Then, to complete my vexations, Maria, my ward, whom I ought to have the power of a father over is determined to turn rebel too, and absolutely refuses the man whom I have long resolved on for her husband — meaning I suppose to bestow herself on his profligate brother.

ROWLEY   You know, Sir Peter, I have always taken the liberty to differ with you on the subject of these two young gentlemen. — I only wish you may not be deceived in your opinion of the elder — for Charles, my life on't! he will retrieve his errors yet. Their worthy father, once my honoured master, was at his years nearly as wild a spark — yet when he died, he did not leave a more benevolent heart to lament his loss.

SIR PETER   You are wrong Master Rowley — on their father's death, you know, I acted as a kind of guardian to them both, till their uncle Sir Oliver's Eastern liberality gave them an early independence. Of course, no person could have more opportunities of judging of their hearts, and I was never mistaken in my life. Joseph is indeed a model for the young men of the age. He is a man of sentiment — and acts up to the sentiments he professes, but for the other, take my word for't, if he had any grains of virtue by descent, he has dissipated them with the rest of his inheritance. Ah! my old friend Sir Oliver will be deeply mortified when he finds how part of his bounty has been misapplied.

ROWLEY   I am sorry to find you so violent against the young man, because this may be the most critical period of his fortune. — I came hither with news that will surprise you.

SIR PETER   What! let me hear.

ROWLEY   Sir Oliver *is* arrived and at this moment in town.

SIR PETER   How!—you astonish me—I thought you did not expect him this month. —

ROWLEY   I did not: but his passage has been remarkably quick.

SIR PETER   Egad I shall rejoice to see my old friend — 'tis sixteen years since we met — we have had many a day together; but does he still enjoin us not to inform his nephews of his arrival?

ROWLEY   Most strictly — he means before it is known to make some trial of their dispositions.

SIR PETER   Ah, there needs no art to discover their merits!—however, he shall have his way—but pray he does know I am married?

ROWLEY   Yes, and will soon wish you joy.

SIR PETER   What, as we drink health to a friend in a consumption! Ah! Oliver will laugh at me—we used to rail at matrimony together— but he has been steady to his text.—Well he must be at my house, tho'—I'll instantly give orders for his reception. But, Master Rowley, don't drop a word that Lady Teazle and I ever disagree.

ROWLEY   By no means.

SIR PETER   For I should never be able to stand Noll's jokes—so I'd have him think, Lord forgive me! that we are a very happy couple.

ROWLEY   I understand you—but then you must be very careful not to differ while he's in the house with you.

SIR PETER   Egad, and so we must—and that's impossible. Ah! Master Rowley, when an old bachelor marries a young wife, he deserves —no—the crime carries the punishment along with it.

Exeunt

End of Act 1st

ACT II

SCENE I

Sir Peter Teazle's house
Enter Sir Peter and Lady Teazle

SIR PETER   Lady Teazle, Lady Teazle, I'll not bear it!

LADY TEAZLE   Sir Peter, Sir Peter, you may bear it or not, as you please, but I ought to have my own way in everything, and what's more, I *will* too—what! tho' I was educated in the country, I know very well that women of fashion in London are accountable to nobody after they are married.

SIR PETER   Very well, Ma'am, very well!—so a husband is to have no influence, no authority?

LADY TEAZLE   Authority! no, to be sure—if you wanted authority over me, you should have adopted me and not married me; I am sure you were old enough.

SIR PETER   Old enough!—aye there it is—well, well, Lady Teazle, tho' my life may be made unhappy by your temper, I'll not be ruined by your extravagance.

LADY TEAZLE   My extravagance—I'm sure I'm not more extravagant than a woman of fashion ought to be.

SIR PETER   No, no, Madam, you shall throw away no more sums on such unmeaning luxury. 'Slife! to spend as much to furnish your dressing-room with flowers in winter as would suffice to turn the Pantheon into a greenhouse and give a *fête champêtre* at Christmas!

LADY TEAZLE   Lord Sir Peter, am I to blame because flowers are dear in cold weather? You should find fault with the climate, and not with me. For my part, I am sure I wish it was spring all the year round, and that roses grew under one's feet!

SIR PETER   Oons! Madam—if you had been born to this, I shouldn't wonder at your talking thus.—But you forget what your situation was when I married you.

LADY TEAZLE   No, no, I don't   'twas a very disagreeable one, or I should never have married *you*.

SIR PETER   Yes, yes, Madam, you were then in somewhat an humbler style — the daughter of a plain country squire. Recollect, Lady Teazle, when I saw you first, sitting at your tambour in a pretty figured linen gown, with a bunch of keys by your side, your hair combed smooth over a roll, and your apartment hung with fruits in worsted, of your own working.

LADY TEAZLE   O yes, I remember it very well, and a curious life I led! —my daily occupation to inspect the dairy, superintend the poultry, make extracts from the family receipt-book, and comb my aunt Deborah's lap-dog.

SIR PETER   Yes, yes, Ma'am, 'twas so indeed.

LADY TEAZLE   And then, you know, my evening amusements — to draw patterns for ruffles which I had not the materials to make— to play Pope Joan with the curate— to read a novel to my aunt—

or to be stuck down to an old spinet to strum my father to sleep after a fox-chase.

SIR PETER   I am glad you have so good a memory. Yes, Madam, these were the recreations I took you from. But now you must have your coach, *vis-à-vis* and three powdered footmen before your chair — and in summer a pair of white cats to draw you to Kensington Gardens. — No recollection I suppose when you were content to ride double behind the butler on a docked coach-horse?

LADY TEAZLE   No—I swear I never did that—I deny the butler, and the coach-horse.

SIR PETER   This, Madam, was your situation — and what have I not done for you? — I have made you a woman of fashion, of fortune, of rank — in short I have made you my wife.

LADY TEAZLE   Well then, and there is but one thing more you can make me to add to the obligation — and that is —

SIR PETER   My widow I suppose?

LADY TEAZLE   Hem! hem!

SIR PETER   Thank you, Madam — but don't flatter yourself, for, tho' your ill-conduct may disturb my peace, it shall never break my heart I promise you: however, I am equally obliged to you for the hint.

LADY TEAZLE   Then why will you endeavour to make yourself so disagreeable to me, and thwart me in every little elegant expense?

SIR PETER   'Slife Madam, I say, had you any of these elegant expenses when you married me?

LADY TEAZLE   Lud, Sir Peter! would you have me be out of fashion?

SIR PETER   The fashion, indeed — what had you to do with fashion before you married me?

LADY TEAZLE   For my part, I should think you would like to have your wife thought a woman of taste.

SIR PETER   Aye — there again — taste! Zounds! Madam, you had no taste when you married *me*!

LADY TEAZLE   That's very true, indeed, Sir Peter! and, *after* having married you, I am sure I should never pretend to taste again! — But now, Sir Peter, if we have finished our daily jangle, I presume I may go to my engagement of Lady Sneerwell's?

SIR PETER   Aye—there's another precious circumstance! —a charming set of acquaintance you have made there.

LADY TEAZLE   Nay, Sir Peter, they are people of rank and fortune, and remarkably tenacious of reputation.

SIR PETER   Yes, egad, they are tenacious of reputation with a vengeance for they don't choose anybody should have a character — but themselves! such a crew! ah! many a wretch has rid on a hurdle who has done less mischief than those utterers of forged tales, coiners of scandal, — and clippers of reputation.

LADY TEAZLE   What! would you restrain the freedom of speech?

SIR PETER   O! they have made you just as bad as any one of the society.

LADY TEAZLE   Why, I believe I do bear a part with a tolerable grace. But
I vow I have no malice against the people I abuse; when I say an
ill-natured thing 'tis out of pure good humour — and I take it for
granted they deal exactly in the same manner with me. But Sir
Peter, you know you promised to come to Lady Sneerwell's too.

SIR PETER   Well, well, I'll call in just to look after my own character.

LADY TEAZLE   Then indeed, you must make haste after me or you'll be
too late — so good-bye to ye.

Exit Lady Teazle

SIR PETER   So, I have gained much by my intended expostulations —
yet with what a charming air she contradicts everything I say, and
how pleasingly she shows her contempt of my authority! well,
tho' I can't make her love me, there is a great satisfaction in quarreling with her, and I think she never appears to such advantage
as when she's doing everything in her power to plague me.   *Exit*

SCENE II

Lady Sneerwell's
*Lady Sneerwell, Mrs. Candour, Crabtree, Sir Benjamin Backbite, and Joseph
Surface*

LADY SNEERWELL   Nay, positively we will hear it.

JOSEPH SURFACE   Yes, yes the epigram by all means.

SIR BENJAMIN   Plague on't, uncle — 'tis mere nonsense.

CRABTREE   No, no, 'fore gad, very clever for an extempore!

SIR BENJAMIN   But ladies, you should be acquainted with the circum-
stances. — You must know that one day last week, as Lady Betty
Curricle was taking the dust in Hyde Park, in a sort of duodecimo
phaëton she desired me to write some verses on her ponies, upon
which I took out my pocket-book and in one moment produced
the following:
"Sure never were seen two such beautiful ponies!
Other horses are clowns — and these — macaronies!
Nay, to give 'em this title I'm sure isn't wrong —
— Their legs are so slim, and their tails are so long."

CRABTREE   There ladies — done in the smack of a whip, and on horseback too!

JOSEPH SURFACE   A very Phoebus, mounted—indeed, Sir Benjamin.

SIR BENJAMIN   O dear sir—trifles—trifles.

Enter Lady Teazle and Maria

MRS. CANDOUR   I must have a copy.

LADY SNEERWELL   Lady Teazle, I hope we shall see Sir Peter.

LADY TEAZLE   I believe he'll wait on your ladyship—presently.

LADY SNEERWELL   Maria my love, you look grave. Come, you shall sit down to cards with Mr. Surface.

MARIA   I take very little pleasure in cards—however I'll do as your ladyship pleases.

LADY TEAZLE [*aside*]   I am surprised Mr. Surface should sit down with *her.* — I thought he would have embraced this opportunity of speaking to me before Sir Peter came.

MRS. CANDOUR [*coming forward*]   Now I'll die but you are so scandalous I'll forswear your society.

LADY TEAZLE   What's the matter, Mrs. Candour?

MRS. CANDOUR   They'll not allow our friend Miss Vermilion to be handsome.

LADY SNEERWELL   O surely she's a pretty woman.

CRABTREE   I am very glad you think so, Ma'am.

MRS. CANDOUR   She has charming fresh colour.

LADY TEAZLE   Yes, when it is fresh put on.

MRS. CANDOUR   O fie! I'll swear her colour is natural—I have seen it come and go.

LADY TEAZLE   I dare swear you have, Ma'am—it goes of a night and comes again in the morning.

MRS. CANDOUR   Ha! ha! ha! how I hate to hear you talk so! but surely now her sister *is*, or *was*, very handsome.

CRABTREE   Who? Mrs. Evergreen?—O Lord, she's six-and-fifty if she's an hour!

MRS. CANDOUR   Now positively you wrong her; fifty-two or fifty-three is the utmost—and I don't think she looks more.

SIR BENJAMIN   Ah! there is no judging by her looks unless one could see her face.

LADY SNEERWELL   Well, well, if Mrs. Evergreen *does* take some pains to repair the ravages of time, you must allow she effects it with great ingenuity—and surely that's better than the careless manner in which the widow Ochre caulks her wrinkles.

SIR BENJAMIN   Nay, now Lady Sneerwell, you are severe upon the widow. Come, come, it is not that she paints so ill—but when she has finished her face, she joins it on so badly to her neck that she looks like a mended statue, in which the connoisseur sees at once that the head's modern tho' the trunk's antique.

CRABTREE   Ha! ha! ha! well said, nephew!

MRS. CANDOUR   Ha! ha! ha! well, you make me laugh but I vow I hate you for't. — What do you think of Miss Simper?

SIR BENJAMIN   Why she has very pretty teeth.

LADY TEAZLE   Yes and on that account, when she is neither speaking nor laughing (which very seldom happens), she never absolutely shuts her mouth but leaves it always on a jar as it were.

MRS. CANDOUR   How can you be so ill-natured?

LADY TEAZLE   Nay I allow even that's better than the pains Mrs. Prim takes to conceal her losses in front. She draws her mouth till it positively resembes the aperture of a poor's-box, and all her words appear to slide out edgeways.

LADY SNEERWELL   Very well Lady Teazle I see you can be a little severe.

LADY TEAZLE   In defence of a friend it is but justice; — but here comes Sir Peter to spoil our pleasantry.

Enter Sir Peter Teazle

SIR PETER   Ladies your most obedient. — Mercy on me, here is the whole set! a character dead at every word I suppose. [*Aside*]

MRS. CANDOUR   I am rejoiced you are come, Sir Peter—They have been *so* censorious. They will allow good qualities to nobody—not even good nature to our friend Mrs. Pursy.

LADY TEAZLE   What, the fat dowager, who was at Mrs. Codille's last night?

MRS. CANDOUR   Nay, her bulk is her misfortune and, when she takes such pains to get rid of it, you ought not to reflect on her.

LADY SNEERWELL   That's very true indeed.

LADY TEAZLE   Yes, I know she almost lives on acids and small whey; laces herself by pulleys; and often, in the noon of summer, you may see her on a little squat pony with her hair plaited up behind like a drummer's, and puffing round the Ring on a full trot.

MRS. CANDOUR   I thank you Lady Teazle for defending her.

SIR PETER   Yes, a good defence truly.

MRS. CANDOUR   But Sir Benjamin is as censorious as Miss Sallow.

CRABTREE   Yes, and she is a curious being to pretend to be censorious! —an awkward gawky, without any one good point under heaven!

MRS. CANDOUR   Positively you shall not be so very severe — Miss Sallow is a relation of mine by marriage and, as for her person, great allowance is to be made, for let me tell you a woman labours under many disadvantages who tries to pass for a girl at six-and-thirty. —

LADY SNEERWELL   Tho' surely she is handsome still—and for the weakness in her eyes, considering how much she reads by candle-light, it is not to be wondered at.

MRS. CANDOUR   True, and then as to her manner, upon my word I think it is particularly graceful, considering she never had the least education; — for you know her mother was a Welsh milliner and her father a sugar-baker at Bristol. —

SIR BENJAMIN   Ah! you are both of you too good-natured!

SIR PETER   Yes, damned good-natured! this their own relation! mercy on me! [*Aside*]

SIR BENJAMIN   And Mrs. Candour is of so moral a turn, she can sit for an hour to hear Lady Stucco talk sentiment.

LADY TEAZLE   Nay, I vow Lady Stucco is very well with the dessert after dinner; for she's just like the French fruit one cracks for mottoes—made up of paint and proverb. —

MRS. CANDOUR   Well, I never will join in ridiculing a friend and so I constantly tell my cousin Ogle, and you all know what pretensions she has to be critical in beauty.

CRABTREE   O to be sure! she has herself the oddest countenance that ever was seen; 'tis a collection of features from all the different countries of the globe.

SIR BENJAMIN   So she has indeed—an Irish front!

CRABTREE   Caledonian locks!

SIR BENJAMIN   Dutch nose!

CRABTREE   Austrian lip!

SIR BENJAMIN   Complexion of a Spaniard!

CRABTREE   And teeth *à la Chinoise*!

SIR BENJAMIN   In short her face resembles a *table d'hôte* at Spa, where no two guests are of a nation—

CRABTREE   Or a congress at the close of a general war—wherein all the members, even to her eyes, appear to have a different interest, and her nose and chin are the only parties likely to join issue.

MRS. CANDOUR   Ha! ha! ha!

SIR PETER   Mercy on my life!—a person they dine with twice a week!
[*Aside*]

MRS. CANDOUR   Nay but I vow you shall not carry the laugh off so — for give me leave to say that Mrs. Ogle—

SIR PETER   Madam, madam, I beg your pardon. There's no stopping these good gentlemen's tongues—but when I tell *you*, Mrs. Candour, that the lady they are abusing is a particular friend of mine —I hope you'll not take her part.

LADY SNEERWELL   Well said, Sir Peter! but you are a cruel creature — too phlegmatic yourself for jest and too peevish to allow wit on others.

SIR PETER   Ah, Madam, true wit is more nearly allied to good nature than your ladyship is aware of.

LADY TEAZLE   True Sir Peter, I believe they are so near akin that they can never be united.

SIR BENJAMIN   Or rather, Madam, suppose them man and wife because one so seldom sees them together.

LADY TEAZLE   But Sir Peter is such an enemy to scandal, I believe he would have it put down by parliament.

SIR PETER   'Fore heaven! Madam, if they were to consider the sporting with reputation of as much importance as poaching on manors, and pass *An Act for the Preservation of Fame*, I believe there are many would thank them for the bill.

LADY SNEERWELL   O lud! Sir Peter, would you deprive us of our privileges?

SIR PETER   Aye Madam, and then no person should be permitted to kill characters or run down reputations but qualified old maids, and disappointed widows.

LADY SNEERWELL   Go, you monster!

MRS. CANDOUR   But sure you would not be quite so severe on those who only report what they hear.

SIR PETER   Yes Madam, I would have law-merchant for them too, and in all cases of slander currency, whenever the drawer of the lie was not to be found, the injured party should have a right to come on any of the indorsers.

CRABTREE   Well, for my part I believe there never was a scandalous tale without some foundation.

LADY SNEERWELL   Come ladies, shall we sit down to cards in the next room?

Enter Servant and whispers Sir Peter

SIR PETER   I'll be with them directly. — [*Exit Servant*] I'll get away unperceived.   [*Aside*]

LADY SNEERWELL   Sir Peter, you are not leaving us?

SIR PETER   Your ladyship must excuse me—I'm called away by partic-ular business—but I leave my character behind me. *Exit Sir Peter*

SIR BENJAMIN   Well certainly, Lady Teazle, that lord of yours is a strange being—I could tell you some stories of him would make you laugh heartily, if he wasn't your husband.

LADY TEAZLE   O pray don't mind that—come, do let's hear them.

[*They join the rest of the company all talking as they are going into the next room*]

JOSEPH SURFACE   [*rising with Maria*] Maria, I see you have no satisfaction in this society.

MARIA   How is it possible I should?—if to raise malicious smiles at the infirmities and misfortunes of those who have never injured us be the province of wit or humour, heaven grant me a double portion of dulness!

JOSEPH SURFACE   Yet they appear more ill-natured than they are. They have no malice at heart.

MARIA   Then is their conduct still more contemptible; for in my opinion, nothing could—excuse the intemperance of their tongues but a natural and ungovernable bitterness of mind.

JOSEPH SURFACE   But can you Maria, feel thus for others, and be unkind to me alone? Is hope to be denied the tenderest passion?

MARIA   Why will you distress me by renewing this subject?

JOSEPH SURFACE   Ah! Maria you would not treat me thus and oppose your guardian, Sir Peter's wishes but that I see that profligate *Charles* is still a favoured rival.

MARIA   Ungenerously urged! but whatever my sentiments of that unfortunate young man are, be assured I shall not feel more bound to give him up because his distresses have lost him the regard even of a brother.

[*Lady Teazle returns*]

JOSEPH SURFACE   Nay but Maria, do not leave me with a frown—by all that's honest I swear—Gad's life here's Lady Teazle. [*Aside*]—You must not—no, you shall not—for tho' I have the greatest regard for Lady Teazle—

MARIA   Lady Teazle!

JOSEPH SURFACE   Yet were Sir Peter to suspect—

LADY TEAZLE   [*coming forward*] What's this pray? do you take her for me?—Child, you are wanted in the next room.—

Exit Maria

What is all this, pray?

JOSEPH SURFACE   O the most unlucky circumstance in nature! Maria has somehow suspected the tender concern I have for your happiness, and threatened to acquaint Sir Peter with her suspicions, and I was just endeavouring to reason with her when you came.

LADY TEAZLE   Indeed!—but you seemed to adopt a very tender method of reasoning—do you *usually* argue on your knees?

JOSEPH SURFACE   O she's a child—and I thought a little bombast—but Lady Teazle, when are you to give me your judgement on my library as you promised?

LADY TEAZLE   No, no—I begin to think it would be imprudent, and you know I admit you as a lover no further than *fashion* requires.

JOSEPH SURFACE   True — a mere Platonic cicisbeo, what every London wife is *entitled* to.

LADY TEAZLE   Certainly one must not be out of the fashion, however I have so much of my country prejudices left—that tho' Sir Peter's ill humour may vex me ever so, it never shall provoke me to—

JOSEPH SURFACE   The only revenge in your power—well I applaud your moderation.

LADY TEAZLE   Go — you are an insinuating wretch! — but we shall be missed—let us join the company.

JOSEPH SURFACE   But we had best not return together.

LADY TEAZLE   Well, don't stay — for Maria shan't come to hear any more of your *reasoning* I promise you.

Exit Lady Teazle

JOSEPH SURFACE   A curious dilemma truly my politics have run me into. — I wanted at first only to ingratiate myself with Lady Teazle that she might not be my enemy with Maria—and I have I don't know how, become her serious lover. Sincerely I begin to wish I had never made such a point of gaining so *very good* a character, for it has led me into so many cursed rogueries that I doubt I shall be exposed at last.   *Exit*

SCENE III

Sir Peter's
Enter Sir Oliver Surface and Rowley

SIR OLIVER   Ha! ha! ha! and so my old friend is married hey?—a young wife out of the country! — Ha! ha! ha! that he should have stood bluff to old bachelor so long and sink into a husband at last!

ROWLEY   But you must not rally him on the subject, Sir Oliver—'tis a tender point I assure you, tho' he has been married only seven months.

SIR OLIVER   Then he has been just half a year on the stool of repentance —poor Peter! But you say he has entirely given up Charles—never sees him, hey?

ROWLEY   His prejudice against him is astonishing — and I am sure greatly increased, by a jealousy of him with Lady Teazle, which he has been industriously led into, by a scandalous society — in the neighbourhood, who have contributed not a little to Charles's ill name; whereas the truth is I believe, if the lady is partial to either of them, his brother is the favourite.

SIR OLIVER   Aye—I know there are a set of malicious, prating, prudent gossips, both male and female, who murder characters to kill time and will rob a young fellow of his good name before he has years to know the value of it. — But I am not to be prejudiced against my nephew by such I promise you! No, no—if Charles has done nothing false or mean, I shall compound for his extravagance.

ROWLEY   Then my life on't, you will reclaim him. Ah sir, it gives me new life to find that *your* heart is not turned against him, and that the son of my good old master has one friend, however, left.

SIR OLIVER   What! shall I forget Master Rowley, when I was at his years myself — egad, my brother and I were neither of us very *prudent* youths — and yet I believe you have not seen many better men that your old master was.

ROWLEY   Sir, 'tis this reflection gives me assurance that Charles may yet be a credit to his family—but here comes Sir Peter.

SIR OLIVER   Egad, so he does.—Mercy on me! He's greatly altered, and seems to have a settled married look—one may read husband in his face at a distance!

Enter Sir Peter Teazle

SIR PETER   Hah! Sir Oliver — my old friend! Welcome to England a thousand times!

SIR OLIVER   Thank you, thank you, Sir Peter—and 'efaith I am glad as glad to find you well, believe me.

SIR PETER   Ah! 'tis a long time since we met — sixteen years I doubt, Sir Oliver, and many a cross accident in the time.

SIR OLIVER   Aye I have had my share—but what! I find you are married, hey, my old boy! — well, well, it can't be helped — and so I wish you joy with all my heart.

SIR PETER   Thank you, thank you, Sir Oliver—yes, I have entered the happy state—but we'll not talk of that now.

SIR OLIVER   True, true, Sir Peter — old friends should not begin on grievances at first meeting—no, no, no.

ROWLEY   [*to Sir Oliver*] Take care pray, sir.

SIR OLIVER   Well, so one of my nephews I find is a wild rogue, hey?

SIR PETER   Wild! ah! my old friend, I grieve for your disappointment there. He's a lost young man indeed — however his brother will make you amends, *Joseph* is indeed what a youth should be — everybody in the world speaks well of him.

SIR OLIVER   I am sorry to hear it—he has too good a character to be an honest fellow. — Everybody speaks well of him! Pshaw! then he has bowed as low to knaves and fools, as to the honest dignity of genius or virtue.

SIR PETER   What, Sir Oliver, do you blame him for not making enemies?

SIR OLIVER   Yes, if he has merit enough to deserve them.

SIR PETER   Well, well, you'll be convinced when you know him. 'Tis edification to hear him converse — he professes the noblest sentiments.

SIR OLIVER   Ah, plague on his sentiments! — if he salutes me with a scrap of morality in his mouth, I shall be sick directly. — But, however, don't mistake me Sir Peter, I don't mean to defend Charles's errors—but before I form my judgement of either of them, I intend to make a trial of their hearts — and my friend Rowley and I have planned something for the purpose.

ROWLEY   And Sir Peter shall own, he has been for once mistaken.

SIR PETER   O my life on Joseph's honour!

SIR OLIVER   Well, come, give us a bottle of good wine, and we'll drink the lads' healths and tell you our scheme.

SIR PETER   *Allons* then!

SIR OLIVER   And don't, Sir Peter, be so severe against your old friend's son. Odds my life! I am not sorry that he has run out of the course a little — for my part I hate to see prudence clinging to the green suckers of youth — 'tis like ivy round a sapling, and spoils the growth of the tree.   *Exeunt*

End of Act the Second

ACT III

SCENE I

Sir Peter's
Sir Peter Teazle, Sir Oliver Surface, and Rowley

SIR PETER   Well then — we will see this fellow first and have our wine afterwards. But how is this, Master Rowley? I don't see the jet of your scheme.

ROWLEY   Why sir, this Mr. Stanley whom I was speaking of, is nearly related to them, by their mother; he was once a merchant in Dublin, but has been ruined by a series of undeserved misfortunes. He has applied by letter since his confinement both to Mr. *Surface* and *Charles*—from the former he has received nothing but evasive promises of future service, while Charles has done all that his extravagance has left him power to do — and he is at this time endeavouring to raise a sum of money, part of which, in the midst of his own distresses, I know he intends for the service of poor Stanley.

SIR OLIVER   Ah! he is my brother's son.

SIR PETER   Well, but how is Sir Oliver personally to—

ROWLEY   Why sir, I will inform Charles—and his brother that Stanley has obtained permission to apply in person to his friends, and as they have neither of them ever seen him let Sir Oliver assume his character, and he will have a fair opportunity of judging at least of the benevolence of their dispositions, and believe me, sir, you will find in the youngest brother one who, in the midst of folly and dissipation, has still, as our immortal bard expresses it—

"a tear or pity, and a hand
Opens as day, for melting charity."

SIR PETER   Pshaw! what signifies his having an open hand or purse either when he has nothing left to give! — well — well — make the trial if you please; but where is the fellow whom you brought for Sir Oliver to examine relative to Charles's affairs?

ROWLEY   Below, waiting his commands, and no one can give him better intelligence. — This, Sir Oliver, is a friendly Jew who to do him justice, has done everything in his power to bring your nephew to a proper sense of his extravagance.

SIR PETER   Pray let us have him in.

ROWLEY   Desire Mr. Moses to walk upstairs.

SIR PETER   But why should you suppose he will speak the truth?

ROWLEY   O, I have convinced him that he has no chance of recovering certain sums advanced to Charles, but thro' the bounty of Sir Oliver, who he knows is arrived; so that you may depend on his fidelity to his interest. I have also another evidence in my power, one Snake, whom I have detected in a matter little short of forgery, and shall shortly produce to remove some of *your* prejudices Sir Peter, relative to Charles and Lady Teazle.

SIR PETER   I have heard too much on that subject.

ROWLEY   Here comes the honest Israelite.

Enter Moses

—This is Sir Oliver.

SIR OLIVER   Sir, I—understand you have lately had great dealings with my nephew Charles.

MOSES   Yes Sir Oliver — I have done all I could for him, but he was ruined before he came to me for assistance.

SIR OLIVER   That was unlucky, truly—for you have had no opportunity of showing your talents.

MOSES   None at all—I hadn't the pleasure of knowing his distresses—till he was some thousands worse than nothing.

SIR OLIVER   Unfortunate indeed! but I suppose you have done all in your power for him, honest Moses?

MOSES   Yes, he knows that. This very evening I was to have brought him a gentleman from the city, who doesn't know him, and will I believe advance him some money.

SIR PETER   What, one Charles has never had money from before?

MOSES   Yes; Mr. Premium, of Crutched Friars—formerly a broker.

SIR PETER   Egad Sir Oliver, a thought strikes me!—Charles, you say, doesn't know Mr. Premium?

MOSES   Not at all.

SIR PETER   Now then Sir Oliver, you may have a better opportunity of satisfying yourself than by an old romancing tale of a poor relation;—go with my friend Moses and represent Mr. *Premium*, and then I'll answer for't, you will see your nephew in all his glory.

SIR OLIVER   Egad, I like this idea better than the other, and I may visit Joseph afterwards, as old *Stanley*.

SIR PETER   True—so you may.

ROWLEY   Well, this is taking Charles rather at a disadvantage to be sure. However, Moses—you understand Sir Peter, and will be faithful.

MOSES   You may depend upon me—this is near the time I was to have gone.

SIR OLIVER   I'll accompany you as soon as you please, Moses; but hold! I have forgot one thing—how the plague shall I be able to pass for a Jew?

MOSES   There's no need   the principal is Christian.

SIR OLIVER   Is he?—I'm sorry to hear it—but then again, an't I rather too smartly dressed to look like a money-lender?

SIR PETER   Not at all; 'twould not be out of character, if you went in your own carriage—would it, Moses?

MOSES   Not in the least.

SIR OLIVER   Well but—how must I talk? there's certainly some cant of usury, and mode of treating, that I ought to know.

SIR PETER   Oh there's not much to learn—the great point as I take it, is to be exorbitant enough in your demands, hey, Moses?

MOSES   Yes, that's a very great point.

SIR OLIVER   I'll answer for't I'll not be wanting in that. I'll ask him eight or ten per cent on the loan at least.

MOSES   If you ask him no more than that, you'll be discovered immediately.

SIR OLIVER   Hey! what the plague! how much then?

MOSES   That depends upon the circumstances. If he appears not very anxious for the supply, you should require only forty or fifty per cent, but if you find him in great distress and want the moneys very bad — you may ask double.

SIR PETER   A good honest trade you're learning, Sir Oliver.

SIR OLIVER   Truly I think so — and not unprofitable.

MOSES   Then you know — you haven't the moneys yourself, but are forced to borrow them for him of a friend.

SIR OLIVER   O I borrow it of a friend, do I?

MOSES   Yes, and your friend is an unconscionable dog, but you can't help it.

SIR OLIVER   My friend is an unconscionable dog, is he?

MOSES   Yes, and he himself hasn't the moneys by him — but is forced to sell stock — at a great loss.

SIR OLIVER   He is forced to sell stock, is he, at a great loss, is he? Well, that's very kind of him.

SIR PETER   Efaith, Sir Oliver — Mr. Premium, I mean — you'll soon be master of the trade. But Moses, wouldn't you have him run out a little against the Annuity Bill? that would be in character I should think.

MOSES   Very much.

ROWLEY   And lament that a young man now must be at years to discretion before he is suffered to ruin himself?

MOSES   Aye, great pity!

SIR PETER   And abuse — the public — for allowing merit to an act whose only object is to snatch misfortune and imprudence from the rapacious relief of usury! and give the minor a chance of inheriting his estate, without being undone by coming into possession.

SIR OLIVER   So, so — Moses shall give me further instructions as we go together.

SIR PETER   You will not have much time for your nephew lives hard by.

SIR OLIVER   O never fear! my tutor appears so able that tho' Charles lived in the next street, it must be my own fault if I am not a complete rogue before I turn the corner.

Exeunt Sir Oliver and Moses

SIR PETER   So — now I think Sir Oliver will be convinced; — you are partial Rowley, and would have prepared Charles for the other plot.

ROWLEY   No, upon my word, Sir Peter.

SIR PETER   Well, go bring me this Snake, and I'll hear what he has to say presently. — I see Maria, and want to speak with her. — [*Exit Rowley.*] I should be glad to be convinced, my suspicions of Lady Teazle and Charles were unjust. I have never yet opened my mind on this subject to my friend *Joseph* — I'm determined I will do it — *he* will give me his opinion sincerely.

Enter Maria

So, child, has Mr. Surface returned with you?

MARIA   No, sir — he was engaged.

SIR PETER   Well, Maria, do you not reflect the more you converse with that amiable young man, what return his partiality for you deserves?

MARIA   Indeed Sir Peter, your frequent importunity on this subject distresses me extremely — you compel me to declare that I know no man who has ever paid me a particular attention whom I would not prefer to Mr. Surface.

SIR PETER   So! — here's perverseness! no, no, Maria, 'tis Charles only whom you would prefer — 'tis evident his vices and follies have won your heart.

MARIA   This is unkind sir — you know I have obeyed you in neither seeing nor corrresponding with him. I have heard enough to convince me that he is unworthy my regard — yet I cannot think it culpable, if while my understanding severely condemns his vices, my heart suggests some pity for his distresses.

SIR PETER   Well, well, pity him as much as you please but give your heart and hand — to a worthier object.

MARIA   Never to his brother!

SIR PETER   Go, perverse and obstinate! but take care Madam, you have never yet known what the authority of a guardian is — don't compel me to inform you of it. —

MARIA   I can only say you shall not have *just* reason. 'Tis true by my father's will I am for a short period bound to regard you as his substitute, but must cease to think you so when you would compel me to be miserable.   *Exit Maria*

SIR PETER   Was ever man so crossed as I am! everything conspiring to fret me! — I had not been involved in matrimony a fortnight before her father — hale and hearty man — died — on purpose I believe, for the pleasure of plaguing me with the care of his daughter. But here comes my helpmate! — She appears in great good humour. — How happy I should be if I could tease her into loving me tho' but a little.

Enter Lady Teazle

LADY TEAZLE   Lud! Sir Peter, I hope you haven't been quarrelling with Maria — it isn't using me well to be ill humoured when I am not by!

SIR PETER   Ah! Lady Teazle, you might have the power to make me good humoured at all times.

LADY TEAZLE   I am sure I wish I had—for I want you to be in charming sweet temper at this moment. Do be good humoured now, and let me have two hundred pounds, will you?

SIR PETER   Two hundred pounds! what, an't I to be in a good humour without paying for it!—but speak to me thus, and efaith there's nothing I could refuse you. You shall have it—but seal me a bond for the repayment.

LADY TEAZLE   O no—there—my note of hand will do as well.

SIR PETER   [kissing her hand] And you shall no longer reproach me with not giving you an independent settlement — I mean shortly to surprise you—but shall we always live thus, hey?

LADY TEAZLE   If you—please—I'm sure I don't care how soon we leave off quarelling, provided you'll own *you* were tired first.

SIR PETER   Well — then let our future contest be, who shall be most obliging.

LADY TEAZLE   I assure you, Sir Peter, good nature becomes you. You look now as you did before we were married!—when you used to walk with me under the elms and tell me stories of what a gallant you were in your youth and chuck me under the chin — you would—and ask me if I thought I could love an old fellow who would deny me nothing—didn't you?

SIR PETER   Yes, yes, and you were as kind and attentive.

LADY TEAZLE   Aye so I was, and would always take your part when my acquaintance used to abuse you and turn you into ridicule.

SIR PETER   Indeed!

LADY TEAZLE   Aye, and when my cousin Sophy has called you a stiff, peevish old bachelor, and laughed at me for thinking of marrying one who might be my father, I have always defended you—and said I didn't think you so ugly by any means and that I dared say you'd make a very good sort of a husband.

SIR PETER   And you prophesied right—and we shall certainly now be the happiest couple—

LADY TEAZLE   And never differ again!

SIR PETER   No, never!—tho' at the same time indeed, my dear Lady Teazle, you must watch your temper very narrowly, for in all our little quarrels — my dear — if you recollect, my love, you always began first.

LADY TEAZLE   I beg your pardon, my dear Sir Peter, indeed you always gave the provocation.

SIR PETER   Now, see my—angel! take care—*contradicting* isn't the way to keep friends.

LADY TEAZLE   Then, don't *you* begin it, my love!

SIR PETER   There now—you—you are going on—you don't perceive, my life, that you are just doing the very thing which you know always makes me angry.

LADY TEAZLE   Nay, you know if you will be angry without any reason—

SIR PETER   There—now you want to quarrel again.

LADY TEAZLE   No, I am sure I don't—but if you will be so peevish—

SIR PETER   There—now who begins first?

LADY TEAZLE   Why you to be sure, I said nothing — but there's no bearing your temper.

SIR PETER   No, no, Madam, the fault's in your own temper.

LADY TEAZLE   Aye, you are just what my cousin Sophy said you would be.

SIR PETER   You cousin Sophy is a forward, impertinent gipsy.

LADY TEAZLE   You are a great bear, I'm sure, to abuse my relations.

SIR PETER   Now may all the plagues of marriage be doubled on me if ever I try to be friends with you any more!

LADY TEAZLE   So much the better.

SIR PETER   No, no, Madam; 'tis evident you never cared a pin for me, and I was a madman to marry you—a pert rural coquette that had refused half the honest squires in the neighbourhood.

LADY TEAZLE   And I am sure I was a fool to marry you—an old dangling bachelor, who was single at fifty only because he never could meet with any one who would have him.

SIR PETER   Aye, aye, Madam, but you were pleased enough to listen to me—*you* never had such an offer before.

LADY TEAZLE   No! didn't I refuse Sir Twivy Tarrier, who everybody said would have been a better match—for his estate is just as good as yours—and he has broke his neck since we have been married!

SIR PETER   I have done with you Madam — you are an unfeeling ungrateful—but there's an end of everything. I believe you capable of anything that's bad—yes Madam I now believe the reports relative to you and Charles — Madam — yes madam, you and Charles—are not without grounds—

LADY TEAZLE   Take—care Sir Peter—you had better not insinuate any such thing! I'll not be suspected *without cause* I promise you.

SIR PETER   Very—well Madam—very well—a separate maintenance as soon as you please. Yes, Madam, or a divorce—I'll make an example of myself for the benefit of all old bachelors. Let us separate, Madam.

LADY TEAZLE   Agreed— agreed— and now, my dear Sir Peter, we are of a mind once more, we may be the *happiest couple,* and *never differ again* you know; ha! ha!— well you are going to be in a passion I see, and I shall only interrupt you—so, bye! bye!   *Exit*

SIR PETER   Plagues and tortures! can't I make her angry neither? O I am the miserablest fellow! — But I'll not bear her presuming to keep her temper — no, she may break my heart but she shan't keep her temper.   *Exit*

SCENE II

Charles's house
Enter Trip, Moses and Sir Oliver Surface

TRIP   Here, Master Moses! if you'll stay a moment, I'll try whether — what's the gentleman's name?
SIR OLIVER   Mr.—. Moses, what *is* my name?   [*Aside*]
MOSES   Mr. Premium. —
TRIP   Premium — very well.

Exit Trip, taking snuff

SIR OLIVER   To judge by the servants, one wouldn't believe the master was ruined. But what! — sure, this was my brother's house?
MOSES   Yes sir; Mr. Charles bought it of Mr. Joseph with the furniture, pictures, &c., just as the old gentleman left — it — Sir Peter thought it a great piece of extravagance in him.
SIR OLIVER   In my mind, the other's economy in *selling* it to him, was more reprehensible by half.
TRIP   My master says you must wait, gentlemen; he has company, and can't speak with you yet.
SIR OLIVER   If he knew *who* it was wanted to see him, perhaps he wouldn't have sent such a message?
TRIP   Yes, yes, sir, he knows *you* are here, I didn't forget little Premium — no, no, no.
SIR OLIVER   Very well — and pray sir, what may be your name?
TRIP   Trip, sir — my name is Trip, at your service.
SIR OLIVER   Well then, Mr. Trip, you have a pleasant sort of place here I guess.
TRIP   Why yes — here are three or four of us pass our time agreeably enough — but then our wages are sometimes a little in arrear — and not very great either — but fifty pounds a year and find our own bags and bouquets.
SIR OLIVER   [*aside*] Bags and bouquets! halters and bastinadoes!
TRIP   But *à propos*, Moses, have you been able to get me that little bill discounted?
SIR OLIVER   [*aside*] Wants to raise money too! — mercy on me! has his

distresses I warrant, like a lord — and affects creditors and duns!

MOSES   'Twas not to be done indeed, Mr. Trip.   [*Gives the note*]

TRIP   Good lack, you surprise me! My friend *Brush* has indorsed it and I thought when he put his mark on the back of a bill 'twas as good as cash.

MOSES   No, 'twouldn't do.

TRIP   A small sum — but twenty pounds. Hark'ee Moses, do you think you couldn't get it me by way of annuity?

SIR OLIVER   [*aside*] An annuity! ha! ha! ha! a footman raise money by way of annuity! Well done luxury, egad!

MOSES   But you must insure your place.

TRIP   Oh, with all my heart — I'll insure my place and my life too, if you please.

SIR OLIVER   [*aside*] It's more than I would your neck.

TRIP   But then, Moses, it must be done before this d — d register takes place — one wouldn't like to have one's name made public you know.

MOSES   No certainly, but is there nothing you could deposit?

TRIP   Why, nothing capital of my master's wardrobe has dropped lately — but I could give you a mortgage on some of his winter clothes with equity of redemption before November — or — you shall have the reversion — of the French velvet — or a post-obit on the blue and silver — these, I should think Moses, with a few pair of point ruffles as a collateral security — hey, my little fellow?

MOSES   Well, well.   [*Bell rings*]

TRIP   Gad, I heard the bell — I believe, gentlemen, I can now introduce you. Don't forget the annuity, little Moses; this way, gentlemen, insure my place! you know

SIR OLIVER   [*aside*] If the man be a shadow of his master, this is the temple of dissipation indeed!

                                                        Exeunt

SCENE III

Charles [Surface], Careless, &C., & C. at a table with wine, & c.

CHARLES SURFACE   'Fore heaven, 'tis true — there's the great degeneracy of the age. Many of our acquaintance have taste, spirit, and politeness — but plague on't, they won't drink.

CARELESS   It is so indeed, Charles — they give in to all the substantial luxuries of the table and abstain from nothing but wine and wit.

CHARLES SURFACE   Oh, certainly society suffers by it intolerably — for now, instead of the social spirit of raillery that used to mantle over a glass of bright Burgundy, their conversation is becoming just like the Spa-water they drink, which has all the pertness and flatulence of champagne without its spirit or flavour.

I GENTLEMAN   But what are *they* to do who love play better than wine?

CARELESS   True — there's Harry diets himself for gaming and is now under a hazard regimen.

CHARLES SURFACE   Then he'll have the worst of it—what, you wouldn't train a horse for the course by keeping him from corn! For my part, egad, I am now never so successful as when I am a little — merry — let me throw on a bottle of champagne and I never lose — at least I never feel my losses which is exactly the same thing.

2 GENTLEMAN   Aye, that I believe.

CHARLES SURFACE   And then, what man can pretend to be a believer in love who is an abjurer of wine? — 'Tis the test by which the lover knows his own heart — fill a dozen bumpers to a dozen beauties, and she that floats at top is the maid that has bewitched you.

CARELESS   Now then Charles, be honest and give us your real favourite.

CHARLES SURFACE   Why, I have withheld her only in compassion to you — if I toast her, you must give a round of her peers — which is impossible on earth!

CARELESS   Oh then we'll find some canonized vestals or heathen goddesses that will do, I warrant!

CHARLES SURFACE   Here then, bumpers, you rogues—bumpers! Maria —Maria—   [*Drink*]

I GENTLEMAN   Maria who?

CHARLES SURFACE   O damn the surname! 'tis too formal to be registered in Love's calendar. But now Sir Toby Bumper, beware—we must have beauty superlative.

CARELESS   Nay, never study Sir Toby — we'll stand to the toast, tho' your mistress should want an eye — and you know you have a song will excuse you.

SIR TOBY   Egad, so I have—and I'll give him the song instead of the lady. —   [*Sings*]

SONG AND CHORUS
Here's to the maiden of bashful fifteen,
Here's to the widow of fifty,
Here's to the flaunting extravagant quean,
And here's to the housewife that's thrifty.
Chorus. Let the toast pass—
Drink to the lass—
I'll warrant she'll prove an excuse for the glass!
Here's to the charmer whose dimples we prize!

> Now to the maid who has none, sir,
> Here's to the girl with a pair of blue eyes,
> —And here's to the nymph with but one, sir!
> *Chorus.* Let the toast pass, &c.
> Here's to the maid with a bosom of snow,
> Now to *her* that's as brown as a berry,
> Here's to the wife with a face full of woe,
> And now for the damsel that's merry.
> *Chorus.* Let the toast pass, &c.
> For let 'em be clumsy or let 'em be slim,
> Young or ancient, I care not a feather,
> —So fill a pint bumper quite up to the brim
> —And let us e'en toast'em together
> *Chorus.* Let the toast pass, &c.

ALL   Bravo! Bravo!

Enter Trip, and whispers Charles Surface

CHARLES SURFACE   Gentlemen, you must excuse me a little. Careless, take the chair, will you?

CARELESS   Nay prithee, Charles, what now?—this is one of your peerless beauties, I suppose, has dropped in by chance.

CHARLES SURFACE   No—faith—to tell you the truth, 'tis a Jew, and a broker, who are come by appointment.

CARELESS   Oh damn it, let's have the Jew in—

1 GENTLEMAN   Aye, and the broker too by all means.

2 GENTLEMAN   Yes, yes, the Jew and the broker.

CHARLES SURFACE   Egad, with all my heart—Trip, bid the gentlemen walk in.—   [*Exit Trip*]
Tho' there's one of them a stranger I can tell you.

CARELESS   Charles, let us give them some generous Burgundy—and perhaps they'll grow conscientious.

CHARLES SURFACE   O hang 'em, no—wine does but draw forth a man's *natural* qualities; and to make *them* drink, would only be to whet their knavery.

Enter Trip, Sir Oliver Surface, and Moses

CHARLES SURFACE   So, honest Moses; walk in—walk in, pray, Mr. Premium—that's the gentleman's name, isn't it, Moses?

MOSES   Yes, sir.

CHARLES SURFACE   Set chairs, Trip—sit down, Mr. Premium. Glasses,

Trip. Sit down, Moses. — Come Mr. Premium, I'll give you a sentiment — here's "Success to usury!" — Moses, fill the gentleman a bumper.

MOSES   Success to usury!

CARELESS   Right, Moses — usury is prudence and industry and deserves to succeed.

SIR OLIVER   Then here's — all the success it deserves!

CARELESS   No, no — that won't do, Mr. Premium. You have demurred to the toast, and must drink it in a pint bumper.

I GENTLEMAN   A pint bumper, at least.

MOSES   O pray, sir, consider — Mr. Premium's a gentleman.

CARELESS   And therefore loves good wine.

2 GENTLEMAN   Give Moses a quart glass — this is mutiny, and a high contempt of the chair.

CARELESS   Here — now for't — I'll see justice done to the last drop of my bottle.

SIR OLIVER   Nay, pray, gentlemen — I did not expect this usage.

CHARLES SURFACE   No, hang it, Careless, you shan't: Mr. Premium's a stranger.

SIR OLIVER   [aside] Odd! I wish I was well out of this company.

CARELESS   Plague on 'em then — if they won't drink, we'll not sit down with 'em; come, Harry, the dice are in the next room; Charles, you'll join us — when you have finished your business with these gentlemen —

CHARLES SURFACE   I will. I will. — [Exeunt.] Careless!

CARELESS   [returning] Well —

CHARLES SURFACE   Perhaps I may want you.

CARELESS   O you know I am always ready — word, note, or bond, 'tis all the same to me.   Exit

MOSES   Sir, this is Mr. Premium, a gentleman of the strictest honour and secrecy — and always performs what he undertakes. Mr. Premium, this is —

CHARLES SURFACE   Pshaw! have done! — Sir, my friend Moses is a very honest fellow, but a little slow at expression; he'll be an hour giving us our titles. Mr. Premium, the plain state of the matter is this — I am an extravagant fellow who wants money to borrow. You I take to be a prudent old fellow, who has got money to lend. I am blockhead enough to give you fifty per cent sooner than not have it, and you I presume are rogue enough to take a hundred if you could get it. Now, sir, you see we are acquainted at once, and may proceed to business without farther ceremony.

SIR OLIVER   Exceeding frank upon my word. I see, sir, you are not a man of many compliments.

CHARLES SURFACE   Oh no, sir—plain dealing in business I always think best.

SIR OLIVER   Sir, I like you the better for't. However you are mistaken in one thing — I have no money to lend. But I believe I could procure some of a friend; but then he's an unconscionable dog— isn't he, Moses? and must sell stock to accommodate you — mustn't he, Moses?

MOSES   Yes, indeed!—you know I always speak the truth, and scorn to tell a lie!

CHARLES SURFACE   Right! People that expect truth generally do — but these are trifles, Mr. Premium. — What! I know money isn't to be bought without paying for't!

SIR OLIVER   Well, but what security could you give—you have no land I suppose?

CHARLES SURFACE   Not a mole-hill, nor a twig, but what's in beau-pots out at the window.

SIR OLIVER   Nor any stock, I presume?

CHARLES SURFACE   Nothing but live stock—and that's only a few point- ers and ponies. But pray Mr. Premium, are you acquainted at all with any of my connections?

SIR OLIVER   Why, to say truth I am.

CHARLES SURFACE   Then you must know that I have a devilish rich uncle in the East Indies, Sir *Oliver Surface*, from whom I have the greatest expectations.

SIR OLIVER   That you have a wealthy uncle I have heard — but how your expectations will turn out is more I believe than you can tell.

CHARLES SURFACE   O no—there can be no doubt of it—they tell me I'm a prodigious favourite – and that he talks of leaving me everything.

SIR OLIVER   Indeed! this is the first I've heard on't.

CHARLES SURFACE   Yes, yes, 'tis just so. Moses knows 'tis true; don't you, Moses?

MOSES   Oh yes—I'll swear to't—

SIR OLIVER   [*aside*] Egad, they'll persuade me presently I'm at Bengal.

CHARLES SURFACE   Now I propose Mr. Premium, if it's agreeable to you, to grant you a post-obit on Sir Oliver's life, tho' at the same time the old fellow has been so liberal to me that I give you my word I should be very sorry to hear anything had happened to him.

SIR OLIVER   Not more than *I* should I assure you. But the bond you mention happens to be just the worst security you could offer me —for I might live to a hundred and never recover the principal.

CHARLES SURFACE   O yes, you would—the moment Sir Oliver dies you know you'd come on me for the money.

SIR OLIVER   Then I believe I should be the most unwelcome dun you ever had in your life.

CHARLES SURFACE   What, I suppose you are afraid now that Sir Oliver is too good a life.

SIR OLIVER   No, indeed I am not—tho' I have heard he is as hale and healthy as any man of his years in Christendom.

CHARLES SURFACE   There again you are misinformed. No, no, the climate has hurt him considerably — poor uncle Oliver — yes, he breaks apace, I'm told—and so much altered lately that his nearest relations don't know him.

SIR OLIVER   No!—ha! ha! ha! so much altered lately that his relations don't know him! Ha! ha! ha! that's droll, egad—ha! ha! ha!

CHARLES SURFACE   Ha! ha! you're glad to hear that, little Premium.

SIR OLIVER   No, no, I'm not.

CHARLES SURFACE   Yes, yes, you are — ha! ha! ha! — you know that mends your chance.

SIR OLIVER   But I'm told Sir Oliver is coming over—nay, some say he is actually arrived.

CHARLES SURFACE   Pshaw! sure I must know better than you whether he's come or not. No, no, rely on't, he is at this moment at Calcutta, isn't he, Moses?

MOSES   Oh, yes, certainly.

SIR OLIVER   Very true, as you say, you must know better than I, tho' I have it from pretty good authority—haven't I, Moses?

MOSES   Yes, most undoubted!

SIR OLIVER   But, sir, as I understand you want a few hundreds immediately, is there nothing you would dispose of?

CHARLES SURFACE   How do you mean?

SIR OLIVER   For instance now — I have heard — that your father left behind him a great quantity of massy old plate.

CHARLES SURFACE   O lud, that's gone, long ago — Moses can tell you better than I can.

SIR OLIVER   Good lack! all the family race-cups and corporation-bowls! [Aside]—then it was also supposed that his library was one of the most valuable and complete—

CHARLES SURFACE   Yes, yes, so it was—vastly too much so for a private gentleman—for my part I was always of a communicative disposition, so I thought it a shame to keep so much knowledge to myself.

SIR OLIVER   [aside] Mercy on me! learning that had run in the family like an heirloom!—[Aloud] Pray, what are become of the books?

CHARLES SURFACE   You must inquire of the autioneer, Master Premium, for I don't believe even Moses can direct you there.

MOSES I never meddle with books.

SIR OLIVER So, so, nothing of the family property left, I suppose?

CHARLES SURFACE Not much indeed, unless you have a mind to the family pictures — I have got a room full of ancestors above — and if you have a taste for old paintings, egad, you shall have 'em a bargain.

SIR OLIVER Hey! and the devil! sure, you wouldn't sell your forefathers, would you?

CHARLES SURFACE Every man of 'em, to the best bidder.

SIR OLIVER What! your great-uncles and aunts?

CHARLES SURFACE Aye, and my great-grandfathers and grandmothers too.

SIR OLIVER Now I give him up! — [Aside] — What the plague, have you no bowels for your own kindred? — Odds life — do you take me for Shylock in the play, that you would raise money of me, on your own flesh and blood?

CHARLES SURFACE Nay, my little broker, don't be angry — what need you care, if you have your money's worth?

SIR OLIVER Well, I'll be the purchaser — I think I can dispose of the family. — [Aside] Oh, I'll never forgive him — this — never!

Enter Careless

CARELESS Come Charles, what keeps you?

CHARLES SURFACE I can't come yet, efaith! we are going to have a sale above — here's little Premium will buy all my ancestors —

CARELESS Oh, burn your ancestors!

CHARLES SURFACE No, he may do that afterwards if he pleases. Stay, Careless, we want you; egad, you shall be auctioneer. So come along with us.

CARELESS Oh, have with you, if that's the case. — I can handle a hammer as well as a dice box!

SIR OLIVER Oh, the profligates!

CHARLES SURFACE Come Moses, you shall be appraiser if we want one. — Gad's life, little Premium, you don't seem to like the business.

SIR OLIVER Oh yes, I do vastly — ha! ha! yes, yes, I think it a rare joke to sell one's family by auction — ha! ha! — [Aside] Oh, the prodigal!

CHARLES SURFACE To be sure! when a man wants money, where the plague should he get assistance, if he can't make free with his own relations?   *Exeunt.*

End of the third Act

ACT IV

SCENE I

Picture-room at Charles's
Enter Charles Surface, Sir Oliver Surface, Moses, and Careless

CHARLES SURFACE   Walk in, gentlemen, pray walk in! — here they are, the family of the Surfaces up to the Conquest.

SIR OLIVER   And, in my opinion a goodly collection.

CHARLES SURFACE   Aye, aye, these are done in true spirit of portrait-painting — no volunteer grace, or expression — not like the works of your modern Raphael, who gives you the strongest resemblance yet contrives to make your own portrait independent of you; so that you may sink the original and not hurt the picture. No, no the merit of these is the inveterate likeness — all stiff and awkward as the originals, and like nothing in human nature beside!

SIR OLIVER   Ah! we shall never see such figures of men again.

CHARLES SURFACE   No, I hope not. You see, Master Premium, what a domestic character I am — here I sit of an evening surrounded by my family. But come, get to your pulpit, Mr. Auctioneer — here's an old gouty chair of my grandfather's — will answer the purpose.

CARELESS   Aye, aye, this will do — but, Charles, I have ne'er a hammer, and what's an auctioneer without his hammer?

CHARLES SURFACE   Egad, that's true. What parchment have we here? [*Takes down a roll*] 'Richard heir to Thomas' — our genealogy in full! Here Careless, you shall have no common bit of mahogany — here's the family tree for you, you rogue — this shall be your hammer, and now you may knock down my ancestors with their own pedigree.

SIR OLIVER   [*aside*] What an unnatural rogue! — an *ex post facto* parricide!

CARELESS   Yes, yes, here's a list of your generation indeed. — Faith Charles, this is the most convenient thing you could have found for the business, for 'twill serve not only as a hammer, but a catalogue into the bargain. — But come, begin — a-going, a-going, a-going! —

CHARLES SURFACE   Bravo, Careless! — well, here's my great uncle Sir Richard Raviline, a marvellous good general in his day I assure you. He served in all the Duke of Marlborough's wars, and got that cut over his eye at the battle of Malplaquet. What say you, Mr. Premium? look at him — there's a hero for you! not cut out of his feathers, as your modern clipped captains are — but enveloped in wig and regimentals — as a general should be. What do you bid?

MOSES Mr. Premium would have you speak.

CHARLES SURFACE Why then, he shall have him for ten pounds and I am sure that's not dear for a staff-officer.

SIR OLIVER Heaven deliver me! his famous uncle Richard for ten pounds! Very well, sir, I take him at that.

CHARLES SURFACE Careless, knock down my uncle Richard. — Here now is a maiden sisten of his, my great-aunt Deborah, done by Kneller, thought to be in his best manner, and a very formidable likeness. There she is, you see, a shepherdess feeding her flock. You shall have her for five pounds ten — the sheep are worth the money.

SIR OLIVER Ah! poor Deborah! a woman who set such a value on herself! — Five pound ten! — She's mine.

CHARLES SURFACE Knock down my aunt Deborah! Here now are two that were a sort of cousins of theirs — you see, Moses, these pictures were done some time ago, when beaux wore wigs, and the ladies wore their own hair.

SIR OLIVER Yes, truly, head-dresses appear to have been a little lower in those days.

CHARLES SURFACE Well, take that couple for the same.

MOSES 'Tis good bargain.

CHARLES SURFACE Careless! — This now is a grandfather of my mother's, a learned judge, well known on the western circuit. What do you rate him at, Moses?

MOSES Four guineas.

CHARLES SURFACE Four guineas! Gad's life, you don't bid me the price of his wig! Mr. Premium, you have more respect for the woolsack do let us knock his lordship down at fifteen.

SIR OLIVER By all means —

CARELESS Gone. —

CHARLES SURFACE And there are two brothers of his, William and Walter Blunt, Esquires, both members of Parliament and noted speakers, and what's very extraordinary, I believe this is the first time they were ever bought and sold.

SIR OLIVER That's very extraordinary, indeed! I'll take them at your own price for the honour of Parliament.

CARELESS Well said, little Premium — I'll knock'em down at forty.

CHARLES SURFACE Here's a jolly fellow — I don't know what relation, but he was mayor of Manchester; take him at eight pounds.

SIR OLIVER No, no — six will do for the mayor.

CHARLES SURFACE Come, make it guineas and I'll throw you the two aldermen there into the bargain.

SIR OLIVER They're mine.

CHARLES SURFACE Careless, knock down the mayor and aldermen.

But, plague on't! we shall be all day—retailing in this manner. Do let us deal wholesale — what say you, little Premium? Give me three hundred pounds for the rest of the family in the lump.

CARELESS   Aye, aye, that will be the best way. —

SIR OLIVER   Well, well, anything to accommodate you; they are mine. But there is one portrait, which you have always passed over.

CARELESS   What, that ill-looking little fellow over the settee?

SIR OLIVER   Yes sir, I mean that, tho' I don't think him so ill-looking a little fellow by any means.

CHARLES SURFACE   What, that? Oh that's my uncle Oliver, 'twas done before he went to India.

CARELESS   Your uncle Oliver! Gad! then you'll never be friends, Charles. That now, to me, is as stern a looking rogue as ever I saw — an unforgiving eye, and a damned disinheriting countenance! an inveterate knave, depend on't. Don't you think so, little Premium?

SIR OLIVER   Upon my soul sir, I do not; I think it is as honest a looking face as any in the room, dead or alive. But I suppose your uncle Oliver goes with the rest of the lumber?

CHARLES SURFACE   No, hang it, I'll not part with poor Noll. The old fellow has been very good to me, and egad, I'll keep his picture while I've a room to put it in.

SIR OLIVER   The rogue's my nephew after all! [*Aside*]—But sir, I have somehow taken a fancy to that picture.

CHARLES SURFACE   I'm sorry for't, for you certainly will not have it. Oons! haven't you got enough of 'em?

SIR OLIVER   I forgive him everything! [*Aside*]—But, sir, when I take a whim in my head I don't value money—I'll give you as much for that as for all the rest.

CHARLES SURFACE   Don't tease me, master broker; I tell you I'll not part with it, and there's an end on't.

SIR OLIVER   How like his father the dog is!—[*Aside*] Well, well, I have done.—I did not perceive it before, but I think I never saw such a resemblance.[*Aside*]—Well, sir—here is a draught for your sum.

CHARLES SURFACE   Why, 'tis for eight hundred pounds!

SIR OLIVER   You will not let Oliver go?

CHARLES SURFACE   Zounds! no! I tell you once more.

SIR OLIVER   Then never mind the difference; we'll balance another time, but give me your hand on the bargain—you are an honest fellow Charles — I beg pardon, sir, for being so free. — Come, Moses.

CHARLES SURFACE   Egad, this is a whimsical old fellow — but hark'ee, Premium, you'll prepare lodgings for these gentlemen.

SIR OLIVER   Yes, yes, I'll send for them in a day or two.

CHARLES SURFACE   But hold—do now—send a genteel conveyance for them, for I assure you they were most of them used to ride in their own carriages.

SIR OLIVER   I will, I will, for all but—Oliver.

CHARLES SURFACE   Aye all, but the little honest nabob.

SIR OLIVER   You're fixed on that—

CHARLES SURFACE   Peremptorily.

SIR OLIVER   A dear extravagant rogue!—Good day!—Come, Moses—let me hear now who dares call him profligate!

Exeunt Sir Oliver and Moses.

CARELESS   Why, this is the oddest genius of the sort I ever saw!

CHARLES SURFACE   Egad, he's the prince of brokers I think. I wonder how the devil Moses got acquainted with so honest a fellow. — Ha! here's Rowley. Do, Careless, say I'll join the company in a moment.

CARELESS   I will—but don't now let that old blockhead persuade you to squander any of that money on old musty debts, or any such nonsense, for tradesmen, Charles, are the most exorbitant fellows!—

CHARLES SURFACE   Very true, and paying them is only encouraging them.

CARELESS   Nothing else.

CHARLES SURFACE   Aye, aye, never fear.—[*Exit Careless.*] So—this was an odd old fellow indeed! Let me see, two-thirds of this is mine by right—five hundred and thirty pounds. 'Fore heaven! I find one's ancestors are more valuable relations than I took 'em for!—Ladies and gentlemen, your most obedient and very grateful humble servant.

Enter Rowley

Ha! Old Rowley, egad, you are just come in time to take leave of your old acquaintance.

ROWLEY   Yes, I heard they were going—but I wonder you can have such spirits under so many distresses.

CHARLES SURFACE   Why there's the point—my distresses are so many that I can't afford to part with my spirits, but I shall be rich and splenetic all in good time. However I suppose you are surprised that I am not more sorrowful at parting with so many near relations; to be sure, 'tis very affecting—but rot 'em, you see they never move a muscle, so why should I?

ROWLEY   There's no making—you serious a moment.

CHARLES SURFACE   Yes faith: I am so now—here, my honest Rowley, here, get me this changed and take a hundred pounds of it immediately to old Stanley.

ROWLEY   A hundred pounds! Consider only—

CHARLES SURFACE   Gad's life, don't talk about it! poor Stanley's wants are pressing—and if you don't make haste, we shall have some one call that has a better right to the money.

ROWLEY   Ah! there's the point—I never will cease dunning you with the old proverb—

CHARLES SURFACE   ''Be *just* before you're *generous*,'' hey!—why, so I would if I could—but Justice is an old lame hobbling beldame and I can't get her to keep pace with Generosity, for the soul of me.

ROWLEY   Yet, Charles, believe me, one hour's reflection—

CHARLES SURFACE   Aye, aye, it's all very true—but hark'ee, Rowley, while I have, by heaven I'll give—so damn your economy and now for hazard.

SCENE II

The Parlour
Enter Sir Oliver Surface and Moses

MOSES   Well sir, I think as Sir Peter said, you have seen Mr. Charles in high glory.—'Tis great pity he's so extravagant.

SIR OLIVER   True, but he wouldn't sell my picture.

MOSES   And loves wine and women so much.

SIR OLIVER   But he wouldn't sell my picture.

MOSES   And game[s] so deep.

SIR OLIVER   But he wouldn't sell my picture. O, here's Rowley.

Enter Rowley

ROWLEY   So, Sir Oliver, I find you have made a purchase.

SIR OLIVER   Yes, yes, our young rake has parted with his ancestors like old tapestry.

ROWLEY   And here has he commissioned me to redeliver you part of the purchase-money—I mean, tho', in your necessitous character of old *Stanley*.

MOSES   Ah! there is the pity of all! he is so damned charitable.

ROWLEY   And I left a hosier and two tailors in the hall, who I'm sure won't be paid, and this hundred—would satisfy 'em.

SIR OLIVER   Well, well, I'll pay his debts—and his benevolence too; but now I am no more a broker and you shall introduce me to the elder brother as old Stanley.—

ROWLEY Not yet awhile; Sir Peter I know means to call there about this time.

Enter Trip

TRIP O gentlemen I beg pardon for not showing you out — this way — Moses, a word.   *Exeunt Trip and Moses*

SIR OLIVER There's a fellow for you! — would you believe it, that puppy intercepted the Jew on our coming and wanted to raise money before he got to his master!

ROWLEY Indeed!

SIR OLIVER Yes, they are now planning an annuity business. Ah! Master Rowley, in my day, servants were content with the follies of their masters when they were worn a little threadbare — but now they have their vices like their birthday clothes with the gloss on.

Exeunt

SCENE III

A library
Joseph Surface and Servant

JOSEPH SURFACE No letter from Lady Teazle?

SERVANT No, sir.

JOSEPH SURFACE [*aside*] I am surprised she hasn't sent if she is prevented from coming! Sir Peter certainly does not suspect me — yet I wish I may not lose the heiress thro' the scrape I have drawn myself in with the wife. However, Charles's imprudence and bad character are great points in my favour.   [*Knocking*]

SERVANT Sir, I believe that must be Lady Teazle.

JOSEPH SURFACE Hold! see — whether it is or not before you go to the door — I have a particular message for you if it should be my brother.

SERVANT 'Tis her ladyship, sir. She always leaves her chair at the milliner's in the next street.

JOSEPH SURFACE Stay, stay — draw that screen before the window — that will do — my opposite neighbour — is a maiden lady of so curious a temper — [*Servant draws the screen and exit.*] I have a difficult hand to play in this affair. Lady Teazle has lately suspected my views on Maria — but she must by no means be let into that secret, at least not till I have her more in my power.

Enter Lady Teazle

LADY TEAZLE   What sentiment in soliloquy! have you been very impatient now?—O lud! don't pretend to look grave. I vow I couldn't come before.

JOSEPH SURFACE   O madam, punctuality is a species of constancy, a very unfashionable quality in a lady.

LADY TEAZLE   Upon my word you ought to pity me. Do you know that Sir Peter is grown so ill-tempered to me of late! and so jealous of *Charles* too—that's the best of the story, isn't it?

JOSEPH SURFACE   [*aside*] I am glad my scandalous friends keep that up.

LADY TEAZLE   I am sure I wish he would let Maria marry him, and then perhaps he would be convinced, don't you, Mr. Surface?

JOSEPH SURFACE   [*aside*] Indeed I do not.—Oh, certainly I do—for then my dear Lady Teazle would also be convinced how wrong her suspicions were of my having any design on the silly girl.

LADY TEAZLE   Well, well, I'm inclined to believe you. But isn't it provoking to have the most ill-natured things said to one? And there's my friend Lady Sneerwell has circulated I don't know how many scandalous tales of me! and all without any foundation too—that's what vexes me.

JOSEPH SURFACE   Aye madam, to be sure that *is* the provoking circumstance — without foundation! yes, yes, there's the mortification, indeed—for when a scandalous story is believed against one, there certainly is no comfort like the consciousness of having deserved it.

LADY TEAZLE   No, to be sure — then I'd forgive their malice — but to attack me, who am really so innocent, and who never say an ill-natured thing of anybody — that is, of any friend — and then Sir Peter too — to have him so peevish, and so suspicious, when I know the integrity of my own heart—indeed 'tis monstrous!

JOSEPH SURFACE   But my dear Lady Teazle, 'tis your own fault if you suffer it — when a husband entertains a groundless suspicion of his wife and withdraws his confidence from her, the original compact is broke and she owes it to the honour of her sex to endeavour to outwit him.

LADY TEAZLE   Indeed! so that if he suspects me without cause, it follows that the best way of curing his jealousy is to give him reason for't.

JOSEPH SURFACE   Undoubtedly — for your husband should never be deceived in you, and in that case it becomes *you* to be frail in compliment to *his* discernment.

LADY TEAZLE   To be sure what you say is very reasonable, and when the consciousness of my own innocence —

JOSEPH SURFACE   Ah, my dear madam, there is the great mistake—'tis this very conscious innocence that is of the greatest prejudice to you. What is it makes you negligent of forms and careless of the world's opinion? why, the *consciousness* of your innocence. What makes you thoughtless in your conduct and apt to run into a thousand little imprudences? why, the *consciousness* of your innocence. What makes you impatient of Sir Peter's temper and outrageous at his suspicions? why, the *consciousness* of your own innocence!

LADY TEAZLE 'Tis very true.

JOSEPH SURFACE Now my dear Lady Teazle, if you would but once make a trifling *faux pas*, you can't conceive how cautious you would grow — and how ready to humour and agree with your husband.

LADY TEAZLE Do you think so?

JOSEPH SURFACE Oh, I'm sure on't—and then you would find all scandal would cease at once, for in short, your character at present is like a person in a plethora, absolutely dying of too much health.

LADY TEAZLE So, so—then I perceive your prescription is—that I must sin in my own defence—and part with my virtue to preserve my reputation.

JOSEPH SURFACE Exactly so upon my credit, ma'am.

LADY TEAZLE Well, certainly this is the oddest doctrine, and the newest receipt for avoiding calumny.

JOSEPH SURFACE An infallible one, believe me. *Prudence*, like *experience*, must be paid for.

LADY TEAZLE Why, if my understanding were once convinced —

JOSEPH SURFACE Oh certainly, Madam, your understanding *should* be convinced—yes, yes—heaven forbid I should persuade you to do anything you *thought* wrong. No, no, I have too much honour to desire it.

LADY TEAZLE Don't you think we may as well leave honour out of the argument?

JOSEPH SURFACE Ah, the ill effects of your country education I see, still remain with you.

LADY TEAZLE I doubt they do, indeed—and I will fairly own to you, that if I could be persuaded to do wrong, it would be by Sir Peter's ill-usage sooner than your honourable logic, after all.

JOSEPH SURFACE Then by this hand which he is unworthy of—

Enter Servant

'Sdeath, you blockhead—what do you want?

SERVANT I beg pardon, sir, but I thought you wouldn't choose Sir Peter to come up without announcing him.

JOSEPH SURFACE Sir Peter!—Oons and the devil!

LADY TEAZLE   Sir Peter! O lud! I'm ruined! I'm ruined!

SERVANT   Sir, 'twasn't I let him in.

LADY TEAZLE   O I'm undone—what will become of me now Mr. Logic?
—O mercy, he's on the stairs—I'll get behind here—and if ever
I'm so imprudent again—   [*Goes behind the screen*]

JOSEPH SURFACE   Give me that book. [*Sits down. Servant pretends to adjust
his hair*]

Enter Sir Peter Teazle

SIR PETER   Aye, ever improving himself!—Mr. Surface, Mr. Surface!—

JOSEPH SURFACE   Oh my dear Sir Peter, I beg your pardon. [*Gaping and
throws away the book*] I have been dozing over a stupid book! well,
I am much obliged to you for this call—you haven't been here I
believe since I fitted up this room. Books you know are the only
things I am a coxcomb in.

SIR PETER   'Tis very neat indeed. Well, well, that's proper—and you
make even your screen a source of knowledge—hung, I perceive,
with maps.

JOSEPH SURFACE   Oh yes, I find great use in that screen.

SIR PETER   I dare say you must—certainly—when you want to find
anything in a hurry.

JOSEPH SURFACE   [*aside*] Aye, or to hide anything in a hurry either.

SIR PETER   Well, I have a little private business—

JOSEPH SURFACE   You needn't stay.   [*To Servant*]

SERVANT   No, Sir.   *Exit.*

JOSEPH SURFACE   Here's a chair, Sir Peter—I beg—

SIR PETER   Well, now we are alone, there is a subject, my dear friend,
on which I wish to unburden my mind to you—a point of the
greatest moment to my peace; in short, my good friend, Lady
Teazle's conduct of late has made me extremely unhappy.

JOSEPH SURFACE   Indeed! I am very sorry to hear it.

SIR PETER   Yes, 'tis but too plain she has not the least regard for me—
but what's worse, I have pretty good authority to suspect she
must have formed an attachment to another.

JOSEPH SURFACE   You astonish me!

SIR PETER   Yes—and, between ourselves—I think I have discovered
the person.

JOSEPH SURFACE   How, you alarm me exceedingly!

SIR PETER   Ah! my dear friend, I knew you would sympathize with
me.

JOSEPH SURFACE   Yes, believe me, Sir Peter, such a discovery would
hurt me just as much as it would you.

SIR PETER   I am convinced of it—ah! it is a happiness to have a friend whom one can trust even with one's family secrets. But have you no guess who I mean?

JOSEPH SURFACE   I haven't the most distant idea — it can't be Sir Benjamin Backbite!

SIR PETER   O no! What say you to Charles?

JOSEPH SURFACE   My brother! impossible! —

SIR PETER   Ah! my dear friend — the goodness of your own heart misleads you — you judge of others by yourself.

JOSEPH SURFACE   Certainly Sir Peter, the heart that is conscious of its own integrity is ever slow to credit another's treachery.

SIR PETER   True — but your brother has no sentiment — you never hear him talk so.

JOSEPH SURFACE   Yet I can't but think Lady Teazle herself has too much principle —

SIR PETER   Aye, but what's her principle — against the flattery of a handsome, lively young fellow?

JOSEPH SURFACE   That's very true.

SIR PETER   And then you know the difference of our ages makes it very improbable that she should have a great affection for me — and if she were to be frail and I were to make it public, why the town would only laugh at me, the foolish old bachelor who had married a girl.

JOSEPH SURFACE   That's true, to be sure — they *would* laugh.

SIR PETER   Laugh! aye — and make ballads — and paragraphs — and the devil knows what of me.

JOSEPH SURFACE   No, you must never make it public.

SIR PETER   But then again — that the nephew of my old friend, Sir Oliver, should be the person to attempt such a wrong, hurts me more nearly.

JOSEPH SURFACE   Aye there's the point; when ingratitude barbs the dart of injury, the wound has double danger in it.

SIR PETER   Aye, I that was in a manner left his guardian — in whose house he had been so often entertained — who never in my life denied him — my advice.

JOSEPH SURFACE   O 'tis not to be credited! There *may* be a man capable of such baseness to be sure, but for my part, till you can give me positive proofs, I cannot but doubt it. — However, if this should be proved on him, he is no longer a brother of mine! I disclaim kindred with him — for the man who can break thro' the laws of hospitality — and attempt the wife — of his friend, deserves to be branded as the pest of society.

SIR PETER   What a difference there is between you! What noble sentiments!

JOSEPH SURFACE   Yet I cannot suspect Lady Teazle's honour.

SIR PETER   I am sure I wish to think well of her — and to remove all ground of quarrel between us. She has lately reproached me more than once, with having made no settlement on her — and in our last quarrel she almost hinted that she should not break her heart if I was dead. Now as we seem to differ in our ideas of expense, I have resolved she shall be her own mistress in that respect for the future — and if I *were* to die, she shall find that I have not been inattentive to her interest while living. Here my friend, are the drafts of two deeds, which I wish to have your opinion on. By one, she will enjoy eight hundred a year independent while I live and by the other, the bulk of my fortune after my death.

JOSEPH SURFACE   This conduct, Sir Peter, is indeed truly generous. — [*Aside*] I wish it may not corrupt my pupil.

SIR PETER   Yes, I am determined she shall have no cause to complain, tho' I would not have her acquainted with the latter instance of my affection yet awhile.

JOSEPH SURFACE   Nor I, if I could help it.   [*Aside*]

SIR PETER   And now my dear friend, if you please we will talk over the situation of your hopes with *Maria*.

JOSEPH SURFACE   [*softly*] No, no, Sir Peter; another time if you please.

SIR PETER   I am sensibly chagrined at the little progress you seem to make in her affection.

JOSEPH SURFACE   I beg you will not mention it — what are my disappointments when your happiness is in debate! [*Softly*] — 'Sdeath, I should be ruined every way!   [*Aside*]

SIR PETER   And tho' you are so averse to my acquainting Lady Teazle with your passion, I am sure she's not your enemy in the affair.

JOSEPH SURFACE   Pray Sir Peter, now oblige me. — I am really too much affected by the subject we have been speaking on to bestow a thought on my own concerns. The man who is entrusted with his friend's distresses can never —

Enter Servant

Well, sir?

SERVANT   Your brother, sir, is speaking to a gentleman in the street, and says he knows you are within.

JOSEPH SURFACE   'Sdeath, blockhead — I'm not within — I'm out for the day.

SIR PETER   Stay — hold — a thought has struck me — you shall be at home.

JOSEPH SURFACE   Well, well, let him up. — *Exit Servant*

He'll interrupt Sir Peter — however —

SIR PETER   Now my good friend, oblige me I entreat you. Before

Charles comes, let me conceal myself somewhere. Then do you tax him on the point we have been talking on, and his answers may satisfy me at once.

JOSEPH SURFACE   O fie, Sir Peter—would you have me join in so mean a trick—to trepan my brother to—!

SIR PETER   Nay, you tell me you are *sure* he is innocent—if so, you do him the greatest service by giving him an opportunity to clear himself, and, you will set my heart at rest. Come, you shall not refuse me — here behind this screen will be [*goes to the screen*] — hey! what the devil! there seems to be *one* listener here already— I'll swear I saw a petticoat.

JOSEPH SURFACE   Ha! ha! ha! — well, this is ridiculous enough. I'll tell you, Sir Peter, tho' I hold a man of intrigue to be a most despicable character, yet you know it doesn't follow that one is to be an absolute Joseph either! Hark'ee! 'tis a little French milliner, a silly rogue that plagues me — and having some character — on your coming she ran behind the screen.

SIR PETER   Ah, you rogue! — but egad, she has overheard all I have been saying of my wife.

JOSEPH SURFACE   O 'twill never go any further, you may depend on't!

SIR PETER   No!—then efaith, let her hear it out.—Here's a closet will do as well.

JOSEPH SURFACE   Well, go in then.

SIR PETER   Sly rogue! sly rogue!   [*Goes into the closet*]

JOSEPH SURFACE   A very narrow escape, indeed! and a curious situation I'm in, to part a man and wife in this manner.

LADY TEAZLE   [*peeping from the screen*] Couldn't I steal off?

JOSEPH SURFACE   Keep close, my angel—

SIR PETER   [*peeping out*] Joseph, tax him home!—

JOSEPH SURFACE   Back, my dear friend!

LADY TEAZLE   [*peeping*] Couldn't you lock Sir Peter in?

JOSEPH SURFACE   Be still, my life—

SIR PETER   [*peeping*] You're sure the little milliner won't blab?

JOSEPH SURFACE   In! in!—my good Sir Peter—'fore gad, I wish I had a key to the door.

Enter Charles Surface

CHARLES SURFACE   Hallo! brother, what has been the matter? Your fellow would not let me up at first. What, have you had a Jew or a wench with you?

JOSEPH SURFACE   Neither brother, I assure you.

CHARLES SURFACE   But—what has made Sir Peter steal off? I thought he had been with you.

JOSEPH SURFACE He was, brother—but, hearing *you* were coming he did not choose to stay.

CHARLES SURFACE What, was the old gentleman afraid I wanted to borrow money of him!

JOSEPH SURFACE No, sir—but I am sorry—to find Charles—that you have lately given that worthy man grounds for great uneasiness.

CHARLES SURFACE Yes, they tell me I do that to a great many worthy men. But how so, pray?

JOSEPH SURFACE To be plain with you, brother, he thinks you are endeavouring to gain Lady Teazle's affections from him.

CHARLES SURFACE Who, I! O lud! not I, upon my word.—Ha! ha! ha! so the old fellow has found out that he has got a young wife, has he?—or what's worse, has her ladyship discovered that she has an old husband?

JOSEPH SURFACE This is no subject to jest on, brother.—He who can laugh—

CHARLES SURFACE True, true, brother, as you were going to say—then seriously, I never had the least idea of what you—charge me with, upon my honour.

JOSEPH SURFACE Well, it will give Sir Peter great satisfaction to hear this. [*Aloud*]

CHARLES SURFACE To be sure I once thought the lady seemed to have taken a fancy to me—but upon my soul, I never gave her the least encouragement.—Besides, you know my attachment to Maria.

JOSEPH SURFACE But sure, brother, even if Lady Teazle had betrayed the fondest partiality for you—

CHARLES SURFACE Why, look'ee, Joseph, I hope I shall never deliberately do a dishonourable action—but if a pretty woman were purposely to throw herself in my way—and that pretty woman married to a man old enough to be her father—

JOSEPH SURFACE Well!—

CHARLES SURFACE Why, I believe I should be obliged to borrow a little of your morality, that's all.—But brother, do you know now that you surprise me exceedingly, by naming *me* with Lady Teazle—for faith, I alway[s] understood *you* were her favourite.

JOSEPH SURFACE O, for shame, Charles—this retort is foolish.

CHARLES SURFACE Nay, I swear I have seen you exchange such significant glances—

JOSEPH SURFACE Nay, nay, sir this is no jest—

CHARLES SURFACE Egad, I'm serious! don't you remember—one day when I called here—

JOSEPH SURFACE Nay, prithee, Charles—

CHARLES SURFACE And found you together—

JOSEPH SURFACE Zounds, sir, I insist—

CHARLES SURFACE   And another time when your sevant—

JOSEPH SURFACE   Brother, brother, a word with you!—[*Aside*] Gad, I must stop him.

CHARLES SURFACE   Informed me, I say, that—

JOSEPH SURFACE   Hush!—I beg your pardon, but Sir Peter has overheard all we have been saying—I knew you would clear yourself or I should not have consented.

CHARLES SURFACE   How, Sir Peter!—where is he?

JOSEPH SURFACE   Softly, there!   [*Points to the closet*]

CHARLES SURFACE   Oh, 'fore heaven, I'll have him out. — Sir Peter, come forth—

JOSEPH SURFACE   No, no—

CHARLES SURFACE   I say, Sir Peter, come into court.—[*Pulls in Sir Peter*] What, my old guardian! — What — turn inquisitor and take evidence incog.?

SIR PETER   Give me your hand, Charles—I believe I have suspected you wrongfully—but you mustn't be angry with Joseph—'twas my plan.

CHARLES SURFACE   Indeed!—

SIR PETER   But I acquit you.—I promise you I don't think near so ill of you as I did. What I have heard has given me great satisfaction.

CHARLES SURFACE   Egad then, 'twas lucky you didn't hear any more— wasn't it, Joseph? [*Half aside*]

SIR PETER   Ah! you would have retorted on him.

CHARLES SURFACE   Aye, aye, that was a joke.

SIR PETER   Yes, yes, I know his honour too well.

CHARLES SURFACE   But you might as well have suspected him as me in this matter, for all that. Mightn't he, Joseph?   [*Half aside*]

SIR PETER   Well, well, I believe you.

JOSEPH SURFACE   Would they were both out of the room!   [*Aside*]

SIR PETER   And in future, perhaps, we may not be such strangers.

Enter Servant who whispers Joseph Surface

JOSEPH SURFACE   Lady Sneerwell!—stop her by all means—[*Exit Servant*] Gentlemen—I beg pardon—I must wait on you downstairs —here's a person come on particular business.

CHARLES SURFACE   Well, you can see him in another room. Sir Peter and I haven't met a long time, and I have something to say to him.

JOSEPH SURFACE   They must not be left together.—I'll send Lady Sneerwell away, and return directly. — [*Aside*] Sir Peter, not a word of the French milliner.

Exit Joseph Surface

SIR PETER   O not for the world! — Ah, Charles, if you associated more with your brother, one might indeed hope for your reformation. He is a man of sentiment — well! there is nothing in the world so noble as a man of sentiment!

CHARLES SURFACE   Pshaw! He is too moral by half, and so apprehensive of his good name, as he calls it, that I suppose he would as soon let a priest into his house as a girl.

SIR PETER   No, no, — come, come, — you wrong him. No, no, Joseph is no rake, but he is not such a saint in that respect either, — I have a great mind to tell him — we should have a laugh!   [*Aside*]

CHARLES SURFACE   Oh, hang him! He's a very anchorite, a young hermit.

SIR PETER   Hark'ee, you must not abuse him. He may chance to hear of it again, I promise you.

CHARLES SURFACE   Why, you won't tell him?

SIR PETER.   No — but — this way. — [*Aside*] Egad, I'll tell him! — Hark'ee! have you a mind to have a good laugh at Joseph?

CHARLES SURFACE   I should like it of all things.

SIR PETER   Then, efaith we will — I'll be quit with him for discovering me. [*Aside*] — He had a girl with him when I called.

CHARLES SURFACE   What, Joseph! you jest.

SIR PETER   Hush! — a little — French milliner — [*whispers*] and the best of the jest is — she's in the room now.

CHARLES SURFACE   The devil she is!

SIR PETER   Hush — I tell you —   [*Points*]

CHARLES SURFACE   Behind the screen — 'slife, let's unveil her!

SIR PETER   No, no! He's coming — you shan't, indeed!

CHARLES SURFACE   O egad! we'll have a peep at the little milliner.

SIR PETER   Not for the world! — Joseph — will never forgive me.

CHARLES SURFACE   I'll stand by you —

SIR PETER   [*struggling with Charles*]   Odds, here he is —

Joseph Surface enters just as Charles throws down the screen

CHARLES SURFACE   Lady Teazle! by all that's wonderful!

SIR PETER   Lady Teazle! by all that's horrible!

CHARLES SURFACE   Sir Peter, this is one of the smartest Frinch milliners I ever saw — egad, you seem all to have been diverting yourselves here at hide and seek — and I don't see who is out of the secret! — Shall I beg your ladyship to inform me! — not a word! Brother, will you please to explain this matter? — what! Morality dumb too? — Sir Peter, tho' I *found* you in the dark, perhaps you are not so now. All mute! Well tho' *I* can make nothing of the affair I suppose you perfectly understand one another — so I'll leave you to yourselves.

—[*Going*] Brother, I'm sorry to find you *have given that worthy man so much uneasiness!* — Sir Peter, there's nothing *in the world so noble as a man of sentiment!*   *Exit Charles*

[*Stand for some time looking at each other*]

JOSEPH SURFACE   Sir Peter — notwithstanding I confess that appearances are against me—if you will afford me your patience—I make no doubt but I shall explain everything to your satisfaction.

SIR PETER   If you please —

JOSEPH SURFACE   The fact is, sir — that Lady Teazle, knowing my pretensions to your ward Maria—I say sir, Lady Teazle being apprehensive of the jealousy of your temper — and knowing my friendship to the family — she, sir, I say — called here — in order that I might explain those pretensions — but on your coming — being apprehensive—as I said of your jealousy—she withdrew — and this, you may depend on't is the whole truth of the matter.

SIR PETER   A very clear account upon my word, and I dare swear the lady will vouch for every article of it.

LADY TEAZLE   [*coming forward*] For not one word of it, Sir Peter.

SIR PETER   How! don't you even think it worth while to agree in the lie?

LADY TEAZLE   There is not one syllable of truth in what that gentleman has told you.

SIR PETER   I believe you, upon my soul, Ma'am!

JOSEPH SURFACE   [*Aside*]'Sdeath Madam, will you betray me?

LADY TEAZLE   Good Mr. Hypocrite, by your leave I will speak for myself.

SIR PETER   Aye, let her alone, sir — you'll find she'll make out a better story than *you* without prompting.

LADY TEAZLE   Hear me, Sir Peter—I came hither, on no matter relating to your ward, and even ignorant of this gentleman's pretensions to her — but I came, seduced by his insidious arguments, at least to listen to his pretended passion, if not to sacrifice *your* honour to his baseness.

SIR PETER   Now I believe, the truth *is* coming indeed —

JOSEPH SURFACE   The woman's mad!

LADY TEAZLE   No, sir — she has recovered her senses, and your own arts have furnished her with the means.—Sir Peter, I do not expect you to credit me—but the tenderness you expressed for me when I am sure you could not think I was a witness to it, has penetrated to my heart and had I left the place without the the shame of this discovery, my future life should have spoke the sincerity of my gratitude. — As for that smooth-tongue hypocrite, who would have seduced the wife of his too credulous friend while he affected honourable addresses to his ward—I behold him now in a light so truly despicable, that I shall never again respect myself for having listened to him.   *Exit*

JOSEPH SURFACE   Notwithstanding all this, Sir Peter, heaven knows—

SIR PETER   That you are a villain! — and so I leave you to your conscience.

JOSEPH SURFACE   You are too rash, Sir Peter—you shall hear me! the man who shuts out conviction by refusing to—

SIR PETER   Oh!

Exeunt, Joseph Surface following and speaking
End of Act 4th.

ACT V

SCENE I

The library
Enter Joseph Surface and Servant

JOSEPH SURFACE   Mr. Stanley! why should you think I would see him? —you *must* know he comes to ask something!

SERVANT   Sir, I should not have let him in, but that Mr. Rowley came to the door with him.

JOSEPH SURFACE   Pshaw! Blockhead! to suppose that I should *now* be in a temper to receive visits from poor relations!—well, why don't you show the fellow up?

SERVANT   I will, sir. — Why, sir, it was not my fault that Sir Peter discovered my lady—

JOSEPH SURFACE   Go, fool!   *Exit Servant*

Sure, Fortune never played a man of my policy such a trick, before —my character with Sir Peter! my hopes with Maria!—destroyed in a moment! — I'm in a rare humour to listen to other people's distresses! — I shan't be able to bestow even a benevolent sentiment on Stanley. — So! here he comes and Rowley with him. I *must* try to recover myself—and put a little charity into my face, however.   *Exit*

Enter Sir Oliver Surface and Rowley

SIR OLIVER   What! does he avoid us?—that was he , was it not?

ROWLEY   It was, sir—but I doubt you are come a little too abruptly—
his nerves are so weak that the sight of a poor relation may be too
much for him.—I should gave gone first to break you to him.

SIR OLIVER   A plague of his nerves! — Yet this is he whom Sir Peter
extols as a man of the most benevolent way of thinking!—

ROWLEY   As to his way of thinking, I cannot pretend to decide; for to
do him justice, he appears to have as much speculative benevolence as any private gentleman in the kingdom, tho' he is seldom
so sensual as to indulge himself in the exercise of it.

SIR OLIVER   Yet has a string of charitable sentiments, I suppose, at his
fingers' ends!

ROWLEY   Or rather at his tongue's end, Sir Oliver, for I believe there
is no sentiment he has more faith in than that 'Charity begins at
home.'

SIR OLIVER   And his, I presume, is of that domestic sort which never
stirs abroad at all.

ROWLEY   I doubt you'll find it so—but he's coming—I mustn't seem
to interrupt you and you know, immediately as you leave him, I
come in to announce—your arrival in your real character.

SIR OLIVER   True—and afterwards you'll meet me at Sir Peter's.

ROWLEY   Without losing a moment.   *Exit Rowley*

SIR OLIVER   So! I don't like the complaisance of his features.

Re-enter Joseph Surface

JOSEPH SURFACE   Sir, I beg you ten thousand pardons, for keeping—
you a moment waiting. Mr. Stanley, I presume.

SIR OLIVER   At your service.

JOSEPH SURFACE   Sir, I beg you will do me the honour to sit down—I
entreat you, sir.

SIR OLIVER   Dear sir—there's no occasion.—Too civil by half!

JOSEPH SURFACE   I have not the pleasure of knowing you, Mr. Stanley
—but I am extremely happy to see you look so well. You were
nearly related to my mother, I think, Mr. Stanley.

SIR OLIVER   I was, sir—so nearly that my present poverty, I fear, may
do discredit to her wealthy children—else I should not have presumed to trouble you.

JOSEPH SURFACE   Dear sir, there needs no apology—he that is in distress, tho' a stranger, has a right to claim kindred with the wealthy.
—I am sure I wish *I* was of that class, and had it in my power to
offer you even a small relief.

SIR OLIVER   If your uncle, Sir Oliver, were here, I should have a friend.

JOSEPH SURFACE   I wish he were, sir, with all my heart—you should
not want an advocate with him, believe me, sir.

SIR OLIVER I should not *need* one — my distresses would recommend me; — but I imagined — his bounty had enabled *you* to become the agent of his charity.

JOSEPH SURFACE My dear sir, you were strangely misinformed. Sir Oliver is a worthy man — a very worthy sort of man — but — avarice, Mr. Stanley, is the vice of age. I will tell you, my good sir, in confidence, what he has done for me has been a mere — nothing, tho' people I know have thought otherwise, and for my part, I never chose to contradict the report.

SIR OLIVER What! has he never transmitted you bullion! rupees! pagodas!

JOSEPH SURFACE O dear sir, nothing of the kind — no, no, a few presents now and then — china — shawls — Congou tea — avadavats, and Indian crackers — little more, believe me.

SIR OLIVER [*aside*] Here's gratitude for twelve thousand pounds — avadavats and Indian crackers!

JOSEPH SURFACE Then, my dear sir, you have heard I doubt not of the extravagance of my brother. There are very few would credit what I have done for that unfortunate young man.

SIR OLIVER Not I, for one!   [*Aside*]

JOSEPH SURFACE The sums I have lent — him — indeed I have been exceedingly to blame — it was an amiable weakness! However, I don't pretend to defend it — and now I feel it doubly culpable, since it has deprived me of the power of serving *you*, Mr. Stanley, as my heart directs.

SIR OLIVER [*aside*] Dissembler! — Then, sir, you cannot assist me?

JOSEPH SURFACE At present it grieves me to say I cannot, but whenever I have the ability, you may depend upon hearing from me.

SIR OLIVER I am extremely sorry —

JOSEPH SURFACE Not more than I am, believe me — to pity without the power to relieve, is still more painful than to ask and be denied.

SIR OLIVER Kind sir, your most obedient humble servant.

JOSEPH SURFACE You leave me deeply affected, Mr. Stanley. — William, be ready to open the door.

SIR OLIVER O dear sir, no ceremony.

JOSEPH SURFACE Your very obedient.

SIR OLIVER Sir, your most obsequious.

JOSEPH SURFACE You may depend upon hearing from me — whenever I can be of service.

SIR OLIVER Sweet sir, you are too good.

JOSEPH SURFACE In the meantime, I wish you health and spirits.

SIR OLIVER Your ever grateful — and perpetual humble servant.

JOSEPH SURFACE Sir, yours as sincerely.

SIR OLIVER Now I am satisfied! [*Exit*]

JOSEPH SURFACE   [*solus*] This is one bad effect of a good character; it invites applications from the unfortunate, and there needs no small degree of address to gain the reputation of benevolence without incurring the expense. The silver ore of pure charity is an expensive article in the catalogue of a man's good qualities — whereas the sentimental French plate I use instead of it, makes just as good a show, and pays no tax. —

Enter Rowley

ROWLEY   Mr. Surface, your servant—I was apprehensive of interrupting you—tho' my business demands immediate attention—as this note will inform you.
JOSEPH SURFACE   Always happy to see Mr. Rowley. — [*Reads*] How! '*Oliver—Surface!*' —My uncle arrived!
ROWLEY   He is indeed — we have just parted — quite well, after a speedy voyage, and impatient to embrace his worthy nephew.
JOSEPH SURFACE   I am astonished! — William! stop Mr. Stanley, if he's not gone.
ROWLEY   O—he's out of reach, I believe.
JOSEPH SURFACE   Why didn't you let me know this when you came in together?
ROWLEY   I thought you had particular—business—but I must be gone to inform your brother, and appoint him here to meet his uncle. He will be with you in a quarter of an hour.
JOSEPH SURFACE   So he says. Well, I am strangely overjoyed at his coming. — [*Aside*] Just at this time!
ROWLEY   You will be delighted to see how well he looks.
JOSEPH SURFACE   O—I'm rejoiced to hear it. —[*Aside*] Just at this time!
ROWLEY   I'll tell him how impatiently you expect him.
JOSEPH SURFACE   Do, do; pray give my best duty and affection. Indeed, I cannot express the sensations I feel at the thought of seeing him. —[*Exit Rowley*] Certainly his coming just at this time is the cruellest piece of ill fortune.   *Exit*

SCENE II

At Sir Peter's

Enter Mrs. Candour and Maid

MAID   Indeed, Ma'am, my lady will see nobody at present.
MRS. CANDOUR   Did you tell her it was her friend Mrs. Candour?

MAID Yes, Madam, but she begs you will excuse her.

MRS. CANDOUR Do go again—I shall be glad to see her if it be only for a moment, for I am sure she must be in great distress. —

Exit Maid

Dear heart, how provoking!—I'm not mistress of half the circumstances!—We shall have the whole affair in the newspapers with the names of the parties at length, before I have dropped the story at a dozen houses.

Enter Sir Benjamin Backbite

O dear Sir Benjamin, you have heard I suppose—

SIR BENJAMIN Of Lady Teazle and Mr. Surface—

MRS. CANDOUR And Sir Peter's discovery—

SIR BENJAMIN O, the strangest piece of business, to be sure!

MRS. CANDOUR Well, I never was so surprised in my life! I am sorry for all parties, indeed I am.

SIR BENJAMIN Now I don't pity Sir Peter at all—he was so extravagantly partial to Mr. Surface.

MRS. CANDOUR Mr. Surface!—why, 'twas with Charles Lady Teazle was detected.

SIR BENJAMIN No such thing—Mr. Surface is the gallant.

MRS. CANDOUR No, no—Charles is the man. 'Twas Mr. Surface brought Sir Peter on purpose to discover them.

SIR BENJAMIN I tell you I have it from one—

MRS. CANDOUR And I have it from one—

SIR BENJAMIN Who had it from one, who had it—

MRS. CANDOUR From one immediately—but here's Lady Sneerwell—perhaps she knows the whole affair.

Enter Lady Sneerwell

LADY SNEERWELL So, my dear Mrs. Candour! Here's a sad affair of our friend Lady Teazle.

MRS. CANDOUR Aye!—my dear friend, who could have thought it.

LADY SNEERWELL Well, there's no trusting appearances, tho' indeed, she was always too lively for me.

MRS. CANDOUR To be sure her manners were a little too free—but she was very young.

LADY SNEERWELL And *had*, indeed, some good qualities.

MRS. CANDOUR So she had indeed!—but have you heard the particulars?

LADY SNEERWELL No—but everybody says that Mr. Surface—

SIR BENJAMIN Aye there, I told you—Mr. Surface was the man.

MRS. CANDOUR   No, no, indeed—the assignation was with Charles.

LADY SNEERWELL   With Charles!—you alarm me, Mrs. Candour.

MRS. CANDOUR   Yes, yes, he was the lover. Mr. Surface—do him justice —was only the informer.

SIR BENJAMIN   Well, I'll not dispute with you, Mrs. Candour, but be it which it may, I hope that Sir Peter's wound will not—

MRS. CANDOUR   Sir Peter's wound!—O mercy! I didn't hear word of their fighting.

LADY SNEERWELL   Nor I, a syllable.

SIR BENJAMIN   No! what, no mention of the duel?

MRS. CANDOUR   Not a word.

SIR BENJAMIN   O Lord — yes, yes — they fought before they left the room.

LADY SNEERWELL   Pray let us hear.

MRS. CANDOUR   Aye, do oblige us with the duel.

SIR BENJAMIN   "Sir" says Sir Peter — immediately after the discovery —"you are a most ungrateful fellow."

MRS. CANDOUR   Aye to Charles—

SIR BENJAMIN   No, no—to Mr. Surface—"a most ungrateful fellow and old as I am, sir," says he, "I insist on immediate satisfaction."

MRS. CANDOUR   Aye, that must have been to Charles for 'tis very unlikely Mr. Surface should go to fight in his house.

SIR BENJAMIN   'Gad's life, Ma'am, not at all—"giving me immediate satisfaction,"—On this, madam, Lady Teazle, seeing Sir Peter in such danger, ran out of the room in strong hysterics, and Charles after her, calling out for hartshorn and water! Then, madam, they began to fight with swords—

Enter Crabtree

CRABTREE   With pistols, nephew—I have it from undoubted authority.

MRS. CANDOUR   O Mr Crabtree, then it is all true!

CRABTREE   Too true, indeed, ma'am, and Sir Peter's dangerously wounded—

SIR BENJAMIN   By a thrust in *seconde* quite through his left side—

CRABTREE   By a bullet lodged in the thorax.

MRS. CANDOUR   Mercy on me! Poor Sir Peter!

CRABTREE   Yes, Ma'am—tho' Charles would have avoided the matter if he could.

MRS. CANDOUR   I knew Charles was the person.

SIR BENJAMIN   Oh, my uncle I see, knows nothing of the matter.

CRABTREE   But Sir Peter taxed him with the basest ingratitude—

SIR BENJAMIN   That I told you, you know.

CRABTREE   Do nephew, let me speak!—and insisted on an immediate
—

SIR BENJAMIN   Just as I said.

CRABTREE   Odds life! Nephew, allow others to know something too—a pair of pistols lay on the bureau—for Mr. Surface, it seems, had come the night before late from Salt-Hill, where he had been to see the Montem with a friend, who has a son at Eton—so unluckily, the pistols were left charged.

SIR BENJAMIN   I heard—nothing of this.

CRABTREE   Sir Peter forced Charles to take one and they fired, it seems pretty nearly together. Charles's shot took place as I told you, and Sir Peter's missed—but what is very extraordinary, the ball struck against a little bronze Pliny that stood over the chimney-piece, grazed out of the window at a right angle, and wounded the postman, who was just coming to the door with a double letter from Northamptonshire.

SIR BENJAMIN   My uncle's account is more circumstantial I must confess—but I believe mine is the true one for all that.

LADY SNEERWELL   [aside] I am more interested in this affair than they imagine and must have better information.   Exit Lady Sneerwell

SIR BENJAMIN   [after a pause looking at each other] Ah!—Lady Sneerwell's alarm is very easily accounted for.

CRABTREE   Yes, yes, they certainly do say—but that's neither here nor there.

MRS. CANDOUR   But, pray, where is Sir Peter at present?

CRABTREE   Oh! they brought him home and he is now in the house, tho' the servants are ordered to deny it.

MRS. CANDOUR   I believe so, and Lady Teazle, I suppose attending him.

CRABTREE   Yes, yes—I saw one of the Faculty enter just before me.

SIR BENJAMIN   Hey! who comes here?

CRABTREE   Oh, this is he—the physician, depend on't.

MRS. CANDOUR   Oh, certainly, it must be the physician and now we shall know.

Enter Sir Oliver Surface

CRABTREE   Well doctor, what hopes?

MRS. CANDOUR   Aye doctor, how's your patient?

SIR BENJAMIN   Now doctor, isn't it a wound with a small-sword?

CRABTREE   A bullet lodged in the thorax, for a hundred!

SIR OLIVER   Doctor!—a wound with a small-sword! and a bullet in the thorax? Oons! are you mad, good people?

SIR BENJAMIN   Perhaps, sir you are not a doctor?

SIR OLIVER   Truly, I am to thank you for my degree, if I am.

CRABTREE   Only a friend of Sir Peter's then, I presume; but, sir, you must have heard of this accident—

SIR OLIVER   Not a word!

CRABTREE   Not of his being dangerously wounded?

SIR OLIVER   The devil he is!

SIR BENJAMIN   Run thro' the body—

CRABTREE   Shot in the breast—

SIR BENJAMIN   By one Mr. Surface—

CRABTREE   Aye, the younger.

SIR OLIVER   Hey! what the plague! you seem to differ strangely in your accounts — however, you agree that Sir Peter is dangerously wounded.

SIR BENJAMIN   Oh, yes, we agree there.

CRABTREE   Yes, yes, I believe there can be no doubt of that.

SIR OLIVER   Then, upon my word, for a person in that situation he is the most imprudent man alive—for here he comes, walking as if nothing at all were the matter.

Enter Sir Peter Teazle

Odds heart, Sir Peter—you are come in good time, I promise you, for we had just *given you over*.

SIR BENJAMIN   Egad, uncle, this is the most sudden recovery!

SIR OLIVER   Why, man, what do you do out of bed with a small-sword through your body, and a bullet lodged in your thorax!

SIR PETER   A small-sword and a bullet—

SIR OLIVER   Aye, these gentlemen would have killed you, without law or physic, and wanted to dub me a doctor — to make me an accomplice.

SIR PETER   Why, what is all this?

SIR BENJAMIN   We rejoice, Sir Peter, that the story of the duel is not true—and are sincerely sorry for your other misfortuncs.

SIR PETER   So, so—all over the town already.   [*Aside*]

CRABTREE   Tho' Sir Peter, you were certainly vastly to blame to marry at all, at your years.

SIR PETER   Sir, what business is that of yours?

MRS. CANDOUR   Tho' indeed, as Sir Peter made so good a husband, he's very much to be pitied!

SIR PETER   Plague on your pity, Ma'am, I desire none of it.

SIR BENJAMIN   However, Sir Peter, you must not mind the laughing and jests, you will meet with on this occasion.

SIR PETER   Sir, I desire to be master in my own house.

CRABTREE   'Tis no uncommon case, that's one comfort.

SIR PETER   I insist on being left to myself; without ceremony, I insist on your leaving my house directly!

MRS. CANDOUR   Well, well, we are going and depend on't we'll make the best report of you we can.

SIR PETER   Leave my house!

CRABTREE   And tell how hardly you have been treated.

SIR PETER   Leave my house!

SIR BENJAMIN   And how patiently you bear it.

SIR PETER   Fiends! vipers! furies! — Oh that their own venom would choke them!

Exeunt Mrs. Candour, Sir Benjamin Backbite, Crabtree, &c.

SIR OLIVER   They are very provoking indeed, Sir Peter.

Enter Rowley

ROWLEY   I heard high words — what has ruffled you, Sir Peter?

SIR PETER   Pshaw, what signifies asking! Do I ever pass a day without my vexations?

SIR OLIVER   Well, I'm not inquisitive — I come only to tell you that I have seen both my nephews in the manner we proposed.

SIR PETER   A precious couple they are!

ROWLEY   Yes, and Sir Oliver is convinced that your judgement was right, Sir Peter.

SIR OLIVER   Yes, I find *Joseph* is indeed the man after all.

ROWLEY   Yes, as Sir Peter says, he's a man of sentiment.

SIR OLIVER   And acts up to the sentiments he professes.

ROWLEY   It certainly is edification to hear him talk.

SIR OLIVER   Oh, he's a model for the young men of the age!—but how's this, Sir Peter!—you don't join in your friend Joseph's praise as I expected.

SIR PETER   Sir Oliver, we live in a damned wicked world, and the fewer we praise the better.

ROWLEY   What, do *you* say so, Sir Peter — who were never mistaken in your life?

SIR PETER   Pshaw! Plague on you both! I see by your sneering you have heard — the whole affair. I shall go mad among you!

ROWLEY   Then to fret you no longer, Sir Peter, we are indeed acquainted with it all. I met Lady Teazle coming from Mr. Surface's, so humbled that she deigned to request *me*, to be her advocate with you.

SIR PETER   And does Sir Oliver know all too?

SIR OLIVER   Every circumstance!

SIR PETER   What, of the closet — and the screen, hey?

SIR OLIVER   Yes, yes, and the little — French milliner. O I have been vastly diverted with the story! ha! ha!

SIR PETER   'Twas very pleasant.

SIR OLIVER   I never laughed more in my life I assure you, ha! ha!

SIR PETER   O vastly diverting! ha! ha!

ROWLEY   To be sure, Joseph with his — sentiments — ha! ha!

SIR PETER   Yes, yes, his sentiments — ha! ha! A hypocritical villain!

SIR OLIVER   Aye, and that rogue Charles — to pull Sir Peter out of the closet — ha! ha!

SIR PETER   Ha! ha! 'twas devilish entertaining to be sure!

SIR OLIVER   Ha! ha! egad, Sir Peter, I should like to have seen your face when the screen was thrown down, ha! ha!

SIR PETER   Yes, yes, my face when the screen was thrown down, ha! ha! O I must never show my head again!

SIR OLIVER   But come, come, it isn't fair to laugh at you neither, my old friend — tho' upon my soul, I can't help it.

SIR PETER   O pray don't restrain your — mirth on my account. — It does not hurt me at all — I laugh at the whole affair myself — yes, yes. I think being a standing jest for all one's acquaintances a very happy situation. O yes, and then of a morning to read the paragraphs about Mr. S—, Lady T—, and Sir P—, will be so entertaining! —

ROWLEY   Without affectation, Sir Peter, you may despise the ridicule of fools. But I see Lady Teazle — going towards the next room. I am sure you must desire a reconciliation as earnestly as she does.

SIR OLIVER   Perhaps my being here, prevents her coming to you. Well, I'll leave honest Rowley to mediate between you — but he must bring you all presently to Mr. Surface's, where I am now returning, if not to reclaim a libertine, at least to expose hypocrisy.

SIR PETER.   Ah! — I'll be present at your discovering yourself there with all my heart — tho' 'tis a vile unlucky place for discoveries!

ROWLEY   We'll follow.   [*Exit Sir Oliver Surface*]

SIR PETER.   She is not coming here, you see, Rowley.

ROWLEY   No, but she has left the door of that room open you perceive. See, she is in tears!

SIR PETER   Certainly a little mortification appears very becoming in a wife! don't you think it will do her good to let her pine a little?

ROWLEY   O, this is ungenerous in you!

SIR PETER   Well, I know not what to think. You remember, Rowley, the letter I found of hers, evidently intended for Charles?

ROWLEY   A mere forgery, Sir Peter — laid in your way on purpose. This is one of the points which I intend *Snake* shall give you conviction on.

SIR PETER   I wish I were once satisfied of that. She looks this way — what a remarkably elegant turn of the head she has! Rowley, I'll go to her.

ROWLEY   Certainly.

SIR PETER   Tho' when it is known that we are reconciled, people will laugh at me ten times more!

ROWLEY   Let — them laugh and retort their malice only by showing them you are happy in spite of it.

SIR PETER   Efaith, so I will — and if I'm not mistaken, we may yet be the happiest couple in the country.

ROWLEY   Nay, Sir Peter — he who once lays aside suspicion —

SIR PETER   Hold, my dear Rowley — if you have any regard for me, never let me hear you utter anything like — a sentiment — I have had enough of *them* to serve me the rest of my life!   *Exeunt*

SCENE III

The library
Joseph Surface and Lady Sneerwell

LADY SNEERWELL   Impossible! Will not Sir Peter immediately be reconciled to *Charles*, and of consequence no longer oppose his union with *Maria*? the thought is distraction to me!

JOSEPH SURFACE   Can passion furnish a remedy?

LADY SNEERWELL   No, nor cunning either — O I was a fool! an idiot! to league with such a blunderer!

JOSEPH SURFACE   Sure, Lady Sneerwell, *I* am the greatest sufferer — yet you see I bear the accident with calmness.

LADY SNEERWELL   Because the disappointment — doesn't reach your *heart*; your *interest* only attached you to Maria. Had you felt for *her*, what *I* have for that *ungrateful* libertine, neither your temper nor hypocrisy could prevent your showing the sharpness of your vexation.

JOSEPH SURFACE   But why should your reproaches fall on *me* for this disappointment?

LADY SNEERWELL   Are you not the cause of it? — what had you to do to bate in your pursuit of Maria to pervert Lady Teazle by the way? Had you not a sufficient field for your roguery in blinding Sir Peter and supplanting your brother? I hate such an avarice of crimes — 'tis an unfair monopoly, and never prospers.

JOSEPH SURFACE.   Well, I admit I have been to blame. I confess I deviated from the direct road of wrong, but I don't think we're so totally defeated neither.

LADY SNEERWELL   No!

JOSEPH SURFACE   You tell me you have made a trial of Snake since we met, and that you still believe him faithful to us.

LADY SNEERWELL   I do believe so.

JOSEPH SURFACE   And that he has undertaken, should it be necessary, to swear and prove that — Charles is at this time contracted by vows and honour to your ladyship — which some of his former letters to you will serve to support?

LADY SNEERWELL   This, indeed, might have assisted.

JOSEPH SURFACE   Come, come; it is not too late yet. — [*Knocking*] But hark! this is probably my uncle, Sir Oliver — retire to that room. We'll consult farther when he's gone.

LADY SNEERWELL   Well! — but if *he* should find you out too —

JOSEPH SURFACE   O, I have no fear of that. Sir Peter will hold his tongue for his own credit['s] sake — and you may depend on't I shall soon discover Sir Oliver's weak side!

LADY SNEERWELL   I have no diffidence of your abilities — only be constant to one roguery at a time.

Exit

JOSEPH SURFACE   I will — I will — So! 'tis confounded hard — after such bad fortune, to be baited by one's confederate in evil. Well at all events, my character is so much better than Charles's that I certainly — hey! what! — this is not *Sir Oliver*, but *old Stanley* again! — Plague on't that he should return to tease me just now — we shall have Sir Oliver come and find him — here — and —

Enter Sir Oliver Surface

Gad's life, Mr. Stanley, why have you come back to plague me just at this time? — you must not stay now, upon my word!

SIR OLIVER   Sir, I hear your uncle Oliver is expected here, and tho' he has been so penurious to *you*, I'll try what he'll do for *me*.

JOSEPH SURFACE   Sir, 'tis — impossible for you to stay now, so I must beg — Come any other time and I promise you, you shall be assisted.

SIR OLIVER   No — Sir Oliver and I must be acquainted.

JOSEPH SURFACE   Zounds, sir! then I insist on your quitting the room directly.

SIR OLIVER   Nay, sir!

JOSEPH SURFACE   Sir, I insist on't — here, William show this gentleman out. Since you compel me, sir — not one moment — this is such insolence!   [*Going to push him out*]

Enter Charles Surface

CHARLES SURFACE   Hey-day! what's the matter now? — what the devil, have you got hold of my little broker here? Zounds, brother — don't hurt little Premium. What's the matter, my little fellow?

JOSEPH SURFACE   So! He has been with you too, has he?

CHARLES SURFACE   To be sure he has! — why, 'tis as honest a little — But sure, Joseph, you have not been borrowing money too, have you?

JOSEPH SURFACE   Borrowing — no! — but brother, you know here we — expect Sir Oliver — every —

CHARLES SURFACE   O gad! that's true—Noll musn't find the little broker here, to be sure.

JOSEPH SURFACE   Yet Mr. *Stanley* insists—

CHARLES SURFACE   Stanley! why his name is *Premium*.

JOSEPH SURFACE   No, no, *Stanley*.

CHARLES SURFACE   No, no, *Premium*.

JOSEPH SURFACE   Well, no matter which—but—

CHARLES SURFACE   Aye, aye, Stanley or Premium, 'tis the same thing, as you say, for I suppose he goes by half a hundred names besides A.B.'s at the coffee-houses.   [*Knock*]

JOSEPH SURFACE   Death! here's Sir Oliver at the door. [*Knocking again*] Now I beg, Mr. Stanley—

CHARLES SURFACE   Aye, and I beg, Mr. Premium—

SIR OLIVER   Gentlemen—

JOSEPH SURFACE   Sir, by heaven you shall go!

CHARLES SURFACE   Aye, out with him certainly.

SIR OLIVER   This violence—

JOSEPH SURFACE   'Tis your own fault.

CHARLES SURFACE   Out with him, to be sure!   [*Both forcing Sir Oliver out*]

Enter Sir Peter and Lady Teazle, Maria, and Rowley

SIR PETER   My old friend, Sir Oliver!—hey—what in the name of wonder!—Here are dutiful nephews!—assault their uncle at the first visit—

LADY TEAZLE   Indeed Sir Oliver, 'twas well we came in to rescue you.

ROWLEY   Truly it was—for I perceive, Sir Oliver, the character of old Stanley was no protection to you.

SIR OLIVER   Nor of Premium, either — the necessities of the *former* couldn't extort a shilling from *that* benevolent gentleman and now, egad, I stood a chance of faring worse than my ancestors, and being knocked down without being bid for.

[*After a pause, Joseph and Charles turning to each other*]

JOSEPH SURFACE   Charles!

CHARLES SURFACE   Joseph!

JOSEPH SURFACE   'Tis now complete!

CHARLES SURFACE   Very.

SIR OLIVER   Sir Peter, my friend, and Rowley too—look on that elder nephew of mine. *You* know what he has already received from my bounty, and you know also, how gladly I would have regarded half my fortune as held in trust for him—judge then my disappointment in discovering him to be destitute of truth — charity — and gratitude.

SIR PETER   Sir Oliver, I should be more suprised at this declaration if I had not myself found him selfish — treacherous and hypocritical!

LADY TEAZLE   And if the gentleman pleads not guilty to these, pray let him call *me* to his character.

SIR PETER   Then I believe we need add no more — if he knows himself, he will consider it as the most perfect punishment, that he is known by the world.

CHARLES SURFACE   [*aside*] If they talk this way to *Honesty*, what will they say to *me* by and by?

SIR OLIVER   As for that prodigal, his brother there —

CHARLES SURFACE   [*aside*] Aye, now comes my turn — the damned family pictures will ruin me.

JOSEPH SURFACE   Sir Oliver! — uncle! — will you honour me with a hearing?

CHARLES SURFACE   [*aside*] Now if Joseph would make one of his long speeches, I might recollect myself a little.

SIR OLIVER   I suppose you would undertake to justify yourself entirely?

JOSEPH SURFACE   I trust I could.

SIR OLIVER   Pshaw! — well, sir — and *you* [*to Charles*] could justify yourself too I suppose?

CHARLES SURFACE   Not that I know of, Sir Oliver.

SIR OLIVER   What! — little Premium — has been let too much into the secret I presume.

CHARLES SURFACE   True, sir — but they were family secrets and should never be mentioned again you know.

ROWLEY   Come, Sir Oliver, I know you cannot speak of Charles's follies with anger.

SIR OLIVER   Odd's heart, no more I can — nor with gravity either. Sir Peter, do you know the rogue bargained with me for all his ancestors — sold me judges and generals by the foot and maiden aunts as cheap as broken china!

CHARLES SURFACE   To be sure Sir Oliver, I did make a little free with the family canvas, that's the truth on't. My ancestors may certainly rise in evidence against me, there's no denying it. But believe me sincere when I tell you — and upon my soul I would not say it if I was not — that if I do not appear mortified at the exposure of my follies, it is because I feel at this moment the warmest satisfaction in seeing you, my liberal benefactor.

SIR OLIVER   Charles — I believe you — give me your hand again. The ill-looking little fellow over the settee has made your peace, sirrah.

CHARLES SURFACE   Then sir, my gratitude to the original is still increased.

LADY TEAZLE [*pointing to Maria*] Yet I believe, Sir Oliver, here is one whom Charles is still more anxious to be reconciled to.

SIR OLIVER O I have heard of his attachment there and with the young lady's pardon, if I construe right that blush —

SIR PETER Well, child, speak your sentiments.

MARIA Sir, I have little to say, but that I shall rejoice to hear that he is happy. For me, whatever claim I had to his affection, I willingly resign it to one who has a better title.

CHARLES SURFACE How, Maria!

SIR PETER Hey-day! what's the mystery now? — while he appeared an incorrigible rake, you would give your hand to no one else, and now that he is likely to reform, I warrant you won't have him!

MARIA His own heart — and Lady Sneerwell know the cause.

CHARLES SURFACE Lady Sneerwell!

JOSEPH SURFACE Brother, it — is with great concern — I am obliged to speak on this point, but my regard to justice compels me — and Lady Sneerwell's injuries can no longer be concealed. [*Goes to the door*]

Enter Lady Sneerwell

SIR PETER So! another French milliner, egad! — He has one in every room in the house, I suppose!

LADY SNEERWELL Ungrateful Charles! — well may you be surprised and feel for the indelicate situation which your perfidy has forced me into.

CHARLES SURFACE Pray, uncle, is this another plot of yours? for as I have life, I don't understand it.

JOSEPH SURFACE I believe, sir, there is but the evidence of one person more necessary to make it extremely clear.

SIR PETER And that person, I imagine, is Mr. Snake. — Rowley, you were perfectly right to bring him with us, and pray let him appear.

ROWLEY Walk in, Mr. Snake.

Enter Snake

SNAKE I thought his testimony — might be wanted, however, it happens unluckily that he comes to confront Lady Sneerwell and not to support her.

LADY SNEERWELL Villain! — treacherous to me at last! [*Aside*] — Speak, fellow, have *you* too conspired against me?

SNAKE I beg your ladyship — ten thousand pardons — you paid me extremely liberally for the lie in question — but I have unfortunately been offered double to speak the truth.

SIR PETER   Plot and counterplot, egad—I wish your ladyship joy of the success of your negotiation.

LADY SNEERWELL   The torments of shame and disappointment on you all!—

LADY TEAZLE   Hold, Lady Sneerwell—before you go, let me thank you for the trouble you and that gentleman have taken in writing letters to me from Charles, and answering them yourself—and let me also request you to make—my respects to the Scandalous College, of which you are president—and inform them, that Lady Teazle, licentiate, begs leave to return the diploma they granted her—as she leaves off practice, and kills characters no longer.

LADY SNEERWELL   You too, Madam!—provoking—insolent!—may your husband live these fifty years!   *Exit*

SIR PETER   Oons! what a fury—

LADY TEAZLE   A malicious creature, indeed!

SIR PETER   Hey—not for her last wish?

LADY TEAZLE   O no—

SIR OLIVER   Well, sir, and what have you to say now?

JOSEPH SURFACE   Sir, I am so confounded to find that Lady *Sneerwell* could be guilty of suborning Mr. *Snake* in this manner to impose on us all, that I know not what to say—however, lest her revengeful spirit should prompt her to injure my brother, I had certainly better follow her directly.   *Exit*

SIR PETER   Moral to the last drop!

SIR OLIVER   Aye, and marry her, Joseph, if you can—Oil and vinegar, egad: you'll do very well together.

ROWLEY   I believe we have no more occasion for Mr. Snake at present.

SNAKE   Before I go, I beg pardon once for all for whatever uneasiness I have been the humble instrument of causing to the parties present.

SIR PETER   Well, well, you have made atonement by a good deed at last.

SNAKE   But I must request of the company that it shall never be known.

SIR PETER   Hey!—what the plague!—are you ashamed of having done a right thing once in your life?

SNAKE   Ah! Sir—consider I live by the badness of my character!—I have nothing but my infamy to depend on! and if it were once known that I had been betrayed into an honest action, I should lose every friend I have in the world.

SIR OLIVER   Well, well, we'll not traduce you by saying anything in your praise, never fear.   *Exit Snake*

SIR PETER   There's a precious rogue—yet that fellow is a writer and a critic!

LADY TAEZLE   See, Sir Oliver, there needs no persuasion now to reconcile your nephew and Maria.   [*Charles and Maria apart*]

SIR OLIVER   Aye, aye, that's as it should—be and egad, we'll have the wedding to-morrow—morning.

CHARLES SURFACE   Thank you, my dear uncle!

SIR PETER   What! you rogue, don't you ask the girl's consent first?

CHARLES SURFACE   O I have done that a long time—above a minute ago —and she has looked yes.

MARIA   For shame, Charles—I protest, Sir Peter, there has not been a word—

SIR OLIVER   Well then, the fewer the better—may your love for each other never know—abatement.

SIR PETER   And may you live as happily together as Lady Teazle and I —intend to do.

CHARLES SURFACE   Rowley, my old friend, I am sure you congratulate me and I suspect that I owe you much.

SIR OLIVER   You do, indeed, Charles.

ROWLEY   If my efforts to serve you had not succeeded you would have been in my debt for the attempt—but deserve to be happy—and you overpay me.

SIR PETER   Aye, honest Rowley always said you would reform.

CHARLES SURFACE   Why as to reforming, Sir Peter, I'll make no promises, and that I take to be a proof that I intend to set about it. But here shall be my monitor—my gentle guide.—Ah! can I leave the virtuous path those eyes illumine?

> Tho' thou, dear maid, shouldst waive thy *beauty's* sway,
> —Thou still must rule, because I *will* obey;
> An humbled fugitive from Folly view,
> No sanctuary near but *Love* and—YOU;

[*To the audience*]

You can, indeed, each anxious fear remove,
For even *Scandal* dies, if *you* approve.

Finis

EPILOGUE
WRITTEN BY G. COLMAN, ESQ.
SPOKEN BY MRS. ABINGTON

I, who was late so volatile and gay,
Like a trade-wind, must now blow all one way;
Bend all my cares, my studies, and my vows,
To one old rusty weathercock—my spouse;—
So wills our virtuous bard!—the motley Bayes
Of crying epilogues and laughing plays.

Old bachelors, who marry smart young wives,
Learn from our play, to regulate your lives;
Each bring his dear to town—all faults upon her—
London will prove the very source of honour:
Plunged fairly in, like a cold bath it serves,
When principles relax—to brace the nerves.
   Such is my case;—and yet I might deplore
That the gay dream of dissipation's o'er;
And say, ye fair, was ever lively wife,
Born with a genius for the highest life,
Like me untimely blasted in her bloom,
Like me condemned to such a dismal doom?
Save money—when I just knew how to waste it!
Leave London—just as I began to taste it!
Must I then watch the early crowing cock,
The melancholy ticking of a clock?
In the lone rustic hall for ever pounded,
With dogs, cats, rats, and squalling brats surrounded?
With humble curates can I now retire,
(While good Sir Peter boozes with the squire,)
And at backgammon mortify my soul,
That pants for loo, or flutters at a vole?
Seven's the main! Dear sound!—that must expire,
Lost at hot cockles, round a Christmas fire!
The transient hour of fashion, too soon spent,
Farewell the tranquil mind, farewell content!
Farewell the plumèd head, the cushioned tête,
That takes the cushion from its proper seat!
That spirit-stirring drum!—card drums I mean,
Spadille—odd trick—pam—basto—king and queen!
And you, ye knockers, that with brazen throat,
The welcome visitor's approach denote;
Farewell! all quality of high renown,
Pride, pomp, and circumstance of glorious town!
Farewell! your revels I partake no more
And Lady Teazle's occupation's o'er—
All this I told our bard—he smiled, and said 'twas clear,
I ought to play deep tragedy next year.
Meanwhile he drew wise morals from his play,
And in these solemn periods stalked away:
"Blest were the fair like you; her faults who stopped,
And closed her follies when the curtain dropped!
No more in vice or error to engage,
Or play the fool at large, on life's great stage."

MODERN AND CONTEMPORARY DRAMA

Each play in this collection of modern and contemporary drama invites us to imagine not only a particular location but also a highly detailed setting within that locale. In the stage directions preceding the first act of *A Doll's House*, for example, Ibsen is not content simply to tell us that the play takes place in the living room of Torvald Helmer's home. He gives us, rather, an elaborate description of that room and all of its furnishings:

> A comfortably and tastefully, but not expensively furnished room. Backstage right a door leads out to the hall; backstage left, another door to Helmer's study. Between these two doors stands a piano. In the middle of the left-hand wall is a door, with a window downstage of it. Near the window, a round table with armchairs and a small sofa. In the right-hand wall, slightly upstage, is a door; downstage of this, against the same wall, a stove lined with porcelain tiles, with a couple of armchairs and a rocking chair in front of it. Between the stove and the side door is a small table. Engravings on the wall. A what-not with china and other bric-à-brac; a small bookcase with leather-bound books. A carpet on the floor; a fire in the stove.

That description is so complete that it asks us even to visualize a fire burning in the stove. And why not, since the action takes place shortly before Christmas? It seems to be a perfectly logical detail for Ibsen to note. But it seems logical to us because as twentieth-century playgoers we have become accustomed to the vividly realistic stage illusions of our present-day theaters.

To Ibsen's audience (which witnessed the first production of *A Doll's House* in 1879) that elaborately realistic set, depicting an upper-middle class interior of the nineteenth century, was almost as revolutionary as his frankly realistic approach to the marital problems of that upper-middle class family. Until the 1850s, in fact, theatrical settings of the nineteenth century consisted largely of painted flats depicting the exotic landscapes of Romantic melodrama. And before the nineteenth century, as we have seen in our introductory notes on classical-through-neoclassical theaters, there were virtually no attempts whatsoever to create a completely detailed visual illusion on stage. Shakespeare's plays were originally staged without sets at all and only a few props. But Ibsen and many dramatists since his time have deliberately aimed to create elaborate settings for their plays, and thus we should be aware of their purposes in doing so. We should not be content simply to attribute those sets to technical advances in the design of theater.

In Ibsen's case that detailed setting is related directly to the naturalistic impulse of his play. Thus, in *A Doll's House* he not only portrays the psychological relationship between Helmer and Nora, but he also displays the environment in which that relationship is rooted. He is, in fact, at such pains to create a total sense of their environment that he turns the stage into a completely furnished living room with a wall at both sides as well as at the back. That box set is also crucial to an experiencing of the play. Were we to witness a production of the play, we would feel as though we were peering in on the characters, as though the space defined by the proscenium arch did not exist for them, as though they were in a room surrounded by four walls, as though they were conducting their personal lives in private.

But beyond having us experience this naturalistic illusion, Ibsen intends us also to see that elaborate set as symbolizing the impact of the Helmers' environment upon their marriage—indeed as symbolizing the very nature of that marriage. That set with all its expensive possessions embodies the profound pressures placed on Helmer and Nora by the material and social conditions of their world. Thus, when we read the play we should keep continually in our mind's eye the rich clutter of that room with its bric-à-brac and its overstuffed chairs that in the end are as stifling—and as deceiving—as the marriage of Nora and Helmer. We should be aware, for example, of how deeply attached Nora is to those possessions in the beginning of the play—like a child, she does not wish to give up the illusions of her doll's house—and thus of how much it takes for her to free herself of their very solid hold on her life: on her physical life *and* on her mental life.

Once we recognize setting as a potentially symbolic element of modern and contemporary drama, we shall find that our reading of plays is enriched when we pay close attention to all the descriptive details concerning the make-up of the set. Dramatists provide those elaborate descriptions not only for the guidance of set designers but also for the enlightenment of readers like us who may not have the opportunity to witness a production of their plays. And as we move from one play to the next, we shall find that the settings enlighten us in quite different ways. Just as dramatists write in different styles, so they use their settings for different symbolic effects. At the beginning of *Major Barbara*, for example, Shaw offers us a relatively sketchy description of the "library in Lady Britomart Undershaft's house in Wilton Crescent," noting merely that it contains a "large and comfortable settee in the middle of the room, upholstered in dark leather," a "writing table" on each side of it, a "window with a window seat," "an armchair" nearby, "books in the library," and "pictures on the walls." From these few details, Shaw does not appear to be interested in providing a naturalistic display of Lady Britomart's environment. Instead, he aims to present her library as an emblem of the traditional aristocratic social values for which she stands, as he makes clear in the remarks he offers about Lady Britomart immediately after the details about her library. He tells us, for example, that she is "a very typical managing matron of the upper class . . . limited in the oddest way with domestic and class limitations, conceiving the universe exactly as if it were a large house in Wilton Crescent." Thus her library with its few typical marks of upper-class privilege is sufficient to stand as a symbol of her aristocratic outlook.

Most settings in modern and contemporary drama are indeed just as richly significant as the actions that take place within them, but that should not surprise us, for we have come to know from our own lives that the environments in which we exist not only influence us but are influenced by us. So it is with the settings and characters of the plays included in this collection. They are inextricably bound up with one another, and thus they can be understood only in relation with one another.

HENRIK IBSEN

1828–1906

Born in Skien, Norway, a small town where his father was then a successful merchant, Ibsen grew up amid the painful circumstances that were brought about by the decline of his father's business, which ended in bankruptcy when Ibsen was eight years old. His family was then forced to move from their large and comfortable home to a small attic apartment, and by the time Ibsen was sixteen he was sent off to another town to make his own way as a druggist's apprentice. When he was twenty-two, he moved to Christiana (now Oslo), hoping to study medicine at the University there, but his failure to gain admission led him to make a career out of the play-writing that he had begun to do several years earlier. During the next six-teen years, he was influenced largely by the nationalistic and romantic movement in Norwegian theater, and thus gave himself over mostly to writing blank verse plays on subjects drawn from Norwegian myth and history. But in 1869, with *The League of Youth*, a play exposing the corruption of provincial politics and politicians, Ibsen began to write realistic prose plays about the social problems of his time. His best-known problem plays—*A Doll's House* (1879) and *Ghosts* (1881)—were highly controversial in his own time, especially among his Norwegian countrymen, who regarded them as attacking such traditional values as marriage and the family. Social reform-ers then and now have hailed them as eloquent pleas in defense of women's rights These plays may also be seen as foreshadowing his late dramatic studies of psychologically troubled men and women in *Rosmers-holm* (1886) and *Hedda Gabler* (1890), and thus he has properly come to be regarded as the father of modern naturalistic drama.

A Doll's House

CHARACTERS

TORVALD HELMER, a lawyer

NORA, his wife

DR. RANK

MRS. LINDE

NILS KROGSTAD, also a lawyer

The HELMERS' three small children

ANNE-MARIE, their nurse

HELEN, the maid

A PORTER

The action takes place in the Helmers' apartment.

ACT I

A comfortably and tastefully, but not expensively furnished room. Backstage right a door leads out to the hall; backstage left, another door to Helmer's study. Between these two doors stands a piano. In the middle of the left-hand wall is a door, with a window downstage of it. Near the window, a round table with armchairs and a small sofa. In the right-hand wall, slightly upstage, is a door; downstage of this, against the same wall, a stove lined with porcelain tiles, with a couple of armchairs and a rocking-chair in front of it. Between the stove and the side door is a small table. Engravings on the wall. A what-not with china and other bric-a-brac; a small bookcase with leather-bound books. A carpet on the floor; a fire in the stove. A winter day.

A bell rings in the hall outside. After a moment, we hear the front door being opened. Nora enters the room, humming contentedly to herself. She is wearing outdoor clothes and carrying a lot of parcels, which she puts down on the table right. She leaves the door to the hall open; through it, we can see a Porter carrying a Christmas tree and a basket. He gives these to the Maid, who has opened the door for them.

Translated by Michael Meyer

NORA   Hide that Christmas tree away, Helen. The children mustn't see it before I've decorated it this evening. [*To the Porter, taking out her purse.*] How much—?

PORTER   A shilling.

NORA   Here's half a crown. No, keep it.

The Porter touches his cap and goes. Nora closes the door. She continues to laugh happily to herself as she removes her coat, etc. She takes from her pocket a bag containing macaroons and eats a couple. Then she tiptoes across and listens at her husband's door.

NORA   Yes, he's here. [*Starts humming again as she goes over to the table, right.*]

HELMER [*from his room*]   Is that my skylark twittering out there?

NORA [*opening some of the parcels*]   It is!

HELMER   Is that my squirrel rustling?

NORA   Yes!

HELMER   When did my squirrel come home?

NORA   Just now. [*Pops the bag of macaroons in her pocket and wipes her mouth.*] Come out here, Torvald, and see what I've bought.

HELMER   You mustn't disturb me! [*Short pause; then he opens the door and looks in, his pen in his hand.*] Bought, did you say? All that? Has my little squanderbird been overspending again?

NORA   Oh, Torvald, surely we can let ourselves go a little this year! It's the first Christmas we don't have to scrape.

HELMER   Well, you know, we can't afford to be extravagant.

NORA   Oh yes, Torvald, we can be a little extravagant now. Can't we? Just a tiny bit? You've got a big salary now, and you're going to make lots and lots of money.

HELMER   Next year, yes. But my new salary doesn't start till April.

NORA   Pooh; we can borrow till then.

HELMER   Nora! [*Goes over to her and takes her playfully by the ear.*] What a little spendthrift you are! Suppose I were to borrow fifty pounds today, and you spent it all over Christmas, and then on New Year's Eve a tile fell off a roof on to my head—

NORA [*puts her hand over his mouth*]   Oh, Torvald! Don't say such dreadful things!

HELMER   Yes, but suppose something like that did happen? What then?

NORA   If anything as frightful as that happened, it wouldn't make much difference whether I was in debt or not.

HELMER   But what about the people I'd borrowed from?

NORA   Them? Who cares about them? They're strangers.

HELMER Oh, Nora, Nora, how like a woman! No, but seriously, Nora, you know how I feel about this. No debts! Never borrow! A home that is founded on debts can never be a place of freedom and beauty. We two have stuck it out bravely up to now; and we shall continue to do so for the short time we still have to.

NORA [goes over towards the stove] Very well, Torvald. As you say.

HELMER [follows her] Now, now! My little songbird mustn't droop her wings. What's this? Is little squirrel sulking? [Takes out his purse] Nora; guess what I've got here!

NORA [turns quickly] Money!

HELMER Look. [Hands her some banknotes] I know how these small expenses crop up at Christmas.

NORA [counts them] One—two—three—four. Oh, thank you, Torvald, thank you! I should be able to manage with this.

HELMER You'll have to.

NORA Yes, yes, of course I will. But come over here, I want to show you everything I've bought. And so cheaply! Look, here are new clothes for Ivar—and a sword. And a horse and a trumpet for Bob. And a doll and a cradle for Emmy—they're nothing much, but she'll pull them apart in a few days. And some bits of material and handkerchiefs for the maids. Old Anne-Marie ought to have had something better, really.

HELMER And what's in that parcel?

NORA [cries] No, Torvald, you mustn't see that before this evening!

HELMER Very well. But now, tell me, you little spendthrift, what do you want for Christmas?

NORA Me? Oh, pooh, I don't want anything.

HELMER Oh, yes, you do. Now tell me, what, within reason, would you most like?

NORA No, I really don't know. Oh, yes—Torvald—!

HELMER Well?

NORA [plays with his coat-buttons; not looking at him] If you really want to give me something, you could—you could—

HELMER Come on, out with it.

NORA [quickly] You could give me money, Torvald. Only as much as you feel you can afford; then later I'll buy something with it.

HELMER But, Nora—

NORA Oh yes, Torvald dear, please! Please! Then I'll wrap up the notes in pretty gold paper and hang them on the Christmas tree. Wouldn't that be fun?

HELMER What's the name of that little bird that can never keep any money?

NORA Yes, yes, squanderbird; I know. But let's do as I say, Torvald; then I'll have time to think about what I need most. Isn't that the best way? Mm?

HELMER [smiles] To be sure it would be, if you could keep what I give you and really buy yourself something with it. But you'll spend it on all sorts of useless things for the house, and then I'll have to put my hand in my pocket again.

NORA   Oh, but Torvald—

HELMER   You can't deny it, Nora dear. [*Puts his arm round her waist.*] The squanderbird's a pretty little creature, but she gets through an awful lot of money. It's incredible what an expensive pet she is for a man to keep.

NORA   For shame! How can you say such a thing? I save every penny I can.

HELMER [*laughs*]   That's quite true. Every penny you can. But you can't.

NORA [*hums and smiles, quietly gleeful*]   Hm. If you only knew how many expenses we larks and squirrels have, Torvald.

HELMER   You're a funny little creature. Just like your father used to be. Always on the look-out for some way to get money, but as soon as you have any it just runs through your fingers, and you never know where it's gone. Well, I suppose I must take you as you are. It's in your blood. Yes, yes, yes, these things are hereditary, Nora.

NORA   Oh, I wish I'd inherited more of Papa's qualities.

HELMER   And I wouldn't wish my darling little songbird to be any different from what she is. By the way, that reminds me. You look awfully—how shall I put it?—awfully guilty today.

NORA   Do I—

HELMER   Yes, you do. Look me in the eyes.

NORA [*looks at him*]   Well?

HELMER [*wags his finger*]   Has my little sweet-tooth been indulging herself in town today, by any chance?

NORA   No, how can you think of such a thing?

HELMER   Not a tiny little digression into a pastry shop?

NORA   No, Torvald, I promise—

HELMER   Not just a wee jam tart?

NORA   Certainly not.

HELMER   Not a little nibble at a macaroon?

NORA   No, Torvald—I promise you, honestly—

HELMER   There, there. I was only joking.

NORA [*goes over to the table, right*]   You know I could never act against your wishes.

HELMER   Of course not. And you've given me your word—[*Goes over to her.*] Well, my beloved Nora, you keep your little Christmas secrets to yourself. They'll be revealed this evening, I've no doubt, once the Christmas tree has been lit.

NORA   Have you remembered to invite Dr. Rank?

HELMER   No. But there's no need; he knows he'll be dining with us. Anyway, I'll ask him when he comes this morning. I've ordered some good wine. Oh, Nora, you can't imagine how I'm looking forward to this evening.

NORA   So am I. And, Torvald, how the children will love it!

HELMER   Yes, it's a wonderful thing to know that one's position is assured and that one has an ample income. Don't you agree? It's good to know that, isn't it?

NORA   Yes, it's almost like a miracle.

HELMER   Do you remember last Christmas? For three whole weeks you shut yourself away every evening to make flowers for the Christmas tree, and all those other things you were going to surprise us with. Ugh, it was the most boring time I've ever had in my life.

NORA   I didn't find it boring.

HELMER *[smiles]*   But it all came to nothing in the end, didn't it?

NORA   Oh, are you going to bring that up again? How could I help the cat getting in and tearing everything to bits?

HELMER   No, my poor little Nora, of course you couldn't. You simply wanted to make us happy, and that's all that matters. But it's good that those hard times are past.

NORA   Yes, it's wonderful.

HELMER   I don't have to sit by myself and be bored. And you don't have to tire your pretty eyes and your delicate little hands—

NORA *[claps her hands]*   No, Torvald, that's true, isn't it—I don't have to any longer? Oh, it's really all just like a miracle. *[Takes his arm]* Now, I'm going to tell you what I thought we might do, Torvald. As soon as Christmas is over— *[A bell rings in the hall.]* Oh, there's the doorbell. *[Tidies up one or two things in the room.]* Someone's coming. What a bore.

HELMER   I'm not at home to any visitors. Remember!

MAID *[in the doorway]*   A lady's called, madam. A stranger.

NORA   Well, ask her to come in.

MAID   And the doctor's here too, sir.

HELMER   Has he gone to my room?

MAID   Yes, sir.

Helmer goes into his room. The Maid shows in Mrs. Linde, who is dressed in traveling clothes, and closes the door.

MRS. LINDE *[shyly and a little hesitantly]*   Good evening, Nora.

NORA *[uncertainly]*   Good evening—

MRS. LINDE   I don't suppose you recognize me.

NORA   No, I'm afraid I— Yes, wait a minute—surely— *[Exclaims.]* Why, Christine! Is it really you?

MRS. LINDE   Yes, it's me.

NORA   Christine! And I didn't recognize you! But how could I—? *[More quietly]* How you've changed, Christine!

MRS. LINDE   Yes, I know. It's been nine years—nearly ten—

NORA   Is it so long? Yes, it must be. Oh, these last eight years have been such a happy time for me!. So you've come to town? All that way in winter! How brave of you!

MRS. LINDE I arrived by the steamer this morning.

NORA Yes, of course—to enjoy yourself over Christmas. Oh, how splendid! We'll have to celebrate! But take off your coat. You're not cold, are you? [Helps her off with it.] There! Now let's sit down here by the stove and be comfortable. No, you take the armchair. I'll sit here in the rocking-chair. [Clasps Mrs. Linde's hands.] Yes, now you look like your old self. It was just at first that—you've got a little paler, though, Christine. And perhaps a bit thinner.

MRS. LINDE And older, Nora. Much, much older.

NORA Yes, perhaps a little older. Just a tiny bit. Not much. [Checks herself suddenly and says earnestly.] Oh, but how thoughtless of me to sit here and chatter away like this! Dear, sweet Christine, can you forgive me?

MRS. LINDE What do you mean, Nora?

NORA [quietly] Poor Christine, you've become a widow.

MRS. LINDE Yes. Three years ago.

NORA I know, I know—I read it in the papers. Oh, Christine, I meant to write to you so often, honestly. But I always put it off, and something else always cropped up.

MRS. LINDE I understand, Nora dear.

NORA No, Christine, it was beastly of me. Oh, my poor darling, what you've gone through! And he didn't leave you anything?

MRS. LINDE No.

NORA No children, either?

MRS. LINDE No.

NORA Nothing at all, then?

MRS. LINDE Not even a feeling of loss or sorrow.

NORA [looks incredulously at her] But, Christine, how is that possible?

MRS. LINDE [smiles sadly and strokes Nora's hair] Oh, these things happen, Nora.

NORA All alone. How dreadful that must be for you. I've three lovely children. I'm afraid you can't see them now, because they're out with nanny. But you must tell me everything—

MRS. LINDE No, no, no. I want to hear about you.

NORA No, you start. I'm not going to be selfish today, I'm just going to think about you. Oh, but there's one thing I must tell you. Have you heard of the wonderful luck we've just had?

MRS. LINDE No. What?

NORA Would you believe it—my husband's just been made manager of the bank!

MRS. LINDE Your husband? Oh, how lucky—!

NORA Yes, isn't it? Being a lawyer is so uncertain, you know, especially if one isn't prepared to touch any case that isn't—well—quite nice. And of course Torvald's been very firm about that—and I'm absolutely with him. Oh, you can imagine how happy we are! He's joining the bank in the New Year, and he'll be getting a big salary, and lots of percentages too. From now on we'll be able to live quite differently—we'll be able to do whatever we want. Oh, Christine, it's such a relief! I feel so happy! Well, I mean, it's lovely to have heaps of money and not to have to worry about anything. Don't you think?

MRS. LINDE   It must be lovely to have enough to cover one's needs, anyway.

NORA   Not just our needs! We're going to have heaps and heaps of money!

MRS. LINDE [smiles]   Nora, Nora, haven't you grown up yet? When we were at school you were a terrible little spendthrift.

NORA [laughs quietly]   Yes, Torvald still says that. [Wags her finger.] But "Nora, Nora" isn't as silly as you think. Oh, we've been in no position for me to waste money. We've both had to work.

MRS. LINDE   You too?

NORA   Yes, little things—fancy work, crocheting, embroidery and so forth. [Casually.] And other things too. I suppose you know Torvald left the Ministry when we got married? There were no prospects of promotion in his department, and of course he needed more money. But the first year he overworked himself quite dreadfully. He had to take on all sorts of extra jobs, and worked day and night. But it was too much for him, and he became frightfully ill. The doctors said he'd have to go to a warmer climate.

MRS. LINDE   Yes, you spent a whole year in Italy, didn't you?

NORA   Yes. It wasn't easy for me to get away, you know. I'd just had Ivar. But of course we had to do it. Oh, it was a marvelous trip! And it saved Torvald's life. But it cost an awful lot of money, Christine.

MRS. LINDE   I can imagine.

NORA   Two hundred and fifty pounds. That's a lot of money, you know.

MRS. LINDE   How lucky you had it.

NORA   Well, actually, we got it from my father.

MRS. LINDE   Oh, I see. Didn't he die just about that time?

NORA   Yes, Christine, just about then. Wasn't it dreadful, I couldn't go and look after him. I was expecting little Ivar any day. And then I had my poor Torvald to care for—we really didn't think he'd live. Dear, kind Papa! I never saw him again, Christine. Oh, it's the saddest thing that's happened to me since I got married.

MRS. LINDE   I know you were very fond of him. But you went to Italy—?

NORA   Yes. Well, we had the money, you see, and the doctors said we mustn't delay. So we went the month after Papa died.

MRS. LINDE   And your husband came back completely cured?

NORA   Fit as a fiddle!

MRS. LINDE   But—the doctor?

NORA   How do you mean?

MRS. LINDE   I thought the maid said that the gentleman who arrived with me was the doctor.

NORA   Oh yes, that's Doctor Rank, but he doesn't come because anyone's ill.

He's our best friend, and he looks us up at least once every day. No, Torvald hasn't had a moment's illness since we went away. And the children are fit and healthy and so am I. [*Jumps up and claps her hands.*] Oh God, oh God, Christine, isn't it a wonderful thing to be alive and happy! Oh, but how beastly of me! I'm only talking about myself. [*Sits on a footstool and rests her arms on Mrs. Linde's knee.*] Oh, please don't be angry with me! Tell me, is it really true you didn't love your husband? Why did you marry him, then?

MRS. LINDE   Well, my mother was still alive; and she was helpless and bedridden. And I had my two little brothers to take care of. I didn't feel I could say no.

NORA   Yes, well, perhaps you're right. He was rich then, was he?

MRS. LINDE   Quite comfortably off, I believe. But his business was unsound, you see, Nora. When he died it went bankrupt, and there was nothing left.

NORA   What did you do?

MRS. LINDE   Well, I had to try to make ends meet somehow, so I started a little shop, and a little school, and anything else I could turn my hand to. These last three years have been just one endless slog for me, without a moment's rest. But now it's over, Nora. My poor dear mother doesn't need me any more; she's passed away. And the boys don't need me either; they've got jobs now and can look after themselves.

NORA   How relieved you must feel—

MRS. LINDE   No, Nora. Just unspeakably empty. No one to live for any more. [*Gets up restlessly.*] That's why I couldn't bear to stay out there any longer, cut off from the world. I thought it'd be easier to find some work here that will exercise and occupy my mind. If only I could get a regular job—office work of some kind—

NORA   Oh but, Christine, that's dreadfully exhausting; and you look practically finished already. It'd be much better for you if you could go away somewhere.

MRS. LINDE   [*goes over to the window*]   I have no Papa to pay for my holidays, Nora.

NORA   [*gets up*]   Oh, please don't be angry with me.

MRS. LINDE   My dear Nora, it's I who should ask you not to be angry. That's the worst thing about this kind of situation—it makes one so bitter. One has no one to work for; and yet one has to be continually sponging for jobs. One has to live; and so one becomes completely egocentric. When you told me about this luck you've just had with Torvald's new job—can you imagine?—I was happy not so much on your account, as on my own.

NORA   How do you mean? Oh, I understand. You mean Torvald might be able to do something for you?

MRS. LINDE   Yes, I was thinking that.

NORA He will too, Christine. Just you leave it to me. I'll lead up to it so delicately, so delicately; I'll get him in the right mood. Oh, Christine, I do so want to help you.

MRS. LINDE It's sweet of you to bother so much about me, Nora. Especially since you know so little of the worries and hardships of life.

NORA I! You say *I* know little of—?

MRS. LINDE [*smiles*] Well, good heavens—those bits of fancy work of yours—well, really—! You're a child, Nora.

NORA [*tosses her head and walks across the room*] You shouldn't say that so patronizingly.

MRS. LINDE Oh?

NORA You're like the rest. You all think I'm incapable of getting down to anything serious—

MRS. LINDE My dear—

NORA You think I've never had any worries like the rest of you.

MRS. LINDE Nora dear, you've just told me about all your difficulties—

NORA Pooh—that! [*Quietly.*] I haven't told you about the big thing.

MRS. LINDE What big thing? What do you mean?

NORA You patronize me, Christine; but you shouldn't. You're proud that you've worked so long and so hard for your mother.

MRS. LINDE I don't patronize anyone, Nora. But you're right—I am both proud and happy that I was able to make my mother's last months on earth comparatively easy.

NORA And you're also proud at what you've done for your brothers.

MRS. LINDE I think I have a right to be.

NORA I think so too. But let me tell you something, Christine. I too have done something to be proud and happy about.

MRS. LINDE I don't doubt it. But—how do you mean?

NORA Speak quietly! Suppose Torvald should hear! He mustn't, at any price—no one must know, Christine—no one but you.

MRS. LINDE But what is this?

NORA Come over here. [*Pulls her down on to the sofa beside her.*] Yes, Christine—I too have done something to be happy and proud about. It was I who saved Torvald's life.

MRS. LINDE Saved his—? How did you save it?

NORA I told you about our trip to Italy. Torvald couldn't have lived if he hadn't managed to get down there—

MRS. LINDE Yes, well—your father provided the money—

NORA [*smiles*] So Torvald and everyone else thinks. But—

MRS. LINDE Yes?

NORA Papa didn't give us a penny. It was I who found the money.

MRS. LINDE You? All of it?

NORA Two hundred and fifty pounds. What do you say to that?

MRS. LINDE But Nora, how could you? Did you win a lottery or something?

NORA [*scornfully*]   Lottery? [*Sniffs.*] What would there be to be proud of in that?

MRS. LINDE   But where did you get it from, then?

NORA [*hums and smiles secretively*]   Hm; tra-la-la-la!

MRS. LINDE   You couldn't have borrowed it.

NORA   Oh? Why not?

MRS. LINDE   Well, a wife can't borrow money without her husband's consent.

NORA [*tosses her head*]   Ah, but when a wife has a little business sense, and knows how to be clever—

MRS. LINDE   But Nora, I simply don't understand—

NORA   You don't have to. No one has said I borrowed the money. I could have got it in some other way. [*Throws herself back on the sofa.*] I could have got it from an admirer. When a girl's as pretty as I am—

MRS. LINDE   Nora, you're crazy!

NORA   You're dying of curiosity now, aren't you, Christine?

MRS. LINDE   Nora dear, you haven't done anything foolish?

NORA [*sits up again*]   Is it foolish to save one's husband's life?

MRS. LINDE   I think it's foolish if without his knowledge you—

NORA   But the whole point was that he mustn't know! Great heavens, don't you see? He hadn't to know how dangerously ill he was. I was the one they told that his life was in danger and that only going to a warm climate could save him. Do you suppose I didn't try to think of other ways of getting him down there? I told him how wonderful it would be for me to go abroad like other young wives; I cried and prayed; I asked him to remember my condition, and said he ought to be nice and tender to me; and then I suggested he might quite easily borrow the money. But then he got almost angry with me, Christine. He said I was frivolous, and that it was his duty as a husband not to pander to my moods and caprices—I think that's what he called them. Well, well, I thought, you've got to be saved somehow. And then I thought of a way—

MRS. LINDE   But didn't your husband find out from your father that the money hadn't come from him?

NORA   No, never. Papa died just then. I'd thought of letting him into the plot and asking him not to tell. But since he was so ill—! And as things turned out, it didn't become necessary.

MRS. LINDE   And you've never told your husband about this?

NORA   For heaven's sake, no! What an idea! He's frightfully strict about such matters. And besides—he's so proud of being a *man*—it'd be so painful and humiliating for him to know that he owed anything to me. It'd completely wreck our relationship. This life we have built together would no longer exist.

MRS. LINDE   Will you never tell him?

NORA [*thoughtfully, half-smiling*]   Yes—some time, perhaps. Years from now, when I'm no longer pretty. You mustn't laugh! I mean of course, when Torvald no longer loves me as he does now; when it no longer amuses him to see me dance and dress up and play the fool for him. Then it might be useful to have something up my sleeve. [*Breaks off.*] Stupid, stupid, stupid! That time will never come. Well, what do you think of my big secret, Christine? I'm not completely useless, am I? Mind you, all this has caused me a frightful lot of worry. It hasn't been easy for me to meet my obligations punctually. In case you don't know, in the world of business there are things called quarterly instalments and interest, and they're a terrible problem to cope with. So I've had to scrape a little here and save a little there as best I can. I haven't been able to save much on the housekeeping money, because Torvald likes to live well; and I couldn't let the children go short of clothes—I couldn't take anything out of what he gives me for them. The poor little angels!

MRS. LINDE   So you've had to stint yourself, my poor Nora?

NORA   Of course. Well, after all, it was my problem. Whenever Torvald gave me money to buy myself new clothes, I never used more than half of it; and I always bought what was cheapest and plainest. Thank heaven anything suits me, so that Torvald's never noticed. But it made me a bit sad sometimes, because it's lovely to wear pretty clothes. Don't you think?

MRS. LINDE   Indeed it is.

NORA   And then I've found one or two other sources of income. Last winter I managed to get a lot of copying to do. So I shut myself away and wrote every evening, late into the night. Oh, I often got so tired, so tired. But it was great fun, though, sitting there working and earning money. It was almost like being a man.

MRS. LINDE   But how much have you managed to pay off like this?

NORA   Well, I can't say exactly. It's awfully difficult to keep an exact check on these kind of transactions. I only know I've paid everything I've managed to scrape together. Sometimes I really didn't know where to turn. [*Smiles*] Then I'd sit here and imagine some rich old gentleman had fallen in love with me—

MRS. LINDE   What! What gentleman?

NORA   Silly! And that now he'd died and when they opened his will it said in big letters: "Everything I possess is to be paid forthwith to my beloved Mrs. Nora Helmer in cash."

MRS. LINDE   But, Nora dear, who was this gentleman?

NORA   Great heavens, don't you understand? There wasn't any old gentleman; he was just something I used to dream up as I sat here evening after evening wondering how on earth I could raise the money. But what does it matter? The old bore can stay imaginary as far as I'm concerned, because now I don't have to worry any longer! [*Jumps up.*] Oh, Christine, isn't it wonderful? I don't have to worry any more! No more troubles! I can play all day with the children, I can fill the house with pretty things, just the way Torvald likes. And, Christine, it'll soon be spring, and the air'll be fresh and the skies blue,—and then perhaps we'll be able to take a little trip somewhere. I shall be able to see the sun again. Oh, yes, yes, it's a wonderful thing to be alive and happy!

The bell rings in the hall.

MRS. LINDE [*gets up*]   You've a visitor. Perhaps I'd better go.
NORA   No, stay. It won't be for me. It's someone for Torvald—
MAID [*in the doorway*]   Excuse me, madam, a gentleman's called who says he wants to speak to the master. But I didn't know—seeing as the doctor's with him—
NORA   Who is this gentleman?
KROGSTAD [*in the doorway*]   It's me, Mrs. Helmer.

Mrs. Linde starts, composes herself and turns away to the window.

NORA [*takes a step towards him and whispers tensely*]   You? What is it? What do you want to talk to my husband about?
KROGSTAD   Business—you might call it. I hold a minor post in the bank, and I hear your husband is to become our new chief—
NORA   Oh—then it isn't—?
KROGSTAD   Pure business, Mrs. Helmer. Nothing more.
NORA   Well, you'll find him in his study.

Nods indifferently as she closes the hall door behind him. Then she walks across the room and sees to the stove.

MRS. LINDE   Nora, who was that man?
NORA   A lawyer called Krogstad.
MRS. LINDE   It was him, then.
NORA   Do you know that man?
MRS. LINDE   I used to know him—some years ago. He was a solicitor's clerk in our town, for a while.
NORA   Yes, of course, so he was.
MRS. LINDE   How he's changed!
NORA   He was very unhappily married, I believe.
MRS. LINDE   Is he a widower now?
NORA   Yes, with a lot of children. Ah, now it's alight.

She closes the door of the stove and moves the rocking-chair a little to one side.

MRS. LINDE   He does—various things now, I hear?
NORA   Does he? It's quite possible—I really don't know. But don't let's talk about business. It's so boring.

Dr. Rank enters from Helmer's study.

RANK [*still in the doorway*]   No, no, my dear chap, don't see me out. I'll go and have a word with your wife. [*Closes the door and notices Mrs. Linde.*] Oh, I beg your pardon. I seem to be *de trop* here too.

NORA   Not in the least. [*Introduces them.*] Dr. Rank. Mrs. Linde.

RANK   Ah! A name I have often heard in this house. I believe I passed you on the stairs as I came up.

MRS. LINDE   Yes. Stairs tire me; I have to take them slowly.

RANK   Oh, have you hurt yourself?

MRS. LINDE   No, I'm just a little run down.

RANK   Ah, is that all? Then I take it you've come to town to cure yourself by a round of parties?

MRS. LINDE   I have come here to find work.

RANK   Is that an approved remedy for being run down?

MRS. LINDE   One has to live, Doctor.

RANK   Yes, people do seem to regard it as a necessity.

NORA   Oh, really, Dr. Rank. I bet you want to stay alive.

RANK   You bet I do. However miserable I sometimes feel, I still want to go on being tortured for as long as possible. It's the same with all my patients; and with people who are morally sick, too. There's a moral cripple in with Helmer at this very moment—

MRS. LINDE [*softly*]   Oh!

NORA   Whom do you mean?

RANK   Oh, a lawyer fellow called Krogstad—you wouldn't know him. He's crippled all right; morally twisted. But even he started off by announcing, as though it were a matter of enormous importance, that he had to live.

NORA   Oh? What did he want to talk to Torvald about?

RANK   I haven't the faintest idea. All I heard was something about the bank.

NORA   I didn't know that Krog—that this man Krogstad had any connection. with the bank.

RANK   Yes, he's got some kind of job down there. [*To Mrs. Linde.*] I wonder if in your part of the world you too have a species of human being that spends its time fussing around trying to smell out moral corruption? And when they find a case they give him some nice, comfortable position so that they can keep a good watch on him. The healthy ones just have to lump it.

MRS. LINDE   But surely it's the sick who need care most?

RANK [*shrugs his shoulders*]   Well, there we have it. It's that attitude that's turning human society into a hospital.

Nora, lost in her own thoughts, laughs half to herself and claps her hands.

RANK   Why are you laughing? Do you really know what society is?

NORA   What do I care about society? I think it's a bore. I was laughing at something else—something frightfully funny. Tell me, Dr. Rank—will everyone who works at the bank come under Torvald now?

RANK   Do you find that particularly funny?

NORA   [smiles and hums] Never mind! Never you mind! [Walks around the room] Yes, I find it very amusing to think that we—I mean, Torvald—has obtained so much influence over so many people. [Takes the paper bag from her pocket.] Dr. Rank, would you like a small macaroon?

RANK   Macaroons! I say! I thought they were forbidden here.

NORA   Yes, well, these are some Christine gave me.

MRS. LINDE   What? I—?

NORA   All right, all right, don't get frightened. You weren't to know Torvald had forbidden them. He's afraid they'll ruin my teeth. But, dash it—for once—! Don't you agree, Dr. Rank? Here! [Pops a macaroon into his mouth.] You too, Christine. And I'll have one too. Just a little one. Two at the most. [Begins to walk round again.] Yes, now I feel really, really happy. Now there's just one thing in the world I'd really love to do.

RANK   Oh? And what is that?

NORA   Just something I'd love to say to Torvald.

RANK   Well, why don't you say it?

NORA   No, I daren't. It's too dreadful.

MRS. LINDE   Dreadful?

RANK   Well, then, you'd better not. But you can say it to us. What is it you'd so love to say to Torvald?

NORA   I've the most extraordinary longing to say: "Bloody hell!"

RANK   Are you mad?

MRS. LINDE   My dear Nora—!

RANK   Say it. Here he is.

NORA   [hiding the bag of macaroons.]   Ssh! Ssh!

Helmer, with his overcoat on his arm and his hat in his hand, enters from his study.

NORA   [goes to meet him]   Well, Torvald dear, did you get rid of him?

HELMER   Yes, he's just gone.

NORA   May I introduce you—? This is Christine. She's just arrived in town.

HELMER   Christine—? Forgive me, but I don't think—

NORA   Mrs. Linde, Torvald dear. Christine Linde.

HELMER   Ah. A childhood friend of my wife's, I presume?

MRS. LINDE   Yes, we knew each other in earlier days.

NORA   And imagine, now she's traveled all this way to talk to you.

HELMER   Oh?

MRS. LINDE   Well, I didn't really—

NORA   You see, Christine's frightfully good at office work, and she's mad to come under some really clever man who can teach her even more than she knows already—

HELMER   Very sensible, madam.

NORA   So when she heard you'd become head of the bank—it was in her local paper—she came here as quickly as she could and—Torvald, you will, won't you? Do a little something to help Christine? For my sake?

HELMER   Well, that shouldn't be impossible. You are a widow, I take it, Mrs. Linde?

MRS. LINDE   Yes.

HELMER   And you have experience of office work?

MRS. LINDE   Yes, quite a bit.

HELMER   Well then, it's quite likely I may be able to find some job for you—

NORA [claps her hands]   You see, you see!

HELMER   You've come at a lucky moment, Mrs. Linde.

MRS. LINDE   Oh, how can I ever thank you—?

HELMER   There's absolutely no need. [Puts on his overcoat.] But now I'm afraid I must ask you to excuse me—

RANK   Wait. I'll come with you.

He gets his fur coat from the hall and warms it at the stove.

NORA   Don't be long, Torvald dear.

HELMER   I'll only be an hour.

NORA   Are you going too, Christine?

MRS. LINDE [puts on her outdoor clothes]   Yes, I must start to look round for a room.

HELMER   Then perhaps we can walk part of the way together.

NORA [helps her]   It's such a nuisance we're so cramped here—I'm afraid we can't offer to—

MRS. LINDE   Oh, I wouldn't dream of it. Goodbye, Nora dear, and thanks for everything.

NORA   *Au revoir.* You'll be coming back this evening, of course. And you too, Dr. Rank. What? If you're well enough? Of course you'll be well enough. Wrap up warmly, though.

They go out, talking, into the hall. Children's voices are heard from the stairs.

NORA   Here they are! Here they are!

She runs out and opens the door. Anne-Marie, the nurse, enters with the children.

NORA   Come in, come in! [Stoops down and kisses them.] Oh, my sweet darlings—! Look at them, Christine! Aren't they beautiful?

RANK   Don't stand here chattering in this draught!

HELMER   Come, Mrs. Linde. This is for mothers only.

Dr. Rank, Helmer, and Mrs. Linde go down the stairs. The Nurse brings the children into the room. Nora follows, and closes the door to the hall.

NORA   How well you look! What red cheeks you've got! Like apples and roses! [*The children answer her inaudibly as she talks to them.*] Have you had fun? That's splendid. You gave Emmy and Bob a ride on the sledge? What, both together? I say! What a clever boy you are, Ivar! Oh, let me hold her for a moment, Anne-Marie! My sweet little baby doll! [*Takes the smallest child from the Nurse and dances with her.*] Yes, yes, Mummy will dance with Bob too. What? Have you been throwing snowballs? Oh, I wish I'd been there! No, don't—I'll undress them myself, Anne-Marie. No, please let me; it's such fun. Go inside and warm yourself; you look frozen. There's some hot coffee on the stove. [*The Nurse goes into the room on the left. Nora takes off the children's outdoor clothes and throws them anywhere while they all chatter simultaneously.*] What? A big dog ran after you? But he didn't bite you? No, dogs don't bite lovely little baby dolls. Leave those parcels alone, Ivar. What's in them? Ah, wouldn't you like to know! No, no; it's nothing nice. Come on, let's play a game. What shall we play? Hide and seek. Yes, let's play hide and seek. Bob shall hide first. You want me to? All right, let me hide first.

Nora and the children play around the room, and in the adjacent room to the left, laughing and shouting. At length Nora hides under the table. The children rush in, look, but cannot find her. Then they hear her half-stifled laughter, run to the table, lift up the cloth and see her. Great excitement. She crawls out as though to frighten them. Further excitement. Meanwhile, there has been a knock on the door leading from the hall, but no one has noticed it. Now the door is half-opened and Krogstad enters. He waits for a moment; the game continues.

KROGSTAD   Excuse me, Mrs. Helmer—

NORA   [*turns with a stifled cry and half jumps up*]   Oh! What do you want?

KROGSTAD   I beg your pardon; the front door was ajar. Someone must have forgotten to close it.

NORA   [*gets up*]   My husband is not at home, Mr. Krogstad.

KROGSTAD   I know.

NORA   Well, what do you want here, then?

KROGSTAD   A word with you.

NORA   With—? [*To the children, quietly.*] Go inside to Anne-Marie. What? No, the strange gentleman won't do anything to hurt Mummy. When he's gone we'll start playing again.

She takes the children into the room on the left and closes the door behind them.

NORA [*uneasy, tense*] You want to speak to me?

KROGSTAD Yes.

NORA Today? But it's not the first of the month yet.

KROGSTAD No, it is Christmas Eve. Whether or not you have a merry Christmas depends on you.

NORA What do you want? I can't give you anything today—

KROGSTAD We won't talk about that for the present. There's something else. You have a moment to spare?

NORA Oh, yes. Yes, I suppose so; though—

KROGSTAD Good. I was sitting in the café down below and I saw your husband cross the street—

NORA Yes.

KROGSTAD With a lady.

NORA Well?

KROGSTAD Might I be so bold as to ask: was not that lady a Mrs. Linde?

NORA Yes.

KROGSTAD Recently arrived in town?

NORA Yes, today.

KROGSTAD She is a good friend of yours, is she not?

NORA Yes, she is. But I don't see—

KROGSTAD I used to know her too once.

NORA I know.

KROGSTAD Oh? You've discovered that. Yes, I thought you would. Well then, may I ask you a straight question: is Mrs. Linde to be employed at the bank?

NORA How dare you presume to cross-examine me, Mr. Krogstad? You, one of my husband's employees? But since you ask, you shall have an answer. Yes, Mrs. Linde is to be employed by the bank. And I arranged it, Mr. Krogstad. Now you know.

KROGSTAD I guessed right, then.

NORA [*walks up and down the room*] Oh, one has a little influence, you know. Just because one's a woman it doesn't necessarily mean that— When one is in a humble position, Mr. Krogstad, one should think twice before offending someone who—hm—

KROGSTAD —who has influence?

NORA Precisely.

KROGSTAD [*changes his tone*] Mrs. Helmer, will you have the kindness to use your influence on my behalf?

NORA What? What do you mean?

KROGSTAD Will you be so good as to see that I keep my humble position at the bank?

NORA   What do you mean? Who is thinking of removing you from your
    position?

KROGSTAD   Oh, you don't need to play the innocent with me. I realize it
    can't be very pleasant for your friend to risk bumping into me; and now
    I also realize whom I have to thank for being hounded out like this.

NORA   But I assure you—

KROGSTAD   Look, let's not beat about the bush. There's still time, and I'd
    advise you to use your influence to stop it.

NORA   But, Mr. Krogstad, I have no influence!

KROGSTAD   Oh? I thought you just said—

NORA   But I didn't mean it like that! I? How on earth could you imagine that
    I would have any influence over my husband?

KROGSTAD   Oh, I've known your husband since we were students together. I
    imagine he has his weaknesses like other married men.

NORA   If you speak impertinently of my husband, I shall show you the door.

KROGSTAD   You're a bold woman, Mrs. Helmer.

NORA   I'm not afraid of you any longer. Once the New Year is in, I'll soon be
    rid of you.

KROGSTAD   [more controlled]   Now listen to me, Mrs. Helmer. If I'm forced to,
    I shall fight for my little job at the bank as I would fight for my life.

NORA   So it sounds.

KROGSTAD   It isn't just the money; that's the last thing I care about. There's
    something else—well, you might as well know. It's like this, you see.
    You know of course, as everyone else does, that some years ago I
    committed an indiscretion.

NORA   I think I did hear something—

KROGSTAD   It never came into court; but from that day, every opening was
    barred to me. So I turned my hand to the kind of business you know
    about. I had to do something; and I don't think I was one of the worst.
    But now I want to give up all that. My sons are growing up; for their
    sake, I must try to regain what respectability I can. This job in the bank
    was the first step on the ladder. And now your husband wants to kick
    me off that ladder back into the dirt.

NORA   But my dear Mr. Krogstad, it simply isn't in my power to help you.

KROGSTAD   You say that because you don't want to help me. But I have the
    means to make you.

NORA   You don't mean you'd tell my husband that I owe you money?

KROGSTAD   And if I did?

NORA   That'd be a filthy trick! [Almost in tears.] This secret that is my pride
    and my joy—that he should hear about it in such a filthy, beastly
    way—hear about it from you! It'd involve me in the most dreadful
    unpleasantness—

KROGSTAD   Only—unpleasantness?

NORA   [vehemently]   All right, do it! You'll be the one who'll suffer. It'll show my husband the kind of man you are, and then you'll never keep your job.

KROGSTAD   I asked you whether it was merely domestic unpleasantness you were afraid of.

NORA   If my husband hears about it, he will of course immediately pay you whatever is owing. And then we shall have nothing more to do with you.

KROGSTAD   [takes a step closer]   Listen, Mrs. Helmer. Either you've a bad memory or else you know very little about financial transactions. I had better enlighten you.

NORA   What do you mean?

KROGSTAD   When your husband was ill, you came to me to borrow two hundred and fifty pounds.

NORA   I didn't know anyone else.

KROGSTAD   I promised to find that sum for you—

NORA   And you did find it.

KROGSTAD   I promised to find that sum for you on certain conditions. You were so worried about your husband's illness and so keen to get the money to take him abroad that I don't think you bothered much about the details. So it won't be out of place if I refresh your memory. Well—I promised to get you the money in exchange for an I.O.U., which I drew up.

NORA   Yes, and which I signed.

KROGSTAD   Exactly. But then I added a few lines naming your father as security for the debt. This paragraph was to be signed by your father.

NORA   Was to be? He did sign it.

KROGSTAD   I left the date blank for your father to fill in when he signed this paper. You remember, Mrs. Helmer?

NORA   Yes, I think so—

KROGSTAD   Then I gave you back this I.O.U. for you to post to your father. Is that not correct?

NORA   Yes.

KROGSTAD   And of course you posted it at once; for within five or six days you brought it along to me with your father's signature on it. Whereupon I handed you the money.

NORA   Yes, well. Haven't I repaid the instalments as agreed?

KROGSTAD   Mm—yes, more or less. But to return to what we were speaking about—that was a difficult time for you just then, wasn't it, Mrs. Helmer?

NORA   Yes, it was.

KROGSTAD   Your father was very ill, if I am not mistaken.

NORA   He was dying.

KROGSTAD   He did in fact die shortly afterwards?

NORA   Yes.

KROGSTAD   Tell me, Mrs. Helmer, do you by any chance remember the date of your father's death? The day of the month, I mean.

NORA   Papa died on the twenty-ninth of September.

KROGSTAD   Quite correct; I took the trouble to confirm it. And that leaves me with a curious little problem— [*Takes out a paper*] —which I simply cannot solve.

NORA   Problem? I don't see—

KROGSTAD   The problem, Mrs. Helmer, is that your father signed this paper three days after his death.

NORA   What? I don't understand—

KROGSTAD   Your father died on the twenty-ninth of September. But look at this. Here your father has dated his signature the second of October. Isn't that a curious little problem, Mrs. Helmer? [*Nora is silent.*] Can you suggest any explanation? [*She remains silent.*] And there's another curious thing. The words "second of October" and the year are written in a hand which is not your father's, but which I seem to know. Well, there's a simple explanation to that. Your father could have forgotten to write in the date when he signed, and someone else could have added it before the news came of his death. There's nothing criminal about that. It's the signature itself I'm wondering about. It *is* genuine, I suppose, Mrs. Helmer? It was your father who wrote his name here?

NORA   [*after a short silence, throws back her head and looks defiantly at him*]   No, it was not. It was I who wrote Papa's name there.

KROGSTAD   Look, Mrs. Helmer, do you realize this is a dangerous admission?

NORA   Why? You'll get your money.

KROGSTAD   May I ask you a question? Why didn't you send this paper to your father?

NORA   I couldn't. Papa was very ill. If I'd asked him to sign this, I'd have had to tell him what the money was for. But I couldn't have told him in his condition that my husband's life was in danger. I couldn't have done that!

KROGSTAD   Then you would have been wiser to have given up your idea of a holiday.

NORA   But I couldn't! It was to save my husband's life. I couldn't put it off.

KROGSTAD   But didn't it occur to you that you were being dishonest towards me?

NORA   I couldn't bother about that. I didn't care about you. I hated you because of all the beastly difficulties you'd put in my way when you knew how dangerously ill my husband was.

KROGSTAD   Mrs. Helmer, you evidently don't appreciate exactly what you have done. But I can assure you that it is no bigger nor worse a crime than the one I once committed, and thereby ruined my whole social position.

NORA   You? Do you expect me to believe that you would have taken a risk like that to save your wife's life?

KROGSTAD   The law does not concern itself with motives.

NORA   Then the law must be very stupid.

KROGSTAD   Stupid or not, if I show this paper to the police, you will be judged according to it.

NORA   I don't believe that. Hasn't a daughter the right to shield her father from worry and anxiety when he's old and dying? Hasn't a wife the right to save her husband's life? I don't know much about the law, but there must be something somewhere that says that such things are allowed. You ought to know about that, you're meant to be a lawyer, aren't you? You can't be a very good lawyer, Mr. Krogstad.

KROGSTAD   Possibly not. But business, the kind of business we two have been transacting—I think you'll admit I understand something about that? Good. Do as you please. But I tell you this. If I get thrown into the gutter for a second time, I shall take you with me.

He bows and goes out through the hall.

NORA   [*stands for a moment in thought, then tosses her head*]   What nonsense! He's trying to frighten me! I'm not that stupid. [*Busies herself gathering together the children's clothes; then she suddenly stops.*] But—? No, it's impossible. I did it for love, didn't I?

THE CHILDREN   [*in the doorway, left*]   Mummy, the strange gentleman's gone out into the street.

NORA   Yes, yes, I know. But don't talk to anyone about the strange gentleman. You hear? Not even to Daddy.

CHILDREN   No, Mummy. Will you play with us again now?

NORA   No, no. Not now.

CHILDREN   Oh but, Mummy, you promised!

NORA   I know, but I can't just now. Go back to the nursery. I've got a lot to do. Go away, my darlings, go away. [*She pushes them gently into the other room, and closes the door behind them. She sits on the sofa, takes up her embroidery, stitches for a few moments, but soon stops.*] No! [*Throws the embroidery aside, gets up, goes to the door leading to the hall and calls.*] Helen! Bring in the Christmas tree! [*She goes to the table on the left and opens the drawer in it; then pauses again.*] No, but it's utterly impossible!

MAID   [*enters with the tree*]   Where shall I put it, madam?

NORA   There, in the middle of the room.

MAID   Will you be wanting anything else?

NORA   No, thank you. I have everything I need.

The Maid puts down the tree and goes out.

NORA [busy decorating the tree]   Now—candles here—and flowers here. That loathsome man! Nonsense, nonsense, there's nothing to be frightened about. The Christmas tree must be beautiful. I'll do everything that you like, Torvald. I'll sing for you, dance for you—

Helmer, with a bundle of papers under his arm, enters.

NORA   Oh—are you back already?

HELMER   Yes. Has anyone been here?

NORA   Here? No.

HELMER   That's strange. I saw Krogstad come out of the front door.

NORA   Did you? Oh yes, that's quite right—Krogstad was here for a few minutes.

HELMER   Nora, I can tell from your face, he's been here and asked you to put in a good word for him.

NORA   Yes.

HELMER   And you were to pretend you were doing it of your own accord? You weren't going to tell me he'd been here? He asked you to do that too, didn't he?

NORA   Yes, Torvald. But—

HELMER   Nora, Nora! And you were ready to enter into such a conspiracy? Talking to a man like that, and making him promises—and then, on top of it all, to tell me an untruth!

NORA   An untruth?

HELMER   Didn't you say no one had been here? [Wags his finger.] My little songbird must never do that again. A songbird must have a clean beak to sing with; otherwise she'll start twittering out of tune. [Puts his arm round her waist.] Isn't that the way we want things? Yes, of course it is. [Lets go of her.] So let's hear no more about that. [Sits down in front of the stove.] Ah, how cosy and peaceful it is here. [Glances for a few moments at his papers.]

NORA [busy with the tree; after a short silence]   Torvald.

HELMER   Yes.

NORA   I'm terribly looking forward to that fancy dress ball at the Stenborgs on Boxing Day.

HELMER   And I'm terribly curious to see what you're going to surprise me with.

NORA   Oh, it's so maddening.

HELMER   What is?

NORA   I can't think of anything to wear. It all seems so stupid and meaningless.

HELMER   So my little Nora's come to that conclusion, has she?

NORA [behind his chair, resting her arms on its back]   Are you very busy, Torvald?

HELMER Oh—

NORA What are those papers?

HELMER Just something to do with the bank.

NORA Already?

HELMER I persuaded the trustees to give me authority to make certain immediate changes in the staff and organization. I want to have everything straight by the New Year.

NORA Then that's why this poor man Krogstad—

HELMER Hm.

NORA [still leaning over his chair, slowly strokes the back of his head] If you hadn't been so busy, I was going to ask you an enormous favour, Torvald.

HELMER Well, tell me. What was it to be?

NORA You know I trust your taste more than anyone's. I'm so anxious to look really beautiful at the fancy dress ball. Torvald, couldn't you help me to decide what I shall go as, and what kind of costume I ought to wear?

HELMER Aha! So little Miss Independent's in trouble and needs a man to rescue her, does she?

NORA Yes, Torvald. I can't get anywhere without your help.

HELMER Well, well, I'll give the matter thought. We'll find something.

NORA Oh, how kind of you! [Goes back to the tree. Pause.] How pretty these red flowers look! But, tell me, is it so dreadful, this thing that Krogstad's done?

HELMER He forged someone else's name. Have you any idea what that means?

NORA Mightn't he have been forced to do it by some emergency?

HELMER He probably just didn't think—that's what usually happens. I'm not so heartless as to condemn a man for an isolated action.

NORA No, Torvald, of course not!

HELMER Men often succeed in re-establishing themselves if they admit their crime and take their punishment.

NORA Punishment?

HELMER But Krogstad didn't do that. He chose to try and trick his way out of it; and that's what has morally destroyed him.

NORA You think that would—?

HELMER Just think how a man with that load on his conscience must always be lying and cheating and dissembling; how he must wear a mask even in the presence of those who are dearest to him, even his own wife and children! Yes, the children. That's the worst danger, Nora.

NORA Why?

HELMER Because an atmosphere of lies contaminates and poisons every corner of the home. Every breath that the children draw in such a house contains the germs of evil.

NORA [comes closer behind him]   Do you really believe that?

HELMER   Oh, my dear, I've come across it so often in my work at the bar. Nearly all young criminals are the children of mothers who are constitutional liars.

NORA   Why do you say mothers?

HELMER   It's usually the mother; though of course the father can have the same influence. Every lawyer knows that only too well. And yet this fellow Krogstad has been sitting at home all these years poisoning his children with his lies and pretences. That's why I say that, morally speaking, he is dead. [Stretches out his hands towards her.] So my pretty little Nora must promise me not to plead his case. Your hand on it. Come, come, what's this? Give me your hand. There. That's settled, now. I assure you it'd be quite impossible for me to work in the same building as him. I literally feel physically ill in the presence of a man like that.

NORA [draws her hand from his and goes over to the other side of the Christmas tree]   How hot it is in here! And I've so much to do.

HELMER [gets up and gathers his papers]   Yes, and I must try to get some of this read before dinner. I'll think about your costume too. And I may even have something up my sleeve to hang in gold paper on the Christmas tree. [Lays his hand on her head.] My precious little songbird!

He goes into his study and closes the door.

NORA [softly, after a pause]   It's nonsense. It must be. It's impossible. It must be impossible!

NURSE [in the doorway, left]   The children are asking if they can come in to Mummy.

NORA   No, no, no; don't let them in! You stay with them, Anne-Marie.

NURSE   Very good, madam. [Closes the door.]

NORA [pale with fear]   Corrupt my little children—! Poison my home! [Short pause. She throws back her head.] It isn't true! It couldn't be true!

ACT II

The same room. In the corner by the piano the Christmas tree stands, stripped and disheveled, its candles burned to their sockets. Nora's outdoor clothes lie on the sofa. She is alone in the room, walking restlessly to and fro. At length she stops by the sofa and picks up her coat.

NORA [drops the coat again]   There's someone coming! [Goes to the door and listens] No, it's no one. Of course—no one'll come today, it's Christmas

Day. Nor tomorrow. But perhaps—! [*Opens the door and looks out.*] No. Nothing in the letter-box. Quite empty. [*Walks across the room.*] Silly, silly. Of course he won't do anything. It couldn't happen. It isn't possible. Why, I've three small children.

The Nurse, carrying a large cardboard box, enters from the room on the left.

NURSE   I found those fancy dress clothes at last, madam.

NORA   Thank you. Put them on the table.

NURSE [*does so*]   They're all rumpled up.

NORA   Oh, I wish I could tear them into a million pieces!

NURSE   Why, madam! They'll be all right. Just a little patience.

NORA   Yes, of course. I'll go and get Mrs. Linde to help me.

NURSE   What, out again? In this dreadful weather? You'll catch a chill, madam.

NORA   Well, that wouldn't be the worst. How are the children?

NURSE   Playing with their Christmas presents, poor little dears. But—

NORA   Are they still asking to see me?

NURSE   They're so used to having their Mummy with them.

NORA   Yes, but, Anne-Marie, from now on I shan't be able to spend so much time with them.

NURSE   Well, children get used to anything in time.

NORA   Do you think so? Do you think they'd forget their mother if she went away from them—for ever?

NURSE   Mercy's sake, madam! For ever!

NORA   Tell me, Anne-Marie—I've so often wondered. How could you bear to give your child away—to strangers?

NURSE   But I had to when I came to nurse my little Miss Nora.

NORA   Do you mean you wanted to?

NURSE   When I had the chance of such a good job? A poor girl what's got· into trouble can't afford to pick and choose. That good-for-nothing didn't lift a finger.

NORA   But your daughter must have completely forgotten you.

NURSE   Oh no, indeed she hasn't. She's written to me twice, once when she got confirmed and then again when she got married.

NORA [*hugs her*]   Dear old Anne-Marie, you were a good mother to me.

NURSE   Poor little Miss Nora, you never had any mother but me.

NORA   And if my little ones had no one else, I know you would—no, silly, silly, silly! [*Opens the cardboard box.*] Go back to them, Anne-Marie. Now I must—Tomorrow you'll see how pretty I shall look.

NURSE   Why, there'll be no one at the ball as beautiful as my Miss Nora.

She goes into the room, left.

NORA [*begins to unpack the clothes from the box, but soon throws them down again*]   Oh, if only I dared go out! If I could be sure no one would come and nothing would happen while I was away! Stupid, stupid! No one will come. I just mustn't think about it. Brush this muff. Pretty gloves, pretty gloves! Don't think about it, don't think about it! One, two, three, four, five, six— [*Cries*] Ah—they're coming—!

She begins to run towards the door, but stops uncertainly. Mrs. Linde enters from the hall, where she has been taking off her outdoor clothes.

NORA   Oh, it's you, Christine. There's no one else out there, is there? Oh, I'm so glad you've come.

MRS. LINDE   I hear you were at my room asking for me.

NORA   Yes, I just happened to be passing. I want to ask you to help me with something. Let's sit down here on the sofa. Look at this. There's going to be a fancy dress ball tomorrow night upstairs at Consul Stenborg's, and Torvald wants me to go as a Neapolitan fisher-girl and dance the tarantella. I learned it on Capri.

MRS. LINDE   I say, are you going to give a performance?

NORA   Yes, Torvald says I should. Look, here's the dress. Torvald had it made for me in Italy; but now it's all so torn, I don't know—

MRS. LINDE   Oh, we'll soon put that right; the stitching's just come away. Needle and thread? Ah, here we are.

NORA   You're being awfully sweet.

MRS. LINDE [*sews*]   So you're going to dress up tomorrow, Nora? I must pop over for a moment to see how you look. Oh, but I've completely forgotten to thank you for that nice evening yesterday.

NORA [*gets up and walks across the room*]   Oh, I didn't think it was as nice as usual. You ought to have come to town a little earlier, Christine. . . . Yes, Torvald understands how to make a home look attractive.

MRS. LINDE   I'm sure you do, too. You're not your father's daughter for nothing. But, tell me. Is Dr. Rank always in such low spirits as he was yesterday?

NORA   No, last night it was very noticeable. But he's got a terrible disease; he's got spinal tuberculosis, poor man. His father was a frightful creature who kept mistresses and so on. As a result Dr. Rank has been sickly ever since he was a child—you understand—

MRS. LINDE [*puts down her sewing*]   But, my dear Nora, how on earth did you get to know about such things?

NORA [*walks about the room*]   Oh, don't be silly, Christine—when one has three children, one comes into contact with women who—well, who know about medical matters, and they tell one a thing or two.

MRS. LINDE [*sews again; a short silence*]   Does Dr. Rank visit you every day?

NORA   Yes, every day. He's Torvald's oldest friend, and a good friend to me too. Dr. Rank's almost one of the family.

MRS. LINDE   But, tell me—is he quite sincere? I mean, doesn't he rather say the sort of thing he thinks people want to hear?

NORA   No, quite the contrary. What gave you that idea?

MRS. LINDE   When you introduced me to him yesterday, he said he'd often heard my name mentioned here. But later I noticed your husband had no idea who I was. So how could Dr. Rank—?

NORA   Yes, that's quite right, Christine. You see, Torvald's so hopelessly in love with me that he wants to have me all to himself—those were his very words. When we were first married, he got quite jealous if I as much as mentioned any of my old friends back home. So naturally, I stopped talking about them. But I often chat with Dr. Rank about that kind of thing. He enjoys it, you see.

MRS. LINDE   Now listen, Nora. In many ways you're still a child; I'm a bit older than you and have a little more experience of the world. There's something I want to say to you. You ought to give up this business with Dr. Rank.

NORA   What business?

MRS. LINDE   Well, everything. Last night you were speaking about this rich admirer of yours who was going to give you money—

NORA   Yes, and who doesn't exist—unfortunately. But what's that got to do with—?

MRS. LINDE   Is Dr. Rank rich?

NORA   Yes.

MRS. LINDE   And he has no dependants?

NORA   No, no one. But—

MRS. LINDE   And he comes here to see you every day?

NORA   Yes, I've told you.

MRS. LINDE   But how dare a man of his education be so forward?

NORA   What on earth are you talking about?

MRS. LINDE   Oh, stop pretending, Nora. Do you think I haven't guessed who it was who lent you that two hundred pounds?

NORA   Are you out of your mind? How could you imagine such a thing? A friend, someone who comes here every day! Why, that'd be an impossible situation!

MRS. LINDE   Then it really wasn't him?

NORA   No, of course not. I've never for a moment dreamed of—anyway, he hadn't any money to lend then. He didn't come into that till later.

MRS. LINDE   Well, I think that was a lucky thing for you, Nora dear.

NORA   No, I could never have dreamed of asking Dr. Rank— Though I'm sure that if I ever did ask him—

MRS. LINDE   But of course you won't.

NORA   Of course not. I can't imagine that it should ever become necessary.

But I'm perfectly sure that if I did speak to Dr. Rank—

MRS. LINDE   Behind your husband's back?

NORA   I've got to get out of this other business; and *that's* been going on behind his back. I've *got* to get out of it.

MRS. LINDE   Yes, well, that's what I told you yesterday. But—

NORA [*walking up and down*]   It's much easier for a man to arrange these things than a woman—

MRS. LINDE   One's own husband, yes.

NORA   Oh, bosh. [*Stops walking.*] When you've completely repaid a debt, you get your I.O.U. back, don't you?

MRS. LINDE   Yes, of course.

NORA   And you can tear it into a thousand pieces and burn the filthy, beastly thing!

MRS. LINDE [*looks hard at her, puts down her sewing and gets up slowly*]   Nora, you're hiding something from me.

NORA   Can you see that?

MRS. LINDE   Something has happened since yesterday morning. Nora, what is it?

NORA [*goes towards her*]   Christine! [*Listens.*] Ssh! There's Torvald. Would you mind going into the nursery for a few minutes? Torvald can't bear to see sewing around. Anne-Marie'll help you.

MRS. LINDE [*gathers some of her things together*]   Very well. But I shan't leave this house until we've talked this matter out.

She goes into the nursery, left. As she does so, Helmer enters from the hall.

NORA [*runs to meet him*]   Oh, Torvald dear, I've been so longing for you to come back!

HELMER   Was that the dressmaker?

NORA   No, it was Christine. She's helping me mend my costume. I'm going to look rather splendid in that.

HELMER   Yes, that was quite a bright idea of mine, wasn't it?

NORA   Wonderful! But wasn't it nice of me to give in to you?

HELMER [*takes her chin in his hand*]   Nice—to give in to your husband? All right, little silly, I know you didn't mean it like that. But I won't disturb you. I expect you'll be wanting to try it on.

NORA   Are you going to work now?

HELMER   Yes. [*Shows her a bundle of papers.*] Look at these. I've been down to the bank— [*Turns to go into his study.*]

NORA   Torvald.

HELMER [*stops*]   Yes.

NORA   If little squirrel asked you really prettily to grant her a wish—

HELMER   Well?

NORA   Would you grant it to her?

HELMER   First I should naturally have to know what it was.

NORA   Squirrel would do lots of pretty tricks for you if you granted her wish.

HELMER   Out with it, then.

NORA   Your little skylark would sing in every room—

HELMER   My little skylark does that already.

NORA   I'd turn myself into a little fairy and dance for you in the moonlight, Torvald.

HELMER   Nora, it isn't that business you were talking about this morning?

NORA   [comes closer]   Yes, Torvald—oh, please! I beg of you!

HELMER   Have you really the nerve to bring that up again?

NORA   Yes, Torvald, yes, you must do as I ask! You must let Krogstad keep his place at the bank!

HELMER   My dear Nora, his is the job I'm giving to Mrs. Linde.

NORA   Yes, that's terribly sweet of you. But you can get rid of one of the other clerks instead of Krogstad.

HELMER   Really, you're being incredibly obstinate. Just because you thoughtlessly promised to put in a word for him, you expect me to—

NORA   No, it isn't that, Helmer. It's for your own sake. That man writes for the most beastly newspapers—you said so yourself. He could do you tremendous harm. I'm so dreadfully frightened of him—

HELMER   Oh, I understand. Memories of the past. That's what's frightening you.

NORA   What do you mean?

HELMER   You're thinking of your father, aren't you?

NORA   Yes, yes. Of course. Just think what those dreadful men wrote in the papers about Papa! The most frightful slanders. I really believe it would have lost him his job if the Ministry hadn't sent you down to investigate, and you hadn't been so kind and helpful to him.

HELMER   But my dear little Nora, there's a considerable difference between your father and me. Your father was not a man of unassailable reputation. But I am; and I hope to remain so all my life.

NORA   But no one knows what spiteful people may not dig up. We could be so peaceful and happy now, Torvald—we could be free from every worry—you and I and the children. Oh, please, Torvald, please—!

HELMER   The very fact of your pleading his cause makes it impossible for me to keep him. Everyone at the bank already knows that I intend to dismiss Krogstad. If the rumor got about that the new manager had allowed his wife to persuade him to change his mind—

NORA   Well, what then?

HELMER   Oh, nothing, nothing. As long as my little Miss Obstinate gets her way—! Do you expect me to make a laughing-stock of myself before my entire staff—give people the idea that I am open to outside influence? Believe me, I'd soon feel the consequences! Besides—there's something else that makes it impossible for Krogstad to remain in the bank while I am its manager.

NORA   What is that?

HELMER   I might conceivably have allowed myself to ignore his moral obloquies—

NORA   Yes, Torvald, surely?

HELMER   And I hear he's quite efficient at his job. But we—well, we were schoolfriends. It was one of those friendships that one enters into over-hastily and so often comes to regret later in life. I might as well confess the truth. We—well, we're on Christian name terms. And the tactless idiot makes no attempt to conceal it when other people are present. On the contrary, he thinks it gives him the right to be familiar with me. He shows off the whole time, with "Torvald this," and "Torvald that." I can tell you, I find it damned annoying. If he stayed, he'd make my position intolerable.

NORA   Torvald, you can't mean this seriously.

HELMER   Oh? And why not?

NORA   But it's so petty.

HELMER   What did you say? Petty? You think I am petty?

NORA   No, Torvald dear, of course you're not. That's just why—

HELMER   Don't quibble! You call my motives petty. Then I must be petty too. Petty! I see. Well, I've had enough of this. [Goes to the door and calls into the hall.] Helen!

NORA   What are you going to do?

HELMER [searching among his papers]   I'm going to settle this matter once and for all. [The Maid enters.] Take this letter downstairs at once. Find a messenger and see that he delivers it. Immediately! The address is on the envelope. Here's the money.

MAID   Very good, sir. [Goes out with the letter.]

HELMER [putting his papers in order]   There now, little Miss Obstinate.

NORA [tensely]   Torvald—what was in that letter?

HELMER   Krogstad's dismissal.

NORA   Call her back, Torvald! There's still time. Oh, Torvald, call her back! Do it for my sake—for your own sake—for the children! Do you hear me, Torvald? Please do it! You don't realize what this may do to us all!

HELMER   Too late.

NORA   Yes. Too late.

HELMER   My dear Nora, I forgive you this anxiety. Though it is a bit of an insult to me. Oh, but it is! Isn't it an insult to imply that I should be frightened by the vindictiveness of a depraved hack journalist? But I forgive you, because it so charmingly testifies to the love you bear me. [Takes her in his arms.] Which is as it should be, my own dearest Nora. Let what will happen, happen. When the real crisis comes, you will not find me lacking in strength or courage. I am man enough to bear the burden for us both.

NORA [*fearfully*]   What do you mean?

HELMER   The whole burden, I say—

NORA [*calmly*]   I shall never let you do that.

HELMER   Very well. We shall share it, Nora—as man and wife. And that is as it should be. [*Caresses her.*] Are you happy now? There, there, there; don't look at me with those frightened little eyes. You're simply imagining things. You go ahead now and do your tarantella, and get some practice on that tambourine. I'll sit in my study and close the door. Then I won't hear anything, and you can make all the noise you want. [*Turns in the doorway.*] When Dr. Rank comes, tell him where to find me. [*He nods to her, goes into his room with his papers and closes the door.*]

NORA [*desperate with anxiety, stands as though transfixed, and whispers*]   He said he'd do it. He will do it. He will do it, and nothing'll stop him. No, never that. I'd rather anything. There must be some escape—! Some way out—! [*The bell rings in the hall.*] Dr. Rank—! Anything but that! Anything, I don't care—!

She passes her hand across her face, composes herself, walks across and opens the door to the hall. Dr. Rank is standing there, hanging up his fur coat. During the following scene it begins to grow dark.

NORA   Good evening, Dr. Rank. I recognized your ring. But you mustn't go in to Torvald yet. I think he's busy.

RANK   And—you?

NORA [*as he enters the room and she closes the door behind him*]   Oh, you know very well I've always time to talk to you.

RANK   Thank you. I shall avail myself of that privilege as long as I can.

NORA   What do you mean by that? As long as you *can?*

RANK   Yes. Does that frighten you?

NORA   Well, it's rather a curious expression. Is something going to happen?

RANK   Something I've been expecting to happen for a long time. But I didn't think it would happen quite so soon.

NORA [*seizes his arm*]   What is it? Dr. Rank, you must tell me!

RANK [*sits down by the stove*]   I'm on the way out. And there's nothing to be done about it.

NORA [*sighs with relief*]   Oh, it's you—?

RANK   Who else? No, it's no good lying to oneself. I am the most wretched of all my patients, Mrs. Helmer. These last few days I've been going through the books of this poor body of mine, and I find I am bankrupt. Within a month I may be rotting up there in the churchyard.

NORA   Ugh, what a nasty way to talk!

RANK   The facts aren't exactly nice. But the worst is that there's so much else that's nasty to come first. I've only one more test to make. When that's done I'll have a pretty accurate idea of when the final disintegration is likely to begin. I want to ask you a favor. Helmer's a sensitive chap, and I know how he hates anything ugly. I don't want him to visit me when I'm in hospital—

NORA   Oh but, Dr. Rank—

RANK   I don't want him there. On any pretext. I shan't have him allowed in. As soon as I know the worst, I'll send you my visiting card with a black cross on it, and then you'll know that the final filthy process has begun.

NORA   Really, you're being quite impossible this evening. And I did hope you'd be in a good mood.

RANK   With death on my hands? And all this to atone for someone else's sin? Is there justice in that? And in every single family, in one way or another, the same merciless law of retribution is at work—

NORA   [holds her hands to her ears]   Nonsense! Cheer up! Laugh!

RANK   Yes, you're right. Laughter's all the damned thing's fit for. My poor innocent spine must pay for the fun my father had as a gay young lieutenant.

NORA   [at the table, left]   You mean he was too fond of asparagus and foie gras?

RANK   Yes; and truffles too.

NORA   Yes, of course, truffles, yes. And oysters too, I suppose?

RANK   Yes, oysters, oysters. Of course.

NORA   And all that port and champagne to wash them down. It's too sad that all those lovely things should affect one's spine.

RANK   Especially a poor spine that never got any pleasure out of them.

NORA   Oh yes, that's the saddest thing of all.

RANK   [looks searchingly at her]   Hm—

NORA   [after a moment]   Why did you smile?

RANK   No, it was you who laughed.

NORA   No, it was you who smiled, Dr. Rank!

RANK   [gets up]   You're a worse little rogue than I thought.

NORA   Oh, I'm full of stupid tricks today.

RANK   So it seems.

NORA   [puts both her hands on his shoulders]   Dear, dear Dr. Rank, you mustn't die and leave Torvald and me.

RANK   Oh, you'll soon get over it. Once one is gone, one is soon forgotten.

NORA   [looks at him anxiously]   Do you believe that?

RANK   One finds replacements, and then—

NORA   Who will find a replacement?

RANK   You and Helmer both will, when I am gone. You seem to have made a start already, haven't you? What was this Mrs. Linde doing here yesterday evening?

NORA   Aha! But surely you can't be jealous of poor Christine?

RANK   Indeed I am. She will be my successor in this house. When I have moved on, this lady will—

NORA   Ssh—don't speak so loud! She's in there!

RANK   Today again? You see!

NORA   She's only come to mend my dress. Good heavens, how unreasonable you are! [Sits on the sofa.] Be nice now, Dr. Rank. Tomorrow you'll see how beautifully I shall dance; and you must imagine that I'm doing it just for you. And for Torvald, of course; obviously. [Takes some things out of the box.] Dr. Rank, sit down here and I'll show you something.

RANK   [sits]   What's this?

NORA   Look here! Look!

RANK   Silk stockings!

NORA   Flesh-coloured. Aren't they beautiful? It's very dark in here now, of course, but tomorrow—! No, no, no; only the soles. Oh well, I suppose you can look a bit higher if you want to.

RANK   Hm—

NORA   Why are you looking so critical? Don't you think they'll fit me?

RANK   I can't really give you a qualified opinion on that.

NORA   [looks at him for a moment]   Shame on you! [Flicks him on the ear with the stockings.] Take that. [Puts them back in the box.]

RANK   What other wonders are to be revealed to me?

NORA   I shan't show you anything else. You're being naughty.

She hums a little and looks among the things in the box.

RANK   [after a short silence]   When I sit here like this being so intimate with you, I can't think—I cannot imagine what would have become of me if I had never entered this house.

NORA   [smiles]   Yes, I think you enjoy being with us, don't you?

RANK   [more quietly, looking into the middle distance]   And now to have to leave it all—

NORA   Nonsense. You're not leaving us.

RANK   [as before]   And not to be able to leave even the most wretched token of gratitude behind; hardly even a passing sense of loss; only an empty place, to be filled by the next comer.

NORA   Suppose I were to ask you to—? No—

RANK   To do what?

NORA   To give me proof of your friendship—

RANK   Yes, yes?

NORA   No, I mean—to do me a very great service—

RANK   Would you really for once grant me that happiness?

NORA   But you've no idea what it is.

RANK   Very well, tell me, then.

NORA   No, but, Dr. Rank, I can't. It's far too much—I want your help and advice, and I want you to do something for me.

RANK   The more the better. I've no idea what it can be. But tell me. You do trust me, don't you?

NORA   Oh, yes, more than anyone. You're my best and truest friend. Otherwise I couldn't tell you. Well then, Dr. Rank—there's something you must help me to prevent. You know how much Torvald loves me—he'd never hesitate for an instant to lay down his life for me—

RANK   [leans over towards her]   Nora—do you think he is the only one—?

NORA   [with a slight start]   What do you mean?

RANK   Who would gladly lay down his life for you?

NORA   [sadly]   Oh, I see.

RANK   I swore to myself I would let you know that before I go. I shall never have a better opportunity. . . . Well, Nora, now you know that. And now you also know that you can trust me as you can trust nobody else.

NORA   [rises; calmly and quietly]   Let me pass, please.

RANK   [makes room for her but remains seated]   Nora—

NORA   [in the doorway to the hall]   Helen, bring the lamp. [Goes over to the stove.] Oh, dear Dr. Rank, this was really horrid of you.

RANK   [gets up]   That I have loved you as deeply as anyone else has? Was that horrid of me?

NORA   No—but that you should go and tell me. That was quite unnecessary—

RANK   What do you mean? Did you know, then—?

The Maid enters with the lamp, puts it on the table and goes out.

RANK   Nora—Mrs. Helmer—I am asking you, did you know this?

NORA   Oh, what do I know, what did I know, what didn't I know—I really can't say. How could you be so stupid, Dr. Rank? Everything was so nice.

RANK   Well, at any rate now you know that I am ready to serve you, body and soul. So—please continue.

NORA   [looks at him]   After this?

RANK   Please tell me what it is.

NORA   I can't possibly tell you now.

RANK   Yes, yes! You mustn't punish me like this. Let me be allowed to do what I can for you.

NORA   You can't do anything for me now. Anyway, I don't need any help. It was only my imagination—you'll see. Yes, really. Honestly. [Sits in the rocking chair, looks at him and smiles.] Well, upon my word you are a fine gentleman, Dr. Rank. Aren't you ashamed of yourself, now that the lamp's been lit?

RANK   Frankly, no. But perhaps I ought to say—*adieu?*

NORA   Of course not. You will naturally continue to visit us as before. You know quite well how Torvald depends on your company.

RANK   Yes, but you?

NORA   Oh, I always think it's enormous fun having you here.

RANK   That was what misled me. You're a riddle to me, you know. I'd often felt you'd just as soon be with me as with Helmer.

NORA   Well, you see, there are some people whom one loves, and others whom it's almost more fun to be with.

RANK   Oh yes, there's some truth in that.

NORA   When I was at home, of course I loved Papa best. But I always used to think it was terribly amusing to go down and talk to the servants; because they never told me what I ought to do; and they were such fun to listen to.

RANK   I see. So I've taken their place?

NORA   [jumps up and runs over to him] Oh, dear sweet Dr. Rank, I didn't mean that at all. But I'm sure you understand—I feel the same about Torvald as I did about Papa.

MAID   [enters from the hall] Excuse me, madam. [Whispers to her and hands her a visiting card.]

NORA   [glances at the card] Oh! [Puts it quickly in her pocket.]

RANK   Anything wrong?

NORA   No, no, nothing at all. It's just something that—it's my new dress.

RANK   What? But your costume is lying over there.

NORA   Oh—that, yes—but there's another—I ordered it specially—Torvald mustn't know—

RANK   Ah, so that's your big secret?

NORA   Yes, yes. Go in and talk to him—he's in his study—keep him talking for a bit—

RANK   Don't worry. He won't get away from me. [Goes into Helmer's study.]

NORA   [to the Maid] Is he waiting in the kitchen?

MAID   Yes, madam, he came up the back way—

NORA   But didn't you tell him I had a visitor?

MAID   Yes, but he wouldn't go.

NORA   Wouldn't go?

MAID   No, madam, not until he'd spoken with you.

NORA   Very well, show him in; but quietly. Helen, you mustn't tell anyone about this. It's a surprise for my husband.

MAID   Very good, madam. I understand. [Goes.]

NORA   It's happening. It's happening after all. No, no, no, it can't happen, it mustn't happen.

She walks across and bolts the door of Helmer's study. The Maid opens the door from the hall to admit Krogstad, and closes it behind him. He is wearing an overcoat, heavy boots and a fur cap.

NORA [*goes towards him.*]   Speak quietly. My husband's at home.

KROGSTAD   Let him hear.

NORA   What do you want from me?

KROGSTAD   Information.

NORA   Hurry up, then. What is it?

KROGSTAD   I suppose you know I've been given the sack.

NORA   I couldn't stop it, Mr. Krogstad. I did my best for you, but it didn't help.

KROGSTAD   Does your husband love you so little? He knows what I can do to you, and yet he dares to—

NORA   Surely you don't imagine I told him?

KROGSTAD   No, I didn't really think you had. It wouldn't have been like my old friend Torvald Helmer to show that much courage—

NORA   Mr. Krogstad, I'll trouble you to speak respectfully of my husband.

KROGSTAD   Don't worry, I'll show him all the respect he deserves. But since you're so anxious to keep this matter hushed up, I presume you're better informed than you were yesterday of the gravity of what you've done?

NORA   I've learned more than you could ever teach me.

KROGSTAD   Yes, a bad lawyer like me—

NORA   What do you want from me?

KROGSTAD   I just wanted to see how things were with you, Mrs. Helmer. I've been thinking about you all day. Even duns and hack journalists have hearts, you know.

NORA   Show some heart, then. Think of my little children.

KROGSTAD   Have you and your husband thought of mine? Well, let's forget that. I just wanted to tell you, you don't need to take this business too seriously. I'm not going to take any action, for the present.

NORA   Oh, no—you won't, will you? I knew it.

KROGSTAD   It can all be settled quite amicably. There's no need for it to become public. We'll keep it among the three of us.

NORA   My husband must never know about this.

KROGSTAD   How can you stop him? Can you pay the balance of what you owe me?

NORA   Not immediately.

KROGSTAD   Have you any means of raising the money during the next few days?

NORA   None that I would care to use.

KROGSTAD   Well, it wouldn't have helped anyway. However much money you offered me now I wouldn't give you back that paper.

NORA   What are you going to do with it?

KROGSTAD   Just keep it. No one else need ever hear about it. So in case you were thinking of doing anything desperate—

NORA   I am.

KROGSTAD   Such as running away—

NORA   I am.

KROGSTAD   Or anything more desperate—

NORA   How did you know?

KROGSTAD   —just give up the idea.

NORA   How did you know?

KROGSTAD   Most of us think of that at first. I did. But I hadn't the courage—

NORA   [*dully*]   Neither have I.

KROGSTAD   [*relieved*]   It's true, isn't it? You haven't the courage either?

NORA   No. I haven't. I haven't.

KROGSTAD   It'd be a stupid thing to do anyway. Once the first little domestic explosion is over. . . . I've got a letter in my pocket here addressed to your husband—

NORA   Telling him everything?

KROGSTAD   As delicately as possibly.

NORA   [*quickly*]   He must never see that letter. Tear it up. I'll find the money somehow—

KROGSTAD   I'm sorry, Mrs. Helmer, I thought I'd explained—

NORA   Oh, I don't mean the money I owe you. Let me know how much you want from my husband, and I'll find it for you.

KROGSTAD   I'm not asking your husband for money.

NORA   What do you want, then?

KROGSTAD   I'll tell you. I want to get on my feet again, Mrs. Helmer. I want to get to the top. And your husband's going to help me. For eighteen months now my record's been clean. I've been in hard straits all that time; I was content to fight my way back inch by inch. Now I've been chucked back into the mud, and I'm not going to be satisfied with just getting back my job. I'm going to get to the top, I tell you. I'm going to get back into the bank, and it's going to be higher up. Your husband's going to create a new job for me—

NORA   He'll never do that!

KROGSTAD   Oh, yes he will. I know him. He won't dare to risk a scandal. And once I'm in there with him, you'll see! Within a year I'll be his right-hand man. It'll be Nils Krogstad who'll be running that bank, not Torvald Helmer!

NORA   That will never happen.

KROGSTAD   Are you thinking of—?

NORA   Now I *have* the courage.

KROGSTAD   Oh, you can't frighten me. A pampered little pretty like you—

NORA   You'll see! You'll see!

KROGSTAD   Under the ice? Down in the cold, black water? And then, in the spring to float up again, ugly, unrecognizable, hairless—?

NORA   You can't frighten me.

KROGSTAD   And you can't frighten me. People don't do such things, Mrs. Helmer. And anyway, what'd be the use? I've got him in my pocket.

NORA But afterwards? When I'm no longer—?

KROGSTAD Have you forgotten that then your reputation will be in my hands? [*She looks at him speechlessly.*] Well, I've warned you. Don't do anything silly. When Helmer's read my letter, he'll get in touch with me. And remember, it's your husband who's forced me to act like this. And for that I'll never forgive him. Goodbye, Mrs. Helmer. [*He goes out through the hall.*]

NORA [*runs to the hall door, opens it a few inches and listens*] He's going. He's not going to give him the letter. Oh, no, no, it couldn't possibly happen. [*Opens the door a little wider.*] What's he doing? Standing outside the front door. He's not going downstairs. Is he changing his mind? Yes, he—!

A letter falls into the letter-box. Krogstad's footsteps die away down the stairs.

NORA [*with a stifled cry, runs across the room towards the table by the sofa. A pause*] In the letter-box. [*Steals timidly over towards the hall door.*] There it is! Oh, Torvald, Torvald! Now we're lost!

MRS. LINDE [*enters from the nursery with Nora's costume*] Well, I've done the best I can. Shall we see how it looks—?

NORA [*whispers hoarsely*] Christine, come here.

MRS. LINDE [*throws the dress on the sofa*] What's wrong with you? You look as though you'd seen a ghost!

NORA Come here. Do you see that letter? There—look—through the glass of the letter-box.

MRS. LINDE Yes, yes, I see it.

NORA That letter's from Krogstad—

MRS. LINDE Nora! It was Krogstad who lent you the money!

NORA Yes. And now Torvald's going to discover everything.

MRS. LINDE Oh, believe me, Nora, it'll be best for you both.

NORA You don't know what's happened. I've committed a forgery—

MRS. LINDE But, for heaven's sake—!

NORA Christine, all I want is for you to be my witness.

MRS. LINDE What do you mean? Witness what?

NORA If I should go out of my mind—and it might easily happen—

MRS. LINDE Nora!

NORA Or if anything else should happen to me—so that I wasn't here any longer—

MRS. LINDE Nora, Nora, you don't know what you're saying!

NORA If anyone should try to take the blame, and say it was all his fault—you understand—?

MRS. LINDE Yes, yes—but how can you think—?

NORA Then you must testify that it isn't true, Christine. I'm not mad—I know exactly what I'm saying—and I'm telling you, no one else knows anything about this. I did it entirely on my own. Remember that.

MRS. LINDE   All right. But I simply don't understand—

NORA   Oh, how could you understand? A miracle—is—about to happen.

MRS. LINDE   Miracle?

NORA   Yes. A miracle. But it's so frightening, Christine. It *mustn't* happen, not for anything in the world.

MRS. LINDE   I'll go over and talk to Krogstad.

NORA   Don't go near him. He'll only do something to hurt you.

MRS. LINDE   Once upon a time he'd have done anything for my sake.

NORA   He?

MRS. LINDE   Where does he live?

NORA   Oh, how should I know—? Oh yes, wait a moment—! [*Feels in her pocket.*] Here's his card. But the letter, the letter—!

HELMER   [*from his study, knocks on the door*]   Nora!

NORA   [*cries in alarm*]   What is it?

HELMER   Now, now, don't get alarmed. We're not coming in; you've closed the door. Are you trying on your costume?

NORA   Yes, yes—I'm trying on my costume. I'm going to look so pretty for you, Torvald.

MRS. LINDE   [*who has been reading the card*]   Why, he lives just round the corner.

NORA   Yes; but it's no use. There's nothing to be done now. The letter's lying there in the box.

MRS. LINDE   And your husband has the key?

NORA   Yes, he always keeps it.

MRS. LINDE   Krogstad must ask him to send the letter back unread. He must find some excuse—

NORA   But Torvald always opens the box at just about this time—

MRS. LINDE   You must stop him. Go in and keep him talking. I'll be back as quickly as I can.

She hurries out through the hall.

NORA   [*goes over to Helmer's door, opens it and peeps in*]   Torvald!

HELMER   [*offstage*]   Well, may a man enter his own drawing room again? Come on, Rank, now we'll see what— [*In the doorway.*] But what's this?

NORA   What, Torvald dear?

HELMER   Rank's been preparing me for some great transformation scene.

RANK   [*in the doorway*]   So I understood. But I seem to have been mistaken.

NORA   Yes, no one's to be allowed to see me before tomorrow night.

HELMER   But, my dear Nora, you look quite worn out. Have you been practising too hard?

NORA   No, I haven't practised at all yet.

HELMER   Well, you must.

NORA   Yes, Torvald, I must, I know. But I can't get anywhere without your help. I've completely forgotten everything.

HELMER   Oh, we'll soon put that to rights.

NORA   Yes, help me, Torvald. Promise me you will? Oh, I'm so nervous. All those people—! You must forget everything except me this evening. You mustn't think of business—I won't even let you touch a pen. Promise me, Torvald?

HELMER   I promise. This evening I shall think of nothing but you—my poor, helpless little darling. Oh, there's just one thing I must see to— [Goes towards the hall door.]

NORA   What do you want out there?

HELMER   I'm only going to see if any letters have come.

NORA   No, Torvald, no!

HELMER   Why, what's the matter?

NORA   Torvald, I beg you. There's nothing there.

HELMER   Well, I'll just make sure.

He moves towards the door. Nora runs to the piano and plays the first bars of the tarantella.

HELMER [at the door, turns]   Aha!

NORA   I can't dance tomorrow if I don't practise with you now.

HELMER [goes over to her]   Are you really so frightened, Nora dear?

NORA   Yes, terribly frightened. Let me start practising now, at once—we've still time before dinner. Oh, do sit down and play for me, Torvald dear. Correct me, lead me, the way you always do.

HELMER   Very well, my dear, if you wish it.

He sits down at the piano. Nora seizes the tambourine and a long multi-coloured shawl from the cardboard box, wraps the latter hastily around her, then takes a quick leap into the center of the room.

NORA   Play for me! I want to dance!

Helmer plays and Nora dances. Dr. Rank stands behind Helmer at the piano and watches her.

HELMER [as he plays]   Slower, slower!

NORA   I can't!

HELMER   Not so violently, Nora.

NORA   I must!

HELMER [stops playing]   No, no, this won't do at all.

NORA [*laughs and swings her tambourine*]   Isn't that what I told you?

RANK   Let me play for her.

HELMER [*gets up*]   Yes, would you? Then it'll be easier for me to show her.

Rank sits down at the piano and plays. Nora dances more and more wildly. Helmer has stationed himself by the stove and tries repeatedly to correct her, but she seems not to hear him. Her hair works loose and falls over her shoulders; she ignores it and continues to dance. Mrs. Linde enters.

MRS. LINDE [*stands in the doorwary as though tongue-tied*]   Ah—!

NORA [*as she dances*]   Christine, we're having such fun!

HELMER   But, Nora darling, you're dancing as if your life depended on it.

NORA   It does.

HELMER   Rank, stop it! This is sheer lunacy. Stop it, I say!

Rank ceases playing. Nora suddenly stops dancing.

HELMER [*goes over to her*]   I'd never have believed it. You've forgotten everything I taught you.

NORA [*throws away the tambourine*]   You see!

HELMER   I'll have to show you every step.

NORA   You see how much I need you! You must show me every step of the way. Right to the end of the dance. Promise me you will, Torvald?

HELMER   Never fear. I will.

NORA   You mustn't think about anything but me—today or tomorrow. Don't open any letters—don't even open the letter-box—

HELMER   Aha, you're still worried about that fellow—

NORA   Oh, yes, yes, him too.

HELMER   Nora, I can tell from the way you're behaving, there's a letter from him already lying there.

NORA   I don't know. I think so. But you mustn't read it now. I don't want anything ugly to come between us till it's all over.

RANK [*quietly, to Helmer*]   Better give her her way.

HELMER [*puts his arm round her*]   My child shall have her way. But tomorrow night, when your dance is over—

NORA   Then you will be free.

MAID [*appears in the doorway, right*]   Dinner is served, madam.

NORA   Put out some champagne, Helen.

MAID   Very good, madam. [*Goes.*]

HELMER   I say! What's this, a banquet?

NORA   We'll drink champagne until dawn! [*Calls.*] And, Helen! Put out some macaroons! Lots of macaroons—for once!

HELMER [*takes her hands in his*]   Now, now, now. Don't get so excited. Where's my little songbird, the one I know?

NORA   All right. Go and sit down—and you too, Dr. Rank. I'll be with you in a minute. Christine, you must help me put my hair up.

RANK [*quietly, as they go*]   There's nothing wrong, is there? I mean, she isn't—er—expecting—?

HELMER   Good heavens no, my dear chap. She just gets scared like a child sometimes—I told you before—

They go out right.

NORA   Well?

MRS. LINDE   He's left town.

NORA   I saw it from your face.

MRS. LINDE   He'll be back tomorrow evening. I left a note for him.

NORA   You needn't have bothered. You can't stop anything now. Anyway, it's wonderful really, in a way—sitting here and waiting for the miracle to happen.

MRS. LINDE   Waiting for what?

NORA   Oh, you wouldn't understand. Go in and join them. I'll be with you in a moment.

Mrs. Linde goes into the dining-room.

NORA [*stands for a moment as though collecting herself. Then she looks at her watch*]   Five o'clock. Seven hours till midnight. Then another twenty-four hours till midnight tomorrow. And then the tarantella will be finished. Twenty-four and seven? Thirty-one hours to live.

HELMER [*appears in the doorway, right*]   What's happened to my little songbird?

NORA [*runs to him with her arms wide*]   Your songbird is here!

ACT III

The same room. The table which was formerly by the sofa has been moved into the centre of the room; the chairs surround it as before. The door to the hall stands open. Dance music can be heard from the floor above. Mrs. Linde is seated at the table, absent-mindedly glancing through a book. She is trying to read, but seems unable to keep her mind on it. More than once she turns and listens anxiously towards the front door.

MRS. LINDE [*looks at her watch*]   Not here yet. There's not much time left. Please God he hasn't—! [*Listens again.*] Ah, here he is. [*Goes out into the hall and cautiously opens the front door. Footsteps can be heard softly ascending the stairs. She whispers.*] Come in. There's no one here.

KROGSTAD [*in the doorway*]   I found a note from you at my lodgings. What does this mean?

MRS. LINDE   I must speak with you.

KROGSTAD   Oh? And must our conversation take place in this house?

MRS. LINDE   We couldn't meet at my place; my room has no separate entrance. Come in. We're quite alone. The maid's asleep, and the Helmers are at the dance upstairs.

KROGSTAD [*comes into the room*]   Well, well! So the Helmers are dancing this evening? Are they indeed?

MRS. LINDE   Yes, why not?

KROGSTAD   True enough. Why not?

MRS. LINDE   Well, Krogstad. You and I must have a talk together.

KROGSTAD   Have we two anything further to discuss?

MRS. LINDE   We have a great deal to discuss.

KROGSTAD   I wasn't aware of it.

MRS. LINDE   That's because you've never really understood me.

KROGSTAD   Was there anything to understand? It's the old story, isn't it—a woman chucking a man because something better turns up?

MRS. LINDE   Do you really think I'm so utterly heartless? You think it was easy for me to give you up?

KROGSTAD   Wasn't it?

MRS. LINDE   Oh, Nils, did you really believe that?

KROGSTAD   Then why did you write to me the way you did?

MRS. LINDE   I had to. Since I had to break with you, I thought it my duty to destroy all the feelings you had for me.

KROGSTAD [*clenches his fists*]   So that was it. And you did this for money!

MRS. LINDE   You mustn't forget I had a helpless mother to take care of, and two little brothers. We couldn't wait for you, Nils. It would have been so long before you'd had enough to support us.

KROGSTAD   Maybe. But you had no right to cast me off for someone else.

MRS. LINDE   Perhaps not. I've often asked myself that.

KROGSTAD [*more quietly*]   When I lost you, it was just as though all solid ground had been swept from under my feet. Look at me. Now I am a shipwrecked man, clinging to a spar.

MRS. LINDE   Help may be near at hand.

KROGSTAD   It was near. But then you came, and stood between it and me.

MRS. LINDE   I didn't know, Nils. No one told me till today that this job I'd found was yours.

KROGSTAD   I believe you, since you say so. But now you know, won't you give it up?

MRS. LINDE   No—because it wouldn't help you even if I did.

KROGSTAD   Wouldn't it? I'd do it all the same.

MRS. LINDE   I've learned to look at things practically. Life and poverty have taught me that.

KROGSTAD   And life has taught me to distrust fine words.

MRS. LINDE   Then it's taught you a useful lesson. But surely you still believe in actions?

KROGSTAD   What do you mean?

MRS. LINDE   You said you were like a shipwrecked man clinging to a spar.

KROGSTAD   I have good reason to say it.

MRS. LINDE   I'm in the same postion as you. No one to care about, no one to care for.

KROGSTAD   You made your own choice.

MRS. LINDE   I had no choice—then.

KROGSTAD   Well?

MRS. LINDE   Nils, suppose we two shipwrecked souls could join hands?

KROGSTAD   What are you saying?

MRS. LINDE   Castaways have a better chance of survival together than on their own.

KROGSTAD   Christine!

MRS. LINDE   Why do you suppose I came to this town?

KROGSTAD   You mean—you came because of me?

MRS. LINDE   I must work if I'm to find life worth living. I've always worked, for as long as I can remember; it's been the greatest joy of my life—my only joy. But now I'm alone in the world, and I feel so dreadfully lost and empty. There's no joy in working just for oneself. Oh, Nils, give me something—someone—to work for.

KROGSTAD   I don't believe all that. You're just being hysterical and romantic. You want to find an excuse for self-sacrifice.

MRS. LINDE   Have you ever known me to be hysterical?

KROGSTAD   You mean you really—? Is it possible? Tell me—you know all about my past?

MRS. LINDE   Yes.

KROGSTAD   And you know what people think of me here?

MRS. LINDE   You said just now that with me you might have become a different person.

KROGSTAD   I know I could have.

MRS. LINDE   Couldn't it still happen?

KROGSTAD   Christine—do you really mean this? Yes—you do—I see it in your face. Have you really the courage—?

MRS. LINDE   I need someone to be a mother to; and your children need a mother. And you and I need each other. I believe in you, Nils. I am afraid of nothing—with you.

KROGSTAD   [clasps her hands]   Thank you, Christine—thank you! Now I shall make the world believe in me as you do! Oh—but I'd forgotten—

MRS. LINDE   [listens]   Ssh! The tarantella! Go quickly, go!

KROGSTAD   Why? What is it?

MRS. LINDE   You hear that dance? As soon as it's finished, they'll be coming down.

KROGSTAD   All right, I'll go. It's no good, Christine. I'd forgotten—you don't know what I've just done to the Helmers.

MRS. LINDE   Yes, Nils. I know.

KROGSTAD   And yet you'd still have the courage to—?

MRS. LINDE   I know what despair can drive a man like you to.

KROGSTAD   Oh, if only I could undo this!

MRS. LINDE   You can. Your letter is still lying in the box.

KROGSTAD   Are you sure?

MRS. LINDE   Quite sure. But—

KROGSTAD [*looks searchingly at her*]   Is that why you're doing this? You want to save your friend at any price? Tell me the truth. Is that the reason?

MRS. LINDE   Nils, a woman who has sold herself once for the sake of others doesn't make the same mistake again.

KROGSTAD   I shall demand my letter back.

MRS. LINDE   No, no.

KROGSTAD   Of course I shall. I shall stay here till Helmer comes down. I'll tell him he must give me back my letter—I'll say it was only to do with my dismissal, and that I don't want him to read it—

MRS. LINDE   No, Nils, you mustn't ask for that letter back.

KROGSTAD   But—tell me—wasn't that the real reason you asked me to come here?

MRS. LINDE   Yes—at first, when I was frightened. But a day has passed since then, and in that time I've seen incredible things happen in this house. Helmer must know the truth. This unhappy secret of Nora's must be revealed. They must come to a full understanding; there must be an end of all these shiftings and evasions.

KROGSTAD   Very well. If you're prepared to risk it. But one thing I can do—and at once—

MRS. LINDE [*listens*]   Hurry! Go, go! The dance is over. We aren't safe here another moment.

KROGSTAD   I'll wait for you downstairs.

MRS. LINDE   Yes, do. You can see me home.

KROGSTAD   I've never been so happy in my life before!

He goes out through the front door. The door leading from the room into the hall remains open.

MRS. LINDE [*tidies the room a little and gets her hat and coat*]   What a change! Oh, what a change! Someone to work for—to live for! A home to bring joy into! I won't let this chance of happiness slip through my fingers. Oh, why don't they come? [*Listens.*] Ah, here they are. I must get my coat on.

She takes her hat and coat. Helmer's and Nora's voices become audible outside. A key is turned in the lock and Helmer leads Nora almost forcibly into the hall. She is dressed in an Italian costume with a large black shawl. He is in evening dress, with a black cloak.

NORA [*still in the doorway, resisting him*]   No, no, no—not in here! I want to go back upstairs. I don't want to leave so early.

HELMER   But my dearest Nora—

NORA   Oh, please, Torvald, please! Just another hour!

HELMER   Not another minute, Nora, my sweet. You know what we agreed. Come along, now. Into the drawing-room. You'll catch cold if you stay out here.

He leads her, despite her efforts to resist him, gently into the room.

MRS. LINDE   Good evening.

NORA   Christine!

HELMER   Oh, hullo, Mrs. Linde. You still here?

MRS. LINDE   Please forgive me. I did so want to see Nora in her costume.

NORA   Have you been sitting here waiting for me?

MRS. LINDE   Yes. I got here too late, I'm afraid. You'd already gone up. And I felt I really couldn't go back home without seeing you.

HELMER [*takes off Nora's shawl*]   Well, take a good look at her. She's worth looking at, don't you think? Isn't she beautiful, Mrs. Linde?

MRS. LINDE   Oh, yes, indeed—

HELMER   Isn't she unbelievably beautiful? Everyone at the party said so. But dreadfully stubborn she is, bless her pretty little heart. What's to be done about that? Would you believe it, I practically had to use force to get her away!

NORA   Oh, Torvald, you're going to regret not letting me stay—just half an hour longer.

HELMER   Hear that, Mrs. Linde? She dances her tarantella—makes a roaring success—and very well deserved—though possibly a trifle too realistic—more so than was aesthetically necessary, strictly speaking. But never mind that. Main thing is—she had a success—roaring success. Was I going to let her stay on after that and spoil the impression? No, thank you. I took my beautiful little Capri signorina—my capricious little Capricienne, what?—under my arm—a swift round of the ballroom, a curtsey to the company, and, as they say in novels, the beautiful apparition disappeared! An exit should always be dramatic, Mrs. Linde. But unfortunately that's just what I can't get Nora to realize. I say, it's hot in here. [*Throws his cloak on a chair and opens the door to his study.*] What's this? It's dark in here. Ah, yes, of course—excuse me. [*Goes in and lights a couple of candles.*]

NORA [*whispers swiftly, breathlessly*]   Well?

MRS. LINDE [*quietly*]   I've spoken to him.

NORA   Yes?

MRS. LINDE   Nora—you must tell your husband everything.

NORA [*dully*]   I knew it.

MRS. LINDE   You've nothing to fear from Krogstad. But you must tell him.

NORA   I shan't tell him anything.

MRS. LINDE   Then the letter will.

NORA   Thank you, Christine. Now I know what I must do. Ssh!

HELMER [*returns*]   Well, Mrs. Linde, finished admiring her?

MRS. LINDE   Yes. Now I must say good night.

HELMER   Oh, already? Does this knitting belong to you?

MRS. LINDE [*takes it*]   Thank you, yes. I nearly forgot it.

HELMER   You knit, then?

MRS. LINDE   Why, yes.

HELMER   Know what? You ought to take up embroidery.

MRS. LINDE   Oh? Why?

HELMER   It's much prettier. Watch me, now. You hold the embroidery in your left hand, like this, and then you take the needle in your right hand and go in and out in a slow, easy movement—like this. I am right, aren't I?

MRS. LINDE   Yes, I'm sure—

HELMER   But knitting, now—that's an ugly business—can't help it. Look— arms all huddled up—great clumsy needles going up and down—makes you look like a damned Chinaman. I say, that really was a magnificent champagne they served us.

MRS. LINDE   Well, good night, Nora. And stop being stubborn. Remember!

HELMER   Quite right, Mrs. Linde!

MRS. LINDE   Good night, Mr. Helmer.

HELMER [*accompanies her to the door*]   Good night, good night! I hope you'll manage to get home all right? I'd gladly—but you haven't far to go, have you? Good night, good night. [*She goes. He closes the door behind her and returns.*]   Well, we've got rid of her at last. Dreadful bore that woman is!

NORA   Aren't you very tired, Torvald?

HELMER   No, not in the least.

NORA   Aren't you sleepy?

HELMER   Not a bit. On the contrary, I feel extraordinarily exhilarated. But what about you? Yes, you look very sleepy and tired.

NORA   Yes, I am very tired. Soon I shall sleep.

HELMER   You see, you see! How right I was not to let you stay longer!

NORA   Oh, you're always right, whatever you do.

HELMER [kisses her on the forehead]   Now my little songbird's talking just like a real big human being. I say, did you notice how cheerful Rank was this evening?

NORA   Oh? Was he? I didn't have a chance to speak with him.

HELMER   I hardly did. But I haven't seen him in such a jolly mood for ages. [Looks at her for a moment, then comes closer.] I say, it's nice to get back to one's home again, and be all alone with you. Upon my word, you're a distractingly beautiful young woman.

NORA   Don't look at me like that, Torvald!

HELMER   What, not look at my most treasured possession? At all this wonderful beauty that's mine, mine alone, all mine.

NORA [goes round to the other side of the table]   You mustn't talk to me like that tonight.

HELMER [follows her]   You've still the tarantella in your blood, I see. And that makes you even more desirable. Listen! Now the other guests are beginning to go. [More quietly.] Nora—soon the whole house will be absolutely quiet.

NORA   Yes, I hope so.

HELMER   Yes, my beloved Nora, of course you do! Do you know—when I'm out with you among other people like we were tonight, do you know why I say so little to you, why I keep so aloof from you, and just throw you an occasional glance? Do you know why I do that? It's because I pretend to myself that you're my secret mistress, my clandestine little sweetheart, and that nobody knows there's anything at all between us.

NORA   Oh, yes, yes, yes—I know you never think of anything but me.

HELMER   And then when we're about to go, and I wrap the shawl round your lovely young shoulders, over this wonderful curve of your neck then I pretend to myself that you are my young bride, that we've just come from the wedding, that I'm taking you to my house for the first time—that, for the first time, I am alone with you—quite alone with you, as you stand there young and trembling and beautiful. All evening I've had no eyes for anyone but you. When I saw you dance the tarantella, like a huntress, a temptress, my blood grew hot, I couldn't stand it any longer! That was why I seized you and dragged you down here with me—

NORA   Leave me, Torvald! Get away from me! I don't want all this.

HELMER   What? Now, Nora, you're joking with me. Don't want, don't want—? Aren't I your husband—?

There is a knock on the front door.

NORA [starts]   What was that?

HELMER [goes towards the hall]   Who is it?

RANK [*outside*]   It's me. May I come in for a moment?

HELMER [*quietly, annoyed*]   Oh, what does he want now? [*Calls.*] Wait a moment. [*Walks over and opens the door.*] Well! Nice of you not to go by without looking in.

RANK   I thought I heard your voice, so I felt I had to say goodbye. [*His eyes travel swiftly around the room.*] Ah, yes—these dear rooms, how well I know them. What a happy, peaceful home you two have.

HELMER   You seemed to be having a pretty happy time yourself upstairs.

RANK   Indeed I did. Why not? Why shouldn't one make the most of this world? As much as one can, and for as long as one can. The wine was excellent—

HELMER   Especially the champagne.

RANK   You noticed that too? It's almost incredible how much I managed to get down.

NORA   Torvald drank a lot of champagne too, this evening.

RANK   Oh?

NORA   Yes. It always makes him merry afterwards.

RANK   Well, why shouldn't a man have a merry evening after a well-spent day?

HELMER   Well-spent? Oh, I don't know that I can claim that.

RANK [*slaps him across the back*]   I can, though, my dear fellow!

NORA   Yes, of course, Dr. Rank—you've been carrying out a scientific experiment today, haven't you?

RANK   Exactly.

HELMER   Scientific experiment! Those are big words for my little Nora to use!

NORA   And may I congratulate you on the finding?

RANK   You may indeed.

NORA   It was good, then?

RANK   The best possible finding—both for the doctor and the patient. Certainty.

NORA [*quickly*]   Certainty?

RANK   Absolute certainty. So aren't I entitled to have a merry evening after that?

NORA   Yes, Dr. Rank. You were quite right to.

HELMER   I agree. Provided you don't have to regret it tomorrow.

RANK   Well, you never get anything in this life without paying for it.

NORA   Dr. Rank—you like masquerades, don't you?

RANK   Yes, if the disguises are sufficiently amusing.

NORA   Tell me. What shall we two wear at the next masquerade?

HELMER   You little gadabout! Are you thinking about the next one already?

RANK   We two? Yes, I'll tell you. You must go as the Spirit of Happiness—

HELMER   You try to think of a costume that'll convey that.

RANK   Your wife need only appear as her normal, everyday self—

HELMER   Quite right! Well said! But what are you going to be? Have you decided that?

RANK   Yes, my dear friend. I have decided that.

HELMER   Well?

RANK   At the next masquerade, I shall be invisible.

HELMER   Well, that's a funny idea.

RANK   There's a big, black hat—haven't you heard of the invisible hat? Once it's over your head, no one can see you any more.

HELMER   [represses a smile]   Ah yes, of course.

RANK   But I'm forgetting what I came for. Helmer, give me a cigar. One of your black Havanas.

HELMER   With the greatest pleasure. [Offers him the box.]

RANK   [takes one and cuts off the tip]   Thank you.

NORA   [strikes a match]   Let me give you a light.

RANK   Thank you. [She holds out the match for him. He lights his cigar.] And now—goodbye.

HELMER   Goodbye, my dear chap, goodbye.

NORA   Sleep well, Dr. Rank.

RANK   Thank you for that kind wish.

NORA   Wish me the same.

RANK   You? Very well—since you ask. Sleep well. And thank you for the light. [He nods to them both and goes.]

HELMER   [quietly]   He's been drinking too much.

NORA   [abstractedly]   Perhaps.

Helmer takes his bunch of keys from his pocket and goes out into the hall.

NORA   Torvald, what do you want out there?

HELMER   I must empty the letter-box. It's absolutely full. There'll be no room for the newspapers in the morning.

NORA   Are you going to work tonight?

HELMER   You know very well I'm not. Hullo, what's this? Someone's been at the lock.

NORA   At the lock—?

HELMER   Yes, I'm sure of it. Who on earth—? Surely not one of the maids? Here's a broken hairpin. Nora, it's yours—

NORA   [quickly]   Then it must have been the children.

HELMER   Well, you'll have to break them of that habit. Hm, hm. Ah, that's done it. [Takes out the contents of the box and calls into the kitchen.] Helen! Helen! Put out the light on the staircase. [Comes back into the drawing room with the letters in his hand and closes the door to the hall.] Look at this! You see how they've piled up? [Glances through them.] What on earth's this?

NORA   [at the window]   The letter! Oh, no, Torvald, no!

HELMER   Two visiting cards—from Rank.

NORA   From Dr. Rank?

HELMER [*looks at them*]   Peter Rank, M.D. They were on top. He must have dropped them in as he left.

NORA   Has he written anything on them?

HELMER   There's a black cross above his name. Look. Rather gruesome, isn't it? It looks just as though he was announcing his death.

NORA   He is.

HELMER   What? Do you know something? Has he told you anything?

NORA   Yes. When these cards come, it means he's said good-bye to us. He wants to shut himself up in his house and die.

HELMER   Ah, poor fellow. I knew I wouldn't be seeing him for much longer. But so soon—! And now he's going to slink away and hide like a wounded beast.

NORA   When the time comes, it's best to go silently. Don't you think so, Torvald?

HELMER [*walks up and down*]   He was so much a part of our life. I can't realize that he's gone. His suffering and loneliness seemed to provide a kind of dark background to the happy sunlight of our marriage. Well, perhaps it's best this way. For him, anyway. [*Stops walking.*] And perhaps for us too, Nora. Now we have only each other. [*Embraces her.*] Oh, my beloved wife—I feel as though I could never hold you close enough. Do you know, Nora, often I wish some terrible danger might threaten you, so that I could offer my life and my blood, everything, for your sake.

NORA [*tears herself loose and says in a clear, firm voice*]   Read your letters now, Torvald.

HELMER   No, no. Not tonight. Tonight I want to be with you, my darling wife—

NORA   When your friend is about to die—?

HELMER   You're right. This news has upset us both. An ugliness has come between us; thoughts of death and dissolution. We must try to forget them. Until then—you go to your room; I shall go to mine.

NORA [*throws her arms round his neck*]   Good night, Torvald! Good night!

HELMER [*kisses her on the forehead*]   Good night, my darling little songbird. Sleep well, Nora. I'll go and read my letters.

He goes into the study with the letters in his hand, and closes the door.

NORA [*wild-eyed, fumbles around, seizes Helmer's cloak, throws it round herself and whispers quickly, hoarsely*]   Never see him again. Never. Never. Never. [*Throws the shawl over her head.*] Never see the children again. Them too. Never. Never. Oh—the icy black water! Oh—that bottomless—that—! Oh, if only it were all over! Now he's got it—he's reading it. Oh, no, no! Goodbye, Torvald! Goodbye, my darlings!

She turns to run into the hall. As she does so, Helmer throws open his door and stands there with an open letter in his hand.

HELMER   Nora!

NORA [*shrieks*]   Ah—!

HELMER   What is this? Do you know what is in this letter?

NORA   Yes, I know. Let me go! Let me go!

HELMER [*holds her back*]   Go? Where?

NORA [*tries to tear herself loose*]   You mustn't try to save me, Torvald!

HELMER [*staggers back*]   Is it true? Is it true, what he writes? Oh, my God! No, no—it's impossible, it can't be true!

NORA   It *is* true. I've loved you more than anything else in the world.

HELMER   Oh, don't try to make silly excuses.

NORA [*takes a step towards him*]   Torvald—

HELMER   Wretched woman! What have you done?

NORA   Let me go! You're not going to suffer for my sake. I won't let you!

HELMER   Stop being theatrical. [*Locks the front door.*] You're going to stay here and explain yourself. Do you understand what you've done? Answer me! Do you understand?

NORA [*looks unflinchingly at him and, her expression growing colder, says*]   Yes. Now I am beginning to understand.

HELMER [*walking round the room*]   Oh, what a dreadful awakening! For eight whole years—she who was my joy and my pride—a hypocrite, a liar—worse, worse—a criminal! Oh, the hideousness of it! Shame on you, shame!

Nora is silent and stares unblinkingly at him.

HELMER [*stops in front of her*]   I ought to have guessed that something of this sort would happen. I should have foreseen it. All your father's recklessness and instability—be quiet!—I repeat, all your father's recklessness and instability he has handed on to you. No religion, no morals, no sense of duty! Oh, how I have been punished for closing my eyes to his faults! I did it for your sake. And now you reward me like this.

NORA   Yes. Like this.

HELMER   Now you have destroyed all my happiness. You have ruined my whole future. Oh, it's too dreadful to contemplate! I am in the power of a man who is completely without scruples. He can do what he likes with me, demand what he pleases, order me to do anything—I dare not disobey him. I am condemned to humiliation and ruin simply for the weakness of a woman.

NORA   When I am gone from this world, you will be free.

HELMER   Oh, don't be melodramatic. Your father was always ready with that kind of remark. How would it help me if you were "gone from this world," as you put it? It wouldn't assist me in the slightest. He can still make all the facts public; and if he does, I may quite easily be suspected of having been an accomplice in your crime. People may think that I was behind it—that it was I who encouraged you! And for all this I have to thank you, you whom I have carried on my hands through all the years of our marriage! Now do you realize what you've done to me?

NORA [*coldly calm*]   Yes.

HELMER   It's so unbelievable I can hardly credit it. But we must try to find some way out. Take off that shawl. Take it off, I say! I must try to buy him off somehow. This thing must be hushed up at any price. As regards our relationship—we must appear to be living together just as before. Only *appear*, of course. You will therefore continue to reside here. That is understood. But the children shall be taken out of your hands. I dare no longer entrust them to you. Oh, to have to say this to the woman I once loved so dearly—and whom I still—! Well, all that must be finished. Henceforth there can be no question of happiness; we must merely strive to save what shreds and tatters— [*The front door bell rings. Helmer starts.*] What can that be? At this hour? Surely not—? He wouldn't—? Hide yourself, Nora. Say you're ill.

Nora does not move. Helmer goes to the door of the room and opens it. The Maid is standing half-dressed in the hall.

MAID   A letter for madam.

HELMER   Give it me. [*Seizes the letter and shuts the door.*]   Yes, it's from him. You're not having it. I'll read this myself.

NORA   Read it.

HELMER [*by the lamp*]   I hardly dare to. This may mean the end for us both. No. I must know. [*Tears open the letter hastily; reads a few lines; looks at a piece of paper which is enclosed with it; utters a cry of joy.*] Nora! [*She looks at him questioningly.*] Nora! No—I must read it once more. Yes, yes, it's true! I am saved! Nora, I am saved!

NORA   What about me?

HELMER   You too, of course. We're both saved, you and I. Look! He's returning your I.O.U. He writes that he is sorry for what has happened—a happy accident has changed his life—oh, what does it matter what he writes? We are saved, Nora! No one can harm you now. Oh, Nora, Nora—no, first let me destroy this filthy thing. Let me see—! [*Glances at the I.O.U.*] No, I don't want to look at it. I shall merely regard the whole business as a dream. [*He tears the I.O.U. and both letters into pieces, throws them into the stove and watches them burn.*] There. Now they're destroyed. He wrote that ever since Christmas Eve you've been—oh, these must have been three dreadful days for you, Nora.

NORA   Yes. It's been a hard fight.

HELMER   It must have been terrible—seeing no way out except—no, we'll forget the whole sordid business. We'll just be happy and go on telling ourselves over and over again: "It's over! It's over!" Listen to me, Nora. You don't seem to realize. It's over! Why are you looking so pale? Ah, my poor little Nora, I understand. You can't believe that I have forgiven you. But I have, Nora. I swear it to you. I have forgiven you everything. I know that what you did you did for your love of me.

NORA   That is true.

HELMER   You have loved me as a wife should love her husband. It was simply that in your inexperience you chose the wrong means. But do you think I love you any the less because you don't know how to act on your own initiative? No, no. Just lean on me. I shall counsel you. I shall guide you. I would not be a true man if your feminine helplessness did not make you doubly attractive in my eyes. You mustn't mind the hard words I said to you in those first dreadful moments when my whole world seemed to be tumbling about my ears. I have forgiven you, Nora. I swear it to you; I have forgiven you.

NORA   Thank you for your forgiveness.

She goes out through the door, right.

HELMER   No, don't go— [*Looks in.*] What are you doing there?

NORA [*offstage*]   Taking off my fancy dress.

HELMER [*by the open door*]   Yes, do that. Try to calm yourself and get your balance again, my frightened little songbird. Don't be afraid. I have broad wings to shield you. [*Begins to walk around near the door.*] How lovely and peaceful this little home of ours is, Nora. You are safe here; I shall watch over you like a hunted dove which I have snatched unharmed from the claws of the falcon. Your wildly beating little heart shall find peace with me. It will happen, Nora; it will take time, but it will happen, believe me. Tomorrow all this will seem quite different. Soon everything will be as it was before. I shall no longer need to remind you that I have forgiven you; your own heart will tell you that it is true. Do you really think I could ever bring myself to disown you, or even to reproach you? Ah, Nora, you don't understand what goes on in a husband's heart. There is something indescribably wonderful and satisfying for a husband in knowing that he has forgiven his wife— forgiven her unreservedly, from the bottom of his heart. It means that she has become his property in a double sense; he has, as it were, brought her into the world anew; she is now not only his wife but also his child. From now on that is what you shall be to me, my poor, helpless, bewildered little creature. Never be frightened of anything again, Nora. Just open your heart to me. I shall be both your will and your conscience. What's this? Not in bed? Have you changed?

NORA [*in her everyday dress*]   Yes, Torvald. I've changed.

HELMER   But why now—so late—?

NORA   I shall not sleep tonight.

HELMER   But, my dear Nora—

NORA [*looks at her watch*]   It isn't that late. Sit down here, Torvald. You and I have a lot to talk about.

She sits down on one side of the table.

HELMER   Nora, what does this mean? You look quite drawn—

NORA   Sit down. It's going to take a long time. I've a lot to say to you.

HELMER [*sits down on the other side of the table*]   You alarm me, Nora. I don't understand you.

NORA   No, that's just it. You don't understand me. And I've never understood you—until this evening. No, don't interrupt me. Just listen to what I have to say. You and I have got to face facts, Torvald.

HELMER   What do you mean by that?

NORA [*after a short silence*]   Doesn't anything strike you about the way we're sitting here?

HELMER   What?

NORA   We've been married for eight years. Does it occur to you that this is the first time that we two, you and I, man and wife, have ever had a serious talk together?

HELMER   Serious? What do you mean, serious?

NORA   In eight whole years—no, longer—ever since we first met—we have never exchanged a serious word on a serious subject.

HELMER   Did you expect me to drag you into all my worries—worries you couldn't possibly have helped me with?

NORA   I'm not talking about worries. I'm simply saying that we have never sat down seriously to try to get to the bottom of anything.

HELMER   But, my dear Nora, what on earth has that got to do with you?

NORA   That's just the point. You have never understood me. A great wrong has been done to me, Torvald. First by Papa, and then by you.

HELMER   What? But we two have loved you more than anyone in the world!

NORA [*shakes her head*]   You have never loved me. You just thought it was fun to be in love with me.

HELMER   Nora, what kind of a way is this to talk?

NORA   It's the truth, Torvald. When I lived with Papa, he used to tell me what he thought about everything, so that I never had any opinions but his. And if I did have any of my own, I kept them quiet, because he wouldn't have liked them. He called me his little doll, and he played with me just the way I played with my dolls. Then I came here to live in your house—

HELMER   What kind of a way is that to describe our marriage?

NORA [*undisturbed*]   I mean, then I passed from Papa's hands into yours. You arranged everything the way you wanted it, so that I simply took over your taste in everything—or pretended I did—I don't really know—I think it was a little of both—first one and then the other. Now I look back on it, it's as if I've been living here like a pauper, from hand to mouth. I performed tricks for you, and you gave me food and drink. But that was how you wanted it. You and Papa have done me a great wrong. It's your fault that I have done nothing with my life.

HELMER   Nora, how can you be so unreasonable and ungrateful? Haven't you been happy here?

NORA   No; never. I used to think I was; but I haven't ever been happy.

HELMER   Not—not happy?

NORA   No. I've just had fun. You've always been very kind to me. But our home has never been anything but a playroom. I've been your doll-wife, just as I used to be Papa's doll-child. And the children have been my dolls. I used to think it was fun when you came in and played with me, just as they think it's fun when I go in and play games with them. That's all our marriage has been, Torvald.

HELMER   There may be a little truth in what you say, though you exaggerate and romanticize. But from now on it'll be different. Playtime is over. Now the time has come for education.

NORA   Whose education? Mine or the children's?

HELMER   Both yours and the children's, my dearest Nora.

NORA   Oh, Torvald, you're not the man to educate me into being the right wife for you.

HELMER   How can you say that?

NORA   And what about me? Am I fit to educate the children?

HELMER   Nora!

NORA   Didn't you say yourself a few minutes ago that you dare not leave them in my charge?

HELMER   In a moment of excitement. Surely you don't think I meant it seriously?

NORA   Yes. You were perfectly right. I'm not fitted to educate them. There's something else I must do first. I must educate myself. And you can't help me with that. It's something I must do by myself. That's why I'm leaving you.

HELMER [*jumps up*]   What did you say?

NORA   I must stand on my own feet if I am to find out the truth about myself and about life. So I can't go on living here with you any longer.

HELMER   Nora, Nora!

NORA   I'm leaving you now, at once. Christine will put me up for tonight—

HELMER   You're out of your mind! You can't do this! I forbid you!

NORA   It's no use your trying to forbid me any more. I shall take with me nothing but what is mine. I don't want anything from you, now or ever.

HELMER   What kind of madness is this?

NORA   Tomorrow I shall go home—I mean, to where I was born. It'll be easiest for me to find some kind of a job there.

HELMER   But you're blind! You've no experience of the world—

NORA   I must try to get some, Torvald.

HELMER   But to leave your home, your husband, your children! Have you thought what people will say?

NORA   I can't help that. I only know that I must do this.

HELMER   But this is monstrous! Can you neglect your most sacred duties?

NORA   What do you call my most sacred duties?

HELMER   Do I have to tell you? Your duties towards your husband, and your children.

NORA   I have another duty which is equally sacred.

HELMER   You have not. What on earth could that be?

NORA   My duty towards myself.

HELMER   First and foremost you are a wife and a mother.

NORA   I don't believe that any longer. I believe that I am first and foremost a human being, like you—or anyway, that I must try to become one. I know most people think as you do, Torvald, and I know there's something of the sort to be found in books. But I'm no longer prepared to accept what people say and what's written in books. I must think things out for myself, and try to find my own answer.

HELMER   Do you need to ask where your duty lies in your own home? Haven't you an infallible guide in such matters—your religion?

NORA   Oh, Torvald, I don't really know what religion means.

HELMER   What are you saying?

NORA   I only know what Pastor Hansen told me when I went to confirmation. He explained that religion meant this and that. When I get away from all this and can think things out on my own, that's one of the questions I want to look into. I want to find out whether what Pastor Hansen said was right—or anyway, whether it is right for me.

HELMER   But it's unheard of for so young a woman to behave like this! If religion cannot guide you, let me at least appeal to your conscience. I presume you have some moral feelings left? Or—perhaps you haven't? Well, answer me.

NORA   Oh, Torvald, that isn't an easy question to answer. I simply don't know. I don't know where I am in these matters. I only know that these things mean something quite different to me from what they do to you. I've learned now that certain laws are different from what I'd imagined them to be; but I can't accept that such laws can be right. Has a woman really not the right to spare her dying father pain, or save her husband's life? I can't believe that.

HELMER   You're talking like a child. You don't understand how society works.

NORA No, I don't. But now I intend to learn. I must try to satisfy myself which is right, society or I.

HELMER Nora, you're ill; you're feverish. I almost believe you're out of your mind.

NORA I've never felt so sane and sure in my life.

HELMER You feel sure that it is right to leave your husband and your children?

NORA Yes. I do.

HELMER Then there is only one possible explanation.

NORA What?

HELMER That you don't love me any longer.

NORA No, that's exactly it.

HELMER Nora! How can you say this to me?

NORA Oh, Torvald, it hurts me terribly to have to say it, because you've always been so kind to me. But I can't help it. I don't love you any longer.

HELMER [controlling his emotions with difficulty] And you feel quite sure about this too?

NORA Yes, absolutely sure. That's why I can't go on living here any longer.

HELMER Can you also explain why I have lost your love?

NORA Yes, I can. It happened this evening, when the miracle failed to happen. It was then that I realized you weren't the man I'd thought you to be.

HELMER Explain more clearly. I don't understand you.

NORA I've waited so patiently, for eight whole years—well, good heavens, I'm not such a fool as to suppose that miracles occur every day. Then this dreadful thing happened to me, and then I knew: "Now the miracle will take place!" When Krogstad's letter was lying out there, it never occurred to me for a moment that you would let that man trample over you. I knew that you would say to him: "Publish the facts to the world." And when he had done this—

HELMER Yes, what then? When I'd exposed my wife's name to shame and scandal—

NORA Then I was certain that you would step forward and take all the blame on yourself, and say: "I am the one who is guilty!"

HELMER Nora!

NORA You're thinking I wouldn't have accepted such a sacrifice from you? No, of course I wouldn't! But what would my word have counted for against yours? That was the miracle I was hoping for, and dreading. And it was to prevent it happening that I wanted to end my life.

HELMER Nora, I would gladly work for you night and day, and endure sorrow and hardship for your sake. But no man can be expected to sacrifice his honor, even for the person he loves.

NORA Millions of women have done it.

HELMER   Oh, you think and talk like a stupid child.

NORA   That may be. But you neither think nor talk like the man I could share my life with. Once you'd got over your fright—and you weren't frightened of what might threaten me, but only of what threatened you—once the danger was past, then as far as you were concerned it was exactly as though nothing had happened. I was your little songbird just as before—your doll whom henceforth you would take particular care to protect from the world because she was so weak and fragile. [*Gets up.*] Torvald, in that moment I realized that for eight years I had been living here with a complete stranger, and had borne him three children—! Oh, I can't bear to think of it! I could tear myself to pieces!

HELMER   [*sadly*]   I see it, I see it. A gulf has indeed opened between us. Oh, but Nora—couldn't it be bridged?

NORA   As I am now, I am no wife for you.

HELMER   I have the strength to change.

NORA   Perhaps—if your doll is taken from you.

HELMER   But to be parted—to be parted from you! No, no, Nora, I can't conceive of it happening!

NORA   [*goes into the room, right*]   All the more necessary that it should happen.

She comes back with her outdoor things and a small traveling-bag, which she puts down on a chair by the table.

HELMER   Nora, Nora, not now! Wait till tomorrow!

NORA   [*puts on her coat*]   I can't spend the night in a strange man's house.

HELMER   But can't we live here as brother and sister, then—?

NORA   [*fastens her hat*]   You know quite well it wouldn't last. [*Puts on her shawl.*] Goodbye, Torvald. I don't want to see the children. I know they're in better hands than mine. As I am now, I can be nothing to them.

HELMER   But some time, Nora—some time—?

NORA   How can I tell? I've no idea what will happen to me.

HELMER   But you are my wife, both as you are and as you will be.

NORA   Listen, Torvald. When a wife leaves her husband's house, as I'm doing now, I'm told that according to the law he is freed of any obligations towards her. In any case, I release you from any such obligations. You mustn't feel bound to me in any way, however small, just as I shall not feel bound to you. We must both be quite free. Here is your ring back. Give me mine.

HELMER   That too?

NORA   That too.

HELMER   Here it is.

NORA   Good. Well, now it's over. I'll leave the keys here. The servants know about everything to do with the house—much better than I do. Tomorrow, when I have left town, Christine will come to pack the things I brought here from home. I'll have them sent on after me.

HELMER   This is the end then! Nora, will you never think of me any more?

NORA   Yes, of course. I shall often think of you and the children and this house.

HELMER   May I write to you, Nora?

NORA   No. Never. You mustn't do that.

HELMER   But at least you must let me send you—

NORA   Nothing. Nothing.

HELMER   But if you should need help—?

NORA   I tell you, no. I don't accept things from strangers.

HELMER   Nora—can I never be anything but a stranger to you?

NORA   [picks up her bag]   Oh, Torvald! Then the miracle of miracles would have to happen.

HELMER   The miracle of miracles?

NORA   You and I would both have to change so much that—oh, Torvald, I don't believe in miracles any longer.

HELMER   But I want to believe in them. Tell me. We should have to change so much that—?

NORA   That life together between us two could become a marriage. Good-bye.

She goes out through the hall.

HELMER   [sinks down on a chair by the door and buries his face in his hands] Nora! Nora! [Looks round and gets up.] Empty! She's gone! [A hope strikes him.] The miracle of miracles—?

The street door is slammed shut downstairs.

OSCAR WILDE
1854–1900

Playwright and poet, novelist and critic, he was born in Dublin. After majoring in Classics at Trinity College, Dublin, he won a scholarship to Oxford University. By the time of his graduation from Oxford in 1878, he was already well known for his commitment to "art for art's sake" and for his eccentricities in dress and manners. Convinced that "industry is the root of all ugliness," he sought to raise the taste of his audiences. Between 1892 and 1895 he wrote a series of comedies for the stage—"trivial comedies for serious people," he called them—whose plots were then regarded as scandalous and whose dialogue glistened with his clever wit. In 1895 he was found guilty of homosexual conduct and sentenced to two years in prison with hard labor. His imprisonment led him to write his poem *The Ballad of Reading Gaol* and his prose confession *De Profundis*. After leaving jail, he emigrated to France, where he spent his last years living under an assumed name. *The Importance of Being Earnest* had its premiere at St. James's Theatre in London on February 14, 1895.

The Importance of Being Earnest

CHARACTERS

JOHN WORTHING, J.P.
ALGERNON MONCRIEFF
REV. CANON CHASUBLE, D.D.
MERRIMAN, butler
LANE, manservant
LADY BRACKNELL
HON. GWENDOLEN FAIRFAX
CECILY CARDEW
MISS PRISM, governess

ACT I

SCENE *Morning room in Algernon's flat in Half-Moon Street. The room is luxuriously and artistically furnished. The sound of a piano is heard in the adjoining room. Lane is arranging afternoon tea on the table, and after the music has ceased, Algernon enters.*

ALGERNON Did you hear what I was playing, Lane?
LANE I didn't think it polite to listen, sir.
ALGERNON I'm sorry for that, for your sake. I don't play accurately —any one can play accurately—but I play with wonderful expres-

sion. As far as the piano is concerned, sentiment is my forte. I keep science for Life.

LANE   Yes, sir.

ALGERNON   And, speaking of the science of Life, have you got the cucumber sandwiches cut for Lady Bracknell?

LANE   Yes, sir. [*Hands them on a salver.*]

ALGERNON   [*inspects them, takes two, and sits down on the sofa*] Oh! . . . by the way, Lane, I see from your book that on Thursday night, when Lord Shoreman and Mr. Worthing were dining with me, eight bottles of champagne are entered as having been consumed.

LANE   Yes, sir; eight bottles and a pint.

ALGERNON   Why is it that at a bachelor's establishment the servants invariably drink the champagne? I ask merely for information.

LANE   I attribute it to the superior quality of the wine, sir. I have often observed that in married households the champagne is rarely of a first-rate brand.

ALGERNON   Good Heavens! Is marriage so demoralizing as that?

LANE   I believe it *is* a very pleasant state, sir. I have had very little experience of it myself up to the present. I have only been married once. That was in consequence of a misunderstanding between myself and a young person.

ALGERNON   [*languidly*] I don't know that I am much interested in your family life, Lane.

LANE   No sir; it is not a very interesting subject. I never think of it myself.

ALGERNON   Very natural, I am sure. That will do, Lane, thank you.

LANE   Thank you, sir.

Lane goes out.

ALGERNON   Lane's views on marriage seem somewhat lax. Really, if the lower orders don't set us a good example, what on earth is the use of them? They seem, as a class, to have absolutely no sense of moral responsibility.

Enter Lane.

LANE   Mr. Ernest Worthing.

Enter Jack. Lane goes out.

ALGERNON   How are you, my dear Ernest? What brings you up to town?

JACK   Oh, pleasure, pleasure! What else should bring one anywhere? Eating as usual, I see, Algy!

ALGERNON   [*stiffly*] I believe it is customary in good society to take some slight refreshment at five o'clock. Where have you been since last Thursday?

JACK [*sitting down on the sofa*] In the country.

ALGERNON What on earth do you do there?

JACK [*pulling off his gloves*] When one is in town one amuses oneself. When one is in the country one amuses other people. It is excessively boring.

ALGERNON And who are the people you amuse?

JACK [*airily*] Oh, neighbors, neighbors.

ALGERNON Got nice neighbors in your part of Shropshire?

JACK Perfectly horrid! Never speak to one of them.

ALGERNON How immensely you must amuse them! [*Goes over and takes sandwich.*] By the way, Shropshire is your country, is it not?

JACK Eh? Shropshire? Yes, of course. Hallo! Why all these cups? Why cucumber sandwiches? Why such reckless extravagance in one so young? Who is coming to tea?

ALGERNON Oh! merely Aunt Augusta and Gwendolen.

JACK How perfectly delightful!

ALGERNON Yes, that is all very well; but I am afraid Aunt Augusta won't quite approve of your being here.

JACK May I ask why?

ALGERNON My dear fellow, the way you flirt with Gwendolen is perfectly disgraceful. It is almost as bad as the way Gwendolen flirts with you.

JACK I am in love with Gwendolen. I have come up to town expressly to propose to her.

ALGERNON I thought you had come up for pleasure? . . . I call that business.

JACK How utterly unromantic you are!

ALGERNON I really don't see anything romantic in proposing. It is very romantic to be in love. But there is nothing romantic about a definite proposal. Why, one may be accepted. One usually is, I believe. Then the excitement is all over. The very essence of romance is uncertainty. If ever I get married, I'll certainly try to forget the fact.

JACK I have no doubt about that, dear Algy. The Divorce Court was specially invented for people whose memories are so curiously constituted.

ALGERNON Oh! there is no use speculating on that subject. Divorces are made in Heaven — [*Jack puts out his hand to take a sandwich. Algernon at once interferes.*] Please don't touch the cucumber sandwiches. They are ordered specially for Aunt Augusta. [*Takes one and eats it.*]

JACK   Well, you have been eating them all the time.

ALGERNON   That is quite a different matter. She is my aunt. [*Takes plate from below.*] Have some bread and butter. The bread and butter is for Gwendolen. Gwendolen is devoted to bread and butter.

JACK   [*advancing to table and helping himself*] And very good bread and butter it is too.

ALGERNON   Well, my dear fellow, you need not eat as if you were going to eat it all. You behave as if you were married to her already. You are not married to her already, and I don't think you ever will be.

JACK   Why on earth do you say that?

ALGERNON   Well, in the first place, girls never marry the men they flirt with. Girls don't think it right.

JACK   Oh, that is nonsense!

ALGERNON   It isn't. It is a great truth. It accounts for the extraordinary number of bachelors that one sees all over the place. In the second place, I don't give my consent.

JACK   Your consent!

ALGERNON   My dear fellow, Gwendolen is my first cousin. And before I allow you to marry her, you will have to clear up the whole question of Cecily. [*Rings bell.*]

JACK   Cecily! What on earth do you mean? What do you mean, Algy, by Cecily! I don't know anyone of the name of Cecily.

Enter Lane.

ALGERNON   Bring me that cigarette case Mr. Worthing left in the smoking room the last time he dined here.

LANE   Yes, sir.

Lane goes out.

JACK   Do you mean to say you have had my cigarette case all this time? I wish to goodness you had let me know. I have been writing frantic letters to Scotland Yard about it. I was very nearly offering a large reward.

ALGERNON   Well, I wish you would offer one. I happen to be more than usually hard up.

JACK   There is no good offering a large reward now that the thing is found.

Enter Lane with the cigarette case on a salver. Algernon takes it at once. Lane goes out.

ALGERNON   I think that is rather mean of you, Ernest, I must say.

[*Opens case and examines it.*] However, it makes no matter, for, now that I look at the inscription inside, I find that the thing isn't yours after all.

JACK   Of course it's mine. [*Moving to him.*] You have seen me with it a hundred times, and you have no right whatsoever to read what is written inside. It is a very ungentlemanly thing to read a private cigarette case.

ALGERNON   Oh! it is absurd to have a hard and fast rule about what one should read and what one shouldn't. More than half of modern culture depends on what one shouldn't read.

JACK   I am quite aware of the fact, and I don't propose to discuss modern culture. It isn't the sort of thing one should talk of in private. I simply want my cigarette case back.

ALGERNON   Yes; but this isn't your cigarette case. This cigarette case is a present from someone of the name of Cecily, and you said you didn't know anyone of that name.

JACK   Well, if you want to know, Cecily happens to be my aunt.

ALGERNON   Your aunt!

JACK   Charming old lady she is, too. Lives at Tunbridge Wells. Just give it back to me, Algy.

ALGERNON   [*retreating to back of sofa*] But why does she call herself little Cecily if she is your aunt and lives at Tunbridge Wells. [*Reading*] ''From little Cecily with her fondest love.''

JACK   [*moving to sofa and kneeling upon it*] My dear fellow, what on earth is there in that? Some aunts are tall, some aunts are not tall. That is a matter that surely an aunt may be allowed to decide for herself. You seem to think that every aunt should be exactly like your aunt! That is absurd. For Heaven's sake give me back my cigarette case. [*Follows Algernon round the room.*]

ALGERNON   Yes. But why does your aunt call you her uncle? ''From little Cecily, with her fondest love to her dear Uncle Jack.'' There is no objection, I admit, to an aunt being a small aunt, but why an aunt, no matter what her size may be, should call her own nephew her uncle, I can't quite make out. Besides, your name isn't Jack at all; it is Ernest.

JACK   It isn't Ernest; it's Jack.

ALGERNON   You have always told me it was Ernest. I have introduced you to everyone as Ernest. You answer to the name of Ernest. You look as if your name was Ernest. You are the most earnest-looking person I ever saw in my lie. It is perfectly absurd your saying that your name isn't Ernest. It's on your cards. Here is one of them [*taking it from case*]. ''Mr. Ernest Worthing, B.4, The Albany.'' I'll keep this as a proof that your name is Ernest if ever you attempt to deny it to me, or to Gwendolen, or to anyone else. [*Puts the card in his pocket.*]

JACK Well, my name is Ernest in town and Jack in the country, and the cigarette case was given to me in the country.

ALGERNON Yes, but that does not account for the fact that your small Aunt Cecily, who lives at Tunbridge Wells, calls you her dear uncle. Come, old boy, you had much better have the thing out at once.

JACK My dear Algy, you talk exactly as if you were a dentist. It is very vulgar to talk like a dentist when one isn't a dentist. It produces a false impression.

ALGERNON Well, that is exactly what dentists always do. Now, go on! Tell me the whole thing. I may mention that I have always suspected you of being a confirmed and secret Bunburyist; and I am quite sure of it now.

JACK Bunburyist? What on earth do you mean by a Bunburyist?

ALGERNON I'll reveal to you the meaning of that incomparable expression as soon as you are kind enough to inform me why you are Ernest in town and Jack in the country.

JACK Well, produce my cigarette case first.

ALGERNON Here it is. [*Hands cigarette case.*] Now produce your explanation, and pray make it improbable. [*Sits on sofa.*]

JACK My dear fellow, there is nothing improbable about my explanation at all. In fact it's perfectly ordinary. Old Mr. Thomas Cardew, who adopted me when I was a little boy, made me in his will guardian to his granddaughter, Miss Cecily Cardew. Cecily, who addresses me as her uncle from motives of respect that you could not possibly appreciate, lives at my place in the country under the charge of her admirable governess, Miss Prism.

ALGERNON Where is that place in the country, by the way?

JACK That is nothing to you, dear boy. You are not going to be invited. . . . I may tell you candidly that the place is not in Shropshire.

ALGERNON I suspected that, my dear fellow! I have Bunburyed all over Shropshire on two separate occasions. Now, go on. Why are you Ernest in town and Jack in the country?

JACK My dear Algy, I don't know whether you will be able to understand my real motives. You are hardly serious enough. When one is placed in the position of guardian, one has to adopt a very high moral tone on all subjects. It's one's duty to do so. And as a high moral tone can hardly be said to conduce very much to either one's health or one's happiness, in order to get up to town I have always pretended to have a younger brother of the name of Ernest, who lives in the Albany, and gets into the most dreadful scrapes.

That, my dear Algy, is the whole truth pure and simple.

ALGERNON   The truth is rarely pure and never simple. Modern life would be very tedious if it were either, and modern literature a complete impossibility!

JACK   That wouldn't be at all a bad thing.

ALGERNON   Literary criticism is not your forte, my dear fellow. Don't try it. You should leave that to people who haven't been at a University. They do it so well in the daily papers. What you really are is a Bunburyist. I was quite right in saying you are a Bunburyist. You are one of the most advanced Bunburyists I know.

JACK   What on earth do you mean?

ALGERNON   You have invented a very useful younger brother called Ernest, in order that you may be able to come up to town as often as you like. I have invented an invaluable permanent invalid called Bunbury, in order that I may be able to go down into the country whenever I choose. Bunbury is perfectly invaluable. If it wasn't for Bunbury's extraordinary bad health, for instance, I wouldn't be able to dine with you at Willis's tonight, for I have been really engaged to Aunt Augusta for more than a week.

JACK   I haven't asked you to dine with me anywhere tonight.

ALGERNON   I know. You are absurdly careless about sending out invitations. It is very foolish of you. Nothing annoys people so much as not receiving invitations.

JACK   You had much better dine with your Aunt Augusta.

ALGERNON   I haven't the smallest intention of doing anything of the kind. To begin with, I dined there on Monday, and once a week is quite enough to dine with one's own relations. In the second place, whenever I do dine there I am always treated as a member of the family, and sent down with either no woman at all, or two. In the third place, I know perfectly well whom she will place me next to, tonight. She will place me next Mary Farquhar, who always flirts with her own husband across the dinner table. That is not very pleasant. Indeed, it is not even decent . . . and that sort of thing is enormously on the increase. The amount of women in London who flirt with their own husbands is perfectly scandalous. It looks so bad. It is simply washing one's clean linen in public. Besides, now that I know you to be a confirmed Bunburyist I naturally want to talk to you about Bunburying. I want to tell you the rules.

JACK   I'm not a Bunburyist at all. If Gwendolen accepts me, I am going to kill my brother, indeed I think I'll kill him in any case. Cecily is a little too much interested in him. It is rather a bore. So I am going to get rid of Ernest. And I strongly advise you to do the same with Mr. . . . with your invalid friend who has the absurd name.

ALGERNON   Nothing will induce me to part with Bunbury, and if you ever get married, which seems to me extremely problematic, you will be very glad to know Bunbury. A man who marries without knowing Bunbury has a very tedious time of it.

JACK   That is nonsense. If I marry a charming girl like Gwendolen, and she is the only girl I ever saw in my life that I would marry, I certainly won't want to know Bunbury.

ALGERNON   Then your wife will. You don't seem to realize, that in married life three is company and two is none.

JACK   [sententiously] That, my dear young friend, is the theory that the corrupt French Drama has been propounding for the last fifty years.

ALGERNON   Yes; and that the happy English home has proved in half the time.

JACK   For heaven's sake, don't try to be cynical. It's perfectly easy to be cynical.

ALGERNON   My dear fellow, it isn't easy to be anything nowadays. There's such a lot of beastly competition about. [The sound of an electric bell is heard.] Ah! that must be Aunt Augusta. Only relatives, or creditors, ever ring in that Wagnerian manner. Now, if I get her out of the way for ten minutes, so that you can have an opportunity of proposing to Gwendolen, may I dine with you tonight at Willis's?

JACK   I suppose so, if you want to.

ALGERNON   Yes, but you must be serious about it. I hate people who are not serious about meals. It is so shallow of them.

Enter Lane

LANE   Lady Bracknell and Miss Fairfax.

Algernon goes forward to meet them. Enter Lady Bracknell and Gwendolen.

LADY BRACKNELL   Good afternoon, dear Algernon, I hope you are behaving very well.

ALGERNON   I'm feeling very well, Aunt Augusta.

LADY BRACKNELL   That's not quite the same thing. In fact the two things rarely go together. [Sees Jack and bows to him with icy coldness.]

ALGERNON   [to Gwendolen] Dear me, you are smart!

GWENDOLEN   I am always smart! Am I not, Mr. Worthing?

JACK   You're quite perfect, Miss Fairfax.

GWENDOLEN   Oh! I hope I am not that. It would leave no room for developments, and I intend to develop in many directions. [*Gwendolen and Jack sit down together in the corner.*]

LADY BRACKNELL   I'm sorry if we are a little late, Algernon, but I was obliged to call on dear Lady Harbury. I hadn't been there since her poor husband's death. I never saw a woman so altered; she looks quite twenty years younger. And now I'll have a cup of tea and one of those nice cucumber sandwiches you promised me.

ALGERNON   Certainly, Aunt Augusta. [*Goes over to tea table.*]

LADY BRACKNELL   Won't you come and sit here, Gwendolen?

GWENDOLEN   Thanks, mamma, I'm quite comfortable where I am.

ALGERNON   [*picking up empty plate in horror*] Good heavens! Lane! Why are there no cucumber sandwiches? I ordered them specially.

LANE   [*gravely*] There were no cucumbers in the market this morning, sir. I went down twice.

ALGERNON   No cucumbers!

LANE   No, sir. Not even for ready money.

ALGERNON   That will do, Lane, thank you.

LANE   Thank you, sir. [*Goes out.*]

ALGERNON   I am greatly distressed, Aunt Augusta, about there being no cucumbers, not even for ready money.

LADY BRACKNELL   It really makes no matter, Algernon. I had some crumpets with Lady Harbury, who seems to me to be living entirely for pleasure now.

ALGERNON   I hear her hair has turned quite gold from grief.

LADY BRACKNELL   It certainly has changed its color. From what cause I, of course, cannot say. [*Algernon crosses and hands tea.*] Thank you. I've quite a treat for you tonight, Algernon. I am going to send you down with Mary Farquhar. She is such a nice woman, and so attentive to her husband. It's delightful to watch them.

ALGERNON   I am afraid, Aunt Augusta, I shall have to give up the pleasure of dining with you tonight after all.

LADY BRACKNELL   [*frowning*] I hope not, Algernon. It would put my table completely out. Your uncle would have to dine upstairs. Fortunately he is accustomed to that.

ALGERNON   It is a great bore, and, I need hardly say, a terrible disappointment to me, but the fact is I have just had a telegram to say that my poor friend Bunbury is very ill again. [*Exchanges glances with Jack.*] They seem to think I should be with him.

LADY BRACKNELL   It is very strange. This Mr. Bunbury seems to suffer from curiously bad health.

ALGERNON   Yes; poor Bunbury is a dreadful invalid.

LADY BRACKNELL   Well, I must say, Algernon, that I think it is high time that Mr. Bunbury made up his mind whether he was going to live or to die. This shilly-shallying with the question is absurd. Nor do I in any way approve of the modern sympathy with invalids. I consider it morbid. Illness of any kind is hardly a thing to be encouraged in others. Health is the primary duty of life. I am always telling that to your poor uncle, but he never seems to take much notice . . . as far as any improvement in his ailments goes. I should be much obliged if you would ask Mr. Bunbury, from me, to be kind enough not to have a relapse on Saturday, for I rely on you to arrange my music for me. It is my last reception, and one wants something that will encourage conversation, particulary at the end of the season when everyone has practically said whatever they had to say, which, in most cases, was probably not much.

ALGERNON   I'll speak to Bunbury, Aunt Augusta, if he is still conscious, and I think I can promise you he'll be all right by Saturday. Of course the music is a great difficulty. You see, if one plays good music, people don't listen, and if one plays bad music, people don't talk. But I'll run over the program I've drawn out, if you will kindly come into the next room for a moment.

LADY BRACKNELL   Thank you, Algernon. It is very thoughtful of you. [*Rising, and following Algernon.*] I'm sure the program will be delightful, after a few expurgations. French songs I cannot possibly allow. People always seem to think that they are improper, and either look shocked, which is vulgar, or laugh, which is worse. But German sounds a thoroughly respectable language, and, indeed I believe is so. Gwendolen, you will accompany me.

GWENDOLEN   Certainly, mamma.

Lady Bracknell and Algernon go into the music room; Gwendolen remains behind.

JACK   Charming day it has been, Miss Fairfax.

GWENDOLEN   Pray don't talk to me about the weather, Mr. Worthing. Whenever people talk to me about the weather, I always feel quite certain that they mean something else. And that makes me so nervous.

JACK   I do mean something else.

GWENDOLEN   I thought so. In fact, I am never wrong.

JACK   And I would like to be allowed to take advantage of Lady Bracknell's temporary absence. . . .

GWENDOLEN   I would certainly advise you to do so. Mamma has a way of coming back suddenly into a room that I have often had to speak to her about.

JACK   [*nervously*] Miss Fairfax, ever since I met you I have admired you more than any girl . . . I have ever met since . . . I met you.

GWENDOLEN   Yes, I am quite aware of the fact. And I often wish that in public, at any rate, you had been more demonstrative. For me you have always had an irresistible fascination. Even before I met you I was far from indifferent to you. [*Jack looks at her in amazement.*] We live, as I hope you know, Mr. Worthing, in an age of ideals. The fact is constantly mentioned in the more expensive monthly magazines, and has reached the provincial pulpits, I am told; and my ideal has always been to love someone of the name of Ernest. There is something in that name that inspires absolute confidence. The moment Algernon first mentioned to me that he had a friend called Ernest, I knew I was destined to love you.

JACK   You really love me, Gwendolen?

GWENDOLEN   Passionately!

JACK   Darling! You don't know how happy you've made me.

GWENDOLEN   My own Ernest!

JACK   But you don't really mean to say that you couldn't love me if my name wasn't Ernest!

GWENDOLEN   But your name is Ernest.

JACK   Yes, I know it is. But supposing it was something else? Do you mean to say you couldn't love me then?

GWENDOLEN   [*glibly*] Ah! that is clearly a metaphysical speculation, and like most metaphysical speculations has very little reference at all to the actual facts of real life, as we know them.

JACK   Personally, darling, to speak quite candidly, I don't much care about the name of Ernest. . . . I don't think the name suits me at all.

GWENDOLEN   It suits you perfectly. It is a divine name. It has a music of its own. It produces vibrations.

JACK   Well, really, Gwendolen, I must say that I think there are lots of other much nicer names. I think Jack, for instance, a charming name.

GWENDOLEN   Jack? . . . No, there is very little music in the name Jack, if any at all, indeed. It does not thrill. It produces absolutely no vibrations. . . . I have known several Jacks, and they all, without exception, were more than usually plain. Besides, Jack is a notorious domesticity for John! And I pity any woman who is married to a man called John. She would probably never be allowed to know the entrancing pleasure of a single moment's solitude. The only really safe name is Ernest.

JACK   Gwendolen, I must get christened at once—I mean we must get married at once. There is no time to be lost.

GWENDOLEN   Married, Mr. Worthing?

JACK   [*astounded*] Well . . . surely. You know that I love you, and you led me to believe, Miss Fairfax, that you were not absolutely indifferent to me.

GWENDOLEN   I adore you. But you haven't proposed to me yet. Nothing has been said at all about marriage. The subject has not even been touched on.

JACK   Well . . . may I propose to you now?

GWENDOLEN   I think it would be an admirable opportunity. And to spare you any possible disappointment, Mr. Worthing, I think it only fair to tell you quite frankly beforehand that I am fully determined to accept you.

JACK   Gwendolen!

GWENDOLEN   Yes, Mr. Worthing, what have you got to say to me?

JACK   You know what I have got to say to you.

GWENDOLEN   Yes, but you don't say it.

JACK   Gwendolen, will you marry me? [*Goes on his knees.*]

GWENDOLEN   Of course I will, darling. How long you have been about it! I am afraid you have had very little experience in how to propose.

JACK   My own one, I have never loved anyone in the world but you.

GWENDOLEN   Yes, but men often propose for practice. I know my brother Gerald does. All my girl friends tell me so. What wonderfully blue eyes you have, Ernest! They are quite, quite blue. I hope you will always look at me just like that, especially when there are other people present.

Enter Lady Bracknell.

LADY BRACKNELL   Mr. Worthing! Rise, sir, from this semi-recumbent posture. It is most indecorous.

GWENDOLEN   Mamma! [*He tries to rise; she restrains him.*] I must beg you to retire. This is no place for you. Besides, Mr. Worthing has not quite finished yet.

LADY BRACKNELL   Finished what, may I ask?

GWENDOLEN   I am engaged to Mr. Worthing, Mamma. [*They rise together.*]

LADY BRACKNELL   Pardon me, you are not engaged to anyone. When you do become engaged to someone, I, or your father, should his health permit him, will inform you of the fact. An engagement should come on a young girl as a surprise, pleasant or unpleasant, as the case may be. It is hardly a matter that she could be allowed to arrange for herself. . . . And now I have a few questions to put to you, Mr. Worthing. While I am making these inquiries, you, Gwendolen, will wait for me below in the carriage.

GWENDOLEN   [*reproachfully*] Mamma!

LADY BRACKNELL   In the carriage, Gwendolen! [*Gwendolen goes to the door. She and Jack blow kisses to each other behind Lady Bracknell's back. Lady Bracknell looks vaguely about as if she could not understand what the noise was. Finally turns round.*] Gwendolen, the carriage!

GWENDOLEN   Yes, Mamma. [*Goes out, looking back at Jack.*]

LADY BRACKNELL   [*sitting down*] You can take a seat, Mr. Worthing. [*Looks in her pocket for notebook and pencil.*]

JACK   Thank you, Lady Bracknell, I prefer standing.

LADY BRACKNELL   [*pencil and notebook in hand*] I feel bound to tell you that you are not down on my list of eligible young men, although I have the same list as the dear Duchess of Bolton has. We work together, in fact. However, I am quite ready to enter your name, should your answers be what a really affectionate mother requires. Do you smoke?

JACK   Well, yes, I must admit I smoke.

LADY BRACKNELL   I am glad to hear it. A man should always have an occupation of some kind. There are far too many idle men in London as it is. How old are you?

JACK   Twenty-nine.

LADY BRACKNELL   A very good age to be married at. I have always been of the opinion that a man who desires to get married should know either everything or nothing. Which do you know?

JACK   [*after some hesitation*] I know nothing, Lady Bracknell.

LADY BRACKNELL   I am pleased to hear it. I do not approve of anything that tampers with natural ignorance. Ignorance is like a delicate exotic fruit; touch it and the bloom is gone. The whole theory of modern education is radically unsound. Fortunately in England, at any rate, education produces no effect whatsoever. If it did, it would prove a serious danger to the upper classes, and probably lead to acts of violence in Grosvenor Square. What is your income?

JACK   Between seven and eight thousand a year.

LADY BRACKNELL   [*makes a note in her book*] In land, or in investments?

JACK   In investments, chiefly.

LADY BRACKNELL   That is satisfactory. What between the duties expected of one during one's lifetime, and the duties exacted from one after one's death, land has ceased to be either a profit or a pleasure. It gives one position, and prevents one from keeping it up. That's all that can be said about land.

JACK   I have a country house with some land, of course, attached to it, about fifteen hundred acres, I believe; but I don't depend on that for my real income. In fact, as far as I can make out, the poachers are the only people who make anything out of it.

LADY BRACKNELL   A country house! How many bedrooms? Well, that point can be cleared up afterwards. You have a town house, I hope? A girl with a simple, unspoiled nature, like Gwendolen, could hardly be expected to reside in the country.

JACK   Well, I own a house in Belgrave Square, but it is let by the year to Lady Bloxham. Of course, I can get it back whenever I like, at six months' notice.

LADY BRACKNELL   Lady Bloxham? I don't know her.

JACK   Oh, she goes about very little. She is a lady considerably advanced in years.

LADY BRACKNELL   Ah, nowadays that is no guarantee of respectability of character. What number in Belgrave Square?

JACK   149.

LADY BRACKNELL   [*shaking her head*] The unfashionable side. I thought there was something. However, that could easily be altered.

JACK   Do you mean the fashion, or the side?

LADY BRACKNELL   [*sternly*] Both, if necessary, I presume. What are your politics?

JACK   Well, I am afraid I really have none. I am a Liberal Unionist.

LADY BRACKNELL   Oh, they count as Tories. They dine with us. Or come in the evening, at any rate. Now to minor matters. Are your parents living?

JACK   I have lost both my parents.

LADY BRACKNELL   To lose one parent, Mr. Worthing, may be regarded as a misfortune; to lose both looks like carelessness. Who was your father? He was evidently a man of some wealth. Was he born in what the Radical papers call the purple of commerce, or did he rise from the ranks of the aristocracy?

JACK   I am afraid I really don't know. The fact is, Lady Bracknell, I said I had lost my parents. It would be nearer to truth to say that my parents seem to have lost me. . . . I don't actually know who I am by birth. I was . . . well, I was found.

LADY BRACKNELL   Found!

JACK   The late Mr. Thomas Cardew, an old gentlemen of a very charitable and kindly disposition, found me and gave me the name of Worthing, because he happened to have a first-class ticket for Worthing in his pocket at the time. Worthing is a place in Sussex. It is a seaside resort.

LADY BRACKNELL   Where did the charitable gentleman who had a first-class ticket for this seaside resort find you?

JACK   [*gravely*] In a handbag.

LADY BRACKNELL   A handbag?

JACK   [*very seriously*] Yes, Lady Bracknell. I was in a handbag—a somewhat large, black leather handbag, with handles on it — an ordinary handbag in fact.

LADY BRACKNELL   In what locality did this Mr. James, or Thomas, Cardew come across this ordinary handbag?

JACK   In the cloakroom at Victoria Station. It was given to him in mistake for his own.

LADY BRACKNELL   The cloakroom at Victoria Station?

JACK   Yes. The Brighton line.

LADY BRACKNELL   The line is immaterial. Mr. Worthing, I confess I feel somewhat bewildered by what you have just told me. To be born, or at any rate bred, in a handbag, whether it had handles or not, seems to me to display a contempt for the ordinary decencies of family life that reminds one of the worst excesses of the French Revolution. And I presume you know what that unfortunate movement lead to? As for the particular locality in which the handbag was found, a cloakroom at a railway station might serve to conceal a social indiscretion—has probably, indeed, been used for that purpose before now—but it could hardly be regarded as an assured basis for a recognized position in good society.

JACK   May I ask you then what you would advise me to do? I need hardly say I would do anything in the world to ensure Gwendolen's happiness.

LADY BRACKNELL   I would strongly advise you, Mr. Worthing, to try and acquire some relations as soon as possible, and to make a definite effort to produce at any rate one parent, of either sex, before the season is quite over.

JACK   Well, I don't see how I could possibly manage to do that. I can produce the handbag at any moment. It is in my dressing room at home. I really think that should satisfy you, Lady Bracknell.

LADY BRACKNELL   Me, sir! What has it to do with me? You can hardly imagine that I and Lord Bracknell would dream of allowing our only daughter—a girl brought up with the utmost care—to marry into a cloakroom, and form an alliance with a parcel. Good morning, Mr. Worthing!

[*Lady Bracknell sweeps out in majestic indignation.*]

JACK   Good morning! [*Algernon, from the other room, strikes up the Wedding March. Jack looks perfectly furious, and goes to the door.*] For goodness' sake don't play that ghastly tune, Algy! How idiotic you are!

The music stops and Algernon enters cheerily.

ALGERNON   Didn't it go off all right, old boy? You don't mean to say Gwendolen refused you? I know it is a way she has. She is always refusing people. I think it is most ill-natured of her.

JACK   Oh, Gwendolen is as right as a trivet. As far as she is concerned, we are engaged. Her mother is perfectly unbearable. Never met such a Gorgon. . . . I don't really know what a Gorgon is like, but I am quite sure that Lady Bracknell is one. In any case, she is a monster, without being a myth, which is rather unfair. . . . I beg your pardon, Algy, I suppose I shouldn't talk about your own aunt in that way before you.

ALGERNON   My dear boy, I love hearing my relations abused. It is the only thing that makes me put up with them at all. Relations are simply a tedious pack of people who haven't got the remotest knowledge of how to live, or the smallest instinct about when to die.

JACK   Oh, that is nonsense!

ALGERNON   It isn't!

JACK   Well, I won't argue about the matter. You always want to argue about things.

ALGERNON   That is exactly what things were originally made for.

JACK   Upon my word, if I thought that, I'd shoot myself. . . . [A pause.] You don't think there is any chance of Gwendolen becoming like her mother in about a hundred and fifty years, do you, Algy?

ALGERNON   All women become like their mothers. That is their tragedy. No man does. That's his.

JACK   Is that clever?

ALGERNON   It is perfectly phrased! and quite as true as any observation in civilized life should be.

JACK   I am sick to death of cleverness. Everybody is clever nowadays. You can't go anywhere without meeting clever people. The thing has become an absolute public nuisance. I wish to goodness we had a few fools left.

ALGERNON   We have.

JACK   I should extremely like to meet them. What do they talk about?

ALGERNON   The fools? Oh! about the clever people, of course.

JACK   What fools.

ALGERNON   By the way, did you tell Gwendolen the truth about your being Ernest in town, and Jack in the country?

JACK   [in a very patronizing manner] My dear fellow, the truth isn't quite the sort of thing one tells to a nice, sweet, refined girl. What extraordinary ideas you have about the way to behave to a woman!

ALGERNON   The only way to behave to a woman is to make love to her, if she is pretty, and to someone else, if she is plain.

JACK   Oh, that is nonsense.

ALGERNON   What about your brother? What about the profligate Ernest?

JACK   Oh, before the end of the week I shall have got rid of him. I'll say he died in Paris of apoplexy. Lots of people die of apoplexy, quite suddenly, don't they?

ALGERNON   Yes, but it's hereditary, my dear fellow. It's a sort of thing that runs in families. You had much better say a severe chill.

JACK   You are sure a severe chill isn't hereditary, or anything of that kind?

ALGERNON   Of course it isn't!

JACK   Very well, then. My poor brother Ernest is carried off suddenly, in Paris, by a severe chill. That gets rid of him.

ALGERNON   But I thought you said that . . . Miss Cardew was a little too much interested in your poor brother Ernest? Won't she feel his loss a great deal?

JACK   Oh, that is all right. Cecily is not a silly romantic girl, I am glad to say. She has got a capital appetite, goes on long walks, and pays no attention at all to her lessons.

ALGERNON   I would rather like to see Cecily.

JACK   I will take very good care you never do. She is excessively pretty, and she is only just eighteen.

ALGERNON   Have you told Gwendolen yet that you have an excessively pretty ward who is only just eighteen?

JACK   Oh! one doesn't blurt these things out to people. Cecily and Gwendolen are perfectly certain to be extremely great friends. I'll bet you anything you like that half an hour after they have met, they will be calling each other sister.

ALGERNON   Women only do that when they have called each other a lot of other things first. Now, my dear boy, if we want to get a good table at Willis's, we really must go and dress. Do you know it is nearly seven?

JACK   [irritably] Oh! it always is nearly seven.

ALGERNON   Well, I'm hungry.

JACK   I never knew you when you weren't. . . .

ALGERNON   What shall we do after dinner? Go to a theater?

JACK   Oh no! I loathe listening.

ALGERNON   Well, let us go to the Club?

JACK   Oh, no! I loathe talking.

ALGERNON   Well, we might trot round to the Empire at ten?

JACK   Oh, no! I can't bear looking at things. It is so silly.

ALGERNON   Well, what shall we do?

JACK   Nothing!

ALGERNON   It is awfully hard work doing nothing. However, I don't mind hard work where there is no definite object of any kind.

Enter Lane.

LANE   Miss Fairfax.

Enter Gwendolen. Lane goes out.

ALGERNON   Gwendolen, upon my word!

GWENDOLEN   Algy, kindly turn your back. I have something very particular to say to Mr. Worthing.

ALGERNON   Really, Gwendolen, I don't think I can allow this at all.

GWENDOLEN   Algy, you always adopt a strictly immoral attitude towards life. You are not quite old enough to do that. [*Algernon retires to the fireplace.*]

JACK   My own darling!

GWENDOLEN   Ernest, we may never be married. From the expression on mamma's face I fear we never shall. Few parents nowadays pay any regard to what their children say to them. The old-fashioned respect for the young is fast dying out. Whatever influence I ever had over mamma, I lost at the age of three. But although she may prevent us from becoming man and wife, and I may marry someone else, and marry often, nothing that she can possibly do can alter my eternal devotion to you.

JACK   Dear Gwendolen!

GWENDOLEN   The story of your romantic origin, as related to me by mamma, with unpleasing comments, has naturally stirred the deeper fibers of my nature. Your Christian name has an irresistible fascination. The simplicity of your character makes you exquisitely incomprehensible to me. Your town address at the Albany I have. What is your address in the country?

JACK   The Manor House, Woolton, Hertfordshire.

Algernon, who has been carefully listening, smiles to himself, and writes the address on his shirt cuff. Then picks up the Railway Guide.

GWENDOLEN   There is a good postal service, I suppose? It may be necessary to do something desperate. That of course will require serious consideration. I will communicate with you daily.

JACK   My own one!

GWENDOLEN   How long do you remain in town?

JACK   Till Monday.

GWENDOLEN   Good! Algy, you may turn round now.

ALGERNON   Thanks, I've turned round already.

GWENDOLEN   You may also ring the bell.

JACK   You will let me see you to your carriage, my own darling?

GWENDOLEN   Certainly.

JACK   [*to Lane, who now enters*] I will see Miss Fairfax out.

LANE   Yes, sir. [*Jack and Gwendolen go off.*]

Lane presents several letters on a salver to Algernon. It is to be surmised that they are bills, as Algernon, after looking at the envelopes, tears them up.

ALGERNON   A glass of sherry, Lane.

LANE   Yes, sir.

ALGERNON   Tomorrow, Lane, I'm going Bunburying.

LANE   Yes, sir.

ALGERNON   I shall probably not be back till Monday. You can put up my dress clothes, my smoking jacket, and all the Bunbury suits . . .

LANE   Yes, sir. [*Handing sherry.*]

ALGERNON   I hope tomorrow will be a fine day, Lane.

LANE   It never is, sir.

ALGERNON   Lane, you're a perfect pessimist.

LANE   I do my best to give satisfaction, sir.

Enter Jack. Lane goes off.

JACK   There's a sensible, intelligent girl! the only girl I ever cared for in my life. [*Algernon is laughing immoderately.*] What on earth are you so amused at?

ALGERNON   Oh, I'm a little anxious about poor Bunbury, that is all.

JACK   If you don't take care, your friend Bunbury will get you into a serious scrape some day.

ALGERNON   I love scrapes. They are the only things that are never serious.

JACK   Oh, that's nonsense, Algy. You never talk anything but nonsense.

ALGERNON   Nobody ever does.

Jack looks indignantly at him, and leaves the room. Algernon lights a cigarette, reads his shirt-cuff, and smiles.

Act Drop

ACT II

Garden at the Manor House. A flight of gray stone steps leads up to the house. The garden, an old-fashioned one, full of roses. Time of year, July. Basket chairs, and a table covered with books, are set under a large yew tree.

Miss Prism discovered seated at the table. Cecily is at the back, watering flowers.

MISS PRISM [*calling*] Cecily, Cecily! Surely such a utilitarian occupation as the watering of flowers is rather Moulton's duty than yours? Especially at a moment when intellectual pleasures await you. Your German grammar is on the table. Pray open it at page fifteen. We will repeat yesterday's lesson.

CECILY [*coming over very slowly*] But I don't like German. It isn't at all a becoming language. I know perfectly well that I look quite plain after my German lesson.

MISS PRISM Child, you know how anxious your guardian is that you should improve yourself in every way. He laid particular stress on your German, as he was leaving for town yesterday. Indeed, he always lays stress on your German when he is leaving for town.

CECILY Dear Uncle Jack is so very serious! Sometimes he is so serious that I think he cannot be quite well.

MISS PRISM [*drawing herself up*] Your guardian enjoys the best of health, and his gravity of demeanor is especially to be commended in one so comparatively young as he is. I know no one who has a higher sense of duty and responsibility.

CECILY I suppose that is why he often looks a little bored when we three are together.

MISS PRISM Cecily! I am surprised at you. Mr. Worthing has many troubles in his life. Idle merriment and triviality would be out of place in his conversation. You must remember his constant anxiety about that unfortunate young man his brother.

CECILY I wish Uncle Jack would allow that unfortunate young man, his brother, to come down here sometimes. We might have a good influence over him, Miss Prism. I am sure you certainly would. You know German, and geology, and things of that kind influence a man very much. [*Cecily begins to write in her diary.*]

MISS PRISM [*shaking her head*] I do not think that even I could produce any effect on a character that according to his own brother's admission is irretrievably weak and vacillating. Indeed I am not sure that I would desire to reclaim him. I am not in favor of this modern mania for turning bad people into good people at a moment's notice. As a man sows so let him reap. You must put away your diary, Cecily. I really don't see why you should keep a diary at all.

CECILY I keep a diary in order to enter the wonderful secrets of my life. If I didn't write them down, I should probably forget all about them.

MISS PRISM Memory, my dear Cecily, is the diary that we all carry about with us.

CECILY Yes, but it usually chronicles the things that have never happened, and couldn't possibly have happened. I believe that Memory is responsible for nearly all the three-volume novels that Mudie sends us.

MISS PRISM   Do not speak slightingly of the three-volume novel, Cecily. I wrote one myself in earlier days.

CECILY   Did you really, Miss Prism? How wonderfully clever you are! I hope it did not end happily? I don't like novels that end happily. They depress me so much.

MISS PRISM   The good ended happily, and the bad unhappily. That is what Fiction means.

CECILY   I suppose so. But it seems very unfair. And was your novel ever published?

MISS PRISM   Alas, no. The manuscript unfortunately was abandoned. [*Cecily starts.*] I used the word in the sense of lost or mislaid. To your work, child, these speculations are profitless.

CECILY   [*smiling*] But I see dear Dr. Chasuble coming up through the garden.

MISS PRISM   [*rising and advancing*] Dr. Chasuble! This is indeed a pleasure.

Enter Canon Chasuble.

CHASUBLE   And how are we this morning? Miss Prism, you are, I trust, well?

CECILY   Miss Prism has just been complaining of a slight headache. I think it would do her so much good to have a short stroll with you in the Park, Dr. Chasuble.

MISS PRISM   Cecily, I have not mentioned anything about a headache.

CECILY   No, dear Miss Prism, I know that, but I felt instinctively that you had a headache. Indeed I was thinking about that, and not about my German lesson, when the Rector came in.

CHASUBLE   I hope, Cecily, you are not inattentive.

CECILY   Oh, I am afraid I am.

CHASUBLE   That is strange. Were I fortunate enough to be Miss Prism's pupil, I would hang upon her lips. [*Miss Prism glares.*] I spoke metaphorically.—My metaphor was drawn from bees. Ahem! Mr. Worthing, I suppose, has not returned from town yet?

MISS PRISM   We do not expect him till Monday afternoon. He is not one of those whose sole aim is enjoyment, as, by all accounts, that unfortunate young man his brother seems to be. But I must not disturb Egeria and her pupil any longer.

MISS PRISM   Egeria? My name is Laetitia, Doctor.

CHASUBLE   [*bowing*] A classical allusion merely, drawn from the Pagan authors. I shall see you both no doubt at Evensong?

MISS PRISM   I think, dear Doctor, I will have a stroll with you. I find I
   have a headache after all, and a walk might do it good.
CHASUBLE   With pleasure, Miss Prism, with pleasure. We might go as
   far as the schools and back.
MISS PRISM   That would be delightful. Cecily, you will read your Political Economy in my absence. The chapter on the Fall of the Rupee
   you may omit. It is somewhat too sensational. Even these metallic
   problems have their melodramatic side. [*Goes down the garden with
   Dr. Chasuble.*]
CECILY   [*picks up books and throws them back on table*] Horrid Political
   Economy! Horrid Geography! Horrid, horrid German!

Enter Merriman with a card on a salver.

MERRIMAN   Mr. Ernest Worthing has just driven over from the station.
   He has brought his luggage with him.
CECILY   [*takes the card and reads it*] "Mr. Ernest Worthing, B.4, The
   Albany, W." Uncle Jack's brother! Did you tell him Mr. Worthing
   was in town?
MERRIMAN   Yes, Miss. He seemed very much disappointed. I men-
   tioned that you and Miss Prism were in the garden. He said he
   was anxious to speak to you privately for a moment.
CECILY   Ask Mr. Ernest Worthing to come here. I suppose you had
   better talk to the housekeeper about a room for him.
MERRIMAN   Yes, Miss. [*Merriman goes off.*]
CECILY   I have never met any really wicked person before. I feel rather
   frightened. I am so afraid he will look just like everyone else.

Enter Algernon, very gay and debonair.

   He does!

ALGERNON   [*raising his hat*] You are my little cousin Cecily, I'm sure.
CECILY   You are under some strange mistake. I am not little. In fact, I
   believe I am more than usually tall for my age. [*Algernon is rather
   taken aback.*] But I am your cousin Cecily. You, I see from your
   card, are Uncle Jack's brother, my cousin Ernest, my wicked cousin
   Ernest.
ALGERNON   Oh! I am not really wicked at all, Cousin Cecily. You
   mustn't think that I am wicked.
CECILY   If you are not, then you have certainly been deceiving us all
   in a very inexcusable manner. I hope you have not been leading
   a double life, pretending to be wicked and being really good all
   the time. That would be hypocrisy.

ALGERNON [*looks at her in amazement*] Oh! Of course I have been rather reckless.

CECILY I am glad to hear it.

ALGERNON In fact, now you mention the subject, I have been very bad in my own small way.

CECILY I don't think you should be so proud of that, though I am sure it must have been very pleasant.

ALGERNON It is much pleasanter being here with you.

CECILY I can't understand how you are here at all. Uncle Jack won't be back till Monday afternoon.

ALGERNON That is a great disappointment. I am obliged to go up by the first train on Monday morning. I have a business appointment that I am anxious . . . to miss!

CECILY Couldn't you miss it anywhere but in London?

ALGERNON No: the appointment is in London.

CECILY Well, I know, of course, how important it is not to keep a business engagement, if one wants to retain any sense of the beauty of life, but still I think you had better wait till Uncle Jack arrives. I know he wants to speak to you about your emigrating.

ALGERNON About my what?

CECILY Your emigrating. He has gone up to buy your outfit.

ALGERNON I certainly wouldn't let Jack buy my outfit. He has no taste in neckties at all.

CECILY I don't think you will require neckties. Uncle Jack is sending you to Australia.

ALGERNON Australia! I'd sooner die.

CECILY Well, he said at dinner on Wednesday night, that you would have to choose between this world, the next world, and Australia.

ALGERNON Oh, well! The accounts I have received of Australia and the next world are not particularly encouraging. This world is good enough for me, Cousin Cecily.

CECILY Yes, but are you good enough for it?

ALGERNON I'm afraid I'm not that. That is why I want you to reform me. You might make that your mission, if you don't mind, Cousin Cecily.

CECILY I'm afraid I've no time, this afternoon.

ALGERNON Well, would you mind my reforming myself this afternoon?

CECILY It is rather Quixotic of you. But I think you should try.

ALGERNON I will. I feel better already.

CECILY You are looking a little worse.

ALGERNON That is because I am hungry.

CECILY How thoughtless of me. I should have remembered that when one is going to lead an entirely new life, one requires regular and wholesome meals. Won't you come in?

ALGERNON   Thank you. Might I have a buttonhole first? I never have any appetite unless I have a buttonhole first.

CECILY   A Maréchal Niel? [*Picks up scissors.*]

ALGERNON   No, I'd sooner have a pink rose.

CECILY   Why? [*Cuts a flower.*]

ALGERNON   Because you are like a pink rose, Cousin Cecily.

CECILY   I don't think it can be right for you to talk to me like that. Miss Prism never says such things to me.

ALGERNON   Then Miss Prism is a shortsighted old lady. [*Cecily puts the rose in his buttonhole.*] You are the prettiest girl I ever saw.

CECILY   Miss Prism says that all good looks are a snare.

ALGERNON   They are the snare that every sensible man would like to be caught in.

CECILY   Oh, I don't think I would care to catch a sensible man. I shouldn't know what to talk to him about.

They pass into the house. Miss Prism and Dr. Chasuble return.

MISS PRISM   You are too much alone, dear Dr. Chasuble. You should get married. A misanthrope I can understand—a womanthrope, never!

CHASUBLE   [*with a scholar's shudder*] Believe me, I do not deserve so neologistic a phrase. The precept as well as the practice of the Primitive Church was distinctly against matrimony.

MISS PRISM   [*sententiously*] That is obviously the reason why the Primitive Church has not lasted up to the present day. And you do not seem to realize, dear Doctor, that by persistently remaining single, a man converts himself into a permanent public temptation. Men should be more careful; this very celibacy leads weaker vessels astray.

CHASUBLE   But is a man not equally attractive when married?

MISS PRISM   No married man is ever attractive except to his wife.

CHASUBLE   And often, I've been told, not even to her.

MISS PRISM   That depends on the intellectual sympathies of the woman. Maturity can always be depended on. Ripeness can be trusted. Young women are green. [*Dr. Chasuble starts.*] I spoke horticulturally. My metaphor was drawn from fruits. But where is Cecily?

CHASUBLE   Perhaps she followed us to the schools.

Enter Jack slowly from the back of the garden. He is dressed in the deepest mourning, with crepe hatband and black gloves.

MISS PRISM   Mr. Worthing!

CHASUBLE   Mr. Worthing?

MISS PRISM   This is indeed a surprise. We did not look for you till Monday afternoon.

JACK   [*shakes Miss Prism's hand in a tragic manner*] I have returned sooner than I expected. Dr. Chasuble, I hope you are well?

CHASUBLE   Dear Mr. Worthing, I trust this garb of woe does not betoken some terrible calamity?

JACK   My brother.

MISS PRISM   More shameful debts and extravagance?

CHASUBLE   Still leading his life of pleasure?

JACK   [*shaking his head*] Dead!

CHASUBLE   Your brother Ernest dead?

JACK   Quite dead.

MISS PRISM   What a lesson for him! I trust he will profit by it.

CHASUBLE   Mr. Worthing, I offer you my sincere condolence. You have at least the consolation of knowing that you were always the most generous and forgiving of brothers.

JACK   Poor Ernest! He had many faults, but it is a sad, sad blow.

CHASUBLE   Very sad indeed. Were you with him at the end?

JACK   No. He died abroad; in Paris, in fact. I had a telegram last night from the manager of the Grand Hotel.

CHASUBLE   Was the cause of death mentioned?

JACK   A severe chill, it seems.

MISS PRISM   As a man sows, so shall he reap.

CHASUBLE   [*raising his hand*] Charity, dear Miss Prism, charity! None of us are perfect. I myself am peculiarly susceptible to draughts. Will the interment take place here?

JACK   No. He seems to have expressed a desire to be buried in Paris.

CHASUBLE   In Paris! [*Shakes his head.*] I fear that hardly points to any very serious state of mind at the last. You would no doubt wish me to make some slight allusion to this tragic domestic affliction next Sunday. [*Jack presses his hand convulsively.*] My sermon on the meaning of the manna in the wilderness can be adapted to almost any occasion, joyful, or, as in the present case, distressing. [*All sigh.*] I have preached it at harvest celebrations, christenings, confirmations, on days of humiliation and festal days. The last time I delivered it was in the Cathedral, as a charity sermon on behalf of the Society for the Prevention of Discontent among the Upper Orders. The Bishop, who was present, was much struck by some of the analogies I drew.

JACK   Ah! that reminds me, you mentioned christenings I think, Dr. Chasuble? I suppose you know how to christen all right? [*Dr. Chasuble looks astounded.*] I mean, of course, you are continually christening, aren't you?

MISS PRISM   It is, I regret to say, one of the Rector's most constant duties in this parish. I have often spoken to the poorer classes on the subject. But they don't seem to know what thrift is.

CHASUBLE   But is there any particular infant in whom you are interested, Mr. Worthing? Your brother was, I believe, unmarried, was he not?

JACK   Oh, yes.

MISS PRISM   [*bitterly*] People who live entirely for pleasure usually are.

JACK   But it is not for any child, dear Doctor. I am very fond of children. No! the fact is, I would like to be christened myself, this afternoon, if you have nothing better to do.

CHASUBLE   But surely, Mr. Worthing, you have been christened already?

JACK   I don't remember anything about it.

CHASUBLE   But have you any grave doubts on the subject?

JACK   I certainly intend to have. Of course I don't know if the thing would bother you in any way, or if you think I am a little too old now.

CHASUBLE   Not at all. The sprinkling, and, indeed, the immersion of adults is a perfectly canonical practice.

JACK   Immersion!

CHASUBLE   You need have no apprehensions. Sprinkling is all that is necessary, or indeed I think advisable. Our weather is so changeable. At what hour would you wish the ceremony performed?

JACK   Oh, I might trot round about five if that would suit you.

CHASUBLE   Perfectly, perfectly! In fact I have two similar ceremonies to perform at that time. A case of twins that occurred recently in one of the outlying cottages on your own estate. Poor Jenkins the carter, a most hard-working man.

JACK   Oh! I don't see much fun in being christened along with other babies. It would be childish. Would half-past five do?

CHASUBLE   Admirably! Admirably! [*Takes out watch.*] And now, dear Mr. Worthing, I will not intrude any longer into a house of sorrow. I would merely beg you not to be too much bowed down by grief. What seem to us bitter trials are often blessings in disguise.

MISS PRISM   This seems to be a blessing of an extremely obvious kind.

Enter Cecily from the house.

CECILY   Uncle Jack! Oh, I am pleased to see you back. But what horrid clothes you have got on. Do go and change them.

MISS PRISM   Cecily!

CHASUBLE   My child! My child! [*Cecily goes toward Jack; he kisses her brow in a melancholy manner.*]

CECILY   What is the matter, Uncle Jack? Do look happy! You look as if you had toothache, and I have got such a surprise for you. Who do you think is in the dining room? Your brother!

JACK   Who?

CECILY   Your brother Ernest. He arrived about half an hour ago.

JACK   What nonsense! I haven't got a brother.

CECILY   Oh, don't say that. However badly he may have behaved to you in the past he is still your brother. You couldn't be so heartless as to disown him. I'll tell him to come out. And you will shake hands with him, won't you, Uncle Jack? [*Runs back into the house.*]

CHASUBLE   These are very joyful tidings.

MISS PRISM   After we had all been resigned to his loss, his sudden return seems to me peculiarly distressing.

JACK   My brother is in the dining room? I don't know what it all means. I think it is perfectly absurd.

Enter Algernon and Cecily hand in hand. They come slowly up to Jack.

JACK   Good heavens! [*Motions Algernon away.*]

ALGERNON   Brother John, I have come down from town to tell you that I am very sorry for all the trouble I have given you, and that I intend to lead a better life in the future. [*Jack glares at him and does not take his hand.*]

CECILY   Uncle Jack, you are not going to refuse your own brother's hand?

JACK   Nothing will induce me to take his hand. I think his coming down here disgraceful. He knows perfectly well why.

CECILY   Uncle Jack, do be nice. There is some good in everyone. Ernest has just been telling me about his poor invalid friend Mr. Bunbury whom he goes to visit so often. And surely there must be much good in one who is kind to an invalid and leaves the pleasures of London to sit by a bed of pain.

JACK   Oh! he has been talking about Bunbury, has he?

CECILY   Yes, he has told me about poor Mr. Bunbury, and his terrible state of health.

JACK   Bunbury! Well, I won't have him talk to you about Bunbury or about anything else. It is enough to drive one perfectly frantic.

ALGERNON   Of course I admit that the faults were all on my side. But I must say that I think that Brother John's coldness to me is peculiarly painful. I expected a more enthusiastic welcome, especially considering it is the first time I have come here.

CECILY   Uncle Jack, if you don't shake hands with Ernest I will never forgive you.

JACK   Never forgive me?

CECILY   Never, never, never!

JACK   Well, this is the last time I shall ever do it. [*Shakes hand with Algernon and glares.*]

CHASUBLE   It's pleasant, is it not, to see so perfect a reconciliation? I think we might leave the two brothers together.

MISS PRISM   Cecily, you will come with us.

CECILY   Certainly, Miss Prism. My little task of reconciliation is over.

CHASUBLE   You have done a beautiful action today, dear child.

MISS PRISM   We must not be premature in our judgments.

CECILY   I feel very happy. [*They all go off except Jack and Algernon.*]

JACK   You young scoundrel, Algy, you must get out of this place as soon as possible. I don't allow Bunburying here.

Enter Merriman.

MERRIMAN   I have put Mr. Ernest's things in the room next to yours, sir. I suppose that is all right?

JACK   What?

MERRIMAN   Mr. Ernest's luggage, sir. I have unpacked it and put it in the room next to your own.

JACK   His luggage?

MERRIMAN   Yes, sir. Three portmanteaus, a dressing case, two hat-boxes, and a large luncheon basket.

ALGERNON   I am afraid I can't stay more than a week this time.

JACK   Merriman, order the dogcart at once. Mr. Ernest has been suddenly called back to town.

MERRIMAN   Yes, sir. [*Goes back into the house.*]

ALGERNON   What a fearful liar you are, Jack. I have not been called back to town at all.

JACK   Yes, you have.

ALGERNON   I haven't heard anyone call me.

JACK   Your duty as a gentleman calls you back.

ALGERNON   My duty as a gentleman has never interfered with my pleasures in the smallest degree.

JACK   I can quite understand that.

ALGERNON   Well, Cecily is a darling.

JACK   You are not to talk of Miss Cardew like that. I don't like it.

ALGERNON   Well, I don't like your clothes. You look perfectly ridiculous in them. Why on earth don't you go up and change? It is perfectly childish to be in deep mourning for a man who is actually staying for a whole week with you in your house as a guest. I call it grotesque.

JACK   You are certainly not staying with me for a whole week as a guest or anything else. You have got to leave . . . by the four-five train.

ALGERNON   I certainly won't leave you so long as you are in mourning. It would be most unfriendly. If I were in mourning you would stay with me, I suppose. I should think it very unkind if you didn't.

JACK   Well, will you go if I change my clothes?

ALGERNON   Yes, if you are not too long. I never saw anybody take so long to dress, and with such little result.

JACK   Well, at any rate, that is better than being always overdressed as you are.

ALGERNON   If I am occasionally a little overdressed, I make up for it by being always immensely over-educated.

JACK   Your vanity is ridiculous, your conduct an outrage, and your presence in my garden utterly absurd. However, you have got to catch the four-five, and I hope you will have a pleasant journey back to town. This Bunburying, as you call it, has not been a great success for you. [*Goes into the house.*]

ALGERNON   I think it has been a great success. I'm in love with Cecily, and that is everything.

Enter Cecily at the back of the garden. She picks up the can and begins to water the flowers.

But I must see her before I go, and make arrangements for another Bunbury. Ah, there she is.

CECILY   Oh, I merely came back to water the roses. I thought you were with Uncle Jack.

ALGERNON   He's gone to order the dogcart for me.

CECILY   Oh, is he going to take you for a nice drive?

ALGERNON   He's going to send me away.

CECILY   Then have we got to part?

ALGERNON   I am afraid so. It's a very painful parting.

CECILY   It is always painful to part from people whom one has known for a very brief space of time. The absence of old friends one can endure with equanimity. But even a momentary separation from anyone to whom one has just been introduced is almost unbearable.

ALGERNON   Thank you.

Enter Merriman.

MERRIMAN   The dogcart is at the door, sir.

[*Algernon looks appealing at Cecily.*]

CECILY   It can wait, Merriman . . . for . . . five minutes.

MERRIMAN   Yes, miss.

Exit Merriman.

ALGERNON   I hope, Cecily, I shall not offend you if I state quite frankly and openly that you seem to me to be in every way the visible personification of absolute perfection.

CECILY   I think your frankness does you great credit, Ernest. If you will allow me, I will copy your remarks into my diary. [*Goes over to table and begins writing in diary.*]

ALGERNON   Do you really keep a diary? I'd give anything to look at it. May I?

CECILY   Oh no. [*Puts her hand over it.*] You see, it is simply a very young girl's record of her own thoughts and impressions, and consequently meant for publication. When it appears in volume form I hope you will order a copy. But pray, Ernest, don't stop. I delight in taking down from dictation. I have reached "absolute perfection." You can go on. I am quite ready for more.

ALGERNON   [*somewhat taken aback*] Ahem! Ahem!

CECILY   Oh, don't cough, Ernest. When one is dictating one should speak fluently and not cough. Besides, I don't know how to spell a cough. [*Writes as Algernon speaks.*]

ALGERNON   [*speaking very rapidly*] Cecily, ever since I first looked upon your wonderful and incomparable beauty, I have dared to love you wildly, passionately, devotedly, hopelessly.

CECILY   I don't think that you should tell me that you love me wildly, passionately, devotedly, hopelessly. Hopelessly doesn't seem to make much sense, does it?

ALGERNON   Cecily.

Enter Merriman.

MERRIMAN   The dogcart is waiting, sir.

ALGERNON   Tell it to come round next week, at the same hour.

MERRIMAN   [*looks at Cecily, who makes no sign*] Yes, sir.

Merriman retires.

CECILY   Uncle Jack would be very much annoyed if he knew you were staying on till next week, at the same hour.

ALGERNON   Oh, I don't care about Jack. I don't care for anybody in the whole world but you. I love you, Cecily. You will marry me, won't you?

CECILY   You silly boy! Of course. Why, we have been engaged for the last three months.

ALGERNON   For the last three months?

CECILY   Yes, it will be exactly three months on Thursday.

ALGERNON   But how did we become engaged?

CECILY   Well, ever since Uncle Jack first confessed to us that he had a younger brother who was very wicked and bad, you of course have formed the chief topic of conversation between myself and Miss Prism. And of course a man who is much talked about is always very attractive. One feels there must be something in him, after all. I daresay it was foolish of me, but I fell in love with you, Ernest.

ALGERNON   Darling. And when was the engagement actually settled?

CECILY   On the 14th of February last. Worn out by your entire ignorance of my existence, I determined to end the matter one way or the other, and after a long struggle with myself I accepted you under this dear old tree here. The next day I bought this little ring in your name, and this is the little bangle with the true lovers' knot I promised you always to wear.

ALGERNON   Did I give you this? It's very pretty, isn't it?

CECILY   Yes, you've wonderfully good taste, Ernest. It's the excuse I've always given for your leading such a bad life. And this is the box in which I keep all your dear letters. [Kneels at table, opens box, and produces letters tied up with blue ribbon.]

ALGERNON   My letters! But, my own sweet Cecily, I have never written you any letters.

CECILY   You need hardly remind me of that, Ernest. I remember only too well that I was forced to write your letters for you. I wrote always three times a week, and sometimes oftener.

ALGERNON   Oh, do let me read them, Cecily?

CECILY   Oh, I couldn't possibly. They would make you far too conceited. [Replaces box.] The three you wrote me after I had broken off the engagement are so beautiful, and so badly spelled, that even now I can hardly read them without crying a little.

ALGERNON   But was our engagement ever broken off?

CECILY   Of course it was. On the 22nd of last March. You can see the entry if you like. [Shows diary.] "Today I broke off my engagement with Ernest. I feel it is better to do so. The weather still continues charming."

ALGERNON   But why on earth did you break it off? What had I done? I had done nothing at all. Cecily, I am very much hurt indeed to hear you broke it off. Particularly when the weather was so charming.

CECILY   It would hardly have been a really serious engagement if it hadn't been broken off at least once. But I forgave you before the week was out.

ALGERNON   [crossing to her, and kneeling] What a perfect angel you are, Cecily.

CECILY   You dear romantic boy. [He kisses her, she puts her fingers through his hair.] I hope your hair curls naturally, does it?

ALGERNON   Yes, darling, with a little help from others.

CECILY   I am so glad.

ALGERNON   You'll never break off our engagement again, Cecily?

CECILY   I don't think I could break it off now that I have actually met you. Besides, of course, there is the question of your name.

ALGERNON   Of course. [*Nervously.*]

CECILY   You must not laugh at me, darling, but it had always been a girlish dream of mine to love someone whose name was Ernest. [*Algernon rises, Cecily also.*] There is something in that name that seems to inspire absolute confidence. I pity any poor married woman whose husband is not called Ernest.

ALGERNON   But, my dear child, do you mean to say you could not love me if I had some other name?

CECILY   But what name?

ALGERNON   Oh, any name you like — Algernon — for instance . . .

CECILY   But I don't like the name of Algernon.

ALGERNON   Well, my own dear, sweet, loving little darling, I really can't see why you should object to the name of Algernon. It is not at all a bad name. In fact, it is rather an aristocratic name. Half of the chaps who get into the Bankruptcy Court are called Algernon. But seriously, Cecily . . . [*moving to her*] if my name was Algy, couldn't you love me?

CECILY   [*rising*] I might respect you, Ernest, I might admire your character, but I fear that I should not be able to give you my undivided attention.

ALGERNON   Ahem! Cecily! [*Picking up hat.*] Your Rector here is, I suppose, thoroughly experienced in the practice of all the rites and ceremonials of the Church?

CECILY   Oh, yes. Dr. Chasuble is a most learned man. He has never written a single book, so you can imagine how much he knows.

ALGERNON   I must see him at once on a most important christening — I mean on most important business.

CECILY   Oh!

ALGERNON   I shan't be away more than half an hour.

CECILY   Considering that we have been engaged since February the 14th, and that I only met you today for the first time, I think it is rather hard that you should leave me for so long a period as half an hour. Couldn't you make it twenty minutes?

ALGERNON   I'll be back in no time. [*Kisses her and rushes down the garden.*]

CECILY   What an impetuous boy he is! I like his hair so much. I must enter his proposal in my dairy.

Enter Merriman.

MERRIMAN A Miss Fairfax just called to see Mr. Worthing. On very important business, Miss Fairfax states.

CECILY Isn't Mr. Worthing in his library?

MERRIMAN Mr. Worthing went over in the direction of the Rectory some time ago.

CECILY Pray ask the lady to come out here; Mr. Worthing is sure to be back soon. And you can bring tea.

MERRIMAN Yes, Miss. [*Goes out.*]

CECILY Miss Fairfax! I suppose one of the many good elderly women who are associated with Uncle Jack in some of his philanthropic work in London. I don't quite like women who are interested in philanthropic work. I think it is so forward of them.

Enter Merriman.

MERRIMAN Miss Fairfax.

Enter Gwendolen. Exit Merriman.

CECILY [*advancing to meet her*] Pray let me introduce myself to you. My name is Cecily Cardew.

GWENDOLEN Cecily Cardew? [*Moving to her and shaking hands.*] What a very sweet name! Something tells me that we are going to be great friends. I like you already more than I can say. My first impressions of people are never wrong.

CECILY How nice of you to like me so much after we have known each other such a comparatively short time. Pray sit down.

GWENDOLEN [*still standing up*] I may call you Cecily, may I not?

CECILY With pleasure!

GWENDOLEN And you will always call me Gwendolen, won't you?

CECILY If you wish.

GWENDOLEN Then that is all quite settled, is it not?

CECILY I hope so. [*A pause. They both sit down together.*]

GWENDOLEN Perhaps this might be a favorable opportunity for my mentioning who I am. My father is Lord Bracknell. You have never heard of Papa, I suppose?

CECILY I don't think so.

GWENDOLEN Outside the family circle, Papa, I am glad to say, is entirely unknown. I think that is quite as it should be. The home seems to me to be the proper sphere for the man. And certainly once a man begins to neglect his domestic duties he becomes painfully effeminate, does he not? And I don't like that. It makes men so very attractive. Cecily, mamma, whose views on education are remarkably strict, has brought me up to be extremely shortsighted; it is part of her system; so do you mind my looking at you through my glasses?

CECILY   Oh! not at all, Gwendolen. I am very fond of being looked at.

GWENDOLEN   [*after examining Cecily carefully through a lorgnette*] You are here on a short visit, I suppose.

CECILY   Oh no! I live here.

GWENDOLEN   [*severely*] Really? Your mother, no doubt, or some female relative of advanced years, resides here also?

CECILY   Oh no! I have no mother, nor, in fact, any relations.

GWENDOLEN   Indeed?

CECILY   My dear guardian, with the assistance of Miss Prism, has the arduous task of looking after me.

GWENDOLEN   Your guardian?

CECILY   Yes, I am Mr. Worthing's ward.

GWENDOLEN   Oh! It is strange he never mentioned to me that he had a ward. How secretive of him! He grows more interesting hourly. I am not sure, however, that the news inspires me with feelings of unmixed delight. [*Rising and going to her.*] I am very fond of you, Cecily; I have liked you ever since I met you! But I am bound to state that now that I know that you are Mr. Worthing's ward, I cannot help expressing a wish you were—well, just a little older than you seem to be—and not quite so very alluring in appearance. In fact, if I may speak candidly—

CECILY   Pray do! I think that whenever one has anything unpleasant to say, one should always be quite candid!

GWENDOLEN   Well, to speak with perfect candor, Cecily, I wish that you were fully forty-two, and more than usually plain for your age. Ernest has a strong upright nature. He is the very soul of truth and honor. Disloyalty would be as impossible to him as deception. But even men of the noblest possible moral character are extremely susceptible to the influence of the physical charms of others. Modern, no less than Ancient History, supplies us with many most painful examples of what I refer to. If it were not so, indeed, History would be quite unreadable.

CECILY   I beg your pardon, Gwendolen, did you say Ernest?

GWENDOLEN   Yes.

CECILY   Oh, but it is not Mr. Ernest Worthing who is my guardian. It is his brother—his elder brother.

GWENDOLEN   [*sitting down again*] Ernest never mentioned to me that he had a brother.

CECILY   I am sorry to say they have not been on good terms for a long time.

GWENDOLEN   Ah! that accounts for it. And now that I think of it I have never heard any man mention his brother. The subject seems distasteful to most men. Cecily, you have lifted a load from my mind. I was growing almost anxious. It would have been terrible if any cloud had come across a friendship like ours, would it not? Of course you are quite, quite sure that it is not Mr. Ernest Worthing who is your guardian?

CECILY   Quite sure. [*A pause.*] In fact, I am going to be his.

GWENDOLEN   [*inquiringly*] I beg your pardon?

CECILY   [*rather shy and confidingly*] Dearest Gwendolen, there is no reason why I should make a secret of it to you. Our little country newspaper is sure to chronicle the fact next week. Mr. Ernest Worthing and I are engaged to be married.

GWENDOLEN   [*quite politely, rising*] My darling Cecily, I think there must be some slight error. Mr. Ernest Worthing is engaged to me. The announcement will appear in the *Morning Post* on Saturday at the latest.

CECILY   [*very politely, rising*] I am afraid you must be under some misconception. Ernest proposed to me exactly ten minutes ago. [*Shows diary.*]

GWENDOLEN   [*examines diary through her lorgnette carefully*] It is very curious, for he asked me to be his wife yesterday afternoon at 5:30. If you would care to verify the incident, pray do so. [*Produces diary of her own.*] I never travel without my diary. One should always have something sensational to read in the train. I am so sorry, dear Cecily, if it is any disappointment to you, but I am afraid I have the prior claim.

CECILY   It would distress me more than I can tell you, dear Gwendolen, if it caused you any mental or physical anguish, but I feel bound to point out that since Ernest proposed to you he clearly has changed his mind.

GWENDOLEN   [*meditatively*] If the poor fellow has been entrapped into any foolish promise I shall consider it my duty to rescue him at once, and with a firm hand.

CECILY   [*thoughtfully and sadly*] Whatever unfortunate entanglement my dear boy may have gotten into, I will never reproach him with it after we are married.

GWENDOLEN   Do you allude to me, Miss Cardew, as an entanglement? You are presumptuous. On an occasion of this kind it becomes more than a moral duty to speak one's mind. It becomes a pleasure.

CECILY   Do you suggest, Miss Fairfax, that I entrapped Ernest into an engagement? How dare you? This is no time for wearing the shallow mask of manners. When I see a spade I call it a spade.

GWENDOLEN   [*satirically*] I am glad to say that I have never seen a spade. It is obvious that our social spheres have been widely different.

Enter Merriman, followed by the footman. He carries a salver, tablecloth, and plate stand. Cecily is about to retort. The presence of the servants exercises a restraining influence, under which both girls chafe.

MERRIMAN   Shall I lay tea here as usual, Miss?

CECILY   [*sternly, in a calm voice*] Yes, as usual. [*Merriman begins to clear table and lay cloth. A long pause. Cecily and Gwendolen glare at each other.*]

GWENDOLEN   Are there many interesting walks in the vicinity, Miss Cardew?

CECILY   Oh! yes! a great many. From the top of one of the hills quite close one can see five counties.

GWENDOLEN   Five counties! I don't think I should like that; I hate crowds.

CECILY   [*sweetly*] I suppose that is why you live in town? [*Gwendolen bites her lip, and beats her foot nervously with her parasol.*]

GWENDOLEN   [*looking around*] Quite a well-kept garden this is, Miss Cardew.

CECILY   So glad you like it, Miss Fairfax.

GWENDOLEN   I had no idea there were any flowers in the country.

CECILY   Oh, flowers are as common here, Miss Fairfax, as people are in London.

GWENDOLEN   Personally I cannot understand how anybody manages to exist in the country, if anybody who is anybody does. The country always bores me to death.

CECILY   Ah! This is what the newspapers call agricultural depression, is it not? I believe the aristocracy are suffering very much from it just at present. It is almost an epidemic amongst them, I have been told. May I offer you some tea, Miss Fairfax?

GWENDOLEN   [*with elaborate politeness*] Thank you. [*Aside.*] Detestable girl! But I require tea!

CECILY   [*sweetly*] Sugar?

GWENDOLEN   [*superciliously*] No, thank you. Sugar is not fashionable any more. [*Cecily looks angrily at her, takes up the tongs and puts four lumps of sugar into the cup.*]

CECILY   [*severely*] Cake or bread and butter?

GWENDOLEN   [*in a bored manner*] Bread and butter, please. Cake is rarely seen at the best houses nowdays.

CECILY   [*cuts a very large slice of cake and puts it on the tray*] Hand that to Miss Fairfax.

Merriman does so, and goes out with footman. Gwendolen drinks the tea and makes a grimace. Puts down cup at once, reaches out her hand to the bread and butter, looks at it, and finds it is cake. Rises in indignation.

GWENDOLEN   You have filled my tea with lumps of sugar, and though I asked most distinctly for bread and butter, you have given me cake. I am known for the gentleness of my disposition, and the extraordinary sweetness of my nature, but I warn you, Miss Cardew, you may go too far.

CECILY   [*rising*] To save my poor, innocent, trusting boy from the machinations of any other girl there are no lengths to which I would not go.

GWENDOLEN   From the moment I saw you I distrusted you. I felt that you were false and deceitful. I am never deceived in such matters. My first impressions of people are invariably right.

CECILY   It seems to me, Miss Fairfax, that I am trespassing on your valuable time. No doubt you have many other calls of a similar character to make in the neighborhood.

Enter Jack.

GWENDOLEN   [*catches sight of him*] Ernest! My own Ernest!

JACK   Gwendolen! Darling! [*Offers to kiss her.*]

GWENDOLEN   [*drawing back*] A moment! May I ask if you are engaged to be married to this young lady? [*Points to Cecily.*]

JACK   [*laughing*] To dear little Cecily! Of course not! What could have put such an idea into your pretty little head?

GWENDOLEN   Thank you. You may! [*Offers her cheek.*]

CECILY   [*very sweetly*] I knew there must be some misunderstanding, Miss Fairfax. The gentleman whose arm is at present round your waist is my dear guardian, Mr. John Worthing.

GWENDOLEN   I beg your pardon?

CECILY   This is Uncle Jack.

GWENDOLEN   [*receding*] Jack! Oh!

Enter Algernon.

CECILY   Here is Ernest.

ALGERNON   [*goes straight over to Cecily without noticing anyone else*] My own love! [*Offers to kiss her.*]

CECILY   [*drawing back*] A moment, Ernest! May I ask you — are you engaged to be married to this young lady?

ALGERNON   [*looking round*] To what young lady? Good heavens! Gwendolen!

CECILY   Yes: to good heavens, Gwendolen, I mean to Gwendolen.

ALGERNON   [*laughing*] Of course not. What could have put such an idea into your pretty little head?

CECILY   Thank you. [*Presenting her cheek to be kissed.*] You may. [*Algernon kisses her.*]

GWENDOLEN   I felt there was some slight error, Miss Cardew. The gentleman who is now embracing you is my cousin, Mr. Algernon Moncrieff.

CECILY   [*breaking away from Algernon*] Algernon Moncrieff! Oh! [*The two girls move towards each other and put their arms round each other's waists as if for protection.*]

CECILY   Are you called Algernon?

ALGERNON   I cannot deny it.

GWENDOLEN   Is your name really John?

JACK   [*standing rather proudly*] I could deny it if I liked. I could deny anything if I liked. But my name certainly is John. It has been John for years.

CECILY   [*To Gwendolen*] A gross deception has been practiced on both of us.

GWENDOLEN   My poor wounded Cecily!

CECILY   My sweet wronged Gwendolen!

GWENDOLEN   [*slowly and seriously*] You will call me sister, will you not? [*They embrace. Jack and Algernon groan and walk up and down.*]

CECILY   [*rather brightly*] There is just one question I would like to be allowed to ask my guardian.

GWENDOLEN   An admirable idea! Mr. Worthing, there is just one question I would like to be permitted to put to you. Where is your brother Ernest? We are both engaged to be married to your brother Ernest, so it is a matter of some importance to us to know where your brother Ernest is at present.

JACK   [*slowly and hesitatingly*] Gwendolen — Cecily — it is very painful for me to be forced to speak the truth. It is the first time in my life that I have ever been reduced to such a painful position, and I am really quite inexperienced in doing anything of the kind. However, I will tell you quite frankly that I have no brother Ernest. I have no brother at all. I never had a brother in my life, and I certainly have not the smallest intention of ever having one in the future.

CECILY   [*surprised*] No brother at all?

JACK   [*cheerily*] None!

GWENDOLEN   [*severely*] Had you never a brother of any kind?

JACK   [*pleasantly*] Never. Not even of any kind.

GWENDOLEN   I am afraid it is quite clear, Cecily, that neither of us is engaged to be married to anyone.

CECILY   It is not a very pleasant position for a young girl suddenly to find herself in. Is it?

GWENDOLEN   Let us go into the house. They will hardly venture to come after us there.

CECILY   No, men are so cowardly, aren't they?

They return into the house with scornful looks.

JACK   This ghastly state of things is what you call Bunburying, I suppose?

ALGERNON   Yes, and a perfectly wonderful Bunbury it is. The most wonderful Bunbury I have ever had in my life.

JACK   Well, you've no right whatsoever to Bunbury here.

ALGERNON   That is absurd. One has a right to Bunbury anywhere one chooses. Every serious Bunburyist knows that.

JACK   Serious Bunburyists? Good heavens!

ALGERNON   Well, one must be serious about something, if one wants to have any amusement in life. I happen to be serious about Bunburying. What on earth you are serious about I haven't got the remotest idea. About everything, I should fancy. You have such an absolutely trivial nature.

JACK   Well, the only small satisfaction I have in the whole of this wretched business is that your friend Bunbury is quite exploded. You won't be able to run down to the country quite so often as you used to do, dear Algy. And a very good thing too.

ALGERNON   Your brother is a little off color, isn't he, dear Jack? You won't be able to disappear to London quite so frequently as your wicked custom was. And not a bad thing either.

JACK   As for your conduct towards Miss Cardew, I must say that your taking in a sweet, simple, innocent girl like that is quite inexcusable. To say nothing of the fact that she is my ward.

ALGERNON   I can see no possible defense at all for your deceiving a brilliant, clever, thoroughly experienced young lady like Miss Fairfax. To say nothing of the fact that she is my cousin.

JACK   I wanted to be engaged to Gwendolen, that is all. I love her.

ALGERNON   Well, I simply wanted to be engaged to Cecily. I adore her.

JACK   There is certainly no chance of your marrying Miss Cardew.

ALGERNON   I don't think there is much likelihood, Jack, of you and Miss Fairfax being united.

JACK   Well, that is no business of yours.

ALGERNON   If it was my business, I wouldn't talk about it. [*Begins to eat muffins.*] It is very vulgar to talk about one's business. Only people like stockbrokers do that, and then merely at dinner parties.

JACK   How you can sit there calmly eating muffins when we are in this horrible trouble, I can't make out. You seem to me to be perfectly heartless.

ALGERNON   Well, I can't eat muffins in an agitated manner. The butter would probably get on my cuffs. One should always eat muffins quite calmly. It is the only way to eat them.

JACK   I say it's perfectly heartless your eating muffins at all, under the circumstances.

ALGERNON   When I am in trouble, eating is the only thing that consoles me. Indeed, when I am in really great trouble, as any one who knows me intimately will tell you, I refuse everything except food and drink. At the present moment I am eating muffins because I am unhappy. Besides, I am particularly fond of muffins. [*Rising.*]

JACK   [*rising*] Well, there is no reason why you should eat them all in that greedy way. [*Takes muffins from Algernon.*]

ALGERNON   [*offering teacake*] I wish you would have teacake instead. I don't like teacake.

JACK   Good heavens! I suppose a man may eat his own muffins in his own garden.

ALGERNON   But you have just said it is perfectly heartless to eat muffins.

JACK   I said it was perfectly heartless of you, under the circumstances. That is a very different thing.

ALGERNON   That may be. But the muffins are the same. [*He seizes the muffin dish from Jack.*]

JACK   Algy, I wish to goodness you would go.

ALGERNON   You can't possibly ask me to go without having some dinner. It's absurd. I never go without my dinner. No one ever does, except vegetarians and people like that. Besides I have just made arrangements with Dr. Chasuble to be christened at a quarter to six under the name of Ernest.

JACK   My dear fellow, the sooner you give up that nonsense the better. I made arrangements this morning with Dr. Chasuble to be christened myself at 5:30, and I naturally will take the name of Ernest. Gwendolen would wish it. We can't both be christened Ernest. It's absurd. Besides, I have a perfect right to be christened if I like. There is no evidence that I have ever been christened by anybody. I should think it extremely probable I never was, and so does Dr. Chasuble. It is entirely different in your case. You have been christened already.

ALGERNON   Yes, but I have not been christened for years.

JACK   Yes, but you have been christened. That is the important thing.

ALGERNON   Quite so. So I know my constitution can stand it. If you are not quite sure about your ever having been christened, I must say I think it rather dangerous your venturing on it now. It might make you very unwell. You can hardly have forgotten that someone very closely connected with you was very nearly carried off this week in Paris by a severe chill.

JACK   Yes, but you said yourself that a severe chill was not hereditary.

ALGERNON   It usen't to be, I know—but I daresay it is now. Science is always making wonderful improvements in things.

JACK   [picking up the muffin dish] Oh, that is nonsense; you are always talking nonsense.

ALGERNON   Jack, you are at the muffins again! I wish you wouldn't. There are only two left. [Takes them.] I told you I was particularly fond of muffins.

JACK   But I hate teacake.

ALGERNON   Why on earth then do you allow teacake to be served up for your guests? What ideas you have of hospitality!

JACK   Algernon! I have already told you to go. I don't want you here. Why don't you go!

ALGERNON   I haven't quite finished my tea yet! and there is still one muffin left.

[Jack groans, and sinks into a chair. Algernon still continues eating.]

ACT III

Morning room at the Manor House. Gwendolen and Cecily are at the window, looking out into the garden.

GWENDOLEN   The fact that they did not follow us at once into the house, as any one else would have done, seems to me to show that they have some sense of shame left.

CECILY   They have been eating muffins. That looks like repentance.

GWENDOLEN   [after a pause] They don't seem to notice us at all. Couldn't you cough?

CECILY   But I haven't got a cough.

GWENDOLEN   They're looking at us. What effrontery!

CECILY   They're approaching. That's very forward of them.

GWENDOLEN   Let us preserve a dignified silence.

CECILY   Certainly. It's the only thing to do now.

Enter Jack followed by Algernon. They whistle some dreadful popular air from a British opera.

GWENDOLEN This dignified silence seems to produce an unpleasant effect.

CECILY A most distasteful one.

GWENDOLEN But we will not be the first to speak.

CECILY Certainly not.

GWENDOLEN Mr. Worthing, I have something very particular to ask. Much depends on your reply.

CECILY Gwendolen, your common sense is invaluable. Mr. Moncrieff, kindly answer me the following question. Why did you pretend to be my guardian's brother?

ALGERNON In order that I might have an opportunity of meeting you.

CECILY [to Gwendolen] That certainly seems a satisfactory explanation, does it not?

GWENDOLEN Yes, dear, if you can believe him.

CECILY I don't. But that does not affect the wonderful beauty of his answer.

GWENDOLEN True. In matters of grave importance, style, not sincerity, is the vital thing. Mr. Worthing, what explanation can you offer to me for pretending to have a brother? Was it in order that you might have an opportunity of coming up to town to see me as often as possible?

JACK Can you doubt it, Miss Fairfax?

GWENDOLEN I have the gravest doubts upon the subject. But I intend to crush them. This is not the moment for German skepticism. [Moving to Cecily.] Their explanations appear to be quite satisfactory, especially Mr. Worthing's. That seems to me to have the stamp of truth upon it.

CECILY I am more than content with what Mr Moncrieff said. His voice alone inspires one with absolute credulity.

GWENDOLEN Then you think we should forgive them?

CECILY Yes. I mean no.

GWENDOLEN True! I had forgotten. There are principles at stake that one cannot surrender. Which of us should tell them? The task is not a pleasant one.

CECILY Could we not both speak at the same time?

GWENDOLEN An excellent idea! I nearly always speak at the same time as other people. Will you take the time from me?

CECILY Certainly. [Gwendolen beats time with uplifted finger.]

GWENDOLEN AND CECILY [speaking together] Your Christian names are still an insuperable barrier. That is all!

JACK AND ALGERNON [speaking together] Our Christian names! Is that all! But we are going to be christened this afternoon.

GWENDOLEN [to Jack] For my sake you are prepared to do this terrible thing?

JACK I am.

CECILY [*to Algernon*] To please me you are ready to face this fearful ordeal?

ALGERNON I am!

GWENDOLEN How absurd to talk of the equality of the sexes! Where questions of self-sacrifice are concerned, men are infinitely beyond us.

JACK We are. [*Clasps hands with Algernon.*]

CECILY They have moments of physical courage of which we women know absolutely nothing.

GWENDOLEN [*to Jack*] Darling!

ALGERNON [*to Cecily*] Darling! [*They fall into each other's arms*]

Enter Merriman. When he enters he coughs loudly, seeing the situation.

MERRIMAN Ahem! Ahem! Lady Bracknell.

JACK Good heavens!

Enter Lady Bracknell. The couples separate in alarm.
Exit Merriman.

LADY BRACKNELL Gwendolen! What does this mean?

GWENDOLEN Merely that I am engaged to be married to Mr. Worthing, mamma.

LADY BRACKNELL Come here. Sit down. Sit down immediately. Hesitation of any kind is a sign of mental decay in the young, of physical weakness in the old. [*Turns to Jack.*] Apprised, sir, of my daughter's sudden flight by her trusty maid, whose confidence I purchased by means of a small coin, I followed her at once by a luggage train. Her unhappy father is, I am glad to say, under the impression that she is attending a more than usually lengthy lecture by the University Extension Scheme on the Influence of a permanent income on Thought. I do not propose to undeceive him. Indeed I have never undeceived him on any question. I would consider it wrong. But of course, you will clearly understand that all communication between yourself and my daughter must cease immediately from this moment. On this point, as indeed on all points, I am firm.

JACK I am engaged to be married to Gwendolen, Lady Bracknell!

LADY BRACKNELL You are nothing of the kind, sir. And now as regards Algernon! . . . Algernon!

ALGERNON Yes, Aunt Augusta.

LADY BRACKNELL May I ask if it is in this house that your invalid friend Mr. Bunbury resides?

ALGERNON   [*stammering*] Oh! No! Bunbury doesn't live here. Bunbury is somewhere else at present. In fact, Bunbury is dead.

LADY BRACKNELL   Dead! When did Mr. Bunbury die? His death must have been extremely sudden.

ALGERNON   [*airily*] Oh! I killed Bunbury this afternoon. I mean poor Bunbury died this afternoon.

LADY BRACKNELL   What did he die of?

ALGERNON   Bunbury? Oh, he was quite exploded.

LADY BRACKNELL   Exploded! Was he the victim of a revolutionary outrage? I was not aware that Mr. Bunbury was interested in social legislation. If so, he is well punished for his morbidity.

ALGERNON   My dear Aunt Augusta, I mean he was found out! The doctors found out that Bunbury could not live, that is what I mean —so Bunbury died.

LADY BRACKNELL   He seems to have had great confidence in the opinion of his physicians. I am glad, however, that he made up his mind at the last to some definite course of action, and acted under proper medical advice. And now that we have finally got rid of this Bunbury, may I ask, Mr. Worthing, who is that young person whose hand my nephew Algernon is now holding in what seems to me a peculiarly unnecessary manner?

JACK   That lady is Miss Cecily Cardew, my ward. [*Lady Bracknell bows coldly to Cecily.*]

ALGERNON   I am engaged to be married to Cecily, Aunt Augusta.

LADY BRACKNELL   I beg your pardon?

CECILY   Mr. Moncrieff and I are engaged to be married, Lady Bracknell.

LADY BRACKNELL   [*with a shiver, crossing to the sofa and sitting down.*] I do not know whether there is anything peculiarly exciting in the air of this particular part of Hertfordshire, but the number of engagements that go on seems to me considerably above the proper average that statistics have laid down for our guidance. I think some preliminary inquiry on my part would not be out of place. Mr. Worthing, is Miss Cardew at all connected with any of the larger railway stations in London? I merely desire information. Until yesterday I had no idea that there were any families or persons whose origin was a Terminus. [*Jack looks perfectly furious, but restrains himself.*]

JACK   [*in a cold, clear voice*] Miss Cardew is the granddaughter of the late Mr. Thomas Cardew of 149 Belgrave Square, S.W.; Gervase Park, Dorking, Surrey; and the Sporran, Fifeshire, N.B.

LADY BRACKNELL   That sounds not unsatisfactory. Three addresses always inspire confidence, even in tradesmen. But what proof have I of their authenticity?

JACK   I have carefully preserved the Court Guides of the period. They are open to your inspection, Lady Bracknell.

LADY BRACKNELL [*grimly*] I have known strange errors in that publication.

JACK Miss Cardew's family solicitors are Messrs. Markby, Markby and Markby.

LADY BRACKNELL Markby, Markby and Markby? A firm of the very highest position in their profession. Indeed I am told that one of the Mr. Markbys is occasionally to be seen at dinner parties. So far I am satisfied.

JACK [*very irritably*] How extremely kind of you, Lady Bracknell! I have also in my possession, you will be pleased to hear, certificates of Miss Cardew's birth, baptism, whooping cough, registration, vaccination, confirmation, and the measles; both the German and the English variety.

LADY BRACKNELL Ah! A life crowded with incident, I see; perhaps somewhat too exciting for a young girl. I am not myself in favour of premature experiences. [*Rises, looks at her watch.*] Gwendolen! the time approaches for our departure. We have not a moment to lose. As a matter of form, Mr. Worthing, I had better ask you if Miss Cardew has any little fortune?

JACK Oh! about a hundred and thirty thousand pounds in the Funds. That is all. Good-bye, Lady Bracknell. So pleased to have seen you.

LADY BRACKNELL [*sitting down again*] A moment, Mr. Worthing. A hundred and thirty thousand pounds! And in the Funds! Miss Cardew seems to be a most attractive young lady, now that I look at her. Few girls of the present day have any really solid qualities, any of the qualities that last, and improve with time. We live, I regret to say, in an age of surfaces. [*To Cecily*] Come over here, dear. [*Cecily goes across.*] Pretty child! your dress is sadly simple, and your hair seems almost as Nature might have left it. But we can soon alter all that. A thoroughly experienced French maid produces a really marvelous result in a very brief space of time. I remember recommending one to young Lady Lancing, and after three months her own husband did not know her.

JACK And after six months nobody knew her.

LADY BRACKNELL [*glares at Jack for a few moments. Then bends, with a practiced smile, to Cecily.*] Kindly turn round, sweet child. [*Cecily turns completely round.*] No, the side view is what I want. [*Cecily presents her profile.*] Yes, quite as I expected. There are distinct social possibilities in your profile. The two weak points in our age are its want of principle and its want of profile. The chin a little higher, dear. Style largely depends on the way the chin is worn. They are worn very high, just at present. Algernon!

ALGERNON   Yes, Aunt Augusta!

LADY BRACKNELL   There are distinct social possibilities in Miss Cardew's profile.

ALGERNON   Cecily is the sweetest, dearest, prettiest girl in the whole world. And I don't care twopence about social possibilities.

LADY BRACKNELL   Never speak disrespectfully of Society, Algernon. Only people who can't get into it do that. [*To Cecily.*] Dear child, of course you know that Algernon has nothing but his debts to depend upon. But I do not approve of mercenary marriages. When I married Lord Bracknell I had no fortune of any kind. But I never dreamed for a moment of allowing that to stand in my way. Well, I suppose I must give my consent.

ALGERNON   Thank you, Aunt Augusta.

LADY BRACKNELL   Cecily, you may kiss me!

CECILY   [*kisses her*] Thank you, Lady Bracknell.

LADY BRACKNELL   You may also address me as Aunt Augusta for the future.

CECILY   Thank you, Aunt Augusta.

LADY BRACKNELL   The marriage, I think, had better take place quite soon.

ALGERNON   Thank you, Aunt Augusta.

CECILY   Thank you, Aunt Augusta.

LADY BRACKNELL   To speak frankly, I am not in favor of long engagements. They give people the opportunity of finding out each other's character before marriage, which I think is never advisable.

JACK   I beg your pardon for interrupting you, Lady Bracknell, but this engagement is quite out of the question. I am Miss Cardew's guardian, and she cannot marry without my consent until she comes of age. That consent I absolutely decline to give.

LADY BRACKNELL   Upon what grounds, may I ask? Algernon is an extremely, I may almost say an ostentatiously eligible young man. He has nothing, but he looks everything. What more can one desire?

JACK   It pains me very much to have to speak frankly to you, Lady Bracknell, about your nephew, but the fact is that I do not approve at all of his moral character. I suspect him of being untruthful. [*Algernon and Cecily look at him in indignant amazement.*]

LADY BRACKNELL   Untruthful! My nephew Algernon? Impossible! He is an Oxonian.

JACK   I fear there can be no possible doubt about the matter. This afternoon during my temporary absence in London on an important question of romance, he obtained admissions to my house by means of the false pretense of being my brother. Under an assumed name he drank, I've just been informed by my butler, an entire pint bottle of my Perrier-Jouet, Brut, '89; wine I was specially reserving for myself. Continuing his disgraceful deception, he succeeded in the course of the afternoon in alienating the affections of my only ward. He subsequently stayed to tea, and devoured every single muffin. And what makes his conduct all the more heartless is, that he was perfectly well aware from the first that I have no brother, that I never had a brother, and that I don't intend to have a brother, not even of any kind. I distinctly told him so myself yesterday afternoon.

LADY BRACKNELL   Ahem! Mr. Worthing, after careful consideration I have decided entirely to overlook my nephew's conduct to you.

JACK   That is very generous of you, Lady Bracknell. My own decision, however, is unalterable. I decline to give my consent.

LADY BRACKNELL   [to Cecily] Come here, sweet child. [Cecily goes over.] How old are you, dear?

CECILY   Well, I am really only eighteen, but I always admit to twenty when I go to evening parties.

LADY BRACKNELL   You are perfectly right in making some slight alteration. Indeed, no woman should ever be quite accurate about her age. It looks so calculating. . . . [In a meditative manner.] Eighteen, but admitting to twenty at evening parties. Well, it will not be very long before you are of age and free from the restraints of tutelage. So don't think your guardian's consent is, after all, a matter of any importance.

JACK   Pray excuse me, Lady Bracknell, for interrupting you again, but it is only fair to tell you that according to the terms of her grandfather's will Miss Cardew does not come legally of age till she is thirty-five.

LADY BRACKNELL   That does not seem to be a grave objection. Thirty-five is a very attractive age. London society is full of women of the very highest birth who have, of their own free choice, remained thirty-five for years. Lady Dumbleton is an instance in point. To my own knowledge she has been thirty-five ever since she arrived at the age of forty, which was many years ago now. I see no reason why our dear Cecily should not be even still more attractive at the age you mention than she is at present. There will be a large accumulation of property.

CECILY   Algy, could you wait for me till I was thirty-five?

ALGERNON   Of course I could, Cecily. You know I could.

CECILY   Yes, I felt it instinctively, but I couldn't wait all that time. I hate waiting even five minutes for anybody. It always makes me rather cross. I am not punctual myself, I know, but I do like punctuality in others, and waiting, even to be married, is quite out of the question.

ALGERNON   Then what is to be done, Cecily?

CECILY   I don't know, Mr. Moncrieff.

LADY BRACKNELL   My dear Mr. Worthing, as Miss Cardew states positively that she cannot wait till she is thirty-five—a remark which I am bound to say seems to me to show a somewhat impatient nature—I would beg of you to reconsider your decision.

JACK   But my dear Lady Bracknell, the matter is entirely in your own hands. The moment you consent to my marriage with Gwendolen, I will most gladly allow your nephew to form an alliance with my ward.

LADY BRACKNELL   [rising and drawing herself up] You must be quite aware that what you propose is out of the question.

JACK   Then a passionate celibacy is all that any of us can look forward to.

LADY BRACKNELL   That is not the destiny I propose for Gwendolen. Algernon, of course, can choose for himself. [Pulls out her watch.] Come, dear [Gwendolen rises], we have already missed five, if not six, trains. To miss any more might expose us to comment on the platform.

Enter Dr. Chasuble.

CHASUBLE   Everything is quite ready for the christenings.

LADY BRACKNELL   The christenings, sir! Is not that somewhat premature?

CHASUBLE   [looking rather puzzled, and pointing to Jack and Algernon] Both these gentlemen have expressed a desire for immediate baptism.

LADY BRACKNELL   At their age? The idea is grotesque and irreligious! Algernon, I forbid you to be baptized. I will not hear of such excesses. Lord Bracknell would be highly displeased if he learned that that was the way in which you wasted your time and money.

CHASUBLE   Am I to understand then that there are to be no christenings at all this afternoon?

JACK   I don't think that, as things are now, it would be of much practical value to either of us, Dr. Chasuble.

CHASUBLE   I am grieved to hear such sentiments from you, Mr. Worthing. They savor of the heretical views of the Anabaptists, views that I have completely refuted in four of my unpublished sermons. However, as your present mood seems to be one peculiarly secular, I will return to the church at once. Indeed, I have just been informed by the pew-opener that for the last hour and a half Miss Prism has been waiting for me in the vestry.

LADY BRACKNELL   [starting] Miss Prism! Did I hear you mention a Miss Prism?

CHASUBLE   Yes, Lady Bracknell. I am on my way to join her.

LADY BRACKNELL   Pray allow me to detain you for a moment. This matter may prove to be one of vital importance to Lord Bracknell and myself. Is this Miss Prism a female of repellent aspect, remotely connected with education?

CHASUBLE   [*somewhat indignantly*] She is the most cultivated of ladies, and the very picture of respectability.

LADY BRACKNELL   It is obviously the same person. May I ask what position she holds in your household?

CHASUBLE   [*severely*] I am a celibate, madam.

JACK   [*interposing*] Miss Prism, Lady Bracknell, has been for the last three years Miss Cardew's esteemed governess and valued companion.

LADY BRACKNELL   In spite of what I hear of her, I must see her at once. Let her be sent for.

CHASUBLE   [*looking off*] She approaches; she is nigh.

Enter Miss Prism hurriedly.

MISS PRISM   I was told you expected me in the vestry, dear Canon. I have been waiting for you there for an hour and three-quarters. [*Catches sight of Lady Bracknell, who has fixed her with a stony glare. Miss Prism grows pale and quails. She looks anxiously round as if desirous to escape.*]

LADY BRACKNELL   [*in a severe, judicial voice*] Prism! [*Miss Prism bows her head in shame.*] Come here, Prism! [*Miss Prism approaches in a humble manner.*] Prism! Where is that baby? [*General consternation. The Canon starts back in horror. Algernon and Jack pretend to be anxious to shield Cecily and Gwendolen from hearing the details of a terrible public scandal.*] Twenty-eight years ago, Prism, you left Lord Bracknell's house, Number 104, Upper Grosvenor Square, in charge of a perambulator that contained a baby of the male sex. You never returned. A few weeks later, through the elaborate investigations of the Metropolitan police, the perambulator was discovered at midnight standing by itself in a remote corner of Bayswater. It contained the manuscript of a three-volume novel of more than usually revolting sentimentality. [*Miss Prism starts in involuntary indignation.*] But the baby was not there. [*Everyone looks at Miss Prism.*] Prism! Where is that baby? [*A pause.*]

MISS PRISM   Lady Bracknell, I admit with shame that I do not know. I only wish I did. The plain facts of the case are these. On the morning of the day you mentioned, a day that is forever branded on my memory, I prepared as usual to take the baby out in its perambulator. I had also with me a somewhat old, but capacious handbag in which I had intended to place the manuscript of a work of fiction that I had written during my few unoccupied hours. In a moment of mental abstraction, for which I can never forgive myself, I deposited the manuscript in the bassinette and placed the baby in the handbag.

JACK   [who has been listening attentively] But where did you deposit the handbag?

MISS PRISM   Do not ask me, Mr. Worthing.

JACK   Miss Prism, this is a matter of no small importance to me. I insist on knowing where you deposited the handbag that contained that infant.

MISS PRISM   I left it in the cloakroom of one of the larger railway stations in London.

JACK   What railway station?

MISS PRISM   [quite crushed] Victoria. The Brighton line. [Sinks into a chair.]

JACK   I must retire to my room for a moment. Gwendolen, wait here for me.

GWENDOLEN   If you are not too long, I will wait here for you all my life. [Exit Jack in great excitement.]

CHASUBLE   What do you think this means, Lady Bracknell?

LADY BRACKNELL   I dare not even suspect, Dr. Chasuble. I need hardly tell you that in families of high position strange coincidences are not supposed to occur. They are hardly considered the thing.

Noises heard overhead as if someone was throwing trunks about. Every one looks up.

CECILY   Uncle Jack seems strangely agitated.

CHASUBLE   Your guardian has a very emotional nature.

LADY BRACKNELL   This noise is extremely unpleasant. It sounds as if he was having an argument. I dislike arguments of any kind. They are always vulgar, and often convincing.

CHASUBLE   [looking up] It has stopped now. [The noise is redoubled.]

LADY BRACKNELL   I wish he would arrive at some conclusion.

GWENDOLEN   This suspense is terrible. I hope it will last.

Enter Jack with a handbag of black leather in his hand.

JACK   [rushing over to Miss Prism] Is this the handbag, Miss Prism? Examine it carefully before you speak. The happiness of more than one life depends on your answer.

MISS PRISM   [calmly] It seems to be mine. Yes, here is the injury it received through the upsetting of a Gower Street omnibus in younger and happier days. Here is the strain on the lining caused by the explosion of a temperance beverage, an incident that occurred at Leamington. And here, on the lock, are my initials. I had forgotten that in an extravagant mood I had them placed there. The bag is undoubtedly mine. I am delighted to have it so unexpectedly restored to me. It has been a great inconvenience being without it all these years.

JACK   [*in a pathetic voice*] Miss Prism, more is restored to you than this handbag. I was the baby you placed in it.

MISS PRISM   [*amazed*] You?

JACK   [*embracing her*] Yes . . . mother!

MISS PRISM   [*recoiling in indignant astonishment*] Mr. Worthing. I am unmarried!

JACK   Unmarried! I do not deny that is a serious blow. But after all, who has the right to cast a stone against one who has suffered? Cannot repentance wipe out an act of folly? Why should there be one law for men, and another for women? Mother, I forgive you. [*Tries to embrace her again.*]

MISS PRISM   [*still more indignant*] Mr. Worthing, there is some error. [*Pointing to Lady Bracknell.*] There is the lady who can tell you who you really are.

JACK   [*after a pause*] Lady Bracknell, I hate to seem inquisitive, but would you kindly inform me who I am?

LADY BRACKNELL   I am afraid that the news I have to give you will not altogether please you. You are the son of my poor sister, Mrs. Moncrieff, and consequently Algernon's elder brother.

JACK   Algy's elder brother! Then I have a brother after all. I knew I had a brother! I always said I had a brother! Cecily, — how could you have ever doubted that I had a brother. [*Seizes hold of Algernon.*] Dr. Chasuble, my unfortunate brother. Miss Prism, my unfortunate brother. Gwendolen, my unfortunate brother. Algy, you young scoundrel, you will have to treat me with more respect in the future. You have never behaved to me like a brother in all your life.

ALGERNON   Well, not till today, old boy, I admit. I did my best, however, though I was out of practice.

[*Shakes hands.*]

GWENDOLEN   [*to Jack*] My own! But what own are you? What is your Christian name, now that you have become someone else?

JACK   Good heavens! . . . I had quite forgotten that point. Your decision on the subject of my name is irrevocable, I suppose?

GWENDOLEN   I never change, except in my affections.

CECILY   What a noble nature you have, Gwendolen!

JACK   Then the question had better be cleared up at once. Aunt Augusta, a moment. At the time when Miss Prism left me in the hand-bag, had I been christened already?

LADY BRACKNELL   Every luxury that money could buy, including christening, had been lavished on you by your fond and doting parents.

JACK   Then I was christened! That is settled. Now, what name was I given? Let me know the worst.

LADY BRACKNELL   Being the eldest son you were naturally christened after your father.

JACK   [*irritably*] Yes, but what was my father's Christian name?

LADY BRACKNELL   [*meditatively*] I cannot at the present moment recall what the General's Christian name was. But I have no doubt he had one. He was eccentric, I admit. But only in later years. And that was the result of the Indian climate, and marriage, and indigestion, and other things of that kind.

JACK   Algy! Can't you recollect what our father's Christian name was?

ALGERNON   My dear boy, we were never even on speaking terms. He died before I was a year old.

JACK   His name would appear in the Army Lists of the period, I suppose, Aunt Augusta?

LADY BRACKNELL   The General was essentially a man of peace, except in his domestic life. But have no doubt his name would appear in any military directory.

JACK   The Army Lists of the last forty years are here. These delightful records should have been my constant study. [*Rushes to bookcase and tears the books out.*] M. Generals . . . Mallam, Maxbohm, Magley — what ghastly names they have — Markby, Migsby, Mobbs, Moncrieff! Lieutenant 1840, Captain, Lieutenant-Colonel, Colonel, General 1869, Christian names, Ernest John. [*Puts book very quietly down and speaks quite calmly.*] I always told you, Gwendolen, my name was Ernest, didn't I? Well it is Ernest after all. I mean it naturally is Ernest.

LADY BRACKNELL   Yes, I remember now that the General was called Ernest. I knew I had some particular reason for disliking the name.

GWENDOLEN   Ernest! My own Ernest! I felt from the first you could have no other name!

JACK   Gwendolen, it is a terrible thing for a man to find out suddenly that all his life he has been speaking nothing but the truth. Can you forgive me?

GWENDOLEN   I can. For I feel that you are sure to change.

JACK   My own one!

CHASUBLE   [*to Miss Prism*] Laetitia! [*Embraces her.*]

MISS PRISM   [*enthusiastically*] Frederick! At last!

ALGERNON   Cecily! [*Embraces her.*] At last!

JACK   Gwendolen! [*Embraces her.*] At last!

LADY BRACKNELL   My nephew, you seem to be displaying signs of triviality.

JACK   On the contrary, Aunt Augusta, I've now realized for the first time in my life the vital Importance of Being Earnest.

TABLEAU

GEORGE BERNARD SHAW

1856–1950

Born and raised in Dublin, Ireland, Shaw was the youngest child of an unhappy marriage between his drunken, joke-telling father and his artistic, undomestic mother. He dropped out of school when he was fifteen, briefly worked at an office job in Dublin, and when he was twenty moved to London, where he lived with his mother who helped to support him out of her income as a private music teacher, while he tried unsuccessfully to make his way as a novelist. During his late twenties, he discovered the economic and political theories of Karl Marx and was so inspired by them that he joined a socialist group, known as the Fabians, and quickly became one of their leading spokesmen, lecturing and writing pamphlets to reform local government, to revise the poor laws, to promote trade unions, and to support women's rights. By his mid-thirties, he had also become a well-known art, literary, and music critic through his reviews for various London newspapers, and he had published his first book, *The Quintessence of Ibsenism* (1891), a manifesto celebrating the socially conscious drama of Ibsen. Having proclaimed the English need for a "new drama" of social ideas, Shaw took up playwriting in 1892, and from then until his death wrote forty-seven full-length plays promoting his ideas and opinions about economics, politics, society, morality, religion, science, and literature. Most of his plays are comedies, which feature witty men and equally witty women who engage in lively debates that illustrate Shaw's belief in "free vitality" and the "life force" as the primary sources of "creative evolution" within human beings and their social institutions. Among his best-known plays are *Candida* (1895), *Man and Superman* (1903), *Major Barbara* (1905), *Heartbreak House* (1919), and *St. Joan* (1923).

Shaw expounded his views not only in his plays but also in prefaces that he wrote for the published versions of his plays. By means of these prefaces, which were sometimes as long as the plays themselves, Shaw used his incisive prose style to explicate his characters, plots, and themes, as well as to gain a wider audience for his ideas than was possible in the theater alone. In his lengthy "Preface to *Major Barbara*," for example, Shaw provides a detailed historical and philosophical rationale for "the gospel of Andrew Undershaft," as well as a sustained attack on "the weaknesses of the Salvation Army" and of "Popular Christianity" in meeting the needs of "real life."

Major Barbara
A Discussion in Three Acts

Preface

FIRST AID TO CRITICS

Before dealing with the deeper aspects of Major Barbara, let me, for the credit of English literature, make a protest against an unpatriotic habit into which many of my critics have fallen. Whenever my view strikes them as being at all outside the range of, say, an ordinary suburban churchwarden, they conclude that I am echoing Schopenhauer, Nietzsche, Ibsen, Strindberg, Tolstoy, or some other her esiarch in northern or eastern Europe.

I confess there is something flattering in this simple faith in my accomplishment as a linguist and my erudition as a philosopher. But I cannot countenance the assumption that life and literature are so poor in these islands that we must go abroad for all dramatic material that is not common and all ideas that are not superficial. I therefore venture to put my critics in possession of certain facts concerning my contact with modern ideas.

About half a century ago, an Irish novelist, Charles Lever, wrote a story entitled A Day's Ride: A Life's Romance. It was published by Charles Dickens in Household Words, and proved so strange to the public taste that Dickens pressed Lever to make short work of it. I read scraps of this novel when I was a child; and it made an enduring impression on me. The hero was a very romantic hero, trying to live bravely, chivalrously, and powerfully by dint of mere romance-fed imagination, without courage, without means, without knowledge, without skill, without anything real except his bodily appetites. Even in my childhood I found in this poor devil's unsuccessful encounters with the facts of life, a poignant quality that romantic fiction lacked. The book, in spite of its first failure, is not dead: I saw its title the other day in the catalogue of Tauchnitz.

Now why is it that when I also deal in the tragi-comic irony of the conflict between real life and the romantic imagination, critics never affiliate me to my countryman and immediate forerunner, Charles Lever, whilst they confidently derive me from a Norwegian author of whose language I do not know three words, and of whom I knew nothing until years after the Shavian *Anschauung* was already unequivocally declared in books full of what came, ten years later, to be perfunctorily labelled Ibsenism? I was not Ibsenist even at second hand; for Lever, though he may have read Henri Beyle, *alias* Stendhal, certainly never read Ibsen. Of the books that made Lever popular, such as Charles O'Malley and Harry Lorrequer, I know nothing but the names and some of the illustrations. But the story of the day's ride and life's romance of Potts (claiming alliance with Pozzo di Borgo) caught me and fascinated me as something strange and significant, though I already knew all about Alnaschar and Don Quixote and Simon Tappertit and many another romantic hero mocked by reality. From the plays of Aristophanes to the tales of Stevenson that mockery has been made familiar to all who are properly saturated with letters.

Where, then, was the novelty in Lever's tale? Partly, I think, in a new seriousness in dealing with Potts's disease. Formerly, the contrast between madness and sanity was deemed comic: Hogarth shews us how fashionable people went in parties to Bedlam to laugh at the lunatics. I myself have had a village idiot exhibited to me as something irresistibly funny. On the stage the madman was once a regular comic figure: that was how Hamlet got his opportunity before Shakespear touched him. The originality of Shakespear's version lay in his taking the lunatic sympathetically and seriously, and thereby making an advance towards the eastern consciousness of the fact that lunacy may be inspiration in disguise, since a man who has more brains than his fellows necessarily appears as mad to them as one who has less. But Shakespear did not do for Pistol and Parolles what he did for Hamlet. The particular sort of madman they represented, the romantic make-believer, lay outside the pale of sympathy in literature: he was pitilessly despised and ridiculed here as he was in the east under the name of Alnaschar, and was doomed to be, centuries later, under the name of Simon Tappertit. When Cervantes relented over Don Quixote, and Dickens relented over Pickwick, they did not become impartial: they simply changed sides, and became friends and apologists where they had formerly been mockers.

In Lever's story there is a real change of attitude. There is no relenting towards Potts: he never gains our affections like Don Quixote and Pickwick: he has not even the infatuate courage of Tappertit. But we dare not laugh at him, because, somehow, we recognize ourselves in Potts. We may, some of us, have enough nerve, enough muscle, enough luck, enough tact or skill or address or knowledge to carry things off better than he did; to impose on the people who saw through him; to fascinate Katinka (who cut Potts so ruthlessly at the end of the story); but for all that, we know that Potts plays an enormous part in ourselves and in the world, and that the social problem is not a problem of story-book heroes of the older pattern, but a problem of Pottses, and of how to make men of them.

To fall back on my old phrase, we have the feeling—one that Alnaschar, Pistol, Parolles, and Tappertit never gave us — that Potts is a piece of really scientific natural history as distinguished from funny story telling. His author is not throwing a stone at a creature of another and inferior order, but making a confession, with the effect that the stone hits each of us full in the conscience and causes our self-esteem to smart very sorely. Hence the failure of Lever's book to please the readers of Household Words. That pain in the self-esteem nowadays causes critics to raise a cry of Ibsenism. I therefore assure them that the sensation first came to me from Lever and may have come to him from Beyle, or at least out of the Stendhalian atmosphere. I exclude the hypothesis of complete originality of Lever's part, because a man can no more be completely original in that sense than a tree can grow out of air.

Another mistake as to my literary ancestry is made whenever I violate the romantic convention that all women are angels when they are not devils; that they are better looking than men; that their part in courtship is entirely passive; and that the human female form is the most beautiful object in nature. Schopenhauer wrote a splenetic essay which, as it is neither polite nor profound, was probably intended to knock this nonsense violently on the head. A sentence denouncing the idolized form as ugly has been largely quoted. The English critics have read that sentence; and I must here affirm, with as much gentleness as the implication will bear, that it has yet to be proved that they have dipped any deeper. At all events, whenever an English playwright represents a young and marriageable woman as being anything but a romantic heroine, he is disposed of without further thought as an echo of Schopenhauer. My own case is a specially hard one, because, when I implore the critics who are obsessed with the Schopenhauerian formula to remember that playwrights, like sculptors, study their figures from life, and not from philosophic essays, they reply passionately that I am not a playwright and that my stage figures do not live. But even so, I may and do ask them why, if they must give the credit of my plays to a philosopher, they do not give it to an English philosopher? Long before I ever read a word by Schopenhauer, or even knew whether he was a philosopher or a chemist, the Socialist revival of the eighteen-eighties brought me into contact, both literary and personal, with Ernest Belfort Bax, an English Socialist and philosophic essayist, whose handling of modern feminism would provoke romantic protests from Schopenhauer himself, or even Strindberg. As a matter of fact I hardly noticed Schopenhauer's disparagements of women when they came under my notice later on, so thoroughly had Bax familiarized me with the homoist attitude, and forced me to recognize the extent to which public opinion, and consequently legislation and jurisprudence, is corrupted by feminist sentiment.

Belfort Bax's essays were not confined to the Feminist question. He was a ruthless critic of current morality. Other writers have gained sympathy for dramatic criminals by eliciting the alleged "soul of goodness in things evil"; but Bax would propound some quite undramatic and apparently shabby violation of our commercial law and morality, and not merely defend it with the most disconcerting ingenuity, but actually prove it to be a positive duty that nothing but the certainty of police persecution should prevent every right-minded man from at once doing on principle. The Socialists were naturally shocked, being for the most part morbidly moral people; but at all events they were saved later on from the delusion that nobody but Nietzsche had ever challenged our mercanto-Christian morality. I first heard the name of Nietzsche from a German mathematician, Miss Borchardt, who had read my Quintessence of Ibsenism, and told me that she saw what I had been reading: namely, Nietzsche's Jenseits von Gut und Böse. Which I protest I had never seen, and could not have read with any comfort, for want of the necessary German, if I had seen it.

Nietzsche, like Schopenhauer, is the victim in England of a single much quoted sentence containing the phrase "big blonde beast." On the strength of this alliteration it is assumed that Nietzsche gained his European reputation by a senseless glorification of selfish bullying as the rule of life, just as it is assumed, on the strength of the single word Superman (Übermensch) borrowed by me from Nietzsche, that I look for the salvation of society to the despotism of a single Napoleonic Superman, in spite of my careful demonstration of the folly of that outworn infatuation. But even the less recklessly superficial critics seem to believe that the modern objection to Christianity as a pernicious slave-morality was first put forward by Nietzsche. It was familiar to me before I ever heard of Nietzsche. The late Captain Wilson, author of several queer pamphlets, propagandist of a metaphysical system called Comprehensionism, and inventor of the term "Crosstianity" to distinguish the retrograde element in Christendom, was wont thirty years ago, in the discussions of the Dialectical Society, to protest earnestly against the beatitudes of the Sermon on the Mount as excuses for cowardice and servility, as destructive of our will, and consequently of our honor and manhood. Now it is true that Captain Wilson's moral criticism of Christianity was not a historical theory of it, like Nietzsche's; but this objection cannot be made to Stuart-Glennie, the successor of Buckle as a philosophic historian, who devoted his life to the elaboration and propagation of his theory that Christianity is part of an epoch (or rather an aberration, since it began as recently as 6000 B.C. and is already collapsing) produced by the necessity in which the numerically inferior white races found themselves to impose their domination on the colored races by priestcraft, making a virtue and a popular religion of drudgery and submissiveness in this world not only as a means of achieving saintliness of character but of securing a reward in heaven. Here was the slave-morality view formulated by a Scotch philosopher of my acquaintance long before we all began chattering about Nietzsche.

As Stuart-Glennie traced the evolution of society to the conflict of races, his theory made some sensation among Socialists — that is, among the only people who were seriously thinking about historical evolution at all — by its collision with the class-conflict theory of Karl Marx. Nietzsche, as I gather, regarded the slave-morality as having been invented and imposed on the world by slaves making a virtue of necessity and a religion of their servitude. Stuart-Glennie regarded the slave-morality as an invention of the superior white race to subjugate the minds of the inferior races whom they wished to exploit, and who would have destroyed them by force of numbers if their minds had not been subjugated. As this process is in operation still, and can be studied at first hand not only in our Church schools and in the struggle between our modern proprietary classes and the proletariat, but in the part played by Christian missionaries in reconciling the black races of Africa to their subjugation by European Capitalism, we can judge for ourselves whether the initiative came from above or below. My object here is not to argue the historical point, but simply to make our theatre critics ashamed of their habit of treating Britain as an intellectual void, and assuming that every philosophical idea, every historic theory, every criticism of our moral, religious and juridical institutions, must necessarily be either a foreign import, or else a fantastic sally (in rather questionable taste) totally unrelated to the existing body of thought. I urge them to remember that this body of thought is the slowest of growths and the rarest of blossomings, and that if there be such a thing on the philosophic plane as a matter of course, it is that no individual can make more than a minute contribution to it. In fact, their conception of clever persons parthenogenetically bringing forth complete original cosmogonies by dint of sheer ''brilliancy'' is part of that ignorant credulity which is the despair of the honest philosopher, and the opportunity of the religious imposter.

THE GOSPEL OF ST ANDREW UNDERSHAFT

It is this credulity that drives me to help my critics out with Major Barbara by telling them what to say about it. In the millionaire Undershaft I have represented a man who has become intellectually and spiritually as well as practically conscious of the irresistible natural truth which we all abhor and repudiate: to wit, that the greatest of our evils, and the worst of our crimes is poverty, and that our first duty, to which every other consideration should be sacrificed, is not to be poor. "Poor but honest," "the respectable poor," and such phrases are as intolerable and as immoral as "drunken but amiable," "fraudulent but a good after-dinner speaker," "splendidly criminal," or the like. Security, the chief pretence of civilization, cannot exist where the worst of dangers, the danger of poverty, hangs over everyone's head, and where the alleged protection of our persons from violence is only an accidental result of the existence of a police force whose real business is to force the poor man to see his children starve whilst idle people overfeed pet dogs with the money that might feed and clothe them.

It is exceedingly difficult to make people realize that an evil is an evil. For instance, we seize a man and deliberately do him a malicious injury: say, imprison him for years. One would not suppose that it needed any exceptional clearness of wit to recognize in this an act of diabolical cruelty. But in England such a recognition provokes a stare of surprise, followed by an explanation that the outrage is punishment or justice or something else that is all right, or perhaps by a heated attempt to argue that we should all be robbed and murdered in our beds if such stupid villainies as sentences of imprisonment were not committed daily. It is useless to argue that even if this were true, which it is not, the alternative to adding crimes of our own to the crimes from which we suffer is not helpless submission. Chickenpox is an evil; but if I were to declare that we must either submit to it or else repress it sternly by seizing everyone who suffers from it and punishing them by inoculation with smallpox, I should be laughed at; for though nobody could deny that the result would be to prevent chickenpox to some extent by making people avoid it much more carefully, and to effect a further apparent prevention by making them conceal it very anxiously, yet people would have sense enough to see that the deliberate propagation of smallpox was a creation of evil, and must therefore be ruled out in favor of purely humane and hygienic measures. Yet in the precisely parallel case of a man breaking into my house and stealing my wife's diamonds I am expected as a matter of course to steal ten years of his life, torturing him all the time. If he tries to defeat that monstrous retaliation by shooting me, my survivors hang him. The net result suggested by the police statistics is that we inflict atrocious injuries on the burglars we catch in order to make the rest take effectual precautions against detection; so that instead of saving our wives' diamonds from burglary we only greatly decrease our chances of ever getting them back, and increase our chances of being shot by the robber if we are unlucky enough to disturb him at his work.

But the thoughtless wickedness with which we scatter sentences of imprisonment, torture in the solitary cell and on the plank bed, and flogging, on moral invalids and energetic rebels, is as nothing compared to the silly levity with which we tolerate poverty as if it were either a wholesome tonic for lazy people or else a virtue to be embraced as St Francis embraced it. If a man is indolent, let him be poor. If he is drunken, let him be poor. If he is not a gentleman, let him be poor. If he is addicted to the fine arts or to pure science instead of to trade and finance, let him be poor. If he chooses to spend his urban eighteen shillings a week or his agricultural thirteen shillings a week on his beer and his family instead of saving it up for his old age, let him be poor. Let nothing be done for "the undeserving": let him be poor. Serve him right! Also—somewhat inconsistently—blessed are the poor!

Now what does this Let Him Be Poor mean? It means let him be weak. Le him be ignorant. Let him become a nucleus of disease. Let him be a standing exhibition and example of ugliness and dirt. Let him have rickety children. Let him be cheap, and drag his fellows down to his own price by selling himself to do their work. Let his habitations turn our cities into poisonous congeries of slums. Let his daughters infect our young men with the diseases of the streets, and his sons revenge him by turning the nation's manhood into scrofula, cowardice, cruelty, hypocrisy, political imbecility, and all the other fruits of oppression and malnutrition. Let the undeserving become still less deserving; and let the deserving lay up for himself, not treasures in heaven, but horrors in hell upon earth. This being so, is it really wise to let him be poor? Would he not do ten times less harm as a prosperous burglar, incendiary, ravisher or murderer, to the utmost limits of humanity's comparatively negligible impulses in these directions? Suppose we were to abolish all penalties for such activities, and decide that poverty is the one thing we will not tolerate — that every adult with less than, say, £365 a year, shall be painlessly but inexorably killed, and every hungry half naked child forcibly fattened and clothed, would not that be an enormous improvement on our existing system, which has already destroyed so many civilizations, and is visibly destroying ours in the same way?

Is there any radicle of such legislation in our parliamentary system? Well, there are two measures just sprouting in the political soil, which may conceivably grow to something valuable. One is the institution of a Legal Minimum Wage. The other, Old Age Pensions. But there is a better plan than either of these. Some time ago I mentioned the subject of Universal Old Age Pensions to my fellow Socialist Cobden-Sanderson, famous as an artist-craftsman in book-binding and printing. "Why not Universal Pensions for Life?" said Cobden-Sanderson. In saying this, he solved the industrial problem at a stroke. At present we say callously to each citizen "If you want money, earn it" as if his having or not having it were a matter that concerned himself alone. We do not even secure for him the opportunity of earning it: on the contrary, we allow our industry to be organized in open dependence on the maintenance of "a reserve army of unemployed" for the sake of "elasticity." The sensible course would be Cobden-Sanderson's: that is, to give every man enough to live well on, so as to guarantee the community against the possibility of a case of the malignant disease of poverty, and then (necessarily) to see that he earned it.

Undershaft, the hero of Major Barbara, is simply a man who, having grasped the fact that poverty is a crime, knows that when society offered him the alternative of poverty or a lucrative trade in death and destruction, it offered him, not a choice between opulent villainy and humble virtue, but between energetic enterprise and cowardly infamy. His conduct stands the Kantian test, which Peter Shirley's does not. Peter Shirley is what we call the honest poor man. Undershaft is what we call the wicked rich one: Shirley is Lazarus, Undershaft Dives. Well, the misery of the world is due to the fact that the great mass of men act and believe as Peter Shirley acts and believes. If they acted and believed as Undershaft acts and believes, the immediate result would be a revolution of incalculable beneficence. To be wealthy, says Undershaft, is with me a point of honor for which I am prepared to kill at the risk of my own life. This preparedness is, as he says, the final test of sincerity. Like Froissart's medieval hero, who saw that "to rob and pill was a good life" he is not the dupe of that public sentiment against killing which is propagated and endowed by people who would otherwise be killed themselves, or of the mouth-honor paid to poverty and obedience by rich and insubordinate do-nothings who want to rob the poor without courage and command them without superiority. Froissart's knight, in placing the achievement of a good life before all the other duties — which indeed are not duties at all when they conflict with it, but plain wickednesses — behaved bravely, admirably, and, in the final analysis, public-spiritedly. Medieval society, on the other hand, behaved very badly indeed in organizing itself so stupidly that a good life could be achieved by robbing and pilling. If the knight's contemporaries had been all as resolute as he, robbing and pilling would have been the shortest way to the gallows, just as, if we were all as resolute and clear-sighted as Undershaft, an attempt to live by means of what is called "an independent income" would be the shortest way to the lethal chamber. But as, thanks to our political imbecility and personal cowardice (fruits of poverty, both), the best imitation of a good life now procurable is life on an independent income, all sensible people aim at securing such an income, and are, of course, careful to legalize and moralize both it and all the actions and sentiments which lead to it and support it as an institution. What else can they do? They know, of course, that they are rich because others are poor. But they cannot help that: it is for the poor to repudiate poverty when they have had enough of it. The thing can be done easily enough: the demonstrations to the contrary made by the economists, jurists, moralists and sentimentalists hired by the rich to defend them, or even doing the work gratuitously out of sheer folly and abjectness, impose only on those who want to be imposed on.

The reason why the independent income-tax payers are not solid in defence of their position is that since we are not medieval rovers through a sparsely populated country, the poverty of those we rob prevents our having the good life for which we sacrifice them. Rich men or aristocrats with a developed sense of life — men like Ruskin and William Morris and Kropotkin — have enormous social appetites and very fastidious personal ones. They are not content with handsome houses: they want handsome cities. They are not content with bediamonded wives and blooming daughters: they complain because the charwoman is badly dressed, because the laundress smells of gin, because the sempstress is anemic, because every man they meet is not a friend and every woman not a romance. They turn up their noses at their neighbor's drains, and are made ill by the architecture of their neighbor's houses. Trade patterns made to suit vulgar people do not please them (and they can get nothing else): they cannot sleep nor sit at ease upon "slaughtered" cabinet makers' furniture. The very air is not good enough for them: there is too much factory smoke in it. They even demand abstract conditions: justice, honor, a noble moral atmosphere, a mystic nexus to replace the cash nexus. Finally they declare that though to rob and pill with your own hand on horseback and in steel coat may have been a good life, to rob and pill by the hands of the policeman, the bailiff, and the soldier, and to underpay them meanly for doing it, is not a good life, but rather fatal to all possibility of even a tolerable one. They call on the poor to revolt, and, finding the poor shocked at their ungentlemanliness, despairingly revile the proletariat for its "damned wantlessness" (*verdammte Bedürfnislosigkeit*).

So far, however, their attack on society has lacked simplicity. The poor do not share their tastes nor understand their art-criticisms. They do not want the simple life, nor the esthetic life; on the contrary, they want very much to wallow in all the costly vulgarities from which the elect souls among the rich turn away with loathing. It is by surfeit and not by abstinence that they will be cured of their hankering after unwholesome sweets. What they do dislike and despise and are ashamed of is poverty. To ask them to fight for the difference between the Christmas number of the Illustrated London News and the Kelmscott Chaucer is silly: they prefer the News. The difference between a stock-broker's cheap and dirty starched white shirt and collar and the comparatively costly and carefully dyed blue shirt of William Morris is a difference so disgraceful to Morris in their eyes that if they fought on the subject at all, they would fight in defence of the starch. "Cease to be slaves, in order that you may become cranks" is not a very inspiring call to arms; nor is it really improved by substituting saints for cranks. Both terms denote men of genius; and the common man does not want to live the life of a man of genius: he would much rather live the life of a pet collie if that were the only alternative. But he does want more money. Whatever else he may be vague about, he is clear about that. He may or may not prefer Major Barbara to the Drury Lane pantomime; but he always prefers five hundred pounds to five hundred shillings.

Now to deplore this preference as sordid, and teach children that it is sinful to desire money, is to strain towards the extreme possible limit of impudence in lying and corruption in hypocrisy. The universal regard for money is the one hopeful fact in our civilization, the one sound spot in our social conscience. Money is the most important thing in the world. It represents health, strength, honor, generosity and beauty as conspicuously and undeniably as the want of it represents illness, weakness, disgrace, meanness and ugliness. Not the least of its virtues is that it destroys base people as certainly as it fortifies and dignifies noble people. It is only when it is cheapened to worthlessness for some and made impossibly dear to others, that it becomes a curse. In short, it is a curse only in such foolish social conditions that life itself is a curse. For the two things are inseparable: money is the counter that enables life to be distributed socially: it *is* life as truly as sovereigns and bank notes are money. The first duty of every citizen is to insist on having money on reasonable terms; and this demand is not complied with by giving four men three shillings each for ten or twelve hours' drudgery and one man a thousand pounds for nothing. The crying need of the nation is not for better morals, cheaper bread, temperance, liberty, culture, redemption of fallen sisters and erring brothers, nor the grace, love and fellowship of the Trinity, but simply for enough money. And the evil to be attacked is not sin, suffering, greed, priestcraft, kingcraft, demagogy, monopoly, ignorance, drink, war, pestilence, nor any other of the scapegoats which reformers sacrifice, but simply poverty.

Once take your eyes from the ends of the earth and fix them on this truth just under your nose; and Andrew Undershaft's views will not perplex you in the least. Unless indeed his constant sense that he is only the instrument of a Will or Life Force which uses him for purposes wider than his own, may puzzle you. If so, that is because you are walking either in artificial Darwinian darkness, or in mere stupidity. All genuinely religious people have that consciousness. To them Undershaft the Mystic will be quite intelligible, and his perfect comprehension of his daughter the Salvationist and her lover the Euripidean republican natural and inevitable. That, however, is not new, even on the stage. What is new, as far as I know, is that article in Undershaft's religion which recognizes in Money the first need and in poverty the vilest sin of man and society.

This dramatic conception has not, of course, been attained *per saltum*. Nor has it been borrowed from Nietzsche or from any man born beyond the Channel. The late Samuel Butler, in his own department the greatest English writer of the latter half of the XIX century, steadily inculcated the necessity and morality of a conscientious Laodiceanism in religion and of an earnest and constant sense of the importance of money. It drives one almost to despair of English literature when one sees so extraordinary a study of English life as Butler's posthumous Way of All Flesh making so little impression that when, some years later, I produce plays in which Butler's extraordinarily fresh, free and future-piercing suggestions have an obvious share, I am met with nothing but vague cacklings about Ibsen and Nietzsche, and am only too thankful that they are not about Alfred de Musset and Georges Sand. Really, the English do not deserve to have great men. They allowed Butler to die practically unknown, whilst I, a comparatively insignificant Irish journalist, was leading them by the nose into an advertisement of me which has made my own life a burden. In Sicily there is a Via Samuele Butler. When an English tourists sees it, he either asks "Who the devil was Samuele Butler?" or wonders why the Sicilians should perpetuate the author of Hudibras.

Well, it cannot be denied that the English are only too anxious to recognize a man of genius if somebody will kindly point him out to them. Having pointed myself out in this manner with some success, I now point out Samuel Butler, and trust that in consequence I shall hear a little less in future of the novelty and foreign origin of the ideas which are now making their way into the English theatre through plays written by Socialists. There are living men whose originality and powers are as obvious as Butler's and when they die that fact will be discovered. Meanwhile I recommend them to insist on their own merits as an important part of their own business.

THE SALVATION ARMY

When Major Barbara was produced in London, the second act was reported in an important northern newspaper as a withering attack on the Salvation Army, and the despairing ejaculation of Barbara deplored by a London daily as a tasteless blasphemy. And they were set right, not by the professed critics of the theatre, but by religious and philosophical publicists like Sir Oliver Lodge and Dr Stanton Coit, and strenuous Nonconformist journalists like William Stead, who not only understood the act as well as the Salvationists themselves, but also saw it in its relation to the religious life of the nation, a life which seems to lie not only outside the sympathy of many of our theatre critics, but actually outside their knowledge of society. Indeed nothing could be more ironically curious than the confrontation Major Barbara effected of the theatre enthusiasts with the religious enthusiasts. On the one hand was the playgoer, always seeking pleasure, paying exorbitantly for it, suffering unbearable discomforts for it, and hardly ever getting it. On the other hand was the Salvationist, repudiating gaiety and courting effort and sacrifice, yet always in the wildest spirits, laughing, joking, singing, rejoicing, drumming, and tambourining: his life flying by in a flash of excitement, and his death arriving as a climax of triumph. And, if you please, the playgoer despising the Salvationist as a joyless person, shut out from the heaven of the theatre, self-condemned to a life of hideous gloom; and the Salvationist mourning over the playgoer as over a prodigal with vine leaves in his hair, careering out-rageously to hell amid the popping of champagne corks and the ribald laughter of sirens! Could misunderstanding be more complete, or sympathy worse misplaced?

Fortunately, the Salvationists are more accessible to the religious character of the drama than the playgoers to the gay energy and artistic fertility of religion. They can see, when it is pointed out to them, that a theatre, as a place where two or three are gathered together, takes from that divine presence an inalienable sanctity of which the grossest and profanest farce can no more deprive it than a hypocritical sermon by a snobbish bishop can desecrate Westminster Abbey. But in our professional playgoers this indispensable preliminary conception of sanct-ity seems wanting. They talk of actors as mimes and mummers, and, I fear, think of dramatic authors as liars and pandars, whose main business is the voluptuous soothing of the tired city speculator when what he calls the serious business of the day is over. Passion, the life of drama, means nothing to them but primitive sexual excitement: such phrases as "impassioned poetry" or "passionate love of truth" have fallen quite out of their vocabulary and been replaced by "passional crime" and the like. They assume, as far as I can gather, that people in whom passion has a larger scope are passionless and therefore uninteresting. Conse-quently they come to think of religious people as people who are not interesting and not amusing. And so, when Barbara cuts the regular Salvation Army jokes, and snatches a kiss from her lover across his drum, the devotees of the theatre think they ought to appear shocked, and conclude that the whole play is an elaborate mockery of the Army. And then either hypocritically rebuke me for mocking, or foolishly take part in the supposed mockery!

Even the handful of mentally competent critics got into difficulties over my demonstration of the economic deadlock in which the Salvation Army finds itself. Some of them thought that the Army would not have taken money from a distiller and a cannon founder: others thought it should not have taken it: all assumed more or less definitely that it reduced itself to absurdity or hypocrisy by taking it. On the first point the reply of the Army itself was prompt and conclusive. As one of its officers said, they would take money from the devil himself and be only too glad to get it out of his hands and into God's. They gratefully acknowl-edged that publicans not only give them money but allow them to collect it in the bar — sometimes even when there is a Salvation meeting outside preaching teetotalism. In fact, they questioned the verisimilitude of the play, not because Mrs Baines took the money, but because Barbara refused it.

On the point that the Army ought not to take such money, its justification is obvious. It must take the money because it cannot exist without money, and there is no other money to be had. Practically all the spare money in the country consists of a mass of rent, interest, and profit, every penny of which is bound up with crime, drink, prostitution, disease, and all the evil fruits of poverty, as inextricably as with enterprise, wealth, commercial probity, and national prosperity. The notion that you can earmark certain coins as tainted is an unpractical individualist superstition. None the less the fact that all our money is tainted gives a very severe shock to earnest young souls when some dramatic instance of the taint first makes them conscious of it. When an enthusiastic young clergyman of the Established Church first realizes that the Ecclesiastical Commissioners receive the rents of sporting public houses, brothels, and sweating dens; or that the most generous contributor at his last charity sermon was an employer trading in female labor cheapened by prostitution as unscrupulously as a hotel keeper trades in waiters' labor cheapened by tips, or commissionaires' labor cheapened by pensions; or that the only patron who can afford to rebuild his church or his schools or give his boys' brigade a gymnasium or a library is the son-in-law of a Chicago meat King, that young clergyman has, like Barbara, a very bad quarter hour. But he cannot help himself by refusing to accept money from anybody except sweet old ladies with independent incomes and gentle and lovely ways of life. He has only to follow up the income of the sweet ladies to its industrial source, and there he will find Mrs Warren's profession and the poisonous canned meat and all the rest of it. His own stipend has the same root. He must either share the world's guilt or go to another planet. He must save the world's honor if he is to save his own. That is what all the Churches find just as the Salvation Army and Barbara find it in the play. Her discovery that she is her father's accomplice; that the Salvation Army is the accomplice of the distiller and the dynamite maker; that they can no more escape one another than they can escape the air they breathe; that there is no salvation for them through personal righteousness, but only through the redemption of the whole nation from its vicious, lazy, competitive anarchy: this discovery has been made by everyone except the Pharisees and (apparently) the professional playgoers, who still wear their Tom Hood shirts and underpay their washerwomen without the slightest misgiving as to the elevation of their private characters, the purity of their private atmospheres, and their right to repudiate as foreign to themselves the coarse depravity of the garret and the slum. Not that they mean any harm: they only desire to be, in their little private way, what they call gentlemen. They do not understand Barbara's lesson because they have not, like her, learnt it by taking their part in the larger life of the nation.

BARBARA'S RETURN TO THE COLORS

Barbara's return to the colors may yet provide a subject for the dramatic historian of the future. To go back to the Salvation Army with the knowledge that even the Salvationists themselves are not saved yet; that poverty is not blessed, but a most damnable sin; and that when General Booth chose Blood and Fire for the emblem of Salvation instead of the Cross, he was perhaps better inspired than he knew:

such knowledge, for the daughter of Andrew Undershaft, will clearly lead to something hopefuller than distributing bread and treacle at the expense of Bodger.

It is a very significant thing, this instinctive choice of the military form of organization, this substitution of the drum for the organ, by the Salvation Army. Does it not suggest that the Salvationists divine that they must actually fight the devil instead of merely praying at him? At present, it is true, they have not quite ascertained his correct address. When they do, they may give a very rude shock to that sense of security which he has gained from his experience of the fact that hard words, even when uttered by eloquent essayists and lecturers, or carried unanimously at enthusiastic public meetings on the motion of eminent reformers, break no bones. It has been said that the French Revolution was the work of Voltaire, Rousseau and the Encyclopedists. It seems to me to have been the work of men who had observed that virtuous indignation, caustic criticism, conclusive argument and instructive pamphleteering, even when done by the most earnest and witty literary geniuses, were as useless as praying, things going steadily from bad to worse whilst the Social Contract and the pamphlets of Voltaire were at the height of their vogue. Eventually, as we know, perfectly respectable citizens and earnest philanthropists connived at the September massacres because hard experience had convinced them that if they contented themselves with appeals to humanity and patriotism, the aristocracy, though it would read their appeals with the greatest enjoyment and appreciation, flattering and admiring the writers, would none the less continue to conspire with foreign monarchists to undo the revolution and restore the old system with every circumstance of savage vengeance and ruthless repression of popular liberties.

The nineteenth century saw the same lesson repeated in England. It had its Utilitarians, its Christian Socialists, its Fabians (still extant): it had Bentham, Mill, Dickens, Ruskin, Carlyle, Butler, Henry George, and Morris. And the end of all their efforts is the Chicago described by Mr Upton Sinclair and the London in which the people who pay to be amused by my dramatic representation of Peter Shirley turned out to starve at forty because there are younger slaves to be had for his wages, do not take, and have not the slightest intention of taking, any effective step to organize society in such a way as to make that everyday infamy impossible. I, who have preached and pamphleteered like any Encyclopedist, have to confess that my methods are no use, and would be no use if I were Voltaire, Rousseau, Bentham, Marx, Mill, Dickens, Carlyle, Ruskin, Butler, and Morris all rolled into one, with Euripides, More, Montaigne, Molière, Beaumarchais, Swift, Goethe, Ibsen, Tolstoy, Jesus and the prophets all thrown in (as indeed in some sort I actually am, standing as I do on all their shoulders). The problem being to make heroes out of cowards, we paper apostles and artist-magicians have succeeded only in giving cowards all the sensations of heroes whilst they tolerate every abomination, accept every plunder, and submit to every oppression. Christianity, in making a merit of such submission, has marked only that depth in the abyss at which the very sense of shame is lost. The Christian has been like Dickens' doctor in the debtor's prison, who tells the newcomer of its ineffable peace and security: no duns; no tyrannical collector of rates, taxes, and rent; no importunate hopes nor exacting duties; nothing but the rest and safety of having no farther to fall.

Yet in the poorest corner of this soul-destroying Christendom vitality suddenly begins to germinate again. Joyousness, a sacred gift long dethroned by the hellish laughter of derision and obscenity, rises like a flood miraculously out of the fetid dust and mud of the slums; rousing marches and impetuous dithyrambs rise to the heavens from people among whom the depressing noise called "sacred music" is a standing joke; a flag with Blood and Fire on it is unfurled, not in murderous rancor, but because fire is beautiful and blood a vital and splendid red; Fear, which we flatter by calling Self, vanishes; and transfigured men and women carry their gospel through a transfigured world, calling their leader General, themselves captains and brigadiers, and their whole body an Army: praying, but praying only for refreshment, for strength to fight, and for needful MONEY (a notable sign, that) preaching, but not preaching submission; daring ill-usage and abuse, but not putting up with more of it than is inevitable; and practising what the world will let them practise, including soap and water, color and music. There is danger in such activity; and where there is danger there is hope. Our present security is nothing, and can be nothing, but evil made irresistible.

WEAKNESSES OF THE SALVATION ARMY

For the present, however, it is not my business to flatter the Salvation Army. Rather must I point out to it that it has almost as many weaknesses as the Church of England itself. It is building up a business organization which will compel it eventually to see that its present staff of enthusiast-commanders shall be succeeded by a bureaucracy of men of business who will be no better than bishops, and perhaps a good deal more unscrupulous. That has always happened sooner or later to great orders founded by saints; and the order founded by St William Booth is not exempt from the same danger. It is even more dependent than the Church on rich people who would cut off supplies at once if it began to preach that indispensable revolt against poverty which must also be a revolt against riches. It is hampered by a heavy contingent of pious elders who are not really Salvationists at all, but Evangelicals of the old school. It still, as Commissioner Howard affirms, "sticks to Moses," which is flat nonsense at this time of day if the Commissioner means, as I am afraid he does, that the Book of Genesis contains a trustworthy scientific account of the origin of species, and that the god to whom Jephthah sacrificed his daughter is any less obviously a tribal idol than Dagon or Chemosh.

Further, there is still too much other-worldliness about the Army. Like Frederick's grenadier, the Salvationist wants to live for ever (the most monstrous way of crying for the moon); and though it is evident to anyone who has ever heard General Booth and his best officers that they would work as hard for human salvation as they do at present if they believed that death would be the end of them individually, they and their followers have a bad habit of talking as if the

Salvationists were heroically enduring a very bad time on earth as an investment which will bring them in dividends later on in the form, not of a better life to come for the whole world, but of an eternity spent by themselves personally in a sort of bliss which would bore any active person to a second death. Surely the truth is that the Salvationists are unusually happy people. And is it not the very diagnostic of true salvation that it shall overcome the fear of death? Now the man who has come to believe that there is no such thing as death, the change so called being merely the transition to an exquisitely happy and utterly careless life, has not overcome the fear of death at all: on the contrary, it has overcome him so completely that he refuses to die on any terms whatever. I do not call a Salvationist really saved until he is ready to lie down cheerfully on the scrap heap, having paid scot and lot and something over, and let his eternal life pass on to renew its youth in the battalions of the future.

Then there is the nasty lying habit called confession, which the Army encourages because it lends itself to dramatic oratory, with plenty of thrilling incident. For my part, when I hear a convert relating the violences and oaths and blasphemies he was guilty of before he was saved, making out that he was a very terrible fellow then and is the most contrite and chastened of Christians now, I believe him no more than I believe the millionaire who says he came up to London or Chicago as a boy with only three half-pence in his pocket. Salvationists have said to me that Barbara in my play would never have been taken in by so transparent a humbug as Snobby Price; and certainly I do not think Snobby could have taken in any experienced Salvationist on a point on which the Salvationist did not wish to be taken in. But on the point of conversion all Salvationists wish to be taken in; for the more obvious the sinner the more obvious the miracle of his conversion. When you advertize a converted burglar or reclaimed drunkard as one of the attractions at an experience meeting, your burglar can hardly have been too burglarious or your drunkard too drunken. As long as such attractions are relied on, you will have your Snobbies claiming to have beaten their mothers when they were as a matter of prosaic fact habitually beaten by them, and your Rummies of the tamest respectability pretending to a past of reckless and dazzling vice. Even when confessions are sincerely autobiographic we should beware of assuming that the impulse to make them was pious or that the interest of the hearers is wholesome. As well might we assume that the poor people who insist on shewing disgusting ulcers to district visitor are convinced hygienists, or that the curiosity which sometimes welcomes such exhibitions is a pleasant and creditable one. One is often tempted to suggest that those who pester our police superintendents with confessions of murder might very wisely be taken at their word and executed, except in the few cases in which a real murderer is seeking to be relieved of his guilt by confession and expiation. For though I am not, I hope, an unmerciful person, I do not think that the inexorability of the deed once done should be disguised by any ritual, whether in the confessional or on the scaffold.

And here my disagreement with Salvation Army, and with all propagandists of the Cross (which I loathe as I loathe all gibbets) becomes deep indeed. Forgiveness, absolution, atonement, are figments: punishment is only a pretence of cancelling one crime by another; and you can no more have forgiveness without vindictiveness than you can have a cure without a disease. You will never get a high morality from people who conceive that their misdeeds are revocable and pardonable, or in a society where absolution and expiation are officially provided for us all. The demand may be very real; but the supply is spurious. Thus Bill Walker, in my play, having assaulted the Salvation Lass, presently finds himself overwhelmed with an intolerable conviction of sin under the skilled treatment of Barbara. Straightway he begins to try to unassault the lass and deruffianize his deed, first by getting punished for it in kind, and, when that relief is denied him, by fining himself a pound to compensate the girl. He is foiled both ways. He finds the Salvation Army as inexorable as fact itself. It will not punish him: it will not take his money. It will not tolerate a redeemed ruffian: it leaves him no means of salvation except ceasing to be a ruffian. In doing this, the Salvation Army instinctively grasps the central truth of Christianity and discards its central superstition: that central truth being the vanity of revenge and punishment, and that central superstition the salvation of the world by the gibbet.

For, be it noted, Bill has assaulted an old and starving woman also; and for this worse offence he feels no remorse whatever, because she makes it clear that her malice is as great as his own. "Let her have the law of me, as she said she would," says Bill: "what I done to her is no more on what you might call my conscience than sticking a pig." This shews a perfectly natural and wholesome state of mind on his part. The old woman, like the law she threatens him with, is perfectly ready to play the game of retaliation with him: to rob him if he steals, to flog him if he strikes, to murder him if he kills. By example and precept the law and public opinion teach him to impose his will on others by anger, violence, and cruelty, and to wipe off the moral score by punishment. That is sound Crosstianity. But this Crosstianity has got entangled with something which Barbara calls Christianity, and which unexpectedly causes her to refuse to play the hangman's game of Satan casting out Satan. She refuses to prosecute a drunken ruffian; she converses on equal terms with a blackguard to whom no lady should be seen speaking in the public street: in short she imitates Christ. Bill's conscience reacts to this just as naturally as it does to the old woman's threats. He is placed in a position of unbearable moral inferiority, and strives by every means in his power to escape from it, whilst he is still quite ready to meet the abuse of the old woman by attempting to smash a mug on her face. And that is the triumphant justification of Barbara's Christianity as against our system of judicial punishment and the vindictive villain-thrashings and "poetic justice" of the romantic stage.

For the credit of literature it must be pointed out that the situation is only partly novel. Victor Hugo long ago gave us the epic of the convict and the bishop's candlesticks, of the Crosstian policeman annihilated by his encounter with the Christian Valjean. But Bill Walker is not, like Valjean, romantically changed from a demon into an angel. There are millions of Bill Walkers in all classes of society today; and the point which I, as a professor of natural psychology, desire to demonstrate, is that Bill, without any change in his character or circumstances whatsoever, will react one way to one sort of treatment and another way to another.

In proof I might point to the sensational object lesson provided by our commerical millionaires today. They begin as brigands: merciless, unscrupulous, dealing out ruin and death and slavery to their competitors and employees, and facing desperately the worst that their competitors can do to them. The history of the English factories, the American Trusts, the exploitation of African gold, diamonds, ivory and rubber, outdoes in villainy the worst that has ever been imagined of the buccaneers of the Spanish Main. Captain Kidd would have marooned a modern Trust magnate for conduct unworthy of a gentleman of fortune. The law every day seizes on unsuccessful scoundrels of this type and punishes them with a cruelty worse than their own, with the result that they come out of the torture house more dangerous than they went in, and renew their evil doing (nobody will employ them at anything else) until they are again seized, again tormented, and again let loose, with the same result.

But the successful scoundrel is dealt with very differently, and very Christianly. He is not only forgiven: he is idolized, respected, made much of, all but worshipped. Society returns him good for evil in the most extravagant overmeasure. And with what result? He begins to idolize himself, to respect himself, to live up to the treatment he receives. He preaches sermons; he writes books of the most edifying advice to young men, and actually persuades himself that he got on by taking his own advice; he endows educational institutions; he supports charities; he dies finally in the odor of sanctity, leaving a will which is a monument of public spirit and bounty. And all this without any change in his character. The spots of the leopard and the stripes of the tiger are as brilliant as ever; but the conduct of the world towards him has changed, and his conduct has changed accordingly. You have only to reverse your attitude towards him—to lay hands on his property, revile him, assault him, and he will be a brigand again in a moment, as ready to crush you as you are to crush him, and quite as full of pretentious moral reasons for doing it.

In short, when Major Barbara says that there are no scoundrels, she is right: there are no absolute scoundrels, though there are impracticable people of whom I shall treat presently. Every reasonable man (and woman) is a potential scoundrel and a potential good citizen. What a man is depends on his character; but what he does, and what we think of what he does, depends on his circumstances. The characteristics that ruin a man in one class make him eminent in another. The characters that behave differently in different circumstances behave alike in similar circumstances. Take a common English character like that of Bill Walker. We meet Bill everywhere: on the judicial bench, on the episcopal bench, in the Privy Council at the War Office and Admiralty, as well as in the Old Bailey dock or in the ranks of casual unskilled labor. And the morality of Bill's characteristics varies with these various circumstances. The faults of the burglar are the qualities of the financier: the manners and habits of a duke would cost a city clerk his situation. In short, though character is independent of circumstances, conduct is not; and our moral judgments of character are not: both are circumstantial. Take any condition of life in which the circumstances are for a mass of men practically alike: felony, the House of Lords, the factory, the stables, the gipsy encampment or where you please! In spite of diversity of character and temperament, the conduct and morals of the individuals in each group are as predictable and as alike in the main as if they were a flock of sheep, morals being mostly only social habits and circumstantial necessities. Strong people know this and count upon it. In nothing have the masterminds of the world been distinguished from the ordinary suburban season-ticket holder more than in their straightforward perception of the fact that mankind is practically a single species, and not a menagerie of gentlemen and bounders, villains and heroes, cowards and daredevils, peers and peasants, grocers and aristocrats, artisans and laborers, washerwomen and duchesses, in which all the grades of income and caste represent distinct animals who must not be introduced to one another or intermarry. Napoleon constructing a galaxy of generals and courtiers, and even of monarchs, out of his collection of social nobodies: Julius Cæsar appointing as governor of Egypt the son of a freedman — one who but a short time before would have been legally disqualified for the post even of a private soldier in the Roman army; Louis XI making his barber his privy councillor: all these had in their different ways a firm hold of the scientific fact of human equality, expressed by Barbara in the Christian formula that all men are children of one father. A man who believes that men are naturally divided into upper and lower and middle classes morally is making exactly the same mistakes as the man who believes that they are naturally divided in the same way socially. And just as our persistent attempts to found political institutions on a basis of social inequality have always produced long periods of destructive friction relieved from time to time by violent explosions of revolution; so the attempt — will Americans please note—to found moral institutions on a basis of moral inequality can lead to nothing but unnatural Reigns of the Saints relieved by licentious Restorations; to Americans who have made divorce a public institution turning the face of Europe into one huge sardonic smile by refusing to stay in the same hotel with a Russian man of genius who has changed wives without the sanction of South Dakota; to grotesque hypocrisy, cruel persecution, and final utter confusion of conventions and compliances with benevolence and respectability. It is quie useless to declare that all men are born free if you deny that they are born good. Guarantee a man's goodness and his liberty will take care of itself. To guarantee his freedom on condition that you approve of his moral character is formally to abolish all freedom whatsoever, as every man's liberty is at the mercy of a moral indictment which any fool can trump up against everyone who violates custom, whether as a prophet or as a rascal. This is the lesson Democracy has to learn before it can become anything but the most oppressive of all the priesthoods.

Let us now return to Bill Walker and his case of conscience against the Salvation Army. Major Barbara, not being a modern Tetzel, or the treasurer of a hospital, refuses to sell absolution to Bill for a sovereign. Unfortunately, what the Army can afford to refuse in the case of Bill Walker, it cannot refuse in the case of Bodger.

Bodger is master of the situation because he holds the purse strings. "Strive as you will," says Bodger, in effect: "me you cannot do without. You cannot save Bill Walker without my money." And the Army answers, quite rightly under the circumstances, "We will take money from the devil himself sooner than abandon the work of Salvation." So Bodger pays his conscience-money and gets the absolution that is refused to Bill. In real life Bill would perhaps never know this. But I, the dramatist whose business it is to shew the connexion between things that seem apart and unrelated in the haphazard order of events in real life, have contrived to make it known to Bill, with the result that the Salvation Army loses its hold of him at once.

But Bill may not be lost, for all that. He is still in the grip of the facts and of his own conscience, and may find his taste for blackguardism permanently spoiled. Still, I cannot guarantee that happy ending. Walk through the poorer quarters of our cities on Sunday when the men are not working, but resting and chewing the cud of their reflections. You will find one expression common to every mature face: the expression of cynicism. The discovery made by Bill Walker about the Salvation Army has been made by everyone there. They have found that every man has his price; and they have been foolishly or corruptly taught to mistrust and despise him for that necessary and salutary condition of social existence. When they learn that General Booth, too, has his price, they do not admire him because it is a high one, and admit the need of organizing society so that he shall get it in an honorable way: they conclude that his character is unsound and that all religious men are hypocrites and allies of their sweaters and oppressors. They know that the large subscriptions which help to support the Army are endowments, not of religion, but of the wicked doctrine of docility in poverty and humility under oppression; and they are rent by the most agonizing of all the doubts of the soul, the doubt whether their true salvation must not come from their most abhorrent passions, from murder, envy, greed, stubbornness, rage, and terrorism, rather than from public spirit, reasonableness, humanity, generosity, tenderness, delicacy, pity and kindness. The confirmation of that doubt, at which our newspapers have been working so hard for years past, is the morality of militarism; and the justification of militarism is that circumstances may at any time make it the true morality of the moment. It is by producing such moments that we produce violent and sanguinary revolutions, such as the one now in progress in Russia and the one which Capitalism in England and America is daily and diligently provoking.

At such moments it becomes the duty of the Churches to evoke all the powers of destruction against the existing order. But if they do this, the existing order must forcibly suppress them. Churches are suffered to exist only on condition that they preach submission to the State as at present capitalistically organized. The Church of England itself is compelled to add to the thirtysix articles in which it formulates its religious tenets, three more in which it apologetically protests that the moment any of these articles comes in conflict with the State it is to be entirely renounced, abjured, violated, abrogated and abhorred, the policeman being a much more important person than any of the Persons of the Trinity. And this is why no tolerated Church nor Salvation Army can ever win the entire confidence of the poor. It must be on the side of the police and the military, no matter what it believes or disbelieves; and as the police and the military are the instruments by which the rich rob and oppress the poor (on legal and moral principles made for the purpose), it is not possible to be on the side of the poor and of the police at the same time. Indeed the religious bodies, as the almoners of the rich, become a sort of auxiliary police, taking off the insurrectionary edge of poverty with coals and blankets, bread and treacle, and soothing and cheering the victims with hopes of immense and inexpensive happiness in another world when the process of working them to premature death in the service of the rich is complete in this.

CHRISTIANITY AND ANARCHISM

Such is the false position from which neither the Salvation Army nor the Church of England nor any other religious organization whatever can escape except through a reconstitution of society. Nor can they merely endure the State passively, washing their hands of its sins. The State is constantly forcing the consciences of men by violence and cruelty. Not content with exacting money from us for the maintenance of its soldiers and policemen, its gaolers and executioners, it forces us to take an active personal part in its proceedings on pain of becoming ourselves the victims of its violence. As I write these lines, a sensational example is given to the world. A royal marriage has been celebrated, first by sacrament in a cathedral, and then by a bullfight having for its main amusement the spectacle of horses gored and disembowelled by the bull, after which, when the bull is so exhausted as to be no longer dangerous, he is killed by a cautious matador. But the ironic contrast between the bullfight and the sacrament of marriage does not move anyone. Another contrast—that between the splendor, the happiness, the atmosphere of kindly admiration surrounding the young couple, and the price paid for it under our abominable social arrangements in the misery, squalor and degradation of millions of other young couples—is drawn at the same moment by a novelist, Mr Upton Sinclair, who chips a corner of the veneering from the huge meat packing industries of Chicago, and shews it to us as a sample of what is going on all over the world underneath the top layer of prosperous plutocracy. One man is sufficiently moved by that contrast to pay his own life as the price of one terrible blow at the responsible parties. His poverty has left him ignorant enough to be duped by the pretence that the innocent young bride and bridegroom, put forth and crowned by plutocracy as the heads of a State in which they have less personal power than any policeman, and less influence than any Chairman of a Trust, are responsible. At them accordingly he launches his sixpennorth of fulminate, missing his mark, but scattering the bowels of as many horses as any bull in the arena, and slaying twentythree persons, besides wounding ninetynine. And all of these, the horses alone are innocent of the guilt he is avenging: had he blown all Madrid to atoms with every adult person in it, not one could have escaped the charge of being an accessory, before, at, and after the fact, to poverty and prostitution, to such wholesale massacre of infants as Herod never dreamt of, to plague, pestilence and famine, battle, murder and lingering death — perhaps not one who had not helped, through example, precept, connivance, and even clamor, to teach the dynamiter his well-learnt gospel of hatred and vengeance, by approving every day of sentences of years of imprisonment so infernal in their unnatural stupidity and panicstricken cruelty, that their advocates can disavow neither the dagger nor the bomb without stripping the mask of justice and humanity from themselves also.

Be it noted that at this very moment there appears the biography of one of our dukes, who, being a Scot, could argue about politics, and therefore stood out as a great brain among our aristocrats. And what, if you please, was his grace's favorite historical episode, which he declared he never read without intense satisfaction? Why, the young General Bonapart's pounding of the Paris mob to pieces in 1795, called in playful approval by our respectable classes "the whiff of grapeshot," though Napoleon, to do him justice, took a deeper view of it, and would fain have had it forgotten. And sinde the Duke of Argyll was not a demon, but a man of like passions with ourselves, by no means rancorous or cruel as men go, who can doubt that all over the world proletarians of the ducal kidney are now revelling in "the whiff of dynamite" (the flavor of the joke seems to evaporate a little, does it not?) because it was aimed at the class they hate even as our argute duke hated what he called the mob.

In such an atmosphere there can be only one sequel to the Madrid explosion. All Europe burns to emulate it. Vengeance! More blood! Tear "the Anarchist beast" to shreds. Drag him to the scaffold. Imprison him for life. Let all civilized States band together to drive his like off the face of the earth; and if any State refuses to join, make war on it. This time the leading London newspaper, anti-Liberal and therefore anti-Russian in politics, does not say "Serve you right" to the victims, as it did, in effect, when Bobrikoff, and De Plehve, and Grand Duke Sergius, were in the same manner unofficially fulminated into fragments. No: fulminate our rivals in Asia by all means, ye brave Russian revolutionaries; but to aim at an English princess! monstrous! hideous! hound down the wretch to his doom; and observe, please, that we are a civilized and merciful people, and, however much we may regret it, must not treat him as Ravaillac and Damiens were treated. And meanwhile, since we have not yet caught him, let us soothe our quivering nerves with the bullfight, and comment in a courtly way on the unfailing tact and good taste of the ladies of our royal houses, who, though presumably of full normal natural tenderness, have been so effectually broken in to fashionable routine that they can be taken to see the horses slaughtered as helplessly as they could no doubt be taken to a gladiator show, if that happened to be the mode just now.

Strangely enough, in the midst of this raging fire of malice, the one man who still has faith in the kindness and intelligence of human nature is the fulminator, now a hunted wretch, with nothing, apparently, to secure his triumph over all the prisons and scaffolds of infuriate Europe except the revolver in his pocket and his readiness to discharge it at a moment's notice into his own or any other head. Think of him setting out to find a gentleman and a Christian in the multitude of human wolves howling for his blood. Think also of this: that at the very first essay he finds what he seeks, a veritable grandee of Spain, a noble, high-thinking, unterrified, malice-void soul, in the guise — of all masquerades in the world! — of a modern editor. The Anarchist wolf, flying from the wolves of plutocracy, throws himself on the honor of the man. The man, not being a wolf (nor a London editor), and therefore not having enough sympathy with his exploit to be made bloodthirsty by it, does not throw him back to the pursuing wolves — gives him, instead, what help he can to escape, and sends him off acquainted at last with a force that goes deeper than dynamite, though you cannot buy so much of it for sixpence. That righteous and honorable high human deed is not wasted on Europe, let us hope, though it benefits the fugitive wolf only for a moment. The plutocratic wolves presently smell him out. The fugitive shoots the unlucky wolf whose nose is nearest; shoots himself and then convinces the world, by his photograph, that he was no monstrous freak of reversion to the tiger, but a good looking young man with nothing abnormal about him except his appalling courage and resolution (that is why the terrified shriek Coward at him): one to whom murdering a happy young couple on their wedding morning would have been an unthinkably unnatural abomination under rational and kindly human circumstances.

Then comes the climax of irony and blind stupidity. The wolves, balked of their meal of fellow-wolf, turn on the man, and proceed to torture him, after their manner, by imprisonment, for refusing to fasten his teeth in the throat of the dynamiter and hold him down until they came to finish him.

Thus, you see, a man may not be a gentleman nowadays even if he wishes to. As to being a Christian, he is allowed some latitude in that matter, because, I repeat, Christianity has two faces. Popular Christianity has for its emblem a gibbet, for its chief sensation a sanguinary execution after torture, for its central mystery an insane vengeance bought off by a trumpery expiation. But there is a nobler and profounder Christianity which affirms the sacred mystery of Equality, and forbids the glaring futility and folly of vengeance, often politely called punishment or justice. The gibbet part of Christianity is tolerated. The other is criminal felony. Connoisseurs in irony are well aware of the fact that the only editor in England who denounces punishment as radically wrong, also repudiates Christianity; calls his paper The Freethinker; and has been imprisoned for "bad taste" under the law against blasphemy.

SANE CONCLUSIONS

And now I must ask the excited reader not to lose his head on one side or the other, but to draw a sane moral from these grim absurdities. It is not good sense to propose that laws against crime should apply to principals only and not to accessories whose consent, counsel, or silence may secure impunity to the principal. If you institute punishment as part of the law, you must punish people for refusing to punish. If you have a police, part of its duty must be to compel everybody to assist the police. No doubt if your laws are unjust, and your policemen agents of oppression, the result will be an unbearable violation of the private consciences of citizens. But that cannot be helped: the remedy is, not to license everybody to thwart the law if they please, but to make laws that will command the public assent, and not to deal cruelly and stupidly with law-breakers. Everybody disapproves of burglars; but the modern burglar, when caught and overpowered by a householder, usually appeals, and often, let us hope, with success, to his captor not to deliver him over to the useless horrors of penal servitude. In other cases the lawbreaker escapes because those who could give him up do not consider his breach of the law a guilty action. Sometimes, even, private tribunals are formed in opposition to the official tribunals; and these private tribunals employ assassins as executioners, as was done, for example, by Mahomet before he had established his power officially, and by the Ribbon lodges of Ireland in their long struggle with the landlords. Under such circumstances, the assassin goes free although everybody in the district knows who he is and what he has done. They do not betray him, partly because they justify him exactly as the regular Government justifies its official executioner, and partly because they would themselves be assassinated if they betrayed him: another method learnt from the official government. Given a tribunal, employing a slayer who has no personal quarrel with the slain; and there is clearly no moral difference between official and unofficial killing.

In short, all men are anarchists with regard to laws which are against their consciences, either in the preamble or in the penalty. In London our worst anarchists are the magistrates, because many of them are so old and ignorant that when they are called upon to administer any law that is based on ideas or knowledge less than half a century old, they disagree with it, and being mere ordinary homebred private Englishmen without any respect for law in the abstract, naïvely set the example of violating it. In this instance the man lags behind the law; but when the law lags behind the man, he becomes equally an anarchist. When some huge change in social conditions, such as the industrial revolution of the eighteenth and nineteenth centuries, throws our legal and industrial institutions out of date, Anarchism becomes aslmost a religion. The whole force of the most energetic geniuses of the time in philosophy, economics, and art, concentrates itself on demonstrations and reminders that morality and law are only conventions, fallible and continually obsolescing. Tragedies in which the heroes are bandits, and comedies in which law-abiding and conventionally moral folk are compelled to satirize themselves by outraging the conscience of the spectators every time they do their duty, appear simultaneously with economic treatises entitled "What is Property? Theft!" and with histories of "The Conflict between Religion and Science."

Now this is not a healthy state of things. The advantages of living in society are proportionate, not to the freedom of the individual from a code, but to the complexity and subtlety of the code he is prepared not only to accept but to uphold as a matter of such vital importance that a lawbreaker at large is hardly to be tolerated on any plea. Such an attitude becomes impossible when the only men who can make themselves heard and remembered throughout the world spend all their energy in raising our gorge against current law, current morality, current respectability, and legal property. The ordinary man, uneducated in social theory even when he is schooled in Latin verse, cannot be set against all the laws of his country and yet persuaded to regard law in the abstract as vitally necessary to society. Once he is brought to repudiate the laws and institutions he knows, he will repudiate the very conception of law and the very groundwork of institutions, ridiculing human rights, extolling brainless methods as "historical,"and tolerating nothing except pure empiricism in conduct, with dynamite as the basis of politics and vivisection as the basis of science. That is hideous; but what is to be done? Here am I, for instance, by class a respectable man, by common sense a hater of waste and disorder, by intellectual constitution legally minded to the verge of pedantry, and by temperament apprehensive and economically disposed to the limit of old-maidishness; yet I am, and have always been, and shall now always be, a revolutionary writer, because our laws make law impossible; our liberties destroy all freedom; our property is organized robbery; our morality is an impudent hypocrisy; our wisdom is administered by inexperienced or malexperienced dupes, our power wielded by cowards and weaklings, and our honor false in all its points. I am an enemy of the existing order for good reasons; but that does not make my attacks any less encouraging or helpful to people who are its enemies for bad reasons. The existing order may shriek that if I tell the truth about it, some foolish person may drive it to become still worse by trying to assassinate it. I cannot help that, even if I could see what worse it could do than it is already doing. And the disadvantage of that worst even from its own point of view is that society, with all its prisons and bayonets and whips and ostracisms and starvations, is powerless in the face of the Anarchist who is prepared to sacrifice his own life in the battle with it. Our natural safety from the cheap and devastating explosives which every Russian student can make, and every Russian grenadier has learnt to handle in Manchuria, lies in the fact that brave and resolute men, when they are rascals, will not risk their skins for the good of humanity, and, when they are not, are sympathetic enough to care for humanity, abhorring murder, and never committing it until their consciences are outraged beyond endurance. The remedy is, then, simply not to outrage their consciences.

Do not be afraid that they will not make allowances. All men make very large allowances indeed before they stake their own lives in a war to the death with society. Nobody demands or expects the millennium. But there are two things that must be set right, or we shall perish, like Rome, of soul atrophy disguised as empire.

The first is, that the daily ceremony of dividing the wealth of the country among its inhabitants shall be so conducted that no crumb shall, save as a criminal's ration, go to any able-bodied adults who are not producing by their personal exertions not only a full equivalent for what they take, but a surplus sufficient to provide for their superannuation and pay back the debt due for their nurture.

The second is that the deliberate infliction of malicious injuries which now goes on under the name of punishment be abandoned; so that the thief, the rufffian, the gambler, and the beggar, may without inhumanity be handed over to the law, and made to understand that a State which is too humane to punish will also be too thrifty to waste the life of honest men in watching or restraining dishonest ones. That is why we do not imprison dogs. We even take our chance of their first bite. But if a dog delights to bark and bite, it goes to the lethal chamber. That seems to me sensible. To allow the dog to expiate his bite by a period of torment, and then let him loose in a much more savage condition (for the chain makes a dog savage) to bite again and expiate again, having meanwhile spent a great deal of human life and happiness in the task of chaining and feeding and tormenting him, seems to me idiotic and superstitious. Yet that is what we do to men who bark and bite and steal. It would be far more sensible to put up with their vices, as we put up with their illnesses, until they give more trouble than they are worth, at which point we should, with many apologies and expressions of sympathy, and some generosity in complying with their last wishes, place them in the lethal chamber and get rid of them. Under no circumstances should they be allowed to expiate their misdeeds by a manufactured penalty, to subscribe to a charity, or to compensate the victims. If there is to be no punishment there can be no forgiveness. We shall never have real moral responsibility until everyone knows that his deeds are irrevocable, and that his life depends on his usefulness. Hitherto, alas! humanity has never dared face these hard facts. We frantically scatter conscience money and invent systems of conscience banking, with expiatory penalties, atonements, redemptions, salvations, hospital subscription lists and what not, to enable us to contract-out of the moral code. Not content with the old scapegoat and sacrificial lamb, we deify human saviors, and pray to miraculous virgin intercessors. We attribute mercy to the inexorable; soothe our consciences after committing murder by throwing ourselves on the bosom of divine love; and shrink even from our own gallows because we are forced to admit that it, at least, is irrevocable — as if one hour of imprisonment were not as irrevocable as any execution!

If a man cannot look evil in the face without illusion, he will never know what it really is, or combat it effectually. The few men who have been able (relatively) to do this have been called cynics, and have sometimes had an abnormal share of evil in themselves, corresponding to the abnormal strength of their minds; but they have never done mischief unless they intended to do it. That is why great scoundrels have been beneficent rulers whilst amiable and privately harmless monarchs have ruined their countries by trusting to the hocus-pocus of innocence and guilt, reward and punishment, virtuous indignation and pardon, instead of standing up to the facts without either malice or mercy. Major Barbara stands up to Bill Walker in that way, with the result that the ruffian who cannot get hated, has to hate himself. To relieve this agony he tries to get punished; but the Salvationist whom he tries to provoke is as merciless as Barbara, and only prays for him. Then he tries to pay, but can get nobody to take his money. His doom is the doom of Cain, who, failing to find either a savior, a policeman, or an almoner to help him to pretend that his brother's blood no longer cried from the ground, had to live and die a murderer.Cain took care not to commit another murder, unlike our railway shareholders (I am one) who kill and maim shunters by hundreds to save the cost of automatic couplings, and make atonement by annual subscriptions to deserving charities. Had Cain been allowed to pay off his score, he might possibly have killed Adam and Eve for the mere sake of a second luxurious reconciliation with God afterwards. Bodger, you may depend on it, will go on to the end of his life poisoning people with bad whisky, because he can always depend on the Salvation Army or the Church of England to negotiate a redemption for him in consideration of a trifling percentage of his profits.

There is a third condition too, which must be fulfilled before the great teachers of the world will cease to scoff at its religions. Creeds must become intellectually honest. At present there is not a single credible established religion in the world. That is perhaps the most stupendous fact in the whole world-situation. This play of mine, Major Barbara, is, I hope, both true and inspired; but whoever says that it all happened, and that faith in it and understanding of it consist in believing that it is a record of an actual occurrence,is, to speak according to Scripture, a fool and a liar, and is hereby solemnly denounced and cursed as such by me, the author, to all posterity.

London, June 1906

POSTSCRIPT 1933. In spite of the emphasis laid both in this preface and in the play on the fact that poverty is an infectious pestilence to be prevented at all costs, the lazy habit still prevails of tolerating it not only as an inevitable misfortune to be charitably patronized and relieved, but as a useful punishment for all sorts of misconduct and inefficiency that are not expressly punishable by law. Until we have a general vital hatred of poverty, and a determination to "liquidate" the underfed either by feeding them or killing them, we shall not tackle the poverty question seriously. Long ago I proposed to eradicate the dangerous disease of hunger among children by placing good bread on public supply like drinking water. No Government nor municipality has yet taken up that very sensible proposal.

CHARACTERS

SIR ANDREW UNDERSHAFT

LADY BRITOMART UNDERSHAFT, his wife

BARBARA, his elder daughter, a Major in the Salvation Army

SARAH, his youngest daughter

STEPHEN, his son

ADOPLPHUS CUSINS, a professor of Greek in love with Barbara

CHARLES LOMAX, young-man-about-town, engaged to Sarah

MORRISON, Lady Britomart's butler

BRONTERRE O'BRIEN ("SNOBBY") PRICE, a cobbler-carpenter down on his luck

MRS. ROMOLA ("RUMMY") MITCHENS, a worn-out lady who relies on the Salvation
    Army

JENNY HILL, a young Salvation Army worker

PETER SHIRLEY, an unemployed coal-broker

BILL WALKER, a bully

MRS. BAINES, Commissioner in the Salvation Army

BILTON, a foreman at Perivale St. Andrews

*Scene: The action of the play occurs within several days in January, 1906. ACT 1: The
library of Lady Britomart's house in Wilton Crescent, a fashionable London suburb. ACT
2: The yard of the Salvation Army shelter in West Ham, an industrial suburb in London's
East End. ACT 3: The library in Lady Britomart's house; a parapet overlooking Perivale
St. Andrews, a region in Middlesex northwest of London.*

ACT I

*It is after dinner in January 1906, in the library in Lady Britomart Undershaft's house in
Wilton Crescent. A large and comfortable settee is in the middle of the room, upholstered
in dark leather. A person sitting on it (it is vacant at present) would have, on his right,
Lady Britomart's writing table, with the lady herself busy at it; a smaller writing table
behind him on his left; the door behind him on Lady Britomart's side; and a window with a
window seat directly on his left. Near the window is an armchair.*

*Lady Britomart is a woman of fifty or thereabouts, well dressed and yet careless of
her dress, well bred and quite reckless of her breeding, well mannered and yet appall-
ingly outspoken and indifferent to the opinion of her interlocutors, amiable and yet
peremptory, arbitrary, and high-tempered to the last bearable degree, and withal a very
typical managing matron of the upper class, treated as a naughty child until she grew
into a scolding mother, and finally settling down with plenty of practical ability and*

worldly experience, limited in the oddest way with domestic and class limitations, conceiving the universe exactly as if it were a large house in Wilton Crescent, though handling her corner of it very effectively on that assumption, and being quite enlightened and liberal as to the books in the library, the pictures on the walls, the music in the portfolios, and the articles in the papers.

Her son, Stephen, comes in. He is a gravely correct young man under 25, taking himself very seriously, but still in some awe of his mother, from childish habit and bachelor shyness, rather than from any weakness of character.

STEPHEN   Whats the matter?

LADY BRITOMART   Presently, Stephen.

Stephen submissively walks to the settee and sits down. He takes up a Liberal weekly called The Speaker.

LADY BRITOMART   Dont begin to read, Stephen. I shall require all your attention.

STEPHEN   It was only while I was waiting—

LADY BRITOMART   Dont make excuses, Stephen.[*He puts down The Speaker*]. Now! [*She finishes her writing; rises; comes to the settee*]. I have not kept you waiting very long, I think.

STEPHEN   Not at all, mother.

LADY BRITOMART   Bring me my cushion. [*He takes the cushion from the chair at the desk and arranges it for her as she sits down on the settee*]. Sit down. [*He sits down and fingers his tie nervously*]. Dont fiddle with your tie, Stephen: there is nothing the matter with it.

STEPHEN   I beg your pardon. [*He fiddles with his watch chain instead*].

LADY BRITOMART   Now are you attending to me, Stephen?

STEPHEN   Of course, mother.

LADY BRITOMART   No: it's not of course. I want something much more than your everyday matter-of-course attention. I am going to speak to you very seriously, Stephen. I wish you would let that chain alone.

STEPHEN   [*hastily relinquishing the chain*]   Have I done anything to annoy you, mother? If so, it was quite unintentional.

LADY BRITOMART [*astonished*]   Nonsense! [*With some remorse*] My poor boy, did you think I was angry with you?

STEPHEN   What is it, then, mother? You are making me very uneasy.

LADY BRITOMART [*squaring herself at him rather aggressively*]   Stephen: may I ask how soon you intend to realize that you are a grown-up man, and that I am only a woman?

STEPHEN [*amazed*]   Only a—

LADY BRITOMART   Dont repeat my words, please: it is a most aggravating habit. You must learn to face life seriously, Stephen. I really cannot bear the whole burden of our family affairs any longer. You must advise me: you must assume the responsibility.

STEPHEN   I!

LADY BRITOMART   Yes, you, of course. You were 24 last June. Youve been at Harrow and Cambridge. Youve been to India and Japan. You must know a lot of things, now; unless you have wasted your time most scandalously. Well, advise me.

STEPHEN [much perplexed]   You know I have never interfered in the household—

LADY BRITOMART   No: I should think not. I dont want you to order the dinner.

STEPHEN   I mean in our family affairs.

LADY BRITOMART   Well, you must interfere now; for they are getting quite beyond me.

STEPHEN [troubled]   I have thought sometimes that perhaps I ought; but really, mother, I know so little about them; and what I do know is so painful! it is so impossible to mention some things to you—[he stops, ashamed].

LADY BRITOMART   I suppose you mean your father.

STEPHEN [almost inaudibly]   Yes.

LADY BRITOMART   My dear: we cant go on all our lives not mentioning him. Of course you were quite right not to open the subject until I asked you to; but you are old enough now to be taken into my confidence, and to help me to deal with him about the girls.

STEPHEN   But the girls are all right. They are engaged.

LADY BRITOMART [complacently]   Yes: I have made a very good match for Sarah. Charles Lomax will be a millionaire at 35. But that is ten years ahead; and in the meantime his trustees cannot under the terms of his father's will allow him more than £800 a year.

STEPHEN   But the will says also that if he increases his income by his own exertions, they may double the increase.

LADY BRITOMART   Charles Lomax's exertions are much more likely to decrease his income than to increase it. Sarah will have to find at least another £800 a year for the next ten years; and even then they will be as poor as church mice. And what about Barbara? I thought Barbara was going to make the most brilliant career of all of you. And what does she do? Joins the Salvation Army, discharges her maid; lives on a pound a week; and walks in one evening with a professor of Greek whom she has picked up in the street, and who pretends to be a Salvationist, and actually plays the big drum for her in public because he has fallen head over ears in love with her.

STEPHEN   I was certainly rather taken aback when I heard they were engaged. Cusins is a very nice fellow, certainly: nobody would ever guess that he was born in Australia; but—

LADY BRITOMART   Oh, Adolphus Cusins will make a very good husband. After all, nobody can say a word against Greek: it stamps a man at once as an educated gentleman. And my family, thank Heaven, is not a pig-headed Tory one. We are Whigs, and believe in liberty. Let snobbish people say what they please: Barbara shall marry, not the man they like, but the man I like.

STEPHEN   Of course I was thinking only of his income. However, he is not likely to be extravagant.

LADY BRITOMART   Dont be too sure of that, Stephen. I know your quiet, simple, refined, poetic people like Adolphus: quite content with the best of everything! They cost more than your extravagant people, who are always as mean as they are second rate. No: Barbara will need at least £2000 a year. You see it means two additional households. Besides, my dear, you must marry soon. I dont approve of the present fashion of philandering bachelors and late marriages; and I am trying to arrange something for you.

STEPHEN   It's very good of you, mother; but perhaps I had better arrange that for myself.

LADY BRITOMART   Nonsense! you are much too young to begin matchmaking: you would be taken in by some pretty little nobody. Of course I dont mean that you are not to be consulted: you know that as well as I do. [*Stephen closes his lips and is silent*]. Now dont sulk, Stephen.

STEPHEN   I am not sulking, mother. What has all this got to do with—with—with my father?

LADY BRITOMART   My dear Stephen: where is the money to come from? It is easy enough for you and the other children to live on my income as long as we are in the same house; but I cant keep four families in four separate houses. You know how poor my father is: he has barely seven thousand a year now; and really, if he were not the Earl of Stevenage, he would have to give up society. He can do nothing for us. He says, naturally enough, that it is absurd that he should be asked to provide for the children of a man who is rolling in money. You see, Stephen, your father must be fabulously wealthy, because there is always a war going on somewhere.

STEPHEN   You need not remind me of that, mother. I have hardly ever opened a newspaper in my life without seeing our name in it. The Undershaft torpedo! The Undershaft quick firer! The Undershaft ten inch! The Undershaft disappearing rampart gun! the Undershaft submarine! and now the Undershaft aerial battleship! At Harrow they called me the Woolwich Infant. At Cambridge it was the same. A little brute at King's who was always trying to get up revivals, spoilt my Bible—your first birthday present to me—by writing under my name, "Son and heir to Undershaft and Lazarus, Death and Destruction Dealers: address, Christendom and Judea." But that was not so bad as the way I was kowtowed to everywhere because my father was making millions by selling cannons.

LADY BRITOMART   It is not only the cannons, but the war loans that Lazarus arranges under cover of giving credit for the cannons. You know, Stephen, it's perfectly scandalous. Those two men, Andrew Undershaft and Lazarus, positively have Europe under their thumbs. That is why your father is able to behave as he does. He is above the law. Do you think Bismarck or Gladstone or Disraeli could have openly defied every social and moral obligation all their lives as your father has? They simply wouldnt have dared. I asked Gladstone to take it up. I asked The Times to take it up. I asked the Lord Chamberlain to take it up. But it was just like asking them to declare war on the Sultan. They wouldnt. They said they couldnt touch him. I believe they were afraid.

STEPHEN   What could they do? He does not actually break the law.

LADY BRITOMART   Not break the law! He is always breaking the law. He broke the law when he was born: his parents were not married.

STEPHEN   Mother! Is that true?

LADY BRITOMART   Of course it's true: that was why we separated.

STEPHEN   He married without letting you know this!

LADY BRITOMART [*rather taken aback by this inference*]   Oh no. To do Andrew justice, that was not the sort of thing he did. Besides, you know the Undershaft motto: Unashamed. Everybody knew.

STEPHEN   But you said that was why you separated.

LADY BRITOMART   Yes, because he was not content with being a foundling himself: he wanted to disinherit you for another foundling. That was what I couldnt stand.

STEPHEN [*ashamed*]   Do you mean for—for—for

LADY BRITOMART   Dont stammer, Stephen. Speak distinctly.

STEPHEN   But this is so frightful to me, mother. To have to speak to you about such things!

LADY BRITOMART   It's not pleasant for me, either, especially if you are still so childish that you must make it worse by a display of embarrassment. It is only in the middle classes, Stephen, that people get into a state of dumb helpless horror when they find that there are wicked people in the world. In our class, we have to decide what is to be done with wicked people; and nothing should disturb our self-possession. Now ask your question properly.

STEPHEN   Mother: have you no consideration for me? For Heaven's sake either treat me as a child, as you always do, and tell me nothing at all; or tell me everything and let me take it as best I can.

LADY BRITOMART   Treat you as a child! What do you mean? It is most unkind and ungrateful of you to say such a thing. You know I have never treated any of you as children. I have always made you my companions and friends, and allowed you perfect freedom to do and say whatever you liked, so long as you liked what I could approve of.

STEPHEN [*desperately*]   I daresay we have been the very imperfect children of a very perfect mother; but I do beg you to let me alone for once, and tell me about this horrible business of my father wanting to set me aside for another son.

LADY BRITOMART [*amazed*]   Another son! I never said anything of the kind. I never dreamt of such a thing. This is what comes of interrupting me.

STEPHEN   But you said—

LADY BRITOMART [*cutting him short*]   Now be a good boy, Stephen, and listen to me patiently. The Undershafts are descended from a foundling in the parish of St Andrew Undershaft in the city. That was long ago, in the reign of James the First. Well, this foundling was adopted by an armorer and gun-maker. In

1118 A COLLECTION OF PLAYS

the course of time the foundling succeeded to the business; and from some notion of gratitude, or some vow or something, he adopted another foundling, and left the business to him. And that foundling did the same. Ever since that, the cannon business has always been left to an adopted foundling named Andrew Undershaft.

STEPHEN   But did they never marry? Were there no legitimate sons?

LADY BRITOMART   Oh yes: they married just as your father did; and they were rich enough to buy land for their own children and leave them well provided for. But they always adopted and trained some foundling to succeed them in the business; and of course they always quarrelled with their wives furiously over it. Your father was adopted in that way; and he pretends to consider himself bound to keep up the tradition and adopt somebody to leave the business to. Of course I was not going to stand that. There may have been some reason for it when the Undershafts could only marry women in their own class, whose sons were not fit to govern great estates. But there could be no excuse for passing over my son.

STEPHEN [*dubiously*]   I am afraid I should make a poor hand of managing a cannon foundry.

LADY BRITOMART   Nonsense! you could easily get a manager and pay him a salary.

STEPHEN   My father evidently had no great opinion of my capacity.

LADY BRITOMART   Stuff, child! you were only a baby; it had nothing to do with your capacity. Andrew did it on principle, just as he did every perverse and wicked thing on principle. When my father remonstrated, Andrew actually told him to his face that history tells us of only two successful institutions: one the Undershaft firm, and the other the Roman Empire under the Antonines. That was because the Antonine emperors all adopted their successors. Such rubbish! The Stevenages are as good as the Antonines, I hope; and you are a Stevenage. But that was Andrew all over. There you have the man! Always clever and unanswerable when he was defending nonsense and wickedness: always awkward and sullen when he had to behave sensibly and decently!

STEPHEN   Then it was on my account that your home life was broken up, mother. I am sorry.

LADY BRITOMART   Well, dear, there were other differences. I really cannot bear an immoral man. I am not a Pharisee, I hope; and I should not have minded his merely doing wrong things: we are none of us perfect. But your father didnt exactly do wrong things: he said them and thought them: that was what was so dreadful. He really had a sort of religion of wrongness. Just as one doesnt mind men practising immorality so long as they own that they are in the wrong by preaching morality; so I couldnt forgive Andrew for preaching immorality while he practised morality. You would all have grown up without principles, without any knowledge of right and wrong, if he had been in the house. You know, my dear, your father was a very attractive man in some ways. Children did not dislike him; and he took advantage of it to put the wickedest ideas into their heads, and make them quite unmanageable. I did not dislike him myself: very far from it; but nothing can bridge over moral disagreement.

STEPHEN   All this simply bewilders me, mother. People may differ about matters of opinion, or even about religion; but how can they differ about right and wrong? Right is right; and wrong is wrong; and if a man cannot distinguish them properly, he is either a fool or a rascal: thats all.

LADY BRITOMART [touched]   Thats my own boy [she pats his cheek]! Your father never could answer that: he used to laugh and get out of it under cover of some affectionate nonsense. And now that you understand the situation, what do you advise me to do?

STEPHEN   Well, what can you do?

LADY BRITOMART   I must get the money somehow.

STEPHEN   We cannot take money from him. I had rather go and live in some cheap place like Bedford Square or even Hampstead than take a farthing of his money.

LADY BRITOMART   But after all, Stephen, our present income comes from Andrew.

STEPHEN [shocked]   I never knew that.

LADY BRITOMART   Well, you surely didnt suppose your grandfather had anything to give me. The Stevenages could not do everything for you. We gave you social position. Andrew had to contribute something. He had a very good bargain, I think.

STEPHEN [bitterly]   We are utterly dependent on him and his cannons, then?

LADY BRITOMART   Certainly not: the money is settled. But he provided it. So you see it is not a question of taking money from him or not: it is simply a question of how much. I dont want any more for myself.

STEPHEN   Nor do I.

LADY BRITOMART   But Sarah does; and Barbara does. That is, Charles Lomax and Adolphus Cusins will cost them more. So I must put my pride in my pocket and ask for it, I suppose. That is your advice, Stephen, is it not?

STEPHEN   No.

LADY BRITOMART [sharply]   Stephen!

STEPHEN   Of course if you are determined—

LADY BRITOMART   I am not determined: I ask your advice; and I am waiting for it. I will not have all the responsibility thrown on my shoulders.

STEPHEN [obstinately]   I would die sooner than ask him for another penny.

LADY BRITOMART [resignedly]   You mean that I must ask him. Very well, Stephen: it shall be as you wish. You will be glad to know that your grandfather concurs. But he thinks I ought to ask Andrew to come here and see the girls. After all, he must have some natural affection for them.

STEPHEN   Ask him here!!!

LADY BRITOMART   Do not repeat my words, Stephen. Where else can I ask him?

STEPHEN   I never expected you to ask him at all.

LADY BRITOMART   Now dont tease, Stephen, Come! you see that it is necessary that he should pay us a visit, dont you?

STEPHEN [*reluctantly*]   I suppose so, if the girls cannot do without his money.

LADY BRITOMART   Thank you, Stephen: I knew you would give me the right advice when it was properly explained to you. I have asked your father to come this evening. [*Stephen bounds from his seat*] Dont jump, Stephen: it fidgets me.

STEPHEN [*in utter consternation*]   Do you mean to say that my father is coming here tonight—that he may be here at any moment?

LADY BRITOMART [*looking at her watch*]   I said nine. [*He gasps. She rises*]. Ring the bell, please. [*Stephen goes to the smaller writing table; presses a button on it; and sits at it with his elbows on the table and his head in his hands, outwitted and overwhelmed*]. It is ten minutes to nine yet: and I have to prepare the girls. I asked Charles Lomax and Adolphus to dinner on purpose that they might be here. Andrew had better see them in case he should cherish any delusions as to their being capable of supporting their wives. [*The butler enters: Lady Britomart goes behind the settee to speak to him*]. Morrison: go up to the drawing room and tell everybody to come down here at once. [*Morrison withdraws. Lady Britomart turns to Stephen*]. Now remember, Stephen: I shall need all your countenance and authority. [*He rises and tries to recover some vestige of these attributes*]. Give me a chair, dear. [*He pushes a chair forward from the wall to where she stands, near the smaller writing table. She sits down; and he goes to the armchair, into which he throws himself*]. I dont know how Barbara will take it. Ever since they made her a major in the Salvation Army she has developed a propensity to have her own way and order people about which quite cows me sometimes. It's not ladylike: I'm sure I dont know where she picked it up. Anyhow, Barbara shant bully me; but still it's just as well that your father should be here before she has time to refuse to meet him or make a fuss. Dont look nervous, Stephen: it will only encourage Barbara to make difficulties. *I* am nervous enough, goodness knows: but I dont shew it.

Sarah and Barbara come in with their respective young men, Charles Lomax and Adolphus Cusins. Sarah is slender, bored, and mundane. Barbara is robuster, jollier, much more energetic. Sarah is fashionably dressed: Barbara is in Salvation Army uniform. Lomax, a young man about town, is like many other young men about town. He is afflicted with a frivolous sense of humor which plunges him at the most inopportune moments into paroxysms of imperfectly suppressed laughter. Cusins is a spectacled student, slight, thin haired, and sweet voiced, with a more complex form of Lomax's complaint. His sense of humor is intellectual and subtle, and is complicated by an appalling temper. The lifelong struggle of a benevolent temperament and a high conscience against impulses of inhuman ridicule and fierce impatience has set up a chronic strain which has visibly wrecked his constitution. He is a most implacable, determined, tenacious, intolerant person who by mere force of character presents himself as—and indeed actually is—considerate, gentle, explanatory, even mild and apologetic, capable possibly of murder, but not of cruelty or coarseness. By the operation of some instinct which is not merciful enough to blind him with the illusions of love, he is obstinately bent on marrying Barbara. Lomax likes Sarah and thinks it will be rather a lark to marry her. Consequently he has not attempted to resist Lady Britomart's arrangements to that end.

All four look as if they had been having a good deal of fun in the drawing room. The girls enter first, leaving the swains outside. Sarah comes to the settee. Barbara comes in after her and stops at the door.

BARBARA   Are Cholly and Dolly to come in?

LADY BRITOMART *[forcibly]*   Barbara: I will not have Charles called Cholly: the vulgarity of it positively makes me ill.

BARBARA   It's all right, mother: Cholly is quite correct nowadays. Are they to come in?

LADY BRITOMART   Yes, if they will behave themselves.

BARBARA *[through the door]*   Come in, Dolly; and behave yourself.

Barbara comes to her mother's writing table. Cusins enters smiling, and wanders towards Lady Britomart.

SARAH *[calling]*   Come in, Cholly. *[Lomax enters, controlling his features very imperfectly, and places himself vaguely between Sarah and Barbara].*

LADY BRITOMART *[peremptorily]*   Sit down, all of you. *[They sit. Cusins crosses to the window and seats himself there. Lomax takes a chair. Barbara sits at the writing table and Sarah on the settee].* I dont in the least know what you are laughing at, Adolphus. I am surprised at you, though I expected nothing better from Charles Lomax.

CUSINS *[in a remarkably gentle voice]*   Barbara has been trying to teach me the West Ham Salvation March.

LADY BRITOMART   I see nothing to laugh at in that; nor should you if you are really converted.

CUSINS *[sweetly]*   You were not present. It was really funny, I believe.

LOMAX   Ripping.

LADY BRITOMART   Be quiet, Charles. Now listen to me, children. Your father is coming here this evening.

General stupefaction. Lomax, Sarah, and Barbara rise; Sarah scared, and Barbara amused and expectant.

LOMAX *[remonstrating]*   Oh I say!

LADY BRITOMART   You are not called on to say anything, Charles.

SARAH   Are you serious, mother?

LADY BRITOMART   Of course I am serious. It is on your account, Sarah, and also on Charles's. *[Silence. Sarah sits, with a shrug. Charles looks painfully unworthy].* I hope you are not going to object, Barbara.

BARBARA   I! why should I? My father has a soul to be saved like anybody else.

He's quite welcome as far as I am concerned. [*She sits on the table, and softly whistles 'Onward Christian Soldiers'*].

LOMAX [*still remonstrant*]   But really, dont you know! Oh I say!

LADY BRITOMART [*frigidly*]   What do you wish to convey, Charles?

LOMAX   Well, you must admit that this is a bit thick.

LADY BRITOMART [*turning with ominous suavity to Cusins*]   Adolphus: you are a professor of Greek. Can you translate Charles Lomax's remarks into reputable English for us?

CUSINS [*cautiously*]   If I may say so, Lady Brit, I think Charles has rather happily expressed what we all feel. Homer, speaking of Autolycus, uses the same phrase. πυκινὸν δόμον ἐλθῖν means a bit thick.

LOMAX [*handsomely*]   Not that I mind, you know, if Sarah dont. [*He sits*].

LADY BRITOMART [*crushingly*]   Thank you. Have I your permission, Adolphus, to invite my own husband to my own house?

CUSINS [*gallantly*]   You have my unhesitating support in everything you do.

LADY BRITOMART   Tush! Sarah: have you nothing to say?

SARAH   Do you mean that he is coming regularly to live here?

LADY BRITOMART   Certainly not. The spare room is ready for him if he likes to stay for a day or two and see a little more of you; but there are limits.

SARAH   Well, he cant eat us, I suppose. *I* dont mind.

LOMAX [*chuckling*]   I wonder how the old man will take it.

LADY BRITOMART   Much as the old woman will, no doubt, Charles.

LOMAX [*abashed*]   I didnt mean—at least—

LADY BRITOMART   You didnt think, Charles. You never do; and the result is, you never mean anything. And now please attend to me, children. Your father will be quite a stranger to us.

LOMAX   I suppose he hasnt seen Sarah since she was a little kid.

LADY BRITOMART   Not since she was a little kid, Charles, as you express it with that elegance of diction and refinement of thought that seem never to desert you. Accordingly—er—[*impatiently*] Now I have forgotten what I was going to say. That comes of your provoking me to be sarcastic, Charles. Adolphus: you will kindly tell me where I was.

CUSINS [*sweetly*]   You were saying that as Mr Undershaft has not seen his children since they were babies, he will form his opinion of the way you have brought them up from their behavior tonight, and that therefore you wish us all to be particularly careful to conduct ourselves well, especially Charles.

LADY BRITOMART [*with emphatic approval*]   Precisely.

LOMAX   Look here, Dolly: Lady Brit didnt say that.

LADY BRITOMART [*vehemently*]   I did, Charles. Adolphus's recollection is perfectly correct. It is most important that you should be good; and I do beg you for once not to pair off into opposite corners and giggle and whisper while I am speaking to your father.

BARBARA   All right, mother. We'll do you credit. [*She comes off the table, and sits in her chair with ladylike elegance*].

LADY BRITOMART   Remember, Charles, that Sarah will want to feel proud of you instead of ashamed of you.

LOMAX   Oh I say! theres nothing to be exactly proud of, dont you know.

LADY BRITOMART   Well, try and look as if there was.

Morrison, pale and dismayed, breaks into the room in unconcealed disorder.

MORRISON   Might I speak a word to you, my lady?

LADY BRITOMART   Nonsense! Shew him up.

MORRISON   Yes, my lady. [*He goes*].

LOMAX   Does Morrison know who it is?

LADY BRITOMART   Of course. Morrison has always been with us.

LOMAX   It must be a regular corker for him, dont you know.

LADY BRITOMART   Is this a moment to get on my nerves, Charles, with your outrageous expressions?

LOMAX   But this is something out of the ordinary, really—

MORRISON [*at the door*]   The—er—Mr Undershaft. [*He retreats in confusion*].

Andrew Undershaft comes in. All rise. Lady Britomart meets him in the middle of the room behind the settee.

Andrew is, on the surface, a stoutish, easygoing elderly man, with kindly patient manners, and an engaging simplicity of character. But he has a watchful, deliberate, waiting, listening face, and formidable reserves of power, both bodily and mental, in his capacious chest and long head. His gentleness is partly that of a strong man who has learnt by experience that his natural grip hurts ordinary people unless he handles them very carefully, and partly the mellowness of age and success. He is also a little shy in his present very delicate situation.

LADY BRITOMART   Good evening, Andrew.

UNDERSHAFT   How d'ye do, my dear.

LADY BRITOMART   You look a good deal older.

UNDERSHAFT [*apologetically*]   I am somewhat older. [*Taking her hand with a touch of courtship*] Time has stood still with you.

LADY BRITOMART [*throwing away his hand*]   Rubbish! This is your family.

UNDERSHAFT [*surprised*]   Is it so large? I am sorry to say my memory is failing very badly in some things. [*He offers his hand with paternal kindness to Lomax*].

LOMAX [*jerkily shaking his hand*]   Ahdedoo.

UNDERSHAFT   I can see you are my eldest. I am very glad to meet you again, my boy.

LOMAX [*remonstrating*]   No, but look here dont you know—[*Overcome*] Oh I say!

LADY BRITOMART [*recovering from momentary speechlessness*]   Andrew: do you mean to say that you dont remember how many children you have?

UNDERSHAFT   Well, I am afraid I—. They have grown so much—er. Am I making any ridiculous mistake? I may as well confess: I recollect only one son. But so many things have happened since, of course—er—

LADY BRITOMART [*decisively*]   Andrew: you are talking nonsense. Of course you have only one son.

UNDERSHAFT   Perhaps you will be good enough to introduce me, my dear.

LADY BRITOMART   That is Charles Lomax, who is engaged to Sarah.

UNDERSHAFT   My dear sir, I beg your pardon.

LOMAX   Notatall. Delighted, I assure you.

LADY BRITOMART   This Stephen.

UNDERSHAFT [*bowing*]   Happy to make your acquaintance. Mr. Stephen. Then [*going to Cusins*] you must be my son. [*Taking Cusins' hands in his*] How are you, my young friend? [*To Lady Britomart*] He is very like you, my love.

CUSINS   You flatter me, Mr Undershaft, My name is Cusins: engaged to Barbara [*Very explicitly*] That is Major Barbara Undershaft, of the Salvation Army. That is Sarah, your second daughter. This is Stephen Undershaft, your son.

UNDERSHAFT   My dear Stephen, I beg your pardon.

STEPHEN   Not at all.

UNDERSHAFT   Mr Cusins: I am much indebted to you for explaining so precisely. [*Turning to Sarah*] Barbara, my dear—

SARAH [*prompting him*]   Sarah.

UNDERSHAFT   Sarah, of course. [*They shake hands. He goes over to Barbara*] Barbara—I am right this time, I hope?

BARBARA   Quite right. [*They shake hands*].

LADY BRITOMART [*resuming command*]   Sit down, all of you. Sit down, Andrew. [*She comes forward and sits on the settee. Cusins also brings his chair forward on her left. Barbara and Stephen resume their seats. Lomax gives his chair to Sarah and goes for another*].

UNDERSHAFT   Thank you, my love.

LOMAX [*conversationally, as he brings a chair forward between the writing table and the settee, and offers it to Undershaft*]   Takes you some time to find out exactly where you are, dont it?

UNDERSHAFT [*accepting the chair, but remaining standing*]   That is not what embarrasses me, Mr Lomax. My difficulty is that if I play the part of a father I shall produce the effect of an intrusive stranger; and if I play the part of a discreet stranger, I may appear a callous father.

LADY BRITOMART   There is no need for you to play any part at all, Andrew. You had much better be sincere and natural.

UNDERSHAFT [*submissively*]   Yes, my dear: I daresay that will be best. [*He sits down comfortably*]. Well, here I am. Now what can I do for you all?

LADY BRITOMART   You need not do anything, Andrew. You are one of the family. You can sit with us and enjoy yourself.

A painfully conscious pause. Barbara makes a face at Lomax, whose too long suppressed mirth immediately explodes in agonized neighings.

LADY BRITOMART [*outraged*]   Charles Lomax: if you can behave yourself, behave yourself. If not, leave the room.

LOMAX   I'm awfully sorry, Lady Brit; but really you know, upon my soul! [*He sits on the settee between Lady Britomart and Undershaft, quite overcome*].

BARBARA   Why dont you laugh if you want to, Cholly? It's good for your inside.

LADY BRITOMART   Barbara: you have had the education of a lady. Please let your father see that; and dont talk like a street girl.

UNDERSHAFT   Never mind me, my dear. As you know, I am not a gentleman; and I was never educated.

LOMAX [*encouragingly*]   Nobody'd know it, I assure you. You look all right, you know.

CUSINS   Let me advise you to study Greek, Mr Undershaft. Greek scholars are privileged men. Few of them know Greek; and none of them know anything else; but their position is unchallengeable. Other languages are the qualifications of waiters and commercial travellers: Greek is to a man of position what the hallmark is to silver.

BARBARA   Dolly: dont be insincere. Cholly: fetch your concertina and play something for us.

LOMAX [*jumps up eagerly, but checks himself to remark doubtfully to Undershaft*]   Perhaps that sort of thing isnt in your line, eh?

UNDERSHAFT   I am particularly fond of music.

LOMAX [*delighted*]   Are you? Then I'll get it. [*He goes upstairs for the instrument*].

UNDERSHAFT   Do you play, Barbara?

BARBARA   Only the tambourine. But Cholly's teaching me the concertina.

UNDERSHAFT   Is Cholly also a member of the Salvation Army?

BARBARA   No: he says it's bad form to be a dissenter. But I dont despair of Cholly. I made him come yesterday to a meeting at the dock gates, and take the collection in his hat.

UNDERSHAFT [*looks whimsically at his wife*]!!

LADY BRITOMART   It is not my doing, Andrew. Barbara is old enough to take her own way. She has no father to advise her.

BARBARA   Oh yes she has. There are no orphans in the Salvation Army.

UNDERSHAFT   Your father there has a great many children and plenty of experience, eh?

BARBARA [*looking at him with quick interest and nodding*]   Just so. How did you come to understand that? [*Lomax is heard at the door trying the concertina*].

LADY BRITOMART   Come in, Charles. Play us something at once.

LOMAX   Righto! [*He sits down in his former place, and preludes*].

UNDERSHAFT   One moment, Mr. Lomax. I am rather interested in the Salvation Army. Its motto might be my own: Blood and Fire.

LOMAX [*shocked*]   But not your sort of blood and fire, you know.

UNDERSHAFT   My sort of blood cleanses: my sort of fire purifies.

BARBARA   So do ours. Come down tomorrow to my shelter—the West Ham shelter—and see what we're doing. We're going to march to a great meeting in the Assembly Hall at Mile End. Come and see the shelter and then march with us: it will do you a lot of good. Can you play anything?

UNDERSHAFT   In my youth I earned pennies, and even shillings occasionally, in the streets and in public parlors by my natural talent for stepdancing. Later on, I became a member of the Undershaft orchestral society, and performed passably on the tenor trombone.

LOMAX [scandalized—putting down the concertina]   Oh I say!

BARBARA   Many a sinner has played himself into heaven on the trombone, thanks to the Army.

LOMAX [to Barbara, still rather shocked]   Yes; but what about the cannon business, dont you know? [To Undershaft] Getting into heaven is not exactly in your line, is it?

LADY BRITOMART   Charles!!!

LOMAX   Well; but it stands to reason, dont it? The cannon business may be necessary and all that: we cant get on without cannons; but it isnt right, you know. On the other hand, there may be a certain amount of tosh about the Salvation Army—I belong to the Established Church myself—but still you cant deny that it's religion; and you cant go against religion, can you? At least unless youre downright immoral, dont you know.

UNDERSHAFT   You hardly appreciate my position, Mr Lomax—

LOMAX [hastily]   I'm not saying anything against you personally—

UNDERSHAFT   Quite so, quite so. But consider for a moment. Here I am, a profiteer in mutilation and murder. I find myself in a specially amiable humor just now because, this morning, down at the foundry, we blew twenty-seven dummy soldiers into fragments with a gun which formerly destroyed only thirteen.

LOMAX [leniently]   Well, the more destructive war becomes, the sooner it will be abolished, eh?

UNDERSHAFT   Not at all. The more destructive war becomes the more fascinating we find it. No, Mr Lomax: I am obliged to you for making the usual excuse for my trade; but I am not ashamed of it. I am not one of those men who keep their morals and their business in water-tight compartments. All the spare money my trade rivals spend on hospitals, cathedrals, and other receptacles for conscience money, I devote to experiments and researches in improved methods of destroying life and property. I have always done so; and I always shall. Therefore your Christmas card moralities of peace on earth and goodwill among men are of no use to me. Your Christianity, which enjoins you to resist not evil, and to turn the other cheek, would make me a bankrupt. My morality—my religion—must have a place for cannons and torpedoes in it.

STEPHEN [coldly—almost sullenly]   You speak as if there were half a dozen moralities and religions to choose from, instead of one true morality and one true religion.

UNDERSHAFT   For me there is only one true morality; but it might not fit you, as you do not manufacture aerial battleships. There is only one true morality for every man; but every man has not the same true morality.

LOMAX [*overtaxed*]   Would you mind saying that again? I didnt quite follow it.

CUSINS   It's quite simple. As Euripides says, one man's meat is another man's poison morally as well as physically.

UNDERSHAFT   Precisely.

LOMAX   Oh, that! Yes, yes, yes. True. True.

STEPHEN   In other words, some men are honest and some are scoundrels.

BARBARA   Bosh! There are no scoundrels.

UNDERSHAFT   Indeed? Are there any good men?

BARBARA   No. Not one. There are neither good men nor scoundrels: there are just children of one Father; and the sooner they stop calling one another names the better. You neednt talk to me: I know them. Ive had scores of them through my hands: scoundrels, criminals, infidels, philanthropists, missionaries, county councillors, all sorts. Theyre all just the same sort of sinner; and theres the same salvation ready for them all.

UNDERSHAFT   May I ask have you ever saved a maker of cannons?

BARBARA   No. Will you let me try?

UNDERSHAFT   Well, I will make a bargain with you. If I go to see you tomorrow in your Salvation Shelter, will you come the day after to see me in my cannon works?

BARBARA   Take care. It may end in your giving up the cannons for the sake of the Salvation Army.

UNDERSHAFT   Are you sure it will not end in your giving up the Salvation Army for the sake of the cannons?

BARBARA   I will take my chance of that.

UNDERSHAFT   And I will take my chance of the other. [*They shake hands on it*]. Where is your shelter?

BARBARA   In West Ham. At the sign of the cross. Ask anybody in Canning Town. Where are your works?

UNDERSHAFT   In Perivale St Andrews. At the sign of the sword. Ask anybody in Europe.

LOMAX   Hadnt I better play something?

BARBARA   Yes. Give us Onward, Christian Soldiers.

LOMAX   Well, thats rather a strong order to begin with, dont you know. Suppose I sing Thourt passing hence, my brother. It's much the same tune.

BARBARA   It's too melancholy. You get saved, Cholly; and youll pass hence, my brother, without making such a fuss about it.

LADY BRITOMART   Really, Barbara, you go on as if religion were a pleasant subject. Do have some sense of propriety.

UNDERSHAFT   I do not find it an unpleasant subject, my dear. It is the only one that capable people really care for.

LADY BRITOMART [*looking at her watch*]   Well, if you are determined to have it, I insist on having it in a proper and respectable way. Charles: ring for prayers. *General amazement. Stephen rises in dismay.*

LOMAX [*rising*]   Oh I say!

UNDERSHAFT [*rising*]   I am afraid I must be going.

LADY BRITOMART   You cannot go now, Andrew: it would be most improper. Sit down. What will the servants think?

UNDERSHAFT   My dear: I have conscientious scruples. May I suggest a compromise? If Barbara will conduct a little service in the drawing room, with Mr Lomax as organist, I will attend it willingly. I will even take part, if a trombone can be procured.

LADY BRITOMART   Dont mock, Andrew.

UNDERSHAFT [*shocked—to Barbara*]   You dont think I am mocking, my love, I hope.

BARBARA   No, of course not; and it wouldnt matter if you were: half the Army came to their first meeting for a lark. [*Rising*] Come along. [*She throws her arm round her father and sweeps him out, calling to the others from the threshold*] Come, Dolly. Come, Cholly.

Cusins rises.

LADY BRITOMART   I will not be disobeyed by everybody. Adolphus: sit down. [*He does not*]. Charles: you may go. You are not fit for prayers: you cannot keep your countenance.

LOMAX   Oh I say! [*He goes out*].

LADY BRITOMART [*continuing*]   But you, Adolphus, can behave yourself if you choose to. I insist on your staying.

CUSINS   My dear Lady Brit: there are things in the family prayer book that I couldnt bear to hear you say.

LADY BRITOMART   What things, pray?

CUSINS   Well, you would have to say before all the servants that we have done things we ought not to have done, and left undone things we ought to have done, and that there is no health in us. I cannot bear to hear you doing yourself such an injustice, and Barbara such an injustice. As for myself, I flatly deny it: I have done my best. I shouldnt dare to marry Barbara—I couldnt look you in the face—if it were true. So I must go to the drawing room.

LADY BRITOMART [*offended*]   Well, go. [*He starts for the door*]. And remember this, Adolphus [*he turns to listen*]: I have a very strong suspicion that you went to the Salvation Army to worship Barbara and nothing else. And I quite appreciate the very clever way in which you systematically humbug me. I have found you out. Take care Barbara doesnt. Thats all.

CUSINS [*with unruffled sweetness*]   Dont tell on me. [*He steals out*].

LADY BRITOMART   Sarah: if you want to go, go. Anything's better than to sit there
as if you wished you were a thousand miles away.

SARAH [*languidly*]   Very well, mamma. [*She goes*].

Lady Britomart, with a sudden flounce, gives way to a little gust of tears.

STEPHEN [*going to her*]   Mother: whats the matter?

LADY BRITOMART [*swishing away her tears with her handkerchief*]   Nothing! Foolishness. You can go with him, too, if you like, and leave me with the servants.

STEPHEN   Oh, you mustnt think that, mother. I—I dont like him.

LADY BRITOMART   The others do. That is the injustice of a woman's lot. A woman
has to bring up her children; and that means to restrain them, to deny them
things they want, to set them tasks, to punish them when they do wrong, to
do all the unpleasant things. And the father, who has nothing to do but pet
them and spoil them, comes in when all her work is done and steals their
affection from her.

STEPHEN   He has not stolen our affection from you. It is only curiosity.

LADY BRITOMART [*violently*]   I wont be consoled, Stephen. There is nothing the
matter with me. [*She rises and goes towards the door*].

STEPHEN   Where are you going, mother?

LADY BRITOMART   To the drawing room, of course [*She goes out. Onward, Christian
Soldiers, on the concertina, with tambourine accompaniment, is heard when the door
opens*]. Are you coming, Stephen?

STEPHEN   No. Certainly not. [*She goes. He sits down on the settee, with compressed
lips and an expression of strong dislike*].

ACT II

*The yard of the West Ham shelter of the Salvation Army is a cold place on a January
morning. The building itself, an old warehouse, is newly whitewashed. Its gabled end
projects into the yard in the middle, with a door on the ground floor, and another in the loft
above it without any balcony or ladder, but with a pulley rigged over it for hoisting sacks.
Those who come from this central gable end into the yard have the gateway leading to the
street on their left, with a stone horse-trough just beyond it, and, on the right, a penthouse
shielding a table from the weather. There are forms at the table; and on them are seated a
man and a woman, both much down on their luck, finishing a meal of bread (one thick slice
each, with margarine and golden syrup) and diluted milk.*

*The man, a workman out of employment, is young, agile, a talker, a poser, sharp enough
to be capable of anything in reason except honesty or altruistic considerations of any kind.
The woman is a commonplace old bundle of poverty and hard-worn humanity. She looks
sixty and is probably forty-five. If they were rich people, gloved and muffed and well
wrapped up in furs and overcoats, they would be numbed and miserable; for it is a grind-*

ingly cold raw January day; and a glance at the background of grimy warehouses and leaden sky visible over the whitewashed walls of the yard would drive any idle rich person straight to the Mediterranean. But these two, being no more troubled with visions of the Mediterranean than of the moon, and being compelled to keep more of their clothes in the pawnshop, and less on their persons, in winter than in summer, are not depressed by the cold: rather are they stung into vivacity, to which their meal has just now given an almost jolly turn. The man takes a pull at his mug, and then gets up and moves about the yard with his hands deep in his pockets, occasionally breaking into a stepdance.

THE WOMAN   Feel better arter your meal, sir?

THE MAN   No. Call that a meal! Good enough for you, praps; but wot is it to me, an intelligent workin man.

THE WOMAN   Workin man! Wot are you?

THE MAN   Painter.

THE WOMAN [*sceptically*]   Yus, I dessay.

THE MAN   Yus, you dessay! I know. Every loafer that cant do nothink calls isself a painter. Well, I'm a real painter: grainer, finisher, thirty-eight bob a week when I can get it.

THE WOMAN   Then why dont you go and get it?

THE MAN   I'll tell you why. Fust: I'm intelligent—fffff! it's rotten cold here [*he dances a step or two*]—yes: intelligent beyond the station o life into which it has pleased the capitalists to call me; and they dont like a man that sees through em. Second, an intelligent bein needs a doo share of appiness; so I drink somethink cruel when I get the chawnce. Third, I stand by my class and do as little as I can so's to leave arf the job for me fellow workers. Fourth, I'm fly enough to know wots inside the law and wots outside it; and inside it I do as the capitalists do: pinch wot I can lay me ands on. In a proper state of society I am sober, industrious and honest: in Rome, so to speak, I do as the Romans do. Wots the consequence? When trade is bad—and it's rotten bad just now—and the employers az to sack arf their men, they generally start on me.

THE WOMAN   Whats your name?

THE MAN   Price. Bronterre O'Brien Price. Usually called Snobby Price, for short.

THE WOMAN   Snobby's a carpenter, aint it? You said you was a painter.

PRICE   Not that kind of snob, but the genteel sort. I'm too uppish, owing to my intelligence, and my father being a Chartist and a reading, thinking man: a stationer, too. I'm none of your common hewers of wood and drawers of water; and dont you forget it. [*He returns to his seat at the table, and takes up his mug*]. Wots your name?

THE WOMAN   Rummy Mitchens, sir.

PRICE [*quaffing the remains of his milk to her*]   Your elth, Miss Mitchens.

RUMMY [*correcting him*]   Missis Mitchens.

PRICE   Wot! Oh Rummy, Rummy! Respectable married woman, Rummy, gittin rescued by the Salvation Army by pretendin to be a bad un. Same old game!

RUMMY What am I to do? I cant starve. Them Salvation lasses is dear good girls; but the better you are, the worse they likes to think you were before they rescued you. Why shouldnt they av a bit o credit, poor loves? theyre worn to rags by their work. And where would they get the money to rescue us if we was to let on we're no worse than other people? You know what ladies and gentlemen are.

PRICE Thievin swine! Wish I ad their job, Rummy, all the same. Wot does Rummy stand for? Pet name praps?

RUMMY Short for Romola.

PRICE For wot!?

RUMMY Romola. It was out of a new book. Somebody me mother wanted me to grow up like.

PRICE We're companions in misfortune, Rummy. Both on us got names that nobody cawnt pronounce. Consequently I'm Snobby and youre Rummy because Bill and Sally wasnt good enough for our parents. Such is life!

RUMMY Who saved you, Mr Price? Was it Major Barbara?

PRICE No: I come here on my own. I'm going to be Bronterre O'Brien Price, the converted painter. I know wot they like. I'll tell em how I blasphemed and gambled and wopped my poor old mother—

RUMMY [shocked] Used you to beat your mother?

PRICE Not likely. She used to beat me. No matter: you come and listen to the converted painter, and youll hear how she was a pious woman that taught me me prayers at er knee, an how I used to come home drunk and drag her out o bed be er snow white airs, an lam into er with the poker.

RUMMY Thats whats so unfair to us women. Your confessions is just as big lies as ours: you dont tell what you really done no more than us; but you men can tell your lies right out at the meetins and be made much of for it; while the sort o confessions we az to make az to be wispered to one lady at a time. It aint right, spite of all their piety.

PRICE Right! Do you spose the Army'd be allowed if it went and did right? Not much. It combs our air and makes us good little blokes to be robbed and put upon. But I'll play the game as good as any of em. I'll see somebody struck by lightnin, or hear a voice sayin "Snobby Price: where will you spend eternity?" I'll av a time of it, I tell you.

RUMMY You wont be let drink, though.

PRICE I'll take it out in gorspellin, then. I dont want to drink if I can get fun enough any other way.

Jenny Hill, a pale, overwrought, pretty Salvation lass of 18, comes in through the yard gate, leading Peter Shirley, a half hardened, half worn-out elderly man, weak with hunger.

JENNY [supporting him] Come! pluck up. I'll get you something to eat. Youll be all right then.

PRICE [rising and hurrying officiously to take the old man off Jenny's hands] Poor old man! Cheer up, brother: youll find rest and peace and appiness ere. Hurry up with the food, miss: e's fair done. [*Jenny hurries into the shelter*]. Ere, buck up, daddy! she's fetchin y'a thick slice o breadn treacle, an a mug o skyblue. [*He seats him at the corner of the table*].

RUMMY [*gaily*]   Keep up your old art! Never say die!

SHIRLEY   I'm not an old man. I'm only 46. I'm as good as ever I was. The grey patch come in my hair before I was thirty. All it wants is three pennorth o hair dye: am I to be turned on the streets to starve for it? Holy God! Ive worked ten to twelve hours a day since I was thirteen, and paid my way all through; and now am I to be thrown into the gutter and my job given to a young man that can do it no better than me because Ive black hair that goes white at the first change?

PRICE [*cheerfully*]   No good jawrin about it. Youre ony a jumped-up, jerked-off, orspittle-turned-out-incurable of an ole workin man: who cares about you? Eh? Make the thievin swine give you a meal: theyve stole many a one from you. Get a bit o your own back. [*Jenny returns with the usual meal*]. There you are, brother. Awsk a blessin an tuck that into you.

SHIRLEY [*looking at it ravenously but not touching it, and crying like a child*]   I never took anything before.

JENNY [*petting him*]   Come, come! the Lord sends it to you: he wasnt above taking bread from his friends; and why should you be? Besides, when we find you a job you can pay us for it if you like.

SHIRLEY [*eagerly*]   Yes, yes: thats true. I can pay you back: it's only a loan. [*Shivering*] Oh Lord! oh Lord! [*He turns to the table and attacks the meal ravenously*].

JENNY   Well, Rummy, are you more comfortable now?

RUMMY   God bless you, lovey! youve fed my body and saved my soul, havnt you? [*Jenny, touched, kisses her*]. Sit down and rest a bit: you must be ready to drop.

JENNY   I've been going hard since morning. But theres more work than we can do. I mustnt stop.

RUMMY   Try a prayer for just two minutes. Youll work all the better after.

JENNY [*her eyes lighting up*]   Oh isnt it wonderful how a few minutes prayer revives you! I was quite lightheaded at twelve o'clock, I was so tired; but Major Barbara just sent me to pray for five minutes; and I was able to go on as if I had only just begun. [*To Price*] Did you have a piece of bread?

PRICE [*with unction*]   Yes, miss; but Ive got the piece that I value more; and thats the peace that passeth hall hannerstennin.

RUMMY [*fervently*]   Glory Hallelujah!

Bill Walker, a rough customer of about 25, appears at the yard gate and looks malevolently at Jenny.

JENNY   That makes me so happy. When you say that, I feel wicked for loitering here. I must get to work again.

She is hurrying to the shelter, when the new-comer moves quickly up to the door and intercepts her. His manner is so threatening that she retreats as he comes at her truculently, driving her down the yard.

BILL   Aw knaow you. Youre the one that took awy maw girl. Youre the one that set er agen me. Well, I'm gowin to ev er aht. Not that Aw care a carse for er or you: see? Bat Aw'll let er knaow; and Aw'll let you knaow. Aw'm gowing to give her a doin thatll teach er to cat awy from me. Nah in wiv you and tell er to cam aht afore Aw cam in and kick er aht. Tell er Bill Walker wants er. She'll knaow wot thet means; and if she keeps me witin itll be worse. You stop to jawr beck at me; and Aw'll stawt on you: d'ye eah? Theres your wy. In you gow. [*He takes her by the arm and slings her towards the door of the shelter. She falls on her hand and knee. Rummy helps her up again*].

PRICE   [*rising, and venturing irresolutely towards Bill*]   Easy there, mate. She aint doin you no arm.

BILL   Oo are you callin mite? [*Standing over him threateningly*]   Youre gowin to stend ap for er, aw yer? Put ap your ends.

RUMMY   [*running indignantly to scold him*]   Oh, you great brute—[*He instantly swings his left hand back against her face. She screams and reels back to the trough, where she sits down, covering her bruised face with her hands and rocking herself and moaning with pain*]

JENNY   [*going to her*]   Oh, God forgive you! How could you strike an old woman like that?

BILL   [*seizing her by the hair so violently that she also screams, and tearing her away from the old woman*]   You Gawd forgimme again an Aw'll Gawd forgive you one on the jawr thetll stop you pryin for a week. [*Holding her and turning fiercely on Price*]   Ev you ennything to sy agen it?

PRICE   [*intimidated*]   No, matey: she aint anything to do with me.

BILL   Good job for you! Aw'd pat two meals into you and fawt you with one finger arter, you stawved cur. [*To Jenny*]   Nah are you gowin to fetch aht Mog Ebbijem; or em Aw to knock your fice off you and fetch her meself?

JENNY   [*writhing in his grasp*]   Oh please someone go in and tell Major Barbara—[*she screams again as he wrenches her head down; and Price and Rummy flee into the shelter*].

BILL   You want to gow in and tell your Mijor of me, do you?

JENNY   Oh please dont drag my hair. Let me go.

BILL   Do you or downt you? [*She stifles a scream*]. Yus or nao?

JENNY   God give me strength—

BILL   [*striking her with his fist in the face*]   Gow an shaow her thet, and tell her if she wants one lawk it to cam and interfere with me. [*Jenny, crying with pain, goes into the shed. He goes to the form and addresses the old man*]. Eah: finish your mess; an git aht o maw wy.

SHIRLEY   [*springing up and facing him fiercely, with the mug in his hand*]   You take a liberty with me, and I'll smash you over the face with the mug and cut your eye out. Aint you satisfied—young whelps like you—with takin the bread out o the mouths of your elders that have brought you up and slaved for you, but you must come shovin and cheekin and bullyin in here, where the bread of charity is sickenin in our stummicks?

BILL [*contemptuously, but backing a little*]   Wot good are you, you aold palsy mag? Wot good are you?

SHIRLEY   As good as you and better. I'll do a day's work agen you or any fat young soaker of your age. Go and take my job at Horrockses, where I worked for ten year. They want young men there: they cant afford to keep men over forty-five. Theyre very sorry—give you a character and happy to help you to get anything suited to your years—sure a steady man wont be long out of a job. Well, let em try you . Theyll find the differ. What do you know? Not as much as how to beeyave yourself—layin your dirty fist across the mouth of a respectable woman!

BILL   Downt provowk me to ly it acrost yours: d'ye eah?

SHIRLEY [*with blighting contempt*]   Yes: you like an old man to hit, dont you, when youve finished with the women. I aint seen you hit a young one yet.

BILL [*stung*]   You loy, you aold soupkitchener, you. There was a yang menn eah. Did Aw offer to itt him or did Aw not?

SHIRLEY   Was he starvin or was he not? Was he a man or only a crosseyed thief an a loafer? Would you hit my son-in-law's brother?

BILL   Oo'see?

SHIRLEY   Todger Fairmile o Balls Pond. Him that won £20 off the Japanese wrastler at the music hall by standin out 17 minutes 4 seconds agen him.

BILL [*sullenly*]   Aw'm nao music awl wrastler. Ken he box?

SHIRLEY   Yes: an you cant.

BILL   Wot! Aw cawnt, cawnt Aw? Wots thet you sy [*threatening him*]

SHIRLEY [*not budging an inch*]   Will you box Todger Fairmile if I put him on to you? Say the word.

BILL [*subsiding with a slouch*]   Aw'll stend ap to enny menn alawv, if he was ten Todger Fairmawls. But Aw dont set ap to be a perfeshnal.

SHIRLEY [*looking down on him with unfathomable disdain*]   You box! Slap an old woman with the back o your hand! You hadnt even the sense to hit her where a magistrate couldnt see the mark of it, you silly young lump of conceit and ignorance. Hit a girl in the jaw and ony make her cry! If Todger Fairmile'd done it, she wouldnt a got up inside o ten minutes, no more than you would if he got on to you. Yah! I'd set about you myself if I had a week's feedin in me instead o two months' starvation. [*He turns his back on him and sits down moodily at the table*].

BILL [*following him and stooping over him to drive the taunt in*]   You loy! youve the bread and treacle in you that you cam eah to beg.

SHIRLEY [*bursting into tears*]   Oh God! it's true: I'm only an old pauper on the scrap heap. [*Furiously*] But youll come to it yourself; and then youll know. Youll come to it sooner than a teetotaller like me, fillin yourself with gin at this hour o the mornin!

BILL   Aw'm nao gin drinker, you oald lawr; bat wen Aw want to give my girl a
bloomin good awdin Aw lawk to ev a bit o devil in me: see? An eah Aw emm,
talkin to a rotten aold blawter like you sted o givin her wot for. [*Working
himself into a rage*] Aw'm gowin in there to fetch her aht. [*He makes vengefully
for the shelter door*].

SHIRLEY   Youre goin to the station on a stretcher, more likely; and they'll take the
gin and the devil out of you there when they get you inside. You mind what
youre about: the major here is the Earl o Stevenage's granddaughter.

BILL [*checked*]   Garn!

SHIRLEY   Youll see.

BILL [*his resolution oozing*]   Well, Aw aint dan nathin to er.

SHIRLEY   Spose she said you did! who'd believe you?

BILL [*very uneasy, skulking back to the corner of the penthouse*]   Gawd! theres no jastice
in this cantry. To think wot them people can do! Aw'm as good as er.

SHIRLEY   Tell her so. It's just what a fool like you would do.

*Barbara, brisk and businesslike, comes from the shelter with a note book, and addresses
herself to Shirley. Bill, cowed, sits down in the corner on a form, and turns his back on
them.*

BARBARA   Good morning.

SHIRLEY [*standing up and taking off his hat*]   Good morning, miss.

BARBARA   Sit down: make yourself at home. [*He hesitates; but she puts a friendly
hand on his shoulder and makes him obey.*] Now then! since youve made friends
with us, we want to know all about you. Names and addresses and trades.

SHIRLEY   Peter Shirley. Fitter. Chucked out two months ago because I was too
old.

BARBARA [*not at all surprised*]   Youd pass still. Why didnt you dye your hair?

SHIRLEY   I did. Me age come out at a coroner's inquest on me daughter.

BARBARA   Steady?

SHIRLEY   Teetotaller. Never out of a job before. Good worker. And sent to the
knackers like an old horse!

BARBARA   No matter: if you did your part God will do his.

SHIRLEY [*suddenly stubborn*]   My religion's no concern of anybody but myself.

BARBARA [*guessing*]   I know. Secularist?

SHIRLEY [*hotly*]   Did I offer to deny it?

BARBARA   Why should you? My own father's a Secularist, I think. Our Father—
yours and mine—fulfils himself in many ways; and I daresay he knew what
he was about when he made a Secularist of you. So buck up, Peter! we can
always find a job for a steady man like you. [*Shirley, disarmed and a little bewildered, touches his hat. She turns from him to Bill*]. Whats your name?

BILL [*insolently*]   Wots thet to you?

BARBARA [*calmly making a note*]   Afraid to give his name. Any trade?

BILL   Oo's afride to give is nime? [*Doggedly, with a sense of heroically defying the*

House of Lords in the person of Lord Stevenage] If you want to bring a chawge agen me, bring it. [*She waits, unruffled*]. Moy nime's Bill Walker.

BARBARA [*as if the name were familiar: trying to remember how*]   Bill Walker? [*Recollecting*] Oh, I know: youre the man that Jenny Hill was praying for inside just now. [*She enters his name in her note book*].

BILL   Oo's Jenny Ill? And wot call as she to pry for me?

BARBARA   I dont know. Perhaps it was you that cut her lip.

BILL [*defiantly*]   Yus, it was me that cat her lip. Aw aint afride o you .

BARBARA   How could you be, since youre not afraid of God? Youre a brave man, Mr Walker. It takes some pluck to do our work here; but none of us dare lift our hand against a girl like that, for fear of her father in heaven.

BILL [*sullenly*]   I want nan o your kentin jawr. I spowse you think Aw cam eah to beg from you, like this demmiged lot eah. Not me. Aw downt want your bread and scripe and ketlep. Aw dont blieve in your Gawd, no more than you do yourself.

BARBARA [*sunnily apologetic and ladylike, as on a new footing with him*]   Oh, I beg your pardon for putting your name down, Mr Walker. I didnt understand. I'll strike it out.

BILL [*taking this as a slight, and deeply wounded by it*]   Eah! you let maw nime alown. Aint it good enaff to be in your book?

BARBARA [*considering*]   Well, you see, theres no use putting down your name unless I can do something for you, is there? Whats your trade?

BILL [*still smarting*]   Thets nao concern o yours.

BARBARA   Just so. [*Very businesslike*] I'll put you down as [*writing*] the man who—struck—poor little Jenny Hill—in the mouth.

BILL [*rising threateningly*]   See eah. Awve ed enaff o this.

BARBARA [*quite sunny and fearless*]   What did you come to us for?

BILL   Aw cam for maw gel, see? Aw cam to tike her aht o this and to brike er jawr for er.

BARBARA [*complacently*]   You see I was right about your trade. [*Bill, on the point of retorting furiously, finds himself, to his great shame and terror, in danger of crying instead. He sits down again suddenly*]. Whats her name?

BILL [*dogged*]   Er nime's Mog Ebbijem: thets wot her nime is.

BARBARA   Mog Habbijam! Oh, she's gone to Canning Town, to our barracks there.

BILL [*fortified by his resentment of Mog's perfidy*]   Is she? [*Vindictively*] Then Aw'm gowin to Kennintahn arter her. [*He crosses to the gate; hesitates; finally comes back at Barbara*]. Are you loyin to me to git shat o me?

BARBARA   I dont want to get shut of you. I want to keep you here and save your soul. Youd better stay: youre going to have a bad time today, Bill.

BILL   Oo's gowin to give it to me? You, preps?

BARBARA   Someone you dont believe in. But youll be glad afterwards.

BILL [*slinking off*]   Aw'll gow to Kennintahn to be aht o reach o your tangue. [*Suddenly turning on her with intense malice*] And if Aw downt fawnd Mog there, Aw'll cam beck and do two years for you, selp me Gawd if Aw downt!

BARBARA [*a shade kindlier, if possible*]   It's no use, Bill. She's got another bloke.

BILL   Wot!

BARBARA   One of her own converts. He fell in love with her when he saw her with her soul saved, and her face clean, and her hair washed.

BILL [*surprised*]   Wottud she wash it for, the carroty slat? It's red.

BARBARA   It's quite lovely now, because she wears a new look in her eyes with it. It's a pity youre too late. The new bloke has put your nose out of joint, Bill.

BILL   Aw'll put his nowse aht o joint for him. Not that Aw care a carse for er, mawnd thet. But Aw'll teach her to drop me as if Aw was dirt. And Aw'll teach him to meddle with maw judy. Wots iz bleedin nime?

BARBARA   Sergeant Todger Fairmile.

SHIRLEY [*rising with grim joy*]   I'll go with him, miss. I want to see them two meet. I'll take him to the infirmary when it's over.

BILL [*to Shirley, with undissembled misgiving*]   Is thet im you was speakin on?

SHIRLEY   Thats him.

BILL   Im that wrastled in the music awl?

SHIRLEY   The competitions at the National Sportin Club was worth nigh a hundred a year to him. He's gev em up now for religion; so he's a bit fresh for want of the exercise he was accustomed to. He'll be glad to see you. Come along.

BILL   Wots is wight?

SHIRLEY   Thirteen four. [*Bill's last hope expires*].

BARBARA   Go and talk to him, Bill. He'll convert you.

SHIRLEY   He'll convert your head into a mashed potato.

BILL [*sullenly*]   Aw aint afride of im. Aw aint afride of ennybody. Bat e can lick me. She's dan me. [*He sits down moodily on the edge of the horse trough*].

SHIRLEY   You aint goin. I thought not. [*He resumes his seat*].

BARBARA [*calling*]   Jenny!

JENNY [*appearing at the shelter door with a plaster on the corner of her mouth*]   Yes, Major.

BARBARA   Send Rummy Mitchens out to clear away here.

JENNY   I think she's afraid.

BARBARA [*her resemblance to her mother flashing out for a moment*]   Nonsense! she must do as she's told

JENNY [*calling into the shelter*]   Rummy: the Major says you must come.

Jenny comes to Barbara, purposely keeping on the side next Bill, lest he should suppose that she shrank from him or bore malice.

BARBARA   Poor little Jenny! Are you tired? [*Looking at the wounded cheek*] Does it hurt?

JENNY   No: it's all right now. It was nothing.

BARBARA [*critically*]   It was as hard as he could hit, I expect. Poor Bill! You dont feel angry with him, do you?

JENNY   Oh no, no, no: indeed I dont, Major, bless his poor heart! [*Barbara kisses her; and she runs away merrily into the shelter. Bill writhes with an agonizing return of his new and alarming symptoms, but says nothing. Rummy Mitchens comes from the shelter].*

BARBARA [*going to meet Rummy*]   Now Rummy, bustle. Take in those mugs and plates to be washed; and throw the crumbs about for the birds.

Rummy takes the three plates and mugs; but Shirley takes back his mug from her, as there is still some milk left in it.

RUMMY   There aint any crumbs. This aint a time to waste good bread on birds.

PRICE [*appearing at the shelter door*]   Gentleman come to see the shelter, Major. Says he's your father.

BARBARA   All right. Coming [*Snobby goes back into the shelter, followed by Barbara*].

RUMMY [*stealing across to Bill and addressing him in a subdued voice, but with intense conviction*]   I'd av the lor of you, you flat eared pignosed potwalloper, if she'd let me. Youre no gentleman, to hit a lady in the face. [*Bill, with greater things moving in him, takes no notice*].

SHIRLEY [*following her*]   Here! in with you and dont get yourself into more trouble by talking.

RUMMY [*with hauteur*]   I aint ad the pleasure o being hintroduced to you, as I can remember. [*She goes into the shelter with the plates*].

SHIRLEY   Thats the—

BILL [*savagely*]   Downt you talk to me, d'ye eah? You lea me alown, or Aw'll do you a mischief. Aw'm not dirt under your feet, ennywy.

SHIRLEY [*calmly*] Dont you be afeerd. You aint such prime company that you need expect to be sought after. [*He is about to go into the shelter when Barbara comes out, with Undershaft on her right*].

BARBARA   Oh, there you are, Mr. Shirley! [*Between them*] This is my father: I told you he was a Secularist, didnt I? Perhaps youll be able to comfort one another

UNDERSHAFT [*startled*]   A Secularist! Not the least in the world: on the contrary, a confirmed mystic.

BARBARA   Sorry, I'm sure. By the way, papa, what is your religion? in case I have to introduce you again.

UNDERSHAFT   My religion? Well, my dear, I am a Millionaire. That is my religion.

BARBARA   Then I'm afraid you and Mr Shirley wont be able to comfort one another after all. Youre not a Millionaire, are you, Peter?

SHIRLEY   No; and proud of it.

UNDERSHAFT [*gravely*]   Poverty, my friend, is not a thing to be proud of.

SHIRLEY [*angrily*]   Who made your millions for you? Me and my like. Whats kep us poor? Keepin you rich. I wouldnt have your conscience, not for all your income.

UNDERSHAFT   I wouldnt have your income, not for all your conscience, Mr Shirley. [*He goes to the penthouse and sits down on a form*].

BARBARA [*stopping Shirley adroitly as he is about to retort*]   You wouldnt think he was my father, would you, Peter? Will you go into the shelter and lend the lasses a hand for a while: we're worked off our feet.

SHIRLEY [*bitterly*]   Yes: I'm in their debt for a meal, aint I?

BARBARA   Oh, not because youre in their debt, but for love of them, Peter, for love of them. [*He cannot understand, and is rather scandalized*] There! dont stare at me. In with you; and give that conscience of yours a holiday [*bustling him into the shelter*].

SHIRLEY [*as he goes in*]   Ah! it's a pity you never was trained to use your reason, miss. Youd have been a very taking lecturer on Secularism.

Barbara turns to her father.

UNDERSHAFT   Never mind me, my dear. Go about your work; and let me watch it for a while.

BARBARA   All right.

UNDERSHAFT   For instance, whats the matter with that outpatient over there?

BARBARA [*looking at Bill, whose attitude has never changed, and whose expression of brooding wrath has deepened*]   Oh, we shall cure him in no time. Just watch [*She goes over to Bill and waits. He glances up at her and casts his eyes down again, uneasy, but grimmer than ever*]. It would be nice to just stamp on Mog Habbijam's face, wouldnt it, Bill?

BILL [*starting up from the trough in consternation*]   It's a loy: Aw never said so. [*She shakes her head*]. Oo taold you wot was in moy mawnd?

BARBARA   Only your new friend.

BILL   Wot new friend?

BARBARA   The devil, Bill. When he gets round people they get miserable, just like you.

BILL [*with a heartbreaking attempt at devil-may-care cheerfulness*]   Aw aint miserable. [*He sits down again, and stretches his legs in an attempt to seem indifferent*].

BARBARA   Well, if youre happy, why dont you look happy, as we do?

BILL [*his legs curling back in spite of him*]   Aw'm eppy enatt, Aw tell you. Woy cawnt you lea me alown? Wot ev I dan to you ? Aw aint smashed your fice, ev Aw?

BARBARA [*softly: wooing his soul*]   It's not me thats getting at you, Bill.

BILL   Oo else is it?

BARBARA   Somebody that doesnt intend you to smash women's faces, I suppose. Somebody or something that wants to make a man of you.

BILL [*blustering*]   Mike a menn o me . Aint Aw a menn? eh? Oo sez Aw'm not a menn?

BARBARA   Theres a man in you somewhere, I suppose. But why did he let you hit poor little Jenny Hill? That wasnt very manly of him, was it?

BILL [*tormented*]   Ev dan wiv it, Aw tell you. Chack it. Aw'm sick o your Jenny Ill and er silly little fice.

BARBARA   Then why do you keep thinking about it? Why does it keep coming up against you in your mind? Youre not getting converted, are you?

BILL [*with conviction*]   Not ME. Not lawkly.

BARBARA   Thats right, Bill. Hold out against it. Put out your strength. Dont lets get you cheap. Todger Fairmile said he wrestled for three nights against his salvation harder than he ever wrestled with the Jap at the music hall. He gave in to the Jap when his arm was going to break. But he didnt give in to his salvation until his heart was going to break. Perhaps youll escape that. You havnt any heart, have you?

BILL   Wot d'ye mean? Woy aint Aw got a awt the sime as ennybody else?

BARBARA   A man with a heart wouldnt have bashed poor little Jenny's face, would he?

BILL [*almost crying*]   Ow, will you lea me alown? Ev Aw ever offered to meddle with you, that you cam neggin and provowkin me lawk this? [*He writhes convulsively from his eyes to his toes*].

BARBARA [*with a steady soothing hand on his arm and a gentle voice that never lets him go*]   It's your soul thats hurting you, Bill, and not me. Weve been through it all ourselves. Come with us, Bill. [*He looks wildly round*]. To brave manhood on earth and eternal glory in heaven. [*He is on the point of breaking down*]. Come. [*A drum is heard in the shelter; and Bill, with a gasp, escapes from the spell as Barbara turns quickly. Adolphus enters from the shelter with a big drum*]. Oh! there you are, Dolly. Let me introduce a new friend of mine, Mr Bill Walker. This is my bloke, Bill: Mr Cusins. [*Cusins salutes with his drumstick*].

BILL   Gowin to merry im?

BARBARA   Yes

BILL [*fervently*]   Gawd elp im! Gaw-aw-aw-awd elp im!

BARBARA   Why? Do you think he wont be happy with me?

BILL   Awve aony ed to stend it for a mawnin: e'll ev to stend it for a lawftawm.

CUSINS   That is a frightful reflection, Mr. Walker. But I cant tear myself away from her.

BILL   Well, Aw ken. [*To Barbara*] Eah! do you knaow where Aw'm gowin to, and wot Aw'm gowin to do?

BARBARA   Yes: youre going to heaven; and youre coming back here before the week's out to tell me so.

BILL   You loy. Aw'm gowin to Kennintahn, to spit in Todger Fairmawl's eye. Aw beshed Jenny Ill's fice; an nar Aw'll git me aown fice beshed and cam beck and shaow it to er. Ee'll itt me ardern Aw itt er. Thatll mike us square. [*To Adolphus*] Is thet fair or is it not? Youre a genlmn: you oughter knaow.

BARBARA   Two black eyes wont make one white one, Bill.

BILL   Aw didnt awst you. Cawnt you never keep your mahth shat? Oy awst the genlmn.

CUSINS [*reflectively*]   Yes: I think youre right, Mr Walker. Yes: I should do it. It's curious: it's exactly what an ancient Greek would have done.

BARBARA   But what good will it do?

CUSINS   Well, it will give Mr Fairmile some exercise; and it will satisfy Mr Walker's soul.

BILL   Rot! there aint nao sach a thing as a saoul. Ah kin you tell wevver Awve a saoul or not? You never seen it.

BARBARA   Ive seen it hurting you when you went against it.

BILL [*with compressed aggravation*]   If you was maw gel and took the word aht o me mahth lawk thet, Aw'd give you sathink youd feel urtin, Aw would. [*To Adolphus*] You tike maw tip, mite. Stop er jawr; or youll doy afoah your tawm [*With intense expression*] Wore aht: thets wot youll be: wore aht. [*He goes away through the gate*].

CUSINS [*looking after him*]   I wonder!

BARBARA   Dolly! [*indignant, in her mother's manner*].

CUSINS   Yes, my dear, it's very wearing to be in love with you. If it lasts, I quite think I shall die young.

BARBARA   Should you mind?

CUSINS   Not at all. [*He is suddenly softened, and kisses her over the drum, evidently not for the first time, as people cannot kiss over a big drum without practice. Undershaft coughs*].

BARBARA   It's all right, papa, weve not forgotten you. Dolly: explain the place to papa: I havnt time. [*She goes busily into the shelter*].

Undershaft and Adolphus now have the yard to themselves. Undershaft, seated on a form, and still keenly attentive, looks hard at Adolphus Adolphus looks hard at him.

UNDERSHAFT   I fancy you guess something of what is in my mind, Mr. Cusins. [*Cusins flourishes his drumsticks as if in the act of beating a lively rataplan, but makes no sound.*] Exactly so. But suppose Barbara finds you out!

CUSINS   You know, I do not admit that I am imposing on Barbara. I am quite genuinely interested in the views of the Salvation Army. The fact is, I am a sort of collector of religions; and the curious thing is that I find I can believe them all. By the way, have you any religion?

UNDERSHAFT   Yes.

CUSINS   Anything out of the common?

UNDERSHAFT   Only that there are two things necessary to Salvation.

CUSINS [*disappointed, but polite*]   Ah, the Church Catechism. Charles Lomax also belongs to the Established Church.

UNDERSHAFT   The two things are—

CUSINS   Baptism and—

UNDERSHAFT   No. Money and gunpowder.

CUSINS [*surprised, but interested*]   That is the general opinion of our governing classes. The novelty is in hearing any man confess it.

UNDERSHAFT   Just so.

CUSINS   Excuse me: is there any place in your religion for honor, justice, truth, love, mercy and so forth?

UNDERSHAFT   Yes: they are the graces and luxuries of a rich, strong, and safe life.

CUSINS   Suppose one is forced to choose between them and money or gunpowder?

UNDERSHAFT   Choose money and gunpowder; for without enough of both you cannot afford the others.

CUSINS   That is your religion?

UNDERSHAFT   Yes.

The cadence of this reply makes a full close in the conversation. Cusins twists his face dubiously and contemplates Undershaft. Undershaft contemplates him.

CUSINS   Barbara wont stand that. You will have to choose between your religion and Barbara.

UNDERSHAFT   So will you, my friend. She will find out that that drum of yours is hollow.

CUSINS   Father Undershaft: you are mistaken: I am a sincere Salvationist. You do not understand the Salvation Army. It is the army of joy, of love, of courage: it has banished the fear and remorse and despair of the old hell-ridden evangelical sects: it marches to fight the devil with trumpet and drum, with music and dancing, with banner and palm, as becomes a sally from heaven by its happy garrison. It picks the waster out of the public house and makes a man of him: it finds a worm wriggling in a back kitchen, and lo! a woman! Men and women of rank too, sons and daughters of the Highest. It takes the poor professor of Greek, the most artificial and self-suppressed of human creatures, from his meal of roots, and lets loose the rhapsodist in him; reveals the true worship of Dionysos to him; sends him down the public street drumming dithyrambs [*he plays a thundering flourish on the drum*].

UNDERSHAFT   You will alarm the shelter.

CUSINS   Oh, they are accustomed to these sudden ecstasies. However, if the drum worries you—[*he pockets the drumsticks; unhooks the drum; and stands it on the ground opposite the gateway*].

UNDERSHAFT   Thank you.

CUSINS   You remember what Euripides says about your money and gunpowder?

UNDERSHAFT   No.

CUSINS [*declaiming*]

> One and another
> In money and guns may outpass his brother;
> And men in their millions float and flow
> And seethe with a million hopes as leaven;
> And they win their will; or they miss their will;
> And their hopes are dead or are pined for still;

> But who'er can know
> As the long days go
> That to live is happy, has found his heaven.

My translation: what do you think of it?

UNDERSHAFT   I think, my friend, that if you wish to know, as the long days go, that to live is happy, you must first acquire money enough for a decent life, and power enough to be your own master.

CUSINS   You are damnably discouraging. [*He resumes his declamation*].

> Is it so hard a thing to see
> That the spirit of God—whate'er it be—
> The law that abides and changes not, ages long,
> The Eternal and Nature-born: these things be strong?
> What else is Wisdom? What of Man's endeavor,
> Or God's high grace so lovely and so great?
> To stand from fear set free? to breathe and wait?
> To hold a hand uplifted over Fate?
> And shall not Barbara be loved for ever?

UNDERSHAFT   Euripides mentions Barbara, does he?

CUSINS   It is a fair translation. The word means Loveliness.

UNDERSHAFT   May I ask—as Barbara's father—how much a year she is to be loved for ever on?

CUSINS   As Barbara's father, that is more your affair than mine. I can feed her by teaching Greek: that is about all.

UNDERSHAFT   Do you consider it a good match for her?

CUSINS [*with polite obstinacy*]   Mr Undershaft: I am in many ways a weak, timid, ineffectual person; and my health is far from satisfactory. But whenever I feel that I must have anything, I get it, sooner or later. I feel that way about Barbara. I dont like marriage: I feel intensely afraid of it; and I dont know what I shall do with Barbara or what she will do with me. But I feel that I and nobody else must marry her. Please regard that as settled.—Not that I wish to be arbitrary; but why should I waste your time in discussing what is inevitable?

UNDERSHAFT   You mean that you will stick at nothing: not even the conversion of the Salvation Army to the worship of Dionysos.

CUSINS   The business of the Salvation Army is to save, not to wrangle about the name of the pathfinder. Dionysos or another: what does it matter?

UNDERSHAFT [*rising and approaching him*]   Professor Cusins: you are a young man after my own heart.

CUSINS   Mr. Undershaft: you are, as far as I am able to gather, a most infernal old rascal; but you appeal very strongly to my sense of ironic humor.

Undershaft mutely offers his hand. They shake.

UNDERSHAFT [*suddenly concentrating himself*]   And now to business.

CUSINS   Pardon me. We are discussing religion. Why go back to such an uninteresting and unimportant subject as business?

UNDERSHAFT   Religion is our business at present, because it is through religion alone that we can win Barbara.

CUSINS   Have you, too, fallen in love with Barbara?

UNDERSHAFT   Yes, with a father's love.

CUSINS   A father's love for a grown-up daughter is the most dangerous of all infatuations. I apologize for mentioning my own pale, coy, mistrustful fancy in the same breath with it.

UNDERSHAFT   Keep to the point. We have to win her; and we are neither of us Methodists.

CUSINS   That doesnt matter. The power Barbara wields here—the power that wields Barbara herself—is not Calvinism, not Presbyterianism, not Methodism—

UNDERSHAFT   Not Greek Paganism either, eh?

CUSINS   I admit that. Barbara is quite original in her religion.

UNDERSHAFT [*triumphantly*]   Aha! Barbara Undershaft would be. Her inspiration comes from within herself.

CUSINS   How do you suppose it got there?

UNDERSHAFT [*in towering excitement*]   It is the Undershaft inheritance. I shall hand on my torch to my daughter. She shall make my converts and preach my gospel—

CUSINS   What! Money and gunpowder!

UNDERSHAFT   Yes, money and gunpowder. Freedom and power. Command of life and command of death.

CUSINS [*urbanely: trying to bring him down to earth*]   This is extremely interesting, Mr. Undershaft. Of course you know that you are mad.

UNDERSHAFT [*with redoubled force*]   And you?

CUSINS   Oh, mad as a hatter. You are welcome to my secret since I have discovered yours. But I am astonished. Can a madman make cannons?

UNDERSHAFT   Would anyone else than a madman make them? And now [*with surging energy*] question for question. Can a sane man translate Euripides?

CUSINS   No.

UNDERSHAFT [*seizing him by the shoulder*]   Can a sane woman make a man of a waster or a woman of a worm?

CUSINS [*reeling before the storm*]   Father Colossus—Mammoth Millionaire—

UNDERSHAFT [*pressing him*]   Are there two mad people or three in this Salvation shelter today?

CUSINS   You mean Barbara is as mad as we are?

UNDERSHAFT [*pushing him lightly off and resuming his equanimity suddenly and com-

pletely] Pooh, Professor! let us call things by their proper names. I am a millionaire; you are a poet; Barbara is a savior of souls. What have we three to do with the common mob of slaves and idolaters? [*He sits down again with a shrug of contempt for the mob*].

CUSINS   Take care! Barbara is in love with the common people. So am I. Have you never felt the romance of that love?

UNDERSHAFT [*cold and sardonic*]   Have you ever been in love with Poverty, like St Francis? Have you ever been in love with Dirt, like St Simeon! Have you ever been in love with disease and suffering, like our nurses and philanthropists? Such passions are not virtues, but the most unnatural of all the vices. This love of the common people may please an earl's granddaughter and a university professor; but I have been a common man and a poor man; and it has no romance for me. Leave it to the poor to pretend that poverty is a blessing: leave it to the coward to make a religion of his cowardice by preaching humility: we know better than that. We three must stand together above the common people: how else can we help their children to climb up beside us? Barbara must belong to us, not to the Salvation Army.

CUSINS   Well, I can only say that if you think you will get her away from the Salvation Army by talking to her as you have been talking to me, you dont know Barbara.

UNDERSHAFT   My friend: I never ask for what I can buy.

CUSINS [*in a white fury*]   Do I understand you to imply that you can buy Barbara?

UNDERSHAFT   No; but I can buy the Salvation Army.

CUSINS   Quite impossible.

UNDERSHAFT   You shall see. All religious organizations exist by selling themselves to the rich.

CUSINS   Not the Army. That is the Church of the poor.

UNDERSHAFT   All the more reason for buying it.

CUSINS   I dont think you quite know what the Army does for the poor.

UNDERSHAFT   Oh yes I do. It draws their teeth: that is enough for me as a man of business.

CUSINS   Nonsense! It makes them sober—

UNDERSHAFT   I prefer sober workmen. The profits are larger.

CUSINS   —honest—

UNDERSHAFT   Honest workmen are the most economical.

CUSINS   —attached to their homes—

UNDERSHAFT   So much the better: they will put up with anything sooner than change their shop.

CUSINS   —happy—

UNDERSHAFT   An invaluable safeguard against revolution.

CUSINS   —unselfish—

UNDERSHAFT   Indifferent to their own interests, which suits me exactly.

CUSINS   —with their thoughts on heavenly things—·

UNDERSHAFT [*rising*]   And not on Trade Unionism nor Socialism. Excellent.

CUSINS [*revolted*]   You really are an infernal old rascal.

UNDERSHAFT [*indicating Peter Shirley, who has just come from the shelter and strolled dejectedly down the yard between them*]   And this is an honest man!

SHIRLEY   Yes; and what av I got by it? [*he passes on bitterly and sits on the form, in the corner of the penthouse*].

Snobby Price, beaming sanctimoniously, and Jenny Hill, with a tambourine full of coppers, come from the shelter and go to the drum, on which Jenny begins to count the money.

UNDERSHAFT [*replying to Shirley*]   Oh, your employers must have got a good deal by it from first to last. [*He sits on the table, with the one foot on the side form. Cusins, overwhelmed, sits down on the same form nearer the shelter. Barbara comes from the shelter to the middle of the yard. She is excited and a little overwrought*].

BARBARA   Weve just had a splendid experience meeting at the other gate in Cripps's lane. Ive hardly ever seen them so much moved as they were by your confession, Mr Price.

PRICE   I could almost be glad of my past wickedness if I could believe that it would elp to keep hathers stright.

BARBARA   So it will, Snobby. How much, Jenny?

JENNY   Four and tenpence, Major.

BARBARA   Oh Snobby, if you had given your poor mother just one more kick, we should have got the whole five shillings!

PRICE   If she heard you say that, miss, she'd be sorry I didnt. But I'm glad. Oh what a joy it will be to her when she hears I'm saved!

UNDERSHAFT   Shall I contribute the odd twopence, Barbara? The millionaire's mite, eh? [*He takes a couple of pennies from his pocket*].

BARBARA   How did you make that twopence?

UNDERSHAFT   As usual. By selling cannons, torpedoes, submarines, and my new patent Grand Duke hand grenade.

BARBARA   Put it back in your pocket. You cant buy your salvation here for two-pence: you must work it out.

UNDERSHAFT   Is twopence not enough? I can afford little more, if you press me.

BARBARA   Two million millions would not be enough. There is bad blood on your hands; and nothing but good blood can cleanse them. Money is no use. Take it away. [*She turns to Cusins*]. Dolly: you must write another letter for me to the papers. [*He makes a wry face*]. Yes: I know you dont like it; but it must be done. The starvation this winter is beating us: everybody is unemployed. The General says we must close this shelter if we cant get more money. I force the collections at the meetings until I am ashamed: dont I, Snobby?

PRICE   It's a fair treat to see you work it, miss. The way you got them up from three-and-six to four-and-ten with that hymn, penny by penny and verse by verse, was a caution. Not a Cheap Jack on Mile End Waste could touch you at it.

BARBARA   Yes; but I wish we could do without it. I am getting at last to think more of the collection than of the people's souls. And what are those hatfuls of pence and halfpence? We want thousands! tens of thousands! hundreds of thousands! I want to convert people, not to be always begging for the Army in a way I'd die sooner than beg for myself.

UNDERSHAFT [*in profound irony*]   Genuine unselfishness is capable of anything, my dear.

BARBARA [*unsuspectingly, as she turns away to take the money from the drum and put it in a cashbag she carries*]   Yes, isnt it? [*Undershaft looks sardonically at Cusins*].

CUSINS [*aside to Undershaft*]   Mephistopheles! Machiavelli!

BARBARA [*tears coming into her eyes as she ties the bag and pockets it*]   How are we to feed them? I cant talk religion to a man with bodily hunger in his eyes. [*Almost breaking down*] It's frightful.

JENNY [*running to her*]   Major, dear—

BARBARA [*rebounding*]   No: dont comfort me. It will be all right. We shall get the money.

UNDERSHAFT   How?

JENNY   By praying for it, of course. Mrs Baines says she prayed for it last night; and she has never prayed for it in vain: never once. [*She goes to the gate and looks out into the street*].

BARBARA [*who has dried her eyes and regained her composure*]   By the way, dad, Mrs Baines has come to march with us to our big meeting this afternoon; and she is very anxious to meet you, for some reason or other. Perhaps she'll convert you.

UNDERSHAFT   I shall be delighted, my dear.

JENNY [*at the gate: excitedly*]   Major! Major! heres that man back again.

BARBARA   What man?

JENNY   The man that hit me. Oh, I hope he's coming back to join us.

Bill Walker, with frost on his jacket, comes through the gate, his hands deep in his pockets and his chin sunk between his shoulders, like a cleaned-out gambler. He halts between Barbara and the drum.

BARBARA   Hullo, Bill! Back already!

BILL [*nagging at her*]   Bin talkin ever sence, ev you?

BARBARA   Pretty nearly. Well, has Todger paid you out for poor Jenny's jaw?

BILL   Nao e aint.

BARBARA   I thought your jacket looked a bit snowy.

BILL   Sao it is snaowy. You want to knaow where the snaow cam from, dresponse downt you?

BARBARA   Yes.

BILL   Well, it cam from orf the grahnd in Pawkinses Corner in Kennintahn. It got rabbed orf be maw shaoulders: see?

BARBARA Pity you didnt rub some off with your knees, Bill! That would have done you a lot of good.

BILL [*with sour mirthless humor*] Aw was sivin anather menn's knees at the tawm. E was kneelin on moy ed, e was.

JENNY Who was kneeling on your head?

BILL Todger was. E was pryin for me: pryin camfortable wiv me as a cawpet. Sow was Mog. Sao was the aol bloomin meetin. Mog she sez "Ow Lawd brike is stabborn sperrit; bat downt urt is dear art." Thet was wot she said. "Downt urt is dear art"! An er blowk—thirteen stun four!—kneelin wiv all is wight on me. Fanny, aint it?

JENNY Oh no. We're so sorry, Mr Walker.

BARBARA [*enjoying it frankly*] Nonsense! of course it's funny. Served you right, Bill! You must have done something to him first.

BILL [*doggedly*] Aw did wot Aw said Aw'd do. Aw spit in is eye. E looks ap at the skoy and sez, "Ow that Aw should be fahnd worthy to be spit upon for the gospel's sike!" e sez; an Mog sez "Glaory Allelloolier!"; and then e called me Braddher, and dahned me as if Aw was a kid and e was me mather worshin me a Setterda nawt. Aw ednt jast nao shaow wiv im at all. Arf the street pryed; an the tather arf larfed fit to split theirselves. [*To Barbara*] There! are you settisfawd nah?

BARBARA [*her eyes dancing*] Wish I'd been there, Bill.

BILL Yus: youd a got in a hextra bit o talk on me, wouldnt you?

JENNY I'm so sorry, Mr Walker.

BILL [*fiercely*] Downt you gow bein sorry for me: youve no call. Listen eah. Aw browk your jawr.

JENNY No, it didnt hurt me: indeed it didnt, except for a moment. It was only that I was frightened.

BILL Aw downt want to be forgive be you, or be ennybody. Wot Aw did Aw'll py for. Aw trawd to gat me aown jawr browk to settisfaw you—

JENNY [*distressed*] Oh no—

BILL [*impatiently*] Tell y' Aw did: cawnt you listen to wots bein taold you? All Aw got be it was bein mide a sawt of in the pablic street for me pines. Well, if Aw cawnt settisfaw you one wy, Aw ken another. Listen eah! Aw ed two quid sived agen the frost; an Awve a pahnd of it left. A mite o mawn last week ed words with the judy e's gowin to merry. E give er wot-for; an e's bin fawnd fifteen bob. E ed a rawt to itt er cause they was gowin to be married; but Aw ednt nao rawt to itt you; sao put anather fawv bob on an call it a pahnd's worth. [*He produces a sovereign*]. Eahs the manney. Tike it; and lets ev no more o your forgivin an pryin and your Mijor jawrin me. Let wot Aw dan be dan an pide for; and let there be a end of it.

JENNY Oh, I couldnt take it, Mr Walker. But if you would give a shilling or two to poor Rummy Mitchens! you really did hurt her; and she's old.

BILL [*contemptuously*] Not lawkly. Aw'd give her anather as soon as look at er. Let her ev the lawr o me as she threatened! She aint forgiven me: not mach.

Wot Aw dan to er is not on me mawnd—wot she [*indicating Barbara*] mawt call on me conscience—no more than stickin a pig. It's this Christian gime o yours that Aw wownt ev plyed agen me: this bloomin forgivin an neggin an jawrin that mikes a menn thet sore that iz lawf's a burdn to im. Aw wownt ev it, Aw tell you; sao tike your manney and stop thraowin your silly beshed fice hap agen me.

JENNY   Major: may I take a little of it for the Army?

BARBARA   No: the Army is not to be bought. We want your soul, Bill; and we'll take nothing less.

BILL [*bitterly*]   Aw knaow. Me an maw few shillins is not good enaff for you. Youre a earl's grendorter, you are. Nathink less than a anderd pahnd for you.

UNDERSHAFT   Come, Barbara! you could do a great deal of good with a hundred pounds. If you will set this gentleman's mind at ease by taking his pound, I will give the other ninety-nine.

Bill, dazed by such opulence, instinctively touches his cap.

BARBARA   Oh, youre too extravagant, papa. Bill offers twenty pieces of silver. All you need offer is the other ten. That will make the standard price to buy anybody who's for sale. I'm not; and the Army's not. [*To Bill*] Youll never have another quiet moment, Bill, until you come round to us. You cant stand out against your salvation.

BILL [*sullenly*]   Aw cawnt stend aht agen music awl wrastlers and awtful tangued women. Awve offered to py. Aw can do no more. Tike it or leave it. There it is. [*He throws the sovereign on the drum, and sits down on the horse-trough. The coin fascinates Snobby Price, who takes an early opportunity of dropping his cap on it*].

Mrs Baines comes from the shelter. She is dressed as a Salvation Army Commissioner. She is an earnest looking woman of about 40, with a caressing, urgent voice, and an appealing manner.

BARBARA   This is my father, Mrs Baines. [*Undershaft comes from the table, taking off his hat with marked civility*]. Try what you can do with him. He wont listen to me, because he remembers what a fool I was when I was a baby. [*She leaves them together and chats with Jenny*].

MRS BAINES   Have you been shewn over the shelter, Mr Undershaft? You know the work we're doing, of course.

UNDERSHAFT [*very civilly*]   The whole nation knows it, Mrs Baines.

MRS BAINES   No, sir: the whole nation does not know it, or we should not be crippled as we are for want of money to carry our work through the length and breadth of the land. Let me tell you that there would have been rioting this winter in London but for us.

UNDERSHAFT   You really think so?

MRS BAINES I know it. I remember 1886, when you rich gentlemen hardened your hearts against the cry of the poor. They broke the windows of your clubs in Pall Mall.

UNDERSHAFT [*gleaming with approval of their method*] And the Mansion House Fund went up next day from thirty thousand pounds to seventy-nine thousand! I remember quite well.

MRS BAINES Well, wont you help me to get at the people? They wont break windows then. Come here, Price. Let me shew you to this gentleman [*Price comes to be inspected*]. Do you remember the window breaking?

PRICE My ole father thought it was the revolution, maam.

MRS BAINES Would you break windows now?

PRICE Oh no, maam. The windows of eaven av bin opened to me. I know now that the rich man is a sinner like myself.

RUMMY [*appearing above at the loft door*] Snobby Price!

SNOBBY Wot is it?

RUMMY Your mother's askin for you at the other gate in Cripps's Lane. She's heard about your confession [*Price turns pale*].

MRS BAINES Go, Mr Price; and pray with her.

JENNY You can go through the shelter, Snobby.

PRICE [*to Mrs Baines*] I couldnt face her now, maam, with all the weight of my sins fresh on me. Tell her she'll find her son at ome, waitin for her in prayer. [*He skulks off through the gate, incidentally stealing the sovereign on his way out by picking up his cap from the drum*].

MRS BAINES [*with swimming eyes*] You see how we take the anger and the bitterness against you out of their hearts, Mr Undershaft.

UNDERSHAFT It is certainly most convenient and gratifying to all large employers of labor, Mrs Baines.

MRS BAINES Barbara: Jenny: I have good news: most wonderful news. [*Jenny runs to her*]. My prayers have been answered. I told you they would, Jenny, didnt I?

JENNY Yes, yes.

BARBARA [*moving nearer to the drum*] Have we got money enough to keep the shelter open?

MRS BAINES I hope we shall have enough to keep all the shelters open. Lord Saxmundham has promised us five thousand pound—

BARBARA Hooray!

JENNY Glory!

MRS BAINES —if—

BARBARA "If!" If what?

MRS BAINES —if five other gentlemen will give a thousand each to make it up to ten thousand.

BARBARA Who is Lord Saxmundham? I never heard of him.

UNDERSHAFT [*who has pricked up his ears at the peer's name, and is now watching Barbara curiously*] A new creation, my dear. You have heard of Sir Horace Bodger?

BARBARA   Bodger! Do you mean the distiller? Bodger's whisky!

UNDERSHAFT   That is the man. He is one of the greatest of our public benefactors. He restored the cathedral at Hakington. They made him a baronet for that. He gave half a million to the funds of his party: they made him a baron for that.

SHIRLEY   What will they give him for the five thousand?

UNDERSHAFT   There is nothing left to give him. So the five thousand, I should think is to save his soul.

MRS BAINES   Heaven grant it may! Oh Mr Undershaft, you have some very rich friends. Cant you help us towards the other five thousand? We are going to hold a great meeting this afternoon at the Assembly Hall in the Mile End Road. If I could only announce that one gentleman had come forward to support Lord Saxmundham, others would follow. Dont you know somebody? couldnt you? wouldnt you? [*her eyes fill with tears*] oh, think of those poor people, Mr. Undershaft: think of how much it means to them, and how little to a great man like you.

UNDERSHAFT [*sardonically gallant*]   Mrs Baines: you are irresistible. I cant disappoint you; and I cant deny myself the satisfaction of making Bodger pay up. You shall have your five thousand pounds.

MRS BAINES   Thank God!

UNDERSHAFT   You dont thank me?

MRS BAINES   Oh sir, dont try to be cynical: dont be ashamed of being a good man. The Lord will bless you abundantly; and our prayers will be like a strong fortification round you all the days of your life. [*With a touch of caution*] You will let me have the cheque to shew at the meeting, wont you? Jenny: go in and fetch a pen and ink. [*Jenny runs to the shelter door*].

UNDERSHAFT   Do not disturb Miss Hill: I have a fountain pen [*Jenny halts. He sits at the table and writes the cheque. Cusins rises to make room for him. They all watch him silently*].

BILL [*cynically, aside to Barbara, his voice and accent horribly debased*]   Wot prawce selvytion nah?

BARBARA   Stop. [*Undershaft stops writing: they all turn to her in surprise*]. Mrs Baines: are you really going to take this money?

MRS BAINES [*astonished*]   Why not, dear?

BARBARA   Why not! Do you know what my father is? Have you forgotten that Lord Saxmundham is Bodger the whisky man? Do you remember how we implored the County Council to stop him from writing Bodger's Whisky in letters of fire against the sky; so that the poor drink-ruined creatures on the Embankment could not wake up from their snatches of sleep without being reminded of their deadly thirst by that wicked sky sign? Do you know that the worst thing I have had to fight here is not the devil, but Bodger, Bodger, Bodger, with his whisky, his distilleries, and his tied houses? Are you going to make our shelter another tied house for him, and ask me to keep it?

BILL   Rotten dranken whisky it is too.

MRS BAINES   Dear Barbara: Lord Saxmundham has a soul to be saved like any of us. If heaven has found the way to make a good use of his money, are we to set ourselves up against the answer to our prayers?

BARBARA   I know he has a soul to be saved. Let him come down here; and I'll do my best to help him to his salvation. But he wants to send his cheque down to buy us, and go on being as wicked as ever.

UNDERSHAFT [*with a reasonableness which Cusins alone perceives to be ironical*]   My dear Barbara: alcohol is a very necessary article. It heals the sick—

BARBARA   It does nothing of the sort.

UNDERSHAFT   Well, it assists the doctor: that is perhaps a less questionable way of putting it. It makes life bearable to millions of people who could not endure their existence if they were quite sober. It enables Parliament to do things at eleven at night that no sane person would do at eleven in the morning. Is it Bodger's fault that this inestimable gift is deplorably abused by less than one per cent of the poor? [*He turns again to the table; signs the cheque; and crosses it*].

MRS BAINES   Barbara: will there be less drinking or more if all those poor souls we are saving come tomorrow and find the doors of our shelters shut in their faces? Lord Saxmundham gives us the money to stop drinking—to take his own business from him.

CUSINS [*impishly*]   Pure self-sacrifice on Bodger's part, clearly! Bless dear Bodger! [*Barbara almost breaks down as Adolphus, too, fails her*].

UNDERSHAFT [*tearing out the cheque and pocketing the book as he rises and goes past Cusins to Mrs Baines*]   I also, Mrs Baines, may claim a little disinterestedness. Think of my business! think of the widows and orphans! the men and lads torn to pieces with shrapnel and poisoned with lyddite! [*Mrs Baines shrinks; but he goes on remorselessly*] the oceans of blood, not one drop of which is shed in a really just cause! the ravaged crops! the peaceful peasants forced, women and men, to till their fields under the fire of opposing armies on pain of starvation! the bad blood of the fierce little cowards at home who egg on others to fight for the gratification of their national vanity! All this makes money for me: I am never richer, never busier than when the papers are full of it. Well, it is your work to preach peace on earth and goodwill to men. [*Mrs Baines's face lights up again*]. Every convert you make is a vote against war. [*Her lips move in prayer*]. Yet I give you this money to help you to hasten my own commerical ruin. [*He gives her the cheque*].

CUSINS [*mounting the form in an ecstasy of mischief*]   The millennium will be inaugurated by the unselfishness of Undershaft and Bodger. Oh be joyful! [*He takes the drum-sticks from his pocket and flourishes them*].

MRS BAINES [*taking the cheque*]   The longer I live the more proof I see that there is an Infinite Goodness that turns everything to the work of salvation sooner or later. Who would have thought that any good could have come out of war and drink? And yet their profits are brought today to the feet of salvation to do its blessed work. [*She is affected to tears*].

JENNY [*running to Mrs Baines and throwing her arms around her*]   Oh dear! how blessed, how glorious it all is!

CUSINS [*in a convulsion of irony*]   Let us seize this unspeakable moment. Let us march to the great meeting at once. Excuse me just an instant. [*He rushes into the shelter. Jenny takes her tambourine from the drum head*].

MRS BAINES   Mr. Undershaft: have you ever seen a thousand people fall on their knees with one impulse and pray? Come with us to the meeting. Barbara shall tell them that the Army is saved, and saved through you.

CUSINS [*returning impetuously from the shelter with a flag and a trombone, and coming between Mrs Baines and Undershaft*]   You shall carry the flag down the first street, Mrs Baines [*he gives her the flag*]. Mr Undershaft is a gifted trombonist: he shall intone an Olympian diapason to the West Ham Salvation March. [*Aside to Undershaft, as he forces the trombone on him*] Blow, Machiavelli, blow.

UNDERSHAFT [*aside to him, as he takes the trombone*]   The trumpet in Zion! [*Cusins rushes to the drum, which he takes up and puts on. Undershaft continues, aloud*] I will do my best. I could vamp a bass if I knew the tune.

CUSINS   It is a wedding chorus from one of Donizetti's operas; but we have converted it. We convert everything to good here, including Bodger. You remember the chorus. "For thee immense rejoicing—immenso giubilo—immenso giubilo." [*With drum obbligato*] Rum tum ti tum tum, tum tum ti ta—

BARBARA   Dolly: you are breaking my heart.

CUSINS   What is a broken heart more or less here? Dionysos Undershaft has descended. I am possessed.

MRS BAINES   Come, Barbara: I must have my dear Major to carry the flag with me.

JENNY   Yes, yes, Major darling.

CUSINS [*snatches the tambourine out of Jenny's hand and mutely offers it to Barbara*].

BARBARA [*coming forward a little as she puts the offer behind her with a shudder, whilst Cusins recklessly tosses the tambourine back to Jenny and goes to the gate*]   I cant come.

JENNY   Not come!

MRS BAINES [*with tears in her eyes*]   Barbara: do you think I am wrong to take the money?

BARBARA [*impulsively going to her and kissing her*]   No, no: God help you, dear, you must; you are saving the Army. Go; and may you have a great meeting!

JENNY   But arnt you coming?

BARBARA   No. [*She begins taking off the silver S brooch from her collar*].

MRS BAINES   Barbara: what are you doing?

JENNY   Why are you taking your badge off? You cant be going to leave us, Major.

BARBARA [*quietly*]   Father: come here.

UNDERSHAFT [*coming to her*]   My dear! [*Seeing that she is going to pin the badge on his collar he retreats to the penthouse in some alarm*].

BARBARA [*following him*]   Dont be frightened. [*She pins the badge on and steps back towards the table, shewing him to the others*] There! It's not much for £5000, is it?

MRS BAINES   Barbara: if you wont come and pray with us, promise me you will pray for us.

BARBARA   I cant pray now. Perhaps I shall never pray again.

MRS BAINES   Barbara!

JENNY   Major!

BARBARA [*almost delirious*]   I cant bear any more. Quick march!

CUSINS [*calling to the procession in the street outside*]   Off we go. Play up, there! Immenso giubilo. [*He gives the time with his drum; and the band strikes up the march, which rapidly becomes more distant as the procession moves briskly away*].

MRS BAINES   I must go, dear. Youre overworked: you will be all right tomorrow. We'll never lose you. Now Jenny: step out with the old flag. Blood and Fire! [*She marches out through the gate with her flag*].

JENNY   Glory Hallelujah! [*flourishing her tambourine and marching*].

UNDERSHAFT [*to Cusins, as he marches out past him easing the slide of his trombone*]   "My ducats and my daughter"!

CUSINS [*following him out*]   Money and gunpowder!

BARBARA   Drunkenness and Murder! My God: why hast thou forsaken me?

She sinks on the form with her face buried in her hands. The march passes away into silence. Bill Walker steals across to her.

BILL [*taunting*].   Wot prawce selvytion nah?

SHIRLEY   Dont you hit her when she's down.

BILL   She itt me wen aw wiz dahn. Waw shouldnt Aw git a bit o me aown beck?

BARBARA [*raising her head*]   I didnt take your money, Bill. [*She crosses the yard to the gate and turns her back on the two men to hide her face from them*].

BILL [*sneering after her*]   Naow, it warnt enaff for you. [*Turning to the drum, he misses the money*] Ellow! If you aint took it sammun else ez. Weres it gorn? Bly me if Jenny Ill didnt tike it arter all!

RUMMY [*screaming at him from the loft*]   You lie, you dirty blackguard! Snobby Price pinched it off the drum when he took up his cap. I was up here all the time an see im do it.

BILL   Wot! Stowl maw manney! Waw didnt you call thief on him, you silly aold macker you?

RUMMY   To serve you aht for ittin me acrost the fice. It's cost y'pahnd, that az. [*Raising a pæan of squalid triumph*] I done you. I'm even with you. Ive ad it aht o y —[*Bill snatches up Shirley's mug and hurls it at her. She slams the loft door and vanishes. The mug smashes against the door and falls in fragments*].

BILL [*beginning to chuckle*]   Tell us, aol menn, wot o'clock this mawnin was it wen im as they call Snobby Prawce was sived?

BARBARA [*turning to him more composedly, and with unspoiled sweetness*]   About half past twelve, Bill. And he pinched your pound at a quarter to two. *I* know. Well, you cant afford to lose it. I'll send it to you.

BILL [*his voice and accent suddenly improving*]   Not if Aw wiz to stawve for it. Aw
aint to be bought.

SHIRLEY   Aint you? Youd sell yourself to the devil for a pint o beer; ony there aint
no devil to make the offer.

BILL [*unshamed*]   Sao Aw would, mite, and often ev, cheerful. But she cawnt baw
me. [*Approaching Barbara*] You wanted maw saoul, did you? Well, you aint
got it.

BARBARA   I nearly got it, Bill. But weve sold it back to you for ten thousand
pounds.

SHIRLEY   And dear at tne money!

BARBARA   No, Peter: it was worth more than money.

BILL [*salvationproof*]   It's nao good: you cawnt get rahnd me nah. Aw downt blieve
in it; and Awve seen tody that Aw was rawt. [*Going*] Sao long, aol soupkitchener! Ta, ta, Mijor Earl's Grendorter! [*Turning at the gate*] Wot prawce selvytion
nah? Snobby Prawce! Ha! ha!

BARBARA [*offering her hand*]   Goodbye, Bill.

BILL [*taken aback, half plucks his cap off; then shoves it on again defiantly*]   Git aht.
[*Barbara drops her hand, discouraged. He has a twinge of remorse*]. But thets aw
rawt, you knaow. Nathink pasnl. Naow mellice. Sao long, Judy. [*He goes*].

BARBARA   No malice. So long, Bill.

SHIRLEY [*shaking his head*]   You make too much of him, miss, in your innocence.

BARBARA [*going to him*]   Peter: I'm like you now. Cleaned out, and lost my job.

SHIRLEY   Youve youth an hope. Thats two better than me.

BARBARA   I'll get you a job, Peter. Thats hope for you: the youth will have to be
enough for me. [*She counts her money*]. I have just enough left for two teas at
Lockharts, a Rowton doss for you, and my tram and bus home. [*He frowns
and rises with offended pride. She takes his arm*]. Dont be proud, Peter: it's sharing between friends. And promise me youll talk to me and not let me cry.
[*She draws him towards the gate*].

SHIRLEY   Well, I'm not accustomed to talk to the like of you—

BARBARA [*urgently*]   Yes, yes: you must talk to me. Tell me about Tom Paine's
books and Bradlaugh's lectures. Come along.

SHIRLEY   Ah, if you would only read Tom Paine in the proper spirit, miss! [*They
go out through the gate together*].

ACT III

*Next day after lunch Lady Britomart is writing in the library in Wilton Crescent. Sarah is
reading in the armchair near the window. Barbara, in ordinary fashionable dress, pale and
brooding, is on the settee. Charles Lomax enters. He starts on seeing Barbara fashionably
attired and in low spirits.*

LOMAX   Youve left off your uniform!

Barbara says nothing; but an expression of pain passes over her face.

LADY BRITOMART [*warning him in low tones to be careful*]   Charles!

LOMAX [*much concerned, coming behind the settee and bending sympathetically over Barbara*]   I'm awfully sorry, Barbara. You know I helped you all I could with the concertina and so forth. [*Momentously*] Still, I have never shut my eyes to the fact that there is a certain amount of tosh about the Salvation Army. Now the claims of the Church of England—

LADY BRITOMART   Thats enough, Charles. Speak of something suited to your mental capacity.

LOMAX   But surely the Church of England is suited to all our capacities.

BARBARA [*pressing his hand*]   Thank you for your sympathy, Cholly. Now go and spoon with Sarah.

LOMAX [*dragging a chair from the writing table and seating himself affectionately by Sarah's side*]   How is my ownest today?

SARAH   I wish you wouldnt tell Cholly to do things, Barbara. He always comes straight and does them. Cholly: we're going to the works this afternoon.

LOMAX   What works?

SARAH   The cannon works.

LOMAX   What? your governor's shop!

SARAH   Yes.

LOMAX   Oh I say!

Cusins enters in poor condition. He also starts visibly when he sees Barbara without her uniform.

BARBARA   I expected you this morning, Dolly. Didnt you guess that?

CUSINS [*sitting down beside her*]   I'm sorry. I have only just breakfasted.

SARAH   But weve just finished lunch.

BARBARA   Have you had one of your bad nights?

CUSINS   No: I had rather a good night: in fact, one of the most remarkable nights I have ever passed.

BARBARA   The meeting?

CUSINS   No: after the meeting.

LADY BRITOMART   You should have gone to bed after the meeting. What were you doing?

CUSINS   Drinking.

LADY BRITOMART	Adolphus!
SARAH	Dolly!
BARBARA	Dolly!
LOMAX	Oh I say!

LADY BRITOMART   What were you drinking, may I ask?

CUSINS   A most devilish kind of Spanish burgundy, warranted free from added alcohol: a Temperance burgundy in fact. Its richness in natural alcohol made any addition superfluous.

BARBARA   Are you joking, Dolly?

CUSINS [*patiently*]   No. I have been making a night of it with the nominal head of this household: that is all.

LADY BRITOMART   Andrew made you drunk!

CUSINS   No: he only provided the wine. I think it was Dionysos who made me drunk. [*To Barbara*] I told you I was possessed.

LADY BRITOMART   Youre not sober yet. Go home to bed at once.

CUSINS   I have never before ventured to reproach you, Lady Brit; but how could you marry the Prince of Darkness?

LADY BRITOMART   It was much more excusable to marry him than to get drunk with him. That is a new accomplishment of Andrew's, by the way. He usent to drink.

CUSINS   He doesnt now. He only sat there and completed the wreck of my moral basis, the rout of my convictions, the purchase of my soul. He cares for you, Barbara. That is what makes him so dangerous to me.

BARBARA   That has nothing to do with it, Dolly. There are larger loves and diviner dreams than the fireside ones. You know that, dont you?

CUSINS   Yes: that is our understanding. I know it. I hold to it. Unless he can win me on that holier ground he may amuse me for a while; but he can get no deeper hold, strong as he is.

BARBARA   Keep to that; and the end will be right. Now tell me what happened at the meeting?

CUSINS   It was an amazing meeting. Mrs Baines almost died of emotion. Jenny Hill simply gibbered with hysteria. The Prince of Darkness played his trombone like a madman: its brazen roarings were like the laughter of the damned. 117 conversions took place then and there. They prayed with the most touching sincerity and gratitude for Bodger, and for the anonymous donor of the £5000. Your father would not let his name be given.

LOMAX   That was rather fine of the old man, you know. Most chaps would have wanted the advertisement.

CUSINS   He said all the charitable institutions would be down on him like kites on a battle-field if he gave his name.

LADY BRITOMART   Thats Andrew all over. He never does a proper thing without giving an improper reason for it.

CUSINS   He convinced me that I have all my life been doing improper things for proper reasons.

LADY BRITOMART   Adolphus: now that Barbara has left the Salvation Army, you had better leave it too. I will not have you playing that drum in the streets.

CUSINS   Your orders are already obeyed, Lady Brit.

BARBARA   Dolly: were you ever really in earnest about it? Would you have joined if you had never seen me?

CUSINS [*disingenuously*]   Well—er—well, possibly, as a collector of religions—

LOMAX [*cunningly*]   Not as a drummer, though, you know. You are a very clear-headed brainy chap, Dolly; and it must have been apparent to you that there is a certain amount of tosh about—

LADY BRITOMART   Charles: if you must drivel, drivel like a grown-up man and not like a schoolboy.

LOMAX [*out of countenance*]   Well, drivel is drivel, dont you know, whatever a man's age.

LADY BRITOMART   In good society in England, Charles, men drivel at all ages by repeating silly formulas with an air of wisdom. Schoolboys make their own formulas out of slang, like you. When they reach your age, and get political private secretaryships and things of that sort, they drop slang and get their formulas out of The Spectator or The Times. You had better confine yourself to The Times. You will find that there is a certain amount of tosh about The Times; but at least its language is reputable.

LOMAX [*overwhelmed*]   You are so awfully strongminded, Lady Brit—

LADY BRITOMART   Rubbish! [*Morrison comes in*]. What is it?

MORRISON   If you please, my lady, Mr Undershaft has just drove up to the door.

LADY BRITOMART   Well, let him in. [*Morrison hesitates*]. Whats the matter with you?

MORRISON   Shall I announce him, my lady; or is he at home here, so to speak, my lady?

LADY BRITOMART   Announce him.

MORRISON   Thank you, my lady. You wont mind my asking, I hope. The occasion is in a manner of speaking new to me.

LADY BRITOMART   Quite right. Go and let him in.

MORRISON   Thank you, my lady. [*He withdraws*].

LADY BRITOMART   Children: go and get ready. [*Sarah and Barbara go upstairs for their out-of-door wraps*]. Charles: go and tell Stephen to come down here in five minutes: you will find him in the drawing room. [*Charles goes*]. Adolphus: tell them to send round the carriage in about fifteen minutes. [*Adolphus goes*].

MORRISON [*at the door*]   Mr Undershaft.

Undershaft comes in. Morrison goes out.

UNDERSHAFT   Alone! How fortunate!

LADY BRITOMART [*rising*]   Dont be sentimental, Andrew. Sit down. [*She sits on the settee: he sits beside her, on her left. She comes to the point before he has time to breathe*]. Sarah must have £800 a year until Charles Lomax comes into his property. Barbara will need more, and need it permanently, because Adolphus hasnt any property.

UNDERSHAFT [*resignedly*]   Yes, my dear: I will see to it. Anything else? for yourself, for instance?

LADY BRITOMART   I want to talk to you about Stephen.

UNDERSHAFT [*rather wearily*]   Dont, my dear. Stephen doesnt interest me.

LADY BRITOMART   He does interest me. He is our son.

UNDERSHAFT   Do you really think so? He has induced us to bring him into the world; but he chose his parents very incongruously, I think. I see nothing of myself in him, and less of you.

LADY BRITOMART   Andrew: Stephen is an excellent son, and a most steady, capable, highminded young man. You are simply trying to find an excuse for disinheriting him.

UNDERSHAFT   My dear Biddy: the Undershaft tradition disinherits him. It would be dishonest of me to leave the cannon foundry to my son.

LADY BRITOMART   It would be most unnatural and improper of you to leave it to anyone else, Andrew. Do you suppose this wicked and immoral tradition can be kept up for ever? Do you pretend that Stephen could not carry on the foundry just as well as all the other sons of the big business houses?

UNDERSHAFT   Yes: he could learn the office routine without understanding the business, like all the other sons; and the firm would go on by its own momentum until the real Undershaft—probably an Italian or a German—would invent a new method and cut him out.

LADY BRITOMART   There is nothing that any Italian or German could do that Stephen could not do. And Stephen at least has breeding.

UNDERSHAFT   The son of a foundling! Nonsense!

LADY BRITOMART   My son, Andrew! And even you may have good blood in your veins for all you know.

UNDERSHAFT   True. Probably I have. That is another argument in favor of a foundling.

LADY BRITOMART   Andrew: dont be aggravating. And dont be wicked. At present you are both.

UNDERSHAFT   This conversation is part of the Undershaft tradition, Biddy. Every Undershaft's wife has treated him to it ever since the house was founded. It is mere waste of breath. If the tradition be ever broken it will be for an abler man than Stephen.

LADY BRITOMART [pouting]   Then go away.

UNDERSHAFT [deprecatory]   Go away!

LADY BRITOMART   Yes: go away. If you will do nothing for Stephen, you are not wanted here. Go to your foundling, whoever he is; and look after him.

UNDERSHAFT   That fact is, Biddy—

LADY BRITOMART   Dont call me Biddy. I dont call you Andy.

UNDERSHAFT   I will not call my wife Britomart: it is not good sense. Seriously, my love, the Undershaft tradition has landed me in a difficulty. I am getting on in years; and my partner Lazarus has at last made a stand and insisted that the succession must be settled one way or the other; and of course he is quite right. You see, I havnt found a fit successor yet.

LADY BRITOMART [obstinately]   There is Stephen.

UNDERSHAFT   Thats just it: all the foundlings I can find are exactly like Stephen.

LADY BRITOMART   Andrew!!

UNDERSHAFT   I want a man with no relations and no schooling: that is, a man who would be out of the running altogether if he were not a strong man. And I cant find him. Every blessed foundling nowadays is snapped up in his infancy by Barnardo homes, or School Board Officers, or Boards of Guardians; and if he shews the least ability he is fastened on by schoolmasters; trained to win scholarships like a racehorse; crammed with secondhand ideas; drilled and disciplined in docility and what they call good taste; and lamed for life so that he is fit for nothing but teaching. If you want to keep the foundry in the family, you had better find an eligible foundling and marry him to Barbara.

LADY BRITOMART   Ah! Barbara! Your pet! You would sacrifice Stephen to Barbara.

UNDERSHAFT   Cheerfully. And you, my dear, would boil Barbara to make soup for Stephen.

LADY BRITOMART   Andrew: this is not a question of our likings and dislikings: it is a question of duty. It is your duty to make Stephen your successor.

UNDERSHAFT   Just as much as it is your duty to submit to your husband. Come, Biddy! these tricks of the governing class are of no use with me. I am one of the governing class myself; and it is waste of time giving tracts to a missionary. I have the power in this matter; and I am not to be humbugged into using it for your purposes.

LADY BRITOMART   Andrew: you can talk my head off; but you cant change wrong into right. And your tie is all on one side. Put it straight.

UNDERSHAFT [disconcerted]   It wont stay unless it's pinned [he fumbles at it with childish grimaces]—

Stephen comes in.

STEPHEN [at the door]   I beg your pardon [about to retire].

LADY BRITOMART   No: come in, Stephen. [Stephen comes forward to his mother's writing table].

UNDERSHAFT [not very cordially]   Good afternoon.

STEPHEN [coldly]   Good afternoon.

UNDERSHAFT [to Lady Britomart]   He knows all about the tradition, I suppose?

LADY BRITOMART   Yes. [To Stephen] It is what I told you last night, Stephen.

UNDERSHAFT [sulkily]   I understand you want to come into the cannon business.

STEPHEN   I go into trade! Certainly not.

UNDERSHAFT [opening his eyes, greatly eased in mind and manner]   Oh! in that case—

LADY BRITOMART   Cannons are not trade, Stephen. They are enterprise.

STEPHEN   I have no intention of becoming a man of business in any sense. I have no capacity for business and no taste for it. I intend to devote myself to politics.

UNDERSHAFT [rising]   My dear boy: this is an immense relief to me. And I trust it may prove an equally good thing for the country. I was afraid you would consider yourself disparaged and slighted [He moves towards Stephen as if to shake hands with him].

LADY BRITOMART [rising and interposing]   Stephen: I cannot allow you to throw away an enormous property like this.

STEPHEN [*stiffly*]   Mother: there must be an end of treating me as a child, if you please. [*Lady Britomart recoils, deeply wounded by his tone*]. Until last night I did not take your attitude seriously, because I did not think you meant it seriously. But I find now that you left me in the dark as to matters which you should have explained to me years ago. I am extremely hurt and offended. Any further discussion of my intentions had better take place with my father, as between one man and another.

LADY BRITOMART   Stephen! [*She sits down again, her eyes filling with tears*].

UNDERSHAFT [*with grave compassion*]   You see, my dear, it is only the big men who can be treated as children.

STEPHEN   I am sorry, mother, that you have forced me—

UNDERSHAFT [*stopping him*]   Yes, yes, yes, yes: thats all right, Stephen. She wont interfere with you any more: your independence is achieved: you have won your latchkey. Dont rub it in; and above all, dont apologize. [*He resumes his seat*]. Now what about your future, as between one man and another—I beg your pardon, Biddy: as between two men and a woman.

LADY BRITOMART [*who has pulled herself together strongly*]   I quite understand, Stephen. By all means go your own way if you feel strong enough. [*Stephen sits down magisterially in the chair at the writing table with an air of affirming his majority*].

UNDERSHAFT   It is settled that you do not ask for the succession to the cannon business.

STEPHEN   I hope it is settled that I repudiate the cannon business.

UNDERSHAFT   Come, come! dont be so devilishly sulky: it's boyish. Freedom should be generous. Besides, I owe you a fair start in life in exchange for disinheriting you. You cant become prime minister all at once. Havnt you a turn for something? What about literature, art, and so forth?

STEPHEN   I have nothing of the artist about me, either in faculty or character, thank Heaven.

UNDERSHAFT   A philosopher, perhaps? Eh?

STEPHEN   I make no such ridiculous pretension.

UNDERSHAFT   Just so. Well, there is the army, the navy, the Church, the Bar. The Bar requires some ability. What about the Bar?

STEPHEN   I have not studied law. And I am afraid I have not the necessary push— I believe that is the name barristers give to their vulgarity—for success in pleading.

UNDERSHAFT   Rather a difficult case, Stephen. Hardly anything left but the stage, is there? [*Stephen makes an impatient movement*]. Well, come! is there anything you know or care for?

STEPHEN [*rising and looking at him steadily*]   I know the difference between right and wrong.

UNDERSHAFT [*hugely tickled*]   You dont say so! What! no capacity for business, no knowledge of law, no sympathy with art, no pretension to philosophy; only a simple knowledge of the secret that has puzzled all the philosophers, baffled all the lawyers, muddled all the men of business, and ruined most of the artists: the secret of right and wrong. Why, man, youre a genius, a master of masters, a god! At twentyfour, too!

STEPHEN [*keeping his temper with difficulty*] You are pleased to be facetious. I pretend to nothing more than any honourable English gentleman claims as his birthright [*he sits down angrily*].

UNDERSHAFT Oh, thats everybody's birthright. Look at poor little Jenny Hill, the Salvation lassie! she would think you were laughing at her if you asked her to stand up in the street and teach grammar or geography or mathematics or even drawing room dancing; but it never occurs to her to doubt that she can teach morals and religion. You are all alike, you respectable people. You cant tell me the bursting strain of a ten-inch gun, which is a very simple matter; but you all think you can tell me the bursting strain of a man under temptation. You darent handle high explosives; but youre all ready to handle honesty and truth and justice and the whole duty of man, and kill one another at that game. What a country! What a world!

LADY BRITOMART [*uneasily*] What do you think he had better do, Andrew?

UNDERSHAFT Oh, just what he wants to do. He knows nothing and he thinks he knows everything. That points clearly to a political career. Get him a private secretaryship to someone who can get him an Under Secretaryship; and then leave him alone. He will find his natural and proper place in the end on the Treasury Bench.

STEPHEN [*springing up again*] I am sorry, sir, that you force me to forget the respect due to you as my father. I am an Englishman and I will not hear the Government of my country insulted. [*He thrusts his hands in his pockets, and walks angrily across to the window*].

UNDERSHAFT [*with a touch of brutality*] The government of your country! *I* am the government of your country: I, and Lazarus. Do you suppose that you and half a dozen amateurs like you, sitting in a row in that foolish gabble shop, can govern Undershaft and Lazarus? No, my friend: you will do what pays us. You will make war when it suits us, and keep peace when it doesnt. You will find out that trade requires certain measures when we have decided on those measures. When I want anything to keep my dividends up, you will discover that my want is a national need. When other people want something to keep my dividends down, you will call out the police and military. And in return you shall have the support and applause of my newspapers, and the delight of imagining that you are a great statesman. Government of your country! Be off with you, my boy, and play with your caucuses and leading articles and historic parties and great leaders and burning questions and the rest of your toys. I am going back to my counting-house to pay the piper and call the tune.

STEPHEN [*actually smiling, and putting his hand on his father's shoulder with indulgent patronage*] Really, my dear father, it is impossible to be angry with you. You dont know how absurd all this sounds to me. You are properly proud of having been industrious enough to make money; and it is greatly to your credit that you have made so much of it. But it has kept you in circles where you are valued for your money and deferred to for it, instead of in the doubtless very old-fashioned and behind-the-times public school and university where I formed my habits of mind. It is natural for you to think that money governs England; but you must allow me to think I know better.

UNDERSHAFT   And what does govern England, pray?

STEPHEN   Character, father, character.

UNDERSHAFT   Whose character? Yours or mine?

STEPHEN   Neither yours nor mine, father, but the best elements in the English national character.

UNDERSHAFT   Stephen: Ive found your profession for you. Youre a born journalist. I'll start you with a high-toned weekly review. There!

Before Stephen can reply Sarah, Barbara, Lomax, and Cusins come in ready for walking. Barbara crosses the room to the window and looks out. Cusins drifts amiably to the armchair. Lomax remains near the door, whilst Sarah comes to her mother.

Stephen goes to the smaller writing table and busies himself with his letters.

SARAH   Go and get ready, mamma: the carriage is waiting. [*Lady Britomart leaves the room*].

UNDERSHAFT [*to Sarah*]   Good day, my dear. Good afternoon, Mr Lomax.

LOMAX [*vaguely*]   Ahdedoo.

UNDERSHAFT [*to Cusins*]   Quite well after last night, Euripides, eh?

CUSINS   As well as can be expected.

UNDERSHAFT   Thats right [*To Barbara*] So you are coming to see my death and devastation factory, Barbara?

BARBARA [*at the window*]   You came yesterday to see my salvation factory. I promised you a return visit.

LOMAX [*coming forward between Sarah and Undershaft*]   Youll find it awfully interesting. Ive been through the Woolwich Arsenal; and it gives you a ripping feeling of security, you know, to think of the lot of beggars we could kill if it came to fighting. [*To Undershaft, with sudden solemnity*] Still, it must be rather an awful reflection for you, from the religious point of view as it were. Youre getting on, you know, and all that.

SARAH   You dont mind Cholly's imbecility, papa, do you?

LOMAX [*much taken aback*]   Oh I say!

UNDERSHAFT   Mr Lomax looks at the matter in a very proper spirit, my dear.

LOMAX   Just so. Thats all I meant, I assure you.

SARAH   Are you coming, Stephen?

STEPHEN   Well, I am rather busy—er—[*Magnanimously*] Oh well, yes: I'll come. That is, if there is room for me.

UNDERSHAFT   I can take two with me in a little motor I am experimenting with for field use. You wont mind its being rather unfashionable. It's not painted yet; but it's bullet proof.

LOMAX [*appalled at the prospect of confronting Wilton Crescent in an unpainted motor*] Oh I say!

SARAH The carriage for me, thank you. Barbara doesnt mind what she's seen in.

LOMAX I say, Dolly, old chap: do you really mind the car being a guy? Because of course if you do I'll go in it. Still—

CUSINS I prefer it.

LOMAX Thanks awfully, old man. Come, my ownest. [*He hurries out to secure his seat in the carriage. Sarah follows him*].

CUSINS [*moodily walking across to Lady Britomart's writing table*] Why are we two coming to this Works Department of Hell? that is what I ask myself.

BARBARA I have always thought of it as a sort of pit where lost creatures with blackened faces stirred up smoky fires and were driven and tormented by my father. Is it like that, dad?

UNDERSHAFT [*scandalized*] My dear! It is a spotlessly clean and beautiful hillside town.

CUSINS With a Methodist chapel? O do say theres a Methodist chapel.

UNDERSHAFT There are two: a Primitive one and a sophisticated one. There is even an Ethical Society; but it is not much patronized, as my men are all strongly religious. In the High Explosives Sheds they object to the presence of Agnostics as unsafe.

CUSINS And yet they dont object to you!

BARBARA Do they obey all your orders?

UNDERSHAFT I never give them any orders. When I speak to one of them it is "Well, Jones, is baby doing well? and has Mrs Jones made a good recovery?" "Nicely, thank you, sir." And thats all.

CUSINS But Jones has to be kept in order. How do you maintain discipline among your men?

UNDERSHAFT I dont. They do. You see, the one thing Jones wont stand is any rebellion from the man under him, or any assertion of social equality between the wife of the man with 4 shillings a week less than himself, and Mrs Jones! Of course they all rebel against me, theoretically. Practically, every man of them keeps the man just below him in his place. I never meddle with them. I never bully them. I dont even bully Lazarus. I say that certain things are to be done; but I dont order anybody to do them. I dont say, mind you, that there is no ordering about and snubbing and even bullying. The men snub the boys and order them about; the carmen snub the sweepers; the artisans snub the unskilled laborers; the foremen drive and bully both the laborers and artisans; the assistant engineers find fault with the foremen; the chief engineers drop on the assistants; the departmental managers worry the chiefs; and the clerks have tall hats and hymnbooks and keep up the social tone by refusing to associate on equal terms with anybody. The result is a colossal profit, which comes to me.

CUSINS [*revolted*]   You really are a—well, what I was saying yesterday.

BARBARA   What was he saying yesterday?

UNDERSHAFT   Never mind, my dear. He thinks I have made you unhappy. Have I?

BARBARA   Do you think I can be happy in this vulgar silly dress? I! who have worn the uniform. Do you understand what you have done to me? Yesterday I had a man's soul in my hand. I set him in the way of life with his face to salvation. But when we took your money he turned back to drunkenness and derision. [*With intense conviction*] I will never forgive you that. If I had a child, and you destroyed its body with your explosives—if you murdered Dolly with your horrible guns—I could forgive you if my forgiveness would open the gates of heaven to you. But to take a human soul from me, and turn it into the soul of a wolf! that is worse than any murder.

UNDERSHAFT   Does my daughter despair so easily? Can you strike a man to the heart and leave no mark on him?

BARBARA [*her face lighting up*]   Oh, you are right: he can never be lost now: where was my faith?

CUSINS   Oh, clever clever devil!

BARBARA   You may be a devil; but God speaks through you sometimes. [*She takes her father's hands and kisses them*]. You have given me back my happiness: I feel it deep down now, though my spirit is troubled.

UNDERSHAFT   You have learnt something. That always feels at first as if you had lost something.

BARBARA   Well, take me to the factory of death; and let me learn something more. There must be some truth or other behind all this frightful irony. Come, Dolly. [*She goes out*].

CUSINS   My guardian angel! [*To Undershaft*] Avaunt! [*He follows Barbara*].

STEPHEN [*quietly, at the writing table*]   You must not mind Cusins, father. He is a very amiable good fellow; but he is a Greek scholar and naturally a little eccentric.

UNDERSHAFT   Ah, quite so. Thank you, Stephen. Thank you. [*He goes out*].

Stephen smiles patronizingly; buttons his coat responsibly; and crosses the room to the door. Lady Britomart, dressed for out-of-doors, opens it before he reaches it. She looks round for the others; looks at Stephen; and turns to go without a word.

STEPHEN [*embarrassed*]   Mother—

LADY BRITOMART   Dont be apologetic, Stephen. And dont forget that you have outgrown your mother. [*She goes out*].

Perivale St Andrews lies between two Middlesex hills, half climbing the northern one. It is an almost smokeless town of white walls, roofs of narrow green slates or red tiles, tall trees, domes, campaniles, and slender chimney shafts, beautifully situated and beautiful in itself. The best view of it is obtained from the crest of a slope about half a mile to the east, where the high explosives are dealt with. The foundry lies hidden in the depths between, the tops of its chimneys sprouting like huge skittles into the middle distance. Across the crest runs an emplacement of concrete, with a firestep, and a parapet which suggests a fortification, because there is a huge cannon of the obsolete Woolwich Infant pattern peering across it at the town. The cannon is mounted on an experimental gun carriage: possibly the original model of the Undershaft disappearing rampart gun alluded to by Stephen. The firestep, being a convenient place to sit, is furnished here and there with straw disc cushions; and at one place there is the additional luxury of a fur rug.

Barbara is standing on the firestep, looking over the parapet towards the town. On her right is the cannon; on her left the end of a shed raised on piles, with a ladder of three or four steps up to the door, which opens outwards and has a little wooden landing at the threshold, with a fire bucket in the corner of the landing. Several dummy soldiers more or less mutilated, with straw protruding from their gashes, have been shoved out of the way under the landing. A few others are nearly upright against the shed; and one has fallen forward and lies, like a grotesque corpse, on the emplacement. The parapet stops short of the shed, leaving a gap which is the beginning of the path down the hill through the foundry to the town. The rug is on the firestep near this gap. Down on the emplacement behind the cannon is a trolley carrying a huge conical bombshell with a red band painted on it. Further to the right is the door of an office, which, like the sheds, is of the lightest possible construction.

Cusins arrives by the path from the town.

BARBARA   Well?

CUSINS   Not a ray of hope. Everything perfect! wonderful! real! It only needs a cathedral to be a heavenly city instead of a hellish one.

BARBARA   Have you found out whether they have done anything for old Peter Shirley?

CUSINS   They have found him a job as gatekeeper and timekeeper. He's frightfully miserable. He calls the time-keeping brainwork, and says he isnt used to it; and his gate lodge is so splendid that he's ashamed to use the rooms, and skulks in the scullery.

BARBARA   Poor Peter!

Stephen arrives from the town. He carries a fieldglass.

STEPHEN [*enthusiastically*]   Have you two seen the place? Why did you leave us?

CUSINS   I wanted to see everything I was not intended to see; and Barbara wanted to make the men talk.

STEPHEN   Have you found anything discreditable?

CUSINS   No. They call him Dandy Andy and are proud of his being a cunning old rascal; but it's all horribly, frightfully, immorally, unanswerably perfect.

Sarah arrives.

SARAH   Heavens! what a place! [*She crosses to the trolley*]. Did you see the nursing home!? [*She sits down on the shell*].

STEPHEN   Did you see the libraries and schools!?

SARAH   Did you see the ball room and the banqueting chamber in the Town Hall!?

STEPHEN   Have you gone into the insurance fund, the pension fund, the building society, the various applications of co-operation!?

Undershaft comes from the office, with a sheaf of telegrams in his hand.

UNDERSHAFT   Well, have you seen everything! I'm sorry I was called away. [*Indicating the telegrams*] Good news from Manchuria.

STEPHEN   Another Japanese victory?

UNDERSHAFT   Oh, I dont know. What side wins does not concern us here. No: the good news is that the aerial battleship is a tremendous success. At the first trial it has wiped out a fort with three hundred soldiers in it.

CUSINS   [*from the platform*]   Dummy soldiers?

UNDERSHAFT   [*striding across to Stephen and kicking the prostrate dummy brutally out of his way*]   No: the real thing.

Cusins and Barbara exchange glances. Then Cusins sits on the step and buries his face in his hands. Barbara gravely lays her hand on his shoulder. He looks up at her in whimsical desperation.

UNDERSHAFT   Well, Stephen, what do you think of the place?

STEPHEN   Oh, magnificent. A perfect triumph of modern industry. Frankly, my dear father, I have been a fool: I had no idea of what it all meant: of the wonderful forethought, the power of organization, the administrative capacity, the financial genius, the colossal capital it represents. I have been repeating to myself as I came through your streets "Peace hath her victories no less renowned than War." I have only one misgiving about it all.

UNDERSHAFT   Out with it.

STEPHEN   Well, I cannot help thinking that all this provision for every want of your workmen may sap their independence and weaken their sense of responsibility. And greatly as we enjoyed our tea at that splendid restaurant— how they gave us all that luxury and cake and jam and cream for threepence I really cannot imagine!—still you must remember that restaurants break up home life. Look at the continent, for instance! Are you sure so much pampering is really good for the men's characters?

UNDERSHAFT   Well you see, my dear boy, when you are organizing civilization you have to make up your mind whether trouble and anxiety are good things or not. If you decide that they are, then, I take it, you simply dont organize civilization; and there you are, with trouble and anxiety enough to make us all angels! But if you decide the other way, you may as well go through with it. However, Stephen, our characters are safe here. A sufficient dose of anxiety is always provided by the fact that we may be blown to smithereens at any moment.

SARAH   By the way, papa, where do you make the explosives?

UNDERSHAFT   In separate little sheds, like that one. When one of them blows up, it costs very little; and only the people quite close to it are killed.

Stephen, who is quite close to it, looks at it rather scaredly, and moves away quickly to the cannon. At the same moment the door of the shed is thrown abruptly open; and a foreman in overalls and list slippers comes out on the little landing and holds the door for Lomax, who appears in the doorway.

LOMAX [*with studied coolness*]   My good fellow: you neednt get into a state of nerves. Nothing's going to happen to you; and I suppose it wouldnt be the end of the world if anything did. A little bit of British pluck is what you want, old chap. [*He descends and strolls across to Sarah*].

UNDERSHAFT [*to the foreman*]   Anything wrong, Bilton?

BILTON [*with ironic calm*]   Gentleman walked into the high explosives shed and lit a cigaret, sir: thats all.

UNDERSHAFT   Ah, quite so. [*Going over to Lomax*] Do you happen to remember what you did with the match?

LOMAX   Oh come! I'm not a fool. I took jolly good care to blow it out before I chucked it away.

BILTON   The top of it was red hot inside, sir.

LOMAX   Well, suppose it was! I didn't chuck it into any of y o u r messes.

UNDERSHAFT   Think no more of it, Mr. Lomax. By the way, would you mind lending me your matches.

LOMAX [*offering his box*].   Certainly.

UNDERSHAFT   Thanks. [*He pockets the matches*].

LOMAX [*lecturing to the company generally*]   You know, these high explosives dont go off like gunpowder, except when theyre in a gun. When theyre spread loose, you can put a match to them without the least risk; they just burn quietly like a bit of paper. [*Warming to the scientific interest of the subject*] Did you know that, Undershaft? Have you ever tried?

UNDERSHAFT   Not on a large scale, Mr. Lomax. Bilton will give you a sample of gun cotton when you are leaving if you ask him. You can experiment with it at home. [*Bilton looks puzzled*].

SARAH   Bilton will do nothing of the sort, papa. I suppose it's your business to blow up the Russians and Japs; but you might really stop short of blowing up poor Cholly. [*Bilton gives it up and retires into the shed*].

LOMAX   My ownest, there is no danger. [*He sits beside her on the shell*].

Lady Britomart arrives from the town with a bouquet.

LADY BRITOMART [*impetuously*]   Andrew: you shouldnt have let me see this place.

UNDERSHAFT   Why, my dear?

LADY BRITOMART   Never mind why: you shouldnt have: thats all. To think of all that [*indicating the town*] being yours! and that you have kept it to yourself all these years!

UNDERSHAFT   It does not belong to me. I belong to it. It is the Undershaft inheritance.

LADY BRITOMART   It is not. Your ridiculous cannons and that noisy banging foundry may be the Undershaft inheritance; but all that plate and linen, all that furniture and those houses and orchards and gardens belong to us. They belong to m e : they are not a man's business. I wont give them up. You must be out of your senses to throw them all away; and if you persist in such folly, I will call in a doctor.

UNDERSHAFT   [*stooping to smell the bouquet*]   Where did you get the flowers, my dear?

LADY BRITOMART   Your men presented them to me in your William Morris Labor Church.

CUSINS   Oh! It needed only that. A Labor Church! [*he mounts the firestep distractedly, and leans with his elbows on the parapet, turning his back to them*].

LADY BRITOMART   Yes, with Morris's words in mosaic letters ten feet high round the dome. NO MAN IS GOOD ENOUGH TO BE ANOTHER MAN'S MASTER. The cynicism of it!

UNDERSHAFT   It shocked the men at first, I am afraid. But now they take no more notice of it than of the ten commandments in church.

LADY BRITOMART   Andrew: you are trying to put me off the subject of the inheritance by profane jokes. Well, you shant. I dont ask it any longer for Stephen: he has inherited far too much of your perversity to be fit for it. But Barbara has rights as well as Stephen. Why should not Adolphus succeed to the inheritance? I could manage the town for him; and he can look after the cannons, if they are really necessary.

UNDERSHAFT   I should ask nothing better if Adolphus were a foundling. He is exactly the sort of new blood that is wanted in English business. But he's not a foundling; and theres an end of it. [*He makes for the office door*].

CUSINS   [*turning to them*]   Not quite. [*They all turn and stare at him*]. I think—Mind! I am not committing myself in any way as to my future course—but I think the foundling difficulty can be got over. [*He jumps down to the emplacement*].

UNDERSHAFT   [*coming back to him*]   What do you mean?

CUSINS   Well, I have something to say which is in the nature of a confession.

SARAH
LADY BRITOMART
BARBARA   Confession!
STEPHEN

LOMAX   Oh I say!

CUSINS   Yes, a confession. Listen, all. Until I met Barbara I thought myself in the main an honorable, truthful man, because I wanted the approval of my conscience more than I wanted anything else. But the moment I saw Barbara, I wanted her far more than the approval of my conscience.

LADY BRITOMART Adolphus!

CUSINS It is true. You accused me yourself, Lady Brit, of joining the Army to worship Barbara; and so I did. She bought my soul like a flower at a street corner; but she bought it for herself.

UNDERSHAFT What! Not for Dionysos or another?

CUSINS Dionysos and all the others are in herself. I adored what was divine in her, and was therefore a true worshipper. But I was romantic about her too. I thought she was a woman of the people, and that a marriage with a professor of Greek would be far beyond the wildest social ambitions of her rank.

LADY BRITOMART Adolphus!!

LOMAX Oh I say!!!

CUSINS When I learnt the horrible truth—

LADY BRITOMART What do you mean by the horrible truth, pray?

CUSINS That she was enormously rich; that her grandfather was an earl; that her father was the Prince of Darkness—

UNDERSHAFT Chut!

CUSINS —and that I was only an adventurer trying to catch a rich wife, then I stooped to deceive her about my birth.

BARBARA [rising] Dolly!

LADY BRITOMART Your birth! Now Adolphus, dont dare to make up a wicked story for the sake of these wretched cannons. Remember: I have seen photographs of your parents; and the Agent General for South Western Australia knows them personally and has assured me that they are most respectable married people.

CUSINS So they are in Australia; but here they are outcasts. Their marriage is legal in Australia, but not in England. My mother is my father's deceased wife's sister; and in this island I am consequently a foundling. [Sensation].

BARBARA Silly! [She climbs to the cannon, and leans, listening, in the angle it makes with the parapet].

CUSINS Is the subterfuge good enough, Machiavelli?

UNDERSHAFT [thoughtfully] Biddy: this may be a way out of the difficulty.

LADY BRITOMART Stuff! A man cant make cannons any the better for being his own cousin instead of his proper self [she sits down on the rug with a bounce that expresses her downright contempt for their casuistry].

UNDERSHAFT [to Cusins] You are an educated man. That is against the tradition.

CUSINS Once in ten thousand times it happens that the schoolboy is a born master of what they try to teach him. Greek has not destroyed my mind: it has nourished it. Besides, I did not learn it at an English public school.

UNDERSHAFT Hm! Well, I cannot afford to be too particular: you have cornered the foundling market. Let it pass. You are eligible, Euripides: you are eligible.

BARBARA Dolly: yesterday morning, when Stephen told us all about the tradition, you became very silent; and you have been strange and excited ever since. Were you thinking of your birth then?

CUSINS When the finger of Destiny suddenly points at a man in the middle of his breakfast, it makes him thoughtful.

UNDERSHAFT   Aha! You have had your eye on the business, my young friend, have you?

CUSINS   Take care! There is an abyss of moral horror between me and your accursed aerial battleships.

UNDERSHAFT   Never mind the abyss for the present. Let us settle the practical details and leave your final decision open. You know that you will have to change your name. Do you object to that?

CUSINS   Would any man named Adolphus—any man called Dolly!—object to be called something else?

UNDERSHAFT   Good. Now, as to money! I propose to treat you handsomely from the beginning. You shall start at a thousand a year.

CUSINS [*with sudden heat, his spectacles twinkling with mischief*]   A thousand! You dare offer a miserable thousand to the son-in-law of a millionaire! No, by Heavens, Machiavelli! you shall not cheat me. You cannot do without me; and I can do without you. I must have two thousand five hundred a year for two years. At the end of that time, if I am a failure, I go. But if I am a success, and stay on, you must give me the other five thousand.

UNDERSHAFT   What other five thousand?

CUSINS   To make the two years up to five thousand a year. The two thousand five hundred is only half pay in case I should turn out a failure. The third year I must have ten per cent on the profits.

UNDERSHAFT [*taken aback*]   Ten per cent! Why, man, do you know what my profits are?

CUSINS   Enormous, I hope: otherwise I shall require twentyfive per cent.

UNDERSHAFT   But, Mr Cusins, this is a serious matter of business. You are not bringing any capital into the concern.

CUSINS   What! no capital! Is my mastery of Greek no capital? Is my access to the subtlest thought, the loftiest poetry yet attained by humanity, no capital? My character! my intellect! my life! my career! what Barbara calls my soul! are these no capital? Say another word; and I double my salary.

UNDERSHAFT   Be reasonable—

CUSINS [*peremptorily*]   Mr Undershaft: you have my terms. Take them or leave them.

UNDERSHAFT [*recovering himself*]   Very well. I note your terms; and I offer you half.

CUSINS [*disgusted*]   Half!

UNDERSHAFT [*firmly*]   Half.

CUSINS   You call yourself a gentleman; and you offer me half!!

UNDERSHAFT   I do not call myself a gentleman; but I offer you half.

CUSINS   This is your future partner! your successor! your son-in-law!

BARBARA   You are selling your own soul, Dolly, not mine. Leave me out of the bargain, please.

UNDERSHAFT   Come! I will go a step further for Barbara's sake. I will give you three fifths; but that is my last word.

CUSINS   Done!

LOMAX   Done in the eye! Why, *I* get only eight hundred, you know.

CUSINS   By the way, Mac, I am a classical scholar, not an arithmetical one. Is three fifths more than half or less?

UNDERSHAFT   More, of course.

CUSINS   I would have taken two hundred and fifty. How you can succeed in business when you are willing to pay all that money to a University don who is obviously not worth a junior clerk's wages!—well! What will Lazarus say?

UNDERSHAFT   Lazarus is a gentle romantic Jew who cares for nothing but string quartets and stalls at fashionable theatres. He will be blamed for your rapacity in money matters, poor fellow! as he has hitherto been blamed for mine. You are a shark of the first order, Euripides. So much the better for the firm!

BARBARA   Is the bargain closed, Dolly? Does your soul belong to him now?

CUSINS   No: the price is settled: that is all. The real tug of war is still to come. What about the moral question?

LADY BRITOMART   There is no moral question in the matter at all, Adolphus. You must simply sell cannons and weapons to people whose cause is right and just, and refuse them to foreigners and criminals.

UNDERSHAFT [*determinedly*]   No: none of that. You must keep the true faith of an Armorer, or you don't come in here.

CUSINS   What on earth is the true faith of an Armorer?

UNDERSHAFT   To give arms to all men who offer an honest price for them, without respect of persons or principles: to aristocrat and republican, to Nihilist and Tsar, to Capitalist and Socialist, to Protestant and Catholic, to burglar and policeman, to black man, white man and yellow man, to all sorts and conditions, all nationalities, all faiths, all follies, all causes and all crimes. The first Undershaft wrote up in his shop IF GOD GAVE THE HAND, LET NOT MAN WITHHOLD THE SWORD. The second wrote up ALL HAVE THE RIGHT TO FIGHT: NONE HAVE THE RIGHT TO JUDGE. The third wrote up TO MAN THE WEAPON: TO HEAVEN THE VICTORY. The fourth had no literary turn; so he did not write up anything; but he sold cannons to Napoleon under the nose of George the Third. The fifth wrote up PEACE SHALL NOT PREVAIL SAVE WITH A SWORD IN HER HAND. The sixth, my master, was the best of all. He wrote up NOTHING IS EVER DONE IN THIS WORLD UNTIL MEN ARE PREPARED TO KILL ONE ANOTHER IF IT IS NOT DONE. After that, there was nothing left for the seventh to say. So he wrote up, simply, UNASHAMED.

CUSINS   My good Machiavelli, I shall certainly write something up on the wall; only, as I shall write it in Greek, you wont be able to read it. But as to your Armorer's faith, if I take my neck out of the noose of my own morality I am not going to put in into the noose of yours. I shall sell cannons to whom I please and refuse them to whom I please. So there!

UNDERSHAFT   From the moment when you become Andrew Undershaft, you will never do as you please again. Dont come here lusting for power, young man.

CUSINS   If power were my aim I should not come here for it. You have no power.

UNDERSHAFT   None of my own, certainly.

CUSINS   I have more power than you, more will. You do not drive this place: it drives you. And what drives the place?

UNDERSHAFT [*enigmatically*]   A will of which I am a part.

BARBARA [*startled*]   Father! Do you know what you are saying; or are you laying a snare for my soul?

CUSINS   Dont listen to his metaphysics, Barbara. The place is driven by the most rascally part of society, the money hunters, the pleasure hunters, the military promotion hunters; and he is their slave.

UNDERSHAFT   Not necessarily. Remember the Armorer's Faith. I will take an order from a good man as cheerfully as from a bad one. If you good people prefer preaching and shirking to buying my weapons and fighting the rascals, dont blame me. I can make cannons: I cannot make courage and conviction. Bah! you tire me, Euripides, with your morality mongering. Ask Barbara: she understands. [*He suddenly reaches up and takes Barbara's hands, looking powerfully into her eyes*] Tell him, my love, what power really means.

BARBARA [*hypnotized*]   Before I joined the Salvation Army, I was in my own power; and the consequence was that I never knew what to do with myself. When I joined it, I had not time enough for all the things I had to do.

UNDERSHAFT [*approvingly*]   Just so. And why was that, do you suppose?

BARBARA   Yesterday I should have said, because I was in the power of God. [*She resumes her self-possession, withdrawing her hands from his with a power equal to his own*]. But you came and shewed me that I was in the power of Bodger and Undershaft. Today I feel—oh! how can I put it into words? Sarah: do you remember the earthquake at Cannes, when we were little children?—how little the surprise of the first shock mattered compared to the dread and horror of waiting for the second? That is how I feel in this place today. I stood on the rock I thought eternal: and without a word of warning it reeled and crumbled under me. I was safe with an infinite wisdom watching me, an army marching to Salvation with me; and in a moment, at a stroke of your pen in a cheque book, I stood alone; and the heavens were empty. That was the first shock of the earthquake: I am waiting for the second.

UNDERSHAFT   Come, come, my daughter! dont make too much of your little tinpot tragedy. What do we do here when we spend years of work and thought and thousands of pounds of solid cash on a new gun or an aerial battleship that turns out just a hairsbreadth wrong after all? Scrap it. Scrap it without wasting another hour or another pound on it. Well, you have made for yourself something that you call a morality or a religion or what not. It doesnt fit the facts. Well, scrap it. Scrap it and get one that does fit. That is what is wrong with the world at present. It scraps its obsolete steam engines and dynamos; but it wont scrap its old prejudices and its old moralities and its old religions and its old political constitutions. Whats the result? In machinery it does very well; but in morals and religion and politics it is working at a loss that brings it nearer bankruptcy every year. Dont persist in that folly. If your old religion broke down yesterday, get a newer and a better one for tomorrow.

BARBARA   Oh how gladly I would take a better one to my soul! But you offer me a worse one. [*Turning on him with sudden vehemence*]. Justify yourself: shew me some light through the darkness of this dreadful place, with its beautifully clean workshops, and respectable workmen, and model homes.

UNDERSHAFT   Cleanliness and respectability do not need justification, Barbara: they justify themselves. I see no darkness here, no dreadfulness. In your Salvation shelter I saw poverty, misery, cold and hunger. You gave them bread and treacle and dreams of heaven. I give from thirty shillings a week to twelve thousand a year. They find their own dreams; but I look after the drainage.

BARBARA   And their souls?

UNDERSHAFT   I save their souls just as I saved yours.

BARBARA [*revolted*]   You saved my soul! What do you mean?

UNDERSHAFT   I fed you and clothed you and housed you. I took care that you should have money enough to live handsomely—more than enough; so that you could be wasteful, careless, generous. That saved your soul from the seven deadly sins.

BARBARA [*bewildered*]   The seven deadly sins!

UNDERSHAFT   Yes, the deadly seven. [*Counting on his fingers*] Food, clothing, firing, rent, taxes, respectability and children. Nothing can lift those seven millstones from Man's neck but money; and the spirit cannot soar until the millstones are lifted. I lifted them from your spirit. I enabled Barbara to become Major Barbara; and I saved her from the crime of poverty.

CUSINS   Do you call poverty a crime?

UNDERSHAFT   The worst of crimes. All the other crimes are virtues beside it: all the other dishonors are chivalry itself by comparison. Poverty blights whole cities; spreads horrible pestilences; strikes dead the very souls of all who come within sight, sound, or smell of it. What y o u call crime is nothing: a murder here and a theft there, a blow now and a curse then: what do they matter? they are only the accidents and illnesses of life: there are not fifty genuine professional criminals in London. But there are millions of poor people, abject people, dirty people, ill fed, ill clothed people. They poison us morally and physically: they kill the happiness of society: they force us to do away with our own liberties and to organize unnatural cruelties for fear they should rise against us and drag us down into their abyss. Only fools fear crime: we all fear poverty. Pah! [*turning on Barbara*] you talk of your half-saved ruffian in West Ham: you accuse me of dragging his soul back to perdition. Well, bring him to me here; and I will drag his soul back again to salvation for you. Not by words and dreams; but by thirtyeight shillings a week, a sound house in a handsome street, and a permanent job. In three weeks he will have a fancy waistcoat; in three months a tall hat and a chapel sitting; before the end of the year he will shake hands with a duchess at a Primrose League meeting, and join the Conservative Party.

BARBARA   And will he be the better for that?

UNDERSHAFT   You know he will. Dont be a hypocrite, Barbara. He will be better fed, better housed, better clothed, better behaved; and his children will be pounds heavier and bigger. That will be better than an American cloth mat-tress in a shelter, chopping firewood, eating bread and treacle, and being forced to kneel down from time to time to thank heaven for it: knee drill, I think you call it. It is cheap work converting starving men with a Bible in one hand and a slice of bread in the other. I will undertake to convert West Ham to Mahometanism on the same terms. Try your hand on my men: their souls are hungry because their bodies are full.

BARBARA   And leave the east end to starve?

UNDERSHAFT [*his energetic tone dropping into one of bitter and brooding remembrance*]   I was an east ender. I moralized and starved until one day I swore that I would be a full-fed free man at all costs; that nothing should stop me except a bullet, neither reason nor morals nor the lives of other men. I said "Thou shalt starve ere I starve"; and with that word I became free and great. I was a dangerous man until I had my will: now I am a useful, beneficent, kindly person. That is the history of most self-made millionaires, I fancy. When it is the history of every Englishman we shall have an England worth living in.

LADY BRITOMART   Stop making speeches, Andrew. This is not the place for them.

UNDERSHAFT [*punctured*]   My dear: I have no other means of conveying my ideas.

LADY BRITOMART   Your ideas are nonsense. You got on because you were selfish and unscrupulous.

UNDERSHAFT   Not at all. I had the strongest scruples about poverty and starvation. Your moralists are quite unscrupulous about both: they make virtues of them. I had rather be a thief than a pauper. I had rather be a murderer than a slave. I dont want to be either; but if you force the alternative on me, then, by Heaven, I'll choose the braver and more moral one. I hate poverty and slavery worse than any other crimes whatsoever. And let me tell you this. Poverty and slavery have stood up for centuries to your sermons and leading articles: they will not stand up to my machine guns. Dont preach at them: dont reason with them. Kill them.

BARBARA   Killing. Is that your remedy for everything?

UNDERSHAFT   It is the final test of conviction, the only lever strong enough to overturn a social system, the only way of saying Must. Let six hundred and seventy fools loose in the streets; and three policemen can scatter them. But huddle them together in a certain house in Westminster; and let them go through certain ceremonies and call themselves certain names until at last they get the courage to kill; and your six hundred and seventy fools become a government. Your pious mob fills up ballot papers and imagines it is governing its masters; but the ballot paper that really governs is the paper that has a bullet wrapped up in it.

CUSINS   That is perhaps why, like most intelligent people, I never vote.

UNDERSHAFT   Vote! Bah! When you vote, you only change the names of the cabinet. When you shoot, you pull down governments, inaugurate new epochs, abolish old orders and set up new. Is that historically true, Mr Learned Man, or is it not?

CUSINS   It is historically true. I loathe having to admit it. I repudiate your sentiments. I abhor your nature. I defy you in every possible way. Still, it is true.

But it ought not to be true.

UNDERSHAFT   Ought! ought! ought! ought! ought! Are you going to spend your life saying ought, like the rest of our moralists? Turn your oughts into shalls, man. Come and make explosives with me. Whatever can blow men up can blow society up. The history of the world is the history of those who had courage enough to embrace this truth. Have you the courage to embrace it, Barbara?

LADY BRITOMART   Barbara: I positively forbid you to listen to your father's abominable wickedness. And you, Adolphus, ought to know better than to go about saying that wrong things are true. What does it matter whether they are true if they are wrong?

UNDERSHAFT   What does it matter whether they are wrong if they are true?

LADY BRITOMART [rising]   Children: come home instantly. Andrew: I am exceedingly sorry I allowed you to call on us. You are wickeder than ever. Come at once.

BARBARA [shaking her head]   It's no use running away from wicked people, mamma.

LADY BRITOMART   It is every use. It shews your disapprobation of them.

BARBARA   It does not save them.

LADY BRITOMART   I can see that you are going to disobey me. Sarah: are you coming home or are you not?

SARAH   I daresay it's very wicked of papa to make cannons; but I dont think I shall cut him on that account.

LOMAX [pouring oil on the troubled waters]   The fact is, you know, there is a certain amount of tosh about this notion of wickedness. It doesnt work. You must look at facts. Not that I would say a word in favor of anything wrong; but then, you see, all sorts of chaps are always doing all sorts of things; and we have to fit them in somehow, dont you know. What I mean is that you cant go cutting everybody; and thats about what it comes to. [Their rapt attention to his eloquence makes him nervous]. Perhaps I dont make myself clear.

LADY BRITOMART   You are lucidity itself, Charles. Because Andrew is successful and has plenty of money to give to Sarah, you will flatter him and encourage him in his wickedness.

LOMAX [unruffled]   Well, where the carcase is, there will the eagles be gathered, dont you know. [To Undershaft] Eh? What?

UNDERSHAFT   Precisely. By the way, may I call you Charles?

LOMAX   Delighted. Cholly is the usual ticket.

UNDERSHAFT [to Lady Britomart]   Biddy—

LADY BRITOMART [violently]   Dont dare call me Biddy. Charles Lomax: you are a fool. Adolphus Cusins: you are a Jesuit. Stephen: you are a prig. Barbara: you are a lunatic. Andrew: you are a vulgar tradesman. Now you all know my opinion; and my conscience is clear, at all events [she sits down with a vehemence that the rug fortunately softens].

UNDERSHAFT   My dear: you are the incarnation of morality. [She snorts]. Your conscience is clear and your duty done when you have called everybody names.

Come, Euripides! it is getting late; and we all want to go home. Make up your mind.

CUSINS   Understand this, you old demon—

LADY BRITOMART   Adolphus!

UNDERSHAFT   Let him alone, Biddy. Proceed, Euripides.

CUSINS   You have me in a horrible dilemma. I want Barbara.

UNDERSHAFT   Like all young men, you greatly exaggerate the difference between one young woman and another.

BARBARA   Quite true, Dolly.

CUSINS   I also want to avoid being a rascal.

UNDERSHAFT [*with biting contempt*]   You lust for personal righteousness, for self-approval, for what you call a good conscience, for what Barbara calls salvation, for what I call patronizing people who are not so lucky as yourself.

CUSINS   I do not: all the poet in me recoils from being a good man. But there are things in me that I must reckon with. Pity—

UNDERSHAFT   Pity! The scavenger of misery.

CUSINS   Well, love.

UNDERSHAFT   I know. You love the needy and the outcast: you love the oppressed races, the negro, the Indian ryot, the underdog everywhere. Do you love the Japanese? Do you love the French? Do you love the English?

CUSINS   No. Every true Englishman detests the English. We are the wickedest nation on earth; and our success is a moral horror.

UNDERSHAFT   That is what comes of your gospel of love, is it?

CUSINS   May I not love even my father-in-law?

UNDERSHAFT   Who wants your love, man? By what right do you take the liberty of offering it to me? I will have your due heed and respect, or I will kill you. But your love! Damn your impertinence!

CUSINS [*grinning*]   I may not be able to control my affections, Mac.

UNDERSHAFT   You are fencing, Euripides. You are weakening: your grip is slipping. Come! try your last weapon. Pity and love have broken in your hand: forgiveness is still left.

CUSINS   No: forgiveness is a beggar's refuge. I am with you there: we must pay our debts.

UNDERSHAFT   Well said. Come! you will suit me. Remember the words of Plato.

CUSINS [*starting*]   Plato! You dare quote Plato to me!

UNDERSHAFT   Plato says, my friend, that society cannot be saved until either the Professors of Greek take to making gunpowder, or else the makers of gunpowder become Professors of Greek.

CUSINS   Oh, tempter, cunning tempter!

UNDERSHAFT   Come! choose, man, choose.

CUSINS   But perhaps Barbara will not marry me if I make the wrong choice.

BARBARA   Perhaps not.

CUSINS [*desperately perplexed*]   You hear!

BARBARA   Father: do you love nobody?

UNDERSHAFT   I love my best friend.

LADY BRITOMART   And who is that, pray?

UNDERSHAFT   My bravest enemy. That is the man who keeps me up to the mark.

CUSINS   You know, the creature is really a sort of poet in his way. Suppose he is a great man, after all!

UNDERSHAFT   Suppose you stop talking and make up your mind, my young friend.

CUSINS   But you are driving me against my nature. I hate war.

UNDERSHAFT   Hatred is the coward's revenge for being intimidated. Dare you make war on war? Here are the means: my friend Mr Lomax is sitting on them.

LOMAX [*springing up*]   Oh I say! You dont mean that this thing is loaded, do you? My ownest: come off it.

SARAH [*sitting placidly on the shell*]   If I am to be blown up, the more thoroughly it is done the better. Dont fuss, Cholly.

LOMAX [*to Undershaft, strongly remonstrant*]   Your own daughter, you know!

UNDERSHAFT   So I see. [*To Cusins*] Well, my friend, may we expect you here at six tomorrow morning?

CUSINS [*firmly*]   Not on any account. I will see the whole establishment blown up with its own dynamite before I will get up at five. My hours are healthy, rational hours: eleven to five.

UNDERSHAFT   Come when you please: before a week you will come at six and stay until I turn you out for the sake of your health. [*Calling*] Bilton! [*He turns to Lady Britomart, who rises*]. My dear: let us leave these two young people to themselves for a moment. [*Bilton comes from the shed*]. I am going to take you through the gun cotton shed.

BILTON [*Barring the way*]   You cant take anything explosive in here, sir.

LADY BRITOMART   What do you mean? Are you alluding to me?

BILTON [*unmoved*]   No, maam. Mr Undershaft has the other gentleman's matches in his pocket.

LADY BRITOMART [*abruptly*]   Oh! I beg your pardon. [*She goes into the shed*].

UNDERSHAFT   Quite right, Bilton, quite right: here you are. [*He gives Bilton the box of matches*]. Come, Stephen. Come, Charles, Bring Sarah. [*He passes into the shed*].

Bilton opens the box and deliberately drops the matches into the fire-bucket.

LOMAX   Oh! I say [*Bilton hands him the empty box*]. Infernal nonsense! Pure scientific ignorance! [*He goes in*].

SARAH   Am I all right, Bilton?

BILTON   Youll have to put on list slippers, miss: thats all. Weve got em inside. [*She goes in*].

STEPHEN [*very seriously to Cusins*]   Dolly, old fellow, think. Think before you decide. Do you feel that you are a sufficiently practical man? It is a huge undertaking, an enormous responsibility. All this mass of business will be Greek to you.

CUSINS   Oh, I think it will be much less difficult than Greek.

STEPHEN   Well, I just want to say this before I leave you to yourselves. Dont let anything I have said about right and wrong prejudice you against this great chance in life. I have satisfied myself that the business is one of the highest character and a credit to our country. [*Emotionally*] I am very proud of my father. I—[*Unable to proceed, he presses Cusins' hand and goes hastily into the shed, followed by Bilton*].

Barbara and Cusins, left alone together, look at one another silently.

CUSINS   Barbara: I am going to accept this offer.

BARBARA   I thought you would

CUSINS   You understand, dont you, that I had to decide without consulting you. If I had thrown the burden of the choice on you, you would sooner or later have despised me for it.

BARBARA   Yes: I did not want you to sell your soul for me any more than for this inheritance.

CUSINS   It is not the sale of my soul that troubles me: I have sold it too often to care about that. I have sold it for a professorship, I have sold it for an income. I have sold it to escape being imprisoned for refusing to pay taxes for hangmen's ropes and unjust wars and things that I abhor. What is all human conduct but the daily and hourly sale of our souls for trifles? What I am now selling it for is neither money nor position nor comfort, but for reality and for power.

BARBARA   You know that you will have no power, and that he has none.

CUSINS   I know. It is not for myself alone. I want to make power for the world.

BARBARA   I want to make power for the world too; but it must be spiritual power.

CUSINS   I think all power is spiritual: these cannons will not go off by themselves. I have tried to make spiritual power by teaching Greek. But the world can never be really touched by a dead language and a dead civilization. The people must have power; and the people cannot have Greek. Now the power that is made here can be wielded by all men.

BARBARA   Power to burn women's houses down and kill their sons and tear their husbands to pieces.

CUSINS   You cannot have power for good without having power for evil too. Even mother's milk nourishes murderers as well as heroes. This power which only tears men's bodies to pieces has never been so horribly abused as the intellectual power, the imaginative power, the poetic, religious power that can enslave men's souls. As a teacher of Greek I gave the intellectual man weapons against the common man. I now want to give the common man weapons against the intellectual man. I love the common people. I want to arm them against the lawyers, the doctors, the priests, the literary men, the professors, the artists, and the politicians, who, once in authority, are more disastrous and tyrannical than all the fools, rascals, and imposters. I want a power simple enough for common men to use, yet strong enough to force the intellectual oligarchy to use its genius for the general good.

BARBARA   Is there no higher power than that [*pointing to the shell*]?

CUSINS   Yes: but that power can destroy the higher powers just as a tiger can
destroy a man: there Man must master that power first. I admitted this when
the Turks and Greeks were last at war. My best pupil went out to fight for
Hellas. My parting gift to him was not a copy of Plato's Republic, but a revolver and a hundred Undershaft cartridges. The blood of every Turk he
shot—if he shot any—is on my head as well as on Undershaft's. That act
committed me to this place for ever. Your father's challenge has beaten me.
Dare I make war on war? I dare. I must. I will. And now, is it all over between
us?

BARBARA [touched by his evident dread of her answer]   Silly baby Dolly! How could it
be!

CUSINS [overjoyed]   Then you—you—you—Oh for my drum! [He flourishes imaginary drumsticks].

BARBARA [angered by his levity]   Take care, Dolly, take care. Oh, if only I could get
away from you and from father and from it all! if I could have the wings of a
dove and fly away to heaven!

CUSINS   And leave me!

BARBARA   Yes, you, and all the other naughty mischievous children of men. But
I cant. I was happy in the Salvation Army for a moment. I escaped from the
world into a paradise of enthusiasm and prayer and soul saving; but the
moment our money ran short, it all came back to Bodger: it was he who saved
our people: he, and the Prince of Darkness, my papa. Undershaft and
Bodger: their hands stretch everywhere: when we feed a starving fellow creature, it is with their bread, because there is no other bread; when we tend the
sick, it is in the hospitals they endow; if we turn from the churches they
build, we must kneel on the stones of the streets they pave. As long as that
lasts, there is no getting away from them. Turning our backs on Bodger and
Undershaft is turning our backs on life.

CUSINS   I thought you were determined to turn your back on the wicked side of
life.

BARBARA   There is no wicked side: life is all one. And I never wanted to shirk my
share in whatever evil must be endured, whether it be sin or suffering. I wish
I could cure you of middle-class ideas, Dolly.

CUSINS [gasping]   Middle cl—! A snub! A social snub to me! from the daughter of
a foundling!

BARBARA   That is why I have no class, Dolly: I come straight out of the heart of
the whole people. If I were middle-class I should turn my back on my father's
business; and we should both live in an artistic drawing room, with you
reading the reviews in one corner, and I in the other at the piano, playing
Schumann: both very superior persons, and neither of us a bit of use. Sooner
than that, I would sweep out the guncotton shed, or be one of Bodger's bar-
maids. Do you know what would have happened if you had refused papa's
offer?

CUSINS   I wonder!

BARBARA   I should have given you up and married the man who accepted it.

After all, my dear old mother has more sense than any of you. I felt like her when I saw this place—felt that I must have it—that never, never, never could I let it go; only she thought it was the houses and the kitchen ranges and the linen and china, when it was really all the human souls to be saved: not weak souls in starved bodies, sobbing with gratitude for a scrap of bread and treacle, but fulfilled, quarrelsome, snobbish, uppish creatures, all standing on their little rights and dignities, and thinking that my father ought to be greatly obliged to them for making so much money for him—and so he ought. That is where salvation is really wanted. My father shall never throw it in my teeth again that my converts were bribed with bread. [*She is transfigured*]. I have got rid of the bribe of bread. I have got rid of the bribe of heaven. Let God's work be done for its own sake: the work he had to create us to do because cannot be done except by living men and women. When I die, let him be in my debt, not I in his; and let me forgive him as becomes a woman of my rank.

CUSINS   Then the way of life lies through the factory of death?

BARBARA   Yes, through the raising of hell to heaven and of man to God, through the unveiling of an eternal light in the Valley of The Shadow. [*Seizing him with both hands*] Oh, did you think my courage would never come back? did you believe that I was a deserter? that I, who have stood in the streets, and taken my people to my heart, and talked of the holiest and greatest things with them, could ever turn back and chatter foolishly to fashionable people about nothing in a drawing room? Never, never, never, never: Major Barbara will die with the colors. Oh! and I have my dear little Dolly boy still; and he has found me my place and my work. Glory Hallelujah! [*She kisses him*].

CUSINS   My dearest: consider my delicate health. I cannot stand as much happiness as you can.

BARBARA   Yes: it is not easy work being in love with me, is it? But it's good for you. [*She runs to the shed, and calls, childlike*] Mamma! Mamma! [*Bilton comes out of the shed, followed by Undershaft*]. I want Mamma.

UNDERSHAFT   She is taking off her list slippers, dear. [*He passes on to Cusins*]. Well? What does she say?

CUSINS   She has gone right up into the skies.

LADY BRITOMART [*coming from the shed and stopping on the steps, obstructing Sarah, who follows with Lomax. Barbara clutches like a baby at her mother's skirt*] Barbara: when will you learn to be independent and to act and think for yourself? I know as well as possible what that cry of "Mamma, Mamma," means. Always running to me!

SARAH [*touching Lady Britomart's ribs with her finger tips and imitating a bicycle horn*] Pip! pip!

LADY BRITOMART [*highly indignant*] How dare you say Pip! pip! to me, Sarah? you are both very naughty children. What do you want, Barbara?

BARBARA   I want a house in the village to live in with Dolly. [*Dragging at the skirt*] Come and tell me which one to take.

UNDERSHAFT [*to Cusins*] Six o'clock tomorrow morning, Euripides.

SAMUEL BECKETT

1906–

Born and raised near Dublin, where his father was a well-to-do purveyor, Beckett was sent to a boarding school at the age of fourteen, and then went on to receive a B.A. at Trinity College, Dublin, where he distinguished himself as a scholar of French and Italian. His academic distinction won him a lectureship in Paris, where he met James Joyce, became his literary disciple, and began writing experimental poetry and fiction. After receiving his M.A. from Trinity College in 1931, he gave up the academic life, returned to the continent and continued to write fiction, while he travelled around France and Germany, leading a vagabond existence. He settled in Paris in 1937, subsequently became a member of the French resistance movement, and at the end of the second world war began writing the plays that were to make him internationally famous as the first and leading practitioner of absurdist drama. His best-known plays, *Waiting for Godot* (1953), *Endgame* (1957), and *Krapp's Last Tape* (1958) repeatedly challenge conventional dramatic expectations through their depiction of bizarre vaudeville-like characters, in outlandish settings, engaged in purposeless activities, exchanging frequently illogical and comically nonsensical dialogue with each other or with themselves. And in challenging traditional forms of theater, they ultimately challenge traditional views of human existence, suggesting that it may be as illogical, as absurd, as the dramatic spectacles they portray.

Krapp's Last Tape
A Play in One Act

A late evening in the future.

Krapp's den.

Front centre a small table, the two drawers of which open towards audience. Sitting at the table, facing front, i.e. across from the drawers, a wearish old man: Krapp.

Rusty black narrow trousers too short for him. Rusty black sleeveless waistcoat, four capacious pockets. Heavy silver watch and chain. Grimy white shirt open at neck, no collar. Surprising pair of dirty white boots, size ten at least, very narrow and pointed.

White face. Purple nose. Disordered grey hair. Unshaven.

Very near-sighted (but unspectacled). Hard of hearing.

Cracked voice. Distinctive intonation.

Laborious walk.

On the table a tape-recorder with microphone and a number of cardboard boxes containing reels of recorded tapes.

Table and immediately adjacent area in strong white light. Rest of stage in darkness.

Krapp remains a moment motionless, heaves a great sigh, looks at his watch, fumbles in his pockets, takes out an envelope, puts it back, fumbles, takes out a small bunch of keys, raises it to his eyes, chooses a key, gets up and moves to front of table. He stoops, unlocks first drawer, peers into it, feels about inside it, takes out a reel of tape, peers at it, puts it back, locks drawer, unlocks second drawer, peers into it, feels about inside it, takes out a large banana, peers at it, locks drawer, puts keys back in his pocket. He turns, advances to edge of stage, halts, strokes banana, peels it, drops skin at his feet, puts end of banana in his mouth and remains motionless, staring vacuously before him. Finally he bites off the end, turns aside and begins pacing to and fro at edge of stage, in the light, i.e. not more than four or five paces either way, meditatively eating banana. He treads on skin, slips, nearly falls, recovers himself, stoops and peers at skin and finally pushes it, still stooping, with his foot over the edge of stage into pit. He resumes his pacing, finishes banana, returns to table, sits down, remains a moment motionless, heaves a great sigh, takes keys from his pockets, raises them to his eyes, chooses key, gets up and moves to front of table, unlocks second drawer, takes out a second large banana, peers at it, locks drawer, puts back keys in his pocket, turns, advances to edge of stage, halts, strokes banana, peels it, tosses skin into pit, puts end of banana in his mouth and remains motionless, staring vacuously before him. Finally he has an idea, puts banana in his waistcoat pocket, the end emerging, and goes with all the speed he can muster backstage into darkness. Ten seconds. Loud pop of cork. Fifteen seconds. He comes back into light carrying an old ledger and sits down at table. He lays ledger on table, wipes his mouth, wipes his hands on the front of his waist-coat, brings them smartly together and rubs them.

KRAPP [*briskly*]   Ah! [*He bends over ledger, turns the pages, finds the entry he wants, reads.*] Box . . . thrree . . . spool . . . five. [*He raises his head and stares front. With relish.*] Spool! [*Pause.*] Spooool! [*Happy smile. Pause. He bends over table, starts peering and poking at the boxes.*] Box . . . thrree . . . thrree . . . four . . . two . . . [*with surprise*] nine! good God! . . . seven . . . ah!
  the little rascal!   [*He takes up box, peers at it.*] Box thrree. [*He lays it on table, opens it and peers at spools inside.*] Spool . . . [*he peers at ledger*] . . . five [*he peers at spools*] . . . five . . . five! . . . ah! the little scoundrel! [*He takes out a spool, peers at it.*] Spool five. [*He lays it on table, closes box three, puts it back with the others, takes up the spool.*] Box thrree, spool five. [*He bends over the machine, looks up. With relish.*] Spooool! [*Happy smile. He bends, loads spool on machine,*

rubs his hands.] Ah! [*He peers at ledger, reads entry at foot of page.*] Mother at rest at last . . . Hm . . . The black ball . . . [*He raises his head, stares blankly front. Puzzled.*] Black ball? . . . [*He peers again at ledger, reads.*] The dark nurse . . . [*He raises his head, broods, peers again at ledger, reads.*] Slight improvement in bowel condition . . . Hm . . . Memorable . . . what? [*He peers closer.*] Equinox, memorable equinox. [*He raises his head, stares blankly front. Puzzled.*] Memorable equinox? . . . [*Pause. He shrugs his shoulders, peers again at ledger, reads.*] Farewell to—[*he turns the page*]—love.

He raises his head, broods, bends over machine, switches on and assumes listening posture, i.e. leaning forward, elbows on table, hand cupping ear towards machine, face front.

TAPE [*strong voice, rather pompous, clearly Krapp's at a much earlier time.*]   Thirty-nine today, sound as a—[*Settling himself more comfortably he knocks one of the boxes off the table, curses, switches off, sweeps boxes and ledger violently to the ground, winds tape back to beginning, switches on, resumes posture.*] Thirty-nine today, sound as a bell, apart from my old weakness, and intellectually I have now every reason to suspect at the . . . [*hesitates*] . . . crest of the wave—or thereabouts. Celebrated the awful occasion, as in recent years, quietly at the Winehouse. Not a soul. Sat before the fire with closed eyes, separating the grain from the husks. Jotted down a few notes, on the back of an envelope. Good to be back in my den, in my old rags. Have just eaten I regret to say three bananas and only with difficulty refrained from a fourth. Fatal things for a man with my condition. [*Vehemently.*] Cut 'em out! [*Pause.*] The new light above my table is a great improvement. With all this darkness round me I feel less alone. [*Pause.*] In a way. [*Pause.*] I love to get up and move about in it, then back here to . . . [*hesitates*] . . . me. [*Pause.*] Krapp.

Pause.

The grain, now what I wonder do I mean by that, I mean . . . [*hesitates*] . . . I suppose I mean those things worth having when all the dust has—when all *my* dust has settled. I close my eyes and try and imagine them.

Pause. Krapp closes his eyes briefly.

Extraordinary silence this evening, I strain my ears and do not hear a sound. Old Miss McGlome always sings at this hour. But not tonight. Songs of her girlhood, she says. Hard to think of her as a girl. Wonderful woman though. Connaught, I fancy. [*Pause.*] Shall I sing when I am her age, if I ever am? No. [*Pause.*] Did I sing as a boy? No. [*Pause.*] Did I ever sing? No.

Pause.

Just been listening to an old year, passages at random. I did not check in the book, but it must be at least ten or twelve years ago. At that time I think I was still living on and off with Bianca in Kedar Street. Well out of that, Jesus yes! Hopeless business. [*Pause.*] Not much about her, apart from a tribute to her eyes. Very warm. I suddenly saw them again. [*Pause.*] Incomparable! [*Pause.*] Ah well . . . [*Pause.*] These old P.M.s are gruesome, but I often find them—[*Krapp switches off, broods, switches on*]—a help before embarking on a new . . . [*hesitates*] . . . retrospect. Hard to believe I was ever that young whelp. The voice! Jesus! And the aspirations! [*Brief laugh in which Krapp joins.*] And the resolutions! [*Brief laugh in which Krapp joins.*] To drink less, in particular. [*Brief laugh of Krapp alone.*] Statistics. Seventeen hundred hours, out of the preceding eight thousand odd, consumed on licensed premises alone. More than 20%, say 40% of his waking life. [*Pause.*] Plans for a less . . . [*hesitates*] . . . engrossing sexual life. Last illness of his father. Flagging pursuit of happiness. Unattainable laxation. Sneers at what he calls his youth and thanks to God that it's over. [*Pause.*] False ring there. [*Pause.*] Shadows of the opus . . . magnum. Closing with a—[*brief laugh*]—yelp to Providence. [*Prolonged laugh in which Krapp joins.*] What remains of all that misery? A girl in a shabby green coat, on a railway-station platform? No?

Pause.

When I look—

Krapp switches off, broods, looks at his watch, gets up, goes backstage into darkness. Ten seconds. Pop of cork. Ten seconds. Second cork. Ten seconds. Third cork. Ten seconds. Brief burst of quavering song.

KRAPP [*sings*]   Now the day is over,
                    Night is drawing nigh-igh,
                    Shadows—

Fit of coughing. He comes back into light, sits down, wipes his mouth, switches on, resumes his listening posture.

TAPE   —back on the year that is gone, with what I hope is perhaps a glint of the old eye to come, there is of course the house on the canal where mother lay a-dying, in the late autumn, after her long viduity [*Krapp gives a start*], and the—[*Krapp switches off, winds back tape a little, bends his ear closer to machine, switches on*]—a-dying, after her long viduity, and the—

Krapp switches off, raises his head, stares blankly before him. His lips move in the syllables of "viduity." No sound. He gets up, goes backstage into darkness, comes back with an enormous dictionary, lays it on table, sits down and looks up the word.

KRAPP [*reading from dictionary*]   State—or condition of being—or remaining—a widow—or widower. [*Looks up. Puzzled.*] Being—or remaining? . . . [*Pause. He peers again at dictionary. Reading.*] "Deep weeds of viduity" . . . Also of an animal, especially a bird . . . the vidua or weaver-bird . . . Black plumage of male . . . [*He looks up. With relish.*] The vidua-bird!

Pause. He closes dictionary, switches on, resumes listening posture.

TAPE   —bench by the weir from where I could see her window. There I sat, in the biting wind, wishing she were gone. [*Pause.*] Hardly a soul, just a few regulars, nursemaids, infants, old men, dogs. I got to know them quite well—oh by appearance of course I mean! One dark young beauty I recollect particularly, all white and starch, incomparable bosom, with a big black hooded perambulator, most funereal thing. Whenever I looked in her direction she had her eyes on me. And yet when I was bold enough to speak to her—not having been introduced—she threatened to call a policeman. As if I had designs on her virtue! [*Laugh. Pause.*] The face she had! The eyes! Like . . . [*hesitates*] . . . chrysolite! [*Pause.*] Ah well . . . [*Pause.*] I was there when— [*Krapp switches off, broods, switches on again*]—the blind went down, one of those dirty brown roller affairs, throwing a ball for a little white dog, as chance would have it. I happened to look up and there it was. All over and done with, at last. I sat on for a few moments with the ball in my hand and the dog yelping and pawing at me. [*Pause.*] Moments. Her moments, my moments. [*Pause.*] The dog's moments. [*Pause.*] In the end I held it out to him and he took it in his mouth, gently, gently. A small, old, black, hard, solid rubber ball. [*Pause.*] I shall feel it, in my hand, until my dying day. [*Pause.*] I might have kept it. [*Pause.*] But I gave it to the dog.

Pause.

Ah well . . .

Pause.

Spiritually a year of profound gloom and indigence until that memorable night in March, at the end of the jetty, in the howling wind, never to be forgotten, when suddenly I saw the whole thing. The vision, at last. This I fancy is what I have chiefly to record this evening, against the day when my work will be done and perhaps no place left in my memory, warm or cold, for the miracle that . . . [*hesitates*] . . . for the fire that set it alight. What I suddenly saw then was this, that the belief I had been going on all my life, namely—[*Krapp switches off impatiently, winds tape forward, switches on again*]— great granite rocks the foam flying up in the light of the lighthouse and the wind-gauge spinning like a propellor, clear to me at last that the dark I have always struggled to keep under is in reality my most—[*Krapp curses, switches off, winds tape forward, switches on again*]—unshatterable association until my dissolution of storm and night with the light of the understanding and the fire—[*Krapp curses louder, switches off, winds tape forward, switches on again*]— my face in her breasts and my hand on her. We lay there without moving. But under us all moved, and moved us, gently, up and down, and from side to side.

Pause.

Past midnight. Never knew such silence. The earth might be uninhabited.

Pause.

Here I end—

Krapp switches off, winds tape back, switches on again.

—upper lake, with the punt, bathed off the bank, then pushed out into the stream and drifted. She lay stretched out on the floorboards with her hands under her head and her eyes closed. Sun blazing down, bit of a breeze, water nice and lively. I noticed a scratch on her thigh and asked her how she came by it. Picking gooseberries, she said. I said again I thought it was hopeless and no good going on, and she agreed, without opening her eyes. [*Pause.*] I asked her to look at me and after a few moments—[*pause*]—after a few moments she did, but the eyes just slits, because of the glare. I bent over her to get them in the shadow and they opened. [*Pause. Low.*] Let me in. [*Pause.*] We drifted in among the flags and stuck. The way they went down, sighing, before the stem! [*Pause.*] I lay down across her with my face in her breasts and my hand on her. We lay there without moving. But under us all moved, and moved us, gently, up and down, and from side to side.

Pause.

Past midnight. Never knew—

Krapp switches off, broods. Finally he fumbles in his pockets, encounters the banana, takes it out, peers at it, puts it back, fumbles, brings out the envelope, fumbles, puts back envelope, looks at his watch, gets up and goes backstage into darkness. Ten seconds. Sound of bottle against glass, then brief siphon. Ten seconds. Bottle against glass alone. Ten seconds. He comes back a little unsteadily into light, goes to front of table, takes out keys, raises them to his eyes, chooses key, unlocks first drawer, peers into it, feels about inside, takes out reel, peers at it, locks drawer, puts keys back in his pocket, goes and sits down, takes reel off machine, lays it on dictionary, loads virgin reel on machine, takes envelope from his pocket, consults back of it, lays it on table, switches on, clears his throat and begins to record.

KRAPP   Just been listening to that stupid bastard I took myself for thirty years ago, hard to believe I was ever as bad as that. Thank God that's all done with anyway. [*Pause.*] The eyes she had! [*Broods, realizes he is recording silence, switches off, broods. Finally.*] Everything there, everything, all the—[*Realizes this is not being recorded, switches on.*] Everything there, everything on this old muckball, all the light and dark and famine and feasting of . . . [*hesitates*] . . . the ages! [*In a shout.*] Yes! [*Pause.*] Let that go! Jesus! Take his mind off his homework! Jesus! [*Pause. Weary.*] Ah well, maybe he was right. [*Pause.*] Maybe he was right. [*Broods. Realizes. Switches off. Consults envelope.*] Pah! [*Crumples it and throws it away. Broods. Switches on.*] Nothing to say, not a squeak. What's a year now? The sour cud and the iron stool. [*Pause.*] Revelled in the word spool. [*With relish.*] Spooool! Happiest moment of the past half million. [*Pause.*]. Seventeen copies sold, of which eleven at trade price to free circulating libraries beyond the seas. Getting known. [*Pause.*] One pound six and something, eight I have little doubt. [*Pause.*] Crawled out once or twice, before the summer was cold. Sat shivering in the park, drowned in dreams and burning to be gone. Not a soul. [*Pause.*] Last fancies. [*Vehemently.*] Keep 'em under! [*Pause.*] Scalded the eyes out of me reading *Effie* again, a page a day, with tears again. Effie . . . [*Pause.*] Could have been happy with her, up there on the Baltic, and the pines, and the dunes. [*Pause.*] Could I? [*Pause.*] And she? [*Pause.*] Pah! [*Pause.*] Fanny came in a couple of times. Bony old ghost of a whore. Couldn't do much, but I suppose better than a kick in the crutch. The last time wasn't so bad. How do you manage it, she said, at your age? I told her I'd been saving up for her all my life. [*Pause.*] Went to Vespers once, like when I was in short trousers. [*Pause. Sings*]

Now the day is over.
Night is drawing nigh-igh,
Shadows—[*coughing, then almost inaudible*]—of the evening
Steal across the sky.

[*Gasping.*] Went to sleep and fell off the pew. [*Pause.*] Sometimes wondered in the night if a last effort mightn't—[*Pause.*] Ah finish your booze now and get to your bed. Go on with this drivel in the morning. Or leave it at that. [*Pause.*] Leave it at that. [*Pause.*] Lie propped up in the dark—and wander. Be again in the dingle on a Christmas Eve, gathering holly, the red-berried. [*Pause.*] Be again on Croghan on a Sunday morning, in the haze, with the bitch, stop and listen to the bells. [*Pause.*] And so on. [*Pause.*] Be again, be again. [*Pause.*] All that old misery. [*Pause.*] Once wasn't enough for you. [*Pause.*] Lie down across her.

Long pause. He suddenly bends over machine, switches off, wrenches off tape, throws it away, puts on the other, winds it forward to the passage he wants, switches on, listens staring front.

TAPE   —gooseberries, she said. I said again I thought it was hopeless and no good going on, and she agreed, without opening her eyes. [*Pause.*] I asked her to look at me and after a few moments—[*pause*]—after a few moments she did, but the eyes just slits, because of the glare. I bent over her to get them in the shadow and they opened. [*Pause. Low.*] Let me in. [*Pause.*] We drifted in among the flags and stuck. The way they went down, sighing, before the stem! [*Pause.*] I lay down across her with my face in her breasts and my hand on her. We lay there without moving. But under us all moved, and moved us, gently, up and down, and from side to side.

Pause. Krapp's lips move. No sound.

Past midnight. Never knew such silence. The earth might be uninhabited.

Pause.

Here I end this reel. Box—[*pause*]—three, spool—[*pause*]—five. [*Pause.*] Perhaps my best years are gone. When there was a chance of happiness. But I wouldn't want them back. Not with the fire in me now. No, I wouldn't want them back.

Krapp motionless staring before him. The tape runs on in silence.

Curtain

TENNESSEE WILLIAMS
1911–

Thomas Lanier Williams, who adopted his college nickname, Tennessee. during the late 1930s, was born in Columbus, Mississippi, where he spent his early childhood, and in 1918 moved to St. Louis, Missouri, an experience that he later described as "tragic." His southern accent, his small town background, his physically weakened condition brought on by diptheria, and his parents' relative poverty altogether made him acutely conscious of being an outsider, a condition that Williams has variously portrayed in virtually all of his plays. Williams' years in St. Louis were also complicated by the emotional pressures of his family—by his overprotective mother, by his domineering father who called him "Miss Nancy" in mockery of his literary interests, and by his psychologically frail sister who gradually withdrew into a permanent state of mental illness. Echoes of Williams' family and of himself can be found in the long-suffering women, the tyrannical men, the artists, the dreamers, and the mentally disturbed persons who figure as characters in all of his major plays, *The Glass Menagerie* (1944), *Streetcar Named Desire* (1947), *Cat on a Hot Tin Roof* (1955), and *The Night of the Iguana* (1961). But Williams' plays are by no means restricted to characters echoing his past, nor are they merely autobiographical even with respect to characters who are based on his personal experience, for Williams has always shaped his characters and plots to reflect and explore the enduring problems of loneliness and illusion in human experience.

The Glass Menagerie

Scene: An Alley in St. Louis. Part 1. Preparation for a Gentleman Caller. Part II. The Gentleman calls. Time: Now and the Past.

THE CHARACTERS

AMANDA WINGFIELD (*the mother*)   A little woman of great but confused vitality clinging frantically to another time and place. Her characterization must be carefully created, not copied from type. She is not paranoiac, but her life is paranoia. There is much to admire in Amanda, and as much to love and pity as there is to laugh at. Certainly she has endurance and a kind of heroism, and though her foolishness makes her unwittingly cruel at times, there is tenderness in her slight person.

LAURA WINGFIELD (*her daughter*)   Amanda, having failed to establish contact with reality, continues to live vitally in her illusions, but Laura's situation is even graver. A childhood illness has left her crippled, one leg slightly shorter than the other, and held in a brace. This defect need not be more than suggested on the stage. Stemming from this, Laura's separation increases till she is like a piece of her own glass collection, too exquisitely fragile to move from the shelf.

TOM WINGFIELD (*her son*)   And the narrator of the play. A poet with a job in a warehouse. His nature is not remorseless, but to escape from a trap he has to act without pity.

JIM O'CONNOR (*the gentleman caller*)   A nice, ordinary, young man.

PRODUCTION NOTES

Being a "memory play," *The Glass Menagerie* can be presented with unusual freedom of convention. Because of its considerably delicate or tenuous material, atmospheric touches and subtleties of direction play a particularly important part. Expressionism and all other unconventional techniques in drama have only one valid aim, and that is a closer approach to truth. When a play employs unconventional techniques, it is not, or certainly shouldn't be, trying to escape its responsibility of dealing with reality, or interpreting experience, but is actually or should be attempting to find a closer approach, a more penetrating and vivid expression of things as they are. The straight realistic play with its genuine Frigidaire and authentic ice cubes, its characters who speak exactly as its audience speaks, corresponds to the academic landscape and has the same virtue of a photographic likeness. Everyone should know nowadays the unimportance of the photographic in art: that truth, life, or reality is an organic thing which the poetic imagination can represent or suggest, in essence, only through transformation, through changing into other forms than those which were merely present in appearance.

These remarks are not meant as a preface only to this particular play. They have to do with a conception of a new, plastic theatre which must take the place of the exhausted theatre of realistic conventions if the theatre is to resume vitality as a part of our culture.

THE SCREEN DEVICE: There is *only one important difference between the original and the acting version of the play* and that is the *omission* in the latter of the device that I tentatively included in my *original* script. This device was the use of a screen on which were projected magic-lantern slides bearing images or titles. I do not regret the omission of this device from the original Broadway production. The extraordinary power of Miss Taylor's performance made it suitable to have the utmost simplicity in the physical production. But I think it may be interesting to some readers to see how this device was conceived. So I am putting it into the published manuscript. These images and legends, projected from behind, were cast on a section of wall between the front-room and dining-room areas, which should be indistinguishable from the rest when not in use.

The purpose of this will probably be apparent. It is to give accent to certain values in each scene. Each scene contains a particular point (or several) which is structurally the most important. In an episodic play, such as this, the basic structure or narrative line may be obscured from the audience; the effect may seem fragmentary rather than architectural. This may not be the fault of the play so much as a lack of attention in the audience. The legend or image upon the screen will strengthen the effect of what is merely allusion in the writing and allow the primary point to be made more simply and lightly than if the entire responsibility were on the spoken lines. Aside from this structural value, I think the screen will have a definite emotional appeal, less definable but just as important. An imaginative producer or director may invent many other uses for this device than those indicated in the present script. In fact the possibilities of the device seem much larger to me than the instance of this play can possibly utilize.

THE MUSIC: Another extra-literary accent in this play is provided by the use of music. A single recurring tune, "The Glass Menagerie," is used to give emotional emphasis to suitable passages. This tune is like circus music, not when you are on the grounds or in the immediate vicinity of the parade, but when you are at some distance and very likely thinking of something else. It seems under those circumstances to continue almost interminably and it weaves in and out of your preoccupied consciousness; then it is the lightest, most delicate music in the world and perhaps the saddest. It expresses the surface vivacity of life with the underlying strain of immutable and inexpressible sorrow. When you look at a piece of delicately spun glass you think of two things: how beautiful it is and how easily it can be broken. Both of those ideas should be woven into the recurring tune, which dips in and out of the play as if it were carried on a wind that changes. It serves as a thread of connection and allusion between the narrator with his separate point in time and space and the subject of his story. Between each episode it returns as reference to the emotion, nostalgia, which is the first condition of the play. It is primarily Laura's music and therefore comes out most clearly when the play focuses upon her and the lovely fragility of glass which is her image.

THE LIGHTING: The lighting in the play is not realistic. In keeping with the atmosphere of memory, the stage is dim. Shafts of light are focused on selected areas or actors, sometimes in contradistinction to what is the apparent center. For instance, in the quarrel scene between Tom and Amanda, in which Laura has no active part, the clearest pool of light is on her figure. This is also true of the supper scene, when her silent figure on the sofa should remain the visual center. The light upon Laura should be distinct from the others, having a peculiar pristine clarity such as light used in early religious portraits of female saints or madonnas. A certain correspondence to light in religious paintings, such as El Greco's, where the figures are radiant in atmosphere that is relatively dusky, could be effectively used throughout the play. (It will also permit a more effective use of the screen.) A free, imaginative use of light can be of enormous value in giving a mobile, plastic quality to plays of a more or less static nature.

Tennessee Williams

SCENE I

The Wingfield apartment is in the rear of the building, one of those vast hive-like conglomerations of cellular living-units that flower as warty growths in overcrowded urban centers of lower middle-class population and are symptomatic of the impulse of this largest and fundamentally enslaved section of American society to avoid fluidity and differentiation and to exist and function as one interfused mass of automatism.

The apartment faces an alley and is entered by a fire escape, a structure whose name is a touch of accidental poetic truth, for all of these huge buildings are always burning with the slow and implacable fires of human desperation. The fire escape is part of what we see—that is, the landing of it and steps descending from it.

The scene is memory and is therefore nonrealistic. Memory takes a lot of poetic license. It omits some details; others are exaggerated, according to the emotional value of the articles it touches, for memory is seated predominantly in the heart. The interior is therefore rather dim and poetic.

At the rise of the curtain, the audience is faced with the dark, grim rear wall of the Wingfield tenement. This building is flanked on both sides by dark, narrow alleys which run into murky canyons of tangled clotheslines, garbage cans and the sinister latticework of neighboring fire escapes. It is up and down these side alleys that exterior entrances and exits are made during the play. At the end of Tom's opening commentary, the dark tenement wall slowly becomes transparent and reveals the interior of the ground-floor Wingfield apartment.

Nearest the audience is the living room, which also serves as a sleeping room for Laura, the sofa unfolding to make her bed. Just beyond, separated from the living room by a wide arch or second proscenium with transparent faded portieres (or second curtain), is the dining room. In an old-fashioned whatnot in the living room are seen scores of transparent glass animals. A blown-up photograph of the father hangs on the wall of the living room, to the left of the archway. It is the face of a very handsome young man in a doughboy's First World War cap. He is gallantly smiling, ineluctably smiling, as if to say "I will be smiling forever."

Also hanging on the wall, near the photograph, are a typewriter keyboard chart and a Gregg shorthand diagram. An upright typewriter on a small table stands beneath the charts.

The audience hears and sees the opening scene in the dining room through both the transparent fourth wall of the building and the transparent gauze portieres of the dining-room arch. It is during this revealing scene that the fourth wall slowly ascends, out of sight. This transparent exterior wall is not brought down again until the very end of the play, during Tom's final speech.

The narrator is an undisguised convention of the play. He takes whatever license with dramatic convention is convenient to his purposes.

Tom enters, dressed as a merchant sailor, and strolls across to the fire escape. There he stops and lights a cigarette. He addresses the audience.

TOM   Yes, I have tricks in my pocket, I have things up my sleeve. But I am the opposite of a stage magician. He gives you illusion that has the appearance of truth. I give you truth in the pleasant disguise of illusion.

To begin with, I turn back time. I reverse it to that quaint period, the thirties, when the huge middle class of America was matriculating in a school for the blind. Their eyes had failed them, or they had failed their eyes, and so they were having their fingers pressed forcibly down on the fiery Braille alphabet of a dissolving economy.

In Spain there was revolution. Here there was only shouting and confusion. In Spain there was Guernica. Here there were disturbances of labor, sometimes pretty violent, in otherwise peaceful cities such as Chicago, Cleveland, Saint Louis . . .

This is the social background of the play.

[*Music begins to play.*]

The play is memory. Being a memory play, it is dimly lighted, it is sentimental, it is not realistic. In memory everything seems to happen to music. That explains the fiddle in the wings.

I am the narrator of the play, and also a character in it. The other characters are my mother, Amanda, my sister, Laura, and a gentleman caller who appears in the final scenes. He is the most realistic character in the play, being an emissary from a world of reality that we were somehow set apart from. But since I have a poet's weakness for symbols, I am using this character also as a symbol; he is the long-delayed but always expected something that we live for.

There is a fifth character in the play who doesn't appear except in this larger-than-life-size photograph over the mantel. This is our father who left us a long time ago. He was a telephone man who fell in love with long distances; he gave up his job with the telephone company and skipped the light fantastic out of town . . .

The last we heard of him was a picture postcard from Mazatlan, on the Pacific coast of Mexico, containing a message of two words: "Hello—Goodbye!" and no address.

I think the rest of the play will explain itself. . . .

Amanda's voice becomes audible through the portieres.

[*Legend on screen:* "Ou sont les neiges?"]

Tom divides the portieres and enters the dining room. Amanda and Laura are seated at a drop-leaf table. Eating is indicated by gestures without food or utensils. Amanda faces the audience. Tom and Laura are seated in profile. The interior has lit up softly and through the scrim we see Amanda and Laura seated at the table.

AMANDA   [*calling*] Tom?

TOM   Yes, Mother.

AMANDA   We can't say grace until you come to the table!

TOM   Coming, Mother. [*He bows slightly and withdraws, reappearing a few moments later in his place at the table.*]

AMANDA   [*to her son*] Honey, don't *push* with your *fingers*. If you have to push with something, the thing to push with is a crust of bread. And chew—chew! Animals have secretions in their stomachs which enable them to digest food without mastication, but human beings are supposed to chew their food before they swallow it down. Eat food leisurely, son, and really enjoy it. A well-cooked meal has lots of delicate flavors that have to be held in the mouth for appreciation. So chew your food and give your salivary glands a chance to function!

Tom deliberately lays his imaginary fork down and pushes his chair back from the table.

TOM   I haven't enjoyed one bite of this dinner because of your constant directions on how to eat it. It's you that make me rush through meals with your
hawklike attention to every bite I take. Sickening—spoils my appetite—all
this discussion of animals' secretion—salivary glands—mastication!
AMANDA   [*lightly*] Temperament like a Metropolitan star!

Tom rises and walks toward the living room.

You're not excused from the table.
TOM   I'm getting a cigarette.
AMANDA   You smoke too much.

Laura rises.

LAURA   I'll bring in the blancmange.

Tom remains standing with his cigarette by the portieres.

AMANDA   [*rising*] No, sister, no, sister—you be the lady this time and I'll be
the darky.
LAURA   I'm already up.
AMANDA   Resume your seat, little sister—I want you to stay fresh and pretty—
for gentlemen callers!
LAURA   [*sitting down*] I'm not expecting any gentlemen callers.
AMANDA   [*crossing out to the kitchenette, airily*] Sometimes they come when
they are not expected! Why, I remember one Sunday afternoon in Blue
Mountain—

She enters the kitchenette.

TOM   I know what's coming!
LAURA   Yes, But let her tell it.
TOM   Again?
LAURA   She loves to tell it.

Amanda returns with a bowl of dessert.

AMANDA   One Sunday afternoon in Blue Mountain—your mother received—
seventeen!—gentlemen callers! Why, sometimes there weren't chairs enough
to accommodate them all. We had to send the nigger over to bring in folding chairs from the parish house.

TOM   [*remaining at the portieres*] How did you entertain those gentlemen callers?

AMANDA   I understood the art of conversation!

TOM   I bet you could talk.

AMANDA   Girls in those days *knew* how to talk, I can tell you.

TOM   Yes?

[*Image on screen*: Amanda as a girl on a porch, greeting callers.]

AMANDA   They knew how to entertain their gentlemen callers. It wasn't enough for a girl to be possessed of a pretty face and a graceful figure—although I wasn't slighted in either respect. She also needed to have a nimble wit and a tongue to meet all occasions.

TOM   What did you talk about?

AMANDA   Things of importance going on in the world! Never anything coarse or common or vulgar.

She addresses Tom as though he were seated in the vacant chair at the table though he remains by the portieres. He plays this scene as though reading from a script.

My callers were gentlemen—all! Among my callers were some of the most prominent young planters of the Mississippi Delta—planters and sons of planters!

Tom motions for music and a spot of light on Amanda. Her eyes lift, her face glows, her voice becomes rich and elegiac.

[*Screen legend: "Ou sont les neiges d'antan?"*]

There was young Champ Laughlin who later became vice-president of the Delta Planters Bank. Hadley Stevenson who was drowned in Moon Lake and left his widow one hundred and fifty thousand in Government bonds. There were the Cutrere brothers, Wesley and Bates. Bates was one of my bright particular beaux! He got in a quarrel with that wild Wainwright boy. They shot it out on the floor of Moon Lake Casino. Bates was shot through the stomach. Died in the ambulance on his way to Memphis. His widow was also well provided-for, came into eight or ten thousand acres, that's all. She married him on the rebound—never loved her—carried my picture on him the night he died! And there was that boy that every girl in the Delta had set her cap for! That beautiful, brilliant young Fitzhugh boy from Greene County!

TOM   What did he leave his widow?

AMANDA   He never married! Gracious, you talk as though all of my old admirers had turned up their toes to the daisies!

TOM   Isn't this the first you've mentioned that still survives?

AMANDA   That Fitzhugh boy went North and made a fortune—came to be known as the Wolf of Wall Street! He had the Midas touch, whatever he touched turned to gold! And I could have been Mrs. Duncan J. Fitzhugh, mind you! But—I picked your *father!*

LAURA   [*rising*]   Mother, let me clear the table.

AMANDA   No, dear, you go in front and study your typewriter chart. Or practice your shorthand a little. Stay fresh and pretty!—It's almost time for our gentlemen callers to start arriving. [*She flounces girlishly toward the kitchenette*] How many do you suppose we're going to entertain this afternoon?

Tom throws down the paper and jumps up with a groan.

LAURA   [*alone in the dining room*]   I don't believe we're going to receive any, Mother.

AMANDA   [*reappearing, airily*]   What? No one—not one? You must be joking!

Laura nervously echoes her laugh. She slips in a fugitive manner through the half-open portieres and draws them gently behind her. A shaft of very clear light is thrown on her face against the faded tapestry of the curtains. Faintly the music of ''The Glass Menagerie'' is heard as she continues, lightly:

Not one gentleman caller? It can't be true! There must be a flood, there must have been a tornado!

LAURA   It isn't a flood, it's not a tornado, Mother. I'm just not popular like you were in Blue Mountain. . . .

Tom utters another groan. Laura glances at him with a faint, apologetic smile. Her voice catches a little:

Mother's afraid I'm going to be an old maid.

The scene dims out with the ''Glass Menagerie'' music.

SCENE II

On the dark stage the screen is lighted with the image of blue roses. Gradually Laura's figure becomes apparent and the screen goes out. The music subsides.
Laura is seated in the delicate ivory chair at the small clawfoot table. She wears a dress of soft violet material for a kimono—her hair is tied back from her forehead with a ribbon. She is washing and polishing her collection of glass. Amanda appears on the fire escape steps. At the sound of her ascent, Laura catches her breath, thrusts the bowl of ornaments away, and seats herself stiffly before the diagram of the typewriter keyboard as though it held her spellbound. Something has happened to Amanda. It is written in her face as she climbs to the landing: a look that is grim and hopeless and a little absurd.

She has on one of those cheap or imitation velvety-looking cloth coats with imitation fur collar. Her hat is five or six years old, one of those dreadful cloche hats that were worn in the late Twenties, and she is clutching an enormous black patent-leather pocketbook with nickel clasps and initials. This is her full-dress outfit, the one she usually wears to the D.A.R. Before entering she looks through the door. She purses her lips, opens her eyes very wide, rolls them upward and shakes her head. Then she slowly lets herself in the door. Seeing her mother's expression Laura touches her lips with a nervous gesture.

LAURA   Hello, Mother I was— [*She makes a nervous gesture toward the chart on the wall. Amanda leans against the shut door and stares at Laura with a martyred look.*]

AMANDA   Deception? Deception? [*She slowly removes her hat and gloves, continuing the sweet suffering stare. She lets the hat and gloves fall on the floor—a bit of acting.*]

LAURA   [*shakily*] How was the D.A.R. meeting?

Amanda slowly opens her purse and removes a dainty white hankerchief which she shakes out delicately and delicately touches to her lips and nostrils.

Didn't you go to the D.A.R. meeting, Mother?

AMANDA   [*faintly, almost inaudibly*] —No.—No. [*then more forcibly:*] I did not have the strength—to go to the D.A.R. In fact, I did not have the courage! I wanted to find a hole in the ground and hide myself in it forever! [*She crosses slowly to the wall and removes the diagram of the typewriter keyboard. She holds it in front of her for a second, staring at it sweetly and sorrowfully— then bites her lips and tears it in two pieces.*]

LAURA   [*faintly*] Why did you do that, Mother?

Amanda repeats the same procedure with the chart of the Gregg Alphabet.

Why are you—

AMANDA   Why? Why? How old are you, Laura?

LAURA   Mother, you know my age.

AMANDA   I thought that you were an adult; it seems that I was mistaken. [*She crosses slowly to the sofa and sinks down and stares at Laura.*]

LAURA   Please don't stare at me, Mother.

Amanda closes her eyes and lowers her head. There is a ten-second pause.]

AMANDA   What are we going to do, what is going to become of us, what is the future?

There is another pause.

LAURA   Has something happened, Mother?

Amanda draws a long breath, takes out the handkerchief again, goes through the dabbing process.

Mother, has—something happened?

AMANDA   I'll be all right in a minute, I'm just bewildered— [*She hesitates.*] —by life. . . .

LAURA   Mother, I wish that you would tell me what's happened!

AMANDA   As you know, I was supposed to be inducted into my office at the D.A.R. this afternoon.

[*Screen image:* A swarm of typewriters.]

But I stopped off at Rubicam's Business College to speak to your teachers about your having a cold and ask them what progress they thought you were making down there.

LAURA   Oh. . . .

AMANDA   I went to the typing instructor and introduced myself as your mother. She didn't know who you were. "Wingfield," she said, "We don't have any such student enrolled at the school!"

I assured her she did, that you had been going to classes since early in January.

"I wonder," she said, "If you could be talking about that terribly shy little girl who dropped out of school after only a few days' attendance?"

"No," I said, "Laura, my daughter, has been going to school every day for the past six weeks!"

"Excuse me," she said. She took the attendance book out and there was your name, unmistakably printed, and all the dates you were absent until they decided that you had dropped out of school.

I still said, "No, there must have been some mistake! There must have been some mix-up in the records!"

And she said, "No—I remember her perfectly now. Her hands shook so that she couldn't hit the right keys! The first time we gave her a speed test, she broke down completely—was sick at the stomach and almost had to be carried into the wash room! After that morning she never showed up any more. We phoned the house but never got any answer"—While I was working at Famous–Barr, I suppose, demonstrating those—

She indicates a brassiere with her hands.

Oh! I felt so weak I could barely keep on my feet! I had to sit down while they got me a glass of water! Fifty dollars' tuition, all of our plans—my hopes and ambitions for you—just gone up the spout, just gone up the spout like that.

Laura draws a long breath and gets awkwardly to her feet. She crosses to the Victrola and winds it up.

What are you doing?

LAURA   Oh! [*She releases the handle and returns to her seat.*]

AMANDA   Laura, where have you been going when you've gone out pretending that you were going to business college?

LAURA   I've just been going out walking.

AMANDA   That's not true.

LAURA   It is. I just went walking.

AMANDA   Walking? Walking? In winter? Deliberately courting pneumonia in that light coat? Where did you walk to, Laura?

LAURA   All sorts of places—mostly in the park.

AMANDA   Even after you'd started catching that cold?

LAURA   It was the lesser of two evils, Mother.

[*Screen image:* Winter scene in a park.]

I couldn't go back there. I—threw up—on the floor!

AMANDA   From half past seven till after five every day you mean to tell me you walked around in the park, because you wanted to make me think that you were still going to Rubicam's Business College?

LAURA   It wasn't as bad as it sounds. I went inside places to get warmed up.

AMANDA   Inside where?

LAURA   I went in the art museum and the bird houses at the Zoo. I visited the penguins every day! Sometimes I did without lunch and went to the movies. Lately I've been spending most of my afternoons in the Jewel Box, that big glass house where they raise the tropical flowers.

AMANDA   You did all this to deceive me, just for deception? [*Laura looks down.*] Why?

LAURA   Mother, when you're disappointed, you get that awful suffering look on your face, like the picture of Jesus' mother in the museum!

AMANDA   Hush!

LAURA   I couldn't face it.

[*There is a pause. A whisper of strings is heard. Legend on screen:* ''The Crust of Humility.'']

AMANDA   [*hopelessly fingering the huge pocketbook*] So what are we going to do the rest of our lives? Stay home and watch the parades go by? Amuse ourselves with the glass menagerie, darling? Eternally play those worn-out phonograph records your father left as a painful reminder of him? We won't have a business career—we've given that up because it gave us nervous indigestion! [*She laughs wearily.*] What is there left but dependency all our lives? I know so well what becomes of unmarried women who aren't prepared to occupy a position. I've seen such pitiful cases in the South—barely tolerated spinsters living upon the grudging patronage of sister's husband or brother's wife!—stuck away in some little mouse-trap of a room—encouraged by one in-law to visit another—little birdlike

women without any nest—eating the crust of humility all their life!
    Is that the future that we've mapped out for ourselves? I swear it's the only alternative I can think of! [*She pauses.*] It isn't a very pleasant alternative, is it? [*She pauses again.*] Of course—some girls *do marry.*

Laura twists her hands nervously.

    Haven't you ever liked some boy?
LAURA   Yes. I liked one once. [*She rises.*] I came across his picture a while ago.
AMANDA   [*with some interest*] He gave you his picture?
LAURA   No, it's in the yearbook.
AMANDA   [*disappointed*] Oh—a high school boy.

[*Screen image:* Jim as the high school hero bearing a silver cup.]

LAURA   Yes. His name was Jim. [*She lifts the heavy annual from the claw-foot table.*] Here he is in *The Pirates of Penzance.*
AMANDA   [*absently*] The what?
LAURA   The operetta the senior class put on. He had a wonderful voice and we sat across the aisle from each other Mondays, Wednesdays and Fridays in the Aud. Here he is with the silver cup for debating! See his grin?
AMANDA   [*absently*] He must have had a jolly disposition.
LAURA   He used to call me—Blue Roses.

[*Screen image:* Blue roses.]

AMANDA   Why did he call you such a name as that?
LAURA   When I had that attack of pleurosis—he asked me what was the matter when I came back. I said pleurosis—he thought that I said Blue Roses! So that's what he always called me after that. Whenever he saw me, he'd holler, "Hello, Blue Roses!" I didn't care for the girl that he went out with. Emily Meisenbach. Emily was the best-dressed girl at Soldan. She never struck me, though, as being sincere . . . It says in the Personal Section—they're engaged. That's—six years ago! They must be married by now.
AMANDA   Girls that aren't cut out for business careers usually wind up married to some nice man. [*She gets up with a spark of revival.*] Sister, that's what you'll do!

Laura utters a startled, doubtful laugh. She reaches quickly for a piece of glass.

LAURA   But, Mother—
AMANDA   Yes? [*She goes over to the photograph.*]
LAURA   [*in a tone of frightened apology*] I'm—crippled!
AMANDA   Nonsense! Laura, I've told you never, never to use that word. Why, you're not crippled, you just have a little defect—hardly noticeable, even!

When people have some slight disadvantage like that, they cultivate other things to make up for it—develop charm—and vivacity—and—*charm!* That's all you have to do! [*She turns again to the photograph.*] One thing your father had *plenty of*—was *charm!*

The scene fades out with music.

SCENE III

Legend on screen: "After the fiasco—"

Tom speaks from the fire escape landing.

TOM   After the fiasco at Rubicam's Business College, the idea of getting a gentleman caller for Laura began to play a more and more important part in Mother's calculations. It became an obsession. Like some archetype of the universal unconscious, the image of the gentleman caller haunted our small apartment. . . .

Screen image: A young man at the door of a house with flowers.

An evening at home rarely passed without some allusion to this image, this specter, this hope. . . . Even when he wasn't mentioned, his presence hung in Mother's preoccupied look and in my sister's frightened, apologetic manner—hung like a sentence passed upon the Wingfields!

Mother was a woman of action as well as words. She began to take logical steps in the planned direction. Late that winter and in the early spring—realizing that extra money would be needed to properly feather the nest and plume the bird—she conducted a vigorous campaign on the telephone, roping in subscribers to one of those magazines for matrons called *The Homemaker's Companion,* the type of journal that features the serialized sublimations of ladies of letters who think in terms of delicate cuplike breasts, slim, tapering waists, rich, creamy thighs, eyes like wood smoke in autumn, fingers that soothe and caress like strains of music, bodies as powerful as Etruscan sculpture.

[*Screen image:* The cover of a glamor magazine.]

Amanda enters with the telephone on a long extension cord. She is spotlighted in the dim stage.

AMANDA   Ida Scott? This is Amanda Wingfield! We *missed* you at the D.A.R. last Monday! I said to myself: She's probably suffering with that sinus condition! How is that sinus condition?

Horrors! Heaven have mercy!—You're a Christian martyr, yes, that's what you are, a Christian martyr!

Well, I just now happened to notice that your subscription to the *Companion*'s about to expire! Yes, it expires with the next issue, honey!—just when that wonderful new serial by Bessie Mae Hopper is getting off to such an exciting start. Oh, honey, it's something that you can't miss! You remember how *Gone with the Wind* took everybody by storm? You simply couldn't go out if you hadn't read it. All everybody *talked* was Scarlett O'Hara. Well, this is a book that critics already compare to *Gone with the Wind*. It's the *Gone with the Wind* of the post-World-War generation!—What?—Burning?—Oh, honey, don't let them burn, go take a look in the oven and I'll hold the wire! Heavens—I think she's hung up!

The scene dims out.

[*Legend on screen:* "You think I'm in love with Continental Shoemakers?"]

Before the lights come up again, the violent voices of Tom and Amanda are heard. They are quarreling behind the portieres. In front of them stands Laura with clenched hands and panicky expression. A clear pool of light is on her figure throughout this scene.

TOM   What in Christ's name am I—
AMANDA   [*shrilly*] Don't you use that—
TOM   —supposed to do!
AMANDA   —expression! Not in my—
TOM   Ohhh!
AMANDA   —presence! Have you gone out of your senses?
TOM   I have, that's true, *driven* out!
AMANDA   What is the matter with you, you—big—big—IDIOT!
TOM   Look!—I've got *no thing*, no single thing—
AMANDA   Lower your voice!
TOM   —in my life here that I can call my OWN! Everything is—
AMANDA   Stop that shouting!
TOM   Yesterday you confiscated my books! You had the nerve to—
AMANDA   I took that horrible novel back to the library—yes! That hideous book by that insane Mr. Lawrence.

Tom laughs wildly.

I cannot control the output of diseased minds or people who cater to them—

Tom laughs still more wildly.

BUT I WON'T ALLOW SUCH FILTH BROUGHT INTO MY HOUSE! No, no, no, no, no!

TOM   House, house! Who pays rent on it, who makes a slave of himself to—
AMANDA   [*fairly screeching*] Don't you DARE to—
TOM   No, no, I mustn't say things! *I've* got to just—
AMANDA   Let me tell you—
TOM   I don't want to hear any more!

He tears the portieres open. The dining-room area is lit with a turgid smoky red glow. Now we see Amanda; her hair is in metal curlers and she is wearing a very old bathrobe, much too large for her slight figure, a relic of the faithless Mr. Wingfield. The upright typewriter now stands on the drop-leaf table, along with a wild disarray of manuscripts. The quarrel was probably precipitated by Amanda's interruption of Tom's creative labor. A chair lies overthrown on the floor. Their gesticulating shadows are cast on the ceiling by the fiery glow.

AMANDA   You *will* hear more, you—
TOM   No, I won't hear more, I'm going out!
AMANDA   You come right back in—
TOM   Out, out, out! Because I'm—
AMANDA   Come back here, Tom Wingfield! I'm not through talking to you!
TOM   Oh, go—
LAURA   [*desperately*] —Tom!
AMANDA   You're going to listen, and no more insolence from you! I'm at the
    end of my patience!

He comes back toward her.

TOM   What do you think I'm at? Aren't I supposed to have any patience to
    reach the end of, Mother? I know, I know. It seems unimportant to you,
    what I'm *doing*—what I *want* to do—having a little *difference* between
    them! You don't think that—
AMANDA   I think you've been doing things that you're ashamed of. That's
    why you act like this. I don't believe that you go every night to the
    movies. Nobody goes to the movies night after night. Nobody in their
    right minds goes to the movies as often as you pretend to. People don't go
    to the movies at nearly midnight, and movies don't let out at two A.M.
    Come in stumbling. Muttering to yourself like a maniac! You get three
    hours' sleep and then go to work. Oh, I can picture the way you're doing
    down there. Moping, doping, because you're in no condition.
TOM   [*wildly*] No, I'm in no condition!
AMANDA   What right have you got to jeopardize your job? Jeopardize the
    security of us all? How do you think we'd manage if you were—
TOM   Listen! You think I'm crazy about the *warehouse*? [*He bends fiercely toward
    her slight figure.*] You think I'm in love with the Continental Shoemakers?
    You think I want to spend fifty-five *years* down there in that—*celotex
    interior!* with—*fluorescent—tubes!* Look! I'd rather somebody picked up a
    crowbar and battered out my brains—than go back mornings! I *go!* Every

time you come in yelling that Goddamn *"Rise and Shine!" "Rise and Shine!"* I say to myself, "How *lucky dead* people are!" But I get up. I *go!* For sixty-five dollars a month I give up all that I dream of doing and being *ever!* And you say self—*self's* all I ever think of. Why, listen, if self is what I thought of, Mother, I'd be where he is—GONE! [*He points to his father's picture.*] As far as the system of transportation reaches! [*He starts past her. She grabs his arm.*] Don't grab at me, Mother!

AMANDA   Where are you going?

TOM   I'm going to the *movies!*

AMANDA   I don't believe that lie!

Tom crouches toward her, overtowering her tiny figure. She backs away, gasping.

TOM   I'm going to opium dens! Yes, opium dens, dens of vice and criminals' hangouts, Mother. I've joined the Hogan Gang, I'm a hired assassin, I carry a tommy gun in a violin case! I run a string of cat houses in the Valley! They call me Killer, Killer Wingfield, I'm leading a double-life, a simple, honest warehouse worker by day, by night a dynamic *czar* of the *underworld, Mother.* I go to gambling casinos, I spin away fortunes on the roulette table! I wear a patch over one eye and a false mustache, sometimes I put on green whiskers. On those occasions they call me—*El Diablo!* Oh, I could tell you many things to make you sleepless! My enemies plan to dynamite this place. They're going to blow us all sky-high some night! I'll be glad, very happy, and so will you! You'll go up, up on a broomstick, over Blue Mountain with seventeen gentlemen callers! You ugly—babbling old—witch. . . . [*He goes through a series of violent, clumsy movements, seizing his overcoat, lunging to the door, pulling it fiercely open. The women watch him, aghast. His arm catches in the sleeve of the coat as he struggles to pull it on. For a moment he is pinioned by the bulky garment. With an outraged groan he tears the coat off again, splitting the shoulder of it, and hurls it across the room. It strikes against the shelf of Laura's glass collection, and there is a tinkle of shattering glass. Laura cries out as if wounded.*]

Music.

[*Screen legend:* "The Glass Menagerie."]

LAURA   [*shrilly*] My glass!—menagerie. . . . [*She covers her face and turns away.*]

But Amanda is still stunned and stupefied by the "ugly witch" so that she barely notices this occurrence. Now she recovers her speech.

AMANDA   [*in an awful voice*] I won't speak to you—until you apologize!

She crosses through the portieres and draws them together behind her. Tom is left with Laura. Laura clings weakly to the mantel with her face averted. Tom stares at her

*stupidly for a moment. Then he crosses to the shelf. He drops awkwardly on his knees
to collect the fallen glass, glancing at Laura as if he would speak but couldn't.*

"The Glass Menagerie" music steals in as the scene dims out.

SCENE IV

*The interior of the apartment is dark. There is a faint light in the alley. A deep-voiced
bell in a church is tolling the hour of five.*

*Tom appears at the top of the alley. After each solemn boom of the bell in the tower, he
shakes a little noisemaker or rattle as if to express the tiny spasm of man in contrast to
the sustained power and dignity of the Almighty. This and the unsteadiness of his
advance make it evident that he has been drinking. As he climbs the few steps to the fire
escape landing light steals up inside. Laura appears in the front room in a nightdress.
She notices that Tom's bed is empty. Tom fishes in his pockets for his door key,
removing a motley assortment of articles in the search, including a shower of movie
ticket stubs and an empty bottle. At last he finds the key, but just as he is about to insert
it, it slips from his fingers. He strikes a match and crouches below the door.*

TOM   [*bitterly*] One crack—and it falls through!

Laura opens the door.

LAURA   Tom! Tom, what are you doing?
TOM   Looking for a door key.
LAURA   Where have you been all this time?
TOM   I have been to the movies.
LAURA   All this time at the movies?
TOM   There was a very long program. There was a Garbo picture and a Mickey
    Mouse and a travelogue and a newsreel and a preview of coming attractions.
    And there was an organ solo and a collection for the Milk Fund—simul-
    taneously—which ended up in a terrible fight between a fat lady and an
    usher!
LAURA   [*innocently*] Did you have to stay through everything?
TOM   Of course! And, oh, I forgot! There was a big stage show! The headliner
    on this stage show was Malvolio the Magician. He performed wonderful
    tricks, many of them, such as pouring water back and forth between
    pitchers. First it turned to wine and then it turned to beer and then it
    turned to whisky. I know is was whisky it finally turned into because he
    needed somebody to come up out of the audience to help him, and I came
    up—both shows! It was Kentucky Straight Bourbon. A very generous fel-
    low, he gave souvenirs. [*He pulls from his back pocket a shimmering rainbow-
    colored scarf.*] He gave me this. This is his magic scarf. You can have it,

LAURA. You wave it over the goldfish bowl and they fly away canaries. . . . But the wonderfullest trick of all was the coffin trick. We nailed him into a coffin and he got out of the coffin without removing one nail. [*He has come inside.*] There is a trick that would come in handy for me—get me out of this two-by-four situation! [*He flops onto the bed and starts removing his shoes.*]

LAURA   Tom—shhh!

TOM   What're you shushing me for?

LAURA   You'll wake up Mother.

TOM   Goody, goody! Pay 'er back for all those "Rise an' Shines." [*He lies down, groaning.*] You know it don't take much intelligence to get yourself into a nailed-up coffin, Laura. But who in hell ever got himself out of one without removing one nail?

As if in answer, the father's grinning photograph lights up. The scene dims out.

Immediately following, the church bell is heard striking six. At the sixth stroke the alarm clock goes off in Amanda's room, and after a few moments we hear her calling: "Rise and Shine! Rise and Shine! Laura, go tell your brother to rise and shine!"

TOM   [*sitting up slowly*] I'll rise—but I won't shine.

The light increases.

AMANDA   Laura, tell your bother his coffee is ready.

Laura slips into the front room.

LAURA   Tom!—It's nearly seven. Don't make Mother nervous.

He stares at her stupidly.

[*beseechingly*] Tom, speak to Mother this morning. Make up with her, apologize, speak to her!

TOM   She won't to me. It's her that started not speaking.

LAURA   If you just say you're sorry she'll start speaking.

TOM   Her not speaking—is that such a tragedy?

LAURA   Please—please!

AMANDA   [*calling from the kitchenette*] Laura, are you going to do what I asked you to do, or do I have to get dressed and go out myself?

LAURA   Going, going—soon as I get on my coat!

She pulls on a shapeless felt hat with a nervous, jerky movement, pleadingly glancing at Tom. She rushes awkwardly for her coat. The coat is one of Amanda's, inaccurately made-over, the sleeves too short for Laura.

Butter and what else?

AMANDA   [*entering from the kitchenette*] Just butter. Tell them to charge it.

LAURA   Mother, they make such faces when I do that.

AMANDA   Sticks and stones can break our bones, but the expression on Mr. Garfinkel's face won't harm us! Tell your brother his coffee is getting cold.

LAURA   [*at the door*] Do what I asked you, will you, will you, Tom?

He looks sullenly away.

AMANDA   Laura, go now or just don't go at all!

LAURA   [*rushing out*] Going—going!

A second later she cries out. Tom springs up and crosses to the door. Tom opens the door.

TOM   Laura?

LAURA   I'm all right. I slipped, but I'm all right.

AMANDA   [*peering anxiously after her*] If anyone breaks a leg on those fire-escape steps, the landlord ought to be sued for every cent he possesses! [*She shuts the door. Now she remembers she isn't speaking to Tom and returns to the other room.*]

As Tom comes listlessly for his coffee, she turns her back to his and stands rigidly facing the window on the gloomy gray vault of the areaway. Its light on her face with its aged but childish features is cruelly sharp, satirical as a Daumier print.

The music of "Ave Maria," is heard softly.

Tom glances sheepishly but sullenly at her averted figure and slumps at the table. The coffee is scalding hot; he sips it and gasps and spits it back in the cup. At his gasp, Amanda catches her breath and half turns. Then she catches herself and turns back to the window. Tom blows on his coffee, glancing sidewise at his mother. She clears her throat. Tom clears his. He starts to rise, sinks back down again, scratches his head, clears his throat again. Amanda coughs. Tom raises his cup in both hands to blow on it, his eyes staring over the rim of it at his mother for several moments. Then he slowly sets the cup down and awkwardly and hesitantly rises from the chair.

TOM   [*hoarsely*] Mother. I—I apologize, Mother.

Amanda draws a quick, shuddering breath. Her face works grotesquely. She breaks into childlike tears.

I'm sorry for what I said, for everything that I said, I didn't mean it.

AMANDA   [*sobbingly*] My devotion has made me a witch and so I make myself hateful to my children!

TOM *No,* you *don't.*

AMANDA I worry so much, don't sleep, it makes me nervous!

TOM [*gently*] I understand that.

AMANDA I've had to put up a solitary battle all these years. But you're my right-hand bower! Don't fall down, don't fail!

TOM [*gently*] I try, Mother.

AMANDA [*with great enthusiasm*] Try and you will *succeed!* [*The notion makes her breathless.*] Why, you—you're just *full* of natural endowments! Both of my children—they're *unusual* children! Don't you think I know it? I'm so—*proud!* Happy and—feel I've—so much to be thankful for but—promise me one thing, son!

TOM What, Mother?

AMANDA Promise, son you'll—never be a drunkard!

TOM [*turns to her grinning*] I will never be a drunkard, Mother.

AMANDA That's what frightened me so, that you'd be drinking! Eat a bowl of Purina!

TOM Just coffee, Mother.

AMANDA Shredded wheat biscuit?

TOM No. No, Mother, just coffee.

AMANDA You can't put in a days' work on an empty stomach. You've got ten minutes—don't gulp! Drinking too-hot liquids makes cancer of the stomach. . . . Put cream in.

TOM No, thank you.

AMANDA To cool it.

TOM No! No, thank you, I want it black.

AMANDA I know, but it's not good for you. We have to do all that we can to build ourselves up. In these trying times we live in, all that we have to cling to is—each other. . . . That's why it's so important to—Tom, I—I sent out your sister so I could discuss something with you. If you hadn't spoken I would have spoken to you. [*She sits down.*]

TOM [*gently*] What is it, Mother, that you want to discuss?

AMANDA *Laura!*

Tom puts his cup down slowly.

[*Legend on screen: "Laura." Music: "The Glass Menagerie."*]

TOM —Oh.—Laura . . .

AMANDA [*touching his sleeve*] You know how Laura is. So quiet but—still water runs deep! She notices things and I think she—broods about them.

Tom looks up.

A few days ago I came in and she was crying.

TOM What about?

AMANDA   You.

TOM   Me?

AMANDA   She has an idea that you're not happy here.

TOM   What gave her that idea?

AMANDA   What gives her any idea? However, you do act strangely. I—I'm not criticizing, understand *that!* I know your ambitions do not lie in the warehouse, that like everybody in the whole wide world—you've had to—make sacrifices, but—Tom—Tom—life's not easy, it calls for—Spartan endurance! There's so many things in my heart that I cannot describe to you! I've never told you but I—*loved* your father. . . .

TOM   [*gently*] I know that, Mother.

AMANDA   And you—when I see you taking after his ways! Staying out late— and—well, you *had* been drinking the night you were in that—terrifying condition! Laura says that you hate the apartment and that you go out nights to get away from it! Is that true, Tom?

TOM   No. You say there's so much in your heart that you can't describe to me. That's true of me, too. There's so much in my heart that I can't describe to *you!* So let's respect each other's—

AMANDA   But, why—*why,* Tom—are you always so *restless?* Where do you *go* to, nights?

TOM   I—go to the movies.

AMANDA   Why do you go to the movies so much, Tom?

TOM   I go to the movies because—I like adventure. Adventure is something I don't have much of at work, so I go to the movies.

AMANDA   But, Tom, you go to the movies *entirely* too *much!*

TOM   I like a lot of adventure.

Amanda looks baffled, then hurt. As the familiar inquisition resumes, Tom becomes hard and impatient again. Amanda slips back into her querulous attitude toward him.

[*Image on screen:* A sailing vessel with Jolly Roger.]

AMANDA   Most young men find adventure in their careers.

TOM   Then most young men are not employed in a warehouse.

AMANDA   The world is full of young men employed in warehouses and offices and factories.

TOM   Do all of them find adventure in their careers?

AMANDA   They do or they do without it! Not everybody has a craze for adventure.

TOM   Man is by instinct a lover, a hunter, a fighter, and none of those instincts are given much play at the warehouse!

AMANDA   Man is by instinct! Don't quote instinct to me! Instinct is something that people have got away from! It belongs to animals! Christian adults don't want it!

TOM   What do Christian adults want, then, Mother?

AMANDA   Superior things! Things of the mind and the spirit! Only animals
have to satisfy instincts! Surely your aims are somewhat higher than
theirs! Than monkeys—pigs—

TOM   I reckon they're not.

AMANDA   You're joking. However, that isn't what I wanted to discuss.

TOM   [*rising*] I haven't much time.

AMANDA   [*pushing his shoulders*] Sit down.

TOM   You want me to punch in red at the warehouse, Mother?

AMANDA   You have five minutes. I want to talk about Laura.

[*Screen legend:* "Plans and Provisions."]

TOM   All right! What about Laura?

AMANDA   We have to be making some plans and provisions for her. She's
older than you, two years, and nothing has happened. She just drifts
along doing nothing. It frightens me terribly how she just drifts along.

TOM   I guess she's the type that people call home girls.

AMANDA   There's no such type, and if there is, it's a pity! That is unless the
home is hers, with a husband!

TOM   What?

AMANDA   Oh, I can see the handwriting on the wall as plain as I see the nose
in front of my face! It's terrifying! More and more you remind me of your
father! He was out all hours without explanation!—Then *left! Goodbye!*
And me with the bag to hold. I saw that letter you got from the Merchant
Marine. I know what you're dreaming of. I'm not standing here blindfolded.
[*She pauses.*] Very well, then. Then *do* it! But not till there's somebody to
take your place.

TOM   What do you mean?

AMANDA   I mean that as soon as Laura has got somebody to take care of her,
married, a home of her own, independent—why, then you'll be free to go
wherever you please, on land, on sea, whichever way the wind blows
you! But until that time you've got to look out for your sister. I don't say
me because I'm old and don't matter! I say for your sister because she's
young and dependent.

I put her in business college—a dismal failure! Frightened her so it made
her sick at the stomach. I took her over to the Young People's League at
the church. Another fiasco. She spoke to nobody, nobody spoke to her.
Now all she does is fool with those pieces of glass and play those worn-
out records. What kind of life is that for a girl to lead?

TOM   What can I do about it?

AMANDA   Overcome selfishness! Self, self, self is all that you ever think of!

*Tom springs up and crosses to get his coat. It is ugly and bulky. He pulls on a cap with
earmuffs.*

Where is your muffler? Put your wool muffler on!

He snatches it angrily from the closet, tosses it around his neck and pulls both ends tight.

> Tom! I haven't said what I had in mind to ask you.

TOM   I'm too late to—

AMANDA   [*catching his arm—very importunately; then shyly*] Down at the ware-house, aren't there some—nice young men?

TOM   No!

AMANDA   There *must* be—*some* . . .

TOM   Mother— [*He gestures.*]

AMANDA   Find out one that's clean-living—doesn't drink and ask him out for sister!

TOM   What?

AMANDA   For *sister!* To *meet!* Get *acquainted!*

TOM   [*stamping to the door*] Oh, my *go-osh!*

AMANDA   Will you?

He opens the door. She says, imploringly:

> Will you?

He starts down the fire escape.

> Will you? *Will* you dear?

TOM   [*calling back*] Yes!

Amanda closes the door hesitantly and with a troubled but faintly hopeful expression.

[*Screen image:* The cover of a glamor magazine.]

The spotlight picks up Amanda at the phone.

AMANDA   Ella Cartwright? This is Amanda Wingfield!
>   How are you, honey?
>   How is that kidney condition?

There is a five-second pause.

> Horrors!

There is another pause.

> You're a Christian martyr, yes, honey, that's what you are, a Christian martyr! Well, I just now happened to notice in my little red book that your subscription to the *Companion* has just run out! I knew that you wouldn't want to miss out on the wonderful serial starting in this new issue. It's by

Bessie Mae Hopper, the first thing she's written since *Honeymoon for Three*. Wasn't that a strange and interesting story? Well, this one is even lovelier, I believe. It has a sophisticated, society background. It's all about the horsey set on Long Island!

The light fades out.

SCENE V

Legend on the screen: "Annunciation."

Music is heard as the light slowly comes on.

It is early dusk of a spring evening. Supper has just been finished in the Wingfield apartment. Amanda and Laura, in light-colored dresses, are removing dishes from the table in the dining room, which is shadowy, their movements formalized almost as a dance or ritual, their moving forms as pale and silent as moths. Tom, in white shirt and trousers, rises from the table and crosses toward the fire escape.

AMANDA   [*as he passes her*] Son, will you do me a favor?
TOM   What?
AMANDA   Comb your hair! You look so pretty when your hair is combed!

Tom slouches on the sofa with the evening paper. Its enormous headline reads: "Franco Triumphs."

    There is only one respect in which I would like you to emulate your father.
TOM   What respect is that?
AMANDA   The care he always took of his appearance. He never allowed himself to look untidy.

He throws down the paper and crosses to the fire escape.

    Where are you going?
TOM   I'm going out to smoke.
AMANDA   You smoke too much. A pack a day at fifteen cents a pack. How much would that amount to in a month? Thirty times fifteen is how much, Tom? Figure it out and you will be astounded at what you could save. Enough to give you a night-school course in accounting at Washington U.! Just think what a wonderful thing that would be for you, son!

Tom is unmoved by the thought.

TOM   I'd rather smoke. [*He steps out on the landing, letting the screen door slam.*]

AMANDA   [*sharply*] I know! That's the tragedy of it. . . . [*Alone, she turns to look at her husband's picture.*]

Dance music: "The World Is Waiting for the Sunrise!"

TOM   [*to the audience*] Across the alley from us was the Paradise Dance Hall. On evenings in spring the windows and doors were open and the music came outdoors. Sometimes the lights were turned out except for a large glass sphere that hung from the ceiling. It would turn slowly about and filter the dusk with delicate rainbow colors. Then the orchestra played a waltz or a tango, something that had a slow and sensuous rhythm. Couples would come outside, to the relative privacy of the alley. You could see them kissing behind ash pits and telephone poles. This was the compensation for lives that passed like mine, without any change or adventure. Adventure and change were imminent in this year. They were waiting around the corner for all these kids. Suspended in the mist over Berchtesgaden, caught in the folds of Chamberlain's umbrella. In Spain there was Guernica! But here there was only hot swing music and liquor, dance halls, bars, and movies, and sex that hung in the gloom like a chandelier and flooded the world with brief, deceptive rainbows. . . . All the world was waiting for bombardments!

Amanda turns from the picture and comes outside.

AMANDA   [*sighing*] A fire escape landing's a poor excuse for a porch. [*She spreads a newspaper on a step and sits down, gracefully and demurely as if she were settling into a swing on a Mississippi veranda.*] What are you looking at?
TOM   The moon.
AMANDA   Is there a moon this evening?
TOM   It's rising over Garfinkel's Delicatessen.
AMANDA   So it is! A little silver slipper of a moon. Have you made a wish on it yet?
TOM   Um-hum.
AMANDA   What did you wish for?
TOM   That's a secret.
AMANDA   A secret, huh? Well, I won't tell mine either. I will be just as mysterious as you.
TOM   I bet I can guess what yours is.
AMANDA   Is my head so transparent?
TOM   You're not a sphinx.
AMANDA   No, I don't have secrets. I'll tell you what I wished for on the moon. Success and happiness for my precious children! I wish for that whenever there's a moon, and when there isn't a moon, I wish for it, too.
TOM   I thought perhaps you wished for a gentleman caller.
AMANDA   Why do you say that?
TOM   Don't you remember asking me to fetch one?

AMANDA   I remember suggesting that it would be nice for your sister if you brought home some nice young man from the warehouse. I think that I've made that suggestion more than once.

TOM   Yes, you have made it repeatedly.

AMANDA   Well?

TOM   We are going to have one.

AMANDA   *What?*

TOM   A gentleman caller!

The annunciation is celebrated with music.

Amanda rises.

[*Image on screen:* A caller with a bouquet.]

AMANDA   You mean you have asked some nice young man to come over?

TOM   Yep. I've asked him to dinner.

AMANDA   You really did?

TOM   I did!

AMANDA   You did, and did he—*accept?*

TOM   He did!

AMANDA   Well, well—well, well! That's—lovely!

TOM   I thought that you would be pleased.

AMANDA   It's definite then?

TOM   Very definite.

AMANDA   Soon?

TOM   Very soon.

AMANDA   For heaven's sake, stop putting on and tell me some things, will you?

TOM   What things do you want me to tell you?

AMANDA   *Naturally* I would like to know when he's *coming!*

TOM   He's coming tomorrow.

AMANDA   *Tomorrow?*

TOM   Yep. Tomorrow.

AMANDA   But, Tom!

TOM   Yes, Mother?

AMANDA   Tomorrow gives me no time!

TOM   Time for what?

AMANDA   Preparations! Why didn't you phone me at once, as soon as you asked him, the minute that he accepted? Then, don't you see, I could have been getting ready!

TOM   You don't have to make any fuss.

AMANDA   Oh, Tom, Tom, Tom, of course I have to make a fuss! I want things nice, not sloppy! Not thrown together. I'll certainly have to do some fast thinking, won't I?

TOM   I don't see why you have to think at all.

AMANDA   You just don't know. We can't have a gentleman caller in a pigsty! All my wedding silver has to be polished, the monogrammed table linen ought to be laundered! The windows have to be washed and fresh curtains put up. And how about clothes? We have to *wear* something, don't we?

TOM   Mother, this boy is no one to make a fuss over!

AMANDA   Do you realize he's the first young man we've introduced to your sister? It's terrible, dreadful, disgraceful that poor little sister has never received a single gentleman caller! Tom, come inside! [*She opens the screen door.*]

TOM   What for?

AMANDA   I want to ask you some things.

TOM   If you're going to make such a fuss, I'll call it off, I'll tell him not to come!

AMANDA   You certainly won't do anything of the kind. Nothing offends people worse than broken engagements. It simply means I'll have to work like a Turk! We won't be brilliant, but we will pass inspection. Come on inside.

Tom follows her inside, groaning.

Sit down.

TOM   Any particular place you would like me to sit?

AMANDA   Thank heavens I've got that new sofa! I'm also making payments on a floor lamp I'll have sent out! And put the chintz covers on, they'll brighten things up! Of course I'd hoped to have these walls re-papered. . . . What is the young man's name?

TOM   His name is O'Connor.

AMANDA   That, of course, means fish—tomorrow is Friday! I'll have that salmon loaf—with Durkee's dressing! What does he do? He works at the warehouse?

TOM   Of course! How else would I—

AMANDA   Tom, he—doesn't drink?

TOM   Why do you ask me that?

AMANDA   Your father *did!*

TOM   Don't get started on that!

AMANDA   He *does* drink, then?

TOM   Not that I know of!

AMANDA   Make sure, be certain! The last thing I want for my daughter's a boy who drinks!

TOM   Aren't you being a little bit premature? Mr. O'Connor has not yet appeared on the scene!

AMANDA   But will tomorrow. To meet your sister, and what do I know about his character? Nothing! Old maids are better off than wives of drunkards!

TOM   Oh, my God!

AMANDA   Be still!

TOM   [*leaning forward to whisper*] Lots of fellows meet girls whom they don't marry!

AMANDA Oh, talk sensibly, Tom—and don't be sarcastic! [*She has gotten a hairbrush.*]

TOM What are you doing?

AMANDA I'm brushing that cowlick down! [*She attacks his hair with the brush.*] What is this young man's position at the warehouse?

TOM [*submitting grimly to the brush and the interrogation*] This young man's position is that of a shipping clerk, Mother.

AMANDA Sounds to me like a fairly responsible job, the sort of job *you* would be in if you just had more *get-up*. What is his salary? Have you any idea?

TOM I would judge it to be approximately eighty-five dollars a month.

AMANDA Well—not princely, but—

TOM Twenty more than I make.

AMANDA Yes, how well I know! But for a family man, eighty-five dollars a month is not much more than you can just get by on. . . .

TOM Yes, but Mr. O'Connor is not a family man.

AMANDA He might be, mightn't he? Some time in the future?

TOM I see. Plans and provisions.

AMANDA You are the only young man that I know of who ignores the fact that the future becomes the present, the present the past, and the past turns into everlasting regret if you don't plan for it!

TOM I will think that over and see what I can make of it.

AMANDA Don't be supercilious with your mother! Tell me some more about this—what do you call him?

TOM James D. O'Connor. The D. is for Delaney.

AMANDA Irish on *both* sides! *Gracious!* And doesn't drink?

TOM Shall I call him up and ask him right this minute?

AMANDA The only way to find out about those things is to make discreet inquiries at the proper moment. When I was a girl in Blue Mountain and it was suspected that a young man drank, the girl whose attentions he had been receiving, if any girl *was*, would sometimes speak to the minister of his church, or rather her father would if her father was living, and sort of feel him out on the young man's character. That is the way such things are discreetly handled to keep a young woman from making a tragic mistake!

TOM Then how did you happen to make a tragic mistake?

AMANDA That innocent look of your father's had everyone fooled! He *smiled* —the world was *enchanted!* No girl can do worse than put herself at the mercy of a handsome appearance! I hope that Mr. O'Connor is not too good-looking.

TOM No, he's not good-looking. He's covered with freckles and hasn't too much of a nose.

AMANDA He's not right-down homely, though?

TOM Not right-down homely. Just medium homely, I'd say.

AMANDA Character's what to look for in a man.

TOM That's what I've always said, Mother.

AMANDA You've never said anything of the kind and I suspect you would never give it a thought.

TOM   Don't be so suspicious of me.

AMANDA   At least I hope he's the type that's up and coming.

TOM   I think he really goes in for self-improvement.

AMANDA   What reason have you to think so?

TOM   He goes to night school.

AMANDA   [*beaming*] Splendid! What does he do, I mean study?

TOM   Radio engineering and public speaking!

AMANDA   Then he has visions of being advanced in the world! Any young man who studies public speaking is aiming to have an executive job some day! And radio engineering? A thing for the future! Both of these facts are very illuminating. Those are the sort of things that a mother should know concerning any young man who comes to call on her daughter. Seriously or—not.

TOM   One little warning. He doesn't know about Laura. I didn't let on that we had dark ulterior motives. I just said, why don't you come and have dinner with us? He said okay and that was the whole conversation.

AMANDA   I bet it was! You're eloquent as an oyster. However, he'll know about Laura when he get here. When he sees how lovely and sweet and pretty she is, he'll thank his lucky stars he was asked to dinner.

TOM   Mother, you mustn't expect too much of Laura.

AMANDA   What do you mean?

TOM   Laura seems all those things to you and me because she our's and we love her. We don't even notice she's crippled any more.

AMANDA   Don't say crippled! You know that I never allow that word to be used!

TOM   But face facts, Mother. She is and—that's not all—

AMANDA   What do you mean "not all"?

TOM   Laura is very different from other girls.

AMANDA   I think the difference is all to her advantage.

TOM   Not quite all—in the eyes of others—strangers—she's terribly shy and lives in a world of her own and those things make her seem a little peculiar to people outside the house.

AMANDA   Don't say peculiar.

TOM   Face the facts. She is.

The dance hall music changes to a tango that has a minor and somewhat ominous tone.

AMANDA   In what way is she peculiar—may I ask?

AMANDA   [*gently*] She lives in a world of her own—a world of little glass ornaments, Mother. . . .

He gets up. Amanda remains holding the brush, looking at him, troubled.

She plays old phonograph records and—that's about all— [*He glances at himself in the mirror and crosses to the door.*]

AMANDA   [*sharply*] Where are you going?

TOM   I'm going to the movies. [*He goes out the screen door.*]
AMANDA   Not to the movies, every night to the movies! [*She follows quickly to the screen door.*] I don't believe you always go to the movies!

He is gone. Amanda looks worriedly after him for a moment. Then vitality and optimism return and she turns from the door, crossing to the portieres.

Laura! Laura!

Laura answers from the kitchenette.

LAURA   Yes, Mother.
AMANDA   Let those dishes go and come in front!

Laura appears with a dish towel. Amanda speaks to her gaily.

Laura, come here and make a wish on the moon!

[*Screen image:* The Moon.]

LAURA   [*entering*] Moon—moon?
AMANDA   A little silver slipper of a moon. Look over your left shoulder, Laura, and make a wish!

Laura looks faintly puzzled as if called out of sleep. Amanda seizes her shoulders and turns her at an angle by the door.

Now! Now, darling, *wish!*
LAURA   What shall I wish for, Mother?
AMANDA   [*her voice trembling and her eyes suddenly filling with tears*] Happiness!
Good fortune!

The sound of the violin rises and the stage dims out.

SCENE VI

The light comes up on the fire escape landing. Tom is leaning against the grill, smoking.

[*Screen image:* The high school hero.]

TOM   And so the following evening I brought Jim home to dinner. I had known Jim slightly in high school. In high school Jim was a hero. He had tremendous Irish good nature and vitality with the scrubbed and polished look of white chinaware. He seemed to move in a continual spotlight. He was a star in basketball, captain of the debating club, president of the senior class and the glee club and he sang the male lead in the annual light operas. He was always running or bounding, never just walking. He seemed always at the point of defeating the law of gravity. He was shooting with such velocity through his adolescence that you would logically expect him to arrive at nothing short of the White House by the time he was thirty. But Jim apparently ran into more interference after his graduation from Soldan. His speed had definitely slowed. Six years after he left high school he was holding a job that wasn't much better than mine.

[*Screen image:* The Clerk.]

He was the only one at the warehouse with whom I was on friendly terms. I was valuable to him as someone who could remember his former glory, who had seen him win basketball games and the silver cup in debating. He knew of my secret practice of retiring to a cabinet of the washroom to work on poems when business was slack in the warehouse. He called me Shakespeare. And while the other boys in the warehouse regarded me with suspicious hostility, Jim took a humorous attitude toward me. Gradually his attitude affected the others, their hostility wore off and they also began to smile at me as people smile at an oddly fashioned dog who trots across their path at some distance.

    I knew that Jim and Laura had known each other at Soldan, and I had heard Laura speak admiringly of his voice. I didn't know if Jim remembered her or not. In high school Laura had been as unobtrusive as Jim had been astonishing. If he did remember Laura, it was not as my sister, for when I asked him to dinner, he grinned and said, "You know, Shakespeare, I never thought of you as having folks!"

    He was about to discover that I did . . .

[*Legend on screen:* "The accent of a coming foot."]

The light dims out on Tom and comes up in the Wingfield living room—a delicate lemony light. It is about five on a Friday evening of late spring which comes "scattering poems in the sky."

Amanda has worked like a Turk in preparation for the gentleman caller. The results are astonishing. The new floor lamp with its rose silk shade is in place, a colored paper lantern conceals the broken light fixture in the ceiling, new billowing white curtains are at the windows, chintz covers are on the chair and sofa, a pair of new sofa pillows make their initial appearance. Open boxes and tissue paper are scattered on the floor.

Laura stands in the middle of the room with lifted arms while Amanda crouches before her, adjusting the hem of a new dress, devout and ritualistic. The dress is colored and designed by memory. The arrangement of Laura's hair is changed; it is softer and more becoming. A fragile, unearthly prettiness has come out in Laura: she is like a piece of translucent glass touched by light, given a momentary radiance, not actual, not lasting.

AMANDA   [*impatiently*] Why are you trembling?

LAURA   Mother, you've made me so nervous!

AMANDA   How have I made you nervous?

LAURA   By all this fuss! You make it seem so important!

AMANDA   I don't understand you, Laura. You couldn't be satisfied with just sitting home, and yet whenever I try to arrange something for you, you seem to resist it. [*She gets up.*] Now take a look at yourself. No, wait! Wait just a moment—I have an idea!

LAURA   What is it now?

[*Amanda produces two powder puffs which she wraps in handkerchiefs and stuffs in Laura's bosom.*]

LAURA   Mother, what are you doing?

AMANDA   They call them "Gay Deceivers"!

LAURA   I won't wear them!

AMANDA   You will!

LAURA   Why should I?

AMANDA   Because, to be painfully honest, your chest is flat.

LAURA   You make it seem like we were setting a trap.

AMANDA   All pretty girls are a trap, a pretty trap, and men expect them to be.

[*Legend on screen: "A pretty trap."*]

Now look at yourself, young lady. This is the prettiest you will ever be! [*She stands back to admire Laura.*] I've got to fix myself now! You're going to be surprised by your Mother's appearance!

Amanda crosses through the portieres, humming gaily. Laura moves slowly to the long mirror and stares solemnly at herself. A wind blows the white curtains inward in a slow, graceful motion and with a faint, sorrowful sighing.

AMANDA   [*from somewhere behind the portieres*] It isn't dark enough yet.

Laura turns slowly before the mirror with a troubled look.

[*Legend on screen: "This is my sister: Celebrate her with strings!" Music plays.*]

AMANDA   [*laughing, still not visible*] I'm going to show you something. I'm going to make a spectacular appearance!

LAURA   What is it, Mother?

AMANDA   Possess your soul in patience—you will see! Something I've resurrected from that old trunk! Styles haven't changed so terribly much after all. . . . [*She parts the portieres.*] Now just look at your mother! [*She wears a girlish frock of yellowed voile with a blue silk sash. She carries a bunch of jonquils —the legend of her youth is nearly revived. Now she speaks feverishly:*] This is the dress in which I led the cotillion. Won the cakewalk twice at Sunset Hill, wore one Spring to the Governor's Ball in Jackson! See how I sashayed around the ballroom, Laura? [*She raises her skirt and does a mincing step around the room.*] I wore it on Sundays for my gentlemen callers! I had it on the day I met your father. . . . I had malaria fever all that Spring. The change of climate from East Tennessee to the Delta—weakened resistance. I had a little temperature all the time—not enough to be serious—just enough to make me restless and giddy! Invitations poured in—parties all over the Delta! "Stay in bed," said Mother, "you have a fever!"—but I just wouldn't. I took quinine but kept on going, going! Evenings, dances! Afternoons, long, long rides! Picnics—lovely! So lovely, that country in May—all lacy with dogwood, literally flooded with jonquils! That was the spring I had the craze for jonquils. Jonquils became an absolute obsession. Mother said, "Honey, there's no more room for jonquils." And still I kept on bringing in more jonquils. Whenever, wherever I saw them, I'd say, "Stop! Stop! I see jonquils!" I made the young men help me gather the jonquils! It was a joke, Amanda and her jonquils! Finally there were no more vases to hold them, every available space was filled with jonquils. No vases to hold them? All right, I'll hold them myself! And then I— [*She stops in front of the picture. Music plays.*]   met your father! Malaria fever and jonquils and then—this—boy. . . . [*She switches on the rose-colored lamp.*] I hope they get here before it starts to rain. [*She crosses the room and places the jonquils in a bowl on the table.*] I gave your brother a little extra change so he and Mr. O'Connor could take the service car home.

LAURA   [*with an altered look*] What did you say his name was?
AMANDA   O'Connor.
LAURA   What is his first name?
AMANDA   I don't remember. Oh, yes, I do. It was—Jim!

Laura sways slightly and catches hold of a chair.

[*Legend on screen: "Not Jim!"*]

LAURA   [*faintly*] Not—Jim!
AMANDA   Yes, that was it, it was Jim! I've never known a Jim that wasn't nice!

The music becomes ominous.

LAURA   Are you sure his name is Jim O'Connor?
AMANDA   Yes. Why?
LAURA   Is he the one that Tom used to know in high school?
AMANDA   He didn't say so. I think he just got to know him at the warehouse.
LAURA   There was a Jim O'Connor we both knew in high school— [*then, with*

effort] If that is the one that Tom is bringing to dinner—you'll have to excuse me, I won't come to the table.

AMANDA   What sort of nonsense is this?

LAURA   You asked me once if I'd ever liked a boy. Don't you remember I showed you this boy's picture?

AMANDA   You mean the boy you showed me in the yearbook?

LAURA   Yes, that boy.

AMANDA   Laura, Laura, were you in love with that boy?

LAURA   I don't know, Mother. All I know is I couldn't sit at the table if it was him!

AMANDA   It won't be him! It isn't the least bit likely. But whether it is or not, you will come to the table. You will not be excused.

LAURA   I'll have to be, Mother.

AMANDA   I don't intend to humor your silliness, Laura. I've had too much from you and your brother, both! So just sit down and compose yourself till they come. Tom has forgotten his key so you'll have to let them in, when they arrive.

LAURA   [*panicky*] Oh, Mother—*you* answer the door!

AMANDA   [*lightly*] I'll be in the kitchen—busy!

LAURA   Oh, Mother, please answer the door, don't make me do it!

AMANDA   [*crossing into the kitchenette*] I've got to fix the dressing for the salmon. Fuss, fuss—silliness!—over a gentleman caller!

The door swings shut. Laura is left alone.

Legend on screen: ''Terror!''

She utters a low moan and turns off the lamp—sits stiffly on the edge of the sofa, knotting her fingers together.

Legend on screen: ''The Opening of a Door!''

Tom and Jim appear on the fire escape steps and climb to the landing. Hearing their approach, Laura rises with a panicky gesture. She retreats to the portieres. The doorbell rings. Laura catches her breath and touches her throat. Low drums sound.

AMANDA   [*calling*] Laura, sweetheart! The door!

Laura stares at it without moving.

JIM   I think we just beat the rain.

TOM   Uh-huh. [*He rings again, nervously. Jim whistles and fishes for a cigarette.*]

AMANDA   [*very, very gaily*] Laura, that is your brother and Mr. O'Connor! Will you let them in, darling?

Laura crosses toward the kitchenette door.

LAURA   [*breathlessly*] Mother—you go to the door!

Amanda steps out of the kitchenette and stares furiously at Laura. She points imperiously at the door.

LAURA   Please, please!
AMANDA   [*in a fierce whisper*] What is the matter with you, you silly thing?
LAURA   [*desperately*] Please, you answer it, *please!*
AMANDA   I told you I wasn't going to humor you, Laura. Why have you chosen this moment to lose your mind?
LAURA   Please, please, please, you go!
AMANDA   You'll have to go to the door because I can't!
LAURA   [*despairingly*] I can't either!
AMANDA   *Why?*
LAURA   I'm *sick!*
AMANDA   I'm sick, too—of your nonsense! Why can't you and your brother be normal people? Fantastic whims and behavior!

Tom gives a long ring.

Preposterous goings on! Can you give me one reason— [*She calls out lyrically.*] Coming! Just one second!—why you should be afraid to open a door? Now you answer it, Laura!
LAURA   Oh, oh, oh . . . [*She returns through the portieres, darts to the Victrola, winds it frantically and turns it on.*]
AMANDA   Laura Wingfield, you march right to that door!
LAURA   Yes—yes, Mother!

A faraway, scratchy rendition of "Dardanella" softens the air and gives her strength to move through it. She slips to the door and draws it cautiously open. Tom enters with the caller, Jim O'Connor.

TOM   Laura, this is Jim. Jim, this is my sister, Laura.
JIM   [*stepping inside*] I didn't know that Shakespeare had a sister!
LAURA   [*retreating, stiff and trembling, from the door*] How—how do you do?
JIM   [*heartily, extending his hand*] Okay!

Laura touches it hesitantly with hers.

JIM   Your hand's cold, Laura!
LAURA   Yes, well—I've been playing the Victrola. . . .
JIM   Must have been playing classical music on it! You ought to play a little hot swing music to warm you up!
LAURA   Excuse me—I haven't finished playing the Victrola. . . . [*She turns awkwardly and hurries into the front room. She pauses a second by the Victrola. Then she catches her breath and darts through the portieres like a frightened deer.*]

JIM   [*grinning*] What was the matter?

TOM   Oh—with Laura? Laura is—terribly shy.

JIM   Shy, huh? It's unusual to meet a shy girl nowadays. I don't believe you ever mentioned you had a sister.

TOM   Well, now you know. I have one. Here is the *Post Dispatch*. You want a piece of it?

JIM   Uh-huh.

TOM   What piece? The comics?

JIM   Sports! [*He glances at it.*] Ole Dizzy Dean is on his bad behavior.

TOM   [*uninterested*] Yeah? [*He lights a cigarette and goes over to the fire-escape door.*]

JIM   Where are *you* going?

TOM   I'm going out on the terrace.

JIM   [*going after him*] You know, Shakespeare—I'm going to sell you a bill of goods!

TOM   What goods?

JIM   A course I'm taking.

TOM   Huh?

JIM   In public speaking! You and me, we're not the warehouse type.

TOM   Thanks—that's good news. But what has public speaking got to do with it?

JIM   It fits you for—executive positions!

TOM   Awww.

JIM   I tell you it's done a helluva lot for me.

[*Image on screen:* Executive at his desk.]

TOM   In what respect?

JIM   In every! Ask yourself what is the difference between you an' me and men in the office down front? Brains?—No!—Ability?—No! Then what? Just one little thing—

TOM   What is that one little thing?

JIM   Primarily it amounts to—social poise! Being able to square up to people and hold your own on any social level!

AMANDA   [*from the kitchenette*] Tom?

TOM   Yes, Mother?

AMANDA   Is that you and Mr. O'Connor?

TOM   Yes, Mother.

AMANDA   Well, you jusk make yourselves comfortable in there.

TOM   Yes, Mother.

AMANDA   Ask Mr. O'Connor if he would like to wash his hands.

JIM   Aw, no—no—thank you—I took care of that at the warehouse. Tom—

TOM   Yes?

JIM   Mr. Mendoza was speaking to me about you.

TOM   Favorably?

JIM   What do you think?

TOM   Well—

JIM   You're going to be out of a job if you don't wake up.

TOM   I am waking up—

JIM   You show no signs.

TOM   The signs are interior.

[*Image on screen:* The sailing vessel with the Jolly Roger again.]

I'm planning to change. [*He leans over the fire-escape rail, speaking with quiet exhilaration. The incandescent marquees and signs of the first-run movie houses light his face from across the alley. He looks like a voyager.*] I'm right at the point of committing myself to a future that doesn't include the warehouse and Mr. Mendoza or even a night-school course in public speaking.

JIM   What are you gassing about?

TOM   I'm tired of the movies.

JIM   Movies!

TOM   Yes, movies! Look at them— [*a wave toward the marvels of Grand Avenue*] All of those glamorous people—having adventures—hogging it all, gobbling the whole thing up! You know what happens? People go to the *movies* instead of *moving*! Hollywood characters are supposed to have all the adventures for everybody in America, while everybody in America sits in a dark room and watches them have them! Yes, until there's a war. That's when adventure becomes available to the masses! *Everyone's* dish, not only Gable's! Then the people in the dark room come out of the dark room to have some adventures themselves—goody, goody! It's our turn now, to go to the South Sea Island—to make a safari—to be exotic, far-off! But I'm not patient. I don't want to wait till then. I'm tired of the *movies* and I am *about* to *move*!

JIM   [*incredulously*] Move?

TOM   Yes.

JIM   When?

TOM   Soon!

JIM   Where? Where?

The music seems to answer the question, while Tom thinks it over. He searches in his pockets.

TOM   I'm starting to boil inside. I know I seem dreamy, but inside—well, I'm boiling! Whenever I pick up a shoe, I shudder a little thinking how short life is and what I am doing! Whatever that means, I know it doesn't mean shoes—except as something to wear on a traveler's feet! [*He finds what he has been searching for in his pockets and holds out a paper to Jim.*] Look—

JIM   What?

TOM   I'm a member.

JIM   [*reading*] The Union of Merchant Seamen.

TOM   I paid my dues this month, instead of the light bill.

JIM   You will regret it when they turn the lights off.

TOM   I won't be here.

JIM   How about your mother?

TOM   I'm like my father. The bastard son of a bastard! Did you notice how he's grinning in his picture in there? And he's been absent going on sixteen years!

JIM   You're just talking, you drip. How does your mother feel about it?

TOM   Shhh! Here comes Mother! Mother is not acquainted with my plans!

AMANDA   [coming through the portieres] Where are you all?

TOM   On the terrace, Mother.

They start inside. She advances to them. Tom is distinctly shocked at her appearance. Even Jim blinks a little. He is making his first contact with girlish Southern vivacity and in spite of the night-school course in public speaking is somewhat thrown off the beam by the unexpected outlay of social charm. Certain responses are attempted by Jim but are swept aside by Amanda's gay laughter and chatter. Tom is embarrassed but after the first shock Jim reacts very warmly. He grins and chuckles, is altogether won over.

[*Image on screen:* Amanda as a girl.]

AMANDA   [coyly smiling, shaking her girlish ringlets] Well, well, well, so this is Mr. O'Connor. Introductions entirely unnecessary. I've heard so much about you from my boy. I finally said to him, Tom—good gracious!—why don't you bring this paragon to supper? I'd like to meet this nice young man at the warehouse!—instead of just hearing him sing your praises so much! I don't know why my son is so stand-offish—that's not Southern behavior!

Let's sit down and—I think we could stand a little more air in here! Tom, leave the door open. I felt a nice fresh breeze a moment ago. Where has it gone to? Mmm, so warm already! And not quite summer, even. We're going to burn up when summer really gets started. However, we're having—we're having a very light supper. I think light things are better fo' this time of year. The same as light clothes are. Light clothes an' light food are what warm weather calls fo'. You know our blood gets so thick during th' winter—it takes a while fo' us to *adjust* ou'selves!—when the season changes . . . It's come so quick this year. I wasn't prepared. All of a sudden—heavens! Already summer! I ran to the trunk an' pulled out this light dress—terribly old! Historical almost! But feels so good—so good an' co-ol, y' know. . . .

TOM   Mother—

AMANDA   Yes, honey?

TOM   How about—supper?

AMANDA   Honey, you go ask Sister if supper is ready! You know that sister is in full charge of supper! Tell her you hungry boys are waiting for it. [*to Jim*] Have you met Laura?

JIM   She—

AMANDA   Let you in? Oh, good, you've met already! It's rare for a girl as
sweet an' pretty as Laura to be domestic! But Laura is, thank heavens, not
only pretty but also very domestic. I'm not at all. I never was a bit. I never
could make a thing but angel-food cake. Well, in the South we had so
many servants. Gone, gone, gone. All vestige of gracious living! Gone
completely! I wasn't prepared for what the future brought me. All of my
gentlemen callers were sons of planters and so of course I assumed that I
would be married to one and raise my family on a large piece of land with
plenty of servants. But man proposes—and woman accepts the proposal!
To vary that old, old saying a little bit—I married no planter! I married a
man who worked for the telephone company! That gallantly smiling gentleman over there! [*She points to the picture.*] A telephone man who—fell
in love with long-distance! Now he travels and I don't even know where!
But what am I going on for about my—tribulations? Tell me yours—I hope
you don't have any! Tom?

TOM   [*returning*] Yes, Mother?

AMANDA   Is supper nearly ready?

TOM   It looks to me like supper is on the table.

AMANDA   Let me look— [*She rises prettily and looks through the portieres.*] Oh,
lovely! But where is Sister?

TOM   Laura is not feeling well and she says that she thinks she'd better not
come to the table.

AMANDA   What? Nonsense! Laura? Oh, Laura!

LAURA   [*from the kitchenette faintly*]   Yes, Mother.

AMANDA   You really must come to the table. We won't be seated until you
come to the table! Come in, Mr. O'Connor. You sit over there, and I'll. . . .
Laura? Laura Wingfield! You're keeping us waiting, honey! We can't say
grace until you come to the table!

*The kitchenette door is pushed weakly open and Laura comes in. She is obviously quite
faint, her lips trembling, her eyes wide and staring. She moves unsteadily toward the
table.*

[*Screen legend: "Terror!"*]

*Outside a summer storm is coming on abruptly. The white curtains billow inward at
the windows and there is a sorrowful murmur from the deep blue dusk.*

Laura suddenly stumbles; she catches at a chair with a faint moan.

TOM   Laura!

AMANDA   Laura!

There is a clap of thunder.

[*Screen legend: "Ah!"*]

[*despairingly*] Why, Laura, you *are* ill, darling! Tom, help your sister into the living room, dear! Sit in the living room, Laura—rest on the sofa. Well! [*to Jim as Tom helps his sister to the sofa in the living room*] Standing over the hot stove made her ill! I told her that it was just too warm this evening, but—

Tom comes back to the table.

Is Laura all right now?
TOM Yes.
AMANDA What *is* that? Rain? A nice cool rain has come up! [*She gives Jim a frightened look.*] I think we may—have grace—now . . .

[*Tom looks at her stupidly.*] Tom, honey—you say grace!
TOM Oh . . . "For these and all thy mercies—"

They bow their heads, Amanda stealing a nervous glance at Jim. In the living room Laura, stretched on the sofa, clenches her hand to her lips, to hold back a shuddering sob.

God's Holy Name be praised—

The scene dims out.

SCENE VII

It is half an hour later. Dinner is just being finished in the dining room, Laura is still huddled upon the sofa, her feet drawn under her, her head resting on a pale blue pillow, her eyes wide and mysteriously watchful. The new floor lamp with its shade of rose-colored silk gives a soft, becoming light to her face, bringing out the fragile, unearthly prettiness which usually escapes attention. From outside there is a steady murmur of rain, but it is slackening and soon stops; the air outside becomes pale and luminous as the moon breaks through the clouds. A moment after the curtain rises, the lights in both rooms flicker and go out.

JIM Hey, there, Mr. Light Bulb!

Amanda laughs nervously.

[*Legend on screen:* "Suspension of a public service."]

AMANDA Where was Moses when the lights went out? Ha-ha. Do you know the answer to that one, Mr. O'Connor?
JIM No, Ma'am, what's the answer?

AMANDA   In the dark!

Jim laughs appreciatively.

> Everybody sit still. I'll light the candles. Isn't it lucky we have them on the table? Where's a match? Which of you gentlemen can provide a match?

JIM   Here.

AMANDA   Thank you, Sir.

JIM   Not at all, Ma'am!

AMANDA   [*as she lights the candles*]   I guess the fuse has burnt out. Mr. O'Connor, can you tell a burnt-out fuse? I know I can't and Tom is a total loss when it comes to mechanics.

They rise from the table and go into the kitchenette, from where their voices are heard.

> Oh, be careful you don't bump into something. We don't want our gentleman caller to break his neck. Now wouldn't that be a fine howdy-do?

JIM   Ha-ha! Where is the fuse-box?

AMANDA   Right here next to the stove. Can you see anything?

JIM   Just a minute.

AMANDA   Isn't electricity a mysterious thing? Wasn't it Benjamin Franklin who tied a key to a kite? We live in such a mysterious universe, don't we? Some people say that science clears up all the mysteries for us. In my opinion it only creates more! Have you found it yet?

JIM   No, Ma'am. All these fuses look okay to me.

AMANDA   Tom!

TOM   Yes, Mother?

AMANDA   That light bill I gave you several days ago. The one I told you we got the notices about?

[*Legend on screen:* "Ha!"]

TOM   Oh—yeah.

AMANDA   You didn't neglect to pay it by any chance?

TOM   Why, I—

AMANDA   Didn't! I might have known it!

JIM   Shakespeare probably wrote a poem on that light bill, Mrs. Wingfield.

AMANDA   I might have known better than to trust him with it! There's such a high price for negligence in this world!

JIM   Maybe the poem will win a ten-dollar prize.

AMANDA   We'll just have to spend the remainder of the evening in the nineteenth century, before Mr. Edison made the Mazda lamp!

JIM   Candlelight is my favorite kind of light.

AMANDA   That shows you're romantic! But that's no excuse for Tom. Well, we got through dinner. Very considerate of them to let us get through dinner before they plunged us into everlasting darkness, wasn't it, Mr. O'Connor?

JIM   Ha-ha!

AMANDA   Tom, as a penalty for your carelessness you can help me with the dishes.

JIM   Let me give you a hand.

AMANDA   Indeed you will not!

JIM   I ought to be good for something.

AMANDA   Good for something? [*Her tone is rhapsodic.*]   You? Why, Mr. O'Connor, nobody, *nobody's* given me this much entertainment in years—as you have!

JIM   Aw, now, Mrs. Wingfield!

AMANDA   I'm not exaggerating, not one bit! But Sister is all by her lonesome. You go keep her company in the parlor! I'll give you this lovely old candelabrum that used to be on the alter at the Church of the Heavenly Rest. It was melted a little out of shape when the church burnt down. Lightening struck it one spring. Gypsy Jones was holding a revival at the time and he intimated that the church was destroyed because the Episcopalians gave card parties.

JIM   Ha-ha.

AMANDA   And how about you coaxing Sister to drink a little wine? I think it would be good for her! Can you carry both at once?

JIM   Sure. I'm Superman!

AMANDA   Now, Thomas, get into this apron!

Jim comes into the dining room, carrying the candelabrum, its candles lighted, in one hand and a glass of wine in the other. The door of the kitchenette swings closed on Amanda's gay laughter; the flickering light approaches the portieres. Laura sits up nervously as Jim enters. She can hardly speak from the almost intolerable strain of being alone with a stranger.

[*Screen legend: "I don't suppose you remember me at all!"*]

At first, before Jim's warmth overcomes her paralyzing shyness, Laura's voice is thin and breathless, as though she had just run up a steep flight of stairs. Jim's attitude is gently humorous. While the incident is apparently unimportant, it is to Laura the climax of her secret life.

JIM   Hello there, Laura.

LAURA   [*faintly*]   Hello.

[*She clears her throat.*]

JIM   How are you feeling now? Better?

LAURA   Yes. Yes, thank you.

JIM   This is for you. A little dandelion wine. [*He extends the glass toward her with extravagant gallantry.*]

LAURA   Thank you.

JIM   Drink it—but don't get drunk!

He laughs heartily. Laura takes the glass uncertainly; she laughs shyly.

Where shall I set the candles?

LAURA   Oh—oh, anywhere . . .

JIM   How about here on the floor? Any objections?

LAURA   No.

JIM   I'll spread a newspaper under to catch the drippings. I like to sit on the floor. Mind if I do?

LAURA   Oh, no.

JIM   Give me a pillow?

LAURA   What?

JIM   A pillow?

LAURA   Oh . . . [*She hands him one quickly.*]

JIM   How about you? Don't you like to sit on the floor?

LAURA   Oh—yes.

JIM   Why don't you, then?

LAURA   I—will.

JIM   Take a pillow!
[*Laura does. She sits on the floor on the other side of the candelabrum. Jim crosses his legs and smiles engagingly at her.*]   I can't hardly see you sitting way over there.

LAURA   I can—see you.

JIM   I know, but that's not fair, I'm in the limelight.

Laura moves her pillow closer.

Good! Now I can see you! Comfortable?

LAURA   Yes.

JIM   So am I. Comfortable as a cow! Will you have some gum?

LAURA   No, thank you.

JIM   I think that I will indulge, with your permission. [*He musingly unwraps a stick of gum and holds it up.*]   Think of the fortune made by the guy that invented the first piece of chewing gum. Amazing, huh? The Wrigley Building is one of the sights of Chicago—I saw it when I went up to the Century of Progress. Did you take in the Century of Progress?

LAURA   No, I didn't.

JIM   Well, it was quite a wonderful exposition. What impressed me most was the Hall of Science. Gives you an idea of what the future will be in America, even more wonderful than the present time is! [*There is a pause. Jim smiles at her.*]   Your brother tells me you're shy. It that right, Laura?

LAURA   I—don't know.

JIM   I judge you to be an old-fashioned type of girl. Well, I think that's a pretty good type to be. Hope you don't think I'm being too personal—do you?

LAURA   [*hastily, out of embarrassment*]   I believe I *will* take a piece of gum, if you—don't mind. [*clearing her throat*]   Mr. O'Connor, have you—kept up with your singing?

JIM   Singing? Me?

LAURA   Yes. I remember what a beautiful voice you had.

JIM   When did you hear me sing?

Laura does not answer, and in the long pause which follows a man's voice is heard singing offstage.

VOICE

O blow, ye winds, heigh-ho,
A-roving I will go!
I'm off to my love
With a boxing glove—
Ten thousand miles away!

JIM   You say you've heard me sing?

LAURA   Oh, yes! Yes, very often . . . I—don't suppose—you remember me—at all?

JIM   [*smiling doubtfully*]   You know I have an idea I've seen you before. I had that idea soon as you opened the door. It seemed almost like I was about to remember your name. But the name that I started to call you—wasn't a name! And so I stopped myself before I said it.

LAURA   Wasn't it—Blue Roses?

JIM   [*springing up, grinning*]   Blue Roses! My gosh, yes—Blue Roses! That's what I had on my tongue when you opened the door! Isn't it funny what tricks your memory plays? I didn't connect you with high school some-how or other. But that's where it was; it was high school. I didn't even know you were Shakespeare's sister! Gosh, I'm sorry.

LAURA   I didn't expect you to. You—barely knew me!

JIM   But we did have a speaking acquaintance, huh?

LAURA   Yes, we—spoke to each other.

JIM   When did you recognize me?

LAURA   Oh, right away!

JIM   Soon as I came in the door?

LAURA   When I heard your name I thought it was probably you. I knew that Tom used to know you a little in high school. So when you came in the door—well, then I was—sure.

JIM   Why didn't you *say* something, then?

LAURA   [*breathlessly*]   I didn't know what to say, I was—too surprised!

JIM   For goodness' sakes! You know, this sure is funny!

LAURA   Yes! Yes, isn't it, though . . .

JIM   Didn't we have a class in something together?

LAURA   Yes, we did.

JIM   What class was that?

LAURA   It was—singing—chorus!

JIM   Aw!

LAURA   I sat across the aisle from you in the Aud.

JIM   Aw.

LAURA   Mondays, Wednesdays, and Fridays.

JIM   Now I remember—you always came in late.

LAURA   Yes, it was so hard for me, getting upstairs. I had that brace on my
leg—it clumped so loud!

JIM   I never heard any clumping.

LAURA   [*wincing at the recollection*]   To me it sounded like—thunder!

JIM   Well, well, well, I never even noticed.

LAURA   And everybody was seated before I came in. I had to walk in front of
all those people. My seat was in the back row. I had to go clumping all the
way up the aisle with everyone watching!

JIM   You shouldn't have been self-conscious.

LAURA   I know, but I was. It was always such a relief when the singing started.

JIM   Aw, yes, I've placed you now! I used to call you Blue Roses. How was it
that I got started calling you that?

LAURA   I was out of school a little while with pleurosis. When I came back you
asked me what was the matter. I said I had pleurosis—you thought I said
Blue Roses. That's what you always called me after that!

JIM   I hope you didn't mind.

LAURA   Oh, no—I liked it. You see, I wasn't acquainted with many—people. . . .

JIM   As I remember you sort of stuck by yourself.

LAURA   I—I—never have had much luck at—making friends.

JIM   I don't see why you wouldn't.

LAURA   Well, I—started out badly.

JIM   You mean being—

LAURA   Yes, it sort of—stood between me—

JIM   You shouldn't have let it!

LAURA   I know, but it did, and—

JIM   You were shy with people!

LAURA   I tried not to be but never could—

JIM   Overcome it?

LAURA   No, I—I never could!

JIM   I guess being shy is something you have to work out of kind of gradually.

LAURA   [*sorrowfully*]   Yes—I guess it—

JIM   Takes time!

LAURA   Yes—

JIM   People are not so dreadful when you know them. That's what you have
to remember! And everybody has problems, not just you, but practically
everybody has got some problems. You think of yourself as having the
only problems, as being the only one who is disappointed. But just look
around you and you will see lots of people as disappointed as you are. For
instance, I hoped when I was going to high school that I would be further
along at this time, six years later, than I am now. You remember that
wonderful write-up I had in *The Torch*?

LAURA   Yes! [*She rises and crosses to the table.*]

JIM   It said I was bound to succeed in anything I went into!

Laura returns with the high school yearbook.

Holy Jeez! *The Torch!*

He accepts it reverently. They smile across the book with mutual wonder. Laura crouches beside him and they begin to turn the pages. Laura's shyness is dissolving in his warmth.

LAURA   Here you are in *The Pirates of Penzance!*

JIM   [*wistfully*]   I sang the baritone lead in that operetta.

LAURA   [*raptly*]   So—*beautifully!*

JIM   [*protesting*]   Aw—

LAURA   Yes, yes—beautifully—beautifully!

JIM   You heard me?

LAURA   All three times!

JIM   No!

LAURA   Yes!

JIM   All three performances?

LAURA   [*looking down*]   Yes.

JIM   Why?

LAURA   I—wanted to ask you to—autograph my program. [*She takes the program from the back of the yearbook and shows it to him.*]

JIM   Why didn't you ask me to?

LAURA   You were always surrounded by your own friends so much that I never had a chance to.

JIM   You should have just—

LAURA   Well, I—thought you might think I was—

JIM   Thought I might think you was—what?

LAURA   Oh—

JIM   [*with reflective relish*]   I was beleaguered by females in those days.

LAURA   You were terribly popular!

JIM   Yeah—

LAURA   You had such a—friendly way—

JIM   I was spoiled in high school.

LAURA   Everybody—liked you!

JIM   Including you?

LAURA   I—yes, I—did, too— [*She gently closes the book in her lap.*]

JIM   Well, well, well! Give me that program, Laura.

She hands it to him. He signs it with a flourish.

There you are—better late than never!

LAURA   Oh, I—what a—surprise!

JIM My signature isn't worth very much right now. But some day—maybe—it
will increase in value! Being disappointed is one thing and being discouraged is something else. I am disappointed but I am not discouraged. I'm
twenty-three years old. How old are you?

LAURA I'll be twenty-four in June.

JIM That's not old age!

LAURA No, but—

JIM You finished high school?

LAURA [*with difficulty*] I didn't go back.

JIM You mean you dropped out?

LAURA I made bad grades in my final examinations. [*She rises and replaces the
book and the program on the table. Her voice is strained.*] How is—Emily
Meisenbach getting long?

JIM Oh, that kraut-head!

LAURA Why do you call her that?

JIM That's what she was.

LAURA You're not still—going with her?

JIM I never see her.

LAURA It said in the "Personal" section that you were—engaged!

JIM I know, but I wasn't impressed by that—propaganda!

LAURA It wasn't—the truth?

JIM Only in Emily's optimistic opinion!

LAURA Oh—

[*Legend:* "What have you done since high school?"]

*Jim lights a cigarette and leans indolently back on his elbows smiling at Laura with a
warmth and charm which lights her inwardly with altar candles. She remains by the
table, picks up a piece from the glass menagerie collection, and turns it in her hands to
cover her tumult.*

JIM [*after several reflective puffs on his cigarette*]   What have you done since high
school?

She seems not to hear him.

Huh?

[*Laura looks up.*]

I said what have you done since high school, Laura?

LAURA Nothing much.

JIM You must have been doing something these six long years.

LAURA Yes.

JIM Well, then, such as what?

LAURA I took a business course at business college—

JIM   How did that work out?

LAURA   Well, not very—well—I had to drop out, it gave me—indigestion—

Jim laughs gently.

JIM   What are you doing now?

LAURA   I don't do anything—much. Oh, please don't think I sit around doing nothing! My glass collection takes up a good deal of time. Glass is something you have to take good care of.

JIM   What did you say—about glass?

LAURA   Collection I said—I have one— [*She clears her throat and turns away again, acutely shy.*]

JIM   [*abruptly*]   You know what I judge to be the trouble with you? Inferiority complex! Know what that is? That's what they call it when someone low-rates himself! I understand it because I had it, too. Although my case was not so aggravated as yours seems to be. I had it until I took up public speaking, developed my voice, and learned that I had an aptitude for science. Before that time I never thought of myself as being outstanding in any way whatsoever! Now I've never made a regular study of it, but I have a friend who says I can analyze people better than doctors that make a profession of it. I don't claim that to be necessarily true, but I can sure guess a person's psychology, Laura! [*He takes out his gum.*]   Excuse me, Laura. I always take it out when the flavor is gone. I'll use this scrap of paper to wrap it in. I know how it is to get it stuck on a shoe. [*He wraps the gum in paper and puts it in his pocket.*]   Yep—that's what I judge to be your principal trouble. A lack of confidence in yourself as a person. You don't have the proper amount of faith in yourself. I'm basing that fact on a number of your remarks and also on certain observations I've made. For instance that clumping you thought was so awful in high school. You say that you even dreaded to walk into class. You see what you did? You dropped out of school, you gave up an education because of a clump, which as far as I know was practically non-existent! A little physical defect is what you have. Hardly noticeable even! Magnified thousands of times by imagination! You know what my strong advice to you is? Think of yourself as *superior* in some way!

LAURA   In what way would I think?

JIM   Why, man alive, Laura! Just look about you a little. What do you see? A world full of common people! All of 'em born and all of 'em going to die! Which of them has one-tenth of your good points! Or mine! Or anyone else's, as far as that goes—gosh! Everybody excels in some one thing. Some in many! [*He unconsciously glances at himself in the mirror.*]   All you've got to do is discover in *what*! Take me, for instance. [*He adjusts his tie at the mirror.*]   My interest happens to lie in electro-dynamics. I'm taking a course in radio engineering at night school, Laura, on top of a fairly responsible job at the warehouse. I'm taking that course and studying public speaking.

LAURA   Ohhhh.

JIM   Because I believe in the future of television! [*turning his back to her.*]   I wish to be ready to go up right along with it. Therefore I'm planning to get in on the ground floor. In fact I've already made the right connections and all that remains is for the industry itself to get under way! full steam—[*His eyes are starry.*]   Knowledge—Zzzzzp! Money—Zzzzzp!—Power! That's the cycle democracy is built on!

His attitude is convincingly dynamic. Laura stares at him, even her shyness eclipsed in her absolute wonder. He suddenly grins.

I guess you think I think a lot of myself!

LAURA   No—o-o-o, I—

JIM   Now how about you? Isn't there something you take more interest in than anything else?

LAURA   Well, I do—as I said—have my—glass collection—

A peal of girlish laughter rings from the kitchenette.

JIM   I'm not right sure I know what you're talking about. What kind of glass is it?

LAURA   Little articles of it, they're ornaments mostly! Most of them are little animals made out of glass, the tiniest little animals in the world. Mother calls them a glass menagerie! Here's an example of one, if you'd like to see it! This one is one of the oldest. It's nearly thirteen.

Music: "The Glass Menagerie."

He stretches out his hand.

Oh, be careful—if you breathe, it breaks!

JIM   I'd better not take it. I'm pretty clumsy with things.

LAURA   Go on, I trust you with him! [*She places the piece in his palm.*]   There now—you're holding him gently! Hold him over the light, he loves the light! You see how the light shines through him?

JIM   It sure does shine!

LAURA   I shouldn't be partial, but he is my favorite one.

JIM   What kind of a thing is this one supposed to be?

LAURA   Haven't you noticed the single horn on his forehead?

JIM   A unicorn, huh?

LAURA   Mmmm-hmmm!

JIM   Unicorns—aren't they extinct in the modern world?

LAURA   I know!

JIM   Poor little fellow, he must feel sort of lonesome.

LAURA   [*smiling*]   Well, if he does, he doesn't complain about it. He stays on a shelf with some horses that don't have horns and all of them seem to get along nicely together.

JIM   How do you know?

LAURA   [*lightly*]   I haven't heard any arguments among them!

JIM   [*grinning*]   No arguments, huh? Well, that's a pretty good sign! Where shall I set him?

LAURA   Put him on the table. They all like a change of scenery once in a while!

JIM   Well, well, well, well— [*He places the glass piece on the table, then raises his arms and stretches.*]   Look how big my shadow is when I stretch!

LAURA   Oh, oh, yes—it stretches across the ceiling!

JIM   [*crossing to the door*]   I think it's stopped raining. [*He opens the fire-escape door and the background music changes to a dance tune.*]   Where does the music come from?

LAURA   From the Paradise Dance Hall across the alley.

JIM   How about cutting the rug a little, Miss Wingfield?

LAURA   Oh, I—

JIM   Or is your program filled up? Let me have a look at it. [*He grasps an imaginary card.*]   Why, every dance is taken! I'll just have to scratch some out.

[*Waltz music:* "La Golondrina."]

Ahhh, a waltz! [*He executes some sweeping turns by himself, then holds his arms toward Laura.*]

LAURA   [*breathlessly*]   I—can't dance!

JIM   There you go, that inferiority stuff!

LAURA   I've never danced in my life!

JIM   Come on, try!

LAURA   Oh, but I'd step on you!

JIM   I'm not made out of glass.

LAURA   How—how—how do we start?

JIM   Just leave it to me. You hold your arms out a little.

LAURA   Like this?

JIM   [*taking her in his arms*]   A little bit higher. Right. Now don't tighten up, that's the main thing about it—relax.

LAURA   [*laughing breathlessly*]   It's hard not to.

JIM   Okay.

LAURA   I'm afraid you can't budge me.

JIM   What do you bet I can't? [*He swings her into motion.*]

LAURA   Goodness, yes, you can!

JIM   Let yourself go, now, Laura, just let yourself go.

LAURA   I'm—

JIM   Come on!

LAURA   —trying!

JIM   Not so stiff—easy does it!

LAURA   I know but I'm—

JIM   Loosen th' backbone! There now, that's a lot better.

LAURA   Am I?

JIM   Lots, lots better! [*He moves her about the room in a clumsy waltz.*]
LAURA   Oh, my!
JIM   Ha-ha!
LAURA   Oh, my goodness!
JIM   Ha-ha-ha!

They suddenly bump into the table, and the glass piece on it falls to the floor. Jim stops the dance.

What did we hit on?
LAURA   Table.
JIM   Did something fall off it? I think—
LAURA   Yes.
JIM   I hope that it wasn't the little glass horse with the horn!
LAURA   Yes. [*She stoops to pick it up.*]
JIM   Aw, aw, aw. Is it broken?
LAURA   Now it is just like all the other horses.
JIM   It's lost its—
LAURA   Horn! It doesn't matter. Maybe it's a blessing in disguise.
JIM   You'll never forgive me. I bet that that was your favorite piece of glass.
LAURA   I don't have favorites much. It's no tragedy, Freckles. Glass breaks so easily. No matter how careful you are. The traffic jars the shelves and things fall off them.
JIM   Still I'm awfully sorry that I was the cause.
LAURA   [*smiling*] I'll just imagine he had an operation. The horn was removed to make him feel less—freakish!

They both laugh.

Now he will feel more at home with the other horses, the ones that don't have horns. . . .
JIM   Ha-ha, that's very funny! [*Suddenly he is serious.*] I'm glad to see that you have a sense of humor. You know—you're—well—very different! Surprisingly different from anyone else I know! [*His voice becomes soft and hesitant with a genuine feeling.*]   Do you mind me telling you that?

Laura is abashed beyond speech.

I mean it in a nice way—

Laura nods shyly, looking away.

You make me feel sort of—I don't know how to put it! I'm usually pretty good at expressing things, but—this is something that I don't know how to say!

Laura touches her throat and clears it—turns the broken unicorn in her hands. His voice becomes softer.

Has anyone ever told you that you were pretty?

There is a pause, and the music rises slightly. Laura looks up slowly, with wonder, and shakes her head.

Well, you are! In a very different way from anyone else. And all the nicer because of the difference, too.

His voice becomes low and husky. Laura turns away, nearly faint with the novelty of her emotions.

I wish that you were my sister. I'd teach you to have some confidence in yourself. The different people are not like other people, but being different is nothing to be ashamed of. Because other people are not such wonderful people. They're one hundred times one thousand. You're one times one! They walk all over the earth. You just stay here. They're common as—weeds, but—you—well, you're—*Blue Roses!*

[*Image on screen:* Blue Roses.]

The music changes.

LAURA   But blue is wrong for—roses. . . .
JIM   It's right for you! You're—pretty!
LAURA   In what respect am I pretty?
JIM   In all respects—believe me! Your eyes—your hair—are pretty! Your hands are pretty! [*He catches hold of her hand.*] You think I'm making this up because I'm invited to dinner and have to be nice. Oh, I could do that! I could put on an act for you, Laura, and say lots of things without being very sincere. But this time I am. I'm talking to you sincerely. I happened to notice you had this inferiority complex that keeps you from feeling comfortable with people. Somebody needs to build your confidence up and make you proud instead of shy and turning away and—blushing. Somebody—ought to—*kiss* you, Laura!

His hand slips slowly up her arm to her shoulder as the music swells tumultuously. He suddenly turns her about and kisses her on the lips. When he releases her, Laura sinks on the sofa with a bright, dazed look. Jim backs away and fishes in his pocket for a cigarette.

[*Legend on screen:* "A souvenir."]

Stumblejohn!

He lights the cigarette, avoiding her look. There is a peal of girlish laughter from Amanda in the kitchenette. Laura slowly raises and opens her hand. It still contains the little broken glass animal. She looks at it with a tender, bewildered expression.

Stumblejohn! I shouldn't have done that—that was way off the beam. You don't smoke, do you?

She looks up, smiling, not hearing the question. He sits beside her rather gingerly. She looks at him speechlessly—waiting. He coughs decorously and moves a little farther aside as he considers the situation and senses her feelings, dimly, with perturbation. He speaks gently.

Would you—care for a—mint?

She doesn't seem to hear him but her look grows brighter even.

Peppermint? Life Saver? My pocket's a regular drugstore—wherever I go. . . . [*He pops a mint in his mouth. Then he gulps and decides to make a clean breast of it. He speaks slowly and gingerly.*]   Laura, you know, if I had a sister like you, I'd do the same thing as Tom. I'd bring out fellows and—introduce her to them. The right type of boys—of a type to—appreciate her. Only —well—he made a mistake about me. Maybe I've got no call to be saying this. That may not have been the idea in having me over. But what if it was? There's nothing wrong about that. The only trouble is that in my case—I'm not in a situation to—do the right thing. I can't take down your number and say I'll phone. I can't call up next week and—ask for a date. I thought I had better explain the situation in case you—misunderstood it and—I hurt your feelings. . . .

There is a pause. Slowly, very slowly, Laura's look changes, her eyes returning slowly from his to the glass figure in her palm. Amanda utters another gay laugh in the kitchenette.

LAURA   [*faintly*]   You—won't—call again?

JIM   No, Laura, I can't. [*He rises from the sofa.*]   As I was just explaining, I've—got strings on me. Laura, I've—been going steady! I go out all the time with a girl named Betty. She's a home-girl like you, and Catholic, and Irish, and in a great many ways we—get along fine. I met her last summer on a moonlight boat trip up the river to Alton, on the *Majestic*. Well—right away from the start it was—love!

[*Legend:* Love!]

Laura sways slightly forward and grips the arm of sofa. He fails to notice, now enrapt in his own comfortable being.

Being in love has made a new man of me!

Leaning stiffly forward, clutching the arm of the sofa, Laura struggles visibly with her storm. But Jim is oblivious; she is a long way off.

The power of love is really pretty tremendous! Love is something that —changes the whole world, Laura!

The storm abates a little and Laura leans back. He notices her again.

It happened that Betty's aunt took sick, she got a wire and had to go to Centralia. So Tom—when he asked me to dinner—I naturally just accepted the invitation, not knowing that you—that he—that I— [*He stops awkwardly.*]   Huh—I'm a stumblejohn!

He flops back on the sofa. The holy candles on the altar of Laura's face have been snuffed out. There is a look of almost infinite desolation. Jim glances at her uneasily.

I wish that you would—say something.

She bites her lip which was trembling and then bravely smiles. She opens her hand again on the broken glass figure. Then she gently takes his hand and raises it level with her own. She carefully places the unicorn in the palm of his hand, then pushes his fingers closed upon it.

What are you—doing that for? You want me to have him? Laura?

She nods.

What for?
LAURA   A—souvenir. . . .

She rises unsteadily and crouches beside the Victrola to wind it up.

[*Legend on screen:* "Things have a way of turning out so badly!" *Or image:* "Gentleman caller waving goodbye—gaily."]

At this moment Amanda rushes brightly back into the living room. She bears a pitcher of fruit punch in an old-fashioned cut-glass pitcher, and a plate of macaroons. The plate has a gold border and poppies painted on it.

AMANDA   Well, well, well! Isn't the air delightful after the shower? I've made you children a little liquid refreshment.

[*She turns gaily to Jim.*]   Jim, do you know that song about lemonade?

"Lemonade, lemonade

Made in the shade and stirred with a spade—
Good enough for any old maid!''

JIM [*uneasily*] Ha-ha! No—I never heard it.

AMANDA Why, Laura! You look so serious!

JIM We were having a serious conversation.

AMANDA Good! Now you're better acquainted!

JIM [*uncertainly*] Ha-ha! Yes.

AMANDA You modern young people are much more serious-minded than my generation. I was so gay as a girl!

JIM You haven't changed, Mrs. Wingfield.

AMANDA Tonight I'm rejuvenated! The gaiety of the occasion, Mr. O'Connor! [*She tosses her head with a peal of laughter, spilling some lemonade.*] Oooo! I'm baptizing myself!

JIM Here—let me—

AMANDA [*setting the pitcher down*] There now. I discovered we had some maraschino cherries. I dumped them in, juice and all!

JIM You shouldn't have gone to that trouble, Mrs. Wingfield.

AMANDA Trouble, trouble? Why, it was loads of fun! Didn't you hear me cutting up in the kitchen? I bet your ears were burning! I told Tom how outdone with him I was for keeping you to himself so long a time! He should have brought you over much, much sooner! Well, now that you've found your way, I want you to be a very frequent caller! Not just occasional but all the time. Oh, we're going to have a lot of gay times together! I see them coming! Mmmm, just breathe that air! So fresh, and the moon's so pretty! I'll skip back out—I know where my place is when young folks are having a—serious conversation!

JIM Oh, don't go out, Mrs. Wingfield. The fact of the matter is I've got to be going.

AMANDA Going, now? You're joking! Why, it's only the shank of the evening, Mr. O'Connor!

JIM Well, you know how it is.

AMANDA You mean you're a young workingman and have to keep workingmen's hours. We'll let you off early tonight. But only on the condition that next time you stay later. What's the best night for you? Isn't Saturday night the best night for you workingmen?

JIM I have a couple of time-clocks to punch, Mrs. Wingfield. One at morning, another one at night!

AMANDA My, but you *are* ambitious! You work at night, too?

JIM No, Ma'am, not work but—Betty!

He crosses deliberately to pick up his hat. The band at the Paradise Dance Hall goes into a tender waltz.

AMANDA Betty? Betty? Who's—Betty!

There is an ominous cracking sound in the sky.

JIM   Oh, just a girl. The girl I go steady with!

He smiles charmingly. The sky falls.

[*Legend:* "The Sky Falls."]

AMANDA   [*a long-drawn exhalation*]   Ohhhh . . . Is it a serious romance, Mr. O'Connor?

JIM   We're going to be married the second Sunday in June.

AMANDA   Ohhhh—how nice! Tom didn't mention that you were engaged to be married.

JIM   The cat's not out of the bag at the warehouse yet. You know how they are. They call you Romeo and stuff like that. [*He stops at the oval mirror to put on his hat. He carefully shapes the brim and the crown to give a discreetly dashing effect.*]   It's been a wonderful evening, Mrs. Wingfield. I guess this is what they mean by Southern hospitality.

AMANDA   It really wasn't anything at all.

JIM   I hope it don't seem like I'm rushing off. But I promised Betty I'd pick her up at the Wabash depot, an' by the time I get my jalopy down there her train'll be in. Some women are pretty upset if you keep 'em waiting.

AMANDA   Yes, I know—the tyranny of women! [*She extends her hand.*]   Good-bye, Mr. O'Connor. I wish you luck—and happiness—and success! All three of them, and so does Laura! Don't you, Laura?

LAURA   Yes!

JIM   [*taking Laura's hand*]   Goodbye, Laura. I'm certainly going to treasure that souvenir. And don't you forget the good advice I gave you. [*He raises his voice to a cheery shout.*]   So long, Shakespeare! Thanks again, ladies. Good night!

He grins and ducks jauntily out. Still bravely grimacing, Amanda closes the door on the gentleman caller. Then she turns back to the room with a puzzled expression. She and Laura don't dare to face each other. Laura crouches beside the Victrola to wind it.

AMANDA   [*faintly*]   Things have a way of turning out so badly. I don't believe that I would play the Victrola. Well, well—well! Our gentleman caller was engaged to be married! [*She raises her voice.*]   Tom!

TOM   [*from the kitchenette*]   Yes, Mother?

AMANDA   Come in here a minute. I want to tell you something awfully funny.

TOM   [*entering with a macaroon and a glass of the lemonade*]   Has the gentleman caller gotten away already?

AMANDA   The gentleman caller has made an early departure. What a wonderful joke you played on us!

TOM   How do you mean?

AMANDA   You didn't mention that he was engaged to be married.

TOM   Jim? Engaged?

AMANDA   That's what he just informed us.

TOM   I'll be jiggered! I didn't know about that.

AMANDA   That seems very peculiar.

TOM   What's peculiar about it?

AMANDA   Didn't you call him your best friend down at the warehouse?

TOM   He is, but how did I know?

AMANDA   It seems extremely peculiar that you wouldn't know your best friend was going to be married!

TOM   The warehouse is where I work, not where I know things about people!

AMANDA   You don't know things anywhere! You live in a dream; you manufacture illusions!

He crosses to the door.

    Where are you going?

TOM   I'm going to the movies.

AMANDA   That's right, now that you've had us make such fools of ourselves. The effort, the preparations, all the expense! The new floor lamp, the rug, the clothes for Laura! All for what? To entertain some other girl's fiancé! Go to the movies, go! Don't think about us, a mother deserted, an unmarried sister who's crippled and has no job! Don't let anything interfere with your selfish pleasure! Just go, go, go—to the movies!

TOM   All right, I will! The more you shout about my selfishness to me the quicker I'll go, and I won't go to the movies!

AMANDA   Go, then! Go to the moon—you selfish dreamer!

Tom smashes his glass on the floor. He plunges out on the fire escape, slamming the door. Laura screams in fright. The dance-hall music becomes louder. Tom stands on the fire escape, gripping the rail. The moon breaks through the storm clouds, illuminating his face.

[*Legend on screen:* "And so goodbye . . ."]

Tom's closing speech is timed with what is happening inside the house. We see, as though through soundproof glass, that Amanda appears to be making a comforting speech to Laura, who is huddled upon the sofa. Now that we cannot hear the mother's speech, her silliness is gone and she has dignity and tragic beauty. Laura's hair hides her face until, at the end of the speech, she lifts her head to smile at her mother. Amanda's gestures are slow and graceful, almost dancelike, as she comforts her daughter. At the end of her speech she glances a moment at the father's picture—then withdraws through the portieres. At the close of Tom's speech, Laura blows out the candles, ending the play.

TOM   I didn't go to the moon, I went much further—for time is the longest distance between two places. Not long after that I was fired for writing a poem on the lid of a shoe-box. I left Saint Louis. I descended the steps of this fire escape for a last time and followed, from then on, in my father's footsteps, attempting to find in motion what was lost in space. I traveled around a great deal. The cities swept about me like dead leaves, leaves that were brightly colored but torn away from the branches. I would have stopped, but I was pursued by something. It always came upon me unawares, taking me altogether by surprise. Perhaps it was a familiar bit of music. Perhaps it was only a piece of transparent glass. Perhaps I am walking along a street at night, in some strange city, before I have found companions. I pass the lighted window of a shop where perfume is sold. The window is filled with pieces of colored glass, tiny transparent bottles in delicate colors, like bits of a shattered rainbow. Then all at once my sister touches my shoulder. I turn around and look into her eyes. Oh, Laura, Laura, I tried to leave you behind me, but I am more faithful than I intended to be! I reach for a cigarette, I cross the street, I run into the movies or a bar, I buy a drink, I speak to the nearest stranger—anything that can blow your candles out!

Laura bends over the candles.

For nowadays the world is lit by lightning! Blow out your candles, Laura— and so goodbye. . . .

She blows the candles out.

EDWARD ALBEE
1928–

Born in Washington, D.C., he attended a series of private schools before graduating from Choate School in Wallingford, Connecticut. He went to Trinity College, Hartford, for eighteen months, then moved to New York City, which became his home. His grim yet frequently humorous plays, usually classified as theater of the absurd, strip their characters of their pretense and hypocrisy and force them to confront less pleasant aspects of their lives. *Who's Afraid of Virginia Woolf?* (1962) remains the most successful of his more than twenty plays. *The Zoo Story*, his first produced play, had its premiere at the Schiller Theater Werkstatt in Berlin on September 28, 1959. It received its first American production four months later at the Provincetown Playhouse in New York City, on a double bill with Samuel Beckett's *Krapp's Last Tape*.

The Zoo Story

PLAYERS

PETER, *a man in his early forties, neither fat nor gaunt, neither handsome nor homely. He wears tweeds, smokes a pipe, carries horn-rimmed glasses. Although he is moving into middle age, his dress and his manner would suggest a man younger.*

JERRY, *a man in his late thirties, not poorly dressed, but carelessly. What was once a trim and lightly muscled body has begun to go to fat; and while he is no longer handsome, it is evident that he once was. His fall from physical grace should not suggest debauchery; he has, to come closest to it, a great weariness.*

SCENE. *It is Central Park; a Sunday afternoon in summer; the present. There are two park benches, one toward either side of the stage; they both face the audience. Behind them: foliage, trees, sky. At the beginning, Peter is seated on one of the benches.*

(*As the curtain rises, Peter is seated on the bench stage-right. He is reading a book. He stops reading, cleans his glasses, goes back to reading. Jerry enters.*)

JERRY   I've been to the zoo. [*Peter doesn't notice.*] I said, I've been to the zoo. MISTER, I'VE BEEN TO THE ZOO!
PETER   Hm? . . . What? . . . I'm sorry, were you talking to me?
JERRY   I went to the zoo, and then I walked until I came here. Have I been walking north?
PETER   [*puzzled*] North? Why . . . I . . . I think so. Let me see.
JERRY   [*pointing past the audience*] Is that Fifth Avenue?
PETER   Why yes; yes, it is.
JERRY   And what is that cross street there; that one, to the right?
PETER   That? Oh, that's Seventy-fourth Street.
JERRY   And the zoo is around Sixty-fifth Street; so, I've been walking north.
PETER   [*anxious to get back to his reading*] Yes; it would seem so.
JERRY   Good old north.
PETER   [*lightly, by reflex*] Ha, ha.
JERRY   [*after a slight pause*] But not due north.
PETER   I . . . well, no, not due north; but, we . . . call it north. It's northerly.
JERRY   [*Watches as Peter, anxious to dismiss him, prepares his pipe.*] Well, boy; *you're* not going to get lung cancer, are you?

PETER [*Looks up, a little annoyed, then smiles.*] No, sir. Not from this.

JERRY No, sir. What you'll probably get is cancer of the mouth, and then you'll have to wear one of those things Freud wore after they took one whole side of his jaw away. What do they call those things?

PETER [*uncomfortable*] A prosthesis?

JERRY The very thing! A prosthesis. You're an educated man, aren't you? Are you a doctor?

PETER Oh, no; no. I read about it somewhere; *Time* magazine, I think. [*He turns to his book.*]

JERRY Well, *Time* magazine isn't for blockheads.

PETER No, I suppose not.

JERRY [*after a pause*] Boy, I'm glad that's Fifth Avenue there.

PETER [*vaguely*] Yes.

JERRY I don't like the west side of the park much.

PETER Oh? [*Then, slightly wary, but interested*] Why?

JERRY [*offhand*] I don't know.

PETER Oh. [*He returns to his book.*]

JERRY [*He stands for a few seconds, looking at Peter, who finally looks up again, puzzled.*] Do you mind if we talk?

PETER [*obviously minding*] Why . . . no, no.

JERRY Yes you do; you do.

PETER [*Puts his book down, his pipe out and away, smiling.*] No, really, I don't mind.

JERRY Yes you do.

PETER [*finally decided*] No; I don't mind at all, really.

JERRY It's . . . it's a nice day.

PETER [*Stares unnecessarily at the sky.*] Yes. Yes, it is; lovely.

JERRY I've been to the zoo.

PETER Yes, I think you said so . . . didn't you?

JERRY You'll read about it in the papers tomorrow, if you don't see it on your TV tonight. You have TV, haven't you?

PETER Why yes, we have two; one for the children.

JERRY You're married!

PETER [*with pleased emphasis*] Why, certainly.

JERRY It isn't a law, for God's sake.

PETER No . . . no, of course not.

JERRY And you have a wife.

PETER [*bewildered by the seeming lack of communication*] Yes!

JERRY And you have children.

PETER Yes; two.

JERRY Boys?

PETER No, girls . . . both girls.

JERRY But you wanted boys.

PETER Well . . . naturally, every man wants a son, but . . .

JERRY [*lightly mocking*] But that's the way the cookie crumbles?

PETER [*annoyed*] I wasn't going to say that.

JERRY And you're not going to have any more kids, are you?

PETER [*a bit distantly*] No. No more. [*Then back, and irksome*] Why did you say that? How would you know about that?

JERRY The way you cross your legs, perhaps; something in the voice. Or maybe I'm just guessing. Is it your wife?

PETER [*furious*] That's none of your business! [*A silence.*] Do you understand? [*Jerry nods. Peter is quiet now.*] Well, you're right. We'll have no more children.

JERRY [*softly*] That *is* the way the cookie crumbles.

PETER [*forgiving*] Yes . . . I guess so.

JERRY Well, now; what else?

PETER What were you saying about the zoo . . . that I'd read about it, or see . . . ?

JERRY I'll tell you about it, soon. Do you mind if I ask you questions?

PETER Oh, not really.

JERRY I'll tell you why I do it; I don't talk to many people—except to say like: give me a beer, or where's the john, or·what time does the feature go on, or keep your hands to yourself, buddy. You know—things like that.

PETER I must say I don't . . .

JERRY But every once in a while I like to talk to somebody, really *talk*; like to get to know somebody, know all about him.

PETER [*lightly laughing, still a little uncomfortable*] And am I the guinea pig for today?

JERRY On a sun-drenched Sunday afternoon like this? Who better than a nice married man with two daughters and . . . uh . . . a dog? [*Peter shakes his head.*] No? Two dogs. [*Peter shakes his head again.*] Hm. No dogs? [*Peter shakes his head, sadly.*] Oh, that's a shame. But you look like an animal man. CATS? [*Peter nods his head, ruefully.*] Cats! But, that can't be your idea. No, sir. Your wife and daughters? [*Peter nods his head.*] Is there anything else I should know?

PETER [*He has to clear his throat.*] There are . . . there are two parakeets. One . . . uh . . . one for each of my daughters.

JERRY Birds.

PETER My daughters keep them in a cage in their bedroom.

JERRY Do they carry disease? The birds.

PETER I don't believe so.

JERRY That's too bad. If they did you could set them loose in the house and the cats could eat them and die, maybe. [*Peter looks blank for a moment, then laughs.*] And what else? What do you do to support your enormous household?

PETER   I . . . uh . . . I have an executive position with a . . . a small publishing house. We . . . uh . . . we publish textbooks.

JERRY   That sounds nice; very nice. What do you make?

PETER   [*still cheerful*] Now look here!

JERRY   Oh, come on.

PETER   Well, I make around eighteen thousand a year, but I don't carry more than forty dollars at any one time . . . in case you're a . . . a holdup man . . . ha, ha, ha.

JERRY   [*ignoring the above*] Where do you live? [*Peter is reluctant.*] Oh, look; I'm not going to rob you, and I'm not going to kidnap your parakeets, your cats, or your daughters.

PETER   [*too loud*] I live between Lexington and Third Avenue, on Seventy-fourth Street.

JERRY   That wasn't so hard, was it?

PETER   I didn't mean to seem . . . ah . . . it's that you don't really carry on a conversation; you just ask questions. And I'm . . . I'm normally . . . uh . . . reticent. Why do you just stand there?

JERRY   I'll start walking around in a little while, and eventually I'll sit down. [*Recalling*] Wait until you see the expression on his face.

PETER   What? Whose face? Look here; is this something about the zoo?

JERRY   [*distantly*] The what?

PETER   The zoo; the zoo. Something about the zoo.

JERRY   The zoo?

PETER   You've mentioned it several times.

JERRY   [*still distant, but returning abruptly*] The zoo. Oh, yes; the zoo. I was there before I came here. I told you that. Say, what's the dividing line between upper-middle-middle-class and lower-upper-middle-class?

PETER   My dear fellow, I . . .

JERRY   Don't my dear fellow me.

PETER   [*unhappily*] Was I patronizing? I believe I was; I'm sorry. But you see, your question about the classes bewildered me.

JERRY   And when you're bewildered you become patronizing?

PETER   I . . . I don't express myself too well, sometimes. [*He attempts a joke on himself.*] I'm in publishing, not writing.

JERRY   [*amused, but not at the humor*] So be it. The truth *is*: I was being patronizing.

PETER   Oh, now; you needn't say that. [*It is at this point that Jerry may begin to move about the stage with slowly increasing determination and authority, but pacing himself, so that the long speech about the dog comes at the high point of the arc.*]

JERRY   All right. Who are your favorite writers? Baudelaire and J.P. Marquand?

PETER   [*wary*] Well, I like a great many writers; I have a considerable

. . . catholicity of taste, if I may say so. Those two men are fine, each in his way. [*Warming up*] Baudelaire, of course . . . uh . . . is by far the finer of the two, but Marquand has a place . . . in our . . . uh . . . national . . .

JERRY   Skip it.

PETER   I . . . sorry.

JERRY   Do you know what I did before I went to the zoo today? I walked all the way up Fifth Avenue from Washington Square; all the way.

PETER   Oh; you live in the Village! [*This seems to enlighten Peter.*]

JERRY   No, I don't. I took the subway down to the Village so I could walk all the way up Fifth Avenue to the zoo. It's one of those things a person has to do; sometimes a person has to go a very long distance out of his way to come back a short distance correctly.

PETER   [*almost pouting*] Oh, I thought you lived in the Village.

JERRY   What were you trying to do? Make sense out of things? Bring order? The old pigeonhole bit? Well, that's easy; I'll tell you. I live in a four-story brownstone rooming-house on the upper West Side between Columbus Avenue and Central Park West. I live on the top floor; rear; west. It's a laughably small room, and one of my walls is made of beaverboard; this beaverboard separates my room from another laughably small room, so I assume that the two rooms were once one room, a small room, but not necessarily laughable. The room beyond my beaverboard wall is occupied by a colored queen who always keeps his door open; well, not always but *always* when he's plucking his eyebrows, which he does with Buddhist concentration. This colored queen has rotten teeth, which is rare, and he has a Japanese kimono, which is also pretty rare; and he wears this kimono to and from the john in the hall, which is pretty frequent. I mean, he goes to the john a lot. He never bothers me, and he never brings anyone up to his room. All he does is pluck his eyebrows, wear his kimono and go to the john. Now, the two front rooms on my floor are a little larger, I guess; but they're pretty small, too. There's a Puerto Rican family in one of them, a husband, a wife, and some kids; I don't know how many. These people entertain a lot. And in the other front room, there's somebody living there, but I don't know who it is. I've never seen who it is. Never. Never ever.

PETER   [*embarrassed*] Why . . . why do you live there?

JERRY   [*from a distance again*] I don't know.

PETER   It doesn't sound like a very nice place . . . where you live.

JERRY   Well, no; it isn't an apartment in the East Seventies. But, then again, I don't have one wife, two daughters, two cats and two parakeets. What I do have, I have toilet articles, a few clothes, a hot plate that I'm not supposed to have, a can opener, one that works with a key, you know; a knife, two forks, and two spoons, one small, one large; three plates, a cup, a saucer, a drinking glass, two picture frames, both empty, eight or nine books, a pack of pornographic playing cards, regular deck, an old Western Union typewriter that prints nothing but capital letters, and a small strongbox without a lock which has in it . . . what? Rocks! Some rocks . . . sea-rounded rocks I picked up on the beach when I was a kid. Under which . . . weighed down . . . are some letters . . . please letters . . . please why don't you do this, and please when will you do that letters. And when letters, too. When will you write? When will you come? When? These letters are from more recent years.

PETER   [Stares glumly at his shoes, then] About those two empty picture frames . . . ?

JERRY   I don't see why they need any explanation at all. Isn't it clear? I don't have pictures of anyone to put in them.

PETER   Your parents . . . perhaps . . . a girl friend . . .

JERRY   You're a very sweet man, and you're possessed of a truly enviable innocence. But good old Mom and good old Pop are dead . . . you know? . . . I'm broken up about it, too . . . I mean really. BUT. That particular vaudeville act is playing the cloud circuit now, so I don't see how I can look at them, all neat and framed. Besides, or, rather, to be pointed about it, good old Mom walked out on good old Pop when I was ten and a half years old; she embarked on an adulterous turn of our southern states . . . a journey of a year's duration . . . and her most constant companion . . . among others, among many others . . . was a Mr. Barleycorn. At least, that's what good old Pop told me after he went down . . . came back . . . brought her body north. We'd received the news between Christmas and New Year's, you see, that good old Mom had parted with the ghost in some dump in Alabama. And, without the ghost . . . she was less welcome. I mean, what was she? A stiff . . . a northern stiff. At any rate, good old Pop celebrated the New Year for an even two weeks and then slapped into the front of a somewhat moving city omnibus, which sort of cleaned things out family-wise. Well no; then there was Mom's sister, who was given neither to sin nor the consolations of the bottle. I moved in on her, and my memory of her is slight excepting I remember still that she did all things dourly: sleeping, eating, working, praying. She dropped dead on the stairs to her apartment, my apartment then, too, on the afternoon of my high school graduation. A terribly middle-European joke, if you ask me.

PETER   Oh, my; oh, my.

JERRY   Oh, your what? But that was a long time ago, and I have no feeling about any of it that I care to admit to myself. Perhaps you can see, though, why good old Mom and good old Pop are frameless. What's your name? Your first name?

PETER   I'm Peter.

JERRY   I'd forgotten to ask you. I'm Jerry.

PETER   [*with a slight, nervous laugh*] Hello, Jerry.

PETER   [*Nods his hello.*] And let's see now; what's the point of having a girl's picture, especially in two frames? I have two picture frames, you remember. I never see the pretty little ladies more than once, and most of them wouldn't be caught in the same room with a camera. It's odd, and I wonder if it's sad.

PETER   The girls?

JERRY   No. I wonder if it's sad that I never see the little ladies more than once. I've never been able to have sex with, or, how is it put? . . . make love to anybody more than once. Once; that's it. . . . Oh, wait; for a week and a half, when I was fifteen . . . and I hang my head in shame that puberty was late . . . I was a h-o-m-o-s-e-x-u-a-l. I mean, I was queer . . . [*very fast*] . . . queer, queer, queer . . . with bells ringing, banners snapping in the wind. And for those eleven days, I met at least twice a day with the park superintendent's son . . . a Greek boy, whose birthday was the same as mine, except he was a year older. I think I was very much in love . . . maybe just with sex. But that was the jazz of a very special hotel, wasn't it? And now; oh, do I love the little ladies; really, I love them. For about an hour.

PETER   Well, it seems perfectly simple to me. . . .

JERRY   [*angry*] Look! Are you going to tell me to get married and have parakeets?

PETER   [*angry himself*] Forget the parakeets! And stay single if you want to. It's no business of mine. I didn't start this conversation in the . . .

JERRY   All right, all right. I'm sorry. All right? You're not angry?

PETER   [*laughing*] No, I'm not angry.

JERRY   [*relieved*] Good. [*Now back to his previous tone*] Interesting that you asked me about the picture frames. I would have thought that you would have asked me about the pornographic playing cards.

PETER   [*with a knowing smile*] Oh, I've seen those cards.

JERRY   That's not the point. [*Laughs.*] I suppose when you were a kid you and your pals passed them around, or you had a pack of your own.

PETER   Well, I guess a lot of us did.

JERRY   And you threw them away just before you got married.

PETER   Oh, now; look here. I didn't *need* anything like that when I got older.

JERRY   No?

PETER   [*embarrassed*] I'd rather not talk about these things.

JERRY   So? Don't. Besides, I wasn't trying to plumb your post-adolescent sexual life and hard times; what I wanted to get at is the value difference between pornographic playing cards when you're a kid, and pornographic playing cards when you're older. It's that when you're a kid you use the cards as a substitute for a real experience, and when you're older you use real experience as a substitute for the fantasy. But I imagine you'd rather hear about what happened at the zoo.

PETER   [*enthusiastic*] Oh, yes; the zoo. [*Then, awkward*] That is . . . if you . . .

JERRY   Let me tell you about why I went . . . well, let me tell you some things. I've told you about the fourth floor of the rooming-house where I live. I think the rooms are better as you go down, floor by floor. I guess they are; I don't know. I don't know any of the people on the third and second floors. Oh, wait! I do know that there's a lady living on the third floor, in the front. I know because she cries all the time. Whenever I go out or come back in, whenever I pass her door, I always hear her crying, muffled, but . . . very determined. Very determined indeed. But the one I'm getting to, and all about the dog, is the landlady. I don't like to use words that are too harsh in describing people. I don't like to. But the landlady is a fat, ugly, mean, stupid, unwashed, misanthropic, cheap, drunken bag of garbage. And you may have noticed that I very seldom use profanity, so I can't describe her as well as I might.

PETER   You describe her . . . vividly.

JERRY   Well, thanks. Anyway, she has a dog, and I will tell you about the dog, and she and her dog are the gatekeepers of my dwelling. The woman is bad enough; she leans around in the entrance hall, spying to see that I don't bring in things or people, and when she's had her midafternoon pint of lemon-flavored gin she always stops me in the hall, and grabs ahold of my coat or my arm, and she presses her disgusting body up against me to keep me in a corner so she can talk to me. The smell of her body and her breath . . . you can't imagine it . . . and somewhere, somewhere in the back of that pea-sized brain of hers, an organ developed just enough to let her eat, drink, and emit, she has some foul parody of sexual desire. And I, Peter, I am the object of her sweaty lust.

PETER   That's disgusting. That's . . . horrible.

JERRY   But I have found a way to keep her off. When she talks to me, when she presses herself to my body and mumbles about her room and how I should come there, I merely say: but, Love; wasn't yesterday enough for you, and the day before? Then she puzzles,

she makes slits of her tiny eyes, she sways a little, and then, Peter
. . . and it is at this moment that I think I might be doing some
good in that tormented house . . . a simple-minded smile begins
to form on her unthinkable face, and she giggles and groans as
she thinks about yesterday and the day before; as she believes
and relives what never happened. Then, she motions to that black
monster of a dog she has, and she goes back to her room. And I
am safe until our next meeting.

PETER   It's so . . . unthinkable. I find it hard to believe that people
such as that really *are*.

JERRY   [*lightly mocking*] It's for reading about, isn't it?

PETER   [*seriously*] Yes.

JERRY   And fact is better left to fiction. You're right, Peter. Well, what
I have been meaning to tell you about is the dog; I shall, now.

PETER   [*nervously*] Oh, yes; the dog.

JERRY   Don't go. You're not thinking of going, are you?

PETER   Well . . . no, I don't think so.

JERRY   [*as if to a child*] Because after I tell you about the dog, do you
know what then? Then . . . then I'll tell you about what happened
at the zoo.

PETER   [*laughing faintly*] You're . . . you're full of stories, aren't you?

JERRY   You don't *have* to listen. Nobody is holding you here; remember
that. Keep that in your mind.

PETER   [*irritably*] I know that.

JERRY   You do? Good. [*The following long speech, it seems to me, should
be done with a great deal of action, to achieve a hypnotic effect on Peter,
and on the audience, too. Some specific actions have been suggested, but
the director and the actor playing Jerry might best work it out for themselves.*] ALL RIGHT. [*As if reading from a huge billboard*] THE STORY OF
JERRY AND THE DOG! [*Natural again*] What I am going to tell you has
something to do with how sometimes it's necessary to go a long
distance out of the way in order to come back a short distance
correctly; or, maybe I only think that it has something to do with
that. But, it's why I went to the zoo today, and why I walked
north . . . northerly, rather . . . until I came here. All right. The
dog, I think I told you, is a black monster of a beast: an oversized
head, tiny, tiny ears, and eyes . . . bloodshot, infected, maybe;
and a body you can see the ribs through the skin. The dog is
black, all black; all black except for the bloodshot eyes, and . . .
yes . . . and an open sore on its . . . *right* forepaw; that is red,
too. And, oh yes; the poor monster, and I do believe it's an old
dog . . . it's certainly a misused one . . . almost always has an
erection . . . of sorts. That's red, too. And . . . what else? . . .
oh, yes; there's a gray-yellow-white color, too, when he bares his

fangs. Like this: Grrrrrrr! Which is what he did when he saw me for the first time . . . the day I moved in. I worried about that animal the very first minute I met him. Now, animals don't take to me like Saint Francis had birds hanging off him all the time. What I mean is: animals are indifferent to me . . . like people [*He smiles slightly.*] . . . most of the time. But this dog wasn't indifferent. From the very beginning he'd snarl and then go for me, to get one of my legs. Not like he was rabid, you know; he was sort of a stumbly dog, but he wasn't half-assed, either. It was a good, stumbly run; but I always got away. He got a piece of my trouser leg, look, you can see right here, where it's mended; he got that the second day I lived there; but, I kicked free and got upstairs fast, so that was that. [*Puzzles.*] I still don't know to this day how the other roomers manage it, but you know what I *think*: I think it had to do only with me. Cozy. So. Anyway, this went on for over a week, whenever I came in; but never when I went out. That's funny. Or, it *was* funny. I could pack up and live in the street for all the dog cared. Well, I thought about it up in my room one day, one of the times after I'd bolted upstairs, and I made up my mind. I decided: First, I'll kill the dog with kindness, and if that doesn't work . . . I'll just kill him. [*Peter winces.*] Don't react, Peter; just listen. So, the next day I went out and bought a bag of hamburgers, medium rare, no catsup, no onion; and on the way home I threw away all the rolls and kept just the meat. [*Action for the following, perhaps.*] When I got back to the roominghouse the dog was waiting for me. I half opened the door that led into the entrance hall, and there he was; waiting for me. It figured. I went in, very cautiously, and I had the hamburgers, you remember; I opened the bag, and I set the meat down about twelve feet from where the dog was snarling at me. Like so! He snarled; stopped snarling; sniffed; moved slowly; then faster; then faster toward the meat. Well, when he got to it he stopped, and he looked at me. I smiled; but tentatively, you understand. He turned his face back to the hamburgers, smelled, sniffed some more, and then . . . RRRAAAA GGGGGHHHH, like that . . . he tore into them. It was as if he had never eaten anything in his life before, except like garbage. Which might very well have been the truth. I don't think the landlady ever eats anything but garbage. But. He ate all the hamburgers, almost all at once, making sounds in his throat like a woman. *Then*, when he'd finished the meat, the hamburger, and tried to eat the paper, too, he sat down and smiled. I think he smiled; I know cats do. It was a very gratifying few moments. Then BAM, he snarled and made for me again. He didn't get me this time, either. So, I got upstairs, and I lay down on my bed and started to think about the dog again. To be truthful, I was offended, and I was damn mad, too. It was six perfectly good hamburgers with not enough pork in them to make it disgusting. I was offended. But, after a while, I decided to try it for a few more days. If you think about it, this dog had what amounted to an antipathy toward me; really. And, I wondered if I mightn't overcome this antipathy. So, I tried it for five more days, but it was always the same: snarl; sniff; move; faster; stare; gobble; RAAGGGHHH; smile; snarl; BAM. Well, now; by this time Columbus Avenue was strewn with hamburger rolls and I was less offended than disgusted. So, I decided to kill the dog. [*Peter raises a hand in protest.*] Oh, don't be so alarmed, Peter; I didn't succeed. The day I tried to kill the dog I bought only one hamburger and what I thought was a murderous portion of rat poison. When I bought the hamburger I asked the man not to bother with the roll, all I wanted was the meat. I expected some reaction from him, like: we don't sell no hamburgers without rolls; or, wha' d'ya wanna do, eat it out'a ya han's? But no; he smiled benignly, wrapped up the hamburger in waxed paper, and said: A bite for ya pussy-cat? I wanted to say: No, not really; it's part of a plan to poison a dog I know. But, you can't say ''a dog I know'' without sounding funny; so I said, a little too loud, I'm afraid, and too formally: YES, A BITE FOR MY PUSSY-CAT. People looked up. It always happens when I try to simplify things; people look up. But that's neither hither nor thither. So. On my way back to the roominghouse, I kneaded the hamburger and the rat poison together between my hands, at that point feeling as much sadness as disgust. I opened the door to the entrance hall, and there the monster was, waiting to take the offering and then jump me. Poor bastard; he never learned that the moment he took to smile before he went for me gave me time enough to get out of range. BUT, there he was; malevolence with an erection, waiting. I put the poison patty down, moved toward the stairs and watched. The poor animal gobbled the food down as usual, smiled, which made me almost sick, and then, BAM. But, I sprinted up the stairs, as usual, and the dog didn't get me, as usual. AND IT CAME TO PASS THAT THE BEAST WAS DEATHLY ILL. I knew this because he no longer attended me, and because the landlady sobered up. She stopped me in the hall the same evening of the attempted murder and confided the information that God had struck her puppy-dog a surely fatal blow. She had forgotten her bewildered lust, and her eyes were wide open for the first time. They looked like the dog's eyes. She sniveled and implored me to pray for the animal. I wanted to say to her: Madam, I have myself to pray for, the colored queen, the Puerto Rican family, the person in the front room whom I've never seen, the woman who cries deliberately behind her closed door, and the rest of the people in all roominghouses, everywhere; besides, Madam, I don't understand how to pray. But . . . to simplify things . . . I told her I would pray. She looked up. She said that I was a liar, and that I probably wanted the dog to die. I told her, and there was so much truth here, that I didn't want the dog to die. I didn't, and not just because I'd poisoned him. I'm afraid that I must tell you I wanted the dog to live so that I could see what our new relationship might come to. [*Peter indicates his increasing displeasure and slowly growing antagonism.*] Please understand, Peter; that sort of thing is important. You must believe me; it *is* important. We have to know the effect of our actions. [*Another deep sigh.*] Well, anyway; the dog recovered. I have no idea why, unless he was a descendant of the puppy that guarded the gates of hell or some such resort. I'm not up on my mythology. [*He pronounces the word myth-o-*logy.] Are you? [*Peter sets to thinking, but Jerry goes on.*] At any rate, and you've missed the eight-thou-sand-dollar question, Peter; at any rate, the dog recovered his health and the landlady recovered her thirst, in no way altered by the bow-wow's deliverance. When I came home from a movie that was playing on Forty-second Street, a movie I'd seen, or one that was very much like one or several I'd seen, after the landlady told me puppykins was better, I was so hoping for the dog to be waiting for me. I was . . . well, how would you put it . . . enticed? . . . fascinated? . . . no, I don't think so . . . heart-shat-teringly anxious, that's it; I was heart-shatteringly anxious to con-front my friend again. [*Peter reacts scoffingly.*] Yes, Peter; friend. That's the only word for it. I was heartshatteringly et cetera to confront my doggy friend again. I came in the door and advanced, unafraid, to the center of the entrance hall. The beast was there . . . looking at me. And, you know, he looked better for his scrape with the nevermind. I stopped; I looked at him; he looked at me. I think . . . I think we stayed a long time that way . . . still, stone-statue . . . just looking at one another. I looked more into his face than he looked into mine. I mean, I can concentrate longer at looking into a dog's face than a dog can concentrate at looking into mine, or into anybody else's face, for that matter. But during that twenty seconds or two hours that we looked into each other's face, we made contact. Now, here is what I had wanted to happen: I loved the dog now, and I wanted him to love me. I had tried to love, and I had tried to kill, and both had been unsuccessful by themselves. I hoped . . .

and I don't really know why I expected the dog to understand anything, much less my motivations . . . I hoped that the dog would understand. [*Peter seems to be hypnotized.*] It's just . . . it's just that . . . [*Jerry is abnormally tense, now.*] . . . it's just that if you can't deal with people, you have to make a start somewhere. WITH ANIMALS! [*Much faster now, and like a conspirator*] Don't you see? A person has to have some way of dealing with SOMETHING. If not with people . . . if not with people . . . SOMETHING. With a bed, with a cockroach, with a mirror . . . no, that's too hard, that's one of the last steps. With a cockroach, with a . . . with a . . . with a carpet, a roll of toilet paper . . . no, not that, either . . . that's a mirror, too; always check bleeding. You see how hard it is to find things? With a street corner, and too many lights, all colors reflecting on the oily-wet streets . . . with a wisp of smoke, a wisp . . . of smoke . . . with . . . with pornographic playing cards, with a strongbox . . . WITHOUT A LOCK . . . with love, with vomiting, with crying, with fury because the pretty little ladies aren't pretty little ladies, with making money with your body which is an act of love and I could prove it, with howling because you're alive; with God. How about that? WITH GOD WHO IS A COLORED QUEEN WHO WEARS A KIMONO AND PLUCKS HIS EYEBROWS, WHO IS A WOMAN WHO CRIES WITH DETERMINATION BEHIND HER CLOSED DOOR . . . with God who, I'm told, turned his back on the whole thing some time ago . . . with . . . some day, with people. [*Jerry sighs the next word heavily.*] People. With an idea; a concept. And where better, where ever better in this humiliating excuse for a jail, where better to communicate one single, simple-minded idea than in an entrance hall? Where? It would be A START! Where better to make a beginning . . . to understand and just possibly be understood . . . a beginning of an understanding, than with . . . [*Here Jerry seems to fall into almost grotesque fatigue*] . . . than with A DOG. Just that; a dog. [*Here there is a silence that might be prolonged for a moment or so; then Jerry wearily finishes his story.*] A dog. It seemed like a perfectly sensible idea. Man is a dog's best friend, remember. So: the dog and I looked at each other. I longer than the dog. And what I saw then has been the same ever since. Whenever the dog and I see each other we both stop where we are. We regard each other with a mixture of sadness and suspicion, and then we feign indifference. We walk past each other safely; we have an understanding. It's very sad, but you'll have to admit that it is an understanding. We had made many attempts at contact, and we had failed. The dog has returned to garbage, and I to solitary but free passage. I have not returned. I mean to say, I have *gained* solitary free passage, if that much further loss can be said to be gain. I have learned that neither kindness nor cruelty by themselves, independent of each other, creates any effect beyond themselves; and I have learned that the two combined, together, at the same time, are the teaching emotion. And what is gained is loss. And what has been the result: the dog and I have attained a compromise; more of a bargain, really. We neither love nor hurt because we do not try to reach each other. And, *was* trying to feed the dog an act of love? And, perhaps, was the dog's attempt to bite me *not* an act of love? If we can so misunderstand, well then, why have we invented the word love in the first place? [*There is silence. Jerry moves to Peter's bench and sits down beside him. This is the first time Jerry has sat down during the play.*] The Story of Jerry and the Dog: the end. [*Peter is silent.*] Well, Peter? [*Jerry is suddenly cheerful.*] Well, Peter? Do you think I could sell that story to the *Reader's Digest* and make a couple of hundred bucks for *The Most Unforgettable Character I've Ever Met*? Huh? [*Jerry is animated, but Peter is disturbed.*] Oh, come on now, Peter; tell me what you think.

PETER [*numb*] I . . . I don't understand what . . . I don't think I . . . [*Now, almost tearfully*] Why did you tell me all of this?

JERRY Why not?

PETER I DON'T UNDERSTAND!

JERRY [*furious, but whispering*] That's a lie.

PETER No. No, it's not.

JERRY [*quietly.*] I tried to explain it to you as I went along. I went slowly; it all has to do with . . .

PETER I DON'T WANT TO HEAR ANY MORE. I don't understand you, or your landlady, or her dog . . .

JERRY *Her* dog! I thought it was my . . . No. No, you're right. It *is* her dog. [*Looks at Peter intently, shaking his head.*] I don't know what I was thinking about; of course you don't understand. [*In a monotone, wearily*] I don't live in your block; I'm not married to two parakeets, or whatever your setup is. I am a *permanent transient,* and my home is the sickening roominghouses on the West Side of New York City, which is the greatest city in the world. Amen.

PETER I'm . . . I'm sorry; I didn't meant to . . .

JERRY Forget it. I suppose you don't quite know what to make of me, eh?

PETER [*a joke*] We get all kinds in publishing. [*Chuckles.*]

JERRY You're a funny man. [*He forces a laugh.*] You know that? You're a very . . . a richly comic person.

PETER [*modestly, but amused*] Oh, now, not really [*still chuckling*].

JERRY Peter, do I annoy you, or confuse you?

PETER   [*lightly*] Well, I must confess that this wasn't the kind of afternoon I'd anticipated.

JERRY   You mean, I'm not the gentleman you were expecting.

PETER   I wasn't expecting anybody.

JERRY   No, I don't imagine you were. But I'm here, and I'm not
leaving.

PETER   [*consulting his watch*] Well, you may not be, but I must be getting home soon.

JERRY   Oh, come on; stay a while longer.

PETER   I really should get home; you see . . .

JERRY   [*Tickles Peter's ribs with his fingers.*] Oh, come on.

PETER   [*He is very ticklish; as Jerry continues to tickle him his voice becomes
falsetto.*] No. I . . . OHHHHH! Don't do that. Stop, Stop. Ohhh,
no, no.

JERRY   Oh, come on.

PETER   [*as Jerry tickles*] Oh, hee, hee, hee. I must go. I . . . hee, hee,
hee. After all, stop, stop, hee, hee, hee, after all, the parakeets
will be getting dinner ready soon. Hee, hee. And the cats are
setting the table. Stop, stop, and, and . . . [*Peter is beside himself
now*] . . . and we're having . . . hee, hee . . . uh . . . ho, ho, ho.
[*Jerry stops tickling Peter, but the combination of the tickling and his
own mad whimsy has Peter laughing almost hysterically. As his laughter continues, then subsides, Jerry watches him, with a curious fixed
smile.*]

JERRY   Peter?

PETER   Oh, ha, ha, ha, ha, ha. What? What?

JERRY   Listen, now.

PETER   Oh, ho, ho. What . . . what is it, Jerry? Oh, my.

JERRY   [*mysteriously*] Peter, do you want to know what happened at
the zoo?

PETER   Ah, ha, ha. The what? Oh, yes; the zoo. Oh, ho, ho. Well, I
had my own zoo there for a moment with . . . hee, hee, the parakeets getting dinner ready, and the . . . ha, ha, whatever it was,
the . . .

ogJERRY   [*calmly*] Yes, that was very funny, Peter. I wouldn't have
expected it. But do you want to hear about what happened at
the zoo, or not?

PETER   Yes. Yes, by all means; tell me what happened at the zoo. Oh,
my. I don't know what happened to me.

JERRY   Now I'll let you in on what happened at the zoo; but first, I
should tell you why I went to the zoo. I went to the zoo to find
out more about the way people exist with animals, and the way
animals exist with each other, and with people too. It probably
wasn't a fair test, what with everyone separated by bars from

everyone else, the animals for the most part from each other, and always the people from the animals. But, if it's a zoo, that's the way it is. [*He pokes at Peter on the arm.*] Move over.

PETER   [*friendly*] I'm sorry, haven't you enough room? [*He shifts a little.*]

JERRY   [*smiling slightly*] Well, all the animals are there, and all the people are there, and it's Sunday and all the children are there. [*He pokes Peter again.*] Move over!

PETER   [*patiently, still friendly*] All right. [*He moves some more, and Jerry has all the room he might need.*]

JERRY   And it's a hot day, so all the stench is there, too, and all the balloon sellers, and all the ice cream sellers, and all the seals are barking, and all the birds are screaming. [*Pokes Peter harder.*] Move over!

PETER   [*beginning to be annoyed*] Look here, you have more than enough room! [*But he moves more, and is now fairly cramped at one end of the bench.*]

JERRY   And I am there, and it's feeding time at the lions' house, and the lion keeper comes into the lion cage, one of the lion cages, to feed one of the lions. [*Punches Peter on the arm, hard.*] MOVE OVER!

PETER   [*very annoyed*] I can't move over any more, and stop hitting me. What's the matter with you?

JERRY   Do you want to hear the story? [*Punches Peter's arm again.*]

PETER   [*flabbergasted*] I'm not so sure! I certainly don't want to be punched in the arm.

JERRY   [*Punches Peter's arm again.*] Like that?

PETER   Stop it! What's the matter with you?

JERRY   I'm crazy, you bastard.

PETER   That isn't funny.

JERRY   Listen to me, Peter. I want this bench. You go sit on the bench over there, and if you're good I'll tell you the rest of the story.

PETER   [*flustered*] But . . . whatever for? What *is* the matter with you? Besides, I see no reason why I should give up this bench. I sit on this bench almost every Sunday afternoon, in good weather. It's secluded here; there's never anyone sitting here, so I have it all to myself.

JERRY   [*softly*] Get off this bench, Peter; I want it.

PETER   [*almost whining*] No.

JERRY   I said I want this bench, and I'm going to have it. Now get over there.

PETER   People can't have everything they want. You should know that; it's a rule; people can have some of the things they want, but they can't have everything.

JERRY [*Laughs*] Imbecile! You're slow-witted!

PETER Stop that!

JERRY You're a vegetable! Go lie down on the ground.

PETER [*intense*] Now *you* listen to me. I've put up with you all afternoon.

JERRY Not really.

PETER LONG ENOUGH. I've put up with you long enough. I've listened to you because you seemed . . . well, because I thought you wanted to talk to somebody.

JERRY You put things well; economically, and, yet . . . oh, what is the word I want to put justice to your . . . JESUS, you make me sick . . . get off here and give me my bench.

PETER MY BENCH!

JERRY [*Pushes Peter almost, but not quite, off the bench.*] Get out of my sight.

PETER [*regaining his position*] God da . . . mn you. That's enough! I've had enough of you. I will not give up this bench; you can't have it, and that's that. Now, go away. [*Jerry snorts but does not move.*] Go away, I said. [*Jerry does not move.*] Get away from here. If you don't move on . . . you're a bum . . . that's what you are. . . . If you don't move on, I'll get a policeman here and make you go. [*Jerry laughs, stays.*] I warn you, I'll call a policeman.

JERRY [*softly*] You won't find a policeman around here; they're all over on the west side of the park chasing fairies down from trees or out of the bushes. That's all they do. That's their function. So scream your head off; it won't do you any good.

PETER POLICE! I warn you, I'll have you arrested. POLICE! [*Pause.*] I said POLICE! [*Pause.*] I feel ridiculous.

JERRY You look ridiculous: a grown man screaming for the police on a bright Sunday afternoon in the park with nobody harming you. If a policeman *did* fill his quota and come sludging over this way he'd probably take you in as a nut.

PETER [*with disgust and impotence*] Great God, I just came here to read, and now you want me to give up the bench. You're mad.

JERRY Hey, I got news for you, as they say. I'm on your precious bench, and you're never going to have it for yourself again.

PETER [*furious*] Look, you; get off my bench. I don't care if it makes any sense or not. I want this bench to myself; I want you OFF IT!

JERRY [*mocking*] Aw . . . look who's mad.

PETER GET OUT!

JERRY No.

PETER I WARN YOU!

JERRY Do you know how ridiculous you look *now*?

PETER [*His fury and self-consciousness have possessed him.*] It doesn't matter. [*He is almost crying.*] GET AWAY FROM MY BENCH!

JERRY   Why? You have everything in the world you want; you've told me about your home, and your family, and *your own* little zoo. You have everything, and now you want this bench. Are these the things men fight for? Tell me, Peter, is this bench, this iron and this wood, is this your honor? Is this the thing in the world you'd fight for? Can you think of anything more absurd?

PETER   Absurd? Look, I'm not going to talk to you about honor, or even try to explain it to you. Besides, it isn't a question of honor; but even if it were, you wouldn't understand.

JERRY   [*contemptuously*] You don't even know what you're saying, do you? This is probably the first time in your life you've had anything more trying to face than changing your cats' toilet box. Stupid! Don't you have any idea, not even the slightest, what other people *need*?

PETER   Oh, boy, listen to you; well, you don't need this bench. That's for sure.

JERRY   Yes; yes, I do.

PETER   [*quivering*] I've come here for years; I have hours of great pleasure, great satisfaction, right here. And that's important to a man. I'm a responsible person, and I'm a GROWNUP. This is my bench, and you have no right to take it away from me.

JERRY   Fight for it, then. Defend yourself; defend your bench.

PETER   You've *pushed* me to it. Get up and fight.

JERRY   Like a man?

PETER   [*still angry*] Yes, like a man, if you insist on mocking me even further.

JERRY   I'll have to give you credit for one thing: you *are* a vegetable, and a slightly nearsighted one, I think . . .

PETER   THAT'S ENOUGH . . .

JERRY   . . . but, you know, as they say on TV all the time—you know —and I mean this, Peter, you have a certain dignity; it surprises me . . .

PETER   STOP!

JERRY   [*Rises lazily.*] Very well, Peter, we'll battle for the bench, but we're not evenly matched. [*He takes out and clicks open an ugly looking knife.*]

PETER   [*suddenly awakening to the reality of the situation*] You are mad! You're stark raving mad! YOU'RE GOING TO KILL ME! [*But before Peter has time to think what to do, Jerry tosses the knife at Peter's feet.*]

JERRY   There you go. Pick it up. You have the knife and we'll be more evenly matched.

PETER   [*horrified*] No!

JERRY   [*Rushes over to Peter, grabs him by the collar; Peter rises; their faces almost touch.*] Now you pick up that knife and you fight with me. You fight for your self-respect; you fight for that goddamned bench.

PETER   [*struggling*] No! Let . . . let go of me! He . . . Help!

JERRY   [*Slaps Peter on each "fight".*] You fight, you miserable bastard; fight for that bench; fight for your parakeets; fight for your cats, fight for your two daughters; fight for your wife; fight for your manhood, you pathetic little vegetable. [*Spits in Peter's face.*] You couldn't even get your wife with a male child.

PETER   [*Breaks away, enraged.*] It's a matter of genetics, not manhood, you . . . you monster. [*He darts down, picks up the knife and backs off a little; he is breathing heavily.*] I'll give you one last chance; get out of here and leave me alone! [*He holds the knife with a firm arm, but far in front of him, not to attack, but to defend.*]

JERRY   [*Sighs heavily.*] So be it! [*With a rush he charges Peter and impales himself on the knife. Tableau: For just a moment, complete silence, Jerry impaled on the knife at the end of Peter's· still firm arm. Then Peter screams, pulls away, leaving the knife in Jerry. Jerry is motionless, on point. Then he, too, screams, and it must be the sound of an infuriated and fatally wounded animal. With the knife in him, he stumbles back to the bench that Peter had vacated. He crumbles there, sitting, facing Peter, his eyes wide in agony, his mouth open.*]

PETER   [*whispering*] Oh my God, oh my God, oh my God . . . [*He repeats these words many times, very rapidly.*]

JERRY   [*Jerry is dying; but now his expression seems to change. His features relax, and while his voice varies, sometimes wrenched with pain, for the most part he seems removed from his dying. He smiles.*] Thank you, Peter. I mean that, now; thank you very much. [*Peter's mouth drops open. He cannot move; he is transfixed.*] Oh, Peter, I was so afraid I'd drive you away. [*He laughs as best he can.*] You don't know how afraid I was you'd go away and leave me. And now I'll tell you what happened at the zoo. I think . . . I think this is what happened at the zoo . . . I think. I think that while I was at the zoo I decided that I would walk north . . . northerly, rather . . . until I found you . . . or somebody . . . and I decided that I would talk to you . . . I would tell you things . . . and things that I would tell you would . . . Well, here we are. You see? Here we *are*. But . . . I don't know . . . could I have planned all this? No . . . no, I couldn't have. But I think I did. And now I've told you what you wanted to know, haven't I? And now you know all about what happened at the zoo. And now you will know what you'll see in your TV, and the face I told you about . . . you remember . . . the face I told you about . . . my face, the face you see right now. Peter

. . . Peter? . . . Peter . . . thank you. I came unto you [*He laughs, so faintly.*] and you have comforted me. Dear Peter.

PETER   [*almost fainting*] Oh my God!

JERRY   You'd better go now. Somebody might come by, and you don't want to be here when anyone comes.

PETER   [*Does not move, but begins to weep.*] Oh my God, oh my God.

JERRY   [*most faintly, now; he is very near death*] You won't be coming back here any more, Peter; you've been dispossessed. You've lost your bench, but you've defended your honor. And Peter, I'll tell you something now; you're not really a vegetable; it's all right, you're an animal. You're an animal, too. But you'd better hurry now, Peter. Hurry, you'd better go . . . see? [*Jerry takes a handkerchief and with great effort and pain wipes the knife handle clean of fingerprints.*] Hurry away, Peter. [*Peter begins to stagger away.*] Wait . . . wait, Peter. Take your book . . . book. Right here . . . beside me . . . on your bench . . . my bench, rather. Come . . . take your book. [*Peter starts for the book, but retreats.*] Hurry . . . Peter. [*Peter rushes to the bench, grabs the book, retreats.*] Very good, Peter . . . very good. Now . . . hurry away. [*Peter hesitates for a moment, then flees, stage-left.*] Hurry away . . . [*His eyes are closed now.*] Hurry away, your parakeets are making the dinner . . . the cats . . . are setting the table . . .

PETER   [*Off stage, a pitiful howl*] OH MY GOD!

JERRY   [*His eyes still closed, he shakes his head and speaks; a combination of scornful mimicry and supplication.*] Oh . . . my . . . God. [*He is dead.*]

CURTAIN

GEORGE RYGA

1932–1987

Born into a Ukrainian family on a marginal homestead in Deep Creek, Alberta, he had only seven years of formal education in a one-room country school before he embarked on a variety of laboring jobs. His first writing consisted of plays for radio and for television, and his apprenticeship in these media prepared him for his prolific career as novelist, poet, and playwright. After 1962 he made his living by writing, and completed three novels and more than forty plays for radio, for television, and for theater. In all his writings, he explored the quality of Canadian life, focusing steadily on the oppressed and the disadvantaged, often Indians and laborers. He found society too preoccupied, too comfortable, and too frightened to confront or to accept its own social responsibilities. His protagonists are often caught and trapped between their own or their tribal ways and the customs and expectations of an alienating society. A committed socialist, he travelled to China to study its society and culture, and recorded his impressions in the somewhat fictionalized *Beyond the Crimson Morning: Reflections from a Journey through Contemporary China* (1979). *The Ecstasy of Rita Joe*, his finest play, had its premiere at the Playhouse Theatre in Vancouver on November 23, 1967.

The Ecstasy of Rita Joe

CHARACTERS

RITA JOE
JAIMIE PAUL
DAVID JOE, Rita's father
MAGISTRATE
MR. HOMER
FATHER ANDREW, a priest
EILEEN JOE, Rita's sister
OLD INDIAN WOMAN
MISS DONAHUE, a teacher
POLICEMAN
WITNESSES
MURDERERS
YOUNG INDIAN MEN
SINGER

SET

A circular ramp beginning at floor level stage left and continuing downward below floor level at stage front, then rising and sweeping along stage back at two-foot elevation to disappear in the wings of stage left. This ramp dominates the stage by wrapping the central and forward playing area. A short approach ramp, meeting with the main ramp at stage right, expedites entrances from the wings of stage right. The magistrate's chair and representation of court desk are situated at stage right, enclosed within the sweep of the ramp. At the foot of the desk is a lip on stage right side.

The singer sits here, turned away from the focus of the play. Her songs and accompaniment appear almost accidental. She has all the reactions of a white liberal folklorist with a limited concern and understanding of an ethnic dilemma which she touches in the course of her research and work in compiling and writing folk songs. She serves too as an alter ego to Rita Joe.

No curtain is used during the play. At the opening, intermission and conclusion of the play, the curtain remains up. The onus for isolating scenes from the past and present in Rita Joe's life falls on highlight lighting.

Backstage, there is a mountain cyclorama. In front of the cyclorama there is a darker maze curtain to suggest gloom and confusion, and a cityscape.

ACT I

The house lights and stage work lights remain on. Backstage, cyclorama, and maze curtains are up, revealing wall back of stage, exit doors, etc.

Cast and singer enter offstage singly and in pairs from the wings, the exit doors at the back of the theatre, and from the auditorium side doors. The entrances are workmanlike and untheatrical. When all the cast is on stage, they turn to face the audience momentarily. The house lights dim.

The cyclorama is lowered into place. The maze curtain follows. This creates a sense of compression of stage into the auditorium. Recorded voices are heard in a jumble of mutterings and throat clearings. The magistrate enters as the clerk begins.

CLERK [*recorded*]   This court is in session. All present will rise. . . .

The shuffling and scraping of furniture is heard. The cast repeat "Rita Joe, Rita Joe." A policeman brings on Rita Joe.

MAGISTRATE   Who is she? Can she speak English?
POLICEMAN   Yes.
MAGISTRATE   Then let her speak for herself.

He speaks to the audience firmly and with reason.

> To understand life in a given society, one must understand laws of that society. All relationships . . .
CLERK [*recorded*]   Man to man . . . man to woman . . . man to property . . . man to state . . .
MAGISTRATE   . . . are determined and enriched by laws that have grown out of social realities. The quality of the law under which you live and function determines the real quality of the freedom that was yours today.

The rest of the cast slowly move out.

> Your home and your well-being were protected. The roads of the city are open to us. So are the galleries, libraries, the administrative and public buildings. There are buses, trains . . . going in and coming out. Nobody is a prisoner here.
RITA [*with humor, almost a sad sigh*]   The first time I tried to go home I was picked up by some men who gave me five dollars. An' then they arrested me.

The policeman retreats into the shadows. The singer crosses down.

MAGISTRATE   Thousands leave and enter the city every day . . .
RITA   It wasn't true what they said, but nobody'd believe me . . .

SINGER   [*singing in recitivo searching for a melody*]
>   Will the winds not blow
>   My words to her
>   Like the seeds
>   Of the dandelion?

MAGISTRATE   [*smiling, as at a private joke*]   Once . . . I saw a little girl in the Cariboo country. It was summer then and she wore only a blouse and skirt. I wondered what she wore in winter?

The murderers hover in the background on the upper ramp. One whistles and one lights a cigarette—an action which will be repeated at the end of the play.

RITA   [*moving to him, but hesitating*]   You look like a good man. Tell them to let me go, please!

The magistrate goes to his podium.

MAGISTRATE   Our nation is on an economic par with the state of Arkansas. . . . We are a developing country, but a buoyant one. Still . . . the summer report of the Economic Council of Canada predicts a reduction in the gross national product unless we utilize our manpower for greater efficiency. Employed, happy people make for a prosperous, happy nation. . . .

RITA   [*exultantly*]   I worked at some jobs, mister!

The magistrate turns to face Rita Joe. The murderers have gone.

MAGISTRATE   Gainful employment. Obedience to the law . . .

RITA   [*to the magistrate*]   Once I had a job . . .

He does not relate to her. She is troubled. She talks to the audience.

>   Once I had a job in a tire store . . . an' I'd worry about what time my boss would come. . . . He was always late . . . and so was everybody. Sometimes I got to thinkin' what would happen if he'd not come. And nobody else would come. And I'd be all day in this big room with no lights on an' the telephone ringing an' people asking for other people that weren't there. . . . What would happen?

As she relates her concern, she laughs. Toward the end of her monologue she is so amused by the absurdity of it all that she can hardly contain herself.

Lights fade on the magistrate who broods in his chair as he examines his court papers.

Lights up on Jaimie Paul approaching on the backstage ramp from stage left. He is jubilant, his laughter blending with her laughter. At the sound of his voice, Rita Joe runs to him, to the memory of him.

JAIMIE   I seen the city today and I seen things today I never knew was there, Rita Joe!

RITA   [*happily*]   I seen them too, Jaimie Paul!

He pauses above her, his mood light and childlike.

JAIMIE   I see a guy on top of a bridge, talkin' to himself . . . an' lots of people on the beach watchin' harbour seals. . . . Kids feed popcorn to seagulls . . . an' I think to myself . . . boy! Pigeons eat pretty good here!

RITA   In the morning, Jaimie Paul . . . very early in the morning . . . the air is cold like at home. . . .

JAIMIE   Pretty soon I seen a little woman walkin' a big black dog on a rope. . . . Dog is mad. . . . Dog wants a man!

Jaimie Paul moves to Rita Joe. They embrace.

RITA   Clouds are red over the city in the morning. Clara Hill says to me if you're real happy . . . the clouds make you forget you're not home. . . .

They laugh together. Jaimie Paul breaks from her. He punctuates his story with wide, sweeping gestures.

JAIMIE   I start singin' and some hotel windows open. I wave to them, but nobody waves back! They're watchin' me, like I was a harbour seal! [*He laughs.*] So I stopped singing'!

RITA   I remember colors, but I've forgot faces already. . . .

Jaimie Paul looks at her as her mood changes. Faint light on the magistrate brightens.

A train whistle is white, with black lines. . . . A sick man talkin' is brown like an overcoat with pockets torn an' string showin.' . . . A sad woman is a room with the curtains shut. . . .

MAGISTRATE   Rita Joe?

She becomes sobered, but Jaimie Paul continues laughing. She nods to the magistrate, then turns to Jaimie Paul.

RITA   Them bastards put me in jail. They're gonna do it again, they said. . . . Them bastards!

JAIMIE   Guys who sell newspapers don't see nothin' . . .

RITA   They drive by me, lookin' . . .

JAIMIE   I'm gonna be a carpenter!

RITA   I walk like a stick, tryin' to keep my ass from showin' because I know what they're thinkin'. . . . Them bastards!

JAIMIE   I got myself boots an' a new shirt. . . . See!
RITA   [*worried now*]   I thought their jail was on fire. . . . I thought it was burning.
JAIMIE   Room I got costs me seven bucks a week. . . .
RITA   I can't leave town. Every time I try, they put me in jail.

A policeman enters with a file folder.

JAIMIE   They say it's a pretty good room for seven bucks a week. . . .

Jaimie Paul begins to retreat backward from her, along the ramp to the wings of stage left. She is isolated in a pool of light away from the magistrate. The light isolation between her and Jaimie Paul deepens, as the scene turns into the coutroom again.

MAGISTRATE   Vagrancy. . . . You are charged with vagrancy.
JAIMIE   [*with enthusiasm, boyishly*]   First hundred bucks I make, Rita Joe . . . I'm
     gonna buy a car so I can take you every place!
RITA   [*moving after him*]   Jaimie!

He retreats, dreamlike, into the wings. The spell of memory between them is broken. Pools of light between her and the magistrate spread and fuse into a single light area. She turns to the magistrate, worried and confused.

MAGISTRATE   [*reading the documents in his hand*]   The charge against you this
     morning is vagrancy. . . .

The magistrate continues studying the papers he holds. She looks up at him and shakes her head helplessly, then blurts out to him.

RITA   I had to spend last night in jail. . . . Did you know?
MAGISTRATE   Yes. You were arrested.
RITA   I didn't know when morning came . . . there was no windows. . . . The
     jail stinks! People in jail stink!
MAGISTRATE   [*indulgently*]   Are you surprised?
RITA   I didn't know anybody there. . . . People in jail stink like paper that's
     been in the rain too long. But a jail stinks worse. It stinks of rust . . . an'
     old hair. . . .

The magistrate looks down at her for the first time.

MAGISTRATE   You . . . are Rita Joe?

She nods quickly. A faint concern shows in his face. He watches her for a long moment.

     I know your face . . . yet . . . it wasn't in this courtroom. Or was it?
RITA   I don't know.

MAGISTRATE   [*pondering*]   Have you appeared before me in the past year?
RITA   [*turning away from him, shrugging*]   I don't know. I can't remember. . . .

The magistrate throws his head back and laughs. The policeman joins in.

MAGISTRATE   You can't remember? Come now. . . .
RITA   [*laughing with him and looking to the policeman*]   I can't remember. . . .
MAGISTRATE   Then I take it you haven't appeared before me. Certainly you
    and I would remember if you had.
RITA   [*smiling*]   I don't remember. . . .

*The magistrate makes some hurried notes, but he is watching Rita Joe, formulating his
next thought.*

RITA   [*naively*]   My sister hitchhiked home an' she had no trouble like I . . .
MAGISTRATE   You'll need witnesses, Rita Joe. I'm only giving you eight hours
    to find witnesses for yourself. . . .
RITA   Jaimie knows . . .

*She turns to where Jaimie Paul had been, but the back of the stage is in darkness. The
policeman exits suddenly.*

Jaimie knew . . .

*Her voice trails off pathetically. The magistrate shrugs and returns to studying his
notes. Rita Joe chafes during the silence which follows. She craves communion with
people, with the magistrate.*

My sister was a dressmaker, mister! But she only worked two weeks in
the city. . . . An' then she got sick and went back to the reserve to help
my father catch fish an' cut pulpwood. [*smiling*]   She's not coming back
. . . that's for sure!
MAGISTRATE   [*with interest*]   Should I know your sister? What was her name?
RITA   Eileen Joe.

Eileen Joe appears spotlit behind, a memory crowding in.

MAGISTRATE   Eileen . . . that's a soft, undulating name.
RITA   Two weeks, and not one white woman came to her to leave an order or
old clothes for her to fix. No work at all for two weeks, an' her money ran
out. . . . Isn't that funny?

The magistrate again studies Rita Joe, his mind elsewhere.

MAGISTRATE   Hmmmmm. . . .

Eileen Joe disappears.

RITA   So she went back to the reserve to catch fish an' cut pulpwood!

MAGISTRATE   I do know your face . . . yes! And yet. . . .

RITA   Can I sit someplace?

MAGISTRATE   [*excited*]   I remember now. . . . Yes! I was on holidays three summers back in the Cariboo country . . . driving over this road with not a house or field in sight . . . just barren land, wild and windblown. And then I saw this child beside the road, dressed in a blouse and skirt, barefooted . . .

RITA   [*looking around*]   I don't feel so good, mister.

MAGISTRATE   My God, she wasn't more than three or four years old . . . walking toward me beside the road. When I'd passed her, I stopped my car and then turned around and drove back to where I'd seen her, for I wondered what she could possibly be doing in such a lonely country at that age without her father or mother walking with her. . . . Yet when I got back to where I'd seen her, she had disappeared. She was nowhere to be seen. Yet the land was flat for over a mile in every direction. . . . I had to see her. But I couldn't. . . .

He stares down at Rita Joe for a long moment.

You see, what I was going to say was that this child had your face! Isn't that strange?

RITA   [*with disinterest*]   Sure, if you think so, mister . . .

MAGISTRATE   Could she have been . . . your daughter?

RITA   What difference does it make?

MAGISTRATE   Children cannot be left like that. . . . It takes money to raise children in the woods as in the cities. . . . There are institutions and people with more money than you who could . . .

RITA   Nobody would get my child, mister!

She is distracted by Eileen Joe's voice in her memory. Eileen's voice begins in darkness, but as she speaks, a spotlight isolates her in front of the ramp, stage left. Eileen is on her hands and knees, two buckets beside her. She is picking berries in mime.

EILEEN   First was the strawberries an' then the blueberries. After the frost . . . we picked the cranberries. . . .

She laughs with delight.

RITA   [*pleading with the magistrate, but her attention on Eileen*]   Let me go, mister . . .

MAGISTRATE   I can't let you go. I don't think that would be of any use in the circumstances. Would you like a lawyer?

Even as he speaks, Rita Joe has entered the scene with Eileen picking berries. The magistrate's light fades on his podium.

RITA   You ate the strawberries an' blueberries because you were always a hungry kid!

EILEEN   But not cranberries! They made my stomach hurt.

Rita Joe goes down on her knees with Eileen.

RITA   Let me pick. . . . You rest. [*holding out the bucket to Eileen*]   Mine's full already. . . . Let's change. You rest. . . .

During the exchange of buckets, Eileen notices her hands are larger than Rita Joe's. She is both delighted and surprised by this.

EILEEN   My hands are bigger than yours, Rita. . . . Look! [*taking Rita Joe's hands in hers*]   When did my hands grow so big?

RITA   [*wisely and sadly*]   You've worked so hard. . . . I'm older than you, Leenie. . . . I will always be older.

The two sisters are thoughtful for a moment, each watching the other in silence. Then Rita Joe becomes animated and resumes her mime of picking berries in the woods.

We picked lots of wild berries when we were kids, Leenie!

They turn away from their work and lie down alongside each other, facing the front of the stage. The light on them becomes summery, warm.

In the summer, it was hot an' flies hummed so loud you'd go to sleep if you sat down an' just listened.

EILEEN   The leaves on the poplars used to turn black an' curl together with the heat . . .

RITA   One day you and I were pickin' blueberries and a big storm came. . . .

A sudden crash of thunder and a lightning flash. The lights turn cold and blue. The three murderers stand in silhouette on a riser behind them. Eileen cringes in fear, afraid of the storm, aware of the presence of the murderers behind them. Rita Joe springs to her feet, her being attached to the wildness of the atmosphere. Lightning continues to flash and flicker.

EILEEN   Oh, no!

RITA   [*shouting*]   It got cold and the rain an' hail came . . . the sky falling!

EILEEN   [*crying in fear*]   Rita!

RITA   [*laughing, shouting*]   Stay there!

A high flash of lightning, silhouetting the murderers harshly. They take a step forward on the lightning flash. Eileen dashes into the arms of Rita Joe. She screams and drags Rita Joe down with her. Rita Joe struggles against Eileen.

Let me go! What in hell's wrong with you! Let me go!
MAGISTRATE   I can't let you go.

The lightning dies, but the thunder rumbles off into the distance. Eileen subsides, and pressing herself into the arms of Rita Joe as a small child to her mother, she sobs quietly.

RITA   There, there. . . . [*With infinite tenderness*] You said to me, "What would happen if the storm hurt us an' we can't find our way home, but are lost together so far away in the bush?"

Eileen looks up, brushing away her tears and smiling at Rita Joe.

RITA and EILEEN   [*in unison*]   Would you be my mother then?
RITA   Would I be your mother?

Rita Joe releases Eileen who looks back fearfully to where the murderers had stood. They are gone. She rises and, collecting the buckets, moves hesitantly to where they had been. Confident now, she laughs softly and nervously to herself and leaves the stage. Rita Joe rises and talks to Eileen as she departs.

We walked home through the mud an' icy puddles among the trees. At first you cried, Leenie . . . and then you wanted to sleep. But I held you up an' when we got home you said you were sure you would've died in the bush if it hadn't been for us being together like that.

Eileen disappears from the stage. The magistrate's light comes up. Rita Joe shakes her head sadly at the memory, then comes forward to the apron of the stage. She is proud of her sister and her next speech reveals this pride.

She made a blouse for me that I wore every day for one year, an' it never ripped at the armpits like the blouse I buy in the store does the first time I stretch. [*She stretches languidly*]   I like to stretch when I'm happy! It makes all the happiness go through me like warm water. . . .

The priest, the teacher, and a young indian man cross the stage directly behind her. The priest wears a Roman collar and a checked bush-jacket of a worker-priest. He pauses before passing Rita Joe and goes to meet her.

PRIEST   Rita Joe? When did you get back? How's life?

Rita Joe shrugs noncommittally.

RITA   You know me, Father Andrew . . . could be better, could be worse. . . .

PRIEST   Are you still working?

Rita Joe is still noncommittal. She smiles at him. Her gestures are not definite.

RITA   I live.
PRIEST   [*serious and concerned*]   It's not easy, is it?
RITA   Not always.

The teacher and the young Indian man exit.

PRIEST   A lot of things are different in the city. It's easier here on the reserve . . .
life is simpler. You can be yourself. That's important to remember.
RITA   Yes, father. . . .

The priest wants to ask and say more, but he cannot. An awkward moment between them and he reaches out to touch her shoulder gently.

PRIEST   Well . . . be a good girl, Rita Joe. . . .
RITA   [*without turning after him*]   Goodbye, Father.
MAGISTRATE   [*more insistently*]   Do you want a lawyer?

The priest leaves stage right. As he leaves, cross light to where a happy Jaimie Paul enters from stage left. Jaimie Paul comes down to join Rita Joe.

JAIMIE   This guy asked me how much education I got, an' I says to him,
"Grade six. How much education a man need for such a job?" . . . An' the
bum, he says it's not good enough! I should take night school. But I got
the job, an' I start next Friday . . like this. . . .

Jaimie Paul does a mock sweeping routine as if he was cleaning a vast office building. He and Rita Joe are both laughing.

Pretty good, eh?
RITA   Pretty good.
JAIMIE   Cleaning the floors an' desks in the building. . . . But it's a government job, and that's good for life. Work hard, then the government give
me a raise. . . . I never had a job like that before. . . .
RITA   When I sleep happy, I dream of blueberries an' sun an' all the nice
things when I was a little kid, Jaimie Paul.

The sound of an airplane is heard. Jaimie Paul looks up. Rita Joe also stares into the sky of her memory. Jaimie Paul's face is touched with pain and recollection. The teacher, Rita Joe's father, an old woman, four young Indian men and Eileen Joe come into the background quietly, as if at a wharf watching the airplane leave the village. They stand looking up until the noise of the aircraft begins to diminish.

JAIMIE   That airplane . . . a Cessna. . . .

He continues watching the aircraft and turns, following its flight path.

She said to me, maybe I never see you again, Jaimie Paul.

There is a faint light on the magistrate in his chair. He is thoughtful, looking down at his hands.

MAGISTRATE   Do you want a lawyer?

RITA   [*to Jaimie Paul*]   Who?

JAIMIE   Your mother. . . . I said to her, they'll fix you up good in the hospital. Better than before. . . . It was a Cessna that landed on the river an' took her away. . . . Maybe I never see you again, Jaimie, she says to me. She knew she was gonna die, but I was a kid and so were you. . . . What the hell did we know? I'll never forget. . . .

Jaimie Paul joins the village group on the upper level.

SINGER   [*singing an indefinite melody developing into a square-dance tune*]
   There was a man in a beat-up hat
   Who runs a house in the middle of town,
   An' round his stove-pipe chimney house
   The magpies sat, just-a-lookin' round.

The Indian village people remain in the back of the stage, still watching the airplane which has vanished. Jaimie Paul, on his way, passes Mr. Homer, a white citizen who has the hurried but fulfilled appearance of the socially responsible man. Mr. Homer comes to the front of the stage beside Rita Joe. He talks directly to the audience.

MR. HOMER   Sure, we do a lot of things for our Indians here in the city at the Center. . . . Bring 'em in from the cold an' give them food. . . . The rest . . . well, the rest kinda take care of itself.

Rita Joe lowers her head and looks away from him. Mr. Homer moves to her and places his hand on her shoulders possessively.

When your mother got sick we flew her out. . . . You remember that, Rita Joe?

RITA   [*nodding, looking down*]   Yes, Mr. Homer. . . . Thank you.

MR. HOMER   And we sent her body back for the funeral. . . . Right, Rita Joe?

The people of the village leave except for the young Indian men who remain and mime drinking.

And then sometimes a man drinks it up an' leaves his wife an' kids and the poor dears come here for help. We give them food an' a place to sleep. . . . Right, Rita?

RITA   Yes.

MR. HOMER   Clothes too. . . . White people leave clothes here for the Indians to take if they need 'em. Used to have them all up on racks over there . . . just like in a store. . . . [*pointing*]   But now we got them all on a heap on a table in the basement.

He laughs and Rita Joe nods with him.

> Indian people . . . 'specially the women . . . get more of a kick diggin' through stuff that's piled up like that. . . .

Mr. Homer chuckles and shakes his head. There is a pale light on the magistrate, who is still looking down at his hands.

MAGISTRATE   There are institutions to help you. . . .

Mr. Homer again speaks to the audience, but now he is angry over some personal beef.

MR. HOMER   So you see, the Center serves a need that's real for Indians who come to the city. [*wagging his finger at the audience angrily*]   It's the do-gooders burn my ass, you know! They come in from television or the newspaper . . . hang around just long enough to see a drunken Indian . . . an' bingo!

JAIMIE   Bingo!

MR. HOMER   That's their story! Next thing, they're seeing some kind of Red Power.

The young Indian men laugh and Rita Joe gets up to join them.

> . . . or beatin' the government over the head! Let them live an' work among the Indians for a few months . . . then they'd know what it's really like. . . .

The music comes up sharply.

SINGER
> Round and round the cenotaph,
> The clumsy seagulls play.
> Fed by funny men with hats
> Who watch them night and day.

The four young Indian men join with Rita Joe and dance. Leading the group is Jaimie Paul. He is drunk, dishevelled. Light spreads before them as they advance onstage. They are laughing rowdily. Rita Joe moves to them.

RITA   Jaimie Paul?

Mr. Homer leaves. Jaimie Paul is overtaken by two of his companions who take him by the arms, but he pushes them roughly away.

JAIMIE   Get the hell outa my way! . . . I'm as good a man as him any time. . . .

Jaimie Paul crosses downstage to confront a member of the audience.

You know me? . . . You think I'm a dirty Indian, eh? Get outa my way!

He puts his hands over his head and continues staggering away.

Goddamnit, I wanna sleep. . . .

The young Indian men and Jaimie Paul exit. Rita Joe follows after Jaimie Paul, reaching out to touch him, but the singer stands in her way and drives her back, singing. . . . Music up tempo and volume.

SINGER
    Oh, can't you see that train roll on,
    Its hot black wheels keep comin' on?
    A Kamloops Indian died today.
    Train didn't hit him, he just fell.
    Busy train with wheels on fire!

The music dies. A policeman enters.

POLICEMAN   Rita Joe!

He repeats her name many times. The teacher enters ringing the school handbell and crosses through.

TEACHER   [*calling*]   Rita Joe! Rita Joe! Didn't you hear the bell ring? The class is waiting. . . . The class is always waiting for you.

The teacher exits.

MAGISTRATE and POLICEMAN   [*sharply, in unison*]   Rita Joe!

The policeman grabs and shakes Rita Joe to snap her out of her reverie.

Light up on the magistrate who sits erect, with authority.

MAGISTRATE   I ask you for the last time, Rita Joe. . . . Do you want a laywer?
RITA   [*defiantly*]   What for? . . . I can take care of myself.

MAGISTRATE   The charge against you this morning is prostitution. Why did you not return to your people as you said you would?

The light on the backstage dies. Rita Joe stands before the magistrate and the policeman. She is contained in a pool of light before them.

RITA   [*nervous, with despair*]   I tried. . . . I tried. . . .

The magistrate settles back into his chair and takes a folder from his desk, which he opens and studies.

MAGISTRATE   Special Constable Eric Wilson has submitted a statement to the effect that on June 18th he and Special Constable Schneider approached you on Fourth Avenue at nine-forty in the evening . . .
POLICEMAN   We were impersonating two deckhands newly arrived in the city . . .
MAGISTRATE   You were arrested an hour later on charges of prostitution.

The magistrate holds the folder threateningly and looks down at her. Rita Joe is defiant.

RITA   That's a goddamned lie!
MAGISTRATE   [*sternly, gesturing to the policeman*]   This is a police statement. Surely you don't think a mistake was made?
RITA   [*peering into the light above her, shuddering*]   Everything in this room is like ice. . . . How can you stay alive working here? . . . I'm so hungry I want to throw up . . .
MAGISTRATE   You have heard the statement, Rita Joe. . . . Do you deny it?
RITA   I was going home, trying to find the highway. . . . I knew those two were cops, the moment I saw them . . . I told them to go f . . . fly a kite! They got sore then an' started pushing me around. . . .
MAGISTRATE   [*patiently now, waving down the objections of the policeman*]   Go on.
RITA   They followed me around until a third cop drove up. An' then they arrested me.
MAGISTRATE   Arrested you. . . . Nothing else?
RITA   They stuffed five dollar bills in my pockets when they had me in the car. . . . I ask you, mister, when are they gonna charge cops like that with contributing to.
POLICEMAN   Your worship . . .
MAGISTRATE   [*irritably, indicating the folder on the table before him*]   Now it's your word against this! You need references . . . people who know you . . . who will come to court to substantiate what you say . . . today! That is the process of legal argument!
RITA   Can I bum a cigarette someplace?
MAGISTRATE   No. You can't smoke in court.

The policeman smiles and exits.

RITA   Then give me a bed to sleep on, or is the sun gonna rise an' rise until it burns a hole in my head?

Guitar music cues softly in the background.

MAGISTRATE   Tell me about the child.
RITA   What child?
MAGISTRATE   The little girl I once saw beside the road!
RITA   I don't know any girl, mister! When do I eat? Why does an Indian wait even when he's there first thing in the morning?

The pool of light tightens around the magistrate and Rita Joe.

MAGISTRATE   I have children . . . two sons . . .
RITA   [*nodding*]   Sure. That's good.

The magistrate gropes for words to express a message that is very precious to him.

MAGISTRATE   My sons can go in any direction they wish . . . into trades or university. . . . But if I had a daughter, I would be more concerned. . . .
RITA   What's so special about a girl?
MAGISTRATE   I would wish . . . well, I'd be concerned about her choices . . . her choices of living, school . . . friends. . . . These things don't come as lightly for a girl. For boys it's different. . . . But I would worry if I had a daughter. . . . Don't hide your child! Someone else can be found to raise her if you can't!

Rita Joe shakes her head, a strange smile on her face.

Why not? There are people who would love to take care of it.
RITA   Nobody would get my child. . . . I would sooner kill it an' bury it first! I am not a kind woman, mister judge!
MAGISTRATE   [*at a loss*]   I see. . . .
RITA   [*a cry*]   I want to go home. . . .

Quick up tempo music is heard. Suddenly, the lights change.

Jaimie Paul and the young Indian men sweep over the backstage ramp, the light widening for them. Rita Joe moves into this railway station crowd. She turns from one man to another until she sees Jaimie Paul.

Eileen Joe and an old woman enter.

RITA   Jaimie!
EILEEN   [*happily, running to him*]   Jaimie Paul! God's sakes. . . . When did you

get back from the north? . . . I thought you said you wasn't coming until breakup. . . .

JAIMIE [*turning to Eileen*] I was comin' home on the train . . . had a bit to drink and was feeling pretty good. . . . Lots of women sleeping in their seats on the train. . . . I'd lift their hats an' say, "Excuse me, lady . . . I'm lookin' for a wife!" [*turning to the old woman*] One fat lady got mad, an' I says to her, "That's alright lady. . . . You got no worries. . . . You keep sleepin'!"

Laughter.

Jaimie Paul and the old woman move away. Eileen sees Rita Joe who is standing watching.

EILEEN Rita! . . . Tom an' I broke up . . . did I tell you?

RITA No, Leenie . . . you didn't tell me!

EILEEN He was no good. . . . He stopped comin' to see me when he said he would. I kept waiting, but he didn't come. . . .

RITA I sent you a pillow for your wedding!

EILEEN I gave it away. . . . I gave it to Clara Hill.

RITA [*laughing bawdily and miming pregnancy*] Clara Hill don't need no pillow now!

JAIMIE [*smiling, crossing to her and exiting*] I always came to see you, Rita Joe.

Rita Joe looks bewildered.

OLD WOMAN [*exiting*] I made two Saskatoon pies, Rita. . . . You said next time you came home you wanted Saskatoon pie with lots of sugar. . . .

Eileen and the old woman drift away. Jaimie Paul moves on to the shadows. The three murderers enter in silhouette; one whistles. Rita Joe rushes to the young Indian men in stagefront.

RITA This is me, Rita Joe, God's sakes. . . . We went to the same school together. . . . Don't you know me now, Johnny? You remember how tough you was when you was a boy? . . . We tied you up in the Rainbow Creek and forgot you was there after recess. . . . An' after school was out, somebody remembered. [*laughing*] And you was blue when we got to you. Your clothes was wet to the chin, an' you said, "That's a pretty good knot. . . . I almost gave up trying to untie it!"

The music continues. Rita Joe steps among the young Indian men and they mime being piled in a car at a drive-in.

Steve Laporte? . . . You remember us goin' to the drive-in and the cold rain comin' down the car windows so we couldn't see the picture show anyhow?

She sits beside Steve Laporte. They mime the windshield wipers.

A cold white light comes up on the playing area directly in front of the magistrate's chair. A male witness of dishevelled, dirty appearance steps into the light and delivers testimony in a whining, defensive voice. He is one of the murderers, but apart from the other three, he is nervous.

FIRST WITNESS   I gave her three bucks . . . an' once I got her goin' she started yellin' like hell! Called me a dog, pig . . . some filthy kind of animal. . . . So I slapped her around a bit. . . . Guys said she was a funny kind of bim . . . would do it for them standing up, but not for me she wouldn't. . . . So I slapped her around. . . .

The magistrate nods and makes a notation. The light on the first witness dies. Rita Joe speaks with urgency and growing fear to Steve Laporte.

RITA   Then you shut the wipers off an' we were just sitting there, not knowing what to do. . . . I wish . . . we could go back again there an' start livin' from that day on. . . . Jaimie!

Rita Joe looks at Steve Laporte as at a stranger. She stands and draws away from him. Jaimie Paul enters behind Rita Joe.

There is a cold light before the magistrate again and another male witness moves into the light, replacing the first witness. He too is one of the murderers. This second witness testifies with full gusto.

SECOND WITNESS   Gave her a job in my tire store . . . took her over to my place after work once. . . . She was scared when I tried a trick, but I'm easy on broads that get scared, providin' they keep their voices down. . . . After that, I slipped her a fiver. . . . Well, sir, she took the money, then she stood in front of the window, her head high an' her naked shoulders shakin' like she was cold. Well, sir, she cried a little an' then she says, "Goddamnit, but I wish I was a school teacher. . . ."

He laughs and everyone onstage joins in the laughter. The light dies out on the second witness. Jaimie Paul enters and crosses to Rita Joe. They lie down and embrace.

RITA   You always came to see me, Jaimie Paul. . . . The night we were in the cemetery . . . you remember, Jaimie Paul? I turned my face from yours until I saw the ground . . . an' I knew that below us . . . they were like us once, and now they lie below the ground, their eyes gone, the bones showin' . . . They must've spoke and touched each other here . . . like you're touching me, Jaimie Paul . . . an' now there was nothing over them, except us . . . an' wind in the grass an' a barbwire fence creaking. An' behind that a hundred acres of barley.

Jaimie Paul stands.

That's something to remember, when you're lovin', eh?

The sound of a train whistle is heard. Jaimie Paul goes and the lights onstage fade. The music comes up and the singer sings. As Jaimie Paul passes her, the singer pursues him up the ramp, and Rita Joe runs after them.

SINGER
    Oh, can't you see that train roll on,
    Gonna kill a man, before it's gone?
    Jaimie Paul fell and died.
    He had it comin', so it's alright.
    Silver train with wheels on fire!

The music dies instantly. Rita Joe's words come on the heels of the music as a bitter extension of the song. She stands before the magistrate, again in the court, but looks back to where Jaimie Paul had been in the gloom. The policeman enters where Jaimie Paul has exited, replacing him, for the fourth trial scene.

RITA Jaimie, why am I here? . . . Is it . . . because people are talkin' about me and all them men. . . . Is that why? I never wanted to cut cordwood for a living. . . . [*with great bitterness*] Never once I thought . . . it'd be like this. . . .

MAGISTRATE What are we going to do about you, Rita Joe? This is the seventh charge against you in one year. . . . Laws are not made to be violated in this way. . . . Why did you steal?

RITA I was hungry. I had no money.

MAGISTRATE Yet you must have known you would be caught?

RITA Yes.

MAGISTRATE Are you not afraid of what is happening to you?

RITA I am afraid of a lot of things. Put me in jail. I don't care. . . .

MAGISTRATE [*with forced authority*] Law is a procedure. The procedure must be respected. It took hundreds of years to develop this process of law.

RITA I stole a sweater. . . . They caught me in five minutes!

She smiles whimsically at this. The magistrate is leafing through the documents before him. The policeman stands to one side of him.

MAGISTRATE The prosecutor's office has submitted some of the past history of Rita Joe. . . .

POLICEMAN She was born and raised on a reservation. Then came a brief period in a public school off the reservation . . . at which time Rita Joe established herself as something of a disruptive influence . . .

RITA What's that mean?

MAGISTRATE [*turning to her, smiling*] A trouble maker!

Rita Joe becomes animated, aware of the trap around her closing even at moments such as this.

RITA Maybe it was about the horse, huh? . . .

She looks up at the magistrate who is still smiling, offering her no help.

There was this accident with a horse. . . . It happened like this . . . I was riding a horse to school an' some of the boys shot a rifle an' my horse bucked an' I fell off. I fell in the bush an' got scratched. . . . The boys caught the horse by the school and tried to ride him, but the horse bucked an' pinned a boy against a tree, breaking his leg in two places. . . .

She indicates the place the leg got broken.

They said . . . an' he said I'd rode the horse over him on purpose!

MAGISTRATE Well . . . did you?

RITA It wasn't that way at all, I tell you! They lied!

The policeman and the singer laugh.

MAGISTRATE Why should they lie, and Rita Joe alone tell the truth? . . . Or are you a child enough to believe the civilization of which we are a part . . .

He indicates the audience as inclusive of civilization from his point of view.

. . . does not understand Rita Joe?

RITA I don't know what you're saying.

MAGISTRATE [*with a touch of compassion*] Look at you, woman! Each time you come before me you are older. The lines in your face are those of . . .

RITA I'm tired an' I want to eat, mister! I haven't had grub since day before yesterday. . . . This room is like a boat on water. . . . I'm so dizzy. . . . What the hell kind of place is this won't let me go lie down on grass?

She doubles over to choke back her nausea.

MAGISTRATE This is not the reservation, Rita Joe. This is another place, another time. . . .

RITA [*straining to remember, to herself*] I was once in Whitecourt, Alberta.

The cops are fatter there than here. I had to get out of Whitecourt, Alberta . . .

MAGISTRATE   Don't blame the police, Rita Joe! The obstacles to your life are here . . . [*He touches his forefinger to his temples.*]   . . . in your thoughts . . . possibly even in your culture. . . .

Rita Joe turns away from him, searching the darkness behind her.

What's the matter?

RITA   I want to go home!

MAGISTRATE   But you can't go now. You've broken a law for which you will have to pay a fine or go to prison. . . .

RITA   I have no money.

MAGISTRATE   [*with exasperation*]   Rita Joe. . . . It is against the law to solicit men on the street. You have to wash. . . .

Rita Joe begins to move away from him, crossing the front of the stage along the apron, her walk cocky. The light spreads and follows her.

You can't walk around in old clothes and running shoes made of canvas . . . . You have to have some money in your pockets and an address where you live. You should fix your hair . . . perhaps even change your name. And try to tame that accent that sounds like you have a mouthful of sawdust. . . . There is no peace in being extraordinary!

The light dies on the magistrate and the policeman.

Rita Joe is transported into another memory. Jaimie Paul enters and slides along the floor, left of centre stage. He is drunk, counting the fingers on his outstretched hands. Mr. Homer has entered with a wagon carrying hot soup and mugs. Four young Indian men come in out of the cold. Mr. Homer speaks to the audience in a matter-of-fact informative way.

MR. HOMER   [*dispensing soup to the young Indian men*]   The do-gooders make something special of the Indian. . . . There's nothing special here. . . . At the Center here the quick cure is a bowl of stew under the belt and a good night's sleep.

JAIMIE   Hey, Mister Homer! How come I got so many fingers? Heh?

He laughs. Mr. Homer ignores Jaimie Paul and continues talking to the audience.

MR. HOMER   I wouldn't say they were brothers or sisters to me . . . no sir! But if you're . . .

Jaimie Paul gets up and embraces Rita Joe.

JAIMIE   I got two hands an' one neck. . . . I can kill more than I can eat. . . . If I
   had more fingers I would need mittens big as pie plates. . . . Yeh?

MR. HOMER   [*to Jaimie Paul*]   Lie down, Jaimie Paul, an' have some more sleep.
   When you feel better, I'll get you some soup.

Rita Joe laughs. Jaimie Paul weaves his way uncertainly to where Mr. Homer stands.

JAIMIE   [*laughing*]   I spit in your soup! You know what I say? . . . I say I spit in
   your soup, Mister Homer. . . .

He comes to Mr. Homer and seems about to do just what he threatens.

MR. HOMER   [*pushing him away with good humour*]   I'll spit in your eyeball if
   you don't shut up!

JAIMIE   [*breaking away from Mr. Homer, taunting*]   You . . . are not Mister Homer!

MR. HOMER   I'm not what?

JAIMIE   You're not Mister Homer. . . . You're somebody wearing his pants an'
   shirt . . . [*stumbling away*]   But you're not Mister Homer. . . . Mister Homer
   never gets mad. . . . No sir, not Mister Homer!

MR. HOMER   I'm not mad. . . . What're you talkin' about?

*Jaimie Paul turns and approaches the young Indian men. He threatens to fall off the
apron of the stage.*

JAIMIE   No . . . not Mister Homer! An' I got ten fingers. . . . How's that?

MR. HOMER   For Chris' sake, Jaimie . . . go to sleep.

*Jaimie Paul stops and scowls, then grins knowingly. He begins to mime a clumsy
paddler paddling a boat.*

JAIMIE   [*laughing again*]   I know you. . . . Hey? I know you! . . . I seen you up
   Rainbow Creek one time . . . I seen you paddling!

He breaks up with laughter.

MR. HOMER   [*amused, tolerant*]   Oh, come on . . . I've never been to Rainbow
   Creek.

JAIMIE   [*controlling his laughter*]   Sure you been to Rainbow Creek. . . . [*He
   begins to mime paddling again.*] Next time you need a good paddler, you
   see me. I have a governmen' job, but screw that. I'm gonna paddle! I
   seen you paddle. . . .

*Again he breaks up in laughter as he once more demonstrates the quality of paddling he
once saw. Rita Joe is fully enjoying the spectacle. So are the young Indian men. Mr.
Homer is also amused by the absurdity of the situation. Jaimie Paul turns, but chokes
up with laughter after saying . . .*

I have seen some paddlers . . . but you!

Jaimie Paul turns and waves his hand derisively, laughing.

MR. HOMER   It must've been somebody else. . . . I've never been to Rainbow
Creek.
JAIMIE   Like hell, you say!

Jaimie Paul paddles the soup wagon out. Guitar music comes in with an upbeat tempo.
Rita Joe and the young Indian men dance to the beat. The young Indian men then drift
after Mr. Homer.

The light fades slowly on centre stage and the music changes.

Rita Joe, happy in her memory, does a circling butch walk in the fading light to the song
of the singer. At the conclusion of the song, she is on the apron, stage right, in a wash of
light that includes the magistrate and the singer.

SINGER
I woke up at six o'clock
Stumbled out of bed,
Crash of cans an' diesel trucks
Damned near killed me dead.

Sleepless hours, heavy nights,
Dream your dreams so pretty
God was gonna have a laugh
An' gave me a job in the city!

Rita Joe is still elated at her memory of Jaimie Paul and his story. With unusual
candor, she turns girlishly before the magistrate, and in mild imitation of her own
moment of drunkenness, begins telling him a story. Faint guitar music in the background
continues.

RITA   One night I drank a little bit of wine, an' I was outside lookin' at the
stars . . . thinking . . . when I was a little girl how much bigger the trees
were . . . no clouds, but suddenly there was a light that made the whole
sky look like day . . .

Guitar out.

. . . just for a moment . . . an' before I got used to the night . . . I saw
animals, moving across the sky . . . two white horses. . . . A man was takin'
them by the halters, and I knew the man was my grandfather. . . .

She stares at the magistrate, unsure of herself now.

MAGISTRATE Yes! Is that all?

RITA No. . . . But I never seen my grandfather alive, and I got so sad thinkin' about it I wanted to cry. I wasn't sure it was him, even. . . . [*She begins to laugh*]. I went an' telephoned the police and asked for the chief, but the chief was home and a guy asks what I want.

MAGISTRATE [*mildly amused*] You . . . called the police?

RITA I told the guy I'd seen God, and he says, "Yeh? What would you like us to do about it?" An' I said, "Pray! Laugh! Shout!"

MAGISTRATE Go on. . . .

RITA He . . . asked where I'd seen God, an' I told him in the sky. He says you better call this number. . . . It's the Air Force. They'll take care of it!

She laughs and the magistrate smiles.

I called the number the guy gave me, but it was nighttime and there was no answer! If God was to come at night, after office hours, then. . . .

A terrible awkwardness sets in. There is a harsh light on her. She turns away, aware that she is in captivity. The magistrate stirs with discomfort.

RITA [*with great fear*] How long will this be? Will I never be able to . . .

MAGISTRATE [*annoyed at himself, at her*] There is nothing here but a record of your convictions . . . nothing to speak for you and provide me with any reason to moderate your sentence! What the hell am I supposed to do? Violate the law myself because I feel that somehow . . . I've known and felt. . . . No! [*turning from her*] You give me no alternative . . . no alternative at all!

The magistrate packs up his books.

RITA I'll go home . . . jus' let me go home. I can't get out of jail to find the highway . . . or some kind of job!

MAGISTRATE [*standing*] Prison and fines are not the only thing. . . . Have you, for instance, considered that you might be an incurable carrier? There are people like that. . . . They cannot come into contact with others without infecting them. They cannot eat from dishes others may use. . . . They cannot prepare or touch food others will eat. . . . The same with clothes, cars, hospital beds!

The magistrate exists. Rita Joe shakes her head with disbelief. The idea of perpetual condemnation is beyond her comprehension. She falls to the floor. Guitar music is heard in the background.

She turns away from the magistrate and the light comes up over the ramp at the back of the stage. Another light comes up on centre stage left. Here, Eileen Joe and the old woman are miming clothes washing using a scrubbing board and placing the wash into woven baskets. The woman and the girl are on their knees, facing each other.

On the ramp above them, Jaimie Paul is struggling with a policeman who is scolding him softly for being drunk, abusive and noisy. Jaimie Paul is jocular; the policeman, harassed and worried. They slowly cross the ramp from stage left.

SINGER
> Four o'clock in the morning,
> The sailor rides the ship
> An' I ride the wind!
>
> Eight o'clock in the morning,
> My honey's scoldin' the sleepyheads
> An' I'm scoldin' him.

JAIMIE   [*to the policeman*]   On the Smoky River . . . four o'clock in the morning . . . hey? There was nobody . . . just me. . . . You know that?
POLICEMAN   No, I don't. Come on. Let's get you home.

Jaimie Paul moves forward and embraces the policeman.

JAIMIE   You wanna see something?

Jaimie Paul takes out a coin to do a trick.

OLD WOMAN   [*to Eileen*]   Your father's been very sick.
EILEEN   He won't eat nothing. . . .
OLD WOMAN   Jus' sits and worries. . . . That's no good.
JAIMIE PAUL   [*finishing his coin trick*]   You like that one? Hey, we both work for the government, eh?

They exit laughing.

> Watch the rough stuff. . . . Just don't make me mad.
OLD WOMAN   If Rita Joe was to come and see him . . . maybe say goodbye to him. . . .
RITA   [*calling from her world to the world of her strongest fears*]   But he's not dying! I saw him not so long ago. . . .

The women in her memory do not hear her. They continue discussing her father.

OLD WOMAN   He loved her an' always worried. . . .
RITA   I didn't know he was sick!
OLD WOMAN   You were smart to come back, Eileen Joe.
RITA   [*again calling over the distance of her soul*]   Nobody told me!

SINGER
>Nine o'clock in the evening,
>Moon is high in the blueberry sky
>An' I'm lovin' you.

JAIMIE [*now passing along the apron beside Rita Joe, talking to the policeman*] You see where I live? Big house with a mongolia in front. . . . Fancy place! You wanna see the room I got?

POLICEMAN [*gruffly, aware that Jaimie Paul can become angry quickly*] When I get holidays, we'll take a tour of everything you've got. . . . but I don't get holidays until September!

From the apron they cross to the stage rear diagonally, between the old woman and Eileen, and Rita Joe.

JAIMIE You're a good man . . . good for a laugh. I'm a good man . . . you know me!

POLICEMAN Sure, you're first class when you're sober!

JAIMIE I got a cousin in the city. He got his wife a stove an' washing machine! He's a good man. . . . You know my cousin maybe?

Fading off. They leave the stage.

The old woman has risen from her knees and wearily collected one basket of clothes. She climbs the ramp and moves to the wings, stage right. Eileen is thoughtful and slower, but she also prepares her clothes wash and follows.

OLD WOMAN Nothing in the city I can see . . . only if you're lucky. A good man who don't drink or play cards . . . that's all.

EILEEN And if he's bad?

OLD WOMAN Then leave him. I'm older than you, Eileen. . . . I know what's best.

The old woman exits. The guitar music dies out. Jaimie Paul's laughter and voice is heard offstage.

JAIMIE [*offstage, loud, boisterous*] We both work for the gov'ment! We're buddies, no? . . . You think we're both the same?

Laughter. The lights on the ramp and centre stage die.

RITA [*following Jaimie Paul's laughter*] Good or bad, what difference? So long as he's a livin' man!

Rita Joe and Eileen giggle. The light spreads around her into pale infinity.

The teacher enters on the ramp. She rings a handbell and stops a short distance from the wings to peer around. She is a shy, inadequate woman who moves and behaves jerkily, the product of incomplete education and poor job placement.

TEACHER   [*in a scolding voice*]   Rita! Rita Joe!

The bell rings.

The class is waiting for you. The class is always waiting.

Rita Joe is startled to hear the bell and see the woman. She comes to her feet, now a child before the teacher, and runs to join Eileen. Jaimie Paul and the young Indian men have entered with the bell and sit cross-legged on the floor as school children.

RITA   The sun is in my skin, Miss Donohue. The leaves is red and orange, and the wind stopped blowin' an hour ago.

The teacher has stopped to listen to this. Rita Joe and Eileen, late again, slip into class and sit on the floor with the others.

TEACHER   Rita! What is a noun?

No answer. The kids poke Rita Joe to stand up.

Did you hear what I asked?
RITA   [*uncertain*]   No . . . yes?
TEACHER   There's a lot you don't know. . . . That kind of behavior is exhibitionism! We are a melting pot!
RITA   A melting pot?
TEACHER   A melting pot! Do you know what a melting pot is?
RITA   It's . . . [*She shrugs.*]   . . . a melting pot!

The class laughs.

TEACHER   Precisely! You put copper and tin into a melting pot and out comes bronze. . . . It's the same with people!
RITA   Yes, Miss Donohue . . . out comes bronze. . . .

Laughter again. The teacher calls Rita Joe over to her. The light fades on the other children.

TEACHER   Rita, what was it I said to you this morning?
RITA   You said . . . wash my neck, clean my fingernails. . . .
TEACHER   [*cagey*]   No, it wasn't, Rita!
RITA   I can't remember. It was long ago.
TEACHER   Try to remember, Rita.
RITA   I don't remember, Miss Donohue! I was thinkin' about you last night, thinkin' if you knew some . . .

TEACHER   You are straying off the topic! Never stray off the topic!

RITA   It was a dream, but now I'm scared, Miss Donohue. I've been a long time moving about . . . trying to find something! . . . I must've lost . . .

TEACHER   No, Rita. That is not important.

RITA   Not important?

TEACHER   No, Rita. . . . Now you repeat after me like I said or I'm going to have to pass you by again. Say after me . . .

RITA   Sure. Say after you . . .

TEACHER   Say after me . . . "A book of verse underneath the spreading bough . . . "

RITA   "A book of verse underneath the spreading bough . . . "

TEACHER   "A jug of wine, a loaf of bread and thou beside me . . . singing in the wilderness."

RITA   [*the child spell broken, she laughs bawdily*]   Jaimie said, "To heck with the wine an' loaf. . . . Let's have some more of this here thou!"

Her laughter dies. She wipes her lips, as if trying to erase some stain there.

TEACHER   [*peevish*]   Alright, Rita. . . . Alright, let's have none of that!

RITA   [*plaintively*]   I'm sorry, Miss Donohue. . . . I'm sure sorry!

TEACHER   That's alright.

RITA   I'm sorry!

TEACHER   Alright. . . .

RITA   Sorry . . .

TEACHER   You will never make bronze! Coming from nowhere and going no place! Who am I to change that?

Rita Joe grips the edge of the desk with both hands, holding on tightly.

RITA   No! They said for me to stay here, to learn something!

TEACHER   [*with exasperation*]   I tried to teach you, but your head was in the clouds, and as for your body. . . . Well! I wouldn't even think what I know you do!

The teacher crosses amongst the other children.

RITA   I'm sorry . . . please! Let me say it after you again . . . [*blurting it out*] "A book of verse underneath the spreading . . . "

TEACHER   Arguing . . . always trying to upset me . . . and in grade four . . . I saw it then . . . pawing the ground for men like a bitch in heat!

RITA   [*dismayed*]   It . . . isn't so!

TEACHER   You think I don't know? I'm not blind . . . I can see out of the windows.

The teacher marches off into the wings and the class runs after her leaving Rita Joe alone onstage.

RITA That's a lie! For God's sake, tell the judge I have a good character. . . . I
am clean an' honest. . . . Everything you said is right, I'm never gonna
argue again. . . . I believe in God . . . an' I'm from the country and lost like
hell! Tell him!

She shakes her head sadly, knowing the extent of her betrayal.

They only give me eight hours to find somebody who knows me. . . . An'
seven and a half hours is gone already!

The light on the scene dies.

SINGER [*recitivo*]
    Things that were . . .
    Life that might have been . . .

*A pale backlight on the back of the ramp comes up. Recorded sounds of crickets and the
distant sound of a train whistle are heard.*

*Rita Joe's father and Jaimie Paul enter on the ramp from stage left. The father leads the
way. Jaimie Paul is behind, rolling a cigarette. They walk slowly, thoughtfully, following the ramp across and downstage. Rita Joe stands separate, watching.*

SINGER
    The blue evening of the first
    Warm day
    Is the last evening.
    There'll not be another
    Like it.
JAIMIE No more handouts, David Joe. . . . We can pick an' can the berries
    ourselves.
FATHER We need money to start a cooperative like that.
JAIMIE Then some other way!

The old man listens, standing still, to the sounds of the train and the night.

FATHER You're a young man, Jaimie Paul . . . young an' angry. It's not good
    to be that angry.
JAIMIE We're gonna work an' live like people . . . not be afraid all the time . . .
    stop listening to an old priest an' Indian Department guys who're work-
    ing for a pension!
FATHER You're a young man, Jaimie Paul. . . .
JAIMIE I say stop listening, David Joe! . . . In the city they never learned my
    name. It was "Hey, fella" . . . or "You, boy" . . . that kind of stuff.

Pause. The sound of the train whistle is heard.

FATHER   A beautiful night, Jaimie Paul.
JAIMIE   We can make some money. The berries are good this year!

Jaimie Paul is restless, edgy, particularly on the train whistle sound.

FATHER   Sometimes . . . children . . . you remember every day with them. . . .
Never forget you are alive with children.

Jaimie Paul turns away and begins to retrace his steps.

JAIMIE   You want us all to leave an' go to the city? Is that what you want?

*The father shakes his head. He does not wish for this, but the generation spread between
them is great now. Jaimie Paul walks away with a gesture of contempt.*

The sounds die. The light dies and isolates the father and Rita Joe.

RITA   You were sick, an' now you're well.
FATHER   [*in measured speech, turning away from Rita Joe, as if carefully recalling
something of great importance.*]   You left your father, Rita Joe . . . never wrote
Eileen a letter that time. . . . Your father was pretty sick man that time . . .
pretty sick man. . . . June ninth he got the cold, an' on June twenty he . . .
RITA   But you're alive! I had such crazy dreams I'd wake up laughing at
myself!
FATHER   I have dreams too. . . .

*Rita Joe moves forward to him. She stops talking to him, as if communicating thoughts
rather than words. He remains standing where he is, facing away from her.*

RITA   I was in a big city . . . so many streets I'd get lost like nothin'. . . . When
you got sick I was on a job . . .
FATHER   June ninth I got the cold . . .
RITA   Good job in a tire store . . . Jaimie Paul's got a job with the government,
you know?
FATHER   Pretty sick man, that time . . .
RITA   A good job in a tire store. They was gonna teach me how to file state-
ments after I learned the telephone. Bus ticket home was twenty dollars.
. . . But I got drunk all the same when I heard an' I went in and tried to
work that day. . . . [*smiling and shaking her head*]   Boy, I tried to work!
Some day that was!
FATHER   I have dreams. . . . Sometimes I'm scared. . . .

They finally look at each other.

RITA   [*shuddering*]   I'm so cold. . . .
FATHER   Long dreams . . . I dream about Rita Joe. . . .   [*sadly*]   Have to get

better. I've lived longer, but I know nothing . . . nothing at all. Only the old stories.

Rita Joe moves sideways to him. She is smiling happily.

RITA   When I was little, a man came out of the bush to see you. Tell me why again!

The father hesitates, shaking his head, but he is also smiling The light of their separate yearnings fades out and the front of the stage is lit with the two of them together. The father turns and comes forward to meet her.

FATHER   You don't want to hear that story again.

He sits on the slight elevation of the stage apron. Rita Joe sits down in front of him and snuggles between his knees. He leans forward over her.

RITA   It's the best story I ever heard!
FATHER   You were a little girl . . . four years old already . . . an' Eileen was getting big inside your mother. One day it was hot . . . sure was hot. Too hot to try an' fish in the lake, because the fish was down deep where the water was cold.
RITA   The dog started to bark.
FATHER   The dog started to bark. . . . How!
FATHER and RITA   [*in unison*]   How! How! How!
FATHER   Barking to beat hell an' I says to myself why . . . on such a hot day? Then I see the bushes moving . . . somebody was coming to see us. Your mother said from inside the house, "What's the matter with that dog?" An' I says to her, "Somebody coming to see me." It was big Sandy Collins, who ran the sawmill back of the reserve. Business was bad for big Sandy then . . . but he comes out of that bush like he was being chased . . . his clothes all wet an' stickin' to him . . . his cap in his hands, an' his face black with the heat and dirt from hard work. . . . He says to me, "My little Millie got a cough last night an' today she's dead." . . . "She's dead," big Sandy says to me. I says to him, "I'm sorry to hear that, Sandy. Millie is the same age as my Rita." And he says to me, "David Joe . . . look, you got another kid coming . . . won't make much difference to you. . . . Sell me Rita Joe like she is for a thousand dollars!"

Rita Joe giggles. The father raises his hand to silence her.

"A thousand dollars is a lot of money, Sandy," I says to him . . . "lots of money. You got to cut a lot of timber for a thousand dollars." Then he says to me, "Not a thousand cash at once, David Joe. First I give you two hundred fifty dollars. . . . When Rita Joe comes ten years old and she's still alright, I give you the next two hundred fifty. . . . An' if she don't die by fifteen, I guarantee you five hundred dollars cash at once!''

Rita Joe and the father break into laughter. He reaches around her throat and draws her close.

So you see, Rita Joe, you lose me one thousand dollars from big Sandy Collins!

They continue laughing. A harsh light on the magistrate, who enters and stands on his podium.

MAGISTRATE   Rita Joe, when was the last time you had dental treatment?

Rita Joe covers her ears, refusing to surrender this moment of security in the arms of her father.

RITA   I can't hear you!

MAGISTRATE   [*loudly*]   You had your teeth fixed ever?

RITA   [*coming to her feet and turning on him*]   Leave me alone!

MAGISTRATE   Have you had your lungs X-rayed recently?

RITA   I was hungry, that's all!

MAGISTRATE   [*becoming staccato, machine-like in his questions*]   When was your last Wasserman taken?

RITA   What's that?

Rita Joe hears the teacher's voice. She turns to see the approaching teacher give the magistrate testimony. The stage is lit in a cold blue light now.

TEACHER   [*crisply to the magistrate as she approaches, her monologue a reading*]   Dear Sir. . . . In reply to your letter of the twelfth, I cannot in all sincerity provide a reference of good character for one Rita Joe. . . .

The witnesses do not see her and the testimony takes on the air of a nightmare for Rita Joe. She is baffled and afraid. The teacher continues to quietly repeat her testimony. Rita Joe appeals to the magistrate.

RITA   Why am I here? What've I done?

MAGISTRATE   You are charged with prostitution.

Her father stands and crosses upstage to the ramp to observe. He is joined by Eileen Joe, and the old woman and the priest. Mr. Homer approaches briskly from stage left.

MR. HOMER   She'd been drinking when she comes into the Center. . . . Nothing wrong in that I could see, 'specially on a Friday night. So I give her some soup an' a sandwich. Then all of a sudden in the middle of a silly argument, she goes haywire . . . an' I see her comin' at me. . . . I'll tell you, I was scared! I don't know Indian women that well!

MAGISTRATE   Assault!

Rita Joe retreats from him. The teacher and Mr. Homer now stand before the magistrate as if they were frozen. Mr. Homer repeats his testimony under the main dialogue. Jaimie Paul staggers in from stage right, over the ramp, heading to the wings of lower stage left.

JAIMIE   [*to himself*]   What the hell are they doing?
RITA   [*running to him*]   Say a good word for me, Jaimie!
JAIMIE   They fired me yesterday. . . . What the hell's the use of living?

Jaimie Paul leaves the stage as the school board clerk enters to offer further testimony to the magistrate.

SCHOOL BOARD CLERK   I recommended in a letter that she take school after grade five through correspondence courses from the Department of Education . . . but she never replied to the form letter the school division sent her. . . .
RITA   [*defending herself to the magistrate*]   That drunken bastard Mahoney used it to light fire in his store. . . . He'd never tell Indians when mail came for us!

SCHOOL BOARD CLERK   I repeat . . . I wish our position understood most clearly. . . . No reply was ever received in this office to the letter we sent Rita Joe!
RITA   One letter . . . one letter for a lifetime?
TEACHER   Say after me! "I wandered lonely as a cloud, that floats on high o'er vales and hills. . . . When all at once I saw a crowd . . . a melting pot . . . "

A policeman and a male witness enter. The priest crosses downstage. The testimonies are becoming a nightmare babble. Rita Joe is slung, stumbling backward from all of them as they face the magistrate with their condemnations.

POLICEMAN   We were impersonating two deckhands. . . .

The priest is passing by Rita Joe. He makes the sign of the cross and offers comfort in a thin voice, lost in the noise.

PRIEST   Be patient, Rita. . . . The young are always stormy, but in time, your understanding will deepen. . . . There is an end to all things.
WITNESS   I gave her a job, but she was kind of slow. . . . I can't wait around, there's lots of white people goin' lookin for work . . . so I figure, to hell with this noise . . .
MAGISTRATE   [*loudly over the other voices*]   Have your ears ached?
RITA   No!
MAGISTRATE   Have you any boils on your back? Any discharge? When did you bathe last?

The murderers appear and circle Rita Joe.

> Answer me! Drunkenness! Shoplifting! Assault! Prostitution, prostitution, prostitution, prostitution!

RITA [*her voice shrill, cutting over the babble*] I don't know what happened . . . but you got to listen to me and believe me, mister!

The babble ceases abruptly. Rita Joe pleads with them as best she knows.

> You got rules here that was made before I was born. . . . I was hungry when I stole something . . . an' I was hollerin' I was so lonely when I started whoring. . . .

The murderers come closer.

MAGISTRATE Rita Joe . . . has a doctor examined you? . . . I mean, really examined you? Rita Joe . . . you might be carrying and transmitting some disease and not aware of it!

RITA [*breaking away from the murderers*] Bastards! [*to the magistrate*] Put me in jail . . . I don't care. . . . I'll sign anything, I'm so goddamn hungry I'm sick. . . . Whatever it is, I'm guilty!

She clutches her head and goes down in a squat of defeat.

MAGISTRATE Are you free of venereal disease?
RITA I don't know. I'm not sick that way.
MAGISTRATE How can you tell?
RITA [*lifting her face to him*] I know. . . . A woman knows them things. . . .

Pause.

MAGISTRATE Thirty days!

The policeman leads Rita Joe off and the house lights come up. The actors and the singer walk off the stage, leaving emptiness as at the opening of the act.

ACT II

The house lights dim. A policeman brings Rita Joe in downstage center. She curls up in her jail cell and sleeps. Rita Joe's father enters on the ramp and crosses down to the audience. The stage work lights die down. Lights isolate Rita Joe's father. Another light with prison bar shadows isolates Rita Joe in her area of the stage.

FATHER   [*looking down on Rita Joe*]   I see no way . . . no way. . . . It's not clear like trees against snow . . . not clear at all. . . .

To the audience.

> But when I was fifteen years old, I leave the reserve to work on a threshing crew. They pay a dollar a day for a good man . . . an' I was a good strong man. The first time I got work there was a girl about as old as I. . . . She'd come out in the yard an' watch the men working at the threshing machine. She had eyes that were the biggest I ever seen . . . like fifty-cent pieces . . . an' there was always a flock of geese around her. Whenever I see her I feel good. She used to stand an' watch me, an' the geese made a helluva lot of noise. One time I got off my rick an' went to get a drink of water . . . but I walked close to where she was watching me. She backed away, and then ran from me with the geese chasin' after her, their wings out an' their feet no longer touching the ground. . . . They were white geese. . . . The last time Rita Joe come home to see us . . . the last time she ever come home . . . I watched her leave . . . and I seen geese running after Rita Joe the same way . . . white geese . . . with their wings out an' their feet no longer touching the ground. And I remembered it all, an' my heart got so heavy I wanted to cry. . . .

The light fades to darkness on the father, as he exits up the ramp and off. Rita Joe wakes from her dream, cold, shaking, desperate.

SINGER
> The blue evening of the
> First warm day
> Is the last evening.
> There'll not be another
> Like it.

The priest enters from darkness with the policeman. He is dressed in a dark suit which needs pressing. He stops in half shadow outside Rita Joe's prison light. The scene between them is played out in the manner of two country people meeting in a time of crisis. Their thoughts come slowly, incompletely. There is both fear and helplessness in both characters.

PRIEST   I came twice before they'd let me see you. . . .

Rita Joe jumps to her feet. She smiles at him.

RITA   Oh, Father Andrew!
PRIEST   Even so, I had to wait an hour.

A long pause. He clumsily takes out a package of cigarettes and matches from his pocket and hands them to her, aware that he is possibly breaking a prison regulation.

I'm sorry about this, Rita.

Rita Joe tears the package open greedily and lights a cigarette. She draws on it with animal satisfaction.

RITA   I don't know what's happening, Father Andrew.

PRIEST   They're not . . . hurting you here?

RITA   No.

PRIEST   I could make an appointment with the warden if there was something . . .

RITA   What's it like outside? . . . Is it a nice day outside? I heard it raining last night. . . . Was it raining?

PRIEST   It rains a lot here . . .

RITA   When I was a kid, there was leaves an' a river. . . . Jaimie Paul told me once that maybe we never see those things again.

A long pause. The priest struggles with himself.

PRIEST   I've never been inside a jail before. . . . They told me there was a chapel. . . .

He points indefinitely back.

RITA   What's gonna happen to me? . . . That judge sure got sore. . . .

She laughs.

PRIEST   [*with disgust, yet unsure of himself*]   Prostitution this time?

RITA   I guess so. . . .

PRIEST   You know how I feel. . . . City is no place for you . . . nor for me. . . . I've spent my life in the same surroundings as your father!

RITA   Sure . . . but you had God on your side!

She smiles mischievously. The priest angers.

PRIEST   Rita, try to understand. . . . Our Lord Jesus once met a woman such as you beside the well. . . . He forgave her!

RITA   I don't think God hears me here. . . . Nobody hears me now, nobody except cops an' pimps an' bootleggers!

PRIEST   I'm here. I was there when you were born.

RITA   You've told me lots of times. . . . I was thinkin' about my mother last night. . . . She died young. . . . I'm older than she was. . . .

PRIEST   Your mother was a good, hard-working woman. She was happy. . . .

A pause between them.

RITA   There was frost on the street at five o'clock Tuesday morning when they arrested me. . . . Last night I remembered things flyin' and kids runnin' past me trying to catch a chocolate wrapper that's blowin' in the wind. . . . [*She presses her hands against her bosom.*] It hurts me here to think about them things!

PRIEST   I worry about you. . . . Your father worries too. . . . I baptized you. . . . I watched you and Leenie grow into women!

RITA   Yes. . . . I seen God in what you said . . . in your clothes! In your hair!

PRIEST   But you're not the woman I expected you to be. . . . Your pride, Rita . . . your pride . . . may bar you from heaven.

RITA   [*mocking him*]   They got rules there too . . . in heaven?

PRIEST   [*angry*]   Rita! . . . I'm not blind . . . I can see! I'm not deaf . . . I know all about you! So does God!

RITA   My uncle was Dan Joe. . . . He was dyin' and he said to me, "Long ago the white man come with Bibles to talk to my people, who had the land. They talk for hundred years . . . then we had all the Bibles, an' the white man had our land. . . ."

PRIEST   Don't blame the Church! We are trying to help . . .

RITA   [*with passion*]   How? I'm looking for the door. . . .

PRIEST   [*tortured now*]   I . . . will hear your confession . . .

RITA   But I want to be free!

PRIEST   [*stiffly*]   We learn through suffering, Rita Joe. . . . We will only be free if we become humble again. [*Pause*]. Will you confess, Rita Joe? [*A long pause*]. I'm going back on the four o'clock bus. [*He begins walking away into the gloom.*] I'll tell your father I saw you, and you looked well.

He is suddenly relieved.

RITA   [*after him as he leaves*]   You go to hell!

The priest turns sharply.

Go tell your God . . . when you see him . . . tell him about Rita Joe an' what they done to her! Tell him about yourself too! . . . That you were not good enough for me, but that didn't stop you tryin'! Tell him that!

The priest hurries away. Guitar in. Rita Joe sits down, brooding.

SINGER
  I will give you the wind and a sense of wonder
  As the child by the river, the reedy river.
  I will give you the sky wounded by thunder
  And a leaf on the river, the silver river.

A light comes up on the ramp where Jaimie Paul appears, smiling and waving to her.

JAIMIE [*shouting*] Rita Joe! I'm gonna take you dancing after work Friday. . . .
  That job's gonna be alright!

Rita Joe springs to her feet, elated.

RITA Put me back in jail so I can be free on Friday!

A sudden burst of dance music. The stage lights up and Jaimie Paul approaches her. They dance together, remaining close in the front center stage.

SINGER
  Round an' round the cenotaph,
  The clumsy seagulls play.
  Fed by funny men with hats
  Who watch them night and day.

  Sleepless hours, heavy nights,
  Dream your dreams so pretty.
  God was gonna have a laugh
  An' gave me a job in the city!

The music continues for the interlude.

Some young Indian men run onto the stage along the ramp and join Jaimie Paul and Rita Joe in their dance. The murderers enter and elbow into the group, their attention specifically menacing towards Jaimie Paul and Rita Joe. A street brawl begins as a policeman passes through on his beat. The murderers leave hastily.

  I woke up at six o'clock,
  Stumbled out of bed.
  Crash of steel and diesel trucks
  Damned near killed me dead.

  Sleepless hours, heavy nights,
  Dream your dreams so pretty.
  God was gonna have a laugh
  An' gave me a job in the city!

Musical interlude. Rita Joe and Jaimie Paul continue dancing languidly. The young Indian men exit.

  I've polished floors an' cut the trees,
  Fished and stooked the wheat.
  Now "Hallelujah, Praise the Lord,"
  I sing before I eat!

Sleepless hours, heavy nights,
Dream your dreams so pretty.
God was gonna have a laugh
An' gave me a job in the city!

Musical interlude.

The music dies as the young Indian men wheel in a brass bed, circle it around and exit. The stage darkens except for a pool of light where Rita Joe and Jaimie Paul stand, embracing. Jaimie Paul takes her hand and leads her away.

JAIMIE   Come on, Rita Joe . . . you're slow.
RITA   [*happy in her memories, not wishing to forget too soon, hesitating*]   How much rent . . . for a place where you can keep babies?
JAIMIE   I don't know . . . maybe eighty dollars a month.
RITA   That's a lot of money.
JAIMIE   It costs a buck to go dancin' even. . . .

They walk slowly along the apron to stage left, as if following a street to Jaimie Paul's rooming house.

It's a good place. . . . I got a sink in the room. Costs seven bucks a week, that's all!
RITA   That's good. . . . I only got a bed in my place. . . .
JAIMIE   I seen Mickey an' Steve Laporte last night.
RITA   How are they?
JAIMIE   Good. . . . We're goin' to a beer parlour Monday night when I get paid . . . the same beer parlour they threw Steve out of! Only now there's three of us goin' in!

They arrive at and enter his room. A spot illuminates the bed near the wings of stage left. It is old, dilapidated. Jaimie Paul and Rita Joe enter the area of light around the bed. He is aware that the room is more drab than he would wish it.

How do you like it? . . . I like it!
RITA   [*examining room critically*]   It's . . . smaller than my place.
JAIMIE   Sit down.

She sits on the edge of the bed and falls backward into a springless hollow. He laughs nervously. He is awkward and confused. The ease they shared walking to his place is now constricted.

I was gonna get some grub today, but I was busy. . . . Here. . . .

He takes a chocolate bar out of his shirt pocket and offers it to her. She opens it, breaks off a small piece, and gives the remainder to him. He closes the wrapper and replaces the bar in his pocket. She eats ravenously. He walks around the bed nervously.

No fat d.p.'s gonna throw me or the boys out of that beer parlour or he's gonna get this!

He holds up a fist in a gesture that is both poignant and futile. She laughs and he glowers at her.

I'm tellin' you!

RITA   If they want to throw you out, they'll throw you out.

JAIMIE   Well, this is one Indian guy they're not pushing around no more!

RITA   God helps them who help themselves.

JAIMIE   That's right! [*laughing*]   I was lookin' at the white shirts in Eaton's and this bugger comes an' says to me, you gonna buy or you gonna look all day?

RITA   [*looking around her*]   It's a nice room for a guy, I guess . . .

JAIMIE   It's a lousy room!

Rita Joe lies back lengthwise in the bed. Jaimie Paul sits on the bed beside her.

RITA   You need a good job to have babies in the city. . . . Clara Hill gave both her kids away they say. . . .

JAIMIE   Where do kids like that go?

RITA   Foster homes, I guess.

JAIMIE   If somebody don't like the kid, back they go to another foster home?

RITA   I guess so. . . . Clara Hill don't know where her kids are now.

JAIMIE   [*twisting sharply in his anger*]   Goddamn it!

RITA   My father says . . .

Jaimie Paul rises, crosses round the bed to the other side.

JAIMIE   [*harshly*]   I don't want to hear what your father got to say! He's like . . . like the kind of Indian a white man likes! He's gonna look wise and wait forever . . . for what? For the kids they take away to come back?

RITA   He's scared . . . I'm scared. . . . We're all scared, Jaimie Paul.

Jaimie Paul lies face down and mimes a gun through the bars.

JAIMIE   Sometimes I feel like takin' a gun and just. . . .

He waves his hand as if to liquidate his environment and all that bedevils him. He turns over on his back and lies beside Rita Joe.

I don't know. . . . Goddamnit, I don't know what to do. I get mad an' then I don't know what I'm doing or thinkin'. . . . I get scared sometimes, Rita Joe.

RITA   [*tenderly*] We're scared . . . everybody. . . .

JAIMIE I'm scared of dyin' . . . in the city. They don't care for one another here. . . . You got to be smart or have a good job to live like that.

RITA   Clara Hill's gonna have another baby . . .

JAIMIE I can't live like that. . . . A man don't count for much here. . . . Women can do as much as a man. . . . There's no difference between men and women. I can't live like that.

RITA   You got to stop worrying, Jaimie Paul. You're gonna get sick worryin'.

JAIMIE You can't live like that, can you?

RITA   No.

JAIMIE I can't figure out what the hell they want from us!

RITA   [*laughing*] Last time I was in trouble, the judge was asking me what I wanted from him! I could've told him, but I didn't!

They both laugh. Jaimie Paul becomes playful and happy.

JAIMIE Last night I seen television in a store window. I seen a guy on television showing this knife that cuts everything it's so sharp. . . . He was cutting up good shoes like they were potatoes. . . . That was sure funny to see!

Again they laugh in merriment at the idea of such a demonstration. Jaimie Paul continues with his story, gesturing with his hands.

Chop . . . chop . . . chop. . . . A potful of shoes in no time! What's a guy gonna do with a potful of shoes? Cook them?

They continue laughing and lie together again. Then Jaimie Paul sobers. He rises from the bed and walks around it. He offers his hand to Rita Joe, who also rises.

JAIMIE [*drily*] Come on. This is a lousy room!

SINGER [*reprise*]
     God was gonna have a laugh,
     And gave me a job in the city!

The light goes down on Rita Joe and Jaimie Paul. The young Indian men clear the bed. Cross fade to the rear ramp of the stage. Rita Joe's father and the priest enter and cross the stage.

PRIEST She got out yesterday, but she wouldn't let me see her. I stayed an extra day, but she wouldn't see me.

FATHER [*sadly*] I must go once more to the city. . . . I must go to see them.

PRIEST You're an old man. . . . I wish I could persuade you not to go.

FATHER You wouldn't say that if you had children, Andrew. . . .

The lights go down on them. The lights come up on center stage front. Three young

Indian men precede Mr. Homer, carrying a table between them. Mr. Homer follows with a hamper of clothes under his arm.

MR. HOMER   Yeh . . . right about there is fine, boys. Got to get the clutter out of the basement. . . . There's mice coming in to beat hell.

Mr. Homer empties the clothes hamper on the table. The young Indian men step aside and converse in an undertone. On the ramp, a young Indian man weaves his way from stage left and down to center stage where the others have brought the table. He is followed by Jaimie Paul and Rita Joe, who mime his intoxicated progress.

MR. HOMER   [*speaking to the audience*]   The Society for Aid to the Indians sent a guy over to see if I could recommend someone who'd been . . . well, through the mill, like they say . . . an' then smartened up an' taken rehabilitation. The guy said they just wanted a rehabilitated Indian to show up at their annual dinner. No speeches or fancy stuff . . . just be there.

The young Indian man lies down carefully to one side of Mr. Homer.

Hi, Louie. Not that I would cross the street for the Society. . . . They're nothing but a pack of do-gooders out to get their name in the papers.

The young Indian man begins to sing a tuneless song, trailing off into silence.

Keep it down, eh, Louie? I couldn't think of anybody to suggest to this guy . . . so he went away pretty sore. . . .

Rita Joe begins to rummage through the clothes on the table. She looks at sweaters and holds a red one thoughtfully in her hands. Jaimie Paul is in conversation with the young Indian men to one side of the table. Mr. Homer turns from the audience to see Rita Joe holding the sweater.

Try it on, Rita Joe. . . . That's what the stuff's here for.

Jaimie Paul turns. He is in a provocative mood, seething with rebellion that makes the humor he triggers both biting and deceptively innocent. The young Indian men respond to him with strong laughter. Jaimie Paul takes a play punch at one of them.

JAIMIE   Whoops! Scared you, eh?

He glances back at Mr. Homer, as if talking to him.

Can't take it, eh? The priest can't take it. Indian Department guys can't take it. . . . Why listen to them? Listen to the radio if you want to hear something.

The young Indian men laugh.

> Or listen to me! You think I'm smart?

YOUNG INDIAN MAN   You're a smart man, Jamie Paul.

JAIMIE   Naw . . . I'm not smart . . . [*pointing to another young Indian man*]   This guy here . . . calls himself squaw-humper . . . he's smart! . . . Him . . . he buys extra big shirts . . . more cloth for the same money. . . . That's smart! [*Laughter.*]   I'm not smart. [*seriously.*]   You figure we can start a business an' be our own boss?

YOUNG INDIAN MAN   I don't know about that. . . .

Jaimie Paul leaves them and goes to lean over the young Indian man who is now asleep on the floor.

JAIMIE   Buy a taxi . . . be our own boss. . . .

He shakes the sleeping young Indian man, who immediately begins his tuneless song.

> Aw, he's drunk. . . .

Jaimie Paul goes over to the table and stares at the young Indian man beyond the table.

JAIMIE   [*soberly*]   Buy everything we need. . . . Don't be bums! Bums need grub an' clothes. . . . Bums is bad for the country, right Mr. Homer?

MR. HOMER   [*nodding*]   I guess so. . . . [*To Rita Joe who is now wearing the old sweater*] Red looks good on you, Rita Joe. . . . Take it!

Jaimie Paul goes over and embraces Rita Joe, then pushes her gently away.

JAIMIE   She looks better in yellow. I never seen a red dandelion before.

He and the young Indian men laugh, but the laughter is hollow.

MR. HOMER   Come on, Jaimie! Leave the girl alone. That's what it's here for. . . . Are you working?

JAIMIE   [*evasive, needling*]   Yeh! . . . No! . . . "Can you drive?" the guy says to me. "Sure, I can drive," I says to him. "Okay," he says, "then drive this broom until the warehouse is clean."

They all laugh.

MR. HOMER   That's a good one. . . . Jaimie, you're a card. . . . Well, time to get some food for you lot. . . .

Mr. Homer leaves. Rita Joe feels better about the sweater. She looks to one of the young Indian men for approval. Jaimie Paul becomes grim-faced.

RITA   Do you like?

YOUNG INDIAN MAN   Sure. It's a nice sweater. . . . Take it.

JAIMIE   Take it where? Take it to hell. . . . Be men! [*pointing after Mr. Homer*] He's got no kids. . . . Guys like that get mean when they got no kids. . . . We're his kids an' he means to keep it that way! Well, I'm a big boy now! [*to Rita Joe*]   I go to the employment office. I want work an' I want it now. "I'm not a goddamned cripple," I says to him. An' he says he can only take my name! If work comes he'll call me! "What the hell is this," I says to him. "I'll never get work like that. . . . There's no telephone in the house where I got a room!"

Mr. Homer returns pushing a wheeled tray on which he has some food for sandwiches, a loaf of bread and a large cutting knife. He begins to make some sandwiches.

RITA   [*scolding Jaimie Paul*]   You won't get work talking that way, Jaimie Paul!

JAIMIE   Why not? I'm not scared. He gets mad at me an' I say to him . . . "You think I'm some stupid Indian you're talkin' to? Heh? You think that?"

Jaimie Paul struts and swaggers to demonstrate how he faced his opponent at the employment office.

MR. HOMER   [*cutting bread*]   You're a tough man to cross, Jaimie Paul.

JAIMIE   [*ignoring Mr. Homer, to the young Indian men*]   Boy, I showed that bastard who he was talkin' to!

RITA   Did you get the job?

JAIMIE   [*turning to her, laughing boyishly*]   No! He called the cops an' they threw me out!

They all laugh. The young Indian men go to the table now and rummage through the clothes.

MR. HOMER   Take whatever you want, boys . . . there's more clothes comin' tomorrow.

Jaimie Paul impulsively moves to the table where the young Indian men are fingering the clothes. He pushes them aside and shoves the clothes in a heap leaving a small corner of the table clean. He takes out two coins from his pockets and spits in his hands.

JAIMIE   I got a new trick. . . . Come on, Mister Homer . . . I'll show you! See this!

He shows the coins, then slams his hands palms down on the table.

      Which hand got the coins?

MR. HOMER   Why . . . one under each hand. . . .

JAIMIE   Right! [*turning up his hands*]   Again? [*He collects the coins and slaps his hands down again.*]   Where are the coins now? Come on, guess!

Mr. Homer is confident now, and points to the right hand with his cutting knife. Jaimie Paul laughs and lifts his hands. The coins are under his left hand.

MR. HOMER   Son of a gun.

JAIMIE   You're a smart man.

He puts the coins in his pockets and, laughing, turns to Rita Joe who stands uncertainly, dressed in the red sweater. She likes the garment, but she is aware Jaimie Paul might resent her taking it. The young Indian men again move to the table, and Mr. Homer returns to making sandwiches.

MR. HOMER   There's a good pair of socks might come in handy for one of you guys!

A young Indian man pokes his thumbs through the holes in the socks, and laughs.

JAIMIE   Sure . . . take the socks! Take the table!

He slaps the table with his hands and laughs.

Take Mister Homer cutting bread! Take everything!

MR. HOMER   Hey, Jaimie!

JAIMIE   Why not? There's more comin' tomorrow, you said!

RITA   Jaimie!

MR. HOMER   You're sure in a smart-assed mood today, aren't you?

JAIMIE   [*pointing to the young Indian man with the socks, but talking to Mr. Homer*] Mister, friend Steve over there laughs lots. . . He figures . . . the way to get along an' live is to grab his guts an' laugh at anything anybody says. You see him laughing all the time. A dog barks at him an' he laughs. . . . [*Laughter from the young Indian man*]   Laughs at a fence post fallin' . . . [*Laughter.*]   Kids with funny eyes make him go haywire. . . . [*Laughter.*] Can of meat an' no can opener. . . .

Mr. Homer watches the young Indian men and grins at Jaimie Paul.

MR. HOMER   Yeh . . . he laughs quite a bit. . . .

JAIMIE   He laughs at a rusty nail. . . . Nice guy . . . laughs all the time.

MR. HOMER   [*to Jaimie Paul, holding the knife*]   You wanted mustard on your bread or just plain?

JAIMIE   I seen him cut his hand and start laughin'. . . . Isn't that funny?

The young Indian men laugh, but with less humor now.

MR. HOMER   [*to Jaimie Paul*]   You want mustard? . . . I'm talkin' to you!

JAIMIE   I'm not hungry.

The young Indian men stop laughing altogether. They become tense and suspicious of Jaimie Paul, who is watching them severely.

MR. HOMER   Suit yourself. Rita?

She shakes her head slowly, her gaze on Jaimie Paul's face.

RITA   I'm not hungry.

Mr. Homer looks from Rita Joe to Jaimie Paul, then to the young Indian men. His manner stiffens.

MR. HOMER   I see. . . .

Jaimie Paul and Rita Joe touch hands and come forward to sit on the apron of the stage, front. A pale light is on the two of them. The stage lights behind them fade. A low light that is diffused and shadowy remains on the table where Mr. Homer has prepared the food. The young Indian men move slowly to the table and begin eating the sandwiches Mr. Homer offers to them. The light on the table fades very low. Jaimie Paul hands a cigarette to Rita Joe and they smoke.

Light comes up over the rear ramp. Rita Joe's father enters onto the ramp from the wings of stage right. His step is resolute. The priest follows behind him a few paces. They have been arguing. Both are dressed in work clothes: heavy trousers and windbreakers.

JAIMIE   When I'm laughing, I got friends.
RITA   I know, Jaimie Paul. . . .
PRIEST   That was the way I found her, that was the way I left her.
JAIMIE   [*bitterly*]   When I'm laughing, I'm a joker . . . a funny boy!
FATHER   If I was young . . . I wouldn't sleep. I would talk to people . . . let them all know!
JAIMIE   I'm not dangerous when I'm laughing. . . .
PRIEST   You could lose the reserve and have nowhere to go!
FATHER   I have lost more than that! Young people die . . . young people don't believe me. . . .
JAIMIE   That's alright . . . that's alright. . . .

The light dies out on Jaimie Paul and Rita Joe. The light also dies out on Mr. Homer and the young Indian men.

PRIEST   You think they believe that hot-headed . . . that troublemaker?
FATHER   [*turning to face the priest*]   Jaimie Paul is a good boy!
PRIEST   David Joe . . . you and I have lived through a lot. We need peace now,

and time to consider what to do next.

FATHER   Eileen said to me last night . . . she wants to go to the city. I worry all night. . . . What can I do?

PRIEST   I'll talk to her, if you wish.

FATHER   [angry] And tell her what? . . . Of the animals there . . . [gesturing to the audience] who sleep with sore stomachs because . . . they eat too much?

PRIEST   We mustn't lose the reserve and the old life, David Joe. . . . Would you . . . give up being chief on the reserve?

FATHER   Yes!

PRIEST   To Jaimie Paul?

FATHER   No . . . to someone who's been to school . . . maybe university . . . who knows more.

PRIEST   [relieved by this, but not reassured] The people here need your wisdom and stability, David Joe. There is no man here who knows as much about hunting and fishing and guiding. You can survive. . . . What does a youngster who's been away to school know of this?

FATHER   [sadly] If we only fish an' hunt an' cut pulpwood . . . pick strawberries in the bush . . . for a hundred years more, we are dead. I know this, here. . . . [He touches his breast.]

The light dies on the ramp. A light rises on stage front, on Jaimie Paul and Rita Joe sitting at the apron of the stage. Mr. Homer is still cutting bread for sandwiches. The three young Indian men have eaten and appear restless to leave. The fourth young Indian man is still asleep on the floor. Rita Joe has taken off the red sweater, but continues to hold it in her hand.

JAIMIE   [to Mr. Homer] One time I was on a trapline five days without grub. I ate snow an' I walked until I got back. You think you can take it like me?

Mr. Homer approaches Jaimie Paul and holds out a sandwich to him.

MR. HOMER   Here . . . have a sandwich now.

Jaimie Paul ignores his hand.

RITA   Mister Homer don't know what happened, Jaimie Paul.

Mr. Homer shrugs and walks away to his sandwich table.

JAIMIE   Then he's got to learn. . . . Sure he knows! [to Mr. Homer] Sure he knows! He's feedin' sandwiches to Indian bums. . . . He knows. He's the worst kind!

The young Indian men freeze and Mr. Homer stops.

MR. HOMER   [coldly] I've never yet asked a man to leave this building.

Rita Joe and Jaimie rise to their feet. Rita Joe goes to the clothes table and throws the red sweater back on the pile of clothes. Jaimie Paul laughs sardonically.

MR. HOMER   [*to Rita Joe*]   Hey, not you, girl. . . . You take it!

She shakes her head and moves to leave.

RITA   I think we better go, boys.

The sleeping young Indian man slowly raises his head, senses there is something wrong, and is about to be helped up when . . .

JAIMIE   After five days without grub, the first meal I threw up . . . stomach couldn't take it. . . . But after that it was alright. . . . [*to Mr. Homer, with intensity*]   I don't believe nobody . . . no priest nor government. . . . They don't know what it's like to . . . to want an' not have . . . to stand in line an' nobody sees you!

MR. HOMER   If you want food, eat! You need clothes, take them. That's all. . . . But I'm runnin' this Center my way, and I mean it!

JAIMIE   I come to say no to you. . . . That's all . . . that's all!

He throws out his arms in a gesture that is both defiant and childlike. The gesture disarms some of Mr. Homer's growing hostility.

MR. HOMER   You've got that right . . . no problems. There's others come through here day an' night. . . . No problems.

JAIMIE   I don't want no others to come. I don't want them to eat here! [*indicating his friends*]   If we got to take it from behind a store window, then we break the window an' wait for the cops. It's better than . . . than this!

He gestures with contempt at the food and the clothes on the table.

MR. HOMER   Rita Joe . . . where'd you pick up this . . . this loudmouth anyway?

RITA   [*slowly, firmly*]   I think . . . Jaimie Paul's . . . right.

Mr. Homer looks from face to face. The three young Indian men are passive, staring into the distance. The fourth is trying hard to clear his head. Jamie Paul is cold, hostile. Rita Joe is determined.

MR. HOMER   [*decisively*]   Alright! You've eaten . . . looked over the clothes. . . . Now clear out so others get a chance to come in! Move!

He tries to herd everyone out and the four young Indian men begin to move away. Jaimie Paul mimics the gestures of Mr. Homer and steps in front of the young Indian men herding them back in.

JAIMIE   Run, boys, run! Or Mister Homer gonna beat us up!

Rita Joe takes Jaimie Paul's hand and tries to pull him away to leave.

RITA   Jaimie Paul . . . you said to me no trouble!

Jaimie Paul pulls his hand free and jumps back of the clothes table. Mr. Homer comes for him, unknowingly still carrying the slicing knife in his hand. An absurd chase begins around the table. One of the young Indian men laughs, and stepping forward, catches hold of Mr. Homer's hand with the knife in it.

YOUNG INDIAN MAN   Hey! Don't play with a knife, Mister Homer!

He gently takes the knife away from Mr. Homer and drops it on the food table behind. Mr. Homer looks at his hand, an expression of shock on his face. Jaimie Paul gives him no time to think about the knife and what it must have appeared like to the young Indian men. He pulls a large brassiere from the clothes table and mockingly holds it over his breasts, which he sticks out enticingly at Mr. Homer. The young Indian men laugh. Mr. Homer is exasperated and furious. Rita Joe is frightened.

RITA   It's not funny, Jaimie!
JAIMIE   It's funny as hell, Rita Joe. Even funnier this way!

Jaimie Paul puts the brassiere over his head, with the cups down over his ears and the straps under his chin. The young Indian men are all laughing now and moving close to the table. Mr. Homer makes a futile attempt at driving them off.

Suddenly Jaimie Paul's expression turns to one of hatred. He throws the brassiere on the table and gripping its edge, throws the table and clothes over, scattering the clothes. He kicks at them. The young Indian men all jump in and, picking up the clothes, hurl them over the ramp.

Rita Joe runs in to try and stop them. She grips the table and tries lifting it up again.

MR. HOMER   [*to Jaimie Paul*]   Cut that out, you sonofabitch!

Jaimie Paul stands watching him. Mr. Homer is in a fury. He sees Rita Joe struggling to right the table. He moves to her and pushes her hard.

You slut! . . . You breed whore!

Rita Joe recoils. With a shriek of frustration, she attacks Mr. Homer, tearing at him. He backs away, then turns and runs. Jaimie Paul overturns the table again. The others join in the melee with the clothes. A policeman enters and grabs Jaimie Paul. Rita Joe and the four young Indian men exit, clearing away the table and remaining clothes.

A sharp, tiny spotlight comes up on the face and upper torso of Jaimie Paul. He is wild with rebellion as the policeman forces him, in an arm lock, down toward the audience.

JAIMIE   [*screaming defiance at the audience*]   Not jus' a box of cornflakes! When I go in I want the whole store! That's right . . . the whole goddamned store!

Another sharp light on the magistrate standing on his podium looking down at Jaimie Paul.

MAGISTRATE   Thirty days!

JAIMIE   [*held by policeman*]   Sure, sure. . . . Anything else you know?

MAGISTRATE   Thirty days!

JAIMIE   Gimme back my truth!

MAGISTRATE   We'll get larger prisons and more police in every town and city across the country!

JAIMIE   Teach me who I really am! You've taken that away! Give me back the real me so I can live like a man!

MAGISTRATE   There is room for dialogue. There is room for disagreement and there is room for social change . . . but within the framework of institutions and traditions in existence for that purpose!

JAIMIE   [*spitting*]   Go to hell! . . . I can die an' you got nothing to tell me!

MAGISTRATE   [*in a cold fury*]   Thirty days! And after that, it will be six months! And after that . . . God help you!

The magistrate marches off his platform and offstage. Jaimie Paul is led off briskly in the other direction offstage.

The lights change. Rita Joe enters, crossing the stage, exchanging a look with the Singer.

SINGER
> Sleepless hours, heavy nights,
> Dream your dreams so pretty.
> God was gonna have a laugh
> An' gave me a job in the city!

Rita Joe walks the street. She is smoking a cigarette. She is dispirited.

The light broadens across the stage. Rita Joe's father and Jaimie Paul enter the stage from the wings of center stage left. They walk slowly toward where Rita Joe stands. At the sight of her father, Rita Joe moans softly and hurriedly stamps out her cigarette. She visibly straightens and waits for the approaching men, her expression one of fear and joy.

FATHER   I got a ride on Miller's truck . . . took me two days. . . .

JAIMIE   It's a long way, David Joe.

The father stops a pace short of Rita Joe and looks at her with great tenderness and concern.

FATHER   [*softly*] I come . . . to get Rita Joe.
RITA   Oh . . . I don't know. . . .

She looks to Jaimie Paul for help in deciding what to do, but he is sullen and uncommunicative.

FATHER   I come to take Rita Joe home. . . . We got a house an' some work
     sometime. . . .
JAIMIE   She's with me now, David Joe.
RITA   [*very torn*] I don't know. . . .
JAIMIE   You don't have to go back, Rita Joe.

Rita Joe looks away from her father with humility. The father turns to Jaimie Paul. He stands ancient and heroic.

FATHER   I live . . . an' I am afraid. Because . . . I have not done everything.
     When I have done everything . . . know that my children are safe . . . then
     . . . it will be alright. Not before.
JAIMIE   [*to Rita Joe*] You don't have to go. This is an old man now. . . . He has
     nothing to give . . . nothing to say!

Rita Joe reacts to both men, her conflict deepening.

FATHER   [*turning away from Jaimie Paul to Rita Joe*] For a long time . . . a very
     long time . . . she was in my hands . . . like that! [*he cups his hands into the
     shape of a bowl.*] Sweet . . . tiny . . . lovin' all the time and wanting love. . . .
     [*he shakes his head sadly.*]
JAIMIE   [*angrily*] Go tell it to the white men! They're lookin' for Indians that
     stay proud even when they hurt . . . just so long's they don't ask for their
     rights!

The father turns slowly, with great dignity, to Jaimie Paul. His gestures show Jaimie Paul to be wrong; the old man's spirit was never broken. Jaimie Paul understands and looks away.

FATHER   You're a good boy, Jaimie Paul . . . a good boy . . . [*to Rita Joe, talking
     slowly, painfully*] I once seen a dragonfly breakin' its shell to get its
     wings. . . . It floated on water an' crawled up on a log where I was sit-
     ting. . . . It dug its feet into the log an' then it pulled until the shell bust
     over its neck. Then it pulled some more . . . an' slowly its wings slipped
     out of the shell . . . like that!

He shows with his hands how the dragonfly got his freedom.

JAIMIE [*angered and deeply moved by the father*] Where you gonna be when they start bustin' our heads open an' throwing us into jails right across the god-damned country?

FATHER Such wings I never seen before . . . folded like an accordion so fine, like thin glass an' white in the morning sun. . . .

JAIMIE We're gonna have to fight to win . . . there's no other way! They're not listenin' to you, old man! Or to me.

FATHER It spread its wings . . . so slowly . . . an' then the wings opened an' began to flutter . . . just like that . . . see! Hesitant at first . . . then stronger . . . an' then the wings beatin' like that made the dragonfly's body quiver until the shell on its back falls off . . .

JAIMIE Stop kiddin' yourself! We're gonna say no pretty soon to all the crap that makes us soft an' easy to push this way . . . that way!

FATHER An' the dragonfly . . . flew up . . . up . . . up . . . into the white sun . . . to the green sky . . . to the sun . . . faster an' faster. . . . Higher . . . higher!

The father reaches up with his hands, releasing the imaginary dragonfly into the sun, his final words torn out of his heart. Rita Joe springs to her feet and rushes against Jaimie Paul, striking at him with her fists.

RITA [*savagely*] For Chris' sakes, I'm not goin' back! . . . Leave him alone. . . . He's everything we got left now!

Jaimie Paul stands, frozen by his emotion which he can barely control. The father turns. Rita Joe goes to him. The father speaks privately to Rita Joe in Indian dialect. They embrace. He pauses for a long moment to embrace and forgive her everything. Then he goes slowly offstage into the wings of stage left without looking back.

FATHER Goodbye, Rita Joe. . . . Goodbye, Jaimie Paul. . . .
RITA Goodbye Father.

Jaimie Paul watches Rita Joe who moves away from him to the front of the stage.

JAIMIE [*to her*] You comin?

She shakes her head to indicate no, she is staying. Suddenly Jaimie Paul runs away from her diagonally across to the wings of rear stage left. As he nears the wings, the four young Indian men emerge, happily on their way to a party. They stop him at his approach. He runs into them, directing them back, his voice breaking with feelings of love and hatred intermingling.

[*shouting at them*] Next time . . . in a beer parlour or any place like that . . . I'll go myself or you guys take me home. . . . No more white buggers pushin' us out the door or he gets this!

He raises his fist. The group of young Indian men, elated by their newly-found determination, surround Jaimie Paul and exit into the wings of the stage. The light dies in back and at stage left.

The magistrate enters. There is a light on Rita Joe where she stands. There is also a light around the magistrate. The magistrate's voice and purpose are leaden. He has given up on Rita Joe. He is merely performing the formality of condemning her and dismissing her from his conscience.

MAGISTRATE   I sentence you to thirty days in prison.

RITA   [*angry, defiant*]   Sure, sure. . . . Anything else you know?

MAGISTRATE   I sentence you to thirty days in prison, with a recommendation you be examined medically and given all necessary treatment at the prison clinic. There is nothing . . . there is nothing I can do now.

RITA   [*stoically*]   Thank you. Is that right? To thank you?

MAGISTRATE   You'll be back . . . always be back . . . growing older, tougher . . . filthier . . . looking more like stone and prison bars . . . the lines in your face will tell everyone who sees you about prison windows and prison food.

RITA   No child on the road would remember you, mister!

The magistrate comes down to stand before her. He has the rambling confidence of detached authority.

MAGISTRATE   What do you expect? We provide schools for you and you won't attend them because they're out of the way and that little extra effort is too much for you! We came up as a civilization having to . . . yes, claw upwards at times . . . There's nothing wrong with that. . . . We give you X-ray chest clinics. . . .

He turns away from her and goes to the apron of the stage and speaks directly to the audience.

We give them X-ray chest clinics and three-quarters of them won't show up. . . . Those that do frequently get medical attention at one of the hospitals . . .

RITA   [*interjecting*]   My mother died!

MAGISTRATE   [*not hearing her*]   But as soon as they're released they forget they're chronically ill and end up on a drinking party and a long walk home through the snow. . . . Next thing . . . they're dead!

RITA   [*quietly*]   Oh, put me in jail an' then let me go.

MAGISTRATE   [*turning to her*]   Some of you get jobs. . . . There are jobs, good jobs, if you'd only look around a bit . . . and stick with them when you get them. But no . . . you get a job and promise to stay with it and learn, and two weeks later you're gone for three, four days without explanation. . . .

Your reliability record is ruined and an employer has to regard you as lazy, undependable. . . . What do you expect?

RITA   I'm not scared of you now, bastard!

MAGISTRATE   You have a mind . . . you have a heart. The cities are open to you to come and go as you wish, yet you gravitate to the slums and skid rows and the shanty-town fringes. You become a whore, drunkard, user of narcotics. . . . At best, dying of illness or malnutrition. . . . At worst, kicked or beaten to death by some angry white scum who finds in you something lower than himself to pound his frustrations out on! What's to be done? You Indians seem to be incapable of taking action to help yourselves. Someone must care for you. . . . Who? For how long?

RITA   You don't know nothin'!

MAGISTRATE   I know . . . I know. . . . It's a struggle just to stay alive. I know . . . I understand. That struggle is mine, as well as yours, Rita Joe! The jungle of the executive has as many savage teeth ready to go for the throat as the rundown hotel on the waterfront. . . . Your days and hours are numbered, Rita Joe. . . . I worry for the child I once saw. . . . I have already forgotten the woman!

He turns away from her and exits into the wings of stage right.

The lights on Rita Joe fade. Lights of cold, eerie blue wash the backdrop of the stage faintly. Rita Joe stands in silhouette for a long moment.

Slowly, ominously, the three murderers appear on the ramp backstage, one coming from the wings of stage right; one from the wings of stage left; and one rising from the back of the ramp, climbing it. One of the murderers is whistling, a soft nervous noise throughout their scene onstage.

Rita Joe whimpers in fear, and as the murderers loom above her, she runs along the apron to stage left. Here she bumps into Jaimie Paul who enters. She screams in fear.

JAIMIE   Rita Joe!

RITA   [terrorized] Jaimie! They're comin'. I seen them comin'!

JAIMIE   Who's coming? What's the matter, Rita Joe?

RITA   Men I once dreamed about. . . . I seen it all happen once before . . . an' it was like this. . . .

Jaimie Paul laughs and pats her shoulders reassuringly. He takes her hand and tries to lead her forward to the apron of the stage, but Rita Joe is dead, her steps wooden.

JAIMIE   Don't worry . . . I can take care of myself!

A faint light on the two of them.

RITA   You been in jail now too, Jaimie Paul. . . .

JAIMIE So what? Guys in jail was saying that they got to put a man behind
bars or the judge don't get paid for being in court to make the trial. . . .
Funny world, eh, Rita Joe?

RITA [*nodding*] Funny world.

The light dies on them. They come forward slowly.

JAIMIE I got a room with a hot plate. . . . We can have a couple of eggs and
some tea before we go to the movie.

RITA What was it like for you in jail?

JAIMIE So so. . . .

*Jaimie Paul motions for Rita Joe to follow him and moves forward from her. The distant
sound of a train approaching is heard. She is wooden, coming slowly after him.*

RITA It was different where the women were. . . . It's different to be a
woman. . . . Some women was wild . . . and they shouted they were riding
black horses into a fire I couldn't see. . . . There was no fire there, Jaimie!

JAIMIE [*turning to her, taking her arm*] Don't worry . . . we're goin' to eat and
then see a movie. . . . Come on, Rita Joe!

*She looks back and sees the murderers rise and slowly approach from the gloom. Her
speech becomes thick and unsteady as she follows Jaimie Paul to the front of the ramp.*

RITA One time I couldn't find the street where I had a room to sleep in . . . forgot
my handbag . . . had no money. . . . An old man with a dog said hello, but
I couldn't say hello back because I was worried an' my mouth was so
sticky I couldn't speak to him. . . .

JAIMIE Are you comin'?

RITA When you're tired an' sick, Jaimie, the city starts to dance. . . .

JAIMIE [*taking her hand, pulling her gently along*] Come on, Rita Joe.

RITA The street lights start rollin' like wheels an' cement walls feel like they
was made of blanket cloth. . . .

*The sound of the train is closer now. The lights of its lamps flicker in the back of the
stage. Rita Joe turns to face the murderers, one of whom is whistling ominously. She
whimpers in fear and presses herself against Jaimie Paul. Jaimie Paul turns and sees
the murderers hovering near them.*

JAIMIE Dont' be scared. . . . Nothing to be scared of, Rita Joe. . . . [*to the
murderers*] What the hell do you want?

*One of the murderers laughs. Jaimie Paul pushes Rita Joe back behind himself. He
moves toward the murderers, taunting them.*

You think I can't take care of myself?

With deceptive casualness, the murderers approach him. One of them makes a sudden lurch at Jaimie Paul as if to draw him into their circle. Jaimie Paul anticipates the trap and takes a flying kick at the murderer, knocking him down.

They close around Jaimie Paul with precision, then attack. Jaimie Paul leaps, but is caught mid-air by the other two. They bring him down and put the boots to him. Rita Joe screams and runs to him. The train sound is loud and immediate now.

One of the murderers has grabbed Rita Joe. The remaining two raise Jaimie Paul to his feet and one knees him viciously in the groin. Jaimie Paul screams and doubles over. The lights of the train are upon them. The murderers leap off the ramp leaving Jaimie Paul in the path of the approaching train. Jaimie Paul's death cry becomes the sound of the train horn. As the train sound roars by, the murderers return to close in around Rita Joe. One murderer springs forward and grabs Rita Joe. The other two help to hold her, with nervous fear and lust. Rita Joe breaks free of them and runs to the front of the stage. The three murderers come after her, panting hard. They close in on her leisurely now, playing with her, knowing that they have her trapped.

Recorded and overlapping voices.

CLERK   The court calls Rita Joe . . .
MAGISTRATE   Who is she? . . . Let her speak for herself . . .
RITA   In the summer it was hot, an' flies hummed . . .
TEACHER   A book of verse, a melting pot . . .
MAGISTRATE   Thirty days!
FATHER   Barkin' to beat hell. . . . How! How!
JAIMIE   [*laughing, defiant, taunting*]   You go to hell!
PRIEST   A confession, Rita Joe . . .

Over the voices she hears, the murderers attack. Dragging her down backwards, they pull her legs open and one murderer lowers himself on her.

RITA   Jaimie! Jaimie! Jaimie!

Rita Joe's head lolls over sideways. The murderers stare at her and pull back slightly.

MURDERER   [*thickly, rising off her twisted broken body*]   Shit . . . she's dead. . . . We hardly touched her.

He hesitates for a moment, then runs, joined by the second murderer.

SECOND MURDERER   Let's get out of here!

They run up onto the ramp and watch as the third murderer piteously climbs onto the dead Rita Joe.

Sounds of a funeral chant. Mourners appear on riser backstage. Rita Joe's father enters from the wings of stage left, chanting an ancient Indian funeral chant, carrying the body of Jaimie Paul. The murderer hesitates in his necrophilic rape and then runs away.

The young Indian men bring the body of Jaimie Paul over the ramp and approach. The body is placed down on the podium, beside Rita Joe's. All the Indians, young and old, kneel around the two bodies. The father continues his death chant. The priest enters from the wings of stage right reciting a prayer. The teacher, singer, policeman and murderers come with him forming the outside perimeter around the Indian funeral.

PRIEST   Hail Mary, Mother of God . . . pray for us sinners now and at the hour of our death.

Repeated until finally Eileen Joe slowly rises to her feet and, turning to the priest and white mourners, says softly . . .

EILEEN   [*over the sounds of chanting and praying*]   No! . . . No! . . . No more!

The young Indian men rise one after another facing the outer circle defiantly and the cast freezes on stage, except for the singer.

SINGER
    Oh, the singing bird
    Has found its wings
    And it's soaring!
    My God, what a sight!
    On the cold fresh wind of morning! . . .

During the song, Eileen Joe steps forward to the audience and as the song ends, says . . .

EILEEN   When Rita Joe first come to the city, she told me . . . the cement made her feet hurt.

SHARON POLLOCK
1936–

Playwright, actress, and director, she was born in Fredericton, New Brunswick. The daughter of a physician, she spent her early years in Quebec's Eastern Townships before returning to Fredericton to attend the University of New Brunswick for two years. She began her acting career in amateur theater in New Brunswick, later moving to Calgary to join the touring company Prairie Players. Her first play, *A Compulsory Option*, won the 1971 Alberta Playwriting Competition. She has written plays for children, several radio and television scripts, and many plays for the theater. Her early plays usually focused on social issues; *The Komagatu Maru Incident*, for example, explored racism in the early twentieth century when a ship filled with Sikh immigrants was denied permission to land in Vancouver. Her more recent plays, such as *Doc*, focus on familial and personal conflicts. She has taught playwriting at the University of Alberta, headed the Playwrights' Colony at the Banff Centre, been playwright-in-residence at Calgary's Alberta Theatre Projects, and served as artistic director of Theatre Calgary. Based loosely on her own familial background, *Doc*, which won the Governor General's Award, had its premiere at Theatre Calgary in April, 1984.

DOC

THE CHARACTERS

EV, an elderly man in his 70's
CATHERINE, his daughter, in her mid-30's
KATIE, Catherine, as a young girl
BOB, Ev's wife, Catherine's mother
OSCAR, Ev's best friend

PLAYWRIGHT'S NOTES

Much of the play consists of the sometimes shared, sometimes singular memories of the past, as relived by Ev and Catherine, interacting with figures from the past. Structurally, shifts in time do not occur in a linear, chronological fashion, but in an unconscious and intuitive patterning of the past by Ev and Catherine. A stage direct [*Shift*] marks these pattern changes which are often, but not always, time shifts as well. In production, music has been used to underscore the pattern shifts, however the characters' shifts from one pattern to another must be immediate. They do not "hold" for the music. The physical blocking must accommodate this immediacy and the stage setting facilitate it.

The "now" of the play takes place in the house in which Catherine grew up and in which Ev now lives alone. The play is most effective when the set design is not a literal one, and when props and furniture are kept to a minimum. I think of the setting as one which has the potential to explode time and space while simultaneously serving certain naturalistic demands of the play.

A kaleidoscope of memory constitutes the dialogue and action of the opening sequence. It is followed by a scene set more firmly in the "now". Ev is "old" during these two segments, as he is at the opening and closing of Act II. Although Ev relives the past as a younger man, we never see Catherine any age but in her mid-thirties. She is able to speak across time to her father, to her mother, and to her younger self. Catherine and Katie blend, sharing a sense of one entity, particularly in the scenes with her father's best friend, Oscar. This should not be interpreted to mean that Catherine and Katie share one mind or are always in accord. They are often in conflict.

Oscar is first seen in the opening sequence wearing a Twenties-era hockey uniform. He is a young man about to enter medical school. Oscar's scenes with Katie cover a four-year period prior to and ending with Bob's death. In the scenes he shares with Bob and Ev there is a longer, more chronological unfolding of time. For the most part, we see him as a man in his mid-thirties.

We see Bob in her mid-twenties to mid-thirties. She wears a dressing gown which has a belt or tie at the waist, and under this she wears a slip. The material of the gown is satin or satin-like; the gown itself has the look of a tailored long dinner gown when appropriately belted. On other occasions, undone and flapping, it has the appearance of a sloppy kimono. Is it necessary to say that her descent into alcoholism, despair, and self-disgust must be carefully charted?

Ev as an old man wears glasses and a worn cardigan sweater.

There are liquor bottles on stage in Act I; they have been removed from the set in Act II. A trunk is useful on stage; it holds photos and memorabilia; as well, it provides a storage place in Act I for Oscar's hockey uniform, and the clothing into which he and Ev will change.

In some productions all characters are always on stage with the exception of Ev, who is free to exit and enter during the play, and Katie, Bob, and Oscar who exit near the end of the play. In other productions there has been a greater freedom of movement re characters' exits and entrances. The script indicates where a character "may enter" or "may exit". If this is not indicated, the character must remain on stage.

ACT I

In the black there is a subtle murmuring of voices, with the odd phrase and word emerging quite clearly. They are repeats of bits and pieces of dialogue heard later in the play. The voices are those of Katie, Oscar, Bob, and the young Ev; they often speak on top of each other.

Light grows on Ev, who is seated by the open trunk. He holds an unopened letter. A match flares as Bob lights a cigarette in the background. Light grows on Bob, on Oscar who is smoothing tape on his hockey stick, and on Katie who concentrates on moving one foot back and forth slowly and rhythmically. Ev slowly closes the trunk, his focus still on the envelope he holds.

Catherine enters. She carries an overnight bag as well as her shoulder bag. She puts the overnight bag down. She sees Katie. She watches Katie for a moment, and then speaks to Katie's rhythmic movement.

CATHERINE   Up-on the carpet . . . you shall kneel . . . while the grass . . . grows in the field

Katie's motion turns into skipping as Katie turns an imaginary skipping rope and jumps to it.

> Stand up straight
> Upon your feet

KATIE   [*speaks with Catherine. The murmuring of voices can still be heard but they are fading*]
> Choose the one you love so sweet
> Now they're married wish them well
> First a girl, gee that's swell

Katie's voice is growing louder, taking over from Catherine.

KATIE & CATHERINE   Seven years after, seven to come
KATIE   [*alone*]
> Fire on the mountain kiss and run
> [*jumps "pepper" faster and faster*]
> Tinker, tailor, soldier, sailor,
> Rich man, poor man, beggar man thief

BOB   Doctor
KATIE   Doc-tor!!! [*stops skipping*]
CATHERINE   [*removing her gloves*] Daddy?
EV   [*looks up from the envelope*] Katie? [*stands up*] Is that you, Katie?
KATIE   [*skipping towards Ev singing*] La da da da daah.

Katie continues her "la dahs" skipping away from Ev as Oscar speaks.

OSCAR   Hey, you and me, Ev.

Ev looks at the letter and sits back down.

> Best friends. Ev and Oscar, Oscar and Ev—and if we weren't—
> I think I'd hate you.

KATIE   [*stops skipping but continues*] La dada da daaah

BOB   Why don't you open it?

OSCAR   You see, Ev—you're just too good at things.

BOB   Go on, open it.

The murmuring voices have faded out.

OSCAR   It makes people nervous.

Sound of an approaching train whistle.

> It makes me nervous.

BOB   Listen.

The train whistle is growing in volume. Katie stops her "la da da dahs".

> Your Gramma, Katie, his mother. She'd set her clock by that train.
> Set her clock by the junction train crossing the railway bridge into
> Devon. Must be what? Three-quarters of a mile of single track
> spanning the river? And midnight, every night, that train coming
> down from the junction—half-way across three-quarters of a mile
> of single track its whistle would split the night . . . and that night
> do you know what she did?

EV   [*his focus on the letter*] No.

BOB   She walked out to meet it.

EV   No.

BOB   You wanna know something, Katie?

KATIE   No.

BOB   Your father's mother, your grandmother, killed herself . . . Katie!

KATIE   What!

BOB   She walked across the train bridge at midnight and the train hit
   her.

KATIE   That's an accident.

BOB   She left a letter, and the letter tells him why she did it.

KATIE   There isn't any letter.

BOB   What's that?

KATIE   Daddy?

BOB   And he won't open it cause he's afraid, he's afraid of what she
   wrote.

KATIE   Is that true, Daddy?

EV   No.

KATIE   Is that the letter?

EV   Your grandmother was walking across the Devon bridge—

KATIE   What for?

EV   Well—it was a kind of short cut.

BOB   Short cut?

EV   And she got caught in the middle of a span and she was hit and killed.

CATHERINE   I stayed with her once when I was little . . . I can hardly remember.

EV   [*continuing to talk to Katie*]   It was after your mother had Robbie.

KATIE   Why didn't I stay with you and Robbie and Mummy?

EV   Your mother was sick so you stayed with your Gramma.

CATHERINE   Yes . . . and she made me soft-boiled runny eggs, and she'd feed me them and tell me stories about Moses in the bull-rushes, and I . . . and I . . . would peel the wallpaper off behind the door, and she'd get angry.

EV   That's right.

CATHERINE   Why didn't she jump?

OSCAR   A hat trick Ev! Everybody screaming—everybody on their feet —what's it feel like, Ev?

BOB   He doesn't care. He doesn't care about anything except his "prac-tice" and his "off-fice" and his "off-fice nurse" and all those stupid, stupid people who think he's God.

EV   [*to Katie*] Don't listen to her.

BOB   You're not God.

EV   Your mother's sick.

KATIE   No she isn't.

OSCAR   God, you're good. You fly, Ev.

KATIE   Why do you keep saying she's sick?

OSCAR   You don't skate, you fly.

KATIE   She's not sick.

EV   Your mother's—

KATIE   Why do you keep saying that!

EV   Katie—

KATIE   No!

CATHERINE   For a long time I prayed to God. I asked him to make her stop. I prayed and prayed. I thought, I'm just a little girl. Why would God want to do this to a little girl? I thought it was a mistake. I thought maybe he didn't know. I don't know what I thought. I prayed and prayed. . . . Now, I don't believe in God.

KATIE   And if there is a God, then I don't like him.

EV   She isn't well.

Bob slowly opens a drawer, feels inside it, and runs her hand along a chair cushion. She continues to quietly, unobtrusively look for something as Katie and Ev speak.

KATIE Tell Robbie that. He wants to believe that. I want the truth.

EV I'm telling you the truth.

KATIE No! Do you know what I did yesterday? She kept going to the bathroom and going to the bathroom and I went in and looked all over and I found it. In the clothes hamper with all the dirty clothes and things. And I took it and I poured it down the sink and I went downstairs and I threw the empty bottle in the garbage so don't tell me she's sick!

BOB It's gone.

Bob looks at Katie. In the following sequence, although Catherine is the speaker, Bob will act out the scene with Katie.

CATHERINE No. No, don't.

BOB It's gone.

CATHERINE No.

BOB You.

CATHERINE No.

BOB You took it and I want it back.

Bob grabs Katie.

I want it back!

CATHERINE It's gone now and you can't have it.

BOB Where? You tell me where?

CATHERINE I poured it out.

BOB No.

CATHERINE Down the sink.

BOB No.

CATHERINE It's gone, forget it.

BOB It's mine, I want it back!

CATHERINE Gone.

BOB No fair!

Bob struggles with Katie.

CATHERINE Let me go!

BOB No right!

CATHERINE Let me go!

BOB You had no right!

Katie strikes Bob, knocking her down.

CATHERINE Daddy!
EV Katie?

Ev gets up from his chair and moves to look for Catherine. Oscar may follow him. Ev does not see Catherine, nor she him.

OSCAR You know my father wishes I were you. He does. He wishes I were you. ''Oscar,'' he says, ''Oscar, look at Ev—why can't you be like Ev.''
BOB Look at what your father did.
KATIE You lie.
OSCAR I say nothing. There's nothing to be said. ''You got to have that killer instinct on the ice,'' he says. I play goalie — what the hell's a killer instinct in a goalie? Then he says, ''Oscar,'' he says, ''Oscar, you are goin' into medicine.''
EV Katie?
OSCAR My Dad's a doctor so I gotta be a doctor.
BOB Your father hit me and I fell.
KATIE You're always lying.
BOB See?
KATIE He didn't hit you.
BOB See?
KATIE I hit you!—Get away from me!
OSCAR What's so funny is you're the one so bloody keen on medicine — you'd kill for medicine. [*laughs*] Hey Ev, kill for medicine, eh. [*laughs*]
BOB Your father's mother, your Gramma, killed herself and he's afraid to open it.
KATIE [*covers her ears*] Now they're married
wish them joy
First a girl for a toy
Seven years after, seven to come,
Fire on the mountain, kiss and run

Ev returns from his search for Catherine. Oscar follows him. Katie sees Catherine, and moves towards her, speaking the verse to her.

KATIE On the mountain berries sweet
Pick as much as you can eat
By the berries bitter bark
Fire on the mountain break your heart
KATIE & CATHERINE Years to come—kiss and run—bitter bark—

Catherine sees Ev, who sees Catherine. Catherine speaks softly, almost to herself.

CATHERINE   Break your heart . . .
   It's me, Daddy.
EV   Katie?
KATIE   When I was little, Daddy.
CATHERINE   It's Catherine now, call me Catherine . . . well . . . aren't you going to say anything?
EV   You're home.
CATHERINE   Ah-huh . . . a hug, a big hug, Daddy, come on.

Catherine and Ev embrace.

   Ooh.
EV   What.
CATHERINE   How long has it been?
EV   Be ah . . .
CATHERINE   Four years, right? Medical convention in where? Vancouver, right?
EV   That's right. Vancouver.
CATHERINE   Montreal, Toronto, Calgary, Van, where haven't we met, eh?
EV   Here.
CATHERINE   Yup. Not . . . not met here.

Catherine notices the envelope in Ev's hand.

   What're you doing with that?
EV   Oh—just goin' through things. Clearin' things out.

Catherine, getting out a cigarette, turns away from Ev.

BOB   Katie's afraid of what she wrote.
KATIE   [*to Catherine*] Is that true?
EV   Are you here for this hoopla tomorrow?
CATHERINE   Not really.
EV   There's gonna be speeches and more speeches. I lay the cornerstone, and dinner I think.
CATHERINE   Ah-huh.
EV   I got it all written down with the times.
CATHERINE   Ah-huh.
EV   I got it downstairs. . . . You wanna take a look? . . . Not here for that, eh?

CATHERINE   No. I came home to see you.

EV   Pretty sad state of affairs when your own daughter's in town and can't attend a sod-turnin' in honor of her father.

CATHERINE   So I'll go, I'll be there.

EV   Coulda sent a telegram, saved the air fare.

CATHERINE   Christ Daddy, don't be so stupid.

EV   Sound like your mother.

CATHERINE   I learnt the four-letter words from you.

EV   Bullshit.

CATHERINE   I said I'd go, I said I'd be there. So. [*pause*] I'm proud of you, Daddy.

EV   Did you know it was a write-in campaign?

CATHERINE   Oh?

EV   The niggers from Barker's Point, the mill workers from Marysville, they're the ones got this hospital named after me. Left to the politicians God knows what they'd have called it.

CATHERINE   Well, I'm proud.

EV   Some goddamn French name I suppose — what?

CATHERINE   Proud, you must be proud having the hospital named after you.

EV   The day I first started practice, that day I was proud. Was the day after you were born. . . . There was a scarlet fever epidemic that year, you remember?

CATHERINE   No Daddy.

EV   Somebody . . . some couple came in, they were carryin' their daughter, what was she? Two, maybe three? I took her in my arms . . . could see they'd left it too late. I remember that child. I passed her back to her mother. Hold her tight, I said. Hold her tight till she goes. . . . Do you remember that woman holdin' that child in the hallway?

CATHERINE   No Daddy.

EV   No. That was your mother . . . that was your mother.

BOB   Blueberries, Katie.

EV   You were just little then.

BOB   Blueberries along the railway tracks, and every year we'd pick them and sell them. I was the youngest, and Mama was always afraid I'd get lost, but I never got lost.

Catherine looks at Bob.

Not once.

Pause

EV   What are you thinkin'?

CATHERINE   [*looks away from Bob*] Nothing. . . . You've lost weight.

EV   Of course I lost. I damn near died. You didn't know that, did you.

CATHERINE   No. No, nobody told me.

EV   Well it was that goddamn heart man. It was him gave me a heart attack.

CATHERINE   Really?

EV   What the hell's his name?

CATHERINE   Whose?

EV   The heart man's!

CATHERINE   I wouldn't know, Daddy.

EV   Demii—no, Demsky. I go to him, I tell him I been gettin' this pain in my ticker, and he has me walkin' up and down this little set a stairs, and runnin' on treadmills. Jesus Christ, I said to him, I'm not tryin' out for a sports team, I'm here because I keep gettin' this pain in my ticker! For Christ's sake, I said, put a stethoscope to my chest before you kill me with these goddamn stairs!

CATHERINE   So how are you now?

EV   It would've served the bastard right if I'd died right there in his office—do you remember how good Valma was with your mother?

CATHERINE   I remember.

EV   Every statutory holiday your mother's killin' herself or seein' things crawlin' on the walls or some goddamn thing or other, and Valma is like a rock, isn't that right?

CATHERINE   I guess so.

EV   So I come home from Demsky's, and I get the pain in my ticker and I wait all night for it to go away, and long about four or four-thirty, I phone Valma. Valma, I say, I'm havin' a heart attack, Valma—and she drops the phone nearly breaking' my ear drum and I can't phone out and I'm damned if I'm gonna get in that car and die all alone on Charlotte Street like that foolish Hazel Arbeton —If you were livin' in town, I'd have phoned you.

CATHERINE   You couldn't if Valma dropped the phone, Daddy.

EV   I'd have phoned you first!

CATHERINE   Would you?

EV   Well if I'd known she was gonna drop that goddamn phone I would have.

CATHERINE   What about Robbie?

EV   Who?

CATHERINE   Your son—Robbie.

EV   I'm not senile, I know who the hell Robbie is, what about him?

CATHERINE   You could have phoned him.

EV   I couldn't phone anyone! I was connected to Valma and I couldn't get disconnected!

CATHERINE   Would you have phoned him if you could?

EV   He wouldn't be home.

CATHERINE   How do you know?

EV   He's never home.

CATHERINE   Do you see him much?

EV   How the hell could I if he's never home?

CATHERINE   Do you *try* to see him!

EV   Of course I try! Have you seen him, phoned him, been over to visit?

CATHERINE   For Christ's sake Daddy, I just got in.

EV   Do you write?

CATHERINE   To Robbie?

EV   Yes to Robbie! You sure as hell don't write to me!

CATHERINE   I don't have the time.

EV   Some people make time.

CATHERINE   Why don't you?

EV   I'm busy.

CATHERINE   So am I.

EV   Mn. [*pause*] Does he ever write you?

CATHERINE   No.

EV   Do you wonder why?

CATHERINE   He's busy! Everyone's busy!

EV   Bullshit. It's that woman of his.

CATHERINE   It isn't.

EV   Paula.

CATHERINE   Who's Paula?

EV   She thinks we're all crazy.

CATHERINE   Well maybe we are, who in hell's Paula?

EV   His wife!

CATHERINE   You mean Corinne.

EV   What did I say?

CATHERINE   You said Paula.

EV   Well I meant Corinne! [*pause*] Paula. Who the hell's Paula? [*pause*]

BOB   Pauline.

EV   Pauline now, that was a friend of your mother's. Died a cancer, died in your room, and where did you sleep?

CATHERINE   In this room

EV   because

CATHERINE   the maid had left

EV   and your mother nursed Pauline right through to the end. Didn't touch a drop for three months.

As Catherine turns away, she sees Bob.

BOB   Not a drop for three months, Katie.

Pause

EV   Best . . . best office nurse . . . I—ever had.
CATHERINE   Who, Mummy?
EV   Not Mummy, no. Valma. She ran that office like Hitler rollin' through Poland, and good with your mother—
CATHERINE   [*turns back to Ev*] I know, forty years like a rock.
EV   That's right, like a rock, but I call her with that heart attack and she goes hysterical. I never saw that in her before. It was a surprise. Is was a goddamn disappointment. She comes runnin' into the house and up the stairs and huffin' and puffin' and blue in the face and—I'm on the bathroom floor by this time. She sees that, and gets more hysterical. She's got to run next door—my phone not workin' bein' connected to her phone which she dropped breakin' my ear drum—and she phones the hospital. And then we sit—I lie, she sits—and we wait for the goddamn ambulance, her holdin' my hand and bawlin'.
CATHERINE   Poor Valma.
EV   Poor Valma be damned! If I'd had the strength I'd have killed her. I kept tellin' her two things, I said it over and over—one, you keep that Demsky away from me—and you know what she does?
CATHERINE   She is sixty-seven.
EV   I'm seventy-three, you don't see me goin' hysterical! And I'm the one havin' the heart attack!
CATHERINE   Alright.
EV   You know the first thing I lay eyes on when I wake up in that hospital bed? Well, do you!
CATHERINE   No, I don't know, no.
EV   First thing I see is that goddamn Demsky hangin' over me like a vulture. Demsky who gave me the heart attack! . . . Next death bed wish I make I sure as hell won't make it to Valma.
CATHERINE   Well . . . it wasn't a real death bed wish, Daddy. You're still here.
EV   No thanks to her!

Pause

CATHERINE   So?
EV   So what?
CATHERINE   Jesus Daddy, so how are you now?
EV   I don't read minds, I'm not a mind reader!

CATHERINE How are you!

EV I'm fine!

CATHERINE Good.

EV What?

CATHERINE I said good. Great. I'm glad that you're fine.

EV Got the nitro pills . . . pop a coupla them. Slow down they say. Don't get excited, don't talk too fast, don't walk too fast, don't, don't, don't, just pop a pill.

CATHERINE Is it hard?

EV Is what hard?

CATHERINE Is it hard to slow down?

EV . . . The nurses could always tell when I'd started my rounds. They could hear my heels hittin' the floor tiles, hear me a wing away.

Oscar starts to laugh quietly.

Did I ever tell you . . .

OSCAR That's what you call a Cuban heel, Ev.

EV . . . 'Bout those white woman's shoes I bought on St. Lawrence?

CATHERINE For the O.R.

EV That's right. They were on sale, real cheap, but they fit my foot cause my foot is so narrow.

OSCAR Still, a woman's shoe, Ev?

EV A good shoe for the O.R. was hard to find then!

CATHERINE So you bought two pair.

EV And I wore them. — How did you know?

CATHERINE You told me.

EV I told you.

CATHERINE Don't you remember? You and Uncle Oscar would act that whole story out. . . . Do you see Uncle Oscar? [*pause*] Daddy? [*pause*] Well . . . anyway . . . so, what was the other thing?

EV Mn?

CATHERINE The other thing. You kept telling Valma two things, Demsky, and what was the other?

EV Don't tell Katie. I musta said that a dozen times. I could hear myself. You're not to tell Katie. You're not to tell Katie.

CATHERINE Why not?

EV Because I didn't want you to know.

CATHERINE Why not?

EV Because I knew, even if you did know, you wouldn't come — and my heart would've burst from that pain.

Catherine and Ev look at each other. Catherine looks away.

Look at me—look at me! . . .

Catherine looks at Ev.

You knew. That goddamn Valma, she told you.

CATHERINE   No—

EV   You think I don't know a lie when I hear it, I see it, right in your goddamn eyes I can see it.

CATHERINE   Alright, alright, Valma did write—

EV   Ignores every goddamn thing I tell her.

CATHERINE   You could have died, Daddy.

EV   If you gave a damn you'd have been here!

CATHERINE   I don't want to fight.

EV   You afraid?

CATHERINE   No.

EV   I'm not afraid.

CATHERINE   God.

EV   Looked death in the face in that goddamn bathroom. It's not easy starin' death down with Valma bawlin' beside you. Every bit a your bein' directed, concentrated on winnin', not lettin' go. . . . [*gets out nitro pills; unscrews top while talking; takes pill by placing it under his tongue during his speech*] Hated, hated losin'! Always. Hockey, politics, surgery, never mattered to me, just *had to win.* Could never let go. Do you know . . . do you know I saved Billy Barnes' life by hangin' onto his hand? I would not let him go till the sulfa took hold. I hung onto his hand, and I said Billy, goddamn it, you fight! And he did. They said it was the sulfa that saved him, miracle drug in those days, but you could never convince Billy of that. "Goddamn it, Doc, it was you!" . . . I opened his belly two or three years ago. Opened his belly and closed his belly. Inoperable carcinoma. . . . "Are you tellin' me this thing is gonna kill me, Doc?" I reached out my hand and he took it. . . . Hung . . . onto my hand. . . .

CATHERINE   I would have come, but you didn't want me to know.

EV   But you did know, didn't you. That goddamn Valma, she told you, and you didn't come.

CATHERINE   I'm here now.

EV   Bit of free time, drop in and see the old man, eh?

CATHERINE   No.

EV   But if this ticker gives out and catches you typin', too bad.

CATHERINE   Don't.

EV   So were you workin' or weren't you workin'?

CATHERINE   I'm always working.

EV   And that's more important than your own father.

CATHERINE   Don't start.

EV   A woman your age should be raisin' a family.

CATHERINE   What family did you ever raise? You were never home from one day to the next so who are you to talk to me about family?

EV   Your father, that's who. The one who damn near died with no one but an office nurse by his side.

CATHERINE   Valma loves you!

EV   That's not what we're talkin' about here. We're talkin' about you and your work and your father dyin', that's what we're talkin' about!

CATHERINE   Are we?

EV   That's what I'm talkin' about—I don't know what the hell you're on about—I don't know what the hell you're doin' here!

CATHERINE   I just came home to see you, I wanted to see you . . . have you got any idea how hard it was for me to come home, to walk in that door, to, to come home? . . . Have you? . . . and when I leave here . . . my plane . . . could fall out of the sky, you could get another pain in your ticker, we could never talk again . . . all the things never said, do you ever think about that?

EV   You mean dyin'?

CATHERINE   No, more than that, I mean . . . I don't know what I mean.

Pause

EV   Are you still with that . . . whatshisname?

CATHERINE   Sort of.

EV   What's his name?

CATHERINE   What's it matter, you never remember.

EV   What's his name? Dugan? or Dougan?

CATHERINE   That was before, years before, Daddy.

EV   You should get one and hang onto one, Katie. Then I'd remember.

CATHERINE   I . . .

EV   What?

CATHERINE   I said it's difficult to keep a relationship goin' when when you're busy, right?

EV   Why don't you marry this whosits?

CATHERINE   Yeah, well. . . . Whosits talks about that.

EV   I'm still waitin' for a grandson you know.

CATHERINE   I'm too old for that.

EV   You're soon gonna be—how old are you anyway?

CATHERINE   Besides I'd only have girls.

EV Robbie's got girls . . . girls are all right. . . . You can have girls if you want.

CATHERINE I said I don't know if I want.

EV But get married first.

CATHERINE Actually—I've been thinking . . . of . . . of maybe calling it quits with whosits.

EV Quits?

CATHERINE Ah-huh.

EV You're callin' it quits.

CATHERINE The work you know. Makes it hard.

EV I thought this was the one. What the hell was his name, Sturgeon or Stefan or—

CATHERINE His name doesn't matter.

EV Stupid goddamn name—an actor, an actor for Christ's sake.

CATHERINE We're not goin' to get into whosits and me and marriage and me and kids and me, all right?

EV You go through men like boxes of kleenex.

CATHERINE I don't want to talk about it!

EV Jesus Christ, I can't keep up.

CATHERINE No you can't! You can't even remember his name!

EV Burgess Buchanan, that was his name! And you sat in the lounge at the Bayside and you said, "Oh Daddy, you just got to meet him, he's such a nice fella, he's so understanding, and he's so this and he's so that and he's. . . . " So explain to me what went wrong this time?

CATHERINE Why do we always end up yelling and screaming, why do we do that?

EV I care 'bout you! . . . I want to see you settled, Katie. Happy. I want you to write, letters, not . . . I want you close.

CATHERINE . . . I do write somebody you know. I write Uncle Oscar . . . every once in while . . . when the spirit moves me.

EV Not often.

CATHERINE No. Not often. But I do. Write letters to someone. I do make the time. I know you and he don't keep in touch any more but I like to.

EV Not lately.

CATHERINE No, not lately. I . . . why do you say that?

EV He was fly-fishin'. He slipped and fell in the Miramichi with his waders on.

CATHERINE [pause] No . . . Did—did you see him?

EV At the morgue when they brought him in.

CATHERINE I mean before. Did you see him before? Were the two of you talking?

Ev shakes his head.

Why not?

EV   Too late.

CATHERINE   Now it's too late.

EV   Too late even then. Even before. Too much had been said.

CATHERINE   I wish you'd have told me.

EV   Would you have come home for him?

CATHERINE   . . . Probably not.

EV   So what difference does it make?

CATHERINE   I like to know these things. Whether I can come or not. I can't help it if I'm in the middle of things.

EV   You make sure you're always in the middle of something. It's an excuse. How old are you now?

CATHERINE   Stop asking me that.

EV   You're gonna end up a silly old woman with nothin' but a cat for company.

CATHERINE   It'll be a live-in cat which is more than you've got with Valma.

EV   If I wanted Valma here, she'd be here.

CATHERINE   So you don't want her here, eh? You like it alone. Sitting up here all alone!

EV   I am not alone!

CATHERINE   You and Robbie, the same city, you never see Robbie!

EV   Go on! Why doncha go on! You got so goddamn much to say, why don't you say it! I am alone and it's you left me alone! My own daughter walkin' out and leavin' her father alone!

CATHERINE   How many years before you noticed my bed wasn't slept in?

EV   Don't go pointin' your finger at me! Look at yourself! What the hell do you do? Work, work, work—at what, for Christ's sake?

CATHERINE   I write! I'm good at it!

EV   Writing, eh Katie?

CATHERINE   Don't call me Katie!

EV   I'll call you by the name we gave you and that name is Katie.

CATHERINE   It's Catherine now.

EV   Oh, it's Catherine now, and you write Literature, don't you? And that means you can ignore your brother and your father and dump this Buchanan jerk and forget kids and family, but your father who gave his life to medicine because he believed in what he was doin' is an asshole!

CATHERINE   I never said that!

EV   My whole family never had a pot to piss in, lived on porridge and molasses when I was a kid.

CATHERINE   Alright!

EV   And fought for every goddamn thing I got!

CATHERINE   And it all comes down to you sitting up here alone with Gramma's letter!

EV   I am goin' through things!

CATHERINE   Why won't you open it?

EV   I know what it says.

CATHERINE   Tell me.

EV   You want it, here, take it.

Catherine grabs letter from Ev. She almost rips it open, but stops and turns it in her hand. Pause.

CATHERINE   Did Gramma really walk out to meet it?

EV   It was an accident.

CATHERINE   What was Mummy?

EV   You blame me for that.

CATHERINE   No.

EV   It was all my fault, go on, say it, I know what you think.

CATHERINE   It was my fault.

EV   Oh for Christ's sake!

Ev moves away from Catherine. He sits, takes off his glasses and rubs the bridge of his nose. He looks at Catherine, then back to the glasses which he holds in his hand.

   . . . Your mother . . .

CATHERINE   Yes?

EV   Your mother and I—

CATHERINE   Tell me. Explain it to me.

BOB   There were eight of us, Katie, eight of us.

OSCAR   [*softly*] Go, go.

BOB   How did my mama manage?

Oscar stands up, holding two hockey sticks. He is looking at Ev, whose back is to him. Ev puts his glasses in his pocket.

OSCAR   Go.

BOB   All older than me, all born before he went to war.

OSCAR   Go.

BOB   Him, her husband, my father, your grandfather, Katie.

OSCAR   Go. Go!

BOB   And her with the eight of us and only the pension.

OSCAR   Go!! Go!!

BOB   How did my mama manage?

Bob may exit. Shift.

OSCAR   Go!!! Go!!!

Oscar throws a hockey stick at Ev who stands, turns, plucking it out of the air at the last minute. They are catapulted back in time, rough-housing after a game.

> Go!!! The Deven Terror has got the puck, out of his end, across the blue line, they're mixing it up in the corner and he's out in front, he shoots! He scores! Rahhhh!

Oscar has ended up on the floor with his hockey sweater pulled over his head. Ev, who's scored, raises his arms in acknowledgement of the crowd's ''Rah!''. Ev helps Oscar up.

> You know somethin' Ev? This is the truth. Honest to God. Are you listenin'?

EV   Yeah.

Ev takes off his ''old man'' sweater and hangs it on the back of a chair. During the following dialogue, Oscar changes out of his hockey clothes, putting them in the trunk. He removes a jacket, pants, and shoes for Ev, and a suit of clothes plus shoes for himself.

OSCAR   When I think of medicine I get sick. Yeah. The thought of medicine makes me ill. Physically ill. Do you think that could be my mother in me?

Ev slips out of his slippers and removes his pants. Oscar will put the pants in the trunk.

EV   Maybe.
OSCAR   My father says it's my mother in me. At least she had the good sense to get out. Leaving me with him. How could she do that?
EV   I dunno. [*puts on suit jacket*]
OSCAR   The old man calls her a bitch. And now nuthin' for it but I got to go into medicine.
EV   So tell him no.
OSCAR   I can't.
EV   Stand up to him.

OSCAR I can't.

EV Just tell him.

OSCAR It'd break his heart.

EV Shit Oscar, it's your life, you can't think about that.

OSCAR Yeah.

EV You just gotta tell him what you really want to do . . . how does that look?

OSCAR Great.

EV Which is?

OSCAR Which is what?

Oscar throws Ev a tie.

EV What you really want to do.

OSCAR Oh.

EV What do you really want to do?

OSCAR I dunno.

EV Come on.

OSCAR Live someplace where it's hot.

EV Come onnn . . .

OSCAR New Orleans, I'd like to live in New Orleans.

EV Oscar—

OSCAR How hot is New Orleans anyway?

EV And *do what*—in New Orleans, Oscar?

OSCAR Do what. I dunno. Something. Anything. Not medicine.

Oscar reties Ev's tie for him.

EV Look, if you're gonna tell your father you don't want to do what he wants you to do, you can't just say your life's ambition is to live someplace where it's hot.

OSCAR What if it is?

EV That is not gonna work, Oscar.

OSCAR You're a lot like my Dad, Ev. The two of you. You're always . . .

EV What?

OSCAR Forging *ahead*.

EV What's wrong with that? [*puts on pants*]

OSCAR Nothing. Forging is fine. I admire forging, I do, I admire it. It's just — not for me, do you think that could be my mother in me?

EV Forget your mother. Concentrate on what you're gonna tell your father—and New Orleans is out.

OSCAR It's honest, don't I get points for honest?

EV   Belt?

OSCAR   No points for honest.

EV   Or suspenders?

OSCAR   What's honest, honest is nothing, nobody wants honest.

EV   Honest is good, New Orleans is bad, belt or suspenders?

OSCAR   Belt.

Oscar throws Ev a belt.

EV   Thanks.

OSCAR   It's not fair.

EV   I don't wanna hear about fair.

OSCAR   Right.

EV   Face it, you're a lazy son of a bitch.

OSCAR   I know.

EV   You've got no drive.

OSCAR   I know.

EV   You've got no push.

OSCAR   I know.

EV   I worked my ass off last summer in construction, what did you do?

OSCAR   I lay in the sun.

EV   That's right.

OSCAR   I'm a loser.

EV   And a whiner.

OSCAR   Right. [*pause*] Why are we friends?

EV   Eh?

OSCAR   I agree with everything you say, it's the truth, what can I say? So why are we friends?—I figure it's the car and the clothes.

Ev puts on shoes. By the end of scene he is dressed in suit, tie, and shoes.

EV   That's a pretty shitty thing to imply.

OSCAR   I wasn't implying, I was just wondering.

EV   You've got other qualities.

OSCAR   Name one.

EV   We grew up together.

OSCAR   Go on.

EV   So we've known each other for a long time.

OSCAR   Yeah.

EV   Since Grade One.

Pause

OSCAR   Well I figure it's the car and the clothes and the fact the old man dotes on you.

EV   Jesus Oscar.

OSCAR   Everybody knows I'm just a—

EV   Don't whine!

OSCAR   I'm not whining. I'm analyzing!

EV   I'm tryin' to help, Oscar. Now you must have some ambition, some desire, something you're at least vaguely interested in, that you could propose to your father as a kinda alternative to medicine, eh?

OSCAR   You mean apart from New Orleans.

EV   That's what I mean.

OSCAR   My mother might have gone to New Orleans.

EV   Forget your mother! Alternative to medicine! Not New Orleans!

OSCAR   Algeria.

EV   Oscar!

OSCAR   I know.

EV   I try to look out for you and it's like pissing on a forest fire.

OSCAR   I'm telling you exactly how I feel. I don't have ambitions and desires and goals in life. I don't need 'em. My old man has my whole life mapped out for me and I know what I'm supposed to do. I'm supposed to read and follow the map. That's it.

Ev moves away from Oscar.

EV   There is no wardrobe and no car and no amount of dotage from your old man that would compensate a person for putting up with you!

Shift

CATHERINE   Uncle Oscar?

Oscar looks at Katie as if it was she who had spoken. Katie holds her shoe out to him.

Fix my shoe.

KATIE   It's got about a million knots—but keep talking.

CATHERINE   I want to know everything.

OSCAR   Construction work in the summer, hockey in the winter, and when we went to McGill, they'd bring him home on the overnight train to play the big games, the important games—and that's how he paid his way through medical school.

KATIE Keep talking.

OSCAR My father was their family doctor — I was there at his house
the night his brother George died from the influenza — and that
left him, and his sister Millie and his Mum and Dad.

CATHERINE My Gramma.

KATIE What was she like?

OSCAR Proper. United Church. Poor and proper.

Oscar gives Katie back her shoe

That's all I remember.

Katie hits Oscar with the shoe.

KATIE Remember more!

OSCAR I think your father got his drive from your Gramma and you
get yours from him.

KATIE Are you saying I'm like her?

OSCAR In some ways perhaps.

KATIE I would never walk across a train bridge at midnight!

OSCAR You might.

KATIE I would not!

OSCAR Well it was an accident she —

KATIE What do you mean I might!

OSCAR It was a short cut.

KATIE I'm not like her! I would never do that!

OSCAR It wasn't anything she did.

KATIE I'm too smart to do that!

OSCAR It was just something that happened.

KATIE You don't know! You don't know anything!

OSCAR Katie —

KATIE Get away from me!

CATHERINE Stop.

Shift

EV If you want to know about this crazy bastard — if you want to
know about him — When I needed a friend at my back, in a fight,
in a brawl? This silly son of a bitch in sartorial splendor has saved
my ass more than once — and me his — I'm gonna tell you a story.
Now listen — we used to drink at this hole in the wall, this waterin'
hole for whores and medical students, eh? An we'd sit there and
nurse a beer all night and chat it up with the whores who'd come
driftin' in well after midnight, towards mornin' really, and this

was in winter, freeze a Frenchman's balls off — and the whores would come in off the street for a beer and we'd sit there all talkin' and jokin' around. They were nice girls these whores, all come to Montreal from Three Rivers and Chicoutimi and a lotta places I never heard tell of, and couldn't pronounce. Our acquaintance was strictly a pub acquaintance, we students preferin' to spend our money on beer thus avoidin' a medical difficulty which intimacy with these girls would most likely entail. So — this night we're stragglin' home in the cold walkin' and talkin' to a bunch a these whores, and as we pass their house, they drop off there up the steps yellin' "Goo-night goo-night". . . . Bout a block further on, someone says: "Where the hell's Oscar?" Christ, we all start yellin': "Where the hell's Oscar? Oscar! Oscar!" Searchin' in gutters, snowbanks and alleys, but the bugger's gone, disappeared! Suddenly it comes to me. Surer than hell he's so pissed he's just followed along behind the girls when they peeled off to go home, and he's back there inside the cat house. So back I go. Bang on the door. This giant of a woman, uglier than sin, opens it up. Inside is all this screamin' and cryin' and poundin' and I say: "Did a kinda skinny fellow" — and she says: "Get that son of a bitch outa here!" "Where is he?" I say. "Upstairs, he's locked himself in one of the rooms with Janette! He's killin' her for Christ's sake!" She takes me up to the room, door locked, girl inside is screamin' bloody murder and I can hear Oscar makin' a kinda intent diabolical ahhhhhin' and oohhhin' sound. "Oscar! Oscar! For Christ's sake, open up!" The girl's pleadin' with him to stop, beggin' him, chill your blood to the bone to hear her. And still that aaahhhhin'! and oohhhhhin'! Nothin' for it but I got to throw myself at the door till either it gives or my shoulder does. Finally Boom! I'm in. I can see Oscar is not. He's got Janette tied to the bed, staked right out, naked and nude. He's straddlin' her but he's fully clothed, winter hat, scarf, boots and all, and he's wieldin' his blue anatomy pencil. He's drawin' all of her vital organs, he's outlinin' them on her skin with his blue anatomy pencil. He's got her kidneys and her lungs, her trachea and her liver all traced out. Takes four of us to pull him off—me and three massive brutes who've appeared. Janette is so upset they sent her back to Rivière-du-Loup for two weeks to recover, Oscar has to turn pimp till he pays back the price of the door, and everyone swears it's the worst goddamn perversion and misuse of a whore ever witnessed in Montreal . . . what in God's name did you think you were doin' that night?

Oscar shrugs and smiles. Ev is taking out a letter and opening it as he speaks.

Jesus Christ . . . silly bastard . . .

Shift

It's from Mum . . . the old man's been laid off.
OSCAR　She sound worried?
EV　She says go ahead with the Royal Vic.
OSCAR　The General would be closer to home.
EV　What good would that do?
OSCAR　I don't know.
EV　No money to be made in post-graduate work anywhere.
OSCAR　I thought moral support, you know, being close.
EV　The Vic's the best in the country.
OSCAR　I know that.
EV　Mum would probably kill me if I gave up the Royal Vic.
OSCAR　She definitely would. . . . What about Millie?
EV　Millie?
OSCAR　Yeah.
EV　What about her?
OSCAR　I guess she could probably help out. Get a job.
EV　There's no jobs anywhere. Besides Millie's still in school.
OSCAR　Will she quit?
EV　What the hell do you want me to do?
OSCAR　I don't want you to do anything. I just wondered if Millie
　　　would quit school to help out at home, that's all.
EV　What the hell're you tryin' to say to me? Are you sayin' I should
　　　quit?
OSCAR　No, I just meant there are hospitals closer to home.

Oscar may exit. Ev calls after him.

EV　You can't be serious. The Vic's the best post-graduate training in
　　　the country. I've worked goddamn hard for it and I won't give it
　　　up—not for Mum if she asked me! Not for Millie! Not for anyone!
CATHERINE　But you did, Daddy.

Ev looks at Catherine.

You gave it up for her.
EV　If . . . if you could have seen her.

Shift. Bob may enter. She carries a music box

BOB　He would step off the elevator—every nurse on the floor, ''Yes

Doctor'' — ''No Doctor'' — ''Is there anything else'' dramatic
pause, sighhhh, ''I can *do* for you, Doctor?'' Even Matron. Yes,
Matron! And the goo-goo eyes — I remember those eyes.

EV   Do you know what they said?

CATHERINE   What did they say?

EV   Forget her, she is immune to the charms of the predatory male.

BOB   They were right.

EV   No fraternization between doctors and nurses on pain of
dismissal.

CATHERINE   So why did you ask her?

EV   I—

BOB   He couldn't resist me — and I —

*Bob passes Catherine the jewellery box to hold. Bob opens the box. It plays
''Smoke Gets in Your Eyes''. Bob takes out a pair of earrings and puts them
on as she's speaking. The lid of the box remains up and the music box plays
during the scene.*

I don't give a fig for regulation or rules, only ones I make myself.
And if in the past I chose to observe that regulation, it was only
because a suitable occasion to break it hadn't arisen.

EV   Be serious.

BOB   My goodness, here I am without two pennies to rub together,
and I rush out and buy a new sweater for a bar date with you, and
you don't call that serious?

EV   When our eyes first met over what? . . . a perforated ulcer, were
you serious then?

BOB   Do you know how many floors my mama scrubbed for that
sweater?

''Smoke Gets In Your Eyes'' played by big band fades in.

CATHERINE   [*closes jewellery box*] Was she really like that?

EV   If you could have seen her.

Oscar may enter

OSCAR   Why risk it?

EV   Wait till you meet her.

Ev moves towards Bob, who is swaying to the music.

OSCAR   I don't need to meet her. For Christ's sake, Ev, you're . . . Ev?
    . . . Ev!

Ev and Bob dance to a medley of Thirties tunes. Oscar watches, drawn into that warm atmosphere. Ev and Oscar take turns cutting in on each other, as they ballroom dance with Bob. They're all very good dancers, and Oscar is as captivated as Ev by Bob. Oscar dances with Bob. She is looking over his shoulder at Ev. Shift

KATIE   [*interrupts, a sudden scream*] Stop that! You stop it!

The dancers stop; a soft freeze.

I know things! I can figure things out!

The soft freeze breaks. Shift.

OSCAR   Have you told your mother?
EV   Not yet.
OSCAR   She had her heart set on a specialist.
EV   She'll settle for a grandson.
CATHERINE   But that's not what you got, you got me.

Shift

KATIE   Why did he marry her?
OSCAR   He loved her.
KATIE   Why didn't you marry her?
OSCAR   She loved him.
KATIE   They didn't want to have me.
OSCAR   That isn't true.
KATIE   Did your mother want to have you?

Shift

BOB   Your mother, ooohhh, your poor father, Ev.
EV   I know.
BOB   And Millie—you never told me about Millie.
EV   I mentioned her once or twice.
BOB   If you were only Catholic she could be a nun.
EV   Don't judge her by what you've seen tonight.
BOB   And your mother could be Pope.
EV   She liked you.
BOB   She hated me.
EV   When you get to know her, it'll be different.
BOB   I don't want to know her. Look at Millie under her thumb.
EV   Millie isn't under her thumb.

BOB   And your father.

There is a sense of intimacy, rather than irritation, between Ev and Bob.

EV   Look, you saw them for the first time for what—four or five hours
—you can't make generalizations based on that.

BOB   You were there. You heard her. "Poor Ev. Giving up the Vic."
You'd think a general practice was the end of the earth — And
why've you fallen so far?

EV   She never said any of those things.

BOB   She implied I'd caught you by the oldest trick in the book.

EV   She didn't.

BOB   "Why does a girl go into nursing?" Why to marry a doctor of
course! And Millie nodding away and your father smiling away
—I wanted to stand up and scream.

EV   You're tired.

BOB   And you, you're there, way up there, the shining light, can do
nothing wrong, except one thing is wrong, we are wrong!

EV   She had certain expectations, I'm not defending her, I'm just
trying to explain how things are, or have been—Bob? . . . Bob!

BOB   For years she's been practising, "I'd like you to meet my son,
The Specialist."

EV   Things haven't been easy, you know. You've seen Dad, he's a
good man but he's — when Georgie died, the old man wept on
her — there was no one for her to weep on. It was hard on her
losin' Georgie, and now all of her hopes for me and for Georgie
are all pinned on me. . . You can understand that.

BOB   She'll be counting the months.

EV   Let her.

Ev kisses Bob.

Again.

Ev kisses Bob.

Again.

BOB   You.

EV   You smile that smile at my Mum and she'll love you. It's a beautiful
smile.

BOB   We aren't wrong, are we?

EV   We'll have a boy and we'll call him George after my brother. She'll
like that.

BOB   Or William, after my brother Bill.

EV   And he'll have a beautiful smile.

BOB   And he'll have a nose like yours.

EV   And he'll . . .

Shift. Ev and Bob may exit.

CATHERINE   I notice this thing about having boys first. I mean what is that all about?

KATIE   Who was I named after?

OSCAR   Kate was your grandmother's name.

KATIE   Nobody calls me Kate.

OSCAR   That's your name.

KATIE   It's an ugly name. Why did they call me that? Couldn't they think of anything else?

OSCAR   Kate isn't ugly.

KATIE   Do I look like a Kate to you?

OSCAR   What's a Kate look like?

KATIE   Do you think names are like dogs?

OSCAR   In what way like dogs?

KATIE   I read dogs start to look like their owners or owners start to look like their dogs. Do you think if you get an ugly name you start to look like your name?

CATHERINE   Or be like who you were named after?

Shift. Ev and Bob may enter. Bob carries Ev's suitcoat. Ev carries a doctor's bag. Bob will help Ev on with his jacket.

BOB   I want to go back to work.

EV   Where would you work?

BOB   I'm an R.N., I'll apply at the hospital.

EV   No.

CATHERINE   Why not?

EV   I don't want her there.

CATHERINE   Why not?

EV   A matter of policy.

CATHERINE   Whose?

EV   What about Katie?

BOB   What about her?

EV   You should be home with her.

BOB   Why?

EV   You're her mother.

BOB   You're her father, you're not home from one day to the next. What am I supposed to do, rattle around with a four-month-old baby to talk to?

EV   So get somebody in.

BOB   Let me work, Ev.

EV   I don't want you down at the hospital.

BOB   Why not?

EV   Because as a surgeon operating out of that hospital, I don't want my wife on staff. I don't want any surgeon's wife on staff. And I don't know any surgeon who wants his wife on staff.

Shift

KATIE   They were fighting last night.

OSCAR   Oh?

KATIE   Do you want to know what they were fighting about, if you don't already know.

OSCAR   How would I know?

KATIE   How do you think! Someone would tell you! Behind Daddy's back they would tell you! They would whisper.

OSCAR   That doesn't happen.

CATHERINE   Then why, Uncle Oscar, did you spend so much time talking to me if you didn't want to find out about them?

Shift

BOB   I could work at the office. [*pours herself a drink*]

EV   No.

BOB   McQuire's wife—

EV   is a silly bitch who keeps McQuire's office in an uproar from the time she comes in in the morning till she leaves at night.

BOB   I'm not Marg McQuire.

EV   I have an office nurse, she does a good job and she needs the job and I don't intend letting her go.

BOB   I could work for somebody else!

EV   I don't know what doctor would hire another doctor's wife as an office nurse.

BOB   Why not?

EV   Look, you're not just an R.N. anymore.

BOB   No.

EV   You're not Eloise Roberts, you're not Bob any more.

BOB   Who am I?

EV   My wife.

CATHERINE   Daddy.

EV   You're working the O.R., the surgeon hits a bleeder, starts scream-ing for clamps, you're slow off the mark, and when the whole mess is under control, he turns round to give you shit, you take

off your surgical mask and who does he see? Not a nurse, another
surgeon's wife. *My* wife. Is he gonna give you shit?

BOB   I'm not slow off the mark in the O.R.

EV   That's not the point, you're my wife, is he gonna give you shit?

BOB   That's his problem, not mine.

EV   I'm in the O.R. I hit a bleeder. I scream for a clamp. I look at the
nurse who's too fuckin' slow and who do I see? My wife!

BOB   I'm not slow! I'm good in the O.R.

EV   That's not the point.

CATHERINE   Why don't you just say you don't want her there instead
of all this bullshit?

EV   Jesus Christ I said it! I don't want her there!

Shift. Katie is holding her wrist. She speaks to Oscar.

KATIE   My father works hard! My father works really hard!

CATHERINE   I know. I know.

KATIE   You don't work as hard as my father. My father is never home.
He goes to the hospital before we're up, and when he comes home
we're asleep.

CATHERINE   Robbie's asleep.

KATIE   I'm surprised Daddy knows who Robbie is. I'm surprised Robbie knows who Daddy is . . . I hate Robbie.

OSCAR   How did this happen?

KATIE   I dunno.

OSCAR   Yes you do.

KATIE   I'm accident-prone. Some people are you know. Accident-
prone. I do dangerous things. I like doing dangerous things.

OSCAR   How'd you do this?

KATIE   It was just something that happened.

OSCAR   Ah-huh.

Oscar is taping Katie's wrist.

KATIE   I do lots of things. Last Sunday when we were supposed to be
in Sunday School, Robbie and I, do you know what we did?

OSCAR   Might hurt.

KATIE   Won't hurt. We went to the freight yards and played. I crawled
under the train cars twice and Robbie crawled over where they're
hitched together. He was too scared to crawl under. I wasn't
scared.

OSCAR   You shouldn't do that.

KATIE   We decided together, Robbie and I. I didn't make him. Do you
believe that?

OSCAR What?

KATIE That Robbie and I decided together to go to the freight yards instead of to Sunday School, do you believe that?

OSCAR No.

KATIE Anyway we had these gloves on. You know the ones Mummy made out of kid or leather the last time she was away? She made about a million pair. She probably gave a pair to you.

Shift

BOB It's not my fault if other people don't know who I am! It's not my fault if all they can see is your wife!

EV Aren't you my wife?

BOB That's not all I am!

EV Don't yell at me.

BOB Who do I yell at?

EV Half the nurses in that goddamn hospital are lookin' for a doctor to marry so they can sit on their ass, and here you are screamin' cause you're not on your feet twelve hours a day bein' overworked and underpaid.

BOB I am on my feet twelve hours a day!

EV So let me get somebody in.

BOB I feel funny with somebody in. . . . If I'm here, I feel I should be doing it.

EV You want to get out more.

BOB I know I'm a good nurse. I'm as good as anyone. When I'm out . . . I'm never sure which fork to use.

EV Who gives a shit which fork you use? Whichever one comes to hand.

BOB When you "go out" that fork's important.

EV Get Oscar to teach you how to play bridge. First year of university that's all he did.

BOB I feel as if I wasted something.

Shift. Katie is still with Oscar.

KATIE I don't know how she's supposed to get better by making gloves and painting pictures. Her pictures are awful. It costs a fortune to send her there and it never works! . . . Anyway . . . I got black all over my gloves and it wouldn't come off so I made Robbie give me his cause Mummy never gets mad at him and that's one of the reasons I hate him, and as soon as we got home do you know what he did?

CATHERINE Told.

KATIE   He told. He said I *made* him go to the freight yards and then I *made* him change gloves. He's always telling and that's another reason I hate him.

OSCAR   You're the oldest—you should look out for Robbie.

KATIE   I am trying to teach Robbie to look out for *himself*! I am! . . . She didn't even ask and he told. She's always saying Robbie's just like her side of the family and I'm just like Daddy's— Have you met my Uncle Bill?

OSCAR   I might have.

KATIE   Well I wouldn't want to be like her side of the family. I'd rather be like his!

Shift

BOB   Nobody else in my family finished high school, did I tell you that?

No one is listening to Bob.

CATHERINE   Was she a good nurse, Daddy?

EV   That's not the point, Katie.

CATHERINE   Was she?

EV   I'm late for my rounds.

BOB   I was the smartest.

EV   You get some sleep now.

Ev may exit.

CATHERINE   Daddy?

BOB   And I always won, Katie! Because I played so hard! Played to win! And school—*first*, always first! "Our valedictorian is Eloise Roberts."

Catherine moves away from Bob, who continues speaking with the drink in her hand.

Eloise Roberts, and they called me Bob, and I could run faster and play harder and do better than any boy I ever met! And my hair? It was all the way down to there! And when I asked my Mama— Mama?— She said, we have been here since the Seventeen Hundreds, Eloise, and in your blood runs the blood of Red Roberts! Do you know who he is? A pirate, with flamin' red hair and a flamin' red beard who harbored off a cove in P.E.I.! A pirate! And inside of me—just bustin' to get out! To reach out! To grow!

. . . And when I sat on our front porch and I looked out—I always looked *up*, cause lookin' up I saw the sky, and the sky went on forever! And I picked and sold berries, and my Mama cleaned house for everyone all around, and my sisters and my one brother Bill, everything for *one thing*. For *me*. For Eloise Roberts. For Bob.

Shift. Ev enters, carrying his bag. He is speaking to Oscar.

EV   You know somethin'!? The goddamn health care services in this province are a laugh!

BOB   Katie?

EV   I had a woman come into my office yesterday. I've never seen her before, but she's got a lump in her breast and she's half out of her mind with worry. Surer than hell it's cancer, but there's nothin' I can do till I damn well find out it *is* cancer. So what do I have to do? I gotta take a section and ship that tissue to Saint John on the bus for Christ's sake! And then what? I got to wait for three days to maybe a week to hear. Do you know how often I get a replay of that scenario? She's a mother or she works for a living or she's at home lookin' after her old man and I can't tell her what's wrong or what we have to do till I get that goddamn report back from Saint John! We need a medical laboratory in this town, and by God, I'm gonna see that we get one!

OSCAR   Have you seen Bob?

EV   When?

OSCAR   Do you know you've a son?

EV   Georgie, we're callin' him Georgie, a brother for Katie. Hell of a good-lookin' boy, have you seen him?

OSCAR   I popped into the nursery.

EV   Looks like his old man.

OSCAR   Where were you?

EV   Had a call in Keswick.

OSCAR   What the hell would take you to Keswick when your wife's in labour?

EV   I hear it went as smooth as silk.

OSCAR   Ev?

EV   . . . Frank Johnston's kid fell under a thresher.

OSCAR   Bad?

EV   Bad as it can get.

OSCAR   You . . . could have sent someone else.

EV   Frank's been a patient of mine since I started practice. Who the hell else could I send?

OSCAR   What about Bob?

EV   Valma was with her.

OSCAR She didn't want Valma, she wanted you.

EV Look, I brought Frank Johnston's kid into the world — and eight hours ago I saw him out, kneelin' in a field, with the kid's blood soakin' my pants. . . . And afterwards, I sat in the kitchen with his mother, and before I left, I shared a mickey of rum with Frank.

OSCAR It was important to Bob you be here, she needed you.

Oscar may exit. Ev calls after him.

EV Well Frank Johnston needed me more!

Ev looks at Catherine.

The last baby I delivered was in a tarpaper shack. They paid me seven eggs, and when the crabapples fall, the mother's bringin' some round. Would you like to talk need to that woman? . . .

Catherine looks away.

She's got the best maternity care this province provides, and the best obstetrician in town. She's got a private nurse, and a baby boy. What the hell else does she want?

Ev carries a chair over near Bob.

CATHERINE She wants you.

EV She's got me.

Ev sits beside Bob. Shift.

BOB I like Robert.

EV I thought it was George or William.

BOB Robbie's better.

EV What's wrong with George?

BOB Nothing's wrong with it, I like Robbie best.

EV George was my brother's name.

BOB I know.

EV Robert George?

BOB Robert Dann.

EV Where the hell did you get that name?

BOB Out of my head.

EV Well, you can stick George in someplace, can't you?

BOB I'm not calling him George.

EV It's my goddamn brother's name!

BOB I know.

EV   It means a lot to my mother.

BOB   I know.

EV   So stick it in someplace!

BOB   No.

EV   Jesus Christ do you have to make an issue outa every little thing?

BOB   I don't like George.

EV   What the hell harm does it do to stick George in somewhere?
Robert Dann George, George Robert Dann, George Damn Robert.

BOB   He's my son.

EV   He's our son.

BOB   So register him whatever you like.

EV   I will. [*stands up*]

BOB   I'm calling him Robbie.

EV   [*returns chair to original position*] I work my ass off. Why do I do
it if it's not for her?

CATHERINE   Why?

EV   For her. Oscar!

Shift. Oscar may enter.

OSCAR   Ah-huh?

EV   What're your evenings like?

OSCAR   What're your evenings like?

EV   I'm doin' rounds at night and squeezin' in house calls after that
—could you drop over to see her till she comes round a bit?

OSCAR   What about my house calls?

EV   You never made a house call in your life.

OSCAR   I made one once.

EV   You lazy son of a bitch. If it weren't for the remnants of your old
man's practice, you'd starve to death. What'll you do when the
last of his patients die off?

OSCAR   Move someplace where it's hot.

EV   Listen, what she needs is someone to talk to, play a little golf,
shit, the Medical Ball's comin' up next month, take her to that.
I'm too goddamn busy.

OSCAR   When do you sleep?

EV   I don't.

OSCAR   How the hell did she ever get pregnant?

EV   I didn't say I never laid down.

Ev may exit with bag. Shift.

BOB   I want to go to New York next month. Go to New York and see
the shows—do you want to do that?

Sound of Forties dance music.

OSCAR   Can Ev get away?
BOB   We'll ask.

Oscar lights Bob's cigarette

> Look around us. Look at all these pursey little lips. Look at all these doctors' wives. Do I look like that? Do I?

OSCAR   Not a bit.

BOB   [*holding glass*] Well thas good. Look at them. . . . D'you know I joined the I.O.D.E.? The I.O.D.E. I joined it. And do you wanna know what's really frightenin'? I could prolly, after a bit, I could prolly achully — forget. I could get to like the I.O.D.E. Isn't tha' frightening? . . . Isn't tha' frightening! . . . Ah, you're as bad as Everett. Whasa matter with doctors, you're a doctor, you tell me, so busy savin' lives you've forgotten how to talk? Talk!

OSCAR   The I.O.D.E. eh?

BOB   Thas right . . . next year I might run as Grand Something. . . . The I.O.D.E. does some very importan' work you know.

Oscar smiles and casually takes the glass from her.

> . . . I don't like anybody here, do you? . . .

Bob takes the glass back as casually, takes a drink.

> Do you know my mother . . . and all my sisters . . . and my one brother Bill who taught me how to fish—hey! We could go fishing some time if you want.

OSCAR   Bob.

BOB   Everett doesn't fish! Everett doesn't do anything except go . . . round . . .

OSCAR   Bob.

BOB   Anyway — so all these people, mother, sisters, Bill, they all worked to put me through nursing, wasn't that wonderful of them? . . . And now Ev, he lent Bill the money for something Bill thinks he wants to do and it'll all be a disaster cause it's about the tenth time he'd done it, but Ev's always giving money to his mother, so I don't care. Why should I care? But you know what I don't like? Do you?

OSCAR   What don't you like?

BOB   I don't like the cleanin' lady. Because every time . . . the cleanin' lady comes in, I think of my Mama who cleaned all around so I could go into nursing

Music out; silence.

and you want to know what's worse? My Mama's so happy I married a doctor. I'm successful you see. I made something of myself. [*moves away smiling; lifting her glass in a toast*] I married a doctor.

Shift. Katie carries a hairbrush.

KATIE Why don't you get married?
OSCAR I'm waiting for you.
KATIE I'm not related to you.
OSCAR No.
KATIE But you're always here, you're always about. . . . Do you love my mother?
OSCAR I love you.
KATIE Do you want to brush my hair?
OSCAR If you want me to.
KATIE You can if you want.

Katie gives Oscar the brush, and sits at his feet. He brushes her hair. She enjoys it for a moment before speaking.

I'm named after my Gramma, but I'm not like my Gramma. . . . I know when trains are coming . . . and when they're coming, I don't go that way then. . . . Do you like brushing my hair?
OSCAR It needs it.
KATIE I don't care if it's messy. It's how you are inside that counts.
OSCAR That's true.
KATIE I'm surprised you don't know that.
CATHERINE Did you love my mother, Uncle Oscar?
OSCAR When your mother's not well, you should think about that.
KATIE About what?
OSCAR How she feels inside.
KATIE . . . I wonder—what my father sees in you. [*grabs the hairbrush*] You're not a very good doctor. What does he see in you?
OSCAR Katie—
KATIE Do you like brushing my hair?
     Do you like brushing my hair!
OSCAR Katie—

KATIE I hate you!

Katie moves away from Oscar, who follows her.   Shift.   Bob moves to the liquor and refills her glass. It is late, and she drinks while she waits.

BOB Ev! . . . is that you, Ev?

Ev may enter. He will sit, his bag at his feet, with his head back and his eyes closed.

EV Yeah.
BOB What time is it? . . . Where were you?
EV Just left the hospital. They brought in some kid with a ruptured spleen . . . car accident . . . took out every guard rail on that big turn on River Road . . . damn near bled out when we got him.
BOB How is he?
EV Mnn?
BOB I said, how is he?
EV Bout half a million pieces . . .
BOB . . . Ev?
EV What time is it?
BOB Late.
EV Takin' out a stomach in the mornin'.
BOB . . . Can we talk?
EV Talk away . . .
BOB I let the maid go today. It wasn't working out—
EV Medjuck call?
BOB What?
EV Did Sam Medjuck call?
BOB I said I let the maid go today—
EV Mn?
BOB [*moves to refill her drink*] Valma phoned and said he'd called her.
EV Christ. [*gets up; picks up his bag*]
CATHERINE Why would he phone Valma's looking for you?
EV He knows her, she kids him along.
CATHERINE Were you over at Valma's?
EV I was takin' out a spleen.
CATHERINE Should I believe that?
EV I was takin' out a spleen!
BOB I said I let the maid go today!
EV How many's that?
BOB She was a smarmy bitch and I fired her!
EV I said how many's that?

Ev may exit.

BOB Where're you going?
EV [*offstage*] House call to Medjuck's!
BOB It's the middle of the night!
EV [*offstage*] It's morning!
BOB Ev! Ev!
CATHERINE He's gone.
BOB You'll fall asleep, Ev! You'll fall asleep and run off the road!
KATIE Shut up Mummy!
BOB Ev!
KATIE Why don't you shut up and let people sleep!
BOB Oscar!
CATHERINE He isn't here, Mummy!
BOB Count on Oscar!
KATIE He's not here, Mummy!
OSCAR When you need me you call, I'll be there.
CATHERINE Daddy!

Ev may enter, isolated on stage. Music filters in, "Auld Lang Syne".

EV Buy a Packard I always say! Best goddamn car on the road!
CATHERINE Do something.
EV I'd be drivin' along, middle of the night—
BOB It's seven maids, that's how many!
EV All of a sudden, swish, swish, swish, tree branches hittin' the car, look. around—
BOB And I'll fire the next seven whenever I damn well feel like it!
CATHERINE Daddy!
EV Car's in the middle of a goddamn orchard.
BOB Oscar!
EV I've fallen asleep and failed to navigate a turn and here's me and the car travellin' through this goddamn orchard.

Bob is joined by Oscar. They dance to "Auld Lang Syne", as Katie watches. Catherine's focus slowly switches, from her father to Bob and Oscar.

BOB Oscar.
EV And me without a clue in the world as to where I'm headed. Black as pitch, not a light to be seen, and me drivin' over bumps and skirtin' fences and tryin' to remember where in the hell I'm goin'. Then I catch a glimpse of this little light, almost like a low-lyin' star in the sky.

Bob kisses Oscar.

EV   . . . head for that—what the hell—could end up on Venus! Door
    opens and someone is standin' there—

Bob sees Katie watching.

    "We been waitin' for you, Doc."
BOB   What do you want?
EV   "Is the coffee hot?"
BOB   What do you want!
EV   "Melt a spoon."
KATIE   [*screams*] Don't! You don't!

Katie launches herself at Oscar and Bob.

EV   "We been waitin' for you, Doc."

*Katie hits Oscar and Bob and Bob steps away from Oscar. During all the
action she continues to scream.*

KATIE   You! You! Get away! Get away! I hate you! I hate you! You
    don't! Get away!

Catherine runs to Katie and tries to restrain her.

CATHERINE   Stop. Stop. Daddy. Daddy!!

Katie collapses against Catherine.

    Help me.

END OF ACT ONE

ACT II

*The house is silent. Ev and Catherine are most prominent on stage. Katie is
not far from Catherine. Bob and Oscar are in the background. Catherine looks
at Ev, who is wearing an old cardigan and glasses. Catherine holds Gramma's
letter.*

CATHERINE   . . . Go on.
EV   . . . When I was little, Katie . . . when I was a kid, I saw my own

father get smaller and smaller, physically smaller, cause he was nothin', no job, no . . . nothin'. I was only a kid but I saw him . . . get smaller like that. . . . Georgie now, he was the one in our family would have gone places.

CATHERINE   Haven't you "gone places"?

EV   Seen half this province from their mother's belly to the grave.

CATHERINE   Was it worth it?

EV   . . . When that goddamn Demsky let me up, I'd wander all round the hospital. I'd look in the wards, Intensive Care. . . . You get to be my age, the only place better than a hospital for meetin' people you know is a mortuary . . . Frank Johnston died while I was there in his room. They had him hooked up to all these goddamn monitors. And do you know how they knew he was dead? Straight lines and the sound from the monitors. Nobody looked down at Frank. Just at the monitors. . . . And that is the kinda hospital they're gonna put my name on? . . . I wouldn't like to go like Frank.

CATHERINE   You won't go for ages, Daddy.

EV   If I can keep away from that Demsky I got a chance . . .

CATHERINE   Daddy?

EV   What?

CATHERINE   About Mummy.

EV . . . If I could—I'm gonna show you somethin', I want you to see this . . . you see this, you'll understand. [opens trunk and begins to sort through it] Six or seven kids standin' by the car, and the car outside this Day Clinic . . . Valma and I, we were doin these check-ups and physicals and what-have-you . . . where the hell . . . we were doin that one day a week in Minto, families a miners, poor goddamn buggers, most of 'em unemployed at the time. And this bunch a little rag-tag snotty-nosed kids, smellin' a wet wool and Javex, were impressed all to hell by the car—and Valma, out with the goddamn camera, and she took this here picture . . . it's in here, where the hell is it? [stops looking for the snapshot] . . . I don't care about this hospital thing, I don't care about . . . I care about those little kids! I looked into their faces, and I saw my own face when I was a kid . . . was I wrong to do that? So goddamn much misery—should I have tended my own little plot when I looked round and there was so damn much to do—so much I could do—I did do! Goddamn it, I did it! You tell me, was I wrong to do that!

Pause. Ev is about to look again for the picture.

CATHERINE   It isn't there, Daddy.

EV   I had to rely on myself cause there was fuckin' little else to rely on, I made decisions when decisions had to be made, I chose a road, and I took it, and I never looked back.

CATHERINE   You've always been so sure of things, haven't you.

Ev watches Catherine as she looks down at the envelope, and turns it over in her hands.

EV   . . . You're like her, Katie.

CATHERINE   Like Gramma?

EV   Like your mother. [*removes his glasses*]

CATHERINE   She always said I was just like you.

EV   Like her.

CATHERINE   Don't say that.

KATIE   Am I like Gramma, Daddy?

EV   You're like yourself, Katie.

KATIE   Why don't you open it, Daddy?

Katie is looking at the letter Catherine holds.

EV   I will.

CATHERINE   When I was little I stayed with her once.

Catherine looks at Katie.

EV   After your mother had Robbie.

KATIE   And I swore, and she said, ''You never say those words, Katie, only in church,'' and when I dropped my prayer book I said, ''Jesus Christ, Gramma'' and she said, ''Ka-Ty!''

CATHERINE   And I said, ''But we are in church, Gramma.''

Katie and Catherine laugh. Ev takes off the old cardigan and hangs it over his chair as he speaks.

EV   She'd write that kinda thing in a letter. That's all that she'd write. That's what's in this letter. [*exits*]

CATHERINE   [*to Katie*] I don't want to be like her, and I don't want to be like Mummy.

KATIE   [*sings to Catherine*] K-K-K-Katie, my beautiful Katie,
You're the only G-G-G-Girl that I adore
When the M-M-M-Moon shines

Katie looks at a note book; she has not carried one before.

I'll be waiting . . .
K-K-K-Katie . . . Katie . . .

Shift. Oscar is watching Katie.

[*to Catherine*] Everything's down in here. I write it all down. And
when I grow up, I'll have it all here.
CATHERINE   Will it be worth it?
KATIE   I used to pray to God, but I don't anymore. I write it all down
in here. I was just little then and now —

Katie senses Oscar is watching her.

Are you interested in this, Uncle Oscar? Cause if you aren't, why
do you listen?
OSCAR   For you.
KATIE   I don't like people doing things for me. I can do things for
myself . . .

Katie starts to write in the book, the only time she does so.

"Now Mummy has a 'medical problem' p-r-ob." Did you know
that, Uncle Oscar? Mummy has a *medical problem* — that's apart
from her *personal problems,* did you know that?

OSCAR   No.
KATIE   Really?

Shift. Ev enters with bag and suit jacket. Oscar may help him on with it.

EV   I thought you knew.
OSCAR   How the hell would I know?
EV   I'm sending her to the Royal Vic.
OSCAR   Who to?
EV   You remember Bob Green from McGill?
OSCAR   Bit quick to cut, isn't he?
EV   You never liked him.
OSCAR   Neither did you.
EV   So he's an asshole, was, is, and will be, but he's goddamn good
at his job.
OSCAR   He's too quick to cut.
EV   And the best gynecologist in the country.
OSCAR   He'll have her in surgery before the ink on her train ticket
dries.

EV   This is your professional opinion, is it, based on your *extensive* practice?

OSCAR   There's gotta be other options.

EV   We could go someplace where it's hot and lie in the sun till she grows a tumor the size of a melon—why don't we do that?

OSCAR   I—

EV   You wanna look at her medical records? Go talk to Barney, tell him I said to pull 'em and show you — fibrous uterus, two opinions.

OSCAR   Green'll go for radical surgery and—

EV   What the hell do you want me to do?

OSCAR   Does she know?

EV   Of course she knows! What the hell do you mean, does she know?

OSCAR   You gotta take some time with her, she's gonna need that.

EV   I got no time.

OSCAR   What's wrong with just takin' off—the two of you go just as soon as she's able.

EV   I can't.

OSCAR   Look, you lie on the sand in the sun and you relax for Christ's sake.

EV   I got patients been waitin' for a bed for months, I can't just leave 'em to whoever's on call.

OSCAR   I'll take 'em, you go.

EV   They count on me bein' there, Oscar.

OSCAR   The population of this province will not wither and die if you take a three-week vacation—I'll handle your patients.

EV   I'd go nuts doin' nothin'.

OSCAR   You're doin' it for her.

EV   I'd go nuts.

OSCAR   You're drivin' her nuts!

EV   Were that to be true, three weeks in the sun wouldn't change it.

OSCAR   Don't think of her as your wife — think of her as a patient who's married to an insensitive son-of-a-bitch.

EV   I was an insensitive son-of-a-bitch when she met me; I haven't changed.

OSCAR   I give up.

EV   O.K. O.K., I'm thinking . . . I'm thinking. . . . I'm thinking you like sand and sun, you could take her.

OSCAR   I didn't marry her.

EV   You like her.

OSCAR   I like her.

EV   She likes you.

OSCAR   Listen to yourself! You're asking me to take your wife on a three-week vacation to recover from major surgery, do you realize that?

EV   She needs to get away, I can't take the time, you can.

OSCAR   It's one thing I'm not gonna do for you.

EV   So do it for her.

OSCAR   No.

EV   It makes sense to me.

OSCAR   No.

EV   Why not?

OSCAR   No, I said no.

EV   You're the one suggested it.

OSCAR   I didn't.

Ev looks at his watch.

We're not leaving it there!

EV   Look. There's an alumnae thing in six or seven months, I can schedule around it and the three of us'll have one hell of a good bash, but right now I cannot get away so I'm askin' you to do me this favour. How often do I ask for a favour? Take her to one of those islands you go to, eat at the clubs, lie in the sun, and — Christ, Oscar, I got to go, so gimme an answer, yes or no? [*pause*] You make the arrangements, I'll pick up the tab.

OSCAR   Half the tab.

EV   Fifty-fifty all the way.

OSCAR   Are you sure you don't want me to check her into the Vic, observe the surgery, hang around the recovery room and generally be there?

EV   I can clear three or four days for that.

Oscar is silent. As Ev is about to leave he notices Oscar's silence and stops.

Say — how did that burn case go?

OSCAR   That was four months ago, Ev.

EV   Seems like yesterday, so how did it go?

OSCAR   Zip, kaput.

EV   What the hell did you do?

OSCAR   Did it ever occur to you that I might find Bob very attractive?

EV   I know she's attractive, hell, I married her, didn't I?

OSCAR   That she might find me very attractive?

EV   Don't let it go to your head.

OSCAR   You know rumours fly.

EV   I'm too damned busy to listen to rumours.

OSCAR   Your mother isn't. She listens. After that, she phones.

EV   Who?

OSCAR   Me. She phones me. To talk about you. She's a remnant of my old man's practice, remember?

EV   Last time I saw her she didn't—

OSCAR   When was that anyway?

EV   Oh I was over—no—ah—

OSCAR   She can't remember either. I've seen you, you son-of-a-bitch, I've seen you take time with some old biddy, you laugh, you hang onto her hand, and she leaves your office thinking she's Claudette Colbert, and has just stolen a night with you at the Ritz—and I—I get the phone calls from your mother who is reduced to writing you letters and crying to me on the phone. You don't call, you don't visit, you don't . . . and now she's got it into her head that . . .

EV   What?

OSCAR   Rumours fly.

EV   So you reassure her. I gotta go, Oscar.

OSCAR   What if I can't reassure her?

EV   Then you laugh, hang onto her hand, and make Mum think she's Claudette Colbert at the Ritz.

OSCAR   It's not that simple.

Ev is moving away from Oscar.

I do find Bob very attractive!

EV   Total agreement.

OSCAR   You never think for one minute there could be one iota of truth in those rumours?

EV   I just don't believe you'd do that to me.

OSCAR   How can you be so sure?

EV   I know you.

OSCAR   Better than I know myself?

EV   I must. [*speaking as he exits*] Barbados eh, or someplace like that.

Shift

BOB   I don't plan on having any more children.

CATHERINE   No more children.

BOB   I didn't plan, didn't.

CATHERINE   No children.

BOB   Don't have to plan now. All taken care of. Are you listenin' to me?

Shift. Katie and Catherine will end up together, a mirror image.

KATIE   I'll tell you what she does. What she does is, she starts doing something. Something big. That's how I can tell. She's all right for awhile — and then she decides she's gonna paint all of the downstairs—or we're gonna put in new cupboards—or knock out a wall! . . . We got so many walls knocked out, the house started to fall down in the middle! Can you believe that?—And we had to get a big steel beam put through in the basement! Can you believe that?

CATHERINE   It's true.

KATIE   And before she gets finished one of those big jobs—she starts.

CATHERINE   And she never finishes. Someone else comes in, and they finish.

KATIE   But that's how I can tell when she's gonna start. And I try to figure out

CATHERINE   I ask myself

KATIE   Does the big job make her start — or does she start the big job because she knows she's gonna start?

CATHERINE   But that's how I could tell, that's the beginning.

Shift

BOB   So . . . why does it . . . why do I feel that it matters? Two were enough, Katie and Robbie, so why do I feel that it matters? I don't want any more . . . Oscar!

OSCAR   I'm here.

BOB   Does it matter?

OSCAR   Well . . . from the medical —

BOB   Medical, medical, medical, I don't wanna talk about medical.

OSCAR   It affects —

BOB   Me! Me! I'm talkin' about me! Why do I feel like, why do I feel —we didn't want any more children! I can't have any more children! Me, the part of me that's important, here, inside here—Me! That's the same. I'm the same. So . . . why do I feel that it matters?

OSCAR   It doesn't matter.

BOB   Why don't you listen? I'm trying to explain. We didn't want any more, I can't have any more, so why does it matter?

OSCAR   It doesn't matter.

BOB   It does matter! . . . I'm the same. Inside I'm the same. I'm Eloise Roberts and they called me Bob and I can run faster and do better than any boy I ever met!

OSCAR   It's all right.

BOB   No.

OSCAR   Come here.

BOB   I try to figure it out and I just keep going round.

CATHERINE   It's all right.

BOB   I need to do more, I need to . . . I need . . .

CATHERINE   Why don't you just do what you want?

BOB   Sometimes I want to scream. I just want to stand there and scream, to hit something, to reach out and smash things—and hit and smash and hit and smash and . . . and then . . . I would feel very tired and I could lie down and sleep.

OSCAR   Do you want to sleep now?

BOB   No. I'm not tired now. I want a drink now. Want a drink, and then we'll . . . what will we do?

CATHERINE   Why couldn't you leave.

BOB   Leave?

CATHERINE   Just leave!

BOB   Katie and Robbie.

CATHERINE   Did you care about them?

BOB   And your father?

Shift. Ev enters, carrying a bag. He is isolated on stage.

EV   We had the worst goddamn polio epidemic this province has seen, eleven years ago. We had an outbreak this year. You are lookin' at the attendin' physician at the present Polio Clinic—it is a building that has been condemned by the Provincial Fire Marshall, it has been condemned by the Provincial Health Officer, it has been condemned by the Victoria Public Hospital, it's infested by cockroaches, it's overrun by rats, it's the worst goddamn public building in this province! When is the government gonna stop building liquor stores and give the doctors of this province a chance to save a few fuckin' lives!

BOB   Haven't you got enough?

EV   Enough what?

BOB   Enough! Enough everything!

EV   You're drunk.

BOB   You'll never get enough, will you?

EV   Did Valma phone?

BOB   I don't answer the phone, just let it ring and ring—

Ev starts to exit.

Where're you going?

EV   Valma's.

BOB   What for?

EV   To pick up the messages that she'd give me by phone if you'd answer the phone.

BOB   Maid could answer it. Does answer it, but she's not good with messages, no.

EV   You run them through the house so goddamn fast they don't have time to pick up a phone. Why don't you get one and keep one?

BOB   Interviewin' them gives me somethin' to do. I enjoy interviewin' them. Purpose and direction to my life! Where're you goin'?

EV   [*exiting*] Valma's.

BOB   Stay.

CATHERINE   Stay.

Ev stops.

Don't go. Sit for a little while.

There is a moment of silence.

CATHERINE   Talk.

EV   If I sit down . . . my head will start to nod.

CATHERINE   That'd be all right. She wouldn't mind. You'd be here.

Ev puts down his bag. He moves to Bob and sits beside her. He takes his hat off and takes her hand. Bob smiles and strokes Ev's hand, then holds it against her face.

BOB   Do you remember . . . sometimes I . . . we had some good times, didn't we?

EV   We can still have good times.

BOB   I don't know.

EV   You've got to get hold of things.

BOB   I try.

EV   I know I'm busy.

BOB   Always busy.

EV   I know.

BOB   If I could do something.

EV   There's the house and the kids. Just tell me what you want and I'll get it.

BOB   I can't do anything.

EV   You can.

BOB   No. There's nothing I can do.

EV   Sure there is.

Bob slowly shakes her head.

> Come on . . . hey, listen, did you know the Hendersons were sellin' their camp on the Miramichi?

Pause

> Well they are. What say we buy it? You'd like that, wouldn't you? You could get away from the kids and the house, do some fishin', you like fishin' don't you?

Bob nods her head.

> Well, that's what we'll do. [*checks his watch*] Shit. You get to bed. Get some sleep. [*exits*]

BOB   Can't sleep.

There is the sound of a train whistle; Bob listens to it. It fades away. Shift.

> . . . Half-way across three-quarters of a mile of single track . . . its whistle would split the night, and that night . . . do you know what she did?

CATHERINE   No, and neither do you.

BOB   She walked out to meet it.

CATHERINE   And you say I'm like his side of the family, you say I'm like her?

BOB   She did.

CATHERINE   I would never do that!

Shift

KATIE   Mummy didn't like her. I could have gone to see her with Daddy, but Daddy was always too busy to go, so it was all his fault I didn't see her. . . . I guess that's true.

CATHERINE   She would phone, she would ask for me.

KATIE   But I could never think of anything to say. . . . They're the ones I'm supposed to like, his side of the family, so it would have been nice to see her . . . was she old? . . .

Catherine doesn't answer

KATIE   Is that what she died of? . . .

Catherine doesn't answer

What did she die of, Uncle Oscar?

OSCAR   It was an accident.

CATHERINE   We know ''accidents'', don't we.

KATIE   I never saw anybody dead before. I don't know if I wanted to see her dead . . . it didn't matter because they didn't take us anyway — I was a bit happy not to go because I don't like to go anywhere with Mummy when she's like that. She said Gramma was a bitch who went around saying bad things about her and Mummy was glad she was dead — and Daddy just kept getting dressed and pretended Mummy wasn't talking — You can only pretend for so long.

CATHERINE   And when they came home he went out.

KATIE   And Mummy phoned all over but he wasn't any place she could find, and . . .

CATHERINE   . . . then she tripped at the top of the stairs and she fell. I went to my bedroom as soon as that happened . . .

KATIE   . . . and Robbie screamed and cried and screamed and cried and . . .

CATHERINE   . . . the maid got up and put her to bed—she'll be leaving soon and we'll get a new one . . .

KATIE   . . . you'd think if a person kept falling down stairs it would hurt them!

CATHERINE   It never did a thing to her.

Shift

BOB   Katie! . . . Katie! You wanna know somethin'?

KATIE   No

BOB   Your father's mother killed herself! . . .

Pause. Katie stares at Bob.

You look at me . . . you look at me and what are you thinking?

KATIE   Nothing.

BOB   This isn't me you know. This isn't really me. This is someone else. . . . What are you thinking?

KATIE   I don't think anything.

BOB   Katie!

CATHERINE   Leave her alone.

BOB   You know what your father's mother said?

CATHERINE   Leave her alone!

BOB   Do you know?

KATIE   No!

BOB   Why would a nurse—to catch a doctor, that's why. Why would he marry me, eh? Why would a brilliant young man, whole life ahead of him, why would he marry me? Eh? Do you know why? Do you know!

KATIE   No.

BOB   Why would he do that?!

KATIE   I don't know.

BOB   Answer me!

KATIE   I don't know!

BOB   No! You don't know! Nobody knows!

KATIE   I know. Inside I know. He had to.

CATHERINE   Don't.

KATIE   Inside I do know. Because of me—and that's what went wrong.

CATHERINE   He loved her and she loved him, Uncle Oscar says.

KATIE   No.

CATHERINE   That's true, Katie!

KATIE   Do you believe that?

Ev enters in his shirt sleeves.

Daddy!

Katie runs to Ev and he puts his arms around her

EV   Your mother sometimes says things that she doesn't mean. She's sick and she—

KATIE   She isn't sick!

EV   She loves you.

KATIE   I don't love her.

Katie quickly moves away. Ev starts after her.

EV   Yes you do.

Shift

BOB   Valma, Valma, Valma, Valma, Valma Valma I am so sick of that woman's name. What're you and her doing, that's what I'd like to know!

EV   Nothing. [*sits*]

BOB   Oooh, you don't tell me that! I know better than that! She's like your right arm, your left arm, part of your leg!

EV   Leave Valma out of it.

BOB   I don't wanna leave Valma out of it! She'd do anything for you

— put your wife to bed, get her up — why does she do that, eh? Tell me why?

EV   She's the best office nurse in the city and I couldn't run that office without her. Why the Christ don't you go to bed?

BOB   Why the Christ don't you go to bed?

EV   Go to bed.

BOB   Gonna go over to Valma's and go to bed? You don't love me, you never loved me! You never loved me.

EV   Go to bed.

BOB   You don't even see me. You look at me and there's nobody there. You don't see anybody but those stupid stupid people who think you're God. You're not God!

Catherine and Katie are together and Bob moves towards them. Bob grabs Catherine's hand.

And it's so funny . . . do you know what he's done, do you know? . . . If I. . . . If I go into the liquor store, do you know what happens? They say . . . sorry, but the Doc says *no*. He says . . . they're not to . . . and they don't. They don't. He tells them don't sell it to her the Doc says don't do that and they don't. But what's so funny is . . . every drunk in the city goes into that office on Saturday and they say . . . "Jeez Chris Doc, spent the whole cheque on booze, the old lady's gonna kill me," and he gives them money. . . . Gives *them* money.

Katie moves away.

And Valma says he says maybe one of them takes it home instead of just buyin' more, can you believe that? . . . And when I go in, they say, "The Doc says no" . . . but I don't have to worry. [*moves to refill her glass*] so long as I keep interviewin' the maids . . . I don't have to worry about a thing.

Shift

KATIE   You don't have any family.

OSCAR   You're my family.

KATIE   I'm not related to you, and you're not related to me, you can't be family, Uncle Oscar.

Shifts

BOB [*leaves her glass*] Hey! Do you want to know what a bastard he is?

Catherine turns her head away as Bob advances on Ev.

Well I don't care if you want to know or not—I'm gonna tell you. I put the clothes out, put the suit out for the cleaners and I went through his pockets, and do you know what I found, do you know? It was something he didn't need for me, something he wouldn't use with me, because I can't have any more, no, I've been fixed like the goddamn cat or the dog so what the hell did you have it for?

EV If you found it, that means I didn't use it, so what the hell's your problem?

Bob runs at Ev.

BOB You bastard!

Bob strikes at Ev's chest. He grabs her wrists.

You bastard you.

Bob attempts to strike Ev several times before collapsing against Ev's chest. He picks her up, carries her to a chair and puts her in it. He looks down at her for a moment, then moves away, to sit isolated on the stage. Oscar joins him. Shift.

OSCAR She tells me you're bangin' Valma.

EV If I wanted to bang someone, it sure as hell wouldn't be Valma.

OSCAR So who are you bangin'?

EV Has she posted that condom story in the staff room, or is it just you she's told?

OSCAR I asked you a question.

EV I'm not bangin' anyone! Who the hell are you bangin'! . . . I . . . I lost Jack Robinson the other night. . . . I felt so goddamn bad. I thought he was gonna make it and then everything started shuttin' down. He gets pneumonia, we get that under control, then his heart starts givin' us problems, we get that solved, then his goddamn kidneys go—I don't know why, just one thing after another. Someone was callin' his name and I couldn't do a damn thing about it . . . and I felt so bad, I thought . . . I don't want to go home, you can see what she's like so . . . you know what I did? I bought a mickey of rum and that goddamn condom and I . . . I drove around for a coupla hours. And that was it. . . . That was it.

OSCAR   Things can't go on.

EV   Don't start on that give her more time shit. Her problem's got nothin' to do with time nor work nor any other goddamn thing.

OSCAR   Her problem is the crazy son-of-a-bitch she's married to.

EV   Who the hell is crazy here? I'm the one can't keep a bottle of booze in the house, I'm the one's gotta put the fear of God in the help so they're too damn scared to buy it for her—and now she's into the vanilla or any other goddamn thing she can pour down her throat! I can't keep pills in the bag and she'd let the kids starve to death if it weren't for the maid! I'm the one goin' eighteen hours a day tryin' to hold the fuckin' fort so I can hear you say what!? . . . That I'm crazy! I'm not a goddamn machine!!! I thought if anyone would understand, it would be you . . . and you . . . [exits]

OSCAR   Ev. Ev!

Oscar may exit after him. Shift. Bob runs her hand along the cushion in the chair. She gets on her knees, lifts the cushion up. Catherine watches her search. Katie too observes, from a distance. Bob continues her search.

BOB   Everyone has something hidden in this house. I hide it and he hides it and you hide it.

CATHERINE   Do something.

BOB   Do something. Just like your father. Do, do, do.

CATHERINE   Just stop!

BOB   Just stop. [finds bottle of pills] Stop doing. [unscrews bottle; pours pills in hand; looks at Catherine] Stop. [swallows pills; settles back in chair; shuts eyes]

Shift. Katie slowly approaches Bob. She and Catherine stand, looking at Bob. Pause.

KATIE   She was blue. . . . I'd never seen anybody blue before. Robbie went in the kitchen and cried. I stood at the bottom of the stairs and watched them bring her down on the stretcher. I didn't cry. . . . I don't know what she took—was it the pills that make her sleep?

CATHERINE   Uncle Oscar said.

KATIE   She was asleep all right. And really blue. I thought . . . I thought . . .

CATHERINE   Go on, you can say it.

KATIE   I thought maybe she was dead. [moves away] . . . and now she's going to Connecticut? Will she be better then?

Catherine joins Katie.

CATHERINE   Uncle Oscar said.
KATIE   All better?

Catherine doesn't answer.

> I wonder . . . do you know what I wonder? I wonder, did she take
> the pills to sleep like she sometimes does, or did she . . .

CATHERINE   It was
KATIE   An accident? . . . Sometimes I look . . .
CATHERINE   . . . in the mirror, I look in the mirror . . .
KATIE   . . . and I see Mummy and I see . . .
CATHERINE   . . . Gramma, and Mummy and me . . .
KATIE   . . . I don't want to be like them.

*Shift. Oscar may enter. Bob is sitting. She will get up and very carefully tie
her gown. There is a certain formality, seriousness, alienation and deliberation
about her. She moves and speaks somewhat slowly. Oscar stands a distance
from her, still and watching.*

BOB   You have to get hold of things. Routine's important. Get out.
Get around. Do things. The I.O.D.E., Bridge. . . . The doctors'
wives have this sort of club and it meets on a regular basis, I . . .
OSCAR   Tired?
BOB   No. Feeling fine. How do I look?
OSCAR   Good.

*Bob moves to another chair and sits. Oscar remains in the same position,
watching her. Bob doesn't speak till seated. She does not look at Oscar.*

BOB   Leisure activity is big. Structured leisure activity. Very big. [*pause*]
Painting. I paint now. You know. [*pause*] Pictures. [*pause; speaks
softly*] What else? [*pause*] Gorgeous place. If you'd been there, it
would have been perfect. [*pause; speaks softly*] What else. [*pause*]
Psychiatrists, psychiatrists. They ask you obvious things and you
give them obvious answers. It's all very obvious. . . . Obvious . . .
[*softly*] what else. [*long pause; softly*] Nothing . . . nothing else . . .
I can't think of . . . anything else.

*Bob sits very still. Oscar stands watching her. Bob begins to rock back and
forth very slightly and sings very softly to herself. She is not singing words,
but merely making sounds. Oscar moves to her. He stands behind her looking
down for a moment. He slowly places a hand on her shoulder. She reaches up*

and holds his hand pressing it to her shoulder. She continues to rock slightly but the words of the song can be heard. She is singing "Auld Lang Syne". Oscar moves around her without letting go of her hand and draws her up to dance, which they do rather formally.

BOB   [*sings*] Should auld acquaintance be forgot
     and never brought to mind
     Should auld acquaintance
     Be forgot—and auld lang syne
     an auld lang syne m'dear
     an auld lang syne

Bob begins to cry but continues singing and dancing.

     Let's drink a cup of kindness up
     For auld lang syne.

Shift. Ev enters. He is isolated on stage. He carries his bag, and his hat is pushed back on his head. There is an air of powerful relaxation and poise about him. He might almost be standing in a glow of golden sunshine. When he speaks Bob and Oscar stop dancing. They turn to stare at him and Oscar will step away from Bob. Bob is drawn towards Ev, who does not acknowledge her.

EV   I say three or four of us go in together. I mean look at the situation now. A patient comes in from Durham Bridge, and has to run all over this Christless city, G.P. here, lab tests there, pediatrician someplace else. I've got my eye on a place on the hill. We renovate it—
BOB   Bar date with him.
EV   And we open a Medical Clinic, lab, X-ray, everything in that one building—
BOB   And you don't call that –
EV   We solicit the best specialists we can to take office space there. We give the people of this goddamn province the medical care they deserve, without havin' to run all over hell and hackety to get it!
BOB   And I laughed—and he said—and it was so funny—such a long time ago . . .

Shift

KATIE   You lied to me.
OSCAR   When?
KATIE   People lie to me quite a bit. They think I don't know it, but I do.

OSCAR I didn't mean to lie.

KATIE You didn't tell the truth.

OSCAR What did I lie about?

KATIE Guess—one guess.

BOB S'funny thing.

KATIE You promised me she'd get better, Uncle Oscar! You promised and you lied.

Shift. Bob lights a cigarette during her speech. By the end of her speech it is apparent she's been drinking.

BOB The more you do of certain things, the less it seems you do. You fill your time up, my time's filled up. I sit at these tea luncheons, s'always . . . sherry. I hate sherry. I never have any sherry. I know what they think, but that's not the reason. I just don't like sherry. No. No sherry. [*pause*] Children are important. [*pause*] And the I.O.D.E . . . I go to —and bridshe, play a lot of bridshe, I'm good at that. Win, always win. . . . I like bridshe. And ahh [*pause*] I don't really like them but — everything's working for them and everything can work for me too. I can be them. It isn't hard, I can do it. If I . . . if I want to.

Bob moves to drawer, opens it and feels inside. She is looking for a bottle, slowly and methodically. She becomes aware of Katie watching her.

BOB What do you want?

KATIE I don't want anything.

BOB What're you doing?

KATIE I'm watching you.

BOB Your father tell you to do that?

KATIE No.

BOB Then why are you watchin'?

KATIE I want to remember.

BOB Remember what?

KATIE Remember you.

BOB I know what you're thinking. It's all right. You can say it . . . do you want me to say it?

KATIE No.

BOB I'm not afraid. I can say it.

KATIE If I were you—I wouldn't let Robbie see me like that. It makes him feel bad. He has to pretend that you're sick.

BOB What do you pretend, Katie?

KATIE I don't have to pretend anymore.

CATHERINE Katie.

Bob stops her search, turns to Katie.

BOB Did you take something of mine?
KATIE Did I?
BOB You took something of mine and I want it back.
KATIE You can't have it back.
BOB I want it back!
KATIE It's gone.
BOB No.
KATIE I poured it out, let go!
BOB Give it back!
CATHERINE Don't.

Bob and Katie struggle.

BOB You had no right you . . .
KATIE Let go!
BOB No.
CATHERINE Let her go.
BOB Give it to me.
KATIE Let go, let go!
BOB You you no right!
KATIE Go!

Katie strikes at Bob, knocking her down.

I'm not gonna cry. I'm not gonna cry!
BOB I tried. I really did try.
CATHERINE I'm not gonna cry.
BOB Listen.

Bob grabs Catherine's hand.

Listen Katie. I want . . . I want to tell you — when — when I was little, do you know, do you know I would sit on our front porch, and I would look up, look up at the sky, and the sky, the sky went on forever. And I just looked up. That was me, Katie. That was me.
CATHERINE I'm holding my breath and my teeth are together and my tongue, I can feel my tongue, it presses hard on the back of my teeth and the roof of my mouth . . .
KATIE . . . and I hang on really tight. Really tight, and then . . . I don't cry.
CATHERINE I never cried . . . [*to Bob*] but I couldn't listen like that.

Bob releases Catherine's hands and moves away from her. Catherine runs after her as she speaks.

CATHERINE   It's one of the things you can't do like that!

KATIE   It's better not to cry than to listen.

CATHERINE   Is it?

KATIE   It's how you keep on. It's one of the ways. I'm surprised you don't know that.

Katie moves away from Catherine, who then follows her. Shift.

EV   Close this time.

OSCAR   How close?

EV   Too damn close. We pumped her stomach and prayed. The kids spent Christmas Day at Valma's. . . . I think . . . I think the psychiatrist she sees is nuttier than she is. . . . I'm alright . . .

Ev sits in the same chair he sat in as "Old Ev", at the start of the play. Pause.

Did you know . . . what the hell is their name . . . live over on King Street, married someone or other, moved to Toronto. . . . I'm alright. [*pause*] Some silly son of a whore didn't look close enough, she kept tellin' him she had this lump in her breast. . . . I'm alright. . . . She's got a three-month-old kid and she's come home to die. . . . Thing is no one's got around to tellin' her that's how it is. They asked me to come over and tell her . . . patients of mine . . . come home to die . . .

Oscar may exit. Pause. Ev takes Gramma's letter out of his pocket and looks at it.

EV   I'm alright . . .

Shift

BOB   Open it! Go on, open it!

EV   You're drunk.

BOB   I'm drunk. So I'm drunk. What the hell are you, what's your excuse? What's his excuse, Katie?

EV   Leave her alone.

BOB   Why don't you open it!

EV   What for?

BOB   To see what it says.

EV   Says nothing.

BOB   Your father's mother killed herself, Katie. She walked across the train bridge at midnight and—

KATIE   That's an accident!

BOB   She left a letter and the letter tells him why she did it.

KATIE   What's in the letter, Daddy?

EV   Your Gramma—

Oscar may unobtrusively enter, and stand silently in the background.

BOB   She killed herself because of him!

KATIE   Because of you!

EV   Your Gramma loved us.

KATIE   Why don't you open it?

EV   She didn't see us so she'd write.

BOB   So open it!

EV   That's all it is.

BOB   Pretending! He's pretending!

KATIE   He is not!

BOB   He pretends a lot!

KATIE   You do!

BOB   Valma! Valma! Valma!

KATIE   I hate you!

BOB   Not afraid to say it!

KATIE   I hate you and I wish that you were dead!

CATHERINE   No.

KATIE   It's true!

CATHERINE   No.

KATIE   I wish and wish and

CATHERINE   No.

KATIE   someday you will be dead and I'll be happy!

OSCAR   It's all right, Katie!

KATIE   [*to Ev*] You all say she's sick, she isn't sick.

BOB   [*to Katie*] Katie!

KATIE   She's a drunk and that's what we should say!

BOB   [*to Catherine*] Katie!?

CATHERINE   Stop.

KATIE   And if I find her next time, I won't call for Daddy!

CATHERINE   No.

KATIE   I won't call for anyone!

CATHERINE   Stop Katie please.

KATIE   [*sits*] I'll go back downstairs and I'll sit in the kitchen and I'll pretend that I don't know, I'll pretend that everything's all right, I'll shut my eyes, and I'll pretend!

BOB   Katie! [*retreats*]

KATIE   [*chants*] Now they're married wish them joy

BOB   Katie. [*exits*]

KATIE   [*puts hands over ears; chants louder*]
    First a girl for a toy
    Seven years after seven to come

BOB   [*voice-over on mike, offstage*] Katie!

KATIE   [*chants louder*] Fire on the mountain
    kiss and run
    on the mountains berries sweet

BOB   [*on mike, offstage*] Katie!

KATIE   [*chants*] Pick as much as you can eat
    By the berries' bitter bark

BOB   [*on mike, offstage*] Katie!

KATIE   [*chants louder*] Fire on the mountain break your heart
    Years to come—kiss and run
    bitter bark—break your heart

Katie slowly takes her hands from her ears. There is silence. Pause.

    I don't hear you! [*pause*] I don't hear you! [*pause*] I don't!

Katie jumps up and whirls around, to look over at where she last saw Bob. Pause.

KATIE   [*softly*] I don't hear you at all.

CATHERINE   You can cry, Katie . . . it's all right to cry . . .

KATIE   Would you want to have me?

CATHERINE   Yes, yes I would.

Shift

EV   All over now.

Ev gets up from chair and moves to the table where Catherine left the jewellery box in Act One. He stands, looking down at it.

CATHERINE   No, Daddy.

OSCAR   When was it we played scrub hockey on the river ice. . . . Ev
    and Oscar, Oscar, Ev. . . . ''We're rough, we're tough, we're from
    Devon, that's enough'' . . .

Ev lifts the lid of the music box. It plays ''Smoke Gets In Your Eyes''

    . . . driving my old man's car, watering his whiskey, Ev and
    Oscar . . .

EV Ever since Grade One.

OSCAR I knew you then, and I knew you after that, and then I got to know you less and less—and here we are. . . . I said why risk it? And I saw her and I knew why . . . well, she's gone now. . . . What the hell does that mean to you, Ev. That's something I want to know. What's it mean? . . . For Christ's sake, say something, say anything.

EV There's nothing to say.

OSCAR It shouldn't have happened.

EV It did. [*closes the music box*]

OSCAR She asked for goddamn little and you couldn't even give her that.

EV You got no more idea of what she wanted than I have.

OSCAR You never knew her and you don't know me.

EV How can you say that? I carried you on my back since Grade One cause I liked you, I loved you, like a brother.

OSCAR I could see it in my father, I can see it in you. You got your eyes fixed on some goddamn horizon, and while you're striding towards that, you trample on every goddamn thing around you!

EV The biggest dream you ever had, what the hell was it? What was it, Oscar? New Orleans! New Orleans.

OSCAR She understood what that meant.

EV Bullshit. You been a pseudo-doctor for your old man, a pseudo-husband to my wife, and a pseudo-father to my kids! I gave you that, Oscar, like I gave you everything else cause I knew you'd never have the goddamn gumption to get it for yourself!

OSCAR I should have taken your wife.

EV My wife wouldn't have you!

Oscar starts to leave. Ev calls after him.

She knew you! She knew what you were! And because of that you say I killed her! It was all my fault?

Oscar stops. Ev moves to him.

Supposin' it were, her death my fault, put a figure on it, eh? Her death my fault on one side—and the other any old figure, thousand lives the figure—was that worth it?

Oscar exits.

Was it? I'm askin' you a question! Was that worth it!

Silence. Shift. Katie approaches Ev. As he removes his overcoat, he speaks to her.

What the hell do you mean?

KATIE   I don't know what I mean.

EV   Where the hell would you go?

KATIE   I don't know. Away. Away to some school.

EV   I don't want you to go.

KATIE   Send me anyway. For me, Daddy. Do it for me.

EV   What if I said no?

KATIE   You won't say no.

EV   You wanna hear me say no!

KATIE   I'm like you, Daddy. I just gotta win — and you just gotta win — and if you say no — you'll have lost. [*exiting as she speaks*] I'll come back . . . every once in a while . . . I'll come back . . .

EV   Katie? [*screams*] Katie!

CATHERINE   I'm here.

Shift. Catherine and Ev are alone on stage. As Catherine speaks, Ev puts on his old cardigan, which was hanging on the back of his chair. He puts on his glasses. Catherine has Gramma's letter.

Do you remember when she gathered together all the photographs and snapshots, all the pictures of her, and she sat in the living room, and she ripped them all up? So . . . after she died, we had no pictures of her. . . . And Oscar, remember Oscar came over with one . . . it was taken at a nightclub somewhere, and she was feeding this little pig — a stupid little pig standing on the table and she — she was feeding it with a little bottle like a baby's bottle . . .

EV   Her with . . .

CATHERINE   . . . a baby bottle feeding the pig with the bottle . . .

EV   [*small chuckle*] Her and Oscar at some goddamn Caribbean night-club feedin' a pig . . .

CATHERINE   Like a baby. She was looking up at the camera. She was smiling a bit. You could see her teeth. She didn't look happy, or unhappy. She looked as if she was waiting. Just waiting.

EV   For what?

CATHERINE   I don't know. But whatever it was, she couldn't grab it.

EV   Do you know what you want?

CATHERINE   . . . Yes . . . Yes, I do.

EV   Then you grab it.

CATHERINE   [*Pause; looks at Gramma's letter, which she is holding in her hand*] What are you gonna do with this?

EV   Do you wanna open it?

CATHERINE   I can. Do you want me to?

EV   I know what's in it.

Pause. Catherine strikes a match. She looks at Ev.

CATHERINE   Should I? . . . should I? . . .

Catherine blows the match out and gives the letter to Ev. He sits looking at it for a moment.

EV   Burn the goddamn thing.

Ev holds the letter out. Catherine sets it on fire and it flares up as Ev holds it.

CATHERINE   Be careful!
EV   I am bein' careful.

Ev drops the burning envelope into an ashtray. Lights are fading.

Two minutes home you're as bad as Valma.
CATHERINE   Bullshit, Daddy.
EV   Jesus Christ I hate to hear a woman talk like that.

As lights fade to black, Catherine looks at Ev and smiles. Black except for the dying flame from the letter.

THE END

LARRY FINEBERG
1945 –

Born in Montreal and educated at McGill University and Emerson College in Boston, Massachusetts, he began his career as an assistant director in London and in New York. He turned to play-writing in the early seventies and returned to Canada in 1972 when his first play, *Stonehenge*, was being produced at the Factory Theatre Lab. Since that time he has written more than a dozen plays that confront the isolation of modern men and women in a seemingly loveless society. In *Death*, spare dialogue and short scenes mirror the emptiness and loneliness of his characters. The Stratford Shakespearean Festival commissioned Fineberg to adapt Constance Beresford-Howe's novel *The Book of Eve* into a successful play titled *Eve*. It has also been produced in the United States, England, and the Netherlands. *Death* had its premiere at the Factory Threatre Lab in December 1972, and was later adapted by Fineberg for CBC television, with Donald Pleasance in the leading role.

Death

CHARACTERS

MAX, 70's. Never whines. Totally devoid of self-pity.
OONA, late 30's. MAX's daughter.
JOHNNY, 16. Unformed. Unemotional.

THE SET

Not proscenium. A garden. A tree. Occasional plant. Wicker table. Chairs. Wrought iron bench. All reasonably sparse. Possible suggestion of forest, in the distance.

NOTES

The style of the piece is meant to be small, and selective. Displays of emotion are to be avoided, except where indicated. If a tree is unavailable, boxes or some anchored neutral object may be substituted. Garden sounds may be used at the director's discretion, but not to excess. Blackouts must be scrupulously observed.

Running time of the play should not exceed thirty-two minutes.

SECTION A

A garden. Plants. A tree. Chairs. Wicker table. Not near it, a wrought iron bench. Farther off, suggestions of a forest. Oona, thirty-five, pretty, slightly worn, enters. Moving backward.

OONA   Come along father. It's only a few more paces. O do keep moving. You
    mustn't stop. [*She crosses backwards*]   Now move. Left foot. Right foot.
MAX   [*Entering on crutches*]   No more, Oona.
OONA   That's very good. Just to the bench. Now.
MAX   I'm falling.
OONA   [*Bright*]   O no, once again. Left. Right.
MAX   [*Small step*]   No.
OONA   Yes. Here. I've got a chocolate biscuit, and there'll be tea.
MAX   [*Walking*]   How far? I can't make it out.
OONA   [*Tapping bench*]   Just here. Our bench.
MAX   I'm falling. [*He does, cleanly*]   I'm not bleeding. The skin isn't broken.
OONA   [*Exiting*]   I'll get the tea.
MAX   [*Softly*]   I've wet my pants.

Blackout

Max and Johnny at table. Chess set.

JOHNNY   [*Holding pawns*]   Which hand?
MAX   Right.
JOHNNY   I go first.
MAX   The men look fuzzy.
JOHNNY   Take your time.
MAX   I don't want to play.
JOHNNY   Shall I read to you?
MAX   No.

Blackout

Max and Oona at table.

OONA   [*Bright*]   And *then* what did you say?
MAX   It doesn't matter.
OONA   There isn't a cloud.
MAX   No.
OONA   Not one.
MAX   Are you leaving?
OONA   Of course not.
MAX   Not going away?
OONA   Not for a bit.
MAX   I was cold last night.
OONA   [*Surprised*]   It's still summer.

Blackout

Max alone. At bench.

MAX   I'm tired of *doing* things.

Johnny enters.

      I don't want a pill.
JOHNNY   What do you want?
MAX   Nothing.
JOHNNY   [*Holding glass and capsule*]   Take this. Shall I leave you alone?
MAX   I don't care.
JOHNNY   Do you want your daughter?
MAX   Don't keep asking me questions. If I need something you'll know soon
      enough. Go away. And stop bothering me.

Johnny starts to exit.

I want a macaroon.

Johnny turns to him.

Blackout

Max and Johnny at table. Chess set.

MAX   [*Hand poised midair with bishop*]   I can't see at all.
JOHNNY   [*Rising*]   What should I do?
MAX   This happens all the time. Sight comes and goes. Guide my hand across
   the board. I'll play by touch.
JOHNNY   [*Guiding*]   These are my men. Knight. Queen. Bishop. Pawn . . .
MAX   I don't care.
JOHNNY   You don't want to play.
MAX   What's that noise?
JOHNNY   I don't hear anything.
MAX   It isn't a bird. It's not the wind. There's something moving.
JOHNNY   Where?
MAX   To your left. Behind the tree.
JOHNNY   [*Going to it*]   It's a new plant. It's tall. [*Kneels*]   How rough the
   leaves are. Thick and spongy. There's a spider, in his web, between leaves
   and branches.
MAX   [*Listening intently*]   There's something with the spider.
JOHNNY   In its web. A wasp. It's been there a while. It's caught in the web.
MAX   Break the web and kill the insects. Step on them.
JOHNNY   Why?
MAX   Do as I say.
JOHNNY   Okay. [*He doesn't move*]   There. Dead.
MAX   You aren't telling me the truth. I can hear everything. Only the wasp's
   head is free. It's all bound up in the web. The spider's advancing to it. It
   jerks forward and back giving quick little bites to the head. One of the
   wasp's eyes is pierced. The wasp can't break free. It's pinioned. It's now
   being stung. It's jerking back and forth. It can't get away. [*Pause*]   I hear
   it screaming. [*Pause*]   It's paralyzed. [*Small pause*]   Kill them. Kill them.
   Will you kill them. Kill them. KILL THEM. NOW!
JOHNNY   [*Breaking the web*]   I wasn't quick enough. The spider got away.
MAX   [*Staccato*]   If you'd been quicker they wouldn't have suffered. They'd
   be dead now. Why wouldn't you tell me the truth?
JOHNNY   How did they suffer?
MAX   The wasp, dying. The spider in putting off its death. Winter's coming.
JOHNNY   That's what they always do. It's instinct. How did they suffer? They're
   bugs.

MAX [*Soft*] I could feel their pain inside me. [*Pause*] Just like humans.
JOHNNY It's instinct.
OONA [*Entering*] What's all the shouting? What's all the trouble here? Father?

Blackout

Max and Oona at the bench.

MAX There are far too many bees this summer. Big fat ones. I've heard them
    buzzing. I don't like bees. In a certain light they look like furry marmalade
    cats. But they aren't. Bees are vicious.
OONA How odd that you've never been stung. How lucky.
MAX It's very odd.
OONA Who'll plant the bulbs, before the earth gets hard?
MAX You know I won't have any bulbs. No flowers. Only plants. Only green
    plants. I'm not taking a chance of being stung.
OONA Shall I help you inside?
MAX I think I can manage. Where's Johnny?
OONA In town. Getting the groceries.

They begin to exit slowly. Oona helping.

    You seem stronger.
MAX I have my good days.
OONA I never know how I'll find you, in the morning.
MAX Neither do I.
OONA Shall we walk around the long way?
MAX I'd rather not.
OONA Let's do. While you're fit you should get the exercise.

Both offstage.

    Damn. There's the telephone. Wait here. It might be Martin.
MAX She's left me. I'm not on my path. I smell yellow flowers. [*Pause*] There's
    buzzing. Bees. [*Pause*] Oona. Oona! OONA!

Blackout

SECTION B

Oona and Johnny facing audience. Max seated, facing upstage.

OONA Father. I can't talk to you this way. Turn and face us.

MAX   The sun is bad for me now. The stings turned into welts. The sun aggravates them.

JOHNNY   It shouldn't.

OONA   The doctor said that sun would dry up the swelling.

MAX   He bandaged my hand where it was stung. Why couldn't he bandage my face?

JOHNNY   Your hand touches more things. It's easier for it to get hurt.

MAX   I know I'm being difficult. I know it doesn't matter. Not now.

OONA   If you're smarting, there's the codeine.

MAX   [*Soft*]   It's all been taken care of.

OONA   I'm looking after you. I'll watch you. I won't allow you to be inconvenienced.

MAX   [*Violent*]   Then how could you allow this to happen? How could you let me be disfigured. [*Pause*]   I have no more trust.

OONA   [*To Johnny—quiet*]   Take him inside.

MAX   [*Turns downstage, face a mass of welts*]   Don't stare at me. I'm accepting it. I'll be good. [*Pause*]   Don't stare.

Blackout

Max at bench.

MAX   Difficult dreams. I was sixteen, and in love. She wore crinolines and was gentle. And soft. And kind. She was human. [*Pause*]   Now I'm awake. [*Pause*]   It's past lunch. She gave me liver and spinach. And tea. I'm hungry again. I can't get enough. Chicken for dinner. Well.

OONA   [*Enters*]   Here's a letter from Martin. He asks for you.

MAX   Which one is he?

OONA   My husband.

MAX   The pretty one?

OONA   Father!

MAX   Is he coming back to you?

OONA   I don't think so.

MAX   That's life.

OONA   He says Random House is publishing his poetry.

MAX   People don't read poetry now.

OONA   He sends his love.

MAX   Does he ask for money?

OONA   No.

MAX   He will, soon.

OONA   We should talk about—financial arrangements.

MAX   I've left everything to Avery.

OONA   Avery is dead.

MAX   So he is.

OONA   Concentrate.

MAX Iris doesn't get a penny. Her husband is a banker.

OONA [*Soft*] I want the house.

MAX I'm not in my grave yet. I should have named you Goneril.

OONA People need to discuss these things.

MAX No.

OONA We'll chat again. When you're feeling fit.

MAX I'm fine.

OONA You have to nap.

MAX You go away.

OONA I'll bring you some tea.

MAX I don't need you.

OONA It's so important you don't exert yourself.

MAX I have the boy.

OONA You don't care for me.

MAX [*Very mild*] I never have.

OONA I wish mother was alive.

MAX Thank God she's dead.

OONA How is your eyesight today?

MAX Never better.

OONA That's good to hear.

MAX I'll outlast you yet.

OONA I wouldn't count on it.

MAX You never know.

OONA [*Pause*] I should think about dinner.

MAX I want the boy to prepare it. I'm going to teach him to cook. Then you
   won't have to do anything.

OONA You go and take your nap!

Blackout

Max and Oona, repositioned.

OONA [*Slow*] It's almost fall.

MAX I keep dreaming.

OONA What about?

MAX Pieces of myself. They're hazy, like fish in a pool. I try to capture them.
   They slip in and out of my fingers.

OONA [*Laughing*] It's very hard to catch a goldfish, father.

MAX That's not what they are.

Blackout

Lights up. Table group. Max. Oona. Johnny pouring tea. Crutches nearby.

OONA Father left all his lunch today. Where's your appetite gone to?

MAX   When you were a little girl I used to hunt. Remember?

Johnny gives him tea.

There was exhilaration, waiting in the brush for game. My old rifle's still in the house. I felt alive. I felt my own blood. I felt a man. Then your mother and I quarrelled. I turned fifty. She died. I moved with less agility. It became more difficult to make a clean kill. A wounded deer that should have been dead looked *through* me with mindless vacant eyes. Insensitive to everything but pain and fear. Sunlight hit the forest trees, and they cast shadows on the winter snow. I saw my own shadow. And the animal's. And his blood. Coming out of his nose with clouds of breath in the air. I wanted to reach inside the creature and feel its heart. I watched it crouching on all fours and the sun shifted and the trees grew longer as dark approached. Shadows of bars, leaf bars, jails. Pain and waste. We were both caged.

That cooked meat bore me ill will. I stopped hunting. But your store food comes wrapped in plastic, and tastes dead. Fish are caught on hooks and have their mouths ripped out. Vegetables taken from the ground have their roots torn and wrenched away.

Every edible thing possesses its own life. It screams at me and says let me be, let me be, let me be.

How am I supposed to live.

Blackout

Oona and Johnny.

OONA   [*Counting money out*]   Twenty, forty, sixty.

JOHNNY   Thank you.

OONA   It's good he's asleep. We can both use a little rest.

JOHNNY   It's five dollars short. Last week he gave me sixty-five.

OONA   I'm sorry. I'll have to get it from inside the house. This can't be pleasant for you. It's no way to spend the summer.

JOHNNY   It doesn't matter.

OONA   We really need a full-time nurse.

JOHNNY   Why! What's wrong with him? Other than being old.

OONA   He's a hemophiliac. Do you know what that means? He can't ever be cut, or bleed or . . .

JOHNNY   Lots of people have that. Not just old people.

OONA   When you get old everything starts to go. Yesterday, for a while he couldn't hear. And he won't eat. And the bedwetting. And . . .

JOHNNY   But it's something else.

OONA   What now? The doctor . . .

JOHNNY   I don't know. He seems so mixed up. Or confused. He's burning up with confusion.

OONA   He's always been like that. I hadn't seen him for five years. I arrived and after a day he was exactly as I'd remembered.

JOHNNY   But can't he be helped?

OONA   That's what happens when you get old.

JOHNNY   No. It doesn't. That's not it at all. It isn't age. It's as though he's *eating* himself instead of other things.

OONA   [*Weary*] I don't know what you mean. He's always been—indifferent to unhappy. He always had money so he never did anything with his life. Not really. He was on boards and things but those were all titular positions. He won't even play games. He hates to compete in any way, with anyone, on any level. It's all so terribly, terribly cold.

JOHNNY   Is that what it is?

OONA   Yes!

JOHNNY   I'm not sure.

Blackout

Max and Johnny. Large box. Johnny handing Max objects.

JOHNNY   I leave next week.

MAX   Is it Labor Day already?

JOHNNY   Next week it is.

MAX   Do you go back to school?

JOHNNY   And work.

MAX   Are your parents poor?

JOHNNY   They're dead. I live with a cousin.

MAX   What kind of work do you do? [*Spots object*] What's that?

JOHNNY   A little box.

MAX   Open it please. What's inside?

JOHNNY   Nothing.

MAX   O. I kept my cocaine inside this. My wife played a game with me. She didn't like my addiction. If she found the box full she emptied it, and put sugar inside. I took to hiding the box. There were months of furtive movements around the house. It was sometimes quite amusing. I believe it prolonged the marriage. Emily was by nature very dull.

JOHNNY   Then why did you marry her?

MAX   One had to marry someone. She was also stunningly attractive. I wanted to sleep with her. Is this embarrassing for you?

JOHNNY   No. Here's a small statue.

MAX   My jade obelisk. It was meant to bring happiness and good luck. So much for superstition. Might as well believe in God. Since I didn't care for Emily, and later disliked her we stopped having sex. What useless memories these are. What's left?

JOHNNY   A gun.

MAX   My hunting rifle. Hasn't been oiled in years. Probably doesn't work. What else?

JOHNNY   This small gold cup. It has writing on it.

MAX   Give it here. This is a trophy I won in a badminton championship in 1923. I remember it very well. I played with great ferocity. If I could walk properly I'd never play again.

JOHNNY   Why not?

MAX   It's competition. Why do we devise so-called games that pit us against each other? That happens more than enough—without games. Do you watch football? I understand Mr. Nixon does. Men plow each other like cattle into the earth for a ball, for a few yards of territory that doesn't matter, broken limbs and pain and mindless cheers from the stadiums as each team suffers a new setback. It's a strange morality we have, condemning those civilizations that had gladiatorial competitions. They at least had some honesty about their own motives. We're more sophisticated. We cloak with such inspired deviousness the impulse to kill. [*The gun is in his lap*] It isn't time for another nap yet, I don't have to be fed, my bladder is quite empty. What can we do to make time pass? You were telling me about your work.

JOHNNY   No I wasn't.

MAX   Well tell me anyway.

JOHNNY   It's just a part-time job, in a meat-packing plant.

MAX   [*Pointing to mementoes*]   Let's have all this destroyed. What do you do?

JOHNNY   I take the pigs, you know, the cut up hogs, and pack the pieces in boxes.

MAX   Why?

JOHNNY   I need the money. It pays more than delivering papers and the abattoir's right near school. And I don't have to talk to anybody. I just do the work. [*Pause*]   I only mind packing the livers. [*Pause*]   I have to go into the cooler and shove my hand into this tall barrel that's piled up to the top with wet pigs' livers. They're partly frozen. I can feel their veins bursting at the touch of my hand. I can't look while I'm doing it. I stare at the cooler walls, all frozen, but I can still see those livers bursting. I see it in my head.

MAX   [*Pause*]   When you aren't working, or at school, what do you do then?

JOHNNY   Nothing. I sleep. Walk a lot. Plan what I have to do on the next day, and the day after that. I hate it when I wake up early in the morning with the whole day ahead. And school. And people. That's what's good about my job. There are people there, but it's like I was alone. I do what I'm supposed to, and nobody touches me.

MAX   Do you see any girls?

JOHNNY   No. There's Sheila.

MAX   She's a friend?

JOHNNY   No. We have sex. That's all.

MAX   [*Cutting him off*]   I understand.

JOHNNY   I guess I don't mind it, or I wouldn't see her. When I do, it's like I'm not even there anyway. I don't know where I am.

MAX [*Long sad pause*] Go inside. I want to rest in the sun, alone, while it's
    still warm. Go inside for a little while. Maybe I'll sleep.
JOHNNY Shall I take all this?
MAX . . . not for awhile.

Johnny leaves, Max feels the gun awhile. Without looking he cocks the trigger.

Blackout

SECTION C

Johnny and Oona. Separately seated. They do not look at each other during this scene.

JOHNNY He tried to take off his bandage last night.
OONA I'd rather place him with trained nurses than tie his hands.
JOHNNY He keeps complaining that the skin itches.
OONA I should have watched more closely. I remembered that rifle was in the
    house.
JOHNNY No oil. Dry barrel. Old bullets. That's why it was only powder burn.
OONA I've got to send him away. Why should *you* have to see this. I don't
    sleep. We fight. He rambles about his dreams. It's wrong. The doctor
    agrees. [*Pause*] I've got to send him away.
JOHNNY It hurts for him to rip at that bandage. Why doesn't he leave himself
    alone?
OONA I don't want this house anymore. Let them sell it. I don't want this
    house. I want to go away.
JOHNNY At night he tears at himself. Thrashes around. Dreams. If I could
    see—*feel*—what he was dreaming. [*Pause*] Something.
OONA Go and check that he's alive! That he hasn't been *at* himself again.
    Don't talk any more about what you see. All of you—Martin, and father,
    and you—all see things. Let's just do what we have to do. Go and check
    that he's alive.

Blackout

*During this scene, the players are to be separated from one another as far as is possible.
They are illuminated only when they speak. No area lighting, unless indicated.*

OONA Soon I'll hear a car in the drive.

Blackout

JOHNNY . . . this empty garden . . .

Blackout

OONA   . . . so it's finished . . . get rid of the furniture . . .

Blackout

JOHNNY   . . . the summer's over . . .

Blackout

OONA   . . . Max . . . best for him.

Blackout

JOHNNY   [*Realization*]   . . . *nothing* in this garden.

Blackout

Max, discovered in wheelchair. Huge bandage covering his face and head. Openings for eyes, nose, mouth.

MAX   Skin itches under this. Can't feel outlines of my face. I'm drugged. Can't see my shadow.

Blackout

Lights up on Oona, alone. We see and hear her pouring water from pitcher into glass. We hear its sound.

Blackout

MAX   I hear them! Shadows in the forest. Hiding in grass and branches.

Blackout

JOHNNY   [*Quiet—calm*]   I wish the summer wasn't over.

Blackout—fraction longer.

Lights up on Oona and Max. Different tempo than before.

OONA   Here's your water, father.
MAX   Back to Martin? To your husband?
OONA   Yes.
MAX   I would hate to be a breathing entity—growing up in that house.

OONA   [*Bland*]   Drink your water.

MAX   . . . with your clinging, driving him out: kisses leaving welts. [*Pause*]
Your marriage is a travesty.

OONA   [*Exploding*]   Leave me be! You and mother better? Living? . . . Dying!
Laziness. Fights. Your addictions. Aloofness. Cold stinging wit. Never
decisions. No passion. No love. [*Pause*]   Where's the man? Where's Max?
Where's my father? [*Pause*]   Who are you?

I hate it, [*Pause*]   I'm like you. [*Pause*]   You're old. [*Pause*]   I can't understand you. [*Pause*]   Why don't you die. Just die. Die. Die. *Die.*

Blackout

MAX   Shadows yelling. In pain. Wandering around dead and bumping into
trees trying to get back to their bodies. How do you catch a shadow? With
water? With blood.

Blackout

OONA   I'm sorry.

Blackout

MAX   Yelling . . . or is it just her men. [*Quiet anger*]   Coming to take me
away . . .

Blackout

*Area lighting on full garden. All furniture has been removed. Max, Oona, Johnny
only, and wheelchair.*

JOHNNY   [*Wishing, knowing it's impossible*]   We should take you inside. Build
a fire. Take your bandage off and burn it up.

MAX   Lose my face? Now? [*Hard*]   Let me see my garden. Wheel me around,
point out plants. Push me, Oona. Welt the garden to my memory.

JOHNNY   I'll do . . .

MAX   Must be Oona. Wheel me. Tell me what to see.

OONA   [*Weary, almost perfunctory*]   Making a circle. Vines—left. Ivy, around.
Green plants, clinging. Don't know all their names. In the middle distance, trees.

MAX   Windy? Clouds?

OONA   Oh yes. Windy and clouds. [*Still wheeling*]   And your tree.

MAX   I'm facing?

OONA   The forest.

MAX   Where's the tree?

OONA   Right behind me. Is that enough?

MAX   More.

OONA   Which direction??

MAX   [*Force and determination*]   Backwards.

He slams her against tree by wheeling his chair. Sets the wheelchair's brake. She is pinioned.

Blackout

Lights up. Max smashing glass against rim of chair. Glass may have been in his lap. We see and <u>hear</u> *it shatter.*

Blackout

Lights up. Max raising hand. Bringing down to glass. When hand almost touching: Blackout.

The above gesture with hand is repeated. Blackout. It's repeated once more. Blackout. On fourth time, Max breaks through bandage, actually doing the smashing. On instant blood flows through Oona yells:

OONA   Johnny!!

Blackout

Lights up. Max's chair has been pushed to one side. He's slumped over, dead. Oona is clutching Johnny in a terrifying hug.

OONA   [*Very soft*]   breakage rupture smashing help. help. help.

Blackout

Lights up. Johnny kneeling, in wheelchair's cast shadow. Max still in chair.

JOHNNY   [*Very soft, to himself*]   She's inside. Hurrying the men.

OONA   [*From inside house*]   It's getting cold. Come inside.

JOHNNY   [*Very soft*]   Soon. Soon.

He has clutched Max's hand. Rubs his face with it. Lets it fall. Blood.

I'm trying to think . . .

Blackout

End

Glossary and Index
of Critical Terms

FICTION

ALLEGORY A story in which the events and characters are symbolic of another order of meaning, in a frame of reference outside that of the fictional world, the way killing a dragon may symbolize defeating the devil. See pp. 13–14.

CHARACTER A name or title and a set of qualities that make a fictional person. See pp. 11–12.

COMEDY The story of a person's rise to a higher station in life through education or improvement of personality. See pp. 8–9.

DESIGN The shape of a story when it is considered as a completed object rather than an ongoing process. See pp. 19–21.

DIALOGUE The parts of a story in which the words of characters are directly reported. See p. 15.

FABULATION Fiction that violates normal probabilities to make some point about the nature of existence. See pp. 23–4.

FACT A thing that has been done, or a true statement. See pp. 3–4.

FANTASY A story of events that violate our sense of natural possibilities in this world; the more extreme the violation, the more fantastic the story. See pp. 5–7.

FICTION Something made up, usually a made-up story. See pp. 3–4.

HISTORY The events of the past, or a re-telling of those events in the form of a story; the most factual kind of fiction. See pp. 5–7.

IRONY The result of some difference in point of view or values between a character in fiction and the narrator or reader. See pp. 15–16.

JUXTAPOSITION The way episodes or elements of a plot are located next to one another to contribute to the design of a story. See pp. 19–21.

1403

METAFICTION   A special kind of fabulation that calls into question the nature of fiction itself. See p. 343.

METAPHOR   The way rich and complex thoughts can be conveyed by the linking of different images and ideas. See pp. 15–19.

NARRATION   The parts of a story that summarize events and conversations. See p. 15.

NARRATOR   The person who tells a story. See p. 15

PATHOS   The emotion generated by the story of a character's fall or persecution through no fault of his own. See pp. 8–9.

PICARESQUE   A kind of story that blends comedy and satire to narrate the adventures of a rogue through a low or debased version of contemporary reality. See p. 9.

PLOT   The order of events in a story as an ongoing process. See pp. 10–11.

POINT OF VIEW   The voice and vision through which the events of a story reach the reader. See pp. 15–19.

REALISM   A mode of fiction that is not specifically factual but presents a world recognizably bound by the same laws as the world of the author. See pp. 7, 147.

REPETITION   The way certain features or elements of a story may be presented more than once to make the thematic point. See pp. 19–21.

ROMANCE   A story that is neither widely fantastic nor bound by the conventions of realism, but offers a heightened version of reality. See p. 7.

SATIRE   A story that offers a world that is debased in relation to the world of the author. See pp. 8–9.

STORY   A complete sequence of events, as told about a single character or group of characters. See p. 4.

STREAM OF CONSCIOUSNESS   A fictional technique in which the thoughts of a character are entirely opened to the reader, usually being presented as a flow of ideas and feelings, apparently without logical organization. See p. 11.

SYMBOL   A particular object or event in a story which acquires thematic value through its function or the way it is presented. See p. 21.

THEME   The ideas, values, or feelings that are developed or questioned by a work of fiction. See pp. 12–14.

TONE   The way in which attitudes are conveyed through language without being presented directly as statements, as in sarcasm. See pp. 15–17.

TRAGEDY   The story of a character's fall from a high position through some flaw of personality. See pp. 8–9.

POETRY

ACCENT   The rhythmical alternation of light and heavy (soft and loud) sounds in verse. See pp. 413–20; see also STRESS.

ALLITERATION   The use of the same sound at the beginning of two or more words in the same line (or two adjacent lines) of verse. See pp. 422–3.

ANIMATION   The endowment of inanimate objects with some of the qualities of living creatures. See p. 405.

BALLAD   A poem that tells a story, usually meant to be sung. See p. 405.

BLANK VERSE   Unrhymed iambic pentameter lines. See pp. 420–1; see also FOOT and LINE.

CAESURA   The point or points within a line of verse where a pause is noticeable. See pp. 420–1.

CONCEIT   An elaborately developed and sometimes farfetched metaphor. See pp. 402–3.

DESCRIPTION   The use of visual images and appeals to other senses in poetry. See pp. 395–7.

DRAMA   The quality of poetry that is like theatrical drama, requiring the reader to grasp the nature of speaker, listener, and situation. See pp. 389–93; see also Drama Glossary.

DRAMATIC MONOLOGUE   A poem in which a single speaker addresses remarks to one or more listeners at some significant moment in the speaker's life. See pp. 390–1.

END-STOPPED   A line of verse that ends where one would normally pause in speech or punctuate in writing. See p. 412.

ENJAMBMENT   The use of run-on lines in verse. See p. 412.

FEMININE RHYME   When rhyme words end in an unaccented syllable, two rhyming sounds are required, as in *yellow* and *fellow*. See pp. 417, 423.

FOOT   A unit of meter or rhythm, of which five kinds are normally recognized: the iamb (da dum), the anapest (da da dum), the trochee (dum da), the dactyl (dum-da-da), and the spondee (dum-dum). See pp. 414–20.

FREE-VERSE   Unrhymed lines in which no particular meter is maintained. See p. 412.

HEROIC COUPLET   A rhymed, iambic pentameter pair of lines, usually both end-stopped, with a period or other full stop at the end of the second line. See pp. 421–2; see also FOOT and LINE.

IMAGERY   The use of sensory details (images) in poetry: sounds, scents, tastes, textures, and especially sights. See p. 401

IRONY   A deliberate gap or disparity between the language in which a thing is discussed and language usually considered appropriate for that particular subject. See pp. 406–9.

LINE   The line of verse as normally printed on a page. Lines may be divided into feet and labeled according to the number of feet per line. In English the most common lines are pentameter (five feet) and tetrameter (four feet). See p. 412; see also FOOT.

MEDITATION   The movement from images to ideas in poetry. See pp. 395–7.

METAPHOR   The discovery of likeness or similarity in different things—a major resource of poetical expression. See pp. 398–402.

METRICS   The part of poetry that has to do with sound rather than sense. See pp. 411–23.

NARRATION   The quality of poetry that is like fiction, requiring the reader to follow shifts in time and space, and to observe significant details, so as to understand a poem as a kind of story. See pp. 392–4.

NARRATOR   One who tells a story. See pp. 392–3.

PERSONIFICATION   The endowment of non-human things or creatures with distinctly human qualities. See pp. 405–6.

PUN   A word used in a context that obliges it to carry two conflicting meanings. See pp. 404–5.

RHYME   A sound pattern in which both vowel and consonant sounds at the end of words match (as in *rhyme* and *chime*), especially when these words come at the end of nearby lines. See pp. 422–3.

RUN-ON   A line of verse that ends where one would not normally pause in speech or punctuate in writing. See p. 412.

SCANSION   To "scan" a poem is to determine its metrical structure and rhyme scheme. See pp. 413–14.

SIMILE   A kind of metaphor in which the likeness of two things is made explicit by such words as *like, as, so*. See pp. 398–9.

SITUATION   In a narrative or dramatic poem, the circumstances of the characters or speaker. See pp. 389–91.

SONNET   A verse form featuring intricate rhyming, usually employing fourteen iambic pentameter lines. See pp. 438–41.

STANZA   A regularly repreated metrical pattern of the same number of lines in groups throughout a poem, sometimes including repeated patterns of rhyme as well. See pp. 417–18.

STRESS   The ways in which verse sounds are accented, of which three types may be recognized in poetry: *grammatical stress*, the normal pronunciation of a word or phrase; *rhetorical stress*, change in pronunciation to emphasize some part of the meaning of an utterance; *poetical stress*, the regular rhythm established in metrical verse. See pp. 413–14.

SYMBOL   An extension of metaphor in which one thing is implicitly discussed by means of the explicit discussion of something else. See pp. 403–4.

TACT   A reader's ability to observe the conventions operating in any particular poem and to pay attention to the idiom of every poet. See pp. 388–9.

DRAMA

ABSURDIST DRAMA   A mode of drama which does not provide any rational source of explanation for the behavior and fate of its characters and thus expresses the possibility that human existence may be meaningless. See pp. 702–4.

BLOCKING   Arrangement of characters on stage during any particular moment in the production of a play. See pp. 690–1.

CHARACTER A dramatic being, known by name, word, and deed. See pp. 709–10.

CHORIC CHARACTER A character who takes part in the action of a play but is not directly involved in the outcome of the action, and thus can provide a source of commentary upon it. See pp. 693–4.

CHORIC COMMENTARY Commentary upon characters and events provided either by a chorus or by choric characters. See p. 693.

CHORUS A group of characters who comment upon the action of a play but do not take part in it. See pp. 693, 712–13.

CLOSET DRAMA Drama written only to be read, rather than to be produced in a theater. See pp. 689–90.

COMEDY Dramatization of a hero's and heroine's change in fortune (from frustration to satisfaction) brought about not only by the effort of the hero and heroine themselves but also by some element of chance, coincidence, or luck. See pp. 640–44, 698–702.

COSTUME A piece of physical apparel worn by actors to create a visual illusion appropriate to the characters they are pretending to be. See pp. 690, 711, 758.

CUE A word, phrase, or statement in the text of a play which provides explicit or implicit information relevant to theatrical production of the play. See pp. 690–1.

DIALOGUE Specialized form of conversation peculiar to drama, in that it is designed to convey everything about the imaginative world of a play, as well as to provide all the cues necessary for production of a play. See pp. 690–1, 692–4, 705–6.

DISCOVERY A change from ignorance to knowledge on the part of a dramatic hero and/or heroine which brings about a significant change in the fortune of the hero and/or heroine. See pp. 700–1, 702; see also REVERSAL.

DRAMA Imitative action created through the words of imaginary beings talking to one another rather than to a reader or spectator. See pp. 689–90, 694–6, 697–9, 705.

DRAMATIC UNIT A segment of the scenario that is determined by the entrance or exit of a character or group of characters. See pp. 707–8; see also SCENARIO.

EXPOSITION Dialogue at the beginning of a play that includes background information about characters and events in the imaginative world of a play. See pp. 692, 708.

GESTURE A physical movement made by actors appropriate to the attitudes and intentions of the characters they are pretending to be. See pp. 690, 711, 786.

INTERACTION Verbal and physical deeds performed by dramatic characters in relation to one another. See pp. 692–3.

INTONATION Particular manner (including pronunciation, rhythm, and volume) in which actors deliver the lines of the characters they are pretending to be. See pp. 690, 711.

MEDITATIVE DRAMA   A form of drama that is primarily concerned with representing the internalized thoughts and feelings of its characters. See
pp. 694–5.

NARRATION   An element in drama that is like the act of storytelling, in that it
tells about characters and events, or comments upon characters and
events, rather than showing them directly. See pp. 692–4; see also CHORIC
CHARACTER, CHORIC COMMENTARY, CHORUS, EXPOSITION, REPORTED ACTION and
RETROSPECTION.

NATURALISTIC DRAMA   A mode of drama which embodies a view of men and
women as being influenced by psychological, social, and economic
forces beyond their control and comprehension. See pp. 702–4.

PACING   Tempo of activity on stage during any particular moment in the production of a play. See p. 690.

PERSUASIVE DRAMA   A form of drama that uses dialogue, plot, and character
primarily as a means of testing ideas, expounding ideas, or demonstrating the superiority of one set of ideas over another. See p. 696.

PLOT   Specialized form of experience peculiar to drama, in that it consists of
a wholly interconnected system of events, deliberately selected and
arranged to fulfill both the imaginative and theatrical purposes of a play.
See pp. 699–702, 705, 707–9; see also SCENARIO.

PROP   Any physical item (other than costume and set) which is used by actors
on stage during the production of a play. See pp. 690, 691, 786, 970.

REPORTED ACTION   Action taking place during the time of the play which is
reported by one or more of the characters rather than being directly
presented. See pp. 692–3, 707–8.

REPRESENTED ACTION   Action taking place during the time of the play which is
directly presented rather than reported by one or more of the characters.
See pp. 689–91, 692–3, 707–8.

RETROSPECTION   Post-expository dialogue in which characters survey, explore,
and seek to understand action which took place well before the time of
the play. See pp. 692–3.

REVERSAL   An incident or sequence of incidents that go contrary to the expectations of a hero and/or heroine. See p. 701.

ROMANCE   A mode of drama that uses characters and events to present an
intensified but not completely idealized view of human excellence. See
pp. 697, 702.

SATIRE   A mode of drama that uses characters and events to present an intensified but not completely negative view of human imperfection. See
pp. 697, 702.

SCENARIO   Action that is directly presented (i.e., on stage), and thus embodies
everything that takes place in the imaginative world of a play (i.e., the
plot). See pp. 707–8.

SCRIPT   Text of a play interpreted as a set of cues for theatrical production.
See p. 690.

SET   Physical construction placed on stage to represent an interior or exterior location in the imaginative world of a play. See pp. 690, 712, 758, 786, 970–2.

SOLILOQUY   Lines spoken by a character that are meant to represent the unspoken thoughts and feelings of the character. See pp. 694–5.

SPECTACLE   Sights and sounds of performance by means of which the imaginative world of a play is brought to life in the theatre. See pp. 690, 711–13, 758, 786, 970–2. See also BLOCKING, COSTUME, GESTURE, INTONATION, PACING, PROP, SET.

TRAGEDY   Dramatization of a hero's or heroine's change in fortune (from prosperity to catastrophe) brought about by some great error in judgment on the part of the hero or heroine. See pp. 698–701, 712–13.

TRAGICOMEDY   A mode of drama that does not embody a clear-cut pattern of catastrophe or rebirth (as in tragedy or comedy), or present clear-cut images of good or evil (as in romance or satire), and thus presents an ambiguous and problematic view of human experience. See pp. 702–4; see also ABSURDIST DRAMA; NATURALISTIC DRAMA.

Index

Names of authors appear in SMALL CAPITALS, titles in *italics,* and first lines of poems in roman type. If title and first line coincide, the title alone is entered; if title begins the first line, it appears in *italics,* the rest of the line in [roman bracketed]. Titles supplied for untitled works appear in [*italic bracketed*].